INFORMATION TECHNOLOGY
FOR MANAGEMENT

▼ INFORMATION TECHNOLOGY For MANAGEMENT

IMPROVING QUALITY AND PRODUCTIVITY

EFRAIM TURBAN
California State University at Long Beach

EPHRAIM MCLEAN
Georgia State University

JAMES WETHERBE
University of Minnesota and University of Memphis

JOHN WILEY & SONS, INC.
New York • Chichester • Brisbane • Toronto • Singapore

ACQUISITIONS EDITOR   Elizabeth Lang Golub
DEVELOPMENTAL EDITOR   Kathleen Dolan
MARKETING MANAGER   Leslie Hines
SENIOR PRODUCTION EDITOR   Tony VenGraitis
DESIGNER   Dawn L. Stanley
MANUFACTURING MANAGER   Mark Cirillo
PHOTO EDITOR   Mary Ann Price
PHOTO RESEARCHER   Elyse Rieder
ILLUSTRATION COORDINATOR   Anna Melhorn
PRODUCTION SERVICES   Ingrao Associates
Cover Photo   © Charles Nes/Liaison International

High-speed trains, such as the one pictured on the cover, are dispatched using sophisticated computer programs. A case study in Chapter 16 examines the computerized expert system in use at the historic Gare de l'Est in Paris, which directs the movement of over 1100 trains each day through the station— a traffic level much higher than those envisioned by the station's designers. The system replaced an outdated manual procedure used until 1989, greatly improving traffic flow and scheduling capabilities.

This book was set in 10/12 Meridien Roman by CRWaldman Graphic Communications and printed and bound by R. R. Donnelley and Sons. The cover was printed by Phoenix Color, Inc.

Recognizing the importance of preserving what has been written, it is a policy of John Wiley and Sons, Inc. to have books of enduring value published in the United States printed on acid-free paper, and we exert our best efforts to that end.

The paper in this book was manufactured by a mill whose forest management programs include sustained yield harvesting of its timberlands. Sustained yield harvesting principles ensure that the number of trees cut each year does not exceed the amount of new growth.

ISBN: 0-471-58059-7

Printed in the United States of America

10 9 8 7 6 5 4 3 2 1

PREFACE

As we approach the end of the century and the millennium, we witness the growing importance of computerized information systems. The number of computers is growing rapidly, as are their applications in business, education, government, the military, medicine, and the home. Computerized systems can be found today in even the smallest businesses. In many cases it is impossible to run a competitive business without a computerized information system.

Global competitive pressures and continuous innovations are forcing many organizations to *rethink* the manner in which they do business and to *reengineer* themselves. Such reengineering requires, in almost all cases, the support of some information technologies. As organizations increasingly depend on computerized information systems, the construction, use, management and maintenance of these systems becomes essential to the welfare or even survival of many organizations.

The unique orientation of this book is reflected in the central model presented in each Part Opener (and discussed in Figure 1.7), which stresses that the purpose of Information Technology is to provide *solutions* to organizational problems and challenges. Our assumption is that it is more important for business students, as future practicing managers, to learn what IT can do for the business rather than learn all the technical details of how systems are built and maintained, or to rehash many of the behavioral and organizational aspects of IT that they learned in introductory management courses.

Many introductory texts on information systems are geared towards yesterday's environment, where the important issues were the technology, the construction of information systems and the support of traditional business functional applications. The approach of this book is different. While recognizing the importance of the technology, system development, and functional transaction processing systems, we emphasize the *innovative* uses of information technology. Such innovations—ranging from a multimedia-based hair salon in Singapore to neural network-based diagnostic work in California hospitals—help organizations to excel in an increasingly competitive global environment.

▶ THEMES

This book is based on the fundamental premise that the major role of information technology is to *provide solutions* to business problems, and to *provide opportunities* for companies by increasing productivity and quality, and enabling business process reengineering. By taking a practical, managerial-oriented approach, the book demonstrates that IT can be provided not only by information systems departments, but by end-users and vendors as well. Managing information resources, new technologies, and communications networks is becoming a—or even *the*—critical success factor in the operations of many companies, and will be essential to the survival of businesses through the 1990s and beyond. This book reflects our vision of where information systems are going and the direction of IS education

v

in business programs. This vision is represented by five overarching themes that we stress throughout the book.

▼ *Real world orientation.* Extensive, vivid examples from large corporations, small businesses, and government and not-for-profit agencies will make concepts come alive by showing students the capabilities of information technology, its cost and justification, and some of the innovative ways real corporations are using IT in their operations.

▼ *A strong emphasis on how IT can improve productivity and quality*, the two areas of top interest to today's managers. Special attention is given to the support IT provides to business process reengineering. The managerial perspective will enable students to see the value of what they are learning and fully appreciate the importance of IT to the organization. Reengineering examples are highlighted with an icon.

▼ *Global perspective.* The importance of global competition, partnerships, and trading is rapidly increasing. IT facilitates export and import, managing multinational companies and trading electronically around the globe. International examples are highlighted with an icon throughout the book and the book closes with five global cases.

▼ *Emphasis on new technologies and applications.* Information technology is driven by innovations. Fuzzy logic, neural computing, hypermedia, and natural language processors have left the laboratory and are being used in businesses today. The text looks at knowledge work and discusses telecommunications applications where appropriate. We also explore some of the ways new technology is being integrated with traditional computer-based information systems, creating new or expanded applications. Examples of emerging technologies are highlighted with an icon.

▼ *Comprehensiveness.* The book provides a solid foundation for both the technical and managerial approaches. All major topics in information technology are covered, allowing for flexibility in use.

▶ ORGANIZATION

This book is divided into five parts. **Part One** introduces the foundations of information systems and their expanding role in the business environment. Particular emphasis is placed on how corporations use information systems to reengineer their business processes. Of special interest is Gordon Davis's definition and categorization of the information systems field.

Part Two delves into the technology of information systems and the IT infrastructure. Hardware, software, data management, and network architecture are discussed in detail. We have also included a unique chapter on human-machine communications (the user interface) that assesses the benefits of advanced communication modes.

In **Part Three** students learn the specifics of system design and development, from analysis to implementation and evaluation. The chapter on information systems planning includes a discussion of the ways IT supports business processes reengineering. End-user and enterprise computing are given special attention in the chapter on corporate information architecture.

Part Four discusses the many ways information systems can be used to support the day-to-day operations of a company, with a strong emphasis on the use of IT in managerial decision making. The four chapters in this part address some of the ways businesses are using information technology to solve specific problems and build strategic, innovative systems that enhance quality and productivity. Special attention is given to innovative applications of telecommunications and intelligent systems.

Part Five explores some of the challenges involved in managing information systems. Topics include operating and maintaining information systems, integration with other systems, and the control and security of information technology. The final chapter is a discussion of the impact of information technology on organizations, individuals, and society, and contains a vision of information technology in the future.

▶ FEATURES OF THE TEXT

We developed a number of pedagogical features to aid student learning and tie together the themes of the book.

▼ *Chapter outline.* The outlines provide a quick indication of the major topics covered.

▼ *Learning objectives.* Learning objectives are provided at the beginning of each chapter to help students focus their efforts and alert them to the important concepts discussed.

▼ *Opening cases.* Each chapter opens with a *real world* example that illustrates the importance of information technology to modern corporations. These cases were carefully chosen to demonstrate the relevance of the topics introduced in the chapter.

▼ *"A Closer Look" boxes.* These contain detailed, in-depth discussions of specific concepts or procedures, often using real world examples. Other boxes enhance the in-text discussion by offering an alternative approach to information technology

▼ *"IT at Work" boxes.* These spotlight some real-world innovations and new technologies that companies are relying on to solve organizational dilemmas or create new business opportunities. Each box concludes with critical thinking questions.

▼ *Highlighted icons.* Icons appear throughout the text and relate the topics covered within each chapter back to the major themes of the book. The icons alert students to three important areas: Reengineering, Emerging Technologies, and Global examples.

▼ *Managerial Issues.* The final section of every chapter explores some of the special concerns managers face as they adapt to an increasingly technological environment. Thought-provoking questions can serve as a springboard for class discussion and challenge business students to consider some of the actions they might take if placed in similar circumstances.

▼ *Key Terms.* All boldfaced, new terms introduced within the chapter appear in a list at the end of the chapter and are defined in the end-of-book glossary.

▼ *Chapter Highlights.* A list of all the important concepts covered. The chapter highlights are linked to the learning objectives introduced at the beginning of each chapter to reinforce the important ideas discussed.

▼ *End of chapter exercises.* Different types of questions measure student comprehension and their ability to apply knowledge. Questions for Review ask students to summarize the concepts introduced. Discussion Questions are intended to promote class discussion and develop critical thinking skills. Exercises are challenging assignments that require students to apply what they have learned. The Group Exercises are class projects designed to foster teamwork.

▼ *Minicases.* Real-world cases that highlight some of the problems encountered by corporations as they develop and implement information systems. Discussion questions and group exercises are included.

▼ *Part ending cases.* Longer real-world cases chosen specifically for their ability to bring together many of the overriding concepts from each part of the text.

▼ *International cases.* Written by prominent international figures in the MIS field, these cases illustrate how IT can be adapted to conform to the cultural and political characteristics of a particular country. Contributors include Kimberly Bechler, International Institute of Management Development (Switzerland), Guy Fitzgerald, University of London (United Kingdom), Young Moo Kang, Dong-A University (Korea), Donald Marchand, International Institute of Management Development (Switzerland), Boon-Siong Neo, Nanyang Technological University (Singapore), Nicolau Reinhard, University of Sao Paulo (Brazil), Leslie Willcocks, Templeton College, Oxford University (United Kingdom), and Ronaldo Zwicker, University of Sao Paulo (Brazil). Additional international cases contributed by Pirkko Walden, Ossi Kokkonen, and Christer Carlsson (Abo Akademi University, Finland), and Chris Sauer (University of New South Wales, Australia) appear at the ends of Parts I and III respectively.

▶ SUPPLEMENTARY MATERIALS

The instructional package consists of:

1. *Instructor's Resource Guide with Test Bank* (ISBN 0471-09204-5). This manual includes sample syllabi, chapter overviews, teaching suggestions, answers to review questions, discussion questions, exercises, and case studies, as well as answers to test questions.

2. *Computerized Test Bank* (ISBN 0471-10324-1). The entire test bank is available in a computerized version, MICROTEST, for use on IBM PC, XT, or AT computers (or compatibles). MICROTEST allows instructors to easily customize and create tests.

3. *Transparency Masters* (ISBN 0471-10315-2). Approximately 100 key text figures are available.

4. *MIS Videotapes* (ISBN 0471-14072-4). A selection of news segments from "Nightly Business Report," the longest-running, most-watched daily business, financial, and economic news program on television, is available as a companion to the text. NBR anchors provide lead-ins to tie the video segments directly to text coverage. In addition, a managerial presentation by Jim Wetherbe is provided.

5. *Software Demonstration* (ISBN 0471-09214-2). Free demonstration software of several popular products, such as Lotus Notes, is available.

▶ ACKNOWLEDGMENTS

Many individuals provided assistance in the creation of the first edition. First, dozens of students participated in class testing of the material and helped develop exercises, find illustrative applications, and contributed valuable suggestions. It is not possible to name all of them, but they certainly deserve recognition and thanks. In particular, we would like to thank the students at the following universities who class tested all or part of the manuscript: California State University-Long Beach, Eastern Illinois University, Nanyang Technological University (Singapore), and the University of Houston.

Faculty feedback was also essential to the development of the book. The following individuals participated in focus groups and/or acted as reviewers:

Mary Anne Atkinson, *University of Delaware*, Benedict Arogyaswamy, *University of South Dakota*, James Carroll, *Georgian Court College*, Paul Cheney, *University of South Florida*, Candace Deans, *Thunderbird School, AGIM*, Bill DeLone, *American University*, Phillip Ein-Dor, *Tel Aviv University (Israel)*, Michael Eirman, *University of Wisconsin-Oshkosh*, Paul Evans, *George Mason University*, Deb Ghosh, *Louisiana State University*, Oscar Gutierrez, *University of Massachusetts-Boston*, Rassule Hadidi, *Sangamon State University*, Fred Harold, *Florida Atlantic University*, Jaak Jurison, *Fordham University*, Astrid Lipp, *Clemson University*, Jo Mae Maris, *Northern Arizona University*, E. F. Peter Newson, *University of Western Ontario*, Michael Palley, *CUNY-Baruch College*, Keri Pearlson, *University of Texas*, Bill Richmond, *George Mason University*, Larry Sanders, *University of Buffalo*, A. B. Schwarzkopf, *University of Oklahoma*, Henk Sol, *Delft Institute of Technology (The Netherlands)*, Timothy Smith, *DePaul University*, Timothy Staley, *DeVry Institute of Technology*, Shannon Taylor, *Montana State University*, Robert Van Cleave, *University of Minnesota*, Kuang-Wei Wen, *University of Connecticut*, Anthony Wensley, *University of Toronto (Canada)*, Jennifer Williams, *University of Southern Indiana*, G. W. Willis, *Baylor University*, Gayle Yaverbaum, *Pennsylvania State University*

Several individuals created portions of chapters or cases, especially international cases. These include:

Kimberly Bechler, *International Institute of Management Development (Switzerland)*
Christer Carlsson, *Abo Akademi University (Finland)*
Gordon Davis, *University of Minnesota*
Lance Eliot, *California State University-Fullerton*
Guy Fitzgerald, *University of London (United Kingdom)*
Young Moo Kang, *Dong-A University (Korea)*
Ossi Kokkonen, *Metsa-Serla Oy (Finland)*
Donald Marchand, *International Institute of Management Development (Switzerland)*
David McDonald, *Georgia State University*
Boon-Siong Neo, *Nanyang Technological University (Singapore)*
Nicolau Reinhard, *University of Sao Paulo (Brazil)*
Chris Sauer, *University of New South Wales (Australia)*
Scott Schneberger, *Georgia State University*
Pirkko Walden, *Abo Akademi University (Finland)*
Leslie Willcocks, *Templeton College, Oxford University (United Kingdom)*
Ronaldo Zwicker, *University of Sao Paulo (Brazil)*

We would like to thank Roy Sprague for creating the instructor's manual and test bank that accompany this book.

Many individuals helped us with the administrative work; of special mention are Karen Hays and Judy Lang, who devoted considerable time to typing and editing, and Gerry Bedore who proofread the pages. Hugh Watson of the University of Georgia, the Information Systems Advisor to Wiley, guided us through various stages of the project. Finally, we would like to thank the dedicated staff of John Wiley & Sons, Andrea Bryant, Leslie Hines, Charlotte Hyland, Anna Melhorn, Mary Ann Price, Dawn Stanley, Matt Van Hattem, and Anthony Vengraitis. A special thank you to Kathleen Dolan and Beth Lang Golub, who contributed their considerable energy, time, and devotion to the success of this project.

We would like to thank those individuals and corporations who helped us to create a book from a collection of data, information, and knowledge.

BRIEF CONTENTS

CONTENTS

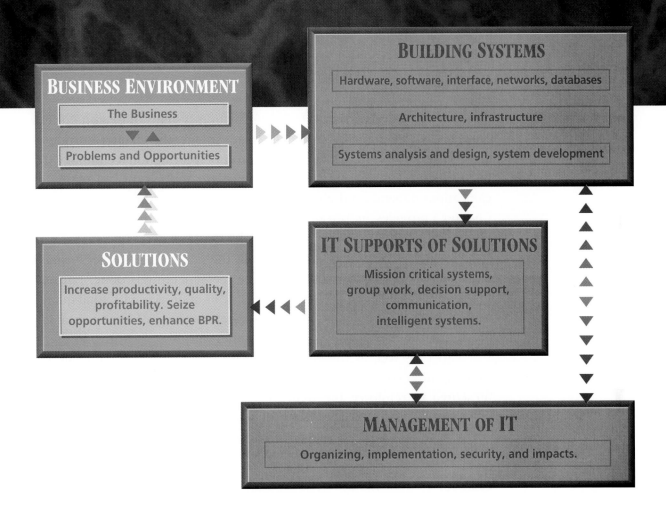

Today's business environment is undergoing rapid changes due to the globalization of business, technological innovations, social and political changes, and increased awareness and demands from customers. These changes result in a tough competitive environment in which many organizations cannot survive. Organizations, private and public, must take measures to increase their productivity, quality of service, and competitive ability. New management approaches—ranging from telecommuting to business processes reengineering—are being used to counter increasing pressures on organizations. The major driving force of many of the changes is information technology, which is also at the core of most of the innovations used by organizations to succeed or even to survive.

Part I places information technology in the context of organizations, focusing on business pressures and the strategies used to counter them.

Chapter 1 provides an overview of business pressures resulting from environmental, organizational, and technological issues. Information systems are viewed as systems that support the critical response activities of organizations, such as increasing productivity, and reducing the business pressures by providing solutions to business problems.

Chapter 2 is dedicated to the various species of information systems. The major categories of systems are those intended to support the functional areas, business transaction processing, and management of the organization. The chapter also outlines the architecture and infrastructure of information technology.

Chapter 3 deals with strategic information systems. Based on Porter's models of value chain and competitive advantage, the chapter introduces several frameworks which illustrate the role of information technology (IT) in supporting strategic initiatives. The welfare and survival of many organizations depend on their ability to reengineer their business processes. Chapter 3 provides an introduction to and overview of the concept of business processes reengineering and the role that IT plays in it.

Chapter 4 concludes Part I. It details the need to reengineer business processes and the manner in which the reengineering is done. Furthermore, the chapter compares and contrasts this approach with total quality management, a complementary management strategy of incremental improvement used by organizations to counter business pressures.

Part I (as well as the entire book) is loaded with real-life examples showing how companies practice what we preach. A Part 1 end case is presented to reinforce the material covered, describing the manner in which Metsä-Serla Corp (of Finland) is using an intelligent decision support system as a strategic management tool. This is an example of a most successful strategic information system.

Chapter 1—Information Systems: Concepts, Trends, and Issues
Chapter 2—Information Technologies: Concepts and Architectures
Chapter 3—Strategic Information Systems and Information Technology for Business Reengineering
Chapter 4—Organizations and Information Technology: Reengineering and Total Quality Management

1

INFORMATION SYSTEMS: CONCEPTS, TRENDS, AND ISSUES

Chapter Outline

Learning Objectives

After studying this chapter, you will be able to:

1. Define computer-based information systems and information technology.

2. Recognize the relationships between business pressures and organizational responses.

3. Describe the major pressures in the business environment.

4. Describe the major changes in organizations and management.

5. Recognize the major trends in information technology.

6. Describe the role of the information system as an enabler to critical response activities.

7. Recognize the importance of information systems and the need to study the field.

▶ 1.1 7-ELEVEN JAPAN: GIVING CUSTOMERS A VOICE

ITO-YOKADO COMPANY IS Japan's most profitable re-tailer. In 1974, Ito-Yokado bought the franchise rights to 7-Eleven in Japan from Southland Corporation (Houston, TX). The first store opened in May 1974, and in 20 years the Japanese franchise grew to about 5,000 stores. In the meantime, 7-Eleven's parent company—Southland—was also expanding its operations. However, heavy debt forced it to seek court protection from its lenders. In an attempt to raise cash, the company was forced to sell assets. In 1990, Ito-Yokado Corporation purchased 70 percent of Southland Corporation.

While 7-Eleven in the United States was losing a con-siderable amount of money, 7-Eleven Japan made over 40 percent profit on its sales ($680 million on sales of $1.44 billion in 1992). Such a high level of profit is ex-tremely unusual, not only in Japan but in other coun-tries. How could a franchiser of 7-Eleven achieve such a high profit margin while its parent company was filing for bankruptcy? The answer is: A *customer-focused* ori-entation based on *information technology*.

7-Eleven Japan created a $200-million information system for its stores in Japan. The purpose of the system was to (1) discover who the customers are and what they want and (2) create a sophisticated product-tracking sys-tem. How does such a system work? Every clerk in every store keys in *customer information*, such as gender and ap-proximate age, at the time purchases are made. In this way, the company knows who buys what, where, and at what time of day, so it can track customer preferences. Clerks also key in information about products requested by customers that are not included in the store's inven-tory. Such information leads to stocking the appropriate products and even to the customization of products, man-ufactured by specially created companies in Japan.

The information system is also used for other pur-poses such as monitoring inventories. By implementing the **"just-in-time" approach**, a minimum inventory is kept on the shelves. However, because stores know cus-tomers' preferences, they seldom run out of stock. In addition, most stores have arrangements for quick deliv-ery of products they sell, and so they do not need large inventories. Other uses of the information system are (1) electronically transmitting orders to distribution cen-ters and manufacturers (via satellite), (2) determining which products to keep in each store (70 percent of the products are replaced each year), (3) determining how much shelf space to allocate to each product, and (4) tracking employee performance (including reward-ing high performers).

In addition, the company maintains a high level of quality. A team of 200 inspectors visit 7-Eleven stores

A 7-Eleven Japan clerk using a computer for a cus-tomer purchase.

regularly. Even the company's president occasionally drops into stores incognito to check quality. Quality con-trol data are collected and analyzed continuously by a computerized decision-support system at headquarters. Brands that do not meet strict quality requirements are immediately discontinued. Quality is extremely impor-tant in Japan, where fresh, hot meals are sold at con-venience stores.

As a result of its information system, 7-Eleven Japan has extensive knowledge of its market. It maximizes sales in limited space and optimizes its inventory level. Also, knowing exactly what the customers want helps the company to negotiate good prices and high quality with its vendors. The company can also maintain extremely close relationships with its vendors who support the just-in-time approach. (About 20 manufacturers have special factories that make only or mostly 7-Eleven products.)

7-Eleven has also created a time-distribution system that changes the product mix on display in its stores every morning and evening, based on careful and continual tracking of customers' needs. The company knows that customers' needs in the morning are com-pletely different from those in the evening. Space is very expensive in Japan, and the stores are small. So the sys-tem allows them to display different items at different hours of the day.

The company is in the process of reshaping its U.S. operations. The Japanese are interested in changing the American way of doing business before they improve the U.S. information systems. Thus, they are concen-trating on transforming 7-Eleven into a high-quality, profitable, and truly *convenience* store operation.

SOURCE: Based on a story in *Business Week*, January 1992, and on information provided by 7-Eleven. See also Forbes, June 21, 1993 pg. 44–45.

▶ 1.2 INFORMATION SYSTEMS AND THE BUSINESS

The case of 7-Eleven illustrates that information systems can be used in one company in different ways to help the company achieve an unusual level of profitability. Using an information system, 7-Eleven was able to *change* the way it was conducting business, enabling the company not only to survive, but to excel.

The information system helped the company to:

▼ *Increase sales* by meeting customers' demands, knowing exactly what the customers want and when.

▼ *Reduce costs* by maintaining low inventory levels, knowing what the customers want and at what time of the day. Also, inventories were kept low due to *electronic communication** with the suppliers, resulting in quick deliveries whenever needed.

▼ *Increase* quality of products, which is especially important when fresh meals are involved.

▼ *Create alliances* with *suppliers* to design special products for 7-Eleven and to deliver them quickly.

▼ *Reduce costs* by negotiating high quality at low prices with suppliers.

▼ *Reduce costs* by optimally utilizing shelf space, knowing when certain products are demanded during the day.

▼ *Increase productivity* by electronically tracking employee performance.

▼ *Concentrate* on its core business, which is a true convenience store operation.

7-Eleven is not the only company that uses information systems to improve its operations. There are very few companies that do not. The annual surveys conducted by *Datamation* (a leading practitioner journal of information systems) indicated in 1993, 1994, and 1995 that the most important role of information systems is to support organizations in their attempt to:

1. Increase productivity (reduce cost, increase effectiveness).
2. Improve quality.
3. Create competitive advantage.
4. Attain company's strategy.
5. Reorganize and reengineer.
6. Make better and more effective decisions.
7. Respond quickly to customer needs and to changes in the business or its environment.
8. Access a wealth of information.
9. Improve creativity and innovation.

We will refer to these activities, some of which are interrelated, as *critical response activities*, since frequently they are done in order to counter the pressures in today's business world. These activities may be performed in some or all of the processes of the organization, from the *mission central* routine processing of payroll to *mission critical* tasks like online order entry, to ad-hoc and strategic systems.

Why is it essential that organizations perform these activities? First, companies want to excel, to do better than other companies. In many cases, however, the reason is that *unless they do so*, they may not even be able to *survive*.

---

*Many terms that are briefly introduced in this chapter will be explained later in the text.

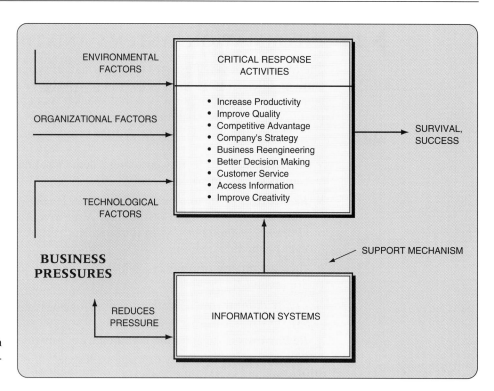

FIGURE 1.1 Information system as a support to critical response activities.

Why is this so? The world is moving into a new industry order where several environmental, organizational, and technological factors create an highly competitive business environment in which customers become extremely important. Furthermore, some of these pressuring factors may change very fast, sometimes in an unpredictable manner (see the MIT Report in Appendix B). So companies need to react frequently and quickly.

The purpose of information systems is to help management execute the previously mentioned activities in an efficient and effective manner. In some cases, information systems are the *only* course of action that management can rely on. Information systems can also be used to directly reduce some of the pressures or respond to them. Finally, information systems themselves, when used by competitors, create additional pressures on organizations. Therefore, it is important to learn and understand information systems, especially since they can be expensive and not all of them may succeed.

The relationships between the pressuring factors, the critical response activities with which organizations respond to these pressures, and the role of information systems are summarized in Figure 1.1. As can be seen in the figure, the pressures are divided into three categories: business environment, organization and management, and information technology. Organizations respond with critical response activities. These responses are enhanced by information systems. Notice that information systems play a dual role. They are part of the pressures (technology), but they can be used to diffuse pressures as well.

The purpose of this book is to teach the manager of the '90s how information systems support management, and how they should be built and managed. Special attention will be given to the support given to the nine critical response managerial activities described earlier. The remainder of this first chapter is divided into four parts: First, some basic definitions are provided. Next, some examples are given that show how information systems support the critical activities. Then, the environmental, organizational, and technological factors are introduced. The chapter ends with a discussion of the value of learning about information systems.

▶ 1.3   INFORMATION SYSTEMS AND INFORMATION TECHNOLOGY

In the previous section, we repeatedly used the term *information systems*. Let's explore the meaning of this term.

WHAT IS AN INFORMATION SYSTEM?

An **information system** (IS) is a collection of components (to be described later) that collects, processes, stores, analyzes, and disseminates information for a specific purpose. Like any other system (see the Appendix at the end of the chapter), an information system includes **inputs** (data, instructions) and **outputs** (reports, calculations). An information system *processes* the inputs and produces outputs that are sent to the user or to other systems. A **feedback** mechanism that controls the operation may be included (see Figure 1.2). Like any other system, an information system operates within an **environment**. The inventory information system at 7-Eleven, for example, may interface with and be affected by a supplier's information system. However, because the vendor cannot manipulate the 7-Eleven system, it is viewed as an environment.

Information systems can be manual or computer-based (some systems are partially computer-based). This book is devoted to the study of **computer-based information systems** (CBIS), which will usually be referred to simply as information systems.

FORMAL AND INFORMAL INFORMATION SYSTEMS. Like any other system, an information system can be formal or informal. Formal systems include agreed upon procedures, standard inputs and outputs, and fixed definitions. Informal systems take many shapes, ranging from an office gossip network to a group of friends exchanging letters electronically. It is important to understand the existence of informal systems. They may consume information resources and sometimes interface with the formal systems. They may also play an important role in resisting and/or encouraging change.

WHAT IS A COMPUTER-BASED INFORMATION SYSTEM?

A CBIS is an information system that uses computer technology to perform some or all of its intended tasks. A CBIS may include a personal computer and software,

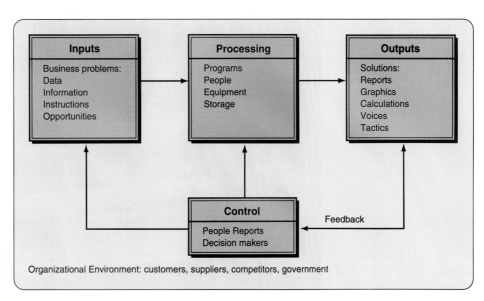

FIGURE 1.2 A schematic view of an information system.

or it may include several thousand computers of various sizes with hundreds of printers, plotters, and other devices, as well as communication networks and databases (see Box 1.1). In most cases a CBIS also includes people. The basic components of information systems are listed below. Note that not every CBIS includes all these components Figure 1.3.

A Closer Look BOX 1.1

THE DIFFERENCE BETWEEN COMPUTERS AND COMPUTER-BASED INFORMATION SYSTEMS

Computers provide effective and/or efficient ways of processing data, and they are a necessary part of a CBIS. A CBIS, however, involves much more than this. A successful application of a CBIS requires understanding of a business (and its environment) that is supported by the CBIS. For example, to build a CBIS that supports transactions executed on the New York Stock Exchange, it is necessary to understand all the procedures related to buying and selling stocks, bonds, options, and so on, including irregular demands on the system. In the New York Stock Exchange situation, CBIS enables the execution of trades on time, without interruptions.

In learning about CBIS, it is not sufficient to learn about computers. Computers are only one part of a complex system that must be designed, operated, and maintained. A public transportation system in a city provides an analogy. Buses are a necessary ingredient of the system, but more is needed. Managers of the transportation system must have knowledge of how buses are operated and maintained. To properly operate the city transportation system, however, managers must know much more. Designing the bus routes, bus stops, different schedules, and so on, requires considerable understanding of customer demand, traffic patterns, city regulations, safety requirements, and the like. Computers, like buses, are only one component in a complex system. The purpose of this book is to acquaint you with computers as well as all other aspects of a CBIS.

▼ *Hardware.* Hardware is a set of devices that accepts data and information, processes them, and displays them.

▼ *Software.* Software is a set of programs that enables the hardware to process data.

FIGURE 1.3 The components of a computer-based information system.

▼ *Database.* A database is a collection of related files, tables, relations, and so on, that stores data and associations among them.

▼ *Network.* A network is a connecting system that permits the sharing of resources by different computers.

▼ *Procedures.* Procedures are the set of instructions about how to combine the previous components in order to process information and generate the desired ouput.

▼ *People.* The people are those individuals that work with the system or use its output. This component is the most intelligent part of the system. In addition, all systems have a purpose and a social context.

▼ *Purpose.* Like any other system, a CBIS has a purpose. A most common purpose is to provide a solution to a business problem. In the 7-Eleven case, the computer helps management increase sales. As explained earlier, CBISs are helpful in enhancing the nine critical response activities such as improving productivity, quality, and competitiveness.

▼ *Social Context.* The *social context of the system,* which involves an understanding of the values and beliefs that determine what is admissible and possible within the culture of the people and groups involved.

WHAT IS INFORMATION TECHNOLOGY?

Information technology (IT), in its narrow definition, refers to the technological side of an information system. It includes hardware, databases, software networks, and other devices. As such, it can be viewed as a subsystem of an information system. Sometimes, the term IT is also used interchangeably with information system, or it may even be used as a broader concept that describes a collection of several information systems, users, and management for an entire organization. In this book, the term IT is used in this broadest sense.

▶ 1.4 INFORMATION SYSTEMS AT WORK WORLDWIDE

Thousands of different information systems are in use throughout the world. The following examples are intended to show the diversity of applications and the benefits provided. At the end of each example, we list the critical response activities supported by the system.

CRIME FIGHTING INFORMATION TECHNOLOGY

EMERGING TECHNOLOGY
...national crime-fighting database

The national Crime Information Center (CIC) in the United States contains a crime-related database operated by the FBI. Every law enforcement agency in the country files all its outstanding arrest warrants on this system. A highway patrol officer can call in a name or driver's license number to find out if a person is wanted, or the officer can use the vehicle ID number to find out if a car is stolen. Some police cars are equipped with devices that read fingerprints and/or take pictures of suspects, transmit them to CIC, and obtain identifications in a matter of seconds.

In February 1993, the system helped the New York police arrest two suspects in the Valentine's Day murder of six people. The suspects used the nicknames Tato and Ding Ding. The police matched the nicknames with the actual names in the database and quickly arrested the suspects. When crime is considered a critical national issue, information systems are certainly an important crime-fighting technique.

Critical response activities supported: customer service, access to information, productivity.

TRACKING UPS PACKAGES WITH PEN COMPUTERS

EMERGING TECHNOLOGY

...the pen computer

More than 65,000 UPS drivers are using hand-held pen computers to improve the accuracy of package delivery records and increase record-keeping efficiency by eliminating paperwork. Each computer has a keypad, infrared bar code scanner, small liquid-crystal display screen, and electronic signature pad for capturing customer signatures. When delivering a package, the driver inputs delivery information via the keypad to the computer. Data is loaded into a PC and forwarded to UPS headquarters (see Figure 1.4). Customers are equipped with software that allows them to electronically access UPS's corporate database and find the status of their packages. Alternatively, the customer can call a UPS customer representative, who will access the database and provide a reply to the customer within a few seconds.

Success response activities supported: customer service, competitive advantage, quality, productivity, access to information.

MERCY HOSPITAL PROVIDES PATIENT-FOCUSED CARE

REENGINEERING

...health care

Health care costs, as well as health care quality, were ranked as the number one concern of people in the United States in 1994. As a result, some hospitals were restructuring their operations and renovating facilities to provide patient-focused care and contain costs. In the patient-focused model, a team of multidisciplinary care givers provides about 80 percent of what patients need. San Diego's Mercy Hospital placed bedside computer terminals in all patients' rooms, allowing the nurses to communicate with doctors, specialists, medical records, laboratories, and so on. Orders for tests, special diets, and medications are all entered from the patient's room. Also, information about the patient, such as nearest relative, can be found in seconds directly from the patient's room. There are no more busy telephone lines, unavailable data, or errors in information. Health team members

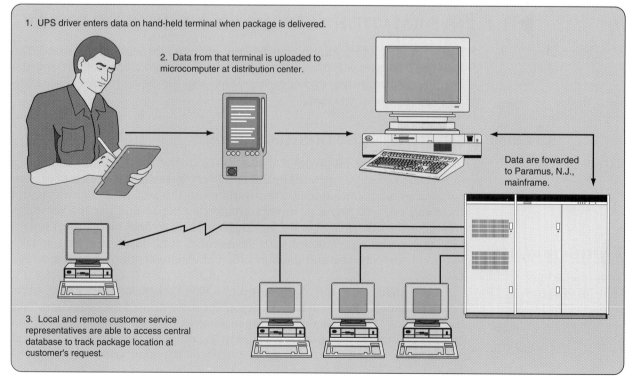

FIGURE 1.4 UPS electronic package tracking system. (SOURCE: Courtesy of United Parcel Service Inc., Atlanta, GA.)

do not have to run to use the computer at the nursing station any more. It is anticipated that this system will reduce operating costs by 10 percent and increase quality of care. Patients, employees, and doctors have expressed enthusiasm for the system, and surveys indicated a 5 to 13 percent improvement in patients' satisfaction. (SOURCE: Condensed from Borzo, G., "Patient-Focused Hospitals Begin Reporting Good Results," *Health Care Strategic Management*, August 1992, pp. 17–22.)

Critical response activities supported: productivity, quality, customer service, company strategy.

WAUBONSEE COMMUNITY COLLEGE: A NEW WAY TO LEARN

*E*MERGING TECHNOLOGY

...the electronic college

Students at Waubonsee Community College (Sugar Grove, IL) are now able to obtain quality education at reduced cost and increased convenience. They do not have to set foot on the prairie campus either to register or take classes. Courses are broadcast via microwave technology from the main campus to high schools near the students' homes. Videotaped courses are also available. Students can submit their assignments directly to professors using electronic mail. The college runs on a sophisticated network of PCs with video monitors displaying important information. A voice response system helps the students check their grades or registration status from a touch-tone phone. The objective of the college is to become more student-centered by providing timely information to students conveniently and by enabling the students to study at home. (SOURCE: Condensed from *IN—The Magazine for the Information Age*, Winter 1991.)

Critical response activities supported: customer service, reengineering.

THE 1990 GOODWILL GAMES: AN INFORMATION SYSTEM FOR TWO WEEKS

The 1990 Seattle Goodwill Games were an international sports competition, one-fourth the size of the Olympics. To manage the event, a computerized system was specially installed which included several applications. A PC-based system scheduled transportation for 10,000 people from 52 countries; a minicomputer security program took care of all planning and scheduling of security; and a mainframe-based system helped in securing accreditation for 2,600 athletes, 1,500 newspeople, and hundreds of coaches and staff support personnel. A special job order program for scheduling the 12,000 volunteers was run on a PC, as was an inventory control system for thousands of items. The organizers also used Apple computers for desktop publishing of newsletters and announcements. Several other applications were used to support the games. "Without computers, this place would have been dead," commented the organizers. To do all the work manually would have required millions of additional dollars, and delays and mistakes would have been daily occurrences. The total effort included 300 PCs, an IBM mainframe, IBM minicomputers, and miles of networks. Seven hundred IS volunteers helped build this system, which was in operation for only two weeks. (SOURCE: Based on a story in *ComputerWorld*, July 16, 1990, pp. 31.)

Critical response activities supported: productivity, quality.

COMPUTERIZED TOTAL QUALITY MANAGEMENT AT FLORIDA POWER AND LIGHT

Florida Power and Light (FPL) is the fourth largest U.S. utility company and has one of the best information systems in the industry. It is also a leader in implementing *total quality management*. It was awarded the prestigious Deming Prize,

Japan's highest award for quality. FPL's IT includes many interesting applications. One is the Generation Equipment Management Systems (GEMS), which tracks generators at 13 oil-fired power plants. When a generator goes down, GEMS diagnoses the problem and recommends a remedy. Once the remedy is approved, GEMS automatically budgets the repair, orders the parts, and issues work orders. GEMS also predicts mechanical breakdowns so preventive maintenance decisions can be made. This cuts downtime from 14 to 8 percent, saving about $5 million per year and also increasing customer satisfaction. FPL has implemented over 20 different quality-control applications. These programs reduced customer complaints by over 50 percent and assisted the company in improving its financial position. Another application that led to increased customer satisfaction is the Trouble Call Management System. It collects complaints from blacked-out customers and analyzes the causes of the malfunction. This analysis has helped to reduce the average black-out time from 70 to 48 minutes. Recognized all over the world for its computerized quality control programs, FPL created a subsidiary, Qualtec Inc., that sells quality control software to other companies, including non-utilities. (SOURCE: Based on information provided by FPL, Miami, FL.)

Critical response factors supported: quality, corporate strategy, decision making, customer service, productivity.

SHARING INFORMATION, TELECOMMUTING, AND SYSTEMS' INTEGRATION PROVIDE HIGH PROFIT

Triange House (Burnemouth, United Kingdom) installed a computerized network and PC applications only to see its productivity declining. A software and services provider, the company is facing a fierce competition. This relatively small company ($15 million annual sales) was on the brink of bankruptcy.

...with on-line information

The solution was found in a radical reengineering of the company supported by Lotus Notes (see Chapter 14). Notes enabled a major cultural change; people are now working together and sharing information. For example, even salaries and expense account information are available to every employee. Half of the company's employees telecommute. Notes is integrated with existing applications and it is used throughout the company. With a mere investment of $30,000 in 1991, net profits quadrupled within two years, resulting in a ROI of 1,666%. (Based on a story in IDC special Report, *Lotus Notes: Agent of Change*, IDS, Framingham MA, 1994).

Critical response activities supported: Productivity, reorganize and reengineer, access information.

▶ 1.5 BUSINESS ENVIRONMENT PRESSURES

To understand the role of information technology in the organization of the '90s, it is useful to review the major business environment factors that create pressures on organizations. The business environment refers to the social, legal, economic, physical, and political activities that impact business activities. Significant changes in the environment are likely to create major changes within organizations. Figure 1.5 presents a schematic view of the five major components of any organization. These components are in equilibrium as long as no significant changes occur in the system. However, as soon as there is a change in the environment, or in any of the internal components, one or more of the components is also likely to be changed significantly. Now let us consider several major environmental factors.

COMPLEX AND TURBULENT ENVIRONMENTS. The environments that surround organizations are increasingly becoming more complex and turbulent. Advancements in communication, transportation, and technology create many changes. Other changes are the result of political or economic activities. Consequently,

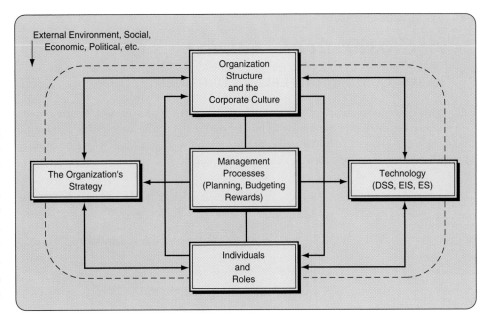

FIGURE 1.5 Framework for organizational and societal impacts of information technology.
(SOURCE: M. Scott Morton, "DSS Revisited for the 1990s," paper presented at *DSS 1986*, Washington, DC, April 1986. Used with permission. Also see Scott-Morton, 1991, p. 20.)

organizations must take actions aimed to improve (or protect) their operations in such volatile environments. These actions may include better scanning of the environment, improved forecasting, flexible and adaptable planning, reengineering of business processes, building business alliances, and quantitative and creative decision making. Organizations also restructure themselves (e.g., become "flatter"). Information technology can be viewed as an *enabler* or supporter of such actions. For example, companies are using so-called executive information systems, which provide them with daily, or even hourly, summaries of sales. Any irregular levels of sales are detected immediately and corrective actions can be taken before it is too late.

STRONG COMPETITION AND A GLOBAL ECONOMY. Pressures from international agencies, deregulation, improved technologies, and increased global communication have increased the level of competition worldwide. An example is the political changes in Eastern Europe, which created a large supply of skilled labor at a cost of $1 to $4 per hour. Inexpensive labor is also available in many countries of South America and Asia (see Box 1.2). In comparison, hourly labor cost in some developed countries ranges from $15 to $25. Companies in developed countries are usually paying high fringe benefits and environmental protection costs. Thus, they have difficulty competing in labor-intensive industries.

Global competition is especially intensified when governments become involved through the use of subsidies, tax policies, and import/export regulations and incentives. The competition is centered not only on prices, but also on quality, service level, and speed of delivery. Therefore, competition, which was previously confined within an industry or a region, is now becoming international.

GLOBAL PERSPECTIVE

...international competition increases use of IT

Rapid and inexpensive communication and transportation increases the magnitude of international trade even further. The nature of the competition is also changing. Competition used to be based on price, quality, and service (after the sale). Now companies compete also on rapid delivery times, and customizing products and services to the customers. Information technology can help companies compete globally (e.g., see the opening case of Chapter 3) and take advantage of globalization. For example, in Box 1.3 we show how a California company is using Russian experts who reside in Moscow. The use of IT to improve productivity, quality, and profitability is the best approach to deal with many of the problems and opportunities of globalization.

A Closer Look   BOX 1.2

LABOR COSTS IN DIFFERENT COUNTRIES

Labor costs differ from one country to another, as shown in the figure below. While the hourly industrial rate (excluding benefits) is over $10 in Western countries, it is only $1 to $2 in many developing countries, including countries in Asia, South America, Eastern Europe, and Africa. The lowest labor cost for industrial employees can be found in China, where the hourly wage rate is 50 cents to $1.00.

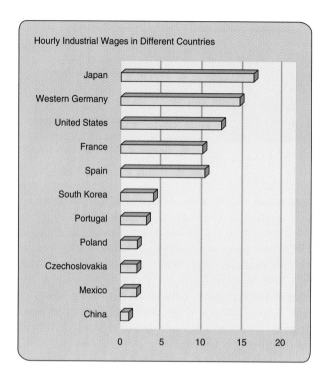

Hourly Industrial Wages in Different Countries

SOURCE: Based on data published by the Institute for the German Economy, 1994.

IT At Work   BOX 1.3

RUSSIANS LIVE IN MOSCOW AND WORK IN CALIFORNIA

Sixty highly computer skilled Russians (some with Ph.D. degrees) live in Moscow but commute electronically to a small software company (Pick Systems) in Irvine, California. The employees work on advanced software projects. Richard Pick, President of Pick Systems, has been using Russian scientists since 1990. The company revealed its Russian venture only in 1994, keeping it secret from its competitors for four years. The communication is done through the Internet global computer network. To exercise management controls, the company is using mirrored systems; what the Russians are doing in Moscow is mirrored in the systems in California.

The Russians are paid low salaries, because there is a huge pool of skilled employees who were laid off from space and military programs after the collapse of the Soviet Union.

Using the Internet and commuting electronically (telecommuting) are described in Chapter 14.

Critical Thinking Issues: What is the advantage of living in Moscow and working in California? Why did the company keep this arrangement a secret? ▲

Table 1.1 Major Areas of Social Responsibility

- **Environmental control** (pollution, noise, trash removal, parks, vegetation, and animals)
- **Equal opportunity** (minorities, women, elderly, physically handicapped, and homosexuals)
- **Employment and housing** (the aged, poor, teenagers, and unskilled)
- **Health, safety, and social benefits to employees** (the role of employer vs. that of the government)
- **Employee education, training, and retraining**
- **External relationships** (community development, political, and other interfaces)
- **Marketing practices** (unfair marketing practices)
- **Privacy and ethics**

SOCIAL RESPONSIBILITY. The interfaces between organizations and society are increasing and changing rapidly. Issues range from the state of the physical environment to the spread of AIDS. Corporations are becoming more aware of these interfaces and are willing to contribute toward improvements. Such a contribution is known as **social responsibility** (see Table 1.1).

Information technology can support many socially responsible activities. Examples include Xerox Corporation of Los Angeles CA, which uses a decision support system to monitor equal opportunity programs, and the U.S. Bureau of Mines, which uses an expert system to improve dust control in U.S. mines. Details of the use of IT to support handicapped at the workplace are provided in Chapter 20.

ETHICAL ISSUES. The use of information technology raised many ethical issues ranging from surveillance of electronic mail to potential invasion of privacy of millions of customers whose data are stored in private and public databases (see Chapter 20). Organizations must deal with ethical issues of their employees, customers, and suppliers. Ethical issues differ from legal issues. Since IT is new and rapidly changing, there is little experience or agreement on how to deal with its ethical issues. Also, as we will show, what is ethical in one country may be unethical in another. Ethical issues are very important since they can damage the image of an organization as well as destroy the morale of the employees.

CHANGING NATURE OF THE WORKFORCE. The workforce is becoming diversified and is changing rapidly. There is an increasing number of female, single parents, minorities, and handicapped persons in all types of positions. Also, many employees continue to work more years than ever before. Information technology is helping the integration of some of these employees into the workforce (e.g., see discussion of telecommuting in Chapter 14, and support to the disabled in Chapter 20).

CONSUMER SOPHISTICATION AND EXPECTATION. The consumer is continuously becoming more knowledgeable about the availability and quality of products and services. This results in a demand for better and customized products and services. For example, buyers of PCs want a computer that includes the options they like. In Japan, for example, a large department store offers refrigerators in 24 different colors with a delivery time of less than two weeks (see Stalk and Weber [1993]).

Consumers also are demanding more detailed information about products and services. They want to know what warranties they receive, what financing is available, and so on, and they want the information quickly. Many companies are starting to treat the customer as a king (see Figure 1.6). Companies need to be able to access information quickly to satisfy the customers.

FIGURE 1.6 The customer is king

TECHNOLOGICAL INNOVATIONS. Technology is playing an increased role in manufacturing and services. New and improved technologies create substitutions for products, alternative service options, and increased quality. Thus, technology accelerates the competitive forces. What is the state of the art today may be obsolete tomorrow. There are many technologies that impact business in areas ranging from genetic engineering to food processing. However, the area that could have the largest overall impact is that of information technologies.

▶ 1.6 ORGANIZATIONS AND MANAGEMENT CHANGES

Changes in the business environment and in technology induce organizations to change the manner in which they operate. It has long been recognized that there are strong relationships among the environment, technology, organizational structure, people in the organization, organizational strategy, and management processes. As discussed earlier, and as was shown in Figure 1.5, significant changes in the environment are likely to change the equilibrium in internal parts of organizations. There is already evidence of some of these changes in many organizations. Changes in one company may impact other companies, creating more business pressures. The major factors that contribute to the pressures are as follows.

BUSINESS ALLIANCES. Many companies realize that alliances with other companies, even competitors, can be very beneficial. There are several types of alliances: sharing resources, establishing permanent supplier-company relationship (as in the case of 7-Eleven), and creating joint research efforts (such as the Micro Electronic Corporation, a joint venture of about 30 large high-technology companies in the United States). One of the most interesting types is the temporary joint venture or strategic alliance, where companies form a special company for a specific, limited-time, mission (see Box 1.4). Such an arrangement is called a **virtual corporation** and, according to Byrne et al. (1993), this could be a typical business organization in the future. More details of virtual corporations and how they are supported by IT are provided in Chapter 17.

A more permanent type of business alliance that links manufacturers, suppliers, and finance corporations is known as *keiretsu* (a Japanese term). This kind of alliance can be heavily supported by information technologies ranging from electronic data interchange to electronic transmission of maps and drawings.

IT At Work BOX 1.4

GLOBAL PERSPECTIVE

IT ENHANCES AN INTERNATIONAL VIRTUAL CORPORATION

An international virtual corporation was established in 1994 in Southeast Asia to set up a satellite-based mobile (wireless) telephone communication system in the region. The one billion dollar project will serve one million subscribers in China, India, Japan, Singapore, Thailand, Malaysia, and other neighboring countries. The international consortium includes companies from the various Asian countries as well as Hughes Communication of the United States. The project is the first of its kind in Asia, and it is scheduled for completion in 1998. The project is expected to increase the competitive edge of the region.

While the project itself is based on IT (telecommunication via satellites), other information technologies will support the project. Due to the different locations of the participating members and vendors, there will be a need to facilitate communication using technologies such as computerized fax, E-mail, and computer conferencing.

Critical Thinking Issues: Why is the idea of a virtual corporation appealing? What role does IT play in supporting the concept? ▲

SOURCE: Based on a story in *The Straits Times*, August 6, 1994.

DECREASED BUDGETS OF PUBLIC ORGANIZATIONS

The U.S. budget deficit sky rocketed in the late '80s and early '90s. At the same time, the U.S. economy entered an economic recession. As a result, there was less funding available from federal, state, and municipal sources. The budget crunch forced organizations to streamline their operations and/or *downsize* them. For example, public universities were forced to reduce course offering. Information technology has become extremely important since it helps to cope with such changes. For example, intelligent computer-aided instruction allows increase in class sizes by over 50 percent without reduction in quality.

BUSINESS PROCESSES REENGINEERING

Business processes reengineering (BPR) refers to a major innovation—a quantum leap of change—in the manner in which organizations conduct their business. Such changes may be needed for increased profitability or mere survival. Business process reengineering involves changes in structure and in processes. The entire technological, human, and organizational dimensions may be changed in BPR (see Hammer and Champy [1993]). Over 70 percent of large U.S. companies claim to be reengineering (*Computerworld*, May 15, 1993, p. 102). As part of BPR, there are management realignments (see Drucker [1988]), mergers, consolidations, operational integrations, and reoriented distribution practices.

IT, as will be shown in Chapters 3, 4, and 17, plays a major role as an enabler of BPR. IT provides automation; allows business to be conducted in different locations; provides flexibility in manufacturing; permits quicker delivery to customers; and supports rapid and paperless transactions among suppliers, manufacturers, and retailers. In brief, it allows an efficient and effective change in the manner in which work is performed.

IMPROVEMENT PROGRAMS: TQM, JIT, AND OTHERS

BPR is a major undertaking. It is frequently compared to surgery, and, like surgery, BPR may be risky. In medicine, there are alternatives and supplements to surgery, such as treating patients with drugs. These alternatives are less costly, take longer time, or have to be taken constantly. Similarly, there are several *continuous improvement programs* that can substitute for or supplement BPR. Two such programs are just-in-time (JIT) and total quality management (TQM).

JUST-IN-TIME. The **just-in-time** (JIT) approach is a comprehensive production scheduling and inventory control system that attempts to reduce costs and improve work flow by scheduling materials and parts to arrive at a work station exactly at the time when they are needed. Such a system minimizes inventories and saves space. It is comprehensive because it includes several other activities such as minimizing waste (see Chapter 17 for details). While just-in-time systems can be managed manually, IT helps the implementation of large and complex JIT systems.

TOTAL QUALITY MANAGEMENT. **Total quality management** (TQM) is an organization-wide commitment to continuous work improvement and meeting customers' needs. It is an organized effort to improve quality wherever and whenever possible. Information technology can enhance TQM by improving data monitoring, collection, summarization, analysis, and reporting. Information technology can also increase the speed of inspection and the quality of testing, and reduce the cost of performing various quality control activities. This topic is developed further in Chapters 4 and 17.

TIME-TO-MARKET. Reducing the time from the inception of an idea until its implementation—**time-to-market**—is an important objective for many organizations because they can be first on the market with a product or they can provide customers with a service or product faster than their competitors do. Information technology can be used to expedite the various steps in the process of product or service development, testing, and implementation. For example, using computer-aided design (CAD) computerized technology, Kodak Corporation was able to win the race to develop the disposable (one time) camera against the Japanese. For other examples, see Box 1.5.

EMERGING TECHNOLOGY
...CAD expedites time to market

EMPOWERMENT OF EMPLOYEES AND COLLABORATIVE WORK. Giving employees the authority to act and make decisions on their own is a strategy used by many organizations as part of their BPR or TQM. **Empowerment** is related to the concept of self-directed teams (see Orsburn et al. [1990], and Shonk [1992]). Management delegates authority to teams who can execute the work faster and with fewer delays. IT enables the decentralization of decision making and authority with a centralized control. It also enables employees to access information they need for making quick decisions. Expert systems, for example, can give experts' advice to team members whenever human experts are not available. In addition, computer networks allow team members to effectively communicate with each other as well as to communicate with other teams. Collaborative work is a very important ingredient in a team-based organization, and it is heavily supported by IT, as will be illustrated in Chapter 14.

CUSTOMER-FOCUSED APPROACH. The 7-Eleven, Mercy Hospital, and other cases demonstrate that companies are becoming more **customer oriented**. They are beginning to pay more attention to customers and their preferences. Companies must reengineer themselves to meet consumer demand. For example, attending to customers' desires can be done by changing manufacturing processes from mass production to **mass customization** (see Pine, [1993]). In mass customization, a company produces large volume. But, in contrast with mass production where all the items are identical, in mass customization, items are made to fit the desires of each customer. Information technology is a major enabler of mass customization (Chapter 17) and other customer-focused approaches.

IT At Work BOX 1.5

IT SPEEDS TIME-TO-MARKET OF NEW DRUGS

THE PROBLEM. The Federal Drug Administration (FDA) must be extremely careful in approving new drugs. At the same time, there is public pressure on the FDA to approve new drugs quickly, especially for cancer and AIDS. The problem is that in order to assure quality, the FDA requires companies to conduct extensive research and clinical testing. The development program of such research and testing, which must be approved by the FDA, covers from 300,000 to 500,000 pages of documentation for each drug. The subsequent results and analysis are reported on 100,000 to 200,000 additional pages. These pages are reviewed by the FDA prior to approval of new drugs. Manual processing of this information significantly delays the work of the FDA, so the total process takes 6 to 10 years.

THE SOLUTION. COMPUTER-AIDED DRUG APPLICATION SYSTEMS (from Research Data Corporation of New Jersey) is a software program that uses a network-distributed document processing system. The pharmaceutical company scans all its related documents into a database. The documents are indexed, and a full text search and retrieval software are attached to the system. Using key words, a user can search the database quickly. The database is also accessible by the FDA employees from their offices, who no longer have to spend hours looking for a specific piece of data (it takes only six to eight seconds to access an image in the database; see screen below). Any viewed information can be processed

or printed at the user's desktop. The system helps not only the FDA, but also the companies' researchers, who have the required information at their fingertips. Remote users can access the system with a computer and a modem. The overall results: reducing the time-to-market of a new drug by up to one year (each week may be translated to $1,000,000 profit and save the lives of many people). The system also reduces the time it takes to patent a new drug.

Critical Thinking Issue: How can IT reduce time-to-market? ▲

SOURCE: Condensed from *IMC Journal* May/June 1993, pp. 23–25.

A screen showing patient information.

IMPROVED PRODUCTIVITY. It is sometimes necessary to completely change the manner in which work is performed by using BPR to significantly improve productivity. Incremental productivity improvement programs have existed for almost a century in the United States, but their improvement magnitude is usually less than 50 percent. Using IT, productivity may increase by several hundred percent even without the need to use BPR. For example, expert systems have reduced complex equipment diagnosis time from 30 minutes to just a few seconds.

▶ 1.7 TRENDS IN INFORMATION TECHNOLOGY

Information Technology contributes to the business pressures on organizations. But it also helps in enhancing organizational response. Therefore, it is important to know the major trends in IT. Imagine this scenario:

It's a Monday morning in the year 2000. Executive Joanne Smith gets into her car, and her voice activates a remote telecommunications access workstation. She requests that all voice and mail messages, open and pending, as well as her schedule for the day be transmitted to her. The office workstation consolidates these items from home and office databases. The "message ordering knowbot" (Knowledge Robot), a computer program Joanne developed, delivers the accumulated messages (in the order she prefers) to the voice-data portable computer in her car. By the time Joanne gets to the office, she has read the necessary messages, sent some replies, revised her day's schedule, and completed a "to-do" list for the week, all of which have been filed in her "virtual database" by her "personal organizer knowbot."

EMERGING TECHNOLOGY

...IT in the not-too-distant future

The "virtual database" has made Joanne's use of IT much easier. No longer does she have to be concerned about the physical location of data. She is working on a large proposal for the Acme Corporation today; and although segments of the Acme file physically exist on several databases, she can access the data from her wireless workstation, wherever she happens to be. To help manage this information resource, Joanne uses an information visualizer that enables her to create and manage dynamic relationships among data collections. This information visualizer has extended the graphical user interface of the early 1990s to a three-dimensional graphic structure. (SOURCE: Benjamin and Blunt [1992], p. 7.)

Hopefully Joanne could do even more work if her car were able to drive itself. While this kind of a car is still in an experimental stage (see Chapter 16), it certainly will be on the road in the twenty-first century.

This "year 2000" scenario is becoming a reality even prior to 2000, owing to important trends in information technology, which are summarized in Table 1.2. These trends are discussed and explained in detail throughout the book.

COST-PERFORMANCE: IMPROVEMENT BY A FACTOR OF AT LEAST 100

In about 10 years, a computer will cost the same as it costs today but will be about 50 times more powerful (in terms of processing speed, memory, and so on). At the same time labor costs could double, so the cost-performance of computers vs. manual work will improve by a factor of 100. This means that computers will have increasingly greater comparative advantages over people. As time passes, more and more tasks will be economically done by a computer rather than by a human.

INFORMATION SUPERHIGHWAYS

EMERGING TECHNOLOGY

...traveling on information superhighways

The U.S. government strongly supports the development of fiber optic national networks, which are called **information superhighways** (or "infobahns"). Communication networks—information highways—are as important to the Information Revolution as canals, bridges, and railroads were to the Industrial Rev-

Table 1.2 **Major Technological Trends**

- The cost-performance advantage of computers over manual labor is increasing.
- Information highways will be available with fiber optics providing large capacities.
- Networked computers and client/server architecture will be the predominant architecture.
- Graphical and other user-friendly interfaces dominate PCs.
- Capacities of storage will increase significantly.
- Multimedia use will increase significantly.
- Emerging computer technologies, especially artificial neural computing and expert systems, will increase in importance.
- Object-oriented programming will be widely accepted.
- Compactness and portability of computers will continue.
- Distributed databases will be an integral part of a corporate-wide client/server computing environment.

olution more than a century ago. Computer networks are facilitating new kinds of markets and new ways to manage organizations all over the world (see Box 1.6).

A Closer Look BOX 1.6

GLOBAL PERSPECTIVE

AN INTELLIGENT COUNTRY

In Singapore, information technology is a top national priority. This country of three million people is preparing itself to be, by the year 2000, the first country with an advanced nationwide information infrastructure, which will connect virtually every home, office, school, and factory. The computer will evolve into an information appliance, combining the functions of the telephone, TV, computers, and more. A nationwide network will provide a wide range of communication means and access to services. Singaporeans will be able to tap into vast reservoirs of electronically stored information and knowledge to improve their businesses and quality of life. Text, sound, pictures, videos, documents, designs, and other forms of media will be transferred and shared through the high capacity of the national fiber optic telecommunication system working in tandem with a pervasive wireless network. A wide range of new infrastructural services—linking government, businesses, and people—will be created to take advantage of new telecommunications. The plan, which has been in implementation for several years as a joint government–industry project, is based on five strategic thrusts:

1. Developing Singapore as a global hub for business, services, and transportation.
2. Improving the quality of life for Singaporeans.
3. Boosting the economic engine, increasing the competitiveness of the island's industries, and decreasing unemployment.
4. Linking communities locally and globally.
5. Enhancing the capabilities of individuals.

IT enables monitoring of operations at Singapore's ports, a major hub for business.

SOURCE: Condensed from "A Vision of an Intelligent Island: The IT 2000 Report," National Computer Board of Singapore, 1992.

NETWORKED COMPUTERS AND CLIENT/SERVER ARCHITECTURE

Client/server architecture, which is the subject of Chapter 10, is predicted to dominate IT. PCs, which are viewed as "clients," are linked to specialized, powerful "servers" (e.g., databases, communication devices, mainframes, and very powerful PCs) which they share, via local or global networks. Such an architecture requires telecommunication standards that will allow interconnection of software and hardware in different computing environments.

GRAPHICAL AND OTHER USER-FRIENDLY INTERFACES WILL DOMINATE PCS

A graphical user interface (GUI) is a set of software features that provides users with direct control of visible objects (such as icons), and actions to replace complex command syntax. GUI allows a user-friendly human–machine interface environment by using icons, pull-down menus, windows, and a mouse. GUI is becoming the major interface in PCs.

The trend is to make the interface as simple as possible. One way to do this is to introduce intelligent interfaces that understand the user's wishes even when expressed in everyday language. To make it even more powerful, the user will use voice to conduct the dialogue with the computer.

STORAGE AND MEMORIES

CD-ROMs and other storage devices will increase secondary storage, thereby enabling a vast amount of information to be stored. Large memories will enable the use of multimedia and emerging computer technologies such as artificial intelligence.

MULTIMEDIA

Computers will play a major role in integrating various types of media (voice, text, graphics, full motion video, and animation) to improve education, training, and decision making.

OBJECT-ORIENTED ENVIRONMENT

An object-oriented environment is an innovative way of programming computers that is expected to significantly reduce both the cost of building and of maintaining information systems. The environment includes object-oriented programming, databases and operating systems that increase the capabilities of IT and its cost effectiveness.

EMERGING TECHNOLOGIES

The increased capabilities of computers enable the implementation of emerging technologies, such as expert systems, natural language processors, and neural computing. These technologies increase productivity and quality and support complex tasks, as well as provide support when the information flow is incomplete or "fuzzy." The emerging technologies can be used individually, but in many cases they are integrated among themselves and with other CBISs. The result is powerful intelligent systems that can support most of the critical response activities described earlier, as well as lessening business pressures.

COMPACTNESS AND PORTABILITY

While the capabilities and the benefit/cost ratio of computers are increasing, the size of computers is decreasing. Compact computers can now be attached to cars, machines, and even consumer products. Because of their small size and the light weight, computers can easily be carried on planes and trains, and in automobiles. The portability of computers allows employees in the field to enter data, thus reducing the time between collection and processing of data.

▶ 1.8 LEARNING ABOUT INFORMATION TECHNOLOGY

This opening chapter introduces the field of information technology. Several examples of organizational use of information technology, nationally and internationally, demonstrate the importance of the field. This section is divided into two parts. First, examples of some unsuccessful systems are presented. Second, employment opportunities in the field are outlined. Finally, managerial issues and concerns are highlighted.

UNSUCCESSFUL SYSTEMS

Information systems may turn out to be unsuccessful, resulting in high cost and layoffs of employees (see Box 1.7). It is essential, therefore, for managers to know about the potential risks and threats associated with information technology so that they can avoid making poor decisions. The box is self-explanatory.

IT At Work BOX 1.7

EXAMPLES OF UNSUCCESSFUL INFORMATION SYSTEMS

BANK OF AMERICA. In 1988, after spending almost a year and $60 million, Bank of America abandoned a computerized system that was supposed to be the "most advanced system in the industry." The system, intended to support the institutional trust division, was unable to produce account statements and crashed frequently, due to its poor design. The bank was forced to abandon the system and subcontract the processing of the data. As a result, the bank lost many customers and substantial layoffs occurred. (SOURCE: California news broadcast.)

LOCKHEED GEORGIA. Lockheed Georgia was one of the first companies to install an information system specifically designed for executives. This executive information system was used extensively for several years. Unfortunately, the system, which was intended to automatically monitor items critical to corporate success, was not designed properly and failed to monitor one critical item. As a result, the company sustained a large loss, estimated at up to $300 million. (SOURCE: Condensed from *PC Week*, January 29 and February 5, 1990.)

CITICORP. Citicorp spends about $1.5 billion each year on computer systems. However, not all systems work as planned. For example, a system that was supposed to sell information on what customers buy at grocery stores was not abandoned after the bank invested over $200 million in the project. A computerized mortgage approval system that was supposed to evaluate a loan request in 15 minutes failed completely. A computerized home banking system was not working either. (SOURCE: Condensed from *Forbes*, June 7, 1993, pp. 110–111.)

THE UNITED STATES SENATE. The U.S. Senate ordered a computer system in 1984 for an initial estimated cost of $12 million. The cost ballooned to about $50 million by 1988 when the system was completed. The cost overrun resulted, in part, from the negligence of the lawmakers to include in the initial estimate a budget for training and maintenance. There was little accountability for what IT senators were purchasing, so there was little planning and budgeting. Despite its huge cost, the system was inferior to the U.S. House system in many respects. The system was so poor that it was unable even to handle the mailing demands of some senators. As a result, several offices returned to their old typewriters. (SOURCE: Based on *Rocky Mountain News*, June 19, 1988.)

THE STATE OF CALIFORNIA SYSTEMS. California's tax computerized accounting system incurred a 75 percent cost overrun ($5.4 million), and its completion was delayed for two years. The problems in the tax system were caused by poor IS planning. These figures are even larger than the 66 percent cost overrun and one-and-a-half year delay, which the state of California experienced on its average IS applications in the late '80s. (SOURCE: Based on *Computerworld*, March 27, 1989, p. 64.)

The Department of Motor Vehicles (DMV) was even more unfortunate. After six years and $44 million, the department abandoned a project to convert the state's 28-year-old DMV database. The agency adopted untested technology that was unable to deal with one million transactions per day. There are 38 million cars in the database and 31 million drivers. (SOURCE: Based on *InformationWeek*, June 13, 1994, p. 72.)

Critical Thinking Issue: If millions of dollars can be lost in unsuccessful systems, how can one guarantee that information systems will be successful? ▲

EMPLOYMENT OPPORTUNITIES IN INFORMATION TECHNOLOGY

Addressing the issues listed in the previous sections requires considerable knowledge about IT. Being knowledgeable about the technology may also increase employment opportunities for graduating students. Even though computerization eliminates some jobs, it also creates many more jobs. For example, it is estimated that the telemarketing industry alone will employ eight million people by the year 2000. Many telemarketing employees will be working with computers (see Box 1.8).

IT At Work BOX 1.8

*R*EENGINEERING

SEARS CATALOG IS REPLACED BY A COMPUTER SYSTEM

The Sears catalog was an "institution" in American society for almost a century. However, in 1993, the Sears catalog business was discontinued as part of the corporate reengineering effort. A major factor in the decision was the introduction of Prodigy. Sears is a partner with IBM in the Prodigy System, a telemarketing mechanism that is based on the PC and a modem instead of a TV and telephone. It allows the user to shop from home by viewing, on their home PCs, catalogs of leading stores such as Sears, JCPenney (see figure below), and K-Mart. Shopping is only one capability available. Users can also create their own travel itinerary, make airline reservations (with 350 airlines), reserve hotel rooms, rent cars, and even charter airplanes.

Critical Thinking Issue: Why is home shopping via computer replacing paper catalogues? Does computer shopping have any advantages over shopping via a TV? ▲

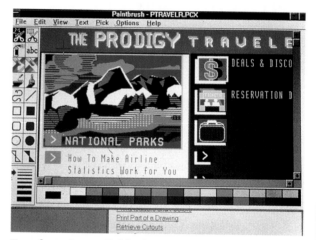

Travel service available through Prodigy.

The demand for the more traditional information technology staff—such as programmers, systems analysts, and designers—is substantial. In addition, many new opportunities are appearing in emerging areas such as client/server, object-oriented programming, telecommunications, artificial intelligence, and multimedia. The U.S. Department of Labor projected that among the 12 fastest expanding employment areas, four will be IT related. They will account for about 50 percent of all additional jobs in these 12 areas by the year 2000. To exploit the well-paid opportunities in IT, one may wish to obtain a college degree in computer science, management information systems (MIS), or a combination of the two. Several schools offer graduate degrees with specialization in information technology. Non-degree programs are also available on hundreds of topics. Majoring in computer information systems (CIS) can be very rewarding. For example, students graduating with BBA degrees from the CIS program at Eastern Illinois University attain the highest starting salaries of all undergraduate business majors. Similarly, MBAs with an undergraduate degree in computer science or CIS have no difficulty getting well-paying jobs, even during recessionary times. Many students select IS as a second major or as an area of specialization.

▶ 1.9 INFORMATION TECHNOLOGY AS AN ENABLER AND THE PLAN OF THE BOOK

In Section 1.2, the reader was introduced to the role of IT as a support mechanism for the critical response activities. How is such support rendered?

The answer is that it is given in many ways, depending on the activity to be supported, on the organization that uses the technology, and on the country in which the organization operates. In addition, the nature of the support is determined by many other factors such as the industry, size of company, and people involved. In most cases, however, IT plays a secondary role of *enabler*. The primary concern is the business, its problems, and opportunities that were created by the three categories of impacting factors described earlier.

A primary purpose of this book is to show how all this is done. We developed a model, which is shown in Figure 1.7. This model has been used as a guide to the composition of this book. The model is composed of five blocks that correspond to the five parts of this book.

> **Block 1:** The core of the model is the *business*, which is surrounded by an environment. There, people perform tasks, different processes exist, transactions are executed, and managers make decisions. Problems and opportunities that are created or intensified by the impacting trends described earlier need to be addressed.

> **Block 2:** Organizations are looking for solutions to problems. Usually they employ some of the nine critical response activities. For example, they may

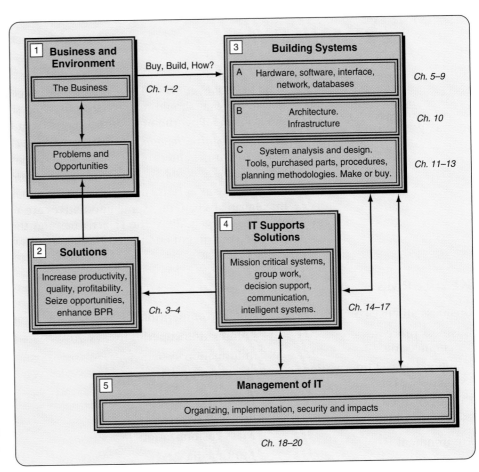

FIGURE 1.7 Information technology as an enabler—a model.

attempt to increase productivity or quality or try to reengineer the business processes.

Block 3: The solutions attempted in Block 2 can be supported by information technology. To do so, we need to build (or buy) specific information systems. In Block 3A we show the basic ingredients of IT: hardware, software, user interface, databases, and networks. In Block 3B we show the IT architecture, which is an integral part of the construction process. The system development methodologies underlying specific applications are shown in Block 3C.

Block 4: The resultant systems constructed can be used to support the day-to-day operations of a company, support communication and decision making in all functional areas of the organization, or build strategic and innovative systems. Of special interest are intelligent systems.

Block 5: The systems developed in Block 4 need to be integrated with other systems, implemented, operated, and maintained. Such systems also need to be secured, and they may have impact on organizations and society.

The specific chapters in the book are related to the blocks as follows:

Part I: Foundations—Chapters 1–4. This part corresponds to Blocks 1 and 2.

Part II: Technology—Chapters 5–9. This part corresponds to Block 3A.

Part III: Development—Chapters 10–13. This part corresponds to Blocks 3B and 3C.

Part IV: Applications—Chapters 14–17. This part corresponds to Block 4.

Part V: Information Systems Management—Chapters 18–20. This part corresponds to Block 5.

▶ MANAGERIAL ISSUES

The following are some managerial issues regarding the topics in this chapter:

1. *How to avoid failures?* The examples provided in Box 1.7 raise a simple question: What should managers do to avoid such problems? The best approach is to follow the procedures suggested in Part 3 of this book.

2. *How to recognize the opportunities for using IT?* The answer to this can be found in most chapters of the book, but especially in Chapters 3 and 11.

3. *Who is going to build, operate, and maintain the information systems?* This is a critical issue because management wants to minimize the cost of IT while maximizing its benefits. Some alternatives are subcontracting (outsourcing) of some, or even all, of the IT activities and the division of work between the MIS department and the end users. Details will be provided in Chapters 12 and 17. ■

KEY TERMS

Business alliances 5

Business processes reengineering 17

Computer-based information system (CBIS) 7

Customer-oriented (focused) 18

Empowerment 18

Environment 7

Feedback 7

Global competition 13

Information superhighways 20

Information system 7

Information technology 9

Inputs 7

Just-in-time (JIT) 18

Mass customization 18

Multimedia 22

Outputs 7

Process 17

Reengineering 17

Social responsibility 15

System(s) 30

Time-to-market 18

Total quality management (TQM) 18

Virtual corporation 16

CHAPTER HIGHLIGHTS *(L-x means learning objective number x)*

▼ An information system collects, processes, stores, and disseminates information for a specific purpose. (L-1)

▼ Information technology sometimes refers to the technology component of an information system. However, the concept is used by many to describe the collection of all information systems in an organization. (L-1)

▼ Many pressures surround the modern organization, which is responding with critical response activities. (L-2)

▼ Information technology is a major enabler of change, supporting critical response activities. (L-2)

▼ The business environment today is characterized by an accelerated rate of change, complexity, and turbulence, and a move toward a global economy. The competition faced by businesses is ever increasing. (L-3)

▼ The world is moving toward a global economy. (L-3)

▼ Corporations are increasingly involved with social responsibility. (L-3)

▼ Business alliances among organizations are spreading largely due to the support of information technology. (L-4)

▼ Organizations are adapting a customer-focused approach in order to succeed. (L-4)

▼ Organizations are reengineering their business processes in order to cope with rapid environmental changes. IT plays an important role in the BPR. (L-4)

▼ Organizations are changing their mode of operation by using IT-supported innovative approaches such as just-in-time, total quality management, and empowerment of employees. (L-4)

▼ The cost-performance advantage of information technology is increasing with time, due to increasing processing speed and storage. (L-5)

▼ Communication networks will be the core of IT in the next century. (L-5)

▼ The most important issues in IT are its use in improving productivity, quality, and competitiveness and in supporting corporate strategy and business processes reengineering. (L-6)

▼ Costs of IT mismanagement can be very high. (L-7)

▼ Employment opportunities in the IT field are rapidly increasing. (L-7)

QUESTIONS FOR REVIEW

1. Define an information system and list its major components.

2. List the nine critical response activities used by organizations.

3. What is an application program? Give a specific example with which you are familiar.

4. What are the major pressures in the business environment?

5. What is a virtual corporation?

6. What is business process reengineering?

7. What do we mean by empowerment of employees?

8. What is meant by total quality management?

9. What is time-to-market? Why is it so important?

10. Describe the concept of mass customization.

11. List the major technological areas of the future.

12. List and briefly discuss the seven categories of the M.I.T. report (see Appendix B, end of chapter).

13. List the major benefits provided by IT.

QUESTIONS FOR DISCUSSION

1. Is Japan's 7-Eleven system infringing on customers' privacy?

2. Describe how information systems can support the just-in-time approach.

3. IBM has been under attack because of its perceived poor leadership. In April 1993, the company replaced its chief executive by hiring the chief executive of RJR Nabisco (a large diversified food and tobacco company). The decision brought immediate debate. Some people felt that a company like IBM needed a technology-oriented chief. Others considered general managerial skills more important than technological experience. Discuss.

4. What are the relationships between increased social responsibility and IT?

5. It is said that IT supports business reengineering. It is also said that IT creates the need for business reengineering. Discuss.

6. Explain the relationship between empowerment of employees and total quality management.

7. Explain why the cost-performance of IT will improve by a factor of 100, while the performance is expected to improve only by a factor of 50.

8. What is the difference between programs such as JIT and TQM and BPR?

9. The MIT report (Appendix B) contains 32 premises in seven categories. Identify the premises you disagree with and state your reasons for disagreement.

10. Is IT a strategic weapon or a survival tool? Discuss.

EXERCISES

1. Review the 7-Eleven case. Identify the environmental factors that are described, as well as the innovative use of information technology.

2. Review the examples of IT applications (Section 1.3), and identify in each example the environmental and organizational factors. Prepare a table that will summarize your findings.

3. Read the findings of the M.I.T. study. Search for a real world story (or stories) in the *Wall Street Journal, Datamation, ComputerWorld* or other journals that confirms or refutes the findings of the study.

4. Review the cases of unsuccessful applications of IT (Box 1.7). Can you find a common cause of these failures?

GROUP ASSIGNMENT

Group members should review the *Wall Street Journal, Fortune, Business Week,* and local newspapers of the last three months to find stories about the use of IT as an enabler in organizations. Each group will prepare a five-page report with at least five applications. The report should emphasize the role of IT and its benefit to the organizations. Issues such as productivity, quality, time-to-market, globalization, and so on, which were discussed in this chapter, should be covered.

Minicase 1

Computers in Mid-Sized Business: A Central Vermont Ski Resort

As baby boomers began to enter their 40s and the number of teenagers shrank, business at many U.S. ski resorts declined. By 1990, the problem got worse in New England because the economy was declining. In addition, nature provided only meager snowfall for several years in a row. Many ski resorts were struggling to survive. One exception was SKI Ltd., which operates a resort in Killington, Vermont. This company stays profitable by using information systems. Here is how IT is used at SKI Ltd.

▼ Sensors track temperature and other weather data in many places around the slopes. Also, sensors collect information about the condition of all equipment (such as snow-making machines and ski lifts). This information is interpreted by computers, thereby helping staff to make quicker and better decisions. Only two people control the entire operation.

▼ The ski season has been extended about one month per year due to computerized planning and scheduling, and the ability to justify the artificial snow by attracting enough customers to the additional period.

▼ SKI Ltd. developed a computerized program that selects seats and prints tickets for the resort's stadium events.

▼ SKI Ltd. modified an existing lodging reservation system to make it more flexible and effective. A customer database of 2.5 million (growing by 200,000 names per year) includes information ranging from the level of skiing ability to skiers' preferences (services desired, times when they ski). This information allows effective advertisement and promotion of special discounts.

▼ The computer monitors the whereabouts of each of the company's 3,000 employees. When an employee arrives at any location, he or she runs a bar-coded ID card through a special device, and the information is transmitted to an IBM AS 400 minicomputer. In this way employees can be quickly located and transferred to areas that need help. This arrangement allows better utilization of personnel and better customer service. The system also tracks employees' hours and jobs for better staffing decisions and improved productivity.

▼ The company developed a customized accounting system in conjunction with a standard off-the-shelf product to create a very sophisticated financial control system. The system provides a detailed picture of each resort's revenue and costs on a *daily* basis. Comparisons with historical data are provided, as well as comparisons of actual results to budgets and plans. The information generated by the system is used at the weekly management meeting.

▼ Since the competitor resorts are also introducing computers, SKI Ltd. created a software division that sells its software products to other ski resorts.

▼ Projects under consideration include: (1) touch-screen "information booths" to be installed at various sites (including locations on the slopes), (2) an automated lodging reservation system (no operators), (3) artificial intelligence systems to assist decision making regarding snow making and staffing, and (4) issuance of "frequent skier" cards.

Questions for Minicase 1

1. Examine the key findings of the M.I.T. report. Which of the issues described in this case are directly related to the seven categories of the report? Be specific.

2. SKI Ltd.'s CEO insists that SKI Ltd. is in no danger of selling off its competitive edge by selling its software to competitors. Do you agree with this statement? Why or why not?

3. The CEO said, "The customer is like a Rubik's Cube. Figuring out and responding to his needs is a complex puzzle, and there is always some better way to solve it." How can IT be utilized to find such a better way?

4. The CEO said that his company "created a culture where people are addicted to information." What does he mean by that, and what are the benefits and drawbacks of such a culture?

5. What kind of trends in the business environment, in management and organizations, and in technology are evidenced in this case?

6. Why is the system considered to be customer-focused?

7. Relate the IT applications to the critical response activities of Section 1.2.

SOURCE: Based on Freedman, D.H. "An Unusual Way to Run a Ski Business." *Forbes ASAP*, December 7, 1992, pp. 27–30.

Minicase 2

Who Needs an Information System?

Sports for All, one of the most successful stores in Middletown, Illinois, is privately owned by Nancy Knowland. It employs 12 people with sales of about $2 million per year. Nancy's family started the sporting goods store over 60 years ago. The store grew slowly over the years, attracting customers from several communities around Middletown. The store's strategy was to provide a large variety of products at low prices. Because of low expenses in Middletown (labor, taxes, rent), the store was able to successfully compete against both K-Mart's and Wal-Mart's sporting goods departments.

Lately, however, the situation has changed. Sports for All was losing customers to Wal-Mart because Wal-Mart was importing extremely inexpensive goods from sources that were not available to Sports for All. Furthermore, several customers opted to travel as much as 150 miles to St Louis and pay high prices for special products that were customized for them by a new and fashionable sporting goods store there.

Nancy became concerned last summer when total sales showed a clear trend of decline for four consecutive quarters. Yesterday, the monthly sales data were compiled and showed the lowest monthly sales level in 10 years. Nancy called in all the key people of the store for an emergency meeting.

Nancy's son, David, an MBA student at the University of Illinois, has been bugging his mother for years to install a modern computerized information system in the store. Last summer, he purchased several computers and an accounting package and transferred most of the manual accounting transactions (billing, purchasing, inventory) to the computer. The store also handles all its correspondence on word processors. Nancy objected to further investment in computer systems, especially since profits were declining.

During the meeting, David proposed the installation of a sophisticated information system that would improve purchasing, inventory management, and customer service. "Some major manufacturers will not sell products to us because we are not on their electronic data interchange (EDI) system. We need to expedite the receipts of shipments and buy directly from manufacturers so we can be more responsive to customers. We also need to control costs and inventories," he explained.

Jim Park, who helps Nancy with finance and marketing, was not too enthusiastic. "David's proposal will cost more than $160,000, and it will not reduce our labor force by even one employee. We are just too small for these fancy machines. We will be better off applying this money toward advertisement and providing special sales to at-tract customers,'' he said.

Questions for Minicase 2

As consultants to Sports for All, complete the following:

1. Prepare a report in which you explain to management

why traditional actions such as an increase in adver-tisement may not be effective.

2. Use the trends described in this chapter and the ca-pabilities of IT to demonstrate to Nancy why she may have to use IT in order to survive.

3. What specific factors need to be considered in order to make a decision on whether or not to accept David's proposal?

REFERENCES AND SUGGESTIONS FOR FURTHER READING

1. Bradley, S.P., et al. (eds), *Globalization, Technology and Competition: The Fusion of Computers and Telecommunications in the 1990s*, Boston: Harvard Business School Press, 1993.

2. Benjamin, R.I., and J. Blunt, ''Critical IT Issues: The Next Ten Years,'' *Sloan Management Review*, Summer 1992.

3. Byrne, J.A., et al., ''The Virtual Corporation,'' *Business Week*, February 8, 1993.

4. Davidow, W., and M.S. Malone, *The Virtual Corporation*, New York: HarperCollins, 1992.

5. Davis, S., and B. Davidson, *2020 Vision*, New York: Simon & Schuster, 1991.

6. Deans, P.C., and M.J. Kane, *International Dimensions of Information Systems and Technology*, New York: PNS-Kent Publishing Co., 1992.

7. Drucker, P.E., ''The Coming of the New Organization,'' *Harvard Business Review*, January/February 1988.

8. Galbraith J.R., and E.E. Lawler III, *Organizing for the Future*, San Francisco: Jossey-Bass, 1993.

9. Hammer, M., and J. Champy, *Reengineering the Corporation*, New York: Harper Business, 1993.

10. Keen, P.G.W., *Shaping the Future*, Boston: Harvard Business School Press, 1991.

11. Martinez E.V., ''Avoiding Large-Scale Information Systems Project Failure: The Importance of the Fundamentals,'' *Project Management Journal*, June 1994.

12. MIT, *The Landmark MIT Study: Management in the 1990s*, MIT in cooperation with Arthur Young, 1989.

13. Neumann, S., *Strategic Information Systems*, New York: Macmillan, 1994.

14. Nirenberg, J., *The Living Organization*, Homewood, IL: Business One IRWIN, 1993.

15. Orsburn, J.D., et al., *Self-Directed Work Teams*, Homewood, IL: Business One IRWIN, 1990.

16. Perry, L.T., et al, *Real-time Strategy*, New York: John Wiley & Sons, 1993.

17. Pine, J.B. II, *Mass Customization*, Boston: Harvard Business School Press, 1993.

18. Quinn, J.B. *Intelligent Enterprise*, New York: The Free Press, 1992.

19. Rhinesmith, S.H., *A Managers Guide to Globalization*, Homewood, IL: Business One IRWIN, 1993.

20. *Scientific American*, September 1991. Special issue dedicated to the impact of computers on organizations and people.

21. Scott Morton, M.S. (ed.), *The Corporation of the 1990s: Information Technology and Organization Transformation*, New York: Oxford University Press, 1991.

22. Shonk, J.H., *Team-Based Organizations*, Homewood, IL: Business One IRWIN, 1992.

23. Stalk, B. Jr., and A.M. Webber, ''Japan's Dark Side of Time,'' *Harvard Business Review*, July/August 1993.

24. Stern, N., and R.A. Stern, *Computing in the Information Age*, New York: John Wiley & Sons, 1993.

25. Van Gigch, J.P., *Applied General Systems Theory*, 2nd ed., New York: Harper and Row, 1978.

26. Whiteley, R.C, *The Customer Driven Company*, Reading, MA: Addison-Wesley, 1991.

27. Zuboff, S., *In the Age of Smart Machines*, New York: Basic Books, 1988.

APPENDIX A: SYSTEMS

A **system** is a collection of elements such as people, re-sources, concepts, and procedures intended to perform an identifiable function or serve a goal. A clear definition of that function is important to the design of an information system. For instance, the purpose of an air defense system is to protect ground targets, not to just destroy attacking aircraft or missiles.

The notion of levels (or a hierarchy) of systems reflects that all systems are actually subsystems, since all are con-tained within some larger system. For example, a bank in-cludes such subsystems as: (1) the Commercial Loan De-partment, (2) the Consumer Loan Department, (3) the Savings Department, and (4) the Operations Department. The bank itself may also be a subsidiary of a holding corporation, such as Bank of America, which is a subsystem of the California banking system, which is a part of the national banking system, which is a part of the national economy, and so on. The interconnections and interactions among the subsystems are termed *interfaces*.

The Structure of a System

Systems are divided into three distinct parts: inputs, processes, and outputs. They are surrounded by an environment and frequently include a feedback mechanism. In addition, a human, the decision maker, is considered a part of the system.

▼ *Inputs* include those elements that enter the system. Examples of inputs are raw materials entering a chemical plant, patients admitted to a hospital, or data inputed into a computer.

▼ All the elements necessary to convert or transform the inputs into outputs are included in the *processes*. For example, in a chemical plant a process may include heating the materials, following operating procedures, operating the materials handling subsystem, and utilizing employees and machines. In a computer, a process may include activating commands, executing computations, and storing information.

▼ *Outputs* describe the finished products or the consequences of being in the system. For example, fertilizers are one output of a chemical plant, cured people are the output of a hospital, and reports may be the output of a computerized system.

   The connections between subsystems are the flow of information and materials between the subsystems. Of a special interest is the flow of information from the output component to a control unit (or a decision maker) concerning the system's output or performance. Based on this information, which is called *feedback*, the inputs or the processes may be modified.

▼ The *environment* of the system is composed of several elements that lie outside it, in the sense that they are not inputs, outputs, or processes. However, they have a significant impact on the system's performance and consequently on the attainment of its goals. One way to identify the elements of the environment is by answering two questions:

   1. Is the element significant to the system's goals?

   2. Is it possible for the decision maker to significantly manipulate this element?

   If, and only if, the answer to the first question is *yes*, but the answer to the second is *no*, the element should be considered part of the environment. Environmental elements can be social, technological, political, legal, physical, and economic. For example, in a decision-support system that deals with capital budgeting, some elements of the environment may be represented by the Dow-Jones database, the manufacturing system, the telecommunications network, and the personnel department.

▼ A system is separated from its environment by a *boundary*. The system is inside the boundary, whereas the environment lies outside. Boundaries may be physical (e.g., the system is a department in Building C) or nonphysical. For example, a system can be bounded by time. In such a case, we may analyze an organization for a period of only one year. When systems are studied, it is often necessary to arbitrarily define the boundaries to simplify the analysis. Such boundaries are related to the concepts of closed and open systems.

Because every system can be considered a subsystem of another, the application of system analysis may never end. Therefore it is necessary, as a matter of practicality, to confine the system analysis to defined manageable boundaries. Such confinement is termed *closing* the system. A *closed system* represents one extreme along a continuum of independence (the *open system** is at the other extreme). A closed system is totally independent, whereas an open system is very dependent on its environment (and/or other systems). The open system accepts inputs (information, energy, materials) from the environment and may deliver outputs into the environment.

When determining the impact of changes on an open system, it is important to check the environment, the related systems, and so on. In a closed system, however, it is not necessary to conduct such checks because it is assumed that the system is isolated. Traditional computer systems like transaction processing systems (TPS) are considered to be closed systems.

System Effectiveness and Efficiency

Systems are evaluated and analyzed with two major classes of performance measurement: effectiveness and efficiency. *Effectiveness* is the degree to which the right goals are achieved. It is concerned with the results or the outputs of a system. The outputs may be the total sales of a company or of a salesperson, for example. *Efficiency* is a measure of the use of inputs (or resources) to achieve results; an example of efficiency might be how much money is used to generate a certain level of sales.

   An interesting way to distinguish between the two terms was proposed by Peter Drucker, who makes the following distinction:

   Effectiveness = Doing the "right" thing

   Efficiency = Doing the "thing" right.

General Systems Theory

The term *general system theory* refers to the discipline that deals with the field of systems and their analysis, design, and improvement. It includes the concepts, methods, and knowledge pertaining to the field of systems and systems thinking. It is an interdisciplinary, holistic approach to the study of systems. For details, see Van Gigch (1978).

---

*The term *open systems* in IT has a different meaning. It refers to the ability of software to run on any hardware.

APPENDIX B: KEY FINDINGS OF THE M.I.T. REPORT ON INFORMATION TECHNOLOGY

The organizational and technological trends discussed in this chapter have been studied extensively by many organizations and research institutions. Of special interest is the Massachusetts Institute of Technology (MIT) research report (1989).

IT is restructuring companies, industries, and markets. IT has a way of "coming in from left field," and within a short time, reworking the status quo beyond recognition. Executives may be blind-sided unless they understand IT's strategic impact, actively support it, and creatively contribute to the use of IT in their firms.

The MIT report is divided into seven categories: Competing well in the 1990s, revising the product life cycle, strategy and innovation, managing human resources, enlarging the scope of business, the promise of integration, and evaluating information technology. Each category is related to information technology. The report itself prescribes actions to be taken and discusses the implications of the role of IT. The key findings regarding the seven categories are presented next.

Category 1. Competing Well in the 1990s

1. Increased competition and globalization call for rapid responses to competitors' actions and for innovative thinking. IT can leverage time and human resources.

2. New IT will be the source of strength to some companies and a source of costly mismanagement to others.

3. Well managed companies will do even better with IT. Poorly managed companies will do worse.

4. Refusing the IT revolution may leave companies behind their competitors.

5. Sustained commitment to IT is necessary for success, especially for complex systems such as computer-integrated manufacturing (CIM) (see Chapter 17).

6. Alignment of strategy, business structure, and IT need to be managed together for success.

7. CIM, in tandem with restructured product development, will decrease the time-to-market, which is a critical success factor* for many companies.

8. Shorter time-to-market is essential and can be achieved by sharing data efficiently among the participants via integrated information and telecommunication systems.

9. Expediting the development of software applications is critical to reducing the time-to-market. Computer-aided system engineering (CASE) technology (see Chapter 13) and object-oriented programming (see Chapter 6) are extremely useful.

Categories 2 and 3. Revising the Product Life Cycle and Providing Strategy and Innovation

1. IT will expand its role from supporting cost reduction and increasing productivity to a strategic role in helping enlarge the scope of the business.

2. Strategic opportunities will be increasingly provided by IT.

3. Strategic management adaptability to changing circumstances is the discipline of the future. It can be greatly enhanced by IT.

4. Introducing new IT will be a *competitive necessity*.

5. Sustained competitive advantage requires *continuous innovations*. IT applications and management are a must.

6. Executive support systems will be commonplace.

7. Eighty percent of results can be quickly achieved through 20 percent of the effort. Simple IT applications can save a lot of money.

8. IT will promote the emergence of strategic alliances among smaller firms in order to compete successfully against larger firms.

Category 4. Managing Human Resources

1. Senior executives who actively encourage the use of IT will see better results.

2. Assimilation of IT requires mutual commitment and cooperation among management, employees, and unions.

3. Motivation, competence, and coordination are needed for effective use of IT (challenge employees, training, retraining).

4. IT "champions" can be extremely useful in any organization.

5. Significant investment in new IT without parallel organizational change is unlikely to yield good results.

6. Desktop computers will raise productivity and expand jobs.

7. Providing training in the use of desktop computers will help companies leap ahead of their competitors.

8. IT projects must be properly managed. High-powered technology in weak hands may damage the organization.

9. The introduction of IT means introduction of change. This change *must* be properly managed.

Category 5. Enlarging the Scope of the Business

1. Internal successful information systems that do not include secret data may be marketable to other companies in the industry (see the Vermont ski resort minicase at the end of this chapter).

---

*The concept of critical success factor and its methodology is described in Chapters 11 and 12.

2. Electronic markets for manufactured goods could be the norm in the '90s.

3. Electronic markets will facilitate the buy (vs. make) option since corporations are exposed to many vendors. At the same time, IT enhances highly focused partnerships (one or a few permanent sub-contractors used in just-in-time management).

Category 6. The Promise of Integration

1. Communication networks will promote productivity within and between organizations. Enterprise-wide systems will be commonplace.

2. Standards are the key to the open systems concept of IT. Competitors should join forces.

Category 7. Evaluating Information Technology

1. The emerging world of IT includes both *enabling* and *inhibiting* factors.

2. Feasibility studies are necessary to assure success.

2

INFORMATION TECHNOLOGIES: CONCEPTS AND ARCHITECTURE

Chapter Outline

Learning Objectives

After studying this chapter, you will be able to:

1. Describe various information systems and their evolution, and identify the category of specific systems you observe.

2. Define a transaction processing system, and relate it to other systems.

3. Describe the value chain model.

4. Explain the functional management information systems (MIS), and analyze their role in supporting functional areas of business.

5. Describe the major support systems, and relate them to managerial functions.

6. Describe operational, managerial, and strategic activities.

7. Discuss information architecture and its importance.

8. Describe information infrastructure, and analyze its role in the delivery of computerized support.

9. Describe the role of legacy systems.

10. Describe the concepts of client/server and enterprise-wide computing and their interrelationship.

▶ 2.1 ENTERPRISE COMPUTING AT PANHANDLE: IMPROVED CUSTOMER SERVICE AND COMPETITIVENESS

PANHANDLE EASTERN CORPORATION (PEC) owns and operates one of the nation's largest natural gas transmission networks. PEC employs 5,000 people in 28 states. The company transports natural gas in underground pipes from sources in the southern United States to markets in the northeastern states. The company is competing with both other natural gas providers and companies that provide other sources of energy.

Information is an essential part of the PEC organization. PEC needs to collect data on gas flows as soon as it is available (real-time data). The company constructed its own electronic communication network, which is based on the latest microwave telecommunication technologies. It enables *enterprise-wide* communication among over 100 different corporate facilities, as well as enables the company to communicate with customers and suppliers and other entities in the outside world. This massive network (see Figure 2.1) supports information processing on projected and actual gas flow, engine availability, personnel, and much more.

Figure 2.1 shows a portion of the information systems architecture of PEC. The core of the system is the corporate network at the headquarters in Houston, TX (shown in red). This network is connected to an IBM mainframe application server, which is also connected via a local area network (LAN) to many small and large computers. The corporate network is connected to seven divisions by a wide area network (WAN). Only one division is shown in the figure (Liberal, KS). Each divisional network is connected to several work areas. Each division and each area has its own LAN structured in a token ring arrangement. Each LAN provides the basis for computing facilities (personal computers, midrange computers, and workstations).

The entire system is connected via telecommunication lines to the outside world. The massive network allows data to be collected daily at more than 13,000 entry locations, then stored in several databases, and processed by more than 3,000 computers. This sophisticated system allows hundreds of software applications

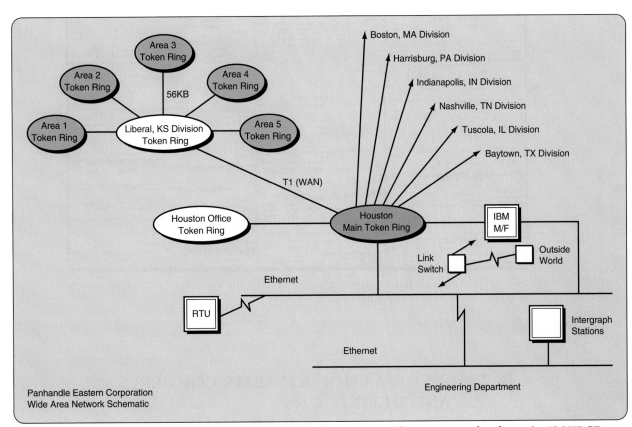

FIGURE 2.1 Panhandle Eastern Corporation wide area network schematic. (SOURCE: Provided by Mark Robben of PEC at Houston, TX.)

to be built by both information system professionals and end users. These applications range from information about the incoming and outgoing gas flow, to information used for making decisions regarding storage of gas and scheduling of personnel. An example of a divisional performance report generated as part of a corporate executive information system, which is accessible to many authorized system users, is shown in Figure 2.2.

The information system includes software applications in all the business's functional areas. There is a comprehensive accounting system with dozens of modules ranging from general ledger to tax-related depreciation schedules. A financial management system handles the corporate lines of credit and sources of financing. Customer files are a part of a marketing system, and a complete inventory control system of all spare parts can be accessed in seconds.

There are many decision support systems constructed by end users and applications of artificial intelligence. Without this kind of information system, PEC would be unable to operate successfully, compete, and meet customers' demand in the 1990s. PEC is considered one of

Panhandle's computer-based pipeline information system.

the best companies in its industry and its stock (traded on the New York Stock Exchange) is performing well.

SOURCE: Based on a term paper written by Mark Robben of PEC at Houston, TX.

FIGURE 2.2 Sample reports (one screen) generated by the executive information system of Panhandle Eastern Corporation.

▶ 2.2 INFORMATION SYSTEMS CONCEPTS AND DEFINITIONS

Information systems are composed of hardware, software, data, database(s), people, procedures, and networks. There are many ways in which a system's components can be put together. Developing an information system is like building housing. Housing can be a single house, or it can be designed for many families as a high-rise building. A house can be small or large, one level or multiple levels. It may include two bedrooms or 25, and it may cost from less than $10,000 to over $10,000,000. It all depends on the purpose of the housing, the availability of money, and constraints such as ecological and environmental factors. Just as there are many different types of housing, there are many different types of information systems.

The opening case illustrates the following information system phenomena that are found in many organizations:

▼ Several different information systems may exist in one organization.

▼ Some of these systems are completely independent; others are interconnected.

▼ A collection of several information systems is referred to as an information system.

▼ Information systems are connected by means of electronic networks. Such an arrangement, when organized as a client/server architecture, is the newest architecture in IT. If the entire company is networked and thereby people can communicate with each other and access information throughout the organization, then the architecture is known as an *enterprise-wide system.*

The purpose of this chapter is to discuss the various types of information systems: according to the organizational levels, to the major functional areas, the type of support they provide, and the information system architecture. Such a classification provides the basis for a better understanding of IT. The classification may help in identifying different systems, analyzing them, planning new systems, planning integration of systems, and making decisions about outsourcing of systems.

▶ 2.3 CLASSIFICATION OF INFORMATION SYSTEMS

Information systems can be classified in several ways. The major classification schemes are described below.

CLASSIFICATION ACCORDING TO ORGANIZATIONAL LEVELS

Organizations are composed of components such as departments, teams, or areas. For example, most organizations have a human resources department, a finance/accounting department, and perhaps a public relations unit. These departments report to a higher organizational level such as a division or a headquarters in a hierarchical manner. This is a traditional *hierarchical* structure with several levels. Although some organizations are reengineering themselves with innovative structures, such as those that are based on teams and networks, and though these innovative structures may be prevalent in the future, the fact is that, today, the vast majority of organizations have a traditional hierarchical structure.

One way to organize information systems is to build them along organizational structure lines. Thus, one can find information systems built for corporate divisions, departments, operating units, and even for individual employees. These systems may stand alone, or they may be interconnected. Note that similar departments may exist in different places in large organizations. For example, a human resources department may exist at the corporate level as well as in each division. Designers of information systems have an option: they can design a divisional information system that includes a human resources subsystem, or design a centralized human resources system for the entire organization. Using the latter approach, the designer builds the system around the organization's functional areas (such as finance or manufacturing).

Typical information systems that follow organizational levels are:

▼ **Departmental information systems.** Frequently, an organization uses several application programs in one functional area. For instance, in managing human resources, it is possible to use a program for screening applicants and a program for monitoring employee turnover. Some applications are completely independent of each other, whereas others are interrelated. The collection of application programs in the human resources area is called a human resources information system. That is, it is referred to as a single information system even though it is made up of many application subsystems.

▼ **Enterprise information systems.** While a departmental IS is usually related to a functional area, one can frequently talk about a collection of applications in several or in all functional areas. Such a collection can be described as an enterprise information system. The city of Los Angeles Information System is an example of such a complex system.

▼ **Interorganizational systems.** Some information systems are complex and involve several organizations. For example, the worldwide airline reservation system is composed of several systems belonging to different airlines. Of these, American Airlines' SABRE system (see Figure 2.3) is the largest.

CLASSIFICATION ACCORDING TO MAJOR FUNCTIONAL AREAS

Departmental information systems follow the traditional functional areas. The major functional information systems are:

▼ the accounting system

▼ the finance system

▼ the manufacturing (operation/production) system

▼ the marketing system

▼ the human resources management system

In each functional area, there are basic computerized tasks that are essential to the operation of the organization and are routine in nature. Preparing a payroll and billing a customer are typical examples. Such tasks are referred to as **mission-central tasks**. The information system that supports these tasks is the **transac-**

FIGURE 2.3 American Airlines' SABRE reservation system. The system is available for travel agents, corporations, and individuals. It is also accessible through the Internet and on-line services such as Prodigy.

tion processing system (TPS). The TPS supports tasks that are performed in all functional areas but especially in accounting and finance.

Note that in each functional area, it is possible to find dozens of IS-specific applications.

CLASSIFICATION ACCORDING TO THE SUPPORT PROVIDED BY THE SYSTEM

A third way to classify information systems is according to the type of support they provide, regardless of the functional area involved. For example, an information system can support office workers in almost any functional area. Similarly managers, regardless of where they work, can utilize computerized decision-making support. The major systems under this classification are:

▼ *Transaction processing system* (TPS)—supports activities central to the mission

▼ *Management information system* (MIS)—supports functional managers

▼ *Office automation system* (OAS)—supports office workers

▼ *Group support system* (GSS)—supports people working in groups

▼ *Decision support system* (DSS)—supports managers and analysts

▼ *Executive information or support system* (EIS)—supports executives

▼ *Intelligent support system*—supports knowledge workers, using **expert systems** (ES) and **artificial neural networks** (ANN).

Brief descriptions of these systems are provided in sections 2.5–2.8.

INTEGRATION. The implementation of a specific application may involve two or more of these systems. For example, a DSS combined with an ES can be built to support a marketing promotion program. Therefore, it is more appropriate to view IS applications as a matrix where the major functional areas are shown on the left side and the entities receiving support on the top. The cells of the matrix are the areas in which specific applications are defined. Such a matrix will be introduced in Section 2.10, when system architecture will be presented.

CLASSIFICATION ACCORDING TO THE INFORMATION SYSTEM ARCHITECTURE

The manner in which an information system is organized depends on what it is intended to support. Therefore, before designing an information system, a key task is to conceptualize the information requirements that relate to the core business of the organization. The conceptualization includes the manner in which requirements are to be met by IT. Such a conceptualization is called an **information architecture**. A related issue is that of the **information infrastructure**, which tells us how computers, networks, databases, and other facilities are arranged and how they are connected, operated, and managed. Architecture and infrastructure are interrelated aspects of IS design. An analogy is the conceptual planning of a house (the architecture) and the physical construction of the foundation, walls, roof, and other components (the infrastructure).

Information systems can be classified according to the system architecture. The following are the major categories:

▼ a mainframe-based system

▼ a stand-alone personal computer (PC)

▼ a distributed system (several variations)

A brief description of these configurations is provided in Sections 2.10–2.12.

▶ 2.4 EVOLUTION OF INFORMATION SYSTEMS

In the previous section, we mentioned several types of IS. To understand what they are, it is useful to describe their evolution over time.

The first computers were designed to compute formulas for scientific and military application, during and immediately after World War II (1940s). The first business application started in the early '50s. The initial applications involved repetitive, large-volume transaction computing. The computers "crunched numbers," summarizing and organizing data. They were justified because of the presence of a large volume of repetitive data, such as preparing a payroll or billing customers. Early TPS* mainly supported the accounting, finance, and personnel areas.

And so the evolutionary path of CBIS began. In addition to the growth of cheaper, friendlier, and better technology, the evolution was the result of organizational learning; people learned the benefits of the technology and the power that it can render. Finally, the evolution was supported by increased computer literacy. Figure 2.4 depicts this evolution from its inception to the '90s.

As the cost of computing decreased and the computers' capabilities increased, it became possible to justify IS for tasks of less repetitive volume. In the 1960s, a new breed of IS started to develop. These were systems that accessed, organized, summarized, and displayed decision-relevant information in the functional areas. Such systems are called **management information systems (MISs),** and they are characterized mainly by their ability to produce **periodic reports** such as a daily list of employees and the hours they work, a weekly report of sales by product, or a monthly report of expenses as compared to a budget. Initially, MIS had a historical orientation; they described events after they occurred. Later, MIS were also used to forecast trends and to support routine decisions. MIS were geared toward middle managers in functional areas, and with the passage of time they became even more diversified. For example, in addition to periodic reports, managers were able to receive special or **ad hoc reports** that were generated on demand. Today MIS reports might include sophisticated statistics as well as sum-

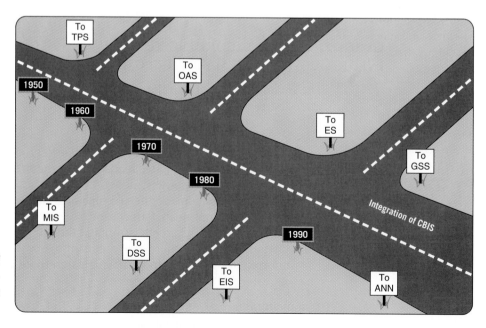

FIGURE 2.4 Evolution of computer-based information systems. (SOURCE: Turban, 1993.)

---

*The acronym TPS can be read either as singular or plural, as can many of the other acronyms related to information systems.

mary reports for periods that are different from the periods of the scheduled reports. The amount of information generated by the MIS grew rapidly. One way to reduce this amount of information is to provide managers with **exception reports**. Such reports are based on the principle of management by exception. For example, in a cost control report, all items whose costs exceeded the budget by 5 percent or more are either highlighted or organized in a special section of the report.

The use of computers expanded in the late 1960s and early 1970s to include electronic communication. Airline reservation systems (see Figure 2.3) are perhaps the best example of this development. The use of electronic communications was only one aspect of what was described as **office automation systems** (OASs). Another aspect of OAS, word processing systems, began to spread in the 1970s into many organizations. At about the same time, computers were introduced to manufacturing environments. Applications ranged from robotics to computer-aided design and manufacturing.

By the early 1970s, the demand for all types of IS started to accelerate. The increased capabilities and reduced costs justified computerized support for an increased number of nonroutine applications. At that time, the discipline of **decision support systems** (DSSs) was initiated. The basic objective of a DSS is to provide computerized support to complex nonroutine and partially structured decisions (see Box 2.1).

IT At Work BOX 2.1 *G*LOBAL PERSPECTIVE

USING DSS IN CHINA TO SUPPORT CHANGING ECONOMY

Dalian Dyestuff is a large chemical plant in China, producing about 100 different kinds of dyes and other chemical products. With economic reforms in China, decision making was decentralized and competition intensified. Important decisions had to be made on both what and how much to produce, and on where to purchase raw materials. In addition, decisions regarding the disposal of environmentally damaging chemicals were needed.

To improve the decision-making process, a DSS was developed and combined with a supportive expert system. It includes five subsystems: production planning, accounting and cost control, finance and budgeting, inventory and materials control, and information services. The DSS employs forecasting and resource allocation models. Two expert systems provide expertise on forecasting demand,

plan production, and analysis of working capital.

The system provides the following benefits:

▼ Increased profits by over $1,000,000 per year (a 10 percent increase)

▼ Improved customer service

▼ Provided flexibility and adaptability to changes

▼ Increased the company's competitive position in the industry

Critical Thinking Issues: Why is it necessary to use a DSS at Dalian? What is the role of the expert systems? ▲

SOURCE: Condensed from Yang, D.L., and W. Mou, "An integrated DSS in a Chinese Chemical Plant," *Interfaces,* November–December, 1993.

At first, the cost of building a DSS prohibited its widespread use. However, the microcomputer revolution, which started around 1980, changed this situation. The availability of desktop machines, which were easily programmable thanks to high-level programming languages, made it possible for a person who knows little about programming to build an IS application. This was the beginning of the era of end user computing. Analysts, managers, many other professionals, and even secretaries started to build their own systems.

By the mid 1980s a new computing discipline emerged: artificial intelligence. **Artificial intelligence** (AI) is the basis of several intelligent systems in the area of knowledge systems. Of special interest were **expert systems** (ESs). These advisory systems were different from the TPS, which centered around data, and the MIS and DSS, which concentrated on processing information. Expert systems use knowledge to diagnose problems, propose solutions to those problems, or train employees (see Box 2.2).

IT At Work BOX 2.2

*E*MERGING TECHNOLOGY

EXPERT SYSTEMS HELPS FARMERS WORLDWIDE

In a world whose population is growing rapidly, food is of major concern. Farmers all over the world are trying to provide this food. One problem is that diseases can reduce crop yields drastically. Small farms and farmers in many developing countries cannot afford to pay the cost of agricultural advisors. Government advisors are too busy. By the time that they come, it may be too late.

ICI is a large international provider of chemicals. Its headquarters are in the United Kingdom (UK). ICI developed an expert system called Wheat Counsellor, which advises on the control of diseases in winter wheat.

Wheat Counsellor first evaluates the risks of fungal diseases in a crop by asking the farmers for information about the variety of wheat being grown, its location, the soil type, local weather, and so on. It then draws on crop-growth data from several organizations, and states the expected loss if no treatment is given. Next, Wheat Counsellor examines the range of fungicides sold by ICI

and other manufacturers and recommends treatment from this range. Finally, it provides costs for these, and states the likely return on investment.

Wheat Counsellor is interesting because it is attached to videotex. ICI uses a private videotex system called Grapevine, which is similar to the public British system Prestel. An ordinary telephone is sufficient to connect an adapted television set or other terminal to Grapevine; Wheat Counsellor can then interact with that terminal. So the farmers can receive advice either over the telephone or on their TV screens.

ICI provides the service free of charge in all countries where ICI products are sold. The company has developed other systems for many vegetables and fruits.

Critical Thinking Issues: How can an expert system provide help to a farmer? Why is the videotex useful? ▲

Extending computer capabilities to knowledge processing became possible only when the power of computers and their storage capabilities reached a high enough level. Similarly, providing extensive capabilities at a reasonable cost resulted in the development of additional systems. For example, **executive information systems** (EIS), which evolved in the late '80s, are designed to support senior executives (see Box 2.3), and **group support systems** (GSS) are available to support the efforts of people working in groups (see Box 2.4).

IT At Work BOX 2.3
*G*LOBAL PERSPECTIVE

EIS HELPS IN MANAGING A GERMAN MULTINATIONAL CORPORATION

Bertelsmann Music Group is a large German conglomerate that owns many companies worldwide. Its U.S. subsidiary, the Bertelsmann Group, owns several entertainment and publishing companies such as RCA Records. To manage all its business units, the company

developed an executive information system (EIS). The main purpose is to provide top-level managers with a system that analyzes trends across business units. The system includes a combination of the traditional EIS for monitoring purposes and a multidimensional spreadsheet (a DSS tool) for conducting trend analysis, comparisons, and evaluations. The system is centered on a mainframe in Indianapolis (Indiana), but controls business units in 39 different countries. The system can track sales on a daily basis, in great detail, by country, by zone, by store, and by product (thanks to the multidimensional software). For example, management knows the daily sales of each album and each book in each store (their customers) worldwide. In the first phase, the system served the 20 top executives of the company.

The EIS is especially helpful for an international company since the data entered in each country are different due to local currency and accounting procedures. EIS enables easy comparisons despite such differences because the spreadsheet, the DSS, and the EIS are from the same vendor (Comshare, Inc.). In phase 2 the system will run on Windows, which will make programming easier, and so more applications and more users will be able to be added to the system.

Critical Thinking Issues: Why is an EIS so important to a multinational corporation? How does the DSS supplement the EIS? ▲

SOURCE: Condensed from *Computerworld*, July 5, 1993, pp. 37, 40.

IT At Work BOX 2.4

◄ GLOBAL PERSPECTIVE

A FRENCH BUILDER IMPROVES COMMUNICATION USING LOTUS NOTES

Profit margins on large construction projects in France are at a low 2 percent. Dalla Vera, a French builder, has responded by subcontracting an ever-increasing percentage of its work. New government regulations require that a prime contractor (Dalla Vera in this case) must now absorb all the risk. How do you manage risk and a large number of subcontractors across 50 building projects per year?

Dalla Vera is a $120 million, 450 employee division of the Bouygues Group in France. The trend toward subcontractors is clearly illustrated in their employment ratios. Five years ago there were 4.5 blue-collar workers for every white-collar worker; now the ratio is one to one.

New regulations that essentially placed all the risk on the prime contractor changed the nature of the contractor relationship. Now the prime contractor has to ensure that subcontractors have all the necessary licenses and insurance prior to initiating work and throughout the contract period.

Prior to adopting Lotus Notes, each building site manager would meet on average three times with each of the 15 contractors. This process was repeated for each of the 50 building sites. These 750 meetings consumed at least 500 days of building site management time. Although a contractor qualified for the initial construction start date, it was all but impossible to track whether his insurance was still good at the end of the construction cycle. Plus each time a contractor was assigned to a building site, he had to go through the same qualification procedure that he may have just gone through at another Dalla Vera site, even a day earlier.

With Notes, Dalla Vera can view documents by contractor so the contractor need not be asked multiple times for the same document at several different building sites. The effect is that overhead for the contractor in dealing with Dalla Vera is reduced, because it takes a contractor one-fifth of the time to find documents currently required than documents required after the job is underway.

Lotus Notes also fosters internal communication among site managers and corporate decision makers. So it is a win–win situation for corporate headquarters, the site managers, and the 560 subcontractors.

Specific Savings. Dalla Vera is saving 50 percent of a secretary's time in contract preparation, and over 500 days per year of job site management time when applied to all their construction sites, plus they have reduced their risk factor by $30,000 per annum. By having a database on all 560 subcontractors, Dalla Vera now selects subcontractors not simply on the basis of who qualifies from a license and insurance perspective, but on additional information that each building site manager can now add that becomes a permanent part of the contractor's record. The rate of return on their IS investment was figured at 101 percent.

Critical Thinking Issue: How can Lotus Notes help in managing risk in a changing business environment? ▲

SOURCE: Compiled from IDC Special Report: *Lotus Notes: Agent of Change* Framingham, MA. 1994, International Data Corporation.

All these systems are very beneficial, but their support is fairly passive and limited. Even expert systems are unable to learn on their own. By the beginning of the 1990s, a new breed of systems emerged, those with learning capabilities. Systems such as *artificial neural networks (ANN)*, *case-based reasoning*, and *genetic algorithms* can learn from historical cases. This capability enables machines to process even vague or incomplete information (see Box 2.5).

IT At Work BOX 2.5

EMERGING TECHNOLOGY

DETECTING BOMBS IN AIRPLANE PASSENGERS' LUGGAGE

The Federal Aviation Administration (FAA) in the United States is making continuous efforts to improve safety and prevent terrorists from sneaking bombs into airplanes. Since it is practically impossible to open and search every piece of luggage, the FAA uses computer technologies in an attempt to find different types of explosives. One approach is to bombard each piece of luggage with gamma rays. These rays are collected by a sensor and then interpreted. The FAA is using statistical analysis and expert systems to conduct the interpretation. However, these technologies cannot detect all types of explosives. Since 1993, artificial neural networks have been used to supplement the traditional technologies.

Artificial neural networks are designed in a manner similar to the way the brain is structured. An ANN includes many interconnected processors whose degree of influence on each other can be changed. An ANN can be trained to detect an explosive (by using actual explosives) even if an explosive is different from the explosives used for training.

The objective is not only to successfully detect explosives, but also to minimize false alarms that result from the fact that many things (including clothing) contain nitrogen, a major component in any bomb.

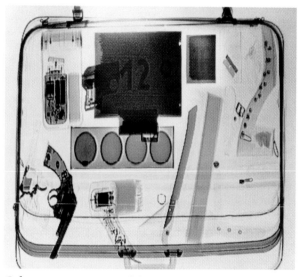

Color x-ray system used for airport security.

Critical Thinking Issues: It is said that two heads are better than one. Can the addition of ANN be considered an extra head? Why? ▲

SOURCE: Informal information provided by Scan-Tech Security, Northvale, NJ, a developer of one of these systems.

Various CBIS may support each other, and frequently they can be integrated. The relationship among the different types of support systems can be summarized as follows:

▼ Each support system has sufficiently unique characteristics so it can be classified as a special entity. Each support system provides a different aspect of support.

▼ The systems are interrelated. For example, an MIS can be based on a TPS; an EIS can be based on TPS and/or MIS. An example of such relationships among TPS, MIS, and EIS is shown in Figure 2.5.

▼ The evolution and creation of the newer types of systems help expand the role of IT for the improvement of management in organizations. (See the M.I.T. Report, Appendix B, Chapter 1.)

▼ The interrelationships and coordination among the different types of systems are still evolving.

▼ In many cases, two or more systems are integrated to form a hybrid information system, as was shown in Box 2.5.

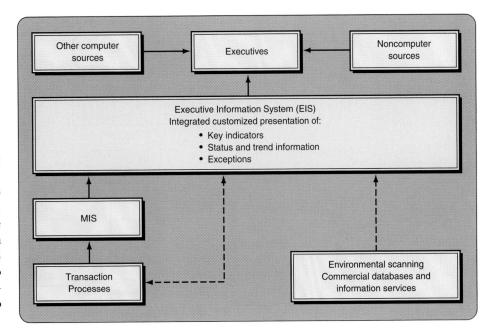

FIGURE 2.5 Role of the EIS. The TPS collects information that is used to build the MIS and EIS. The information in the MIS as well as information that flows from other CBIS can be used as an input to the EIS. (SOURCES: Millet et al., 1991; see also Millet, 1992.)

▶ 2.5 TRANSACTION PROCESSING SYSTEMS

Now that we have introduced the different types of systems involved in the evolution of IS, let us look at some of the key systems in more detail.

The earliest information systems built in many organizations were the *transaction processing systems* (TPS). A TPS (in many organizations, actually several systems) supports the monitoring, collection, storage, processing and dissemination of the organization's basic business transactions. It also provides the backbone for many applications involving the other support systems such as DSS. The transaction processing systems are considered critical to the success of any organization since they support the mission-central operations, such as purchasing of materials, billing customers, preparing a payroll, or shipping goods to customers.

Any organization that performs financial, accounting, and other daily business activities faces routine, repetitive tasks. For example, employees are paid at regular intervals, customers place purchase orders and are billed periodically, and expenses are monitored and compared to the budget. Figure 2.6 depicts typical daily business transactions in a manufacturing company. Table 2.1 presents a partial list of related business transactions.

As can be seen in Figure 2.6, manufacturing organizations base their production and inventory levels on actual orders by customers and/or a forecasted demand. When a customer enters an order, the customer's credit is checked. If credit is approved, an order is issued to ship the merchandise. First, a search is made to determine if there is enough quantity on hand (inventory). If there is enough inventory, then the order is transferred to the shipping department for delivery to the customer. If there is not sufficient inventory, an order to manufacture the product(s) is made. In such a case, the necessary raw materials are allocated from a stock, or they are purchased. Then, the product(s) is manufactured and moved to shipping for delivery to the customer. In any of the above cases, all relevant information is transferred to product pricing and accounting. Shipping may use a carrier to deliver the goods to customers, or they may use their own trucks. In either case, cost information is provided to product pricing and accounting. Also, information for payroll is continuously generated. Accounting manages the accounts receivable (from customers) and accounts payable (to

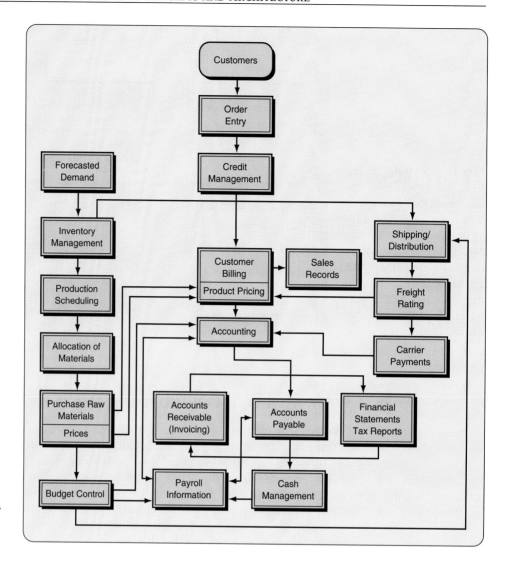

FIGURE 2.6 Daily business transactions in a manufacturing company. (SOURCE: Dr. C.J. Walter, Dean, College of Business Administration, California State University, Long Beach.)

vendors). Money is collected and dispensed by the cash management activities, and financial statements are generated periodically.

The TPS generates documents and reports, but it can also provide data to other types of information systems such as marketing information systems or a decision support system. The TPS collects data continuously, frequently on a daily basis; or even in real time (as soon as they are generated, as in the PEC case). Most

---

Table 2.1 **Business Transactions in a Factory**

Payroll
  Employee time cards
  Employee pay and deductions
  Payroll checks
Purchasing
  Purchase orders
  Deliveries
  Payments (accounts payable)
Sales
  Sales records
  Invoices and billings
  Accounts receivable
  Sales returns
  Shipping

Manufacturing
  Production reports
  Quality-control reports
Finance and accounting
  Financial statements
  Tax records
  Expense accounts
Inventory management
  Material usage
  Inventory levels

of these data are stored in the corporate databases and are available for processing. The raw data, as well as the processed data (e.g., summaries, comparisons), are distributed to interested parties and stored in databases for future reference. A TPS that handles customers' orders in real time is shown in Box 2.6. The system not only improves customers' satisfaction, but also collects data for marketing analysis. Further details on TPS are provided in Chapter 17.

IT At Work BOX 2.6

DOMINO'S PIZZA MATCHES CUSTOMERS' CALLS TO THE CLOSEST DOMINO'S OUTLET

Domino's Pizza and AT&T teamed up to create a service that speeds up the ordering and delivery of pizzas to customers' homes, and reduces transportation costs to the customers. To begin the process, the customer dials a special number (see the figure, step 1). The calls are received at the AT&T Store Locator Service Node (step 2). Using an automatic number identification system, the Store Locator finds the address of the caller. The computer then matches the caller's address with the nearest open Domino's Pizza restaurant (step 3) and dials that restaurant (step 4). The entire process takes 7 to 11 seconds. An employee at the restaurant picks up the phone, talks with the customer, and arranges the delivery. The system is especially useful in large cities. For example, in Los Angeles there are over 300 restaurants, and many customers do not know which restaurant is nearest to them or which one is open for business at certain hours.

Domino's is facing competitive pressures, especially from Pizza Hut. Domino's share of the pizza delivery market has declined from close to 100 percent to less than 50 percent in less than 10 years. The new service changes fundamentally the manner in which pizzas are being ordered. Also, the system is used to generate bills immediately and to store market information about customers (e.g., for the purpose of issuing sales coupons). Using this technology, the company hopes to increase customers' loyalty and ultimately its market share. (Pizza Hut's reply to this innovation was to set up an ordering system on the Internet.)

AT&T plans to create similar alliances with other national businesses that depend on a network of outlets. Rental car agencies, florists, clothing stores, repair shops, insurance companies and auto dealerships would be the most likely participants.

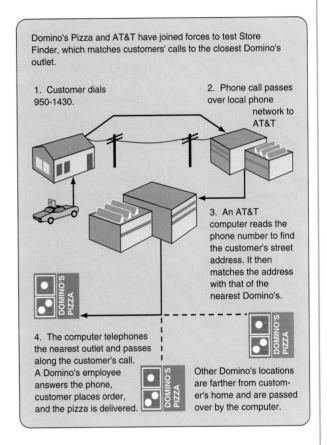

Domino's Pizza and AT&T have joined forces to test Store Finder, which matches customers' calls to the closest Domino's outlet.

1. Customer dials 950-1430.

2. Phone call passes over local phone network to AT&T

3. An AT&T computer reads the phone number to find the customer's street address. It then matches the address with that of the nearest Domino's.

4. The computer telephones the nearest outlet and passes along the customer's call. A Domino's employee answers the phone, customer places order, and the pizza is delivered.

Other Domino's locations are farther from customer's home and are passed over by the computer.

Critical Thinking Issues: How did the new service reengineer the delivery of pizza? How can the information collected be used to improve marketing and customer service? ▲

SOURCE: Condensed from *The New York Times*, September 9, 1991.

▶ 2.6 THE VALUE CHAIN MODEL

To better understand the manner in which organizations operate and the role of MIS in supporting such operations, we begin this section by examining the value chain model.

VALUE CHAIN ANALYSIS MODEL

According to the **value chain model** (Porter [1985]), the activities conducted in any organization can be divided into two parts: *primary activities* and *support activities*. Figure 2.7 depicts the model. Five primary activities can be observed: (1) inbound logistics (inputs), (2) operations (manufacturing and processing), (3) outbound logistics (storage and distribution), (4) marketing and sales, and (5) service. The primary activities are sequenced. The incoming materials are processed (in receiving, storage, etc.) and so value is added to them, in what is called inbound logistics. Then, the materials are used in operations, where more value is added in making products. The products need to be prepared for delivery (e.g., packaging, storing, shipping), and so more value is being added. Then, marketing and sales deliver the products to customers. Finally, a service to the customer is performed. All these activities result (hopefully) in profit. These primary activities are supported by (1) firm infrastructure (accounting, finance, management), (2) human resource management, (3) technology development, and (4) procurement. Each support activity can support any and/or all primary activities; they may also support each other.

A firm's value chain is part of a larger stream of activities, termed by Porter as a **value system**. A value system includes both the suppliers that provide the inputs necessary to the firm and their value chains. Once the firm creates products, they pass through the value chains of distributors (that also have their own value chains), all the way to the buyers (customers), who also have their value chains. Gaining and sustaining a competitive advantage and supporting the advantage by IT require understanding of the entire value system.

The value chain and value system concepts can be drawn for both products and services and for any organization, private or public. Although the major purpose of the value chain model was to analyze the internal operation of a corporation to increase its efficiency, effectiveness, and competitiveness, we will use the model as a basis for explaining the support IT can provide.

The value chain model and system may determine the nature of the IT in the organization in the following manner. The use of the value chain approach forces an organization to examine its primary and support activities to determine which ones contribute most to the profit margins. Such analysis may result in restructuring of the organization and its processes so that the ones that contribute

FIGURE 2.7 Porter's value chain model for a manufacturing firm. (SOURCE: Reprinted with permission of The Free Press, a Division of Simon & Schuster Inc. from Competitive Advantage: Creating and Sustaining Superior Performance by Michael E. Porter. Copyright © 1985 by Michael Porter.)

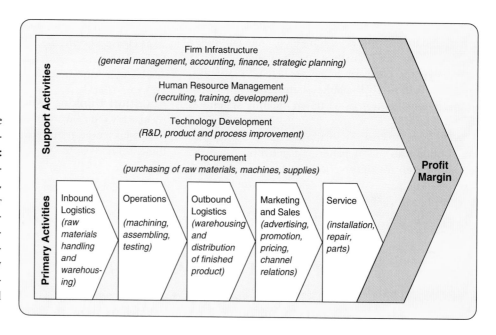

the most value survive and those that make little or no contribution are eliminated. Information systems are enablers to the various activities identified in the models and are developed accordingly.

Therefore, it makes sense to develop information systems according to the value chain model. Most organizations do it in the following way. First, they determine the departments that will execute the primary and support activities (see Box 2.7). Then, they build the information systems needed to support tasks carried out in these departments. As will be shown in Chapter 3, there is another approach to the execution of the value chain activities, organizing according to a business process. In such a case, the IT support will align itself with a process rather than a department. But first let us examine what is done by most organizations in the traditional functional departments.

A Closer Look BOX 2.7

MAJOR DEPARTMENTS (FUNCTIONAL AREAS) IN A TYPICAL ORGANIZATION

Departments for Executing Primary Activities

Manufacturing
Material Management (Logistics)
Engineering
Testing and Quality Control
Maintenance and Service
Marketing and Sales

Departments for Executing Support Activities

Accounting
Finance
Strategic Planning
Human Resources Management (HRM)
Research and Development
Procurement (Purchasing)
Public Relations
Information Systems

 ## 2.7 MANAGEMENT INFORMATION SYSTEMS

The primary and support activities in organizations are performed in departments or organizational units known as *functional areas*. Each of these departments executes a large number of tasks. For example, the human resources management (HRM) department hires, councils, and trains people. Each of these tasks can be divided into subtasks. Training may involve selecting topics to teach, selecting people to participate, scheduling classes, finding teachers, and preparing class materials; and each subtask adds some value. A human resources information system (HRIS) can support one or several of these tasks and subtasks. This support can be performed by one unified system such as that of Federal Express. (For the details of this system, see Palvia et al. [1992] and Minicase 1 in Chapter 17.) Alternatively, the support can be done by several independent applications such as one for recruiting, one for performance evaluation, and one for a fringe benefit system.

WHAT IS A MIS?

The systems that support the management of the functional areas are referred to as management information systems.* A MIS provides periodic information to functional managers and other employees on such routine topics as operational efficiency, effectiveness, and productivity.

*The term MIS here refers to a specific application in a functional area. MIS is also used to describe information systems management (see section 2.13).

A typical MIS extracts information from the corporate database and processes it according to the needs of the user. For example, an HRIS can provide that department's manager with a daily report of the percentage of people who were on vacation or called in sick. The report can compare actual to forecasted figures. Further comparisons such as to a previous week or to an industry average can also be made. MIS are used for planning, monitoring, and control. For example, a sales forecast by region is shown in Figure 2.8.

Functional information systems are put in place to ensure that business strategies come to fruition in an efficient manner. For example, the report shown in Figure 2.8 can help the marketing manager make better decisions regarding advertisements and pricing of products. Functional information systems or portions of them can be constructed by end users. Also, functional information systems (or portions of them) can be combined to form special applications.

▶ 2.8 GENERAL SUPPORT SYSTEMS

The major purpose of a MIS is to support the management of a specific functional area. Other technologies and systems are intended to support other categories of employees, and these employees can be in *any* functional area. The main general support systems that are described in this book are shown in Table 2.2 together with the employees they support and the chapters in which they are described.

In the next section, we will provide more detail on the relationships between these systems and the activities and people they support.

▶ 2.9 OPERATIONAL, MANAGERIAL, AND STRATEGIC SYSTEMS

Another important way to classify information systems is by the nature of the activity supported, which can be either operational, managerial, or strategic.

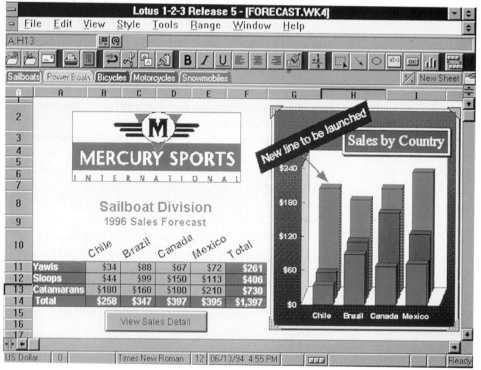

FIGURE 2.8 Sales forecast by region generated by marketing MIS.

Table 2.2 **Main General Support Systems**

System	Employee Supported	Detailed Discussion in:
Office automation	Office workers	Chapters 14, 17
Communication	All employees	Chapter 14
Group support system	People working in groups	Chapters 14, 15
Decision support system	Decision makers, managers	Chapter 15
Executive information or support systems	Executives, top managers	Chapter 15
Expert systems	Knowledge workers, professionals	Chapter 16
Neural networks	Knowledge workers, professionals	Chapter 16

OPERATIONAL SYSTEMS

Operational systems deal with the day-to-day operations of an organization such as assigning employees to tasks and recording the number of hours they work. Another example is placing a purchase order. Operational decisions are of short-term nature. The information systems that support operational activities are mainly transaction processing, routine reporting, and repetitive decision support. Operational systems are used by supervisors (first-line managers), operators, and clerical employees.

MANAGERIAL SYSTEMS

Managerial systems, also called tactical systems, deal with middle management activities such as short-term planning, organizing, and control. Frequently, managerial systems are equated with MIS, because of the need for data summarization. Middle managers also like to get quick answers to queries. Managerial systems, in contrast to operational systems, are broader in scope, but like operational systems, they mainly use internal sources of data. Managerial systems provide the following types of support.

▼ ***Statistical summaries.*** Statistical reports include summaries of raw data such as daily production, weekly absenteeism rate, and monthly usage of electricity.

▼ ***Exception reports.*** To relieve managers from the information-overload syndrome, an information system can extract (or highlight) exceptions. For example, in a report that compares expenses to a budget, all expense items that exceed the budget by more than 5 percent are underlined, colored, or separated from the rest of the items.

▼ ***Periodic and ad hoc reports.*** Both statistical summaries and exception reports can be done on a routine periodic basis or on demand by users (ad hoc). Ad hoc reports are requested because they contain information not available in the routine reports or because the users cannot wait for the scheduled time of the periodic report. As technology improves, the ability to request and receive ad hoc reports will improve. Managers will be able to view current or even real-time information at any time they wish to do so.

▼ ***Comparative analysis.*** Managers like to see performance values and other information compared to their competitors, past performance, or industry standards.

▼ ***Projections.*** In contrast to an operational system, which has a historical orientation, managerial information systems provide standard projections, such as trend analysis, projection of future sales, projection of cash flows, or forecasting of market share.

▼ *Early detection of problems.* By comparing and analyzing data, managerial systems can detect problems in their early stages. For example, statistical quality-control reports can reveal if a trend for reduced quality is developing.

▼ *Routine decisions.* Middle managers are involved in many routine decisions. They schedule employees, order materials and parts, and decide what and when to produce. Standard computerized mathematical, statistical, and financial models are available for the execution of these activities.

STRATEGIC SYSTEMS

Strategic systems deal with long-term situations and with decisions that significantly change the manner in which business is being done. Traditionally, strategic systems implied only long-range planning. Today, however, strategic systems help organizations in two other ways.

Strategic response systems are intended to respond to a competitor's action or to any other significant change in the environment of the enterprise. Such responses are not included in the long-range plan because they are unpredictable. Sometimes they can be planned for as a set of contingencies. Many times the change itself is related to IT (e.g., a new technological development by a competitor). These responses are considered strategic because their organizational impact is very significant. IT is often used to decide on the response or to provide the response itself. An example is Kodak's entry to the disposable camera market. When Kodak learned that the Japanese were developing such a camera, Kodak decided to do it too. However, the Japanese were already in the middle of the development process. By using computer-aided design and other information technologies, Kodak was able to cut the design time and beat the Japanese in the race to be first in retail outlets.

Instead of waiting for a competitor to introduce a major change or innovation, an organization can be the initiator of change. Such initiation results in situations not included in the long-range plan. This is a case of proactive strategic systems, and it is frequently supported by IT. Federal Express's package tracing system is an example of a proactive strategic system supported by IT. Idea-generation software (see Chapters 14 and 15) can be used to support proactive strategic systems.

RELATIONSHIP OF SUPPORT SYSTEMS TO MANAGERIAL LEVELS AND THEIR DECISIONS

Strategic decisions are usually made by top management, and they can be supported by EIS. Managerial decisions are made by middle managers, and they are supported mainly by MIS. Finally, operational decisions are made by line managers and operators, and they are supported mainly by the TPS. The relationships between the support systems, the managerial levels, and the type of decisions are shown in Figure 2.9. The figure is organized as a triangle to illustrate the volume involved. Top managers are few, and they sit at the top of the triangle.

As can be seen in the figure, an additional level of staff support is introduced between top and middle management. These are professional people (such as financial and marketing analysts). They act as advisors to both top and middle management, and they are supported by DSS, ES, and ANN.

Many of these professional workers are **knowledge workers**. A knowledge worker is a person who *creates* information and knowledge as part of her work and integrates it into the business. Knowledge workers are engineers, financial and marketing analysts, production planners, lawyers, and accountants, to mention just a few. Knowledge workers are characterized by their post–high school education (a university, polytechnic) and by their membership in a recognized

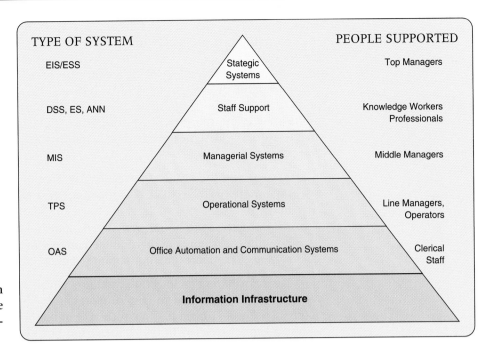

TYPE OF SYSTEM

| | | PEOPLE SUPPORTED |

EIS/ESS — Stategic Systems — Top Managers

DSS, ES, ANN — Staff Support — Knowledge Workers Professionals

MIS — Managerial Systems — Middle Managers

TPS — Operational Systems — Line Managers, Operators

OAS — Office Automation and Communication Systems — Clerical Staff

Information Infrastructure

FIGURE 2.9 Information systems support of people and activities in organizations.

profession or professional society. Knowledge workers are responsible for finding or developing external knowledge for the organization and integrating the new knowledge with the existing information. Therefore they must keep abreast of all developments and events related to their profession. They also act as advisors and consultants to the members of the organizations. Finally, they act as change agents, by introducing new procedures, technologies, or processes to the organization. In developed countries knowledge workers comprise 70–80% of all workers.

Knowledge workers can be supported by a large variety of information systems ranging from ES and ANN that help them scan information and interpret it, to CAD and hypertext that help them increase their productivity and quality.

Another class of employees consists of clerical people. They support all the managerial levels and, therefore, they are placed at the bottom of the triangle. Among clerical workers, there is a special class of those who use, manipulate, or disseminate information. They are referred to as *data workers*. These include book-keepers, secretaries who work with wordprocessors, electronic file clerks, and insurance claim processors. Clerical employees are supported by office automation and communication systems including document management, workflow, E-mail, and coordination software. Employees of any of the levels described, when working in groups (which may cut across managerial levels and/or functional areas), are supported by group support systems (also called groupware).

All the systems in the triangle are built on the information infrastructure, which is described in the next section.

▶ 2.10 INFORMATION ARCHITECTURE AND INFRASTRUCTURE

Recall that an *information architecture** is a high-level map (or plan) of the information requirements in organizations. It also relates the information resources and their utilization to the provision of support for the information requirements.

---

*Information architecture needs to be distinguished from computer architecture. For example, architecture for a computer may involve several processors, or special features to increase speed (such as reduced instructions set computing, or RISC). Our interest here is in information architecture only.

Thus, it assures us that the organization's IT meets the strategic business needs of the corporation. It is a guide for current operations and a blueprint for future directions.

Remember the analogy of the architecture for a house. The architect prepares a conceptual high-level drawing of the house. The architect needs to know the purpose of the house, the requirements of the dwellers, the constraints (time, money, etc.), and the preferences of the dwellers. In preparing an information architecture, the designer needs similar information, which can be divided into two parts:

1. Recognizing the business needs for information; that is, understanding the organizational objectives and problems and the contribution that IT can make.

2. Knowing the information systems that already exist in an organization and how these systems can be combined among themselves and/or with future systems to support the information needs.

The information architecture produces a plan that shows how information systems will be organized to best support the organization. It is clear that the potential users of IT must play a critical role in the first part of design process. An architect cannot excel without knowing the purpose of the house and the requirements of the owners.

In the previous sections, we classified information systems according to functional and general support information systems. When we relate the two categories, a matrix is produced, as shown in the center of Figure 2.10; this matrix can be viewed as the tabulation of all IS applications in the organization. For example, the Chinese DSS (Box 2.1) could be placed in the cell at the intersection of POM and DSS. To develop and use these applications, we need an infrastructure that surrounds all applications. An *information infrastructure* refers to the physical facilities, the services, and the management that support all computing resources in an organization. There are five major infrastructures: computer hardware, general purpose software, networks and communication facilities, databases, and information management personnel. Infrastructure includes these resources and their integration, operation, documentation, maintenance, and management. Infrastructures support all types of applications anywhere in the corporation. The

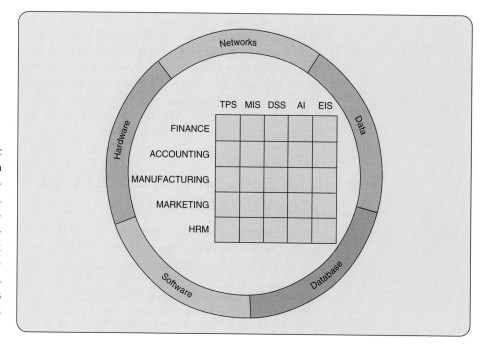

FIGURE 2.10 Schematic view of the information architecture, which combines the functional areas, the general support system, and the infrastructure. The inside matrix includes specific applications in an organization. The outside ring includes the computing resources of the infrastructure.

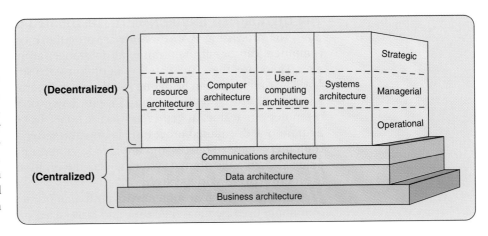

FIGURE 2.11 The information architecture model. (SOURCE: W.R. Synnott, *The Information Weapon: Winning Customers and Markets with Technology*, p. 199. Copyright © 1987 John Wiley & Sons. Reprinted by permission of John Wiley & Sons, Inc.)

information architecture combines the requirements (application matrix) together with the infrastructure (outer circle) as shown in Figure 2.10.

A system's architecture cannot be completed until the planning for the business is complete. However, IT architecture and business planning, for either a new business or the restructuring of an existing organization, are interrelated. This important topic will be revisited in Chapters 4, 11, and 12.

CONTENT OF THE INFORMATION ARCHITECTURE

The information architecture, according to Synnott (1987), deals with designing a conceptual framework for the organizational IT infrastructure. It is a plan for the structure and integration of the information resources in the organization. Synnott proposes a model for information architecture as shown in Figure 2.11.

Synnott's model divides the information architecture into two major parts. The centralized portion serves the entire organization and includes the business architecture (information needs of the organization), the data architecture, and the communications architecture. The decentralized (upper) portion focuses on an organizational function or on some service or activity (e.g., human resources, computers, end-user computing, and systems). In some organizations, the decentralized modules (except end-user computing) can be centralized.

TYPES OF INFORMATION ARCHITECTURES

There are several types of information architectures, and they keep changing. One way to classify an architecture is by the role that the hardware plays. It is possible to distinguish two extreme cases: (1) a mainframe environment and (2) a PC environment. The combination of these two creates a family of a third type of architecture, the *distributed environment.*

MAINFRAME ENVIRONMENT. In the mainframe environment, the processing is done by a mainframe computer. The users work with passive (or "dumb") terminals. The terminals are used to enter or change data and access information from the mainframe. This was the dominant architecture until the late 1980s. Very few organizations use this type of architecture exclusively in the 1990s. An extension of this is an architecture where PCs are used as smart terminals.

PC ENVIRONMENT. In the PC configuration, only PCs form the hardware information architecture. The PCs are independent of each other. An extension of this is an environment where the PCs are connected via electronic networks. This architecture is common for many small- to medium-sized organizations.

THE DISTRIBUTED ENVIRONMENT. **Distributed processing** involves distributing the processing work between two or more computers. The participating computers can be all mainframe, all midrange, all micros, or a combination of sizes. Therefore, there are many configurations of distributed systems (see Chapter 10). The computers can be in one location or in several. **Cooperative processing** is a type of distributed processing in which two or more *geographically dispersed* computers are teamed together to execute a specific task. Another important configuration of distributed processing is the *client/server* arrangement, where several computers share resources and are able to communicate with many other computers. When a distributed system covers the entire organization it is referred to as an **enterprise-wide system**.

A distributed environment with both mainframe and PCs is very flexible and commonly used by most medium- and large-sized organizations. This basic classification is analogous to the manner in which transportation systems are designed. Traveling can be done in three ways. First, the commuter can use public transportation, such as a train or a plane. In this case, several riders share the vehicle. The riders need to come to the vehicle at specific times and locations and obey certain rules. Second, the commuter can use the automobile. This private vehicle is used at the rider's wish. Third, one can use both; for example, a person can use the automobile to drive to the train station and from there use the train to commute to work, or he can drive to the airport and take a plane for a vacation. The car can be viewed as a PC, while the train or the plane is the mainframe. Such an arrangement is flexible, providing the benefits of the two extreme systems.

Distributed systems involve networks and telecommunication. The Panhandle case is an example of a distributed *client/server enterprise-wide* system. It involves both local area networks (at the various areas and divisions) and wide area networks (that connect the divisions to headquarters).

▶ 2.11 LEGACY SYSTEMS

Legacy systems refer to older or mature information systems, some of which were installed 20 or 30 years ago. Such systems are pure mainframe systems or distributed systems where the mainframe plays the major role and the PCs are smart terminals (for uploading and downloading data and doing local analysis). Newer legacy systems may include one or more LANs.

Legacy systems were developed from the late '50s to the early '90s. They were developed for general-purpose business use in medium- to large-size companies where they were the primary computers for large processing applications.

Legacy systems are housed in a secured and costly data (or computer) center. They occupy one or several rooms. They are operated by professional staff rather than by end users. Much of their work is routine, such as preparing the payroll or billing customers.

Some of the legacy systems are very large including hundreds of remote terminals linked or networked to the mainframe processor. The terminals can be at the same or different locations.

▶ 2.12 NEW ARCHITECTURES: CLIENT/SERVER ARCHITECTURE AND ENTERPRISE-WIDE COMPUTING

Two major architectural concepts provide the foundation of the newest IT architecture: **client/server architecture** and **enterprise-wide computing**. Together, they form the enterprise-wide client/server computing environment. The principles of these two concepts are briefly explained in this section, while the details are provided in Chapter 10.

CLIENT/SERVER ARCHITECTURE

A client/server arrangement divides networked computing units into two major categories: clients and servers. A **client** is a computer such as a PC or a workstation attached to a network, which is used to access *shared* network resources. A **server** is a machine that provides clients with services. Example of servers are the database server that provides a large database (such as a mainframe) and the communication server that provides connection to another network, to commercial databases, or to a powerful processor.

The purpose of such a division is to maximize the utilization of computer resources. A client/server architecture provides a way for different computing devices to work together, each doing the job for which it is best suited. Thus, the role of each machine is not fixed. A workstation, for example, can be client in one task and a server in another. Another important element is *sharing*. The clients, which are usually inexpensive PCs, share more expensive devices (the servers).

Client/server architecture gives a company as many access points to data as there are PCs on the network. It also lets a company use more tools to process data and information. The client/server architecture has changed the way people work in organizations; for example, people are empowered to access databases at will.

ENTERPRISE-WIDE CLIENT/SERVER ARCHITECTURE

Client/server computing can be practiced in a small work area or in one department on a LAN. The main benefit is the sharing of resources within a department. However, many users frequently need access to corporate data, applications, services, electronic-mail, and real-time flows of data, so they can improve productivity and competitiveness. The solution is to deploy an enterprise-wide client/server architecture, that is, to combine the two concepts to form a cohesive, flexible, and powerful computing environment. An example of such an architecture is provided in the PEC opening case and in Box 2.8.

IT At Work BOX 2.8

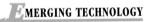 EMERGING TECHNOLOGY

A CLIENT/SERVER SYSTEM AT BURLINGTON, INC.

Burlington Inc. operates 190 textile retail stores and two distribution centers in various parts of the United States. The headquarters are in New Jersey. The company runs its entire business off an enterprise-wide client/server system. The figure to the right shows how the system works.

The cash registers and other PCs are networked to a main processor (a Sun workstation) in each store, which acts as a file server for the registers. It also acts as a communication gateway to the corporate mainframe computers for processing. The communication is done via a WAN using satellite technology. At headquarters, data can be processed or moved to several destinations such as the VISA/MasterCard system for credit card transactions. Routine transactions are executed on the corporate

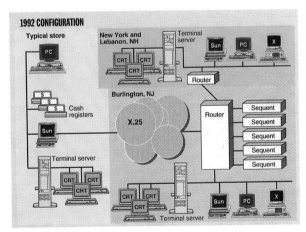

Burlington's client/server system.

Sequent computers, which process the transactions in parallel. Users can feed information from the corporate databases into spreadsheets or word processors on their desktop computers for end-user computing. The system handles everything from conveyor-belt scanners that generate database transactions, to PCs with a graphical user interface, where users can enter queries. The ter-minal servers shown in the figure enable data entry and queries from workstations.

Critical Thinking Issue: How would Burlington be conducting its business today if it had not adopted a client/server enterprise-wide architecture? ▲

SOURCE: Condensed from *Byte*, June, 1993, p. 99.

An enterprise-wide client/server architecture, according to Sybase Inc. (1993), provides total integration of departmental and corporate IS resources, thereby allowing for a new class of applications that span the enterprise and bene-fit both the corporate central management (providing controls) and end-user sys-tems (providing empowerment). It also provides better control and security over data in a distributed environment. By implementing client/server computing as the architecture for enterprise-wide information systems, organizations maximize the value of information by increasing its availability. Enterprise-wide client/ server computing enables organizations to reengineer business processes, to dis-tribute transactions, to streamline operations, and to provide better and newer services to customers. In short, by using an enterprise-wide client/server architec-ture, a corporation can gain a significant competitive advantage, a topic we will discuss in the next chapter.

▶ 2.13 INFORMATION SYSTEMS MANAGEMENT AS A FIELD: A CONCEPTUAL FRAMEWORK*

INTRODUCTION

The infrastructure, applications, IS personnel and other related resources need to be managed. The field that deals with it is referred to as *information management*. A distinction can be made between information management as a specialized or-ganization function (such as the IS department) and the organization's informa-tion system that results from the work of this function.

The conceptual framework that is presented in this section defines infor-mation management from both perspectives via an input-process-output model. This framework provides a set of principles and concepts which form the theory base of the field.

The **organization information management system** provides informa-tion and communication services and resources for the products and services, op-erations, management and control activities, and cooperative work of an organi-zation. The system consists of information technology infrastructures to provide the organization with capabilities and capacity for communication and informa-tion processing, and for *application systems* (programs) for applying information technology capabilities to human-machine systems for specific tasks and activities. *Application systems* (referred to as *applications*), can be a payroll system, vehicle scheduling, or a university registration system. The set of applications in an or-ganization is referred to as the *portfolio of applications*.

The *information management organization function* (IS department) plans, de-velops, implements, operates, and maintains the organization's information tech-

---

*Condensed from Gordon Davis, "Defining information management as a field of professional work and an academic field," unpublished paper. University of Minnesota. Reproduced with the permission of the author.

nology infrastructures and the organization's portfolio of applications. It also provides support and advisory services for systems developed and operated by individuals and organization units.

AN INPUT-PROCESS-OUTPUT MODEL FOR DEFINING THE FIELD

▼ *Outputs.* The unique, specialized outputs include a strategy for information management in the organization, information infrastructures, application systems, organization process changes, services from operation of systems, and information and management advisory services.

▼ *Inputs.* The inputs to information management as a functional system are personnel with information management skills, information and communication (Networks) technology, organization data and external databases, and system analysis and development methods and technologies.

▼ *Processes.* The specialized processes of the information management function include strategic information planning, system building and maintenance, change management, system operation, and providing information management advisory services.

The description of outputs, inputs, and processes emphasizes those characteristics of the IS field that are specialized and unique. Brief discussion of some of these follows.

OUTPUTS AND THEIR VALUE

The first step in developing a conceptual framework is to examine *why* the outputs are needed or *how* they add value to an organization.

▼ *Systems and processes.* Productivity in a task is improved by establishing routines that minimize unnecessary activities, reduce cognitive load on participants by routinizing some activities, and reducing communication requirements with others who provide inputs to, and use outputs from, the task. Routines also reduce cost and improve effectiveness of training. Design or redesign of systems and processes in an organization can improve productivity and reduce cycle times by increasing scope and responsibility through improved availability of information, increasing information and communication in order to allow parallel activities, and increasing the speed of communication among those involved in the system or process. Systems and processes depend upon information processing, communications, and information.

▼ *Information processing.* Information processing is required because organization processes store, retrieve, and manipulate data in performing organization activities. Information processing may be part of an application system provided by the organization or may be performed by users employing the information retrieval and processing facilities available through the information technology infrastructure.

▼ *Communication services.* Organizations require communication among individuals in the same organization, among groups and teams, and with external organizations such as suppliers, vendors, and creditors. Communication is required for obtaining information, coordinating activities, negotiating, obtaining orders for goods and services, instructing suppliers, and so forth.

▼ *Information.* Information is required for analysis, evaluation, and decision making at all levels in the organization. Providing correct and complete information when needed, where needed, and in a form that is useable adds value to an organization. Information is also important to negotiation and decision making by external organizations. Information can be differentiated as data, information, and knowledge, although the terms are often used interchangeably.

–*Data.* Data items about things, events, activities, and transactions are recorded, classified and stored, but are not organized to convey any specific meaning. Data items can be numeric, alphanumeric, figures, sounds or images. A *database* of stored data items organized for retrieval adds value as a general information resource available for many possible uses.

–*Information.* Information is data that has been organized so that it has meaning to the recipient. It confirms something the recipient knows or may have "surprise" value by telling something not known. The recipient interprets the meaning and draws conclusions and implications. Data items processed by an *application* so that the results are meaningful for an intended action or decision represent a more specific use and a higher value added relative to that use than simply access to the database. For example, the total weekly wages paid last week.

–*Knowledge.* Knowledge consists of data items that are organized and processed to convey *understanding, experience, accumulated learning,* and *expertise* as they apply to a current problem or activity. A set of data items processed to extract critical implications and to reflect past experience and expertise provides the recipient with organizational knowledge and a very high potential value added. Knowledge can be the application of data and information to make a decision.

THE INPUTS TO INFORMATION MANAGEMENT

The inputs to information management as a functional system are personnel with information management skills, information and communication technology, organization data and external databases, and system analysis and development methods and technologies. These inputs will be discussed in Chapters 8, 9, 11–14 and 18.

THE PROCESSES OF INFORMATION MANAGEMENT

The unique processes of the information management function include strategic information planning, system building and maintenance, change management, system operation, and information management advisory services.

▼ ***Strategic information planning.*** There are four strategic planning processes for information management: information technology scanning, participation in organization strategy planning, information infrastructures planning, and application portfolio planning. They depend upon an understanding of organization requirements and opportunities for communications, information processing, and information.

–*Information technology scanning.* This is a specialized planning process to prepare those in the information management function to provide inputs about technology opportunities and threats to the other planning processes. It involves tracking current developments in information technology, projecting current trends, and identifying ways in which new technology developments can provide opportunities or can threaten existing assets.

–*Participation in organization strategy planning.* The organization strategic planning process benefits from inputs about information technology opportunities and threats and assessments of current information technology use. The organization strategy process may suggest needs and opportunities; the information management function provides input on how information technology can be applied to meet them.

–*Information infrastructures planning.* The information infrastructures of an organization provides capacity and capabilities for information management activities across the organization. The infrastructure planning and application portfolio planning interact because the portfolio depends on appropriate infrastructures.

–*Application portfolio planning.* The information infrastructures provide general capacity and capabilities. The capabilities are utilized by applications developed by individuals, departments, and the information management function. The information management function has responsibility for building (or acquiring) a portfolio of major applications that meet the important needs of the organization. The *core applications* of an organization should be integrated to support information sharing and use of data across applications. Other applications depend on the existence of the core applications and transaction databases derived from them.

▼ *System building and maintenance.* Information systems are designed and built to meet organization requirements. Once built and implemented, systems must be maintained by making corrections and enhancements. The requirements process precedes both original system building and maintenance of existing systems. Following requirements determination, there are building and maintenance processes for the computer and communication infrastructure systems, the system of databases, the system of information management personnel, and applications.

–*Requirements determination.* The organization requirements are determined during strategic planning plus organization requirements determination processes. Application requirements arise from innovations to incorporate more information or information processing, in products or services, by incorporating information or information processing in business process design or redesign, and by applications to support management processes. Requirements determination processes for individual applications are described in Chapter 13.

–*Building and maintaining the computer and communication infrastructure systems.* The design of the computer and communication infrastructures reflects both organizational and technical considerations. The extent to which the organization is centralized or decentralized will affect the infrastructure design. Examples of other organizational factors are maturity of information technology use, industry practice, and customer and supplier technology use. Technical considerations include conformance with hardware and software standards, effect of new technology on existing systems, and technical performance.

–*Building and maintaining the system of databases.* Most organizations have several databases. Databases serving users across the organization are considered part of the database infrastructure. The system may include databases supplied by or accessed through external vendors. The databases are based on organization requirements plus technical considerations to support efficient access. The building of the infrastructure databases involves requirements analysis, data modeling, logical database design, physical database design, and implementation. External databases require analysis and design to fit access into organization procedures.

–*Building and maintaining the system of information management personnel.* The information management personnel infrastructure includes personnel within the information management function and personnel who perform information management activities but are part of other organization functions or units. The allocation of activities among the locations where personnel may be assigned is part of the infrastructure planning.

–*Building and maintaining applications.* Applications are designed for specific needs in products or services, business processes, and knowledge work activities. Applications may be acquired from outside vendors or developed internally. Development technology and methodologies are employed in building and maintaining applications.

▼ *Change management.* Managing change is an important process for information management because the use of IT involve changes in processes, procedures, jobs, responsibilities, and organization structures (see Figure 1.5). The information infrastructures enable organization changes because they provide the organization with increased information processing and communication capabilities. Use of information technology may increase scope and responsibility for business processes and reduce cycle time through improved information access and communication. Applications of information technology to knowledge work activities may change the way the work is done and expectations about the work. Change management is based on principles of socio-technical design of systems, participation by system users, and involvement of all stakeholders.

▼ *Information management operations.* The information management function manages the day-to-day computer and communication infrastructures. The operation of core applications includes transaction processing, supporting access to databases, producing transaction documents and reports, and maintaining databases. The function also has responsibility for security and backup protection for core applications and databases (see Chapters 18 and 19).

▼ *Information management advisory services.* Not all information processing and data are under the direct control and supervision of the information management function. Individual users have responsibility for their personal computers and the data they maintain on their systems. Departments may operate small, departmental systems. Client/server systems may store and make available all software and data needed by a workgroup or a department. The dispersion of computing resources in support of knowledge workers often means that the information management function has the reponsibility for formulating standards so that individual systems fit within the corporate systems and for providing assistance to individual users in configuring, purchasing, and installing systems and software. Ongoing assistance may need to be provided as problems arise.

KNOWLEDGE REQUIREMENTS FOR INFORMATION MANAGEMENT

The five unique processes of the information management function (strategic information planning, system building and maintenance, change management, system operation, and information management advisory services) plus the issues associated with the management of the function are the basis for knowledge requirements for those in the field. In order to perform the five processes of information management, expert knowledge is required in information technology as applied in organizations, and processes for development of systems and effecting changes required by them. These two areas of expert knowledge are supported by knowledge of organizations and organization processes.

1. *Expert information technology application knowledge.* The technology employed in information management includes a broad range of computer and communications technologies, usually described as *information technologies* (or tools). Technology knowledge includes technologies incorporated in systems (such as analytical models and methods for building expertise into systems) and technologies employed in developing and implementing systems. The

information management function has expertise in these technologies. The depth of expertise supports the design and development of systems employing the technology rather than the design or invention of new technologies. The requirement is expertise to understand and employ state-of-the-art, commercially available hardware, software, and communications technologies in systems and in building systems.

2. ***Expert knowledge of system development and change processes.*** Although many persons in an organization may participate at some time in a system development project or change process, the information management function provides ongoing expertise. The expertise extends to both small, personal systems and corporate-wide applications. Included in the domain of system development knowledge are methodologies and development technologies. Change management required by new or redesigned systems involve an understanding of change processes for both individuals and organizations.

3. ***Broad knowledge of organization strategies and structures.*** There is an interaction between information systems and other uses of information technology in an organization and the strategies and structures of the organization. The information systems may reflect organization strategies and structure or they can be the basis for innovations and changes in strategies and structures. Information management personnel should have sufficient knowledge of strategies and structures to participate effectively in the design of new information infrastructures and systems to support changes and innovations.

4. ***Broad knowledge of organization systems and processes.*** Building systems, providing consultation to the organization on information technology, and building and operating information infrastructures and systems, demands a knowledge of the organization systems and processes being supported. This knowledge should be sufficient to interact with and understand the requirements of functional specialists and to integrate requirements across the organization. The knowledge includes the purposes and processes for transaction processing, reporting systems, analysis and decision making, and strategic planning. In support of their project activities, information management personnel need a good understanding of project management, service quality, interpersonal relationships in organizations, and budgeting and reporting.

INFORMATION MANAGEMENT AS AN ORGANIZATION FUNCTION

Organizations create specialized functions when a specialized expertise is required. The use of information technology is so pervasive that a certain level of expertise must be distributed broadly across the organization. Individuals and workgroups within the other organization functions may have significant responsibility for their own information management activities or local systems involving information technology.

However, the information management function has responsibility for maintaining expertise sufficient to assist individuals, groups, departments, and functions in their information management, to provide integration across the organization, and build and maintain the corporate information infrastructures and standards necessary for integrated information processes. The same concept can be observed in other functions. For example, budgeting and analysis of financial results must be applied by many individuals and groups in an organization, but the accounting function has responsibility for establishing standards, providing expertise to the organization, and consolidating and interpreting results at the organization level.

Table 2.3 **Corporate Versus Information Management Function Views**

Corporate View of Any Function	View of Information Management Function
Structural Preconditions	**Structural Preconditions**
Management/managers	Management/managers for the function of information management
Strategy	Information management strategy
Business process infrastructure	Information management infrastructure
Abstract	Abstract
Organization, procedures, and routines	Organization, procedures, and routines
Concrete	Concrete
Technology and systems	Technology (hardware, communications, system software)
	Databases
	Applications
Personnel	Information management personnel
Operations	**Operations**
Operational processes	Data processing operations
	Database access operations
	Communications operations
Operational management	Information operations management
Management control	Information management control

The structural preconditions and information management operations are directly analogous to the rest of the organization as shown in Table 2.3.

An organization must build, maintain, and rebuild its business processes and information systems. Every business function has a role in these activities. However, the information management function has a more active role because many of the processes and systems incorporate information technology. Although each business function should be involved in the design and development of its processes and systems, the complete information system expertise needed for such development is not normally present in a function. Also, many systems cross functions, so no single function can define the requirements for these systems. The information management function has special expertise for business process and system development for the functions of an organization and for cross functional systems. Unlike other functions where the activities are periodic, the information management function has an ongoing expert role in business process and system development. A unique role of information management is integration, both in development and information operations. This cross functional, integrative role makes information management very broad in its domain of interest, dynamic, and demanding.

▶ MANAGERIAL ISSUES

FROM LEGACY SYSTEMS TO CLIENT/SERVER

A major issue confronting many companies is if and when to move from their legacy system to a client/server enterprise-wide architecture. While the general trend is to do it, there have been several unsuccessful transformations. Client/server and enterprise computing are relatively new, and so there are several unresolved issues regarding implementation of these systems. Moving to the new architecture requires new infrastructure, and it may have a considerable impact on people, quality of work, and budget. This important issue is discussed in detail in Chapter 10.

HOW MUCH INFRASTRUCTURE?

Justifying information system applications is not an easy job due to the intangible benefits and the rapid changes in technologies that often make them obsolete. Justifying infrastructure is even more difficult since the infrastructure (such as corporate databases, networks, and data centers) is shared by many users and applications. This makes it almost impossible to quantify the benefits. Basic architecture is a necessity, but there are some options. An interesting approach is proposed by Weill and Broadbent (1994). ■

KEY TERMS

Ad hoc report *40*

Application systems *39*

Artificial intelligence *41*

Artificial neural networks (ANN) *44*

Client/server architecture *56*

Cooperative processing *56*

Data *60*

Decision support system (DSS) *41*

Distributed processing *56*

Enterprise-wide computing *56*

Enterprise-wide system *56*

Exception report *41*

Executive information system (EIS) *42*

Expert system (ES) *42*

Group support system (GSS) *42*

Information *60*

Information architecture *39*

Information infrastructure *54*

Intelligent support systems *39*

Knowledge *60*

Knowledge workers *52*

Legacy system *56*

Management information system (MIS) *40*

Mission-central tasks *38*

Office automation system (OAS) *41*

Periodic report *40*

Transaction processing system (TPS) *45*

Value chain model *48*

Value system *48*

CHAPTER HIGHLIGHTS *(L-x means learning objective number x)*

▼ Information systems can be organized according to business functions, the people they support, or both. (L-1)

▼ The transaction processing system (TPS) covers the mission-central repetitive organizational transactions such as purchasing, billing, or payroll. (L-2)

▼ The data collected in TPS are used to build other systems. (L-2)

▼ The activities performed in any organization should add value to a product or service. They are interrelated as in a value chain. (L-3)

▼ The major functional information systems in an organization are accounting, finance, manufacturing (operations), human resources, and marketing. (L-4)

▼ The main general support systems are OAS, DSS, GSS, EIS, ES, and ANN. (L-5)

▼ Managerial activities and decisions can be classified as operational, managerial, and strategic. (L-6)

▼ An information architecture provides the conceptual foundation for building the information infrastructure and specific applications. It maps the information requirements as they relate to information resources. (L-7)

▼ There are three major configurations of an information architecture: the mainframe environment, the PC environment, and the distributed environment. (L-7)

▼ The information infrastructure refers to the shared information resources (such as corporate database) and their linkages, operation, maintenance, and management. (L-8)

▼ Legacy systems are older systems in which the mainframe is at the core of the system. (L-9)

▼ In a client/server architecture, several PCs (the clients) are networked among themselves and are connected to databases, telecommunications and other providers of services (the servers). (L-10)

▼ An enterprise-wide information system is a system that provides communication among all the organization employees. It also provides accessibility to any data or information needed by any employee at any location. (L-10)

QUESTIONS FOR REVIEW

1. Describe a TPS.

2. What is an MIS?

3. Explain the role of the DSS.

4. What is the purpose of an EIS?

5. Describe operational, managerial, and strategic activities.

6. Define data, information, and knowledge.

7. What information systems support the work of groups?

8. What is an enterprise-wide system?

9. What is an information architecture?

10. Describe information infrastructure.

11. Discuss the evolution of CBIS.

12. Distinguish among periodic, ad hoc, and exception reports.

13. Define business transactions and give some examples.

14. Which business functions are considered primary activities and which are support activities in the value chain model?

15. Distinguish between a mainframe and a distributed environment.

16. Describe a legacy system.

17. What is a client/server system?

QUESTIONS FOR DISCUSSION

1. Review the analogy between means of transportation and an information architecture. Show the equivalence and indicate the major advantages and disadvantages for each of the three subsystems.

2. Discuss the logic of building information systems in accordance with the organizational hierarchical structure.

3. Distinguish between information architecture and information infrastructure.

4. Information systems evolved over time starting with TPS. What is the logic of such evolution?

5. Explain how operational, managerial, and strategic activities are related to general support systems.

6. Relate the following concepts: client/server, distributed processing, and enterprise-wide computing.

7. Some believe that a client/server architecture when organized in an enterprise-wide setting is the most desirable option for many companies. Explain why.

8. Explain how an enterprise-wide system can be related to the Porter's value system model. (Consult Figure 2-1 in Porter's book [1985]).

EXERCISES

1. Classify the following systems into one (or more) of the general support systems:
   a. A student registration system in a university
   b. A system that advises farmers about which fertilizers to use
   c. A hospital patient's admission system
   d. A system that provides a marketing manager with demand reports regarding the sales volume of specific products
   e. A robotic system that paints cars in a factory

2. Develop conceptual value chains for the following situations:
   a. Manufacturing cars
   b. Shipping cargo to a foreign country
   c. Searching for a missing child
   d. Domino's delivery business (Box 2.6)

3. Use the value chain model to describe the operation of your organization or an organization with which you are familiar. How is IT related to its primary activities?

4. Review the following systems in Chapter 1 and classify each of them according to the inside matrix in Figure 2.10. Try to match each system with at least one cell of the matrix. Note that one system can be classified in several ways. The systems in Chapter 1 are:

7-Eleven
UPS (Figure 1.4)
Crime Information System
Waubonsee College
The 1990 Goodwill Games
Florida Power and Light
Triange House
FDA (Box 1.3)
SKI Ltd. (Minicase 1)

5. Review the following systems in this chapter and classify each of them according to the triangle of Figure 2.9.

Panhandle Eastern
Dalian plant (Box 2.1)
ICI Ltd. (Box 2.2)
BMG (Box 2.3)
Dalla Vera (Box 2.4)
Detecting bombs (Box 2.5)
Domino Pizza (Box 2.6)
Burlington Inc. (Box 2.8)
Atlantic Electric (Minicase 1)

GROUP ASSIGNMENT

Observe a checkout counter in a supermarket that uses a scanner to identify the items checked out. Find some material that describes how the scanned code is translated into the price that the customers pay.

1. Identify the following components of the systems: inputs, processes, outputs, feedback.

2. What kind of a system is this: TPS, DSS, EIS, MIS, etc.? Why?

3. Having the information electronically in the system may provide opportunities for additional managerial uses. Identify such uses.

4. Find material about how such systems will be operating in the future. Describe it.

Minicase 1

Information Technology Helps Atlantic Electric Co. Survive

Atlantic Electric Co. of New Jersey is losing the monopoly it once held. Some of its clients are already buying electricity from a new, unregulated brand of competitor—an independent cogenerator that generates its own electricity and sells its additional capacity to other companies at low prices. The competitor finds easy-to-serve commercial accounts. Atlantic Electric Company may even lose its residential customer base since the local regulatory commission could rule that the customers would be better served by another utility.

In order to survive, the company must be the least expensive provider in its territory. One way to do it is to provide employees with the information they need to make more up-to-date and accurate business decisions. The current IT includes a mainframe and a corporate network for mainframe access. The users use both dumb and smart terminals. However, this system was unable to meet the new challenge. It is necessary to develop user applications, in a familiar format, and to do it rapidly with minimum cost. This can be done on PCs but not on the mainframe.

Some of the needed applications include the following:

1. a database and decision support system for fuel purchasing,

2. a database for customers and their electricity usage pattern, and DSS for customized rates,

3. a DSS for substations design and transmission, and

4. cash management DSS for the treasury department.

The company decided to explore an enterprise-wide option, with departmental LANs connected to the corporate network. The estimated cost of the proposed system is $1.5 million.

Questions for Minicase 1

1. Is an enterprise-wide option the best in this case? Why?

2. Should the option be a client/server?

3. The existing mainframe system is using the networks as a traditional distributed system, where people can download and upload information with their PCs. Why not modify this system rather than using a client/server option? (You may want to consult Chapter 10 for a good answer.)

4. The concern of Atlantic Electric Company is survival. What kind of information technologies can be used to help survival in this case?

5. Identify some of the pressures described in Chapter 1.

SOURCE: Based on Goff, L. "Old Game, New Rules," *InfoWorld Direct*, May 1993, p. 30.

REFERENCES AND SUGGESTIONS FOR FURTHER READING

1. Aituv N., et al., "Factors Affecting the Policy of Distributed Computing Resources," *MIS Quarterly*, December 1989.

2. Bolt, R.C., and P. Wallace, "Data Dippers," *Corporate Computing*, August 1992.

3. Clark, M., "Creating Customer Value: Information-chain Based Management," *Information Strategy: The Executive's Journal*, Fall, 1993.

4. Davis, S., and B. Davidson, *2020 Vision*, New York: Simon & Schuster, 1991.

5. *Datamation*, special supplement on the best in client/server computing, October 1, 1991.

6. *Datamation*, special supplement on client/server computing, June 15, 1993.

7. Khama, R., *Distributed Computing Implementation and Management Strategy*, Englewood Cliffs, NJ: Prentice Hall, 1994.

8. Millet, I., et al., "Executive Information Systems," *DSS 91 Transactions*, Zigurs I. (ed.), Providence, RI: The Institute of Management Sciences, 1991.

9. Millet, I. and C.H. Mawhinney, "Executive Information Systems," *Information & Management*, Volume 23, 1992.

10. Palvia, P.C., et al, "The Prism System: A Key to Organizational Effectiveness at Federal Express Corporation," *MIS Quarterly*, September 1992.

11. Porter, M.E., *Competitive Advantage: Creating and Sustaining Superior Performance*, New York: The Free Press, 1985, p. 37.

12. Shapiro, J.F., et al., "Optimizing the Value Chain," *Interfaces*, March–April 1993.

13. Sinha, A., "Client-server Computing," *Communications of the ACM*, July 1992.

14. Sybase Inc., "A Special Advertising Report," *Network Computing*, May 1993.

15. Synnott, W.R., *The Information Weapon*, New York: John Wiley & Sons, 1987.

16. Turban, E., *Decision Support and Expert Systems* (3rd ed.), New York: Macmillan, 1993.

17. Ullman, E., "Client/Server Frees Data," *Byte*, June 1993.

18 Weill, P., and M. Broadbent, "Infrastructure goes industry specific," *MIS* (Australia), July 1994.

3

Strategic Information Systems and Information Technology for Business Reengineering

Chapter Outline

Learning Objectives

After studying this chapter, you will be able to:

1. Define strategic information systems and explain their advantages.

2. Describe the value chain model and its relationship to information technology.

3. Describe Porter's competitive forces model and how information technology helps companies improve their competitive positions.

4. Describe several frameworks that show how IT supports the attainment of competitive advantage.

5. Describe representative strategic information systems.

6. Understand the major implementation and managerial issues of strategic information systems.

7. Describe the concept of business processes reengineering and contrast it with continuous improvement.

8. Discuss the role of IT as an enabler to business processes reengineering.

9. Discuss the relationship between strategic information systems and business processes reengineering.

▶ 3.1 OPENING CASE: CATERPILLAR CO. FENDS OFF JAPANESE COMPETITION

REENGINEERING

CATERPILLAR INC. (CAT) OF Peoria, Illinois, is a world leader in manufacturing heavy machinery. In 1982, the company entered a difficult period of competition. Komatsu of Japan, a major competitor, offered bulldozers in the United States for 40 percent less than CAT's. Caterpillar was forced to cut prices. A poor economy and a lengthy labor strike worsened the situation. By 1985, the accumulated losses amounted to $953 million. Caterpillar, which sells its products all over the world, responded to the downturn in all the usual ways: they closed plants, laid off workers, and slashed expenses. But the usual ways did not work: market share declined and losses increased. Management decided that the only solution lay in information technology. CAT realized it would not be globally competitive without state-of-the-art information technology. The information technology project lasted eight years and cost $2 billion. What did the project accomplish?

Computer-integrated manufacturing (CIM) (see Chapter 17), a dream of many companies, is a reality at CAT. Robots, computer-aided design, and computer-aided manufacturing are functioning throughout the various plants. These and other computerized systems resulted in in-process inventory reductions by 60 percent and savings of several million dollars. Nonessential labor was eliminated, production processes were simplified, plants and warehouses were closed, lead time to build a product was reduced to 10 days from 45 days, and on-time deliveries to customers increased by 70 percent. Modern management techniques, such as a computerized MRP II (see Chapter 17), were installed, and computerized purchasing and logistics systems were placed in operation. A sophisticated system for providing replacement parts to dealers was installed. This sophisticated system enabled dealers to provide parts to their clients quickly, yet maintain low inventories. Although each of CAT's 17 divisions operates as an autonomous business unit, the IT project was the responsibility of a centralized IS group.

Some other important IT applications are:

▼ A global network with 7,000 terminals connects 50,000 employees and 180 dealers in 1,000 locations (Caterpillar uses both its fiber optic network and a leased satellite service).

Employees at Caterpillar Inc.

▼ An executive information system enables business units to analyze data, identify trends, and evaluate the dealers' performance.

▼ CAT's dealers and suppliers are on electronic data interchange (EDI) system. An EDI is a sophisticated electronic communication systems used for intercompany transaction processing (see Chapter 14).

▼ The telecommunication system includes a "CAT TV" program to dealers, as well as audio and video teleconferencing capabilities.

▼ Ninty percent of the company's employees can access data on the company's enterprise-wide system.

For its efforts, CAT was a winner of *InformationWeek's* 1991 "Excellence in IS" award. The IT project supported a massive restructuring of the company. Such a massive effort can be considered as the *reengineering* of the corporation.

The results: By 1993, Caterpillar had become stronger than its competitors, controlling more than 30 percent of the U.S. construction equipment market. Caterpillar was able to export more than half of its sales to foreign buyers, yet was able to keep the manufacturing plants and the jobs in the United States.

And what about CAT's chief rival, Komatsu of Japan? Komatsu shifted its construction-equipment strategy away from bulldozers in order to avoid head-to-head competition with CAT.

SOURCE: Condensed from Bartolomew D; "Caterpillar Digs in" *InformationWeek*, June 7, 1993, pp. 36–41.

▶ 3.2 WHAT IS A STRATEGIC INFORMATION SYSTEM?

A study conducted by *Datamation* in 1994 (*Datamation*, January 15, 1994) concluded that the use of IT to increase the **competitive advantage** of organizations is the third most important issue faced by directors of information systems departments. (The first two were productivity and quality.)

The Caterpillar case illustrates the use of information systems to achieve a strategic advantage. Such systems are known as **strategic information systems** (SIS).

Strategic information systems can be defined as systems that support or shape a business unit's competitive strategy (Wiseman [1988]). An SIS is characterized by the system's ability to *significantly* change the manner in which the business supported by the system is done. This occurs through its contribution to the strategic goals of an organization and/or its ability to significantly increase performance and productivity. Neumann (1994) maintains that some conventional information systems that are used in innovative ways can become strategic. Originally, strategic systems were considered to be *outwardly* aiming at direct competition in their industry, for example by providing new services to customers and/or suppliers with the specific objective of beating their competitors. But starting in the late '80s, strategic systems were also viewed *inwardly*: they were focused on enhancing the competitive position of the firm by supporting the **business processes reengineering** (BPR) of companies, increasing employees' productivity, improving teamwork, and enhancing communication. Caterpillar combined the outward and inward orientations to its advantage. In addition, it used IT to support its BPR efforts. Strategic systems are critical to the attainment of strategic goals. For example, Caterpillar is using the EDI and the CAT TV programs to increase their direct competitive advantage against the Japanese (another outward approach). They also reengineered their manufacturing processes by using various computer-integrated manufacturing (CIM) tools.

In addition to the inward and outward approaches, there is another dimension to SIS, **strategic alliances**, where two or more companies share a strategic information system. For example, many banks share the same ATM network. Strategic alliances were described in Chapter 1 and will be revisited throughout this book.

In this chapter, we provide an overview of SIS. In addition, we will provide an introduction to BPR and discuss its relationship with SIS.

ASPECTS OF STRATEGIC MANAGEMENT

Strategic management has long been associated with long-range planning. Today, however, strategic management includes three complementary aspects: long-range planning, response management, and innovation (see Figure 3.1).

The traditional way of introducing significant changes into organizations involved a **long-range planning** approach. Moving to a new product line, expanding the business by acquiring supporting businesses, and moving to foreign

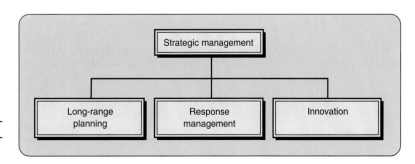

FIGURE 3.1 Strategic management has three complementary elements.

countries are prime examples. A long-range planning document outlines strategies and plans for 5 or even 10 years. From this plan, companies derive their shorter period planning, budgeting, and resources' allocation.

Response management is a strategy that focuses on an organization's quick reaction to protect itself against a competitor's action or some change in the environment. The response is considered to be strategic if the change that triggers it is so significant that unless a quick response is undertaken, the well-being, or even the survival, of the organization may be in jeopardy.

In contrast to a response management, organizations may use a proactive strategy. That is, companies introduce innovative changes that give them a competitive advantage in the short run. **Innovation** is considered as one of the four most important business concepts for the 1990s (see Davenport [1993]).

Companies today are engaged in all aspects of strategic management. As a matter of fact, when a major innovation is introduced by one company other companies in the industry need to *respond* to the threat. Innovation is strongly related to information technologies (creativity and idea generation), as will be illustrated in Chapters 14 and 15 and is shown in Table 3.1.

Information technology contributes to strategic management in many ways. Consider these three:

1. Information technology creates applications that provide direct strategic advantage to organizations. For example, Federal Express was the first company in its industry to use information technology to track the location of every package in its system.

2. IT supports strategic changes such as reengineering. For example, information technology allows efficient decentralization by providing speedy communication lines, and it streamlines and shortens product design time by using computer-aided engineering tools. For example, Kodak designed the disposal camera with CAD tools and was able to put the camera in stores before the Japanese.

3. IT provides *business intelligence* by collecting and analyzing information about innovations, markets, competitors, and environmental changes. Such information provides strategic advantage because, if a company knows something

Table 3.1 **Areas of IT Related to Technological Innovations**

Innovation	Advantage
New products	Constantly innovating with new competitive products and services. Electronic Art is introducing CD ROM-based video games.
Extended products	Leveraging old products with new competitive extensions. A Korean company was the first to introduce fuzzy logic to its washing machines, sales went up 50% in a few months.
Differentiated products	Gaining advantage through unique products or added value. Compaq computers become the leading PC seller after providing self-diagnostic disks with their computers.
Super systems	Erecting competitive barriers through major system developments that cannot be easily duplicated. American Airlines Reservation System became so comprehensive that it took years to duplicate; a super system always stays ahead of the competition.
Customer terminals	Putting computer terminals in customer spaces (locking out the competition). See American Hospital Supply in Section 3.9.
Electronic delivery	Using EDI as a substitute for paper transactions and as a mean of global expansion.
Computer-aided sales	Offering systems that provide computer-supported to marketing and sales. For example, providing sales people with wireless hand-held computers that allow them to provide quotation on the customer's situation.

EMERGING TECHNOLOGY
...inducing innovations

SOURCE: Based on Synnott, 1987.

important before its competitors, or if it can make the correct interpretation of the information before its competitors, then it can introduce changes and benefit from them (see Box 3.1).

A Closer Look BOX 3.1

COMPETITIVE INTELLIGENCE—A KEY TO SUCCESS

Information about the competition can mean the difference between winning or losing a business battle. Many companies continuously monitor the activities of their competitors. For example, Frito Lay distributors, when they deliver to a store, will count what their competitors have on the shelves, enter the information into hand-held computers, and transmit it to the corporate database within minutes. An executive information system at Hertz monitors car rental prices of their competitors, on a daily basis. An EIS at Kraft, the giant food maker, closely monitors the performance of their competitors. Such activities are part of *competitive intelligence*, which drives business performance by increasing market knowledge, internal relationships, and the quality of strategic planning. Research indicates that the percentage of companies using CBIS to support competitive intelligence has increased from 31 percent in 1993 to about 50 percent in 1995.

Information about markets, technologies, and government's actions is also collected by competitive intelligence. Several information technologies can be used for collecting such information, ranging from text retrieval to optical character recognition. Analyzing and interpreting the information is as important as collecting it. Here, one can use spreadsheets and expert systems. For example, Chase Manhattan Bank (New York) uses expert systems to track several sources of information to determine impacts on the bank, the customers, and the industry.

Competitive intelligence is looking at internal sources as well. There is a lot of informal information that can be collected and stored in what some companies call "institutional memory" or "corporate knowledge base." Competitive intelligence can be enhanced by several information technologies, including intelligent agents (Chapter 16).

Subscribing to newswire alert services is another way to collect information. Such services monitor hundreds of databases to find the relevant information for their subscribers.

There is another aspect to competitive intelligence: espionage. Spies are looking especially for marketing plans, cost analysis, new products/services, and strategic plans. For example, in a well-known case, an employee who left Borland International to work for a competitor, Symentac, transferred (electronically) Borland's trade secrets regarding strategic planning to Symentac (see details in Chapter 20). Such espionage can be unfair or even illegal. Another problem is the theft of portable computers at conferences, which is spreading all over the world. Most of the thieves are interested in the information stored in the computers, not in the computers themselves.

Protecting against such activities is important and is discussed in Chapter 19.

SOURCE: *Based in part on Wreden W.,* "Get Smart—Competitive Intelligence Networks," *Beyond Computing,* January/February 1994.

Before presenting a framework for SIS and illustrating its applications, we will clarify the relationships between competitive advantage and strategic advantage.

COMPETITIVE ADVANTAGE VERSUS STRATEGIC ADVANTAGE

Competition, according to Porter (1985), is at the core of a firm's success or failure. **Competitive strategy** is the search for a **competitive advantage** in an industry, either by controlling the market or by enjoying larger than average profits. Such a strategy aims to establish a profitable and sustainable position against the forces that determine industry competition. SIS are designed to provide or support competitive strategy. Indeed, during the '70s and '80s, we witnessed the implementation of a large number of SIS applications. Now during the 1990s, as a result of advancements in technology, it has become difficult to *sustain* an advantage for an extended period. Competitors can imitate systems in months rather than in years. New technological innovations today make yesterday's innovations obsolete. Furthermore, experience indicates that information systems, by themselves, can rarely provide a sustainable competitive advantage.

Only when SIS are combined with structural changes in the organization can they be very beneficial in providing a *strategic advantage*. For example, PRISM is a comprehensive strategic information system used by Federal Express to better manage human resources, and increase the effectiveness and efficiency of their operation (see Minicase 1 in Chapter 17). It does not compete directly with any company (like their package tracking system did), but it provides a strategic advantage by building and maintaining first–class personnel. The shift of corporate operations from a *competitive* to a *strategic* orientation (of which competition is only one aspect) is fundamental. Some studies (e.g., Andersen Consulting, see McNurlin [1991]), show that fewer top executives of the 1990s (as compared to the '80s) feel that IT holds the key to competitive advantage. However, more than 90 percent of these top executives strongly agree that IT has a significant impact on the profitability of an organization and even upon its *survival* (see Box 3.2).

IT At Work BOX 3.2

REENGINEERING

MCKESSON DRUG COMPANY'S ECONOMOST

McKesson Drug Company is a wholesale drug distributor, known for its extensive use of IT in a very competitive market. One example is Economost, its electronic order entry system for drug distribution.

McKesson had an important motivation to install Economost in 1975. Its primary customers were small, independent pharmacies which were at risk of going out of business because they were unable to compete with the large pharmacy chains. Economost was aimed at giving these pharmacies many of the advantages enjoyed by the large chains, thereby preserving their business.

Here is how the system works. The customer's order is phoned in, faxed, or transmitted electronically to McKesson's data center. The order is then entered into a computer and acknowledged. Next, the orders are transferred to an IBM 3090 mainframe for storage. Regional distribution centers pull their shipment orders from the mainframe at regular intervals and deliver the drugs quickly.

The IT has been combined with structural changes. The distribution centers are designed for maximum efficiency. For example, "pickers" walk through McKesson's warehouses, pushing carts on rollers and filling the orders. Warehouse shelves are arranged to correspond to pharmacy departments and are laid out to minimize the effort of shelf pickers. Also, each distribution center has a minicomputer that runs the entire operation from bar code order identification labels which are used to sort and route the products. Distant customers not tied directly to a warehouse are served from "mother trucks," which are sent to switching points where their content is transferred into smaller trucks for local deliveries.

Benefits accrued to both customers and McKesson.

BENEFITS TO CUSTOMERS (Small Pharmacies)

▼ More reliable order filling

▼ Reduced transaction costs

▼ Reduced inventory holding costs

▼ Increased management support

▼ Faster delivery service

BENEFITS TO McKESSON

▼ Rapid, reliable, and cost-effective customer order entry. The number of order-entry clerks has been reduced from 700 to 15.

▼ Sales personnel are no longer primarily order takers. The number of sales personnel has been cut in half.

▼ Productivity of warehouses' staff has increased by 17 percent.

▼ Purchasing has been reorganized to tightly match actual sales.

▼ Customers are tied to McKesson because they want to enjoy their benefits.

The impact of Economost for McKesson has been significant. Although the company's total market share has not increased significantly, Economost changed the manner in which business is done such that both McKesson and its customer pharmacies have been able to survive.

Critical Thinking Issue: Does Economost provide McKesson with a sustainable competitive advantage? Why or why not? ▲

SOURCE: Based on Clemons and Row, *Planning Review*, 1988.

3.3 COMPETITIVE ADVANTAGES OF STRATEGIC INFORMATION SYSTEMS

The use of an SIS can be important to a business in many ways. The most obvious is that it can give a firm a competitive advantage in the marketplace. Here are five ways an SIS can offer a competitive advantage (Sass and Keefe [1988]):

1. Creating barriers to competitors' entry into the market as illustrated in the Caterpillar and the McKesson cases.
2. Building of customers' switching costs (cost of switching suppliers) and/or operational dependence, e.g., by using EDI, to discourage customers from changing suppliers. An example is McKesson, which provided its customers with many benefits.
3. Completely changing the basis of competition by offering new services, products, or information not offered by competitors. For example, Citicorp was the first bank in New York to introduce ATM machines for their customers.
4. Completely changing the organization's operations in such a way as to change the nature or environment of the business. Sears closed its century-old catalog business and moved to Prodigy, a system that allows electronic shopping from home.
5. Precipitating a business process, such as pricing, that allows the firm to choose an optimal pricing strategy for products and services. Computerized frequent flyer or frequent user programs allow companies to provide discounts and special services to the customers with a high volume of business (see Box 3.3).

IT At Work BOX 3.3   ◄ **G**LOBAL PERSPECTIVE

SMART CARDS MOVE SHOPPERS TO THE TWENTY-FIRST CENTURY

Takashimaya is a giant retailer based in Japan with stores in Asia, Europe, and America. The company was the first to introduce an international smart credit card in Singapore. The card called Takashimaya VISA Smart card (TVS) can be used as a regular credit card worldwide. The smart card also features a microchip that stores bonus points a cardholder earns while shopping at Takashimaya department store in Singapore. Cardholders can redeem these bonus points for privileges like free car parking, free delivery, lucky draws, gifts, and gift coupons. The card also stores information about the cardholder's shopping habits as well as about target direct mail programs.

The smart card system consists of an electronic data capture terminal, a card reader, and a printer. It is integrated with the point of sale (POS) terminal and a handheld scanner.

The information collected is used to create a customer information system. The card also includes the customer address, age, and shopping preferences. A similar system is used by most major airlines for their frequent flyer programs, but the airlines do not use smart cards. Mr. Chen Seong Leng, the MIS Manager at Takashimaya Singapore, said that "at today's competitive environment, a retailer has to find better means of identifying shopping trends and habits." Retailers must know exactly who bought what merchandise (recall the 7-Eleven case in Chapter 1).

The system saves time for cashiers, who now make one entry instead of two (one at the POS, the other one for a credit payment). The Singapore store is located on Orchard Road, one of the most competitive shopping streets in the world. Since the introduction of smart card, business is booming as never before. The information collected is also processed by a DSS for pricing, making advertisements, and other promotion decisions.

Critical Thinking Issue: Are competitors likely to copy this innovation? What can Takashimaya do in response? ▲

SOURCE: Based on a story in *ITAsia*, December, 1993.

Another advantage was proposed by Parson (1983): Substituting IT for labor. This can reduce production and distribution costs. Hence, cost to the customer or delivery time can be reduced. For example, the Port of Singapore is using expert systems to plan the loading and unloading of containers from hundreds of vessels each week. The systems resulted in reducing the number of planners by 90 percent (a saving of several hundred employees and millions of dollars), enabling the port to charge lower fees and also shorten the time the ship is at the port. This allows the port to compete with ports in Indonesia and Malaysia, making it the second largest container port in the world.

Many other benefits can be realized by using IT as an enabler to support competitive advantage, as will be illustrated throughout this book.

▶ 3.4 STRATEGIC INFORMATION SYSTEMS FRAMEWORKS

A framework is a descriptive structure of SIS that helps us understand and classify the relationship among strategic management, competitive strategy, and information technology. A framework is basically a classification language, a subjective conceptual model that helps us understand how IT can support the business. One reason for the abundance of frameworks is that there are many different information systems, as was shown in Chapter 2. Also, different frameworks developed at different times. Neumann (1994) advocates the use of strategic information systems frameworks and provides a detailed description of (and references for) the most important ones. In this book we will present only a few frameworks, basically to illustrate their role in the study of information technology.

Many of the SIS frameworks are derived from the work of Michael Porter. In this chapter the following frameworks will be introduced:

▼ Porter's **value chain model**, which was introduced in its generic format in Chapter 2, is revisited in Section 3.5. Porter and Millar created a framework based on this model that shows how to exploit opportunities that information technologies create.

▼ Porter's **competitive forces model** (again, a generic model) is introduced in Section 3.6 to illustrate specific areas and strategies where information technologies can be helpful in supporting Porter's competitive strategies.

▼ Frameworks that are directly related to Porter's models are presented in Section 3.7.

▼ A global business drivers' framework for multinational corporation is presented in Section 3.8.

▼ A customer resource life cycle framework is presented in Chapter 11.

▶ 3.5 HOW INFORMATION TECHNOLOGY AFFECTS COMPETITION: PORTER'S VALUE CHAIN MODEL

Porter's value chain model, which was introduced in Chapter 2, can serve as a framework to illustrate how IT affects competition. The value chain analysis helps explain how organizations reason. As shown in Figure 3.2, organizational activities are divided into nine activities, of which five are classified as **primary activities** and four as **support activities.** The primary activities are linked together in a chain, and each activity adds *value* to the product or service under consideration. By examining each of the cells and the links in the chain, one can identify ways to increase competitive advantage. In Figure 3.2, one can find representative technologies that can be used to support each cell of the matrix.

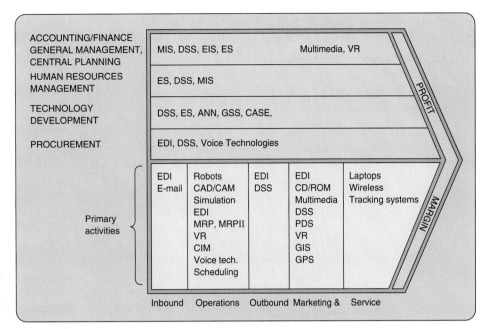

FIGURE 3.2 Representative technologies in a firm's value chain. (VR refers to virtual reality (see Chapter 7))

In this book, we use this framework to introduce specific information technologies, which can be used to support the nine activities of the model. Throughout the book, we will demonstrate how the technologies add *value* to the processes. For example, Federal Express was the first company in its industry to use a tracking system to improve the service to its customers, being able to tell them the status of each package at any given time.

Porter and Millar (1985) concluded that competition has been affected by IT in three vital ways. First, industry structure and rules of competition have changed. Second, organizations have outperformed their competitors by using IT. Finally, organizations have created new business by using IT. Porter and Miller also suggested five steps (see Box 3.4) that organizations can take to exploit the strategic opportunities that IT creates. Not all the steps must be followed.

A Closer Look BOX 3.4

PORTER AND MILLAR'S FIVE-STEP PROCESS

Step 1. *Assess information intensity.* Organizations need to assess the information intensity of each link in each of their value chains. Higher intensity implies greater opportunity. If the customers or suppliers with which the organization deals are highly dependent on information, or if the product or service is mainly information-related, then intensity is high and strategic opportunity is likely to exist.

Step 2. *Determine the role of IT in the industry structure.* An organization needs to know how buyers, suppliers, and competitors might be affected by and react to IT. New strategies may be necessary to retain industry position in some circumstances.

Step 3. *Identify and rank the ways in which IT can create competitive advantage.* An organization must analyze how

particular links of the value chain might be affected by IT. Links that represent high cost or critical areas of business activity are targets for the IS manager to focus his or her efforts.

Step 4. *Investigate how IT might spawn new businesses.* Excess computer capacity or large corporate databases, or special strength in some aspect of IT, may provide opportunities for spin-off businesses. Organizations should answer the following three questions:

a. What information generated (or potentially generated) by the business could be sold?

b. What information-processing capacities exist internally to start a new business?

c. Does IT make it feasible to produce new items related to the organization's current products?

Step 5. *Develop a plan for taking advantage of IT.* To take advantage of strategic opportunities that IT presents one must have a plan that assigns priorities to the strategic investments that the organization needs to make. The process of developing such a plan should be business–driven rather than technology-driven.

SOURCE: Drawn from Porter and Millar, *Havard Business Review,* 1985.

Porter and Millar's model offers a framework whereby managers can assess the information intensity and role of IT in their businesses, thus setting priorities for using IT to achieve a competitive advantage. The basic idea is to determine how specific information technologies can enhance various links in the chain. The enhancements can be to internal operations or the external marketplace. The framework relates the information intensity of a product's value chain to the **information content** of products. The framework can be used to identify opportunities for using IT to enhance value-added activities. Porter and Millar have developed a matrix that indicates the high and low values of the interrelated information. The authors used the matrix to identify the role that information plays in product offerings, as well as the process used to deliver the product to customers.

Several companies have used this model successfully (e.g., Benetton Corporation, see Box 3.5).

IT At Work BOX 3.5

GLOBAL PERSPECTIVE

BENETTON SPA—A SUCCESS STORY

Benetton SPA, a highly successful Italian fashion retailer, has effectively exploited the information-intensive nature of the retail fashion industry to its own benefit. Though its products have very low information content, its production and marketing processes, which are part of its value chain, are highly information-intensive (Step 1 in Porter and Millar's model).

As much as 20 percent of new fashion ideas depend on previous fashion ideas. Thus, the process of designing new clothes is highly information-intensive. Benetton has been able to leverage its expertise in information systems by recording its previous fashions on a laser disc-based computer database, which can be accessed by personal computers. Through this easily accessible database, Benetton can further reduce the time spent in designing new clothes, hence improving response time to customers (Step 2 in the model).

By virtue of its innovative investments in information technology for production and marketing processes, Benetton has been able to respond to changes in fashion trends faster than anyone else in the industry. Its ability to provide overnight adjustments of production, via its highly computerized manufacturing environment, allows its worldwide licensees to receive items within two to three weeks from the time of ordering (Step 3 in the model).

Benetton developed a plan (Step 5 in the model) that enabled it to take advantage of IT. The company can delay production of garments until an order is placed by a franchisee, thereby eliminating inventory costs. The flexibility offered by the computerized manufacturing system allows Benetton to respond quickly to changes in fashion trends. It can delete slow-selling items from its product lines and expand production of fast-selling clothes.

By utilizing the information-intensive nature of the fashion industry, Benetton achieved tremendous success. From a meager $2,000 investment in 1955, Benetton has become a company with sales of $2.5 billion in 1987, and its sales in 1995 were over $4.0 billion.

Critical Thinking Issues: What makes Benetton's business amenable to IT? What is the advantage of the utilization of Porter and Millar's model? ▲

SOURCE: Condensed from Martin J. ''Benetton's IS instinct,'' *Datamation,* July 1, 1989 pp. 15–16.

▶ 3.6 ANALYZING COMPETITIVENESS: PORTER'S COMPETITIVE FORCES MODEL

One of the most well-known frameworks for analyzing competitiveness is Porter's **competitive forces model** (1985). This model has been used to develop strategies for companies to increase their competitive edge. It has also been used to demonstrate how IT can enhance the competitiveness of corporations. The model proposes five forces that could endanger a company's position in a given industry (see Figure 3.3). Although the details of the model differ from one industry to another, the five forces can be generalized as follows:

1. The threat of entry of new competitors.
2. Bargaining power of suppliers.
3. Bargaining power of customers (buyers).
4. The threat of substitute products or services.
5. Rivalry among existing firms.

The strength of each force is determined by several factors of the industry structure, which are also shown in Figure 3.3.

The forces and determining factors that were identified in the early '80s are related to today's pressures identified in Chapter 1 (Sections 1.6–1.8). Porter suggested how to develop a *strategy* aimed at establishing a profitable and sustainable

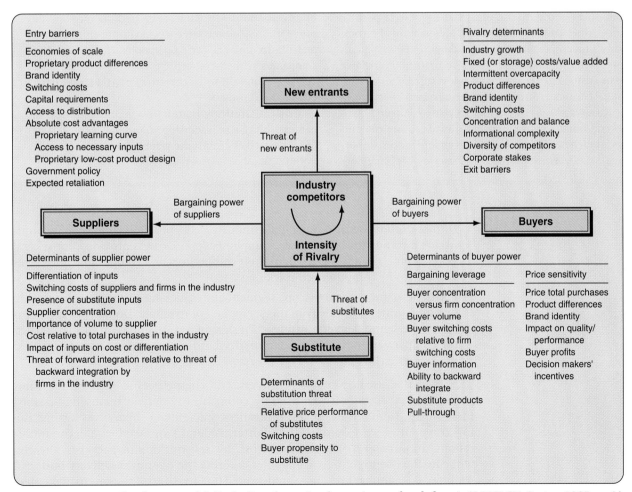

FIGURE 3.3 Porter's five forces model (including the major determinant of each force). (SOURCE: Porter, 1985, p. 6.)

position against these forces. He explained how a company can influence the industry structure for its benefit. Porter suggested three strategies that organizations can use for achieving above-average performance in an industry:

▼ **Cost Leadership:** Producing products and/or services at the lowest cost in the industry. An example is Wal-Mart, which through business alliances supported by computers and by computerized purchasing and inventory management was able to provide low-cost products at its stores. Other examples are given in Box 3.6.

IT At Work BOX 3.6

TRUCKING COMPANIES USE IT FOR GAINING COST LEADERSHIP

The trucking business is very competitive. Here are some examples of how IT helps in significant cost cuts.

J. B. Hunt of Lowell, Arkansas, is a large truckload carrier. The corporate PCs are connected into the fuel commodity market in a real-time fashion. This allows a minute-by-minute monitoring of the greatly fluctuating fuel prices and purchase of fuel at the lowest possible prices (fuel costs represent 18–35 percent of the company's total operating cost). In addition, the system allows J. B. Hunt to pass on a very accurate fuel surcharge to its customers; the company tailors surcharges to individual customers on a percent-per-mile basis every week.

Roadway Express, another trucking company, owns several hundred gas pumps nationwide. Using computers, the company compares six vendors' prices to purchase the least expensive gas. Leaseway Trucking does not own pumps, but centrally controls the purchasing of gas by over 10,000 drivers. The company saves about 10 percent of fuel cost by instructing drivers where to purchase gas any time they need a refill.

Computers are also used by large companies to monitor drivers' and trucks' productivity. Using telecommunication and satellites, companies can monitor thousands of drivers and trucks (study their performance and improve it). In addition, large trucking companies use DSS and EIS to optimize their operations. IT provides large companies with a competitive edge against the small companies and allows truckers to survive in an extremely competitive business.

Critical Thinking Issues: How do the trucking companies achieve cost leadership? Can smaller truckers defend themselves against the giants? How? ▲

SOURCE: Based on *Computerworld*, April 7, 1991, p. 59.

▼ **Differentiation:** Being unique in the industry, e.g., providing high-quality products at a competitive price. For example, Federal Express provided, for several years, a much better service than their competitors at a competitive price. This was due to its computerized tracking system.

▼ **Focus:** Selecting a narrow-scope segment and achieving either a cost leadership or a differentiation strategy in this segment. For example, Domino's Pizza dominates the home delivery business. To sustain a differentiation in the market, the company introduced the computerized ordering system that was described in Chapter 2, Box 2.6.

IT can be used by suppliers, buyers, and competitors to increase the competitive forces. IT can also be used by companies to defend themselves against these forces. Here are examples of businesses defending themselves against the five competitive forces proposed by Porter: Federal Express offers telecommunications software to its clients at no cost, for self-tracking of packages, thereby reducing the chance of new companies entering the overnight delivery business. Automobile manufacturers use sophisticated quality-control systems to make steel producers (the suppliers) more conscious of quality. Allowing suppliers of funds to financial institutions (depositors, investors) to electronically transfer funds rapidly and easily is an example of increased bargaining power of suppliers by the use of IT. Many banks, national and international, use electronic data interchange as a substitute for paper transactions. Frequent flyer programs in the airline industry and discount brokering in the securities industry have significantly changed rivalries among existing firms. The use of IT for strategic planning is revisited in Chapter 11.

▶ 3.7 ILLUSTRATIVE STRATEGIC INFORMATION SYSTEMS FRAMEWORKS

Several frameworks have been developed using Porter's ideas to identify how to use IT for achieving competitive advantage. Two are discussed here: the Wiseman and MacMillan framework, and the Bakos and Treacy framework. Other frameworks are based on different approaches (see Chapter 11).

WISEMAN AND MACMILLAN: STRATEGIC THRUST–STRATEGIC TARGET

Wiseman and MacMillan (1984) and Wiseman (1988) added the following to Porter's basic defense strategies: innovation, growth, alliance, and time. Their framework attempts to show how to identify the opportunities available in gaining a competitive advantage via innovative use of IT. The framework also uses three of Porter's five forces (see top of Table 3.2) to form the matrix, as shown in Table 3.2. Each cell in the matrix relates the available strategies for each external target.

For example, EDI can be used to form an alliance with the supplier, a strategy used by Wal-Mart and Sears. The cash management system, described in Section 3.9, is an example of differentiation designed to provide an advantage over the competitor. McKesson's inventory system saves cost to their customers and ties the customers to McKesson.

As a matter of fact, it is possible to find many applications in several of the cells in one company. The question is how to identify such applications. An example of a company that used this framework successfully is GTE Corporation. The company used a brainstorming procedure to identify more than 300 ideas on strategic applications of IT in the various cells of the matrix (see Box 3.7).

Table 3.2 **Wiseman/MacMillan's Matrix: Example of Technologies Are Listed in the Cells**

Strategic Thrusts	Supplier	Customer	Competitor
Differentiation	Not applicable	IT-supported mass customization	Cash management
Cost	Not applicable	Computerized inventory system	Expert systems (reduce cost)
Innovation	Lotus Notes	Use of Geographical information systems for quick response	Intelligent systems
Growth	Lotus Notes	Empower customers to do own enquiries	Not applicable
Alliance	EDI	EDI	E-mail
Time	EDI, electronic transfer of funds	E-mail	CAD

SOURCE: Based on Wiseman and MacMillan, 1984. Technologies inserted by the authors.

IT At Work BOX 3.7

GTE IDENTIFIES HUNDREDS OF STRATEGIC INFORMATION SYSTEMS APPLICATIONS

To find applications for SIS, GTE, a large telecommunication company, used a five-phase process following the Wiseman and MacMillan framework. The process relies on continuous idea-generation activities and training and education of the employees participating in the search. The participants were presented with the matrix and were encouraged to fill in the cells with ideas. The phases are:

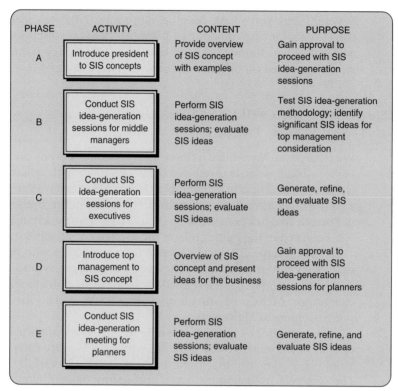

The SIS planning and implementation process

If this process would have to be repeated today, one could have used the group DSS idea-generation software, or any other creativity software to enhance the identification of SIS applications, in addition to the inducement provided by the matrix.

Critical Thinking Issues: What benefits did the Wiseman and Macmillan approach provide to GTE? Are there any other ways that you can think of to identify applications for SIS? ▲

SOURCE: Table reprinted from ''Information Systems for Competitive Advantage: Implementation of a Planning Process.'' Reprinted with permission from the *MIS Quarterly*.

BAKOS AND TREACY: BARGAINING POWER AND COMPARATIVE EFFICIENCY

According to Bakos and Treacy's framework (1986), the two major sources of Porter's competitive advantage are bargaining power and comparative efficiency (see Figure 3.4). These sources are determined by five specific activities: search-related costs, unique product features, switching costs, internal efficiency, and interorganizational efficiency. Initially, IT efforts were aimed at increasing comparative efficiency. Lately, however, IT is also dealing with enhancing bargaining power activities.

Let us consider some ways in which IT can support the five activities that drive bargaining power and comparative efficiency.

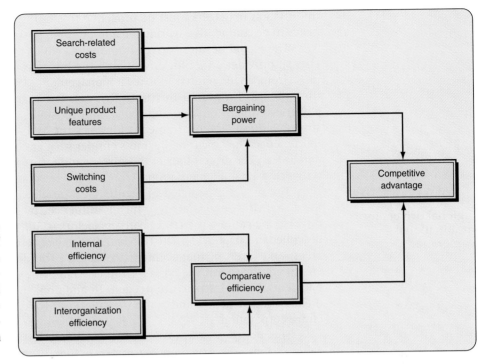

FIGURE 3.4 Bakos and Treacy's causal model of competitive advantage. (SOURCE: Figure 1. "Information Technology and Corporate Strategy: A Research Perspective," Reprinted with permission from the *MIS Quarterly*.)

1. Increasing the cost for a company's customer to search for other suppliers. If customers will have to pay a high cost to switch, they will not do it. For example, Procter & Gamble runs the inventory system of Wal-Mart for their products such as Pampers. Thus, it would cost Wal-Mart too much to move to another supplier.

2. Create unique product features. IT can provide unique features (e.g., see the Merrill Lynch case in Section 3.9—the computerized cash management system was a unique product, which increased the company stronghold on its customers).

3. **a.** Increase customer switching costs; e.g., by placing terminals at customers' sites (see American Hospital Supply case in Section 3.9), it became difficult for customers to move to other suppliers.

   b. Decrease the corporate switching costs from one supplier to another. For example, an organization can use IT to become its own supplier, or use E-mail to do business with international suppliers. Thus, the company may increase its bargaining power with suppliers.

4. Internal efficiency can be increased by reduced costs and/or increased productivity. IT is known for its effectiveness in this area. Several examples are provided throughout the book.

5. Increase interorganizational efficiency through *synergy*. IT enhances business partnerships, joint ventures, and other alliances. For example, EDI is a critical success factor in many partnerships. The topic of business alliances is covered in Chapters 14 and 17.

▶ 3.8 A FRAMEWORK FOR MULTINATIONAL CORPORATIONS

THE IVES, JARVENPAA, AND MASON GLOBAL BUSINESS DRIVERS FRAMEWORK

The success of multinational firms in a highly competitve global market is strongly dependent on the alignment of a global information system and business strategy.

Information managers must be proactive to identify the IT solutions that a firm needs to be competitive worldwide and tie them to strategic business imperatives.

The global business driver framework, which was developed by Ives et al. (1993), provides a tool for envisioning the business entities that will benefit the most from an integrated global IT management. The basic idea is to apply IT through a firm's **global business drivers**. These are entities that benefit from global economies of scale and scope, and thus add value to the global business strategy. These drivers are means for assessing high-level global information requirements. They focus on business entities such as customers, suppliers, projects, and orders. The drivers look at the current and future information needs and focus on worldwide implementation.

The model is depicted in Figure 3.5. The global drivers are determined by the global vision and strategy, which is influenced by globalization. To identify the drivers, one can use the critical success factors (CSF) methodology (which will be described in Chapter 11). The CSFs can be applied across country units, functional areas, and levels of management to produce the drivers. Once the drivers are identified, they form the basis for the IT strategy as well as the specific data, applications, and infrastructure needed. In addition, they determine the necessary organization structure and communication networks for sharing data across the entire corporation.

The model can address both the firm's internal value chain and its external value system (e.g., suppliers, customers). The authors developed questions that may be asked in order to uncover global drivers and their importance. These are shown, together with the business drivers and examples, in Table 3.3.

> **GLOBAL PERSPECTIVE**
>
> ...global drivers for multinational corporations

▶ 3.9 REPRESENTATIVE STRATEGIC INFORMATION SYSTEMS APPLICATIONS

The applications presented in this section are divided into two categories. The first three systems center around outward orientation, whereas the last three center around inward orientation.

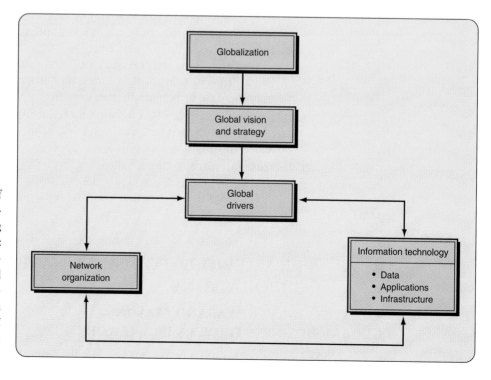

FIGURE 3.5 Alignment of global vision with information technology using global drivers. (SOURCE: Ives, et al., 1993. Copyright © 1993 International Business Machines Corporation. Reprinted with permission from *IBM Systems Journal*, Vol. 32, No. 1.)

Table 3.3 **Analysis of Some Global Business Drivers**

Global Business Drivers	Analysis Questions	Examples of Entities
Joint Resources	Can you electronically move work to countries with a highly skilled workforce and favorable wage levels? Can you compose and manage work teams with globally dispersed members? Do you manage human resources skills on a global level?	Employee location, employee skill, employee position, work assignments, employee compensation, standard work tools, relationship history between customers and employees
Rationalized and flexible operations	Can you move production around the world? Can you rapidly move knowledge work around the world? Can you share production resources across country boundaries? Are you optimizing plant locations and production planning on a global scale?	Production plan, production schedule, product demand, plant capacity, vehicles, storage facilities
Risk reduction	Do you manage your monetary flows and the associated risks on a daily and hourly basis at the global level? Are you vulnerable to political and economic conditions in particular countries?	Investments, pending investments, foreign exchange, assets, safety of assets
Global products	Are there opportunities for global products and brands? Do you need to launch synchronized product introductions on a global basis?	Product standards, process standards, legal requirements, repair records, marketing plans
Quality	Can you identify the source of a defective component on a global basis? Are you conducting competitive benchmarking on a worldwide basis?	Competitive benchmarks, internal performance standards
Suppliers	Can volume discounts be negotiated on a global scale? Do you know your global position with a major supplier?	Supplier information, parts and material, procurement standards, innovations
Corporate customers	Are your leading-edge customers becoming global? Can you ensure consistent product and service regardless of the location? Can you provide seamless worldwide ordering, order tracking, and billing? Do the needs of global customers provide new business opportunities?	Customer information, customer quality standards, customer product specification, local preferences, preorder history, order status

SOURCE: Ives et al., 1993. Copyright © 1993 International Business Machines Corporation. Reprinted with permission from *IBM Systems Journal*, Vol. 32, No. 1.

OUTWARD SYSTEMS

*R*EENGINEERING

...computerize your clients

COMPUTER TERMINALS AT CUSTOMERS' LOCATIONS: THE AMERICAN HOSPITAL SUPPLY CASE. American Hospital Supply (AHS, now a part of Baxter International Corporation) installed computer terminals on their clients' premises 20 years ago. The terminals were connected to an AHS computer, so that customers could order supplies electronically. Quick deliveries allow the customers to maintain low inventories. According to Wysocki and Young (1990), this arrangement represents a commitment on the part of both the customer and AHS that has had a powerful effect on the hospital supply business. It has significantly reduced the time between order placement and order delivery, essentially eliminating one person in the vendor-customer relationship in each hospital and has given the customer more control over sources of supply. Even more significantly, it has controlled a channel of distribution and placed AHS in a position of considerable strategic advantage. Others have emulated AHS's system, but the company still maintains a significant market advantage over its competitors. Details of the system and its development over the years are given in Chapter 1 of Neumann (1994).

MERRILL LYNCH'S CASH MANAGEMENT ACCOUNTS SYSTEM. Merrill Lynch bundled together a number of financial services (brokerage, deposit account, money market funds, and so on), resulting in a single combined monthly statement for each customer. The company achieved a **differentiation** strategy by delivering a service not provided by any competitor. The individual services were not new, but bundling them together was a unique idea.

It took the competitors several years to imitate the system, since they did not have the necessary integrated technology infrastructure. (*Note:* Today, such a system could have been duplicated in only a few months.)

REENGINEERING

...airline reservations via desktop

AMERICAN AIRLINES' COMPUTERIZED RESERVATION SYSTEM. The SABRE system was developed by American Airlines in the early 1960s. By the mid-1970s, the company began installing SABRE in travel agencies across the country. Despite the fact that there were several attempts to copy it, SABRE continued to dominate the market. In fact, rather than developing their own reservation systems, many airline carriers now subscribe to SABRE.

The system did not show a profit until 1983, but it has sustained its competitive advantage by continually adding capabilities. For example, the airline created an office automation software package for travel agencies called Agency Data Systems, which enables travel agents to manage their office and communicate with airlines and clients. SABRE now encompasses hotel reservations, car rentals, train schedules, theater tickets, and limousine rental. It even has a feature that lets travelers use the system interactively.

Despite SABRE's comprehensiveness, several airlines do have similar reservations systems. Therefore, American Airlines must continue to look for further enhancements to SABRE to maintain its role as an industry leader.

INWARD SYSTEMS

HOW A DANISH SHIPYARD BUILT THE LARGEST THING THAT MAN MOVES WITH THE WORLD'S SMALLEST OBJECTS. Odense shipyard in Denmark was faced with strong competition from South Korean companies where labor costs are about one-third less, and from the former East Germany where the government subsidizes the shipyards. Yet, they compete successfully, especially in their area of specialty—building the largest ships. Information technology makes the difference between winning and losing.

GLOBAL PERSPECTIVE

...competing against cheap labor

Using IT, Odense was able to win a construction contract for a supertanker against the Japanese. IT also helped in cutting costs. A special department was established to find ways of using IT, plant automation, and robots. One hundred fifty special computer-aided design (CAD) machines help in expediting design by as much as 600%. In addition, CAD allows the creation of alternative designs that can be evaluated quickly for durability and efficiency. Additional software assists with labor and logistic decisions (there are more than 400,000 different parts in a large ship). IT also allows for just-in-time, a concept (see Ch. 17) that enables operations with very little inventory. Many more things are done with computers such as costing, scheduling, and project management.

IT is not only a condition for survival, but it also helped in capturing 20% of the world market of container ships, and 10% of the supertanker market. (Based on *Forbes, ASAP*, December 5, 1994.)

CUSTOMER-ORIENTED COMMUNICATION AND DECISION-MAKING SYSTEM AT DELL COMPUTERS. The $50 billion-a-year PC industry is most competitive, and giants such as IBM and Apple are competing with several dozen smaller companies. Dell is a relative newcomer in this industry. Dell invests $50 million annually in IT, without which the company simply could not exist.

Dell, a direct-sales company, receives over 35,000 telephone calls, faxes, and E-mail messages every day from potential buyers and existing customers. All calls are received by employees who work on PCs linked to a powerful parallel processing computer. The computer contains over one million records about existing customers. Each call is stored in a database, which is shared by all departments. The company analyzes the stored data to learn such things as the following: "if Dell uses a yellow background on a catalog cover, the response rate will be 30% lower than a cover with green."

The company's objective is to be responsive to customer needs, by tailoring responses to customers' wishes. Thus, a mailing is much more effective. As soon as a representative receives a call and types it into the computer, the computer automatically generates sales hints about the calling customer. As a result, sales of certain products jumped 1,000 percent. The large database helps in developing new models, and consumer trends are monitored and analyzed constantly. The result—Dell commands a 4 percent market share, which is outstanding for a company that was started by two college students about 10 years ago (for details see Sherman [1993]).

REENGINEERING

...working more productively from home

PRODUCTIVITY GAINS AT AMERICAN EXPRESS BY TELECOMMUTING. Travel counselors at American Express in Houston, Texas, do not have to commute two to three hours a day anymore. American Express, which spends over $1 billion annually on IT, allows these counselors to work from their home (for a discussion of telecommuting, see Chapter 14) using telephones and computers to communicate with customers. The company has invested $1,300 worth of computerized equipment in each employee who works at home. Supervisors are able to monitor the work of these employees. Another savings is that less office space is needed (a potential savings of $4,400/per person/per year). Astounding productivity gains were also achieved. A typical counselor can handle 26 percent more business from home, and less commuting time makes employees healthier, happier, and better performers. Revenues per counselor increased by 46 percent in the travel booking area, resulting in higher profits to the company. IT changed the manner in which the company conducted its business for the benefit of all (for details see Sherman [1993]).

CONCLUSION

Strategic information systems support or shape the business competitive advantage by changing the manner in which business is done. However, there are other approaches that can do the same, sometimes in conjunction with SIS. Such approaches are described in the remaining part of this chapter and in Chapter 4.

▶ 3.10 INCREMENTAL IMPROVEMENTS AND BUSINESS REENGINEERING

Achieving competitive advantage can be done in two major ways. First it can occur through a systematic incremental improvement program. Some people describe such an approach as **life-cycle reengineering**; others call it an incremental improvement program. For example, quality circles is a program intended to involve employees in activities designed to continuously improve quality. The second approach is to *completely change the manner in which business is done*. Such a change can be in response to a crisis, when the old business processes are crumbling under the weight of demands and pressure, or it can be a goal-oriented change such as moving to become an industry leader. This second approach is termed **business reengineering**, **business processes reengineering (BPR)**, or just **reengineering**.

Strategic information systems can be used to support some incremental improvement programs. However, when a company is considering BPR, the use of IT as an enabler is required in almost all cases.

Business reengineering may be necessary for a company to maintain its competitive advantage or even for it to survive. Though life-cycle reengineering is beneficial, it is not always sufficient. An analogy can be made with people who are ill. Exercising and taking drugs can help some people, but not all of them. Therefore, surgery is sometimes the only means for survival. BPR can be viewed as surgery. In the forthcoming three sections, we will describe the fundamentals of business reengineering and the role of IT in supporting BPR.

▶ 3.11 WHAT IS BUSINESS REENGINEERING?

The pressures described in Chapter 1 create a business environment in which many companies as well as public organizations have difficulty operating or even surviving. The reason is that both the magnitude and pace of the changes around the business are much stronger and faster than ever before. Organizations used to conduct business in a certain manner for many years, and they excelled in what they were doing. When rapid and strong changes occurred, many organizations found themselves unable to cope with the new conditions. The reason for this, according to Hammer and Champy (1993), is that the principles of the classical American corporation are sadly obsolete. The only way that companies can survive is by rapidly changing the manner in which they conduct their business. The method that Hammer and Champy proposed to execute such change was BPR, which means starting all over, starting from scratch. The authors feel that at the heart of BPR lies the notion of *discontinuous thinking*, namely identifying and abandoning the outdated rules that underlie current business operations. These rules of business operations started in 1776, when Adam Smith documented the principle of division of labor and specialization. This was the beginning of the Industrial Revolution, which moved the developing countries into high productivity and steadily increased the standard of living. Several principles were created over the years that enhanced the development of the Industrial Revolution. The most important principles are:

▼ Specialization of employees

▼ Specialization of support functions (e.g., marketing, finance)

▼ Mass production (producing large quantities, storing them, selling them at a later time)

▼ Hierarchical organizational structure with top-down lines of authority

▼ Assembly lines that bring the work to the worker whenever possible

▼ Complex support systems for planning and budgeting, resource allocation, and control

The foregoing principles are no longer working for many companies because of the pressures cited in Chapter 1. The major pressures are summarized by Hammer and Champy (1993) as three Cs: *customers, competition,* and *change*.

▼ Customers today know what they want, what they are willing to pay, and how to get products and services on their own terms.

▼ Competition is continuously increasing with respect to price, quality, selection, service, and promptness of delivery. Removal of trade barriers, international cooperation, and technological innovations cause competition to intensify.

▼ Change will continue to occur. Markets, products, services, technology, the business environment, and people keep changing, frequently in an unpredictable manner.

Incremental improvements provided by automation, computerization, method improvements, incentive programs, and other productivity and quality programs that were very useful in the past have proven to be, in the 1990s, only a temporary relief in many cases. Once the improvements have been executed, additional environmental changes result in new problems. Therefore, the only solution may be to reengineer the organization. It is not possible to achieve breakthroughs in performance by cutting fat or automating existing processes. Rather, it is necessary to challenge old assumptions and shed the old rules that made the business underperform in the first place. If this occurs we envision an **organization transformation**, where the entire processes, organization climate and organization structure are changed. The following definitions are provided by Hammer and Champy (1993):

▼ *Reengineering* is the fundamental rethinking and radical redesign of business processes to achieve dramatic improvements in critical contemporary measures of performance such as cost, quality, service, and speed.

▼ *Business process* is a collection of activities that takes one or more kinds of inputs and creates an output that is of value to the customer. For example, accepting an application for a loan, processing it, and approving (or rejecting) it, is a process in a bank (see Box 3.8).

A Closer Look BOX 3.8

WHAT IS A BUSINESS PROCESS?

The following are some examples of business processes:

1. *Credit card approval.* An applicant submits an application. The application is reviewed first to make sure that the form has been completed properly. If not, it is returned for completion. The complete form goes through a verification of information. This is done by ordering a report from a credit company (e.g., TRW) and calling references. Once the information is verified, an evaluation is done. Then, a decision (yes or no) is made. If the decision is negative, an appropriate rejection letter is composed. If the decision is positive, an account is opened, and a card is issued and mailed to the customer. The process, which may take a few weeks due to work load and waiting time for the verifications, is usually done by several individuals.

2. *Processing an expense form.* An employee submits a form for expense reimbursement. The form is checked for completeness (receipts? signature? dates?). The eligibility is checked together with the nature of the receipts and the limits of expenses by category. A certain amount is then approved for reimbursement with explanation of amount denied. An authorization to pay is made. A check is issued and sent to the payee. Appropriate bookkeeping takes place. If the payee is not happy, further explanation and negotiation take place. An adjustment may be made.

3. *Renewal of a driver's license.* The applicant fills out a form. Then he is given a written test of driving rules. The test is checked. If the applicant passes, he takes a vision test. Then a picture is taken, the appropriate fee is collected, and a temporary license is issued. The information is entered into a database, and a permanent license is issued and mailed to the applicant. (In some states a permanent license is issued on the spot.)

▶ 3.12 PRINCIPLES OF BUSINESS REENGINEERING

To understand the principles that are being used in reengineering, it is beneficial to analyze the differences between reengineering and incremental improvement programs. According to Davenport (1993), reengineering is a part of **process innovation**, which involves stepping back from a process to inquire into its overall business objectives, and then effecting creative and radical change to realize order-of-magnitude improvements in the way that the objective is accomplished. The term process innovation encompasses the envisioning of new work strategies, the actual process design activity, and the implementation of the change in all its complex technological, human, and organizational dimensions.

The differences between process innovation and incremental improvement are shown in Table 3.4.

THE PRODUCT–PROCESS CHANGE FRAMEWORK

A framework called the *product-process change matrix* was developed by Boynton et al. (1993). It can help managers do the following: (1) assess their competitive position by understanding where their firms have been in the past, (2) build a vision of where their firms must be in the future, and (3) create a transformation strategy to turn that vision into reality. Two new organizational designs are emerging. The first, *mass customization*, competes under dynamic product change and stable process change. The mass customizer combines the product variety of the invention designer with the production efficiency of the mass producer. The second organizational design, *continuous improvement*, competes under conditions of stable product change and dynamic process change. The synergy between mass customization and continuous improvement, referred to as dynamic stability, may define the basis of competition into the next century.

CHARACTERISTICS OF BUSINESS PROCESSES REENGINEERING

According to Hammer and Champy (1993), certain common characteristics exist in business reengineering, most of which are enhanced by IT. The major characteristics are:

1. Several jobs are combined into one.
2. Employees make decisions (empowerment of employees). Decision making becomes part of the job.
3. Steps in the business process are performed in a natural order, and several jobs get done simultaneously.

Table 3.4 Process Innovation vs. Incremental Improvement

	Process Innovation	*Incremental Improvement*
Change	Abrupt, volatile	Gradual, constant
Effects	Immediate, dramatic	Long-term, more subtle
Involvement	A few champions	From few to everybody
Investment	High initially, less later	Low initially, high to sustain
Orientation	Technology	People
Focus	Profits	Processes

SOURCE: Merlyn V., Ernst and Young, private communication.

IT At Work BOX 3.9

IBM CREDIT CORPORATION REDUCED CYCLE TIME BY 90 PERCENT

IBM Credit Corp. provides credit to customers who purchase IBM computers. The process of credit approval used to take an average of seven days. Because of the long processing time, salespeople felt that they were losing many potential customers; therefore, reducing processing time became critical.

Old Process

Step 1: The IBM salesperson telephones in, requesting credit approval.

Step 2: A clerk logs the call on paper; a messenger takes it to the credit department.

Step 3: A specialist enters the data into the computer, checks creditworthiness of the potential customer, and prepares a report.

Step 4: The report is physically moved to the business practices department.

Step 5: The business practices department modifies a standard loan to fit the customer's needs.

Step 6: Using a spreadsheet, a pricer determines the appropriate interest rate and payment schedule. Another piece of paper is added to the application.

Step 7: An administrator uses the information to develop a quote letter.

Step 8: The quote letter is delivered to the salesperson, who submits it to the customer.

Attempts to incrementaly increase productivity improved some of the activities, but the overall time reduction was minimal.

Reengineered Process

One person, called a deal structurer, conducts all the above steps. One generalist replaces four specialists.

IT Support

To enable one person to execute the above steps, a simple DSS provides the deal structurer with the guidance needed. The program guides the generalist in finding information in the databases, plugging numbers into an evaluation model, and pulling boilerplate clauses from a file. For difficult situations, the generalist can get the help from a specialist. The communication can be done by telephone or by E-mail.

Results: The turn-around time has been slashed from seven days to four hours! Furthermore, IBM credit can handle a volume of business 100 times larger now.

Critical Thinking Issues: Why is this change considered a BPR? What role did IT play in introducing the change? ▲

SOURCE: Based on Hammer and Champy, 1993.

---

4. Processes have multiple versions. This enables the economies of scale that result from mass production, yet allows customization of products and services.

5. Work is performed where it makes the most sense, including at the customers' or suppliers' sites. Thus, work is shifted across organizational and international boundaries (see Boxes 1.3 and 1.4 in Chapter 1).

6. Controls and checks and other non-value added work are minimized.

7. Reconciliation is minimized by cutting back the number of external contact points and by creating business alliances (see the 7-Eleven case in Chapter 1).

8. A single point of contact is provided to customers (called a "case manager" or a deal structurer (see Box 3.9)).

9. A hybrid centralized/decentralized operation is used.

CHANGES IN WORK PRACTICES

The characteristics of BPR can lead to a new world of work. The major differences between this new world and the conventional world are summarized in Table 3.5. Details can be found in Hammer and Champy (1993).

Table 3.5   Changes in the World of Work

From conventional	To BPR
Functional departments	Process teams
Simple tasks (division of labor)	Empowered employees
Controlled people (by management)	Multidimensional work
Training of employees	Education of employees
Compensation for skill and time spent	Compensation for results
Pay raises based on promotions and seniority	Low pay plus high performance-related bonuses
Advancement based on ability	Advancement based on performance
Protective organizational culture	Productive organizational structure
Managers supervise and control	Managers coach and advise
Hierarchical organizational structure	Horizontal (flat) structure
Executives as scorekeepers	Executives as leaders
Separation of duties and functions	Cross-functional teams
Linear and sequential processes	Parallel processes
Mass production	Mass customization

*R*EENGINEERING

...for results

SOURCE: Based on Hammer and Champy, 1993.

3.13   THE ENABLING ROLE OF INFORMATION TECHNOLOGY

According to Robert L. Stark, President of the Personal Communications Group of Hallmark Cards, a company that successfully reengineered its business processes, information technology was a vital ingredient to the corporate reengineering efforts. Hammer and Champy (1993) and Currid et al. (1994) believe that IT is an *essential enabler* that is part of any reengineering effort. Davenport (1993) shows that IT is the cornerstone to reengineering dramatic results. IT has been used for several decades to improve productivity and quality by automating existing processes. However, when it comes to reengineering, it is necessary to view the role of IT from a different perspective. Most importantly, the traditional process of looking at problems first and then seeking technology solutions for them needs to be reversed. It is necessary to first recognize a powerful solution, and then seek the problems it might solve. Such an approach requires *inductive* rather than *deductive* thinking. It requires innovation, since a company may be looking for problems it does not even know exist. In some cases, such a process means entirely new classes of applications.

IT can break old rules that limit the manner in which work is performed, thus enabling process reengineering. Typical examples compiled mainly from Hammer and Champy (1993) are given in Table 3.6. McKesson Water Products Co. is another example that shows how a water products company applied several information technologies in support of a comprehensive reengineering project (see Box 3.10).

Hundreds of cases can be used to demonstrate the role of IT in BPR and SIS. For this reason, we elected to distribute the many examples throughout the book.

MANAGERIAL ISSUES

CREATIVITY

Innovation has been recognized as a major element in strategic management and as a key to BPR. Therefore, there is a need to develop conditions that nurture

Table 3.6 **Changes Brought by IT**

REENGINEERING

...new rules of
business with IT

Old Rule	Intervening Technology	New Rule
Information appears in only one place at one time	Shared databases, client/ server architecture, electronic mail	Information appears simultaneously wherever needed
Only an expert can perform complex work	Expert systems, neural computing	Novices can perform complex work
Business must be either centralized or decentralized	Telecommunication and networks: client/server	Business can be both centralized and decentralized
Managers make all decisions	Decision support systems, enterprise support systems, expert systems	Decision making is part of everyone's job
Field personnel need offices to receive, send, store, and process information	Wireless communication and portable computers, information highways, electronic mail	Field personnel can manage information from any location
The best contact with potential buyers is a personal contact	Interactive videodisk, desktop teleconferencing, electronic mail	The best contact is the one that is most cost effective
You have to locate items manually	Tracking technology, groupware, workflow software, client/server	Items are located automatically (see Mark III, Minicase 3)
Plans get revised periodically	High-performance computing systems	Plans get revised instantaneously whenever needed
People must come to one place to work together	Groupware and group support systems, telecommunication, electronic mail, client/server	People can work together while at different locations
Customized products and services are expensive and take a long time to develop	CAD-CAM, CASE tools, on-line systems for JIT decision making, expert systems	Customized products can be made fast and inexpensively (mass customization)
A long period of time is spanned between the inception of an idea and its implementation (time-to-market)	CAD-CAM, electronic data interchange, groupware, imaging (document) processing	Time-to-market can be reduced by 90 percent
Information-based organizations and processes	Artificial intelligence, expert systems	Knowledge-based organizations and processes
Move labor to countries where labor is inexpensive (off-shore production)	Robots, imaging technologies, object-oriented programming, expert systems, geographical information systems (GIS)	Work can be done in countries with high wages and salaries (see Caterpillar's case)

SOURCE: Compiled from Hammer and Champy, 1993.

IT At Work BOX 3.10

REENGINEERING

MCKESSON WATER PRODUCTS CO. (PASADENA, CA) REENGINEERS OPERATIONS

McKesson, the number one supplier of noncarbonated bottled water in the United States (no connection with McKesson Drug Co. in Box 3.2), went through a $5 million reengineering effort of several business processes. New computer systems were installed to integrate sales, service, and customer relations into a new teleservice center. Route management was greatly enhanced through the use of a GIS, and hand-held terminals with wireless communication links to the central database greatly improved inventory control, distribution, and overall efficiency. The January 1994 earthquake in Los Angeles put McKesson's new systems to the test, which it passed with flying colors. This is why:

1. ***IT supports changes in the organization structure.***
   The sales organization, service, and customer re-

lations were consolidated in a single location by installing a computerized telephone switch that routed calls from seven regional offices into a new teleservice center. A new telemarketing department was established to utilize the new teleservice center.

2. ***IT supports changes in the business process.*** The teleservice center staff now combines the functions of sales, service, and customer relations. A geographical information system (GIS) was installed to optimize the process of adding new customers to existing routes. Previously 100,000 addresses had to be looked up manually on keymaps, to allow them to be added to the appropriate route of the delivery people. With the new GIS, route allocation is fully automatic, while the entire route structure can be redesigned to achieve better efficiency and improve resource utilization.

Hand-held wireless terminals and alpha numeric pagers provide the staff with instant information, and allow the central database to be updated at all times from all locations, without depending on public telephones, paper records, redundant data entry, and inevitable human errors.

Automation and integration resulted in a fixed cost reduction of $7 million, while staffing was reduced by 60 percent.

3. ***IT supports shortening the time-to-market.*** The new teleservice center installed a standard software package, which enabled automatic telephone number identification and allowed customer's background information to appear on the staff member's screen. This technology made data in-stantly available to the service representatives, and therefore to the customer. Since all data was available on-line, immediate follow-up activities could be carried out, resulting in drastically reduced delivery times.

4. ***IT supports customer-centered organizations.*** The newly integrated customer service center is focusing on improving customer satisfaction; faster order processing at lower cost, with instant information available to the customer at each phase of the process. The automatic telephone number identification system enables a much more focused, and therefore efficient, customer service operation.

5. ***IT enhances empowerment of employees.*** Empowerment was supported by making all sales, service, and customer service information available to all service center employees involved in the operations. Enhanced team operations resulted in greater productivity, employee morale, and independence.

6. ***IT enhances TQM programs.*** The new integrated systems guaranteed consistent, timely, and verifiable data, and therefore resulted in a greatly improved quality of the process and an optimization of the resources needed.

Critical Thinking Issues: Why do we consider this use a BPR? What role did IT play in supporting the change? ▲

SOURCE: Condensed from D. Bartholomew, "Keeping Water Flowing in L.A.," *InformationWeek*, February 14, 1994.

creative performance in the design of IT solutions and the implementation of SIS and BPR. How to develop such conditions is an important topic that requires a book of its own. However, IT itself can be used to enhance creativity, as will be shown in Chapters 14 and 15. Managers must realize the value of promoting creativity, without which innovation will not flourish.

STRATEGIC INFORMATION SYSTEMS PLANNING

The planning of SIS is a major concern of organizations, according to Earl (1993). This topic is part of IS planning and will be visited in Chapter 11. It is interesting to note that the Porter and Millar framework is one of several methods that can be used to plan and develop a strategy of how to use SIS.

Earl (1993) surveyed 27 companies and reported on five major SIS planning approaches. Exploiting IT for competitive advantage can be viewed as one of four major activities of SIS planning. The other three (which will be discussed later on) are aligning investment in IS with business goals, directing efficient and effective management of IS resources, and developing technology policies and architecture.

WHEN TO USE A BPR

As indicated earlier, an analogy to BPR is surgery. So a question can be raised: to operate, or not to operate? It is a major decision and a very expensive one. Unfortunately, there are sometimes unsuccessful surgeries. The failure rate of BPR is very high (some estimate as high as 75–85%). One reason for such failures is the inability to properly align BPR and IT and the large expenses that are necessary to reengineer the information infrastructure and applications to support the new processes. Also, organizational resistance can be a large factor.

ETHICAL ISSUES

Gaining competitive advantage by the use of IT may involve unethical or even illegal actions. Companies use IT to monitor the activities of other companies and may invade the privacy of individuals. In using business intelligence (spying on competitors) companies may be engaged in many unethical tactics such as pressuring competitor's employees to reveal information or using software which is the intellectual property of other companies (frequently without the knowledge of these other companies). Many such actions are not illegal, due to the fact that IT is new and its legal environment is not well developed as yet. (See Chapter 20 for details.) ■

KEY TERMS

Business reengineering *88*

Business process reengineering (BPR) *71*

Competition *73*

Competitive advantage *71*

Competitive forces model *76*

Competitive strategy *73*

Cost leadership *80*

Differentiation *80*

Focus *80*

Global business drivers *84*

Information content *78*

Innovation *72*

Life-cycle reengineering *88*

Long-range planning *71*

Organization transformation *89*

Primary activities *76*

Process innovation *90*

Reengineering *88*

Response management *72*

Strategic information systems (SIS) *71*

Strategic alliances *71*

Support activities *76*

Value-chain model *76*

CHAPTER HIGHLIGHTS

▼ Strategic information systems (SIS) support or shape competitive strategy. (L-1)

▼ SIS can be outward (customer)-oriented or inward (organizational)-oriented. (L-1)

▼ Strategic management involves long-range planning, response management, and technological innovation. (L-1)

▼ SIS not only help companies to perform above average, but they may also help companies to survive tough competition. (L-1)

▼ The value chain model can be used to identify areas in which IT can be used to provide strategic advantage. (L-2)

▼ Porter's model of competitive industry forces is frequently used to explain how SIS works. (L-3)

▼ Cost leadership, differentiation, and focus are Porter's major strategies for gaining a competitive advantage. (L-3)

▼ Different frameworks can be used to describe the relationship between IT and attainment of competitive advantage. (L-4)

▼ Multinational corporations need to use a special approach to support their business strategies. (L-5)

▼ Some SIS are expensive and difficult to justify, and others turn out to be unsuccessful. Therefore, careful planning and implementation are essential. (L-6)

▼ To increase productivity, quality, and profitability—or even to survive, it is necessary either to use continuous improvement programs or fundamentally reengineer the organization. (L-7)

▼ Information technology is the major enabler of BPR. (L-8)

▼ SIS can be part of a BPR project. In many cases, SIS are evidenced in situations where major changes in organizational structure and processes occurred. (L-9)

QUESTIONS FOR REVIEW

1. What is a SIS?

2. Describe the three dimensions of strategic management.

3. List the major benefits of SISs.

4. Describe Porter's value chain model and its view regarding competition.

5. List Porter and Millar's steps of exploiting strategic opportunities.

6. Describe Porter's competitive forces model.

7. Explain the meaning of cost leadership, differentiation, and focus.

8. Describe the global business drivers model.

9. Describe how innovation can be enhanced by information technology.

10. List all the major variables in the Bakos and Treacy model that provide a competitive advantage.

11. Define business processes reengineering.

12. Distinguish between BPR and incremental improvements.

13. List the five principles of BPR.

QUESTIONS FOR DISCUSSION

1. Review the opening case and identify all the "outward looking" and "inward looking" aspects of Caterpillar's system.

2. Identify the processes that were reengineered by Caterpillar and identify the information technologies that supported the reengineered processes.

3. A prominent IT researcher said that "now that Caterpillar has strengthened its market leadership, cheaper labor is no longer the biggest issue. It is service, quality, mass customization, and lead time that count." Explain this statement.

4. Review the opening case (and read the original article if possible). Explain how the use of IT can help Caterpillar in its mass customization approach.

5. Compare the inward versus outward competitive orientations.

6. Examine Box 3.2. Identify all the BPR activities and describe the information technologies used to support these activities.

7. Discuss the idea that IS by itself can rarely provide a sustainable competitive advantage.

8. Give examples that show how IT can help a company *reduce* the impact of the five forces in Porter's model.

9. Give examples of how companies can use IT to *increase* the impact of the five forces in Porter's model.

10. Explain the relationship between Wiseman and MacMillan's model and Porter's model.

11. Why is it so difficult to justify SIS and why is it that some systems may not work?

12. Explain what unique aspects are provided by the global business drivers model.

13. Identify the BPR activities at Dell Computers and at IBM Credit Corp.

14. List and discuss the principles of reengineering as suggested by Hammer and Champy.

15. Provide examples that will illustrate the changes in the corporate workplace due to reengineering.

16. Explain why IT is such an important reengineering enabler.

17. Some people say that BPR is a "capital-labor struggle in disguise." Comment.

18. It is said that implementing SIS requires aligning the investment in IS with business goals. Identify all the places in this chapter where such an alignment is considered.

19. Some people say that BPR is a special case of SIS, whereas others say that the opposite is true. Comment.

20. The introduction of BPR requires a fundamental rethinking; relate BPR to the concept of creativity.

EXERCISES

1. Review the applications of Section 3.9 and relate them to Porter's five forces.

2. Describe a situation in which a company enjoyed some of Sass and Keefe's benefits (from your own experience or from a magazine article).

3. Draw a flowchart that shows how McKesson Drug uses IT for both themselves and their customers. Show how the processes are connected.

4. Go to a supermarket and buy at least 10 items. Examine the in-store coupon given to you together with your receipt. Try to find a connection between the coupon and your purchases (see Minicase 2).

5. Carlson Travel Network of Minneapolis is the second largest travel agency in the United States. It provides an agentless service to corporate clients, the first of which was General Electric Company, in April 1993. A computerized system allows GE employees to book trips by filling out a form on their PCs. The system is available 24 hours a day. It is connected with the computer reservation systems of major airlines, car rental companies, and hotel chains. The automated system generates detailed spending reports, enabling GE to negotiate special rates for their employees. Complex travel itineraries are still handled manually, but they account for less than five percent of the total trips. The system saves GE several million dollars each year.
   a. Identify the process reengineering activities.
   b. Describe the support provided by IT.

GROUP ASSIGNMENT

Review Porter's competitive model in Figure 3.3. Relate the model to the pressuring factors of Chapter 1. Each group member is assigned to one industry for executing the comparisons. The industries to be investigated are: banking, airlines, retailers, and toys.

Once a comparison is completed by each member, the group will synthesize the findings into one report.

MINICASE 1

The Robot Music Store Competes with Retail Stores*

You do not have to go to a retail store (e.g., Warehouse) to buy CDs anymore. You can buy them from a vending machine. All you do is make a selection from over 5,000 titles, and pay cash or use a credit card. In contrast with vending machines that usually charge you more than the supermarket, the Robot Music Store will charge you the same price as a record store. You can even listen to a 40-second sample of music from any CD, at superb sound.

The Robot Music Store occupies only 140 square feet, and it can be found in the downtown Minneapolis Mall (see picture) and in other shopping centers.

The customer can see a full-face view of the 500 best sellers and a side view of more than 4,500 other CDs. (For rare or obscure CDs, you will have to go to a record store.) Using a touch screen, the customer is first prompted to select a category (e.g., country music, classical). Then, she is directed to key in the first two letters of the artist's name. A list appears, which the customer can scroll through, until the desired title is found. Another touch on the screen will show the price, song list, and a brief review.

Once you make a selection and pay, the robot retrieves the selected CD and delivers it with change and a receipt through a dispensing slide. Restocking is done by a robot, and a person comes only once a week to collect the money and bring new CDs. The owner automatically receives a daily sales report. Since only one person has access to the inventory, shrinkage is nonexistent (in retail stores, theft by employees and customers can be a big problem). The computer automatically places a title on the list for special sale if it fails to move after a certain length of time.

The Robot Music Store.

Conventional stores use buyers to determine what to purchase for display. The Robot Music Store's computer tracks the actual sales to determine the inventory level. The computer also examines national trends and lists published in the trade publication *Billboard* in order to determine which CDs to stock and how many of each.

Questions for Minicase 1

1. Where can one buy a CD today? Prepare a list of all such possibilities. Compile a list of advantages and disadvantages of each. What is the role of IT in each?

2. What competitive advantages can you identify in the Robot Music Store (as compared to other distribution channels identified in question 1)?

*Minicase 1 is designed as a group exercise.

3. What problems and limitations can you foresee?

4. What are some of the implications of management's decision not to cut prices (as compared to Warehouse)?

5. Explain why the concept of this store can be considered as a BPR of purchasing CDs.

6. Home shopping using a computer, such as Prodigy, may be a strong competitor to the Robot Music Store, as well as to Warehouse. What information technologies can be used by the Robot Music Store to increase its competitive advantage against such a threat?

7. Prepare a presentation for the class.

SOURCE: Condensed from *Chain Store Age Executive*, April 1990, p. 60. See also *Fortune*, February, 7, 1994.

Minicase 2

Atlantic and Pacific Tea Company Competes Using Information Technology

The Great Atlantic and Pacific Tea Company (A&P), a large supermarket chain, uses point-of-sale scanning technology and frequent-shopper programs to build a sophisticated customer database. Customers at participating A&P stores are invited to sign up for free Bonus Saver cards, which entitle them to check-cashing and other privileges. Each week hundreds of items are marked with special discounts for cardholders. A cashier runs the card through a special card-reading device connected to the cash register and the discount is computed automatically. The card-reading machine transmits the customer's identity and a full list of purchases to an in-store computer that saves the information.

This information is instantaneously used by the computer to issue the in-store coupons the customer receives along with the receipt. Incidently, these coupons, which are also issued by most other stores, are tailored to a customer's purchases. For example, a woman buying diapers might receive coupons for baby food. This information is then transmitted to a mainframe computer at A&P's headquarters in Montvale, New Jersey, for further analysis. The Bonus Saver program allows the central-office merchandise buyers to know the detailed characteristics of who is buying what products, at which price, and in which store.

By combining the frequent-shopper database with demographic and life-style data, and cooperating with store managers, merchandise buyers at company headquarters can select products and prices tailored to customers' preferences at each store and region. Furthermore, A&P can use customer purchasing profiles to aim promotions at individual customers and eventually reach households with direct marketing. Building a customer database will enable A&P to form long-term relationships with its customers and to focus its marketing efforts, while gaining competitive advantage over smaller competitors. A&P's extensive customer data-base allows it to embark on a strategy of accurate and centralized buying, which in turn gives A&P greater buying clout with its suppliers through greater volume purchases. In addition, A&P achieves greater efficiency in inventory management, reduces the number of buying personnel, and sharpens advertising activities.

Questions for Minicase 2

1. Relate Porter's forces model to the actions taken by A&P and explain what kind of strategic advantages are provided for the company and against whom.

2. In Long Beach, California, there is strong competition between four large supermarkets: Alpha Beta, Lucky, Ralph's and Vons. Only Vons was using the innovations used by A&P, by the end of 1993. In your opinion, why are many major retailers not using these innovations?

3. What can small independent supermarkets do to protect themselves from the IT-based competition described in this case?

4. Would you consider this case as the use of IT to support business processes reengineering?

SOURCE: Condensed from Bessen (1993).

Minicase 3

High-Tech Integration Drives Van Conversions

Mark III is the world's largest van conversion company (Ocala, FL). The company converts old vans and pickup trucks by stripping them of everything except the engine, body, chassis, seats, and air conditioning. Then, a conversion is made into luxury vehicles with plush interiors and high-tech sound systems. The conversion is usually made to a customer's order. Luxuries may include Nintendo games, cocktail bars, vacuum cleaners, and fancy computers. Every day more than 300 vehicles enter the plant. For many years, the data on each arriving car were entered by hand, creating a two-to-three-day paperwork lag before the company even knew a vehicle had entered the conversion parking lot. But today, IT helps change the manner in which business is done.

Using hand-held bar code data-collection equipment, the vehicle identification number, location, date, and time received for each vehicle is inputted. This information is then downloaded into a computer system, which integrates engineering, manufacturing, financial management, and management reporting. This system was designed to support business processes reengineering.

Using an expert system, the company quickly produces a customized manufacturing order for each entering van. This allows the company to offer a large number of configurations to its dealers as well as to quickly produce special orders. For example, a German customer gave Mark III seven days to build a special van and put it on a boat bound for Germany. Not only was the company able to fulfill the order because the work started immediately, but also, because it used an integrated client/server architecture with object-oriented programming and graphical user interface, the company was able to design and follow the order on a moment-by-moment basis.

Using the bar codes on each van, the company tracks what is going on in each workstation automatically using a wireless radio frequency bar code. These data are entered into a database allowing salespeople instant access to the status of each order. Since most of the components are manufactured in-house, it is critical for Mark III to have complete control of its processes. Using its information systems, the company can solve any logistic, accounting, or technical problem immediately. Using a just-in-time approach, the company assures that all parts, materials, and tools are in place when the vehicle arrives. There are no inventories since there is no need for buffer stocks.

The IS integration allows quick and accurate payroll, which includes a productivity incentive pay. It also integrates the production and inventory MRP systems with a quality-control system.

Finally, the system is used to enhance customers' service after the vehicles are sold. Using the system, customer service operators can answer the more than 10,000 weekly calls from customers quickly and accurately. Having a file on each vehicle helps in identifying the replacement parts. If a customer needs a replacement part, the service center finds the correct part in seconds and prepares an order to the warehouse, right from the screen. Shipment is made in less than 24 hours compared with three days using the old process.

Dealers are also served better with the new systems. For example, dealers are now reimbursed for parts and labor made under warranties in less than 10 days (it used to take 20–30 days). The results—the company is able to maintain its top-ranked position in the industry, keep profitability at a high level, and increase its production from 70,000 vehicles in 1993 (prior to the reengineering) to over 100,000 vehicles in 1994 (after the reengineering).

Questions for Minicase 3

1. Why are the activities described in this case considered reengineering and not incremental improvements?

2. Identify the various reengineering activities described in this case.

3. Identify the various information technologies used to support the reengineering efforts.

4. The client/server system is extended to dealers as well. What are some of the benefits of such an extension?

5. How would you visualize the database in this case?

6. How would you visualize the telecommunications network in this case?

(SOURCE: Condensed from C. Thomas , ''High Tech Integration Drives Van Conversions,'' *APICS*, October 1993, p. 70.

REFERENCES AND BIBLIOGRAPHY

1. Adcock, K., M. M. Helms, and W. J. K. Jih, ''Information Technology: Can It Provide a Sustainable Competitive Advantage?'' *Information Strategy, The Executive Journal*, Spring 1993.

2. Allen, T. J., and M. Scott Morton, *Information Technology and the Corporation of the 1990s*, Oxford: Oxford University Press, 1993.

3. Bakos, J. Y., and M. W. Treacy, "Information Technology and Corporate Strategy: A Research Perspective," *MIS Quarterly*, June 1986.

4. Banker, R. D., et al. (eds.), *Strategic Information Technology Management*, Harrisburg, PA: The Idea Group, 1993.

5. Bergerson, F., et al., "Identification of Strategic Information Systems Opportunities: Applying and Comparing Two Methodologies," *MIS Quarterly*, March 1991.

6. Bessen, J., "Riding the Marketing Information Wave," *Harvard Business Review*, September/October 1993.

7. Boynton, A. C., et al., "New Competitive Strategies: Challenges to Organizations and Information Technologies," *IBM Systems Journal*, Vol. 32, No. 1, 1993.

8. Clemons, E. K., and M. Row, "A Strategic Information System: McKesson Drug Company's Economost," *Planning Review*, September/October 1988.

9. Currid, C., et al., *Computing Strategies for Reengineering Your Organization*, Rocklin, CA: Prima Publishing, 1994.

10. Davenport, T. H., *Process Innovation: Reengineering Work Through Information Technology*, Boston: Harvard Business School Press, 1993.

11. Earl, M. J., "Experiences in Strategic Information Systems Planning," *MIS Quarterly*, March 1993.

12. Ghoshal, S., and S. K. Kim, "Building Effective Intelligence Systems for Competitive Advantage," *Sloan Management Review*, Fall 1986.

13. Hooly, G. J., et al., *Competitive Position*, Englewood Cliffs, NJ: Prentice-Hall, 1993.

14. Hornby, R. E., and P. A. Golder, "SDP: A Strategic DSS," *MIS Quarterly*, March 1994.

15. Hammer, M., and J. Champy, *Reengineering the Corporation*, New York: Harper Business, 1993.

16. Hammer, M., "Reengineering Work: Don't Automate, Obliterate," *Harvard Business Review*, July–Aug. 1990.

17. Ives, B., et al., "Global Business Drivers: Aligning IT to Global Business Strategy," *IBM Systems Journal*, Vol. 32, No. 1, 1993.

18. Katz, A. I., "Measuring Technology's Business Value," *Information Systems Management*, Winter 1993.

19. Katzenback, J. R., and D. K. Smith, *The Wisdom of Teams*, Boston: Harvard Business School Press, 1993.

20. Kettinger, W. J., et al., "Strategic Information Systems Revisited: A Study in Sustainability and Performance," *MIS Quarterly*, March 1994.

21. King, W. R., et al., "Using Information and Information Technology for Sustainable Competitive Advantage," *Journal of Management Information Systems*, Summer 1988.

22. McFarlan, W. E., "Information Technology Changes the Way You Compete," *Harvard Business Reviews*, May–June 1984.

23. McNurlin, B. (ed.), *Trends in Information Technology*, Chicago, IL: Andersen Consulting, Fall 1991.

24. NCR, "Assessing the Value of Information Technology," NCR's Strategic Consulting Group, Dayton, OH, March 1992.

25. Neumann, S., *Strategic Information Systems—Competition Through Information Technologies*, New York: Macmillan, 1994.

26. Oster, S. M., *Modern Competitive Analysis* (2nd ed.), Oxford: Oxford University Press, 1993.

27. Palvia, P. C., J. A. Perkins, and S. M. Zeltmann, "The Prism System: A Key to Organizational Effectiveness at Federal Express Corporation," *MIS Quarterly*, December 1992.

29. Parsons, G., "Information Technology: A New Competitive Weapon," *Sloan Management Review*, Fall 1983.

30. Porter, M. E., "Competitive Advantage: Creating and Sustaining Superior Performance," New York: *Free Press*, 1985.

31. Porter, M. E., and V. E. Millar, "How Information Gives You Competitive Advantage," *Harvard Business Review*, July–August, 1985.

32. Primozic, K., et al., *Strategic Choices: Supremacy, Survival, or Sayonara*, New York: McGraw-Hill, 1991.

33. Rockoff, N., et al., "Information Systems for Competitive Advantage: Implementation of a Planning Process," *MIS Quarterly*, Dec. 1985 pp. 285–94.

34. Saas, C. J., and T. A. Keefe "MIS for Strategic Planning," *Journal of Systems Management*, June 1988.

35. Shank, J. K., and V. Govindarajan, "Strategic Cost Analysis of Technological Investments," *Sloan Management Review*, Fall 1992.

36. Sherman, S., "How to Bolster the Bottom Line," *Fortune*, Special Issue: 1994 Information Technology Guide, Autumn 1993.

37. Synnott, W. R., *The Information Weapon: Winning Customers and Markets with Technology*, New York: John Wiley & Sons, 1987.

38. Teng, J. T. C, et al., "Re-designing Business Processes with Information Technology," *Long Range Planning*, February, 1994.

39. Tuggle, F. D., and H. A. Naphir, "Modeling the Development and Use of Strategic Information Systems," *Information Resources Management Journal*, Fall 1994.

40. Wiseman, C., *Strategic Information Systems*, Homewood, IL: Dow Jones-Irwin, 1988.

41. Wiseman, C. and I. MacMillan, "Creating Competitive Weapons from Information Systems," *Journal of Business Strategy*, Fall 1984.

42. Wysocki, R. K., and J. Young, *Information Systems: Management Principles in Action*, New York: John Wiley & Sons, 1990.

ORGANIZATIONS AND INFORMATION TECHNOLOGY: REENGINEERING AND TOTAL QUALITY MANAGEMENT

Chapter Outline

Learning Objectives

After studying this chapter, you will be able to:

1. Understand competitive forces facing organizations.

2. Discuss why traditional organizations have difficulties competing.

3. Discuss the legacy of organizational design.

4. Discuss the fragmented, complex, suboptimized nature of hierarchical organizations.

5. Understand how technique lags behind technology.

6. Define the information-based, networked organization.

7. Relate quality improvement to business reengineering.

8. Discuss leadership and self-directed teams.

9. Understand cultural change and organizational changes.

10. Discuss the new paradigm for work and organizations.

11. Describe the process of reengineering and its major activities.

▶ 4.1 ALMOST EVERY INSURANCE COMPANY

NICK SIMMONS HAD been an executive at the Chrysler Corporation in Detroit for over 25 years. After he made a decision to accept an executive position with Honeywell in Minneapolis, he contacted his insurance company in Detroit. He had been a customer for the past 25 years and wanted to transfer his insurance to Minneapolis. He explained that he wanted to keep the same life, health, personal liability, and auto insurance. The only difference would involve purchasing a new house, and he would deal with that issue later. Specifically, Nick wanted to avoid the process of filling out new forms and making decisions again about which features of insurance, deductibles, and so on he would have in his policies. He wanted the same insurance in Minneapolis that he had in Detroit.

Much to Nick's disappointment, he found that he would have to contact an agent when he arrived in Minneapolis and reapply for insurance, which would involve filling out all the forms to establish the policies. Nick asked his agent in Detroit if she could at least give him the name of a good agent to contact in Minneapolis. He was told the best thing to do would be to look up an agent in the Yellow Pages.

Nick found this whole process unbelievable. He had been a loyal customer for over 25 years and was trying to remain a customer. Yet, it was as if the insurance company was deliberately trying to alienate him.

Transferring insurance is not always as easy as a phone call.

Nick decided he would shop around for an insurance company when he arrived in Minneapolis and check competitive rates. After making that evaluation, he ended up selecting a new insurance company. Ironically, the very insurance company that seemed to abandon him in Detroit contacted him two years after his move to Minneapolis in an effort to telemarket insurance services to him. There was little chance of that happening.

▶ 4.2 ORGANIZATIONS: WHAT IT TAKES TO BE COMPETITIVE

Organizations are human-designed and human-controlled systems. They are systems made of people, equipment, inventory, and procedures arranged to interact to accomplish one or more objectives. For example, in a profit-oriented business organization, objectives typically include the production of goods or services, organization survival and growth, social responsibility, and profitability.

Assuming an insurance company is concerned about retaining customers, the opening case of this chapter illustrates an organization that is probably not accomplishing its objectives very well. Indeed, a thought-provoking question that organizations can ask themselves is, "If we were deliberately trying to fail, how would we go about doing business?" The way Nick Simmons was treated by his insurance company is indicative of an organization that is not operating in a way that is consistent with providing customer service, retaining customers, and ultimately being profitable. Research shows that it is from five to six times more difficult to *obtain* a new customer than it is to *retain* an existing customer. Yet companies are losing customers, and they face great difficulty in gaining new ones. The way this insurance company was operating clearly works against retaining existing customers.

As you will see in this chapter, organizations in all industries (banking, airlines, hotels, universities, and so on) often behave in ways that are not consistent with retaining existing customers or obtaining new ones. Such types of behavior do not make sense in what has become an extremely competitive marketplace. Such organizations and industries need to be reengineered to perform differently by behaving and operating differently.

As described in Chapter 1, the world has moved to a global economy and competition has become intense. Therefore, many traditionally successful organizations are being eliminated in this competitive wake.

Some organizations do know what it takes to succeed. A good agenda for any organization attempting to compete in the 1990s, as discussed in Chapter 1, would include these elements:

▼ *Nimbleness*—rapid spotting and response to changing conditions and competition.

▼ *Speed*—dramatic compression of the time it takes to complete a task for key business processes.

▼ *Compression*—cutting major chunks of cost and capital throughout the value chain.

▼ *Flexibility*—adaptive processes and structures.

▼ *Quality*—obsession with superior service and value to the customer.

▼ *Innovation*—leadership through imaginative change.

▼ *Productivity*—being effective and efficient.

▼ *Customer focus*—the customer is king.

The pace of change and the degree of uncertainty in tomorrow's competitive environment will continue to accelerate. Therefore, as described in Chapter 1, organizations are going to be under increasing pressure to provide more, using fewer resources. We saw organizations such as IBM, GM, and DEC eliminating over 100,000 jobs during the early 1990s in an attempt to get "lean and mean" and be ready to respond to—and survive in—the marketplace.

During the 1980s and early 1990s, customers in almost every area of business became very disillusioned with the types of service they were receiving from most organizations. Figure 4.1 indicates what customers often find as they try to receive

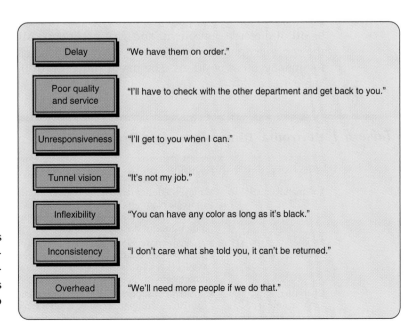

FIGURE 4.1 Organizations need to be more responsive than ever to customers to succeed in today's environment. But what do we often find?

service from many organizations. What went wrong with organizations? And what reengineering needs to be done to correct the problem?

▶ 4.3 TECHNIQUES LAG BEHIND TECHNOLOGY

One of the fundamental problems is that the ways we do things do not keep up with technology: *techniques lag behind technologies*. This has always been true. For example, in history books you see pictures of soldiers lined up shoulder-to-shoulder, several layers deep, marching through meadows in bright uniforms, white pants, black boots, and bright red jackets. Did you ever think about how someone was able to convince those soldiers to be on the front line dressed as if they were a bull's-eye? And whose idea was it to line up like this and march at people who were shooting rifles? Interestingly enough, this organizational technique was derived during the sword-and-shield era of technology. In hand-to-hand combat, it can be very useful to group together when approaching an enemy. You can help each other, protect each other's backside, as well as look intimidating. The introduction of the rifle made this technique devastatingly obsolete. However, it took quite some time before people abandoned the old technique and began hiding behind objects, out of the line of fire, thereby finally adapting rifle technology into military organizations.

Similarly, many of the approaches that are being used by organizations today were developed before computing technology and, more recently, network technology. During the Industrial Revolution, the notions of specializing and dividing and conquering were prevalent as organizations developed what is now called the **hierarchical organization**, as illustrated in Figure 4.2. In this hierarchical or pyramidal structure, ultimate authority and responsibility reside at the top. Authority and responsibility flow down through ever-widening successions of levels to the bottom of the organization.

All organizations have both horizontal and vertical dimensions. The horizontal dimensions are defined by the organization's layers or hierarchical structures; the vertical dimensions are defined by the organization's departments or subunits.

HORIZONTAL DIMENSIONS

The horizontal dimension of an organization can be broadly categorized as top, middle, and operating management. In Figure 4.2, top management includes the board of directors, president, and vice-presidents. Middle management includes the controller and various directors. Operating management includes the remaining management positions. The major functions of these levels are illustrated in Table 4.1.

Table 4.1 **Horizontal Dimensions of an Organization**

Management Level	Function
Top management	Management defines overall organizational objectives and formulates strategic plans and policies to achieve objectives. Management allocates the required financial and human resources among the vertical dimensions of the organization.
Middle management	Management develops, directs, and controls departmental objectives and plans policies consistent with overall organizational objectives and available resources. Management integrates and coordinates the vertical dimensions of the organization.
Operating management	Management supervises the daily production of goods and/or services consistent with performance criteria established by middle management.

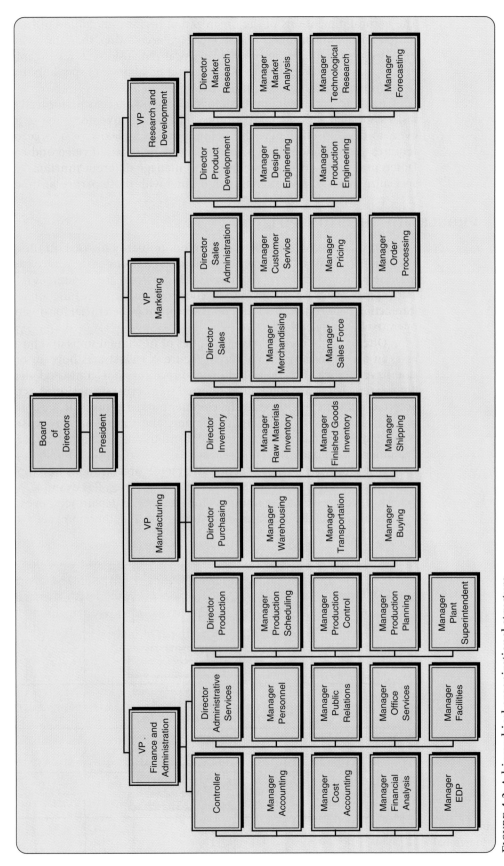

FIGURE 4.2 A hierarchical organizational structure.

VERTICAL DIMENSIONS

The vertical dimensions of the organization perform the different **functions** required for the organization to operate (e.g., accounting, manufacturing, marketing, and research). The number of vertical dimensions in an organization is a function of the differentiation (i.e., division of labor) and specialization required to perform the various tasks in the organization.

In a small, one-owner proprietorship, the owner may perform all the various tasks associated with sales, accounting, purchasing, inventory, and so forth. However, to develop efficiency, the volume and complexity of a large corporation requires specialization; that is, various tasks must be "divided and conquered." Different departments are established to manage different functions, and people specialize in performing the tasks associated with those particular functions.

PROBLEM OF THE STOVEPIPE

The vertical dimension of the organization, primarily focused on functional specialization, has caused many problems in organizations as they have tried to move into the information-based economy; such problems are sometimes referred to as "stovepipes" because of the lack of cooperation between functional areas. The interaction between vertical functions turns out to be crucial for organizations to operate efficiently and effectively.

Often, the difference between duties of functional units and business processes in an organization is confused. Figure 4.3 illustrates how an organization can have vertical functions but have processes that transcend departmental boundaries. These are sometimes referred to as **cross-functional activities**. As depicted in Figure 4.3, product development, order processing, customer service, market management, planning, resourcing, and control are **processes** that can transcend the functional boundaries of distribution, purchasing, research and development, manufacturing, and sales.

Historically, as we have seen in Chapter 2, organizations have operated and built information systems along functional boundaries. For example, a budgeting system was perceived to be primarily for the finance department, even though all functional areas of the organization do budgeting and, therefore, need information

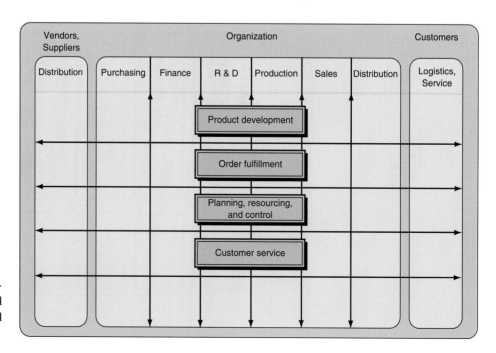

FIGURE 4.3 Business processes across functional areas and organizational boundaries.

system support. In fact, one of the reasons why spreadsheet software became so popular is that it allows functional managers outside finance to obtain reports that are helpful for them in managing their respective departmental budgets. Traditionally, budget reports focused on control and checking balances; they looked similar to what customers receive in account statements from banks. Such statements are useful for reconciliation purposes, but one wouldn't want to manage one's checking account on a day-to-day basis with only a monthly statement. Likewise, operating managers needed more timely information, presented in different ways, than the once-a-month report they were receiving from the finance department.

▶ 4.4 FRAGMENTED PIECEMEAL SYSTEMS

The net effect of focusing on vertical functions and on information systems to support the business has been fragmented, piecemeal information systems, and organizations that operate in a way in which the "left hand doesn't know what the right hand is doing." For example, one insurance company made a judgment call and cancelled the insurance of a teenager after learning that the teenager had received his third speeding ticket. The cancellation seemed like a good idea until the insurance company found out that the teenager was the son of the owner of a company that was one of their largest customers. The father was so irritated by the insurance company's decision that he cancelled his entire corporate insurance with the unsuspecting company. The insurance company handled consumer insurance policies and commercial insurance policies as separate functions, and there was no interaction between those two organizational activities. Therefore, no one was able to understand the complete relationship of a customer to the company. This is a prevalent problem in organizations, and it is based on the problem of organizational structure and technique lagging behind organizational technology. In this case, as information technology came into the insurance organization, the information systems applications were built according to how the company had historically been organized and operated, which was functional rather than cross-functional. Automating in this manner is referred to as "automating history," which is a very bad idea.

A BANKING EXAMPLE

As a vivid illustration of how organizations develop functional, nonintegrated systems, let us track the evolution of information systems in typical banks. Historically, banks have been organized along different types of accounts such as checking or savings accounts, installment loans, mortgage loans, trust accounts, retirement accounts, and so forth. They have been organized this way for many decades—certainly prior to the Information Technology Revolution. Consider a bank that installs its first computer system. The largest and most cost-effective application to computerize is its demand-deposit accounting (DDA) or checking accounts. A systems analyst is assigned to work with users (i.e., bank employees working in DDA) to automate this system. DDA is a highly structured process that lends itself well to computer processing. Account numbers can be used as record identifiers, and the data to be stored in computer files is primarily the data that was used in the manual system, with some enhancements. Figure 4.4 depicts the data contained in a DDA file. Once stored in the computer system, the DDA file can be used to generate a variety of reports and/or terminal displays associated with the management and control of DDA.

During the two-year project to develop and implement the DDA system, the bank decides to begin implementation of a computer-based savings accounting system. Another systems analyst is assigned to work with users to automate this system. Input transactions, reports, and files are designed based on the manual

1. Account number
2. Name
3. Spouse's name
4. Social security number
5. Telephone number
6. Date of birth
7. Sex
8. Marital status
9. Number of children
10. Number of dependents
11. Rent or own home
12. Occupation code
13. Years employed
14. Income range
15. Credit rating
16. Line of credit
17. Officer code
18. Date DDA opened
19. Current balance
20. Last statement date
21. Balance forward — last statement
22. Amount of credits — current period
23. Number of credits — current period
24. Amount of debits — current period
25. Number of debits — current period
26. Number of returned checks year-to-date
27. Date of last deposit
28. Service charge
29. Date of last overdraft
30. Amount of last overdraft
31. Number of overdrafts

FIGURE 4.4 Contents of a DDA file.

savings accounting system, with several enhancements. The contents of a file designed for the savings accounting system are shown in Figure 4.5a.

Over the next few years, the bank continues its development of computer-based information systems by automating its installment loan system and its mort-

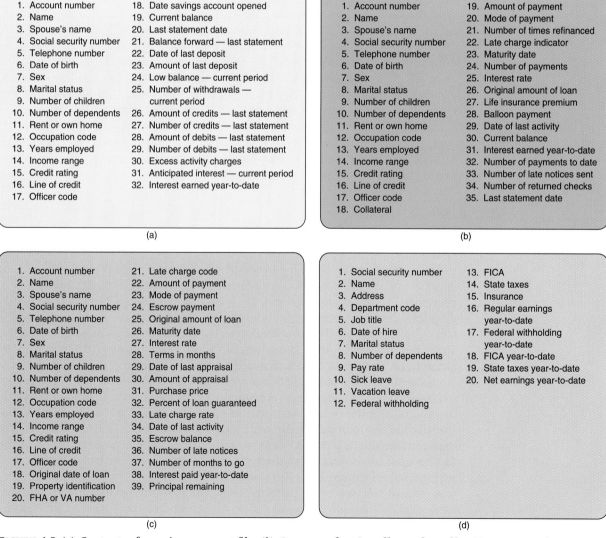

(a)

1. Account number
2. Name
3. Spouse's name
4. Social security number
5. Telephone number
6. Date of birth
7. Sex
8. Marital status
9. Number of children
10. Number of dependents
11. Rent or own home
12. Occupation code
13. Years employed
14. Income range
15. Credit rating
16. Line of credit
17. Officer code
18. Date savings account opened
19. Current balance
20. Last statement date
21. Balance forward — last statement
22. Date of last deposit
23. Amount of last deposit
24. Low balance — current period
25. Number of withdrawals — current period
26. Amount of credits — last statement
27. Number of credits — last statement
28. Amount of debits — last statement
29. Number of debits — last statement
30. Excess activity charges
31. Anticipated interest — current period
32. Interest earned year-to-date

(b)

1. Account number
2. Name
3. Spouse's name
4. Social security number
5. Telephone number
6. Date of birth
7. Sex
8. Marital status
9. Number of children
10. Number of dependents
11. Rent or own home
12. Occupation code
13. Years employed
14. Income range
15. Credit rating
16. Line of credit
17. Officer code
18. Collateral
19. Amount of payment
20. Mode of payment
21. Number of times refinanced
22. Late charge indicator
23. Maturity date
24. Number of payments
25. Interest rate
26. Original amount of loan
27. Life insurance premium
28. Balloon payment
29. Date of last activity
30. Current balance
31. Interest earned year-to-date
32. Number of payments to date
33. Number of late notices sent
34. Number of returned checks
35. Last statement date

(c)

1. Account number
2. Name
3. Spouse's name
4. Social security number
5. Telephone number
6. Date of birth
7. Sex
8. Marital status
9. Number of children
10. Number of dependents
11. Rent or own home
12. Occupation code
13. Years employed
14. Income range
15. Credit rating
16. Line of credit
17. Officer code
18. Original date of loan
19. Property identification
20. FHA or VA number
21. Late charge code
22. Amount of payment
23. Mode of payment
24. Escrow payment
25. Original amount of loan
26. Maturity date
27. Interest rate
28. Terms in months
29. Date of last appraisal
30. Amount of appraisal
31. Purchase price
32. Percent of loan guaranteed
33. Late charge rate
34. Date of last activity
35. Escrow balance
36. Number of late notices
37. Number of months to go
38. Interest paid year-to-date
39. Principal remaining

(d)

1. Social security number
2. Name
3. Address
4. Department code
5. Job title
6. Date of hire
7. Marital status
8. Number of dependents
9. Pay rate
10. Sick leave
11. Vacation leave
12. Federal withholding
13. FICA
14. State taxes
15. Insurance
16. Regular earnings year-to-date
17. Federal withholding year-to-date
18. FICA year-to-date
19. State taxes year-to-date
20. Net earnings year-to-date

FIGURE 4.5 (a) Contents of a savings account file; (b) Contents of an installment loan file; (c) Contents of a mortgage loan file; (d) Contents of a payroll file.

gage loan system. Existing accounting numbers are used for each system, and existing data-capture methods are expanded to obtain all the data shown in Figures 4.5b and 4.5c.

The bank also automates its payroll system. The file for this system includes the data shown in Figure 4.5d.

The development of these five information systems has spanned several years and cost several million dollars. Bank employees and managers responsible for DDA have their own information systems. For example, bank employees and managers responsible for savings accounts have their own information system, and so forth. Each system was developed as an independent subsystem; no thought was given to interfacing the subsystems to provide integrated processing or reporting. This is a common problem of many banks today, as evidenced by how they typically send the customer a separate envelope for each of his accounts.

REDUNDANCY

The first problem with the bank's information systems is that there is a great deal of **redundancy in the data** collected, stored, and processed. Consider a bank customer who has a checking account, a savings account, an installment loan, and a mortgage loan. Though the bank is dealing with one customer, its information systems treat this customer as four customers. The customer has four account numbers (one in each information system).

Specifically, data elements 1 through 16 are identical in each of four files (see Figures 4.4 and 4.5.)* If a customer has more than one checking account, savings account, or loan, the redundancy becomes even greater. This redundancy creates the following problems.

1. Customers are required to supply duplicate data for each account they open, even when some or all of the data needed have been collected previously.
2. Storage space is wasted because the same data are stored in different places in the same file and/or in different files.
3. Processing time is wasted. For example, a customer's address may, due to redundancy, be stored in eight different places in the bank's computer files. If the customer's address changes, all eight addresses must be updated to keep the data current in all information systems.
4. Inconsistencies and/or other errors develop in data files. The majority of information systems fail to update all redundant data. For example, a customer's address may be updated in the DDA file but not in the savings accounting or loan files. Consequently, there are inconsistencies concerning the address of that customer.

INTEGRATION

Besides creating inefficient redundancies, the independent subsystem structure causes difficulties in the **integration** of information. The systems and files have been developed along departmental or functional boundaries. The account numbers are not logically related and cannot be used for cross-referencing a customer's accounts. This seriously limits reporting capabilities. For example, a loan officer may want to check information pertaining to a loan applicant's checking and savings accounts. However, there is no linkage to these data from the loan system. Indeed, the loan officer may have to ask the loan applicant if she has checking and/or savings accounts with the bank and what her account numbers are.

Consider a case where the management of the bank wants to increase mortgage loans to offset several large savings deposits. Management decides to send

---

*These data elements were made identical for the purposes of this example. In actuality, the systems would share many common data elements, but files would tend to vary some in their names, sequence, and inclusion of elements.

letters encouraging specific customers to consider buying homes, using convenient financing available through the bank. Management also decides that the best customers to send such letters are these:

1. Customers who do not have mortgage loans.
2. Customers who have good checking account records (i.e., few or no overdrafts).
3. Customers with sufficient funds in their savings accounts to make a down payment on a home.
4. Customers who have good payment records on any installment loans with the bank.

Though the data necessary to identify such customers are available in different files of different information systems (see Figures 4.4 through 4.5), there is no convenient way to integrate them. Instead, extensive programming and clerical work are required to satisfy such an information request. Management is understandably disappointed and unable to function effectively.

The problem is that the bank's information systems were not designed to integrate information to serve management's needs. Integration of information is more readily achievable when it is considered prior to developing and implementing systems. After the fact, integration can be unwieldy; it usually requires new systems development.

Not all organizational information needs to be integrated. For example, the contents of the payroll file in Figure 4.5d are independent of the contents of the other files, described in Figures 4.4 and 4.5a, 4.5b, and c. However, it may make sense to integrate payroll with other personnel-related data (bonus plans, vacation time, annual reviews, and so forth).

The situation at the bank is caused by lack of foresight, lack of planning, and automating history. Originally, systems were developed in a fragmented, piecemeal manner with no thought given to eventual integration requirements. Figure 4.6 shows the relationships of the data contained in the bank's five files. Box 4.1 portrays what can happen in such an environment.

The scenario of the bank can be translated into other organizational settings. For example, let's consider a university. Student data, course data, faculty data, and classroom facilities data should all be integrated. Student demand for classes needs to be related to faculty and classroom availability. Every semester, many students suffer the consequences because this information is not handled optimally. Another example is a manufacturing plant, where sales data, inventory data, production resources data, and purchasing data should all be integrated.

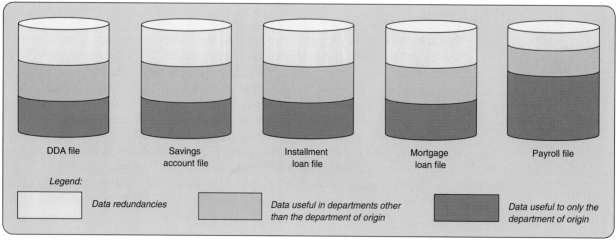

DDA file   Savings account file   Installment loan file   Mortgage loan file   Payroll file

Legend:

Data redundancies

Data useful in departments other than the department of origin

Data useful to only the department of origin

FIGURE 4.6 The relationship of data in a bank's files.

IT At Work BOX 4.1

NORTHWESTERN BANK

Susan Kirk had been a customer of Northwestern Bank for 15 years. She started banking there when she was a student, and as her career blossomed and her income increased, she established several accounts including savings, bond, and trust accounts. She also established her checking account there and obtained her car loans. Then, Susan decided to purchase a retirement property. It was a repossession from a bank in Florida. She was able to buy the property for 50 cents on the dollar, which resulted in a total purchase price of $82,000. Her income during the next two years would actually allow her to pay for this property during that period, so she was not interested in establishing a conventional mortgage loan for the property. She did not want to go through the transaction costs, closing costs, appraisals, origination fees, and so on.

Susan went to the bank and expressed her interest in having an $82,000 line of credit loan established through their executive banking services. When she described what she wanted, the bank officer perceived that what she wanted was a mortgage loan and told her she should go to the mortgage loan department. She explained that she didn't want a mortgage loan because of the transaction costs and that she intended to pay the loan off very quickly. Then, she was told to check with the installment loan people for a shorter term loan. Again, she saw no reason to do that because she was not interested in set-

ting up the property as collateral, having an appraisal, and so forth. She felt that her standing with the bank and her income were sufficient to warrant a line of credit. Susan was bounced around to several departments to fill out forms as the banking personnel struggled with exactly how to handle a situation like hers.

She became totally frustrated and walked across the street to another bank where she explained her predicament. She was sent to a new service that the bank had set up called Private Banking for customers who had incomes in excess of $150,000 a year and net worth exceeding $500,000. That service was immediately able to establish a line of credit loan for her at $1\frac{1}{2}$ percent above prime using her signature as collateral. She was so pleased with the service that she transferred all her accounts from her old bank. One month later, the old bank noticed that Susan Kirk was no longer doing banking with them and contacted her to see what had happened. She explained her experience. The vice president was shocked at her treatment and offered to try and remedy it. At this point, however, Susan had gone through the time and effort of moving all her banking relationships to a new bank and really wasn't interested in yet more change.

Critical Thinking Issues: What role does IT play in this case? (Think hard.) How can file integration eliminate some of Susan's problems? ▲

▶ 4.5 FAILURE TO INTEGRATE

In retrospect, it is not difficult to see that, when appropriate, information systems must be integrated. However, few organizations attempted such integration in their initial attempts to develop computer-based information systems. The failure to approach information systems in an integrated fashion illustrates a key concept discussed throughout this book. Many information systems are developed as high-speed, automated versions of existing manual systems. Since manual systems did not typically lend themselves to integration with other manual systems, the original computer versions of these systems have retained this nonintegrated orientation. The opportunity to integrate the manual systems as they are computerized was not exploited. The cost of correcting this problem can be staggering. Instead, the personnel developing the systems reacted to management's demands for integrated information after it became apparent that there was a structural deficiency within the initial development.

Most organizations realized the deficiency and have now attempted to integrate their information systems either initially or during revisions of their initial systems. Though their insight and efforts have enabled them to more readily integrate data and therefore reduce redundancies, they still encounter problems. The programming of data relationships that transcend departmental or functional

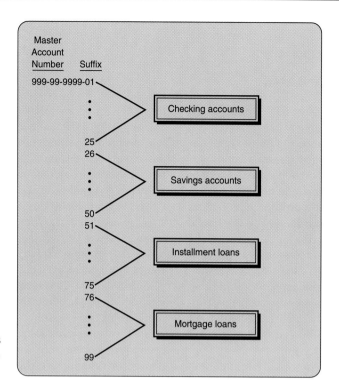

FIGURE 4.7 Use of suffixes to achieve centralized account numbers at a bank.

boundaries is extremely complex. Integration requires consolidation of files and/ or linking of data stored in separate files.

In our bank example, four systems of the bank (DDA, savings accounting, installment loans, and mortgage loans) can be integrated. One way this can be accomplished is by assigning a master account number to each customer and then using suffixes to designate the various accounts the customer has within the bank. Figure 4.7 illustrates such a customer account structure. Note that a customer can have several checking accounts, savings accounts, and loans. The unique identity provided for each customer account allows the accounts to be consolidated as shown in Figure 4.8. By organizing the bank data as depicted in Figure 4.8, the bank can reengineer itself to be more customer oriented as well as reduce cost.

Figure 4.9 depicts what a customer would go through in a traditional bank to establish several accounts. Each time the customer would have to give out the same demographic information, and each time each department would view the same customer as a separate customer.

Figure 4.10 depicts a reengineered bank. Note that the customer can open all accounts—and have accounts marketed to them—with one-stop shopping.

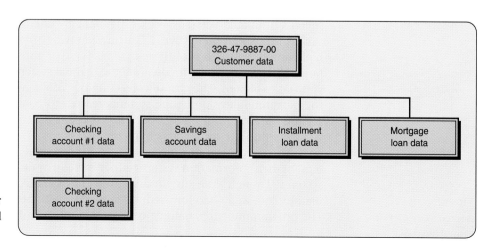

FIGURE 4.8 A customer record from a consolidated bank file.

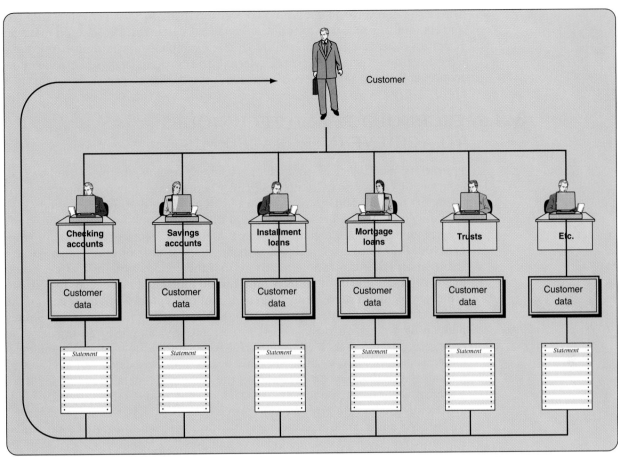

FIGURE 4.9 Bank before reengineering—customer has to go to every department and gets different statements.

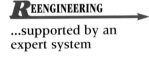

REENGINEERING

...supported by an
expert system

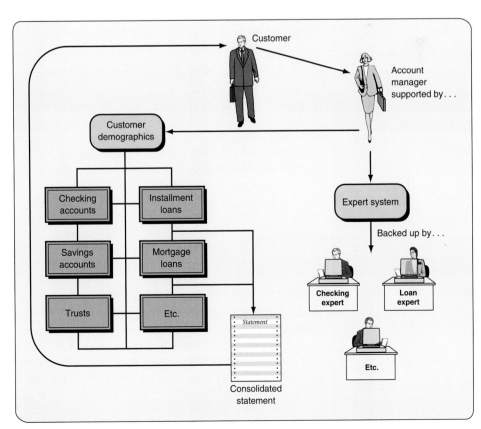

FIGURE   4.10   Reengi-
neered bank with inte-
grated system.

They also can resolve all questions and problems with one account representative, and get only one monthly consolidated financial statement. The account manager is not a genius; she is supported by IT. For example, she can derive functional expertise from expert systems, and effective and efficient databases provide information both about the customers and about the bank's services.

▶ 4.6 TECHNOLOGY AND TECHNIQUES TO ACHIEVE INTEGRATED MIS

Prior to the availability of database management systems, the programming necessary to link files was extremely difficult. The implementation of database management systems and computer-assisted systems design (CASE) products—including code generators, as discussed in Chapters 6 and 8—greatly reduced the programming task of integrating systems. A database management system, however, does not provide integrated systems. A great deal of effort must go into information systems planning to ensure that the various systems that get developed within an organization over time can be integrated as needed. In order to achieve integration successfully, a great deal of conceptual work must go into the various functions and files that make up the database of an organization. Simply purchasing a database management system and installing it in an organization only gives programmers a more powerful access technique for their fragmented, piecemeal information systems. A database is a concept; a database management systems is a technology. To fully exploit the technology, database planning is required as well as database technology. And, of course, integrated systems, including decision support, are required to provide the capabilities really necessary to support top and middle management. It is through well-integrated information systems with on-line decision-support capabilities that management expectations can begin to be met. Planning techniques and decision techniques for achieving integrated systems and decision-support systems are provided in Chapters 11 and 15.

Integration can be achieved more easily in a corporate-wide client/server architecture, as will be illustrated in Chapter 10. Also, groupware software such as Lotus Notes can provide the skeleton around which integrated applications are constructed, as will be described in Chapter 14.

▶ 4.7 FROM HIERARCHY TO NETWORK

How should contemporary organizations be organizing and using their information systems? Early in the chapter, we talked about how techniques lag behind technology. When new technologies come along, organizations tend to try to use them in old ways; only later do they realize the need to change the way things are done. Interestingly, when computers first came into business use, they were hierarchical in the way that they operated, just like the organizations. The mainframe computer was at the top of the hierarchy with everything else connected to it. Eventually, when computer users moved to on-line systems, they had terminals, but these were called "dumb" terminals. Organizations didn't even realize these terminals were dumb until much later, when smart terminals were introduced. The smart terminals evolved into what are now known as personal computers (PCs) or microcomputers; most recently, we have moved to client/server technology.

The movement away from the mainframe, or hierarchical, view of technology had a serious impact on a lot of computer vendors (it was almost like the realization that the sun was not really the center of the universe). Many organizations considered the mainframe to be the center of the information-processing universe. Reality has since indicated that information processing has evolved to networks. Organizations that are becoming highly effective operationally are be-

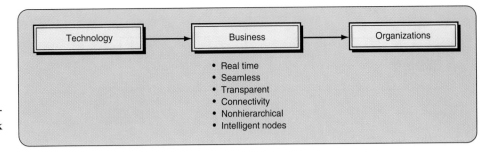

FIGURE 4.11 How organizations adapt to network technology.

ginning to mirror these networks. Figure 4.11 portrays this evolution. First the technology exists, and it gets incorporated into the business. Later, the organization modifies itself to fully absorb the benefit of the technology. Recall earlier that rifles were added to the existing way of organizing for battle; later, the military changed the way it was organized. So, what are the characteristics of network technology, and how should organizations mirror them? As portrayed in Figure 4.11, **networks** are real-time, seamless, and transparent. They have connectivity, are nonhierarchical, and have intelligent nodes in the network. Intelligent nodes means that nodes have computer processing ability and data.

How would an organization behave if it had these characteristics? Consider the case study at the beginning of the chapter where Nick Simmons was moving from Detroit to Minneapolis. If the insurance company had behaved like a network, it could simply have told Nick that the transaction was taken care of. Operationally, this would mean that the different regional insurance offices were operating from a common database. For every account Nick Simmons had with the insurance company, the company would have linked to a master account number to understand the entirety of those relationships and access them. From the standpoint of global competition, a customer would be able to move to any city in the world, and the insurance company could handle the transaction on a real-time, seamless, and transparent basis. Such a capability becomes particularly important when you consider what type of person moves from one city to another city, worldwide. Typically, this is a high-income, professional person—the type of person an insurance company would want to retain as a customer.

If we were to apply these network characteristics to the bank example, anyone at the bank would be able to view the entirety of someone's relationship with the bank. If a bank employee wanted to open a new account for a customer, he would simply add the suffix for that account to the master account number, as opposed to having the customer provide demographic information over again. It would also mean that the bank would be able to send the customer a consolidated financial statement of his or her entire relationship with the bank instead of separate information for each account.

▶ 4.8 REENGINEERING THE ORGANIZATION

Though changing the insurance and/or banking organizations to behave in the manner described seems straightforward and simple from a customer standpoint, the internal organizational gyrations are not trivial. To transform an organization from a traditionally hierarchical organization to an information-based network organization—**to reengineer**—is difficult.

The fundamental problem with the hierarchical approach is that any time a decision needs to be made it must climb up and down the hierarchy. All it takes is one person who doesn't understand the issues to say "no," and everything comes to a screeching halt. Also, if information is required from several "functions," getting all the right decision making coordinated can be a time-consuming and frustrating process to employees and customers alike.

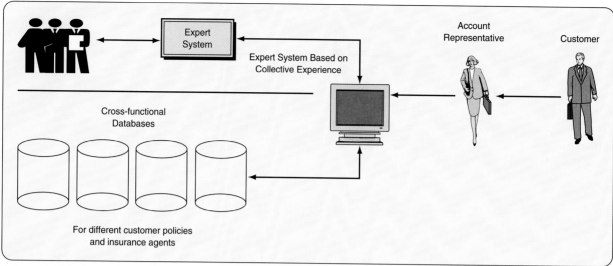

FIGURE 4.12 Information and organization model for customer service.

REENGINEERING

...through a single contact

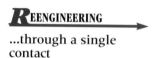

Figure 4.12 represents a model of how both the bank and insurance organizations described can be reengineered. Note that the single point of contact (account representative) need not be the same person if this contact has access to all customer profiles and historical information. Box 4.2 illustrates how a single contact can in fact be several people. In the case of the insurance company, a customer locating to a different city can be transferred to a new agent, who would become the customer's new single contact. Note that all agents have access to all customer data. Another model used by companies such as the highly successful USAA, Otis elevators (see case at end of the book) is to have all agents located in one city and give customers an 800, toll free number. In this model, the agents can respond like the travel agents discussed in Box 4.2. However, if personal, face-to-face contact is important, locating the agents near customers is preferable. This illustrates the need to reengineer in a way that mirrors how an organization wants to conduct business.

IT At Work BOX 4.2

TRAVEL COMPANY

James Williams made extensive use of the Travel Company to coordinate his various speaking and consulting engagements. Because of his specific travel requirements, he always liked to deal with Kathy, a senior travel agent. Kathy was familiar with Mr. Williams's travel requirements. She knew that when he said "book a flight" he meant a Northwest Airlines flight and to be sure to use his Gold Card discount. For any other airline he might use, she knew all his frequent flyer numbers to ensure he received any discounts or frequent flyer mileage. She also knew that he preferred direct flights. If he wanted to rent a car, she knew to reserve a full-size car and to get it from National Car Rental. She made sure that he had an aisle seat and ordered a low-cal, low-fat meal. Any time he wanted a limousine booked in a city, she would know the appropriate service to use.

The problem was that when Jim called the Travel Company, Kathy was usually on the line with another customer. He would leave a message for her to call him back, but then he would be tied up. So telephone tag inevitably developed, which is a typical frustration of dealing with any travel company.

One day Jim called in to book a flight; as usual, Kathy was tied up, so he left a message for her to return his call. The individual taking the message said, "Mr. Williams, how was your flight to London last week?"

Jim said, "Fine."

She said, "Did you receive an aisle seat and a low-cal, low-fat meal as requested?" He said he did. She asked "Was the limo service there to pick you up as arranged?"

He said, "Yes," and then inquired, "Who is this?"

The individual on the other end said, "This is Mary."

Jim replied, "Well, perhaps you could help me."

Without any coaxing on the part of the Travel Company, Jim was now willing to talk to any agent who picked up the phone at the company. The company had installed call-center technology, which brought up on the computer's screen, a complete customer profile and history anytime a customer called in. That meant that any travel agent who picked up the phone could be as personal as Kathy, the agent who had been dealing with the caller exclusively, and give the same customized service. Customer service improved while the costs of the Travel Company declined and the productivity of agents increased. This is because instead of having five people waiting to talk to one travel agent, while other agents were sitting idle, the work load could now be distributed to all employees at the Travel Company.

Critical Thinking Issues: Why is IT important in this case? Some people suggest that you really do not need a travel agency; you can use Compuserve or Prodigy to make reservations on your own. Can Jim get the customer service he gets now from the travel agency from a do-it-yourself system? ▲

Reengineering is not limited to a banking organization. As a matter of fact, studies indicate that 70 percent of all large U.S. corporations are reengineering or considering reengineering. In addition, the public sector, including the U.S. federal government, is implementing reengineering (see Box 4.3).

IT At Work BOX 4.3

REENGINEERING THE FEDERAL GOVERNMENT WITH INFORMATION TECHNOLOGY

The impact of information technology and reengineering is not limited to corporations. The Federal Government is using IT to streamline bureaucracy and improve public services. Although not fully implemented, the program has strong backing with Vice President Al Gore as leader of the National Performance Review (NPR) team. The team's plan is to create an "electronic government," moving from the Industrial Age to the Information Age.

Information technology is playing a key role in this reengineering of government operations and services. The information technology team is providing the direction and getting the various agencies to work to a common technology. As with any project, top management support is vital. In the case of this project, the president has issued direction that agencies should cooordinate new programs for distributing information to the public through the IT team. This helps provide central direction and continuity in the services provided.

The IT team describes the new electronic government systems as a "virtual agency" in which information is shared throughout the government. The U.S. Department of Agriculture already distributes food stamps electronically. Medicare and Social Security payments may also be integrated. Other services being proposed by the NPR team include a national network serving law enforcement and public safety agencies; electronic linkage of tax files at federal, state, and local agencies; and international trade data system; a national environmental data index; government-wide electronic mail; and an integrated information infrastructure, including consolidated data centers. The IT team is also looking at client/server networks to eliminate the need for large mainframe data centers.

It is encouraging to see the federal government entering the Information Age to improve public services. The government is renowned for being slow to change. However, with the rapid growth in technology and the support from the president, this administration may make some major improvements in government services.

NPR IT SUGGESTIONS. The following are information technology recommendations from the National Performance Review (NPR):

Overall:

▼ Provide strong leadership to integrate information technology into the business of government.

Develop these *"electronic government" applications*:

▼ Integrated system for electronic benefits transfer.

▼ Electronic access to government data and services via 800 numbers, "kiosks," and electronic bulletin boards.

▼ National network for law enforcement and public safety.

▼ Intergovernmental tax filing, reporting, and payment processing.

▼ International trade data system.

▼ National environmental data system.

▼ Government-wide electronic mail.

Establish these frameworks:

▼ Integrated information infrastructure, including consolidated data centers.

▼ Systems and mechanisms to ensure privacy and security, including a Privacy Protection Board, privacy standards, and a digital signature standard for unclassified data.

▼ Improved methods for information technology acquisition.

▼ Incentives for innovation, including performance-based contracting and a government-wide venture capital fund for innovative information technology projects.

▼ Information technology training for federal employees; required certification for information technology managers.

Critical Thinking Issues: Why is the system referred to as an electronic agency? Is so much computerization of the government beneficial? Why or why not? ▲

SOURCE: Condensed from G.H. Anthes, ''Feds to downsize with IT,'' *Computerworld*, September 13, 1993.

▶ 4.9 NETWORK IS NOT JUST ABOUT TECHNOLOGY

Information technology facilitates movement to the information-based networked organization. Nevertheless, *approaches to management* have had to adapt in order to use information technology to achieve network-style organization. This evolution is discussed next.

APPROACHES TO MANAGEMENT

During recent years, a transformation of management has occurred as many people attempted to determine the best way to manage organizations. Broadly speaking, existing management approaches form a continuum between two extreme positions with respect to management: the classical or hierarchical approach and the approach of networks and **self-directed teams**. The primary management concepts within each approach are listed in Figure 4.13.

The hierarchical and network approaches to management obviously present significant contrast. Both approaches have been used with success in some organizations and have been unsuccessful in others. Understandably, the results have

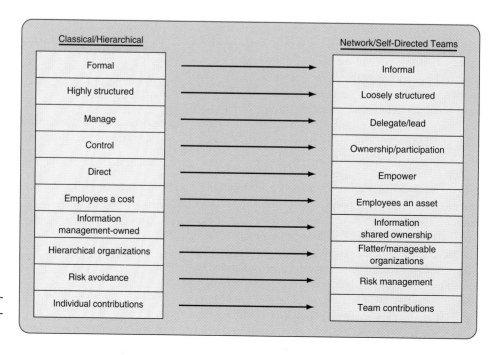

Classical/Hierarchical	Network/Self-Directed Teams
Formal	Informal
Highly structured	Loosely structured
Manage	Delegate/lead
Control	Ownership/participation
Direct	Empower
Employees a cost	Employees an asset
Information management-owned	Information shared ownership
Hierarchical organizations	Flatter/manageable organizations
Risk avoidance	Risk management
Individual contributions	Team contributions

FIGURE 4.13 Transformation of managerial approaches.

created confusion and debate as to which approach is the better way to manage organizations.

CONTINGENCY MANAGEMENT

Actually, there is no single, best way to manage all organizations. Rather, the best management approach is *contingent* on characteristics of the organization being managed. This concept is referred to as **contingency management**. It attempts to recognize organizational differences and propose management approaches that best fit those differences.

For example, the organizational characteristics of an assembly line in a manufacturing plant are different from the organizational characteristics of a group of research scientists. Assembly-line work can be characterized as routine and repetitive, whereas research work is creative and diverse. To be effective, each group of workers should be structurally set up and managed differently. The management challenge becomes one of systematically identifying relevant differentiating characteristics and then applying appropriate management techniques to each group.

TECHNOLOGY AND ENVIRONMENT

The contingency theory of management has established that the technology and environment of an organization are the key variables that characterize the organization. *Technology* is defined as the human and mechanical processes by which an organization produces its goods and/or services. *Environment* is defined as all relevant factors external to the organization. An organization's environment includes such things as customers, competitors, and government regulations. The technology and environment of an organization establish the organization's position on a continuum, ranging from closed/stable/mechanistic to open/adaptive/organic.

A closed/stable/mechanistic organization has a predominantly routine and predictable situation. Productivity is a major objective. In this type of organization, technology and environmental forces are relatively stable and certain. Consequently, decision making tends to be straightforward and programmable. An example of a closed/stable/mechanistic organization is the can manufacturing industry. It has used a relatively stable technology and encountered a relatively stable environment for decades.

Alternatively, an organization that is open/adaptive/organic is involved with activities other than just the routine. Creativity and innovation are required. Technology and environmental forces tend to be volatile and present considerable uncertainty. Problems encountered are complex, presenting conflict and unclear courses of action. Decision-making processes are characterized as risky, and few optimum decisions are possible. An example of an open/adaptive/organic organization is the personal computer industry; it has had an extremely dynamic technology and environment.

The realization that organizations vary in form, from closed/stable/mechanistic to open/adaptive/organic, in order to accommodate their technology and environment, provides the basic framework for contingently applying managerial approaches. A management style aligned with the hierarchical approach tends to be effective in relatively closed/stable/mechanistic organizations. Management can operate in a structured, centralized, and process-oriented mode. Conversely, the approach of network management (self-directed team) tends to be effective in open/adaptive/organic situations where employees are coping with greater uncertainty and complexity. Management must provide a more autonomous and participative setting for what is generally a more sophisticated level of staff. Of course, within subsystems (suborganizations or departments) within an organization, you find varying degrees of closed/stable/mechanistic vs. open/adaptive/organic tendencies. For example, accounting will typically be more stable and mechanistic, and marketing will be more open and adaptive.

▶ 4.10 SITUATIONAL LEADERSHIP AND NETWORK MANAGEMENT

Today there is a clear trend away from the traditional hierarchical organization toward the networked organization. This trend is being brought on by the evolution from industrial-based economy to the information-based economy. In the industrial economy, emphasis was on division and specialization of labor into hierarchical, stable, mechanistic processes. This approach worked fine for low-skilled labor.

Now, however, less than 15 percent of the workforce is involved in specialized, traditional labor, much of which has been automated. Today, most people do what is called *knowledge work.* Knowledge work includes any job in which the primary emphasis is information processing: engineers, financial analysts, market researchers, salespeople, professors, lawyers, authors, systems analysts, scientists, clerks, and so on. In knowledge work, the intellectual context of the work increases to the point where the subordinate usually has more expertise than his "hierarchical" supervisor. Consequently, management cannot be effective dictating to lower levels in the organization. Rather, managers should be open to suggestions and solutions, and empower their employees.

Figure 4.14 portrays the continuum from the hierarchical approach to the network approach. Note that in the middle is the **flattened organization**, which has fewer layers of management and broader spans of control.

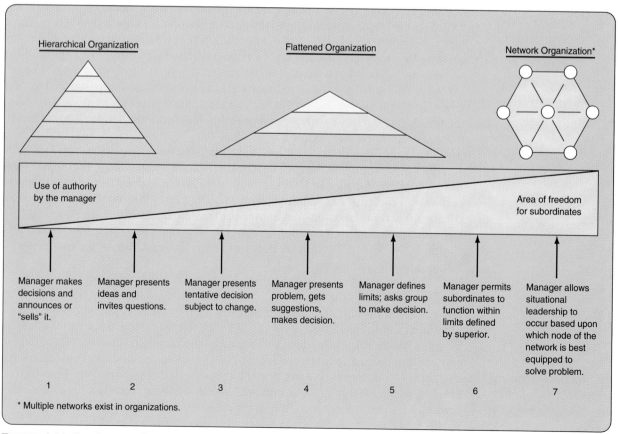

FIGURE 4.14 Continuum of organizations.

If managers knew "everything," they could tell employees what to do, how to do it, and when to do it. They could get by with hierarchical approaches and announce or sell a decision. But when managing physicians, scientists, engineers, and similar groups, such an approach would be a mistake. The employees or "nodes" in this organizational network are not "dumb" terminals like those in the original hierarchical mainframe computers. Each employee or node has special expertise and information. Therefore, it is better to view the information-based organization as a client/server network. The best "node" should be used to solve the problem.

As a straightforward example of a network approach to problem solving, let's say a student in class began to have cardiac arrest. What should happen? If one student in the class knows CPR, she should become a situational leader and configure a team to solve the problem. That person is the best equipped "node" in the network. Note that she might be temporarily hierarchical in behavior. For example, she might tell one person to call 911, another to get some blankets, and another to keep the hallways clear for the ambulance personnel. The professor of the course should relinquish authority, and those people assigned tasks by the CPR expert should not argue about who should call 911! The goal is to recognize the most important task. In this case, saving a life preempts teaching, and the situational leader needs to emerge from the network.

Traditional, multilevel hierarchies can become too bureaucratic and slow to be responsive to dynamic problem solving. In an organization, situational networks might configure to solve a technical problem with a product, overcome sales resistance from a key account, or deal with an employee turnover problem.

In the network organization, there are fewer layers of management and broader spans of control. In the United States, close to 2 million middle management positions have been eliminated. Why are these jobs not needed? A nationwide recession and competition forced these initial staffing reductions in order to survive. The result has been improvements in information management and more empowered and knowledgeable employees working with less supervision.

Organizations, like networks, need to be able to quickly reconfigure themselves to solve a problem. Workers need to quickly organize and work together to solve issues such as customer service, engineering, or product problems. IT plays a major role, enabling team members to do just that. This will be shown in Chapters 14 and 17. Organizations should have standing teams that exist over time, as well as ones that are quickly created and dissolved to solve temporary problems (think of a pick-up basketball game.) Figure 4.15 provides a graphic portrait of the network organization for a division of British Petroleum. Note the standing teams of Engineering Resources, Technology Development, and Business Services. The 16 independent clusters represent "pick-up teams" assigned to solve problems that develop. An interesting application of team-based organization is illustrated in Box 4.4.

IT At Work BOX 4.4

 **G**LOBAL PERSPECTIVE

HOW GE OF CANADA SUPPORTS ITS TEAMS WITH IT

One of the most publicized examples of a company that transformed itself to a self-directed team structure is GE of Canada. Being relatively small (360 employees) and in the financial services industry made it easier to reengineer the company. The company now is composed of 20 teams (see figure that follows) who are heavily supported by IT.

The steering committee that planned the BPR recognized from the beginning that IT is a critical factor in the transformation—both for communication among teams, for information sharing, and as a tool to support the work of the team members. Here are some of the IT applications.

1. Since all secretarial and administrative resources were eliminated, it was necessary to provide productivity software support applications (such as word processing and electronic calendars).

2. Special applications were written for user-friendly access to databases. For example, an on-line access to financial data was created to facilitate data analysis by the payroll and control teams. Downloading data from the mainframe was made simple and easy.

3. Employees were empowered to make their own travel arrangements by electronically accessing available information, and by electronically making reservations. (GE has an agreement with a large travel agency that allows these activities.)

4. Robots were installed to deliver mail and supplies.

5. E-mail, voice mail, and fax were made available to all employees.

6. Training in spreadsheet software (Lotus 1-2-3) and in downloading data to the spreadsheet was provided.

7. Special hardware and software requested by specific teams for improving productivity, quality, or communication, was provided (e.g., scanners, imaging technology). As a matter of fact, employees were *encouraged* to find ways in which IT could be of help.

The results of the GE transformation were dramatic indeed. The number of employees was reduced by 40 percent, while the productivity of the group and its quality (especially in terms of customers' service) were drastically improved.

Critical Thinking Issues: Who is the boss in this structure? How are employees empowered and how can one control such an organization? ▲

SOURCE: Condensed from Applegate L. H., and J. J. Cash "G.E. Canada: Designing a New Organization," Harvard Business School Case 9-189-138, 1989.

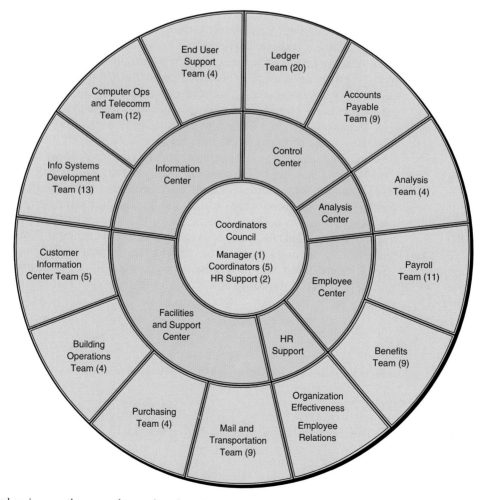

*Note: The numbers in parentheses are the number of employees in each team.

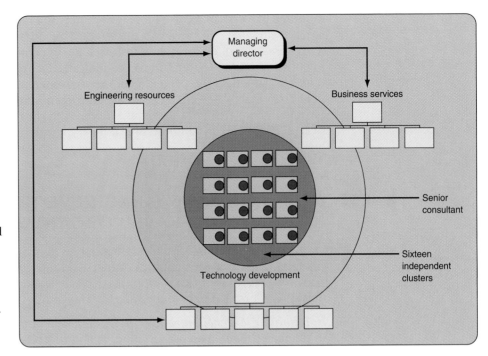

FIGURE 4.15 British Petroleum Engineering networked with self-directed teams. (SOURCE: Mills, Quinn D., *Rebirth of the Corporation*. Copyright © 1991 John Wiley & Sons, Inc. Reprinted by permission of John Wiley & Sons, Inc.)

▶ 4.11 HOW TO REWARD WITHOUT PROMOTION

A common issue that comes up as organizations move to the networked, self-directed team situation is how to reward employees without promotion. In the hierarchical model, one of the key goals for employees was to climb the corporate ladder to higher level positions of authority. Many organizations in transition from hierarchies to networks find one of the biggest sources of employee resistance to the change is fear of lost power and status. This fear can be actual or imaginary.

In contrast, organizations that have dealt with work of high intellectual content for years have already moved away from placing a premium value on position in the hierarchy. For example, consider the medical or academic communities. Most physicians, given a choice, would prefer to be the best neurosurgeon or best cardiovascular surgeon as opposed to being chief of staff. Faculty usually prefer to be the best researcher as opposed to being department chairperson or dean. Why? As the intellectual content of work goes up, the work itself becomes quite interesting, self-gratifying, and motivating. Administration, on the other hand, remains relatively stable, dealing with budgets, office space, and things of that nature. If we are talking about manual, menial tasks—say digging ditches—clearly it is preferable to be in management. On the other hand, if we are talking about interesting work, the administrative aspect of it can be less appealing. A good example in the computing industry is a company named Cray Research, a leader in the supercomputers field. Seymour Cray, a leading computer designer who had left Control Data Corporation, was instrumental in setting up Cray Research, but he was never president of the company. He was in charge of research. John Rollwagon was brought in as the president, even though someone in the lab was the namesake of the company.

In the networked, self-directed world, employee status comes from being chosen first to be a member of a team because of the value the team contributes. The recognition and camaraderie individuals receive from team members become substitutes for promotion and a key part of the reward system. In this sense, it is very much like a sports team in which there are key athletes who are the "superstars," highly recognized by any team. As in the medical or academic communities, players can receive more recognition and higher compensation than the coach, who would be viewed as the typical "hierarchical leader."

Research on self-directed transformation of organizations—from hierarchies to networks and self-directed teams—indicates that there is generally a period of transition in which the people who lose their management or supervisory positions are unhappy and often even leave the organization. Within a couple of years, however, there are indications that everybody in the organization feels more motivated, and their contributions are better recognized than when they were in the hierarchical model.

▶ 4.12 REENGINEERING TO ACHIEVE THE NETWORK INFORMATION-BASED ORGANIZATION

Transforming organizations from hierarchies to networks involves significant changes. Often it means cultural changes, changes in attitudes, and changes in skills required in an organization, particularly leadership skills. Some key tasks that an organization must undertake to achieve this new organization follow:

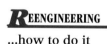

REENGINEERING

...how to do it

▽ *Eliminate layers of management.* As discussed in this chapter, the more layers of management in an organization, the more levels of approval required before action can be taken. A key dimension of a networked information-based organization is that the organization is flattened.

▽ *Ensure cross-functional, interorganizational use of information.* The key issue here is that the left hand must know what the right hand is doing. Things such as just-in-time inventory are achieved only when there is free flow of information from one function to another and from one organization to another.

▽ *Replace need-to-know with need-to-enrich.* One might argue that airline agents at a counter would not "need to know" that the customer standing in front of them flies over 350,000 miles a year with their airline and has done so for the past 10 years. However, it can clearly be in the best interest of the airline for the counter agent to know this information when handling any problems that the passenger has encountered.

▽ *Reward without promotion.* By flattening an organization, there is obviously less opportunity for traditional hierarchical promotion. A mind-set change must occur here. People must place value in being a treasured team member—a team member who is quickly selected any time a "pick-up basketball game" needs to be played to solve an organizational problem.

▽ *Focus on results, not activities.* Traditionally hierarchical management has played a key role in overseeing activities of subordinates. In the network paradigm of organization, you rely more on team members to put pressure on other team members to help contribute to get problems solved. Therefore, there can be a much greater focus on the team's results rather than on observing individual work behaviors. For the team to succeed, team members must contribute. This tends to create sufficient regulation of team members' behavior within the team, and less supervision is needed.

Organizations that fully achieve this new organizational paradigm can expect to reap the following benefits:

▽ *Simultaneous independence and interdependence of business units.* For example, in the case of the insurance company discussed at the beginning of the chapter, each agent should be able to respond to customers and each city should be able to respond to customers within the metro area; but the organization should also be able to transfer customers from one city to another city, achieving interdependence of business units.

▼ *Multiple concurrent modes of operation (by customer, by market, by product, by geography, and so on.).* For example, a credit card company should be able to identify all customers who have been making international travel arrangements during the past year and know which airlines they have been using most often in an effort to market a frequent flyer program to them.

▼ *Business processes that are horizontal and parallel, not vertical and sequential (no stovepipes).* This is achieved by ensuring cross-functional and interorganizational use of information so that the left hand knows what the right hand is doing.

▼ *Organizational change without permanent physical structural change to the organization.* The key issue is for the organization to be able to reconfigure its resources to solve problems differently. Organizational participants should still have a sense of what their primary areas of expertise are and what the home of that expertise is (e.g., information technology expertise). But they should be very fluid in their ability to become team members to solve different organizational challenges.

▼ *Both uniformity and flexibility.* Of concern here is the ability to ensure good-quality products but not make them all one size and one color. By good use of cross-functional interorganizational information, companies can achieve what is referred to as mass customization. Mass customization involves the ability to let customers have economy-of-scale prices yet be able to select specific features desirable to them. This concept is explored more in the strategic planning discussion in Chapter 11 under the topics of customer resource life cycle and future perfect. It is also considered in Chapter 17, where mass customization is compared with mass production.

▼ *Complete communication independent of geography and time.* One of the early leaders in achieving this type of capability has been the credit card industry, where if you lose a credit card in a foreign country you can have your credit card replaced almost immediately. This can be achieved only by having a networked information-based organization.

▼ *Failures.* A word of caution: One of the lessons of IT history is that very big systems have a tendency to fail when requirements and vision exceed real capabilities. For example, many of the early MRP systems (see Chapter 17), artificial intelligence, and complex transaction processing systems (see Chapter 1) never worked. BPR and some TQM are no exception. They do fail for many reasons. One of the reasons for failure is miscalculation of the required IT. It simply may be too expensive to rebuild and reengineer the IT infrastructure and applications that are necessary for BPR. The solution may be to defer the BPR and use incremental improvement instead, or to reengineer the critical processes only. A medium-sized professional services company in southern California decided to defer for five years the replacement of its mainframe with a client/server, which was needed for reengineering. Instead, the mainframe operations were improved. The CEO reasoned that the client/server technology was too new (this was 1994), and since it was necessary for the BPR, he would play it safe and invest money in upgrading the mainframe, so it would do an adequate job for five years.

▶ 4.13 TOTAL QUALITY MANAGEMENT AND REENGINEERING

Throughout this chapter, we have been focusing on improving organizational performance through better use of information technology. A very important concept has emerged during the past two decades which is very complementary to the notion of the reengineered information-based network organization: **Total Quality Management (TQM)**. Although quality of Japanese products had actually been a problem during the 1950s and 1960s, the Japanese made a very strong commitment to TQM in the late '60s and early '70s, which resulted in their producing products that were often superior to what was being manufactured elsewhere in the world. This was particularly demonstrated in the areas of consumer electronics and automobiles. Interestingly, the TQM movement in Japan was initiated by an American professor by the name of Deming, who found U.S. companies uninterested in this quality technique.

As a result of the Japanese success, products in Europe and the United States began to be considered inferior in quality to the Japanese. Therefore, during the 1980s a strong movement was initiated in Europe and the United States to achieve what had become a higher standard for world-class quality.

TQM is a concept by which all employees in the organization consider quality to be part of their responsibility. Early attempts at quality, particularly in the United States, consisted of setting up a separate quality department whose job was to audit, teach, and possibly implement systems for quality throughout organizational processes. Note that this tendency is very much like the stovepipe, non-cross-functional perspective which was typical of the piecemeal approach to organization and management. The TQM concept is very compatible with the network approach to organization in that every node in the network, every team involved in organizational processes, takes on quality as an agenda item. The result of TQM programs in organizations has been a significant increase in quality. In fact, today most customers take quality as a given; they simply will not accept products that are not of world-class quality. To be competitive, organizations often have to go beyond quality and get into reengineering in order to achieve dramatic improvements through radical change in management organization. In other words, total quality programs tend to achieve incremental improvements, whereas reengineering efforts achieve dramatic improvements.

This is not to say that reengineering and TQM programs are incompatible concepts. Indeed, they are quite complementary. Figure 4.16 portrays the similarities between total quality management and reengineering. Both have a strong customer focus and require strong, visible, consistent leadership from the top. They both also use problem-solving methods, goals, and measures.

The truly significant difference between TQM and reengineering is the degree of change that can be achieved from the two approaches. This notion is portrayed in Figure 4.17. Note in the figure that TQM offers a sustained, continued improvement in terms of impact on quality products or service. A business reengineering effort results in a dramatic increase. What an organization should be doing is have ongoing quality improvement programs, but be prepared to do something dramatically different when the opportunity arises or when pressured to do so by competition.

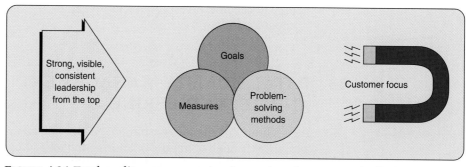

FIGURE 4.16 Total quality management and reengineering—some similarities.

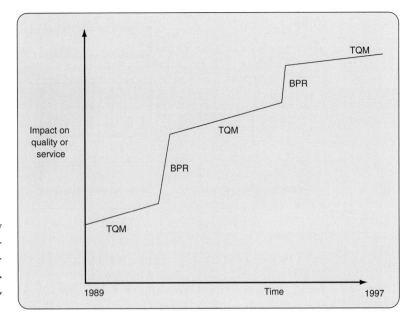

FIGURE 4.17 Total quality management and reengineering—synergy. (Copyright © 1992 by James C. Wetherbe and CSC Index, Inc. All rights reserved.)

NOTHING HAPPENS UNTIL YOU MEASURE IT

Whether involved in TQM or business reengineering, a key issue is "nothing happens until you measure it." Keeping score is necessary in order to achieve improvements in organizational performance. Keeping score also simply makes things more interesting and challenging. Consider, for example, that you are at a football or basketball game. It is very important to know what the score is. Imagine if there were no scoreboards at sports events. A great deal of the entertainment value would be lost. Let's consider a second example. If you have ever exercised on a treadmill, exercise bike, rowing machine, or stair climber that had a feedback mechanism, you may have noticed something very interesting. First, when you are exercising against some type of performance monitor (e.g., rowing against another boat on a computer graphic), you generally put in more effort and the exercise is more interesting. Have you also noticed that when you participate in sports such as ping pong, tennis, and basketball, people typically warm up for a while before someone says the magic words "let's keep score"? At that point, effort and intensity increase, as does performance. A key concept for improving performance is, in fact, "keeping score." Not keeping score is like hitting golf balls into the dark. Imagine going out and hitting 50 golf balls in a totally dark driving range. It would not be very interesting or motivating, would it? Nor would it be enough for someone to say, "Just number the golf balls from 1 to 50, hit them tonight, and we'll check it out tomorrow and let you know how you did." The important point here is that feedback needs to be timely enough to allow for corrective adjustments to be made in order for performance to improve.

Of course, in order to have a scoreboard, feedback is required. Figure 4.18 provides a basic model for feedback. Note that we look at organizational processes as having inputs and outputs, such as filling an order or manufacturing a product. Notice that the process must have a sensor to sense something and compare it to some standard, in order to allow the process to change its behavior. A simple example of feedback would be a thermostat, which senses the temperature in the room, compares it to the thermostat setting, and activates the air-conditioning accordingly. This feedback loop could also provide individual workers or a work team with some type of measurement on how well they are performing in comparison to some manufacturing standard. This basic feedback model should be driven by an overall vision of a goal as it relates to the organizational process. A

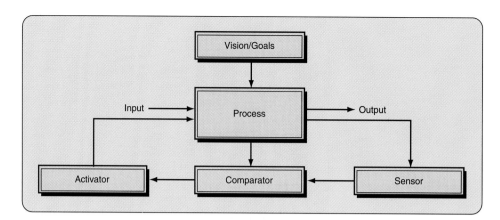

FIGURE 4.18 Feedback model.

key that we learn from reengineering and TQM is that feedback should not just be about one individual box—what we called "stovepiping" earlier in the chapter. Instead, processes need cross-functional feedback to determine how their behavior is affecting other organizational processes. This concept is portrayed in Figure 4.19. Note that in this illustration, feedback moves backward and forward between organizational processes.

An example can illustrate how this concept works. Suppose we have a company that manufactures weightlifting equipment. Box A in Figure 4.19 would represent the manufacturing process, box B the warehouse, box C the retailer, and box D the customer. The customer has purchased a piece of weightlifting equipment and is assembling it in her home. During assembly, she notices that two bearings are missing for the weight stacks. There are supposed to be eight bearings, and there are only six. The instructions include the name of the manufacturer, so the customer calls the manufacturer directly to explain the predicament. The manufacturer tells the customer, "Maybe it won't make that much difference. Why don't you just try assembling it with six bearings?" The customer complains, saying she paid for eight bearings, the specifications say eight, and she doesn't want to take it apart again if it doesn't work well without eight bearings. The manufacturer finally tells the customer to go back to the retailer and ask for two bearings out of another unit. The customer does this, but when she does, she notices that there are only four bearings in the newly opened unit. The customer asks about this, and the retailer explains that all units come with only six. Another customer has already been back to pick up two more bearings for another unit, so this unit is left with only four.

Now, what needs to happen here? Who needs feedback? Who is "hitting golf balls in the dark"? The people who put bearings in the box, for some reason, are putting in six instead of eight. Perhaps they misunderstood their instructions, forgot, or are confused. Whatever the case may be, until these people get feedback

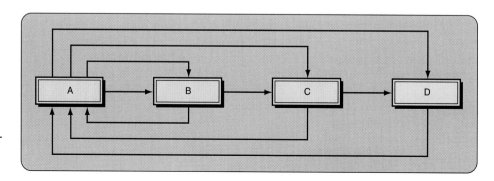

FIGURE 4.19 Feedback and measurement involving multiple or cross-functional processes.

that six bearings is incorrect, they will continue to put six bearings in each box. Note that it would be much more cost effective to have the feedback get to the bearing packers and have the problem corrected at its source than to continually be raiding boxes at the retail level. Eventually the retailer would have to come back to the manufacturer to correct the problem. This is the source of the classic argument in the TQM literature that "quality is free." The notion is that it is much less expensive to do something "right the first time" than to have to correct it later and also change several organizational processes.

Historically, in organizations without TQM, people had a tendency to point fingers at others. For example, the retailer would say it is not his fault, he didn't pack the box, and thus no corrective action would be taken. A key concept for TQM is the way you actually score organizational processes. For example, in the case of the exercise equipment problem, scoring would work as follows (see Figure 4.19). Box A, the manufacturer, would receive three defect points. Why? Because it had done something that adversely affected the warehouse, the retailer, and the customer (boxes B, C, and D). The warehouse, box B, would receive two defect points. Why? Because a mistake got through and adversely affected a retailer and a customer. How many defect points would box C receive? The answer is one, because it was involved in something that adversely affected a customer. Now suppose that each organization is rewarded by how few defect points it has. Then, there will be an incentive for the retailer, the warehouse, and the manufacturer to work together to resolve the problem so they all can avoid defect points. Also note that the primary cause of the problem, manufacturing, receives the heaviest penalty in terms of defect points. This type of scoring is a key concept of TQM and has encouraged organizational participants to behave much more like a team—as in our networked, self-directed team example—so that organizational performance is improved. Traditionally, stovepipe behavior is discouraged.

Notice that this time, team members will be from three different organizations. TQM teams, of course, are frequently in the same organization, but in different departments. In either case, they need to receive feedback and communicate. This is where IT acts as an enabler by facilitating timely, effective, and efficient communication, as will be shown in Chapter 14.

An example of how scoreboards have helped major U.S. industries improve their performance and quality is the Federal Aviation Administration (FAA) keeping score on airline arrival performances. During the mid 1980s, arrival performance had become terrible for U.S. airlines. The FAA, in essence, started keeping track of arrival performance for all airlines, ranked airlines based on their performance, and published the rankings once a month. These lists are very popular news items for newspapers such as *USA Today*. Once airlines saw how they ranked with other airlines, they were all motivated and have achieved much better arrival performance since the late 1980s.

Another classic example is J. D. Powers and Associates, a consumer advocate company that collects information on quality of automobiles. It keeps statistics on such things as how often you have to take a car back for repairs, how serious the repair was, how the repair was handled, what types of service you received, and so on. It then began ranking automobiles in terms of quality. The net effect? Quality in all auto manufacturers improved because anyone who did not fare well by the J. D. Powers scoreboard became much less attractive to consumers. A positive result is that automobile manufacturers and dealers have started working much more closely together to solve problems with cars. Before the quality programs, there was a tendency for manufacturers to let cars leave the plant with problems, assuming that "they'll fix it at the dealership." Dealers would often let a customer take a car, figuring that if he did not like it, he could bring it back. But once J. D. Powers started keeping meaningful scoreboards and statistics on quality, this type of behavior did not allow manufacturers or dealers to remain competitive. They would lose customers.

As stated earlier, total quality programs tend to result in incremental improvements. As an example, suppose a door handle is occasionally coming off cars when used repeatedly by customers. It turns out that the door handle can be put on in two different ways. One way, it stays on. The other way is incorrect, and eventually the handle comes loose. By providing this feedback to engineering, the door handle can be redesigned so that it can go in only one way—the correct way. This is an example of nice, helpful, straightforward incremental improvement—nothing radical, nothing dramatic, just an ongoing continuous effort to "make sure the bearings are in the box," to make sure that over time, the products gets better and better.

RELEVANCE OF INFORMATION SYSTEMS IN TQM

Information systems play four key roles in total quality management (see Box 4.5). These roles are to provide feedback, to provide better quality processes through use of information technology, to ensure that quality information systems are built, and to facilitate communication among the TQM team members. These roles are discussed in the following.

A Closer Look BOX 4.5

TOTAL QUALITY MANAGEMENT AND IT

There are several definitions of TQM. A common definition is that TQM is a focused management philosophy for providing the leadership, training, and motivation to continuously improve an organization's management and product-oriented processes in order to satisfy internal and external customers. The objectives of implementing TQM are defect-free performance, timeliness to schedule, cycle-time reduction, and lower cost. What distinguishes TQM from previous quality programs is its focus on the *process* rather than the product, on *prevention* rather than inspection, on *involvement* of employees at all levels of the company, and on long-term *commitment* to continuous improvement and customer satisfaction.

The TQM system embraces new ideas and concepts in three areas: (1) people working within teams and partnerships, (2) disciplined systems and process, and (3) a supportive cultural environment. The human relationships concepts include employee empowerment, suppliers as partners, the ability to work as a team, and a coaching, nonauthoritative leadership style. Training in people skills is as important as training in job performance skills.

Top management has the responsibility to develop, support, and communicate the vision of TQM; to empower the employees in the performance of their assignments using a set of disciplined processes; and to support the employees with the necessary tools and training to do their jobs. TQM is a total organizational approach directed at continuous improvement of both customer satisfaction and team productivity. Top management must establish a new culture that is supportive of the continual change that is a part of TQM.

TQM consists of following a seven-step process, which has striking similarities to the generic strategic planning process and the general design process used in BPR.

1. Establish the management and cultural environment.
2. Define the mission of each component.
3. Set performance improvement goals.
4. Establish improvement projects and action plans.
5. Implement projects using improvement methodologies.
6. Evaluate performance.
7. Review and repeat.

The process of continuous improvement relies on documentation and performance measurement. Performance deficiencies are uncovered and root causes determined by careful selection and timely tracking of the critical performance measures.

TQM is a disciplined methodology built on a number of tools and techniques that have been successfully used in the past. Included among these tools and techniques are benchmarking (comparing your performance to that of "world-class" competitors), cause and effect diagrams (also known as "fishbone" diagrams), statistical process control, nominal group technique, team building, Pareto diagrams (which are used to isolate the "critical few" causes), and workflow analysis. These tools and techniques have been acquired from diverse fields.

It is apparent that IT plays a vital role in many aspects of TQM (e.g., see Ayers [1993]). For example, advances in computer-aided design, manufacturing, and logistics (CAD/CAM/CAL) have made it possible to implement concurrent engineering, a process for reducing the product development cycle time by including manufacturing, suppliers, and product support early in the product development process. State-of-the-art 3-D, "solid" modeling utilizing color and shading, has greatly improved the transfer of ideas among the design team. The computer database allows all participants in the design process access to current information including design definition, bill of materials, building instructions, schedules, and operating instructions. The computer database is the modern equivalent of gathering around the design engineer's board.

A large part of quality is repeatability, being able to produce parts to close tolerance. Robotics, computer-controlled machines, and other IT applications have resulted in significant reductions in product variability and increased shop floor efficiency.

Implementing the TQM seven-step process is dependent on gathering and analyzing data about product quality and work performance. These data must be accurate, timely, and gathered at minimum overhead cost. IT makes it possible to efficiently collect the performance measures and turn them into tables and graphs which employees can see to continually make adjustments to the process and monitor the results of their actions. For further details, see Mathieson and Wharton (1993).

If you want things to improve, measurement is critical. Information systems can play a key role in the measurement process by providing feedback systems. These can be straightforward systems such as providing feedback on production defects, output by department, output per employee, and so on. They can also be used to provide compiled statistics to an organization. Systems such as the J. D. Powers's and the FAA's systems discussed earlier are able to tabulate their reports through information systems. More significantly, organizations should be providing their own feedback loops through information technology to avoid "hitting golf balls in the dark." Procter & Gamble, GE, and Pillsbury are examples of organizations that have made strong use of information technology to provide them with good feedback loops. All three companies put toll-free 800 numbers on their products so that customers can call in with complaints or problems they are having. In addition to resolving problems for customers, all three organizations collect, categorize, summarize, analyze, and report information generated from complaints and problems as a feedback process throughout all functions of their companies in order to improve their products. Notice how the telephone call for the "missing bearings" should have been feedback to the "bearing packer." A key TQM element is the use of periodic meetings of people from one or several departments, sometimes referred to as "quality circles," where employees brainstorm about problems they are having within their departments or problems that are occurring cross-functionally. Meetings, typically held on a weekly basis, are a key part of a continuous improvement program. Quality circles helped the Japanese change the quality of their products from extremely poor in the 1960s to world class in the 1970s.

The second role information systems can play in a total quality program is to improve quality through information systems themselves. The examples of the insurance company and bank discussed earlier in the chapter illustrate how customer service can be improved through better systems. Another good example is Digital Equipment Corporation (DEC). DEC has always done a lot of customized configuration of computer systems for customers. The difficulty was that achieving these configurations correctly was complex. Often customers would receive their equipment, but there would be an incorrect cable or interface board. By developing an expert system to configure every order, DEC was able to virtually eliminate these errors and save the company millions of dollars per year.

Information systems must also deal with a third key issue in the quality area—to make sure that the systems themselves are developed with quality software. Techniques of providing feedback and using new software to allow people to develop better software all play a role in improving software development itself. As an example, Motorola, the first winner of the prestigious, U.S. national Malcolm Baldridge Quality award, decided that they wanted to achieve dramatic improvements in software development. They set as their scoreboard, or benchmark, development of a million lines of code in 90 days, defect free. They realized they would not be able to do this with humans writing code and using the traditional COBOL methods they had been using for years. This resulted in their moving into code generators and object-oriented programming to achieve the same high quality levels in software that they had achieved in their manufacturing processes. Chapter 13 goes into the quality issues in developing software and discusses some of the techniques such as design overviews, structured walkthroughs, and code inspections which are used to improve quality in software.

The final role that information systems can play is to enhance communication among TQM team members, especially if they are in different locations. As will be demonstrated in Chapter 14, it is possible to improve communication by using groupware software such as desktop teleconferencing, screen sharing of documents, and workflow software for tracking what is going on with respect to tasks, people, products, or processes.

AND WHAT IF TQM WON'T GET YOU THERE?

TQM is an accepted management practice that has helped organizations internationally. But some organizations are finding that incremental improvement is not enough. For example, they find that someone else is producing a product twice as good for 25 percent of the cost. A dramatic improvement is thus required, which necessitates radical change. This, of course, takes us into a situation where reengineering is required. Even the Japanese realized in the mid '90s that incremental improvement may be insufficient, and they are resorting to BPR (see Box 4.6).

A Closer Look BOX 4.6 ◄*G*LOBAL PERSPECTIVE

REENGINEERING IN JAPAN

Japanese companies are seizing on reengineering—a Western management concept—but they add to it a distinctly Eastern approach. The Japanese enthusiastically embrace reengineering and adapt it to their unique social and cultural environment. This adaptation could make Japan a leader of the reengineering movement. Here are some aspects of the Japanese reengineering plans:

1. Instead of cutting jobs, the Japanese, who believe that corporations must sustain their long-term commitment to employees, are concentrating on creating new added-value opportunities for employees.

2. Because there are so many traditional obstacles and limitations in Japanese industry, it must take a "creative destruction" in order to forge a new path to prosperity. They plan to use *mugin soi* (limitless creativity).

3. The Japanese plan to fix their weakest points, which are weak white-collar and service sectors and inefficient distribution systems. Although the Japanese own most of the largest banks in the world, for example, they run them very inefficiently, using some nineteenth-century methods.

4. The Japanese will use their strengths in reengineering corporations, namely a long-term perspective; em-

ployees who are accustomed to teamwork, job rotation, process orientation, and ongoing training and education; experience with continuous incremental improvement programs (such as "quality circles"); and absence of old front-office automation.

5. They will focus on value creation rather than on cost reduction.

6. They will use technology leapfrogging in office automation.

7. They will revolutionize the distribution channels, which will be combined with Japan's traditional commitment to customer service and quality.

8. In contrast to a top-down approach used in U.S. reengineering, the Japanese top management leave the details to middle and low-level management, emphasizing a team-building approach.

9. The Japanese recognize that traditional improvement methods are not sufficient, so reengineering may be the only way to stay competitive.

10. The Japanese are looking for visionary CEOs to lead the reengineering movement.

SOURCE: Compiled from Petro, F., "Reengineering II: Made in Japan," and Takeuchi, H., Interview, *Insights Quarterly*, Spring 1994.

Table 4.2 Comparing TQM and Reengineering

	TQM	Reengineering
Case for action	Assumed to be necessary	Compelling
Goals	Small-scale improvements in many places with cumulative effects	Outrageous
Scope and focus	Attention to tasks, steps, and processes across the board	Select but broad business processes
Degree of change	Incremental and continual	Order of magnitude and periodic
Senior management involvement	Important up front	Intensive throughout
Role of information technology	Incidental	Cornerstone

SOURCE: Gulden and Ewers, 1991, p. 11.

A comparison between TQM and reengineering is provided in Table 4.2. The details of the comparison can be found in Gulden and Ewers (1991).

FROM TQM TO TOTAL PRODUCT AND SERVICE IMPROVEMENT

Incremental improvement of quality is necessary, but not sufficient. Quality is clearly necessary, but customers want the products and services that they like best, and they want them fast. Furthermore, they do not want to pay more than they would pay for similar products. Therefore, it is necessary to complement TQM with other incremental improvement programs. And indeed, companies are continuously striving to reduce cost, speed up delivery times, assure that products and services are customized, and develop new and improved products and services. While TQM receives lots of publicity, organizations have been engaged in cost and productivity improvements and other programs for decades. Some of these programs are formal; others informal. What is new is the role of IT in supporting such programs. As will be demonstrated in Chapter 17, IT plays a major role in all types of productivity improvement programs and in all activities of the value chain processes.

As stated earlier, continuous improvement programs may not be sufficient, and this is where BPR is needed. However, as portrayed in Figure 4.17, once a BPR is completed, an organization should return to TQM and other incremental improvement programs. This type of effort is required to fully enjoy the benefits of business reengineering, which is revisited next.

▶ 4.14   THE 3 Rs OF REENGINEERING

*R*EENGINEERING

...redesign, retool & reorchestrate

We have defined reengineering as achieving dramatic performance improvements through radical change in organizational processes. This really means the rearchitecting of business and management processes. It involves the redrawing of organizational boundaries, the reconsideration of jobs, tasks, and skills. Reengineering means redefining the ambitions of the organization. It literally means "rethinking everything." It is also important to understand what reengineering is not. Reengineering is not across-the-board cuts in employees or blind head count reduction; and, as we've discussed many times in this chapter, it is not "automating history." The key steps of reengineering are referred to as the **3 Rs of Reengineering**, which includes *redesign*, *retool*, and *reorchestrate*. Each of these steps is briefly discussed in the following section.

REDESIGN

The redesign of an organization must, first of all, focus on perspective. Reengineering requires a cross-functional scope. Reengineering is not about improving a department or a function; it is always about improving cross-functional activities. The perspective must be ambitious. Typically, an organization that tries to cut costs by 5 to 10 percent often compromises services. However, organizations that try to cut costs by 50 percent often end up improving service. Why? Because you can save 5 to 10 percent by compromising customer service. But a 50 percent cut will require a new process. For example, consider the travel company in Box 4.2 as an example of how an organization can dramatically cut cost and at the same time improve customer service.

Another key perspective of redesign involves breaking rules or breakthrough thinking as discussed earlier: *techniques lag behind technology.* Nowhere is the need to break rules more true than the rules that organizations impose upon themselves. As a simple example, Federal Express, like many organizations, had rules that any expenditures must be approved by a supervisor. This interfered with customer service and situations where the customer had a small claim. Fred Smith, the founder of Federal Express, said that they should be able to trust any employee to make decisions on customer complaints up to $100. Consequently, whenever a claim is made for less than that amount, any employee is authorized to handle it on the spot and send the check to the customer.

A key component of reengineering is that it must focus on an outcome that the organization needs to achieve. The outcome should, of course, be an ambitious outcome. Examples of ambitious outcomes are 24-hour delivery to any customer anywhere in the world, approval of mortgage loans within 60 minutes of application, or ability to have on-line access to a patient's medical records no matter where they are in any major city in the world. These types of visionary goals require rethinking the way most organizations do business, they will need very sophisticated supporting information systems.

Redesign involves making basic changes to current organizational processes. These moves can be conveniently referred to as ''ing'' words, since they all end in ''ing.'' These moves are listed and illustrated as follows:

▼ *Challenging.* This involves holding nothing sacred in the current organizational process. Everything the organization currently does in any process should be highly scrutinized to see if it is still necessary. As an example, one manufacturer found that by challenging their warehousing function, it could be eliminated through the use of just-in-time inventory with computerized on-line entry of all orders and tracking distribution at the retail level. No one had challenged the concept of the warehouse for years because it just seemed logical that you needed a place to store things. But in reality, just-in-time inventory eliminated the need for the warehouse completely, cutting overall operating costs by 50 percent.

▼ *Eliminating.* After challenging organizational processes, eliminate steps that are not necessary—for example, eliminating the warehouse as discussed above or eliminating the need for supervisors' approval on claims of less than $100 as illustrated in the Federal Express example. Using an on-line ordering, approval, and payment system may eliminate half the steps in an order processing system.

▼ *Flattening.* As discussed earlier in this chapter, the need exists to eliminate hierarchical levels of management so that an organization can be more responsive.

▼ *Simplifying.* A key issue here is simplifying the relationship of the customer, or supplier, to the organization. In the examples of the insurance company and the bank discussed earlier in this chapter, it is much simpler for the customer to have a single point of contact in dealing with either institution. Many business processes can be simplified by making them shorter, by providing clear instruction (e.g., by using computerized help desk), or by eliminating unnecessary steps.

▼ *Standardizing.* The key issue here is trying to achieve uniformity in a way that improves customer service. For example, standardizing a customer with multiple accounts to one account number with suffixes, allows great performance improvement in terms of customer service and operating cost.

▼ *Paralleling.* There are two ways we have made computers faster. One is to reduce the distance the electronic impulse has to travel; the other is by doing more than one thing at one time. Typically in organizations, market research, product design and development, production, distribution, and selling are separate, sequential steps. Parallel processing involves, for example, doing market research every time a product is sold. This is a technique used by visionary retailers such as Wal-Mart and JCPenney. Every time an inventory item is sold, that information is fed back to the distributor, manufacturer, and designer so they know what items are popular with customers on a day-to-day basis, thus improving feedback. They no longer wait until the end of the year or the end of the month to find out what items are popular. Many companies reduce their design time, as will be shown in Chapter 17, both by using automation and executing several tasks in parallel.

▼ *Empowering.* The concept of empowering was illustrated earlier in the Federal Express example. Key ways to achieve reengineering are to accept that there are "intelligent nodes" in the network and to trust employees to do the right thing. The role of IT in empowerment is described in Chapter 17.

▼ *Informating.* Informating simply means sharing information cross-functionally so that the left hand knows what the right hand is doing. By sharing information interorganizationally (i.e., with their suppliers) on men's suits sales, for example, JCPenney has been able to improve profit margins by 80 percent and greatly improve stocking items that customers prefer. Sam Walton, the founder of Wal-Mart, said the great secret behind Wal-Mart's success was that he substituted *information* for *inventory*. IT plays an extremely important role in information sharing. Tools such as Lotus Notes provide efficient and effective enterprise-wide information sharing capabilities.

▼ *Monitoring.* Monitoring means continually tracking and providing feedback on key organizational performance issues. This can also be very helpful interorganizationally; for example, a supplier might monitor a customer's inventory and automatically replenish it as necessary. This has been done between Procter & Gamble and Wal-Mart, and between Ford Motor Company and their key suppliers. Again, IT plays a major role in reporting transactions in real time and lets business partners access databases from remote locations.

▼ *Partnering.* Forming strategic alliances is another key strategy. This has been accomplished, for example, where airlines have partnered with credit card companies to offer frequent flyer programs as an incentive to use both the credit card and the airline. There are several types of partnerships which can be supported by different information technologies.

▼ *Outsourcing.* This involves letting another organization perform services you used to perform but that you no longer consider to be mainstream for your organization. For example, some organizations such as Kodak have outsourced their operation and management of computing facilities to IBM and DEC. Many companies have outsourced their warehousing and even order entry systems to Federal Express and located their warehouses in Memphis, which is the major hub for Federal Express. In so doing, someone who wants shoes from Nike can place an order before 6:00 P.M. and have them by 10:00 A.M., the next day. The shoes go directly from Memphis to the customer. JCPenney, for example, processes credit cards for thousands of retailers. Without high-speed transaction processing capabilities, efficient processing of such a large number of retailers and bills would have been impossible.

▼ *Prescheduling.* The key issue in the area of "left hand not knowing what the right is doing" is letting someone know in advance when you might need something. For example, the typical textbook is not available for several months after the writing is complete. The biggest problem is that authors typically are not reliable in their estimates of when they are going to be finished writing. So, everyone waits until the manuscript is ready and then the production process is scheduled. Another example is Levi Strauss Co. which allows its suppliers to enter its database so a supplier can see Levi's sales and preschedule the delivery of the needed raw materials.

Each of the "ing" words discussed previously can be used as ways to brainstorm about redesign moves to achieve reengineering. The key things to keep in perspective are the cross-functional scope, being ambitious, being willing to break rules, and focusing on outcomes. For an example of redesign, see Box 4.7. Once redesign issues have been investigated, reengineering can move to the next step: retooling.

IT At Work BOX 4.7

BOISE CASCADE IMPROVES EFFICIENCY AND EFFECTIVENESS WHILE PLEASING CUSTOMERS

The Boise Cascade Timber and Wood (BCTW) Products Division in Boise, Idaho, had a problem, a big problem! Its customers were not satisfied with the length of time it took to access data necessary for internal and external operations. A new process was needed to eliminate this time disparity.

BCTW wanted to improve the efficiency (performing tasks with the least amount of effort) and effectiveness (reducing the number of problems and improving the results for customers) of the notification and scheduling of freight-on-board mill loads and prepaid truck-ready shipments from the mill. Information from the customers was essential. Customer requests for information on order status were not easy to fulfill because forecasting records were cumbersome and not always readily available.

A "tiger team" was organized to evaluate customer and internal needs. The team eliminated processes that were redundant or unnecessary and took full advantage of the computer network, which was vastly underutilized. The computer system was updated to handle the new information capacity and storage requirements, and the system was put to the test.

Using cross-functional teams and IT, the company was able to eliminate steps and simplify activities in the customer ordering process, reducing it from 52 steps to 7 (see figure at top of page 137.).

The most notable indicator of improvement was the average pickup time after an order was ready, which was reduced from 3.25 days to 1.39 days. Tasks once handled manually were now processed by the information system electronically. The new organization and information flow greatly improved production planning and inventory management. Better access to information has reduced the time needed to check order status, eliminated much duplication or order traces, and minimized the related interruptions to the mills. At one location, overtime costs were reduced by 70 percent. Better information systems and improved practices in all critical functional areas have resulted in substantial savings for Boise Cascade.

Once again, IT to the rescue! BCTW had an information-handling problem. Full utilization of a computer-aided information system improved customer satisfaction and efficiency and effectiveness and has made BCTW Products Division more competitive from both cost and customer satisfaction points of view. BCTW realized that customers must be an important business concern, because without them there is no business.

Critical Thinking Issues: From what you learned in this chapter can you guess the role of the cross-functional teams? How could IT have helped the functional teams? ▲

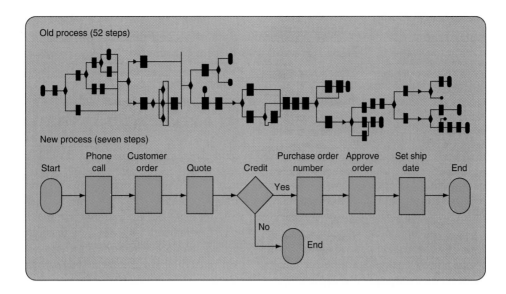

RETOOLING IT

Retooling focuses on making sure the IT systems development process will be responsive to the reengineering effort. Many organizations, such as the insurance company illustrated at the beginning of this chapter, found that once they realized they had a problem and wanted to do something about it, their information systems function could not be responsive. They were being "held hostage" by their information systems department. For example, a government agency in Singapore decided to defer a badly needed BPR project when they discovered that it would cost over $15 million to rewrite all their application programs.

To retool for reengineering, the key issue is getting a good understanding of the current installed base of information systems applications and databases (see Rose, 1995). It is also important to understand the existing infrastructure in terms of computing equipment networks, and the like, and their relationships to the current available software, procedures, and data. The key is an assessment of what the ideal IT architecture would be for the organization in terms of hardware and software, as well as an appropriate information architecture. The concept of information architecture is expanded in Chapters 10 and 11.

During this stage, it is very important to benchmark the technology being used in the organization vs. what the best competitors are using. It is also imperative to find out what the latest technologies are and do some enabled visioning to determine in what direction the organization needs to go. For example, many organizations are moving from mainframe computers to client/server architectures as they reengineer. These issues will be expanded upon further in Chapters 10–13, which focus on the systems development process.

The organization must decide on what upgrading or reengineering needs to be done on their information systems tools and applications so they can properly support the proposed reengineering projects. An example of a massive IT retooling in a public agency is provided in Box 4.8. In this case, the technology enabled the company to reengineer all its major business processes.

IT At Work BOX 4.8

THE NATIONAL HOUSING BOARD IN SINGAPORE RETOOLS ITS IT

More than 87 percent of the population in Singapore live in housing units provided by the government. A government agency called the Housing Development Board (HDB) is managing over a million properties. HDB must be responsive to its customers, business partners, and changing government policies. The organization faces shortage of manpower. Thus, it has been facing many of the business pressures described in Chapter 1.

Due to its rapid growth rate, HDB was unable to meet all its demands without reengineering its business processes. To succeed in its reengineering efforts, HDB decided to retool its information services department. In a period of about four years, the IT area was retooled to become one of the most sophisticated IT-based organizations in the world. Furthermore, HDB is creating in a process of continuously improving its IT tools, which will enable HDB to undergo a transformation that will make it perhaps the best housing authority in the world in a few years. The technology retooling completed by 1995 includes:

▼ A sophisticated graphical-based property database.

▼ A large resident database.

▼ 200 CAD workstations that increased productivity of office drawing.

▼ More than 2,600 users of Lotus Notes.

▼ An integrated Land Information System.

▼ A voice response system that serves about a million customers (residents) 24 hours a day.

▼ Electronic hand-held terminals that enable HDB's parking wardens to print parking violation notices on site.

▼ An integrated payment collection system that includes conveniently located payment kiosks for electronic transfer of funds by residents.

▼ Sophisticated local area and wide area networks connecting 3,400 workstations in hundreds of HDB and business partner cities throughout Singapore. These networks are ISDN-based (see Chapter 9) and are part of Singapore's Information Highway System.

▼ An elevator telemonitoring system that handles 1,400 calls per day. If rescue is needed, it is provided in less than 30 minutes.

▼ A client/server technology that is replacing many of the mainframe applications.

▼ EDI technology to reengineer business processes with partners.

▼ Imaging and workflow applications.

In the immediate future, the IT retooling will include:

▼ Transacting with residents at their homes (using interactive TV).

▼ Smart customer information cards that store all pertinent customer information on one card. By running the card through an input device, all the necessary information appears on a screen. No more keying in information or filling out forms.

Other measures in the IT retooling include a new management team, staff development, a quality management system, and the creation of a users' steering committee.

The IT retooling enabled HDB to improve its operations and to reengineer its business processes. For example, customer service improved by a quantum leap (waiting time was reduced from several hours to less than 5 minutes), and customers enjoy one-stop service. The automated voice response system serves 30,000 callers per day (the same as 200 telephone operators). The retooling paid for itself very quickly. Every dollar spent returned $2.53 in less than four years.

Critical Thinking Issues: Why does HDB need all this technology? How can an IT retooling help BPR? ▲

SOURCE: Condensed from *Vision 2000, HDB's Strategic IT Plan.* HDB Corporate Internal Report Singapore, 1994.

REORCHESTRATE

Reorchestration concerns bringing about the organizational change necessary to achieve reengineering. It is important to point out that there are really two levels of reengineering. There can be an overall organizational transformation from traditional hierarchical to network-type organizations, which has a very broad, total impact on organizations. There can also be more isolated, specific reengineering efforts pertaining to one (or a few) cross-functional organizational process. In this chapter, we have been focusing more on *organizational transformations*. However, in many organizations, it is much more palatable to deal with a single organizational process or to achieve broader organizational transformation into a network-type organization by going through a series of reengineering efforts each at the single organizational process level.

Whether it be at the organization or process levels, a reengineering effort requires radical change to achieve success. In any case, the principles of reorchestration are applicable. Key principles to achieve reorchestration are as follows:

▼ Visible and passionate leadership is necessary to achieve organizational commitment.

▼ A reengineering effort must be consistent with the underlying beliefs and values of the organization to ensure broad organizational acceptance. For example, if loyalty to the company and respect for the individual are values of an organization, these must be considered when reengineering.

▼ Incentives must be developed for the reengineering change. For example, in the case of the insurance company, it would be important that insurance agents be rewarded when a customer moves from one city to another and remains with the insurance company.

▼ Business process change must be balanced with cultural change. If an organization is attempting to change its culture to one that is more customer driven, that cultural change must occur at the same time as the systems supporting customer service are implemented.

▼ Accountabilities must be changed to support the new process. For example, a bank that is going to have single contacts for customers must change accountabilities to support this new working arrangement.

▼ The campaign must be treated like a religious crusade. In this sense, committing to something like having same-day shipment to any customer in the world must become a passion within the organization.

▼ During reengineering, senior management must communicate, communicate, and communicate. Experience shows that nobody has ever overestimated the amount of communicating and training needed for reengineering success.

▼ Organizational participants must be able to be comfortable with ambiguity. A key issue here is to let people know that new approaches will be tried. If they work, they will be adopted; if they don't, they will be changed. Otherwise, any change tends to be resisted because individuals are fearful that if it doesn't work, they will be stuck with a bad situation.

▼ Obstacles that stand in the way of change must be removed. For example, a rule such as only a supervisor can approve expenditures over a certain amount may have to change in order to empower employees.

▼ Success must be celebrated. Reengineering efforts will often involve false starts and failures. It is crucial that when success occurs, it is celebrated and rewarded.

An example of how reengineering efforts were reorchestrated at an insurance company is illustrated in Box 4.9.

IT At Work BOX 4.9   R*EENGINEERING*

HOW BPR WAS ORCHESTRATED AT MUTUAL BENEFIT LIFE

Mutual Benefit Life (MBL) is a mid-sized U.S. insurance company (4,700 employees) located both in Kansas City and Newark. Starting in 1988, one of the most successful publicized BPR in the USA was orchestrated. Customers' satisfaction and employee productivity are critical success factors to any service company, and as discussed earlier, a traditional hierarchical organizational structure was ineffective and inefficient in the highly competitive insurance industry. Here are some of the changes that were introduced in MBL.

▼ The company was transformed to a networked organization, composed of a set of small business units.

▼ The use of PCs was championed by the CEO to increase creativity and productivity.

▼ A major cultural change occurred in the organization where employees are encouraged to further their education, participate in volunteer work, and attend recitals during lunchtime. Art and music came to play a major role in corporate life.

▼ A creative atmosphere was institutionalized.

▼ Case managers (a concept described earlier in the chapter) who worked with powerful workstations became a center of the BPR, achieving in hours what used to take days, or even weeks, to accomplish.

▼ The case managers were empowered to make important decisions. They were authorized to access databases and were entrusted with personal computers that were connected to local area networks.

▼ The case managers' responsibilities were expanded. Previously, they did all the office work to back up policy underwriters. Now, they were trained to write certain insurance policies as well.

▼ The case managers were organized in teams with business specialists. A team was capable of handling the entire process of writing and managing insurance policies.

▼ The human resources department was reengineered to match the new culture and structure. The department now oversees a range of educational, cultural, and health-related programs.

▼ A new reward system was installed. The reward is directly related to performance as well as to the knowledge base of the employees.

▼ A less obtrusive control system was installed.

The results were astonishing. MBL, which had been struggling through a series of crises during the '80s turned the corner. Furthermore, everyone was enthusiastic about the change.

Critical Thinking Issues: Do you agree that a BPR was done at MBL? Why? Why was the traditional structure ineffective in this case, and what contribution did IT make? Are these changes likely to sustain MBL's turnaround? ▲

SOURCE: Compiled from a Harvard Business School Case 9-492-015 by J. P. Berkley, (1992).

▶ 4.15   ARE YOU REALLY REENGINEERING?

One of the biggest problems with reengineering is that people start off with ambitious plans, but these can quickly be compromised as people try to come up with change that they are more comfortable with. A reduction of the scope of the goals will ultimately compromise the reengineering effort. Therefore, it is crucial during the reengineering effort to continually assess what is really happening by asking the following questions:

▼ Is the reengineering effort truly transformational?

▼ Will the reengineering effort improve the relationship with the customer?

▼ Are the right players involved to bring about a change?

▼ Has the reengineering effort cut across the organization?

▼ Is information technology playing an integral role in the reengineering solution?

▼ Does it hurt?

The last point is, unfortunately, necessary. Reengineering efforts involve dramatic changes in people's jobs and working relationships. Often jobs are eliminated. Changes of this nature can be very painful. It is one of the reasons that organizations often put off reengineering until it becomes radical and painful. As we have seen, organizations in the late 1980s and 1990s had to lay off thousands of people in order to remain competitive. This clearly indicates that remaining competitive often does involve pain. However, the pain of reengineering is much less than the pain of being completely eliminated as a viable business.

A statement by Pablo Picasso puts into perspective the meaning of reengineering organizations to become information based networks: *"Every act of creation is first of all an act of destruction."*

▶ 4.16   LIKE AN ORCHESTRA: A LAST NOTE ON REENGINEERING

The new paradigm of the reengineered organization is like a symphony orchestra. An orchestra is a flat organization with a conductor directing a span of control that can often be more than a hundred people. Note that in an orchestra, everyone has been "informated" in that they all have the necessary music to perform their roles in the organization.

If the orchestra operated like a hierarchy, there would be a conductor. There would be directors of flutes, oboes, cellos, and so on, then supervisors, then unit supervisors, and so on. Every time the conductor wanted a particular note played, he would have to instruct each manager to instruct their supervisors, and so on down the line. On a note-by-note basis, this would create a rather prolonged and worthless performance.

By allowing everyone in the orchestra organization to prepare in individual groups, which are much like self-directed teams, the conductor can, with one sweep of the hand, have all the musicians do what they are supposed to do on cue.

A fascinating illustration of the orchestra paradigm is provided by an episode involving the Minnesota Orchestra. Several years ago, the orchestra was between conductors and operating with an interim conductor. The well-known author Robert Fulghum, who had written the books *All I Really Need to Know I Learned in Kindergarten*, and *Uh-Oh!*, had mentioned previously in an interview that his lifetime dream had been to conduct a symphony orchestra. The Minnesota Orchestra picked up on this and thought it would make an enjoyable and interesting attraction to have Fulghum conduct the orchestra. He readily accepted the invitation.

Fulghum came to Minneapolis to work with the interim conductor to prepare for conducting the orchestra. It quickly became clear that he had no music background whatsoever, other than waving his arms around in his living room while listening to symphony music. Astonished, the interim conductor of the Minnesota Orchestra asked, "What made you think you could conduct a symphony orchestra?"

Fulghum replied, "I never said I thought I could. I just said I always wanted to." They both realized that they were in deep trouble.

Fulghum was given a crash course in conducting. In a typical symphony movement, the conductor plays a critical role about 30 to 40 times, when he must change tempo, bring in the correct instruments, and so on. If these tasks are not done correctly, the performance will suffer.

As it turned out, Robert Fulghum was able to conduct the symphony orchestra with great grace, style, and dignity, and the orchestra successfully executed his piece. After the performance, the interim conductor was mystified. He told Fulghum that he had done an excellent job, but one thing really baffled him. He couldn't understand how he was able to conduct the orchestra while paying so little attention to the score or music. The interim conductor commented that when he conducts the orchestra, he needs the score to know when to bring in the different instruments. Fulghum smiled and said, "Well, that's very interesting. I didn't need the score to know when they needed to come in. They signaled me. For example, when the violins are ready to come in, they all lift their instruments in unison. So did the flutes and everybody else. All I did was wave my hand at them when they brought their instruments up and they came in when they were supposed to." This rather amusing illustration points out something that we have been talking about throughout this chapter on achieving the information-based network organization. If you pay attention to the nodes in the network, they can tell you what needs to be done. If you aren't observing or paying attention to them, you'll probably miss it.

▶ MANAGERIAL ISSUES

Ethical issues. Conducting a BPR may result in a need to layoff, retrain, or transfer employees. Should management notify the employees in advance regarding such possibilities? And what about those older employees who are difficult to retrain? Other ethical issues may involve sharing of personal information which may be part of the new organizational culture. Finally, individuals may have to share computer programs that they designed for personal use. Such programs may be the intellectual property of the individuals.

BPR implementation. While large numbers of companies report reengineering their processes, only a few conduct a true company-wide BPR. Most companies reengineer only a few processes or accelerate incremental improvement programs.

BPR tools. BPR utilizes tools and techniques that were in existence for generations. What is new is the framework that recognizes BPR as a major reorganization effort, undertaking with clear objectives.

Role of IT. Almost all major BPR examples use IT as a major enabler. However, it is important to remember that in most cases the technology plays a secondary role, and the primary role is organizational and managerial in nature.

Incremental improvement programs. Incremental improvement programs do not require fundamental rethinking or radical redesign, and they do not result in rapid and dramatic improvements, but they are useful for the welfare of many organizations.

TQM and BPR. Although TQM is not BPR, it is related to it. In a TQM environment it may be easier to launch a BPR. Information technology enhances both TQM and BPR. ■

KEY TERMS

Business function *106*

Business process *106*

Contingency management *119*

Cross-functional systems *106*

Flattened organization *120*

Hierarchical organization *104*

Integration *109*

Networks *115*

Organization *102*

Real-time business process *115*

Redundancy (of data) *109*

Reengineering *115*

Self-directed teams *118*

Total quality management (TQM) *126*

3 Rs of Reengineering *133*

CHAPTER HIGHLIGHTS *(L-x means learning objective number x)*

▼ Most organizations are built on the Industrial Revolution model of division of labor and specialization. (L-1, L-2)

▼ Many business processes are performed in more than one functional area.

▼ Initial computing technology was hierarchical in nature like a mainframe processor, but now technology is moving toward a networked, client/server configuration. (L-6)

▼ Hierarchical organizations have difficultly responding to cross-functional needs. (L-3, L-4)

▼ Hierarchical organizations tend to be bureaucratic and inflexible and need to be reengineered. (L-4)

▼ Techniques lag behind technology. Organizing is a technique, and many organizations lag behind information technology. (L-5)

▼ The trend is for organizations to be reengineered to behave like networks and operate in an on-line, real-time, seamless, empowered mode of operation. (L-6)

▼ Network organizations are flattened and make extensive use of self-directed teams. (L-6)

▼ Managers of networked, flattened organizations have broad spans of control. Instead of managing an average of six people, they have spans of control ranging from 30 to 150 people. (L-6)

▼ Self-directed teams can be permanent teams, or they can be quickly configured teams that solve specific problems and are then dissolved. (L-8)

▼ In the network paradigm, organizations tend to reward individuals in ways other than through promotion. (L-8, L-9)

▼ The goal of using information technology and the new network organizational paradigm is to allow customers to have straightforward, simple contact with organizations, even though the organizations internally may be quite complex and extensive; networking may be necessary to solve a problem for the customer. (L-6, L-10)

▼ Total quality programs are complementary to reengineering efforts. Both are focused on customers and require visionary leadership. They involve cross-functional efforts, and measurement plays a key role in assessing progress. The key difference between total quality and reengineering is that TQM typically involves incremental, continuous change whereas reengineering involves radical change. (L-7)

▼ Achieving reengineering involves the 3 Rs of reengineering, which are redesign, retool, and reorchestrate. (L-11)

▼ Reengineering is a painful but necessary process to ensure the long-term viability of organizations. (L-11)

QUESTIONS FOR REVIEW

1. How did organizations arrive at the hierarchical structure?

2. What are the limitations of the hierarchical structure in service organizations, such as banks, from a customer's perspective? from an organization perspective?

3. What is meant by the concept that techniques lag behind technology? Give examples.

4. Explain how a bank could end up with fragmented information systems so that one customer with several accounts may be perceived as several customers? What would a reengineered bank be like from a customer perspective?

5. If you receive a separate envelope and statement for every account that you have with a bank, what does that tell you about the bank's information systems and how the bank perceives you as a customer? What type of statement would you expect to receive from a reengineered bank?

6. What are the characteristics of a network? How would those characteristics be applied to an organization if it were trying to mirror networks?

7. Explain the role of the self-directed team in the context of a network organization.

8. Contrast the difference between a standing team and a pick-up team.

9. Why do employees accept lack of promotion as part of the reward system in the network organization?

10. What is the difference between TQM and reengineering? Are they complementary?

11. What are the 3 Rs of reengineering?

QUESTIONS FOR DISCUSSION

1. For the case that opened the chapter, discuss how the insurance company could have ended up with information systems that had the limitations described.

2. What are some quick intermediate steps that could have been taken to solve the problem that Nick Simmons was facing? Consider something that could be implemented in a week or two to provide some value-added services to customers.

3. The solution proposed in the chapter to solve the banking problem—for a customer to have a master account number with suffixes for individual accounts—is a fairly simple idea. Discuss why banks didn't do that originally but are doing it retroactively.

4. Discuss the transformation in management approaches from the classical hierarchical to the network, self-directed team. Discuss which approach would make you most productive in doing your career or schoolwork.

5. Try to recall situations where a pick-up team was put together to solve a particular problem, either at work or even in a social situation, where leadership was determined by situational capabilities as opposed to appointment.

6. Discuss with your instructor if he has aspirations to be a department chair or a dean and his reasons for that decision.

7. Discuss what it would be like if the registration process and class scheduling process were reengineered to an on-line, real-time, seamless basis with good connectivity and good empowerment in the university organization.

8. Review Box 4.4. What are the strengths and weaknesses of the new organizational design at GE Canada?

9. Review Box 4.5. Compare some of the features and characteristics of TQM and those of BPR.

EXERCISES

1. In the opening case of ''Almost Every Insurance Company,'' two key issues had to be dealt with: the difficultly in moving from one geographical region to another and an individual having different types of insurance policies (auto, life, health). Discuss what types of information capabilities would be necessary to address both issues.

2. Contact several banks about opening up multiple accounts (checking, savings, installments, and so on), and ask them to send you the necessary applications for opening the accounts. Assess if the banks are moving toward an integrated network organization.

3. Contact a stock brokerage house and ask how the company ascertains the type of relationship a potential customer would have with it. Also, discuss what the company does to try to provide an integrated service to that customer.

4. If you were to redesign your organization into a ''horizontal organization'' with self managing teams as the main operating units, how would you do it? What issues will you have to address? Which groups will like the new design? Which groups will resist it?

5. Read the story of Citibank (Matteis, 1979). Are the actions take by the bank considered BPR? Why or why not?

GROUP ASSIGNMENT

1. *Literature Review*
   a. Review the literature of the last 12 months and look for actual cases of BPR (good sources are *Industrial Engineering, InformationWeek* and *Forbes ASAP*).
   b. Each group member should find three such cases.
   c. In addition, each group member should find one case of actual TQM application.
   d. Based on the information collected, the group prepares a report that includes:
      (1) The organizational changes that occurred as a result of the BPR and the TQM.
      (2) A list of all information technologies used to support the BPR.
      (3) A description and possibly a diagram that shows, for each case, how IT was used as an enabler (similar to Figure 4.12).

2. *Improving Hotel Operations*
   A major hotel chain attempting to explore ways to improve its competitiveness in the marketplace recognized that business travelers constitute the largest por-

tion of their guests. Aware that airlines had success in offering special services to frequent flyers such as free upgrades to first class, the hotel chain decided to conduct a focus group comprised of business travelers. This group would explore issues important to frequent business travelers that were not being well-addressed by the hotel industry. It turned out that the single biggest complaint that business travelers expressed was the inflexibility of check-out time, which was typically twelve noon or one o'clock. Business travelers often arrive at a hotel late in the evening, conduct business generally until late afternoon, and then have to catch a flight to another destination. Ideally, they would like to be able to return to the hotel and change into more comfortable travel clothes rather than travel in their professional attire. Given that the business travelers weren't arriving until, in most cases, after seven or eight o'clock in the evening, they did not understand why they had to give up their room at noon. It seemed that as long as there was a four-hour window to clean the room, that should be sufficient for most hotels.

The main argument is, why should check-out time be enforced at 12 o'clock? A hotel cannot clean every room at 12 o'clock. All business travelers expressed that they would give strong consideration to a hotel that provided flexibility in check-out time. The hotel decided to explore how they could improve their check-in/check-out process and room cleaning in a way that could accommodate this important requirement for business travelers.

a. Contact some hotels. Ask them about their check-out policy and explore with them why they can't offer more flexibility. See what types of responses you can get.

b. Consider the important decisions that a hotel must make and the basic operations of check-in/check-out and cleaning the rooms. Also, consider what information would be necessary to deal with a flexible check-in/check-out process. How might they recognize a VIP or frequent customer? Discuss how the process could be reengineered to accommodate the business traveler.

c. How can IT be used to support new or improved business processes?

d. Prepare a report to top management. Is this a BPR? Outline your proposal. Make a five-minute presentation to the class.

Minicase 1

High Tech Manufacturing

High Tech manufacturing had a problem. The very thing that had made the company successful—allowing small entrepreneur mini-companies to develop under the umbrella of High Tech—was now working against it. Because High Tech always felt that bureaucracy would stifle innovation and creativity, it allowed engineers and marketing people with good ideas to create their own little companies and "run with them." Market penetration had been a great success.

Now, however, customers were beginning to complain that High Tech had so many different companies that often they would get called on by several salespeople during the same month. Customers were asking why High Tech couldn't get its act together and have one representative present the entire product line. Customers were also frustrated because when they had technical problems with products, they often would have to navigate through the different mini-companies of High Tech to get answers.

As High Tech struggled with this issue, it finally recognized that it needed a consolidated sales force representing multiple product lines from the different mini-companies. However, High Tech also recognized that there were all sorts of separate customer files and market analyses built into each mini-company. High Tech quickly realized that not only did it need to reorganize, but it also had to change its information systems.

Questions for Minicase 1

1. Discuss the information systems implications of the changes that High Tech manufacturing wants to make.

2. High Tech has recognized the need to consolidate the sales activity, but are there any other organizational activities that it might consider consolidating to be responsive to customer issues?

3. What would be the roles of self-directed teams in setting up this type of organization? For example, how might the sales force deal with specific technical questions that could arise during marketing efforts?

Minicase 2

Boston Chicken Uses IT to Improve Productivity and Quality and to Reengineer

Boston Chicken, the nation's largest restaurant chain specializing in rotisserie-roasted poultry, uses IT to both reengineer processes and improve performance on a continuous basis. The company's IS structure uses distributed computing, with a variety of client/server configurations for specialty applications. This configuration allows rapid development of end user applications, such as a modified POS system for their drive-up window and a touch screen application to obtain real-time customer feedback. Sophisticated GIS systems are used in new location selections and are an essential tool for speedy in-house demographic research. IS staff developed a brand new concept called "intellistore." The system has an enterprise-wide, open architecture and uses a universal modular terminal design that allows complete interchangeability of all terminal types used in the organization. Extensive use of touch screens, graphical user interface (GUI), and multimedia technologies ensure maximally user-friendly systems, while maintaining total flexibility. Internal help desks maximize data and information propagation within the organization. By developing an object-oriented library of marketing data, Boston Chicken is able to adapt to rapidly changing market conditions and customer preferences. This ability is vital in an industry in which leadership depends on how fast one can adapt to changes in the external business environment.

How did IT support changes in the organization structure? By designing a universal set of systems, supporting specialty operations, Boston Chicken was able to expand more than 100 percent in one year. The concept of "market partners" allowed this rapid expansion without significantly expanding their corporate infrastructure and staffing levels. Outsourcing of IT specialty functions, such as the operation of a help desk, allowed Boston Chicken to obtain the benefit of the latest technology without any investment.

How did IT support changes in the business process? By introducing the principle of universal modular applications, which are fully portable within the organization's terminals, the staff became truly multifunctional and was able, supported by IT, to be allocated to any task within the restaurant process.

How did IT support shortening the time-to-market? By implementing real-time feedback from customers through touch screen terminals, a rapid response to changing customer preferences was facilitated. By having a fully IT-supported, flexible, easily adaptable business process, Boston Chicken was able to stay ahead of the competition through rapid innovation and adaptation to changing market conditions.

How did IT support joint ventures, virtual corporations, and business alliances? By creating an IT-based restaurant "machine," the company was able to contract with market partners, for rapid expansion in a specific geographic area. This resulted in a much greater efficiency than having to deal with single outlets.

How did IT support mass customization? Sophisticated POS systems using GUI and multimedia technology facilitate mass customization without the traditional infrastructure required to implement "custom cooking."

How did IT support customer-centered organizations? The restaurant business is uniquely focused on customer satisfaction, and all IT systems within Boston Chicken are designed to achieve a maximum level of customer satisfaction, service, and feedback.

How did IT enhance empowerment of employees? By designing a total open system, which allows all operations to be performed from any terminal location, employees no longer have traditional barriers to becoming multifunctional. As a result, enhanced team operation resulted in greater productivity, employee morale, and independence.

How did IT enhance quality? On-line management access to information on business aspects such as staffing levels, sales, and customer feedback resulted in a greatly improved quality of the restaurant process and an optimization of resource utilization.

Questions for Minicase 2

1. Identify the reengineering activities and segregate them according to the 3 Rs of BPR.

2. Are there any TQM activities?

3. Identify regular activities of continuous improvement.

4. Identify the specific processes that were reengineered and describe the role of IT in each.

SOURCE: Compiled from L. Wilson, "Atop the Rotisserie League," *InformationWeek*, Jan. 3, 1994.

Minicase 3

Harry Burkstaller's Health Care Problem

Harry Burkstaller had experienced a series of serious headaches, and one day he actually passed out at work. He was rushed to the emergency room, and exams were conducted. No problem could be identified at the time, and the physicians thought the problems were most likely stress related. Nevertheless, they wanted to conduct more tests before they would feel comfortable with that conclusion. Harry, however, had an extensive travel schedule for his consulting work. In fact, he had to make a trip to the West Coast early the following week. The doctors felt comfortable enough to allow him to make the trip.

When Harry arrived at the client site, he was again experiencing headaches and concerned that he might again pass out. He did not want to trouble his client by relating his medical crisis. But at the same time, he was concerned that if he should lose consciousness and be rushed to a hospital, his clients would have no knowledge or record of what had transpired—the tests that had already been done and the tentative conclusions. This troubled Harry greatly. He wondered why a person could handle an airline transaction or credit transaction from anywhere in the world, but something much more crucial such as medical status was totally fragmented and piecemeal. This inadequacy could put someone's life—his life—at risk.

Since his company specialized in information systems consulting, Harry began to ponder what type of information system and what type of organization would need to be created in order to deal with such an issue.

Questions for Minicase 3

1. Discuss the type of information system Harry Burkstaller wanted that does not exist today.

2. What type of information system would be necessary to allow people to travel around the world yet have their medical records readily available should they be needed?

3. What type of networked organizations would be necessary to facilitate the system of question 2?

REFERENCES AND BIBLIOGRAPHY

1. Applegate, L., "IBM Canada, Ltd.: Restructuring for the 1990's," Harvard Business School, April 1990 (mimeo). See also Tom Corcoran, "And Now for the E Word," *Dialogue*, IBM Corporation, 1989; see also Applegate, L. and J. J. Cash, Case #9-189-138 of Harvard Business School.

2. Ayers, B., "TQM and Information Technology: Partners for Profit," *Information Strategy, The Executive Journal*, Spring 1993.

3. Bashein, B. J., Markus, L., and P. Riley, "Business Reengineering Preconditions for BPR Success and How to Prevent Failure," *Information Systems Management*, Spring 1994.

4. Bounds, G., et al.; *Beyond Total Quality Management* New York: McGraw Hill, 1994.

5. Byrne, J. A., "The Horizontal Corporation," *Business Week*, December 20, 1993.

6. Davenport, T., *Process Innovation: Re-engineering Work through Information Technology*, Boston, HBS Press, 1993.

7. Davenport, T., and Nitin Nohria, "Case Management and the Integration of Labor," *Sloan Management Review*, Winter 1994.

8. Dixon, J. R., et al., "Business Process Reengineering: Improving in Low Strategic Directions," *California Management Review*, Summer 1994.

9. Garvin, D. A., "Building a Learning Organization," *Harvard Business Review*, Vol. 71, No. 4, 1993, p. 78.

10. Gulden, G. K., and D. E. Ewers, "Is Total Quality Enough?" *INSIGHTS*, Fall 1991.

11. Hall, G., J. Rosenthal, and J. Wade, "How to Make Reengineering Really Work," *Harvard Business Review*, November–December 1993.

12. Hamel, G., and C. K. Prahalad, "Competing for the Future," *Harvard Business Review*, July–August 1994.

13. Hammer, M., and J. Champy, *Re-engineering the Corporation*, New York: Harper Business, 1993.

14. Harrarr, G., "Outsourcing Tale," *Forbes ASAP*, June 7, 1993, p. 36.

15. Harrison, D. B., and M. D. Pratt, "A Methodology for Reengineering Business," *Planning Review*, Vol. 21, No. 2, 1993, p. 6.

16. Henderson, J., and N. Venkatraman, "Strategic Alignment: Leveraging IT for Transforming Organizations," *IBM Systems Journal*, January 1993.

17. Hunt, V. D., *Managing for Quality*, Homewood, IL: Business One Irwin, 1993.

18. Katzenbach, J. R., and D. K. Smith, "The Discipline of Teams," *Harvard Business Review*, March–April 1993.

19. Kirkpatrick, D., "Making It All Worker-Friendly," *Fortune*, Vol. 128, No. 7, 1993, p. 44.

20. Malone, T. W., and J. F. Rockart, "Computers, Networks and the Corporation," *Scientific American*, September 1991.

21. Moad, J., "Does Reengineering Really Work?" *Datamation*, Vol. 39, No. 15, 1993, p. 22.

22. Neo, B. S., and L. Gilbert, "Business Process Reengineering: Conceptual Antecedents and Current Practice," *Accounting and Business Review*, July 1994.

23. Riffkin, G., "Reengineering Aetna," *Forbes ASAP*, June 7, 1993, p. 78.

24. Rose 1., "Retooling the information systems profession," *Journal of Systems Management*, January/February 1995.

25. Saylor, James H., *TQM Field Manual*, New York: McGraw-Hill, 1992.

26. Scott, G. M., "Downsizing, Business Process Reengineering, and Quality Improvement Plans: How Are They Related?" *Information Strategy: The Executives Journal*, Spring 1995.

27. Stow, R. P., "Reengineering by Objectives," *Planning Review*, Vol. 21, No. 3, 1993, p. 14.

WOODSTRAT: A SUPPORT SYSTEM FOR STRATEGIC MANAGEMENT

PIRKKO WALDEN AND CHRISTER CARLSSON
Institute for Advanced Management Systems Research
Åbo Akademi University (Finland)

AND OSSI KOKKONEN
Metsä-Serla Oy (Finland)

The Corporation and the Competitive Environment

Today, Finland has more forests than it has had for the last several hundred years. This is due to the ecological concept of *sustainable development*, in which a considerable part of the forest's natural growth remains unexploited. Although Finnish pine and spruce forests are only about 1 percent of the total resources in the world, Finland has been able to build a leading position among the forest industry nations.

Metsä-Serla is a Finnish forest products group with 1993 net sales of FIM 8,239 million (U.S. $881 million). It is the fourth-largest forest products company in Finland; its operating profit was FIM 964 million (U.S. $220 million) and the consolidated financial result was over FIM 550 million (U.S. $126 million) better than in 1992. This shows an impressive recovery from a severe recession in the Finnish forest industry. The year 1993 will be remembered "as one in which, in real terms, prices for several forest products on world markets fell to their lowest level in 20 years" (Timo Poranen, president and CEO of Metsä-Serla). In its eight divisions, which operate rather independently, Metsä-Serla processes wood raw material into paper and paperboard, corrugated board, and tissue as well as sawn goods, pulp, and chemicals. It has production and marketing operations in Europe and sells its products worldwide; exports from Finland and sales through foreign subsidiaries together contribute 84 percent of net sales. Metsä-Serla's basic strategy is to expand and strengthen its market positions in carefully selected core businesses (Metsä-Serla, *Annual Report 1993*). In 1993, the number of employees was approximately 8,700, of whom almost 30 percent worked outside Finland.

Metsä-Serla has undertaken a rapid and thorough adaptation to the emerging characteristics of its European markets. It was one of the first companies in Finland to adopt modern environmental values and has actively developed proenvironmental technology and products. "We see it as a trend that we should be directly involved in, right from the start," says Timo Poranen. "We are concentrating on manufacturing the type of products that best bring out the excellent properties of primary fiber; an additional factor is that products should be well suited to recycling and processes should consume as little energy as possible." Strategic thinking has a long history in the corporation and new ideas have, on many occasions, been very successfully implemented.

In the corporation, strategic planning used to be rather a formal exercise. This is the case in most forest industry corporations, where the pressures of rapidly changing markets and strong competition quickly make most strategic plans obsolete. Ossi Kokkonen, a senior vice president, did not feel very happy with the way things were done. He heads a division with nine small business units (SBUs) representing sawn goods, pulp, and building materials. These SBUs operate with multiple products in different markets and market segments. Softwood and hardwood pulps are mainly sold to Metsä-Serla's other mills, and fluff pulp (a speciality that is used as raw material for hygiene products) is marketed mainly to European and North American manufacturers. Important segments for the sawn goods are joinery, planing mill, furniture, packaging, and construction industry. Sawn goods are marketed through the division's own sales offices in Denmark, the United Kingdom, France, and Switzerland; in the other markets, sales are taken care of by local agents. Building materials—windows, doors, log houses, and saunas—are distributed to European markets, but also remote markets such as the Japanese have been attractive for log houses. Ossi Kokkonen's view on traditional strategic planning is that the process offers very little substance to its participants. He elaborates as follows:

My vision is that the process should be a dynamic one, sensitive to changes in the competitive context and aimed at creating strategic advantages. I want more effective strategic management processes, as I expect my people to be well prepared to face drastic changes and new challenges in the markets. I am not too sure that my managers are practicing customer-oriented thinking, which is one of the cornerstones in my management philosophy [forest industry companies have traditionally been production oriented]. I have my doubts about how knowledgeable my SBU teams are about assessing their expected market shares, developing their competitiveness, and attaining expected sales margins of their segments or markets. I am looking for ways to make the strategic planning knowledge based, dynamic, interactive, and more insightful—at least in my own division. This is why I formed the Woodstrat consortium together with the Institute for Advanced Management Systems Research [IAMSR] and Kymmene [another major Finnish forest industry corporation].

The consortium has developed a new technology for building and implementing support systems for strategic management in the forest industry; this support system is called *Woodstrat* and is a knowledge-based system, built as a hybrid of an object-oriented expert system and a hyperknowledge[1] user interface. Kokkonen explains that ''in the beginning, I had the feeling that the Woodstrat concept was far too theoretical and abstract. We proposed to link market and competitive visions to profitability, and I thought it was—if not impossible—at least far too advanced for practical purposes. But the relationships turned out to be almost self-evident for my SBU managers, and now I feel a little bit ashamed to confess it.''

The first version of the *Woodstrat* support system was done with a Lisp-based expert system shell which turned out to be too restrictive and was quickly followed with a full-scale system in PC ToolBook (by Asymetrix). The most recent version is built with Visual Basic (version 3.0 by Microsoft Corporation), in which all the expert systems and hyperknowledge features of the Lisp and ToolBook versions have been constructed as objects, with their elements designed to jointly perform the hyperknowledge functions. The system is run on portable PCs that allow users to spend time with the system out of the office. The end result is that the Woodstrat system is actually run by SBU managers; it is extensively used as a support system in strategic management; and users are actively improving the system while they use it.

The Woodstrat System

Strategic management is commonly understood to cover both the strategic planning process and implementation of its results. Metsä-Serla quickly found out that we needed a more formal description of the concept. *Stratetgic management* is the process through which a SBU, for a chosen planning period, (1) defines its operational context; (2) outlines and decides upon its strategic goals and long-term objectives; (3) explores and decides upon its strengths, weaknesses, opportunities, and threats; (4) formulates its sustainable competitive advantages; and (5) develops a program of action that exploits its competitive advantages and ensures profitability, financial balance, adaptability to sudden changes, and sound development of its capital structure. This requires an advanced support system, and the technology developed in Woodstrat became fairly advanced but also very supportive for users.

Technology is, however, not enough. There were some practical issues that needed to be tackled and solved satisfactorily: (1) where to get reliable external data, (2) how to find enough information about strengths and weaknesses of key competitors, (3) how to determine the effects of perceived competitive advantages on competitive positions in key market segments, and (4) how to combine and transform the results of strategic decisions into estimates of profitability, financial positions, and capital structure for the strategic planning period. Metsä-Serla has resolved these issues using Woodstrat, which became a natural and logical basis for the strategic planning process.

Ossi Kokkonen explained the evolution of the system at Metsä-Serla:

In the beginning of the project, we were far too eager to create a system for all aspects of the strategic arena. But as we went along with the development process, we were able to separate important strategic issues from those of minor interest; this made the system more easy to grasp. My managers do not accept a system which they do not fully understand. Implementing traditional profitability measures is, of course, easy and understandable, but implementing nontraditional measurements, such as customer satisfaction, is hard to do and even harder to link to profitability in any intuitively understandable way.

We succeeded, and in my division from now on we can do more effective and efficient planning. Of course, my SBU managers are now forced to learn more about their business, as they have to take into account many

---

[1]Hyperknowledge is represented by a system of concepts, in which the use of a concept triggers another concept in a theoretically correct and meaningful way (see Chang et al. [1993] and Walden and Carlsson [1994]).

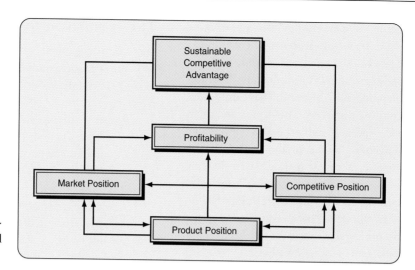

FIGURE 1 Strategic management: a conceptual framework.

more factors than before. They must consider different scenarios and visions and, of course, Woodstrat gives me the possibility to demand a greater knowledge about our markets, competitors, and customers. I have started to think of Woodstrat as a multidimensional navigation chart (I am a sailor) for my division. It means I can plot a course for the years ahead and locate my division in terms of positions (market, competitive, and production); profitability; and sustainable competitive advantages [see Figure 1].

In Woodstrat, these conceptual constructs are linked with functions and logistical connectives to form a *hyperknowledge* system—a context in which they interact to form a synthesis that represents possible variations of sustainable competitive advantages. The support system was implemented in all nine SBUs, with some variations to account for differences in markets and competition.

The status and expected developments of an SBU are defined by its strategic *market position*, in which expected net sales (defined by forecasts of sales volumes and prices) is determined. The market position is influenced by the competitive position and the production position, which both determine the profitability. The market position is built with knowledge-based (KB) links among several different conceptual constructs. Countries are described with economic indicators, and markets/segments are characterized by market share, competitive ability, profitability, and volume and price development (see Figure 2). Woodstrat helps the SBU management teams work out the potential of all the markets/segments in which they operate in terms of forecasted demand and their share of it as well as expected price development and changes in currency exchange rates. This process also shows the management team where they are missing data about the market, where they need more knowledge about their customers

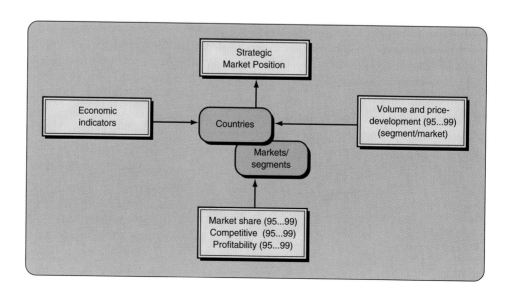

FIGURE 2 Market position.

and the competition and so on. Woodstrat initiated bench-marking studies in key markets. In order to enhance market knowledge, the system will also be distributed to all sales offices in Europe, which will be an effective way to update and develop the knowledge base on the markets.

The strategic market position is partially determined by the *competitive position*, which covers the same countries, markets, segments, and product groups (see Figure 3). Hyperknowledge links give access to the same background information as in the market position module. Woodstrat is supported by a rather extensive database with country and market forecasts.

In order to determine their competitive position, SBU managers are expected to assess their price competitiveness, their competitive advantages (with support from KB-links to models of critical success factors for the segments), the threat from entries of new products in the segments, viable market strategies, and the influence of their corresponding market position on the competitive position. Assessment of the competitive position is consolidated from all individual assessments. Factors defining the competitive position may change among the SBUs, and the hyperknowledge environment allows for changes and adaptive actions concerning the background information given the managers.

After deciding their own competitive positions, SBU managers select their main competitors and assess both their critical success factors and the expected development of competitive status for the planning period. The competitive positions (their own, competitors) are evaluated for each country, market/segment, and product group.

They are then consolidated to give the overall competitive position for the SBU. The overall position is used to modify the overall market position (with KB-links) and to modify the forecasts of net sales and operational costs (with another set of KB-links).

Here, Woodstrat produced an unexpected bonus: the management teams were able—in many cases, for the first time—to assess their critical success factors and determine their competence in them. It turned out that, for the first time, they also could compare themselves with key competitors in a systematic way. In many cases, they realized that they did not know enough about the competition, and sales offices were activated to find out more. Links to the market position and the possibility to determine how volume and price developments are influenced by the competition were considered to be very useful.

Sustainable competitive advantages are also defined by the *production position*. This is the SBU manager's assessment of the potential development of the unit's overall productivity as a function of several factors: (1) quality of raw material, (2) availability of energy, (3) skill level of personnel, and (4) quality level of production technology. The overall productivity level, when consolidated from these factors, will improve both market and competitive positions (through a system of KB-links). The productivity will also define parts of the operating costs (through another set of KB-links), which are very sensitive to changes in the productivity levels (see Figure 4).

Decisions on major process investments and assessment of their impact on production technology and productivity are part of the production position. In this way, investment decisions are evaluated properly. With the

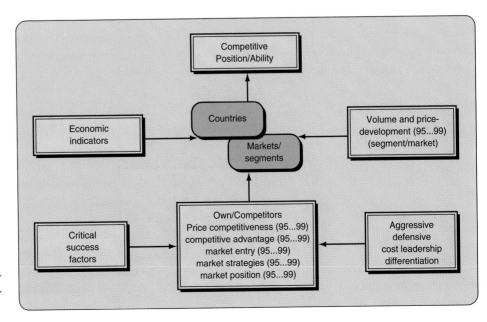

FIGURE 3 Competitive positions: own vs. key competitors.

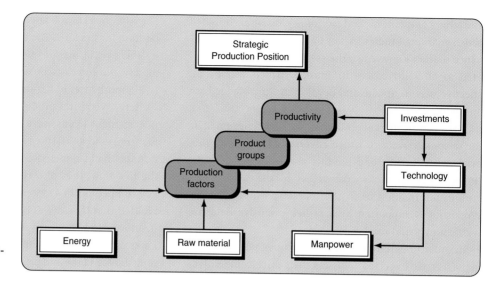

FIGURE 4 Production position.

help of KB-links, their impact on the sustainable competitive advantages is assessed, and their effects on both operating costs and financing are worked out in detail.

Productivity is enhanced with cost-effective production technology and by the use of full production capacity to produce competitively priced products that completely cover the SBUs' share of the market demand. Thus, productivity is influenced by the customers' demand patterns, the competition, and the price/cost relationships between products and production factors. Productivity is supported or enhanced with investments in production technology, which influence product quality and costs. Needless to say, the cause–effect relationships involved are complex, and Woodstrat—probably for the first time—offered a means for figuring out the interdependencies of productivity as well as market and competitive positions for an individual SBU.

The market, competitive, and production positions are linked to the *profitability and financing positions*, which shows the forecasts of income, positive and negative cash flows, capital structure, and profitability for the planning period. As the linking is done with KB-links, it has been possible in Woodstrat to ensure that the impacts of the various factors are theoretically correct, intuitively understandable, and supportable with empirical data.

The process described in Figure 5 is a simple and practical way to work out the financial implications of strategic visions, which is a necessary but rather difficult task. Much of the work done in careful strategic planning is simplified away when it should be evaluated in terms of financial consequences. The integrated evaluation introduced in Woodstrat gained immediate acceptance among the SBU managers as it eliminated a tedious, time-consuming and uninspiring phase of the planning process.

In addition, Woodstrat proved to offer more thorough and systematic information on the consequences of various market and competitive assessments, and the analysis carried out was more thorough, more detailed, and faster than before. The managers were confident that they could gain advantages relative to their competitors because they had a better understanding of their customers and their markets but also because they could guess the competi-

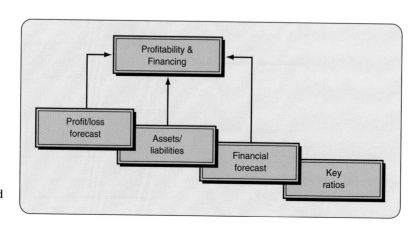

FIGURE 5 Profitability and financing position,

tors' next strategic moves on the market with support from their own knowledge base. Ossi Kokkonen sums up his feelings on the system this way:

> Woodstrat has given me a fair basis for evaluating my SBU-managers' level of knowledge, and it has created a very natural, on-going need to improve it. Now, I really have the feeling that we have done the basic work as it should be done. We have cut off all matters of minor importance for strategic management, and we have realized that we should concentrate on the customers who are really important to us.
>
> Even with this much more detailed and systematic planning process, I am not going to need more planning staff in my division; I will need more portable PCs for my managers who are doing the planning. Woodstrat has been able to make many key decision processes faster because all the important external and internal information is available on the spot. If any information in the system proves to be wrong, the message to my managers is to correct it on the spot. Now I believe that we have a system to make strategic management an effective, dynamic process in my division. With Woodstrat, I am able to quickly and thoroughly communicate strategic shifts and changes with all my SBUs, and I have an effective instrument for continuous and systematic evaluation of how successful my strategic decisions have been.
>
> The future is also very straightforward, from Kokkonen's point of view: Woodstrat will be an ongoing development process. The knowledge base should be even more profound and the system should be enlarged to cover the sales offices abroad. We will next look into possibilities to link all the SBUs and the sales offices in a corporate-wide, European LAN in which to consolidate the knowledge, assessments, updates, decisions, plans, and conclusions that we make with Woodstrat. I am going to establish a training program in order to make the use of Woodstrat routine.

Conclusions

The Woodstrat system was built and implemented in all nine SBUs during 1992 and 1993; the development work was done in close cooperation with the SBU management teams as a series of prototypes. The system was tested by managers during the entire development process on a continuous basis. The system contains the knowledge and experience of the SBU managers because they had the opportunity to participate in the development process. The managers feel that Woodstrat is their own system. "The reason why the managers have accepted the system

is because they were allowed to play an active part in its development process, and I am convinced that this is the only successful way to build support systems for upper-level managers," Kokkonen said—with a smile.

With Woodstrat, management team members work through their business more carefully in several ways: (1) they are guided to determine their own market positions in all their markets/segments in a number of countries; (2) they assess their own competitive positions in the same markets/segments by determining how good they are going to be on critical success factors, both independently and in relation to the competition; (3) they evaluate their production technology and productivity, and compare themselves with their competitors; (4) they work out the necessary investment plans and their corresponding financial plans; and (5) they work out a profitability position, a forecast of the capital structure, the long-term cash flows, and key ratios.

The support system received quick and easy acceptance. Between 1992 and 1994, managers were tested on several points: (1) their cognitive maps of strategic management as compared with the strategic planning documents prior to Woodstrat; (2) the minimum knowledge base for effective strategic management; (3) the effectiveness of strategic planning with Woodstrat; (4) the effectiveness of group processes supported with Woodstrat; and (5) their insights on the critical elements that form the sustainable competitive advantages. Results so far show definite improvements in the quality of some key elements of the strategic management process.

Case Study Questions

1. What are the key elements to assess when building strategic plans?

2. Explain how computer support could be used to enhance the process of building strategic plans.

3. Examine Figure 3 and explain how you would visualize the role of hyperknowledge links in accessing information.

4. Explore the potential of some innovations in information technology to be used for building support systems in strategic management.

5. Explore the use of hypermedia as a basis for group support systems.

References and Bibliography

CARLSSON, C., "New Instruments for Management Research," *Human Systems Management*, Vol. 10, No. 3, 1991, pp. 203–220.

CARLSSON, C., "Expert Systems as Conceptual Frameworks and Management Support Systems for Strategic Management," *International Journal of Information Resource Management,* Vol. 2, No. 4, 1991, pp. 14–24.

CARLSSON, C., "Knowledge Formation in Strategic Management," In *Proceedings of the Twenty-Seventh Annual Hawaii International Conference on System Sciences, Information Systems: DSS/Knowledge-Based Systems,* Eds. Jay F. Nunamaker, Jr., and Ralph H. Sprague, Vol. III, 1994, pp. 221–230.

CHANG, A. M., C. W. HOLSAPPLE, and A. B. WHINSTON, "Model Management Issues and Directions," *Decision Support Systems,* Vol. 9, 1993, pp. 19–37.

WALDEN, P., and C. CARLSSON, "Enhancing Strategic Market Management with Knowledge-Based Systems," In *Proceedings of the Twenty-Sixth Annual Hawaii International Conference on System Sciences, Information Systems: DSS/Knowledge-Based Systems,* Eds. Jay F. Nunamaker, Jr., and Ralph H. Sprague, Vol. 3, 1993, pp. 240–248.

WALDEN, P., and C. CARLSSON, "Strategic Management with a Hyperknowledge Support System," In *Proceedings of the Twenty-Seventh Annual Hawaii International Conference on System Sciences, Information Systems: DSS/Knowledge-Based Systems,* Eds. Jay F. Nunamaker, Jr., and Ralph H. Sprague, Vol. 3, 1994, pp. 241–250.

PART II

INFORMATION SYSTEMS TECHNOLOGY

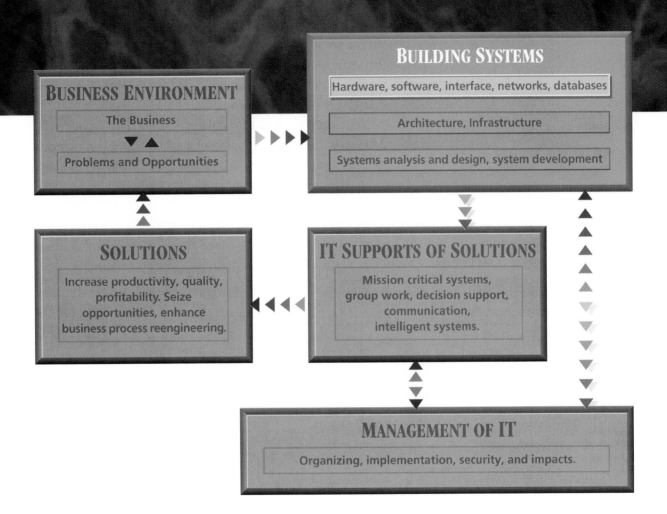

Information technology is based on computer technology and information systems, whose foundations are presented in Part II. Understanding the technology is essential for managers, because decisions regarding investments in IT and the manner in which it is used can make or break organizations.

The technology is divided into five chapters. The first four chapters describe the basic components of information systems: hardware, software, the user interface, and databases. Computer networks, which connect individual computers to form information systems as well as enable systems to communicate with each other, are described in the fifth chapter.

Chapter 5 offers a review of computer hardware. A basic computer literacy is provided along with an explanation of the role of hardware in information systems and its role in emerging technologies and trends in hardware development.

Chapter 6 deals with software and programming. In addition to providing descriptions of various types of software, this chapter focuses on emerging trends and innovations in software, and on software development and management.

Chapter 7 introduces the reader to a large variety of devices and features which constitute the environment within which people communicate with computers. In addition to regular input and output devices, the chapter highlights emerging user interface and graphics features. These includes multimedia, hypermedia, geographical information systems, visual simulation, virtual reality, and natural language processing.

Chapter 8 is dedicated to data and data management. In addition to basic computer literacy concepts of file and database organizations, the chapter presents emerging concepts such as object-oriented and multimedia databases, as well as intelligent databases. Important issues in administering databases are also discussed.

Chapter 9 closes the technology section by presenting an overview of telecommunication and networks. The technology of communication networks is presented, including all major hardware and software components.

Part II end case deals with the ABC Company, a fictionalized company that is in the automotive retail industry. It is facing many of the organizational and technological choices detailed in this part.

Chapter 5—Processing the Information: Computer Hardware
Chapter 6—Processing the Information: Computer Software
Chapter 7—User Interface: Enabling Human-Computer Communication
Chapter 8—Data and Data Management
Chapter 9—Data Communication and Network Architecture

5

PROCESSING THE INFORMATION: COMPUTER HARDWARE

Chapter Outline

Learning Objectives

After studying this chapter, you will be able to:

1. Understand the development of computers from a historical perspective.

2. Identify and distinguish among the different types of computers.

3. Identify and describe the key components of computer hardware, and explain their roles.

4. Classify computer hardware by commonly used measures.

5. Distinguish among the key features of computer architecture, and explain the purpose of each.

6. Identify emerging features of computer hardware and how they will affect future performance.

Case

▶ 5.1 LIGHTS! CAMERAS! COMPUTERS!

MANY MOVIEGOERS LOVE visual special effects and flock to movies like *Terminator 2* or *Jurassic Park*, but these movies cost fortunes to make. Therefore, to meet the demand for these special effects, Hollywood is turning to supercomputers.

Traditionally, special effects have been extremely hard and time-consuming to produce. Creating them meant tediously filming many different parts of a scene using blue screen backgrounds that can be optically erased, then layering the film images together precisely—individually, frame by frame, separated by hand-drawn light-blocking "mattes." These combined images were then rephotographed with an optical printer. A single special-effects scene lasting just a few seconds on film could take weeks of work and cost hundreds of thousands of dollars. One brief space battle scene in *Return of the Jedi* required combining 70 separate shots. Not only was it costly, but each layer added to image blurring.

Now, by scanning images into digital form, a filmmaker can combine, crop, color, matte, and retouch them (to remove wires, forgotten soda cans, or intruding microphones) at a single computer workstation. No need to hand draw mattes or feed image sandwiches through an optical printer. Moreover, there is no blurring or loss of resolution. Robin Williams flew so gracefully through the set of *Hook* because his heavy cable harness was electronically erased by a computer. Coca-Cola made Paula Abdul seem to dance around a reincarnated Gene Kelly in Coke commercials.

Although digital special effects and movie editing have been around for a while in cruder forms, the surprise is how rapidly supercomputer technology is remaking the film business. "I'm excited," said filmmaker James Cameron who directed *Terminator 2* and *The Abyss*. "Things never before possible will be, and what was possible will be cheaper."

"[Computers] will do for filmmaking what the PC did for writing," declared Ed Jones, who won an Oscar award for his work on the animated movie *Who Framed Roger Rabbit*?

Some of the "objects" we now see in movies do not even exist, except as data in someone's computer. Rather than photograph real objects, digitize them, and then manipulate the images, some computer animation shops simulate three-dimensional objects in a computer, light them from a certain direction, and then make them sing and dance like the cups and saucers in *Beauty and the Beast* or the "morph" from liquid metal to robot in *Terminator 2*. The herds of rocket-equipped penguins in *Batman Returns* were drawn on a computer, programmed to waddle, and then placed into a digital set.

Lead digital artist Michelle Moen at Boss Film Studio.

"We don't have to blow up real helicopters and buildings or even models of them anymore," notes David B. Brown, president of Blue Sky Productions.

The main difficulty Hollywood has faced with digitally producing special effects is having enough computer power and storage to cope with the high-resolution levels needed for a film to be shown on a big screen. An IBM supercomputer used for special effects by Los Angeles' Boss Film Studios contains 32 computer chips working simultaneously in tandem to do 2.5 billion computations per second. A single 35-mm frame contains up to 20 million bytes of information. At 24 frames a second, a 90-minute movie requires the equivalent storage of 2 trillion textual characters—enough data to fill over 10,000 common personal computers' hard drives. Even with data compression techniques, it will be a while before an entire movie is digitized.

Although primarily used within studios for special effects, this type of power and storage potential could usher in wide changes in the movie industry. Movies—once they are entirely digitized—could be distributed digitally by fiber-optic cables or beamed by satellites instead of through costly celluloid film copies manually transported to theaters. Movies could be shown on brilliant electronic screens or in personal wraparound helmet viewers with thundering stereo sound. In fact, these digital movies could be instantly altered for tailored viewing by certain age, ethnic, or religious groups or become interactive with the viewer for personalized plots and action.

SOURCE: Norman, J. R., *Forbes*, October 26, 1992.

▶ 5.2   UNDERSTANDING COMPUTER TECHNOLOGY

When early attempts were made to use the first generations of computers for business purposes (as opposed to military or scientific purposes), a high level of computer technology understanding was required. Data processing managers, or "DP managers" as they were called, had to master both the hardware and software in order to develop business applications for their companies. Computers were hard to operate and harder to program; and considerable training in the technology was necessary in order to be successful as a DP manager.

With time, all this changed. Advances in hardware and software sophistication, coupled with an increased availability of computer professionals trained in university programs in computer science, computer engineering, and other computer-related disciplines, allowed managers to focus more on the application of computer technology than on the technology per se. At the same time, the advent of microcomputers or "personal computers" and easy-to-use software put the power of computing in the hands of literally millions of people. These developments have led to the widespread feeling that "I don't need to know about how computers work, only how to use them." In reality, an understanding of both is necessary.

Although the main thrust of this book is managerial, this chapter and the other chapters in Part II provide the necessary technical background to complement the managerial focus. Even if you will never program a computer or manage an information systems department, a knowledge of the underlying concepts of computer technology will be invaluable. With computers touching virtually all parts of organizations today, both public and private, the informed manager has a distinct advantage over his or her less well versed co-workers.

▶ 5.3   A BRIEF HISTORY OF COMPUTERS

When filmmakers such as Boss Film Studios talk of using supercomputers to perform 2.5 *billion* computations per second to achieve movie special effects, it is hard to appreciate that computers, as we know them today, have been in existence for barely 40 years. The UNIVAC I, the first computer in commercial use, operated at *millisecond* (thousandth of a second) speeds—over a million times more slowly than Boss Film's computers. Understanding the evolution of computers can help us understand the processes that define them. Although this evolution spans many millennia, it has been most noticeable during the past half century. Today, what guides spacecraft millions of miles in space, creates previously unimaginable movie images, or processes our words as we write, started with simple arithmetic computing devices.

EARLY COMPUTING DEVICES

Perhaps the earliest computing device (besides our fingers) is the **abacus** (see Figure 5.1). The ancient Chinese used this device to represent numbers and perform calculations. It was simple to learn and use, and it was very fast in skilled hands. It is so simple and effective, in fact, that the abacus is still a dominant computing device in Asia today.

It was some time before the first mechanized calculating devices were created. A French mathematician, Blaise Pascal, invented a gear-driven calculating machine in 1642 that was capable of addition, subtraction, and multiplication. It was complicated and only improved the performance of a single processing step. But other mathematicians continued Pascal's work on mechanical calculating machines, improving on his invention by adding more functionality.

FIGURE 5.1 An abacus.

Many years later, for a completely different application, the evolution of computers took a giant step. In 1801, Joseph Jacquard designed a loom that could use a series of punched wooden cards to control the weaving process. The holes in the cards activated mechanical fingers that determined which threads were to appear in the fabric. The sequencing of the cards could produce a large number of patterns and designs. This invention was carefully guarded because it was felt to be so important to France's "competitive advantage" in the international weaving industry. The penalty for disclosing to a foreign power how the Jacquard loom worked was death! The concept of punched cards to control a process was utilized by most modern-day computers well into the 1970s.

In 1822, an English mathematician named Charles Babbage combined the control principles of the Jacquard loom with mechanisms of his own devising to perform numeric calculations. He developed a machine that could take a series of *stored* computing steps and process data automatically. Babbage called his device a **difference engine** and used it to calculate logarithm tables. He later devised an even more comprehensive machine, which he called an **analytic engine**. Unfortunately, the analytic engine design was beyond the manufacturing capability of the day and was never built.

Supporting Babbage throughout much of his work, both intellectually and financially, was the wife of an English country squire, Lord Lovelace. Her name was Ada, Lady Lovelace, and she corresponded extensively with Babbage, although they never met. (For those interested in literary figures, she was also the daughter of Lord Byron, the English poet.) She explained, should his analytic engine be built, how it could be programmed. Based on her writings, she has often been called "the world's first programmer." One of the most powerful modern-day programming languages is named Ada for her.

The principles embodied in Babbage's analytic engine, even though it was never operational, are almost identical to those in today's electronic computers. It is interesting to note that from Babbage's day until the end of World War II, the term *computer* referred to a *person* performing calculations, not the *device* being used.

The 1880s saw a huge influx of immigrants to the United States. To reduce the time needed to record and tabulate information about these new Americans, Herman Hollerith, a U.S. Census Bureau employee, developed a tabulating machine that used machine-readable cards, similar in concept to the wooden cards used in the Jacquard loom. These cards provided a convenient and reliable way to record and input data for census calculations. This machine was so successful in accurately recording data that the U.S. government used it for its 1890 national census. The company Hollerith founded to produce these tabulating machines is today known as the International Business Machine Corporation (IBM). These punched cards, once known as "Hollerith cards," later came to be known as "IBM cards."

THE FIRST COMPUTER

The first truly electronic computing device was developed at the Moore School of Electrical Engineering at the University of Pennsylvania by a team of engineers led by John W. Mauchly and J. Presper Eckert, Jr., during the latter days of World War II. The U.S. Army Ordnance Corps funded their work for calculating mathematical tables of artillery trajectories. The resulting ENIAC (electronic numerical integrator and calculator) computer used vacuum tubes for electronic switching and was controlled by manually plugging and unplugging connecting wires.

Mauchly and Eckert left the university in 1951 to form the first company to develop an electronic computer, the UNIVAC I (universal automatic computer), for commercial use. The U.S. government used a UNIVAC I for the 1950 national census. Another UNIVAC I became the first computer used to predict a presidential

FIGURE 5.2
The UNIVAC I.

election when, in 1952, it predicted Eisenhower would defeat Stevenson when only 5 percent of the vote had come in (see Figure 5.2).

In 1954, the General Electric Company in Louisville, Kentucky, installed the UNIVAC I for the first computerized payroll processing system—the first commercial use of computers. Most early commercial applications of computers were for accounting or financial functions (for example, payroll, accounts receivable/payable, general ledger). Although these financial applications continue to be important, computers now touch all parts of business—marketing and sales, logistics, and operations—and at all levels—operational, managerial, and strategic. Nevertheless, because of the early use of computers for accounting purposes, many corporate computer departments still report to their company's chief financial officer (CFO). Understanding this historical background helps us understand the current organizational arrangements for providing computing services.

The vacuum tubes used in the early computers were notoriously unreliable, generated huge amounts of heat, and required many tons of air-conditioning capacity to keep them from exploding. With the development of the **transistor** at Bell Laboratories in New Jersey in 1947, a new era began, commonly referred to as "the second generation of computing." Transistors, also known as *solid-state devices* or *semiconductors*, allowed for great advances in the construction of computers. They were smaller, faster, generated less heat, and most importantly, cheaper. Correspondingly, the number of machines bought by companies grew dramatically. Companies' uses for computers expanded from accounting functions to sales management, manufacturing control, inventory control, and product design. Most company employees became familiar with some computer functions like payroll, but few ever saw the computer itself and most knew almost nothing about how computers worked. These first computers were called **mainframes**.

THE DEVELOPMENT OF MICROCOMPUTERS

The next truly significant evolutionary—some say revolutionary—step in computers came with the development of microcomputers in the 1970s. The rate of microcomputer development since then has been astounding and unparalleled in modern life. About every three years, microcomputers have gone through a significant improvement—doubling their computation power every 18 months—

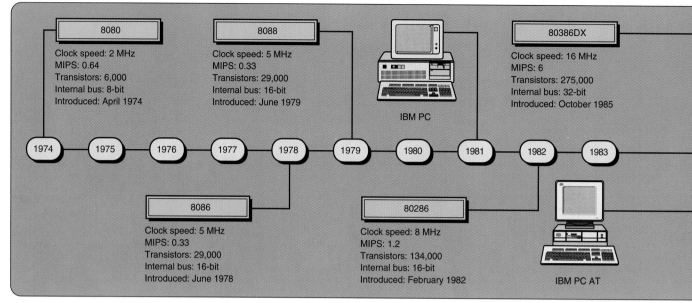

FIGURE 5.3 The lineage of Intel microprocessors. (SOURCE: *PC Magazine*, April 27, 1993)

while becoming less and less expensive to own and operate. This continual evolution has made the microcomputer an almost omnipresent device in modern society—found in everything from offices to wrist watches.

In 1971, Robert Noyce, who founded Intel Corporation, developed the first miniature electronic circuitry used in the microcomputer. The first microprocessor, called the Intel 4004, could process only four binary digits of information at a time; but the microprocessor "chip" was the size of a fingernail, required only a few volts of electricity, and could be mass-produced. In 1974, the Intel 8080 provided enough speed and power for developing a truly personal computer. Successively more powerful and faster microprocessors were introduced in 1978, 1982, 1985, 1986, and 1993 (see Figure 5.3)

The Altair 8800 was the first commercially available microcomputer. First marketed in 1975 by Ed Roberts, the Altair was sold for $395 as a computer kit for electronics hobbyists. At the other extreme was the IBM 5100, which came complete with screen, keyboard, internal storage for 16,000 characters, and either APL or BASIC (two computer languages) built-in for a price of nearly $25,000. The revolutionary aspect of the Altair was that the general public could purchase, program, and use a device that previously only large corporations or governments could own.

Soon after, in 1977, Steven Jobs and Stephen Wozniak, working out of their garage, founded Apple Computer Corporation. The Apple computer was the first widely sold microcomputer preassembled and delivered with monitors and keyboards (see Figure 5.4). In less than seven years, Apple Computer Corporation produced and sold hundreds of thousands of computers, particularly to schools and colleges, and became a *Forbes 500* company. IBM introduced its Personal Computer or "PC" in 1982. The IBM PC quickly set the standard in the business community for desktop computing and launched many efforts to "put a PC on every desk." Computing was controlled and done by workers themselves, rather than by computer technicians.

FIGURE 5.4 The original Apple II.

COMPUTER HARDWARE GENERATIONS

The evolution of computers can be examined within specific phases or generations. These generations are determined largely by the technology used to construct the computers (see Table 5.1).

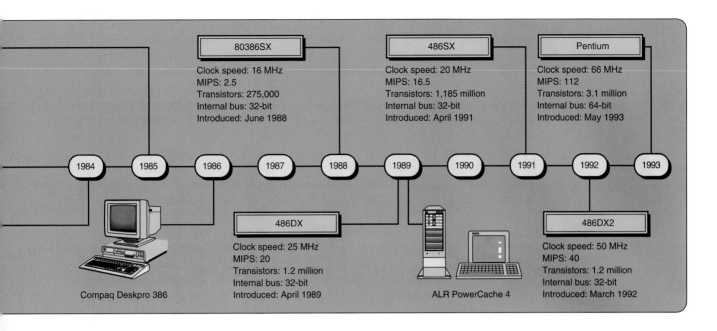

Table 5.1 Hardware Generations

Feature	Generations			
	1st	*2nd*	*3rd*	*4th*
Circuitry	Vacuum tubes	Transistors	Integrated circuits	LSI and VLSI
Primary storage	2 KB	64 KB	4 MB	16 MB
Cycle times	100 millisecs	10 microsecs	500 nanosecs	800 picosecs
Average cost	$2.5 million	$250 thousand	$25 thousand	$2.5 thousand

FIRST GENERATION: VACUUM TUBE SYSTEMS (1951–1958). First-generation computers were characterized by their use of vacuum tubes for data storage and processing; magnetic drums for primary storage; punched cards for input, output, and secondary storage; and programs written in machine language (see Chapter 6 on software). These computers were very large, slow, unreliable, expensive, and tedious to program.

SECOND GENERATION: TRANSISTOR SYSTEMS (1958–1964). Transistors replaced vacuum tubes in the second generation. As a result, second-generation computers were smaller, easier, and cheaper to use than first-generation computers. The internal memory of these machines was composed of tiny, doughnut-shaped magnetic cores strung on thin, intersecting wires. Magnetic tape and paper cards were devices for input and output, and printers with speeds of up to 600 lines per minute were developed. There were also improvements in software with the development of programming languages such as FORTRAN and COBOL, and the invention of operating systems (see Chapter 6).

THIRD GENERATION: INTEGRATED CIRCUITS (1964–1971). As a direct by-product of the space program, integrated circuits were developed that contained transistors photochemically etched into silicon chips. Third-generation computers used integrated circuits and displayed marked increases in speed with corresponding decreases in physical size. Major developments also occurred in the capabilities of peripheral devices and in the operating system. Multiprogramming operating systems with time-sharing capabilities were developed (see Chapter 6).

In 1960, the then three-year-old Digital Equipment Corporation (DEC) brought out the first minicomputer using integrated circuits—the PDP-1. The PDP product line grew; and the PDP-11, introduced in 1969, became the best-selling general-purpose minicomputer ever produced. In 1964, IBM introduced the System/360 family of computers, consisting of six computers with memory sizes ranging from 16 kilobytes (16 thousand) to over 1 megabyte (1 million). These computers were enormously successful because customers could upgrade from one member of the family to another without changing their application software. In the mainframe market, IBM, with the success of its System/360 family of computers, captured a 60 to 70 percent share of the market for large computers.

FOURTH GENERATION: LARGE-SCALE INTEGRATED CIRCUITS (1971–PRESENT). The fourth generation is usually understood to coincide with the development of the *large-scale integrated* circuit (LSI) and the *very large-scale integrated* circuit (VLSI). LSI is a single chip containing thousands of transistors; thus it is possible to place a complete central processing unit (CPU) on one very small chip. VLSI chips contain millions of transistors and usually combine the circuitry of different processing chips into one. Microcomputers were first introduced during this period.

A FIFTH GENERATION? Dispute exists about whether the fifth generation of computer hardware has yet arrived. As the very large-scale integrated circuits have become larger still, with tens of millions of circuit elements on a single chip—sometimes called very, very large-scale integrated circuits (VVLSI)—some claim this has ushered in the fifth generation. Others look at the developments in massively parallel computers (see Box 5.1) or neural networked computers and believe that these will be the hallmarks of the fifth generation.

A Closer Look BOX 5.1

 EMERGING TECHNOLOGY

PARALLEL PROCESSING

Parallel processing literally means executing several processing instructions at the same time (in parallel) rather than one at a time (serial or sequential processing), as happens in conventional computers. However, true parallel processing refers to the use of a number of general-purpose processors working together simultaneously.

Parallel processing architectures can be divided into two broad areas: *single instruction/multiple data* (SIMD) and *multiple instruction/multiple data* (MIMD). SIMD computers execute the same instruction on many data values simultaneously. An example is an *array processor*, which calculates a large two-dimensional matrix of values in parallel by applying the same operation to every element, such as in weather forecasting. MIMD, on the other hand, connects a number of processors that run different programs or parts of programs on different data sets. MIMD computers can be further subdivided into shared-memory and distributed-memory machines.

In shared-memory MIMD computers, all processors have access to a common memory pool via a shared high-speed bus or interconnection. This makes communication between processes easy; each processor leaves its answer in memory and tells another processor the address at which to find this answer. The only problem is that with many processors sharing the same bus, the whole system can be brought to a crawl by a processor having to wait to use the bus. This problem—called *bus contention*—limits the number of processors that can be supported. However, because they share a common address space, shared-memory systems are, for the most part, transparent to application programs. Thus, they are easier to program than other types of parallel machines.

In distributed-memory systems, each processor has its own memory store and communicates via high-speed links. In other words, every computing *node* is a complete computer, each with its own local memory. These machines are often referred to as *multicomputers*. Because a node cannot see into another node's private memory space, results must be passed between nodes over a communication network. The problems associated with the multicomputer are similar to that of the shared-memory MIMD; here, however, the speed of the network, rather than bus contention, is the primary determinant of performance.

Scalability is the biggest advantage of the distributed-memory systems over shared-memory systems. As we have noted, as shared-memory machines increase the numbers of processors, the overall system performance may suffer due to bus contention. With multicomputers, increasing the number of processors can almost linearly increase the computing power; 10 times more processors result in a comparable 10-fold increase in throughput.

The biggest problem with distributed-memory machines is the tremendous difficulty in programming them. This is the primary reason that the multicomputer market has been limited to the high-end realm of government and university research labs. One company, NCUBE, is exploring ways in which multicomputers may become commercially viable by using them as a database and computational server in the local area network marketplace.

With application needs becoming more complex, parallel computing seems to be the next logical step in fulfilling future computing requirements.

*E*MERGING TECHNOLOGY

...optical and biological computers

Finally, laboratory experiments with optical and biological computers hold promise for a true break with the past. Optical computers would use switched lasers rather than electronic circuit elements to control processing in the CPU, thereby achieving significant improvements in processing speeds. The inherent advantage in using light is that, unlike electricity, many light beams or circuits can cross and intermingle without any interference or heat generation. Biological computers would be "grown" from microorganisms rather than assembled from electronic transistors; still further reductions in processing size and increased functionality would result. History will have to be the judge as to which of these developments eventually becomes the fifth generation of computers.

▶ 5.4 CLASSIFYING COMPUTER HARDWARE

In attempting to understand computer hardware, a number of schemes or organizing approaches can be used. Computers can be analog or digital, big or small, old or new. Each of these ways of looking at computers will be examined in turn.

ANALOG VERSUS DIGITAL

Digital and analog computers differ in the way they represent data internally. **Digital** computers "count" discretely (using 0s and 1s), whereas analog computers "measure" continuously. A conventional clock face with rotating hands displays time in an analog fashion; a clock displaying discrete numbers is digital. Digital computers are much more widely used in businesses and homes than analog computers. They are faster, more accurate, and easier to program than analog computers and are a prime component of virtually all information systems.

In a digital computer, the binary number system is used to represent data; voltage is in either an "on" state (represented by the binary digit 1) or in an "off" state (represented by the binary digit 0). All data in a digital computer are stored, transmitted, and processed as ones and zeroes.

An **analog** computer, on the other hand, represents data through continuous measurement of some physical property such as voltage level, temperature, or pressure. Analog computers are used almost exclusively in process control and scientific applications. For example, analog computers are used in hydroelectric power stations to monitor the flow of water to the turbines that produce electricity and in oil refineries to control the "cracking" (refining) process. Even these applications, however, are yielding ground to the lower costs and ease of use of digital computers.

SIZE AND COMPUTING POWER

Because successive generations of computers have shrunk in size even as they have grown in computing power (and decreased in price), classifying computers by size has been somewhat straightforward; but classifying computers by computing power must be a *relative* exercise. After all, the largest computers of four decades ago have only a tiny fraction of the computing power of today's smallest palmtop computers. What is considered the most powerful processor today will certainly not be so in the future. It is common business practice, however, to position ideas or items on a scale. Thus, computing power scales for computers can be useful.

FIGURE 5.5 A Cray supercomputer.

SUPERCOMPUTERS. In a relative sense, **supercomputers** (see Figure 5.5) have the most processing power of computers generally available. The primary application of supercomputers has been in scientific and military work, but their use is growing rapidly in business as supercomputer prices come down. Supercomputers are especially valuable for large simulation models of real-world phenomena, where complex mathematical representations and calculations are required, or for image creation and processing as described in the case on moviemaking at the beginning of this chapter. Federal agencies use supercomputers to model the world's weather system in order to improve weather predictions. A simulation of a model as large and complex as this requires enormous speed and processing power. Supercomputers generally operate at 4 to 10 times faster than the next most powerful computer class, the mainframe. In an effort to increase processing speeds even further, some computer companies are linking together individual or *serial* processors into *multiprocessor* or **parallel processing** systems. These are discussed in greater detail in Box 5.1.

MAINFRAMES. **Mainframes** (see Figure 5.6) are not as powerful, generally not as large, and typically not as expensive as supercomputers. Mainframe computers are most often used by large corporations where data processing is centralized and large databases are maintained. Applications that run on a mainframe can be large and complex, allowing for data and information to be shared throughout the organization. A mainframe system may have anywhere from 8 to 200 megabytes (MB) of primary storage. On-line secondary storage may be achieved using high-capacity magnetic and optical storage media with capacities in the gigabyte (billions) to terabyte (trillions) range. Additionally, off-line storage is often accomplished through high-capacity magnetic tape systems. Typically, several hundreds or even thousands of on-line terminals can be linked to a mainframe.

MINICOMPUTERS. A **minicomputer**, also called a **midrange computer**, is a relatively small, cheap, and compact computer that performs the same functions

FIGURE 5.6 A mainframe computer.

FIGURE 5.7 A minicomputer.

as the larger mainframe computer, but to a limited extent (see Figure 5.7). Minicomputers are usually designed to accomplish specific tasks such as process control, scientific research, and engineering applications. For example, large insurance companies may off-load all printing tasks to a specialized print shop driven by a minicomputer. For this specific task, the print shop does not require as large a CPU or primary and secondary storage as does the company's mainframe.

Many larger companies find greater corporate flexibility by *distributing* data processing with smaller computers throughout organizational units instead of *centralizing* computing at one location. Minicomputers can allow a firm to distribute data processing throughout remote locations connected to each other through telecommunication links. Also, the minicomputer is capable of meeting the needs of many smaller organizations that would be wasting valuable corporate resources by purchasing larger systems.

WORKSTATIONS. For many years, scientists and engineers were dependent on mainframes, or in some cases *super minicomputers*, to support their research and design work. With the advent of microcomputers and personal computers (PCs), however, vendors began creating desktop engineering workstations, or **workstations** for short, to provide the high levels of performance demanded by these users. These workstations are typically based upon a RISC (reduced instruction set computer) architecture (described in detail in Section 5.5) and provide both very high-speed calculations and high-resolution color displays. They have found widespread acceptance within the scientific community and, more recently, within the business community (see Figure 5.8).

Wall Street investment firms are providing their quantitatively oriented analysts—sometimes called "rocket scientists"—with workstations in order to analyze trends in the financial markets and to identify promising investment opportunities. Market research organizations are similarly analyzing marketing data and evaluating alternative marketing strategies.

With the ever-increasing demand for computing power by users of all sorts, the distinction between workstations and personal computers is rapidly blurring. The latest PCs have the computing power of yesterday's workstation. Indeed, a low-end workstation is indistinguishable from a high-end PC.

FIGURE 5.8 A workstation.

FIGURE 5.9 Desktop, portable, laptop/notebook, and palmtop microcomputers.

MICROCOMPUTERS. The smallest and least expensive category of general-purpose computers is called **microcomputers**, **micros**, or **personal computers**. They may be subdivided into four classifications based on their size: desktops, portables, laptops and notebooks, and palmtops (see Figure 5.9).

A **desktop personal computer** is the archetypal microcomputer system. It is usually modular in design, with separate but connected monitor, keyboard, and CPU. A **portable computer** is a small, easily transportable micro that is rapidly being replaced by the **laptop** or **notebook** computer—a lightweight micro that fits easily into a briefcase. Portables, laptops, and notebooks are designed for maximum convenience and transportability, allowing users to have access to processing power and data without being bound to an office environment. Finally, the **palmtop computer** is a hand-held micro, small enough to carry in one hand. Although still capable of general-purpose computing, the palmtop is usually configured for specific applications and limited in the number of ways it can accept user input and provide output.

In general, micros have between 2 and 8 megabytes (MB) of primary storage, but it is not uncommon to find 16 megabytes of memory in many systems. Microcomputers typically have one or two floppy disk drives, one to accommodate a standard 3.5-in. disk and often a second one for the older 5.25-in. size, and one hard disk drive with 200 or more megabytes in storage capacity. More than any other computer category, the microcomputer has experienced the largest growth in both processing power and primary and secondary storage capacity—while simultaneously realizing the largest decrease in cost. As a result, the use of micros in both home and business environments has increased at a phenomenal rate, (see Box 5.2).

IT At Work BOX 5.2

A PC SYSTEM SIMPLIFIES CREDIT CARD PROCESSING

With credit card purchases topping 11.5 billion transactions in 1992, it appears that future growth in retailing must include processing sales and customer information as efficiently and quickly as possible. With the increase in computer technology creating a decrease in PC prices, even small businesses are finding that affordable systems can be purchased. Even companies that had previously been using scan-type credit card processors are finding advantages in changing to PC-based systems.

For a small wine accessory company called International Wine Accessories (IWA), electronic credit processing has replaced the equivalent of 2 employees (out of a total of 12 employees), thus saving the company over $50,000 per year. In addition, the new system enters the sales and customer information at the time of the sale and reduces the redundancy of copying the information two or three different times.

For the system used by International Wine Accessories, a clerk passes the card through a reader and inputs the sale price. The information is then sent through a network to a host computer of the credit processing company. The host computer relays the message that the card has been accepted or denied. The company uses the electronic draft recapture feature and therefore receives payment immediately. This saves valuable time that would be lost because of all the paperwork that was necessary

under the older, manual system.

Doug Walz, International Wine Accessories' product manager, stated that batch processing under the old system took half a day to process all the credit charges. The new system can handle 250 charges in 20 minutes. The new system not only saves valuable time but also reduces the three separate entry processes to one (eliminating costly errors) and integrates the information into the company accounting software. The time savings in the prompt processing of charge information has been estimated to save the company over 10 percent in bank fees under the new system. Utilization of this system has allowed International Wine Accessories to reduce expenses, reduce input errors, and speed payment and approval times.

This example shows how the use of a PC-based system can save companies both time and money. The same type of technology is also being used with ATM cards, bringing retail firms even closer to a paperless business. Technology will allow consumers to spend cash without actually carrying any, and retailers will decrease bad debt expense by collecting funds immediately.

Critical Thinking Issue: What impediments are there to firms like IWA adopting this new technology? ▲

SOURCE: Condensed from Lawton, G., "Make Credit Card Processing Easy," *PC Today*, September 1993.

A *personal digital assistant* (PDA) is a palmtop computer that combines a fast processor with a multitasking operating system using a pen rather than keyboard input (Figure 5.10). PDAs differ from other personal computers in that they are usually very specialized for individual users. In some sense, the PDA may be thought of as a computing appliance, rather than a general-purpose computing device.

EMERGING TECHNOLOGY

...computers that fit in your hand

The PDA case is very small, usually only four inches wide by eight inches long, and it weighs less than a pound. To facilitate input with such a small unit, PDAs are designed to work with handwriting recognition as well as software that may anticipate a user's intentions. For example, a user with a PDA simply has to jot down "Call John" for the PDA to bring up an address book with phone numbers for all entries with the name John. By selecting the appropriate entry, a

FIGURE 5.10 A personal digital assistant.

wireless link can be used to make the connection. Wireless connections are also used to link into a wide array of services such as electronic mail (E-mail), electronic information sources, and electronic paging. Infrared connection to local area networks may also be accomplished with PDAs. An even smaller form of computer is the smart card described in Box 5.3, and discussed in Chapter 7.

IT At Work BOX 5.3

"SMART" CARDS

One result of the continual shrinkage of integrated circuits is the "smart" card. Similar in size and thickness to ordinary plastic credit cards, they contain a small processor, memory, and an input/output device that allow these "computers" to be used in everyday activities such as personal identification and banking. In such applications, the processor's usual role is to act as a gateway to the card's memory.

Originally developed in France in the early 1980s, smart cards have evolved to the point where international standards are now in place and millions of cards are used for a variety of purposes (see also Box 3.3). Data can be continuously changed according to an algorithm in the card; and the password, known only to the cardholder, must match the password contained in the memory of the card. Knowing the password is not enough; having the card is not enough. Thus, one of the advantages of smart cards is that they are virtually tamperproof.

Uses for these smart cards are appearing rapidly. People are using them as checkbooks; a bank ATM (automatic teller machine) can "deposit money" into the card's memory for "withdrawal" at retail stores. Many states and private health maintenance organizations are issuing smart health cards that contain the owner's complete health history, emergency data, and health insurance policy data. Smart cards are being used to transport data between computers, replacing floppy disks. Adding a small transmitter to a smart card can allow businesses to locate any employee and automatically route phone calls to the nearest telephone.

A variety of smart cards from around the world.

Another form of smart card has become common with laptop and palmtop computers—the Personal Computer Memory Card International Association (PCMCIA) card. With computers that have corresponding PCMCIA connectors, these cards allow users to add capabilities such as faxing and connections to networks, to add more primary memory, or to run specialized application software.

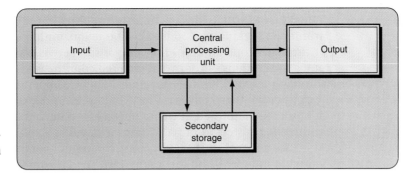

FIGURE 5.11 The hardware components of a computer system.

5.5 COMPUTER HARDWARE COMPONENTS

A **computer** is an electronic device capable of storing and manipulating data and instructions. A computer, or more accurately a **computer system**, is composed of **hardware**—physical equipment; media; and attached input, output, and storage devices—and **software**—instructions or coding that manipulates the hardware. Viewing a computer from a systems perspective, the hardware components may be classified according to their role: for *inputting* into the system, for *processing* or manipulating programs and data, for *storing* programs and data, or for *outputting* from the system (Figure 5.11). Software may be similarly classified by its purpose: to operate and control the hardware or to provide some useful result or functionality directly to the computer user.

Any system may be viewed in one of two ways: (1) looking at the inputs to the system and the desired outputs; or (2) knowing the internal processes or operations of the system. The first method is often called the **black box** approach; the second is the **white box** approach. For most people, a computer system is a black box. They know what they enter into the computer and what they expect to get from it, but they know little of the internal mechanisms that process the data into useful information. In this chapter, we will transform the view of a computer from a black box to a white box or, maybe more appropriately, to a transparent box, where we shall be able to examine and understand these internal mechanisms.

THE CENTRAL PROCESSING UNIT

The **central processing unit (CPU)** is the center of all computer processing activities. It is here that all processing is controlled, all data are manipulated, arithmetic computations are performed, and logical comparisons are made. The most important components of the CPU (Figure 5.12) are the **processor**, comprised of the arithmetic/logic unit (ALU), the control unit (CU), and primary storage or "memory."

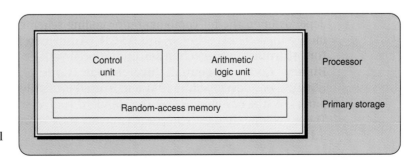

FIGURE 5.12 A central processing unit.

THE PROCESSOR. The **arithmetic/logic unit** (ALU) performs the four basic arithmetic operations of addition, subtraction, multiplication, and division, as well as the logical operations of the comparison between two pieces of data. *All* computer applications—from weather prediction to word processing—are achieved through these five simple operations. The ALU operations are performed serially (one after another), based on instructions from the control unit. For these operations to be performed, the data must first be moved from primary storage to the arithmetic registers in the ALU (registers will be explained shortly).

The **control unit** regulates the computer operations much as a "traffic cop" would. It interprets and carries out instructions contained in computer programs, selecting program statements from primary storage or memory, moving them to the instruction registers in the control unit, and then carrying them out. It controls input and output devices and data-transfer processes from and to memory. The control unit does not actually change or create data; it merely directs the data flow within the central processing unit. The control unit can execute only one instruction at a time, but it can execute instructions so quickly (millions per second) that it can appear to do many different things simultaneously.

PRIMARY STORAGE. **Primary storage**, or **main memory**, stores data and program statements for the CPU. It has four basic purposes:

1. To store data that have been input until they are transferred to the arithmetic/logic unit for processing.
2. To store data and results during intermediate stages of processing.
3. To hold data after processing until they are transferred to an output device.
4. To hold program statements or instructions received from input devices and from secondary storage.

Over the years, many methods of primary storage have been used. The first computer systems used vacuum tubes or magnetic drums. These devices were later replaced by magnetic ferrite cores—tiny doughnuts of iron about the size of the head of a pin with wires through their centers. Data were stored by directionally passing an electric current through the wires to "positively" or "negatively" charge the cores. Magnetized clockwise, the wires would represent an "on" state (binary 1), and magnetized counterclockwise, an "off" state (binary 0).

Today, **integrated circuits**, with millions of subminiature transistors, have replaced magnetic cores. Integrated circuits are interconnected layers of etched semiconductor materials forming electrical transistor memory units with "on–off" positions that direct the electrical current passing through them. Millions of these tiny transistors can be placed on a single circuit chip less than an inch square. Experimental work is being conducted with optical and laser memories to provide even greater storage capacities.

The "on–off" states of the transistors are used to establish a binary 1 or 0 for storing one **binary digit**, or **bit**. A sufficient number of bits to represent specific characters—letters, numbers, and special symbols—is known as a **byte**, usually 8 bits. Because a bit only has two states, 0 or 1, the 8 bits comprising a byte can represent any of 2^8, or 256, unique characters. Which character is represented depends upon the bit combination or coding scheme used. The two most commonly used coding schemes are **ASCII (American National Standard Code for Information Interchange)**, pronounced "ask-ee," and **EBCDIC (Extended Binary Coded Decimal Interchange Code)**, pronounced "eb-sa-dick." EBCDIC was developed by IBM and is used primarily on large, mainframe computers. ASCII has emerged as the standard coding scheme for microcomputers. These coding schemes, and the characters they represent, are shown in Figure 5.13.

Character	EBCDIC Code	ASCII Code	Character	EBCDIC Code	ASCII Code
A	11000001	10100001	S	11100010	10110011
B	11000010	10100010	T	11100011	10110100
C	11000011	10100011	U	11100100	10110101
D	11000100	10100100	V	11100101	10110110
E	11000101	10100101	W	11100110	10110111
F	11000110	10100110	X	11100111	10111000
G	11000111	10100111	Y	11101000	10111001
H	11001000	10101000	Z	11101001	10111010
I	11001001	10101001	0	11110000	01010000
J	11010001	10101010	1	11110001	01010001
K	11010010	10101011	2	11110010	01010010
L	11010011	10101100	3	11110011	01010011
M	11010100	10101101	4	11110100	01010100
N	11010101	10101110	5	11110101	01010101
O	11010110	10101111	6	11110110	01010110
P	11010111	10110000	7	11110111	01010111
Q	11011000	10110001	8	11111000	01011000
R	11011001	10110010	9	11111001	01011001

FIGURE 5.13 Internal computing coding schemes.

RANDOM-ACCESS MEMORY (RAM). Primary storage or memory that may be read or written to is known as **random-access memory (RAM)**. This is the place in which the CPU stores the instructions and data it is processing. The larger the memory area, the larger the programs that can be stored and executed. With newer computer operating system software, more than one program may be operating at a time, each occupying a portion of RAM. Most personal computers today have a minimum of 1,048,576 bytes of storage, normally referred to as 1 megabyte (MB) of RAM. (1 MB = 1,048,576 bytes = 2^{20} bytes.) With the wide adoption of Microsoft's Windows software, which requires substantial amounts of storage, it is common to find personal computers with at least 4 MB of RAM.

The latest trend in computing combines sound, graphics, animation, and video. Collectively known as "multimedia," these applications require substantial amounts of memory. As multimedia becomes more prevalent in the marketplace, personal computers will need a minimum of 8 MB of RAM, with 16 MB a more typical configuration.

The advantage of RAM is that it is very fast in storing and retrieving any type of data, whether textual, graphical, sound, or animation-based. Its disadvantages are that it is relatively expensive; and it is *volatile* or *dynamic*, that is, all data and programs stored in RAM are lost when the power is turned off. To lessen this potential loss of data, many of the newer application programs perform periodic automatic "saves" of the data.

Because RAM contains both data and instruction, various arrangements have been made to allocate storage between the two. In Box 5.4, there is a discussion of how storage is made available for the *disk operating system (DOS)*, the control software necessary for the operation of microcomputers (operating systems software is discussed in more detail in Chapter 6).

READ-ONLY MEMORY (ROM). We often need to be able to restore a program or data after the computer has been turned off or, as a safeguard, to prevent a program or data from being changed. For example, the instructions needed to start, or "boot," a computer must not be lost when it is turned off. **Read-only memory** (ROM) is used to fulfill these requirements. ROM cannot be changed or erased; if instructions or data change, a new ROM must be created to replace the old. This type of storage is *nonvolatile*; that is, the program instructions are continually retained within the ROM, whether power is supplied to the computer or not.

A Closer Look BOX 5.4

DISK OPERATING SYSTEM (DOS) MEMORY

In the early days of personal computers, most machines could access only 64 kilobytes (KB) of memory—65,536 actual bytes—due to a limitation of the early CPU chips. For several years, this was not a problem because the software programs of the day were not very large. However, introduction of the first IBM personal computer changed everything. This machine used the Intel 808X family of CPU chips (the 8080, the 8085, the 8086, and the 8088); the 808X family of chips could address up to 1 MB of memory, even though these early microcomputers rarely had more than 256 KB of memory actually installed. With this extra potential memory to work with, programmers began developing larger and markedly more sophisticated application packages. Users soon discovered their programs were running up against the 808X limit of 1 MB of addressable memory. This was especially so because the design of early microcomputers reserved some of the RAM storage for the CPU to communicate with input and output devices such as disk drive controllers and video display cards. Thus, substantially less than a million bytes were actually available to the user.

CONVENTIONAL AND HIGH MEMORY AREAS. The one megabyte of addressable memory available in the 808X chip was divided into two regions: a 640 KB portion commonly referred to as low DOS memory or *conventional memory*; and an upper 407 KB portion known as high DOS memory area or *high memory area*.

Conventional memory typically fills up very quickly. It is used by most application programs. Also, some specialized programs, known as *memory resident* programs, remain in conventional memory in order to be available to the user from within other applications. Furthermore, parts of the DOS program itself occupy conventional memory. Specialized programs that control specific pieces of hardware, called *device drivers*, reside in conventional memory. All the programs can be loaded into the high memory area, however, with the aid of special software known as a "memory manager."

However, before a memory manager can relocate these programs into high memory, other considerations must be taken into account. A system program that contains the *basic input/output system* (BIOS) for the computer is already located in the uppermost 64 KB portion of high memory. This BIOS contains code that runs when the computer is first turned on or when the system is reset. It also provides access to various hardware devices. Add-on cards, such as network interface boards and video boards, use high memory for the logical and physical interface needed for DOS.

EXPANDED MEMORY. After loading in the operating system, the device drivers, the memory resident programs, and the BIOS, more than half of the original megabyte of memory is filled and, thus, unavailable for application programs. Since more than 512 KB are necessary for many of today's more sophisticated applications, new technologies are needed to allow for the growth of software development.

The computer industry attempted to develop methods for going beyond the one megabyte barrier. The most successful, the result of a collaboration between Microsoft, Intel, and Lotus, was called *expanded memory specification* (EMS), which makes additional memory accessible from *within* the first megabyte. With the proper hardware and software, it became possible to add as much as 32 MB of expanded memory to any microcomputer.

EMERGING TECHNOLOGY

...users can now program—and reprogram—their own ROM chips

ROMs are manufactured by exposing a photosensitive material through a mask that contains the desired circuit pattern and then etching away the exposed surface. Once the mask is created, ROM chips are much easier and less expensive to produce than their RAM counterparts. However, sometimes it is desirable to make changes for a particular client or configuration. The **programmable ROM (PROM)** memory chip was invented to fulfill this need. A PROM can be programmed once (and only once) by a customer, thereby reducing the necessity of having to wait for a manufacturer to produce a special mask and production run for a customized chip.

Soon after the invention of the PROM, chip developers came out with the **erasable PROM (EPROM)**, which could not only be programmed in the field but also be erased for reprogramming. EPROMs require a special chamber that exposes the chip to a strong ultraviolet light to erase the settings of the chip. The **electrically erasable PROM (EEPROM)**, the latest development in programmable ROMs, overcomes this limitation by allowing the chip to be altered by applying electrical pulses, rather than exposure to ultraviolet light.

REGISTERS. Registers are specialized, high-speed memory areas for storing temporary results of ALU operations as well as for storing certain control information. One register, the *program counter*, is used to point to the next instruction to be executed (the term is really a misnomer as nothing is actually counted). The **instruction register** is a register designed to hold the instruction currently being executed. Two other registers in the control unit are the *memory address register* and the *memory buffer register*. When data or an instruction are needed from memory, the control unit places the address of the sought **word** (a logical grouping of bits in memory) into the memory address register and sends a "read" signal to the memory. The desired word is then retrieved from memory and placed in the memory buffer register, where the control unit can make use of it. Similarly, to write a word to memory, the control unit places the address for the word to be stored in the memory address register and the actual word of data in the memory buffer register.

THE CLOCK. The central processing unit, the arithmetic/logic unit, RAM, and ROM must work in perfect synchronization. The component that provides the timing for all processor operations is the **clock**, located within the control unit. Perhaps slightly misnamed, the clock does not provide the correct time of day to processing components—it provides only a steady beat to which components harmonize. Thus, it is really more like a metronome than a clock. The beat frequency of the clock (measured in megahertz [MHz] or millions of cycles per second) determines how many times per second the processor performs operations. All things being equal, a processor that uses a 40-MHz clock operates at twice the speed of one that uses a 20-MHz clock.

The design and makeup of the central processor components determine how fast the processor can operate. The size of the integrated circuit transistors on a chip directly affects the speed at which a transistor can switch from one state to another; all things being equal, the smaller the transistor, the faster it can switch. Furthermore, the more densely packed the transistors, the shorter the distance electrons must travel (about 11 inches in a nanosecond, or billionth of a second); the shorter the distance, the less time it takes for electrons to travel. Therefore, the smaller and the closer the transistors are, the higher the clock frequency that can be used. Chip designers are not just thinking of advantages in computer packaging when they squeeze more and more into smaller and smaller spaces; their main goal is to increase processing speed. The ever-increasing speeds of microcomputer chips are a testimony to the designers' success. Box 5.5 describes how a program actually executes within a CPU.

INPUT/OUTPUT

The **input/output (I/O) devices** of a computer are not part of the central processing unit; rather, they are channels for communicating between the external environment and the CPU. Data and instructions are entered into the computer through input devices; processing results are provided through output devices. Some of the most widely used I/O devices are the cathode-ray tube (CRT) or visual display unit (VDU), magnetic storage media, printers, keyboards, "mice," and image-scanning devices. I/O devices are controlled directly by the CPU or indirectly through special processors dedicated to input and output processing. Generally speaking, I/O devices are subclassified into secondary storage devices (primarily disk and tape drives) and peripheral devices (any input/output device that is attached to the computer). Peripheral devices are more fully explored in Chapter 7; secondary storage devices are described below.

A Closer Look BOX 5.5

HOW DOES THE CPU EXECUTE A PROGRAM?

PROGRAMMING INSTRUCTIONS. A program, containing the set of instructions a computer is to follow, is entered into the computer's primary memory. Each instruction—whether to add, subtract, move data, or compare—is stored in sequential memory locations. Programming instructions have several parts. In some languages, such as assembler (described in Chapter 6), the first part of the instruction, called an *operation code* or *op code*, directs the machine to carry out specific actions, such as add or compare data. The second part of the instruction, the *operand*, describes the locations where data will be found or where the results will be sent.

MACHINE CYCLES. Procedures for executing programming instructions involve two cycles that are synchronized by pulses from the cycle clock. These cycles are (1) the *instruction cycle*, which sets up circuitry to perform a required operation, and (2) the *execution cycle*, during which the operation is actually carried out.

There are two distinct steps in the instruction cycle: *fetch* and *decode*. With a "fetch," the computer locates an instruction in memory and places it in the control unit. The operation code is sent to the instruction register and the operand to the address register. During the decode step, the op code is decoded and sent to the ALU, along with any necessary data. The address counter is then incremented, informing the computer of the location of the next instruction.

In the execution cycle, data specified in the op code are manipulated by the computer. The data specified by the operand are taken from storage and sent to the proper device by the circuitry initiated by the op code. Manipulated data operations include adding, subtracting, or multiplying numbers, and moving data from primary storage to registers and vice versa. The results of these manipulations are placed either in other registers or in storage.

After the execution cycle, the process begins anew with the next instruction. This continues until the last instruction of the program has been executed.

SECONDARY STORAGE

Secondary storage is separate from primary storage and the CPU, but directly connected to it. It stores data in a format that is compatible with data stored in primary storage, but secondary storage provides the computer with vastly increased potential for storing and processing large quantities of software and data for long periods. Whereas primary storage is fixed in size and volatile, secondary storage is not. Whereas primary storage is contained in memory chips, secondary storage can be on many different forms of media, most of them much less expensive than primary storage. However, while primary memory is very fast in storing and retrieving data, secondary storage is relatively slower. These advantages and disadvantages are weighed when considering how and where to store programs and data.

Historically, secondary storage media included Jacquard's wooden cards, Hollerith's paper cards, and, later, punched paper tape. Today's storage media are almost exclusively magnetic or optical.

MAGNETIC TAPE STORAGE. In the earlier days of computing, **magnetic tape** (see Figure 5.14) was the most commonly used medium for input and secondary storage, especially with large computers. Magnetic tape units, referred to simply as *tape drives*, are used to read and record magnetic tape. They are similar to common audio tape drives.

Magnetic tape is kept on a large reel or in a small cartridge or cassette. The tape on reels is usually half an inch wide and 2,400 feet long. Today, cartridge

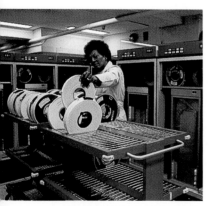

FIGURE 5.14 Magnetic tape drives.

tape is rapidly replacing the reel systems, which many organizations utilize. Tape in a cartridge or cassette is smaller and easier to use than the older reel-to-reel systems. Magnetic tape is a plastic ribbon coated on one side with an iron-oxide material that can be magnetized by electromagnetic pulses. Data are recorded as tiny magnetized spots on the iron-oxide side of the tape and may be played back many times or erased and reused.

The main disadvantage of magnetic tape is its potentially slow response time, since data are stored continuously on a tape which must be searched sequentially from the beginning to find the desired data. Even though many other types of secondary storage (see Box 5.6) have become competitive with magnetic tape, many systems managers are reluctant to change. Besides being a medium they feel comfortable with, tape systems are highly reliable. More importantly, tapes are one of the least expensive solutions to batch processing systems. Tape also is the medium of choice for the transfer of large quantities of data.

A Closer Look BOX 5.6

EMERGING TECHNOLOGY

NEW MAGNETIC TAPE STORAGE TECHNOLOGIES

Three new magnetic tape scanning formats (collectively known as *helical scan*) have recently been introduced. The first format is 4-mm digital audio tape (DAT), which has a much larger capacity than standard audio cassette quarter-inch tapes. Because it uses a smaller medium, there is a correspondingly a lower cost per megabyte; but DAT is still too expensive to supplant the current market for quarter-inch tape. The second format is identical to that used in household VCRs—the familiar 13-mm VHS format. The third format is an 8-mm cartridge tape format similar to that used in video camcorders.

MAGNETIC DISKS. Because magnetic tapes store data in a linear fashion and searches have to start at the beginning and sequentially examine each item of data to locate the item sought, researchers have been encouraged to find a faster means of storing and retrieving data. With magnetic tapes, it is not uncommon for a data retrieval search to take minutes or even hours, if many different tapes have to be searched. Moreover, tapes are very fragile and can be damaged easily when not properly wound on their reels; manual handling of tape reels can be costly and error prone. Because of this, developers sought a way to assign specific address locations for data on a magnetic medium, so that they could go directly to the address space (analogous to a street address in our postal delivery system) without having to go through intervening locations looking for the right data to retrieve.

The answer was found in magnetic disks, now commonly known as **hard disks** (see Figure 5.15). A hard disk is somewhat like an old phonograph record but is made of metal and coated with magnetic material. A *hard disk drive* is like a phonograph containing one or more of these metal-coated platters (usually permanently mounted). Each platter is divided into addressable concentric rings—known as **tracks**—with each track divided into addressable **sectors**, or sections of track. Magnetic read-write "heads," attached to arms, hover over the rapidly spinning platters. To locate an address for storing or retrieving data, the head

FIGURE 5.15 A magnetic disk drive.

moves inward or outward to the correct track, then waits for the correct sector to fly by underneath. When it does, the head "reads" the existing magnetic spots or "writes" new ones onto the revolving surface. High storage "density" and fast disk access times can achieve remarkable speeds.

In 1958, IBM marketed the first hard disk drive. The IBM RAMAC 305 consisted of 50 22-in. disks, capable of storing 5 million characters, or 5 MB. By 1980, Seagate Technology was able to fit the same storage capacity onto a single 5.25-in. disk. By 1990, a single 5.25-in. disk could store 1.2 billion bytes (or gigabytes). Data compression techniques are increasingly being used to double or triple these capacities without any physical modification to the disk or disk drive. In the meantime, typical disk access speeds have gone from tenths of a second to less than 10 milliseconds (thousandths of a second or milliseconds). Furthermore, since magnetic platters do not have to be thin enough to travel around tape capstans and rollers, as is the case with magnetic tape, disks can be made "hard" and thus less vulnerable to handling damage.

Unfortunately, magnetic disks are susceptible to head "crashes" because the head "floats" just above the platter surface. The heads of the IBM 3380 magnetic disk drive, for example, skim the surface at a distance of only 0.25 *micrometers* (millionths of a meter). At that distance, a tiny dust particle can appear to be a huge boulder to the drive head. Even though the technology that produces these low-floating heads on magnetic drives is fairly reliable, *disk crashes*, where the head actually touches the surface thereby damaging both the head and disk surface, still occur.

Most computers today—from supercomputers to laptop-size microcomputers—rely on hard disks for retrieving and storing large amounts of instructions and data in a nonvolatile (not lost when power is shut off) and rapid manner. When most computers are switched on or restarted, the CPU gets the bulk of its start-up instructions from magnetic hard disks.

In contrast to the large fixed disk drives of the past, a new approach is to combine a large number of small disk drives developed originally for microcomputers. These devices are called **RAID** (Random Arrays of Inexpensive Disks). Because data are stored across many drives, the overall impact on system performance is greatly lessened when one drive malfunctions. Also, multiple drives provide multiple data paths, thus improving performance. Finally, because of manufacturing efficiencies of small drives, the cost of RAID devices is significantly lower than the cost of large disk drives of the same capacity.

MAGNETIC DISKETTES. Even though hard disks are fast and effective, they are not very practical for transporting data or instructions from one personal computer to another. When developing the microcomputer, computer technologists turned to a soft or "floppy" version of the hard disk, usually called a **diskette** or simply a **floppy disk**.

Like the hard disk, the floppy disk is widely used, but it is found exclusively in workstations and personal computers. The floppy disk is a small, removable, flexible magnetic platter encased in a plastic housing. Similar to the hard disk, the floppy disk is also divided into concentric tracks, each of which is subdivided into sectors. However, unlike the hard disk drive, the read/write head of the floppy disk drive actually touches the surface of the disk. As a result, the speed of the floppy drive is much slower, with an accompanying reduction in data transfer rate. However, the diskettes themselves are very inexpensive (often less than 25 cents each for the somewhat older 5.25-in. diskettes), thin enough to be slipped into books or mailed, and able to store relatively large amounts of data. Like hard disks, they have evolved over the years, continually getting smaller while storing even more data (see Box 5.7). Presently 3.5-in. diskettes store 1.44 MB of data and cost less than $1 each (see Figure 5.16).

A Closer Look BOX 5.7

NEW FLOPPY DISK TECHNOLOGIES

New floppy disk drives are entering the market. These have capacities ranging from 5.25 gigabytes (billions of bytes or GB) for 3.5-in. disks to 9 GB for 5.25-in. disks, data transfer rates of approximately 2 million bits per second, and access times as fast as 6 milliseconds. Most improvements have come from increasing both the recording density and number of tracks per disk. Although backwardly compatible with today's current floppy formats, the high storage capacities of these new drives can be achieved only with a special metal floppy disk. These dramatic improvements in storage densities have resulted in considerable savings for the pioneering companies that have adopted them.

Some vendors are introducing robotic devices such as the one pictured to handle these new diskettes automatically, thus further increasing speed of access.

Robotic system automates cartridge handling.

OPTICAL TECHNOLOGY. Computer technologists, in their attempts to store even more data on smaller spaces for computer access, have recently concentrated on *optical* storage technology. The primary advantage of optical devices is extremely high storage density. Typically, much more information can be stored on an optical disk than on a comparably sized magnetic disk. Since a highly focused laser beam is used to read or write information encoded on tracks of an optical disk, the tracks can be placed much closer together. In addition, the amount of physical disk space needed to record an optical bit is much smaller than that usually required by magnetic media.

*E*MERGING TECHNOLOGY

...optical storage technology offers high reliability and capacity

Another advantage of optical storage is that the media itself is less susceptible to contamination or deterioration. First, the recording surfaces (on both sides of the disk) are protected by two plastic plates, which keep dust and dirt from contaminating the substrate surface. Second, only a laser beam of light comes in contact with the recording surface, not a flying head; the head of an optical disk drive comes no closer than 1 mm from the disk surface. Optical drives are also far less

FIGURE 5.16 8-in., 5.25-in., and 3.5-in. magnetic diskettes.

fragile, and the disks themselves may easily be loaded and removed. Three common types of optical drive technologies are discussed next: CD-ROM, WORM, and rewritable optical.

CD-ROM. **CD-ROM** (compact disk read-only memory) is the oldest of the optical technologies for computer storage. A close cousin to audio compact disks, CD-ROM technology is well established and refined. Whether used to carry audio or computer data, the format has been standardized by the pioneers in CD technology, Sony and Phillips. The disks themselves are made in much the same way as phonograph records—injection-molded in dies where all the format and data marks appear as raised surfaces on the interior faces. Because of their great capacity and low cost, they have become quite popular for a number of computer secondary storage purposes (see Box 5.8). One of the most exciting uses of CD-ROM is to provide high-resolution images and even full-motion video for multimedia applications. Multimedia is discussed in detail in Chapter 7.

IT At Work BOX 5.8

CD-ROM HELPS A SMALL COMPANY TO SURVIVE

Tom Kazalski, a sales engineer for CP Equipment Sales, uses the CD-ROM systems in his laptop computer to gain an advantage over the competition. He uses a program called Bookshelf, which contains *The Concise Columbia Encyclopedia*, *The American Heritage Dictionary*, *Roget's Thesaurus*, *Bartlett's Familiar Quotations*, *Hammond Atlas*, and *The World Almanac and Book of Facts*. If a letter needs to be written, Tom checks his spelling and adds a quotation to make the letter more memorable, to set it apart from others being written by competitors.

Tom also uses a disk called the *DeLorme Street Atlas U.S.A.* Because he travels three days a week, obtaining information on different areas within seconds makes him more efficient. The CD-ROM provides directions when an address is entered into the system. He can also find areas of interest, hotels, restaurants, gas stations, and other necessities while on the road. This type of technology saves him valuable time that was previously spent looking through maps, calling for directions, or driving around back streets. He uses the time saved to call on new prospective clients.

Other CD-ROMs used by CP Equipment Sales include *The National Yellow Pages Directory*, *Thomas's Register* (a directory of American manufacturers), *Accumail* (con-

taining ZIP codes for the entire nation, along with mailing information), and *Grolier's Encyclopedia* (21 volumes with 33,000 articles on one disk). This type of data would normally take up over 40 feet of shelf space, but with a CD-ROM system, a few diskettes hold all this information and sit on the employee's desktop.

The major advantage of CD-ROM technology for companies like CP Equipment Sales is the fact that an immense amount of data can be at the fingertips of any employee within seconds. Where it once took hours to search for particular information on an industry or company that the firm wished to solicit, the computer can now search for relevant information in a matter of minutes with a CD-ROM system. Tom Kazalski estimated that without the CD-ROM system, the company would have to hire an additional five or six employees to accomplish the same amount of work. This system has saved his company both time and money by speeding up the searching process and allowing three people to do the work of nine.

Critical Thinking Issue: What other kinds of information would be useful to put onto CD-ROMs? ▲

SOURCE: Condensed from Gutman, D., "Database in Your Briefcase," *Success*, October 1993.

WORM. CD-ROMs are very effective and efficient for mass producing optical disks, but are generally too expensive for unique, one-of-a-kind applications. For these situations, **WORM** (write once, read many) technology is more practical.

WORM technology is not as standardized as that of CD-ROMs. One format features an organic film containing a dye that absorbs a strong laser pulse, causing local vaporization and a bubble in the absorbing layer above the active layer. In another common design, a laser creates a pit in the material, exposing a highly reflective metal film below the active layer. Change in the amount of reflection is used to sense the absence or presence of a pit or bubble. Another design uses a stronger laser beam to melt a metal film surface, creating a hole (or pit) in the film that solidifies when it cools. In all cases, the storage capacity and access time are virtually the same as those with CD-ROMs.

EMERGING TECHNOLOGY

...users can now write onto as well as read CDs

REWRITABLE OPTICAL DISKS. CD-ROMs are best suited for mass producing many copies of large amounts of information that does not need to be changed. But often information needs to be changed or updated, and companies do not want to incur the expense of mastering and producing a new CD-ROM. In these situations, **rewritable optical disks** are needed.

Though many technical solutions are being developed, *magneto-optical disks*, similar to WORM disks, use the only approach that is commercially viable. When first manufactured, magneto-optical disks have a magnetic material with uniform magnetic orientation. At room temperatures, this material is insensitive to normal magnetic fields. However, when the material is heated to a higher temperature, it can be altered magnetically. To write to the disk, the optical drive head heats the target area with a laser beam and then applies a magnetic field to alter the magnetic orientation. When the disk area cools down, the data are "locked in" as varying magnetic orientations. The disk can be erased and overwritten, but overwriting with new data requires two passes: one to erase the data and another to write the new data. Unfortunately, this two-pass system makes typical write times twice as long as read times (typically 100 milliseconds).

To read information from this type of medium, a laser beam is focused on the recording layer. The magnetic orientation of the disk area changes the polarity of the reflected light—known as the *Kerr Effect*. By sensing light polarity, the optical drive is able to distinguish binary marks from spaces. The main problem with optical devices, however, is their slow access time. The large head used by optical devices is larger than CD-ROM or WORM heads, typically resulting in access times of about 100 milliseconds.

DATA CHANNELS

The CPU is connected to primary storage and to input/output devices (including secondary storage) through a series of parallel wires known as a **bus**. A bus may be thought of as a multilane highway through which data and instructions are carried to and from the CPU; each wire carries one bit of information. Data buses are usually identified by the number of bits they carry at one time (the most common personal computer bus is 16 bits). Furthermore, buses are classified by their function: address bus, data bus, or control bus.

Matching the CPU to its computer bus can affect performance significantly. In some personal computers, the CPU is capable of handling 32 bits at a time, but the data buses are only 16 bits wide. In this case, the CPU must send and receive each 32-bit word in two 16-bit chunks, one at a time. This effectively doubles data transmission times. The newest challenge to Intel's dominance in the microprocessor industry is the Power PC, described in Box 5.9.

A Closer Look BOX 5.9

EMERGING TECHNOLOGY

THE POWERPC

The PowerPC is a relatively new computer that combines the power of the workstation with the ease of use of a personal computer. In 1991, a team of computer architects from Apple, IBM, and Motorola worked to define a single architecture that would pave the way for future computing in everything from small portable computers to the most powerful supercomputers. The result of this work was the PowerPC architecture introduced in October 1991. IBM owns the rights to the PowerPC architecture and licenses it to Apple, Motorola, and other companies. In the marketplace, both IBM and Apple have released their own versions of the PowerPC. Internally, both are very similar. The PowerPC uses a new Motorola 6XX CPU, which is based on the RISC (reduced instruction set computer) chips IBM uses in its RS/6000 Unix workstations. The first four chips developed for the PowerPC were the Motorola 601, 603, 604, and 620. The first PowerPCs produced commercially by Apple used the 601 chip, running at 60 MHz. The standard configuration came with 8 MB of main storage, a 2.8MB floppy drive, and built-in support for a 16-bit color display.

The most significant enhancement introduced by the PowerPC over the RISC-based RS/6000 architecture was the extension to 64 bits. To review briefly, the smallest piece of information stored within a computer is called a bit. These bits are grouped into bytes (8 bits), half words (16 bits), words (32 bits), and double words (64 bits) to form the computer's representation of numbers, letters of the alphabet, memory addresses, instructions in a program, and so forth. The extension to 64 bits means that the all-important general registers within the microprocessor are now capable of holding 64 bits. Since programming instructions act (i.e., move, add, and so on) on the contents of registers, bigger registers mean that more information can be processed by each instruction. Additionally, 64-bit registers enable computer systems to manage more main storage.

▶ 5.6 COMPUTER ARCHITECTURES

The arrangement of components and their interactions is often called an architecture. **Computer architecture** descriptions, as opposed to information architectures (discussed in Chapter 2 and 10), include the instruction set and the number of the processors, the structure of the internal buses, the use of caches, and the types and arrangements of I/O device interfaces. The first three will be discussed in this chapter; I/O devices are covered in Chapter 7. The remainder of Section 5.6 will focus on the microcomputer, since personal computer architectures are more prevalent and thus likely to be more meaningful to the reader.

PROCESSOR INSTRUCTION SETS

Every processor comes with a unique set of operational codes or commands, such as ADD, STORE, or LOAD, that represents the computer's **instruction set**. An instruction is made up of *operations* (or operation codes or op codes), which specify the functions to be performed, and *operands*, which represent what is to be operated on. Today, two instruction set strategies, **complex instruction set computer** (CISC) and **reduced instruction set computer** (RISC), dominate the processor instruction sets of computer architectures. These two strategies differ by the number of operations available and how and when operands are moved into memory.

Originally, computers had relatively few instructions built-in; but as applications and application programming languages became more complex, there was a corresponding demand to enlarge the computer's instruction set. New commands were added as new requirements arose. In time, these came to be called CISC processors.

With a CISC processor, there are upwards of 200 unique coded commands, one for virtually every type of operation. The CISC design goal is for its instruction set to look like a sophisticated programming language. Inexpensive hardware can then be used to replace expensive software, thereby reducing the cost of developing software. The penalty exacted for this ease of programming is that CISC processor-based computers have increased architectural complexity and decreased overall system performance. In spite of these drawbacks, most computers in the marketplace—micros, minis, and mainframes alike—still use CISC processors.

The other, more recent, approach is RISC processors, which, as the name implies, eliminate many of the little-used codes found in the complex instruction

*E*MERGING TECHNOLOGY

...RISC architecture
offers better cost/
performance

set. Underlying RISC design is the claim that a very small subset of instructions accounts for a very large percentage of all instructions executed. The instruction set, therefore, should be designed around a few simple "hard-wired" instructions that can be executed very quickly. The rest of the needed instructions can be created in software. These will be somewhat slower than built-in instructions, but they are typically used so seldom that it does not matter.

This theory has been supported in practice; and RISC processor-based computers are known for their significantly higher speeds of execution. Because of this performance gain, the market trend is toward RISC processor-based computers—especially as designers approach what is felt to be the physical limits of further CISC performance. Many of the computers known as workstations are RISC-based.

BUS CONNECTIONS

The bus, together with the bit-size capacity of the CPU, is another important factor in a computer's architecture. The most common system architecture for personal computers, the **Industry Standard Architecture (ISA)**, originated with a 16-bit central processor and a 16-bit bus. Although processor power increased beyond 16 bits, the 16-bit bus remained. As a result, the newer, more powerful processors were bogged down with a "hurry up and wait" situation. More and more often, the processor was ready to carry out instructions, but the bus was not able to deliver the next instruction quickly enough. This led to the development of **Extended Industry Standard Architecture (EISA)** used by many personal computer manufacturers (except IBM) and **Micro Channel Architecture (MCA)** (which is IBM's approach). Both are somewhat successful in addressing the bottlenecks of ISA, but they still fail to overcome the constraints on certain speed-critical peripherals, such as graphic-intensive high-resolution color monitors.

As CPU speeds continue to increase, too much peripheral activity can bog down the CPU bus, causing something like highway gridlock. By separating the CPU bus from a high-performance *local bus*, speed-critical functions such as graphics and disk drive interfaces do not impede CPU performance. Local bus architecture is somewhat of a misnomer, since the use of a local bus actually occurs within one of the existing industry standards, that is, ISA, EISA, or MCA.

CACHE MEMORY

Many software programs are larger than the internal, primary storage (RAM) available to store them. To get around this limitation, some programs are divided into smaller *blocks*, with each block loaded into RAM only when necessary. However, depending on the program, continuously loading and unloading blocks can slow down performance considerably, especially since secondary storage is so much slower than RAM. As a compromise, some architectures use high-speed **cache memory** as a temporary storage for the most often used blocks, RAM to store the next most often used blocks, and secondary storage for the least used blocks.

Since cache memory operates at a much higher speed than conventional memory (i.e., RAM), this technique greatly increases the speed of processing because it reduces the number of times the program has to fetch instructions and data from RAM and secondary storage. Cache memory can be so important to performance that processors are often labeled as to their manufacturer, their clock speed, and the cache size within the processor. For example, a computer advertisement might state: "486/50MHz/256KB." This translates into an Intel 80486 microprocessor running at a clock speed of 50 MHz and utilizing 256 KB of cache memory as part of the processor. Box 5.10 gives additional information on the difference between clock speed and processor speed.

A Closer Look BOX 5.10

MEASURING A COMPUTER'S PERFORMANCE

Computer performance is generally rated by two dimensions: the clock speed of the processor, measured in megahertz (millions of cycles per second or MHz), and the rate at which instructions can be moved to and from the CPU along a data or I/O pathway. The clock speed determines how many operations the central processor can accomplish per second. Each operation, such as fetching an instruction, takes one or more cycles to complete. The term used to denote processor speed when actually *executing* instructions within a computer is millions of instructions per second, or more commonly, **MIPS**. In 1971, an Intel-based

personal computer performed at 4 MHz and less than 0.1 MIPS. Today's Intel-based personal computers can operate at 66 MHz and 100 MIPS.

Comparing computers by MIPS can be misleading, however, depending on *which* instructions were executed during performance testing. Many standardized performance test procedures exist to "level the playing field" for comparison purposes. And because those tests may be very different from everyday computing, MIPS numbers should be used only as a guideline to actual performance.

▶ MANAGERIAL ISSUES

A number of managers believe that, with the many advances in information technology, it is no longer necessary—or even possible—for them to learn about all the details of computer hardware and software. They feel that such knowledge can—and must—be left to technical specialists, while they concentrate on the business applications of the technology.

This is a dangerous position to take. Not to minimize in any way the importance of understanding the business needs for computing, an understanding of the technology that makes those applications possible is also essential. The challenge for managers in the 1990s, as their companies become more and more dependent on computers and information processing technology, is to become *more* knowledgeable about this technology, not less.

The material presented in this chapter is a beginning for such an understanding, but only a beginning. You, as managers, will be faced with many decisions in your careers that have technical components and, in some cases, are centrally dependent on making choices among competing and/or emerging technologies. Without an understanding of at least the principles that underlie information technology, you will be at the mercy of either your technical support staff or your vendor. The information in this chapter and the next four should help to put you on a more even footing, providing that you use it as a base upon which to build your knowledge. ■

KEY TERMS

Abacus *159*

American National Standard Code for Information Interchange (ASCII) *172*

Analog *165*

Analytic engine *160*

Arithmetic/logic unit (ALU) *172*

Binary digit/bit *172*

Black box *171*

Bus *180*

Byte *172*

Cache memory *183*

CD-ROM *180*

Central processing unit (CPU) *171*

Clock *175*

Complex instruction set computer (CISC) *182*

Computer *171*

Computer architecture *182*

Computer system *171*

Control unit *172*

Desktop personal computer *168*

Difference engine *160*

Digital *165*

Diskette/floppy disk *178*

CHAPTER HIGHLIGHTS *(L-x means learning objective number x)*

▼ The first truly electronic computer was developed in the late 1940s. The first commercial use of an electronic computer was by General Electric in 1954. The first commercially available microcomputer was marketed in 1975. (L-1)

▼ The four main types of computers are supercomputers, mainframes, minicomputers or midrange computers, and microcomputers or "personal computers." (L-2)

▼ A computer is an electronic device capable of storing and manipulating data and instructions. (L-3)

▼ The key computer hardware components are the central processing unit, input and output devices, secondary storage, and the data bus. (L-3)

▼ The key parts of the central processing unit are the processor; the arithmetic/logic unit; the control unit, including the clock; and primary storage. (L-3)

▼ The two main types of secondary storage media are magnetic (tape, hard disk, and floppy disk) and optical (CD-ROM, WORM, and rewritable optical disk). (L-3)

▼ The three most common approaches to classifying computer hardware are as analog or digital, by size and computing power, and by generation. (L-4)

▼ Computer architecture is concerned with the processor instruction set, the internal buses, and the use of memory caches. (L-5)

▼ Increased microprocessor computing speeds, the development of massively parallel computing architectures, and inexpensive RAID storage devices are some of the emerging hardware features that will enhance future performance. (L-6)

QUESTIONS FOR REVIEW

1. What *is* a computer?

2. What was Charles Babbage's contribution to computer development?

3. Who is considered to be the world's first programmer?

4. What is a Hollerith card?

5. Explain the significance to computers of the invention of the transistor.

6. What are the components of a computer?

7. What are the components of the central processing unit (CPU), and what functions are performed by each?

8. Explain the difference between RAM and ROM. Why do computers have both?

9. What function do registers play in a computer?

10. Describe the differences between primary and secondary storage.

11. What are the relative advantages and disadvantages of magnetic tapes and disks?

12. What are the relative advantages and disadvantages of magnetic and optical disks?

13. Define a bus, and explain how it affects microcomputer execution times.

14. What is a complex instruction set computer (CISC)? A reduced instruction set computer (RISC)? What advantages are claimed for each? Why?

15. Describe cache memory. Why have it?

16. What is the difference between analog and digital computers? Why have the latter obtained dominance for most applications?

17. List and explain the differentiating factors among the generations of computers.

QUESTIONS FOR DISCUSSION

1. Discuss the factors to consider when deciding what type of computer to acquire for a small business and for a large, multidivision firm.

2. What are some factors to consider in choosing a type of secondary storage for company data? When should a company keep data on-line and when can it access them in some other form? Will the prediction of a "paperless" office ever become a total reality? Why or why not?

3. Computing power is doubling about every 18 months.

Of those business areas that have not traditionally been computerized, which might have high potential in the near future, given the availability of lower-cost computing?

4. With computer technology improving as fast as it has, how can a company keep abreast of the latest in "high tech"? What factors should be considered when weighing choices between upgrading older equipment and investing in new equipment?

EXERCISES

1. Read a current edition of a popular business magazine (e.g., *Forbes*). Note those articles that focus on computer hardware or the results of business use of computer hardware.

2. Contact a local business. Ask if its computer hardware investment (in dollars) has been going up or down over the past few years. Ask them the reason why the business could be spending less because hardware prices are going down or more because it is buying even more equipment, lower prices not withstanding.

3. Look at a popular computer periodical (e.g., *BYTE*) from 10 years ago. What computer hardware capabilities were being predicted then for today? In what ways were the predictions correct? In what ways were they wrong?

GROUP ASSIGNMENT

No one type of computer is right for all applications. Different organizations require different types of systems depending upon their size, business, geographical dispersion, and so on. Consider the following three organizations.

▼ A medical group practice of five physicians.

▼ An independent men's clothing shop.

▼ A small, private, liberal arts college.

Have each class group form into two teams. Each team will then independently study and recommend a computer system for one or more of these organizations. Make whatever assumptions are needed, but be sure to document them. Prepare a final report specifying the system chosen, the approximate costs, and the rationale for the choice. Then have the teams exchange their reports and provide a brief critique of each other's report.

Minicase 1

Reengineering Aetna with Information Technology

Aetna Insurance Company has been one of the preeminent insurers in the United States since the Civil War. Currently, it is the nation's largest publicly traded insurance company, with $90 billion in assets. So Aetna must have been doing *something* right all those years. But "Mother Aetna," as it has fondly been called over the decades, is junking its past to save its future; it is turning to information technology to reengineer itself. Some of the initiatives, among dozens, are described in the following.

▼ A computer system that is linked to vendors allows Aetna employees to order their own supplies from their desktop terminals and have those orders processed and paid for centrally, without the need for the traditional costly, time-consuming review by the purchasing department. Aetna saved $20 million in 1992 and expects these savings to increase annually.

▼ The small business marketing group, which sells group life and health insurance to small businesses, started using laptop computers and new software to enroll prospective members at their own site and print out ID cards instantly. The entire process now takes less than half a day. Previously, the process required mailing handwritten applications to the home office and took two months. The company estimates it will save $700,000 annually, just in productivity gains.

▼ Aetna is installing image-processing technology at its Health Plan Service Center. Claims received by mail, which used to sit in limbo for a week or more, are scanned into a network of personal computers. Claims can be called up instantly by a service representative fielding questions from a customer. Lost files and end-

less paper shuffling are being dramatically reduced. After the claim is processed, the data are transferred to rewritable optical disks for permanent storage, and retrieval if needed.

Questions for Minicase 1

1. What type of secondary storage is likely used with the laptops in selling group life and health insurance to small businesses? What is an advantage of storing company data on a hard drive? On a floppy disk?

2. What is the technical advantage of having claims converted from paper to digitized imagery? What might be a disadvantage?

3. Why would Aetna use optical disks for permanent storage? Why use rewritable disks and not CD-ROMs?

4. Not all of the proposed changes have been enthusiastically adopted at Aetna. What might be some reasons for this?

SOURCE: Rifkin, G., "Reengineering Aetna," *Forbes ASAP*, June 7, 1993.

Minicase 2

Technology Enables Change at Fannie Mae

The Federal National Mortgage Association, commonly known as Fannie Mae, was founded by the U.S. Congress in 1938. Its purpose was to bolster the home mortgage industry by buying mortgages from banks and other issuers. In 1968, it assumed another mission: to make a profit as a shareholder-owned company. This dual role means that it must contend with government oversight as well as private company competition. In 1992, Fannie Mae bought about $76 billion worth of mortgages (making Fannie Mae the largest issuer of debt outside the U.S. Treasury) and made $1.6 billion in profit.

In the early 1980s, Fannie Mae executives recognized that information technology was becoming the strategic battleground for business. Like many others at the time, the company decided to build a single, enormous, mainframe-based system capable of providing virtually everything that everyone wanted. It took eight years and $100 million, but Fannie Mae persisted until development of its LASER system—the world's largest loan-accounting system—was finished. The problem was that LASER no longer addressed most of Fannie Mae's pressing business needs.

Its business had changed significantly. When the LASER project began, Fannie Mae was losing $1 million a day buying and selling mortgages. To turn things around, it started issuing mortgage-backed securities, having investors share the interest rate risk, to help smooth out earnings. To attract more buyers, Fannie Mae

started offering a wide array of security variations, "high-tech derivative securities," which were spun off of simple home loans. And it *worked*. By 1986, Fannie Mae had sold $61 billion of mortgage-backed securities. But that is not what LASER was designed and built for. In the meantime, Fannie Mae's main competitor was using a supercomputer to do sophisticated financial modeling and consistently beating Fannie Mae's prices.

This time, Fannie Mae turned to workstations interconnected so that their processing power could be pooled into more than an equivalent supercomputer. Accessed by microcomputers throughout the company, mortgage buyers can get real-time pricing data on securities. Within seconds, the system can calculate the highest possible price on which Fannie Mae is likely to profit, based on up-to-the-minute data. The system is so current, in fact, that it automatically invalidates a price offer if the buyer doesn't decide within 60 seconds. This system cost $3 million and took six months to develop.

Fannie Mae did not stop there. It developed a workstation-based financial analyst system, a "risk sharing" system, a "lender evaluation" system, and a "distressed assets" system. "I expect our systems to have a lifetime of about three years," said Franklin Raines, Fannie Mae's vice chairman. "By that time, they'll have been so heavily modified that they'll essentially be new systems. We shouldn't ever have to rebuild the entire platform."

Questions for Minicase 2

1. What could be the reasons Fannie Mae first turned to mainframes for the LASER system?

2. For what reasons do you think Fannie Mae later turned to workstations? Were there developmental reasons as well as technical reasons?

3. How could the systems based on workstations be as powerful as a supercomputer but cost so much less? What other types of benefits could the workstation approach provide?

4. What use is there for the LASER system as presently implemented?

SOURCE: Freedman, D. H., "Fannie Mae's Fast Footwork," *Forbes ASAP*, June 7, 1993.

REFERENCES AND BIBLIOGRAPHY

1. Freedman, D. H., "Fannie Mae's Fast Footwork," *Forbes ASAP*, June 7, 1993

2. Gutman, D. "Database in Your Briefcase," *Success*, October 1993.

3. Lawton, G., "Make Credit Card Processing," *PC Today*, September 1993.

4. Norman, J. R., *Forbes*, October 26, 1992.

5. Rifkin, G., "Reengineering Aetna," *Forbes ASAP*, June 7, 1993.

▶6

PROCESSING THE INFORMATION: COMPUTER SOFTWARE

Chapter Outline

Learning Objectives

After studying this chapter, you will be able to:

1. Define software in your own words, and explain the two major classes of software.

2. Explain what a programming language is, and differentiate among the generations of programming languages.

3. Name six common types of application software packages, and describe the functionality each provides to users.

4. State the purpose of systems software and its three major functional categories.

5. Describe operating system software and its three major functions.

6. Identify the different types of operating systems.

7. Describe the software development process and some of the tools used.

8. Explain the issues involved with software licensing.

▶ 6.1 "KILLER SOFTWARE" AT CYPRESS SEMICONDUCTOR

IMAGINE YOU ARE a manager at Cypress Semiconductor Corporation—a manufacturer of computer chips. A product you ordered from an outside supplier fails to arrive on time, but no one explains to you or senior management why it is late. As a result, a software program shuts down all the computer systems in the purchasing department. To get the systems back on-line, purchasing has to get a new commitment for delivery and explain the situation to you and the chief financial officer.

To many business people, the foregoing situation would seem a draconian, if not self-destructive, solution to solving internal problems. But this is not the view of Cypress Semiconductor Corporation, which has installed "killer software" in its systems to improve productivity based on the threat of a shutdown. Cypress managers maintain that the benefits gained from increased productivity outweigh the costs of an occasional shutdown. They believe that their manufacturing processes are so complex and interdependent that minor slipups can have enormous complications. Killer software, they say, draws everyone's attention to a problem right away to prevent a minor problem from becoming a major one.

The corporate systems at Cypress are based on "groupware"—software that lets employees working at computers share files and data, and continuously interact electronically. Groupware allows practically no secrets; what happens in one unit is not only accessible via the software to all others, it is often broadcast. Employee activities are monitored so closely, performance is measured in such detail, and data are shared so widely that vice presidents and managers can minutely review the

Computer usage at Cypress Semiconductor.

progress of nearly 11,000 workers—every employee except factory workers and laborers.

The unorthodox killer software, as well as a "take no prisoners" corporate culture, has made the computer chip maker a hot player. In the first year after the company installed killer programs, Cypress's record for on-time shipments rose from 65 percent to 90 percent. No raw materials remain in inventory longer than 10 days, as compared to as much as 18 months previously. By making sure that people get credit for what they do, the system, managers say, actually boosts morale. After visiting Cypress to see the system in action, one visiting engineering director said, "I was impressed by the enthusiasm of the people there. They're really focused on getting things done." Small wonder, with computer software bloodhounds at their heels.

SOURCE: Adapted from *BusinessWeek*, December 9, 1991, p. 70, and *InformationWeek*, January 6, 1992, pp. 22–28.

▶ 6.2 TYPES OF SOFTWARE

In the preceding chapter, computer hardware and its internal components were discussed. But computer hardware, by itself, is merely a collection of circuitry. It is not capable of performing a single act without instructions. These instructions are known as **software** or **programs**. If a computer system can be likened to a car, then the software functions as the driver.

The Cypress Semiconductor case gives a good example of how sophisticated software can be. Not only does the software process basic business transactions—inventory, purchasing, manufacturing—but, when things go wrong, it brings the problem to management's attention in a very dramatic way. It shuts down the application in question!

Software, in a very real sense, is at the heart of all computer applications. Computer hardware is, by design, general purpose; only with software can you tailor computers to provide specific business value. The chapters in Part IV give extensive examples of these applications, ranging from electronic mail to expert systems. To appreciate these applications, however, it is first necessary to understand the nature of software itself and the different types.

An **application program** is a set of computer instructions written in a programming language, the purpose of which is to provide *functionality* to a user. That functionality may be very broad, such as general word processing, or very narrow, such as a retailer's payroll program. Another example of a narrow, or "vertical," application program is one that is written solely to process student registrations at a university. It provides functionality (e.g., record keeping, file searching, and printing transcripts) for users (e.g., the registrar). An application program *applies* a computer to a need. *Application programming* is either the creation or the modification and improvement of application software. Performing application programming requires the use of programming languages. They are discussed in the following section.

Systems software is a set of instructions that act primarily as an intermediary between computer hardware and application programs (see Figure 6.1). Systems software may also be directly manipulated by knowledgeable users—as if the user were an application program. Systems software provides important self-regulatory functions for computer systems such as loading itself when the computer is first turned on, managing hardware resources such as secondary storage for all applications, and providing commonly used sets of instructions for all applications to use. *Systems programming* is either the creation or maintenance of systems software.

Application programs primarily manipulate data or text to produce and provide information, whereas systems programs primarily manipulate computer hardware resources. The systems software available on a computer system provides the capabilities (and limitations) within which the application software can operate.

Unlike computer hardware, which can be designed and manufactured on automated assembly lines, software must be engineered painstakingly by hand. Whereas computer hardware power grows roughly by a factor of two every 18 months, computer software power barely doubles in eight years! This lag presents a great challenge to software development and to information systems use in general.

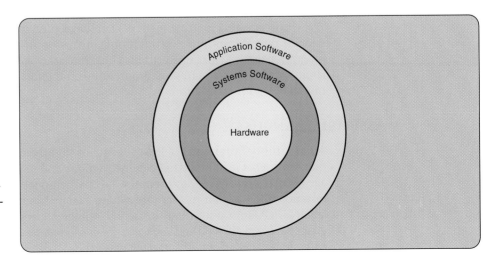

FIGURE 6.1 Systems software serves as intermediary between hardware and functional applications.

▶ 6.3 PROGRAMMING LANGUAGES

Programming languages are the basic building blocks for all software, both systems and applications software. They are the means by which programmers create software. Even though the distinction between programming languages as systems software and programming languages as application software is somewhat blurred—and some authors even claim that programming languages are a third class of software altogether—the function of programming languages is clear. Programming languages allow people to tell computers what to do. They are the means by which systems are developed.

Some people also regard certain general-purpose software, such as database management systems, as development software. This is so because applications are written using a programming language that is an integral part of the database management system. It is not unusual to find accounting applications and other business applications created through the use of a database management program.

Programming languages such as BASIC, COBOL, FORTRAN, Pascal, C, and C++ are examples of software used to develop business applications. Programming languages range in complexity from "low level" to "high level." The lowest-level computer language is machine code—the actual instructions understood and directly executable by the central processing unit.

MACHINE LANGUAGE

As discussed in the last chapter, digital computers represent and process data and instructions as binary numbers—as 0s or 1s. Combinations of these binary digits (or **bits**) are called **bytes**. This internal representation of instructions and data is **machine language**, that is, the instructions that are built into the computer. A program using this lowest level of coding is called a *machine language program* and represents the *first generation of programming languages*. A computer's central processing unit is capable of executing only machine language programs; machine language programs, in turn, are *machine-dependent* (the machine language for one model of central processor may not run at all on other models).

Because of its low level, machine language is extremely difficult to understand and use by programmers. As a result, increasingly more user-oriented languages have been developed. These languages make it much easier for people to program, but they are impossible for the computer to execute without first translating the program into machine language. The set of instructions written in a user-oriented language is called a **source program**. The set of instructions produced after translation into machine language is called the **object program** (see Figure 6.2).

Programming in a higher-level language (i.e., more user-oriented) is easier and less time-consuming, but additional processor time is required to translate the program before it can be executed. Thus, one trade-off in the use of higher-level languages is a decrease in programmer time and effort for an increase in processor time needed for translation.

ASSEMBLY LANGUAGE

An **assembly language** is a lower-level but slightly more user-oriented language that represents machine language instructions and data locations in primary storage by using *mnemonics,* or memory aids, which people can more easily use. For instance, the location in memory where "labor hours worked" is stored can be labeled HOURS, rather than the actual storage address—143,252. Assembly languages are considered the *second generation of computer languages*. Compared to machine language, assembly language eases the job of the programmer considerably. However, one statement in an assembly language is still translated into one state-

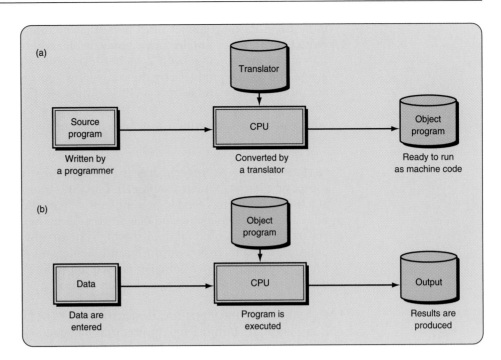

FIGURE 6.2 The translation process.

ment in machine language. Since machine language is hardware dependent and since an assembly language program is translated mostly on a one-to-one statement basis, an assembly language is still unique to a particular computer or series of processors.

Translating an assembly language program into machine language is accomplished by a systems software program called an **assembler**. An assembler accepts a source program as input and produces an object program as output. Translating the program is called *assembling* the program (see Figure 6.2).

HIGH-LEVEL LANGUAGES

PROCEDURAL LANGUAGES. *High-level languages* were the next step in the evolution of user-oriented programming languages. High-level languages are much closer to natural language and therefore easier to write, read, and alter. Moreover, one statement in a high-level language is translated into a number of machine language instructions, thereby making programming more productive. In general, high-level languages are more like natural language than assembly language, and they use common words rather than abbreviated mnemonics.

The two most commonly used high-level languages on mainframe computers are FORTRAN and COBOL. On microcomputers, BASIC, C (and C++), and Pascal are widely used. These languages are known as **procedural languages** because they require the programmer to specify—step by step—exactly how the computer must accomplish a task. Another type of high-level language, however, is **nonprocedural**; it allows the user to specify the desired result without having to specify the detailed procedures needed for achieving the result. A procedural language is oriented toward *how* a result is to be produced; a nonprocedural language is oriented toward *what* is required. An advantage of nonprocedural languages is that they may be manipulated by nontechnical users to carry out specific functional tasks.

COMPILATION. The translation of a high-level language program to object code is accomplished by a software program called a **compiler**; the translation process is termed *compilation* (see again Figure 6.2). Thus, to translate a program written in Pascal, a Pascal compiler must be available. Similarly, to translate a program written in C, a C compiler must be available. Although fewer source program statements are required with a higher-level language than with assembly language, the coding produced by the compiler is likely to be less efficient than with assembly language and *much* less efficient than with machine language. The main advantages of higher-level languages over assembly languages lie in the ease with which the user can write a program, make modifications to the program, and debug (fix errors).

INTERPRETERS. An **interpreter** is a compiler that translates and executes one source program statement at a time. Because this translation is done one statement at a time, interpreters tend to be simpler than compilers. Owing to this simplicity, more extensive debugging and diagnostic aids are frequently available. Interpreters are most often used on time-sharing systems and on microcomputers. Sometimes an interpreter is used during the debugging and testing phase of, say, a BASIC program. Then, a compiler is used to produce a more efficient object program for continuing use in a production environment.

EXAMPLES OF PROCEDURAL LANGUAGES. FORTRAN (**For**mula **Tran**slator) is an algebraic, formula-type procedural language (see Figure 6.3a). FORTRAN was developed to meet typical scientific processing requirements, such as matrix manipulation, precision calculations, iterative processing, expressing and resolving mathematical equations, and so on. FORTRAN is popular with mathematicians and engineers who write programs to meet their specialized scientific needs.

    COBOL (**Co**mmon **B**usiness **O**riented **L**anguage) was developed as a programming language for the business community (see Figure 6.3b). It is still one of the most widely used languages in the world today. The original intent of the developers of COBOL was to make its instructions approximate the way they would be expressed in natural English. In this way, the programs would be "self-documenting." Although COBOL is a very powerful language, many programmers consider it to be excessively wordy. Still, COBOL has over 30 years of acceptance and use; it will not be easily replaced in the foreseeable future. Since many busi-

---

A Closer Look BOX 6.1

MERGING TECHNOLOGY

OBJECT-ORIENTED COBOL

For 30 years, COBOL has been the dominant language in the mainframe community. Millions of applications have been written in COBOL, and it shows no sign of going away. What then is next? Developers at Micro Focus Corporation in California are bringing an object orientation to COBOL. They hope to have a formal standard for object-oriented COBOL approved by the American National Standards Institute (ANSI) by 1997. A PC version is being released in late 1994.

    One of the key benefits of an object-oriented approach to programming is the concept of usability. Code "objects" are created that can be used over and over again, thus lessening the burden on application developers. Mike West, a vice president at the Gardner Group, predicts busi-

nesses will use object-oriented COBOL as "a reengineering tool that will take libraries of existing COBOL applications and reengineer them with object-oriented assets, which can become a part of future architectures."

    This means programmers can use a building-block approach when they create new COBOL applications; they can reuse the vast amounts of COBOL code that has already been written. Object-oriented COBOL will enable businesses to take mission-critical applications that are now on mainframes and migrate them to client/server environments.

SOURCE: Adapted from "What's Next for COBOL?" *Information Week*, February 21, 1994.

nesses use COBOL as a common language for government reporting requirements, there are more COBOL programs currently in use than any other computer language. With developments like those described in Box 6.1 (see page 194), it is likely to be around well into the next century.

```
C   ***                        PAYCHECK PROGRAM                        ***
C   ***                                                                ***
C   *** This program calculates an employee's paycheck based on the    ***
C   *** number of hours the employee worked and base pay per hour.     ***
C   ********************************************************************

program Paychk

character * 12 Name
real Gross, Hours, PayRat
C
C  Prompt the user for the employee's name, hours worked, and rate of
C  pay per hour.
C
print*, '     PAYCHECK PROGRAM'
print*
print*
print*, 'Enter the employee''s name:  '
read*, Name
print*, 'Enter the hours worked:'
read*, Hours
print*, 'Enter the hourly pay rate:'
read*, PayRat
C
C  Calculate gross pay.
C
Gross = Hours * PayRat
C
C  Print the results of the paycheck calculations for this employee.
C  Then quit.
C
print*, 'Employee Name        ', Name
print*, '   Hours Worked       ', Hours
print*, '   Pay Rate           ', PayRat
print*, '   Gross Pay          ', Gross

stop
end
```

FIGURE 6.3 (*a*) A sample FORTRAN program that calculates each employee's paycheck amount.

```
                 IDENTIFICATION DIVISION.
                 PROGRAM-ID. SAMPLE.
                 ENVIRONMENT DIVISION.
                 INPUT-OUTPUT SECTION.
                 FILE-CONTROL. SELECT EMPLOYEE-DATA    ASSIGN TO DISK.
                               SELECT PAYROLL-LISTING ASSIGN TO SYSLST.
                 DATA DIVISION.
                 FILE SECTION.
                 FD  EMPLOYEE-DATA          LABEL RECORDS ARE STANDARD.
                 01  EMPLOYEE-RECORD.
                     05  EMPLOYEE-NAME-IN      PICTURE X(20).
                     05  HOURS-WORKED-IN       PICTURE 9(2).
                     05  HOURLY-RATE-IN        PICTURE 9V99.
                 FD  PAYROLL-LISTING       LABEL RECORDS ARE OMITTED.
                 01  PRINT-REC.
                     05                        PICTURE X(21).
                     05  NAME-OUT              PICTURE X(20).
                     05                        PICTURE X(10).
                     05  HOURS-OUT             PICTURE 9(2).
                     05                        PICTURE X(8).
                     05  RATE-OUT              PICTURE 9.99.
                     05                        PICTURE X(6).
                     05  WEEKLY-WAGES-OUT      PICTURE 999.99.
                 WORKING-STORAGE SECTION.
                 01  ARE-THERE-MORE-RECORDS   PICTURE XXX VALUE 'YES'.
                 PROCEDURE DIVISION.
                 100-MAIN-MODULE.
                     OPEN INPUT EMPLOYEE-DATA
                          OUTPUT PAYROLL-LISTING.
                     READ EMPLOYEE-DATA
                          AT END MOVE 'NO ' TO ARE-THERE-MORE-RECORDS.
                     PERFORM 200-WAGE-ROUTINE
                          UNTIL ARE-THERE-MORE-RECORDS = 'NO '.
                     CLOSE EMPLOYEE-DATA
                          PAYROLL-LISTING.
                     STOP RUN.
                 200-WAGE-ROUTINE.
                     MOVE SPACES TO PRINT-REC.
                     MOVE EMPLOYEE-NAME-IN TO NAME-OUT.
                     MOVE HOURS-WORKED-IN TO HOURS-OUT.
                     MOVE HOURLY-RATE-IN TO RATE-OUT.
                     MULTIPLY HOURS-WORKED-IN BY HOURLY-RATE-IN
                          GIVING WEEKLY-WAGES-OUT.
                     WRITE PRINT-REC.
                     READ EMPLOYEE-DATA
                          AT END MOVE 'NO ' TO ARE-THERE-MORE-RECORDS.
```

FIGURE 6.3 (*b*) An excerpt from a COBOL program that also calculates paychecks. Note that the COBOL program is different from the others—it operates on any number of data items, whereas the others just operate on one set of data.

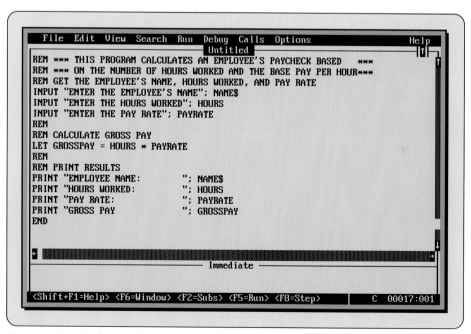

FIGURE 6.3 (*c*) This is the same payroll program written in BASIC. Notice that this version of BASIC does not require numbered lines; some other versions do.

```
program Paycheck (input, output);

{ *** This program calculates an employee's paycheck based on  ***
  *** the number of hours the employee worked and the base pay ***
  *** per hour.                                                 ***  }

var
   Name : string;
   Hours, PayRate, GrossPay : real;

begin   { Paycheck }

   { Prompt the user to enter name, hours worked and hourly rate. }
   write ('Enter the employee''s name: ');
   readln (Name);
   write ('Enter the number of hours worked: ');
   readln (Hours);
   write ('Enter the hourly pay rate: ');
   readln (PayRate);

   { Calculate gross pay.}
   GrossPay := Hours * PayRate;

   { Print the results of the paycheck calculations for this employee.
     Then quit. }

   writeln ('Employee Name:        ', Name);
   writeln ('Hours Worked:         ', Hours:8:2);
   writeln ('Pay Rate:             ', PayRate:8:2);
   writeln ('Gross Pay:            ', GrossPay:8:2);

end.    { Paycheck }
```

FIGURE 6.3 (*d*) A sample PASCAL program that calculates employee pay.

```
/***                        PAYCHECK PROGRAM                        ***/
/***                                                                ***/
/*** Program Paycheck calculates an employee's paycheck based on the ***/
/*** number of hours worked and base pay per hour.                  ***/
/********************************************************************/

main()
{
char    Employee_Name[40];
float   Gross_Pay;
float   Pay_Rate;
float   Hours_Worked
int     Temp;
char    c;
/* ---------------------------------------------------------------- */

    /* Prompt the user for the employee's name, hours worked, and rate
       of pay per hour. */
printf ("                        PAYCHECK PROGRAM\n");
printf ("Enter the employee's name: ");
    /* read characters into name array, one at a time  */
for (Temp = 0; (Temp < 40) && ((c = getchar()) != '\r') && (c != '\n');
   Temp++) Employee_Name[Temp] = c;
Employee_Name[Temp] = '\0';     /* put in end of string character */
printf ("\n");                  /* write a new line to screen     */

printf ("Enter the number of hours worked: ");
scanf ("%f", &Hours_Worked); /* read number of hours from standard input*/
printf ("Enter the hourly pay rate: ");
scanf  ("%f", &Pay_Rate);   /* read pay rate from standard input        */

    /* Calculate gross pay. */

Gross_Pay = Hours_Worked * Pay_Rate;

    /* Print the results of the paycheck calculations for this employee.
          Then quit. */

printf ("\n\n");
printf ("Employee Name          %s\n",    Employee_Name);
printf ("   Hours Worked         %8.2f\n", Hours_Worked);
printf ("    Pay Rate            %8.2f\n", Pay_Rate);
printf ("    Gross Pay           %8.2f\n", Gross_Pay);

}
```

FIGURE 6.3 (*e*) C program. Not as readable, but translation to machine language is easier.

BASIC (**B**eginners **A**ll-purpose **S**ymbolic **I**nstruction **C**ode), developed in 1964, is the primary programming language on millions of personal computers (see Figure 6.3c). Since 1981, it has been "bundled with" (i.e., comes with) the most popular microcomputer operating system, MS-DOS. It is not limited, however, to personal computers; BASIC can also be found on many mainframe computers. BASIC is a very easy language to learn and use.

Pascal, a programming language named after the seventeenth-century French mathematician Blaise Pascal, experienced tremendous growth in the 1970s and 1980s (see Figure 6.3d). Pascal has power, flexibility, and a self-documenting structure that makes it an attractive choice for academic, business, and scientific applications. In fact, many colleges and universities have used Pascal as the foundation of their computer science and information system programs. Many of their students graduate with a knowledge and preference for Pascal; however, it has not had widespread adoption for business applications.

The **C** programming language experienced the greatest growth of any language in the 1990s (see Figure 6.3e). A recent employment survey shows C programmers to be those most sought after by corporate America. Developers of proprietary software are interested in C because it is considered more transportable than other languages. A C program written for one type of computer can generally be run on another type of computer with little or no modification. When faced with the time-consuming and expensive task of translating programs to run on a dozen different micros and mainframes, C becomes an attractive choice. Additionally, the C language is easily modified. With object-oriented software development becoming more prevalent (see Section 6.6, on object-oriented programming), a superset of the C language, called **C++**, has been developed to support this new development paradigm.

NONPROCEDURAL LANGUAGES

A major development in computer-assisted programming is the emergence of non-procedural, or **fourth-generation languages** (4GL). These types of programming languages allow nontechnically trained users, as well as professional programmers, to specify the results they want and let the computer determine the sequence of instructions that will accomplish those results. In contrast, traditional programming languages require users and programmers to develop the exact sequence of instructions the computer must follow to achieve the desired result. Fourth-generation languages greatly simplify and accelerate the programming process as well as reduce the number of coding errors.

Application or program generators are also considered to be fourth-generation languages, as are query (e.g., MPG's RAMIS), report generator (e.g., IBM's RPG), and data manipulation languages (e.g., ADABASE's Natural) provided by most database management systems. They allow users and programmers to interrogate and access computer databases using statements that resemble natural language.

The term *fourth-generation language* is used to differentiate these languages from machine languages (first generation), assembly languages (second generation), and procedural, high-level languages (third generation). For a summary of the differences, see Table 6.1.

Natural language programming languages (for example, English or Spanish as opposed to "formal languages" like mathematics) are the next evolutionary step (see Section 7.12). Computer scientists have long sought to develop a programming language that could be used as easily as one's natural language.

These are sometimes known as **fifth-generation languages**. Translator programs to translate natural languages into a structured, machine-readable form are extremely complex, however, and require a large amount of computer re-

Table 6.1 Language Generation Table

Language generation	Features				
	Portable (machine independent)?	Concise (one-to-many)?	Use of mnemonics & labels?	Procedural?	Structured?
1st—Machine	no	no	no	yes	yes
2nd—Assembler	no	no	yes	yes	yes
3rd—High level	yes	yes	yes	yes	yes
4th—4GL	yes	yes	yes	no	yes
5th—Natural language	yes	yes	yes	no	no

sources. Nevertheless, their benefits to nontechnically trained individuals could be enormous. As indicated in Box 6.2, programming by nonprogrammers is rapidly becoming a reality.

A Closer Look BOX 6.2

 **E**MERGING TECHNOLOGY

PROGRAMMING BY NONPROGRAMMERS

Software developers have long argued about involving everyday users in the development of complex software programs. To some, everyday users are not sufficiently knowledgeable about software design and coding, let alone about which features to use or avoid using. To others, users are the ultimate authority on the intended functionality of the software; therefore, they should not only be involved but should drive the development process. Frustrated with costly development efforts and poorly functioning software, some software users are taking the matter into their own hands.

Fourth-generation languages and associated "productivity tools" allow them to do just that with minimal software training. General managers and information workers can design and program specific-function applications that incorporate their experience and specialized expertise. The

more scarce professional programming resources can be left to focus on critical, businesswide applications.

Programming languages and tools being used include those based on *visual programming*; Visual BASIC is one widely used example. With visual programming, users need not understand the vocabulary, syntax, or grammar rules of ordinary programming languages. Instead, they use a mouse to point, move, and assemble into a functioning program such "objects" as screens, data tables, decision points, or other program elements. The user neither sees nor needs to understand the resulting code created by the programming software. Altering or maintaining the resulting program is also done visually. Although the resulting software may not be efficient in terms of execution, it can be developed very quickly and used effectively in specific, ad hoc situations.

▶ 6.4 APPLICATION SOFTWARE

Application software consists of instructions that direct a computer system to perform specific information processing activities and provide functionality for users. Because there are so many different uses for computers, there is a commensurate number of different application programs available (see Table 6.2). These are special-purpose programs or "packages" that are tailored for a specific purpose, for example, inventory control or order entry. The word *package* is a commonly used term for a computer program (or group of programs) that has been developed by a vendor and is available for purchase in a prepackaged form. In addition, there are general-purpose application programs that are not linked to any specific busi-

Table 6.2 **Some Common Software Applications**

Accounts receivable and payable
Cost control and reporting systems
Cost flow analysis
Electronic data interchange
General ledger systems
Inventory control
Material equipment planning
Order entry
Payroll
Personnel administration
Project management and scheduling
Sales analysis
Sales forecasting

ness function, but instead support general types of processing. Seven widely used types of such application packages are *spreadsheet, data management, word processing, desktop publishing, graphics, multimedia,* and *communications.* Box 6.3 details some novel approaches that are being introduced in the selling of software packages.

IT At Work BOX 6.3

TEST-DRIVING SOFTWARE

International Business Machines (IBM) announced plans in mid-1993 to sell software through a novel approach. Intended to increase efficiency and cost savings for software publishers, the approach allows customers to walk into a store and pick up a CD-ROM containing 100 different software programs. Instead of buying individual boxes of software and returning some of them after fully evaluating them, customers can go home, evaluate any or all the programs on the CD-ROM, and decide which program to "buy." The purchase is made by calling an 800 number and receiving a decrypting code to "unlock" the product from the CD-ROM after proper information, including billing, is provided by the customer. Elaborate security systems will prohibit customers from turning around and lending their code and the CD-ROM to friends. IBM hopes it will be the next advance in selling computer software.

But the idea has perplexed distributors and industry observers. Some distributors see it as an effort to eliminate them. Distributors *want* people to spend a lot of time in their stores. And think of the administrative headaches as a result of keeping track of CD-ROM disks and updating them as individual software packages improve.

Industry analysts say most people like to go to a store to buy things and would have to go back to the store anyway to get newer versions. They doubt that dealers will carry the CD-ROMs. "[IBM is] doomed to failure," says one computer industry consultant. "It's not the way people like to shop. I think there will be a little bubble of excitement and then [it] will die."

Critical Thinking Issue: *Is* IBM "doomed to failure?" Try to find the answer by talking with salespeople in software stores. ▲

SOURCE: Adapted from *The Wall Street Journal*, July 19, 1993, p. B7.

SPREADSHEETS

In 1978, a Harvard Business School student named Dan Brickland enlisted some graduate students from the Massachusetts Institute of Technology to create a program that resembled an accountant's spreadsheet to run on a microcomputer. That software, called VisiCalc, became the first computer spreadsheet program. Not only did VisiCalc provide significant new capabilities for creating, manipulating, and printing spreadsheets, but it also revolutionized the way people perceived personal computers. Along with word processors, computer spreadsheets showed the business world that the personal computer was no longer a hobbyist's toy; it was a valuable asset to the organization.

Computer **spreadsheet** software transforms a computer screen into a ledger sheet, or grid, of coded rows and columns (see Figure 6.4). Users can enter numeric or textual data into each grid location—called a **cell**. They can then format the cells for appearance and perform mathematical functions on individual cells (or on rows or columns of cells). Most importantly, a formula or macro can also be entered into a cell to obtain a calculated answer displayed in that cell's location. The term **macro**, from the Greek meaning "large," is used to refer to a single instruction or formula that combines a number of other simpler instructions. Thus a user-defined macro can be used to enhance and extend the basic instructions and commands that are furnished with the spreadsheet. In general usage, spreadsheet packages are considered electronic versions of a pencil, paper, and calculator. In reality, they provide far more mathematical and formatting capabilities than are practical with paper and pencil. In essence, spreadsheets and the data displayed become *soft*. They become instantly malleable or changeable with built-in arithmetic and statistical functions.

Perhaps the most important feature of spreadsheet packages is the ability to store and retrieve cell calculations and formulas that they give the user. Since these formulas or macros can use information stored in other cells, a change in the value of one cell can cause all other related cells to be automatically updated accordingly. A macro may include arithmetic operations, statistical functions, logical operations, and textual operations. Thus, spreadsheet packages have an important "what-if" capability. Moreover, they give everyday users the ability to "program" their computers for unique tasks using simple, common accounting-like procedures and arithmetic formulas. In some cases, "intelligence" has been added to make the software even more valuable (see Box 6.4).

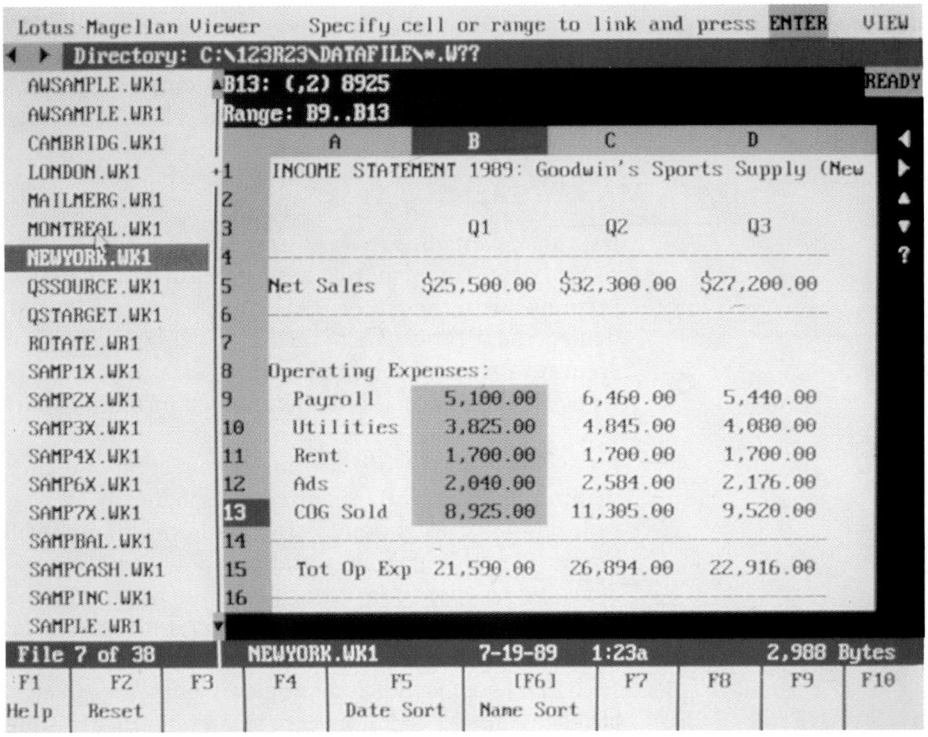

FIGURE 6.4 A Lotus 1-2-3 spreadsheet.

A Closer Look BOX 6.4

INTELLIGENT SOFTWARE AND PROGRAMMING AGENTS

Intelligent software agents are software components that communicate with their peers by exchanging messages in an expressive agent communication language. Agents have the potential to participate actively in accomplishing tasks, rather than serving as passive tools as do today's software applications. An example of an intelligent agent is the Wizard feature, found in Microsoft's Excel.

The Wizard is a built-in package capability that "watches" users and offers suggestions as they attempt to perform tasks by themselves. For example, suppose you are trying to format a group of spreadsheet cells or locations in a particular manner. If you are not adept at using the spreadsheet package, you might try to format each cell individually. A much faster method is to select the entire group of designated cells and then conduct the format once for all the selected locations.

Suppose a friend of yours was watching you format a task and noted that you worked on an individual cell basis. Suppose further that your friend was more of an expert on the software package than you were. Presumably, your friend would tell you that you were formatting unproductively. In a similar sense, the Wizard can detect your laborious, repetitive attempts and notify you that a better way exists or even take the next step and offer to complete the remainder of the formatting tasks for you.

In addition to generic agents such as Wizards, it is possible to program agents to do special jobs. Such tailoring is needed to empower people, to improve learning, and to increase productivity and quality. At the present time such custom programming is available only in research laboratories. However, in the future it is expected that both tools and procedures will be available for end users to build their own agents. A popular way to program agents is to code them in General Magic's Telescript language.

Whereas Wizard is an independent agent, other software agents work cooperatively; they can help exchange information and services with other software programs and thereby solve problems that cannot be solved alone. They can also execute tasks more efficiently.

Computer spreadsheet packages are used primarily for financial information, such as income statements or cash flow analysis. However, they also are relevant for many other types of data that can be easily organized into rows and columns. Another type of data manipulation is achieved through data management software.

Although products such as Lotus Corporation's 1-2-3 are thought of as primarily spreadsheets, they are actually much more. In addition to the spreadsheet functions, 1-2-3 contains data management and graphical capabilities (which are discussed next). Thus, it is more properly called an *integrated package*.

DATA MANAGEMENT

Data management software supports the storage, retrieval, and manipulation of related data. There are two basic types of data management software: simple filing programs patterned after traditional, manual data filing techniques and database management programs that take advantage of a computer's extremely fast and accurate ability to store and retrieve data in primary and secondary storage. Both types are introduced here and covered in more detail in Chapter 8.

FILES SYSTEMS. A **file** is a simple collection of related records organized in some manner. Files can be organized alphabetically, chronologically, or hierarchically in levels—just as is done using common, manual filing cabinets. An employee master file, for example, could contain records on each employee; an inventory file could have records on each inventory item. File-based data management software is typically very simple to use and often very fast, but it is difficult or time consuming to modify because of the structured manner in which files are created.

The most significant problems with file-based data management software packages are the isolation, repetition, and inconsistency of data. Comparing data between files is usually difficult because of the many data filing approaches (chronological vs. hierarchical), different data structures (e.g., employees filed by department in one case and filed by pay scale in another), and different data formats (e.g., measurement in inches in one file and meters in another) available. As a consequence, data are often repeated or duplicated in multiple files that are developed and used for different purposes. Database management software was largely developed to rectify such problems with file-based data management software.

DATABASE MANAGEMENT SOFTWARE. A **database** is a collection of files serving as the data resource for computer-based information systems. In a database, all data are integrated with established relationships. Thus, most of the problems that occur with separate file-based software packages are avoided.

Data redundancy is minimized since identical information need not be duplicated in multiple files. This reduces inconsistency as well as overall storage requirements. Because the data in the database are available in one location, accessing and maintaining them is much easier and can be done in a more consistent manner. Users do not need to be trained in six different file-based systems; they need only be trained in one database system. As a result, operational expenses can be significantly less in supporting, maintaining, and providing training for one database, as opposed to doing so for many individual files. Functionality is also increased considerably; data that used to be in disparate files and very difficult to compare can, with a database, be analyzed as a group for a number of possible relationships.

There is, however, an inherent problem with databases—data security. With all information in one location and potentially accessible in a common way to all users, invasion of privacy and other information abuses can occur unless proper procedures are established and enforced. These are discussed in more detail in Chapter 19. Also, those with access authority can alter information at will, unless proper safeguards are in place. Whereas file-based systems are local in character—designed and programmed for one particular purpose—database systems, because of their more global character, may lead to misuse unless special precautions are taken.

Another problem with database systems is the built-in complexity of the database. Most database management systems software (discussed in detail in Chapter 8) insulates users from this complexity, but database design and implementation can require specialized training and careful design efforts. On the whole, however, database software has enabled many organizations to move from traditional file organization to database organization, thereby enjoying the benefits of reduced data redundancy, improved data shareability, and increased data integrity.

In the microcomputer environment, database packages like dBASE, Foxpro, Paradox, and Access (see Figure 6.5) provide users with powerful tools for organizing, storing, and retrieving data and information. In fact, users can build many applications entirely within a database package, without the need to resort to programming languages like BASIC or Pascal.

WORD PROCESSING

Word processing software allows the user to manipulate text rather than just numbers. Earlier in the development of computers, this type of software was referred to as a **text editor**. Most of these early text editors were little more than computerized typewriters, but usually more difficult to use. Today's word processors, however, contain many productive writing features. These applications enable the user to prepare stylized reports, bulletins, letters, or other written documents easily and quickly (see Figure 6.6).

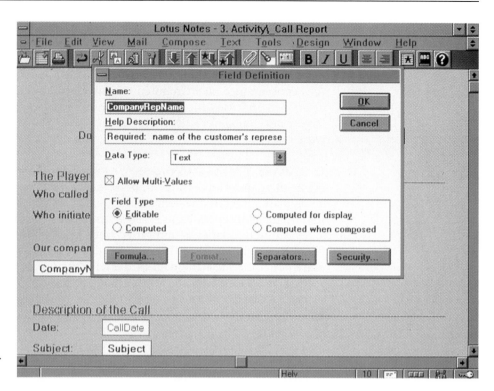

FIGURE 6.5 Database software.

A typical word processing software package, such as WordPerfect or Word for Windows, consists of an integrated set of programs including an editor program, a formatting program, a print program, a dictionary, a thesaurus, a grammar checker, and a mailing list program. Indeed, some of the better word processing programs now have integrated graphics, charting, and drawing programs. Most popular packages now provide menus and icons to help the user easily select commands, as well as built-in tutorials to train a user on how to best use the package's features. **Menus** are *lists* of options available to the user, and **icons** are *pictures* of these same features or functions.

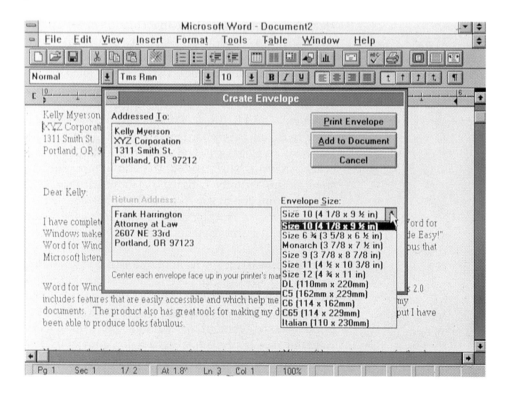

FIGURE 6.6 Word processing software.

Word processors are particularly valuable when extensive editing or revisions are needed. Text to be "processed" by the word processor is typed in without regard to line width or spacing; these are taken care of automatically by the software. Words, phrases, or sentences can be replaced, rearranged, or deleted by the user. At the press of a key or the click of a mouse, the text can be printed out as a draft or final copy. The printed text can be done using different formats, fonts, line widths, and page depths. Word processors can automatically center lines, provide page numbers, insert headers and footnotes, and create a table of contents or an index.

WYSIWYG (**W**hat **Y**ou **S**ee **I**s **W**hat **Y**ou **G**et) word processors have the added advantage of displaying the text material on the screen exactly—or almost exactly—as it will look on the final printed page (based on the type of printer connected to the computer). Thus, the document will appear on the video monitor with such features as indentations, line widths, variable spacing, character size and font, underlining, boldface, italics, and graphics. Once the user is satisfied with the appearance, the document can be stored on the computer's secondary, or long-term, storage for retrieval at a later time.

DESKTOP PUBLISHING

A level of sophistication beyond regular word processing is **desktop publishing**. In the past, newsletters, announcements, advertising copy, and other specialized documents had to be laid out by hand and then typeset. Now, special desktop software allows microcomputers to perform these tasks directly. Photographs, diagrams, and other images can be combined with text, including several different font styles, to produce a finished, camera-ready document. When printed on a high-resolution laser printer (described in Chapter 7), the output is difficult to detect from that which was produced by a professional typesetter (see Figure 6.7).

GRAPHICS

Graphics software allows the user to create, store, and display or print charts, graphs, maps, and drawings. Many users maintain that more information can be absorbed more quickly, relationships and trends in data can be spotted more easily, and selling points can be made more emphatically through the use of graphics. To help users create graphics, there are three basic categories of graphics software packages: presentation graphics, analysis graphics, and computer-aided design software.

Presentation graphics software allows users to create pseudo three-dimensional images, superimpose multiple images, highlight certain aspects of a drawing, and create freehand drawings. These packages typically contain drawing tools, presentation templates, various font styles, spell-checking routines, charting aids, and tools to aid in assembling multiple images into a complete presentation. Recent graphics packages are designed for everyday users as much as for trained graphics designers. Most even have extensive built-in tutorials and libraries of **clip art**—pictures that can be electronically "clipped out" and "pasted" into the finished image (see Figure 6.8).

Analysis graphics applications additionally provide the ability to convert previously analyzed data—such as statistical data—into graphic formats like bar charts, line charts, pie charts, and scatter diagrams. The charts may also include elements of different textures, labels, and headings. Some packages prepare three-dimensional displays. The quality of the display depends on the capability of the specific output unit used (monitor or printer) as well as the program. Once the display has been generated, it can be edited and modified as needed. The finished display can be displayed in different sizes, widths, or colors.

First Impressions

Summer 1994 | **Issue: Three**

A Link to the Future of Printing

Looking for an easy way to print high-quality materials directly from your computer, more quickly and less expensively than with other types of printing? Then the RISO Publisher is worth looking into.

The RISO Publisher is a Risograph digital printer linked to either a PC or Macintosh computer. This powerful combination offers three important document processing capabilities...high speed printing, input scanning, and stand-alone copy/duplicating. The RISO Publisher is a high-production system that allows you to achieve the real potential of desktop publishing...creating colorful documents in-house and on demand.

RISO's Computer Interface, which links the Risograph to your computer, makes printing easy because it allows the Risograph to emulate the HP LaserJet III™ and the Apple LaserWriter™. Therefore, you can print from virtually any popular software program. The Computer Interface uses the Microsoft True Image Postscript™ interpreter and supports the HP PCL 5™ printer language. There are also 35 Postscript and 22 PCL fonts resident in the Computer Interface, providing a faster printing

speed because these fonts don't have to be downloaded.

When using the RISO Publisher, you control copy count and color separations right from your software program. Because data is sent from the computer directly to the Risograph, you will obtain a noticeable improvement in the quality of the output. You can also use the Risograph's built-in scanner to scan images into your computer such as logos, line art, or photographs, then incorporate the images into your document. You simply re-size, re-position, add text or color, then print the finished piece.

The RISO Publisher does not require any special training. You print from your computer to a Risograph just as you would print to a laser printer. Print faster — 2 pages per second; more economically — as low as a third of a cent per page, and in color — 12 colorful inks available. And because you have the flexibility of a Risograph, you can print on a variety of paper stocks, weights, and textures.

The RISO Publisher will change the way you think about putting ink on paper. ≈

Risograph Tips and Tricks

One challenge that Risographers sometimes encounter is eliminating unwanted ink transfer or "setoff" on the back of their printed sheets. David Murphy, RISO district sales manager for the Western Region, provides the following tips.

1 Use the right paper.
There are some paper stocks that work best for photocopiers, others that are perfect for offset presses, and still others designed specifically for laser printers. The Risograph is no different. Although the Risograph handles nearly all paper stocks and weights up to 110 lbs., jobs containing heavy solids or requiring two-sided printing may need a more porous paper to absorb the ink. Other jobs may run beautifully on very smooth paper, a finish that produces superb image quality. By testing a variety of paper stocks, you can get the right paper for the right job. (See Issue 1 and 2 for additional information on paper.)

2 Adjust the scanning mode and density dial properly.
Originals with large text or dense graphics may cause setoff on some jobs. Fortunately, the Risograph is extremely flexible and allows the user to make adjustments to the scanning density. There is a **scanning** control dial for adjusting the density

(continued on page 2)

FIGURE 6.7 A newsletter created with desktop publishing.

Computer-aided design (CAD) software, used for designing items for manufacturing, allows designers to design and "build" production prototypes in software, "test" them as a computer object under given parameters (sometimes called **computer-aided engineering** or **CAE**), compile parts and quantity lists, outline production and assembly procedures, and then transmit the final design directly to milling and rolling machines (see Figure 6.9). **Computer-aided manufacturing (CAM)** software uses digital design output, such as that from a CAD system, to control production machinery directly. **Computer-integrated machinery (CIM)** software is embedded within each automated production machine to produce a product. In the aggregate, a design from CAD software is used by CAM software to control individual CIM programs in individual machines. Used effectively, CAD/CAM/CIM software can dramatically shorten development time and give firms the advantage of economies of scope. (For additional discussion of CAD, see Chapter 17.)

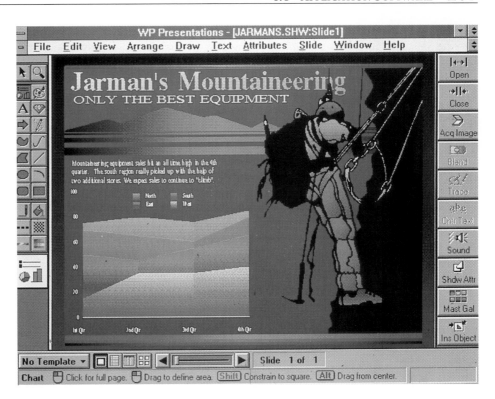

FIGURE 6.8 Presentation graphics.

MULTIMEDIA

Multimedia goes beyond just text and data. Multimedia is the combination of at least two media for input or output of data; these media include audio (sound), voice, animation, video, text, graphics, and images (see Section 7.8 in Chapter). Multimedia can also be thought of as the combination of spatial-based media (such as text and images) with time-based media (such as sound and video). This mix of computer media is revolutionary when compared to earlier computer input and output, which was limited to just one medium. Actually, motion pictures and television are types of multimedia; this section, however, focuses on *computer-based* multimedia—when computer software creates or controls multiple computer media. It is likely that *all* software would have used multimedia techniques had the technology that now makes them possible been available from the beginning of electronic computers. With recent technological advances, all software will likely

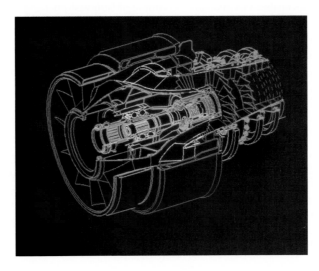

FIGURE 6.9 Computer-aided design.

FIGURE 6.10 A multimedia information kiosk.

be multimedia software in the future, at least to some extent. Box 6.5 shows how multimedia is helping in such areas as language learning.

There are two general types of multimedia software: presentation and interactive. **Presentation software** presents a sequential procession of information similar to a movie or television show. The order of events is fixed, although the presentation can be stopped and started. Speakers and trade show booths often use multimedia for marketing purposes. **Interactive software** allows a user to alter the sequence or flow of information—similar to looking at an encyclopedia or a photo album. Educational, interactive multimedia products are popular at museums or at information kiosks and show great potential for public and private education both within and outside of the classroom (see Figure 6.10). In the personal computer realm, Harvard Graphics, Freelance Graphics, PowerPoint, WordPerfect Presentations, ToolBook, and Hypercard are just a few examples of presentation packages that are available in the marketplace.

COMMUNICATIONS

Computers are often interconnected in order to share or relate information. Distributed computing, in fact, relies on many smaller computers sharing information over electronic networks rather than storing all the information in one central location. To exchange information, computers rely on communications software. **Communications software** allows computers located close together or thousands of miles apart to exchange data over dedicated or public cables, telephone lines, satellite relay systems, or microwave circuits. When the network is at one location, it is called a *local area network* (LAN); when dispersed across many locations, it is a *wide area network* (WAN). These networks are discussed in greater detail in Chapter 9.

IT At Work BOX 6.5

 **GLOBAL PERSPECTIVE**

LANGUAGE SOFTWARE

A small but growing number of people are learning or relearning to read and speak foreign languages from computers. Language educators are taking advantage of powerful new multimedia-capable PCs that include color, sound, and motion to design training programs that go far beyond both earlier generations of technology, such as cassette tapes, and older computer programs that replaced flash cards in drill-and-practice vocabulary building.

Most of the foreign language training programs speak words aloud while displaying the word or phrase and a related picture. They will repeat the word as often as the user clicks the mouse; they will jump forward or back; and they will display a translation on demand without thumbing through a dictionary. They will also never criticize. Some quiz the user and keep score, thereby making the students aware of their progress.

Col. Donald C. Fischer, head of the U.S. Defense Language Institute in Monterey, California, says his staff of

700 teachers is creating computer-assisted language teaching and refresher courses in languages from Arabic to Tagalog. Col. Fischer says, "The miracle is that, for a couple of hundred bucks, we can turn every word processor [in the Defense Department] into a multimedia language training device."

Many language training or refresher computer packages are commercially available for less than $400. Although the programs do not magically shorten the learning process, they are extremely convenient to use anytime and anywhere there is a properly configured microcomputer and a willing student.

Critical Thinking Issue: Do you think that, on your next trip to a foreign country, you can take a friendly computer with you as a translator (not just to act as a dictionary)? ▲

SOURCE: Adapted from *The Wall Street Journal*, January 25, 1993, p. B4.

When communications software exists in both the sending and receiving units, computers are able to establish and relinquish electronic links, code and decode data transmissions, verify transmission errors (and often correct them automatically), compress data streams for more efficient transmission, and manage the transmission of documents. Communications software establishes the switched routings needed to ensure successful "end-to-end" transmissions, establishes electronic contact ("handshaking") between distant computers, and assures that data will be sent in the proper format and at the proper speed. It detects transmission speeds and codes, and routes information to the appropriate hardware. Communications software checks for and handles transmission interruptions or conflicting transmission priorities.

Communications software provides functionality far beyond numeric computation, textual editing, and graphics. It provides access to a virtually unlimited amount of information from almost anywhere on Earth (and in space!).

Another type of communication-based software that is gaining increased popularity is known as **groupware**, an example of which was described in the Cypress Semiconductor case at the beginning of this chapter. Using packages such as Lotus Notes, groups of users working together on projects are able to see each other's screens, share data, and exchange ideas and notes in an interactive mode. Such capabilities greatly leverage the productivity of work groups.

▶ 6.5 SYSTEMS SOFTWARE

Systems software is the class of programs that controls and supports the computer system and its information processing activities. Systems software also facilitates the programming, testing, and debugging of computer programs. It is more general than applications software and is usually independent of any specific type of application. Systems software programs support application software by directing the basic functions of the computer. For example, when the computer is turned on, an initialization program (a systems program) prepares and readies all devices for processing. Systems software can be grouped into three major functional categories:

▼ **System control programs** are programs that control the use of the hardware, software, and data resources of a computer system during its execution of a user's information processing job. An operating system is the prime example of a system control program.

▼ **System support programs** are programs that support the operations, management, and users of a computer system by providing a variety of support services. System utility programs, performance monitors, and security monitors are examples of system support programs.

▼ **System development programs** are programs that help users develop information processing programs and procedures and prepare user applications. Major development programs are language compilers, interpreters, and translators.

Each of these types of systems software will be discussed in turn.

SYSTEM CONTROL PROGRAMS

OPERATING SYSTEMS. The main component of systems software is a program known as the **operating system**. The operating system supervises the overall operation of the computer, including such tasks as monitoring the computer's status, handling executable program interruptions, and scheduling of operations, which include the controlling of input and output processes.

On mainframes and minicomputers, which may perform several tasks at the same time, the operating system controls which particular task has access to the various resources of the computer. At the same time, the operating system controls the overall flow of information within the computer. In a sense, the operating system is like a traffic cop, controlling the flow of information.

On a microcomputer, the operating system controls the computer's communication with its display, printer, and storage devices. It also receives and directs inputs from the keyboard and other data input sources. The operating system is designed to maximize the amount of useful work the hardware of the computer system accomplishes.

Programs running on the computer use various resources controlled by the operating system. Examples of such resources are CPU time, primary storage or memory, input/output devices, and so forth. The operating system attempts to allocate the use of these resources in the most efficient manner possible.

The operating system also provides an interface between the user and the hardware itself. By masking many of the hardware features, both the professional and end-user programmer is presented with a system that is easier to use.

An increasingly desirable characteristic of operating systems is portability. **Portability** means that the same operating system software can be run on different computers. Portability has been partially achieved on microcomputers and small minicomputers. An example of a portable operating system, originally developed by AT&T, is the Unix system. Versions of Unix can run on hardware produced by a number of different vendors. Because of the various "dialects" of Unix however, there is no one standard version that will run on all machines.

The operating system itself consists of a set of interacting programs. The total set may occupy a relatively large amount of storage space. As a result, the total operating system is not placed in primary storage all at one time. The entire system, however, must be stored on a secondary storage device so that it can be brought into primary storage when needed.

OPERATING SYSTEM FUNCTIONS. The operating system performs three major functions in the operation of a computer system: job management, resource management, and data management.

Job management is the preparing, scheduling, and monitoring of jobs for continuous processing by the computer system. A **job** is a unit of work within a program. A **job control language (JCL)** is a special computer language found in the mainframe computing environment that allows a programmer to communicate with the operating system. Commands in a job control language are read by the supervisor, checked for errors, and then carried out by the operating system at the appropriate time. The job management function is provided by an integrated set of programs that schedules and directs the flow of jobs through the computer system. Job management activities include interpreting job control language statements, scheduling and selecting jobs for execution by the computer system, initiating the processing of each job, terminating jobs, and communicating with the computer operator.

Resource management is controlling the use of computer system resources employed by the other systems software and application software programs being executed on the computer. These resources include primary storage, secondary storage, CPU processing time, and input/output devices. Since these resources must be managed to accomplish various information processing tasks, this function is also called *task management*.

Data management is the controlling of the input/output of data as well as their location, storage, and retrieval. Data management programs control the allocation of secondary storage devices, the physical format and cataloging of data storage, and the movement of data between primary storage and secondary storage devices. Since most business computer applications require a great deal of input/ output and secondary storage activity, the use of data management programs greatly simplifies the job of programming business applications.

THE SUPERVISOR. The **supervisor** is a control program in the operating system that acts as an overall coordinating program. The supervisor, sometimes called the *executive* or *kernel*, directs the operations of the entire computer system by controlling and coordinating the (1) other operating system programs, (2) other systems and application software packages, and (3) activities of all of the hardware components of the system. Part of the supervisor resides in primary storage whenever the computer is operating; these programs are collectively termed *resident*. Other components of the supervisor are transferred back and forth between main storage and a secondary storage device. These programs, not permanently resident, are known as the *transient* portion of the operating system. It is easy to see that, if a large portion of the operating system is resident, there will be little time spent in retrieving additional components from a secondary storage device. However, a large resident segment will occupy a large amount of area in primary storage. Therefore, only the most frequently used programs of the operating system are made resident.

The supervisor monitors input/output activities and handles interrupt conditions (i.e., the temporary halt of a program execution to fulfill a system requirement, such as accessing a disk file), job scheduling and queuing, program fetching, and primary storage allocation.

A variety of operating systems are in use on computers today. Each has its own advantages and disadvantages. The operating system used on most personal computers is called **MS-DOS**, for **Microsoft-Disk Operating System**. Many minicomputers use the UNIX operating system. Mainframes use primarily the operating systems called **virtual memory system (VMS)** or **multiple virtual system (MVS)**.

Although operating systems are designed to aid the user in utilizing the resources of the computer, instructions or commands necessary to accomplish this are often quite cryptic. For instance, when the DOS prompt "C:\>" appears on the screen, it means "enter the name of the program you wish to execute." Mainframe operating systems are even more obscure with "= = =>" being just one example of a user-*un*friendly prompt. Needless to say, such commands are hardly intuitive, and a fair amount of time is needed to master them.

One of the appeals of the operating system on the Apple Corporation's Macintosh computer is that, through the use of menus and icons, the system is easy to learn and users can become proficient fairly quickly. This easy-to-use interface was originally developed at Xerox's Palo Alto Research Center (PARC) and used in their Star line of computers. It was first adopted by Apple in their Lisa microcomputers and later popularized in the Macintosh.

To provide a similar "user-friendly" interface to the user of DOS, Microsoft Corporation created a program that "sits on top of" DOS and provides a graphical interface similar to those of Xerox and Apple. It is called **Windows**; and, although it appears to function like an operating system, it is merely the front-end to DOS. Thus, it accepts inputs from the user by means of a mouse or keyboard and then must pass these on to DOS to be executed. With the development of Windows NT and Windows 95, DOS is now no longer necessary, for these versions of Windows are true operating systems, not merely "front-ends" to DOS. With the increased power and sophistication of these new operating systems, many companies are designing new networks, creating the client/server systems such as those described in Chapter 9.

SYSTEM SUPPORT PROGRAMS

SYSTEM UTILITY PROGRAMS. **System utilities** are programs that have been written to accomplish common tasks such as sorting records or copying disk files onto magnetic tape for backup. All operating system software includes utility programs of various kinds. For example, the MS-DOS operating system package includes utilities to check the integrity of magnetic disks, to create directories and subdirectories, to restore accidentally erased files, to locate files within the directory structure, to manage memory usage, to redirect output, and many others. These utilities have become indispensable in utilizing the computer.

SYSTEM PERFORMANCE MONITORS. *System performance monitors* are programs that monitor the processing of jobs on a computer system. They monitor computer system performance and produce reports containing detailed statistics concerning the use of system resources, such as processor time, memory space, input/output devices, and system and application programs. Such reports are used to plan and control the efficient use of the computer system resources. They are used primarily on large mainframe systems.

SYSTEM SECURITY MONITORS. *System security monitors* are programs that monitor the use of a computer system to protect it and its resources from unauthorized use, fraud, or destruction. Such programs provide the computer security needed to allow only authorized users access to the system. For example, identification codes and passwords are frequently used for this purpose. Security monitors also control use of the hardware, software, and data resources of a computer system. For example, even authorized users may be restricted from calling up certain devices, programs, and data files. Lastly, such programs monitor use of the computer and collect statistics on attempts at improper use.

SYSTEM DEVELOPMENT PROGRAMS

As discussed in the earlier section on programming languages, it is necessary to translate or convert user programs written in source code into object or machine code. This translation process requires the use of compilers or interpreters, which are examples of *system development programs*. Other examples are CASE programs, standing for computer-aided software engineering, which are discussed later in this chapter.

TYPES OF OPERATING SYSTEMS

To perform the many functions described previously, different types of operating systems have evolved. Some are used only in large computers or mainframes—for instance, time-sharing and virtual machine operating systems—while other types are applicable across a wide range of computers (see Box 6.6). The systems discussed next are multiprogramming and multiprocessing, time-sharing, virtual memory, and virtual machine.

MULTIPROGRAMMING AND MULTIPROCESSING. To increase the efficiency and utilization of computer systems, **multiprogramming** systems were developed. Multiprogramming involves two or more application modules or programs placed into main memory at the same time. The first module is executed until an *interrupt* occurs, such as a request for input. The input request is initiated and handled while the execution of a second application module is started. The execution of this second module continues until another interruption occurs, when execution of a third module begins. When the processing of the interrupt has been completed, control is returned to the program that was interrupted, and the cycle

A Closer Look BOX 6.6

OPERATING SYSTEMS BATTLE IT OUT

The first commercially successful microcomputer operating system was Digital Research's CP/M (Control Program/ Microcomputers). However, when IBM threw its marketing weight behind an operating system developed by the fledgling Microsoft Corporation, CP/M went the way of the dinosaurs. Although another start-up company, Apple Computer, had developed its own operating system, the real power in the marketplace was Microsoft's MS-DOS. Eight out of every ten application programs for the microcomputer were developed to run under MS-DOS. The choice of operating system drastically limited the choice of application programs. For a decade, Microsoft held virtual monopoly power in the PC world.

Today, all this is changing, with competition once again prevalent in the operating system market. Windows NT, Windows 95, Unix, NextStep, OS/2, System 7, and Workplace OS are all vying to dominate, but application programs are no longer locked to a particular operating system.

While Windows can't yet run Unix applications, some Unix vendors are convinced they need the ability to run Windows application software. This ability has been made available by certain third-party software emulation specialists like Insignia, which allows for Windows emulation on Mac, Sun, IBM, Next, and Silicon Graphics Unix workstations.

However, the most aggressive approach to bringing Windows and Unix together comes from Sun Micro-

systems' SunSelect division, which has developed Wabi. Whereas Insignia's SoftWindows product uses recompiled Windows source code from Microsoft, Wabi is an attempt to reverse-engineer Windows based on its functional specification. All operating-system-related functions (e.g., display, memory management, and interprocess communication) are handled by Unix. Instead of the Windows desktop, each Windows application running under Wabi appears in its own window and uses the Motif or Open-Look screen appearance rather than that of Microsoft Windows.

Not to be outdone, Apple is working on its own Mac translator to run both Unix and Windows applications. The first version, Macintosh Application Services (MAS), will run on PowerPC-based workstations running the PowerOpen system software. MAS will let PowerOpen workstations run standard Unix, Windows, or Macintosh applications. MAS will appear as a "Macintosh window" on PowerOpen-based PowerPCs. Macintosh applications in this environment will still have the distinctive look and feel of a Mac.

The real impact of these changes in operating systems will be on the user, in the form of easier access to a wider range of application and system software. This may not be the best news for some operating system and application software vendors; for users who have needed software they could not previously run, however, this new freedom of choice is a welcome change.

repeats. Because switching among programs occurs so rapidly, all programs appear to be executing at the same time. However, since there is only one processor (i.e., one CPU), only one can actually be in execution mode at any one time. This is called **concurrent execution**.

Multiprogramming is clearly different from **multiprocessing**. In a multiprocessing system, more than one processor—or CPU—is involved. Input/output devices may be shared by the processors, although each processor may also control some devices exclusively. In some cases, all processors may share primary memory (see Box 5.1). As a result, more than one CPU operation can be carried on at exactly the same time; that is, each processor may execute an application module or portion of an application module *simultaneously*. Multiprogramming is implemented entirely by software, whereas multiprocessing is primarily a hardware implementation, aided by fairly sophisticated software.

TIME-SHARING. Time-sharing is really an extension of multiprogramming. In this mode, a number of users operate on-line with the same CPU, but each uses a different input/output terminal. An application module of one user is placed into a partition (i.e., a reserved section of primary storage). Execution is carried on for a given period of time, called a *time slice*, or until an input/output request (an interrupt) is made. As in multiprogramming, modules of other users have also been placed into primary storage in other partitions. Execution passes to another application module at the end of a time slice and rotates among all users.

At times, there may be more users than there are partitions in main memory. When this occurs, an application module may be swapped out of memory after execution during its time slice. This means that the status of the module will be copied onto a secondary storage device and the partition filled with the next module in the queue. When a module is swapped out, the contents of any data-holding memory locations and of various registers showing the current status of the program are also saved. A copy of the original module is already contained on the secondary storage device, so it does not have to be copied. When it is required again, the module is loaded back into a partition, and the data-holding memory locations and registers are restored to their previous settings.

VIRTUAL MEMORY. Before beginning any discussion of virtual memory, it is first important to understand the concept of *paging*. In a paged system, an application program or module is divided into fixed-length portions called **pages**. Primary memory is divided into the same size areas as the pages. Such an area of primary memory is called a *page frame*. Thus, a page is placed into a page frame. The operating system maintains a *page frame table* that contains the current availability of all page frames. Additionally, a page table is maintained for each application module, indicating the locations in primary memory of each of its pages.

Since all pages are the same size and will fit into any page frame, memory allocation consists merely of determining the availability of the required number of page frames.

Virtual memory allows the user to write a program as if primary memory were larger than it actually is. The user is provided with "virtually" all the primary storage he needs. It is implemented by means of the paging system just described. With virtual memory, all the pages of an application module need not be loaded into primary memory at the same time. As the program executes, control passes from one page to another. If the succeeding page is already in primary memory, execution continues. If the succeeding page is not in primary memory, a delay occurs until that page is loaded. In effect, primary memory is extended into a secondary storage device. This allows the user to work with a pseudo, or virtual, memory that is larger than the physical memory. The disadvantage is that some delay will be encountered when unavailable pages must be loaded from secondary storage into primary storage.

A trade-off exists on the selection of page size. If the page size is large, then a poorer utilization of primary memory results, since fewer application modules may have pages residing in primary memory. For an individual application module, however, there will be less loading of pages from secondary storage. If the page size is small, better utilization of primary memory results, but more pages must be described in page tables and a higher paging rate may be required.

VIRTUAL MACHINE OPERATING SYSTEM. A **virtual machine** is a computer system that appears to the user as a real computer but, in fact, has been created by the operating system. A *virtual machine operating system* makes a single real machine appear as multiple machines to its users, each with its own unique operating system.

Each user may choose a different operating system for her virtual machine. As a result, multiple operating systems may exist in the real machine at the same time. Different versions of the same operating system may appear in different virtual machines. The most popular virtual machine operating system is IBM's VM. A control program supervises the real machine and keeps track of each virtual machine's operation. MVS and DOS are two other IBM operating systems. Each divides primary memory into partitions to hold different jobs. The *conversational monitoring system (CMS)* is a system that provides the user with a highly interactive environment coupled with somewhat easier access to translators, editors, and various debugging aids. VM may also be chosen to run in a virtual machine under the control program. VM offers greater flexibility to its users than prior mainframe operating systems and also gives each user the illusion of a machine solely dedicated to his or her work. However, compared to the strides made in personal computer operating systems, the VM system must still be considered a user-*un*friendly operating system.

With the advent of the Intel 80X86 and Motorola 60X40 CPU architectures, personal computer operating systems, such as Windows, Deskview, System 7, and OS/2, began to proliferate. These operating systems, combined with network operating systems such as Novell, Banyon Vines, and Lantastic, allowed for networked users to couple the VM advantages of a mainframe computer to the ease of use of the personal computer.

▶ 6.6 SOFTWARE DEVELOPMENT

Most programming today is done by taking a large process and breaking it down into smaller, more easily comprehended modules. This method is commonly described as *top-down programming, step-wise refinement*, or *structured programming*. These terms are essentially synonymous, all describing a basic approach to program organization and development. They describe a commitment to a logical, unidirectional program flow. Structured programming is part of a larger concept, called *structured design*. This is discussed in greater detail in Chapter 12.

Structured programming models a system similar to a layered set of functional modules. These modules are built up in a pyramid-like fashion, each layer a higher-level view of the system. Even with this approach, however, many systems have evolved into complex behemoths. Thousands of modules with cross-links between them are often dubbed "spaghetti code." Programmers have long sought assistance in improving software code organization; one answer has been the development of CASE technologies.

CASE

Computer-aided software engineering (CASE) is a tool for programmers, systems analysts, business analysts, and systems developers to help automate software development and at the same time improve software quality. CASE helps managers and analysts plan future systems, design the structure of these systems, and translate them into workable code.

CASE is a combination of software tools and structured software development methods. The tools automate the software development process, while the methodologies help identify those processes to be automated with the tools. A CASE tool can be described as any software tool that provides automated assistance for software development, maintenance, or project management activities. CASE tools often use graphics or diagrams to help describe and document systems and to clarify the interfaces or interconnections among the components (see Figure 6.11). They are generally integrated, thereby allowing data to be passed from tool to tool. They also capture system information and store it in a computerized depository known as the **data repository**. As modules are added, this data repository must be constantly updated for CASE to be effective.

Sometimes a distinction is made between "uppercase" CASE tools, which focus on the first steps in the systems development process of analysis and requirements definition, and "lowercase" CASE tools, which focus on the latter phases of detailed design and the construction of code.

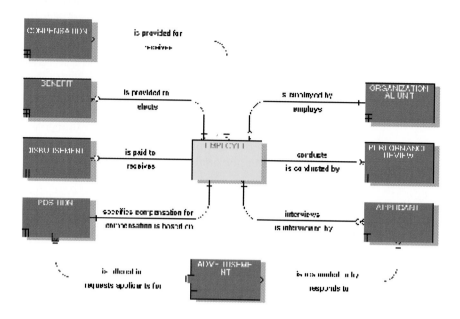

FIGURE 6.11 A CASE display.

CASE tools may be broken down into two subcategories: tool kits and work benches. A **tool kit** is a collection of software tools that automates one type of software task or one phase of the software development process. An example might be software to aid in specifically designing graphical user interfaces. A CASE **work bench** is a collection of software tools that are interrelated based on common assumptions about the development methodology being employed (see Chapters 12 and 13). A work bench also uses the data repository containing all technical and management information needed to build the software system. Ideally, work benches provide support throughout the entire software development process and help produce a documented and executable system.

ADVANTAGES AND DISADVANTAGES. What are the benefits of using CASE? Several major advantages have been cited:

1. CASE improves productivity by helping the analyst understand the problem and how to solve it in an organized manner.
2. CASE facilitates joint application and design (JAD) sessions, resulting in better interaction among users and information system professionals.
3. CASE makes it easier to create prototypes, so that users can see what they are going to get at an early stage in the development process.
4. CASE makes it easier to make system design changes as circumstances change.

REENGINEERING

...CASE tools help with business reengineering

Well-designed software engineering tools help improve the productivity, effectiveness, and quality of information systems by saving time. Tasks that are repeated may be automated with CASE tools, for example, drawing data flow diagrams (a graphical technique for representing the system under development) or drawing system charts. *Effectiveness* results from forcing the developer to do the task in an organized, consistent manner as dictated by the CASE tool. A useful by-product is greater accuracy, since all tasks are examined by the tool for correctness and completeness. As a consequence, if CASE improves the processes that make up an information system, then the *quality* of the information system will also be improved.

Because of the graphical nature of most CASE tools and the ability to produce working prototypes quickly, nontechnically trained users can participate more actively in the development process. They can see what the completed system will look like before it is actually constructed, resulting in fewer misunderstandings and design mistakes.

Using CASE can help make revising an application easier. When revisions are needed, one needs only change specifications in the data repository rather than the source code itself. This also enables prototype systems to be developed more quickly and easily. Some CASE tools help generate source code directly, and the benefits can be significant. Not only is there time saved by not having to create or maintain source code, but there are also added benefits such as standardization and consistency. Modules created by this method are more likely to be compatible with other modules and work together more harmoniously.

On the downside, a lack of management support for CASE within organizations can be a problem. CASE is very expensive to install, train developers on, and use properly. Many companies do not know how to measure quality or productivity in software development and therefore find it difficult to justify the expense of implementing CASE. Moreover, receptivity of professional programmers can greatly influence the effectiveness of CASE. Many programmers who have mastered one approach to development are hesitant to shift to a new method.

Additionally, the insistence on one structured method in a CASE program can be a double-edged sword: good for standardization but potentially stifling for creativity and flexibility. If an analyst is in an organization that does not use a structured methodology to accompany CASE, then the effectiveness of CASE will be greatly reduced. Creating software often entails imaginative solutions to procedural problems; being constrained to one methodology and the tools included in the CASE package can be constricting. On the other hand, some CASE tool kits are only graphic drawing programs or limited documentation tools. Vendors frequently claim that their CASE tool kits will support more functions than they actually do, or vendors promise more productivity improvements than their tool kits can achieve. Finally, and not surprisingly, CASE tools cannot overcome poor, incomplete, or inconsistent specifications. It is possible to use CASE software to produce a program efficiently that will ultimately be unusable by the user.

OBJECT-ORIENTED PROGRAMMING

Structured programming models a system's *behavior*. **Object-oriented programming** (often called OOP) models a system as a set of cooperating objects. Like structured programming, object-oriented programming tries to manage the behavioral complexity of a system, but it goes beyond structured programming in also trying to manage the informational complexity of a system. Because object-oriented programming models both the behavioral and informational complexity of a system, the system can be much better organized than if it were simply well structured. Systems that are better organized are easier to understand, control, and evolve. Thus, using an object-oriented approach goes far beyond mere programming. It involves the operating systems environment, object-oriented databases, and even a whole new way of looking at business applications.

THE OBJECT MODEL. An **object** is an entity that represents people, places, concepts, or things—either abstract or concrete. The characteristics of these objects are referred to as attributes and methods. **Attributes** describe an object; attribute values give the state of that object. For example, serial number, model, color, and year are just a few attributes for an object called "Honda"; the state of this object would be a serial number M345Z45, Accord, red, and 1994. **Methods** are the procedures or behaviors performed by an object that will change the state of that object (i.e., change the attribute values). Methods are sometimes referred to as the operations that manipulate the object.

Objects within a program must cooperate. To help accomplish coordination, methods also produce **messages**, which are sent to other objects. These messages may activate methods in the recipient objects; in turn, the activated methods of recipient objects may produce messages for still other objects. A message allows for one object to communicate and interact with another object.

A **class** is a group of objects that share the same attributes and behaviors. Every object is an instance or member of some class (even a class of one). Classes may also be thought of as templates for a set of similar objects; classes may be part of a hierarchical structure from which super- and subclasses are defined. For instance, an "automobile" class may have a superclass called "vehicle" and a subclass called "convertible."

One strength of object-oriented programming is the mechanisms that promote reusability. Thus an object, once created, can be used again and again, substantially increasing the productivity of the development staff. **Inheritance** is the concept that any class, once defined, may derive subclasses that inherit all the attributes, methods, and messages of the superclass. The subclass can override or add to the definitions of the superclass attributes and methods. In other words, subclasses do not have to be redefined from scratch—they can inherit all the characteristics of higher level classes in a hierarchy. For example, knowing that an automobile has four wheels means that a convertible will inherit this attribute—it need not be respecified.

Another strength of object-oriented programming is the concept of **encapsulation**. Encapsulation places all procedures *and* the data needed by these procedures together in an object. Data direct the flow of procedures, while the proce-

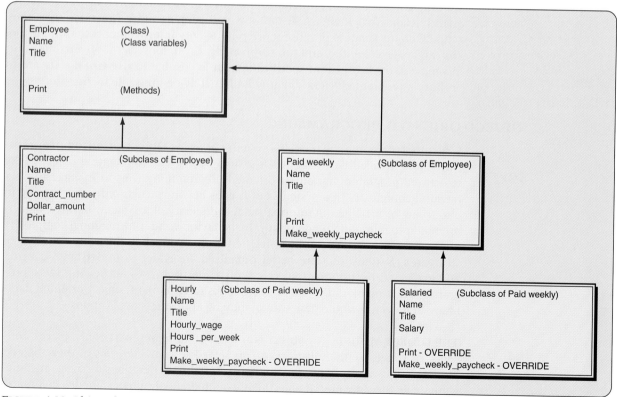

FIGURE 6.12 Object classes, subclasses, inheritance, and overriding. (Copyright © Apple Corporation. Used with permission.)

dures manipulate and shape the values of data. When data and procedures are separate, there is always the possibility that the correct procedure may call the wrong data or the wrong procedure may call the correct data. Figure 6.12 is an example of object-oriented programming using employee data.

Certain programming languages have emerged, such as C++ and Smalltalk, that are well suited to object-oriented development. However, similar to CASE tools, there has been some resistance to the use of object-oriented programming languages and approaches. More than just learning a new language, OOP requires a whole new conceptualization of how systems are constructed. However, for pioneers like American Airlines (see Box 6.7), the benefits have been substantial.

IT At Work BOX 6.7

SMALLTALK FOR BIG APPLICATIONS

Until recently, the ground-breaking, object-oriented programming language developed in the 1970s by Alan C. Kay—called Smalltalk—was something used only by computer scientists, academics, and some daring customers. Originally developed to build computers even children could program, Smalltalk has now hit it big with major corporations.

Enabling large programs to be built from pretested software objects, Smalltalk can provide ten-fold gains in programmer productivity and software quality. Programs are completed sooner, work better, and can withstand repeated and radical change. Moreover, Smalltalk programs deal in terms nontechnical people can understand. Where most programming languages deal in *subroutines* and *do-loops*, an object created in Smalltalk can be a shipping schedule or an invoice.

In 1991, American Airlines wanted a new system to help track and dispatch crew, meals, and other resources for 2,600 interconnecting flights a day. A team of three programmers wrote the system in Smalltalk in eight months and discovered only two errors. This was "a remarkable turnaround time," said an American Airlines software project manager. First Boston Corporation uses a version of Smalltalk to model new financial instruments in days instead of months. Smalltalk experts are in such demand on Wall Street that the best ones command as much as $2,000 a day.

The most promising application of Smalltalk may be in business modeling. Using objects to represent business functions, managers who want to reengineer their company can try out ideas in software first before rearranging people and other assets. Big effects from Smalltalk.

Critical Thinking Issue: Without knowing much about Smalltalk or C++, why do you think it is possible to write programs in them so fast? ▲

SOURCE: Adapted from *BusinessWeek*, April 19, 1993, pp. 111–112.

SOFTWARE LICENSING

An increasing number of software users are opting to buy commercial software packages instead of developing their own. However, licensing a product that is extremely easy to copy and distribute presents problems for software vendors and for purchasers.

Software users are held responsible by producers for protecting software ownership rights. However, users also need to protect their investments, which often requires them to make backup copies of operational software. But software vendors must also protect their investments in software development, which involves restricting copying. Issues of software copying and licensing have become very controversial; many cases are being addressed through legislation or tested in court.

The software industry maintains that software should be protected under federal copyright laws. Software vendors claim that these laws and their license agreements, which are descriptions of how software can be used or copied, are frequently being violated. License agreement statements are usually located on the outside of the software container or under the shrink-wrapping of the software. Copyright laws allow the owner of a program to make backup copies. Licensed programs remain under vendor ownership, however. Unless the licensed user has written permission to make copies other than for backup, duplicating software is a violation of federal law.

When a user unwraps the shrink-wrap covering or breaks the seal on a software package to gain access to the program, this means the user accepts the terms of the license. Yet enforcing this agreement is difficult, especially in a multiterminal environment or a computer system in which many computers are connected or networked. License agreements usually require an application program to be purchased for each microcomputer using the software. To prevent organizations from being tempted to violate license agreements and make a copy of the purchased program for each computer, some vendors offer site licenses. These agreements allow an organization to pay a single fee covering the copying of a program for all computers within the organization.

To ensure adherence to the law, many organizations have instituted policies that give management, not end users, the responsibility for making backup copies of software. Software inventories are to be maintained and periodically audited to prevent any violation of stated policies. To monitor compliance, many software vendors have banded together to form an organization that searches for illegal copying and presents evidence for government prosecution. When purchasing commercial software, organizations need to consider licensing agreements closely and their potential ramifications for company and personal culpability.

▶ MANAGERIAL ISSUES

The proper use of licensed software, as discussed previously, is just one of the issues facing corporate management. Companies want to take maximum advantage of the software they purchase, whether mainframe or microcomputer based. Vendors want to be sure *they* are properly compensated for the software they provide. Companies must be careful to guard against unauthorized copying of licensed software, whether for business or personal (home) use. In either case, the company could be liable for substantial fines if copying is discovered.

Management must also address the basic make-vs.-buy decision on software. There is a tendency in many companies, particularly within the information services department, to want to develop their own software in-house. Any purchased software, they argue, requires that certain compromises must be made. Either the software will have to be modified—an expensive and potentially risky undertaking—or the organization may be forced to change its procedures—a potentially disruptive occurrence.

A third area that demands management's attention is the choice of a software development platform. What operating systems should be chosen—Windows 95, OS/2 WARP, or Unix—and if Unix, which version? For application development, should an object-oriented approach be taken, using Smalltalk, C++, or some vendor's proprietary language? If a new approach *is* used, what about the huge investment in legacy systems programmed in COBOL? Who will maintain them if all the new applications, and the application programmers, work in, for example, C++? These questions cannot be left to technicians to answer; the implications for the success of the business are too important. ■

KEY TERMS

Analysis graphics *205*	Assembly language *192*	Bits *192*
Application software *191*	Attribute *217*	Bytes *192*
Assembler *193*	BASIC *198*	C *198*

CHAPTER HIGHLIGHTS *(L-x means learning objective number x)*

▼ A program or software is the set of instructions linked together to accomplish a particular result. There are two broad classes of software: application software and systems software. (L-1)

▼ Application software directs a computer to perform specific processing activities and provides functionality for users. (L-1)

▼ Programming languages, which are used to create and maintain software, range from low-level machine and assembly code to high-level procedural language code to nonprocedural fourth-generation code. (L-2)

▼ There are six widely used types of application software packages: spreadsheets, data managers, word processing, graphics, multimedia, and communications. (L-3)

▼ Database management software reduces file sys-

tem redundancy and data inconsistency while increasing functionality. (L-3)

▼ Presentation graphics and analysis graphics software allow users to create, store, and display charts, graphs, maps, and drawings. (L-3)

▼ Multimedia software combines at least two media (audio, voice, animation, video, text, graphics, or images) for input and output. (L-3)

▼ Systems software acts as an intermediary between computer hardware and application programs; it controls and supports the computer system and its information processing activities. (L-4)

▼ The main component of system software is the operating system that performs three major functions: job management, resource management, and data management. (L-5)

▼ Types of operating systems are single program,

multiprogramming (concurrent execution), time-sharing, and multiprocessing. (L-6)

▼ Software development is normally done in a top-down fashion called structured programming. CASE tools help managers and analysts plan, design, and code software systems. (L-7)

▼ Object-oriented programming builds software packages by using re-usable modular objects that

contain their code and needed data. Assembling and testing object-oriented programs can be done quickly. (L-7)

▼ Software licensing is an important issue for those purchasing commercial software packages. Software producers and vendors depend on copyright laws to prevent illegal copying and resale. (L-8)

QUESTIONS FOR REVIEW

1. What is the difference between systems software and application software?

2. Describe the different generations of programming languages.

3. What is the purpose of assemblers and compilers?

4. How does an interpreter differ from a compiler?

5. What is a spreadsheet program? What types of applications are appropriate for use with a spreadsheet program?

6. What advantages do database management programs have over file systems?

7. Explain a word processing menu and an icon.

8. Define WYSIWYG. Why is it valuable?

9. What is multimedia, and how does it differ from previous types of software?

10. What is the purpose of an operating system? What are its three primary functions?

11. Give some examples of system support software.

12. Explain multiprogramming and multiprocessing. Why were they developed?

13. What is virtual memory? What problem is it designed to solve, and how does it work?

14. What is a virtual machine?

15. Explain CASE and its importance.

16. What is object-oriented programming? What are the benefits claimed for it?

QUESTIONS FOR DISCUSSION

1. Will application software tend to become more integrated in the future or more specialized?

2. In general, is software becoming less expensive per functionality, more expensive, or remaining the same?

3. Are first- and second-generation languages still being used for programming? If so, why?

4. Why is it that companies might not embrace fourth-generation languages entirely for all programming?

5. What does software maintenance mean?

6. What are the differences between something that is mechanically controlled (like an old spring-and-gear watch) and something that is software-controlled (like a digital watch)?

EXERCISES

1. Look over some issues of *InfoWeek* or *Computerworld* from 15 and 10 years ago (presumably from a library). What types of software were most discussed—application or systems? What were some of the issues?

2. Study a local business that has more than 10 employees

and at least one computer. How many and what types of software applications do they use? About how many and what types did they use 5 or 10 years ago? In what ways, if any, is the business different now?

GROUP ASSIGNMENT

Each of the class groups should contact a local firm that is in the process of considering whether to develop or purchase a new computer application. After the group has determined the purpose of the application and the desired features from the company's standpoint, each member of the group should investigate a different software package as to its suitability for meeting the company's requirements. Such issues as cost, features, flexibility, support, and vendor's reputation are among the items to be considered in making this evaluation.

Once each of the evaluations has been completed, the group should then construct an overall evaluation table, comparing and weighing the features of each of the competing packages. Finally, using agreed-upon criteria, the group should select one (or at most two) as their recommendation and be prepared to make a presentation to the company and defend its decision.

Minicase 1

Computer Games at Work

With a few minutes on her hands, an office worker at New Jersey's Department of Environmental Protection recently commanded her personal computer to pull up the game of Solitaire. The computer gave her this message: "Sorry, department policy prohibits the use of this program."

ZAP! Employers across the country are firing a new volley in their war to stamp out game playing and other unauthorized use of office computers. With the help of new network management programs that control which software programs can be used and when, managers can hunt down and neutralize game players before any triggers are pulled.

These measures represent managers' latest attempt to regain control over the very technologies they introduced to their offices. Purchased as productivity enhancers, items such as the latest souped-up PCs, color monitors, sophisticated software, and high-speed modems have simultaneously enhanced workers' abilities to goof off.

Indeed, games often come bundled free with office software these days. Solitaire and Minesweeper, for example, are included with copies of Microsoft Windows to provide new owners with a nonthreatening way to learn to use a mouse device. But these, as well as other non-educational games like Doom, have addicted thousands of workers.

At the same time, managers say unauthorized copying of games and other programs has exposed companies to copyright-infringement suits, computer viruses, and system overloads, not to mention the long hours spent fixing computer glitches that result. Aggravated executives have responded by imposing strict antigame rules. Most recently, the governor of Virginia banned game playing on all state-owned computers. A recent poll of large cor-

porations conducted by CIMI Corporation, a strategic planning consulting firm, found that 11 percent have policies of erasing game programs on company computers, while 4 percent have reprimanded or fired game-playing employees.

But short of sneaking up on unsuspecting workers and catching them in the act, managers have had little success. To make matters worse, many games now come equipped with *boss keys*, which hide the programs behind phony spreadsheets and other applications with the touch of a button.

Questions for Minicase 1

1. Are management's attempts to stamp out their employees' use of computer games justified? Using an informal survey of local companies, find out how widespread such game playing is and what actions, if any, companies are taking to stop such practices.

2. Should employees be allowed to play computer games on their own time (i.e., during lunch and/or breaks)? Why or why not?

3. Given the increased familiarity with microcomputers on the part of managers and clerical workers alike, is there any longer a justification for using computer games as "a nonthreatening way to learn to use a mouse device"?

4. If games such as Solitaire and Minesweeper come bundled with Microsoft Windows operating systems, what steps should management take when installing Windows? Remove the games from the software? Leave the games in place but caution employees not to use them on company time? Do nothing?

SOURCE: Adapted from "Employers Sabotage Office Computer Games," *The Wall Street Journal*, February 6, 1995.

Minicase 2

Old Dogs and New Tricks

Many old-line corporations are making wholesale conversions from systems that are mainframe-based with single operating systems to corporate systems consisting of many networks of distributed personal computers with multiple operating systems and graphical user interfaces. In the midst of these changes, many mainframe systems

analysts and programmers are having to face up to the task of relearning a trade or changing careers. As one partner of an IS placement firm put it, "If you don't want to practice your graphical front-end development, practice 'Would you like fries with that burger?'"

But mainframe old-timers are also learning that their

mainframe system management skills are in high demand. Skills with such basics as system security, system testing, backup, disaster recovery, documentation, version control, and data integrity are becoming increasingly valuable in complex computing environments—where system management is just as necessary but harder to ensure. "Mainframe people are used to looking at what the whole group is doing, the whole organization," said an IS manager, "while people who only worked on a PC . . . don't think like that."

Moreover, experienced mainframe people have valuable business and corporate experience that can be leveraged. "Do you go with someone who knows your business inside out?" asked another IS manager. "Or do you take a young whippersnapper, fresh out of college, who has learned the tools but doesn't have a clue about your business?" Retraining mainframers, however, can be expensive. Some companies balk at spending upward of $20,000 to retrain systems analysts and programmers who may then simply leave for higher-paying jobs.

The smartest old dogs may be the ones that merge their old tricks with the new ones.

SOURCE: Condensed from "IS Veterans Retool Talents For '90s," *PCWeek*, April 11, 1994, pp. 1, 12.

Questions for Minicase 2

1. What incentives can a company offer a 20-year mainframe veteran to learn a whole new set of skills *and* stay with the company? What sorts of conditions might serve as disincentives?

2. Who should manage new development in the new computing environment: old-timers who don't understand the new technology but have plenty of experience managing projects, or youngsters who have little management/corporate experience but understand the underlying technology that is to be implemented? Are there alternatives? Does it have to be one *or* the other?

3. How can "young whippersnappers" best be taught the basic systems management skills that the mainframers have?

4. Do employers *owe it* to their loyal mainframers to retrain them in the radically new technological skills? To what degree is retraining the responsibility of the mainframers themselves?

REFERENCES AND BIBLIOGRAPHY

1. *Business Week*, December 9, 1991, p. 70

2. *InformationWeek*, January 6, 1992, pp. 22–28.

3. "What's Next for COBOL?" *InformationWeek*, February 21, 1994.

4. *The Wall Street Journal*, January 25, 1993, p. B4.

5. *Business Week*, April 19, pp. 111, 112.

6. "How to Bolster the Bottom Line," *Fortune 1994 Information Technology Guide*, Vol 128, no. 7, Autumn 1993, pp. 22–24.

7. "IS Veterans Retool Talents for '90s," PCWeek, April 11, 1994, p. 1, 12.

8. Employers Sabotage Office Computer Games, *The Wall Street Journal*, February 6, 1995, pp. B1, B5.

USER INTERFACE: ENABLING HUMAN-COMPUTER COMMUNICATION

Chapter Outline

Learning Objectives

After studying this chapter, you will be able to:

1. Describe a user interface and understand its importance.

2. Discuss various input and output devices.

3. Compare the various interface modes.

4. Explain the role of graphics in user interfaces.

5. Analyze the value of a graphical user interface in computerized systems.

6. Analyze the role of multimedia and hypermedia in computer-based information systems.

7. Describe geographical information systems and analyze their importance.

8. Analyze the role of visual interactive technologies in decision making.

9. Analyze the potential contribution of virtual reality to the business world.

10. Describe the potential of voice technologies and natural language processing.

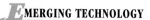

7.1 THE IMAGING SYSTEM AT UNITED SERVICES AUTOMOBILE ASSOCIATION

UNITED SERVICES AUTOMOBILE Association (USAA) is a large insurance company (San Antonio, TX) serving about 2 million military officers, former officers, and their dependents. The company does not have any field agents, so all communication between the company and its clients is done via the mail or the telephone.

USAA's objective is to be transformed into a completely paperless company in an environment called Automated Insurance Environment (AIE). All human-machine interface will be done electronically. The company processes about 100,000 documents every workday.

In the 1980s, the company employed 120 clerks whose only job was to search files (which occupied 39,000 square feet) for information when needed. Searches for one document took anywhere from an hour to two weeks, and some documents were never found. Since 1993, employees scan about 45 million pieces of mail per year into a computer database. Then agents, using special imaging terminals, access the database to process information and assist customers. Customers can now obtain *instant* answers to questions such as the following: "Is the car we bought an hour ago insured against theft?" The system is also used to expedite the treatment of claims. When a customer calls to report a car accident, the telephone call is digitized and stored. Subsequently, all documents (photos, doctors' reports, appraisers' reports, and so on) are scanned into the computer. Once the case is closed, it is stored on a CD-ROM for future reference.

Here is how the data entry works. Each day the company receives almost 20,000 letters as well as thousands of telephone calls; each day the company sends over 50,000 letters and policies. All the documents are indexed on an IBM mainframe, and then are scanned to create a digital electronic picture of all documents. The imaged documents can then be accessed from anywhere in the company for processing. Special high-resolution terminals are used for displaying and printing the image documents. The company uses *electronic forms* to expedite the preparation of standard documents.

The system improves productivity of employees, reduces cost of storing documents (most paper documents are destroyed), and improves customer service. What follows is an example of how the system saves money for USAA.

Employee productivity is improved by eliminating the time necessary to search for the appropriate documents. With the new system, all pertinent data can be

The imaging system at United Services Automobile Association.

called to the user's screen within 6 minutes of issuing the request. With the old system, document collection required an average of .5 manhours. (If any of the documents were not housed in the local facility, the document collection averaged 1.2 hours.) The average hourly cost of $15 for document handlers results in the following calculations:

Document in local facility:
0.5 manhours × 90% = .45 hours

Document in nonlocal facility:
1.2 manhours × 10% = .12 hours

Average hours per search (one document) in the old method   Total .57 hours

Average hours per search using the new method   .10 hours

Average savings in manhours per document   .47 hours

Average cost saved per search $7.05

Annual savings for the 10,000,000 documents handled by USAA each year: $70,500,000

Most users find the imaging system easier to work with than the old paper-clogged system. The system provides employees with scanned documents, so they do not have to deal with paper. Furthermore, it is now possible to find the status of any document in a matter of seconds. The system is also used for scheduling work and monitoring work flow.

SOURCE: Based on stories in *Best's Review Magazine*, May 1993; *Datamation*, May 15, 1990. *MIS Quarterly*, December 1991; and *IBM Systems Journal*, vol. 29, no. 3, 1990.

▶ 7.2 OVERVIEW OF USER INTERFACES

The USAA opening case demonstrates the advantages of scanning data into computers by using **imaging technology** for storing and presenting information and electronic forms to expedite data entry. Scanning, electronic forms, and imaging are examples of efficient and attractive user interfaces.

Most computer users have limited computer experience. Inexperienced users are not prepared to learn the computer-oriented details typically required of experienced users. Often, inexperienced users expect to use an application as easily as they use the telephone or ride an elevator. However, most operating systems and other software that support applications were developed for users accustomed to carrying out complicated computerized tasks. The desire to meet the needs of users who demand power without complication has made the computer industry increasingly sensitive to the design of the user interface. The study of user interface is a subset of a field called human-computer interaction, which is the study of people, computer technology, and the ways these influence each other (see Dix et al. [1993]).

User interface is the hardware and software that enable communication and interaction between the user and the computer. The user interface may be thought of as a surface through which data pass back and forth between user and computer. Physical aspects of the user interface (see Figure 7.1) include the user; input devices such as a mouse, microphone, video camera, or keyboard; and display devices such as a monitor, printer, or speaker. The user begins an interaction by entering data into the computer. The data displayed on the monitor provides a context for interaction and gives cues for action by the user. The user formulates a response and takes an action. Data then passes back to the computer through the interface. The cyclical process shown in Figure 7.1 consists of the following elements:

1. *Dialogue.* Dialogue is an observable series of interchanges or interactions between the human and the computer.

2. *Action language.* A user's **action language** can take various shapes, ranging from selecting an item from a menu to answering a question, moving a display window, or typing in a command. One or more **input devices** are used to execute actions. It deals with flows of information from the user to the computer, via an input device.

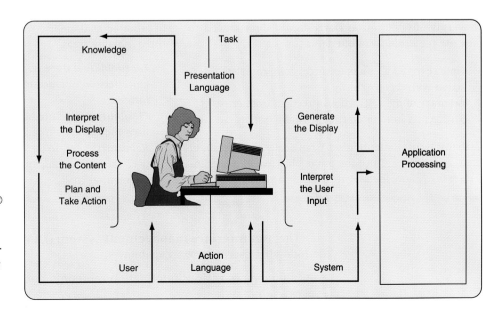

FIGURE 7.1 The process of user–computer interfacing. (Source: Bennett, 1986 pg. 65. Copyright © 1986 International Business Machine Corporation. Reprinted with permission from *IBM Systems Journal*, Vol. 25, Nos. 3 and 4.)

3. *Knowledge.* Knowledge is what the user must have in order to communicate with the computer. The knowledge may be expertise possessed by the user, or it may be included in a reference card or in a series of "help" messages available on request.

4. *User's reaction.* The user interprets the display, processes the content, and plans an action.

5. *Computer.* The computer interprets the user's action (input), executes a task (e.g., computation), and generates a display that is basically the presentation language or the output of the computer.

6. *Presentation language.* **Presentation language** is the information displayed to the user via a variety of **output devices**. It can be shown as display menus, icons, or text. It can be static or dynamic, numeric or symbolic. It can appear on the monitor, or be presented as voice or printout. A variety of studies have shown that the presentation provided has an impact on the quality of the decisions made and the user's perception of the system. It is important to provide output that is appropriate for the users of the systems and the decisions being supported.

These elements can be designed and used in different ways.

The quality of the interface, from the user's perspective, depends on what the user sees or senses, what the user must know to understand what is sensed, and what actions the user can (or must) take to obtain needed results (see Box 7.1). Providing a quality interface is a complex task due to technological, psychological, physical, and other influencing factors. Following are some of the important issues in building a user interface: screen design, human-machine interaction sequence, use of colors, information density, use of icons and symbols, information display format, and choice of input and output devices. Some of these issues are handled by the user interface management system, a concept similar to a database management system (see Chapter 8).

A Closer Look BOX 7.1

MEASURING THE USABILITY OF A USER INTERFACE

Meera Blattner from the Lawrence Livermore National Laboratory (Livermore, CA) and Eugene Schultz from the University of California at Davis suggest three criteria to measure the *usability* of interfaces.

▼ Time required by users to successfully complete interaction with the system.
▼ Accuracy of the interactions (freedom from errors).
▼ Satisfaction from interacting with the system.

Usability focuses attention on what really matters about the user interface. Since the prime objective of a user interface is to allow the user to achieve particular goals, the

interface must be usable. Dix et al. (1993) developed design principles that can be applied to an interactive system to promote its usability. These principles have impact on three usability areas.

▼ *Learnability* is the ease with which new users can begin effective interaction and achieve maximum performance.
▼ *Flexibility* is measured by the multiplicity of ways the user and the system can exchange information.
▼ *Robustness* refers to the level of support provided to the user in determining successful achievement and assessment of goals.

The **user interface management system (UIMS)** is software that provides the following user interface capabilities.

▼ Accommodates various information representations of the system (voice, images, etc.).

▼ Accommodates the action language that enables the user to manage the computer inputs and outputs.

▼ Interacts in several different interface styles.

▼ Captures, stores, and analyzes dialogue usage (tracking), which can be used for improving the interface system.

▼ Gives users "help" capabilities, prompting, diagnostic and suggestion routines, or any other flexible support.

▼ Provides user interface with the database and other components of the CBIS.

▼ Creates data structures to describe outputs (output formatter).

▼ Stores input and output data.

▼ Provides color graphics, three-dimensional graphics, or data plotting.

▼ Has windows to allow multiple functions to be displayed concurrently.

▼ Supports communication among and between users and builders of CBIS.

▼ Provides training by examples (guiding users through the input and modeling process).

There is much interest in the subject of human-computer interfaces at this time, and literature is emerging on this subject (see Harrison and Hix [1989] and Dix et al. [1993]). Some of the *interface* modes used in UIMS are presented in Section 7.5.

 ## 7.3 INPUT DEVICES

Users can command the computer and communicate with it by using one or more input devices to trigger the action language. Each input device accepts a specific form of data; for example, keyboards transmit typed characters while handwriting recognizers "read" handwritten characters. Users want communication with computers to be simple, fast, and error free. Therefore, a variety of input devices fits the needs of different individuals and applications. A list of input devices is provided in Table 7.1, and some of the devices are portrayed in Figure 7.2. The high-

Table 7.1 **Representative Input Devices**

Keying devices
 Punched card reader
 Keyboard
 Point-of-sale terminal

Pointing devices (devices that point to objects on the computer screen)
 Mouse (including rollerballs and trackballs)
 Touch screen
 Light pen
 Joy stick

Optical character recognition (devices that scan characters)
 Bar code scanner
 Wand reader
 Optical mark reader
 Optical character readers
 Cordless reader

Handwriting recognizers

Voice recognizers (data are entered by voice)

Other devices
 Magnetic ink character devices
 Automatic teller machines (ATM)
 Digitizers (for maps, graphs, etc.)
 Cameras
 Smart cards
 Telephone

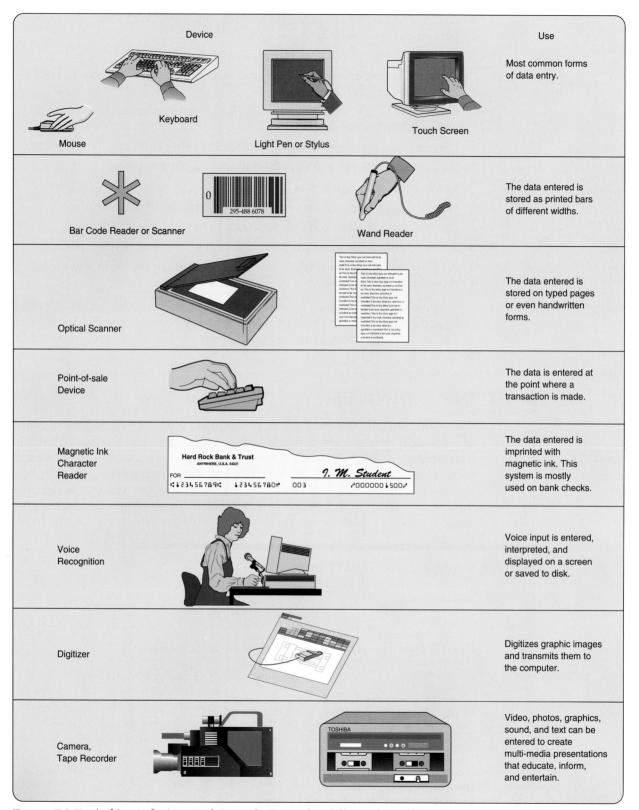

FIGURE 7.2 Typical input devices. Each input device reads a different form of data for processing by the CPU. (Source: Stern and Stern, 1993, p. 172. Copyright © 1983 John Wiley and Sons, Inc. Reprinted by permission of John Wiley and Sons, Inc.)

lights of major devices are presented next. For detailed descriptions, see Chapter 5 of Stern and Stern (1993) and Dix et al. (1993).

KEYING DEVICES

In keying devices, the information or data are typed in by users. The major devices are are follows:

PUNCHED CARD READERS. The initial input device to computers was an 80-column card in which holes were punched in different configurations to represent numbers or letters. The cards were punched on a special machine and then fed to a card reader, which sensed the holes and translated them to the original characters so that the computer could "understand" the data. Punched cards are used by very few companies today because of the bulkiness, slowness, cost, and high error rate. They can be found in any computer museum.

KEYBOARDS. The most common input device is the keyboard. The keyboard is designed like a typewriter but with many additional specialized keys. Most users utilize keyboards regularly.

POINT-OF-SALE TERMINALS. Whenever you pay at your favorite supermarket, pizza place, retail store, or other places that sell a product or service, the data of your transaction are likely entered into the computer via a **point-of-sale (POS) terminal**. The POS terminal has a specialized keyboard. For example, when you go to McDonald's, you can see that the terminal includes all the items on the menu. The touch of one key will create an entry in your bill and frequently transmit your order to the kitchen. A POS terminal in a retail store is equipped with a scanner that reads the bar-coded sales tag. POS devices increase the speed of data entry and reduce the chance of errors. POS terminals may include many features such as scanner, printer, voice synthesis, and accounting software (see Figure 7.3).

FIGURE 7.3 POS terminal increases speed of data entry.

POINTING DEVICES

A variety of devices is available for pointing to objects on the computer screen. They improve speed and/or ease of use as compared to keying devices. The major pointing devices are as follows:

MOUSE. The **mouse** is a hand-held device used to point a cursor at a desired place on the screen, such as an icon, a cell in a table, an item in a menu, or any other object. Once an object is reached, the user clicks a button on the mouse, instructing the computer to take some action. The use of the mouse reduces the need to type in information or use the slower arrow keys. Special types of mice are **rollerballs** and **trackballs**, used in many portable computers. Trackballs are frequently used in military aircraft to identify target points on a radar display for the pilots. The cursor can also be controlled by a finger. A new technology called *glide-and-tap* allows fingertip cursor control.

TOUCH SCREEN. An alternative to the mouse or other screen-related devices is a **touch screen**. You can activate an object on the screen by touching it with your finger.

LIGHT PEN. Instead of using your finger, you can use a special device with a light-sensing mechanism to touch the screen. Pointing with a **light pen** is more accurate because you can point at very small objects. The light pen is connected to the computer by a cable.

JOY STICKS. **Joy sticks** are used primarily at workstations that can display dynamic graphics. They are also used to play video games. The joy stick moves and positions the cursor at a desirable object on the screen. For example, joy sticks can be used to rotate a 3-D representation of objects in simulations.

OPTICAL CHARACTER RECOGNITION (OCR)

Several types of **optical character recognition** devices are available to scan data or pictures so that they do not have to be typed in. The devices optically scan documents and convert them to machine-readable form (see the opening case). The scanned material is stored as a bit-map representation in memory (see Box 7.2).

A Closer Look BOX 7.2

SCANNING AND OPTICAL CHARACTER RECOGNITION

Optical scanners are used to store hard-copy documents on a computer. Typically an optical scanner will take a picture of a document and store that picture in computer memory in bit-map form. A bit-map is a pictorial representation in a computer as opposed to a file.

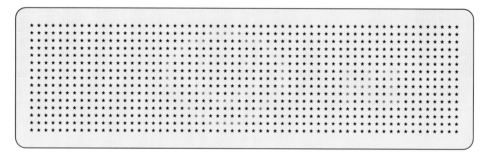

A bit-map is composed like the picture in the box. In our example, it is a 15 row by 40 columns = 600-pixel image. We entered a smiley face and an HI on the bit-map. When it is coded, a star will be zero, and a covered area will be one. Thus the binary code of this picture will look like this:

row 1 = all zeros

row 2 = 00000000000011111110000
00000000000000000

. . . .

. . . .

row 15 = all zeros

This kind of representation is used for image information for several techniques such as digital fax, and object-oriented graphics.

Data stored in a bit-map form take up a lot of computer memory. However, data in bit-map form can be used only as a picture in a database. It would be much more useful to us if we could convert any pictures of words that appear in the bit-map into a file of words. This way we could edit, search, or dynamically link the file into a database. This is where *optical character recognition* software plays a big role.

Optical character recognition software scans a bit-map looking for pictures of letters, numbers, and other text characters. When the OCR finds a character, it converts it into the corresponding ASCII character and puts it into a file. This process is continued until all the characters in the bit-map have been placed into the file. After the bit-map file is scanned by the OCR and an output file is created, the user can open the output file with an editor and make modifications to the file, just as if it had been created on a computer.

Character recognition is one of the areas where artificial intelligence is helpful. Some of the more advanced OCR software packages use neural computing or fuzzy logic (see Chapter 16) to resolve problems that arise in scanning both printed and handwritten characters. The computer is given certain rules that describe each character. It evaluates the character based on the rules and makes a guess based on the results. These rules may relate to many aspects of the document including character formation, context, and grammatical appropriateness, to name just a few.

BAR CODE SCANNERS. **Bar code scanners** are most visible in the checkout counters of the supermarket. They scan the black-and-white bars written in a code called the Universal Product Code (UPC). This code specifies the name of the product and its manufacturer. Bar codes are used in hundreds of situations, ranging from airline stickers on luggage to blood samples in laboratories. They are especially useful in high-volume tracking where keyboard entry is too slow and/or inaccurate. Other applications are the tracking of moving items, such as packages tracked by Federal Express; railroad cars tracked at various locations; and cars at the Mark III plant (see Minicase 3 in Chapter 3).

WAND READER. The **wand reader** is a special hand-held bar code reader. It can read codes that are also readable by people.

OPTICAL MARK READER. The **optical mark reader** is a special scanner for detecting the presence of pencil marks on a predetermined grid, such as multiple-choice answer sheets. It is also used in casinos to mark selections in a game called keno.

OPTICAL CHARACTER READER (OR OPTICAL SCANNER). With an **optical scanner**, source documents such as reports, typed manuscripts, or even books can be entered directly into a computer without the need for keying. An optical scanner converts text and images on paper into digital form and stores the data on disk or other storage media. Optical scanners are available in different sizes and for different types of applications. Small hand-held units for PCs cost only several hundred dollars and can process a few pages a minute. More sophisticated scanners for larger computers can process hundreds of pages a minute at a cost of thousands of dollars or more, depending on the speed and capability of the device.

The publishing industry is a leading user of optical scanning equipment. Publishers scan printed documents and convert them to electronic databases that can be referenced as needed. Similarly, they may scan manuscripts instead of retyping them in preparation for the process that converts them into books or magazines. Considerable time and money are saved, and the risk of introducing typographical errors is reduced. Scanners are becoming increasingly more reliable. Some are sophisticated enough to read not only text but visuals such as photos, illustrations, and graphs.

CORDLESS READER. This bar code reader, which can be 100 ft or more away from a computer, is useful in warehouses and other places where it is inconvenient to carry cables.

HANDWRITING RECOGNIZERS

The dream of any post office in the world is to be able to automate the reading of handwritten addresses on all letters, regardless of their shape. Today's scanners are good at "reading" typed or published material (see Box 7.3), but, they are not very good at handwriting recognition. **Handwriting recognition** is supported by technologies such as expert systems and neural computing (see Chapter 16) and is available in some **pen-based computers**. When you receive an overnight letter or a traffic violation ticket, you will probably sign for it on the screen of a pen-based computer. Clerks in stores take inventories with these portable devices. Users make selections from checklists, enter text, and even enter sketches and drawings using pen-based computers.

A Closer Look BOX 7.3

HOW HANDWRITING RECOGNITION WORKS

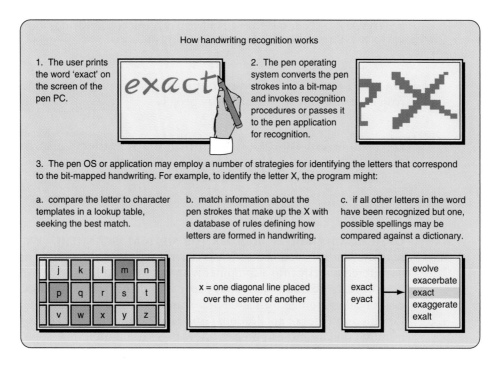

SOURCE: Mobile Computing, *PCWeek Supplement*, April 19, 1993.

Scanners that can interpret handwritten input are subject to considerable error. To minimize mistakes, handwritten entries should follow very specific rules. Some scanners will flag handwritten entries that they cannot interpret or will automatically display for verification all input that has been scanned. Because handwritten entries are subject to misinterpretation and typed entries can be smudged, misaligned, erased, and so forth, optical scanners have an error rate considerably higher than the error rate for keyed data.

Handwriting interfaces are especially popular with slow typers. Of special interest are products such as Apple's Newton Personal Data Assistant (see Chapter 5, pp. 169–170).

VOICE RECOGNIZERS

The most natural way to communicate with computers is by voice, using a natural language. **Voice recognition** devices are extremely important because they are fast, free the user's hands, and result in few entry errors. They also allow people with visual or other disabilities to communicate with computers (see Chapter 20). When voice technology is used in combination with telephones, people can call their computers from almost any location. While voice technologies have certain limitations such as the size of the vocabulary, they are improving with time, and some software products are already available on the market (see Box 7.4).

IT At Work BOX 7.4

DESKTOP DICTATING MACHINE ENABLES REENGINEERING THE PROCESSING OF MEDICAL REPORTS

Personal Dictation Systems (shown in the picture at right) from IBM enables users to talk to their computers and enter data at a speed of about 100 words per minute. The system is very accurate (95 to 98 percent). Both the accuracy and speed are expected to improve, while the cost (about $1000) will certainly decrease. People speak at about 100 to 120 words per minute, which is much faster than typing. Using mathematical algorithms to isolate, identify, and decipher the sound patterns of individual voices, the system converts words into text. However, the system has to be trained to recognize an individual voice. It takes only 90 minutes for the system to learn the user's dialect, pitch, and voice fluctuations. As the user speaks, the system can backtrack and correct mistakes made in previous words. The system's vocabulary is approximately 32,000 words.

An interesting application is reported in Singapore, where doctors are using a software called *DragonDictate* to prepare medical records. Previously a doctor would dictate his findings to an audio typist, who then typed the document, returned it to the doctor for checking, and made amendments requested by the doctor. The document was then returned to the doctor for a final read and signature. The process took about a week (it takes up to two weeks in the United States). The report is needed for

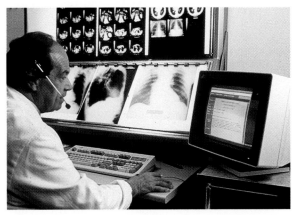

With an IBM personal dictation system, reports can be prepared in under two days.

filing insurance claims, and legal and medical purposes. The new process has reduced the cycle to one or at most two days. The cost is under $1300 and the system's vocabulary includes over 30,000 words.

Critical Thinking Issue: Can the medical application in Singapore be considered a business processing reengineering? ▲

SOURCE: Based on publicity material from IBM, *Datamation*, January 7, 1994, and *ITAsia*, July 1994.

OTHER DEVICES

Several other devices have been developed to act as input devices. They meet the diversified needs of various organizations and individuals. Typical devices are discussed as follows.

MAGNETIC INK CHARACTER READERS. Magnetic ink character readers (MICR) read information printed on checks in magnetic ink. This information identifies the bank and the account number. On a canceled check, the amount is also readable after it is added in magnetic ink.

AUTOMATED TELLER MACHINES. Automated teller machines are everywhere. This popular interactive input/output device enables you to get cash in thousands of locations and updates your bank account instantly. ATMs can handle a variety of banking transactions, including the transfer of funds to specified accounts. One drawback of the ATM is its vulnerability to computer crimes (see Chapter 19) and to attacks made on customers as they approach outdoor ATMs.

DIGITIZERS. Digitizers are devices that convert drawings made with a pen on a sensitized surface to machine-readable input. As drawings are made, the images are transferred to the computer. This technology is based on changes in electrical charges that correspond to the drawings. Digitizers are used by designers, engineers, and artists.

CAMERAS. Regular video cameras can be used to capture pictures that are digitized and stored in computers. Special cameras are used to transfer pictures and images to storage on a CD-ROM. A digital camera can take photos and load them directly from the camera, digitally, to a main storage or to a secondary storage device.

EMERGING TECHNOLOGY

...chip on a card

SMART CARDS. **Smart cards** closely resemble credit cards, but the plastic strip on a smart card contains a built-in microprocessor and storage on a silicon chip (see Box 5.3 in Chapter 5). This card is used for several applications. For example, the smart card described in Box 3.3 (Chapter 3) is a credit card and a debit card. It accumulates bonus points, stores the entire purchasing history, and includes other information about the shopper. Kaiser Permenente, the largest HMO in America, has each patient carry a smart card that includes the patient's complete medical history, including X-rays. Simpler cards can be purchased for making telephone calls. Each time a telephone call is made, the card is read by a verifying device and the balance is reduced by the amount of the call. Many libraries sell smart cards for their copying machines. There is an increasing number of new applications for smart cards, ranging from paying highway tolls to executing purchases and banking transactions.

THE TELEPHONE. A **telephone** can be used as an input device in several ways. First, the user can respond to a voice query and then push certain numbers, letters, or symbols to designate a certain answer or request. For instance, by entering a particular code (using the keyboard or voice), users can activate a computer search of a database. A voice response is then provided on issues ranging from the balance in a checking account to the price of a stock on the New York Stock Exchange.

DEVICES OF THE FUTURE. Experiments are being conducted in several countries to enable people, especially the disabled, to command computers using brainpower (see Box 7.5). Incidently, as will be shown in Chapter 20, computers can be used to support disabled people in carrying out many tasks. One example is an OCR machine that allows blind people to read books by scanning the text and

---

A Closer Look BOX 7.5

USING BIOELECTRIC SIGNALS TO COMMUNICATE WITH COMPUTERS

BioControl Systems of Palo Alto, California, has developed a special-purpose device that allows paralyzed or physically impaired persons to communicate with computers using eye, muscle, or brain signals. This device meets the difficult requirements of the Americans with Disabilities Act (see Chapter 20).

The device, called Biomouse, is based on research done at Stanford University. It maps the body's bioelectric signals and uses them, as a computer uses a mouse or keystroke, to move a cursor on the computer screen. The user "interfaces" with a computer via head set, wrist band, or electrodes, which then map and transmit neural messages onto a computer screen. By moving the cursor, or "eyecon" (for eye controller), a person can "type" words or perform other functions on a computer.

BioControl Systems' technology also creates computer-simulated environments, but through the use of the user's own bioelectric signals rather than through an external device like a joystick, 3-D headset, or virtual reality gloves.

Using brainwaves to communicate with computers is a topic related to virtual reality (see Section 7.11).

then transmitting the text using voice technology (a system from Kurzwil Systems Corporation). Another device is the gloves of virtual reality, which are used to command a computer.

7.4   OUTPUT DEVICES

The output generated by a computer can be transmitted to the user via several devices and media. The presentation of information is extremely important in encouraging users to embrace computers. This section presents the major output devices (see Figure 7.4). The forthcoming sections present several technologies that can be used to present output information.

MONITORS

The data entered into the computer can be visible on the computer monitor, which is basically a video screen that displays both input and output. Monitors come in different sizes, ranging from inches to feet, and in different colors. The major benefit is the interactive nature of the device. Monitors display information in a **softcopy** form, and they are used in most of the interface modes (see Section 7.5). A common technology is the *cathode ray tube* (CRT), an inexpensive device that resembles a TV screen. Portable computers use a flat screen consisting of a liquid crystal display (LCD), which is also used in several other products such as digital wristwatches and pocket calculators.

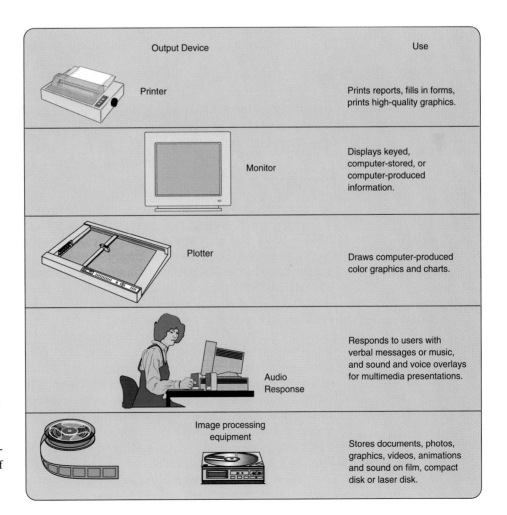

FIGURE 7.4 Representative output devices and their use. (Source: Stern and Stern, 1993, p. 199. Copyright © 1993 John Wiley and Sons, Inc. Reprinted by permission of John Wiley and Sons, Inc.)

PRINTERS

A printer is commonly used to create a hard copy of the computer output. There are several types of printers, and they can be divided into two major categories: impact and nonimpact printers.

IMPACT PRINTERS. Like typewriters, impact printers use some form of striking action to press a carbon or fabric ribbon against paper to create a character. **Serial printers** print one character at a time. The most common serial printers are the dot matrix, daisy wheel, and line. *Dot matrix* printers create characters by using a rectangular grid of pins. The pins strike against a carbon ribbon to print on paper, one character at a time. *Daisy wheel printers* have a mechanism that positions the daisy wheel so that the required character for each letter lines up with an electromagnetic hammer. The hammer then strikes against a carbon ribbon to print on paper one character at a time. *Line printers* print one line at a time; therefore, they are faster than other serial printers. They also appear in several shapes, such as a chain, drum, or band.

NONIMPACT PRINTERS. Impact printers are slow and noisy, cannot do high-resolution graphics, and are often subject to mechanical breakdowns. Nonimpact printers overcome these deficiencies, but they are more expensive. **Laser printers** are higher speed, high-quality devices that use laser beams to write information on photosensitive drums, whole pages at a time; then the paper passes over the drum and picks up the image with toner. Because they produce "print" quality text and graphics, laser printers are used in desktop publishing and even in reproduction of artwork. *Thermal printers* create whole characters on specially treated paper that responds to patterns of heat produced by the printer. *Ink-jet printers* shoot tiny dots of ink onto paper. Sometimes called bubble jet, they are relatively inexpensive and are especially suited for graphical applications when different colors of ink are required.

PLOTTERS. **Plotters** are printing devices using computer-driven pens for creating high-quality black-and-white or color *graphic* images—charts, graphs, and drawings (even large ones). They are used in complex, low-volume situations.

VOICE OUTPUT

Some devices provide output via voice—synthesized voice. This refers to the technology by which computers "speak." The synthesis of voice by computer differs from a simple playback of a prerecorded voice by either analog or digital means. As the term "synthesis" implies, the sounds that make up words and phrases are constructed electronically from basic sound components and can be made to form any desired voice pattern. **Voice synthesis** has already come of age. There are several good, commercially available voice synthesis packages that work on limited domains and encompass phonetic rules.

The quality of synthesized voice is currently very good, and the cost is already low (you can buy a voice output card for your PC for less than $100). The anticipated improved performance of synthetic voice in the near future will encourage more widespread commercial applications. The opportunities for its use will encompass almost all applications that can provide an automated response to a user, such as inquiries by employees pertaining to payroll and benefits. Several banks already offer a voice service to customers, informing about their balance, which checks were cashed, and so on. Another example is synthesized voice response to requests for telephone numbers.

Voice response units are frequently combined with a telephone in a technology called *voice response systems*. For example, when you call for assistance in finding a telephone number, you speak to an operator, but the response is provided electronically. Digital voice messages are played back on command of the operator, similar to what is done in a voice mail system. Computerized voice response applications are frequently combined with voice input applications (see Box 7.6).

AT At Work BOX 7.6

SAMPLE OF VOICE TECHNOLOGY APPLICATIONS

Company	Applications
Scandinavian Airlines, other airlines	Answering inquiries about reservations, schedules, lost baggage, etc.[a]
Citibank, many other banks	Informing credit card holders about balances and credits, providing bank account balances and other information to customers[a]
Delta Dental Plan (CA)	Verifying coverage information[a]
Federal Express	Requesting pickups
Illinois Bell, other telephone companies	Giving information about services, receiving orders[a]
Domino's Pizza	Enabling stores to order supplies, providing price information[a,b]
General Electric, Rockwell International, Austin Rover, Westpoint Pepperell, Eastman Kodak	Allowing inspectors to report results of quality assurance tests[b]
Cara Donna Provisions	Allowing receivers of shipments to report weights and inventory levels of various meats and cheeses[b]
Weidner Insurance, AT&T	Conducting market research and telemarketing[b]
U.S. Department of Energy, Idaho National Engineering Laboratory, Honeywell	Notifying people of emergencies detected by sensors[a]
New Jersey Department of Education	Notifying parents when students are absent and about cancellation of classes[a]
Kaiser-Permanente Health Foundation (HMO)	Calling patients to remind them of appointments, summarizing and reporting results[a]
Car manufacturers	Activating radios, heaters, and so on, by voice[b]
Texoma Medical Center	Logging in and out by voice to payroll department[b]
St. Elizabeth's Hospital	Prompting doctors in the emergency room to conduct all necessary tests, reporting of results by doctors[a,b]
Hospital Corporation of America	Sending and receiving patient data by voice, searching for doctors, preparing schedules and medical records[a,b]

Critical Thinking Issue: What other applications are possible with voice technology?

SOURCE: Based on Turban, 1992.

[a]Ouput device
[b]Input device

PRESENTATION SCREENS

There are several types of large presentation screens for public view. For example, a four-by-eight-foot LCD screen is available for presenting computer output in a meeting. A *data show* is another popular presentation device. It allows you to project the image of the computer output on a regular screen using an overhead projector as an intermediary.

▶ 7.5 INTERFACE MODES

The combination of presentation and action languages is referred to as an *interface-mode (style)*. Interface modes are used in the interactive communication between a user and a computer. The interface mode determines how information is entered and displayed. It also determines the ease and simplicity of learning and using the system. This section considers the following styles: menu interaction, command language, questions and answers, form interaction, natural language, and object manipulation.

MENU INTERACTION

Menu interaction means that the user selects from a list of possible choices (the menu) which function is to be performed. For example, a user may choose which application to use or whether or not to exit a program. The choice is made by use of input devices. Menus appear in a relational order, starting with a main menu and going on to submenus. Menu items can include commands that appear in separate submenus or in the menus with noncommand items. Menus can become tedious and time-consuming when complex situations are analyzed, since it may take several menus to build or use a system, and the user must shift back-and-forth among the menus.

A **pull-down menu** is a submenu that appears as a superimposed drop-down window on the screen, usually after an entry has been made in a higher level menu. It is very popular in the graphical interface environment.

COMMAND LANGUAGE

In the **command language** mode, the user enters a command such as "print," "run," or "plot." Many commands are composed of a verb–noun combination (e.g., "plot sales"). Some commands can be executed with the function keys (F1, F2, and so on) on the keyboard. Another way to simplify commands (or even a series of commands) is to use macros. Commands can also be entered by voice.

QUESTIONS AND ANSWERS

The **questions and answers** mode begins with the computer asking the user a question. The user answers the question with a phrase or a sentence. The computer may prompt the user for clarification and/or additional input. A question may involve the presentation of a menu from which the answer is to be selected. In certain applications, the sequence of questioning may be reversed: the user asks a question and the computer gives an answer. In some expert systems, for example, instead of being asked to answer one question at a time, the user is asked to answer several questions at once (using a checklist).

FORM INTERACTION (ELECTRONIC FORMS)

In **form interaction**, the user enters data or commands into predesignated spaces (fields) in a form (see Figure 7.5). The headings of the form serve as a prompt for the input. The computer may produce some output after an input is made, and the user may be requested to continue the form interaction process. **Electronic forms** can alleviate many of the resource-intensive steps of processing forms. Traditional typesetting and printing steps become unnecessary. Distribution and storage requirements are streamlined when forms are handled electronically. Processing centers do not need to rekey data from paper-based forms, since the data remains in electronic format throughout the process (see the USAA opening case).

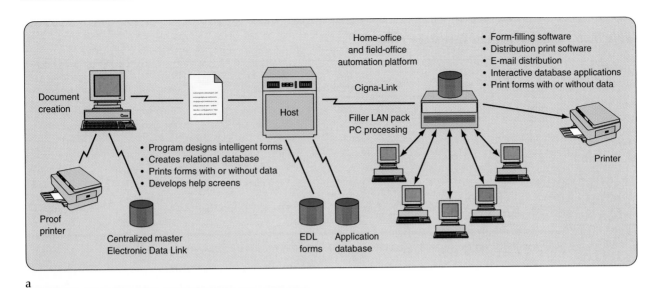

a

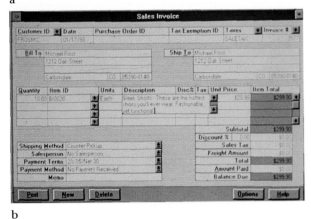

b

FIGURE 7.5 Form interaction. The upper part shows the process of using electronic forms while a form is shown in the lower part. (a) An intelligent electronic form processing (paperless). (Source: Reprinted with permission from the November 1993 issue of BYTE Magazine, © by McGraw-Hill, Inc., New York, NY. All rights reserved.) (b) A standard "service invoice" form. The form appears on-line to the user who fills in the appropriate information. The program executes automatic routing computations (such as sales tax).

NATURAL LANGUAGE PROCESSING

Natural language processing refers to a human-computer interaction that is similar to a human–human dialogue. Today, natural language dialogue is done mainly via the keyboard. In the future such dialogue will be conducted using voice as input and output. The major limitation of using natural language processing is essentially the inability of the computer to *understand* much of a natural language (such as English or Japanese). However, advances in AI (artificial intelligence) increasingly enhance the natural language dialogue. For example, natural language processors are used to access databases (see Chapters 8 and 16).

OBJECT MANIPULATION

In the **object manipulation** mode, objects, usually represented as icons (or symbols), are directly manipulated by the user. For example, the user can point the mouse or the cursor at an icon (or use a command) to move it, enlarge it, or show the details behind it. This mode is further discussed in the graphical user interface section (see Section 7.7).

CHOOSING AN APPROPRIATE INTERFACE MODE

Several studies have been conducted to determine the efficiency and accuracy of some interface modes. A summary of the research in this area is shown in Table 7.2. Some computer programs leave the choice of mode to the user by offering

Table 7.2 **Comparison of Interface Modes**

Dimensions	Menu Interaction	Fill in the Blanks (Forms)	Command Language	Object Manipulation	Questions and Answers
Speed	Slow at times	Moderate	Fast	Could be slow	Slow at times
Accuracy	Few errors	Moderate	Many errors	Few errors	Moderate
Training time	Short	Moderate	Long	Short	Short
User preference	Very high	Low	Prefer (if trained)	High	High
Power	Low	Low	Very high	Moderate-high	Moderate
Flexibility	Limited	Very limited	Very high	Moderate-high	High (if open ended)
Control	The system	The system	The user	The system and the user	The system

SOURCE: Based, on Majchrzak et al., (1987) and on Turban (1992).

alternate modes. For example, in many cases one can use either the regular menu or object manipulation. In other cases, the command language is available as an alternative to a menu interaction (programmers generally prefer command language). Filling in the blanks of forms is used by many companies that process large numbers of forms (e.g., insurance claims). Questions and answers are common in expert systems applications.

 ## 7.6   COMPUTER GRAPHICS

Graphics enable the presentation of information in a way that more clearly conveys the meaning of data and permits users to visualize relationships. The value of charts and graphs in the communication of numeric data has long been recognized (see the Wharton Experiment in Box 7.7).

A Closer Look BOX 7.7

THE WHARTON EXPERIMENT

In a study conducted by the Wharton School, University of Pennsylvania, overhead projection was shown to significantly influence how decisions were reached at meetings, how the presenter of the information was perceived by meeting participants, and whether the deciding group could quickly reach a consensus. In the six-month study, candidates for a master's degree in business administration assumed the roles of corporate decision makers grappling with a major marketing decision.

METHOD. The students were divided into 36 groups of three or four people each and given the task of making a decision on whether to introduce a new product, "Crystal, a light beer." The groups were urged to reach a consensus decision on whether or not to market the beer—"go" or "no go."

Student presenters, playing the role of marketing experts, then gave opposing viewpoints for and against the product: one used overhead transparencies, and the other used a white board to emphasize certain points. In one third of the meetings, the presenters in favor of a marketing decision used transparencies; in one third, those against it used transparencies; and in one third, no transparencies were used.

RESULTS. Regardless of which side they were favoring, presenters were able to convince more people when they used transparencies than when they did not. Sixty-seven percent agreed with the presenter promoting a "go" decision using visuals, and the same percent agreed when the presenter using visuals argued for a "no go" decision. When no overhead projector was used, a deadlock at 50–50 occurred. In addition, the presenters who used transparencies were rated as significantly better prepared, more professional, more persuasive, more credible, and more interesting than those who did not use transparencies.

Finally, the study indicated that the leader of the group that used graphics achieved consensus in a meeting time that was 28 percent shorter than those without graphics.

NOTE: A 28 percent reduction in meeting length could produce savings for American business equal to several billion dollars a year or a time savings of up to 42 extra working days per year for executives who spend an average of half their time in business meetings.

SOURCE: Condensed from Oppenheim L., et al., "A Study of the Effects of the Use of Overhead Transparencies on Business Meetings," Report of the Applied Research Center of the Wharton School, University of Pennsylvania, October 1981.

Graphics can be produced by two methods: traditional and computerized. The traditional method employs graphic artists who produce visuals for meetings and formal presentations. The major deficiencies of this method are long production time, difficulties in making changes, and significant associated cost. The second method, which overcomes the deficiencies of the first, is referred to as computer graphics. **Computer graphics** permit the user to quickly and inexpensively generate graphic information even without a graphic artist. Furthermore, this information can even be presented in an animated mode.

GRAPHICS SOFTWARE

The primary purpose of graphics software is to present visual images of information on a computer monitor, a printer/plotter, or both. The information presented may be constructed from numeric data and shown as graphs or charts, or it may be generated from text and symbols and expressed as drawings or pictures. The boundaries between drawing-oriented applications and chart applications using numeric data are often hazy, and many software products support both. The graphics software can be a stand-alone package, or it can be integrated with other software packages (e.g., with a database management system). Integrated software packages allow managers to create graphic output directly from databases or spreadsheets in a nontechnical and user-friendly way.

Stand-alone graphics are usually more powerful than integrated ones. They permit a larger variety of graph styles. They can often handle more data than the integrated graphics products. Another capability of some stand-alone packages is that several graphs can be combined on one screen, compared with the one-graph-at-a-time capability of many integrated packages. Often there are interfaces to import graphics into other programs. Of course, with the integrated package, one does not have to buy the extra software. Representative business graphics software packages are Harvard Graphics, SAS Graph, Lotus Freelance, DrawPerfect, Microsoft's PowerPoint, WordPerfect Presentations, and Tell-a-Graph.

THE ROLE OF COMPUTER GRAPHICS IN BUSINESS

For almost two decades, supporters of computer graphics systems have been urging the use of graphics for business management purposes. Graphics may be especially important for business problem solving and decision making because they help managers "visualize" data, relationships, and summaries. A wide variety of graphics can be generated by computers (see Table 7.3 and Figure 7.6).

Here are some of the ways that people in business use various types of graphics in a computerized environment.

REPORTS. Graphics are widely used in reports, such as those prepared for management. Perhaps the most common graphs are bar charts and time-series charts.

PRESENTATIONS. Graphics are used in 35-mm slides, overhead transparencies, and computer projection for presentation of information at briefings, meetings,

Table 7.3 **Types of Computer Graphics**

- ***Text*** plays a critical role in graphics—listing points that the speaker is discussing, showing subject titles, identifying components and values of a chart, and so on.
- ***Time-series charts*** show the value of one or more variables over time.
- ***Bar and pie charts*** can be used to show total values (by the size of the bar or pie slice), as well as component values, such as breakdowns of, for example, "source of money received."
- ***Scatter diagrams*** show the relationship between two variables, such as the number of air travelers who fly on Mondays, Tuesdays, and so on.
- ***Maps*** can be two- or three-dimensional. Two-dimensional maps are useful for showing spatial relationships; for example, the locations of customers in relation to the locations of a company's customer service facilities. Three-dimensional maps show surface contours.
- ***Layouts*** of rooms, buildings, or shopping centers convey much information in relatively simple diagrams.
- ***Hierarchy charts***, such as organizational charts, are widely used.
- ***Sequence charts***, such as flowcharts, show the necessary sequence of events and activities which can or must be done in parallel.
- ***Motion graphics***, such as motion pictures and television, clearly will continue to perform vital functions.
- ***Desktop publishing***—in-house computerized publishing systems that have extensive graphic capabilities (e.g., transferring a picture into the computer, laying it in a desirable position, and then printing it)—are gaining popularity.
- ***Project management charts*** such as critical path, planning, and monitoring.

SOURCE: Compiled from Sprague, R. H. and B. McNurlin, (1993), p. 401. Reprinted by permission of Barbara McNurlin from R. V. Sprague, Jr. and B. C. McNurlin, Information Systems Management in Practice, Prentice-Hall, 1993.

FIGURE 7.6 Representative examples of presentation graphics.

and conferences. By means of networks, displays can be made in several locations simultaneously.

ANALYSIS, PLANNING, AND SCHEDULING. Certain types of graphics have proved to be very helpful for supporting management decisions. *Geographical information systems* (see Section 7.9) are one type applicable to analysis, planning, and scheduling. Critical path charts (such as PERT and CPM) have been effective in vividly showing the critical activity path of projects.

COMMAND, CONTROL, AND COMMUNICATION. Although not often found in business and industry, communication, command, and control centers are widely used in the military. Some local governments also use them for controlling the operations of police, fire, and other vital public services. Maps and other graphic techniques play a key role in these centers by enabling rapid response to emergencies.

MANUFACTURING CONTROL CENTERS. Incorporating graphics with various computerized manufacturing systems for production-equipment experimentation and control is becoming popular. This combination permits dynamic modeling and what-if analysis. The graphic outputs help visualize both the problem and the potential solutions.

INTEGRATING GRAPHIC FORMULAS. It is now possible to purchase off-the-shelf software packages that integrate several graphic formats. One common application of such software is in planning and scheduling. In some planning and scheduling software packages (like Open Plan, Primavera, or Artemis), critical paths, sequences, hierarchies, and time-series charts can be displayed from different information in the database. What makes this truly a powerful tool is that the software maintains the correlation of the data between the different output formats.

OTHER USES. One of the main uses of graphics is to provide design, engineering, and production drawings for the manufacturing of products. Computer-aided design and computer-aided manufacturing (see Chapter 17) systems are receiving much attention these days (see Minicase 1 in Chapter 3). Graphics are used in teleconferencing and videotext systems as well. Graphics can also be used in dynamic modeling. Of special interest are animation, visual interactive modeling, and virtual reality, which are presented later in this chapter.

▶ 7.7 GRAPHICAL USER INTERFACE

The **graphical user interface (GUI)** is a system in which users have direct control of visible objects (such as icons) and actions that replace complex command syntax. The most well known GUIs are Windows from Microsoft Corporation and the built-in interfaces in Apple's computers. Experiments indicate that GUIs have significant benefits. For example, novice users work faster with GUI, their productivity is higher, and their level of frustration is lower, as compared to character-based interfacing. Users just touch or aim at visual areas to interact with the computer (see Figure 7.7). The next generation of GUI technology will incorporate elements such as virtual reality, head-mounted displays, sound and speech, pen and gesture recognition, animation, multimedia, artificial intelligence, and highly portable computers with cellular/wireless communication capabilities.

Table 7.4 compares current interface technology with next generation interfaces along 12 dimensions, ranging from user focus to software packaging. Future computer interface will be much friendlier than even the next generation shown in the table.

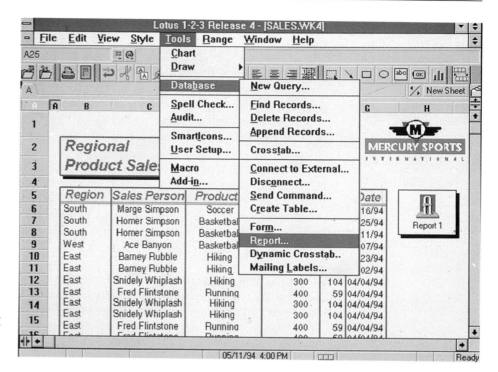

FIGURE 7.7 A typical GUI (from Lotus 1-2-3 for Windows)

The GUI combined with object-oriented programming has evolved from Xerox's Star and Apple's Lisa into a most powerful programming tool, especially for PCs. The major elements that the user touches or sees are windows, icons, menus and pointing devices (WIMP); pull-down menus; smart icons; colors; and dialogue boxes. GUI enables quick *customization of interfaces*. It permits selection from different colors and font sizes, different icons (to match culture, maturation, training, etc.), different levels and sequences of menu commands, and multiple hardware interfaces (input/output devices) to match the task and the individual.

GUI users point at an object on the screen with a mouse and then take action on that object by "clicking" on the mouse. For example, if a word processor changes a word to a boldface type, that word immediately appears bold on the

---

Table 7.4 **Comparison Between the Current Generation of Command-Based Interfaces and the Potential Next Generation of Interfaces Across 12 Dimensions**

Dimension	Current Interface Generation	Next-Generation Interfaces
User focus	Controlling computer	Controlling task domain
Computer's role	Obeying orders literally	Interpreting user actions and doing what it deems appropriate
Interface control	By user (i.e., interface is explicitly made visible)	By computer (since user does not worry about the interface as such)
Syntax	Object-action composites	None (no composites since single user token constitutes an interaction unit)
Object visibility	Essential for the use of direct manipulation	Some objects may be implicit or hidden
Interaction stream	Single device at a time	Parallel streams from multiple devices
Bandwidth	Low (keyboard) to fairly low (mouse)	High to very high (virtual realities)
Tracking feedback	Possible on lexical level	Needs deep knowledge of object semantics
Turn-taking	Yes; user and computer wait for each other	No; user and computer both keep going
Interface locus	Workstation screen, mouse, and keyboard	Embedded in user's environment, including entire room and building
User programming	Imperative and poorly structured macro languages	Programming-by-demonstration and nonimperative, graphical languages
Software packaging	Monolithic applications	Plug-and-play modules

SOURCE: Nielson (1993), p. 86. Copyright © 1993, Association for Computing Machinery, Inc.

Table 7.5 **Representative Graphical User Interface**

Product	Vendor
DeskMate	Tandy Corporation
DOS 5.0 and up	Microsoft Corporation
GeoWorks Ensemble	GeoWorks Corporation
Indigo Magic	Silicon Graphics
Macintosh	Apple Computer
Motif (for UNIX)	Open Software
New Wave	Hewlett-Packard
NEXTStep GUI	NEXT Computer Corporation
OpenLook	Sun Microsystems
Presentation Manager	IBM/Microsoft
Windows	Microsoft Corporation
X Window	A consortium of companies

screen, and it can be printed exactly as displayed. Many GUI products are available on the market (see Table 7.5 for a representative sample of GUI builders) and the capabilities of GUIs are increasing constantly.

In the GUI environment, the answer to the question "What do I do next?" is always on the screen, and it is frequently a picture of the result. In the GUI environment, you are always presented with options of how to proceed; this is in contrast to the character interface where you have to remember what to enter and the correct way to enter it. It is a well-supported fact that humans interpret pictures faster and more accurately than they can interpret text. To enhance the representations (primarily in the form of icons) and to present the options available to the user, every attempt is made to make the icon reflect an image of what the user is considering. For example, the user may wish to convert a regular font to italics; the icon would be an italicized letter. If a user wants to convert data into a pie chart, the icon would be a small pie chart.

MAJOR COMPONENTS OF GUI

The major components of GUIs are windows, icons, and hot spots. A brief description of each follows.

A **window** is an area of the computer screen that behaves as if it were an independent terminal. It may contain text, graphics, motion pictures, or other windows. It can be resized or moved. Several windows can appear on one screen, and so the user can see presentations from several tasks (generated by databases, other computers, etc.). Windows can overlap each other and are associated with devices such as **scrollers**, which allow the user to manipulate the content of a window.

Note: The concept of windows is prevalent in the GUI environment. However, there are windowing products that do not have any of the GUI characteristics (e.g., Desqview from Quarterdeck Software). The one thing that windowing does have in common with GUI is intent. Both are designed to make computing more analogous to the way humans think. The concept of windows addresses the characteristic of human thinking that allows a human to do several things at once.

An **icon** is a small picture that represents a window, a command, or some other action that is currently not shown. However, the user knows what the icon represents. When working with GUI, the user can see many icons on the screen. Icons are used for several purposes. In some cases, they represent commands. In other cases, clicking on an icon activates a related window, expanding it to full size. Windows are temporarily shrunk to an icon when the user does not want to follow a particular thread of dialogue or to see certain data. These icons are referred to as **smart icons**. Icons represent other objects, such as unwanted files or items on menus, and can take many forms.

Hot spots are objects on a window that contain additional information that cannot be seen unless activated. When a point cursor "touches" a hot spot, a text, a picture, or other presentation is activated.

WYSIWYG ENVIRONMENT

In a **what-you-see-is-what-you-get (WYSIWYG)** environment (see Chapter 6), the user works with multiple overlapping windows and other GUI parts, and is able to move text and graphics seamlessly across applications. WYSIWYG is a display mode primarily concerned with the relationship between screen presentation and hard-copy presentation.

▶ 7.8 MULTIMEDIA, HYPERMEDIA, AND HYPERTEXT

User interfaces can be enriched by the use of multimedia. Computerized systems employ several multimedia technologies such as virtual reality and hypertext as presentation or navigation devices. Multimedia can also be an integral part of information processing and decision making.

MULTIMEDIA

Multimedia refers to a pool of human-machine communication media (see Chapter 6), some of which can be combined in one application. In information technology, an *interactive multimedia approach* involves the use of computers to improve human–machine communication by using several items of the media pool (Table 7.6) with the computerized system as the center of the application. Such integration allows the combination of the strengths of voice, GUI, and other media. The construction of an application is called *authoring*. An example of a complex input/output system is shown in Figure 7.8. Multimedia can merge the

---

Table 7.6 **Communication Media**

Computer	**Projected still visuals**
CRT and terminals	Slide
CD-ROM	Overhead
Computer interactive videodisc	**Graphic materials**
Digital video interactive	Pictures
Compact disc interactive	Printed job aids
Computer simulation	Visual display
Teletext/videotext	**Audio**
Intelligent tutoring system	Tape/cassette/record
Hypertext	Teleconference/audioconference
Image digitizing	Sound digitizing
Scanners	Microphone
Screen projection	Compact disc
Object-oriented programming	Music
Motion image	**Text**
Videodisc (cassette)	Printouts
Motion pictures	
Broadcast television	
Teleconference/videoconference	
Animation	
Virtual reality	

SOURCE: Based on Chao P., et al., "Using Expert Systems Approaches to Solve Media Selection Problems: Matrix Format," *Proceedings of the Association of Computer Interface System*, November 1990, IEEE.

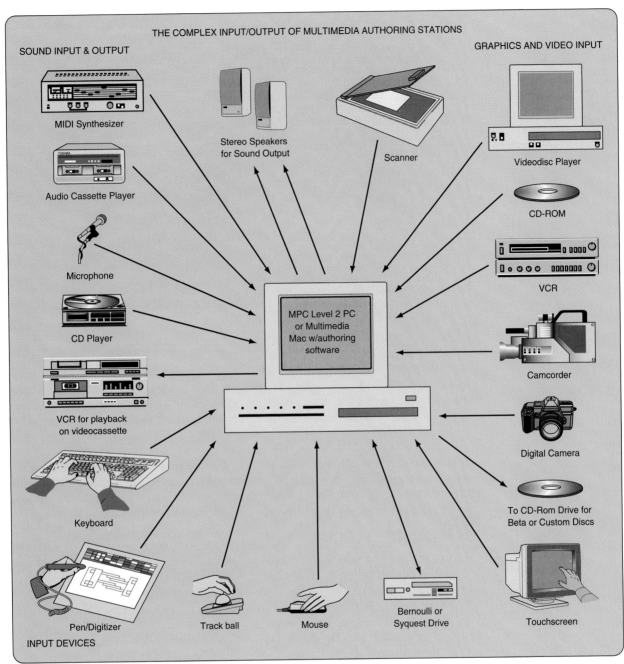

THE COMPLEX INPUT/OUTPUT OF MULTIMEDIA AUTHORING STATIONS

SOUND INPUT & OUTPUT

GRAPHICS AND VIDEO INPUT

MIDI Synthesizer

Stereo Speakers
for Sound Output

Scanner

Videodisc Player

Audio Cassette Player

CD-ROM

Microphone

VCR

MPC Level 2 PC
or Multimedia
Mac w/authoring
software

CD Player

Camcorder

VCR for playback
on videocassette

Digital Camera

Keyboard

To CD-Rom Drive for
Beta or Custom Discs

Pen/Digitizer

Track ball

Mouse

Bernoulli or
Syquest Drive

Touchscreen

INPUT DEVICES

FIGURE 7.8 Multimedia authoring system with a great variety of input sources and output displays. (Source: *Reseller Management*, November, 1993. Copyright 1993 with the permission of *Reseller Management* from the 11/93 VAR Workbook Series by John McCormick and Tom Fare, Multimedia Today Supplement: VAR Workbook Series, pgs 4–5, 7.)

capabilities of computers with TVs, VCRs, CD players, and other entertainment devices. An example of a commercial multimedia development tool is shown in Figure 7.9.

HYPERTEXT AND HYPERMEDIA*

Multimedia software is mainly used for making dynamic presentations—providing information or computer-based training in an interactive and exciting manner that

---

*This section is from Stern and Stern (1993) pp. 276–277.

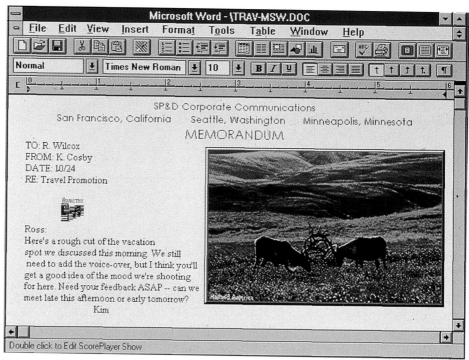

FIGURE 7.9 Microsoft Multimedia Viewer, an authoring tool for building multimedia applications. With *Microsoft Multimedia Viewer*, you can create on-line publications (titles) that use sophisticated searching and hypermedia links—connecting text, graphics, and video—to make communication and learning more natural, productive, and enjoyable.

makes use of video, sound, animation, and graphics as well as text. Multimedia software tools use a *hypermedia* navigational technique incorporated into a wide variety of products. Hypermedia itself is based on *hypertext* navigation, which was text-based but incorporated innovative mechanisms for interacting with a computer.

Hypertext software is a dynamic approach to navigating, or moving, through a database where information is linked together and is accessible in any form desired, regardless of its location. With hypertext, some links lead to other links, which further link to other topics, and so forth. Suppose you are interested in information about display terminals. You can go to a reference book, look up the topic in the index, and then read the pages cited. This would be a basic hypertext search. But the pages to which you were referred may also discuss associated subjects such as menus, prompts, icons, and mice. These subjects might be helpful as well; they may be cited in other places in the book. It would be difficult to navigate through the book looking for all topics that relate to display terminals.

By using software that contains hypertext components, however, you can select a topic, read about it, and then easily choose related subtopics from a menu. The context-sensitive help function provided by many software packages has hypertext tools to enable users to find the level of help they desire. As an author using hypertext software, you can build connections between ideas and concepts, and structure your ideas in a number of meaningful ways.

The basic concept behind hypertext is not new. Think of an encyclopedia. An article in an encyclopedia often ends with a series of subtopics that relate to the article. Each subtopic may also have reference points, including information specifically related to the subtopic and to more general topics. Using hypertext, however, it is possible to ''jump'' directly to a desired specific screen display. This is much easier than flipping through volumes of an encyclopedia in search of such topics.

Hypermedia improves on the hypertext concept by linking together not only text but also graphics, sound, animation, and even video (see Box 7.8). The major benefit of computerized hypermedia is that readers do not need to know the physical location (analogous to a page number) of data. They simply select the links they desire. Suppose you are at your computer reading about activities at your college or university from a manual available on-line. You come across the term *physical fitness* and it is highlighted, which means that more information is available. You can move the cursor to this item or use your mouse to click on it. The screen will be created, and an animated description of how to stay fit will appear. From here, you can select information about your school's exercise equipment, and a video may be played demonstrating how to use the equipment.

A Closer Look BOX 7.8

HYPERMEDIA SAVES TIME AND MAKES IMPRESSIVE PRESENTATIONS

Hypertext allows navigation through huge text files. For example, if you are designing a software manual or other complex documents, you can provide ways for people to jump quickly from one part to another. Many products make the creation of hypertext links smooth and easy by simply highlighting a word or phrase, choosing a file you wish to link to, and executing your command! Hypermedia software can link text to graphics and even to sound files, making it a hypermedia. In the picture at right, a product called Hyperwrite (from Looking Glass Software) was used to bring up text and graphics related to the term Christopher Columbus. Sound can be added as well.

SOURCE: Condensed from *PC World*, April 1993.

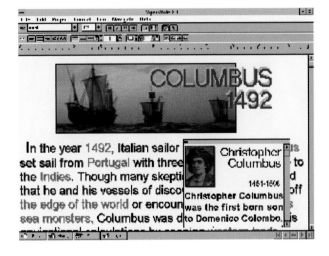

Some hypermedia products allow you to interact with them. For example, you can test your understanding of a topic, or you can enter values to see how they would affect results. Such interactive techniques make hypermedia tools ideal for on-line tutorials and other computer-based training applications. Many software packages have hypertext or hypermedia features added on for navigating through the package or for getting on-line help. QuickBASIC and QBASIC (supplied with MS-DOS 5.0 and higher), for example, are two such products.

Hypermedia techniques include the following:

▼ Paging or navigating through a lesson or inquiry that includes text, graphics, video, animation, and sound.

▼ Leaving ''bookmarks'' to return to specific pages for references.

▼ Going directly to any new concept without having to sequentially scroll through a text.

▼ Taking tests at any point and getting results immediately.

▼ Viewing a map of all linkages to obtain an overview of the structure of the topic investigated.

▶ 7.9 GEOGRAPHICAL INFORMATION SYSTEMS

A **geographical information system (GIS)** is a computer-based system for capturing, storing, checking, integrating, manipulating, and displaying spatial data using digitized maps. In a GIS, every record or digital object has an identified geographical location. This property is the most distinguishing characteristic of a GIS. By integrating maps with spatially oriented (geographical location) databases, users can increase their productivity and quality. GIS can provide access to types of information not otherwise available. GIS is basically a decision-support system that integrates spatially referenced data in a problem-solving environment. Therefore, GIS has many applications (see Box 7.9 and Minicase 2).

▶ 7.10 VISUAL INTERACTIVE MODELING AND SIMULATION

Visual interactive modeling (VIM) uses computer graphic displays to represent the impact of different management decisions on goals such as profit or market share. VIM differs from regular graphics in that the user can intervene in the decision-making process and see the results of the intervention. A visual model is much more than a communication device since it is used as an integral part of the decision making and/or problem solving.

A VIM can be used both for supporting decisions and training (see Box 7.10). It can represent a static or dynamic system. Static models display a visual image of the result of one decision alternative at a time. (With computer windows, several results can be compared on one screen.) Dynamic models display systems that evolve over time; the evolution is represented by animation or motion pictures.

IT At Work BOX 7.9

SAMPLE OF GIS APPLICATIONS

▼ Demographic maps of customers and neighborhoods.

▼ Locational information for retail outlets.

▼ Information for travelers (e.g., in National Parks).

▼ Real estate maps for tax collection.

▼ Locating homes for possible purchase.

▼ Disaster management (e.g., tracking of Hurricane Andrew's damage areas).

▼ Tracking fleets of trucks to determine delivery zones, scheduling, and regulatory compliance.

▼ Mapping of natural resources (e.g., gold, timber).

▼ Exhibition of electricity and other utility lines.

▼ Land use as a base for zoning, and tax collection.

▼ Identifying the density of crimes and allocating police accordingly.

▼ Soil and vegetation surveys.

▼ Environmental monitoring/control (e.g., oil spills).

▼ Urban planning.

▼ Site selection (for a warehouse, manufacturing plant, retail store, and so on).

▼ Sales support.

▼ Fleet management.

▼ Military applications (e.g., targeting decisions).

An example of how a land developer could use a GIS is shown in the figure on the next page (Courtesy of MapInfo Corporation, Troy, NY). The map uses shading, symbols, and grid patterns to show occupied properties, undeveloped land, and land under construction. By clicking on a street—in this case, Broadway—a listing of all properties in the street segment appears in a window. Additional information, such as demographic data, could be overlaid on this map.

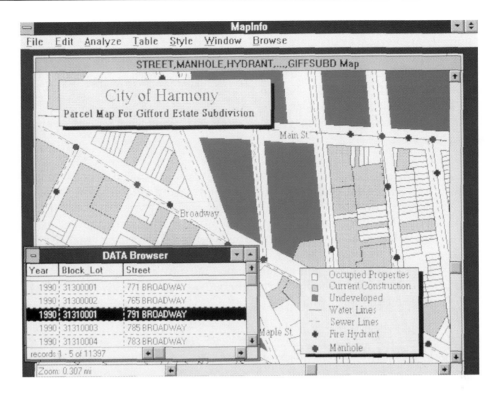

Critical Thinking Issue: How can a land developer benefit from a map like the one shown in the above figure? ▲

A Closer Look BOX 7.10

HOW CAN VISUAL INTERACTIVE DECISION MAKING HELP A MANAGER?

The first exposure to visual interactive modeling (VIM) positions the manager on unfamiliar ground. A large color screen lights up with a graphic display which may include moving icons and blinking colors. The first response is usually to make a comparison with a video game and, indeed, the program creating the display has much in common with game software. The comparison is, however, short lived. The power of the technique emerges in stages.

1. Managers recognize the screen display as a graphic representing a familar process or situation.
2. Managers observe the screen carefully, perhaps several other screen displays also, and accept the picture(s) as a sufficiently detailed image of the real process, with any motion showing realistic process evolution.
3. Managers interact with the model and observe that the screen image responds in accordance with their understanding of the real system.
4. Through experimentation and observation, managers gain confidence in the visual model and become convinced that the model producing the displays is a valid representation of the real system.

5. Once convinced of the validity of the visual model, managers can begin to ask "what-if" questions, and the visual model becomes a powerful decision-making aid.

The power of VIM as a decision-making tool comes from the *confidence* in the model that grows as managers see the model confirm their understanding of the real system.

Managerial validation of the model occurs because:

▼ A picture is recognizable as a model of the real world more readily than a table of numbers; a street map of a city is easier to recognize as the city than a list of the coordinates of street intersections.

▼ A visual model is not a "black box." The interior workings of the model are in full view and nothing has to be taken on trust.

▼ Dynamic visual models show the same transient behavior of the process that the manager sees every day, rather than a static view that represents average behavior over a long period of time.

▼ VIM enables the manager to interact directly with the model rather than work with a mathematical model through an analyst.

The manager chooses experiments to be conducted and evaluates them using results provided by the model. Explicit measures of the performance and quality of alternative solutions can be incorporated into the model. For example, in a bus-routing problem, it may be desirable to keep the routes as short as possible; after changing stops around, the total length of the routes can be computed and displayed. Optimization procedures can also be built into the model. For example, when a stop is moved from one route to another, the routes can be redrawn to minimize the distance traveled.

SOURCE: Condensed from Bell et al. (1984).

One of the most developed areas in dynamic VIM is **visual interactive simulation (VIS)**. The basic philosophy of VIS is that decision makers will be able to interact with a simulated model and watch the results developing over time in an animated form. This is achieved by using a visual display unit (see Box 7.11 on page 253).

General-purpose, dynamic VIM software is commercially available for both mainframe and microcomputers. For a representative list of packages with animation, see Swain, 1993.

▶ 7.11 VIRTUAL REALITY

3-D PRESENTATIONS

An increasing number of today's computer applications have 3-D graphical user interfaces. Such presentation is especially important in the manufacturing and marketing environments. The 3-D user interface offers rich opportunities for powerful interactions that use the mind's natural experiences in spatial perception. However, in 3-D environments, which are shown on flat 2-D screens, we see only 2-D projections of 3-D objects. The user must therefore use such views to deduce geometric properties and spatial relationships. 3-D viewing helps with depth perception, but to grasp a complex screen fully, it is best to let the user move freely about the objects by manipulating a virtual camera or eye. The implementation of such 3-D user interface is, therefore, difficult and expensive. One of the most interesting implementations of such 3-D user interface is *virtual reality*.

WHAT *IS* VIRTUAL REALITY?

There really is no standard definition of **virtual reality (VR)**. The most common definitions usually imply that virtual reality is interactive, computer-generated, three-dimensional graphics, and delivered to the user through a head-mounted display. Defined technically, virtual reality is an "environment and/or technology that provides artificially generated sensory cues sufficient to engender in the user some willing suspension of disbelief." So in virtual reality, a person "believes" that what she is doing is real, even though it is artificially created. Several people and large groups can potentially share and interact in the same environment. Because of this ability, VR can be a powerful medium for communication, entertainment, and learning. With virtual reality, instead of looking at a flat computer screen, the user interacts with a 3-D computer-generated environment (see Box 7.12). To see and hear the environment, the user wears stereo goggles and a 3-D headset. To interact with the environment (control objects or move around), the user wears a computerized behavior-transducing head-coupled display and hand position sensors (gloves). Virtual reality displays achieve the illusion of a surrounding medium by updating the display in real time. The user can grasp and move virtual objects.

IT At Work BOX 7.11

VISUAL INTERACTIVE SIMULATION AT WEYERHAEUSER CO.

Weyerhaeuser Company (Tacoma, WA) is a large timber processor. The company developed several applications of visual interactive simulation, including a log-cutting system.

Timber processing involves harvesting trees that are delimbed and topped. The resulting "stems" are crosscut into logs of various lengths. These logs are allocated among different mills, each of which makes a different end product (e.g., plywood, lumber, paper). For each tree, there may be hundreds of reasonable cutting combinations. The decisions are made on a stem-by-stem basis, because each tree is physically different from every other tree. The cutting decisions are the major determinant of revenues. Because costs are not affected much by these decisions, the larger the revenue generated, the larger the profit.

Management scientists developed a theoretical optimization model for the cutting and allocating decisions. However, employees in the field were reluctant to use solutions that resulted from an unfamiliar, somewhat intimidating, "black box" algorithm. The *visual decision simulator* allows operators to deal with the proposed optimization solutions on their own terms. The simulator allows the operator to roll, rotate, cut, and allocate each stem right on the computer screen. He can see the end product and the resultant profit contribution of the suggested solution. He can then compare it with the profit resulting from the recommendation of the dynamic programming model. If not satisfied, the operator can recut the same stem repeatedly (on the computer screen, of course) to explore alternate decisions. The final decision, how to cut, is always made by the operator; therefore, the system is nonthreatening. Furthermore, the repeated cutting experimentation on the screen is well documented and has led to improved decision-making skills in the field.

Critical Thinking Issue: Why are the employees in favor of VIS, and why is the system nonthreatening? ▲

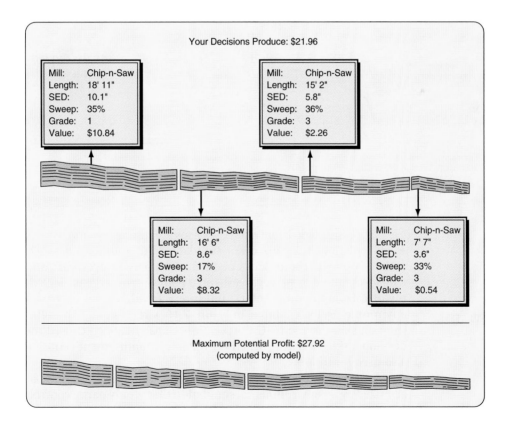

SOURCE: Abstracted from Lembersky and Chi (1986).

A Closer Look BOX 7.12

HOW DOES VR WORK?

In a typical virtual reality system (see figure below), the user views the virtual world with either a head-mounted display or on a screen (with or without 3-D shutter glasses). Delivered over headphones or speakers, 3-D sound provides realistic audio. A tracking system receiver and one or more transmitters tell the computer where the user is looking and where the 3-D controller is in space.

These connect to the computer through either a serial port or a special interface card. The computer contains the graphics subsystem, spatialized audio subsystem, the databases of the geometry of the objects in the world, the world database (which defines the environment and how objects in it relate to each other), and the sound database.

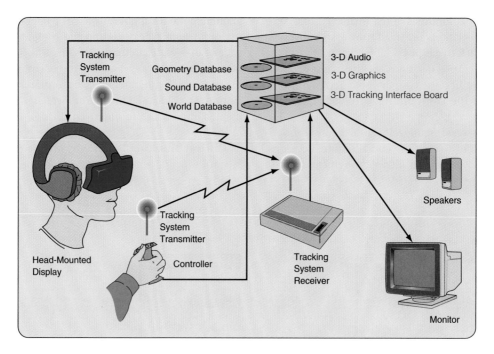

SOURCE: Reproduced from *New Media*, (Aug. 1994), p. 45.

...virtual skiing in Japan

Sophisticated virtual reality systems are interactive and usually simulate real-world phenomena. They often simulate sight, sound, and touch and combine these senses with computer-generated input to users' eyes, ears, and skin. By using a head-mounted display, gloves, and a bodysuit, or large projected images in simulator cabs, users can ''enter'' and interact with virtual or artificially generated environments. For example, in Figure 7.10, virtual skiing is presented. The picture shows a skiier in the NEC Corporation (Japan) Lab. NEC used the laboratory to develop a ski simulator, which is available in amusement centers. The product is also used for training.

In a broad historical perspective, VR can be seen as a form of *interface* characterized by an environmental simulation that is only partly controlled by the user. VR may also be characterized by the reality being depicted. The work currently in progress on virtual reality falls on a continuum from the development of computer-mediated realities to computer-developed alternative realities. Moving along the continuum, there are efforts such as remote-controlled undersea or interplanetary robots that provide computer-mediated realities. Another charac-

FIGURE 7.10 Developing virtual skiing in Japan.

teristic of virtual reality is its natural user involvement. Some virtual realities are indistinguishable from reality.

Currently, virtual reality is available in some games and in limited commercial applications (see Table 7.7). Within several years, however, there will be many commercial applications (e.g., making purchasing decisions by observing virtual products).

Table 7.7 **Examples of Virtual Reality Applications**

Industry	*Application*
Automotive and heavy equipment	• Design testing • Virtual prototyping • Engineering analysis • Ergonomic analysis • Virtual simulation of assembly, production, and maintenance
Architecture	• Design of building and other structures
Military	• Training (pilots, astronauts, drivers) • Battlefield simulations
Medicine	• Training surgeons (with simulators) • Planning surgeries • Physical therapy
Research/education	• Virtual physics lab • Hurricane studies • Galaxy configurations • Representation of complex mathematics
Amusement	• 3-D race car games (on PC) • Air combat simulation (on PC) • Virtual reality arcades • Virtual reality parks • Ski simulator

SOURCE: Compiled from Adam (1993) and updated.

▶ 7.12 NATURAL LANGUAGE PROCESSING

...soon computers will be able to understand what you say

Natural language processing (NLP) refers to communicating with a computer in English or other spoken languages. Today, computer commands are usually typed on the keyboard, once they are organized in a special manner understood by the computer. In responding to a user, the computer outputs symbols or short cryptic notes of information or direction.

To use a computer properly, one must learn special commands, languages, and jargon. This usually takes considerable time and practice, and it is the main reason why computers have been called "unfriendly." Menus and icons with pointing devices like light pens, mice, and touch screens help, of course, but they are not perfectly natural.

Many problems would be minimized or even eliminated if we could communicate with the computer in our own language. We would simply type in directions, instructions, or information. The computer would be smart enough to interpret the input regardless of its format. An even better alternative would be to give the computer voice instructions in a natural language.

To understand a natural language inquiry, a computer must have sufficient knowledge to analyze the input in order to interpret it. This may include linguistic knowledge about words, domain knowledge, common sense knowledge, and even knowledge about users and their goals. NLP must understand grammar and definitions of words. Once the computer understands the input, it can take the desired action.

In addition to *natural language understanding*, there is also *natural language generation*. Once the computer takes action, it will usually provide some output, preferably in a natural language. These topics are discussed further in Chapter 16.

▶ MANAGERIAL ISSUES

IMPORTANCE OF THE USER INTERFACE

The ease of communication between people and the computer is critical for achieving widespread use of computers. Resistance to computers may be reduced if the user interface improves. MIS experts may not appreciate this point and therefore build applications that the user may reject. Much research is being done on user interface, and improved devices arrive all the time.

SUBJECTIVITY

Different people prefer different user interfaces. Adding interface options may seem a waste of money, but in many cases increasing the flexibility of interface modes may be a worthwhile investment, especially when the cost of adding more options is not too high.

THE WORLD OF GUI

The computing industry is moving into the world of GUI. Management will have to make difficult decisions regarding the available products. For example, should you use Macintosh, Windows, or something else? Advances in the GUI field are very rapid and must be taken into consideration in IT planning. Products such as Windows 95 include more options, but they do not come free.

JUSTIFICATION AND COST–BENEFIT ANALYSIS

Justification of user-friendly interfaces as well as graphics and multimedia is difficult owing to the mostly intangible benefits and the newness of the technology. Colors and graphics are pleasant and entertaining, but not necessarily effective.

ELECTRONIC DOCUMENT MANAGEMENT

Many of the important business processes in organizations are based on or driven by documents. Dramatic improvements in operations can be achieved if the documents are stored in computers for future processing.

EMERGING INTERFACE TECHNOLOGIES

Recognizing the importance of user interface, companies are developing new interface products. However, management should be careful in adopting those products. While virtual reality, for example, can be extremely impressive in the arcade, it may be a poor investment for use in advertising men's suits.

VOICE TECHNOLOGIES

Despite their current limitations, such as difficulty in understanding continuous speech, voice technologies are extremely important because they are natural and provide fast data entry. Management should monitor new developments and introduce these technologies as they become cost effective.

MULTIMEDIA

Many people underestimate the power of multimedia for presenting information in training, education, entertainment, and advertisement. Management must investigate the current state of the art and introduce multimedia applications whenever they become economically feasible. Again, justification is a major issue; but ignoring the technology may cause a company to lag behind its competitors.

HEALTH AND SAFETY ISSUES

Several input and output devices, such as the keyboard and the monitor, may be hazardous to people's health and safety. Therefore, appropriate design and use of these devices is important. Many lawsuits have been filed against employers. This issue is further explored in Chapter 20.

ETHICAL ISSUES

Can virtual reality (VR) be used for unethical (or even illegal) purposes? Rheingold (1991) thinks that the difference between reality and simulation created by VR is so small that the users may not know the difference and could be manipulated to act destructively, thinking that they are in the imaginary world.

Also, presentations in general influence people, and computer presentations can be so vivid that people may be led to believe in things that they should not.

How can management ensure that presentations will be used ethically? Can management control its salespeople and avoid abusive presentations?

INTERNATIONAL ISSUES

User interface considerations may become more complicated when international aspects are added. For example, inputting and outputting Asian scripts using a regular keyboard is feasible today, but it may slow data entry (see Box 7.13). ■

A Closer Look BOX 7.13

*G*LOBAL PERSPECTIVE

SOME INTERNATIONAL ASPECTS OF USER INTERFACE

How can you use your PC to type in Chinese?

There are several methods. Here is one that combines Microsoft Word with a package from China, called Cstar, which contains about 15,000 Chinese characters in its database. As an example, let us look at the words *School of Management*. In Chinese, this is written by four characters: two describe *management* (on the left), two describe *school* (on the right).

管 理 学 院 (School of Management)
Guan Li Xue Yuan

The pronunciation of these four characters is shown below the characters.

You take the first character, *guan*, and type it. When you do, the computer will come up with about eight Chinese characters, all of which are pronounced *guan*. You select the one that describes the first part of *management*. Then you type in *Li*; again you will get several possibilities from which you select the second character for *management*. You continue in this manner until you type all the characters. This lengthy job can be made shorter. For example, if you use the word *management* often, then you associate it with *gl* (for *guan li*) and put it in the database. So, when you type *gl*, the word *management* will appear.

Other methods break the Chinese characters into standard vowels and consonants using a one-to-one code; each of these corresponds to a letter or a number. This method is slow, but shortcuts are available. Voice technologies, of course, will solve the problem and greatly expedite data entry in Chinese or any other language.

When the Thai language needed to be computerized, we faced different problems. In contrast to Chinese, where each symbol has a meaning, the Thai language uses complex letters. The long word shown below is written in the Thai language. It means "welcome to beautiful Thailand." The symbols appear in four levels: lowercase, centered regular symbols (in the middle), upper small symbols, and lower small symbols.

ขอต้อนธับสู่ดวามสวย-
งามของเมืองไทยและ

Sometimes there are even five levels. To begin with, it is difficult to place five levels in a computer. Furthermore, there are 46 regular letters in the Thai alphabet, which are combined to create very long words. Finally, the meaning of many words in Thai depends on the voice level at which these words are spoken.

Voice technologies will be able to expedite the problem of data entry of Asian languages. However, using voice understanding or even voice synthesis devices may create problems for pitch-sensitive languages.

KEY TERMS

CHAPTER HIGHLIGHTS *(L-x means learning objective number x)*

▼ The user interface is critical to the success of any information system. (L-1)

▼ An interface is the hardware, software, and procedures that provide human-machine communication. (L-1)

▼ An interface is composed of action and presentation languages, computer hardware and software, and procedures. (L-1)

▼ Major input devices are keying devices, the mouse, light pens, touch screens, optical character recognizers, and handwriting and voice recognition devices. (L-2)

▼ Major output devices are monitors, printers, plotters, and voice. (L-2)

▼ Major interface modes (styles) are menu interaction, command language, questions and answers, form interaction, object manipulation, and natural language processing. They provide flexibility and choice in human-machine interface. (L-3)

▼ Graphics play a major role in CBIS, both as a presentation language and in supporting active user interface. (L-4)

▼ The GUI enables the user to control visible objects

and actions, thereby minimizing the use of command language. (L-5)

▼ Multimedia is utilized in managerial decision making, both for presentation and actions such as expediting a search using hypertext. (L-6)

▼ A geographical information system captures, stores, manipulates, and display data using digitized maps. (L-7)

▼ Visual interactive modeling is an implementation of GUI that is usually combined with simulation and animation. (L-8)

▼ Virtual reality is implementation of GUI in three dimensions. It includes audio, sensors, and other features that take the user into an almost-real environment. (L-9)

▼ Natural language processing provides an opportunity for a user to communicate with a computer in a day-to-day spoken language. (L-10)

▼ Speech understanding, which enables people to communicate with the computer by voice, has many benefits. (L-10)

▼ Voice synthesis is the transformation of computerized output to voice. (L-10)

QUESTIONS FOR REVIEW

1. What are the major elements of a user interface?

2. Describe the various modes of interfaces.

3. List the major types of graphics.

4. Define graphical user interface (GUI).

5. What does WYSIWYG mean? Why is it useful?

6. Define a user interface management system (UIMS).

7. How does hypertext work? What is its major advantage?

8. Define presentation and action languages.

9. What are the major advantages of a natural language?

10. List the major input devices.

11. List the major output devices.

12. Define virtual reality and list its major benefits. Any drawbacks?

13. Explain multimedia and hypermedia.

14. Distinguish between voice recognition and voice synthesis.

15. List the major advantages of voice recognition.

16. What is a geographical information system?

17. Explain visual simulation.

18. What is visual interactive modeling?

19. List the major managerial issues in building a user interface.

20. List the major benefits of using graphics.

QUESTIONS FOR DISCUSSION

1. Research results indicate that graphical presentation is not more effective than tabular presentation. Practitioners disagree; they claim that graphics are superior. Explain why such differences may occur.

2. Discuss the role of graphics in CBIS. How can graphics support decisions?

3. Discuss the major benefits of GUI.

4. Explain how handwriting recognition works. Will it one day eliminate the keyboard? Alternatively, would it be eliminated by voice entry devices? Discuss.

5. Discuss the role of UIMS.

6. Some say that the interface is the most important component of a CBIS. Explain why.

7. Explain the *process* of user–computer interaction (per Figure 7.1).

8. Geographical information systems are receiving great recognition (e.g., see Tetzeil [1993]). Why is this so? Will they eliminate the spreadsheet?

9. Menu interaction is probably the most well-liked interface style. Explain why.

10. Why is a command language the preferred style of many experienced users?

11. What are the commonalities between VR and VIM? What are the differences?

12. Describe a combination of menus and commands from your own experience.

13. What is the difference between voice recognition and voice understanding?

14. Give five examples where voice recognition can be applied today, and list the benefit(s) in each case. Be specific.

15. Several computer games, such as Flight Simulation II and GATO, can be considered visual interactive simulation. Explain why.

16. It is said that VIM is particularly helpful in implementing recommendations derived by computers. Explain why.

17. The Wharton Experiment (see Box 7.7) has far-reaching implications for computers. Give three examples that convey this concept.

18. Provide several examples of how new technologies in input devices can help disabled workers interact with computers.

19. Why is the popularity of GUI on the increase?

20. Discuss the relationships between multimedia, hypertext, and hypermedia.

21. Explain the benefits of multimedia.

EXERCISES AND APPLICATIONS

1. What input and output devices would you use for the following systems? For each, compare and contrast at least two alternatives.
   a. A peopleless spaceship communication with Earth.
   b. A tourist information kiosk, located on a mountain and having no employees.
   c. An information and help desk at a hospital where an employee is using a computer to advise patients and their relatives.
   d. A designer in an engineering company working on a workstation.
   e. Remodeling of a house.

2. Virtual reality is moving into the business world. Find evidence for recent commercial applications, and explain the benefits generated by the technology in each case.

3. Multimedia, hypertext, and hypermedia may have specific applications in the college classroom. Detail some examples that you find interesting.

GROUP ASSIGNMENT

Each group member will interview five computer users, at school, work, or home. For each user, identify the three interface modes preferred by the user, ranked in descending order. Also, the interviewer needs to find the reasons why people prefer a particular interface mode. Then, the group will consolidate the findings of its members and prepare a report that will guide a novice computer user to the interface(s) with which he should become familiar.

Minicase 1

An Electronic Job Search System in Illinois

Illinois was the first state to introduce an electronic system to eliminate long lines at its unemployment offices and reengineer its operations. The goal of the system, which was tested in 1993 and 1994, is to transform the paper-intensive bureaucracy of the Department of Employment Security into a computerized system that will help find jobs for people and eliminate time-consuming tasks.

Job seekers are communicating with the computer system using computers in self-service kiosks, which are networked. There is a touch-screen monitor in each kiosk, but management wants to add more input/output devices to improve the user interface.

Here are some data about the state's unemployment system: (1) six million pieces of paper are generated each year for the purpose of processing claims and hunting for jobs, (2) many people in the state do not understand English, (3) each unemployment claim involves four forms, and (4) many applicants cannot type. The basic idea is to transfer work currently done by the state's employees to the applicants. To assist customers, kiosks will be placed in shopping malls, schools, and public libraries.

Since the budget is limited, management cannot offer too many input and output devices. Specifically, management would like you to rank the options in each of the following categories:

▼ *Input devices:* keying devices, pointing devices, OCR, voice recognizer, handwriting recognizer, and "brain-wave" devices.

▼ *Output devices:* monitors, printers, and voice synthesizers.

▼ *Interface modes:* menus, fill-in-the-blanks (forms), command, questions and answers, and GUI.

Questions for Minicase 1

1. In each category, rank the *three* devices or interface modes you recommend by order of importance. Consider ease of use, accuracy, speed, and cost in your answer (you need to conduct some research regarding the cost of the devices).

2. Describe the major benefits of your proposal.

3. Can this case be considered an example of BPR?

Minicase 2

Geographical Information System at Dallas Area Rapid Transit

Public transportation in Dallas and its neighboring communities is provided by the Dallas Area Rapid Transit (DART), which operates buses and vans and plans to operate a light-rail system by 1996. The service area has grown very fast. By the mid-'80s, the agency was no longer able to properly respond to customer requests, make rapid changes in scheduling, plan properly, or manage security. The solution to these problems was discovered in geographical information systems (GIS). A GIS digitizes maps (see the picture that follows) and maplike information, integrates it with other database information, and uses the combined information for planning, problem solving, and decision making.

DART maintains a centralized graphical database of every object for which DART is responsible.

The GIS presentation makes it possible for DART's managers, consultants, and customers to view and analyze data on digitized maps. Previously, DART manually created service maps showing bus routes and schedules. The maps were updated and redistributed several times a year, at a high cost. The manual method made it difficult to quickly and accurately respond to about 5000 customer inquiries each day. For example, to answer a question concerning one of the more than 200 bus routes or a specific schedule, it was often necessary to look at several maps and routes. Planning a change was also a time-consuming task. Analysis of the viability of bus route alternatives made it necessary to photocopy maps from map books, overlay tape to show proposed routes, and spend considerable time gathering information on the demographics of the corridors surrounding the proposed routes. The GIS includes attractive and accurate maps that interface with a database containing information about bus schedules, routes, bus stops (in excess of 13,500), traffic surveys, demographics, and addresses on each street in the database. The system allows DART employees to:

▼ Respond rapidly to customer inquiries (reducing response time by at least 33 percent).

▼ Provide accurate information to customers.

▼ Plan services (e.g., new and modified routes, schedules).

▼ Perform the environmental impact studies required by the city.

▼ Cut costs of generating bus schedules.

▼ Track where the buses are at any time (using Global Positioning System, a satellite-based navigation system, which is accurate within 10 ft).

▼ Improve security on buses.

▼ Monitor subcontractors quickly and accurately.

▼ Analyze the productivity and use of existing routes.

For instance, a customer wants to know the closest bus stop and the schedule of a certain bus to take her to a certain destination. The GIS automatically generates the answer when the caller says where she is by giving an address, a name of an intersection, or a landmark. The computer can calculate the travel time to the desired destination as well. Currently, the system is used by operators who answer the telephone calls. In the future, it will be used directly by the caller (either by using a computer or a telephone with a voice response arrangement).

Analyses, which previously took days to complete, are now executed in less than an hour. Preparation of special maps, which previously took up to a week to produce at a cost of $13,000 to $15,000 each, are produced in five minutes at the cost of three feet of plotter paper.

SOURCE: Condensed from *GIS World*, July 1993.

Questions for Minicase 2

1. What kind of user interface is provided by the GIS?

2. Which of DART's system capabilities and benefits are directly related to user interface?

3. Comment on the following statement: "Using GIS, one can improve not only the inputing of data but also its use."

A representative map in DART's database.

REFERENCES AND BIBLIOGRAPHY

1. Adam, J., "Virtual Reality is Real," *IEEE Spectrum*, October 1993. (VR special report)

2. Antonoff, M., "Living in a Virtual World," *Popular Science*, June 1993.

3. Bell, P. C., et al., "Visual Interactive Problem Solving— A New Look at Management Problems," *Business Quarterly*, Spring 1984.

4. Bennett, J. L., "Tools for Building Advanced User Interfaces." *IBM Systems Journal*, No. 3/4, 1986.

5. Dix, A. et al., *Human-Computer Interaction*, New York: Prentice Hall, 1993.

6. "Geographical Information Systems: A New Way to Look At Business Data," *I/S Analyzer*, January 1994.

7. Grimshaw, D. J., *Bringing Geographical Information Systems into Business*, Essex, England, Longman Scientific and Technical, 1994

8. Grupe, F. H., "A GIS for County Planning," *Information Systems Management*, Winter 1992.

9. Harrison, H. R., and D. Hix, "Human-Computer Interface Development: Concepts and Systems for Its Management," *ACM Computing Surveys*, Vol. 21, No. 1, March 1989.

10. *Hypermedia*, Special issue of *Communication of ACM*, February 1994.

11. Lansdale, M. W., and T. C. Ormerod, *Understanding Interfaces: A Handbook of Human-Computer Dialogue*, San Diego: Academic Press, 1994.

12. Lembersky, M. R., and U. H. Chi, "Decision Simulators Speed Implementation and Improve Operations," *Interfaces*, July–August 1984 (see also January–February 1986).

13. Majchrzak, A., et al., *Human Aspects of Computer-Aided Design*. Philadelphia: Taylor and Francis, 1987.

14. Marcus, A., "User-Interface Developments for the Nineties," *Computer*, September 1991.

15. Milheim, W. D., "Computer-Based Voice Recognition," *Performance Improvement Quarterly*, Vol. 6, No. 1, 1993.

16. Nielson, J. "Noncommand User Interfaces," *Communications of the ACM*, April 1993. (GUI special issue).

17. Neuman, W. A., and F. J. Brock, "Graphical User Interfaces in the 90's," *Information Executive*, Winter 1991.

18. Pimentel, K., and K. Teixeira, *Virtual Reality—Through the New Looking Glass*, New York: McGraw-Hill, November 1992 (easy to read introductory book).

19. Patel, H., and R. Cardinali, "Virtual Reality Technology in Business" *Management Decision*, Vol. 32, #7, 1994

20. Pracht, W. E., "Model Visualization: Graphical Support for DSS Problems Structuring and Knowledge Organization," *Decision Support Systems*, Vol. 6, 1990.

21. Ravden, S., and G. Johnson, *Evaluating Usability of Human–Computer Interfaces: A Practical Method*. New York: Wiley, 1989.

22. Rheingold, H., *Virtual Reality*, New York: Summit Books, 1991.

23. Stern N., and R. A. Stern, *Computing in the Information Age*, New York: Wiley, 1993.

24. Sprague, R. H., Jr., "Electronic Document Management," *MIS Quarterly*, March 1995.

25. Sprague, R. H., Jr., and B. McNurlin, *Information Systems Management in Practice*, Englewood Cliffs, NJ: Prentice-Hall, 1st ed. 1986, 3rd ed. 1993.

26. Swain, J. J., "Simulation Software Survey," *OR/MS Today*, Dec. 1993.

27. Tetzeil, R., "Mapping for Dollars," *Fortune*, October 18, 1993.

28. *The Benefits of the Graphical User Interface*, Special Report, Lexington, MA: Temple, Barker, and Stone, Inc., Spring 1990.

29. Turban, E., *Expert Systems and Applied Artificial Intelligence*, New York: Macmillan, 1992.

30. *Virtual Reality 93—Special Report*, published by *AI Expert*, 1993.

31. Watt, A., *Fundamentals of Three-Dimensional Computer Graphics*, Boston: Addison-Wesley, 1990.

32. Woolley, B., *Virtual Worlds: A Journey in Hype and Hyperreality*, Cambridge, MA: Blackwell, 1992.

8

DATA AND DATA MANAGEMENT

Chapter Outline

Learning Objectives

After studying this chapter, you will be able to:

1. Describe the two most basic types of computer-based information organization—files and databases—and their relative advantages and disadvantages.

2. Explain how data are organized logically into databases as well as differentiate between the four basic structural models.

3. Describe how data are organized and manipulated physically in databases by software packages, by manipulation languages, and by topology.

4. Describe the three ways data are stored and accessed in databases.

5. Explain what a logical database view is and its benefits.

6. Explain the role and responsibilities of a database administrator.

▶ 8.1 KNOW YOUR CUSTOMER—DATABASES MAKE IT EASIER

DELL COMPUTER CORPORATION has been the world's largest direct-sale vendor of personal computers. One way the company distinguishes itself from other suppliers of PCs is by acting quickly on the masses of data it gathers from customers (the company receives 35,000 telephone calls or electronic mail messages daily). "Information is a valuable competitive weapon," says Tom Thomas, the chief information officer. "Our whole business system is geared to collect it."

Many of the calls are from potential customers who dial 800 numbers to reach the company's sales representatives; the rest are from current users of Dell machines asking the technical support staff for help. The employees who take these calls work on PCs linked to a computer that contains the company's customer database, which has well over one million entries. The telephone representatives enter information about each call as it occurs, recording names and addresses along with product preferences and/or technical problems. The company stores all this information and much more in a single database shared by employees in departments from marketing to product development to customer service.

The data yield significant marketing and sales guidelines. Says Tom Martin, Dell's chief marketer, "We know that if we use a yellow background on a catalog cover, we'll get a 30 percent lower response rate than with gray." The company tailors its mailings ever more precisely to each recipient. The rate of response to its small-business mailings rose 250 percent once Dell used customer feedback to refine its pitch. At a mailing price of 50 cents to $3 per piece, the benefits of accurate targeting add up quickly.

Experience from the database also guides the sales representatives who receive calls. As they enter information about each caller, sales suggestions automatically pop up on their computer screens. Dell had a 10-

Dell phone representatives using the computer database.

fold increase in sales of three-year warranties after prompting representatives to pitch them to all callers buying systems costing more than a certain dollar amount.

Routine analysis of customer and sales data allows Dell to spot consumer trends like a shift to larger hard disk drives. At one time, when Dell was shipping most of its systems with drives capable of storing over 120 million characters (120 MB), the customer database alerted them to the fact that new orders were rapidly climbing for drives with nearly twice the storage capability. Dell buyers rushed out, negotiated volume discounts from large disk drive manufacturers, and locked in deliveries before other Dell competitors.

"Know your customer" is tried-and-true business wisdom, and Dell gets the most they can out of it through customer databases.

SOURCE: Adapted from *Fortune 1994 Information Technology Guide,* August 1993.

▶ 8.2 THE NEED TO ORGANIZE

Business managers, like those at Dell, are constantly making business decisions based on information that is increasingly being stored and manipulated using computers. As the old axiom goes, information is power. Computerized information can, indeed, be powerful when it is organized properly and easily accessible in the right form, at the right time, and at the right place.

Businesses are increasingly dependent on information. However, they must first be able to get at information when it's needed, where it's needed, and in the form in which it's needed. To be useful, data must be well organized, stored, and managed. The field of information sciences and all libraries are based on this simple premise. Computer-based information is no exception to this premise; computer-based information systems must be able to organize, store, and manage data for the data to be useful to businesses. Computers themselves may have nearly perfect internal storage and incredible speed; but disorganized data perfectly retrieved in milliseconds is still disorganized data and, thus, most likely to be useless. Moreover, in a dynamic business environment, there are many unanticipated needs for information. Business information not only must be well organized and managed, but it must also be easily and flexibly accessible to a wide range of users. *How* to organize, store, retrieve, and manage computer-based data are the subjects of this chapter.

People have found many ways to organize data, such as alphabetically (e.g., telephone directory books), chronologically (e.g., historical records), by subject (e.g., this textbook), and by source (e.g., bibliographies). Usually the method chosen is tailored to the expected method of accessing the data, as well as to what is already known and what is needed. For example, telephone directory books are usually alphabetized because people are readily familiar with the order of letters of the alphabet. Also, they usually know a name (based on letters) but not the telephone number. On the other hand, when someone knows a telephone number but not the associated name, the telephone directory is usually too difficult to use because the information in it is not organized according to that user's purpose. (It is for this reason that telephone companies also offer—for an extra price—directories that are organized by telephone number or by address rather than name.) Likewise, computer-based information systems need the capability to organize, store, and manage data in many different ways—based on the expected method of accessing that data, what the user already knows, and what the user seeks to know.

This chapter describes two main types of computer-based information organization—*files* and *databases*—and their relative advantages and disadvantages. It next discusses how data are organized *logically* and *physically*—the various *models* used to organize data and the ways these models are implemented and used in actual (physical) information systems. Finally, the chapter addresses the process of *managing* computer-based information, including designing logical and physical database systems.

Data are the foundation of information systems and the foundation of a knowledge-based business and society. A business specialist's—or programmer's or analyst's—knowledge of how computer-based data are organized, accessed, and managed is increasingly critical to business success.

▶ 8.3 FILES: THE TRADITIONAL APPROACH

As with many aspects of human life, most data have some commonality and some form of natural order among them. Data with some form of commonality are usually grouped into what are generally called **files**. People have made and kept files for countless reasons for millennia; they are the simplest and historically the most prevalent way of organizing data. Files were a mainstay in businesses long before the advent of electronic computers.

DATA COMMONALITY AND ORDER

Files contain **entities**—things about which we want to collect, store, and maintain information. For example, people are entities, and many different types of files are kept on them—files on students, teachers, families, tax payers, medical patients, and so on. Likewise, files are kept on products, resources, inventory, sales, purchases, and cash balances. What entities we choose to keep in files normally depends on our intended use of the data. How we organize the data on these entities often depends on the inherent order of the data.

Within files, subsets of the data on a particular entity are usually called **records** (data are an *instance* or *occurrence* of an entity). For example, in a file on university students, a record would be a group of data about each university student; a file on 200 students would have 200 records. In an analogy to a common filing cabinet, there would be 200 folders—one for each student record. Each unique type of information or *characteristic* about the entity is called a **field**. Each record, therefore, consists of many fields of data. In the student file example, there might be fields for a student's name, address, date of birth, sex, academic major, and so on. In the aggregate, therefore, files are composed of records which are, in turn, composed of fields of data.

In manual-based files, data are kept in cabinets, drawers, folders, and on sheets of paper in a hierarchical fashion. In computer-based files, data (as described in Chapter 5) are physically stored in *bytes* (equivalent to letters, numbers, or other characters) which are composed of *bits* (digital 1s and 0s). A computer-based file, therefore, has the natural hierarchy shown in Figure 8.1. Bits are grouped into bytes, bytes are grouped into fields, fields are grouped into records, and records are grouped into files.

FILING PROBLEMS

Although files based on commonality among entities and organized by some form of natural hierarchy are relatively simple to conceive and easy to implement, there are problems with this approach—problems that are exacerbated when files are computer based. These problems can be categorized as problems with filing programs, data redundancy, data sharing, and data consistency.

Computer-based files, stored as electronic 1s and 0s, are unintelligible to humans and, therefore, depend entirely on the electronic means of storing and accessing the data. Flipping through a telephone book or a paper file is relatively easy for humans; "flipping" through electronic bits is not. The means of accessing computer-based data is through *software* (introduced in Chapter 6) or *programs*. Ever since data have been computerized, software programs have been written to organize, store, retrieve, and manage data files. In the early days of computer-based data files, customized programs were written for each file, which structured how data were to be used, stored, and managed. Returning to our university example, there would be a student registration program for a student file, an accounting program for a student accounts file, and a sports participation program for a student sports file. Each program and its respective file would be used by different university offices, uniquely designed for their individual needs (as shown in Figure 8.2).

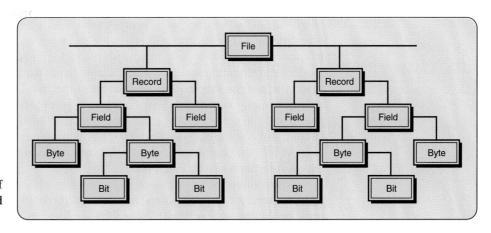

FIGURE 8.1 Hierarchy of data for a computer-based file.

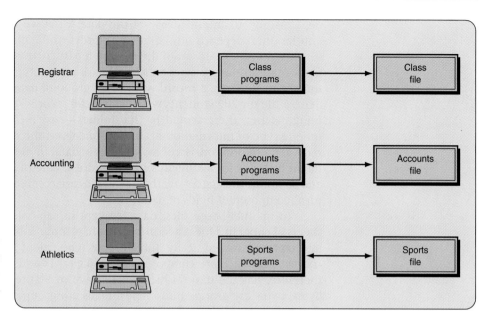

FIGURE 8.2 Computer-based files of this type cause problems such as redundancy, inconsistency, and data isolation.

Problems with file programs are apparent in Figure 8.2. All the file programs in this university example would share some common core functions, such as input, report generation, querying, and data browsing. Most likely, however, these common functions would be designed, coded, documented, and tested—at great expense—for *each* program. Moreover, users must be trained to use each different program. A clerk moving from the registrar's office to the accounting office, for example, would likely have to be fully trained on a new filing program with different procedures, screen images, data formats, and detailed functionality. Many systems for computer-based files can waste valuable resources creating and maintaining similar programs as well as in training users how to use them.

Data redundancy problems can also be seen in this example and in Figure 8.2. Each file will contain records about students, many of whom will be represented in other files. This means that student files in the aggregate will contain some amount of duplicate data. For example, all student records are likely to have a field for name, student identification number, address, telephone number, and so on. It is not uncommon with computer-based files for a new student to have to give his name, address, phone number, and so forth half a dozen times to different campus offices—the same information over and over! This is wasteful not only of physical computer storage media and of students' time and effort, but also of all the clerks' time needed to enter and maintain the data.

Perhaps the biggest problem with files, however, is that the data in them cannot readily be shared or related. With files uniquely designed and implemented, data are likely organized differently, stored in different formats (e.g., height in inches vs. height in centimeters), and often physically inaccessible to other file programs. In the university file example, an administrator who wanted to know which students taking advanced courses were also starting players on the football team would most likely not be able to get the answer from the computer-based file system. Printed output data from the two files would most likely have to be manually compared. This could be accomplished, of course, but doing so would take a great deal of time and effort. It would also ignore the greatest strengths of computers—fast processing and accurate storage. Keeping data in the form of files on computers seriously limits the productive potential of computers and of information system users.

Maintaining duplicate data in many files also raises the problem of **data inconsistency** with computer-based data files. With duplicate data, all changes must be duplicated everywhere the data are located. A student whose telephone number changes must ensure that the telephone number is changed in every file that contains it. Moreover, the student must ensure that the change is made correctly in every file. This problem intensifies problems of data sharing and relating among files. Even if data in files could be shared or related somehow electronically, any inconsistency among the files would prevent it from occurring. Searching for student information by student identification number in different files, for example, requires identical student identification numbers in each file.

The First Commandment of Data Organization, therefore, could be stated as follows:

"Thou shalt have one datum in only one place at only one time."

Programming, data redundancy, data sharing, and data inconsistency problems with computer-based files led to the development of *databases.*

▶ 8.4 DATABASES: THE MODERN APPROACH

A **database** is a superset of related files. In a database, data are integrated and related so that one set of software programs provides access to all the data. Therefore, data redundancy is minimized, data can be shared among all users of the data, and data inconsistency is minimized. The software program (or group of programs) that provides access to a database is known as a **database management system (DBMS)**. A database with a DBMS for the university example used previously is shown in Figure 8.3.

ADVANTAGES OF DATABASE MANAGEMENT SYSTEMS

With a database, only one program—the DBMS with any special subprograms written with the DBMS—needs to be written or purchased. Furthermore, only one overall program needs to be maintained, documented, or learned by users. With a common database, users can share all data files, relate data among files, enter data just once, and change data once. Redundancy and inconsistency, therefore, are greatly reduced with a database approach. Access is available to many, but the integrity of confidential data can still be preserved through a security system.

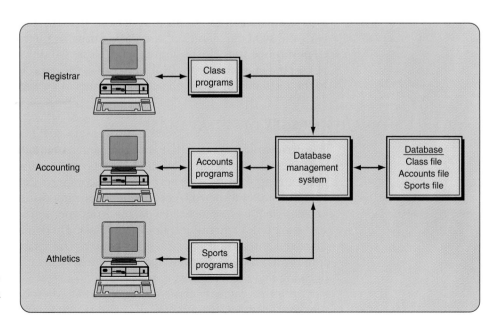

FIGURE 8.3 Database management system provides access to all data in the database.

A database management system allows users much greater access to organizational information. Most organizations have accumulated a wealth of data, but translating these data to meaningful information has, at times, proven difficult. This is especially true in a traditional file environment. Under these circumstances, an organization may be data rich, but information poor; a database can turn a wealth of data into a wealth of information. The structure of an integrated database provides tremendous flexibility regarding types of reports that can be generated and types of on-line inquiries that can be made. This expanded scope of available information enables management to make more informed, and therefore better, decisions than they might make without it.

Most databases are independent of the programs that use them and the hardware on which they are located. Information in the files is organized in a way that allows for generalized access. This means sets of data can be reached via programs written in many different computer languages. The same database can also be accessed through an elementary language, designed to be simpler to learn and use than a traditional programming language. Finally, updating and maintenance is simplified because all data are collected, managed, updated, and purged through one software program.

Even though redundancy is minimized with a database, some data redundancy must be maintained to enhance processing efficiency. This *controlled data redundancy* is miniscule, however, when compared to the costly redundancy of a traditional file environment. By minimizing data redundancy, data collection and update procedures are simplified. **Data integrity**, or the accuracy and accessibility of data, is enhanced because all the information about an event or entity is updated in only one place—the central database.

A database and a DBMS allow programmers and systems analysts to perform their functions more easily and efficiently. The database environment provides information that would be too time consuming or impractical to obtain using traditional file organization. The programming task is simplified with a DBMS because data are more readily available.

In a database, data are *independent* of the application programs. That is, fields can be added, changed, and deleted from the database without necessarily affecting existing application programs. Adding a field to a record of a traditional file may require modification and testing of dozens, perhaps even hundreds, of programs dependent on the old file structure. With a DBMS, programs can be changed without the data storage being changed, and data storage can be changed without the programs being changed. As shown in Figure 8.3, the DBMS serves as an interface between programs and data so that the programs are concerned only with the symbolic names of the data, not with their physical storage. **Data independence** frees the programmer and user from the detailed and complex task of keeping up with the physical structure of the data. This contributes significantly to the flexibility of the application programs in a DBMS environment.

DISADVANTAGES OF A DATABASE

The disadvantages of database management systems are relatively few; in the long run, they are outweighed by the advantages. One disadvantage is that databases and DBMS programs can become quite complex. Relating multiple files can be complicated, and the concepts can be confusing to users. Therefore, managing a database requires sophisticated database designers and administrative personnel— and sometimes extensive training for users. These are discussed in the database management section later in this chapter. The current database programming trend is to produce database management systems that are easy for users to understand and organizations to maintain.

Another database disadvantage is that DBMS software creates additional system overhead because it generally requires more processing than file programs

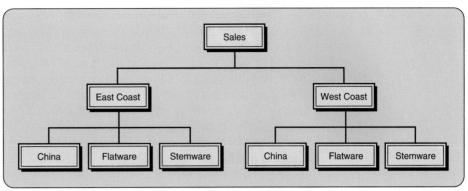

FIGURE 8.4 Hierarchical database model.

A clerk accessing a database.

and more disk space for software storage (files and data relating the files). Similarly, as with other complex software systems, the cost—in terms of hardware, software, and personnel—can be expensive for small organizations.

Finally, when all users must access files through the DBMS, that DBMS presents a single point of failure for the organization. When the DBMS fails to work, no one may be able to access the database. Additionally, when only one DBMS is used within an organization, all users are restricted to the capabilities of that DBMS. The benefit from data sharing does have a potential downside—the shared limitations of the DBMS being used and the database design being employed in the application under development.

8.5 LOGICAL DATA ORGANIZATION

Just as there are many ways to structure business organizations, there are many ways to structure the data those organizations need. A manager's ability to use a database is highly dependent on how the database is structured logically and physically, just as a clerk's ability to find a personnel file depends on how personnel file cabinets are organized. In *logically* structuring a database, businesses need to consider the characteristics of the data and how the data will be accessed. In the example of the clerk's file cabinet, a personnel file can be logically structured based on name, department or division, pay grade, or even office telephone number. Accessing files by name, however, implies a file structured sequentially by name in alphabetical order.

There are four basic models for logically structuring databases: *hierarchical, network, relational,* and *object oriented.* Using these models, database designers can build *logical* or conceptual views of data that can then be *physically* implemented into virtually any database with any DBMS. Hierarchical, network, and object-oriented DBMSs usually tie related data together through linked lists. Relational DBMSs relate data through information contained in the data.

HIERARCHICAL DATABASE MODEL

The **hierarchical model** relates data by rigidly structuring data into an inverted "tree" in which records contain two elements:

1. A single root or master field, often called a **key**, which identifies the type, location, or ordering of the records.
2. A variable number of subordinate fields that defines the rest of the data within a record.

As a rule, while all fields have only one "parent," each parent may have many "children." An example of a hierarchical database is shown in Figure 8.4.

The hierarchical structure was developed simply because hierarchical relationships are commonly found in many traditional business organizations and processes. For example, organization charts most often describe a hierarchical relationship—top management at the highest level, middle management at lower levels, and other employees at the lowest levels. Within each hierarchy, each level of management may have many employees or levels of employees beneath it, but each employee has only one manager. The hierarchical structure is characterized by this one-to-many relationship among data.

A hierarchical approach is very simple for users to design and understand since it is usually patterned after real-world organizations. But perhaps the strongest advantage of the hierarchical model is the speed and efficiency with which it can be searched for data. Why? Because so much of the database is eliminated in the search with each "turn" going down the tree. As shown in Figure 8.4, half the records in the database (East Coast sales) are eliminated once the search turns toward West Coast sales, and two-thirds of the West Coast sales are eliminated once the search turns toward stemware. For this reason, many computer software operating systems use a hierarchical approach to keep track of files in directories and subdirectories; it is a simple approach that can be very fast and efficient for searching—assuming, of course, that the hierarchy has been properly set up.

Finally, due to the explicit relationships in a hierarchical model, the integrity or "wholeness" of the database is strongly maintained. After all, every child in a hierarchical database *must* belong to a parent, and if a parent is eliminated from the database, all its children automatically become children of the parent's parent.

But there are problems with the hierarchical approach. In the hierarchical model, each relationship must be *explicitly* defined when the database is created. Each record in a hierarchical database can only contain one key field, and only one relationship is allowed between any two fields. This can create a problem because real-world data do not always conform to such a strict hierarchy. For example, in a matrix organization, an employee might report to more than one manager; this would be awkward for a hierarchical structure to handle. Moreover, all data searches must originate at the top or "root" of the tree and work downward from parent to child. Additionally, the fact that this database is restricted to one-to-many relationships can make some searches very awkward, especially if the explicit structure of the database is not known to a user.

Another significant disadvantage of the hierarchical model is the fact that it is difficult to relate "cousins" in the tree. In the example shown in Figure 8.4, there is no direct relationship between china sales on the East Coast and china sales on the West Coast. A comparison of company-wide china sales would entail two separate searches and then another step combining the search results.

THE NETWORK DATABASE MODEL

The **network model** creates relationships among data through a linked list structure in which subordinated records (called *members*, not children) can be linked to more than one parent (called an *owner*). Similar to the hierarchical model, the network model uses explicit links, called **pointers**, to link subordinates and parents. That relationship is called a **set**. Physically, pointers are storage addresses that contain the location of a related record. With the network approach, a member record can be linked to an owner record and, at the same time, can itself be an owner record linked to other sets of members (see Figure 8.5). In this way, many-to-many relationships are possible with a network database model—a significant advantage of the network model over the hierarchical model.

Compare Figure 8.5 to Figure 8.4. In Figure 8.5, sales information about china, flatware, and stemware is in one subordinate or member location. Information about each has two parents or owners, East Coast and West Coast. The problem of getting a complete picture of nationwide china sales that exists with the hierarchical model does not occur with the network model. Moreover,

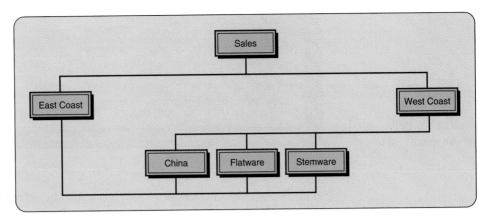

FIGURE 8.5 Network data-base model.

searches for data do not have to start at a root—there may not even *be* a single root to a network—which gives much greater flexibility for data searches.

The network model essentially places no restrictions on the number of relationships or sets in which a field can be involved. This is more consistent with real-world business relationships where, for example, vendors have many customers and customers have many vendors. For flexibility and adaptability to real-world situations, however, network databases have a price to pay in terms of complexity. For every set, a pair of pointers must be maintained. As the number of sets or relationships increases, the overhead becomes substantial. The network model is by far the most complicated type of database to design and implement.

THE RELATIONAL DATABASE MODEL

While most business organizations have been organized in a hierarchical fashion, most business data have traditionally been organized into simple tables of columns and rows, especially accounting and financial data. Tables allow quick comparisons by row or column, and items are easy to retrieve by finding the point of intersection of a particular row and column. The **relational model** is based on the simple concept of tables in order to capitalize on characteristics of rows and columns of data. This, too, is often more consistent with real-world business situations. Some firms, for example, are based on a project or matrix structure where an employee may "belong" to many supervisors at the same time and cross lines of authority.

In a relational database, these tables on entities are called **relations**, and the model is based on the mathematical theory of sets and relations. In this model, each row of data is equivalent to a record, and each column of data is equivalent to a field. In the relational model terminology, a row is called a **tuple**, and a column is called an **attribute**. A relational database is not always, however, one big table (usually called a *flat file*) consisting of all attributes and all tuples. That design would likely entail far too much data redundancy. Instead, a database is usually designed as many related tables.

There are some basic principles in a relational database. First, the order of tuples or attributes in a table is irrelevant. This is because their position relative to other tuples and attributes is irrelevant in finding data based on specific tuples and attributes. Second, each tuple must be uniquely identifiable by the data within the tuple—some sort of *primary key* data (e.g., a social security number or employee number). Third, each table must have a unique identifier—the name of the relation. Fourth, there can be no duplicate attributes or tuples. Finally, there can only be one value in each row-column "cell" in a table.

One of the greatest advantages of the relational model is its conceptual simplicity and the ability to link records in a way that is not predefined (that is, they are not *explicit* as in the hierarchical and network models). This provides great flexibility. The relational or tabular model of data can be used in a variety of

East Coast Mgrs.			
NAME	TITLE	AGE	DIVISION
Smith, A.	Dir., Accntg	43	China
Jones, W.	Dir., TQM	32	Stemware

FIGURE 8.6 Relational database model—a table.

applications. Most people can easily visualize the relational model as a table, but the model does use some unfamiliar terminology.

Consider the relational database table example on East Coast managers shown in Figure 8.6. The table contains data about the entity called East Coast managers. Attributes or characteristics about the entity are name, title, age, and division. The tuples, or occurrences of the entity, are the two records on A. Smith and W. Jones. The links among the data—and among tables—are *implicit*, as they are not necessarily physically linked in a storage device but implicitly linked by the design of the tables into rows and columns.

This property of implicit links provides perhaps the strongest benefit of the relational model—flexibility in relating data. Unlike the hierarchical and network models, where the only links are those rigidly built into the design, *all* the data in a table and between tables can be linked, related, and compared. This gives the relational model much more *data independence* than the hierarchical and network models. That is, the logical design of data into tables can be more independent of the physical implementation. This gives much more flexibility in implementing and modifying the logical design. Of course, as with all tables, a searcher for data need only know two things: the identifier(s) of the tuple(s) to be searched and the desired attribute(s). Database searches with even less information are possible (see Box 8.1 for an explanation of one method).

The relational model is currently the most popular of the four database structures because it provides the most flexibility and ease of use. But there are some

A Closer Look BOX 8.1

 EMERGING TECHNOLOGY

DEDUCTIVE DATABASES

Hierarchical, network, and relational DBMSs have been used for decades to facilitate data access by users. Users, of course, must understand what they are looking for, the database they are looking at, and at least something about the information sought (like a key and some field or attribute about a record). This approach, however, may not be adequate for some knowledge-based applications that require deductive reasoning for searches. As a result, there is interest in what are called deductive database systems.

Deductive database systems are formulated on harmonious cooperation between logical inference and database querying techniques. This is especially essential for very large databases, where a user is increasingly likely to be unfamiliar with the entire scope of data available to search.

A deductive database system applies mathematical logic to database management, both in representing and manipulating data. Essentially, a deductive database system can derive and provide users with new implicit data from data explicitly stored.

For example, a table on competitors that includes their types of products or services could recursively deduce other relationships, such as who their vendors are and which vendors are competitors themselves. All vendors are also customers to some extent; these relationships can be derived through deductive databases. Marketing organizations can make extensive use of deductive databases on potential customers based on demographics, income, family size, and so on.

disadvantages. Because large-scale databases may be composed of many interrelated tables, the overall design may be complex and therefore have slower search and access times (as compared to the hierarchical and network models). Such processing inefficiencies, however, are continually being reduced through improved database design and programming. Second, data integrity is not as inherently a part of this model as with hierarchical and network models. Therefore, it must be enforced with good design principles. The primary means of enforcing data integrity on relational databases is through *normalization*.

NORMALIZATION. **Normalization** is a method for analyzing and reducing a relational database to its most parsimonious or streamlined form for minimum redundancy, maximum data integrity, and best processing performance. Specifically, normalization has several goals:

▼ Eliminate redundancy caused by fields repeated within a file, fields that do not directly describe the entity, and fields that can be derived from other fields.

▼ Avoid update anomalies (i.e., errors from inserting, deleting, and modifying records).

▼ Represent accurately the items being modeled.

▼ Simplify maintenance and information retrieval.

All the tables in a database must be looked at closely to detect violations of normalization rules. A table in the *first normal form* abides by the relational database principle of only one value per cell, and no repeating attributes can be used to get around that restriction. For example, let's consider a personnel table on employees with the usual attributes of name, age, social security number, and so forth. Each employee has only one value for each of these attributes, but what about an attribute of children's names, when an employee may have more than one child? If their names are stored in a list of fields such as CHILD1, CHILD2, and so on, the principle of only one value per cell is kept, but the table would be unworkable. A table with four CHILD attributes, for example, would fail for a family with five, and setting aside attributes for perhaps twelve children would be grossly wasteful of storage resources since the average number of children in a U.S. family is two. Moreover, to search for a child by name would mean searching all CHILD fields. Similarly, counting the number of children requires checking all CHILD fields. In a large database, many passes through the table for data like this can convert a simple query into a complex task—tying up computer resources.

The problem lies in the fact that children of an employee are not simply attributes of the employee, but constitute another entity by themselves which is related to the employee's. As a normalization solution, a table called CHILDREN would be created to store the names of the children. This table would be linked to the PERSONNEL table using a key that would occur in both tables as an attribute—for example, the parent's social security number.

A table is said to be in *second normal form* when it meets the qualifications for first normal form and reduces data unnecessarily stored in multiple files. This most subtle normalization goal is to eliminate attributes that can be derived from other attributes. If, for example, the CHILDREN file contains the parent's social security number *and* the parent's name, one of those attributes is redundant. Obviously, if one knows a parent's social security number, one can look up the corresponding name from the PERSONNEL file. Storing the parent's name in the CHILDREN file wastes space and introduces the possibility of inconsistency.

Similarly, one field should not be a computed field of another. In a personnel database, for example, one might want to have an attribute for the number of years an employee has worked for the company. However, since there is already an attribute for the hiring date, a years-worked attribute should not be created because one could simply calculate seniority by subtracting the date hired from the present date. Furthermore, if there was such a computed attribute field, the database would have to be updated perpetually on the anniversary of every employee's hiring date.

Another common normalization problem is table duplication—two or more tables that essentially track the same entity. A real estate sales system, for example, may have separate tables for office buildings, retail spaces, warehouses, and residential properties. All these tables really contain the same entities: properties. Keeping separate files for different types of property makes searches for a particular building more difficult. To find the property at 123 Main Street, one might have to search all four tables if the type of property is not known. If a property is rezoned from office to retail, the record would have to be deleted from the office table and entered into the retail table. These tasks can be simplified by combining the four tables into one and adding a new field to show the property type. An example of a popular DBMS for personal computers is described in Box 8.2.

A Closer Look BOX 8.2

A PERSONAL COMPUTER DBMS

Of the many popular database management systems software packages available for personal computers, Microsoft's Access is a typical example of the growing sophistication of database software for microcomputer users.

Access is a relational DBMS that operates under the Microsoft Windows environment. (Whether or not a particular DBMS is *truly* relational is often contentious among academics, database purists, and software developers; most general practitioners see the question as a matter of degree and would likely agree that Access generally qualifies as a bona fide relational DBMS.) It is graphically oriented. Users can select and execute commands using a pointing device like a mouse; users are presented with graphical portrayals of related tables; multiple tables can be displayed at the same time by either overlapping them or displaying them in separate portions of the display area; and most functions can be selected by "clicking" a pointing device on top of graphical icons or buttons. Moreover, all the graphical services generally available to Windows applications are available to Access users (such as being able to copy and "paste" graphical images to and from Access).

Access allows users to query databases by using the simple query-by-example format—yet gives them powerful functions for ordering, rearranging, filtering, and adding calculated fields. Query results (in table format) can be used subsequently as the basis for further queries or reports. Queries can also be made using the popular structured query language (SQL) for querying Access or external databases.

Reports can be easily designed graphically in a what-you-see-is-what-you-get (WYSIWYG) environment, with extensive control over fonts, font sizes, arrangement of data, shading, and highlighting. Reports can include images such as identification photos of individuals in a per-

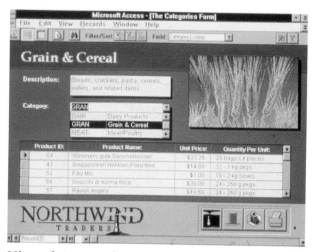

Microsoft Access software.

sonnel database and graphics such as bar graphs and scatter plots of financial or production data.

Sophisticated tasks can be automated either by writing statements in a programming language (a version of BASIC) or by simply having Access "record" a user's manual steps for later "playback."

Finally, the range of help features for a confused user rivals the complexity of the DBMS functions available. Help programs built into the DBMS include extensive "how-to" guides and function reference material which is indexed and searchable by key words. A feature called Cue Cards is available at all times; cue cards provide step-by-step instructions with graphical examples, guidance, and transfers to additional reference material.

For a few hundred dollars (or less in many cases), businesses can provide a sophisticated DBMS right on an employee's desktop or even in a notebook computer while she is away from the office.

THE OBJECT-ORIENTED DATABASE MODEL

The most recent development in databases is the **object-oriented model**. Although no common definition for this model has yet emerged, there is agreement as to some of its features. Terminology in the object-oriented model, similar to object-oriented programming languages (see Chapter 6), consists of objects, attributes, classes, methods, and messages.

An **object** is similar to an entity in that it is the embodiment of a person, place, or thing. Similarly, *attributes* are characteristics that describe the *state* of that object—the attribute values for an object at a given period in time (e.g., the age of an employee). A **method** is an operation, action, or a behavior the object may undergo (e.g., a product may be sold). *Messages* from other objects activate operations contained within the object. Once an operation is activated, it will often send another message to a third object, which, in turn, may activate methods within that object and so on. Significantly, all the data that an object needs in order to perform an operation are logically contained *within* the object. **Encapsulation** is the termed used to describe the fact that an object contains all the data and operations necessary to carry out some action.

Every object is an instance of some **class**. An object's class defines all the messages to which the object will respond, as well as the way in which objects of this class are implemented. Classes are typically arranged in a tree-like structure, connecting superclasses to their subclasses. The links or relationships between a superclass and a subclass is often called an *IS-A* link. The IS-A chain shows that all subclasses **inherit** all behaviors and attributes defined by its superclass as well as any additional behaviors and attributes of its own. For example, an object of trucks is a subclass of an object of motor vehicles; a truck "IS-A" motor vehicle.

Object-oriented databases can be particularly helpful in heterogeneous (multimedia) environments such as in many manufacturing sites. Data from design blueprints, photographic images of parts, operational acoustic signatures, test or quality control data, and geographical sales data can all be combined into one object, itself consisting of structures and operations. For companies with widely distributed offices, an object-oriented database can provide users with a transparent view of data throughout the overall system.

Object-oriented databases can be particularly useful in supporting temporal and spatial dimensions. All things change; sometimes keeping track of temporal and spatial changes—rather than just the latest version—is important. Related but slightly different versions of an object can easily be maintained in an object-oriented database.

Object-oriented databases allow firms to structure their data and use it in ways that would be impossible, or at least very difficult, with other database models. One example of a business using an object-oriented database is presented in Box 8.3.

▶ 8.6 PHYSICAL DATA ORGANIZATION

Once a database is logically structured, based on its characteristics, relationships, and access methodology it must be physically implemented with specific software and hardware so that business managers and planners can access data in real-world applications. Data organized into databases are usually stored and accessed through database management systems, which are themselves organized under various processing arrangements or *topologies*. Each database management system uses one or more of the various digital storage and access methods; this can significantly affect the amount of required storage space and the speed of data retrieval.

IT At Work BOX 8.3

OBJECT-ORIENTED DATABASE AT DAIMLER-BENZ

Daimler-Benz, the German automobile and aerospace multinational corporation known for its Mercedes cars, is a pioneer in the use of object-oriented databases for business applications. The company uses this emerging technology to integrate data stored worldwide throughout the enterprise and to expedite decision making. Cooperating with a small software vendor, Daimler-Benz integrated object databases with its existing or "legacy" information systems for distributed network applications. The new technology enables Daimler-Benz to tie its diverse database systems together and link to customers and suppliers in a network-based, distributed on-line information system.

Object-oriented databases have been around since the mid-1980s, but they were used primarily for computer-aided design and graphical information systems. Since the early 1990s, object-oriented databases have become popular for many other business applications, due to their integration with existing relational and hierarchical databases, and with networks.

This is why Daimler-Benz pioneered the large-scale use of the technology. The distributed network-based environment gives a global view of all Daimler-Benz data available worldwide. The company maintains an object database of product-model data, based on an automotive industry standard. The databases are used in design, manufacturing, and sales of both automobile and aerospace products. One reason why Daimler-Benz was willing to invest heavily in the emerging technology was that it could meet its business goals of high productivity and quality and at the same time leverage the high investment it had in existing legacy information systems.

Critical Thinking Issues: Object-oriented databases were used originally for pictures and graphs. Why is Daimler-Benz interested in their capabilities, and why do they want to integrate them with their legacy systems? ▲

SOURCE: Compiled from *InformationWeek*, November 7, 1994.

DATABASE MANAGEMENT SYSTEMS

Database management system software has enabled many organizations to move from a traditional file approach to a database approach, thereby enjoying the benefits of a higher level of data access, less data redundancy, less data inconsistency, and greater ease in programming. A database management system (DBMS) is software that organizes, manipulates, and retrieves data stored in a database. A DBMS provides users with tools to add, delete, maintain, display, print, search,

A data storage device for a mainframe.

select, sort, and update data. These tools range from easy-to-use natural language interfaces to complex programming languages used for developing sophisticated database applications.

Database management systems are installed in a broad range of information systems. Some are loaded on a single user's personal computer and used in an ad hoc manner to support individual decision making. Others are located on several interconnected mainframe computers and are used to support large-scale transaction processing systems, such as order entry and inventory control systems. Still others are interconnected throughout an organization's local area networks, giving individual departments access to corporate data. Because a DBMS need not be confined to storing just words and numbers, firms use them to store graphics, sounds, and video as well.

There are many specialized databases, depending on the type or format of data stored. For example, a *geographical information database* may contain locational data for overlaying on maps or images; one could spatially view customer and vendor locations instead of simply reading textual addresses. A *knowledge database* can store decision rules used to evaluate situations and help users make decisions like an expert. A *multimedia database* can store data of many media—sounds, video, images, graphic animation, and text.

Database management systems are designed to be relatively invisible to the user. To interact with them, however, one needs to understand the procedures for interacting, even though much of their work is done behind the scenes and is therefore invisible or "transparent" to the end user. Most of this interaction occurs by using DBMS *languages*.

DATABASE LANGUAGES. Conceptually, a database management system uses two languages—a **data definition language (DDL)** and a **data manipulation language (DML)**. The DDL is essentially the link between the logical and physical views of the database. ("Logical" refers to the way the user views data; "physical" refers to the way the data are physically stored and processed.) A DBMS user defines views or **schemas** using the DDL. There may be many users and application programs utilizing the same database; therefore many different **sub-schemas** or "user views" can exist. Each user or application program utilizes a set of DDL statements to construct a subschema for those data elements that are of interest.

The DDL is used to define the physical characteristics of each record; the fields within a record; and each field's logical name, data type, and character length. A field's logical name (such as EMPNAME for an employee's name field) is used by both application programs and users to refer to the field for retrieving or updating the data in it. The DDL is also used to specify relationships among the records. Other primary functions of the DDL are the following:

▼ Provide a means for associating related data

▼ Indicate the unique identifiers (or keys) of the records

▼ Set up data security access and change restrictions

The data manipulation language provides users with the ability to retrieve, sort, display, and delete the contents of their databases. The DML generally includes a variety of manipulation verbs (e.g., CREATE, MODIFY, DELETE) and operands for each verb. Furthermore, most data manipulation languages interface with high-level programming languages such as COBOL or C. These languages enable a programmer to perform additional data manipulation that the DBMSs DML does not allow.

A principle feature of a DML is that it uses logical names as operands (such as STUDENTNO for student number) when referring to data instead of physical storage locations. This capability is possible since the data definition language provides linkages between the logical view of data and their physical storage. This allows programmers and system operators to modify physical data storage, conduct database maintenance, or even change data storage devices without disturbing users or user DML programs.

STRUCTURED QUERY LANGUAGE (SQL). Requesting information from a database is the most commonly performed operation. Because one cannot generally request information in a natural language form, query languages (essentially DMLs) form an important component of a DBMS. **Structured query language**, more commonly referred to as **SQL**, is the most popular relational database language, combining both DML and DDL features. To illustrate SQL, Figure 8.7 shows a question in English followed by the same question paraphrased in SQL.

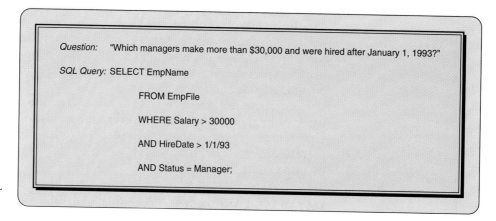

FIGURE 8.7 A typical SQL query on employees.

In this example, SELECT specifies the field to be retrieved, FROM identifies the file to search, and the remaining three statements specify which records can satisfy the conditions of the question.

SQL offers the ability to perform quite complicated searches with relatively simple statements. Standard matching conditions include EQUAL TO, GREATER THAN, and LESS THAN as well as the logical operators AND, OR, and NOT. By combining logical operators with selection criteria, the user can perform quite complex queries. Moreover, these queries can be made against many files simultaneously—an action called a JOIN. A user can search for information in one file based on information in other files or can search for composite information from many files. Besides being relatively easy to learn and use, SQL is widely available in DBMSs that operate on systems from microcomputers to mainframes. Furthermore, SQL is fairly well standardized so that SQL users of one DBMS can easily use SQL with another DBMS (see Box 8.4).

A Closer Look BOX 8.4

SQL STANDARDS

For over ten years, SQL (structured query language) has been the de facto standard database description and manipulation language for relational databases. A big problem with the SQL standard, however, is that there are too many of them.

No fewer than eight standardizing efforts were underway in 1993 to create a standard SQL. International or-

ganizations were working on it as well as industry consortia and individual companies with SQL products to offer. Every SQL database management system speaks its own SQL dialect, with its own unique extensions or "improvements" to the language. Lack of one widely accepted standard drives up the cost of databases and related tools, and makes maintaining a seamless environment among database management systems complex and difficult. What is the difference between no standard and too many standards? Not much.

Many companies, not waiting for standard-setting efforts to bear fruit, are launching their own attempts to create de facto standards in the marketplace. The more their product sells, the closer it comes to being *the* standard. Others say that an SQL standard is not the real issue; efforts should be focused on the application programming interface (API) software that directly interacts with a user to generate SQL database commands. Others promote "intelligent drivers" which act as intermediaries between applications (generating one of the many SQL formats) and databases expecting one particular SQL format. The driver translates and tailors the SQL statements for the database management software. Such intermediary software is sometimes referred to as "middleware."

QUERY-BY-EXAMPLE (QBE). Most database languages for personal computers use a query method called **query-by-example** or **QBE**. To perform a query with QBE, the user simply chooses which table(s) to ask questions of, selects the fields to be included in the answer, and then enters an *example* of the data wanted. The QBE feature gives the answer based on the example. Figure 8.8 demonstrates how the previous SQL query about managers would be performed using QBE. Notice that the tables are represented graphically by field, with the names of the tables labeled in the left-most column (i.e., EMPFILE and ANSWER). A "P." is placed in the columns of the fields that are to be part of the output, while examples of the selection criteria are placed in the appropriate columns. The result is given in table form (the table "ANSWER"), and only the field(s) that had a "P." in them are found in the search table(s). If, in addition, we had wished to see a listing of salaries along with the manager names in the result, we merely would have placed "P. > 30000" in the SALARY column.

EMPFILE	EMPNO	EMPNAME	ADDRESS	SALARY	STATUS	HIREDATE
		P.		> 30000	Manager	> 1/1/93

ANSWER	EMPNAME
	Sally Jones
	John Drake
	Susan White
	Peter Smith

FIGURE 8.8 The arrangement of tables and fields in query-by-example.

NATURAL LANGUAGE INTERFACES. The easiest way to manipulate data in a database, of course, would be to do so using natural language—the way one requests information from another person. A **natural language** interface lets a user retrieve data with simple, language-like commands. For example, a query using this type of interface might be:

"Give me the names of all persons with sales of more than $100,000 in 1994."

In SQL, this query would be:

SELECT Name FROM AnnualSales WHERE Sales > 100000 AND Year = 1994;

In actual word length, these two queries are not too different; but for general users, a natural language interface is far easier to learn and use.

A natural language interface is programmed to accept queries in the same manner in which most of us listen—by looking for key words in sentences. In the previous query, the key words would be *names, sales, 100,000,* and *1994.* Natural language systems usually come with a predefined dictionary or *lexicon* of common user terminology. If it cannot match a key word to a synonym, it may ask the user to give another word or select from several choices that are probable synonyms. In this way, the system keeps track of key words and their synonyms for each user. The synonyms would then be used to interpret the query and to select appropriate relationships and data items.

For many people, natural language database access evokes a scenario out of *Star Trek* or *2001: A Space Odyssey,* where users simply talk out loud to ubiquitous computers that understand what is sought or have the apparent wisdom to ask for clarification. Although perhaps ideal, such systems are impractical at present for most applications. Although computers are extremely precise, human speech patterns and language usage are not; they thus require a tremendous amount of processing for an acceptable level of accuracy in everyday situations. Some limited natural language interfaces are available today. An example is the Intellect system of Artificial Intelligence, Inc. (now Trinzic Corporation). Its use is described in Box 8.5. However, widespread use of such interfaces for general applications, particularly those involving very large databases, is still in the future.

IT At Work BOX 8.5

FRIENDLY COMPUTERS KEEP DOWN RUMORS

In a community college district near Los Angeles, the president wanted to get a better idea of how well his district was doing, and—with impending budget cuts—what the future might hold. He wanted to get answers to such questions as which academic departments had the largest average class sizes, which departments had the largest number of canceled classes, which classes drew students most heavily from adjacent college districts (and thus represented a source of additional revenue), which classes cost the most to offer, and so forth.

He knew the data were available somewhere in the system because he had asked for such special reports in the past. After several days—or weeks—of manual effort, the information had always finally been provided. Often, merely *asking* for such information caused concern—even apprehension—on the part of the departments involved, even if no subsequent action were ever taken.

The president asked his staff if there weren't some way that he could get the desired information more quickly and on his own, without the intervention of the college information systems staff. He was, however, very unsophisticated as far as computers and databases were concerned. "I want to be able to ask questions in English—or something very close to it," he said.

The answer the staff came up with was Intellect. This database software package allowed the president to pose questions like those listed previously without having to let anyone know the sorts of questions that were on his mind. Moreover, he became a hands-on user of the system with less than a day of training.

Now he peruses the database to his heart's content, secure in the knowledge that his most outrageous or outlandish questions will not be misinterpreted or become a source of alarm to those involved. However, the use of Intellect places high demands on campus computer resources. Therefore, the president restricts his use of the system to evenings and other after-hours periods.

Critical Thinking Issue. How does having a natural-language-like interface help the president find answers to his queries? ▲

SOURCE: Personal interview.

DATA DICTIONARIES. In ordinary language, a dictionary is a reference book containing words, arranged alphabetically, that gives information about their form, origin, function, meaning, and syntax. In a DBMS, a **data dictionary** is a comprehensive list or collection of information, usually arranged alphabetically, that gives the form, function, meaning, and syntax of the data in a database. Data dictionaries describe standard field sizes, coding schemas, and the kind and type of data to be included in the system.

Data dictionaries are a prerequisite to setting up a properly functioning, manageable system. They establish consistency and eliminate repetitions and omissions. They may also contain a security function; i.e., they define which files or fields may be accessed, changed, or modified by specific users. They are an essential part of both logical and physical data organization.

DATABASE TOPOLOGY

A database, as we have seen, is a collection of related files that need not be in one physical location. Where those related files are located can greatly affect user accessibility, query response times, data entry, security, and cost. In general, database files can be centralized, distributed, or external.

A **centralized database** has all the related files in one physical location (see Figure 8.9). Centralized database files on large, mainframe computers were the main database topology for decades, primarily because of the enormous capital and operating costs of other alternatives. Not only do centralized databases save the expenses associated with multiple computers, but they also provide database administrators with the ability to work on a database as a whole at one location. Files can generally be made more consistent with each other when they are physically kept in one location because file changes can be made in a supervised and orderly fashion. Files are not accessible except via the centralized host computer; they can be protected more easily from unauthorized access or modification. Recovery from disasters can be more easily accomplished at a central location. Like all centralized systems, however, they are vulnerable as a single point of failure. When the central database computer fails to function properly, all users suffer. Additionally, access speed is often a problem when users are widely disbursed and must do all of their data manipulations from great distances, thereby incurring transmission delays.

A **distributed database** has complete copies of a database, or portions of a database, in more than one location which is usually close to users (see Figure 8.10). A *replicated* database has complete copies of the entire database in many locations, primarily to alleviate the single point-of-failure problems of a centralized database as well as to increase user access responsiveness. There is significant overhead, however, in maintaining *consistency* among replicated databases as records

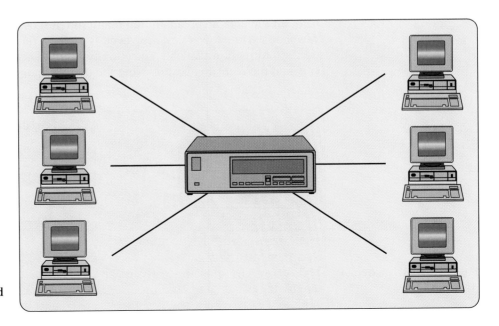

FIGURE 8.9 Centralized database.

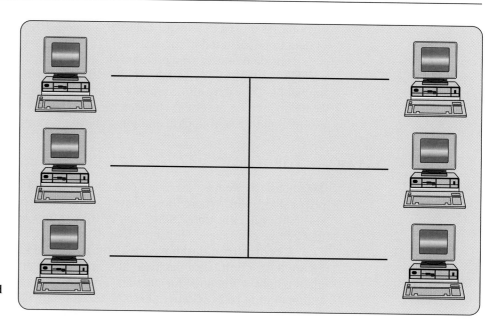

FIGURE 8.10 Distributed database.

are added, modified, and deleted. A *partitioned* database is subdivided, so that each location has a portion of the entire database (usually the portion meeting users' local needs). This type provides the response speed of localized files without the need to replicate all changes in multiple locations. One significant advantage of a partitioned database is that data in the files can be entered more quickly and kept more accurate by the users immediately responsible for the data. On the other hand, widespread access to potentially sensitive company data can significantly increase corporate security problems. Telecommunications costs and associated time delays can also be major factors.

An **external database** is considerably different from the previous two; it is a database wholly outside the organization but accessible via communications (see Figure 8.11). Hundreds of public and commercially available databases are accessible to anyone with only a personal computer, a modem, and a telephone line. Commercial databases are generally available on a fee basis for the time connected. For pennies, however, a firm can do extensive marketing research using demographic databases; operations planning with geographic or property databases; or financial scheming with banking, commerce, and commodity databases. Perhaps the greatest advantage of external databases is that the cost to collect, store, and maintain the data is spread among many (often tens of thousands) of users. This ease of access and lower cost, however, is partially offset by the potential limits to specific information available, uncertainty over the accuracy and timeliness of the data, and the recurring cost of using the databases on an ongoing basis.

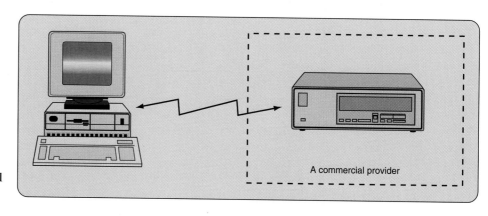

A commercial provider

FIGURE 8.11 External database.

PHYSICAL DATA STORAGE

Just as databases can be physically structured into various topologies, data can be stored and accessed in various ways. Three prominent methods of physical data storage are *direct* (also sometimes referred to as *random*), *sequential*, and *indexed-sequential*. Each method has its own processing advantages and disadvantages; which method is used to implement a database can significantly affect a database user's efficiency and effectiveness.

An important concern with business information systems is how to access individual *records* within files. To do so, one must be able to identify each unique record. This is done with a record identifier called a **primary key**, which is a field that uniquely identifies the record and thus distinguishes it from all other records in the file. For example, a business personnel file might contain each employee's social security number, which would adequately serve as the primary key, since each social security number is different from all other social security numbers in the file. Normally, users or programs identify or select individual records by supplying the primary key to the DBMS. In this manner, records are accessed *directly*, similar to the way a courier picks up a letter or parcel directly from a location based on its unique address. This method of database storage is highly efficient for access to isolated records when speed is essential.

In addition to using primary keys, other fields can be used to construct an *index* for the database. An **index** is an ordered listing of certain fields used to aid the DBMS in locating particular records even more quickly. A database index is similar to an index in a book. Finding the particular text location of a name or topic is usually faster if one uses the book's index rather than searches through the entire book. Likewise, a courier can more quickly locate a business based on its unique address if all the business addresses are in order.

Not all databases physically store records using primary keys or storage addresses; some simply store records one after another. This type of technique is called *sequential* storage. **Sequential** database access starts at the beginning of the database, "examining" each record in turn until the one sought is found. In the courier example above, this would be similar to requiring the courier to go from door to door inquiring at every business, one after another, until the right business is located. On the surface, this would appear to be a highly inefficient way of storing data in a database. However, it is sometimes more efficient than direct access, especially when the sequential file is ordered, or sorted, by the field to be searched; when a large number of records will be accessed at one time; or when the records sought are at the beginning of the database storage area.

For example, if a courier had to deliver a package to each of the publishing firms in a city, it would obviously be faster and easier if the publishing firms were lined up next to each other instead of scattered all over town. Weekly payroll processing, when all records are accessed, is most likely done on employee records that are sequentially stored.

The third primary method of physically storing database records is the **indexed sequential access method (ISAM)**—a combination or compromise between direct and sequential storage. An ISAM file consists of two files: the data file containing the full records stored sequentially and a much smaller index file containing locations or addresses of certain blocks of the sequential file. A request for a particular record is first directed to the index file which, in turn, "points" to the beginning of the block containing the record. The block is then searched sequentially for the particular record. This would be comparable to using a telephone book with an index showing the page numbers of each alphabetic block of listings. One would find the telephone number of Ann Jones by first finding the page number of the beginning of the Js, then searching sequentially for Jones, Ann. The number and size of blocks of sequential records in an ISAM database can be adjusted for the most efficient balance between requirements for direct access—

with its faster access time—and requirements for sequential access—with its greater processing efficiency.

LOGICAL VERSUS PHYSICAL

As mentioned earlier, the key benefits from a database (as opposed to multiple unrelated files) come from the ability of many different users to share data and process resources. But as there can be many different users, there are many different database needs. How can a single, unified database meet the differing requirements of so many users? For example, how can a single database be structured so that sales personnel can see customer, inventory, and production schedule data without requiring them to wade through production maintenance data and while maintaining restricted access to private personnel data?

A DBMS minimizes these problems by providing two "views" of the database data: a *physical view* and a *logical view*. The **physical view** deals with the actual, physical arrangement and location of data in the direct access storage devices (DASD). Database specialists use this view to make efficient use of storage and processing resources. Users, however, may wish to see data differently from how it is stored, and they do not want to know all the technical details of physical storage. After all, a business user is primarily interested in *using* the information, not in how it is stored.

The **logical view**, or *user's view*, of a database represents data in a format that is meaningful to a user and to the software programs that process that data. One strength of a DBMS is that while there is only one physical view of the data, there can be an endless number of different logical views—one specifically tailored to every individual user, if necessary. Salespeople can see the sales data they want—and no more—in the way they want it. Production, human resources, or financial database users can do the same. This allows users to see database information in a more business-related way rather than from a technical, processing viewpoint. Clearly, users must adapt to the technical requirements of database information systems to some degree, but DBMS logical views allow the system to adapt to the business needs of the users.

▶ 8.7 DATABASE MANAGEMENT

Access to databases is essential for managers today.

Organizing, implementing, and operating a database efficiently and effectively require sound database management. Database management, outside of purely technical hardware and software considerations, consists primarily of two functions: *database design and implementation*, and *database administration*.

In designing and implementing databases, specialists should carefully consider the individual needs of all existing and potential users in order to design and implement a database which optimizes both processing efficiency and user effectiveness. The process usually starts by analyzing what information each user (or group of users) needs and then producing logical views for each. These logical views are analyzed as a whole for similarities that can lead to simplification, and then related so that a single, cohesive logical database can be formed from all the parts. This logical database is implemented with a particular DBMS in a specific hardware system.

To what degree should the user, with business knowledge, or the database specialist, with technical system knowledge, be the driving force behind database design and implementation? The answer is problematic but highly important. Clearly, a highly efficient database that does not meet the business needs of the users is useless. But so is a database, however well designed from the user's standpoint, that runs so poorly as to be unusable. Business managers need to ensure that database efficiency and effectiveness requirements are appropriately weighted during design and implementation. Good business process management applies to databases as well as to business in general.

Database administration (DBA) of an implemented database can also present a significant challenge in trying to meet the organization's operational and strategic business goals. **Database administrators** are responsible for ensuring that the database fulfills the user's business needs, in terms of functionality as well for the data itself. User needs, like business in general, do not remain constant. As the business environment changes, and organizational goals and structures react, the database that the firm depends on must also change to remain effective. The computer hardware on which the DBMS software is installed must change to meet changing environments or to take advantage of new technology. This brings concomitant constraints and/or new opportunities for the DBMS processing performance.

Further, database administrators need to ensure the reliability of databases under their care by managing daily operations, including planning for emergency contingencies by providing backup data and systems to ensure minimal loss of data in the event of a disaster. Security is always a data administration concern when there are multiple accesses to databases that contain all the corporate data. Administrators must balance the business advantages of widespread access with the threat of corporate espionage, sabotage by disgruntled employees, and database damage due to negligence. Database administrators play a significant role in training users about what data is available and how to access it. Finally, administrators are responsible for ensuring that the data contained in the database are accurate, reliable, verifiable, complete, timely, and relevant—a daunting task at best. Otherwise-brilliant business decisions, based on wrong information, can be disastrous in a highly competitive market. Box 8.6 discusses some problems that managers and database administrators face when dealing with modern DBMSs.

A Closer Look BOX 8.6

DATA MANAGEMENT—SOME VERY REAL PROBLEMS

Today, most corporations realize that information is a corporate asset and, as such, needs to be managed like any other asset. It has become clear to IS managers that they need efficient and cost-effective technology to collect, organize, and query massive amounts of information. But these new information technologies, though needed and welcome, can pose some real challenges for an implementing organization.

One very real problem is what to do with the mass of information stored in a variety of formats, often known as the *legacy data acquisition* problem. Data in older, perhaps obsolete, databases still needs to be available to newer database management systems. Many of the legacy application programs used to access the older data simply cannot be converted into new computing environments without both transparent and procedural access to critical data remaining in the legacy environment.

Additionally, the legacy data problem has slowed utilization of newer relational database systems. According to the Gartner Group, 85 percent of the data in a typical organization resides in legacy, nonrelational data formats.

The challenge of concurrent relational and nonrelational-data access often must be met before database computing can be extended across the enterprise.

Basically, there are three approaches to solving this problem. One is to create a database front-end that can act as a translator from the old system to the new. The second is to migrate applications into the new system, so that data can be seamlessly accessed in the original format. The third is to migrate the data into the new system by reformatting it.

Another problem, closely related to the legacy data problem, is how to move data efficiently around an enterprise. The inability to communicate among different groups in different geographical locations is a serious roadblock to implementing distributed applications properly, especially given the many remote sites and mobility of today's workers.

Finally, human resource talent becomes an issue when it is hard to find technicians who know enough details about the various databases that need to be accessed.

Information *is* a source of advantage when it is well organized and readily available to users in the form, at the time, and in the place needed. Data and data management can provide that advantage. Indeed, the motto might well be:

Data—any place, any time, any way, and in any form.

▶ MANAGERIAL ISSUES

A number of challenges face companies that are undertaking a database management approach.

Where to locate data physically? Should data be distributed close to the sources of the data, thereby potentially speeding up their entry and updating but increasing problems of data security and backup? Or should data be centralized for easier control, security, backup, and disaster recovery, though they will be more distant from users and create a single point-of-failure location?

Internal or external? Should a firm invest in internally collecting, storing, maintaining, and purging its own databases of information? Or should it pay to subscribe to external databases, where providers are responsible for all data management and data access? Can an external data provider gain (and possibly market) competitive data about a subscribing firm or exercise some indirect form of control by manipulating or limiting data access? On the other hand, does maintaining data internally really contribute to the firm's strategic business goals?

Disasters. Can an organization's business processes that have become dependent on its databases recover and sustain operations after a natural or other type of information system disaster?

Data security and ethics. Are a company's competitive data safe from external snooping or sabotage? Are confidential data, such as personnel details, safe from improper or illegal access and alteration? Are confidential personnel data verified and corrected when found inaccurate?

Data purging. When is it beneficial to "clean house" and purge information systems of obsolete or non-cost-effective data? Although electronic data storage can be relatively inexpensive, there is a point at which continued storage is not worth the expense of hardware, new software, or migrating data from older formats to newer formats. ■

KEY TERMS

Attribute *275*

Centralized database *285*

Class *279*

Data definition language (DDL) *281*

Data dictionary *284*

Data inconsistency *270*

Data independence *272*

Data integrity *272*

Data manipulation language (DML) *281*

Data redundancy *270*

Database *271*

Database administrator *289*

Database management system (DBMS) *271*

Distributed database *285*

Encapsulation *279*

Entities *268*

External database *286*

Field *269*

Files *268*

Hierarchical model *273*

Index *287*

Indexed sequential access method *287*

Inheritance *279*

Key *273*

Logical view *288*

Method *279*

Natural language *283*

Network model *274*

Normalization *277*

Object *279*

Object-oriented model *279*

Physical view *288*

Pointers *274*

Primary key *287*

Query-by-example (QBE) *283*

Records *269*

Relations *275*

Relational model *275*

Schema *281*

Sequential *287*

Set *274*

Structured query language (SQL) *282*

Subschema *281*

Tuple *275*

CHAPTER HIGHLIGHTS *(L-x means learning objective number x)*

▼ There are two main types of data organization: files and databases. (L-1)

▼ Computer-based files are kept on information in the form of records, which are themselves composed of fields, which are composed of bytes, which are composed of bits. Significant programming, redundancy, data inconsistency, and inefficiency problems can occur with computer-based files. (L-2)

▼ A database is a group of related files in which one program, a database management system, provides access to all files; file data can be shared among users; and data redundancy and inconsistency are minimized. (L-2)

▼ There are four basic models for logically structuring databases: hierarchical, network, relational, and object-oriented. The hierarchical model is simple and fast for searching; the network model is more flexible for real-world situations; the relational model is easy to use and highly flexible;

and the object-oriented model can link autonomous objects of code and data. (L-2)

▼ Database management systems provide data definition and manipulation languages for physically implementing and using databases. The most prevalent languages are structured query language (SQL), query-by-example, and natural language. (L-3)

▼ Each of the three types of databases—centralized, distributed (replicated and partitioned), and external—has advantages and disadvantages. (L-3)

▼ Data are stored and accessed either directly, sequentially, or indexed-sequentially. (L-4)

▼ DBMS logical views allow many users to get the most out of one physical view of data. (L-5)

▼ Database administrators play a crucial role in designing and administering enterprise databases. (L-6)

QUESTIONS FOR REVIEW

1. What are the advantages and disadvantages of a file-based system of organizing data?

2. What are the advantages and disadvantages of a computer-based database system?

3. What is the natural hierarchy of data in a computer-based database?

4. Describe the hierarchical, network, relational, and object-oriented database models. What are the relative advantages and disadvantages of each?

5. What is normalization, and why is it done?

6. What is the difference between a data definition language and a data manipulation language? Name and describe three types of database languages.

7. Describe the three basic types of database topologies. What are some of the advantages and disadvantages of each?

8. What is the practical difference between sequentially and randomly accessed data that are physically stored in a database?

9. What is a database administrator, and what are some of her responsibilities?

QUESTIONS FOR DISCUSSION

1. Will society ever reach the point where *all* information is instantly available to *everyone*? What are some of the reasons arguing against this happening? Can governmental forces legislate it? If it could happen, what would be some of the disadvantages?

2. Since consolidating files into databases has so many advantages, should all databases be further consolidated into related *super*-databases? If not, at what point is file and/or database consolidation counterproductive?

3. As the demand for databases and instant access to large amounts of data increases, will databases proliferate or

consolidate? Will telecommunication requirements increase or decrease? Will DBMS development increase or decrease?

4. What are the ideal characteristics of a database administrator? Of a database designer? Of a database user?

5. As databases grow in size, will the error rate—the number of factual mistakes in the database in relation to its size—increase or decrease? What can be done to identify errors and decrease the error rate of databases? Can something be done to at least insulate users from database errors?

EXERCISES

1. Visit a major library (e.g., a university or city library) and determine what on-line databases the library has access to, the scope of information available to library users, the costs or fees for accessing these databases, and the cost of the equipment needed to use the databases. In general, how extensively are these on-line databases used?

2. Visit a local retailer with less than 50 employees who has a computer-based database system (e.g., a local automobile parts store). What type of database model is used (hierarchical, network, relational, or object-ori-ented)? How many different files are maintained? What DBMS is used? Who logically designed the database and who physically implemented it? What language is used to query the database?

3. Visit a local company with hundreds of employees, many databases, and a full-time database administrator. Determine the DBA's responsibilities to the firm and to the firm's users, whether or not the DBA logically de-signs databases, and in what ways the DBA modifies the databases. In what ways will DBAs' responsibilities change in the future?

GROUP ASSIGNMENT

Many organizations have not yet adopted a database ap-proach for managing their corporate data. Have each of the groups in the class contact a local firm and find out how it is currently managing its data.

a. If the company is using a database management system, have the team investigate how well the DBMS is work-ing and what new applications have been undertaken or made possible because of the use of the DBMS. Through interviews, attempt to find out how business was conducted differently—if at all—prior to the adop-tion of the DBMS. Document the benefits that have re-sulted from the use of the DBMS.

b. If the company is not yet using a DBMS, have the team investigate the current portfolio of computer-based ap-plications and see if it is possible to modify them to op-erate under a DBMS. Identify a commercially available DBMS that might be suitable for use within the com-pany. Document the potential benefits of such a con-version, as well as the costs. Develop an implementation plan for moving from the present system to the one us-ing the DBMS approach.

*M*inicase 1

Global "Libraries"—Pros and Cons

Businesses are finding that on-line wide area information services (WAIS) can be an extremely economical way to gather and trade information. For as little as $1 an hour, a subscriber to the Internet (described in Chapter 7) can sit at a personal computer in his office, issue a request for information, and have the network route his request to libraries around the globe. In a matter of seconds, the sys-tem will retrieve a collection of card-catalog citations from thousands of libraries. Citations, however, are not what people are generally after; they want the information con-tained in the sources cited.

Full-text digital library retrieval is around the corner. When it comes, many analysts say, the local library as we know it will all but disappear. In lieu of brick and mortar libraries, we will have full-text databases of books, mag-azine articles, video clips, sound recordings, imagery, and graphics. Instead of traditional librarians, we will have da-tabase experts and very smart database management sys-tems.

The new library system database software will be "like a research librarian who watches you read through a stack of information, taking notes on what you looked at first and set aside for future reference, and what information

you threw away," explains Brewster Kahle whose firm helps organizations set up electronic libraries. Moreover, these programs will automatically search for related words. Ask for information about freight trains, for ex-ample, and they will also offer you information about boxcars, tank cars, flat loaders, and so on.

Futurists dream of an interlibrary loan system on a grand scale—where there is only one digitized copy of every book or magazine known. That one copy could be used electronically around the globe by many people at the same time and would never be lost, damaged, or over-due. To the consternation of authors and publishers, how-ever, that electronic book could also be easily duplicated.

Some of the 152,000 librarians in the United States may also resist this idea for personal reasons. The thought of either losing their jobs or having to learn a new, com-puter-based career could easily be frightening to them. The idealism of providing instant access to an enormous amount of material might be balanced with a desire to control it. Furthermore, digitizing existing books is an enormous, if not impractical, undertaking. The Library of Congress, for example, contains over 22 million volumes that would have to be digitally scanned page by page. Almost all newly published works, however, are already digitized. Most newly published works are set in print with digital typesetting machines using digitized text from popular word processing software programs (as was this book).

Questions for Minicase 1

1. How could publishers protect their publishing investments with electronically available text? Could publishers become extinct as authors sell their products directly to database providers?

SOURCE: Adapted from "Good-bye, Dewey Decimals," *Forbes*, February 15, 1993.

2. What sorts of services could a library provide when full-text retrieval is available to everyone electronically?

3. What sorts of services could an entrepreneur offer the public based on public-domain material in digitized databases?

4. How might full-text retrieval of books—including illustrations and even multimedia material—change our higher education system?

Minicase 2

Prospecting the Modern Way

More and more nonprofit groups are targeting potential donors by maintaining and comparing databases containing information on wealthy people. They are hiring prospect researchers, skilled in using computer databases, to provide detailed biographical, financial, and sometimes psychological profiles to interested fund-raisers.

And it works. By knowing that a prospective donor just took $10 million in stock options when his company went public, fund-raisers can instantly identify an opportunity for giving. One fund director had a list of 100,000 possible donors but did not really know anything about them. Wanting to cull out the best prospects, she turned to a firm that compared this list with their database on wealthy people. The fund director learned that 250 people on her list were multimillionaires and another 2,500 were in the millionaire category. "After one year," she said, "we've already raised over $2 million; and we've only contacted one quarter of the people at the top of the list."

Prospect researchers fill their databases with demographic information based on magazine subscriptions, car ownership, and other indicators of wealth. Some check records on individual credit history, real estate transactions, divorce settlements, boat and airplane registrations, and even probate settlements for picking up newly rich heirs. One firm specializes in making psychological profiles of potential donors by statistically examining all the information about them. Neodata provides such services to nonprofit and for-profit organizations. Neodata's relational database was built to store demographic, psychographic, and synchographic information (data tied to major events in people's lives) on 22 million consumers in the United States.

Most prospect researchers figure that, as long as they find out details about prospects from public sources in legal ways, they are doing worthy work for a worthy cause. Others are doubtful. Mary Culnan, a business professor specializing in privacy, told a meeting of prospect researchers that she was "appalled at what's going on" and that the group "represents the worst fears of the privacy advocates." The chief counsel to the House Subcommittee on Government Information added, "People are not likely to be happy about the collation of information about themselves without their knowledge."

Questions for Minicase 2

1. What effects (good and evil) could prospect research organizations have on *private individuals*?

2. At what point is a firm "stepping across the line" in using public information about private individuals? How could this be regulated?

3. People gathering or entering data into computerized databases can make mistakes. How can firms specializing in collecting information about individuals be certain that the information is accurate? What sort of liability problems could an information database service company face? How would an individual find out that incorrect information had been electronically replicated and disseminated to other databases?

4. Database searches often depend on unique identifiers for each record (primary keys). Is it possible to do business today without being uniquely identified by credit card, social security number, bank account, or driver's license number?

SOURCE: Adapted from "Nonprofits Dig Into Databases for Big Donors," *The Wall Street Journal,* September 8, 1992, and "Getting a Read on the Customer," *InformationWeek,* May 3, 1993.

REFERENCES AND BIBLIOGRAPHY

1. Date, C. J., *An Introduction to Database Systems*, 5th ed., Reading, MA: Addison–Wesley, 1990.

2. Orli, Richard J., "Modeling Data for the Summary Database," *DATABASE*, Spring 1990, pp. 11–18.

3. *Reengineering Information Systems for Document Management*, white paper, Boston: Delphi Consulting Group, 1994.

4. Ullman, Jeffrey D., *Principles of Database Systems*, Rockville, MD: Computer Sciences Press, 1980.

DATA COMMUNICATION
AND NETWORK ARCHITECTURE

Chapter Outline

Learning Objectives

After studying this chapter, you will be able to:

1. Describe and differentiate among the most common types of data communications media.

2. Identify data communications transmission modes and common types of hardware used in data communications.

3. Explain the differing communication network architectures, including the common network topologies and their advantages/disadvantages, the different scopes of architectures, and some of the systems used in network architecture.

4. Outline the data communications process, including interfaces, synchronization, protocols, and standards.

5. Describe the types of communications providers and different data routing techniques.

6. Identify and describe the most common data communications applications.

7. Describe the use of wireless and mobile computing.

▶ 9.1 ON-LINE COMPANY ON THE ROAD

HATIM TYABJI, CHAIRMAN, president and CEO of Veri-Fone, was on the last leg of a business trip that took him from San Francisco to customers and corporate employees in Hong Kong, Bangalore (India), Marseilles (France), Copenhagen (Denmark), and Washington, D.C.—in nine days. Although the round-the-world trip was long, he did not fear returning to an office cluttered with mail, memos to answer, phone messages to act on, reports to read, or meeting-hungry managers vying for his time. "Being at headquarters is irrelevant to me," he says. Pointing to his laptop computer, he adds, "There is my office." VeriFone, a maker of credit card verification equipment, is competing against several U.S., Japanese, and European companies to control the global market.

Most of VeriFone's 1,500 employees are expected to be wherever the customers are, ferreting out their needs and responding rapidly to opportunities. That mandate is so strong that Tyabji and his associates are constantly traveling around the world; about one-third of all employees are on the road more than half the time. "There's no opportunity we don't find out about before our competitors do," says Tyabji, who himself logs about 400,000 air miles a year visiting every major and many minor prospects and customers on a regular basis. Furthermore, there are no secretaries at VeriFone; responding directly to customers and prospects is expected of all managers.

But what's great for marketing might be a formula for managerial chaos if it weren't for the fact that everyone at VeriFone is on-line with each other almost all of the time. New VeriFone employees get laptop computers equipped for telecommunications before they even get desks, and they quickly learn that it's in their best interest to plug into the corporate network at airports, hotel rooms, and customer's offices—even at pay telephones on the street. As one manager put it, they constantly tap in "or they die."

VeriFone managers get an average of 60 messages a day over the company's electronic mail system and the Internet—sometimes over 200. Paper mail, called *P-mail* at VeriFone, is literally banned internally. Even customers are encouraged to communicate with VeriFone staff

Hatim Tyabji, president and CEO of VeriFone.

members by electronic mail (E-mail). With E-mail, VeriFone also can take advantage electronically of time zone differences. When a group at one facility working on a time-critical proposal is ready to go home, they electronically hand off everything to a group that is perhaps eight hours earlier in its day. By passing work from, say, San Francisco to Taipei to London and back to San Francisco, VeriFone can work on a project an extra 18 hours a day, while competitors are literally sleeping.

VeriFone managers cite an example: A complete marketing program, with special lease packages and detailed sales presentations, took shape over the company network with inputs from around the world in less than a week—even with many of the key players traveling. "At any other company, it would have taken at least a quarter to put the plan together," said Roger Bertman, general manager and vice president of marketing. By the end of that quarter, the new plan already had brought in $2.7 million in sales.

SOURCE: Adapted from "Culture of Urgency," *Forbes ASAP*, September 13, 1993.

▶ 9.2 THE NEED TO COMMUNICATE

Communication implies an exchange of information between at least two parties. This exchange may be in the form of words, letters, messages, drawings, body movements, or any other symbols that strive to represent the ideas we wish to make known to others. Communication also suggests a system of routes or paths through which information travels from party to party.

People need to communicate; computer users are no exception, as VeriFone executives obviously appreciate. People need to transmit and receive data and information among themselves and their computer systems. This was difficult in the early years of computing when the computer resources of an organization were located in a room separate from corporate users. But today's computing environment is quite a bit different. Mainframe computers, computer terminals, and personal computers are everywhere. They are dispersed both geographically and organizationally. As a result, *data communications* takes on a significant role within an organization.

Data communications entails electronically exchanging data or information. In today's computing world, data refers to facts, statistics, pictures, voice, and other information that is *digitally coded* and intelligible to a variety of electronic machines. *Data communications systems* facilitate transmitting data over communication links between one or more computer systems and a variety of input/output devices. These links can range from simple telephone communication connections to complex communications control computers.

The term **telecommunication** generally refers to all types of long-distance communication through the use of **common carriers**, those businesses which supply high speed voice and data communication services. As telecommunication costs are often a significant part of an organization's operating expenses, many traditional telephone and mail systems have been redesigned to take advantage of today's computing power. Providers of these communication services are also working to meet the demands created by the use of computers in the office. Computer-controlled voice messaging systems, telephone conferencing, videoconferencing, and networking are just a few of the developments that organizations are experiencing.

In most modern organizations, computing and communication functions are blurred. The integration of communications technologies and the computer has broadened the scope of the role of information systems. These innovations, coupled with the deregulation of the communication industry and the resulting competitive environment, have left many managers overwhelmed and confused. Moreover, businesses are finding electronic communications essential in today's global marketplace to minimize terrestrial time and distance limitations. The story of VeriFone at the beginning of this chapter highlights the key role data communications can play when customers, suppliers, vendors, and regulators are multinational in a world that is continuously awake and doing business, somewhere, on a 24-hour-a-day basis.

To understand data communications—its capabilities as well as limitations—we need to understand communications *media* (the physical media through which data are transferred, including wireless media), communications *hardware* (the systems used in data communications), communications *networks* (the linkages among computers and communications devices), the communications *process* (how data communication occurs), data communications *providers* (regulated utilities and private firms), and communications *applications* used in today's computing environment. These topics are presented in this chapter along with some issues of telecommunication management.

▶ 9.3 COMMUNICATIONS MEDIA AND CHANNELS

For data to be communicated from one location to another, some form of pathway or *medium* must be used. This book, for example, is using paper and ink as its medium. Centuries ago, data was often communicated by semaphore or flashing lights (and still is on naval vessels at sea). But fast, accurate, and long distance data communication was first made possible by electrical circuits using wire (such as with a telegraph). Before delving into the different types of media, it is important to understand the two basic types of signals that the media can carry, especially when discussing ways to connect computer-based information systems.

SIGNALS

Analog signals are continuous waves that "carry" information by altering the characteristics of the waves. Voice and all sound is analog, traveling to human ears in the form of waves—the higher the wave (or amplitude), the louder the sound; the more closely packed, the higher the frequency or pitch. The amplitude and frequency of an irate senior executive can certainly convey meaning to a subordinate! Radio, telephones, and recording equipment historically have been analog, but they are beginning to change—due largely to computers—to the other type of signal, *digital.*

Digital signals are discrete on-off pulses that convey information in terms of 1s and 0s—just like the central processing unit in computers (see Chapter 5). While prevalent in computer-based devices, digital signaling is by no means modern technology. Flashing light and telegraph messages are on-off pulses—just not normally in binary code (in Morse code, for telegraph).

Digital signals have some especially appealing advantages over analog signals. First, digital signals tend to be less affected by interference or "noise." Noise (e.g., "static") can seriously alter the information-carrying characteristics of analog signals, while it is generally easier, in spite of noise, to distinguish between an "on" and an "off." Because of this, digital signals can be repeatedly strengthened for long distances without ever accumulating noise. Second, since computer-based systems "think" digitally, digital communications among computers requires no conversion from digital to analog to digital.

CABLES

In most organizations, data transfers occur over common twisted pairs of copper wire or over coaxial cable, but the use of glass fiber cables is increasing significantly.

Twisted-pair wire is the most prevalent form of communications wiring, since it is used for almost all business telephone wiring. It is relatively inexpensive to purchase, widely available, and easy to work with; and it can be made relatively unobtrusive by running it inside walls, floors, and ceilings. But there are some important disadvantages. Twisted-pair wire emits electromagnetic interference, is subject to interference from other electrical sources, and can be easily "tapped" for gaining unauthorized access to data by unintended receivers. In some appli-

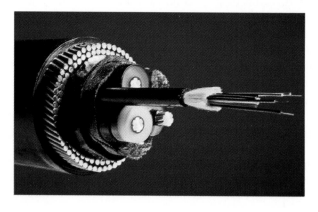

A coaxial cable.

cations, such as on a ship, the sheer weight of copper cabling and its ability to conduct heat during fires may negate its advantages in cost and simplicity.

Coaxial cable is also metallic cable, but it is much less susceptible to electrical interference and can carry much more data than twisted-pair wire. For these reasons, it is commonly used to carry high-speed data traffic as well as television signals (thus, the term *cable TV*). However, coaxial cable is more expensive, more difficult to work with, and relatively inflexible. Coaxial cable can cost from 10 to 20 times more than twisted-pair wire and—because of its inflexibility—can drive up the cost of installation or recabling due to corporate changes. This is a significant limitation in office environments where there are frequent equipment moves or reorganizations. The costs of connecting (see Box 9.1) can quickly drive up the costs of data communication.

A Closer Look BOX 9.1

MORE ABOUT THE COSTS OF CONNECTING

The cost of connecting can be alluringly deceptive. While most individuals today are familiar with the cost of general telephones (about $30 for a plain model), they have little appreciation for the cost of the circuits connecting telephones. In general, it is about 50 times the cost of the telephone; a telephone customer's share of a phone company's wires and switching gear amounts to about $1,500.

While the ratio is not quite that high between computers and computer networks that connect them, it is very easy to spend more on the connections among computers than on the computers themselves. This ratio is increasing as computers become quicker at processing data (and as they become cheaper). The stronger the computer user's hunger for data or the computer's ability to transfer data to other computers, the higher the demands placed on data communications connections and the higher the costs.

A recent survey of *Fortune 1000* companies found that support costs for connecting computers within a firm amounts to an average of more than $1,270 per user, per year, with some organizations spending $3,900 per user. But most of this amount was *not* for sophisticated communications hardware—it was for staff. At the firms studied, there was one dedicated data communications specialist for every 50 interconnected computer users, at an average cost of $61,000 per specialist per year. The cost of these specialists, including recurrent training, can easily drive up the cost of connecting computers. Indeed, 59 percent of the $1,270 cost per year went to staff members—only 22 percent was spent on the communications equipment itself.

SOURCE: adapted from ''The Heavy Burden of LAN Costs,'' *Datamation*, June 1, 1993.

Development of fiber-optic technology combined with the invention of the semiconductor laser has provided the means to transmit information through cables in the form of light waves, instead of electric current. Presently, the largest growth area for fiber-optic systems is in replacing conventional copper wiring in telephone cable networks.

Fiber-optic cables consist of thousands of very thin filaments of glass fibers which can conduct light pulses generated by lasers at transmission frequencies that approach the speed of light. Besides significant size and weight reductions over traditional cable media, fiber-optic cables provide increased speed, greater data-carrying capacity, and greater security from interference and tapping. A single hair-like glass fiber can carry up to 30,000 simultaneous telephone calls, compared to about 5,500 calls on a standard metallic coaxial cable.

EMERGING TECHNOLOGY
... fiber-optic cables are rapidly expanding

Fiber optics are beginning to be installed on a scale large enough to be economically practical. Until recently, the costs of fiber and difficulties in installing fiber-optic cable slowed its growth. While joining the ends of metallic wires is fairly simple and reliable, joining fiber-optic cables with little or no loss of signal can be very difficult—especially in cable tunnels, closets, and ceilings.

A fiber-optic bundle.

▶ 9.4 WIRELESS COMMUNICATIONS AND MOBILE COMPUTING

The communication media described in the previous section involves various types of physical wires or cables. The problem with cables is that they may be very expensive to install and change; with the exception of fiber-optic cables, they also have a fairly limited capacity. The alternative is **wireless communication**, which is still slow and expensive, but is predicted to be a major, perhaps, *the* major communication media of the future.

A common Madison Avenue image of today's business "road warrior" is one overflowing with communications technology. Besides a textual or audio message pager—perhaps one that receives its signals directly from orbiting satellites—this perpetually-in-motion company representative will also have the quintessential cellular pocket telephone. With some form of computing device such as a notebook or palmtop computer, this person will pause in airport waiting lounges to transmit or receive (via the cellular phone) electronic mail, spreadsheets, and faxes. The key to all this communication-on-the-go is electromagnetic media— the "airwaves" as they used to be called. Although wireless radio transmissions were used commercially from the outset of their invention, large-scale electromagnetic communications began with the use of microwave transmissions.

MICROWAVE

A microwave relay tower.

Microwave systems were first used extensively to transmit very high frequency radio signals in a line-of-sight path between relay stations spaced approximately 30 miles apart (due to the earth's curvature). To minimize line-of-sight problems, microwave antennas were usually placed on top of buildings, towers, and mountain peaks. Microwave systems were adopted by long distance telephone carriers because they generally provide about 10 times the data-carrying capacity of wire without the significant efforts necessary to string or bury wire. Compared to 30 miles of wire, microwave communications can be set up much more quickly (within a day) at much less cost.

But the fact that microwave requires line-of-sight transmission severely limited its usefulness as a practical large-scale solution to data communication needs, especially over very long distances. Additionally, microwave transmissions are susceptible to environmental interference during severe weather such as heavy rain or snow storms. Although still fairly widely used, long distance microwave data communications systems have been replaced largely by satellite communications systems.

SATELLITES

In addition to fiber optics, another major advance in communications in recent years is the use of **communication satellites** for digital transmissions. Although the radio frequencies used by satellite data communication transponders are also line-of-sight, the enormous "footprint" of a satellite's coverage area from such high altitudes overcomes the limitations of microwave data relay stations. It is not uncommon for one communication satellite to be able to cover 30 percent of the earth's surface. There are now dozens of communication satellites from several nations in stationary "geosynchronous" orbits, hovering approximately 22,000 miles above the equator. A comparison of transmission rates is shown in Table 9.1.

Table 9.1 **Typical Media Transmission Speeds**

Medium	*Typical transmission speeds*
Metallic wire	.0012 Mbps–10 Mbps
Microwave and satellite	.256 Mbps–100 Mbps
Fiber optics	.5 Mbps–1,000 Mbps

Satellites have a number of unique characteristics. Some of these are advantages that make communication satellites not only practical but also attractive for certain specific applications. Others are restrictions that make satellite use either impractical or impossible for other applications.

Advantages of communication satellites include the following:

▼ The cost of transmission by satellite is the same regardless of the distance between the sending and receiving stations within the footprint of a satellite. A transmission from New York to Los Angeles can be sent as cheaply as one from New York to Philadelphia.

▼ The cost of a satellite transmission remains the same regardless of the number of stations receiving that transmission. Everyone within the satellite footprint can receive a transmission simultaneously.

▼ Satellite systems have the ability to carry very large amounts of data.

▼ Satellite systems are extraterrestrial, that is, there is no need to dig trenches as with cabling systems, especially in rough terrain.

▼ Satellite transmissions can easily cross or span political borders, often with minimal government regulation.

▼ Transmission errors in a digital satellite signal occur almost completely at random. Thus, statistical methods for error detection and correction can be applied efficiently and reliably.

▼ Satellite users can be highly mobile while sending and receiving signals (e.g., a ship at sea or a tank in battle).

Disadvantages of communications satellites include the following:

▼ Because of the great distance from the ground to a satellite in geosynchronous orbit, any one-way transmission over a satellite link has an inherent propagation delay of approximately one-quarter of a second. This delay makes the use of satellite links inefficient for some data communication needs. For example, voice communications—especially when there are multiple "hops" up and down with more than one satellite for very long distance calls—can become more than just irritating with one-second lags. When not accustomed to these propagation delays, people tend to interrupt inadvertently or preempt each other's speech.

▼ Because of weight limitations for launching into orbit, satellites can carry or generate very little electrical power. The low power of satellite signals combined with the great distances the signals must span can result in an extremely weak signal at the receiving earth station.

▼ Satellite signals are inherently not secure because they are available to all receivers within the footprint—intended or not. Any receiving station within sight of the satellite can intercept its signals when tuned to the proper frequency.

▼ Some frequencies used for satellite signals are susceptible to interference from bad weather; others are susceptible to interference from ground-based microwave signals.

RADIO

Radio electromagnetic data communications does not have to depend on microwave or satellite links, especially for short ranges such as within an office setting. Radio is being used increasingly to connect computers and peripheral equipment or computers and local area networks.

Radio data communications, like other electromagnetic media, have some distinct advantages for data communications. The simplest but perhaps greatest advantage is that no metallic wires are needed; equipment connected by radio can be highly mobile without being leashed to a wall. Radio waves tend to propagate easily through normal office walls, allowing for officewide data accessibility. Radio communication devices are fairly inexpensive and easy to install (especially without cabling). Finally, radio allows for high data rates, typically in the lower megabit per second range.

On the other hand, radio media are susceptible to electrical interference problems—an ever growing problem in offices filled with electrical equipment like telephones, computers, copy machines, facsimile machines, and so on. Radio data transmitters can also add to the interference problems of all other electronic devices. Finally, data transmitted via radio are susceptible to snooping by anyone with a similar device tuned to the appropriate frequency within range of the transmitter—sometimes as far as 2,000 feet away.

INFRARED

Another increasingly popular data communications medium is *infrared* radiation. **Infrared** light is red light below what is commonly visible to human eyes, but light nonetheless that can be modulated or pulsed for conveying information. Probably the most universal application of infrared light is with television or videocassette recorder remote control units. With computers, infrared transmitters and receivers (or "transceivers") are being used for short distance connections between computers and peripheral equipment, or between computers and local area networks.

Infrared light has some distinct advantages for data communications. Like electromagnetic media, no metallic wires are needed; equipment can be highly mobile without being tethered to a wall. There are no electrical interference problems with infrared communications—a growing problem in offices filled with electrical equipment. Because of this, no Federal Communications Commission permission is required to operate an infrared transmitter, and no certification is needed before selling an infrared device. Infrared devices are fairly inexpensive and easy to install. Finally, infrared allows for very high data rates, typically in the megabit per second range.

On the other hand, infrared media are susceptible to fog, smog, smoke, dust, rain, and air temperature fluctuations. When they are used indoors with a local area network, however, most of those problems are minimal. But infrared energy doesn't always "bounce" well; units often need to be within line-of-sight of each other.

CELLULAR RADIO TECHNOLOGY

A businessman using a cellular phone.

*G*LOBAL PERSPECTIVE

... European cellular service goes digital

Cellular radio technology, while introduced for mobile telephone voice conversations, is increasingly being used (by telephone users) for data communications. The basic concept of **cellular radio technology** is relatively simple. The Federal Communication Commission (FCC) has defined geographic cellular service areas; each cellular coverage area is then subdivided into hexagonal cells that fit together like a honeycomb to form the backbone of that area's cellular radio system. The number of cells per system is not predefined; the cellular service provider can split, section, or combine cell groups and add or borrow channels as needed. This allows cellular systems to grow to a virtually infinite number of cells, each cell subdividing into smaller and smaller cells.

Located at the center of each cell (hexagon) is a radio transceiver and a computerized cell-site controller that handles all cell-site control functions. All of the cell sites are connected to a mobile telephone switching office that provides the connections from the cellular system to a wired telephone network and transfers calls from one cell to another as a user travels out of the cell serving one area and into another (see Figure 9-1). While cell coverage is not nearly complete, especially in remote areas, all major U.S. and European cities have cellular telephone coverage.

At the present time, cellular service in the United States is primarily analog, like ground-based telephones, while in Europe it is digital. Digital transmission offers the potential of much greater traffic capacity within each cell, less susceptibility to interference, greater voice clarity, and fewer data errors. A conversion to digital is underway in the United States.

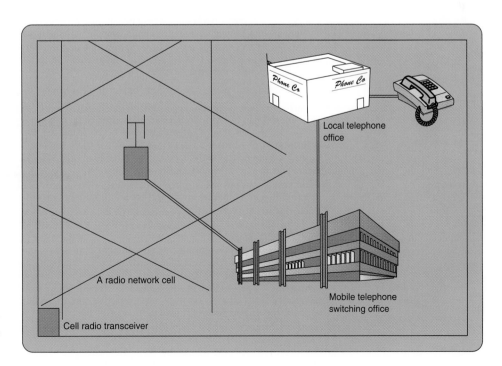

FIGURE 9.1 How a cellular telephone connects to a wired telephone.

MOBILE COMPUTING

Wireless communication provides for mobile computing devices. **Mobile computing** refers to the use of portable computer devices that can be used in multiple places. Computers can be connected to the network through wired ports or through wireless connections. Mobile computing, especially if wireless, provides for many applications (see Table 9.2). Many people, including Judy Hamilton, president and CEO of Dataquest (a large computing research company), believes that mobile computing will revolutionize the computer industry and is likely to be viewed as more important than the PC was in the 1980s.

Table 9.2 **Mobile and Wireless Applications**

Mobile computing enables existing and entirely new kinds of applications, for example:

- **Mobile personal communications capabilities,** such as the new personal digital assistants (PDAs), for networked communications and applications (a networked extension of the portable palmtop style of computing).
- **On-line transaction processing,** for example, where a salesperson in a retail environment can enter an order for goods and also charge a customer's credit card to complete the transaction.
- **Remote database queries,** for example, where a salesperson can use a mobile network connection to check an item's availability or the status of an order, directly from the customer's site.
- **Dispatching,** which means any kind of dispatching application such as air traffic control, rental car pick up and return, delivery vehicles, trains, taxis, cars, and trucks.
- **Front-line IT applications,** where instead of the same data being entered multiple times as it goes through the value chain, it is entered only once, typically at the beginning of the cycle or where first created.

Wireless communications enables both mobile computing applications and low cost cable replacement applications, for example:

- Temporary offices can be set up quickly and inexpensively by using wireless network connections (often just running the wires to a standard office can cost hundreds of dollars).
- Wireless connections to permanent office locations are often practical in difficult wiring environments, e.g., in historic buildings where installed wired connections could cause damage, or in buildings where there is asbestos insulation, and wire installation could produce a health risk.
- Campus area network backbones where installing a wireless connection can replace leased lines that are used to connect LANs, thus eliminating the costs of monthly line leases.
- Preconfigured LAN installations, where the software and the network is preconfigured, preloaded, and pretested as a sort of LAN-in-a-box so that anyone can install the network instead of having to use an expensive network installation specialist.

There are mobile and wireless application opportunities in many industries, such as:

- **Retail**—the most successful application to date, particularly in department stores where there are frequent changes of layout; retail sales personnel could conduct inventory enquiries or even sales transactions on the retail floor with wireless access from their PCs.
- **Wholesale/distribution**—many distributors currently use wireless networking for inventory picking in warehouses with PCs mounted directly on forklifts and for delivery and order status updates, with PCs inside distribution tractor trailers.
- **Field service/sales**—dispatching, on-line diagnostic support from customer sites, and parts ordering/inventory queries are typical applications in all types of service and sales functions.
- **Factories/manufacturing**—process control, hostile environments, clean rooms; applications could include mobile shop-floor quality control or wireless applications that give added flexibility for temporary setups.
- **Healthcare/hospitals**—healthcare personnel need to access and send data to patient records or consult comparative diagnosis databases wherever the patient or the healthcare worker may be located (different hospital rooms, departments, outpatient sites, and so forth).
- **Education**—interesting pilot applications involve equipping students with PCs in the lecture halls, linked by a wireless network, for interactive quizzes, additional data and graphics lecture support, and on-line hand-out materials.
- **Banking/finance**—mobile transactional capabilities can assist in purchasing, selling, inquiry, brokerage, and other dealings.

Source: Advertisement from the Digital Equipment Corporation

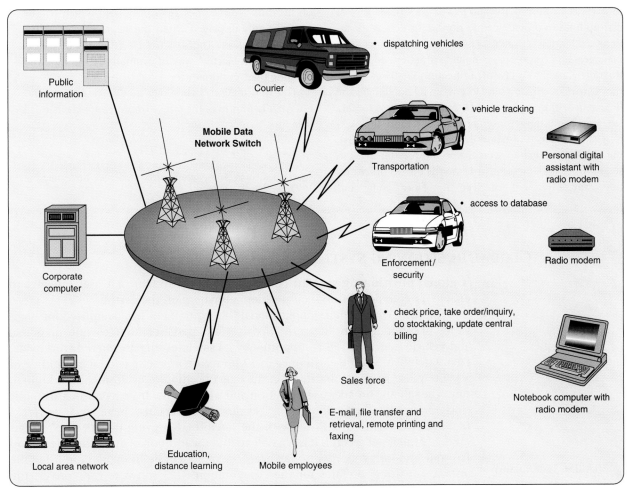

FIGURE 9.2 Applications of mobile computing.

Mobile computing applications are available not only in the corporate environment but in the public arena as well (see Figure 9.2). Several of these applications were presented in Chapters 1-4 and more are illustrated in Chapters 14 and 17. An example of wireless applications is provided in Box 9.2, while a presentation of an emerging application—a global positioning system—follows.

IT At Work BOX 9.2

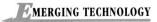

EMERGING TECHNOLOGY

ARMOUR CORPORATION USES WIRELESS RADIO NETWORKS TO INCREASE PRODUCTIVITY

Armour Swift-Eckrich, a food manufacturer, is turning to the latest in mobile computing technology to track minute, constantly changing details from store to store. The company's relatively new retail operation needed to collect data at the store level and get it back to headquarters as quickly as possible. Its field representatives employ Poqet hand-held PCs and wireless radio networks to feed data from the store shelves to a corporate host database. Weighing just 1.5 pounds, the Poqet is a DOS-based palmtop that can operate for 16 to 48 hours

using a rechargeable nickel-cadmium battery. Before the company adopted Poqet, the 150 Armour merchandising representatives nationwide spent from 4 to 6 hours a week manually creating reports from data collected from individual stores. Now, they electronically capture pertinent product information on the spot and then upload it via a wireless network to Fastech's proprietary sales information system database. Access is available over public wide area telephone service (WATS) lines. Armour uses a combination of systems network architecture (SNA) connectivity and PC-based Crosstalk over dial-up links to provide connections to its PCs, workstations, and dumb terminals. This system enables regional managers and corporate headquarters' staff to download the sales data into a PC spreadsheet or database, where they can analyze it and send follow-up instructions to the field staff within 24 hours. The real-time access to data lets merchandising representatives spend more time visiting stores instead of laboring over reports. In the past, the only way to get answers to specific questions was to send a voice mail message or fax to the district office and hope the sales rep received it before going out

on his calls. Now, a message can be sent which will be automatically displayed when the sales rep gets to the store in question. The system also provides managers with a more objective way of evaluating sales reps and tracking their performance.

The information technology in this case, Poqet PC Plus, really improves the way Armour conducts its retail business. ▲

SOURCE: Condensed from LaPlante, A., "Armour Deploys Strategic Sales Force Automation," *ComputerWorld*, November 29, 1993.

GLOBAL POSITIONING SYSTEMS

A **global positioning system (GPS)** is a wireless system that uses satellites to enable users to determine their position anywhere on the earth.

Starting with military applications, GPS equipment has been used for navigation of commercial airlines and ships. It is also used for land surveying, mapping, and vehicle tracking. GPS is supported by 24 satellites that are shared worldwide. Each satellite orbits the earth once in 12 hours, on a precise path at an altitude of 10,900 miles. At any point in time, the exact position of each satellite is known, since the satellite broadcasts its position and a time signal from its on-board atomic clock, accurate to one-billionth of a second. Receivers also have accurate clocks that are synchronized with those of the satellites. Knowing the speed of signals (186,272 miles per second) it is possible to find the location of any receiving station (latitude and longitude) within an accuracy of 50 feet by triangulation, using the distance of three satellites for the computation. GPS software can convert the latitude and longitude computed to an electronic map. Box 9.3 shows how GPS can be used in the trucking industry.

*E*MERGING TECHNOLOGY

... satellites allow for pinpoint positioning

IT At Work BOX 9.3

USING GPS TO IMPROVE SALES AND SERVICE

Imagine that a truck, carrying hazardous material on a lonely interstate road at night, is starting to have engine problems. The temperature gauge shoots up and the engine seizes. The driver tries to call for help on his cellular phone, but the phone is not working since the truck is too far from a major metropolitan area. The driver then pushes an emergency button and a signal is sent to a satellite. Within 30 seconds, the communication system of Boyle Transportation (Billerica, MA), the owner of the truck, receives the signal and calculates its exact location. Seconds later, Boyle's dispatcher contacts the state police, who arrive at the scene within minutes with appropriate fire-fighting and other equipment. A potential disaster has been prevented.

Boyle Transportation is a relatively small U.S. trucker (75 trucks) that hauls hazardous material nationwide. The need to be constantly in touch with the drivers is

obvious. Before GPS, drivers had to call headquarters every few hours. It was an onerous requirement for the drivers, forcing them to pull over to find pay phones on the road. And the home office still had no idea where its trucks were the rest of the time.

Boyle developed a special information system, called transportation operations management system (TOMS). TOMS is constructed with a relational database at its center, containing information about customers, pickups, deliveries, truck locations, and truck statuses. The database accepts information from the trucks, collected by satellite feed, and automatically updates each truck's pickup and delivery information. The database also takes newly entered customer order data and matches it to the nearest available truck, based on positioning information received from the satellite. The database then generates schedules and notifies the designated truck driver to make the new pickup, giving him the exact address. The software then calculates an estimated time of arrival. The database enables Boyle to know—in almost real time—where every truck is, where it is going, and what it is carrying. The system can also generate tariffs which are used in the company electronic data interchange (EDI) system.

The system is fully backed up for security purposes and the results are gratifying. In addition to improved customer service and safety, dispatchers' productivity grew by 80 percent, drivers no longer waste time searching for pay phones, and the administrative staff handles 35 percent more business with the same number of employees.

Boyle's system was custom-made and the first of its kind in the trucking industry. Boyle is considering the development of TOMS as a commercial software package to sell to other trucking companies.

Critical Thinking Issues: Why is the integration of telecommunication and database vital for a trucking company, and why was satellite technology selected for TOMS? ▲

SOURCE: Condensed from Radding A., "With Satellites, Boyle Keeps Trucking All Night Long," *InfoWorld*, October 17, 1994.

▶ 9.5 COMMUNICATIONS HARDWARE

Clearly, wires or radios are not enough by themselves to allow computer users to share data or equipment. Specialized communications systems must be used to take advantage of communications media, manage the media, and ensure satisfactory communications. This section deals with the most common equipment used in data communications and their use—modems, transmission modes, transmission accuracy, and communications processes.

MODEMS

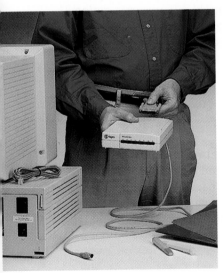

An external modem.

The public telephone system was designed as an analog network to carry voice signals or sounds in an analog wave format. In order for this type of circuit to carry digital information, that information must be converted into an analog wave pattern. The conversion from digital to analog is called **modulation**, and the reverse is **demodulation**. The device that does this is called a **modem**, a contraction of the terms **mo**dulate/**dem**odulate. Modems are always used in pairs. The unit at the sending end converts digital information from a computer into analog signals for transmission over analog lines; at the receiving end, another modem converts the analog signal back into digital signals for the receiving computer.

Like most communications equipment, a modem's transmission speed is measured in bits-per-second, usually expressed as bps. Typical modems have speeds of 9,600, 14,400, and 28,800 bps; even home computer users can purchase inexpensive 14,400 bps modems. Obviously, a receiving modem must be capable of handling data at a speed equal to or greater than the sending modem.

The amount of data actually transferred from one system to another in a fixed length of time is only partially dependent on the transmission speed. Actual throughput speed, or the *effective throughput* speed, varies with a number of factors and is usually measured in characters per second (cps). Data compression, for example, can reduce the number of characters in a message, essentially increasing the effective throughput rate for the message even though the transmission rate is held constant. On the other hand, electrical noise, resulting in frequent retransmissions, can decrease effective throughput.

Transmission speeds of modems, while normally the largest factor in actual throughput speed, sometimes get too much attention. Effective throughput should be the overriding business criteria. For example, people rarely take jet flights for 10 mile trips even though jets are very, very fast; the effective travel speed is significantly reduced by the trip to and from an airport, the boarding process, and so on. Another important factor in effective throughput is the transmission mode.

TRANSMISSION MODES

Data transmission, as in all communications, occurs in one of three modes: *simplex, half-duplex,* or *full-duplex.* A **simplex** data transmission uses one circuit in one direction only—similar to a doorbell or a public announcement system. It is simple and relatively inexpensive but very constraining, since communication is one way only (much the same as broadcast television or radio).

A **half-duplex** transmission also uses only one circuit, but it is used in both directions—one direction at a time. This is similar to an intercom or a citizen's band radio where users can receive or transmit but not do both simultaneously. Half-duplex can be much more useful than simplex because of two-way data transfer, but half-duplex communications can be very difficult to coordinate, especially if the coordination has to be done using the same single channel.

Full-duplex transmission uses two circuits for communications—one for each direction simultaneously (for example, a common telephone). This mode is clearly easier to use than half-duplex, but the cost of two circuits can be significant, especially over long distances. Most data devices operate at both half- and full-duplex modes, although a simplex mode may be used to turn a device on or off at certain predefined times. Cost and ease of use are two of the key factors in choosing what transmission mode to use in data communications.

TRANSMISSION ACCURACY

An electrical communications line—whether using cable or radio—can be subject to interference from storms, signals from other lines, and other phenomena that introduce errors into a transmission. Telephone line cables may be mishandled by repair personnel, accidentally cut by construction workers, or subjected to power surges while data are being transmitted. These events might cause one bit or several bits to be "dropped" during transmission, thus corrupting the integrity of the information. Since there are usually thousands of bits traveling over the line every second, and since the loss of even one of them could alter a character or control code, data transmission requires accuracy controls. These controls consist of bits called **parity bits** that are like check sums added to characters and/or blocks of characters at the sending end of the line. Parity bits are checked and verified at the receiving end of the line to determine whether bits were lost during transmission.

There are two general types of actions taken to deal with these communication errors once detected—backward error correction and forward error correction. **Backward error correction** (BEC) entails going "back" to the sender and requesting retransmission of the entire data stream or of a particular part, if it can be identified. **Forward error correction** (FEC) uses knowledge about the message stream and mathematical algorithms to allow the receiver to correct the received data stream without having to go back to the sender. BEC is much simpler and less expensive to use when there are few errors or when time delays are not crucial. FEC is more complex but may be necessary over long distances when retransmissions are costly.

PROCESSORS

There are many types of data communications hardware devices specifically designed to process data communications rapidly and to manage circuits. These include devices known as multiplexors, concentrators, communications controllers, cluster controllers, protocol converters, data encryptors, communications processors, and front-end processors. Most of these devices are beyond the scope of this book. Multiplexors and front-end processors, however, are so common that a brief discussion of both is warranted.

MULTIPLEXORS. A **multiplexor** is an electronic device that allows a single communications channel to carry data transmissions simultaneously from many sources. The objective of a multiplexor is to lower communication costs by allowing the more efficient use of circuits through sharing. Traffic over a communication channel is rarely smooth and continuous; communication channels have traffic peaks and valleys. Adding more capacity to a communication circuit in order to deal with peaks may be highly inefficient for use at all other times. Another solution involves more efficient use of the existing channel through multiplexing.

Typically, a multiplexor merges the transmissions of several terminals at one end of a communications channel, while a similar unit separates the individual transmissions at the receiving end. Technically, this is accomplished through *frequency division multiplexing* (FDM), where a multiplexor divides a high-speed channel into multiple slow-speed channels; *time division multiplexing* (TDM), where the multiplexor divides the time each terminal can use a high-speed line into very short time slots or time frames; and *statistical time division*, which dynamically allocates time slots to terminals based on priorities.

FRONT-END PROCESSORS. With most computers, the CPU has to communicate with several devices or terminals at the same time. Routine communication tasks can absorb a large proportion of the CPU's processing time, leading to degraded performance on more important jobs. In order not to waste this precious CPU time, many computer systems have a small secondary computer dedicated solely to communication. Known as a **front-end processor**, this specialized computer manages all routine communications with peripheral devices.

For large mainframe installations, a front-end processor is typically a special-purpose minicomputer. Its function may include coding and decoding data, error detection, recovery, recording, interpreting, and processing of the control information which is transmitted. It can also *poll* remote terminals to determine if they have a message to send or are ready to receive a message. In addition, a front-end processor has the responsibility of controlling access to the network, assigning priorities to messages, logging all data communications activity, computing statistics on network activity, and routing and rerouting messages among alternative communication links. Front-end processors can provide up to 30 percent additional processing time for the mainframe.

▶ 9.6 NETWORK ARCHITECTURE

When a building is constructed, its architecture is the plan or structure by which the component parts are related. It guides a designer or builder to ensure that everything fits together as a unified whole. It also imposes order on a system to help guarantee that system components can interact properly. When connecting computing devices for data communications, how the connections are structured can be significant in terms of capabilities, cost, flexibility to changes, data security, and reliability. The next section in the text will discuss some common computer network architectures (or topologies), the two main types of networks in terms of scope, and common network processing arrangements.

NETWORK TOPOLOGY

A network's **topology** is the physical and logical arrangement of its parts relative to one another. Each part is commonly called a **node**, which is any device on a network with the ability to exchange control and data transmissions with other nodes on the network. There are three basic network topologies: *bus, ring,* and *star* (see Figure 9.3).

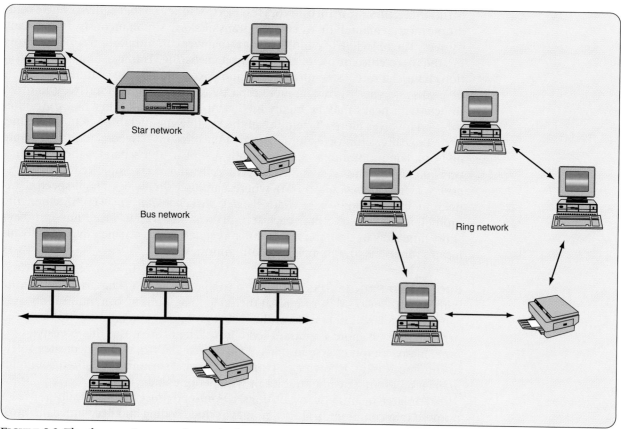

FIGURE 9.3 The three main network topologies.

In a **bus** topology, nodes are arranged along a single length of cable that can be extended at the ends. In a **ring** topology, nodes are arranged along the transmission path so that a signal passes through one station at a time before returning to its originating node; the nodes, then, form a closed circle. A **star** network has a central node that connects to each of the other nodes by a single, point-to-point link. Any communication between one node and another in a star topology must pass through the central node.

In all three topologies, transmissions are broadcast to all nodes even though only intended for specific recipients. Any signal transmitted on the network passes to all the network's nodes; it is then up to the receiving node to determine for whom the message is intended. In a ring topology, the message passes through each node on its way to the recipient; in a star topology, the message passes through the central node. With a bus topology, all nodes receive the message simultaneously, and each node must compete for use of the bus since only one message at a time can be on the bus. With star and ring topologies, there can be many messages in transit simultaneously. In all cases, each receiving node recognizes its address in a given signal and copies only signals that are its own. In star networks, signals sent through the central node are switched to the proper receiving station over a permanently or temporarily dedicated physical path.

Each topology has strengths and weaknesses. For example, communications using the bus topology can be relatively fast, since all nodes have instant access to the bus and all nodes receive every message simultaneously, without intermediaries. But a bus network's performance can quickly degrade as the number of active nodes increases since all nodes must compete to use the bus. When an organization is choosing a topology, it should consider such performance issues as delay, throughput, reliability, and the network's ability to continue through—or recover after—the failure of one or more of its nodes. The company should also consider such physical constraints as the maximum transmission speed of the circuit, the distances between nodes, the circuit's susceptibility to errors, and the overall system costs (such as those pointed out in Box 9.1).

NETWORK SCOPE

Because people need to communicate over long as well as short distances, the scope of data communications networks is important. There are two general network scopes: *wide area* and *local area* (a "metropolitan" area network is a hybrid somewhere between the two). While similar conceptually, they can be very different in practice.

WIDE AREA NETWORKS. Wide area networks (WANs) are networks that generally span distances greater than one city—they include regional networks such as telephone companies or international networks such as global communications services providers. They usually have very large capacity circuits with many communications processors to use these circuits efficiently. Some WANs are commercial, regulated networks, while others are privately owned—usually by large businesses that can afford the costs. Some WANs, however, are "public" in terms of their management, resources, and access. One such WAN that is increasingly being used by businesses is the Internet (see Box 9.4 and Chapter 14). Hailed by many as the foundation of a forthcoming worldwide **information superhighway**, Internet proponents praise its independent, distributed management; its enormous store of diverse and extensive information; its ability to link users using electronic mail; and its wide and relatively easy geographical availability.

A Closer Look BOX 9.4

 **G**LOBAL PERSPECTIVE

MORE ABOUT THE INTERNET

The Internet is one of the largest, most widely-used wide area networks in the world not owned by a regulated or private commercial carrier. The Internet links millions of users around the world, and is often described as the prototype for a worldwide information "superhighway." It is touted by political activists as an international town hall—a center of emerging democracy—and yet it isn't really owned or managed by anyone.

In 1969 the Internet was developed by the Department of Defense and named ARPANET (Advanced Research Project Agency Network) for use as a way to link, over dedicated phone lines, large computer data bases to be shared by military and government officials and by academic researchers. Today, it is a formless, mostly unregulated system for linking thousands of big server computers all over the world holding data on many subjects with thousands of users attached to each server. A large part of the system is now run by the National Science Foundation, but most of it is self-managed by the server institutions.

The Internet has recently grown explosively as businesses have begun to use it as well. (VeriFone, the company highlighted in the case study at the beginning of this chapter, uses the Internet for electronic mail on a global basis.)

People around the world routinely send and receive E-mail over the Internet, including those accessing it via commercial services such as MCI Mail. Much of the news available to the world concerning the attempted Soviet coup in 1991 came via the Internet and facsimile networks. Another major use of the Internet is the posting of public messages in electronic discussion groups called "news groups." These are like international bulletin boards or public forums for discussing everything from TV shows to politics. The Internet is also used to tap into thousands of large databases and search through them. Most university libraries offer database search services using the Internet.

Although the Internet is not very user friendly by today's standards for networks, it is a true wide area network for millions of users everyday.

To some extent, the Internet WAN analogy to a highway is apt; the vast U.S. system of roads is locally funded and built (with federal guidance and partial funding) and easily accessed. Whether envisioned to promote scientific research, provide entertainment on demand, or permit long-distance education, information superhighway champions seek nothing less than "any information, anywhere, anytime." This concept is much broader than simply a "telephone system for computers," and the specifics about its architecture, management, and accessibility have yet to be decided. A number of emerging issues concerning existing and proposed "public" WANS can be significant to business computing. Among the leading issues are funding and access, privacy, criminal activity, information overload, and telecommuting.

Some information superhighway advocates attribute the U.S.'s present worldwide telecommunications leadership to the existence of competing commercial communications firms (such as AT&T, MCI, and Sprint) and their push for the commercialization of national and global communication networks.

WANs can use the three basic types of network topologies, but most generally use the star topology in order to more tightly control the network. A common WAN spanning the continental U.S. may have a dozen or more "hubs" to form a very complex star or group of stars. The services these WANs can provide are discussed in more detail in Section 9.9. The benefits of WAN and LAN are illustrated in Box 9.5.

IT At Work BOX 9.5

LAN AND WAN INCREASE PRODUCTIVITY

The Seattle-based advertising agency, Cole & Weber ($100 million in annual revenues) had a previous LAN that could not handle effectively the large volume of graphics output that is critical to the productivity and success of an advertising agency. It was not uncommon that when a 200 MB graphics file was sent, the entire LAN would, as one employee put it, "screech to a halt." The company's IS director believes that management's earlier goal of saving money resulted in the inexpensive network cards being "blown away." This resulted in a lot of downtime, something that is lethal in a graphics-intensive, deadline-driven environment such as an advertising agency, where graphic materials have to be modified and remodified until deadline time.

The production department was running illustrations—drawing and photo-imaging packages that clogged the wires—users "maxed-out" the Ethernet server by quickly reaching its 10 Mb-per-second limit.

Under the previous system, when ads had to be changed at the last minute, employees were stressed and frazzled during the process, and this lead to high error rates. New materials had to be sent to clients by Federal Express or even read over the phone to someone whose ability to make the proper copy changes was unreliable.

Last year, Cole & Weber spent $200,000 to upgrade its network infrastructure and to implement a comprehensive system which now handles everything from customer billing to the scheduling and trafficking of ads. The changes included the installation of an HP 3000 minicomputer, adding a 486 file server, and boosting overall throughput. Cole & Weber has also built a WAN to connect its Portland, Oregon satellite office and has provided an Internet connection to its 124 Portland employees.

The network was remapped and split into two segments, with the graphics and multimedia files running on one part and spreadsheet and word processing files running on the other. Other network upgrades followed, and the office standardized by using Microsoft desktop applications such as Word, Excel, Powerpoint, and Mail.

Agency management believes that their new electronic production facilities have become a key element in the agency's improved service levels. As a service business, maintaining and augmenting service is a distinct competitive advantage. Now, last-minute production changes can be whisked to clients via modem. The investment in this technology is credited with Cole & Weber winning the Microsoft account.

Critical Thinking Issues: How can an integrated LAN/WAN system increase productivity? How can all this contribute to increased service levels? ▲

SOURCE: Condensed from "Ad Agency Overhauls LAN to Escape Net Gridlock," *InfoWorld*, February 28, 1994.

LOCAL AREA NETWORKS. A **local area network** (**LAN**) is a system for interconnecting two or more communicating devices within 2,000 feet—usually intraorganizational, privately owned, internally administered, and not subject to regulation by the FCC—which supports full connectivity so that every user device on the network has the potential to communicate with any other device. LANs are generally medium to high speed, typically supporting transfer rates ranging from 3 to 100 Mbps. A LAN allows a large number of intelligent devices to share corporate resources (such as storage devices, printers, programs, and data files) and integrates a wide range of functions into a single system.

The most common commercial LAN is the **Ethernet**. The Ethernet is a standardized package of hardware, communications media, and system software using a single cable. Ethernet networks can transmit data at 10 Mbps, and some versions can increase this to 100 Mbps. As with other networks, the Ethernet allows a user to query others on the network, move data from one point to another, or direct information to be printed on any printer connected to the system.

In an office, a local area network can give users fast and efficient access to a common bank of information (such as customer lists, schedules, and document formats) while also allowing the office to pool other resources, such as printers and facsimile machines. A well-constructed LAN can also eliminate the need to circulate paper documents by distributing electronic memos and other material to each worker's terminal.

PRIVATE BRANCH EXCHANGE. Similar to a LAN, a **private branch exchange** (**PBX**) is a unifying medium for diverse communicating machines. Like a star LAN, a PBX is the central point of control for an intrafirm telecommunication network; i.e., all devices in the network are connected to it. Once used solely to switch voice telephone lines, PBXs now support both voice and data traffic, allowing data terminal and telephone users to share a common network of telephone lines.

PBXs can provide a very low cost method of connecting computing devices by using existing corporate phone wiring. Their transmission speed, however, is usually considerably less than with a true local area network. For very occasional data communications of low volume data, or for combining voice and digital data (such as digitized voice mail services), a PBX can offer advantages.

NETWORK DISTRIBUTED PROCESSING

Distributed data processing is a form of information processing made possible by a network of dispersed computers. Distributed data processing is a movement away from a *centralized* processing approach, which relies on large central computers (usually mainframes). *Decentralized* processing, on the other hand, involves completely independent user computer systems with independent databases, programs, applications, budgets, and information system personnel.

Distributed data processing has some strong advantages. Real-time applications processing is more feasible since data can be entered locally and used immediately. User response and turnaround time are improved because processing is carried out at the user's location. Computer applications can be more flexible and tailored to the user's requirements, since hardware and software can be developed to fit the user's organizational and operational requirements. Finally, input errors are minimized, because local users control data entry.

Distributed data processing systems can cost less to operate—for most applications—than centralized systems, since the processors are significantly less expensive for the same total processing power. There is also less likelihood of a total network breakdown or failure, since processing is spread among many computers. Furthermore, replacing one failed, small processor is much easier than the large, single processor.

But distributed systems also have limitations. Although there is less likelihood of a total system failure, the use of many communication links as a network increases the chances of subsystem failures. If not managed properly, data processing costs can rise substantially due to too many users or too many data transactions. Building and coordinating a distributed processing network for an entire organization can be a very complex task. Inefficient use and unnecessary duplication of information processing resources may occur. Controls are needed to preserve the integrity of the distributed databases in the organization. Last, training users and providing adequate documentation and other forms of user support can be difficult.

The structure of the distributed processing network can significantly affect its functionality, cost, reliability, and performance. The first distributed processing architecture using network data communications was the *file server* approach. Its limitations gave rise to the now very popular approach called *client/server*—the structure widely used by businesses to downsize from centralized mainframe computer processing. The third common approach is *peer-to-peer*. These three distributed processing network methods will be discussed next.

FILE SERVER ARCHITECTURE. **File server** distributed processing is the simplest approach for a relatively large number of network processors to share data. Enterprise-wide data are digitally stored in a designated file server processor connected to the network. When an application at any node needs to perform processing on data contained in a file, the application requests the file from the file server. The file server then responds by transmitting the entire file to the requesting node processor, and the requesting node performs the necessary processing locally.

Limitations of this arrangement can be significant. First, large files can electronically choke the network whenever they are transmitted to a node for processing, especially if they are transmitted often to a large number of nodes. Second, many nodes can be simultaneously altering the same file—thereby creating chaos when the file is "returned" to the file server. Alternatively, the file server can only allow one node at a time to update a file, but then one node can tie up a file needed by other nodes. These problems helped spur the development of the client/server computing architecture.

CLIENT/SERVER ARCHITECTURE. In a **client/server** approach, the server not only has the data files, it also contains the application software as well. Each node is a client of the server, calling upon the server for services rendered by the application software. When a node needs information based on files in the server, the node sends a message (or **remote procedure call**) requesting the information from the server. The server processes file data and provides the information—not the entire file(s)—to the node.

This arrangement has clear advantages. The network is not overloaded with entire files being transferred back and forth through the network circuits for processing at each remote terminal. Moreover, the integrity of the files is much easier to maintain, since only the server actually updates the files. In addition, file security is easier to maintain with the server in full control of file data.

*E*MERGING TECHNOLOGY

... client/server systems improve network processing

These benefits have contributed to a significant computing trend in the 1990s based on the client/server networking approach. Louis Gerstner, chairman and CEO of IBM, called the wholesale movement toward client/server computing as a "sea of change in our industry." In a survey of 400 CEOs by Deloitte & Touche, client/server applications accounted for almost 30 percent of all application software in use during 1993 and were expected to account for 50 percent of all applications in 1995. While many information systems executives say that expected lower processing costs are the driving force behind client/server adoption, many others say that productivity benefits—regardless of costs—are the determinants.

The movement to a client/server architecture from mainframe or other LAN architectures has been dubbed by many as "downsizing" or "rightsizing."

PEER-TO-PEER ARCHITECTURE. Peer-to-peer network architecture treats all processors equally as users and file servers. Each node has transparent access (as assigned for security or integrity purposes) to all files on all other nodes. All storage devices on all nodes appear to reside in each node for accessing files. This sounds ideal, but in practice the response time for files maintained at other nodes can be impractical. A common peer-to-peer network will use serial transmission (one byte at a time); even at 100 Mbps, corporate files (especially those containing graphics, images, sound, or video) can take many minutes to transfer in bulk.

This approach is more robust than the simple file server approach, however, since there is not a single point of failure for file storage; files can be geographically scattered, including duplicate copies for backup purposes. Updating files can be quicker than with a file server approach, since the updated file can be kept locally. The peer-to-peer architecture is generally not as efficient as the client/server approach, however. Files are still transferred to distant users en masse, sometimes choking the network circuitry; and a user updating a file can block usage from all other nodes.

▶ 9.7 COMMUNICATIONS PROCESS

Now that the reader understands the need for business information systems to communicate with other systems, the various media and hardware used in data communications, and the architectures used to connect computer equipment, it is time to examine the process of communicating data. That process includes interfacing computers and the concepts of bandwidth, synchronization, protocols, and communications standards.

INTERFACES

An interface is a physical connection between two communications devices. One important concept of interfacing concerns the types of data transfer—parallel or serial. *Parallel* data transfer, most often used for local communications, employs a communication interface with a series of dedicated wires, each serving one purpose. In parallel communication, both data and control signals are transmitted simultaneously. A typical parallel communications cable will have control and data wires equal to the number of bits that can be transmitted at one time, in parallel.

A *serial* data transfer, most often used for long-distance communications, is bit by bit rather than many bits in parallel. Serial communication requires certain impositions to be made on a data stream; the serial bit stream must be broken up into individual characters with coded bits placed around each character. Most data communications devices transmit in serial fashion. While much slower than parallel data transfer, serial transfer is simpler and requires much less on the part of the receiving system.

BANDWIDTH

For our purposes, **bandwidth** refers to the range of frequencies available in any communication channel. Bandwidth is a very important concept in communications because the transmission capacity (stated in bits per second) is largely dependent on its bandwidth. In general, the greater the bandwidth, the greater the channel capacity.

For many communications applications, a small bandwidth is usually adequate. For example, linking a student personal computer to a university mainframe is typically done at 2,400 to 14,400 bps. In communication terms, this is comparable to a telephone channel. On the other hand, graphical information displayed on a video screen requires a greater bandwidth than does textual data. A typical color TV picture, for example, is made up of 1 million bits of information or pixels. To achieve the illusion of motion, individual pictures or *frames* are transmitted at a rate of 30 frames per second. Sending a television signal requires a bandwidth measured in millions of bits per second or Mbps. Although it would be possible to send video signals over a 2,400 bps channel, it would hardly make for interesting viewing since the bandwidth of the channel would be too narrow to create the illusion of motion on the screen.

Channel capacity is subdivided into three bandwidths: narrowband, voiceband, and broadband channels. Slow, low-capacity transmissions, such as those transmitted over telegraph lines, make use of narrowband channels while telephone lines utilize voiceband channels. The channel bandwidth with the highest capacity is broadband, used by microwave, cable, and fiber-optic lines. A discussion of one bandwidth issue concerning baseband vs. broadband circuits is found in Box 9.6.

A Closer Look BOX 9.6

MORE ABOUT BASEBAND VERSUS BROADBAND

Two very different transmission techniques with very similar-sounding names can have significantly different effects in communications effectiveness: *baseband* and *broadband* circuits.

Baseband communication uses one signal at a time on a single communication channel. Digital information is sent across a baseband circuit in serial fashion, that is, one bit at a time. Since a baseband circuit has a single channel limitation, it is not possible to integrate parallel signals composed of voice, data, and video over a baseband cable. Also, baseband LANs (i.e., those which use baseband cabling) are generally restricted to 1,500 feet without further amplification. However, one advantage of baseband cabling is that it is easy to tap into this cable in order to connect or disconnect workstations.

Broadband channels can carry many signals at a time, with each signal occupying a different frequency band. While data rates currently practical on any one channel of a broadband network are somewhat lower than those available with baseband transmission—between 1 and 5 Mbps—the availability of up to 20 or 30 channels on a single cable greatly increases the total amount of data the medium can carry. Signals on a broadband network are always *analog*, represented by variations in the strength or frequency of a carrier signal. LANs utilizing broadband cabling can share a cable with other analog signals such as cable television channels—all operating at different frequencies.

Broadband technology offers some strong benefits. First, it is an old technology, well established and mature. Second, although a single broadband channel transmits slower than a baseband channel, the total capacity of a broadband system is much greater. For example, cable TV systems with more than 100 channels have been installed. Each television channel occupies a bandwidth of approximately 6 MHz, the same as typically is allocated to each channel of a broadband network. Third, the maximum distance of a broadband network has an upper limit of about 40 miles, greatly exceeding the 1,500 foot limitation of a baseband cabled network. Finally, and perhaps most significantly, broadband cabled networks can accommodate the transmission of voice, video, and data, *simultaneously*.

SYNCHRONIZATION

Data transmissions may be either **asynchronous** or **synchronous**. In an asynchronous transmission, only one character is transmitted or received at a time. During transmission, the character is preceded by a start bit and followed by a stop bit that lets the receiving device know where a character begins and ends. There is typically idle time between transmission of characters, so synchronization is maintained on a character-by-character basis. Asynchronous transmission is inherently inefficient due to the additional overhead required for start and stop bits, and the idle time between transmissions. It is therefore generally used for only relatively low-speed data transmissions (up to 28,800 bps).

In a synchronous transmission, a group of characters is sent over a communications link in a continuous bit stream while data transfer is controlled by a timing signal initiated by the sending device. The sender and receiver must be in perfect synchronization to avoid the loss or gain of bits; therefore data blocks are preceded by unique characters called *sync* bits that are encoded into the information being transmitted. The receiving device recognizes and synchronizes itself with a stream of these characters. Synchronous transmission is generally used for higher-speed data transfers.

▶ 9.8 ENTERPRISE NETWORKING AND OPEN SYSTEMS

INTRODUCTION

Most organizations have several LANs; if they are geographically dispersed, they may have one or more WANs. Organizations have other computing resources including a data center and several types of hardware and software. In many cases, it makes sense to connect all the computing resources in an organization together to form an enterprise entity. Tying all the computing resources together can be done in several different configurations, as will be shown in Chapter 10. Each configuration has advantages and limitations. In this section we will describe the major concepts and issues that are common to most enterprise networking and especially to those architectures that involved distributed processing, such as client/server architectures.

The most important concept related to enterprise networking is that of open systems. An enterprise network and the way that such a system is connected is shown in Fig. 9.4. This is the system of Nanyang Technological University (NTU) in Singapore. Notice that the many LANs are connected by a broadband network. Several components are connected to other systems using WAN by various connecting devices such as *bridges, routes,* and *gateways* (see Box 9.7).

A Closer Look BOX 9.7

NETWORK GLOSSARY

Network terms

Media—the physical cabling, satellite, or microwave circuit over which the data pass. Common network media are coaxial and fiber-optic cable, twisted-pair wiring, and telephone circuits.

Metropolitan area network (MAN)—a voice/video/data transmission facility connecting sites that are geographically separated by no more than 50 km (30 miles) and operate at speeds in excess of 100 MBS. It is larger than a LAN and smaller than a WAN. The MAN standard is IEEE 802.6.

Protocol—the language or rules a network uses to pass information through the various computers and other hosts, such as gateways and terminal servers.

System/network management—the products and services that enable customers to design, control, direct, and support the entire network.

Network Devices

Bridge—a device that connects two network segments using the same medium. Bridges operate at layer 2 (data link) of the Open System Interconnection (OSI) model and are protocol sensitive.

Cluster control unit—a communications controller that has up to 32 terminal devices attached. The cluster control unit connects to a data communications circuit and communicates with the mainframe computer through the front-end processor.

Router—a device that can interconnect network segments over long distances and usually over different media. This term generally refers to a network routing device that supports multiple protocols.

Gateway—a router that handles traffic of different protocol types and supports connection of several media to form a heterogeneous network. Gateways and routers operate at layer 3 (network) of the OSI model and are protocol sensitive.

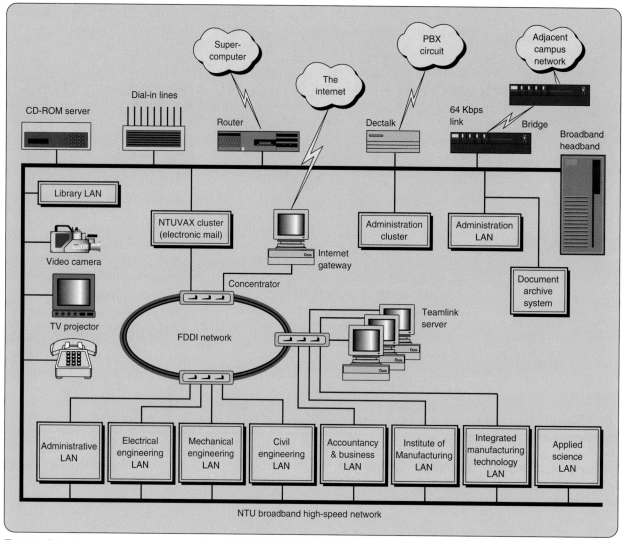

FIGURE 9.4 An enterprise network. (Courtesy of Nanyang Technological University.)

The most important concept related to enterprise networking is that of open systems.

THE PHILOSOPHY OF OPEN SYSTEMS

The philosophy of **open systems** is based on the notion of moving away from a one-vendor IT environment to a multiple-vendors, multiple-products IT environment. The key benefits of this philosophy are the flexibility in implementing IT solutions, the optimization of computing effectiveness, and the ability to provide new levels of integrated functionality to meet user demands. Thus, IT can best meet the enterprise needs on a global basis and allow the enterprise to handle the pressures discussed in Chapter 1.

When different products from different vendors are being placed together, it is obvious that some compatibility problems could develop. In other words, open systems require **connectivity** among the various components of the system; but some connectivity problems are likely. Connectivity is the ability of the various computer resources to communicate with each other. This communication is done through network devices, such as bridges, without human intervention.

CONNECTIVITY AND ITS PROBLEMS

Connectivity holds the promise of several capabilities. Most important are application portability, interoperability, and scalability.

Portability refers to the ability to move applications, data, and even people from one system to another with minimal adjustments. For example, you develop a financial spreadsheet application on your PC at home and run it on the Macintosh at work.

Interoperability refers to the ability of systems to work together by sharing applications, data, and computer resources. It is the intelligent exchange of data among systems and networks. It is the capability for people and applications working in one computing environment to access and use data created and stored in another computing environment.

Scalability refers to the ability to run applications software unchanged on any open system where the hardware can range from a laptop PC to a supercomputer.

Connectivity enables applications portability, interoperability, and scalability on a vendor-independent basis. However, connectivity is not easy to achieve for the following reasons.

▼ Mainframe to PC connections can be difficult to build. Even the downloading of information from the mainframe's database to a PC can be difficult.

▼ Some companies have several E-mail systems that cannot communicate with each other (Chapter 14).

▼ Often, it is difficult to share data and applications among PCs from different vendors.

▼ Many organizations cannot share information among their different functional areas (e.g., accounting and manufacturing).

▼ Different hardware devices, even from the same vendor, may not exchange information among themselves.

Such problems are most serious in older systems, which were built over a long time. For many years, buyers of computer equipment were mainly interested in efficiency of computations and/or cost. No one was thinking about enterprise computing.

To achieve connectivity, it is necessary to evaluate all the components of open systems: operating systems, programming languages, data management technologies, graphical user interface, and computer networking. In each of these components, it is necessary to use communication standards and protocols to achieve connectivity.

PROTOCOLS

In human communication, those engaged in conversation must agree (even if unconsciously) to a set of rules or limits in language and flow of speech in order to have some level of mutual understanding. Eye contact generally means "I'm listening, go ahead" and head-nodding means "I understand what you're saying." These types of rules are collectively called a **protocol**. Communications protocols range from single character-by-character transmissions with no error checking to complex transmissions moving large amounts of data among many devices.

In general, data communications protocols fall into three major areas: the method in which data is represented and coded (e.g., in ASCII or EBCDIC; see Chapter 5); the method in which the codes are transmitted and received (asynchronously or synchronously); and nonstandard information exchanges by which two devices establish control, detect failures or errors, and initiate corrective action. Protocols are essential to communications because they establish procedures—so essential that unless the sending and receiving protocols match or are compatible, effective data communications will not occur. This constraint has encouraged the use of communications standards.

COMMUNICATIONS STANDARDS

Underlying the development of any network are certain standards and prerequisites for communication. In a data communications network, devices communicating with each other must speak the same language and follow the same rules; there must also be some mechanism in place to ensure that data sent from one device to another have been transmitted without errors. Unfortunately, commercially available data communication devices speak a variety of tongues and follow a number of different rules, and this has caused substantial confusion among data communications users.

TYPES OF STANDARDS. Since open systems involve several components, it is necessary to develop standards for all of them. In this section, we will describe mainly networking and transmission standards.

Attempts at standardizing data communications have been somewhat successful, but standardization in the United States has lagged behind other countries where the communication industry is more closely regulated. Various organizations, including the Electronic Industries Association (EIA), the Consultative Committee for International Telegraph and Telephone (CCITT), and the International Standards Organization (ISO) have developed electronic interfacing standards that are widely used within the industry.

NETWORKING STANDARDS—THE OSI. Typically, the protocols required to achieve communication on behalf of an application are actually multiple protocols existing at different levels or layers. Each layer defines a set of functions that are provided as services to upper layers, and each layer relies on services provided by lower layers. At each layer, one or more protocols define precisely how software on different systems interact to accomplish the functions for that layer. This layering notion has been formalized in several architectures. The most widely known is the reference model of **Open Systems Interconnection (OSI)**, depicted in Figure 9.5. The figure indicates that there is a peer-to-peer communication between software at each layer and a reliance on underlying layers for services to accomplish communication.

The OSI model has seven layers, each having its own well-defined function.

Layer 1: Physical layer. This layer is concerned with transmitting raw bits over a communication channel. Its purpose is to provide a physical connection for the transmission of data among network entities and the means by which to activate and deactivate a physical connection.

Layer 2: Data link layer. This layer is responsible for providing a reliable means of transmitting data across a physical link. It breaks up the input data into data frames sequentially and processes the acknowledgment frames sent back by the receiver.

Layer 3: Network layer. The network layer routes information from one network computer to another. These computers may be physically located within the same network or within another network that is interconnected

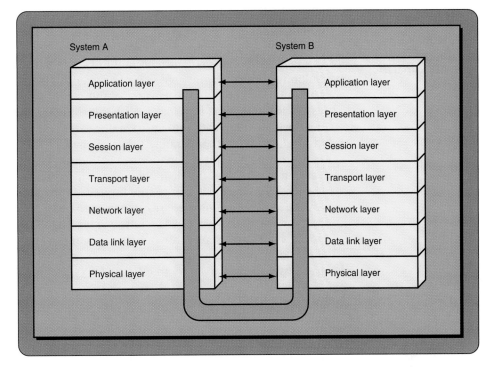

FIGURE 9.5 The reference model for open systems interconnection. (SOURCE: Singelton and Schwartz, 1994, p. 309. Copyright © 1994 International Business Machines Corporation. Reprinted with permission from *IBM Systems Journal*, Vol. 33, No. 2.)

in some fashion. It accepts messages from the source host and sees to it that they are directed towards the destination.

Layer 4: Transport layer. The purpose of the transport layer is to provide a network-independent transport service to the session layer. The basic function of the transport layer is to accept data from the session layer, split it up into smaller units as required, pass these to the network layer, and ensure that all the pieces arrive correctly at the other end.

Layer 5: Session layer. The session layer is the user's interface into the network. It is at this layer that the user must negotiate to establish a connection with a process on another machine. Once the connection has been established the session layer can manage the dialogue in an orderly manner.

Layer 6: Presentation layer. Here, messages are translated to and from the format used in the network to a format used at the application layer.

Layer 7: Application layer. The application layer includes activities related to users, such as supporting file transfer, handling messages, and providing security.

TRANSMISSION STANDARDS. Although today's general purpose networks are too slow for advanced computing applications, a number of network bandwidth boosters are coming into their own and may provide solutions to this problem. These technologies include FDDI (fiber distributed data interface), ATM (asynchronous transfer mode), switching hubs, and ISDN (integrated services digital network).

Like token-ring networks, FDDI passes data around a ring but with a bandwidth of 100 Mbps—far faster than a standard 10-13 Mbps token-ring or bus network. Although the FDDI standard can use any transmission medium (such as twisted-pair wire), it is based on the high-speed, high-capacity capabilities of fiber optics (hence its name). While FDDI can significantly boost network performance, FDDI networks are about 10 times more expensive to implement than most LAN networks.

EMERGING TECHNOLOGY

... new technologies
significantly increase
network capacities

ATM networks (not to be confused with banking ATMs or automated teller machines) are based on switched technologies, allowing for almost unlimited bandwidth. For example, the public telephone system utilizes switching when a call is made, so that a dedicated line links two parties through various switches. Millions of calls may be going on concurrently. Even though the telephone lines have a low bandwidth, the capacity of this *switched* network, i.e., its *aggregate bandwidth*, is huge. ATM provides high bandwidth on demand. It is a *packet-switched* network, dividing data into very small clusters, called packets, and moving them around the network separately (in parallel when there are multiple channels) for reassembling at their destinations. ATM allows channel mixing and matching of varying bandwidths and data types (e.g., video, data, and voice) and much higher speeds since the data is more easily "squeezed" in among other very small packets. Switched hub technologies are often used to boost local area networks. A switched hub can turn many small LANs into one big LAN. A network need not be rewired nor adapter cards replaced when changes are made; all that is needed is the addition of a switching hub. Switched hub technology can also add an ATM-line packet switching capability to existing LANs, essentially doubling bandwidth.

OTHER STANDARDS

There are several other standards for open systems. Of special interest are the software standards. In order to have an open system, it is necessary to have three types of software standards: *operating systems standards, graphical user interface (GUI) standards*, and *software application standards*.

OPERATING SYSTEMS. Of all the various types of operating systems, Unix can operate on computers of many sizes and hardware types. However, it has not been recognized yet as *the standard*. For instance, Microsoft is pushing their Windows NT, IBM is pushing their OS/2, and several other companies are pushing OSF (Open Software Foundation). All this results in many differing versions of operating systems.

GRAPHICAL USER INTERFACE STANDARD. X Windows is considered the zstandard for GUI. It runs on all types of computers and is used with Unix and the DEC VAX/VMS operating systems. It permits one display of several applications on one screen and allows one application to use several windows.

SOFTWARE APPLICATION STANDARDS. The U.S. government is attempting to establish a standard for all its systems. The standard will cover operating systems, DBMS, user interfaces, programming languages, electronic data interchange, and so on.

▶ 9.9 TRANSMISSION PROVIDERS

Data transmission facilities include the routes, circuit switching systems, and communication media used to transmit data among local and geographically dispersed equipment. Organizations that offer transmission facilities are called *providers*. Communications providers that offer facilities to the public for a fee and are controlled by state or federal regulations are called **common carriers** (e.g., AT&T, MCI, BellSouth, and PacTel).

VALUE-ADDED NETWORKS.

Some communications providers—sometimes called **value-added networks (VANS)**—add communications services to existing common carriers. VANs can add message storage, tracking, and relay services; teleconferencing services; and more closely tailor communications capabilities to specific business needs. A leased telephone line is one such value-added service that telephone companies provide for a fixed fee. This is a private line dedicated to a specific organization for its individual communications needs.

A leased line may handle digital data only, or it may be capable of handling both voice and digital data just as a standard telephone line does. When leased lines have been designed specifically for data transmission, they produce less static and fewer transmission errors than regular telephone lines—and they are more secure from wiretapping and other security risks. Most importantly, the central processor is always accessible through the leased line; and the line usually transmits data at speeds faster than a standard telephone line. Like any other lease, customers do not have to invest in their own network medium and software, nor do they need to maintain the network facilities. Finally, they do not have to perform error checking, editing, routing, and protocol conversion. Therefore, VAN is a viable alternative for companies that do not own their own network systems (see the opening case in Chapter 2). A major provider of VANs is GE Information Services.

VIRTUAL PRIVATE NETWORKS

Not all common carriers are alike in terms of resources, management, and accessibility; Box 9.8 notes some of the difficulties with European carriers. In order to solve the difficulties of European and other international customers, an inexpensive service called a **virtual private network (VPN)** is available. This private service is of high quality, and customers are billed in currencies of their choice. Communication is provided over public phone lines, which make the service inexpensive, yet the computers and software provide quality similar to private lines.

A Closer Look BOX 9.8

GLOBAL PERSPECTIVE

MORE ABOUT EUROPEAN CONNECTIONS

Connecting computers across Europe can be mind-boggling to Americans. Major technological and legal barriers face U.S. firms seeking to build or expand computer networks in Europe—even as Europe is attempting to unify. Some of the obstacles are the following.

▼ Unreliable and inconsistent telecommunications services between individual countries and cities.

▼ Conflicting standards for everything from formats to equipment.

▼ Monopolistic, government-controlled communication services providers that limit vendor service and equipment choices.

▼ Unpredictable installation and service "turn-on" target dates.

▼ Widely varying government regulations and tariff structures.

▼ Competing arrays of national guidelines for data security and privacy.

▼ Language barriers and different business practices.

▼ A bewildering set of alliances, coalitions, joint ventures, and projects among vendors and government agencies.

Although analysts say that telecommunications reforms are spreading across Europe, the reforms are not coming fast enough, they say, for expanding business links. Because of the many potential problems, many U.S. firms expanding into Europe are outsourcing some or all of their European telecommunications operations. Outsourcing to established European firms with local know-how not only saves a lot of time but also prevents a lot of expensive mistakes. According to communications consultants, those firms that want to build or expand European networks but do not want to outsource should do the following.

▼ Think "European" in customs, labor practices, languages, and culture.

▼ Be realistic about what services are available; the differences between neighboring countries can be enormous.

▼ Be flexible and ready with "work-arounds" when installing and running the network.

▼ Allow plenty of time for delays—from vendors and governments.

▼ Check all equipment for compliance with local regulations.

▼ Keep up with changing regulations.

According to *InformationWeek*, the eight major problems of running an international network (in descending order of importance) are costs and tariffs, network management, graphical expansion, installation delays, poor quality of services, regulatory constraints, changing user requirement, and standardization issues.

SOURCE: Thyfault, M. E., "Virtual Europe," *InformationWeek*, November 14, 1994.

Most frequently, the transmission facility will be public telephone lines consisting of copper wire, but they may also be fiber-optic or coaxial cable, or satellite, microwave, or cellular radio. The major types of long-distance routing facilities are circuit-switched (dial-up), private line (leased), and packet-switched.

A **circuit-switched** network is composed of analog channels and is used mainly for low-speed, intermittent transmissions, as it is the most prone to errors. It is used by many parties at once, and users are charged only for their time on the line. Of course, one might encounter a busy signal when attempting to make a call on a switched facility.

A **private line** facility is an analog or digital line that is rented exclusively to one customer for voice and/or data communications. Facility providers are usually able to "condition" the line, making it less prone to errors and thus better suited for data transmission. Private lines are much more expensive than having access to switched lines, but there are no busy signals with a private line!

Packet switching, a service available from various common carriers, is used on data networks for connecting geographically dispersed organizations. On a packet-switched network, data are sent in groups of characters in which control information has been added to the beginning and end of the group. The character group and control information are collectively called a "packet," comparable to an "envelope" around a letter that is not "opened" until it reaches its destination. With packet switching, messages are broken into packets that are transmitted in short bursts over a communication network to a specified address, where they are reassembled into the original message. Packets are dynamically routed though a network, i.e., they are sent over the most efficient path to their destination. This means that packets of one message may be sent via different routes.

Whereas circuit switching makes a physical connection between two points, packet switching makes a *virtual* connection. By sending data in small packets, each with its own address, bandwidth can be allocated more effectively. Moreover, a large number of packets can be multiplexed onto a single channel. Many small packets can be routed over many different paths on the network, instead of large messages being routed over a single path. If errors occur, usually only a single packet of data is lost instead of the entire message. If different paths in the network go down, packets can easily be rerouted because no physical connection has been established, only a virtual connection.

▶ 9.10 COMMUNICATIONS APPLICATIONS

Like computer applications in general, communications applications allow us to *do* something functionally that takes advantage of data communications. The number of applications is growing rapidly as organizations not only depend more and more on data communications but also take advantage of new business opportunities made possible through data communications. Some of the most prevalent or up-and-coming applications are electronic mail, facsimile (fax), video teleconferencing, electronic data interchange, and electronic funds transfer. These subjects are discussed further in Chapter 14. One of the problems associated with these communications applications is discussed in Box 9.9. Some of the most common applications are the following.

A Closer Look BOX 9.9

MORE ABOUT COMMUNICATIONS SPYING

Pierre Marion, the former head of French Intelligence, admitted that his country had been regularly spying on IBM, Texas Instruments, and Corning for 10 years, putting their trade secrets in the hands of competitors and costing the victims billions of dollars. While these and many other large firms spend large amounts to secure their data centers, new forms of communications are increasingly nullifying their efforts. Most data leaks, security experts say, occur because companies ignore "low-tech" communications links: cellular phones, fax machines, wireless phones and networks, and E-mail.

Today's employees regularly hand out their fax machine numbers and pass documents back and forth across unsecured lines, while corporate business travelers routinely speak about sensitive business matters over hotel, auto, and airline cellular phones. Executives hail the access they have to corporate files, reports, and memos while on the road—but rarely think about the ease with which that same data can be accessed by freelance corporate spies or companies.

Cellular phones are considered the weakest link in many corporate networks. "They're essentially FM radios," says Robert Edwards, president of a risk management consultancy. "You don't have to be a rocket scientist to scan an FM frequency band." McCaw Cellular Communications warns its customers that anyone with a scanner, available for $100, can eavesdrop on cellular calls. This will change in the future, analysts say, when cellular systems go digital and an eavesdropper will have to unscramble 1s and 0s.

Wireless telephones are also very easy to monitor. Upcoming digitized wireless phones will increase wireless phone security, as will "spread spectrum" technology that can continually break up the signal among many frequencies—making it hard to track and combine into one coherent signal. Wireless local area networks face the same problems as wireless phones, even though the data is in 1s and 0s. At least one wireless local area network manufacturer is moving to spread spectrum protection for security.

Fax machines are considered easy marks for spies. They are as easy to tap as phone lines but much more lucrative because they provide documents—often signed. Bank of Boston has a fax policy: "Always assume the other end is insecure and that everything you fax could go to the local newspaper." For sensitive documents, they prefer courier services. Their policy toward electronic mail is similar: "Assume that what you send over public E-mail is nearly public information."

ELECTRONIC MAIL

Computer-based messages can be electronically manipulated, stored, combined with other information, and transmitted through telephone wires or wireless networks. With **electronic mail** (popularly called **E-mail**), the sender inputs the message at a terminal and includes data on the intended recipient(s). Any other electronic objects, such as graphic, sound, motion, text, or application files may be attached to the message. The system then automatically routes the message to the recipient(s). At the receiving end, a recipient can read the message on a computer terminal, print it, file it, edit it, and/or pass it on to other people.

Electronic mail can be sent simultaneously to many people. Data can be received at one point, revised or updated, and sent on to other points. Perhaps most significantly, electronic mail eliminates time delays and other problems associated with physically delivered mail. Electronic mail users need not be concerned with the equivalent of "phone tag" when the recipient is not physically present at the moment a message is sent. And receivers can go through their mail in batches, when it is convenient to do so.

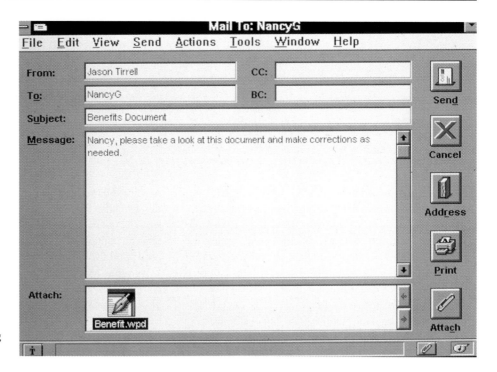

An E-mail message using Novell's Group Wise.

VIDEOCONFERENCING

Videoconferencing allows two or more people to have "face-to-face" communications with a group in another location(s) without having to be present in person. In essence, videoconferencing is a multiple-input television session. Although limited by the inherent limitations of audio and video, these visual conferences may save time (and expenses) that otherwise would be spent in travel. Simultaneous computer-to-computer connections during the teleconferences also allow participants to confer over text or images shown at all locations—like a shared chalk board or paper easel. Videoconferencing is much more expensive than an audio-line (e.g., telephone) conference because it requires more expensive equipment to capture and transmit video images, and telephone charges are higher due to the slow transportation speed. However, communications research shows that much information communicated between individuals in person is communicated by *nonverbal* means (e.g., head and eye movements or body language). Therefore, videoconferencing may be able to provide a much richer means of communicating than text or audio alone.

ELECTRONIC DATA INTERCHANGE (EDI)

Much commercial transaction data is generated by computer systems for other computer systems (e.g., an invoice from company A's purchasing system to company B's sales system). Unfortunately, transaction data is often manually entered into information systems several times over along the way. Very often, computerized data is converted to paper, then entered again as data after a decision is made. Direct computer-to-computer data exchange is much more efficient and less prone to data entry mistakes.

Electronic data interchange (EDI) is the electronic transmission of routine, repetitive business documents directly between business computer systems of separate companies doing business with each other. EDI offers both direct and indirect benefits. Eliminating manual paper processing results in direct savings. Faster, more complete information transmission results in indirect savings and performance improvements. Lead time (the time between when an order decision is made and when the order is received and available for use) is often significantly reduced, permitting lower safety stocks and increasing inventory savings. Also, the use of EDI results in a more complete use of the information that is transmitted. With paper transmittals, documents received from many sources are not uniform, and much of the decision making must be done manually. EDI enables all transmitted data to be entered, and entered consistently.

ELECTRONIC FUNDS TRANSFER (EFT)

The banking industry has particularly benefited from the growth of data communications. **Electronic funds transfer (EFT)** is now widely used—with funds, debits and credits, and charges and payments electronically routed among banks and between banks and customers. EFT is fast; it eliminates delays associated with sending hard-copy documents. It has become the *only* practical way to handle the large volume of financial transactions generated daily by the banking industry. Data communications adds flexibility to banking; automated teller machines (ATMs) using EFT communication links are increasingly prevalent in shopping centers and business areas, allowing individuals to make deposits or withdrawals from their accounts 24 hours a day.

On the other hand, electronic communication has been historically notorious for being susceptible to wiretapping or fraudulent use. How can a business ensure that a hacker isn't bilking corporate accounts by electronically transferring funds, or that competitive snoops aren't gaining a complete picture of corporate financial assets? After all, electrical 1s and 0s traveling at almost the speed of light are extremely hard to monitor and control. Security is a serious topic with EFT, and Box 9.10 discusses one of the issues of EFT security.

A Closer Look BOX 9.10

 EMERGING TECHNOLOGY

MORE ABOUT EFT SECURITY—DIGITAL SIGNATURES

Special seals or handwritten signatures have, for centuries, served as proof of authorship or authority on documents. While not completely unforgeable, they have been essential for government, business, and personal legal documents. But what about "signing" a digital stream of 1s and 0s in a computer-generated document? When one receives an E-mail message containing critical information, how does one *know* who it's from? How does one *know* that the content hasn't been altered? Even if some form of signature—like the graphical image of a thumbprint—were attached, it could easily be "lifted" digitally and reused since bit streams are easy to copy and move from one document to another. With transactions totaling about $30 trillion a day being transmitted digitally over circuits within the United States, the need for secure signatures is enormous.

Digital signatures attempt to create documents that can be mathematically traced to their authors or authorizers. A digital signature is a stream of bits attached to an electronic document generated by the signer based on both the document's data and the person's secret password. Someone who receives the document can prove that the signer

actually signed the document and that the document was not altered.

One of the most promising techniques for doing this is *public-key cryptography*. Public-key cryptography uses special encryption algorithms with two different keys: a public key that everyone knows, and a private key known only to the holder. Public-key algorithms encrypt the contents of an electronic document using *both* keys. Because one of the keys is completely private, the data is secure. Because one of the keys is public, anyone knowing the public key can verify the file's authenticity. Moreover, it is computationally infeasible (within thousands of years at present) to calculate the private key from the public key and a sample of encrypted data.

The procedure works like this. The sender passes a document through a reducing or "hashing" algorithm to produce a message digest which is then encoded with the private key to form the digital signature. This signature is then attached to the original document and transmitted to the recipient. Upon receiving the document, the recipient uses the same hashing algorithm to create a new message digest of the document while using the originator's public key to decode the digital signature. The resulting message digest and the decoded signature are then compared for authenticity. If they don't match, either the signature is bogus or the document was altered.

Proponents of digital signatures say that public-key digital signatures will soon be standard in software products and mostly invisible to users. Many software vendors are working to build digital signature capabilities into their products.

FACSIMILE

Facsimile (fax) equipment may use either analog or digital encoding. Analog encoding converts the white and black areas of a page into encoded sine waves—just as today's television cameras do. These modulated signals are then converted back into white and black areas for printing by the receiving facsimile machine. Digital encoding converts a page's white and black areas into binary 1s and 0s. The primary advantage of using digital encoding is that digital streams of 1s and 0s are very easy to compress—especially with textual documents that contain large amounts of white (blank) areas. Compressing fax documents at the ratio of 20:1 is common with digitally encoded fax machines; the result is that one page can be transmitted within 5 to 10 seconds instead of the two to six minutes it takes with analog encoding.

Fax machines using analog or digital encoding can transmit documents over either analog circuits—such as common telephone voice lines—or purely digital circuits, depending on the built-in capabilities of the particular device. Those that transmit over analog circuits must use modem features to convert the digital encoding into analog signals; the receiving fax must then reconvert the analog signals back into digital encoding for printing. Although these machines are the most prevalent in business use today, due mainly to the common use of analog telephone circuits, analog-encoding fax machines are becoming increasingly obsolete. Digitally-encoded fax machines that can use digital circuits are the fastest of all; text can be highly compressed, and there is no analog conversion.

▶ MANAGERIAL ISSUES

1. *Speed vs effective throughput.* Data transmission speed depends on the type of media (e.g., copper, wire, or fiber optic), distance, hardware (e.g., modems), and architecture (e.g., ring, star, or bus topology). Effective throughput depends on circuit reliability, data compression, the point of transaction data entry, and protocol standards.

2. *Reliability.* Data communications reliability depends on the reliability of the media and hardware, the volume of data, the expertise and diligence of communications specialists designing and maintaining a system, and the degree to which one controls the communications circuits (i.e., owned, leased, or outsourced).

3. *Data security.* Security of communicated data relies on the form of the data (analog or digital), the circuit media used, whether or not data encryption is used, the architecture and where nodes are located and controlled, secure operating procedures (e.g., password protection), and the degree of circuit ownership.

4. *Standards.* Standards can affect effective throughput, development costs, circuit media and hardware, training costs, and data entry/access.

5. *Information vs noise.* Too much low-value information can mask important high-value information. Effective communications depends on source data accuracy, filtering out low-value information, fusing related low-value data

into high-value information, correctly formatting data for presentation, and managing personnel time.

6. *Virtual office organization.* How to manage workers not physically present can present organizational, career, and personal challenges, while leveraging their accessibility to those outside the firm can provide significant business advantages.

7. *Speed and capacity.* Both are necessary for many data-intensive applications. Increasing speed and capacity means higher cost. Some of the promising technologies such as fiber channels, fast Ethernet, and ATM (asynchronous transfer mode) are expensive and plagued by system incompatibilities. So, care must be taken in installing these promising techniques. Of special interest is ATM, which provides high-speed transmission of data, voice, and video over a single network. ■

KEY TERMS

Analog signals *298*

Asynchronous *316*

Backward error correction *308*

Bandwidth *315*

Bus topology *310*

Cellular radio technology *303*

Circuit-switched *324*

Client/server *314*

Coaxial cable *299*

Common carriers *297*

Communication satellites *301*

Connectivity *319*

Data communications *297*

Demodulation *307*

Digital signals *298*

Distributed data processing *313*

Electronic data interchange (EDI) *326*

Electronic funds transfer (EFT) *327*

Electronic mail (E-mail) *325*

Ethernet *313*

Facsimile (fax) *328*

Fiber-optic cables *299*

File server *314*

Forward error correction *308*

Front-end processor *309*

Full-duplex *308*

Global positioning system (GPS) *306*

Half-duplex *308*

Information superhighway *311*

Infrared *302*

Local area network (LAN) *313*

Microwave *300*

Mobile computing *304*

Modem *307*

Modulation *307*

Multiplexor *309*

Node *309*

Open systems interconnection (OSI) *320*

Open systems *318*

Packet switching *324*

Parity bits *308*

Peer-to-peer *315*

Private branch exchange (PBX) *313*

Private line *324*

Protocol *319*

Remote procedure call *314*

Radio *302*

Ring topology *310*

Simplex *308*

Star topology *310*

Synchronous *316*

Telecommunication *297*

Topology *309*

Twisted-pair wire *298*

Value-added network *322*

Videoconferencing *326*

Virtual private networks *323*

Wide area network (WAN) *311*

Wireless communication *300*

CHAPTER HIGHLIGHTS *(L-x means learning objective number x)*

▼ Data communications entails media (the physical media through which data are transferred), hardware (the systems used in data communications), networks (the linkages among computers and communications devices), the communications process (how data communication occurs), communications providers (regulated utilities and private firms), and communications applications. (L-1)

▼ The pathway or medium through which data are

communicated is commonly cable (metallic or glass fiber) or electromagnetic (i.e., radio) waves in the form of microwave, satellite, and cellular circuits. (L-2)

▼ A network topology is the physical and logical arrangement of its parts relative to one another; the most common are star, ring, and bus. A node is any device on a network. Networks are also identified by their scope: wide area and local area. (L-3)

▼ The process of communicating data includes interfacing computers and the concepts of bandwidth, synchronization, protocols, and communications standards. (L-4)

▼ Data communications providers include the routes, circuit-switched systems, and communication media used to exchange data; regulated providers are called common carriers. (L-5)

▼ Communications applications provide computer users with data communications functionality, including electronic mail, facsimiles, videoconferencing, electronic data interchange, and electronic funds transfer. (L-6)

▼ Wireless and mobile computing can take many forms, including microwave, satellites, radio, infrared, and cellular technology. (L-7)

QUESTIONS FOR REVIEW

1. What are data communications? What are the issues involved in data communications?

2. Describe the two main types of data transmission media. What are three common electromagnetic media, and what are the advantages of each?

3. What purpose do modems serve? What is the difference between simplex, half-duplex, and full-duplex transmissions? What is a multiplexor, and why is it used?

4. Explain a network topology. What are the three common network topologies, and what are the relative advantages/disadvantages of each? What purpose does a PBX serve?

5. What is bandwidth, and why is it important? What are the two types of data transmission synchronization, and how are they different? What is a data communications protocol?

6. What is a common carrier? What is packet switching, and how does it work?

7. What are some of the differences between paper mail and electronic mail? What is electronic data interchange, and why is it used? What is electronic funds transfer, and what industry is most likely to use it?

8. Distinguish between a value-added network and a virtual private network.

9. What is a global positioning system, and how is it used?

10. What is an open system?

QUESTIONS FOR DISCUSSION

1. Which transmission media would be the best for ships at sea? For a banking or automatic teller network? For remote news service providers?

2. Some scientists recommend flip-flopping how people normally communicate—they recommend that voice communication move from phone line (e.g., cable) to radio and that radio/television move from radio to cable. What might be advantages to this? Disadvantages?

3. What type of network topology might be best for an all-campus network? For a departmental network? For a hospital network?

4. Under what conditions should a firm install a PBX instead of a local area network?

5. Which is more important, bandwidth or protocol? Why or when?

6. Why has the data communications industry expanded so rapidly in the last 10 years? Why are there so many new providers?

7. Under what conditions might (textual) electronic mail be better than a facsimile? When would a facsimile be better than electronic mail?

8. Relate the concept of open system to connectivity and Microsoft's Windows.

EXERCISES

1. Contact a local business that uses a local area network of at least 15 nodes (e.g., terminals, computers, and printers). Identify and quantify the resources expended to manage the network on a per-node basis. What is the per-node variable cost of the network vs the per-node fixed cost?

2. Imagine you are designing a corporate information network for a fast food chain with 1,200 sites in 16 Eastern states. You hope to be able to predict customer demand and react to customer preferences better by acting collectively on all site sales data. What kind of network topology would be best for this situation? Should the network use the services of a common carrier for circuits, or should it manage its own communications circuits? What kind of communications applications should the network be capable of handling?

3. Find five recent applications of global positioning systems in air, sea, and land situations. Prepare a report that outlines the benefits and the interfaces with other information systems.

GROUP ASSIGNMENTS

1. Each member of the group is to be assigned to a company, government agency, or other organization. Each member will conduct an interview and identify the current and future applications of wireless communication. The group will compile the applications and make a class presentation.

2. Divide the class into two groups: one group advocating commercial development and management of a U.S. information superhighway, and the other group advocating government development and management (either federally or locally). Have group representatives give the respective business benefits of each option.

MINICASE 1

Full-Featured Network Connects a City

Community leaders in Cupertino, California, have launched plans to build what may be the nation's first citywide computer network linking residents, government, schools, and local corporations. For a $20 annual fee, any of Cupertino's residents with a computer and phone line will be able to shop, job hunt, or obtain information about city programs and services. Local residents will no longer have to visit a city office in person to pick up a form or communicate with local officials. The network will also provide a channel for the city to disseminate information to citizens.

While a handful of U.S. communities have established electronic networks, these have been limited to single applications such as electronic bulletin boards. Cupertino's network, however, will be full featured. Cupertino schools are expected to be the first on-line with access to database services and the Internet. The plan will eventually include all key institutions that people generally consult for information—schools, libraries, city government,

the chamber of commerce, and major employers in the area. Costs?—about $20,000 including hardware, software development, and initial deployment.

Questions for Minicase 1

1. Could security or privacy problems arise through use of the Cupertino network?

2. How could town managers effectively manage the information available over the network—making sure that it is accurate, complete, and timely?

3. How could town businesses use the network?

4. People go to city offices for more than just information (e.g., driver's license renewal, marriage certificates, and building permits). Could these public transactions also take place over the network? What about civic equivalents of bank automatic teller machines for those without home computers?

Source: Adapted from "Town Crier Goes On Line," *InformationWeek*, May 10, 1993.

MINICASE 2

Should the Hotel Chain Go Open System?

Eurotel is a large chain of hotels in Europe. Its hotels are scattered all over the continent. The company is using an aged IBM mainframe at its headquarters. Most of its 68 hotels use regular telephones line to transmit information. Fax and express mail are used frequently. Headquarters feels that it needs to track numerous individual hotel functions closely. The existing system was found to be ineffective since data arrive too late, information is incomplete, and E-mail communication is incompatible with some hotels.

Stephen Class, the IS director, was looking for an improvement. Here are some of the possibilities he considered.

1. Scrap the old system, and move to an enterprise open system environment. This option will require finding a Unix-based hotel management system (several exist), a Unix-based DBMS, and 4GL modeling language, and Unix-based hardware (minicomputers, mainframe) for both the individual cities and the ho-

tels. The problem with this option is that it will be necessary to rewrite all the applications, including the reservation system. The connectivity problems in the existing components are just too big, so scrapping is the only solution. A large investment will be required, and the projected time for the completion of the project is three to four years.

2. Upgrade the existing mainframe system. This solution will not solve the problem completely, but there will be some improvements. In a few years, there will be a need for more improvements. The cost is minimal, and upgrading can be done within a month.

3. Develop a corporate telecommunications network using LAN, WAN, and so on; use as much of the old equipment as possible; and invest money in solutions for the connectivity problem.

Questions for Minicase 2

1. What kind of telecommunication system would you suggest to build for alternative #1? (provide a figure).

2. What are the major differences between alternatives #2 and #3?

3. Prepare a list of the major advantages and disadvantages with each alternative.

REFERENCES AND BIBLIOGRAPHY

1. Black, U., *Data Networks*, Englewood Cliffs, NJ: Prentice Hall, 1989.

2. "Culture of Urgency," *Forbes ASAP*, September 13, 1993.

3. Derfler, F. J., Jr., "Linking LANs," *PC Magazine*, March 16, 1993.

4. Fitzgerald, J., *Business Data Communications: Basic Concepts, Security, and Design*, 4th Ed., New York: John Wiley & Sons, 1993.

5. Gilder, G., "Into the Telecosm," *Harvard Business Review*, March/April 1991.

6. Harvey, G., "Making the Information Highway Work," *Business Quarterly*, Spring 1994.

7. "The Heavy Burden of LAN Costs," *Datamation*, June 1, 1993.

8. Keen, P. G. W., *Shaping the Future: Business Design Through Information Technology*, Cambridge, MA: Harvard Business School Press, 1991.

9. "Quick Response to Nervous Tummies," *Information Week*, June 15, 1992.

10. Roche, E. M., *Telecommunications and Business Strategy*, Chicago: The Dryden Press, 1991.

11. Rockart, J. F., "The Line Takes the Leadership—IS Management in a Wired Society," *Sloan Management Review*, Summer 1988.

12. Rowe, S. H. II., *Business Telecommunications*, New York: Macmillan, 1991.

13. Schroth, R., et al., "Wireless and the Untethered Organization," *Insights Quarterly*, Summer 1993.

14. Singleton, J. P., and M. M. Schwartz, "Data Access Within the Information Warehouse Framework," *IBM Systems Journal*, Vol. 33, No. 2, 1994.

15. Springs, J. D., et al., *Telecommunications Protocols and Design*, Reading, MA: Addison-Wesley, 1992

16. Stewart, T. A., "Managing in a Wired Company," *Fortune*, July 11, 1994.

17. Strauss, P., "Write Your Own Wireless Applications," *Datamation*, September 15, 1994.

18. "Town Crier Goes On Line," *InformationWeek*, May 10, 1993.

ABC, INC. CAR DEALERSHIPS: ENABLING BUSINESS WITH IT

ABC, Inc. is a 20-year-old firm with 184 car dealerships in eight southeastern states. Founded as Scott's Auto in 1948 with one outlet, it steadily grew to 15 dealerships, then merged with six other dealership organizations in 1975 to form the Automobile Buying Consolidated, Inc., headquarted in Atlanta, Georgia.

When ABC was formed, the IS organization was functionally centralized at Atlanta, while the seven merged firms retained operational computer systems at their respective regional offices, tied electronically to the main office in Atlanta. Each regional IS office operated independently to meet its own business needs, but transferred financial data nightly to the central office; ABC headquarters in turn sent summary financial data (as well as payroll) weekly to the regional sites.

By 1990, this IS arrangement had become untenable to corporate executives, dealership managers, vendors, IS personnel, and even customers. Specifically, there were problems with the databases, processing, telecommunications, software applications, user access, and IS staff training and retention—to mention just a few!

There were 11 separate databases at the eight sites (seven at regional offices and four at the headquarters) using three different database management system software packages. Although the headquarters databases contained data from the regional sites, it only contained summary data, not the detailed data needed by corporate officers. There was, therefore, no single database that contained all the financial, marketing, sales, inventory, service, and personnel data for ABC. Moreover, there was no practical way to bring the data together. One region might have car parts that other regions had on back-order; customers moving from one region to another were "lost"; executives could not closely manage cash flows among the regions; vendors had to negotiate with each region; and IS personnel were besieged with requests for cross-comparisons of data in the various databases.

Processing was similarly dispersed. All IS sites had centralized computer system architectures based on mainframe computers—from three different computer vendors. These large computers, with dozens of terminals attached to each, had computing power to spare when they were first installed; but recently, system response times to users were often more than twenty seconds at

some sites. Users were demanding more terminals than IS was willing to provide due to the additional costs and the further degrading effects on response time. Moreover, the corporate CFO (Chief Financial Officer) warned that sufficient funds would not be available to purchase additional or replacement mainframe computers.

Telecommunications costs between the regional sites and headquarters were becoming overbearing, especially in light of slower response times. Each regional site had dedicated, private analog lines connecting them with headquarters. These lines were leased from the regional telephone company and were billed for continuous use even though there were times (like during lunch or late at night) when they were hardly used. Furthermore, regional sites could only share data with headquarters and not among themselves. Allowing vendors or users to have direct access to data—like inventory levels or part availability—was out of the question.

The applications running on the mainframe systems were displayed on "dumb" terminals—monochrome (green) displays incapable of fine resolution graphics or the use of color. All interaction with users was through a keyboard and special function keys whose functions changed depending on which program was running. Except for some IS personnel, all users from executives to regional administrative staff members thought the terminals and the applications were "stone age" compared to the PCs and colorful graphic programs they were familiar with or used at home with their children. More importantly, users could only do rigidly programmed functions; they couldn't tailor programs to their individual needs or changing business needs. And when they asked IS to modify them for crucial new needs, IS seemed to simply sigh and add one more request to a long list of "required" changes.

Even those who found value in the applications had trouble getting access to them due to the limited number of terminals. Office automation work like word processing was done on PCs; corporate work had to be done on separate mainframe terminals that were centrally located in clusters in each office so that everyone could have access to them. Users would sometimes have to juggle work on their desktop PC with work on a terminal in another room, provided no one came along and usurped their work on the terminal. Data from the terminal had to be retyped into a PC program, and vice versa. The terminals and the PCs were almost completely different in how they worked. Phone calls generally went unanswered whenever someone was fortunate enough to get a terminal; and when a terminal went "down," they all went down.

On top of all this, IS retention was plummeting. IS personnel felt overcome by user demands for new software, for faster response times, and for new technology while facing a steady IS budget. They felt undertrained in the newer technologies and avoided user questions. It was getting harder to hire newly graduated computer technologists for working with what they regarded as "ancient" systems.

In frustration, corporate executives hired an outside consulting service to provide recommendations on how to improve IS support of ABC business needs as thoroughly, rapidly, and cheaply as possible. Three basic plans developed—one from the headquarters IS director (in reaction to the corporate executives hiring the outside consulting company), the recommendation from the consulting company, and one unsolicited development plan from a group of vendors.

Plan A came from the Director of Corporate IS, George Bedrock (favorite saying: "If it ain't broke, don't fix it"). George felt that the firm's investment in mainframe computers, legacy software applications, computer operations spaces, and technologist experience was far too valuable to jeopardize, let alone throw away. George believed the existing system should be leveraged with enhancements. He recommended:

▼ Increasing the breadth and amount of data each region transmitted to headquaters, that is, *all* regional data. A new database at headquarters would be developed based on the existing summary database. This database, containing corporate-wide financial, sales, inventory, and service data, would be accessible by all headquarters personnel. Corporate summary data would be transmitted to all regional sites weekly. This would provide centralized control and security for corporate data, especially sensitive financial and personnel data.

▼ Leasing a new, much more powerful mainframe (with new terminals) for processing the new database and sending summarized data to the regional sites. A new, powerful minicomputer would be leased for each regional site to improve regional system response times. Existing applications would run on either the old mainframes or the new minicomputer. When business needs changed, additional minicomputers could be leased or purchased while existing mainframes could continue to provide service for many years. Additional programmers would be hired to alleviate the backlog of application software enhancements.

▼ Reducing the bandwidth of the telecommunications circuits to save money. Headquarters would closely schedule, monitor, and manage all telecommunications sessions to prevent traffic congestion. Regional data uploading and downloading would be spread out during each 24-hour period, with scheduled overflow periods for contingencies.

Plan B, from the consulting firm, took a more state-of-the-art approach while capitalizing on the existing mainframe computers and their infrastructure. This plan recommended:

▼ Consolidating the data in each regional database into a data warehouse at headquarters, which would be accessible by headquarters and all regional sites. Regional data would be entered and maintained locally while copies of all new regional data would be transmitted to the warehouse database automatically every hour. There the data would be converted into the headquarters database format and checked for consistency with other data. Nightly batch transmissions of summary data would no longer be necessary, and everyone would have access to all corporate data that was up to date within an hour.

▼ A three-tiered client/server system architecture: *client processors* (PCs) at almost every desk (executives, sales, administration, service, parts, personnel, etc.), *application servers* (powerful PCs) with consistent, graphically oriented business and office automation applications, and *data repositories* (on the existing mainframe computers). Almost all user work would be shouldered by the client and application servers, while the mainframes woud only have to maintain data files and provide data to the application servers. When business needs changed, client and application servers could be easily added or removed; off-the-shelf applications could likewise be added to these processors. Existing mainframes could continue to provide service for many years, and could be supplemented with cheaper, higher-end workstations or minicomputers when needed.

▼ All client and application processors would be connected with local area networks within each site and a wide area network among the sites, allowing all users to communicate seamlessly with all local and regional users. Local area networks would include wireless gateways to allow roving sales and service personnel to access databases on site at all times. Local area networks would provide access to telephone lines for shared facsimile transmissions and receipt, telephone data transmissions with sales or vendor representatives off site, and centralized voice-mail services. The wide area network would use frame relay protocols using two commercial value-added telecommunications vendors (for redundancy); telecommunication usage would be charged based on actual usage, not dedicated line capacity. Moreover, line capacity could instantly respond to increased needs.

Plan C, from a group of vendors, sought to push the limits of technology to make ABC, Inc. "the leader of the pack." This plan recommended:

▼ Replacing all databases with one "virtual" database distributed among the regional sites and headquarters. Exactly where this data would reside at any moment was up to the database management system software running at headquarters; it would use neural-network technology to disperse the data optimally among all the processors and secondary storage devices to take advantage of slack processing and storage capacity. Access to data would appear seamless to all corporate users regardless of where the data are actually located. All corporate data would be entered directly into this database by users responsible for the data; all corporate data would be as current as it would be entered locally. All existing database applications would have to be replaced, with new applications designed and developed using the latest CASE tools and written using 4GL languages. Application programs would be very user-friendly with colorful graphics and touch screens for user interaction. As business needs change, alterations to the application software could be developed much more rapidly, using prototyping to define requirements. All existing legacy corporate data would be converted to the new database format by contractors off site and added to the new database as archived data.

▼ A "virtual parallel" system of computer processors would be installed at all sites, replacing all mainframes and terminals. This system of processors would be centrally managed by a supervisory processor using neural-network technology to partition and assign processing work continuously based on current and projected processing loads. Any "user" computer can quickly change roles to a "server" computer (and vice versa) as necessary to optimize processing power and response times. Processing would be primarily the responsibility of powerful workstations used by financial, advertising, and technical workers; application interaction with all other users would be primarily done with PCs. When business needs change, workstations and PCs could be easily added or removed by updating the configuration files of the supervisory processor. All processors would provide the latest technology (such as CD-ROM drives) and provide a much higher MIPS-to-price ratio than mainframe or minicomputers. Moreover, they could be capitalized more rapidly for more frequent replacement to take advantage of newer technology.

▼ All client and application processors would be connected with local area networks within each site and a wide area network among the sites, allowing all users to communicate seamlessly with all local and regional users. Local area networks would include wireless gateways to allow roving sales and service personnel to access databases at all times on site. Local area networks would provide access to telephone lines for shared facsimile transmissions and receipt, telephone data transmissions with sales or vendor representatives off site, and centralized voice-mail services. The wide area network would include access to the Internet; potential customers could browse, query, even order cars and parts over the World Wide Web from almost anywhere in the world. The wide area network would use *Asynchronous Transfer Mode* (ATM) protocols using two commercial value-added telecommunications vendors (for redundancy). Telecommunication usage would be charged based on actual usage, not dedicated line capacity. Moreover, line capacity could instantly respond to increased needs.

Corporate executives felt so overwhelmed by the task of choosing the best proposed plan that they hired an independent consultant to summarize the benefits and costs of each plan. They were very apprehensive of all three plans and sought to avoid a quick decision. They also talked to counterparts they were familiar with at other large dealerships in the United States for their experiences and advice.

Case Study Questions

1. Which plan would you have chosen, and why? Which plan would regional IS directors most likely choose or avoid? Everyday users?

2. Which plan would have had the shortest payback period, and why?

3. Which plan would best meet business goals centered around meeting customer needs? Which would best meet business goals to increase benefits to stockholders? Which plan would best meet business goals to attain and retain the best employees?

4. Which plan would best allow ABC, Inc. to react to changing business needs and new opportunities?

5. Which plan would have resulted in the widest use of corporate data? Which plan would have provided the strongest data security, consistency, or easiest data recovery?

6. Which plan is the riskiest, overall, to ABC, Inc.? Why?

PART III

INFORMATION SYSTEMS DEVELOPMENT

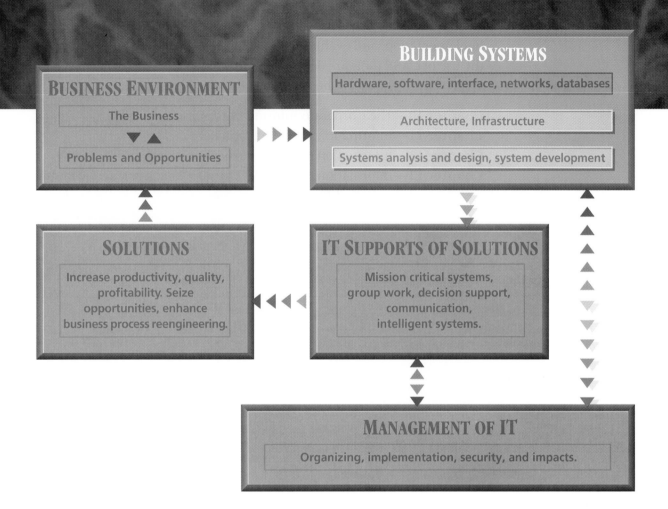

BUSINESS ENVIRONMENT

The Business

▼ ▲

Problems and Opportunities

BUILDING SYSTEMS

Hardware, software, interface, networks, databases

Architecture, Infrastructure

Systems analysis and design, system development

SOLUTIONS

Increase productivity, quality, profitability. Seize opportunities, enhance business process reengineering.

IT SUPPORTS OF SOLUTIONS

Mission critical systems, group work, decision support, communication, intelligent systems.

MANAGEMENT OF IT

Organizing, implementation, security, and impacts.

A key factor for the success of information systems in organizations is the architecture of the corporate information system and the development of the infrastructure and the specific information systems applications.

Part III covers the many topics related to the planning and executing of the architecture, infrastructure, and specific system development.

Chapter 10 describes the traditional mainframe-based centralized architecture and then it contrasts it with client/server architecture. The chapter also discusses the role of the information warehouse in an organization (as part of the architecture) and the issue of outsourcing.

The process of planning, both for the entire information infrastructure and for specific applications, is the topic of Chapter 11. The chapter introduces some important planning models and deals with the important issue of information systems payoffs and justification.

Developing information systems can be a lengthy process and can be done in different ways. Poorly constructed systems will not work properly causing major damage to organizations. This topic is described in two chapters. Chapter 12 is centered around the first steps of the system development life cycle: problems identification, system analysis, and determination of information requirements. Chapter 13 deals with the final steps: design, implementation, and evaluation. Important topics such as prototyping and the use of CASE tools are described in these two chapters which also relate systems development to business processes reengineering.

Chapter 10—The Corporate Information Architecture
Chapter 11—Information Systems Planning
Chapter 12—Information Systems Analysis and Design
Chapter 13—Information Systems Design, Development, Implementation, and Evaluation

THE CORPORATE INFORMATION ARCHITECTURE

Chapter Outline

Learning Objectives

After studying this chapter, you will be able to:

1. Describe the three fundamental IT architectures, and explain why IT architecture is an important IT issue.

2. Explain the concept of centralized computing, the role mainframe computers play in centralized computing, and the issues surrounding centralized legacy systems.

3. Describe the most common types of noncentralized computing architectures and the advantages and disadvantages of distributed computing.

4. Define client/server computing, including client/server tools.

5. Characterize end-user computing—its opportunities and risks, information centers, and IT architectural implications.

6. Describe an information warehouse and its potential IT benefits, and explain how to organize one.

7. Define IT outsourcing and its potential benefits, as well as IT architectural issues.

► 10.1 DISTRIBUTED PROCESSING AND RISK

AMERISURE IS A $500 million insurance company, with 1,300 employees in 12 large regional offices and three smaller branch offices, that sell property, casualty, and commercial insurance. In the early 1990s, Amerisure was feeling the pinch from a sagging real estate market and decreased investment income. In response, they felt they needed to generate incremental income, cut costs, and bolster flattening profits.

They decided to build a new distributed information system and reengineer some key business processes to take advantage of new technology. Basically, they wanted to restructure their information system and their business processes to combine marketing and under-writing into one job. They hoped this would allow Amerisure sales agents to spend more time servicing ex-isting customers and pursuing new opportunities. With the old information system, Amerisure sales agents re-questing a quote for customers on a policy might have to wait days for the information—and weeks for the fi-nal policy if they closed a deal.

Amerisure started by purchasing a popular, off-the-shelf software package that allowed field agents to do everything from rate insurance policies to print out the final policy with portable printers right on the spot. This package alone reduced certain agent tasks from weeks to one or two days. But it was unable to take full ad-vantage of the company's existing mainframe process-ing, something the company wanted to leverage. So the company development team developed its own "mid-dleware" software to link agent software with the cor-porate mainframe and its database. Then they started adding sophisticated communications packages that would work with the agent software. Finally, they cus-tomized a popular user interface package with icons to initiate computer processes quickly.

In the meantime, they started to build a technical in-frastructure to handle the evolving client/server system. They recruited people who had strong line-of-business skills and who seemed to have some technical inclina-tion; they wanted personnel who could better match technology with business needs. They trained technical staff on the new technologies, agents on how to use the new software, and management on what the system could do. Three years later, the 100-person development team put the finishing touches on the new distributed client/server system. But not without some difficulties.

While they were not exactly exploring new technical frontiers, they were "out there where it hurts a little," according to their technical services manager. First, the odyssey was more time-consuming and expensive than

An insurance agent talking with clients.

they had expected. "When we started this, we thought it would take 18 months," he said. "All the hidden time and costs of client/server you read about—they aren't hidden to us now." The biggest mistake, he says, was that they made a number of technical decisions before they had completed making business process reengi-neering decisions. It took time to iron out dysfunctional decisions and mismatches. Another mistake was that they underestimated the time it would take to educate technical personnel on newer languages, system archi-tectures, and development tools. Finally, they under-estimated the time it would take to train field agents to use the personal computers and new software, and thus be able to take advantage of the new technology.

The other major problem is a continuous one: secu-rity. Protecting company proprietary and personal cus-tomer data is all the more difficult with distributed data-bases and their easy access for agents out in the field. Moreover, Amerisure has many security packages, at many levels of the system, that must be dealt with one by one. Each Amerisure agent, for example, must use three different codes and procedures to access data on the mainframe, the local area network, and the data base.

On the positive side, the company estimates the new system and business processes save workers "tremen-dous amounts of time" and add value to their product. As a side benefit, the project made their programmers much more productive; whereas the first version of a system management package took about a year to de-velop, the second version took three months.

SOURCE: Adapted from "Illuminating the Way," *Computer-World*, November 1994.

▶ 10.2 OVERVIEW OF INFORMATION TECHNOLOGY ARCHITECTURE

As the Amerisure story illustrates, piecing together information systems closely tied to business processes can be a very complex and demanding task. A complete corporate information system not only includes hardware and software—as the Amerisure technical services manager pointed out—but data and people as well. The organizational challenge is to arrange those pieces in the most efficient and effective way.

This architectural challenge, of course, is not unlike that faced by those designing buildings, bridges, or breweries—or any other complex system with interdependent parts. **Information technology architecture** is the field of study and practice devoted to understanding and deploying information systems components in the form of an *organizational infrastructure*. The architectural infrastructure is meant to deal appropriately with the use and management of information processing technology in order to meet organizational goals.

In its simplest view, IT architecture consists of the combination of hardware, software, data, personnel, and telecommunications elements used by an organization along with procedures to employ them. A small company might have a handful of IBM-compatible PCs linked together via a local area network using low-end word processing and spreadsheet software, an archived digital file of correspondence and accounting data, and one or two technical specialists for a dozen system users. A large company—with the same basic items—might have numerous mainframe computers, hundreds of midrange computers, thousands of PCs of all kinds, hundreds of different software packages for running the business, dozens of major databases, an elaborate network of wide area and local area communications systems for national and international networking needs, and an information systems staff numbering in the hundreds.

An information technology architecture is conceptually similar to *information architecture* that is described in Chapter 2. Information architecture is a high-level plan of the information requirements and the structures or integration of information resources needed to meet those requirements. *Information infrastructure* also described in Chapter 2 is most similar to the information technology architecture discussed in this chapter.

FUNDAMENTAL ARCHITECTURES

There are three fundamental architectures which this chapter will describe in detail. The following brief introduction to each can help the reader more fully appreciate the underlying IT architectural issues.

CENTRALIZED ARCHITECTURE. For most of the history of electronic computing, *centralized* computer systems were modeled on the basis of a **master–slave relationship** (illustrated in Figure 10.1). ''Slaves'' were devices that were not usually self-contained computer processors. They were merely machines through which information was entered, distributed, stored, or communicated. There are five basic types of these devices: *terminals* for direct, temporary interaction with people (usually using a typewriter-like keyboard and an electronic monitor or screen); *output devices* like printers for permanent output such as paper; *input devices* like bar scanners for inputting data; *communications devices* for exchanging data with other computer systems; and *storage devices* for electronically storing data. (See Chapter 5 for a review of computer hardware.) In each case, the ''master'' or ''host'' (usually a *mainframe* computer) was the machine capable of and responsible for computer processing; and it was centrally connected directly to each slave device. All activity was orchestrated by the master, and much of it was carried out by the slaves. This arrangement was simple, direct, and easily controlled.

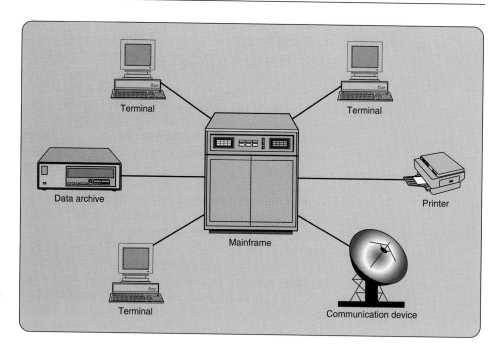

FIGURE 10.1 An example of a centralized architecture.*

PEER-TO-PEER ARCHITECTURE. As smaller, midrange computers appeared (commonly called *minicomputers*) and businesses wanted computer systems to be able to share information and resources, computing evolved into more of a **peer-to-peer relationship** (see Figure 10.2). In this architecture, one computing resource would deal with processing equally in conjunction with another computing resource. As peers, they share devices and data with each other, although one ''peer'' may be ''more equal'' than another for certain tasks or for controlling devices such as printers. Such a peer-to-peer relationship became even more pronounced as PCs began to proliferate in offices and as they were used to communicate with each other.

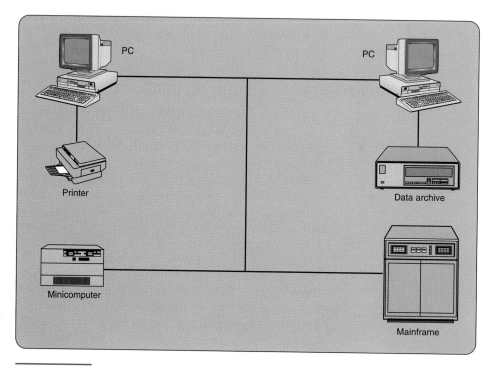

FIGURE 10.2 An example of a peer-to-peer architecture.

*Figures appearing in Chapters 10–13 are adapted by permission from James C. Wetherbe and Nicholas P. Vitalari, *Systems Analysis and Design: Best Practices*, 1994 (St. Paul, MN: West Publishing). Copyright 1994 West Publishing Co.

EMERGING TECHNOLOGY

...client/server
architectures

CLIENT/SERVER ARCHITECTURE. As various linkages of computers evolved—mainframe-to-mainframe, mainframe-to-midrange, midrange-to-midrange, midrange-to-PC, PC-to-mainframe, and PC-to-PC—different types of relationships matured. The most advanced use of computing has evolved to a relationship called **client/server** (see Figure 10.3). In one sense, it is the blending of the master–slave and peer-to-peer relationships. In the client/server model, servers with a peer-to-peer relationship meet the data and processing needs of clients, but clients are themselves fully capable computer processors who have peer-to-peer relationships among themselves as well. Strict distinctions between master–slave and peer-to-peer roles have become more balanced with respect to the computing power found in computing systems of today. A client can bring locally controlled computing directly to a user's desktop—while still sharing computing, device, and data resources with other users.

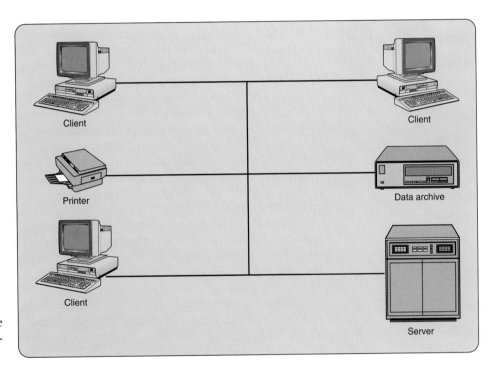

FIGURE 10.3 An example of a client/server architecture.

THE NEED

Notice that the definition of IT architecture emphasizes the need to deal appropriately with the information needs of the business. A poorly organized IT architecture can disrupt a business by hindering or misdirecting information flows. Each organization—even within the same industry—has its own particular needs and preferences for information, and therefore requires an IT architecture specifically designed and deployed for its use.

Unfortunately, many organizations have allowed their IT architecture to evolve over time without a systematic and explicit blueprint of what the architecture should be. In many organizations today, you may find a wide mixture of IT components which do not fit well together and do not fit well with the needs of the business. Moreover, architecture patching and fixing may continue to occur even though the business is highly dependent on that architecture to keep things running. Businesses often do not have the luxury of stopping midstream and "starting clean" with the development of a brand new IT architecture.

Historically, IT architecture was a somewhat mundane and arcane issue. It merely involved deciding upon a desirable configuration, with a mainframe as a centralized computing device and terminals for access to this centralized mainframe. Decisions on hardware, software, databases, and telecommunication were all made periodically, based upon the notion that the centralized system was the key to running the business and dealing with its information needs. With client/ server architectures, however, this is clearly not the case; and IT architecture decisions are now much more complex and far reaching.

Another important facet of IT architecture deals with using and managing information. Indeed, technology should not be selected and adopted by an organization merely to have technology in place, but rather to accomplish desired business goals (such as ensuring that information flows through functional areas of the business or between customers and suppliers). Otherwise, an organization can end up with costly equipment that provides little return to the business for the technology investments made.

Specialists who concern themselves with designing and deploying IT architecture are often called information engineers. Information engineering is a top-down approach to information planning and implementation that will also examine, describe, revamp or reengineer (as necessary), and guide the direction of an existing IT architecture on an ongoing basis.

IT architecture is as much a managerial-based issue as it is a technology-based issue. A wide array of important management issues must be confronted when designing, deploying, and maintaining an IT architecture. Failure to deal with managerial issues will lead even the best information architecture technology into a hopeless morass of components which do not fit the needs of the business. IT architecture should be viewed from an enterprise computing perspective, concerned with IT on an organization-wide basis and connecting with stakeholders outside the business such as customers and suppliers (review Chapter 2 about enterprise-wide and departmental computing). Box 10.1 addresses meeting enterprise-wide information processing needs.

Managers discussing
their IT architecture.

In today's computing environment, IT architectures are becoming increasingly more complex, yet they still must be responsive to changing business needs. These requirements call for tough decisions about a number of architectural issues. The rest of this chapter is organized around these fundamental IT architectural issues: *centralized vs. noncentralized computing, end-user and enterprise computing, information warehouses,* and *IT outsourcing.* Moreover, these issues are not independent. For example, on a daily basis, you might have a financial analyst deciding which PC to acquire and which database management software package to use. While a division chief is deciding which local area network to use within the division, the firm's top executives are deciding how to distribute data across the entire organization. At the same time, IT specialists are deciding which overall technical standards to adopt for data communication nationally and internationally.

Downsizing and *reengineering* are two processes for changing an IT architecture or a business process in order to take advantage of IT. These closely related architectural issues are discussed in Chapters 4 and 11 and will be referred to in this chapter when appropriate.

Centralized computing has been the foundation of corporate computing for 30 years. With client/server systems, however, its role has now shifted toward a more collaborative relationship with other computing resources used within an organization. Although some proponents of PCs claim that the mainframe is dead as a computing resource, most experts agree that the mainframe is likely to exist for many years, particularly as a repository for data that can be centrally maintained for enterprise-wide use.

As computing has spread throughout organizations—especially with distributed processing arrangements—users themselves increasingly have taken on the duties and responsibilities of IT specialists. This phenomenon, commonly called end-user computing, is a field of study and practice that focuses on users and their means to cope directly with IT.

A Closer Look BOX 10.1

ENTERPRISE ARCHITECTURE PRINCIPLES

Business needs and opportunities are changing rapidly. To deal with rapid change, many organizational structures have evolved toward ad hoc project teams or cross-functional groups. Similarly, IT structures are becoming more dynamic in order to provide flexibility and yet be stable in terms of direction to meet future needs. To help ensure an IT architecture can achieve these often-conflicting goals, some argue that IT architectures must be *principle-based* enterprise architectures. These enterprise IT principles concern *organization, applications, data,* and *infrastructure.* The following are some examples of enterprise IT principles in each of the four areas.

ORGANIZATION PRINCIPLES. All IT professionals in each business unit need to report either directly or indirectly to the person responsible for the IT function in that business unit. Technology areas need to collaborate in order to provide the best service possible in application development and support—and to eliminate artificial internal competition. The IT function in a business unit must be organized to make IT a strategic tool, and IT professionals need to acquire the necessary skills to use and exploit IT as a strategic asset for the business.

APPLICATIONS PRINCIPLES. Information systems planning needs to be an integral part of the strategic business planning process. Information systems need to be de-

veloped using formal planning and software engineering methodologies. Successful projects require proactive user and sponsor involvement to ensure proper functionality and ultimate business success. Information systems need to be developed for portability across various hardware and software systems. Information systems need to be periodically reviewed as to their ability to meet business needs and their technological obsolescence. Information systems should be managed as an enterprise asset.

DATA PRINCIPLES. Data should be viewed as a corporate asset and managed as such. Enterprise data plans need to be developed and maintained independent of the applications and the storage technology. The user of an application should be responsible for the content and consistency of the data that the application provides or uses. The steward of an application is responsible for the security of the data that the application processes.

INFRASTRUCTURE PRINCIPLES. A model-based infrastructure architecture can facilitate information system development and data sharing. A high level of connectivity and compatibility among all hardware, software, and communications components is needed.

SOURCE: Richardson, G. L., B. M. Jackson, and G. W. Dickson, "A Principles-Based Architecture," *MIS Quarterly*, December 1990.

The notion of treating data or information as an item of inventory has led to a movement toward warehousing. Drawing upon the principles of inventory management, we can apply warehousing techniques to the timely and proper collection, maintenance, distribution, and cleansing of data and information.

Finally, sometimes an organization may find it too costly or distracting to deal with their IT architecture themselves. Thus, some organizations have contracted with outside vendors to handle a portion or all of their IT architecture. This process of outsourcing the IT architecture carries both benefits and risks and demands careful analysis.

▶ 10.3 CENTRALIZED COMPUTING

The issue of **centralized computing** vs. noncentralized (or decentralized) computing is perhaps the foremost IT architectural issue with the most far-reaching effects on other issues. Centralized computing has been the foundation of corporate computing for over 30 years. The centerpiece of this architecture is the *mainframe* or *minicomputer,* centrally connected to many user terminals and peripherals (such as printers). Even as businesses migrate from centralized computing with mainframes to noncentralized architectures (usually with smaller computers), they generally have to deal with centralized systems, which have become *legacy* systems—hardware, software, and databases on which the company has become dependent. (Legacy systems are discussed in Chapter 2.)

This section deals with issues of centralized computing mainframes in today's business environment and the reengineering of centralized systems that have become corporate legacy systems.

MAINFRAMES

Chapter 5 briefly described the history of corporate computing and the type of computer known as a *mainframe* computer. **Mainframe computers** are relatively large computers built to handle corporate-size databases (such as airline reservations), thousands of user terminals with fast response times, and millions of transactions (such as those occurring in a credit card company's files). Mainframes have been responsible for the far-reaching growth in business computing and for bringing about the Information Age (as well as establishing the computer hardware and software industry). But mainframe computing—as a technology and as a concept—is changing.

As previously stated, for over 30 years mainframes have represented the centralized form of computing; but now minicomputers, workstations, and powerful PCs are challenging that dominance. Centralized computing, as an architecture, can consist of *all* sizes of computer processors, including a conglomeration of computers acting in parallel. Mainframes, by themselves, no longer "rule the roost"; but they are an important part of IT architecture together with all other computers, right down to palmtops. Whereas architectural decisions were relatively simple with one computer—the mainframe—they are now much more varied and complex with a wide range of computers available.

Mainframe computers can still play a key role in distributed, client/server architecture. In a client/server model, the mainframe could be a large-scale file server, processing server, database server, or printing server. In other words, the mainframe—like other types of computers—can be assigned to specific kinds of information-processing tasks that are appropriate for the type of IT being used and the business needs being fulfilled. Mainframes, like all computers, are good when properly applied.

A typical mainframe computer room.

Mainframes have traditionally been expensive to purchase, operate, and maintain. Indeed, the cost of a mainframe is the primary reason industry analysts predict its demise. But the acquisition and operational costs of mainframes are being reduced, partly because of technological improvements (such as cheaper, more efficient components and peripheral equipment) and production cost reductions (encouraged by low-cost PCs). Operational costs have also been reduced through these same technological improvements, and they can be further reduced by using modern managerial techniques such as "lights out" automated operations, which reduce the need for personnel to maintain the mainframe system. Built-in monitoring tools allow for control of the mainframe and problem detection without the need of a human presence.

Mainframe systems have traditionally required a number of IT specialists in systems software, storage devices, and environmental control. These specialists, who once knew only the mainframe and its needs, are gradually finding themselves limited (in terms of career opportunities and pay) as businesses move away from mainframe dominance. The many years of mainframe stability can make it difficult for these specialists to adjust to significant technological shifts that require retraining and organizational changes. Today, well-rounded IT specialists learn the full range of IT technologies and then specialize in particular areas, as necessary.

There are still business applications in which mainframes reign. For high-volume, rapid-pace, transaction-based applications—such as airline reservation systems or stock trading systems—the mainframe still plays a vital role. The requirements of continuous availability and rapid response as well as the safety of reliability and security are all part of the typical mainframe package, making it worthy of ongoing attention. Whether mainframe sales will continue to fall, however, is the topic described in more detail in Box 10.2.

Many of the lessons learned by using and maintaining mainframes are now being translated into similar approaches for smaller, more distributed computing resources. For example, change management on a mainframe has evolved to track

A Closer Look BOX 10.2

ARE MAINFRAMES BECOMING DINOSAURS?

1993 was a good year for IBM's mainframe computer sales; it sold out its entire year's stock by the third quarter. This was good news for a company that receives over half its profits from mainframes and related software. 1994 revenues were projected to be down for the year, although it was less than the 40 percent drop experienced the previous year.

To extend the mainframe's life, IBM introduced a new series of mainframes based on—with obvious irony—PC technology. Using PC-type chips, these new mainframes do only specific tasks such as transaction processing or database queries. The new models cost at least 25 percent less to produce than traditional mainframes, but they cost only a little less to purchase. As a result, older more general-purpose mainframes were selling fast while the new ones weren't. The new machines cost about $28,000 per million instructions per second (MIPS) capability; high-

end workstations sell for only about $19,000 per MIPS, while ordinary desktop PCs sell for about $2000 per MIPS.

Moreover, it may take IBM up to 30 months to work the new technology into its product line. Key software—such as a version of IBM's DB2 database program—wouldn't be ready for another year.

While the mainframe is not yet extinct, many industry analysts say mainframe producers like IBM aren't doing enough to reverse their slide into extinction. Some businesses will depend on the massive capabilities of mainframes for some time, and some businesses will probably eke out a bit more of their mainframe investments. But there is little on the horizon to suggest their resurgence as "king of the beasts."

SOURCE: Adapted from "Return of the Dinosaurs," *BusinessWeek*, August 1, 1994.

changes made to applications and data. Unfortunately, the same principles and practices of change management are not yet completely adhered to in the PC environment; thus organizations are discovering the trauma associated with unknown or untrackable changes that are made to their PC systems (in the same way they were experienced in the early days of mainframe systems). Applying seasoned, managerial wisdom to new architectures gained from over 30 years of mainframe computing can be a significant challenge—but highly beneficial to the organization.

REENGINEERING LEGACY SYSTEMS

REENGINEERING

...legacy systems present a reengineering challenge

Legacy systems, older systems that have become keystones for business operations, may still be capable of meeting business needs (and might not require any immediate changes) or may be in need of reengineering to meet current business needs (and require significant changes). Each legacy system has to be examined for its own merits, and a judgment must be made regarding the ongoing and future value of the legacy system to the organization. This type of decision—to keep, improve, or replace—can present management with agonizing alternatives. On one hand, keeping a legacy system going presents stability and investment return ("if it ain't broke, don't fix it"). On the other hand, increasing processing demands and high operational costs make replacement seem attractive if not imperative. Newer systems, however, may be more risky and less robust.

Suppose a payroll application exists on a mainframe in an organization. This legacy application may or may not be suitable for the company's ongoing needs (you cannot immediately assume that it is or is not). If the cost of processing the payroll is higher due to higher mainframe hardware costs or software licensing fees (as opposed to doing the payroll on a midrange system or PCs), then a business case could be made to reengineer the payroll application. If the payroll application simply does not properly calculate the payroll anymore, then you could also make a business case to reengineer the payroll application. But if the legacy system meets current needs and the cost of reengineering is far more than rising operational costs, a case should be made for deferring reengineering.

Reengineering is the process of examining legacy systems to determine their present status, to determine what changes are warranted in order to allow the system to meet current and future business needs, and to redesign and redevelop the legacy system accordingly. Often, specialized tools are used to examine legacy software applications and determine their overall status. Some of the most important legacy application reengineering issues are examined in Box 10.3.

A Closer Look BOX 10.3

REENGINEERING

SOME REENGINEERING CHALLENGES

Many businesses recognize that more recent software applications provide functionality and ease of use that have not been available in older mainframe environments, especially graphical user interfaces (GUI) with icons and screen pointers. Rather than extend the life of mainframe applications written 10 to 30 years ago, these businesses are increasingly choosing either to shelve the older mainframe applications or rewrite them for smaller, less expensive hardware like desktop PCs.

Most applications that are rewritten (or "rehosted") are legacy applications that have become crucial to business

applications and are too unique to replace with generally available packages. Rehosting can allow a business to leverage its existing software assets and at the same time provide users greater functionality and allow a growth path for future enhancements.

But rehosting can be difficult, time-consuming, and expensive. Moreover, the migration should be done in such a way that the benefits of control and robustness that came with the mainframe environment will not be lost, and there will be minimum amount of disruption. To do so, industry analysts highlight the following rehosting issues.

APPLICATION SELECTION. Some applications are harder and riskier to rewrite. One approach is to first re-host those applications that lend themselves to the new computing environment while other, less time-critical programs remain on the mainframe. This can be costly (maintaining two environments), but it is a less risky path for users, especially with large, complex information systems.

TARGET PLATFORM. The application requirements should not outpace the hardware capabilities or fall short of the business requirements. Requirements, hardware seection, and the rehosted software in development should be continually reevaluated for fit. The weak point in many distributed hardware configurations is network capacity sufficient to handle high volume transactions and large numbers of users.

PERSONNEL SKILLS. Mainframe environment personnel may thoroughly understand the original application but lack any knowledge of the new environment. Programmers skilled in dealing with the new environment may know almost nothing about the application's purpose and functionality. Getting a good blend of old and new skills can be a personnel challenge—especially since the

mainframe personnel are likely more senior in terms of company time. Good communications and strong training are usually required.

DATA. Businesses must ensure that historic enterprise data is readily available in the new, rehosted environment. Electronic data storage devices, formats in which data are stored, and organization of the stored data can be significantly different in the new environment.

MIGRATION TOOLS. Despite vendor promises, few migration software tools exist, and those that do can be exorbitantly expensive.

ORGANIZATIONAL STRUCTURE. Moving applications from a centralized computing structure to a distributed computing structure will likely require a similar IT personnel organizational restructuring. The IT organization should fit the user requirements and the computing environment.

SOURCE: Adapted from Van Hook, H., "Rehosting Mainframe Applications" and Hoffman, T., "Getting There" *ComputerWorld Client/Server Journal.*

It should be noted that legacy systems are not confined just to mainframe platforms. A legacy system might be a system of PC applications that needs to be reengineered and "ported" to a mainframe (sometimes called **upsizing** the system). Or a legacy system might be a mainframe application that needs to be reengineered and rehosted on PCs (often called **downsizing** the system). In each instance, a business is trying to "rightsize" effectively a legacy system that will meet evolving business requirements.

Finally, but perhaps most importantly, legacy system reengineering should be done in concert with business process reengineering. Changes made to the computerized or automated side of a business should be kept in synchronization with the rest of the business processes. While legacy reengineering might be justified solely on a cost or efficiency basis, significant business gains can also be made when it is a coordinated part of reengineering the entire business in an effort to improve efficiency and effectiveness.

▶ 10.4 NONCENTRALIZED COMPUTING

Noncentralized computing architectures are *decentralized* or *distributed*. Decentralized computing breaks centralized computing into functionally equal parts, with each part essentially a smaller, centralized subsystem. Almost all telephone utilities operate this way. Local switching stations contain local, centralized computers for the telephones in their immediate areas—each switching center is functionally identical. **Distributed computing**, on the other hand, breaks centralized computing into many computers that may not be (and usually are not) functionally equal. For a bank with many regional headquarters, for example, one site may process all loan applications, another foreign currency transactions, and another all business and individual accounts. All banks could provide and access all data, but certain computing functions would be distributed across different regional sites.

This section of the chapter discusses issues revolving around distributed computing and the currently most popular form of distributed computing, the client/server model.

DISTRIBUTED COMPUTING

There is nothing inherently good or bad about a decision to centralize vs. a decision to distribute in an IT architecture. Instead, there are benefits and limitations to each approach. Most organizations would normally be categorized somewhere along a continuum between the extremes of completely centralized and completely distributed architectures.

All business computing started out centralized, but most older organizations have either evolved toward distributed computing in some way or started their information systems based on distributed computing. True to form with any decision based on relative advantages and disadvantages, some organizations that completely abandoned centralized computing are now finding that their move was ill-timed. Likewise, some firms that fully embraced distributed computing wonder how anyone could operate otherwise. A hybrid approach, such as that shown in Figure 10.4, may well be the most reasoned route.

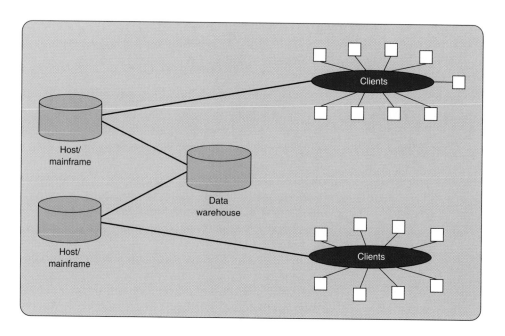

FIGURE 10.4 Hybrid mainframe-client/server example.

CENTRALIZED ADVANTAGES/DISTRIBUTED DISADVANTAGES. Centralized approaches can exploit the economies-of-scale that arise whenever you have a large number of uses for an entity. It may be more cost-effective to have one large-scale computing resource that is used by many, than it is to have many small-scale computing resources that are used by many. The cost of a centralized facility can be divided among many users, usually reducing duplication of effort and more efficiently managing an operation (this applies to housing the computing, providing support services, and so on.).

Centralized approaches can also offer easier control from an enterprise perspective. If important corporate data are stored on a centralized computing platform, a company is able to impose strict physical access controls and preserve the data. When data are spread throughout an organization, securing and preserving data becomes much more difficult.

DISTRIBUTED ADVANTAGES/CENTRALIZED DISADVANTAGES. A distributed approach argues that needs and choices for computing are best handled at the point of the computing need; individual needs are best met with individualized computing. The rise in popularity of PCs, with their decreasing costs and increasing performance, has led many organizations to embrace decentralized computing, giving users direct control over their own computing. Additionally, system data can be entered, verified, and maintained closer to its source.

Distributed computing can also offer a high degree of flexibility and system redundancy. When an organization expands, it may be much easier and less expensive to add another local, distributed processor than to replace a centralized mainframe with an even larger mainframe. Moreover, a malfunctioning distributed computer ordinarily does not prevent other distributed computers from data processing, especially if data are partially or fully duplicated around the system. A centralized approach, however, provides a single point of failure—the central computer. When it goes down, no one computes.

Finally, if the centralized computer is some distance away from a user, response time may be much slower than it would be with a localized computer.

Distributed computing brings enterprise-wide information to the desktop.

BLENDING CENTRALIZED AND DISTRIBUTED COMPUTING. As noted earlier, computing does not have to be entirely centralized or entirely decentralized—it can be a blending of the two models. In some circumstances, the mainframe (centralized resource) is viewed as a kind of peripheral device for other (distributed) computing resources. The mainframe can be a large file server that offers the economies-of-scale and data control that are desirous in most organizations, and yet still allow processing and handling of local needs via the distributed computing resources. *What* to distribute *where* (and what not to distribute) then become key issues.

CLIENT/SERVER ARCHITECTURE

There is no single, accepted definition of client/server, since it is such a recent and booming phenomenon. A client is generally agreed to be any system or process that can request and make use of data, services, or access to other systems provided by a server. This arrangement is illustrated in Figure 10.5. An example of a client might be a desktop PC used by a financial analyst to request data from a corporate mainframe. Or it might be a laptop used by a salesman to get pricing and availability information from corporate systems and then calculate, print an invoice, and order goods directly—all from a client's office.

A server is generally agreed to be any system or process that provides data, services, or access to other systems for clients, most often for multiple clients simultaneously (as a shared resource). In order to serve multiple clients, most servers are considerably more powerful than individual clients—mainframes, minicomputers, workstations, and sometimes high-end PCs. An example of a server

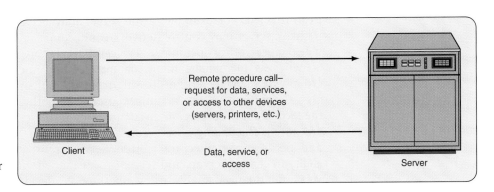

Remote procedure call—
request for data, services,
or access to other devices
(servers, printers, etc.)

Client

Data, service, or
access

Server

FIGURE 10.5 Client/server relationship.

might be a powerful PC that controls network traffic in an office setting or an IBM AS/400 midrange machine that provides access to a corporate database.

There is a working relationship among clients and servers, whereby requests for service from clients go to servers that attempt to fulfill those requests. Neither clients nor servers are "masters" or "slaves" in any sense; they process independently but in conjunction with one another. Thus, we normally refer to this integral relationship by denoting it as "client/server" (as opposed to "client or server" or "client and server"). This may appear to be only a subtle difference, but it is an important one architecturally. Independence in a practical sense gives client/server systems the ability to be reconfigured rapidly—clients and servers can be easily added or subtracted, giving IT managers previously unheard-of architectural flexibility. As a result of this flexibility and high degree of functionality at a user's desk, client/server implementation has grown rapidly—a "sea of change" in computing, as the CEO of IBM called it. Some data on its growth are given in Box 10.4.

A *Closer Look* BOX 10.4

THE GROWTH OF CLIENT/SERVER APPLICATIONS

In the early 1990s, client/server systems were primarily used for non-mission-critical applications due to experiences with—or fears of—poor system stability and robustness. This appears to have changed recently.

Studies by International Data Corporation (IDC) and IDC Research Services in early 1994 showed a significant increase in the number and size of installed business client/server systems—especially for critical on-line transaction processing.

IDC's study of 200 IS organizations found that 36 percent had large-scale client/server applications—those with more than 50 users and dealing with applications critical to the organization. IDG found that 62 percent of 100 IS organizations surveyed were developing or planning to develop mission-critical applications in client/server environments. Finally, another IDC survey found that 31 percent of 280 organizations were using or developing mission-

critical, on-line transaction processing client/server applications.

The studies also showed some interesting facts. The first IDC survey found that financial applications were the most prevalent client/server application, with operations, manufacturing, sales and marketing, human resources, and executive support following. The assumption was that financial applications were the most prevalent to begin with, but it also pointed out the degree of confidence organizations had in client/server systems.

Another interesting finding concerned changes or improvements that organizations wanted most to see in their client/server systems. First on the list was ease of use, followed by compatibility, lower cost, improved support, speed or performance, and finally documentation.

SOURCE: Adapted from "Client/Server Applications Grow Up," *ComputerWorld,* August 1994.

SPECIALIZATION. Because servers may have to handle the needs of many clients in diverse operational conditions, they tend to be specialized in the types of services provided. For example, a file server may be used to manage data files, a network server may control network connections, and an image server may provide digitized office documents. Typically, servers are singularly dedicated to such activities as file management, database management, network management, groupware management, processing/transaction management, and so on.

Computing clients are not supposed to be bothered by server details, such as the location of the server, internal processes of the server, or how and where data are stored. This hiding of server details is referred to as "service transparency"— and it is a good architectural feature. Service transparency gives IT managers the ability to change servers and server processing without affecting clients, and vice versa. If a financial analyst using a desktop PC decides to access a file server that contains accounting data, the analyst should not be required to specify the physical location of the server nor the physical location of the data on the server. Instead, he should only have to send a request for the required data and have the server (whichever one it is and however it does it) respond appropriately. Clients and servers are, therefore, scalable. Upgrading a client to a more powerful machine is called *horizontal scaling*; upgrading a server is called *vertical scaling*.

CLIENT/SERVER RESPONSIBILITIES. Decisions must be made regarding the amount of work to be performed on a client versus the amount of work to be performed on a server. In any given setup, more work performed on one side is referred to as "fat" for the corresponding side. For example, if a client were a desktop PC for a financial analyst that calculated various financial reports on the PC and simply used the server to briefly upload/download data, the client would be considered a "fat client" since most of the work is done by a client processor. On the other hand, if the processing burden were shifted to the server, allowing the financial reports to be calculated on the server and then merely displayed on the client, it would be called a "fat server." Where to distribute processing "fat" is not only a technically important processing question, but one that can also have significant practical implications for users. The goal of IT managers is a "balanced" system. One example of a client/server application is described in Box 10.5.

IT At Work BOX 10.5

REENGINEERING

CLIENT/SERVER ARCHITECTURE FOR CUSTOMER LOAN OPERATIONS AT HOUSEHOLD FINANCE

It is lunch time, and Josephine Customer has only 30 minutes to resolve a home loan problem. Clutching a Household Finance Corporation loan statement indicating that they never received her last mortgage payment, Josephine goes to their office. After waiting in line for the only teller not at lunch, the teller cuts her off in midsentence, saying she must talk to a customer-account representative. After waiting patiently for the account representative (but keeping a wary eye on her watch), Josephine finally has the opportunity to explain the problem. The representative responds, "We'll check into this, and then call you in a day or so." Four days later, a fourth HFC representative leaves Josephine a message telling her to ignore the loan statement; the agency had received the payment after all.

To minimize these types of customer problems and the delays in resolving them, HFC reengineered their IT architecture, moving from a centralized mainframe architecture to a client/server architecture. The effort is intended to place corporate loan information at the fingertips of branch representatives as well as speed up new loan applications.

By 1996, HFC's 1.7 million customers will be served by a single customer representative at any of 467 branch HFC offices or over the telephone—with all loan information instantly available to all representatives over a client workstation. Questions like Josephine's, which used to take four days, will be answered in minutes. Loans and underwriting will be accomplished in two hours instead of the previous average—18 days.

Critical Thinking Issue. Why is the new client/server architecture able to do what the previous mainframe system was unable to do? ▲

SOURCE: *InformationWeek*, November 7, 1994.

A distributed application (such as the financial analysis program previously mentioned or a loan application program such as HFCs) can be split in various ways across a client/server setup. Data can reside on the server and be used by a client, or they can reside on the client and be only partially shared (or not shared at all) with the server. Application processing can take place on the client, or it can take place on one or more servers—or both. Displaying computational or analytical results usually takes place on the client, the device directly interfacing

Client/server systems require careful attention.

EMERGING TECHNOLOGY

...Middleware facilitates client/server interaction

with a human user, but even this can be partially split with the server by having the server determine what is displayed or by controlling the display shown on the client.

If this sounds complex—it *is*. Like most things, the advantage of flexibility brings the baggage of complexity. While client/server architectures give IT managers unprecedented flexibility to "tune" their systems and adjust to changing business needs, that flexibility also carries the burden of dealing with highly complex systems—planning, documenting, implementing, and maintaining them. Client/server systems put a premium on good IT management principles, people, and execution.

CLIENT/SERVER TOOLS. To help IT managers deal with a complex web of client/server hardware and software components, various hardware and software specialized components and tools are used. A client may need a special operating system, a special hardware network connection card, and other components to participate in the client/server architecture. The server may likewise need a special operating system, special hardware networking features, and other components to participate in the client/server architecture. These added layers of capability come at a cost and must be monitored and maintained in order to ensure ongoing functioning of the client/server setup.

In order to help ensure the proper interaction between clients and servers, a new type of software has been developed that is often called "middleware." **Middleware** can translate client requests into a form that certain servers can better understand and translate server responses into a form a client can better understand. Middleware can monitor system performance, alerting system operators to problems or realigning processing responsibilities on its own. Middleware can aid application software developers and maintainers to plan, document, and code software for clients and servers. In effect, middleware is in a gray area between doing work that a client or a server should do and work that some sort of system "overseer" should do. Again, it is part of the continuum of roles between clients and servers and the fact that there is no single master controlling slaves. A given client/server setup, however, may not have any distinguishable middleware at all. The clients and servers may deal with any necessary translation themselves. In general, however, most client/server systems do use some sort of middleware. More detail on client/server tools is provided in Box 10.6.

A Closer Look BOX 10.6

CLIENT/SERVER TOOLS

These are the most prevalent types of client/server tools used to develop or support client/server applications.

QUERY AND REPORTING TOOLS. These tools are used to create basic data access applications and reports quickly with little or no coding. They can reduce the cost of IS operations by off-loading some of the development to the end user, provide ad hoc access to business data, and provide strong links to other personal productivity products such as spreadsheets, word processors, and charting applications.

EIS/DSS TOOLS. Similar to query and reporting tools, executive information and decision support system tools

provide strong support for legacy and on-line data sources—especially for strategic applications. These tools allow knowledge workers to traverse large amounts of data easily looking for trends or other unexplored relationships, thus converting data into information. Some others contain sophisticated graphic functions.

FRONTWARE. Frontware tools allow developers to create appealing graphical user interfaces for existing mainframe programs, without the much greater expense of having to change the mainframe code. They can provide a good bridge between a client/server system and a centralized system or help acclimate users to the eventual migration to client/server.

CLIENT/SERVER DEVELOPMENT. These tools are cross-platform development environments for creating high performance client/server applications. Some can be used for object-oriented and object-relational databases. They are also useful for porting programs across platforms or downsizing legacy systems.

CASE TOOLS. These tools, either component CASE (computer-aided software engineering) tools or fully in-

tegrated CASE tools, support the rapid generation and maintenance of applications. CASE tools guide analysts and programmers through development and maintenance cycles, support automated documentation, and even write code based on documented requirements and development designs.

SOURCE: Adapted from "Walking Through C/S Tool Taxonomy," *Application Development Trends*, August 1994.

In summary, client/server architectures offer the potential to use resources to their fullest (such as a client desktop PC using its full processing power for calculations, but using the tailored functionality of a file server to deal with file handling). They also facilitate resource sharing (perhaps so that other clients can make use of a server or share data with other clients via a server). The client/server model fits well in an environment of disparate computing needs that are distributed throughout an organization, in an environment that is unstable or changes often, and in an environment characterized by risk and uncertainty. In today's business environments, we can fully expect that client/server architectures will continue to increase in popularity and sophistication.

▶ 10.5 END-USER AND ENTERPRISE COMPUTING

IT executives, managers, and technical specialists can never forget the *people* using an information system—as this book so often points out. Whereas the previous sections of this chapter have mainly dealt with the physical arrangement of a system's technology, this section focuses on the primary users—often called *end users*—of a system, management issues, and relevant architectural issues.

OPPORTUNITIES FROM END-USER COMPUTING

Despite much discussion of end-user computing in the academic and popular press, no definition is generally agreed upon. In this book, **end-user computing** is defined as the use and/or development of information systems by the principal users of the systems' outputs or by their staffs. The extent of end-user computing has grown for several reasons.

1. Many applications, especially those that are retrieval- and analysis-oriented, may readily be done by the user.
2. Lead times on development requests may be shorter when end users develop their own systems.
3. End users may have more control over system development and use.
4. IS department procedures may not be appropriate for small applications.
5. The IS department may not be perceived as being concerned about users' needs.
6. End users may want to learn more about computing.
7. End users have better knowledge of business processes and needs.
8. Costs may be lower when end users develop their own systems.

The rapid and continued growth in end-user computing is evidence that users believe the benefits from doing their own computing are substantial.

Besides the advantages for users, there may also be benefits for an IS department. First, the shortage of systems development personnel can be relieved.

This allows IS executives to use their expensive human resources on larger, more technical development projects. Second, if users know their requirements, they can implement them directly into a system and thus avoid the time-consuming and error-prone process of communicating requirements to an outside developer. Finally, systems implementation becomes the responsibility of the users. Their committed ownership of the system is thereby ensured, and a major stumbling block to successful system implementation can be removed. Taken together, these benefits to both users and the MIS department are substantial.

RISKS OF END-USER COMPUTING

Unfortunately, end-user computing also has a downside. An organization's hardware, software, and data are valuable resources that can be lost or diminished if they are not properly developed and protected. End users, acting independently, cannot always be expected to use these resources in ways that are optimum for the whole organization. And since end-user computing bypasses the monitoring and control mechanisms built into the IS department, there is no formal check on user behavior. To illustrate these risks, consider three scenarios where end-user computing leads to problems for three unwary firms.

1. A faulty corporate financial model developed by an end user leads to a disastrous acquisition that later forces the firm into bankruptcy.
2. Errors by an end user in retrieving data for an analysis cause a substantial underestimation of the cost of introducing a new employee benefit. The actual costs are so high that the firm is forced to cancel the program, with disastrous results for employee relations.
3. An employee who developed an important end-user application leaves the company to establish her own business. Since the system was not documented, no one in the organization knows how to use or maintain it.

Problems with inadequate documentation, poor data, faulty backup procedures, and a lack of data security can be common with end-user applications.

IS executives might argue that they should not be held accountable for end-user mistakes and failures. For certain kinds of computing and certain knowledgeable end users, this argument may be defensible. In the majority of cases, however, the expertise and experience of the IS department make it the obvious organizational unit for protecting the computing and information resources of the firm. Top management reasonably looks to the IS department for leadership in computing and information systems, no matter who develops or uses the system. Most firms will find it too dangerous to ignore these risks.

DIVIDING COMPUTING RESPONSIBILITIES

A management strategy to encourage the beneficial aspects of end-user computing and to minimize its risks is to divide computing responsibilities among groups—including the IT or IS group. This is a shared task for end users and IT departments. One approach is first to brainstorm a list of required computing activities, making the list as long as possible before eventually cutting it down to the most important activities. These activities should then be defined as clearly as possible, since the formal definition will prevent questions later about what was actually meant by the assignment of an activity. Each activity is then assigned to either an IT group or to end users. Some types of activities that should be examined for divisional responsibilities are listed in Table 10.1. Box 10.7 describes how 3M Corporation divided some of its computing activity responsibilities.

Table 10.1 **Computing Activities for Divided Responsibility Decisions**

- Standards for hardware and software acquisition.
- Purchase authority for hardware and software.
- Economic cost-justification standards and procedures.
- Responsibility for developing and maintaining types of applications.
- Data security, integrity, and privacy.
- Electronic access to local and corporate data.
- Authority and responsibility for entering and modifying data.

IT At Work BOX 10.7

END-USER SUCCESS AT 3M

3M is an excellent example of well managed end-user computing. Recognized by Tom Peters and Robert Waterman in their book on outstanding management, *In Search of Excellence*, 3M has a corporate culture that encourages entrepreneurship. This is possible because the more than 60 divisions operate like small, independent companies. But 3M wants the advantage of a large company's corporate-wide financial and human resource management and corporate-wide career path planning to benefit from economies-of-scale. What 3M does not want is a central bureaucracy to inhibit the competitiveness of its divisions.

3M resolved this situation by having a centralized system and staff for financial and human resource systems, and a decentralized system and staff for logistical and operational systems. However, all decentralized technology is as compatible as possible, in order to help technology transfer and allow staff to be reassigned without being retrained.

For the logistical and operational systems, the corporate IS staff plays a key role in planning and coordinating. These staffers facilitate the technology transfer of applications between divisions.

At 3M, there is one function of IS that is close to sacrosanct and will likely never be decentralized: planning. They can decentralize hardware, software, data, and technical staff, but they will probably never completely decentralize planning; it is too easy to miss opportunities for shared efforts and resources.

Critical Thinking Issues. Relate 3M's IT architecture to its organizational structure and mode of operation. How does IT contribute to 3M being recognized as a well-managed company? ▲

Problems can result from giving *too* much computing responsibility to end users. End-user organizations, for example, may overly stress localized system and database development—to the detriment of other corporate users. Business unit managers may be more inclined to experiment with risky, unproven technologies, especially since they are not so likely to have much technical expertise in complex systems development, operation, and maintenance. Finally, end-user computing development may be inefficient from a corporate perspective, with a group in one division developing a system identical to one being developed (and paid for) by another group—perhaps in the same division. One piece of good advice is to disseminate computing responsibility incrementally and under centralized guidance and monitoring.

End users will regularly need help carrying out their agreed-upon responsibilities. The most common approach to delivering help is with an *information center*—described in Chapter 18. With support, end users can indeed be more self-sufficient, which leverages the expertise of the IS staff. The old saying *"Catch a fish for a friend and you feed him for a day; teach him how to fish and you feed him for a lifetime"* is quite applicable to end-user computing.

INFORMATION ARCHITECTURES AND END-USER COMPUTING

Like a personal automobile, a personal computer gives its user great flexibility, power, and freedom. But just as the user of an automobile needs access to an infrastructure of highways, the user of a personal computer needs access to an infrastructure of databases and communication networks. Creating an architecture for end-user computing invariably addresses PC linkage issues.

There are five basic configurations of PCs for end users.

1. Centralized computing with end users using a "dumb terminal."
2. A single-user PC not connected to any other device.
3. A single-user PC connected to other PCs or systems using ad hoc telecommunications (such as dial-up telephone connections).
4. Multiuser PCs.
5. Distributed computing with many PCs fully connected by a network.

The managerial key is to have the technical architecture support the divisions of responsibility previously agreed upon by IS and user groups. If centralized, corporate control of data is paramount (perhaps for high security reasons), then an architecture leaning toward centralized computing is appropriate. On the other hand, if data access and sharing is preeminent (perhaps among sales and production staffs), then a distributed architecture is probably better.

There are clear benefits and risks, but end-user computing with desktop PCs is inevitable. The key for IT executives and managers is to maximize corporate business benefits and, at the same time, minimize risks and undue constraints on user initiative, business knowledge, and unity.

▶ 10.6 THE INFORMATION WAREHOUSE

Data or information can be viewed as a tangible asset that needs to be stored, tracked, and made readily available to those who need it when they need it—just as any physical asset of an organization should be stored, tracked, and made available. Borrowed from the principles and practices used in the warehousing of physical assets, the field of study and practice within the IT area is known as *data warehousing* or *information warehousing*. This section will discuss what an information warehouse is, its potential benefits, and how to organize one as a part of an overall IT structure.

DEFINITION

Although definitions vary, an **information warehouse** is generally thought of as a decision-support tool, collecting information from multiple sources and making that information available to end users in a consolidated, consistent manner. The concept started in the 1970s, when corporations realized they had isolated "islands" of information systems that could neither share information nor project an enterprise-wide picture of corporate business. Recently, there has been a resurgence of interest in this concept, as corporations seek distributed computing architectures while they leverage isolated legacy systems. Rather than trying to unite all the systems into one or linking all systems in terms of processing, why not just combine the *data* in one place and make it available to all systems?

In most cases, a data warehouse is a consolidated database maintained separately from an organization's production system databases. It is significantly different from a design standpoint. Production databases are organized around business functions or processes such as payroll and order processing. Many organizations have multiple production databases, often containing duplicate data. A data warehouse, in contrast, is organized around informational subjects rather than specific business processes. The data warehouse, then, is used to store data fed to it from multiple production databases in a format that is more readily accessed and interpreted by end users.

For example, separate production systems may track sales and coupon mailings. Combining data from these different systems may yield insights into the cost-efficiency of coupon sales promotions that would not be immediately evident from the output data of either system alone. Integrated within a data warehouse, however, such information could be easily extracted.

INFORMATION WAREHOUSE BENEFITS

One immediate benefit of data warehousing is the one previously described in the example about sales and marketing data. Providing a consolidated view of corporate data is better than many smaller (and differently formatted) views. Another benefit, however, is that data warehousing allows information processing to be off-loaded from individual (legacy) systems onto lower-cost servers. Once done, a significant number of end-user information requests can be handled by the end users themselves, using graphical interfaces and easy-to-use query and analysis tools. Accessing data from an updated information warehouse should be much easier than doing the same thing with older, separate systems. Furthermore, some production system reporting requirements can be moved to decision support systems—thus freeing up production processing.

Additionally, the performance of a database for production processing will likely be optimized for its particular type of processing—typically for simple and frequent transactional updating. Information warehouse databases, on the other hand, could also be optimized for ad hoc, complex queries such as those needed by decision makers. It would likely be very difficult, if not impossible, to optimize existing databases for both operational production purposes and for decision-making needs.

HOW TO ORGANIZE AN INFORMATION WAREHOUSE

The first step in organizing an information warehouse is to identify and analyze all operational production databases that will be consolidated. Data entities, relationships, and formats must be identified. This information is then used, as in the normal database design discussed in Chapter 8, to design a logical and physical database for the information warehouse.

Next, data *extraction* tools are used to convert data from separate databases and transform them (i.e., get rid of duplicates, resolve inconsistencies, convert different units of measurement) into data to be stored in the information warehouse. Fortunately, data warehousing management software is now available to simplify data extraction and transformation processes, and to help document them. These programs usually run on the production systems to extract relevant data into a large file or set of files to be loaded into the information warehouse database.

An example of building an information warehouse in the retail industry is described in Box 10.8.

Information warehousing can be an important part of an IT architecture, determining who will have access to what information when and how. Implementing information warehousing may require dramatic changes to the IT architecture, or it may be implemented via gradual, minor changes—depending on the scope and current IT architecture in place. IT specialists known as data or database administrators play an important role in helping to design and implement an information warehousing approach.

IT At Work BOX 10.8

MINIMIZING RISK WITH DATA WAREHOUSING

A key issue in retail stores is managing valuable shelf space—placing one product in any one space displaces other potential products. Profits can be maximized by clearly understanding the trade-offs between the number of products available and the shelf space given to them.

The 7-Eleven Company (Japan) wanted to forecast product sales better to deal with these trade-offs and cut expenses through better distribution and delivery management. They had point-of-sale (POS) data collection, but data were maintained by separate departments on separate computer systems—making it difficult to cross-correlate sales information and forecast overall sales trends. They decided to implement a data warehouse.

With the new scheme, POS data from separate mainframe systems are extracted and transformed prior to being loaded into a warehouse database. Additional data sources for the warehouse database include regional data, climate data (certain items sell better in certain weather), business information (perhaps on their competitors), and administrative information.

By having all this data in one database, 7-Eleven executives are able to forecast sales of new products (including seasonality) based on historical sales of similar existing products. They can adjust inventory levels based on weather forecasts. They can even forecast sales of potential new stores with reasonable accuracy. And they can better match their distribution and delivery needs to actual sales demands.

Critical Thinking Issues. Why is the concept of data warehousing becoming popular? How does it relate to forecasting? ▲

▶ 10.7 IT OUTSOURCING

There are many business functions or services regularly purchased from vendors outside a firm. For example, a business may contract out for a janitorial service, security guards, lawyers, accountants, and even executives. IT provides a service that may also be contracted out to vendors. Using outside vendors to create, maintain, or reengineer IT architectures is called **IT outsourcing**.

Outsourcing might be done for hardware and software elements (e.g., let someone else buy and maintain expensive hardware and software in return for a lease fee), for telecommunications equipment (e.g., leasing phone company lines rather than building a corporate communications network), for managing an IT architecture (e.g., hiring IT consultants to find processing bottlenecks), or for designing and developing entirely new systems. Today, most organizations choose to outsource selectively, and then only those pieces of the IT architecture they believe warrant being outsourced.

Deciding what and when to outsource may not be easy because of the potential advantages (see Table 10.2) and disadvantages. Advantages include the potential for cost reduction due to economies-of-scale gained by the outsourcer, removal of day-to-day problems maintaining an IT architecture, and exploiting the use of newer technology or techniques that the outsourcer may already have implemented. Outsourcing may also free up capital that would have been spent on expensive hardware and software, opting, instead, to use operational funds during high revenue periods. Companies may feel that their prime business mission is being distracted by IT requirements; outsourcing may allow a firm to concentrate on its core business needs. See Table 10.2 for additional benefits.

One disadvantage of outsourcing, like the disadvantage of leasing instead of owning, is the danger that the organization may become too reliant upon the outsourcer for its IT architectural needs—especially if the outsourcer turns out to be less than completely supportive or is inflexible to changing business needs. A firm undertaking outsourcing may also pay more than if the IT architecture were efficiently designed from the start and operated within its own organization. More-

Table 10.2 **Potential Outsourcing Benefits**

Financial
- Avoid heavy capital investment, thereby releasing funds.
- Improve cash flow and cost accountability.
- Cost benefits from economies-of-scale, sharing computer housing, hardware, software, and personnel.
- Release expensive office space.

Technical
- More freedom to choose software due to wider range of hardware.
- Technological improvements gained more easily.
- Greater access to technical skills.

Management
- Management concentrates on developing and running core business activity.
- IT development (design, production, acquisition, and so on) and operational responsibility delegated to the supplier.
- No need to recruit and retain competent IT staff.

Human
- Specialist skills available from a pool of expertise, when needed.
- Enriched career development and opportunities for staff.

Quality
- Clearly defined service levels.
- Improved performance accountability.
- Quality accreditation.

Flexibility
- Rapid response to business demands.
- Better ability to handle IT demand peaks and valleys.

over, a company may risk loss of proprietary business information by using an outsourcer with links to competitors or vendors. Some benefits of outsourcing IT telecommunications are described in Box 10.9.

A Closer Look BOX 10.9

SOME BENEFITS OF NETWORK OUTSOURCING

The concept of outsourcing, using outside vendors for communications services, is not new. Businesses have relied on public utility telegraph and telephone companies for over a hundred years. But relying on outsourcing for wide area networking is gaining popularity with firms trying to link widely dispersed business units, customers, and suppliers.

A Forrester Research study, published in May 1994, concluded that communications outsourcing is rapidly rising. Seventy-two percent of randomly contacted *Fortune* 1000 companies indicated that they used telecommunications outsourcing. That is nine percent more than in December 1992. Networking installation and management outsourcing doubled from 18 percent in December 1992 to 36 percent in May 1994. Moreover, 62 percent believed their outsourcing was beneficial and successful.

The study indicated a number of reasons for the increase in telecommunications outsourcing. One was to "add personnel" quickly in the face of corporate hiring-freezes while attempting to expand IS services. Another was to bring needed skills into IT organizations without long-term financial career commitments. The study also revealed that cost reduction was a major goal but that vendor responsiveness and quality of vendor service are also itical factors.

One telecommunications outsourcer said that they find the customers' number one benefit is the ability to consolidate IT needs, where a single organization provides cross-trained individuals in a changing market. Also, the rise in telecommunications outsourcing has grown in proportion to the move by companies to client/server environments—which are communications intensive. Businesses have often found that vendors that design, build, and sell telecommunications *equipment* do not provide services to design, build, and operate telecommunications *networks*.

SOURCE: Condensed from "Take This Network and Run It!", *Managing Automation*, November 1994.

IT outsourcing experts generally agree that any organization that makes use of IT on a truly strategic, competitive basis is less likely to find it advantageous to outsource than will organizations where IT is less strategically used. In other words, businesses should focus on their core competencies; the other functions should be candidates for outsourcing. IT outsourcing is still controversial, and organizations should evaluate their needs based on their own situations.

▶ MANAGERIAL ISSUES

1. *Fitting the IT architecture to the organization.* Management of an organization may become concerned that their IT architecture is not suited to the needs of the organization. In such a case, there has likely been a failure on the part of the IT technicians to determine properly the requirements of the organization. Perhaps there has also been a failure on the part of management to understand the type and manner of IT architecture that they have allowed to be fostered or that they need.

2. *IT architecture planning.* IT specialists versed in the technology of IT must meet with business users and jointly determine the present and future needs for the IT architecture. In some cases, IT should lead (e.g., when business users do not understand the technical implications of a new technology); in others cases, users should lead (e.g., when technology is to be applied to a new business opportunity). Plans should be written and published as part of the organizational strategic plan and as part of the IT strategic plan. Plans should deal with training, career implications, and other generated infrastructure requirements.

3. *IT policy.* IT architectures should be based on corporate guidelines or principles laid out in policies. These policies should include the roles and responsibilities of IT personnel and users, security issues, cost-benefit analyses when considering IT, and IT architectural goals. Policies should be communicated to all personnel who are managing or directly affected by IT. ■

KEY TERMS

Centralized computing *345*

Client/server *343*

Distributed computing *349*

Downsizing *349*

End-user computing *355*

Information technology architecture *341*

Information warehouse *358*

IT outsourcing *360*

Legacy systems *348*

Mainframe computers *346*

Master-slave relationship *341*

Middleware *354*

Peer-to-peer relationship *342*

Reengineering *348*

Upsizing *349*

CHAPTER HIGHLIGHTS *(L-x means learning objective number x)*

▼ The three fundamental IT architectures are master-slave, peer-to-peer, and client/server. The IT architecture can significantly affect the usefulness of an information system. IT architecture is an important issue for companies increasingly dependent on IT as they strive to meet rapidly changing business needs. (L-1)

▼ Centralized computing is based on one computer (usually a mainframe) directly controlling all other information system devices. Legacy systems are older systems that have become essential to business operations but may need replacing or up-

grading. Reengineering legacy systems can be very risky and costly, but it can provide considerable compensating business benefits. (L-2)

▼ There are two primary types of noncentralized computing architectures: decentralized and distributed. Distributed computing can offer users more direct control over their computing, better data input, and a high degree of flexibility to deal with changing business needs. The client/server is based on one or more servers providing computational, data, or service access to one or more clients, usually operated directly by end users. Client/server tools primarily help IT managers deal with the complexity of client/server development, documentation, and maintenance. (L-3)

▼ End-user computing benefits include faster application development by those with the greatest business expertise; less work by IT personnel on routine queries or report generation; greater IT awareness by users (including executive management), with resulting wider support for IT benefits; and better accountability for IT by users. Some of its risks include shoddy application development, duplication of development work, and poor testing and documentation of applications. The rights and responsibilities of end-user computing should be wisely divided between professional IT personnel and end users, with an IT architecture that is appropriately positioned between completely centralized and completely distributed. (L-4)

▼ An information warehouse is a collection of information from many sources made available to end users in a consolidated, consistent manner. Information warehouses can simplify access to data from disparate source systems, provide an enterprise-wide view of business data, and optimize IT hardware and software for a firm's particular needs. When organizing one, IT information specialists should identify and analyze existing databases, design a logical and physical consolidated database, and move the data from the source systems into the warehouse database. (L-5)

▼ IT outsourcing uses outside vendors to create, maintain, and/or reengineer IT systems or services. It potentially frees a business to concentrate on its core competencies, taking advantage of economies-of-scale for decreased IT costs and allowing for more rapid adoption of new technology. Outsourcing also has a downside. Companies should closely examine IT outsourcing benefits and costs, based on their individual company situation—especially if IT is used for strategic business advantages. (L-6)

QUESTIONS FOR REVIEW

1. What is information technology architecture, and why is it important?

2. What are the three fundamental IT architectures, and what are their primary differences?

3. What are the advantages and disadvantages of centralized computing architectures?

4. What are some types of noncentralized computing architectures? What are their advantages and disadvantages compared to centralized computing architectures?

5. What is a legacy system? Why do companies have legacy systems?

6. Describe the client/server model and how it works.

7. What is end-user computing? What are the advantages and disadvantages of end-user computing? What are the five basic end-user computing configurations?

8. What are the typical services provided by an information center?

9. What is an information warehouse? What are the prime benefits of having one?

10. What is IT outsourcing? Give some examples.

QUESTIONS FOR DISCUSSION

1. Why were most information systems based on the master-slave arrangement for the first 30 years of business computing? What factors might lead to a resurgence of master-slave arrangements?

2. What factors should a firm consider when evaluating a move from a mainframe computing system to a client/server system? What factors should not be considered?

3. Will mainframes ever go away completely? Why or why not?

4. What should come first in corporate reengineering efforts involving IT—business process reengineering or IT reengineering? Why?

5. How can firms minimize the risks of end-user computing?

6. Should there be a correlation between a firm's human organization architecture and its IT architecture (e.g., centralized IT for a centralized company organization)?

7. What are some of the risks (like data security) of an information warehouse? How can they be minimized?

8. When is IT outsourcing avoiding management responsibilities?

EXERCISES

1. Describe the IT architecture at your university. Determine the reasons behind the architecture. Are they still valid?

2. If your university has a mainframe, interview IT managers to determine why. Are there plans to stop using a mainframe? If so, why; if not, why not?

3. If your university has a client/server system, interview IT managers to determine the main problems managing it.

4. Identify and interview some administrative end users of your university IT. In what ways do they control the information systems they use? What things do they not control?

5. Should your university's IT be outsourced? If only parts of it should be, which parts and why?

GROUP ASSIGNMENT

Divide into groups of six people or less. Each group will be entrepreneurs attempting to start a nation-wide company of its choice. Each group should describe the IT architecture it would build, as well as expected benefits from and potential problems with the IT architecture.

Minicase 1

Cruising with Distributed Computing

The Norwegian Cruise Line and Royal Cruise Line divisions of Kloster Cruise Ltd. were facing an ocean of red ink and stiff competition. Setting course for what it believes will be smoother computing waters, the company is chucking overboard its ten-year-old, homegrown reservations system and its host mainframe computer—replacing both with modified packaged software running in a distributed computing environment. To do so, it turned to a computer services organization for a multimillion dollar, five-year systems development and management contract.

High on Kloster's development priority list are a new reservation system, a yield management system, and direct computer links with travel agents. Kloster was booking almost all of its cruises through agents calling in reservations over the telephone. By modifying reservation systems software developed by the United State's two largest computerized reservation systems—Apollo and SABRE—it hopes to make Kloster cruises more appealing to travel agents than other cruise lines that still have to receive reservations by telephone. "If I don't have to sit on the phone, but can make bookings interactively, that will boost my profitability," says a senior vice president with a major travel company. Agents will also be able to search for passenger-specific options more quickly and easily.

Kloster outsourced development of the new systems because it expected that the $8.6 billion-a-year developer—with its purchasing clout and expertise in systems development and management could save Kloster $10 million over the life of the contract. The cruise company is trying to raise capital for more modern ships. Kloster will retain ownership of its data center in Coral Gables, Florida, but the computer services company will consolidate Kloster's San Francisco data center into the Coral Gables center. Eventually, all Kloster systems will migrate to a distributed computing environment supporting 600 users in Coral Gables, London, and Oslo, Norway.

Questions for Minicase 1

1. What benefits does Kloster expect to receive by moving from a centralized to a distributed computing environment? Could it achieve the same benefits with a new or upgraded mainframe?

2. Who are the end users of the new distributed system? How might computing responsibilities be divided between the computer centers and end users?

3. How could Kloster set up information centers or their equivalent for end users—including those at sea?

4. What are some of the risks of Kloster using the Apollo or SABRE software as the foundation of the reservation system? How can it minimize those risks?

5. What are some of the pros and cons of Kloster outsourcing their systems—in particular, their reservations system? What appears to have been the prime motive(s)? What should have been the prime motive(s)?

SOURCE: Condensed from "Open Systems On Open Seas," *InformationWeek*, December 19, 1994.

Minicase 2

Data Warehouse Paybacks

Hughes Aircraft's Aerospace and Defense Sector expects to recover the development costs of its materiel data warehouse within one year. Fingerhut Corporation calculates that its data warehouse project will pay for itself within two years—with a "big payback." Finally, GE Appliances anticipates a three-to-one payback on its data warehousing project based on its prototype used by 100 decision makers. These projects range from $250,000 to over $5 million.

"Companies that implement a data warehouse begin to understand their business better," says an information systems consultant. "This allows for more intelligent business process reengineering that improves the bottom line." In many cases, there are substantial time savings as well.

Before Hughes built its materiel data warehouse, its Aerospace and Defense Sector had nine full-time people manually assembling information about suppliers and commodity purchases across its three business units. Now, users can get that information themselves at their desktops. The data warehouse also cut costs dramatically, by reducing paper reports from 480,000 pages to 150,000 per month. Buyers can negotiate better prices and put together more effective purchase agreements by instantly getting data on previous purchases.

GE Appliances also expects to redeploy information intermediaries as a result of its data warehousing project. "In some cases, they are financial analysts who have been spending their time providing data instead of analyzing it," said the project director. By gaining immediate access to sales-trend information, sales staffers have eliminated weeks spent reading and analyzing data reports during a year. Salespeople can immediately identify dealer customers whose sales are down and determine which products are responsible for the drop. And by integrating information about technical service, service contracts, parts, and appliances, they can better profile consumers.

Fingerhut salespeople can now see sales figures on a weekly basis and look at information they were never able to see before. Analysts have gained access to financial data that was formerly trapped in different mainframe systems. The director of Fingerhut's information services says the new data warehouse is "taking the cobwebs off of our heads."

Questions for Minicase 2

1. What were some of the expected benefits from data warehousing by these three companies? Could they have gained these benefits without using a data warehouse? If so, how?

2. How can a company apply cost-benefit analysis in deciding whether or not to build a data warehouse? How could it measure the anticipated benefits and costs? How will the company know later on if the data warehouse was worth it?

3. Can end users have too much data "at their fingertips"? Will end users like the salespeople at GE and Fingerhut know what to do with the information available?

SOURCE: Condensed from "Expecting a Huge Payback," *Open Computing*, October, 1994.

REFERENCES AND BIBLIOGRAPHY

1. Gray, P., King, W. R., McLean, E. R., and Watson, H. J., *Management of Information Systems*, Chicago: Dryden Press, 1989, 1994.

2. McLean, E. R., "End-Users as Application Developers," *MIS Quarterly*, December 1979, pp. 37–46.

3. McNurlin, B. C., and Sprague, R. H., Jr. (eds.), *Information Systems Management in Practice* (2nd ed.), Englewood Cliffs, NJ: Prentice-Hall, 1989.

4. Peters, T., and Waterman, R., *In Search of Excellence: Lessons from America's Best Run Companies*, New York: Harper Collins, 1982.

11

INFORMATION SYSTEMS PLANNING

Chapter Outline

Learning Objectives

After studying this chapter you will be able to:

1. Describe the evolution of information systems planning.

2. Discuss the major problems of information systems planning.

3. Explain the four-stage model of information systems planning.

4. Discuss several different methodologies for conducting strategic information systems planning.

5. Review the processes necessary to establish an information architecture.

6. Define the approaches for allocating information systems resources.

7. Review the approaches to project planning, and discuss their applicability.

8. Apply specific guidelines to establish what information systems planning is needed in an organization.

11.1 UTILITIES: PLANNING FOR CHANGE

THINGS ARE CHANGING rapidly for the staid electric and natural gas utilities. The new business climate of deregulation—intended to force open competition—could be a death knell for utilities that don't adjust. Information technology will likely play a significant role in determining success or failure.

For starters, IS must provide flexible systems to keep up with new regulations—changing accounting practices, metering and billing procedures, and supply contracting. IS will support customer service improvements in order to retain existing customers and attract new business. Business processes will need to be reengineered to achieve improved cost efficiencies and customer service effectiveness. Adding to the challenge, IS will have to fight for limited capital improvement dollars as the entire industry retools. How will IS planners meet this challenge? How can they plan new architectures now to meet future regulatory, technology, and business climate changes?

One example of this kind of IS planning was done, beginning in 1993, by the director of MIS at ARKLA, part of the third largest natural gas distribution company in the United States. ARKLA first decided to take advantage of the architectural flexibility of client/server systems in lieu of its relatively inflexible, centralized mainframe computer system. They predicted that a client/server system would be more capable of accommodating regulatory changes and the faster pace of market forces. But when it came time to design systems such as contracting, accounting, order confirmation, billing, and others, the company needed to know specifically what the regulators had in mind. "The Federal Energy Regulatory Commission was issuing rules while we were in the process of design," said the MIS director. "We were literally designing to our best guess of what the business regulations would be. In some cases, our best guesses were wrong." Fortunately, such missteps were corrected with relatively little difficulty because the client/server system allowed the company to make changes rapidly.

Providing and marketing innovative services posed another new planning challenge for utilities. Histori-

A natural gas storage plant.

cally, utilities have limited marketing experience and have not been overly concerned about getting to know their customers' needs in detail. "That is one of the processes [our planning is] going to focus on," said the director of business process improvement at Florida Power. The electric utility's databases contain a wealth of customer information—such as consumption rates, bill-paying history, and peak usage times—which has not heretofore been used to identify and target customers for marketing programs. Customer service representatives need to have this information at their fingertips when responding to service calls. Moreover, utilities are even thinking of venturing into cable television programming and other information products such as on-line information services. Designing or redesigning databases to meet these changes can involve much more than just "tweaking."

Meeting constantly changing regulatory requirements, creating innovative value-added services, and maintaining existing support simultaneously can present IS planners with enormous business (and career) challenges and opportunities.

SOURCE: Frabris, P., "Power Surge," *CIO*, March 1, 1995.

11.2 PLANNING—A CRITICAL ISSUE

As the IS planners in the utility industry know full well, planning and forecasting are not the same thing. **Forecasting** is *predicting* the future; **planning** is *preparing* for that future. Given the many changes that are occurring in the utility industry, not the least of which are changing federal and state regulations, forecasting is particularly difficult. But just because the future is very uncertain and forecasting it a daunting task, it does not mean that IS planning can be deferred or neglected. Certain assumptions about the environment—and about technology—must be made, even if some of them prove to be wrong, as was the case at ARKLA.

Improving the planning process for information systems has consistently ranked as one of the top concerns of IS executives (see Wetherbe, 1991). Top management, often baffled by information technology, has historically been standoffish toward IS but, at the same time, has been increasingly concerned with escalating IS budgets. For their part, IS professionals have historically experienced difficulty relating IS technology to key business issues.

This chapter focuses on the critical issue of planning. The evolution of information systems planning is described first. Then, a four-stage model of information systems planning is presented: strategic planning, requirements analysis, resource allocation, and project planning. Methodologies for operationalizing the model are discussed next, with primary emphasis placed on the stages of strategic planning and requirements analysis. In addition, a number of specific planning approaches are described. Finally, there is a discussion of guidelines for IS planning.

▶ 11.3 EVOLUTION OF INFORMATION SYSTEMS PLANNING

Initial efforts to establish planning and control systems for information systems started in the late 1950s and early 1960s. During the early stages, information technology resources were expended on developing new applications and revising existing operation applications systems. These two areas became focal points for the first planning and control systems. Methodologies for developing systems were adopted, and project management systems were installed to assist with planning new applications. These included the use of well-defined project phases, specified deliverables, formal user reviews, and sign-off procedures. Additionally, attention was focused on the efficient process of completed systems. High availability and reliability were emphasized, and computer operations planning and scheduling by computer were initiated.

These initial mechanisms addressed *operational* information systems planning. As organizations became more sophisticated in their use of information systems, emphasis shifted to *managerial* IS planning, or resource allocation control. A manifestation of this shift was the organization of the IS function into a corporate computing utility. A form of charge-out (i.e., users pay for the computing and information services they use) was implemented in an attempt to shift accountability for IS expenditures to users. Some questioned the effectiveness of charge-out as a cost-control tool; but at least in theory, charge-out fostered greater user attention to benefits versus costs and resulted in more effective planning and utilization.

Collectively, these measures had an effect on planning, and a process for identifying demands for information services was developed. Typically, annual planning cycles were established to identify potentially beneficial IS services, to perform cost-benefit analyses, and to subject the portfolio of potential projects to resource allocation analysis. Often the entire process was conducted by an IS **steering committee** composed of key managers representing major functional units within the organization. The steering committee was created to oversee the IS function, to ensure that adequate planning and control processes were present, and to focus IS activities on long-range organizational objectives and goals (see Table 11.1). The steering committee reviewed the project portfolio, approved projects considered to be beneficial, and assigned relative priorities. The approved

Table 11.1 IS Steering Committee Functions

1. To *educate* members of the committee on the strengths and weaknesses, opportunities and threats (SWOPs) of the use of information technology.
2. To *communicate* the status and plans for use of IT within the organization among the members of the committee and their respective functional units.
3. To *allocate* available resources among competing IS projects, setting priorities as needed.
4. To *evaluate* overall performance and success of the IS function and of the systems in operation and under development.

projects were then mapped onto a development schedule, usually encompassing a one- to three-year time frame. This schedule became the basis for determining IS support requirements such as long-range hardware, software, personnel, facilities, and financial requirements.

The planning process just described, typical of the traditional approaches to IS planning, is currently practiced by many organizations today. Specifics of the IS planning process, of course, will vary among organizations. For example, not all organizations have a high-level IS steering committee. Project priorities may be determined by the IS manager, by her superior, by company politics, or even on a first come-first served basis. Organizations with decentralized IS functions often employ integrative mechanisms, such as formal review and consolidation meetings, to determine their overall IS plan. In cases of strong divisional autonomy, no centralized planning may be attempted; rather, a process similar to that just described may be utilized by each divisional IS group.

▶ 11.4 PROBLEMS OF INFORMATION SYSTEMS PLANNING

The most common problems with traditional information systems can be summarized in four categories, each of which will be discussed individually.

1. Aligning the IS plan with the overall strategies and objectives of the organization.
2. Designing an information system architecture for the organization in such a way that various databases can be integrated.
3. Allocating information systems development and operations resources among competing applications.
4. Completing information system projects on time and according to budget.

ALIGNMENT OF THE IS PLAN WITH THE ORGANIZATIONAL PLAN

The first problem in the IS planning process is to identify and select information systems applications that fit the priorities established by the organization. Surprisingly, organizational strategies and plans are often not in writing, or they may be formulated in terms that are not useful for information system planning. Therefore, it is often difficult to ascertain the strategies and goals to which the information system plan should be aligned. Nevertheless, without this alignment, the information systems plan will not obtain long-term organizational support. If selection and scheduling of information systems projects is based only on proposals submitted by users, the projects will reflect existing computer-use biases in the organization, managers' aggressiveness in submitting proposals, and various aspects of organizational power struggles, rather than the overall needs and priorities of the organization.

DESIGN OF AN INFORMATION SYSTEM ARCHITECTURE

As discussed in Chapters 2 and 10, the term *information system architecture,* or **information architecture**, refers to the overall structure of all of the information systems in an organization. This structure consists of applications for various managerial levels of the organization (operations, management control, and strategic planning) and applications oriented to various management activities such as marketing, R&D, production, and distribution. The information architecture also includes databases and supporting software. An information systems architecture for an organization should guide long-range development as well as allow responsiveness to diverse, short-range information systems demands.

Failure to have good architectural planning is best illustrated by the problem facing most banks today. Their various systems, such as checking, savings, installment loans, mortgage loans, and IRAs, are not usually integrated. Consequently, their various systems treat one customer with several accounts as several different customers instead of as one customer with several relationships. These problems are elaborated in Chapter 4.

ALLOCATION OF DEVELOPMENT RESOURCES

Rational, optimum allocation of the resources of information systems development among competing organizational units is difficult. This is especially true if the portfolio of potential applications does not fit into an overall organizational plan, and if the functional/organizational unit requirements do not fit into some orderly framework that establishes completeness and priority. Sometimes organizational dynamics such as relative power, and aggressiveness are used in place of rational allocation. The result may result in a precarious political situation for IS management.

COMPLETION OF PROJECTS ON TIME AND ACCORDING TO BUDGET

Few information system projects are completed on time or within budget. Consequently, organizational performance and IS management's credibility suffer. Project plans are seldom accurate, as time and resource requirements are generally underestimated.

Often, under the pressure to finish a project on time and/or within budget, certain promised features are allowed to slip. This reduction in system quality frequently leads to user dissatisfaction with the resultant systems. Missing or inadequate features must be added later in what is usually called "system maintenance." Proper project planning would avoid such a sequence of mishaps.

11.5   BASIC FOUR-STAGE MODEL OF IS PLANNING

A generic information systems planning model called the **four-stage model of planning** has been formulated based on an observation of planning efforts, promotional literature, and an analysis of the methodologies being used in the planning process. The basic IS planning model, depicted in Figure 11.1 and described

FIGURE 11.1 Basic four-stage model of IS planning.

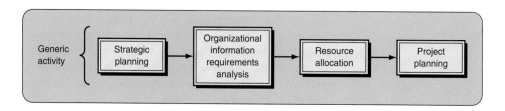

Table 11.2 Description of IS Planning Stages

Major IS planning activity	Description
Strategic planning	Establishing the relationship between the overall organizational plan and the IS plan.
Organizational information requirements analysis	Identifying broad, organizational information requirements to establish a strategic information architecture that can be used to direct specific application system development projects.
Resource allocation	Allocating both IS application development resources and operational resources.
Project planning	Developing a plan that expresses schedules and resource requirements for specific information system projects.

in Table 11.2, consists of four major, generic activities: strategic planning, requirements analysis, resource allocation, and project planning.

Most organizations engage in each of the four stages, but their involvement tends to be random and influenced by problems as they occur rather than in a stage-by-stage process. During these stages, planning methodologies are often chosen based on the persuasive power of developers rather than on a reasonable choice, given the stage of IS planning.

The basic IS planning model presented here provides a framework for study and evaluation of the IS planning process and for mapping methodologies to the basic activities.

The general four-stage model can be expanded to include major activities and outputs of the four stages as shown in Figure 11.2. With additional detail, the

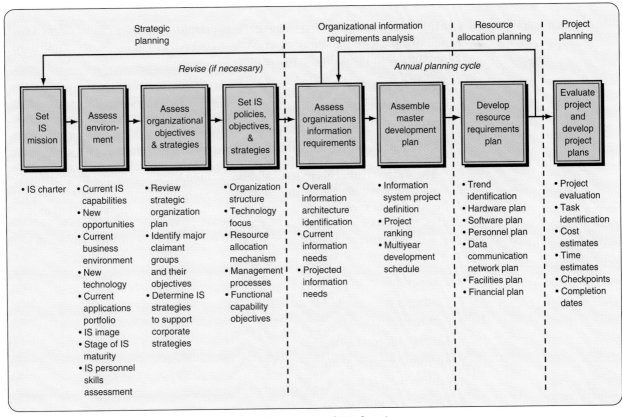

FIGURE 11.2 Major activities and outputs in the four stages of IS planning.

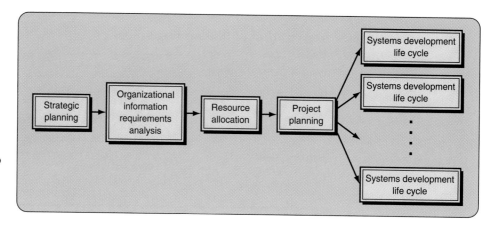

FIGURE 11.3 Relationship of the planning model to the system development life cycle.

model moves from a high level of abstraction to a more concrete formulation of IS planning activities. The expanded methodologies useful for conducting each planning stage are discussed in the following pages.

The four-stage planning model is the foundation for the development of different information systems. Since several systems will usually be under development at one time, there is a relationship between the four-stage planning model and the system development life cycle (SDLC), which is portrayed in Figure 11.3. The system development life cycle pertains to the steps (i.e., analysis, design, development, and implementation) used to construct a specific information system. The SDLC is discussed in detail in Chapters 12 and 13.

▶ 11.6 STRATEGIC IS PLANNING

Strategic planning, the first stage of the IS planning model, must be aligned with overall organizational planning (see McLean & Soden, 1977). To accomplish this, the organization must do the following.

▼ Set the IS mission.

▼ Assess the environment.

▼ Assess organizational objectives and strategies.

▼ Set IS policies, objectives, and strategies.

The output from this process should include the following: a new or revised IS charter and assessment of the state of the IS function; an accurate perception of the strategic aspirations and directions of the organization; and a statement of policies, objectives, and strategies for the IS effort.

The following methodologies are very useful for IS planning. They will each be described in an individual section.

▼ Competitive strategy.

▼ Customer resource life cycle (CRLC).

▼ Future perfect.

▼ Strategy set transformation.

▼ Business systems planning (BSP).

▼ Critical success factors (CSFs).

▼ Stages of IS growth.

▼ Ends/means (E/M) analysis.

COMPETITIVE STRATEGY

Much of the current work on strategic use of information systems has evolved from Michael Porter's work on **competitive strategy** described in detail in Chapter 3. Competitive strategy does not focus specifically on IS strategies; rather, it focuses on general corporate strategy. Many organizations have found, however, that this competitive strategy framework is particularly useful as a means to determine how information systems can contribute to corporate strategy.

Competitive strategy identifies five major competitive forces faced by all organizations.

1. Threat of new competitors.
2. Intensity of rivalry from existing competitors.
3. Pressure from substitute products.
4. Bargaining power of buyers.
5. Bargaining power of suppliers.

Porter proposes that organizations wishing to gain a strategic advantage should consider building defenses against competitive forces by formulating specific courses of action that can directly influence them. Following are three generic approaches that an organization may use to formulate a competitive strategy.

1. *Be a low-cost supplier.* Information systems technology can be very helpful by reducing clerical, scheduling, and inventory costs, and so forth.
2. *Differentiate products or services.* Information systems technology can help by adding features to products or services. For example, a pharmacy may check two different prescriptions from two different doctors for a customer to make sure that no unhealthy combination of drugs has been inadvertently prescribed. The pharmacy can also keep records for customers on all tax-deductible purchases and supply customers with this information for use in preparing tax forms.
3. *Focus on a specialized niche.* Information systems technology can help by identifying specific customers with specific needs. For example, frequent flyer programs allow airlines to identify their most important customers and offer them special packages for travel, hotels, rental cars, and so on.

The main advantages of using IS for strategic advantage are through differentiation and to create product niches. Additionally, cost reduction can be a useful by-product of the innovative use of technology. Based on Porter's work, the following questions can be used to generate strategic ideas for the use of information systems.

▼ Can IS be used to provide a unique product or service? For example, one retailer has a gift suggestion system available to customers. The customer enters into a PC the demographics of the gift recipient such as age, sex, hobbies, and place of residence. The gift giver also indicates an acceptable price range. Based upon market research and store availability, the system gives the customer a list of gift suggestions and their location in the store.

▼ Can IS reduce cycle time? For example, writing a book is significantly faster as a result of word processing and desktop publishing, which eliminate many intermediate clerical and production steps. The apparel industry is another example. In general, $26 billion is lost annually in unsold goods because purchasing agents must buy one year in advance and frequently misjudge customers' tastes. Response to trends is also critical. For example, in 1988, 10 percent of men's suits had pleated trousers. By fall of 1989, the figure had skyrocketed to 90 percent. Additionally, demand for suits with an athletic cut jumped from

5 percent to 30 percent during the same year. Retailers who could not respond quickly to these trends lost out.

▼ Can a more customized product or service be provided? JCPenney responded to trends in men's suits by using information systems to order customized men's suits. Systems linking JCPenney, distributors, garment makers, and textile mills allow customers to select fabric, cut, and size at a JCPenney store and get a custom-made suit in a week. This is an interorganizational system that reduces cycle time and provides customization. The garment manufacturer makes the suits using CAD-CAM systems. This allows the manufacturer to run off an economical order quantity of an hour's worth of suits rather than a month's worth. The distributor can monitor orders regionally and adjust stock to reflect local tastes. For example, a fabric that sells downtown may not sell well in the suburbs. Rather than have one purchasing agent making blanket decisions a year in advance, the process is highly customized.

▼ Can IS be used to open new channels and market niches? ICI, an international manufacturer of fertilizer, uses an expert system to provide direct ordering, thus replacing the normal distribution channel. The normal distribution channel is the feed lot, where the product sits with other competing products that employees sell like commodities. With ICI's expert system, farmers using a PC at home can review last year's planting, examine soil and climate conditions, look at market futures, and order products directly. The system suggests crop rotation strategies and provides a customized fertilization program, adjusting for soil conditions, elevation, and other geographic factors. ICI's highly tailored process provides a strategic advantage and a direct marketing channel to the customer.

▼ Can IS be used to produce higher-quality results? The key here is tracking. Companies need a systematic way of gathering key measurements (such as customer complaints) and keeping a scoreboard on their performance. Procter & Gamble includes a toll-free consumer-affairs number on its products. The company systematically logs, categorizes, and summarizes customer problems, and then solves them.

▼ Can IS be used to fill product position gaps? Bookseller B. Dalton's computer-based inventory system carries twice as many titles as other stores and can let customers know exactly in which store a book is located. B. Dalton, the first book retailer to use computer-based inventorying, is four times as likely to have a title than its competitors because of increased inventory and inventory that is demographically tuned to its geographical area. In book retailing, there are no substitutes. If you are looking for the latest whodunit, you don't want *War and Peace* instead.

▼ Can IS be used to block channel access? Otis Elevator's toll-free maintenance service number and self-diagnosing elevators blocked third-party maintenance organizations from the lucrative elevator maintenance business. With its on-line customer service system, Otis can quickly troubleshoot calls because it has access to an elevator's maintenance history. It can locate and dispatch the appropriate mechanic from virtually anywhere in the country, and it records the mechanic's work for future troubleshooting purposes. Otis subsequently installed telephones on elevators for direct maintenance communications, which further blocked third-party maintenance efforts.

▼ Can IS be used to raise buyer switching costs? American Hospital Supply's ASAP system was the first on-line order entry system provided for hospital supply customers. Their customers soon found it difficult to do business with other suppliers. Switching suppliers meant learning a new system, which was inconvenient. Furthermore, competitors were blocked from offering price advantages. American Hospital Supply had struck deals with suppliers two years earlier, and thus the company had price advantages and product-line breadth unmatched by its competitors. It took competitors years to imitate the technology, but by then it was too late. "Why should I learn a new system when you can only offer me 70 percent of the inventory carried on ASAP?" customers asked. By being first to market with ASAP, American Hospital Supply locked in a captive audience based on convenience and price, which translated into prohibitively high switching costs. The fact that ASAP was so successful was one of the main reasons that Baxter later acquired American Hospital Supply in a corporate takeover.

CUSTOMER RESOURCE LIFE CYCLE

The **customer resource life cycle (CRLC)** is an innovative framework (Ives and Learmonth, 1984) that focuses directly on the relationship with the customer. The idea behind CRLC is that an organization differentiates itself from its competition in the eyes of the customer. Therefore, concentrating on the relationship to the customer is the key to achieving a strategic advantage. CRLC postulates that the customer goes through 13 fundamental stages in its relationship with a supplier and that each stage should be examined to determine if information systems can be used to achieve a strategic advantage. The 13 stages and examples are described next.

1. **Establish customer requirements.** Owens-Corning Fiberglass uses data on energy efficiency to help builders evaluate insulation requirements for new building designs. Evaluations meeting minimum standards of energy efficiency are provided free of charge to builders—provided they agree to purchase their insulation from Owens-Corning.

2. **Specify customer requirements.** A greeting card distributor developed a system for automatic reordering, which frees retailers from involvement in manual reordering. When a particular card is sold out, the retailer returns the reorder ticket at the back of the stack. The system determines the type of card (e.g., father's birthday) and resupplies, not necessarily with the same card but with one specified by the system, usually the best-selling card in the particular category.

3. **Select a source (match customer with supplier).** The customer must locate an appropriate source for the required resource. The ASAP system of American Hospital Supply Company (now Baxter) allows customers to determine immediately if a necessary supply is available.

4. **Place an order.** Distributors such as Baxter, McKesson Pharmaceuticals, General Electric Supply Company, and Arrow Electronics have all established sophisticated round-the-clock order entry systems that accept a customer-entered order without human intervention.

5. **Authorize and pay for goods or services.** Gas stations are using a debit card network that immediately debits customer bank accounts for purchases made with debit cards. The customer is provided with the convenience of a credit card and also receives the same per-gallon discount that a cash purchase would offer. The retailer is spared most of the additional work and inconvenience of credit card sales.

6. **Acquire goods or services.** Automated teller machines not only deliver money to customers, but they also dispense airline and ski-lift tickets and store coupons.

7. **Test and accept goods or services.** Western Union provides a service for matching freight shippers with motor-freight carriers and also checks to ensure that responding carriers have appropriate authority and insurance to qualify for the prospective load.

8. **Integrate into and manage inventory.** General Electric Supply Company assists customers in inventory management by making a commitment to stock, for a specified time, a prearranged quantity of items that are purchased repetitively. The distributor, in effect, keeps inventory for customers.

9. **Monitor use and behavior.** ARA Services distributes magazines to a variety of retail establishments. Unsold magazines are returned to ARA for a refund. Returns are machine processed, which permits ARA to monitor sales information and make appropriate decisions regarding future magazine stock. For instance, they are aware that *Sports Illustrated* will sell six times as many copies of the "swimsuit" edition than other issues.

10. **Upgrade if needed.** Bergen Brunswig monitors product sales data for druggists and uses the data to supports its Space Management product. For a monthly fee, customers are advised on shelf arrangement and potential upgrades related to product choice.

11. **Maintenance.** Sears uses information systems to support its maintenance contracts. The system alerts management when maintenance contracts are about to expire. It also informs management of customers who have not purchased maintenance contracts. Then, Sears is able to offer special package deals to customers who have made multiple appliance purchases but have not purchased maintenance contracts. The program has boosted service revenues and benefited marketing by improving customer service.

12. **Transfer or dispose.** The Washington Hotel in Tokyo is using an automated registration robot to check in guests with no human assistance. Upon checkout, the robot will "eat the key and inform guests of how much is owed for cold drinks and telephone calls."

13. **Accounting for purchases.** American Express Company (AmEx) has combined traditional credit services with the functions of a travel agency. Large corporations can obtain travel services from American Express Travel Related Services, pay with a corporate credit card, and receive reports from AmEx on how travel funds are being spent. Also, many retail pharmacies, as a service to their customers, provide detailed accounting of their customers' drug purchases for income tax purposes. Even a small local pharmacy, with the aid of a personal computer, can offer this competitively attractive service.

FUTURE PERFECT

Future perfect, which is based on Stanley Davis's book of the same title, is a simple but powerful concept. The basic tenet of future-perfect vision is that technology is getting better and better, which means that business processes can get better and better. Taken to its logical conclusion, technology will get perfect. Therefore, companies should develop a business vision of perfection.

What does "perfection" look like? Customers get what they want *anytime*, *anyplace*, and *anyway* they want it. Consider, for example, obtaining cash from a bank. Perfection would be to snap one's fingers at any time, anywhere, and receive the exact amount of desired cash. Customers used to be restricted to banking hours before automatic teller machines (ATMs) came into existence—which, at first, were only available inside banks. There is a tendency to use new technologies in old ways. ATMs have progressed, however, from being *in* banks, to 24-hour ATMs *outside* of banks, to ATMs throughout metropolitan areas, to national and international ATM networks. Each step gets closer to perfection. The idea is that when a new technoogy comes along, one should already know what to do with it: give the customer perfection, within the limitations of the technology.

National Car Rental is another example of the concept of future perfect. The company has a system that allows customers to walk up to a terminal, look at pictures of available cars, select a car, and make a credit card-style transaction.

National Car Rental eliminated the clerical job of assigning cars and, at the same time, enhanced customer service by allowing customers to have the car they want. This concept is discussed further in Box 11.1.

IT At Work BOX 11.1

GREEN MEANS GO: STRATEGIC PLANNING AT NATIONAL CAR RENTAL

National Car Rental has been an innovator in using information technology to become competitive in the car rental business. Research into issues that most concerned customers revealed that customers were tired of long delays, waiting in line, and providing the same information again and again (drivers license, car preferences, features in rental cars, and so on). Customers were also frustrated because cars were assigned to them; they could not select the exact model, color, or features. When customers tried to specify car model or color, it resulted in delays and upset other customers waiting in line.

After conducting a strategic planning exercise using the techniques discussed in this chapter—competitive strategy, customer resource life cycle, and future perfect—National Car Rental came up with an innovation called the Emerald Card. The Emerald Card prequalifies customers for renting cars; customers simply make a reservation, skip the line, and select a car of their choice from the rental lot. When they leave the lot, they use the Emerald Card as documentation to show that they rented a car and are leaving with it. When customers return a car, they again use the Emerald Card to indicate the return and an invoice is generated automatically.

Critical Thinking Issues: How can the Emerald Card help in providing customers' choices? What are the benefits to National? ▲

A music store in Los Angeles keeps sheet music on disk and prints out customized scores in the key requested by the customer. By storing sheet music electronically, the store can have a much greater inventory offering. The next step is to have customers log onto the store's network and access music from home. This service will move the business closer to the concept of perfection and keep the company ahead of customer expectations.

Combining the concept of "perfect" with the customer resource life cycle yields an additional framework based on the matrix shown in Figure 11.4. The matrix offers a way to pinpoint areas where technology can be applied for com-

	ANY TIME	ANY PLACE	ANY WAY
1. Establish customer requirements.			
2. Specify customer requirements.			
3. Select a source.			
4. Place an order.			
5. Authorize and pay for goods and services.			
6. Acquire goods or services.			
7. Test and accept goods or services.			
8. Integrate into and manage inventory.			
9. Monitor use and behavior.			
10. Upgrade if needed.			
11. Maintain.			
12. Transfer or dispose.			
13. Account for purchases.			

FIGURE 11.4 Framework formed by the customer resource life cycle and the concept of future perfect.

petitive advantage. Different areas are addressed at different times on an ongoing basis, thereby forming a continuous improvement process.

Using the matrix, an organization can define specific areas of competitive advantage in each cell of the matrix and assess the organization's performance in each of them. Each cell can be proportionally shaded in, according to its status: 20 percent if just begun, for example, or 100 percent if complete. The objective, over time, is to have every cell completely shaded in.

For example, banks could focus on integrating and monitoring activity at any time. This could mean providing 24-hour access to account balances over the phone. Or a hotel could study how to "select and order" any time. This might mean analyzing reservation and check-in procedures for round-the-clock service. The hotel could install a voice mail system that would handle such requests as directions to the hotel and room reservations. Customers would save time by not being put on hold during peak calling periods. To make a reservation, a customer would enter his credit card number over the phone; the number would trigger the customer's frequent hotel number, credit information, and any discounts. The hotel could also use kiosks and credit cards for check-in. Upon arrival, a customer would insert his credit card into a kiosk, have his billing information linked to his reservation, get his room number and directions to the room, and have the credit card become the room key. At check-out, a customer would insert the credit card into the kiosk, get a final bill, and deactivate the card as a room key. Such a streamlined process would eliminate waiting for reservationists as well as carrying room keys.

This framework, formed by the customer resource life cycle and future perfect, can be used to identify the key competitive areas on which a company should focus.

STRATEGIC PLANNING RETREAT

The best approach to using methodologies such as competitive strategy, customer resource life cycle, and future perfect is to have an annual planning retreat where senior executives and customers brainstorm to arrive at new directions in the application of technology. (Box 11.1 provides an illustration of what happened at National Car Rental as a result of such a retreat.)

STRATEGY SET TRANSFORMATION

One expert, William R. King, proposes an approach to the strategic phase of IS planning that he terms **strategy set transformation**. The overall organizational strategy is viewed as an information set consisting of the mission, objectives, strategies, and other strategic variables (e.g., managerial sophistication, proclivity to accept change, important environmental constraint, and so on). Strategic IS planning is the process of transforming the organizational strategy set into an IS strategy set consisting of IS system objectives, constraints, and design strategies.

BUSINESS SYSTEMS PLANNING (BSP)

Business systems planning or **BSP**, one of the oldest IS planning methodologies, has influenced other planning efforts such as Anderson Consulting's Method 1 and Martin and Finkelstein's Information Engineering. At its core, BSP has two main building blocks: business processes and data classes. **Business processes** are groups of logically related decisions and activities required to manage the resources of the business. Recognition that *processes* (such as filling a customer order) are a more fundamental aspect of business than departments or other organizational arrangements is at the heart of much of the current business process reengineering activity discussed in Chapter 4. Similarly, data classes and the data elements of which they are comprised form the basis of much of the data-driven application development work of the last two decades. A **data class** is a basic item of data which underlies the business, such as an *employee* or an *order*. A **data element** is a more detailed part of a data class, such as an employee's name or social security number. Taken together, they are used to define an *information architecture*. Figure 11.5 shows the steps in the BSP process.

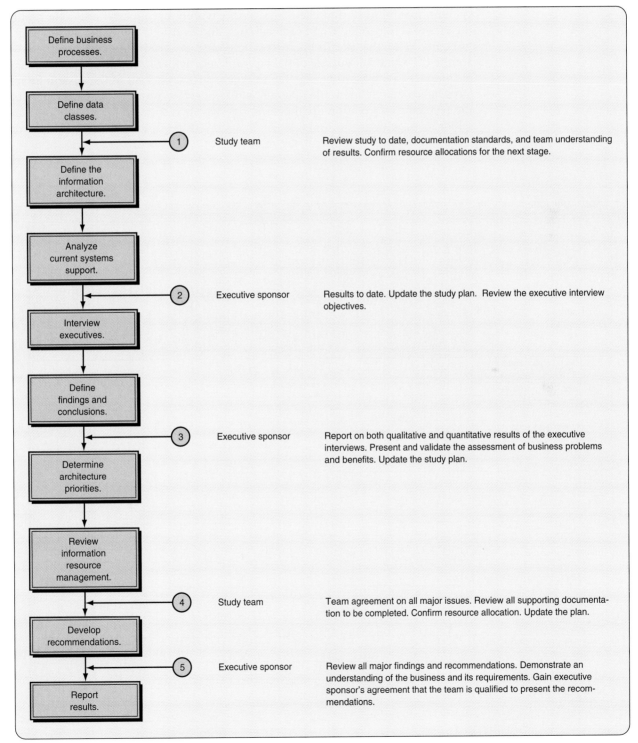

FIGURE 11.5 BSP study control points.

To illustrate how this information architecture is constructed, Figures 11.6a, b, c, and d show the four main stages. In figure 11.6a, certain processes create—"C"—(and use) certain data classes. Other processes use—"U"—data created by other processes. For instance, the business process "Forecasts production requirements" *creates* (and uses) "Product forecasts" data and *uses* "Objectives," "Shipment," and "Customer order" data created by other processes. Similarly, the "Buy finished goods" and "Plan seasonal production" processes use "Product forecast" data created by the "Forecast product requirement" process.

In Figure 11.6b, processes and data are arranged into logical groupings or systems, making sure that each data class is within a group and only one group (i.e., there is only one "C" in each column, and every "C" is within a grouping). In Figure 11.6c, the interfaces among the groups or systems are identified. These are the "U"'s that fall outside of the box and help define how one system is linked or interfaced with another. Finally, in Figure 11.6d, after all of the system interfaces have been defined, the diagram is rearranged to produce a stylized view of the resultant information architecture, one which is suitable for presentation to senior management.

Business processes \ Data classes	Objectives	Policies & procedures	Organization unit desc	Product forecasts	Bldg & real estate reqt	Equipment requirements	Organization unit budget	G/L accounts desc & budget	Long-term debt	Employee requirements	Legal requirements	Competitor	Marketplace	Product description	Raw material description	Vendor description	Buy order	Product warehouse inventory	Shipment	Promotion	Customer description	Customer order	Seasonal production plan	Supplier description	Purchase order	Raw material inventory	Production order	Equipment description	Bldg & real estate desc	Equipment status	Accounts receivable	Product profitability	G/L accounts status	Accounts payable	Employee description	Employee status
Establish business direction	C	C	C								U	U	U																			U	U			
Forecast product requirements	U			C															U			U														
Determine facility & eqt reqts	U		U		C	C	U																					U	U	U						
Determine & control fin reqts	U		U				C	C	C																								U			
Determine personnel reqts		U	U			U	U	U	U	C	U																									U
Comply with legal reqts		U							U		C			U																					U	U
Analyze marketplace	U											C	C								U															
Design product	U										U	U		C	C						U															
Buy finished goods			U											U			C	C																U		
Control product inventory														U			U	C	U								U									
Ship product														U				C				U						U								
Advertise & promote product													U	U					U	C												U				
Market product (wholesale)													U	U	U				U		U	C	U													
Enter & cntrl customer order														U							U	U			U	C					U					
Plan seasonal production			U											U									C				U	U							U	U
Purchase raw materials															U									C	C									U		
Control raw materials inventory															U										U	C	U									
Schedule & control production														U	U								U			U	C	U			U				U	U
Acquire & dispose fac & eqt					U	U																						C	C							
Maintain equipment																											U	U		C						U
Manage facilities																													U							
Manage cash receipts																					U	U									C					
Determine product profitability							U					U	U						U									U	U			C	U		U	U
Manage accounts								U								U									U						U		C	U		U
Manage cash disbursements								U							U	U	U							U	U									C	U	U
Hire & terminate personnel		U	U				U			U	U																								C	U
Manage personnel		U																																	U	C

FIGURE 11.6a Business process/data class matrix.

CRITICAL SUCCESS FACTORS (CSFS)

A framework advocated by J. F. Rockart argues that the information needs for top managers can be derived from **critical success factors (CSFs)**. These are the key activities for any organization in which performance must be satisfactory if the business is to survive and flourish. Critical success factors differ among industries and for individual firms within a particular industry.

As an example, Rockart cites the four industry-based CSFs for supermarkets: (1) have the right product mix available at each store; (2) keep it on the shelves; (3) provide effective advertising to attract shoppers to the store; and (4) develop correct pricing. Because these areas of activity are major determinants of a supermarket chain's success, the status of performance in these areas should be continually measured and reported.

Rockart has identified four primary sources of CSFs.

1. Industry-based factors.
2. Competitive strategy, industry position, and geographical location factors.

Business processes \ Data classes	Objectives	Policies & procedures	Organization unit desc	Product forecasts	Bldg & real estate reqt	Equipment requirements	Organization unit budget	G/L accounts desc & budget	Long-term debt	Employee requirements	Legal requirements	Competitor	Marketplace	Product description	Raw material description	Vendor description	Buy order	Product warehouse inventory	Shipment	Promotion	Customer description	Customer order	Seasonal production plan	Supplier description	Purchase order	Raw material inventory	Production order	Equipment description	Bldg & real estate desc	Equipment status	Accounts receivable	Product profitability	G/L accounts status	Accounts payable	Employee description	Employee status
Establish business direction	C	C	C								U	U	U																			U	U			
Forecast product requirements	U		C																		U		U													
Determine facility & eqt reqts	U		U		C	C	U																					U	U	U						
Determine & control fin reqts	U		U				C	C	C																							U				
Determine personnel reqts		U	U		U	U	U	U		C	U																									U
Comply with legal reqts		U						U				C		U																					U	U
Analyze marketplace	U											C	C								U															
Design product	U										U	U		C	C						U														U	
Buy finished goods			U											U		C	C								U							U				
Control product inventory														U			U	C	U							U										
Ship product																		U	C			U					U									
Advertise & promote product													U	U					U	C															U	
Market product (wholesale)												U	U	U						U	C	U														
Enter & cntrl customer order														U						U	U	U	C								U					
Plan seasonal production		U												U									C				U		U						U	U
Purchase raw materials															U									U	C	C	U								U	
Control raw materials inventory															U										U	C	U									
Schedule & control production														U	U								U		U	C	U								U	U
Acquire & dispose fac & eqt					U	U																						C	C							
Maintain equipment																											U	U		C						U
Manage facilities																													U							
Manage cash receipts																			U	U											C					
Determine product profitability								U						U	U						U						U	U				C	U		U	U
Manage accounts									U							U											U				U	C	U			U
Manage cash disbursements									U							U	U	U						U	U									C	U	U
Hire & terminate personnel		U	U				U			U	U																								C	U
Manage personnel		U																																	U	C

FIGURE 11.6*b* Process groupings.

3. Environmental factors.

4. Temporal factors.

The CSF approach involves a series of interviews conducted in two or three sessions. In the first session, the manager is queried as to her goals and the CSFs that underlie those goals. Considerable discussion may be required to ensure that the analyst thoroughly understands the interrelationships between the goals and CSFs. Every effort is made to combine or eliminate similar CSFs, and an initial set of performance measures is developed. The second session is a review of the first; it primarily focuses on identification of specific performance measures and possible reports. Additional sessions are held as necessary to obtain agreement on the CSF measures and the reports for tracking them. The reports and related information systems required to provide them are then designed by the IS group (Table 11.3).

STAGES OF IS GROWTH

Considerable insight on both the impact of computer-based information systems and the need for improved organization, planning, and control has resulted from research efforts headed by Richard L. Nolan. These research findings indicate that organizations go through six **stages of IS growth**, as portrayed in Figure 11.7.

Business processes \ Data classes	Objectives	Policies & procedures	Organization unit desc	Product forecasts	Bldg & real estate reqt	Equipment requirements	Organization unit budget	G/L accounts desc & budget	Long-term debt	Employee requirements	Legal requirements	Competitor	Marketplace	Product description	Raw material description	Vendor description	Buy order	Product warehouse inventory	Shipment	Promotion	Customer description	Customer order	Seasonal production plan	Supplier description	Purchase order	Raw material inventory	Production order	Equipment description	Bldg & real estate desc	Equipment status	Accounts receivable	Product profitability	G/L accounts status	Accounts payable	Employee description	Employee status
Establish business direction	C	C	C									U	U	U																			U	U		
Forecast product requirements	U		C															U					U													
Determine facility & eqt reqts	U		U		C	C		U																				U	U	U						
Determine & control fin reqts	U		U				C	C	C																								U			
Determine personnel reqts		U	U			U	U	U	U		C	U																							U	U
Comply with legal reqts		U						U			C			U																					U	U
Analyze marketplace	U										C	C						U																		
Design product	U							U	U			C	C															U								
Buy finished goods			U						U			C	C																			U				
Control product inventory								U			C	C						U								U										
Ship product																	U	C				U								U						
Advertise & promote product								U	U				U			C												U								
Market product (wholesale)								U	U	U											U	C	U							U						
Enter & cntrl customer order								U							U	U		U	C							U										
Plan seasonal production			U					U															C					U	U						U	U
Purchase raw materials								U							U	C	C	U							U						U					
Control raw materials inventory								U								U	C	U																		
Schedule & control production								U	U							U	C	U	U									U							U	U
Acquire & dispose fac & eqt					U	U																		C	C											
Maintain equipment																		U						U		C										U
Manage facilities																										U										
Manage cash receipts																				U	U									C						
Determine product profitability								U				U	U					U										U	U		C	U	U	U		
Manage accounts				U												U									U		C	U		U	U					
Manage cash disbursements				U												U	U						U		U								C	U	U	
Hire & terminate personnel		U	U				U			U	U																								C	U
Manage personnel		U																																	U	C

FIGURE 11.6c Interfaces among process groupings.

Table 11.3 Steps in the Critical Success Factor Approach

1. What *objectives* are central to your organization?
2. What *critical success factors* are essential to meeting these objectives?
3. What *decisions* or *actions* are key to these critical success factors?
4. What *variables* underlie these decisions, and how are they measured?
5. What *information systems* can supply these measures?

In each stage, four processes are active, to varying degrees. They are the application portfolio, users' role and awareness, IS resources, and management planning and control techniques.

The *application portfolio* is the mix of computer applications that the IS department has installed or is in the process of developing on behalf of the company. The *user's role and awareness* is the extent to which the user community is actively involved in identifying and promoting IS applications in its areas of responsibility. The *IS resources* are the hardware, software, staff, and management available to provide information services to the company. Lastly, *management planning and con-*

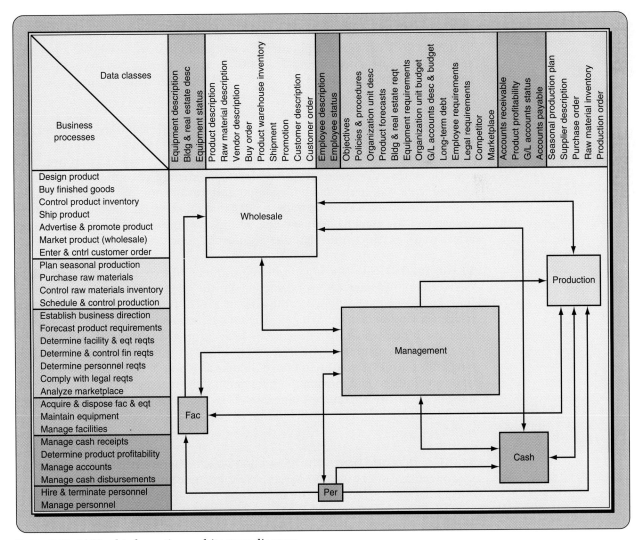

FIGURE 11.6*d* Final information architecture diagram.

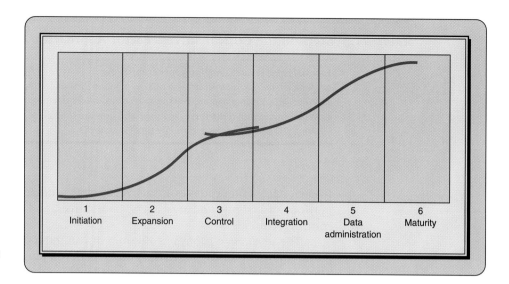

FIGURE 11.7 Nolan's six stages of IS growth.

trol is the various tools and techniques, such as long-term or strategic planning and charge-out schemes, used to manage the IS function. Each of the stages and these processes are discussed in the following section.

STAGE 1: INITIATION. In this stage, the computer is introduced within the organization. Users are encouraged to use the system but, due to unfamiliarity, they do not yet flock to request applications. Applications that are developed are simple and, typically, of an accounting or financial nature. During this stage, the IS organization is often centralized because its members, like the users, must also learn the new technology.

STAGE 2: EXPANSION. Soon, users become enthusiastic about the computer and request the development of all sorts of applications. Computer services are often "free" to them since computing expenses are generally carried as an overhead expense during this stage, and new developments are encouraged. Pressure is exerted by IS staff to expand both computer hardware and computer staff during this stage in order to keep up with the demand for services. The budget in the IS department rises rapidly. Management of the computer department can be characterized as lax, since little planning is done and much control is lacking.

STAGE 3: CONTROL. The organization has entered the control stage when senior management becomes very concerned about the level of benefits being received from computer applications vs. the cost of the IS function. When this occurs, budget expansion is called to a halt. The total IS budget is either held constant, or the growth rate is sharply reduced. The focus is on giving to the department the type of professional management found in other parts of the organization. Planning and control systems are initiated. Emphasis is placed upon documenting existing applications and moving them toward middle management and away from a focus on strictly operational functions. It is also during this stage that charge-out systems are introduced—an attempt to make users accountable for their computer use.

STAGE 4: INTEGRATION. The integration stage is characterized by an attempt to take advantage of new technology, typically database and telecommunications, by integrating existing systems. The IS function is set up to service users much as is a utility. Once this stage is reached, according to Nolan, there is a significant transition point in an organization's computer use.

STAGE 5: DATA ADMINISTRATION. In the data-administration stage, database technology is in place and a data-administration function is created to plan and control the use of the organization's data. But this time, users are effectively accountable for computer-resource use, and the emphasis is placed upon common, integrated systems in which data are shared by means of telecommunications among the various functions in the organization.

STAGE 6: MATURITY. When an organization reaches maturity (and few have), it has truly integrated the computer into its managerial processes. The data resource is meshed with the strategic planning process of the organization. Joint-use and data-processing accountability exist regarding allocation of computing resources within the organization.

ENDS/MEANS (E/M) ANALYSIS

Ends/means (E/M) analysis is a planning technique developed by Wetherbe and Davis. It can be used to determine information requirements at the organizational, departmental, or individual manager level.

Based upon general systems theory, this technique focuses first on the *ends*, or outputs (goods, services, and information), generated by an organizational process. Next, the technique is used to define the *means* (inputs and processes) used to accomplish the ends.

The ends or outputs from one process—whether viewed as an organizational, departmental, or individual process—are the inputs to some other process. For example, the inventory process supplies parts to the production process, the accounting process generates budget information for other organizational processes, and the marketing process offers products to customer processes.

Ends/means analysis is concerned with both the effectiveness and efficiency of generating outputs from processes. *Effectiveness* refers to how well outputs from a process fill the input requirements of other processes. *Efficiency* refers to the resources required and the use of these resources to transform an input into an output.

A model of ends/means analysis is provided in Figure 11.8. As shown in the model, *effectiveness* information is based on (1) what constitutes output effectiveness and (2) what information, or feedback, is needed to evaluate this effectiveness. *Efficiency* information is based on (1) what constitutes input and transformation efficiency and (2) what information, or feedback, is needed to evaluate this efficiency.

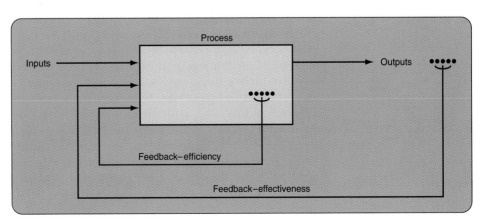

FIGURE 11.8 Model of ends/means analysis.

As an example of information requirements in ends/means analysis, an inventory manager might specify the following.

1. *Ends specification.* The output, or end result, of the inventory management function is an inventory kept as low as possible but at an acceptable level of availability.

2. *Means specification.* The inputs and processes to accomplish the ends are the following:
   ▼ Forecasts of future needs.
   ▼ Amounts on hand and on order.
   ▼ Items that are obsolete or in unusable condition.
   ▼ Stock safety policy.
   ▼ Demand variations.
   ▼ Cost of ordering and holding inventory.
   ▼ Cost of items.
   ▼ Stock-outs.

3. *Efficiency measures* needed for inventory management are the following:
   ▼ Number and cost of orders placed.
   ▼ Cost of holding inventory.
   ▼ Loss from disposal of obsolete or unusable inventory.

4. *Effectiveness measures* needed for inventory management are the following:
   ▼ Number of stock-outs.
   ▼ Seriousness of stock-outs.

Ends/means analysis has been used in diverse industrial settings with positive results. Information requirements determined by this means are usually more extensive than those generated using other techniques. The problem with most information planning tools is that they usually result in information systems that provide only efficiency-oriented information. However, managers agree that it is more important to be effective than to be efficient. Ends/mean analysis brings out effectiveness information requirements. Such requirements typically transcend departmental boundaries, and, therefore, ends/means analysis is especially useful for a database planning effort.

▶ 11.7 ORGANIZATIONAL INFORMATION REQUIREMENTS ANALYSIS

The second stage of the model for information systems planning, **organizational information requirements analysis (OIRA)**, is to ensure that various information systems and databases can be integrated to support decision making and operations. Such integration requires an information architecture to be in place.

The first phase of OIRA consists of assessing current and projected information needs to support decision making and operations of the organization. Do not confuse this effort with the detailed information requirements analysis associated with specifications for application systems (e.g., report and terminal display layouts), which will be discussed in Chapter 12. Rather, OIRA is a higher level of information requirements analysis, aimed at developing an overall information architecture for the organization or a major sector of the corporation.

The second phase of OIRA consists of assembling a master development plan. This plan is derived from the information architecture and defines specific information system projects, the ranking of projects, and a development schedule.

One of the main objectives of an OIRA is to avoid the fragmented, nonintegrated systems described in Chapter 4. Recall the banking example, where a customer with multiple accounts is viewed as multiple customers.

BUILDING AN OIRA

Figure 11.9 presents a five-step model for developing an information architecture. To make the process concrete, the results of a case study are used to illustrate information generated from an OIRA. This case study is based on a real-estate leasing firm that leases single-family dwellings throughout the United States.

STEP 1: DEFINE UNDERLYING ORGANIZATIONAL SUBSYSTEMS. The first step of an OIRA is to define underlying organizational processes. An organizational process is the fundamental organizational activity necessary for the operation of the organization. For the real estate leasing company, these are the major processes.

▼ Leasing.

▼ Maintenance.

▼ Accounts receivable.

▼ Credit.

▼ Evictions/delinquencies.

▼ Inspection.

▼ Inventory.

▼ Marketing.

▼ Advertising.

▼ Insurance

▼ Sales.

▼ Audit.

▼ Appraisal.

▼ Personnel administration.

▼ Legal.

▼ Market and product analysis.

▼ Corporate accounting.

▼ Client reporting.

These processes were obtained by an iterative process by discussing all organizational activities and arranging them into broad categories of processes. As new activities are considered, they should be placed either in previously defined or in newly created categories.

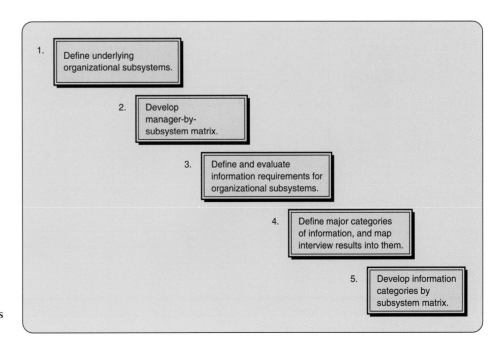

1. Define underlying organizational subsystems.

2. Develop manager-by-subsystem matrix.

3. Define and evaluate information requirements for organizational subsystems.

4. Define major categories of information, and map interview results into them.

5. Develop information categories by subsystem matrix.

FIGURE 11.9 Planning model for organizational information requirements analysis.

STEP 2: DEVELOP SUBSYSTEM MATRIX. Once the underlying organizational processes are defined, the next phase of the OIRA planning exercise is to relate specific managers to organizational processes. The resulting document, called a *manager by process*, is illustrated in Figure 11.10. Note that the processes in the left column of the matrix are the same as those identified in Step 1.

The matrix is developed by reviewing the major decision responsibilities of each middle to top manager and relating them to specific processes. The matrix indicates the managers who have major decision-making responsibility for each specific process. Note that personnel changes or organizational changes can easily be reflected in an adjusted matrix.

STEP 3: DEFINE AND EVALUATE INFORMATION REQUIREMENTS FOR ORGANIZATIONAL SUBSYSTEMS. In this phase of the planning model, managers with major decision-making responsibility for each process are interviewed in groups in order to obtain the information requirements of each organizational process. Interview methods are described in Chapter 12. The interviews used for OIRA and systems design can be business systems planning, critical success factors, and/or ends/means analysis.

STEP 4: DEFINE MAJOR INFORMATION CATEGORIES AND MAP INTERVIEWS INTO THEM. The process of categorizing information categories is done in the same way that the data dictionary for an information system was factored into entities and attributes (see Chapter 8). The difference is that the task is much larger when you are doing an organization-wide entity-attribute analysis. By placing the information categories (defined from organizational process interviews) into broad, generic categories of information, an overall profile of necessary information categories can be developed. Broad categories of information that can be identified as entities (i.e., customers, contracts, vendors) and attributes (i.e., names, addresses, phone numbers) are categorized within their respective entities.

Organizational processes	Managers				
	Manager 1	Manager 2	Manager 3	Manager 4	Manager n
Leasing					
Maintenance					
Accounts receivable	X				
Credit	X	X			
Evictions/delinquencies		X		X	
Inspection				X	
Inventory					
Marketing			X		
Advertising					
Insurance					
Sales					
Audit					X
Appraisal			X		
Personnel/administration					X
Legal					X
Market and product analysis			X		
Corporate accounting					X
Client reporting			X		

FIGURE 11.10 Manager-by-process matrix.

STEP 5: DEVELOP INFORMATION/SUBSYSTEM MATRIX. By mapping information categories against organizational subsystems, an information-categories-by-organizational-process matrix can be developed. Figure 11.11 illustrates such a matrix for the real-estate leasing firm.

Note that at the intersections of information categories and organizational processes there are coded values defined in the following manner. During the interview, managers are asked about both the *importance* and the current *availability* of different types of information. Responses for both importance and availability are recorded as high, medium, or low.

	LOW	MEDIUM	HIGH
Importance	1	2	3
Availability	3	2	1

A score is computed for each category of information, according to the following formula:

$$\text{Score} = \text{Importance} \times \text{Availability}$$

Note that the reversed scaling of responses results in information categories with the highest importance and lowest availability getting the highest score (e.g., $S = 3 \times 3 = 9$). Conversely, information that is least important and readily available gets the lowest score (e.g., $S = 1 \times 1 = 1$).

This scoring procedure gives a good indication of the value of a category of information to a single business subsystem. The composite score can be a rough indicator of the value provided by any organization subsystem that intersects with the information category.

Organizational processes	Contract	Policy training	Customer financial	Customer demographics	Complaint	Leasing/ transactions	Vendor	A/P	A/R	Maintenance	Warranty	Inventory
Leasing	9	9	6	6	4	4				9		9
Maintenance	9	9			9		9	2	1	9	2	4
Accounts receivable	9	6	3	4	4	9	4	1	3	9		2
Credit	9	9	9	4		6				3		
Evictions/delinquencies	9	9	9	6	6		9	2	3			9
Inspection	4	9			9		6			9	2	6
Inventory	6		9	9	6		6		4	9	3	6
Marketing	9	9										9
Advertising	2		9	9			9	6				4
Insurance	9	9			4		2		3	9	3	
Sales	9	9	9	9	9		3	1	4	9	2	3
Audit	6	9	4		9	4	2	6	9	9	2	
Appraisal	9	9			2		6	6		4		
Personnel/administration		9			2			9				
Legal	9	4			6	2	6	2	6	1		1
Market and product analysis	9	4	6	9	9					4		6
Corporate accounting	9	4			6	3	6	3	6	4	2	9
Client reporting	9	4			9	2			3	4	9	
Total score	135	121	64	56	94	30	68	41	46	94	16	68

FIGURE 11.11 Information categories by organizational processes matrix.

USE OF THE OIRA PLANNING RESULTS

The results of the OIRA exercise are twofold. It identifies high-payoff information categories and provides an architecture for information projects.

IDENTIFYING HIGH PAYOFFS. By evaluating composite scores for information categories, you can select those categories with the highest scores to consider first in feasibility studies. Note that the information-categories-by-organizational process matrix does not tell if it is technically, economically, or operationally feasible to improve an information category. The matrix merely indicates relative values of information. Feasibility studies and project definitions must still be performed, as described in Chapter 12.

PROVIDING ARCHITECTURE. By clearly defining the intersection of information and subsystems, an organization will not build separate, redundant information systems for different organizational processes, as occurred in the banking example described in Chapter 4. When an organization decides to improve information for one organizational process, other processes that need such information can be taken into consideration. This avoids building separate information systems for each subsystem, which often requires reworking or duplicating what has already been done. By completing the conceptual work first, an organization can identify information system projects that will offer the most benefit and lead to cohesive, integrated systems. The resulting systems will be far better than the fragmented, piecemeal systems that are continually being reworked or abandoned because they do not mesh with the organization's general requirements. This requires planning from the top down rather than randomly from the bottom up.

Think about how an architecture such as that portrayed in Figure 11.11 could have kept the bank (discussed in Chapter 4) from developing nonintegrated systems. For example, when the bank developed a savings account system, it would have been obvious that checking, installment loans, and mortgage-loan decision makers needed access to savings account information.

Perhaps the best way to illustrate the value of organizational information architecture for IS is by quoting the president of the real-estate leasing firm one year after he personally led the development of the firm's information architecture.

> I had worked in top management in one of our other subsidiaries and experienced the disappointment that comes from developing systems in the traditional FIFO [first in, first out], piecemeal way with the consequences of redundant, nonintegrated, and inaccessible information.
>
> When I took over the new subsidiary, I decided there must be a better way. There was. By developing an information architecture before developing systems, we have been able to pull all our systems together. Our short-run system decisions are dovetailing into our long-range systems. We know where we are going and [we are] getting there.
>
> Beyond that, just the process of going through an organizational information requirements analysis gave me and my management invaluable insight into our business.

▶ 11.8 RESOURCE ALLOCATION

Resource allocation, the third stage of the model for information systems planning, consists of developing the hardware, software, data communications, facilities, personnel, and financial plans needed to execute the master development plan defined in the OIRA. This stage provides the framework for technology procurement, personnel planning, and budgeting to provide appropriate service levels to users.

RETURN ON INVESTMENT (ROI)

Return on investment (ROI) is a cost-benefit analysis technique widely used in a variety of planning applications. Variations of ROI include internal rates of return and net present values on discounted cash flows. Typically, projects are ranked in descending order by ROI, and the highest-ranked projects that provide an acceptable rate of return are selected. For example, a project offering an ROI of 15 percent would be ranked over a project offering 10 percent. Considerations other than ROI—such as resource constraints, organizational priorities, or politics—may alter the selection process.

Many corporations apply ROI analysis to information systems projects in an attempt to make them pass the same criteria as other organizational undertakings. To the extent that costs and benefits are quantifiable, ROI is a useful planning tool. Unfortunately, information systems projects often do not lend themselves to easy quantification and estimation of costs and benefits. The costs and benefits of such projects are variable, complex, interrelated, and difficult to estimate, and thus they often preclude a meaningful ROI analysis.

CHARGE-OUT

Some form of **charge-out** system is frequently used as a basis for planning and controlling information systems. In large corporations, the IS function is often organized as a service bureau or utility, charged with providing information services to all organizational subunits. Fee schedules are developed for each unit of service (e.g., processing time, data storage, data transmission, and so on) with the objective of recovering (or partially recovering) IS expenditures. Users are charged for the information services rendered for their subunits. In theory, holding users responsible for the cost of their information systems fosters greater planning and control of those systems.

Charge-out-based planning systems are typical of the traditional approach to IS planning which was discussed in the beginning of the chapter. In addition to a charge-out system, the traditional approach usually includes guidelines, procedures, and schedules to specifically direct planning efforts. The focus, however, is frequently on justifying costs relative to the benefits of proposed information systems. Planning and decision making are decentralized to the user department. This decentralization tends to limit the search for beneficial new information systems, especially with integrated systems affecting multiple departments and applications areas with intangible benefits. A number of other problems are associated with charge-out-based planning, including high expense (in terms of both administration and computer-processing overhead), complexity, and market imperfections.

The nature of charge-out-based planning systems varies among organizations. However, without specific procedures to the contrary, there are no systematic mechanisms that link information system planning based on charge-out to broader organizational strategy and objectives. This may result in strictly bottom-up development of information systems with short-range time horizons.

▶ 11.9 JUSTIFYING IT INVESTMENTS

Much has been written about measuring the value of information technology—positively and negatively. Some laud IT for transforming business practice, making goods and services possible that would otherwise be unfeasible. However, others charge that organizations are not enjoying productivity gains commensurate with the investments being made in technology. Since many of the latter charges originate from upper management, it should come as no surprise that these managers are requiring information technology investments to pass more rigorous justifications. Unfortunately, it has long been a struggle for IS organizations to come up with concrete financial justifications for information technology.

Acquiring information technology requires significant resources in terms of time, personnel, and money—money for hardware and software acquisition, application development, training, and follow-up maintenance. At the same time, adoption of information technology offers two major benefits: increased efficiency and increased effectiveness. In justifying the acquisition of information technology, the task is to try to predict what costs will be incurred, quantify them, and match them with the predicted benefits (quantified, of course). At this point, the decision is very simple. If quantified benefits outweigh quantified costs, the acquisition of information technology is justified. If faced with multiple information technology alternatives, one should choose the alternative with the largest benefit-to-cost "delta." And, of course, if the costs outweigh the benefits, information technology acquisition is not justified.

This section outlines five perspectives, each with a different view on the justification challenge.

1. The cost-benefit perspective.
2. The management accounting perspective.
3. The financial analysis perspective.
4. The information economics perspective.
5. The business orientation perspective.

THE COST-BENEFIT PERSPECTIVE

This is the simplest approach to cost justification, with five basic variations.

1. Direct output model. Hard, identifiable dollar costs are compared with hard, identifiable dollar benefits. Although simple and widely used, this model excludes all intangible costs or benefits. It may cause many attractive IT investments to be excluded from consideration.

2. Inferred output model. Where hard figures are difficult to obtain, ranges of predicted costs and benefits are quantified through a group-consensus-building process; then analysis proceeds in the same manner as the direct output model. What this model lacks in simplicity, it makes up for in increased comprehensiveness.

3. Direct input model. It focuses on the costs (inputs) incurred by the organization and ignores the outputs when they are hard to quantify. Outputs are held constant, and the inputs required to produce the outputs are reduced due to the presence of information technology.

4. Inferred input model. This is similar to the direct input model except the inputs (costs) required to perform activities are estimated first *without* information technology, and then the inputs required to do the same activities *with* information technology are predicted or inferred. It can be overly subjective, and people can be poor estimators when predicting costs.

5. Bayesian theory. This model is based on the assumption that the probability of making good decisions can be determined by past success or failure. If it is assumed that IT will allow an organization to make better decisions, the probability of making good decisions should increase. By comparing "before" and "after" decision making, coupled with the respective quantified costs and benefits, the organization should, in theory, be able to place a dollar cost or benefit on the use of information technology.

THE MANAGEMENT ACCOUNTING PERSPECTIVE

Management accounting techniques include *transfer pricing* (i.e., charge back) and *budget variance analysis* with an underlying focus on cost control. The charge-back system serves as the foundation for these techniques, providing a vehicle to charge user departments for the information technology resources they use.

However, there are many problems with these techniques. The first problem is that accounting techniques are focused primarily on tangible costs related to the information technology investment; intangible costs such as downtime are not typically considered. Also, with the rise of departmental systems based on LAN technologies, it is becoming increasingly difficult to identify specific user costs. Similarly, the intangible benefits from IT investments escape this analysis.

Another problem relates to how IT investments are valued and accounted for—book value or as expenses? Also, the underlying purpose of charge-back systems can be called into question; is it to allocate IS costs to the true users, or is it to alter the behavior of users and make them more accountable for their resource usage?

Finally, it should be asked how many resources and how much time are consumed in providing and managing the charge-back function. Maintaining and managing charge backs may not be worth the time and expense necessary to produce the charges.

THE FINANCIAL ANALYSIS PERSPECTIVE

This perspective is a return-based analysis—return on assets, equity, or investment (ROA, ROE, or ROI) as discussed earlier. These are concepts that upper management readily understands, but they are also not without their problems.

Similar to management accounting techniques, the manner in which information technology investments are accounted for has a profound effect on the outcome of return-based analysis techniques; and intangible costs and benefits are often excluded in the ROA, ROE, and ROI analyses. In essence, ROA, ROE, and ROI are primarily backward-looking techniques; they perform well when analyzing historic costs and benefits. In order to get a feel for the benefits that can be derived from the *next* dollar invested in information technology, creative assumptions may be more appropriate.

THE INFORMATION ECONOMICS PERSPECTIVE

This approach is based on economic theory and principles. One theoretical model is called the enterprise-wide information management (EWIM) model (Parker and Benson, 1989), designed to help IS managers focus on organizational goals.

This model uses a continuum of potential applications for information technology within an organization as well as the justification techniques that might be applied with each type of application (Figure 11.12). At one end of the contin-

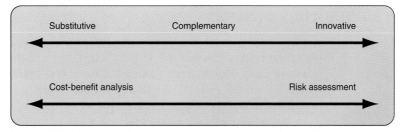

FIGURE 11.12 Enterprisewide information economic continuum.
(SOURCE: Adapted from Parker and Benson, 1989)

uum, information technology can take the form of substitutive applications whereby technology is used as a substitute for human resources. Since the primary benefit in this area is cost avoidance, and most costs as well as benefits can be easily quantified, traditional cost-benefit analyses are recommended. In the middle of the continuum, information technology can take the form of complementary applications. Here, technology complements employees by improving their productivity. Since the benefits here are beginning to get more intangible and difficult to measure, Parker and Benson recommend two approaches. First, much like the inferred input model mentioned earlier, they suggest trying to evaluate the value of the particular job functions that will benefit from the technology. Second, they suggest considering how the realized benefits will be accomplished within the organization and then quantifying the time value of these benefits accordingly. At the other end of the information technology continuum, information technology takes the form of innovative applications. Here, technology is used to maintain or develop a competitive edge. Since the benefits here are highly intangible and speculative, Parker and Benson recommend justifying these investments with risk assessment techniques—evaluating the potential risks or rewards of undertaking the information technology initiative and assigning probabilities to them.

Much of the theory and analyses behind information economics provide descriptive and/or explanatory power. Unfortunately, little—if any—of the economic theory applied to information technology investments is such that it provides much in the way of predictive power. As a result, it has achieved little actual use in practice.

THE BUSINESS ORIENTATION PERSPECTIVE

The business orientation perspective centers around the idea of measuring IS inputs (tools, people, training, and so on) and connecting them to business outputs (customer satisfaction, improved quality, and so on). The key difference lies in the methodology employed to make these connections. Business orientation measures the "yield" of information technology investments as a function of the delivered value versus the expected value—taking into account the level of customer satisfaction. Since delivered value can only be measured after the fact, the yield measure or index is primarily retrospective in nature.

Like the information economics perspective, the business orientation perspective is attractive in that it focuses on the broader benefits related to an organization's strategy. However, it has two primary weaknesses. First, the framework or indexes do not really help in addressing future investment decisions. Second, the dimensions of the indexes are not intuitively obvious or stated in general business terms. As a result, they would be difficult to operationalize and would ultimately not provide much explanatory power to upper management.

THE CHANGING NATURE OF INFORMATION TECHNOLOGY BENEFITS

In the early days of information technology, information systems typically provided more *efficient* solutions. Usually, the system automated a manual process. As a result, head counts were reduced. These "cost takeout" benefits were typically narrow in scope—that is, it was clear where to look for them. In addition, measuring the amount of those benefits was usually straightforward.

More recently, the potential benefits of information technology are enhanced *effectiveness.* They are becoming increasingly intangible with little, if any, direct bottom-line impact on costs. As a result, benefits are not only more difficult to identify, they are also difficult to quantify. Furthermore, process-related benefits can be realized anywhere throughout the process—not just in the area of information technology intervention. Moreover, efficiency-related benefits are also synergistic in nature. That is, a significant benefit, derived from one information technology initiative, may couple with an insignificant benefit from another information technology initiative, to produce a benefit with a level of significance that is much more than the sum of its less-insignificant parts.

Another characteristic of many of today's information technology benefits is that it enables an organization to realize additional benefits. These *enabling benefits* may allow the organization to lever future technologies and be more responsive to demands of the marketplace as well as to competitive threats. When taken into account, these benefits alone may provide adequate justification.

The result of this evolution in the nature of benefits is that organizations must be more creative and spend more time looking for hidden benefits. In particular, organizations need to investigate the hidden effects of information technology on worker productivity, looking not only for the obvious productivity boosts, but also for second-order gains which follow from first-order gains. For process-related benefits, firms need to examine the entire process for evidence of information technology's benefits. Finally, companies should consider the synergistic and enabling benefits of information technology—potential interactions of these benefits with other benefits in existing or future information technology platforms.

▶ 11.10 PROJECT PLANNING

The fourth and final stage of the model for information systems planning, **project planning**, provides an overall framework with which the system development life cycle can be planned, scheduled, and controlled. The fundamental tools of project management include milestones; critical path method (CPM), also known as program evaluation and review technique (PERT); and Gantt charts.

MILESTONES

Milestone planning techniques allow projects to evolve as they are developed. Rather than try to predict all project requirements and problems in advance, management allows the project to progress at its own pace. **Milestones**, or checkpoints, are established to allow periodic review of progress so that management can determine if a project merits further commitment of resources, if it requires adjustments, or if it should be discontinued.

Milestones can be based on time, budget, or deliverables. For example, a project's progress might be evaluated weekly, monthly, or quarterly (i.e., time). It might be evaluated after a certain amount of resources are used, such as $50,000 (i.e., budget). However, milestones are most effective when they identify that certain deliverables are completed or events occur, such as the completion of the preliminary study. Figure 11.13 illustrates the simplicity of a milestone chart. Remember, each milestone can be based on time, budget, and/or deliverables.

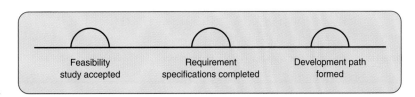

FIGURE 11.13 Milestones.

CRITICAL PATH METHOD (CPM)

A commonly used planning technique is **CPM (critical path method)**. A CPM diagram represents the network of tasks required to complete a project (hence, it is sometimes referred to as a *network chart*). It explicitly establishes sequential de-

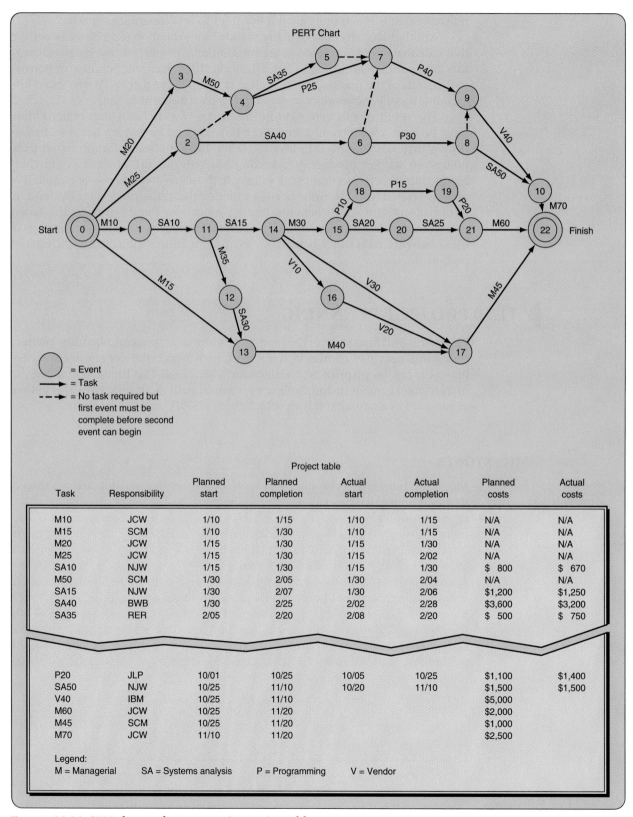

FIGURE 11.14 CPM chart and accompanying project table.

pendencies and relationships among the tasks. A CPM diagram consists of both *activities* and *events*. Activities are defined as time- and resource-consuming efforts required to complete a segment of the total project. Events are the completion of segments, or parts of segments, of the project. Activities are represented by solid lines with directional arrows; events are represented by circles. Dotted lines represent sequential dependencies where they exist, but where no task has to be performed to progress from the first event to the second one. Activities and events are coded or described to designate their functions in the overall project.

Figure 11.14 shows a CPM chart and an accompanying project table that defines the responsible personnel, planned times and costs, as well as the actual times and costs, so management can monitor and control project performance.

A final advantage of CPM is that total time required to complete the project can be determined by locating the longest path (in terms of time) in the chart. This path is referred to as the *critical path*. For scheduling purposes, any delay of tasks in the critical path results in an corresponding delay on the overall project.

GANTT CHART

The **Gantt chart** is a planning technique that, like CPM, provides definitions of tasks to be performed and specifies when they are to start and finish (Figure 11.15). A Gantt chart does not show sequential dependencies, as a CPM chart does. For example, in Figure 11.15, the chart does not show that analysis must be completed before design can begin. Consequently, a Gantt chart does not have as much information as a CPM chart, but it is much easier to prepare.

A particularly good feature of Gantt charts is that a macro-Gantt chart can be factored into one or more levels of micro-Gantt charts. For example, in Figure 11.15, the line labeled "Analysis" could be made into a separate Gantt chart consisting of the subtasks that constitute analysis (e.g., feasibility study, interviews, process modeling). Such microcharts provide more detail, allow for specific assignment of responsibility, and facilitate better estimation of time requirements.

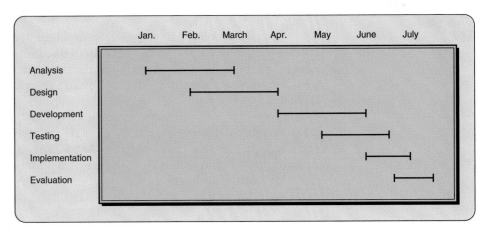

FIGURE 11.15 Gantt chart.

PROJECT PRIORITIES AND PROPERTIES

Setting budget and time frames prior to defining the system constrains design is perhaps the greatest mistake made in project planning. For example, management may decide to install a new order entry system in nine months and is willing to spend $1 million. This leaves one important issue undefined—what will the new system do? By default, management has constrained the limits of the new system.

The proper sequence for managing a project is *first* to get a good functional definition of what the system is to do, and then have people with experience and expertise in information systems project management develop a budget and schedule. If management cannot accept the schedule or budget, then reductions in capability of the new system can be made to improve the schedule and/or budget.

In developing a budget, schedule, and specifications for a system, several properties of projects and their management should be understood and considered. These five project properties most significantly influence the overall nature of a project.

1. **Predefined structure.** The more predefined structure a project has, the more easily it can be planned and controlled. For example, transaction-processing applications inherently have a great deal of predefined structure. Their structure reduces the difficulty of designing computer applications to process them. Conversely, decision-support systems (e.g., a market-forecast system) are not usually well structured. They require considerable definition and structuring before they can be computerized.

2. **Stability of technology.** The greater the experience with a given technology to be used for a new system, the more predictable the systems development process is. On the other hand, when a new information system is to use new and unproven hardware and/or software, many unforeseen problems may arise that will impede the development process.

3. **Size.** There is an inverse relationship between project size in terms of years and costs, and the ability to plan accurately the number of years and the costs that will be required to complete the project. In other words, the larger the project, the more difficult it is to estimate the resources required to complete it.

4. **User proficiency.** The more knowledgeable and experienced users and managers are in their functional areas and in developing systems, the higher their "user proficiency" will be and the easier it will be to develop a system for them. Lack of knowledge and experience among users results in greater difficulty in developing systems.

5. **Developer proficiency.** The more knowledge and experience the systems analyst assigned to a project has, the easier the project will go, and vice versa.

Any given project can possess any variation of each of the preceding properties. For example, a project can have predefined structure but use unstable technology, or it can be a massive undertaking and have low user and developer proficiencies (e.g., most initial on-line airline reservations systems could be described in this fashion).

The properties of a very straightforward project are the following: (1) predetermined structure, (2) use of stable technology, (3) small project size, and (4) high user and developer proficiency. The more any of these properties deviates in the opposite direction, the less straightforward the project, and therefore, the more difficult it will be to plan.

PROJECT PROPERTIES AND TECHNIQUES

The techniques for managing information systems, discussed earlier in this chapter, can be categorized as informal (milestone), formal (CPM), and in-between (Gantt). The technique appropriate for a given project is contingent upon the properties or characteristics of the project. Informal project management techniques are appropriate for projects that are neither straightforward nor predictable. Formal techniques are better suited for projects that are relatively straightforward and predictable.

Inappropriate application of formal or informal project management techniques can have unfortunate consequences, including project failure. The use of informal techniques for a straightforward project needlessly forgoes planning definition and control. For example, CPM and Gantt planning techniques provide structure for time and cost estimates. To forgo such planning is unfair to the organization and to the systems developers, whose performance cannot be evaluated as accurately as is possible when more formal techniques are used.

The use of formal techniques for projects that are not straightforward and predictable generally puts dysfunctional constraints on what should be a relatively innovative and creative process. Systems developers are often forced to cut corners and stifle innovative processes in order to keep the project on schedule and within budget. When approaching new areas of systems development, there must be sufficient slack allowed to nurture innovation.

Techniques used for projects can be combinations of formal and informal techniques. For example, if the specific project tasks and their sequential dependencies are known, but it is not known how long they will take or how much they will cost, a CPM chart can be constructed without time and cost estimates. Such an approach provides more definition than a milestone approach, without unduly constraining project time or producing cost estimates that may be unrealistic. Figure 11.16 illustrates the relationship between project characteristics and the selection of project planning techniques.

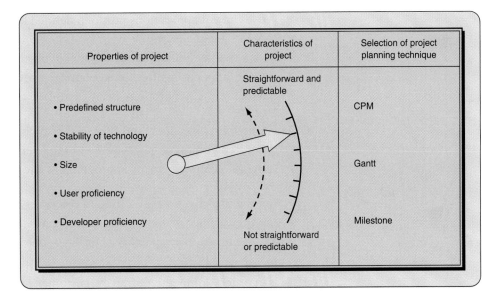

FIGURE 11.16 Effect of properties of project on selection of project planning technique.

▶ 11.11 GUIDELINES FOR IS PLANNING

At the beginning of this chapter, the major problems of information systems planning were identified. These problems are addressed directly by the four-stage planning model. Within the framework of the model, a set of appropriate methodologies is applied to each stage.

Look to the model for practical guidance in IS planning. The model can help you recognize the nature of planning problems in a specific project as well as select the appropriate stage of planning. Too often, this is not done. For example, some organizations view their IS function as making minimal contributions to strategic organizational objectives. In seeking to resolve this problem, some organizations have installed a charge-out system (resource allocation planning) to make IS pay its own way. Other organizations have conducted an OIRA planning exercise to resolve the same problem. Although these activities may result in improved IS services, the IS planning model suggests they are probably not the appropriate methodologies for the given situation. If the IS is not responsive to the organization, the four-stage IS planning model indicates that a *strategic-oriented planning effort* should precede OIRA and resource allocation planning exercises.

To determine the IS planning needed, an organization should assess the extent to which each stage of IS planning has been accomplished. This assessment can be performed by analyzing major activities and outputs according to the four-stage planning model depicted in Figure 11.3. After the IS planning needs at each stage have been determined, appropriate methodologies can be selected.

STAGE ASSESSMENTS

STRATEGIC PLANNING. Each of the four stages of the IS planning model suggest specific questions. In assessing the strategic planning stage, the following questions should be asked.

1. Is there an IS mission clearly expressed in an IS charter?
2. Is there a comprehensive assessment of the environment?
   - ▼ Are IS capabilities adequately assessed?
   - ▼ Are new opportunities identified?
   - ▼ Is the current business environment understood?
   - ▼ Is the current applications portfolio defined and documented?
   - ▼ Is the IS image healthy?
3. Is there a clear definition of organizational objectives and strategies?
   - ▼ Has the strategic organizational plan been reviewed?
   - ▼ Have strategic applications been identified to improve strategic advantage?
4. Are IS policies, objectives, and strategies established?
   - ▼ Is the IS organization appropriate to the overall organization?
   - ▼ Is the IS technology focus appropriate to the technology focus of the organization?
   - ▼ Are the objectives for allocating IS resources appropriate?
   - ▼ Are the IS management processes appropriate?
   - ▼ Are the functional capability objectives appropriate?

If answers to these questions indicate a weakness at this stage, a strategic planning exercise is in order. Competitive strategy, customer resource life cycle, and future perfect offer formal methodologies for conducting such an exercise.

ORGANIZATIONAL INFORMATION REQUIREMENTS ANALYSIS. To conduct an assessment of the OIRA stage, an organization should ask the following questions.

1. Is there an adequate assessment of organizational information requirements?
   - ▼ Is the overall organizational information architecture identified?
   - ▼ Is there a good understanding of current information needs of the organization?
   - ▼ Is there a good understanding of projected information needs of the organization?
   - ▼ Are the major databases and their relationships defined?
2. Is there a master IS development plan?
   - ▼ Are IS projects defined?
   - ▼ Are projects ranked by priority?
   - ▼ Is there a multiyear development schedule?

If an organization does not have acceptable answers to these questions, an OIRA planning exercise is in order.

RESOURCE ALLOCATION. To assess the resource allocation stage, an organization should ask the following questions.

1. Does the organization have a resource requirements plan?
- ▼ Are trends identified?
- ▼ Is there a hardware plan?
- ▼ Is there a software plan?
- ▼ Is there a data management plan?
- ▼ Is there a data communications plan?
- ▼ Is there a personnel plan?
- ▼ Is there a facilities plan?
- ▼ Is there a financial plan?

2. Does the organization have an adequate procedure for resource allocation?

If an organization does not have acceptable answers to these questions concerning the resource allocation stage, a resource allocation planning exercise is in order. Formal planning methodologies available to conduct such an exercise are charge-out and investment analysis.

PROJECT PLANNING. To assess the status of project planning, an organization should ask the following questions.

1. Is there a procedure for evaluating projects in terms of difficulty or risk?
2. Are project tasks usually identified adequately?
3. Are project cost estimates generally accurate?
4. Are project time estimates generally accurate?
5. Are checkpoints defined to monitor progress of projects?
6. Are projects generally completed on schedule?

If an organization does not get satisfactory answers to the project planning questions, a review of project planning techniques is in order. Techniques available to improve project planning include CPM, Gantt charts, and milestones.

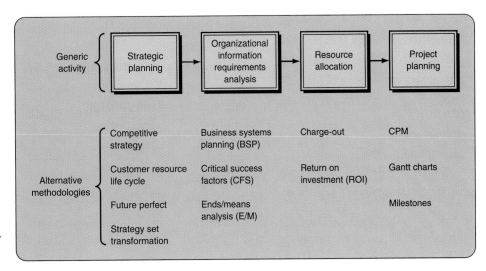

FIGURE 11.17 Alternative IS planning methodologies classified by stage of the IS process.

SELECTING A METHODOLOGY

Revisiting the model (Figure 11.17), each of the methodologies that have been discussed are associated with a particular stage in the planning process. The four-stage planning model provides considerable insight into IS planning issues. Following the model reduces confusion about competing planning methodologies. For example, an organization that follows the planning model can avoid using a resource allocation methodology when an OIRA or strategic methodology is more appropriate. Keep in mind, however, that the planning model does not indicate which of several methodologies categorized within a planning stage should be used for any particular planning stage. Most organizations find using the methodologies in a combination provides different, useful perspectives that are missed when only one methodology is used.

▶ MANAGERIAL ISSUES

Getting ready for the future—that is, planning—is one of the most challenging tasks facing all of management, and IS management is no different. Each of the four steps of the IS strategic planning process—setting the mission; assessing the environment; assessing the organization's goals and objectives; and, finally, setting the IS objectives, strategies, and policies—provides its own unique problems.

What *should* be the role of the IS function? How should it be organized? staffed? funded? What of the environment? the competition? the economy? governmental regulations? emerging technologies? What is the strategic direction of the host organization? What are its key objectives? Are they agreed upon and clearly stated? Finally, within these strategies and objectives and the larger environment, what strategies and objectives should IS pursue? What policies should it establish? What should the information architecture look like? How should investments in IT be justified?

The answer to each of these questions must be tailored to the particular circumstances of the IS function and the larger organization of which it is a part. Thus, what has been presented in this chapter are not answers but rather frameworks and methodologies for addressing these questions. ■

KEY TERMS

Business processes *378*

Business systems planning (BSP) *378*

Charge-out *391*

Competitive strategy *373*

Critical path method (CPM) *396*

Critical success factors (CSFs) *381*

Customer resource life cycle (CRLC) *375*

Data class *379*

Data element *379*

Ends/means analysis *385*

Forecasting *367*

Four-stage model of planning *370*

Future perfect *376*

Gantt chart *397*

Information architecture *370*

Milestones *395*

Organizational information requirements analysis (OIRA) *386*

Planning *367*

Project planning *395*

Resource allocation *390*

Return on investment *391*

Stages of growth *382*

Steering committee *368*

Strategic planning *372*

Strategic set formation *378*

CHAPTER HIGHLIGHTS *(L-x means learning objective number x)*

▼ Information systems planning has evolved from fragmented, piecemeal activities to a more structured approach. (L-1) (L-2)

▼ Information systems planning problems involve strategy, architecture, resource allocation, and time and budget issues. (L-2)

▼ Information systems planning works best in a four-stage model. (L-3)

▼ Strategic planning involves using methodologies such as competitive strategy, customer resource life cycle, and future perfect. (L-4)

▼ Other planning methodologies include critical success factors, business systems planning, and ends/means analysis. (L-4)

▼ Information architectures ensure integration of organizational information. (L-5)

▼ Resource allocation involves selecting from project candidates which are derived from strategic planning and information architecture planning. (L-6) (L-7)

▼ Tools for project planning include CPM, Gantt charts, and milestones. (L-7)

▼ Project planning must be adjusted to the properties or characteristics of the project. (L-7) (L-8)

▼ Practical guidelines can be used to select the appropriate planning tools. (L-8)

QUESTIONS FOR REVIEW

1. Briefly discuss the evolution of IS planning.

2. What are the problems commonly associated with IS planning?

3. Define and discuss the four-stage model of IS planning.

4. Identify the methods used for strategic planning, and review their characteristics.

5. Define and discuss the steps necessary to build an information architecture.

6. Discuss the pros and cons of using charge-out to allocate IS resources.

7. Identify and discuss project planning methods. Under what circumstances might you choose one over another?

QUESTIONS FOR DISCUSSION

1. Discuss how a strategic planning exercise, as described in this chapter, could help an electric utility plan its future.

2. How might an organization with a good strategic idea be limited in ability to implement that idea if it has an inferior information architecture? Provide an example.

3. What type of problems might an organization encounter if it focuses only on resource allocation planning and project planning?

4. Why might charge-out be counterproductive to achieving integrated cross-functional information systems?

5. Discuss the risks of applying CPM project techniques to an ill-defined project using a new, unstable technology with inexperienced users.

6. What are the risks of using a milestone approach to a straightforward, low-risk information systems project?

EXERCISES

1. Using the competitive strategy, customer resource life cycle, and future perfect methods of strategic planning, determine new strategic initiatives that a utility might make using information technology.

2. Based on the strategic planning methods in Exercise 1, discuss how a university might improve its admission and registration processes.

3. Visit with managers of an information systems function (perhaps the university's), and assess what stage they are in with regards to the four-stages of information systems planning.

GROUP ASSIGNMENT

Have teams from the class visit project development efforts at local companies. The team members should interview members of the project team to ascertain the following information.

a. How will the project contribute to the goals and objectives of the company?

b. Is there an information architecture in place? If so, how does this project fit into that architecture?

c. How was the project justified?

d. What planning approach, if any, was used?

e. What is the "risk profile" of the project?

f. How is the project being managed?

Minicase 1

Denver Airport—When IT Plans Fail

IT trade journals like to publish IT success stories, and readers can learn much from these experiences. Rarely, however, are IT *failures* presented for planners to learn from; businesses don't like having their mistakes publicized even though learning from mistakes can sometimes be more instructive than learning from successes. Studies show that for every three large-scale IT systems put into operation, one other is canceled prior to completion because of deficiencies. One particular IT planning failure that has not escaped media attention, however, is Denver's new airport baggage handling system.

When Denver's new airport opened in February of 1995, it was 16 months late and $3 billion over budget because its computerized baggage system failed miserably to deliver bags to the right destination—if it delivered them at all. Delays in opening cost the city of Denver $1.1 million a day while the system's developer, BAE Automated Systems, worked out the bugs. How could this happen? BAE had previously built the world's largest computerized baggage system in Frankfurt, Germany, and Denver's planners were closely monitoring that airport's progress.

There appears to be sufficient blame for all parties. To begin with, industry analysts say, the Denver system was more than an order of magnitude larger than the Frankfurt system and far more complex due to Denver's distributed computer architecture. Neither BAE nor Denver apparently appreciated that magnitude. "This is an enormous system," said BAE's president. "Along the way it became apparent that this would be a lot more difficult to do than we thought." Denver planners assumed BAE would have benefited from its Frankfurt experience and would be even more efficient building Denver's airport.

Denver authorities made the situation even more difficult. To begin with, they gave BAE only two years to design, develop, test, and implement the system—less time than BAE had for the smaller Frankfurt system. BAE says they weren't given anywhere near sufficient time to develop the software that controls baggage cart movement. Denver officials blamed BAE for agreeing to the contract in the first place.

In actual practice, BAE wasn't even given the full two years. Denver authorities saddled BAE with $20 million worth of changes to the design long after construction had begun, making it virtually impossible to complete the system on time. Denver said that the problem the system was supposed to solve changed while it was being built; BAE assumed once their design was approved, they'd be left in peace to build it.

For the airport's opening day, only a small-scale version was operating at just one concourse and for only one airline. Denver's Deputy Director of Aviation admitted the system's problems weren't over. "We relied on technology that was ahead of its time," she said. Or behind, depending on how one looked at it.

Questions for Minicase 1

1. Based on the planning methodologies presented earlier in this chapter, could BAE have done anything to prevent the time and cost overrun? If so, what? If not, why not?

2. What were some of the IT planning guidelines that BAE and Denver failed to follow? If they had, do you think the system would still have been late and over budget?

3. If BAE had *expected* requirements to change while the system was being built, how could they have adequately planned for those changes?

4. Some authors highlight three constraining "legs" of development: cost, requirements, and time. To reduce time, one must reduce the requirements or increase the cost; to save on the cost, one must reduce requirements or increase the time allotted. Likewise, to increase requirements, one must increase time or cost. From this perspective, what happened in the case of Denver's new airport baggage system?

5. Group discussion question: Could BAE, other potential contractors, and the Denver authorities have planned the baggage system development *together before* the contract was signed? Would that have helped ensure the airport opened on time and within budget?

SOURCES: Violino, R., and P. Kapustka, "Is It Really Ready to Fly?" *InformationWeek,* March 13, 1995.

Minicase 2

Methodist Hospital

It was the third time in 14 months that John Henderson had to go to Methodist Hospital. He had broken a wrist playing basketball 14 months ago, only to break an ankle 6 months later playing volleyball. Now this past week, he experienced chest pains that turned out to be a pulled muscle in his chest as a result of weightlifting at the gym.

John found it incredible that each time he went to the hospital he was a complete stranger. Each time he had to provide a medical history, insurance information, employment information, and demographic information. It took up to an hour to get all of this data recorded and for him to be admitted. Finally, in a moment of extreme frustration during his third attempt to get admitted, he said "Don't you people have any corporate memory? Don't you have any way to determine or keep track of the fact that I have been here before?"

Wendy Brown, a physician overhearing the comments, brought up the issue at a staff meeting the following week. The hospital was interested in what it might do to avoid such frustration to patients and reduce the cost of having to capture information over and over again every time a patient was admitted. As a result, the staff met with the information systems group to determine what could be done to improve the admission process.

Questions for Minicase 2

1. Use the strategic planning methods of competitive strategy, customer resource life cycle, and future perfect to determine what Methodist Hospital should do to improve its competitive position.

2. Based on the ideas that you came up with in Question 1, decide how these ideas might be assessed and selected. What types of project planning might be appropriate for proceeding with them?

REFERENCES AND BIBLIOGRAPHY

1. *Business Systems Planning—Information Systems Planning Guide*, Application Manual GE20-0527-3, Third Edition, IBM Corporation, July 1981.

2. Davis, S. M., *Future Perfect*, Reading, MA: Addison-Wesley, 1987.

3. Ives, B., and Learmouth, G. P., "The Information System as a Competitive Weapon," *Communications of the ACM*, Vol. 27, No. 12, December 1984, pp. 1193-1201.

4. King, W. R., "Strategic Planning for Management Information Systems," *MIS Quarterly*, Vol. 2, No. 1, March 1978, pp. 27-37.

5. McLean, E. R., and Soden, J. V., *Strategic Planning for MIS*, Wily-Interscience, 1977.

6. Nolan, R. L., "Managing the Computer Resource: A Stage Hypothesis," *Communications of the ACM*, Vol. 16, No. 3, March 1973, pp. 399-405.

7. Nolan, R. L., "Managing the Crises in Data Processing," *Harvard Business Review*, March/April 1979, pp. 81-91.

8. Parker, M. M., and Benson, R. J., *Information Economics*, Englewood Cliffs, NJ: Prentice-Hall, 1988.

9. Porter, M. E., *Competitive Advantage: Creating and Sustaining Superior Performance*, New York: Free Press, 1985.

10. Rockart, J. F., "Chief Executives Define Their Own Data Needs," *Harvard Business Review*, March/April 1979, pp. 81-93.

11. Wetherbe, J. C., "Executive Information Requirements: Getting It Right," *MIS Quarterly*, Vol. 15, No. 1, March 1991, pp. 51-65.

12. Wetherbe, J. C., "Four-Stage Model of MIS Planning Concepts, Techniques, and Implementation," *Strategic Information Technology Management: Perspectives on Organizational Growth and Competitive Advantage*, R. Banker, R. Kaufman, and M. Mahmood, (Eds.) Harrisburg, PA: Idea Group Publishing, 1993.

13. Wetherbe, J. C., and Davis, G. B., "Strategic MIS Planning Through Ends/Means Analysis," University of Minnesota, *Management Information Systems Research Center Working Paper Series*.

12

INFORMATION SYSTEMS ANALYSIS AND DESIGN

Learning Objectives

After studying this chapter, you will be able to:

1. Explain the first three stages of the system development life cycle and how they relate to the subsequent four stages.

2. Explain the best way to uncover information systems problems, identify the true underlying cause of a problem, conduct a feasibility study for an information systems project, and establish a project team.

3. Describe the various methodologies for gathering information about existing and proposed information systems, and explain how to document them graphically.

4. Explain three common methodologies for determining information requirements.

5. Describe the concept of reengineering a business process.

▶ 12.1 RIGORS OF REGISTRATION

A STUDENT AT a major state university was going through registration. Because she was married to a faculty member, she was entitled to have the out-of-state tuition charge waived. As she was processed through the graduate school, she was asked to prove that her husband was on the faculty. (Do you find it interesting that the employer was asking the spouse to do the proving?) She was required to get a letter from the department chairperson documenting employment—it took two hours.

When she went to the registrar's office, she was again asked to prove that her husband was on the faculty. Would they accept the letter on file at the graduate school? Of course not! A form had to be filled out by the dean of the business school. More hours for more paperwork.

Next she went to the bursar's office. As she tried to pay her fees, she again had to prove her husband's faculty appointment. At this point, she gave them two alternatives—the letter on file at the graduate school or the form on file at the registrar's office. Unfortunately, they had their own procedure, involving yet another form, and more hours were spent getting it filled in and signed.

Registration can require considerable "running around."

In total, an entire day of this student's life was taken from her as she repeatedly proved the same fact to different parts of the same organization. No one at the university was aware of the total system requirements and their absurdity.

▶ 12.2 OVERVIEW OF THE SYSTEMS DEVELOPMENT LIFE CYCLE

As the opening case illustrates, bad systems make for bad experiences. But how are good systems developed, and who develops them? In this chapter and the next, the **systems development life cycle (SDLC)** process is discussed. Figure 12.1 provides a basic graphic model of the steps involved in the systems development and shows how they are divided between Chapter 12 and Chapter 13. Note that more emphasis is placed on the first three stages by allocating an entire

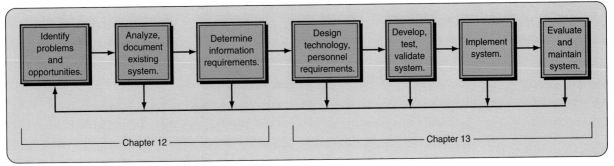

FIGURE 12.1 Systems development life cycle overview.

chapter to them. This is because the first three stages of systems development ensure that the systems development effort is focusing on the "right things"—the managerial issues. Subsequent steps of systems development focus on making sure that "things are done right." These steps include technical issues that would be covered in detail in a text on systems construction and implementation.

The steps in the cycle are not completely discrete, one-time processes. Rather, the systems development cycle is iterative and evolutionary. They do, however, retain a basic sequential flow from the point of origin to "identify new problems and opportunities." Each step represents a major checkpoint, or milestone, and has identifiable deliverables that symbolize completion. At any step in the cycle, previously unidentified problems and/or opportunities may be discovered. In such cases, it is important to ensure proper integration of a solution to the new problem and/or new opportunity.

Making even a minor change to a system without proper consideration of what has been previously established can cause unanticipated and undesirable rippling effects. These effects can seriously damage the operation of the system. Therefore, as Figure 12.1 shows, all steps of the systems development cycle allow return to the point of origin at any time. This feature causes the life cycle to exhibit a "spiraling" or "whirlpool" characteristic rather than a purely sequential or "waterfall" characteristic.

The "waterfall" model (as shown in Figure 12.2)—the traditional life cycle model—has come under increasing criticism for being too inflexible to respond to today's changing business climate. With its natural movement "downward," it implies that returning "upward" to previous steps is unnatural, undesirable, and to be avoided. The rapid pace of business change, however, suggests a model that facilitates if not encourages revisiting previous steps to ensure system viability and reduce subsequent changes downstream. The model shown in Figure 12.2 more aptly supports this view.

The time required to complete the cycle for a given problem or opportunity may range from a few hours to many years, depending on the complexity of the task. A brief overview of each of the seven steps of the SDLC is provided next. The remainder of the chapter will focus on the first three stages of the SDLC.

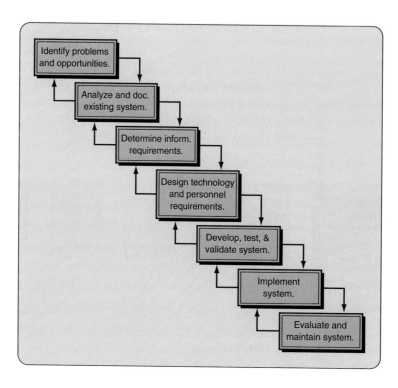

FIGURE 12.2 "Waterfall" system development life cycle model.

▶ 12.3 THE SYSTEMS DEVELOPMENT LIFE CYCLE

STEP 1: IDENTIFY PROBLEMS AND OPPORTUNITIES

As shown in Figure 12.1, the impetus for initiating a systems development cycle is to identify new problems and opportunities. For example, a wholesale distributor may receive customer complaints concerning late order deliveries, resulting in lost orders and customer goodwill. Action is necessary to solve these problems and take advantage of opportunities for improvement. To understand clearly the exact nature of the problem requires a thorough analysis and understanding of the existing system.

STEP 2: ANALYZE AND DOCUMENT EXISTING SYSTEMS

Existing systems—including manual, paper-based information systems—need to be thoroughly analyzed and documented before designing, developing, and implementing changes (or a totally new system). In the late delivery example just discussed, management might initiate a project team (or task force) to analyze the existing order-processing system. Analyzing the existing system involves activities such as the following.

▼ Review work flow

▼ Define decision making associated with the work flow.

▼ Review current information available to support decision making (e.g., transactions and reports).

▼ Isolate deficiencies in the existing information system.

Once analyzed, the existing information system is documented for further analysis and for communication purposes.

STEP 3: DETERMINE INFORMATION REQUIREMENTS

Once deficiencies in the information system have been determined and the existing system is thoroughly analyzed and documented, information requirements can be determined. Since the end result of an information system is the provision of information necessary for decision making, solutions to information problems can be defined in terms of the inclusion or structure of information.

In the case of a wholesale distributor, it might be determined that historical information about customers' orders would facilitate better inventory forecasting. This solution would require including new information in the system. Often, the solution involves simply restructuring existing information such as providing a summarized average-demand-by-month report. Note that in the opening case, information needed to confirm that the student's spouse was on the faculty was already available in the organization's personnel file—it was just not accessible to those who needed it.

STEP 4: DESIGN TECHNOLOGY AND PERSONNEL REQUIREMENTS

Design of information and processing requirements establishes the criteria for identifying alternative means for solution achievement. That is, while the previous step defines *what* is desired, this step defines *how* to do it. Viable technologies and personnel are identified that, if included in the system, can be structured to support the solution defined in the previous step. Generally, several alternatives, offering varying degrees of solution achievement, are available.

For example, a wholesale distributor may currently post customer orders to an inventory file weekly. The inventory file and inventory reports are updated once a week. The problem with this system is that inventory information can be up to one week old. Consequently, sales personnel might overcommit existing inventory. Also, the need to reorder out-of-stock items is not detected until the weekly processing has been completed. One means for improving the timeliness of inventory reporting is to restructure the existing system to expedite the current processing procedure. Within this alternative, varying degrees of expedition are possible. Transaction posting could be done immediately (in real time).

Inclusion of a new technology is another possibility. For example, an expert system could be used to allocate inventory using criteria such as which customer needs inventory the most, promised delivery dates, available credit, order history, and shipping schedules.

STEP 5: DEVELOP, TEST, AND VALIDATE SYSTEM

At this point, desired solutions and the means of achieving them have been identified. The actual development and testing of the system is now possible. This step consists of installing any additional hardware or software required and generating and testing computer programs where necessary. Software may be purchased as a completed system requiring some customization, or it may be developed by the organization. The end product of this step is an operable and reliable system that actualizes the original design objectives in solving a problem or taking advantage of an opportunity.

STEP 6: IMPLEMENT SYSTEM

After the new system has been developed and tested, conversion from the old system to the new system can occur. A key part of the implementation process is dealing with organizational and behavioral issues that often arise. Implementing new information systems usually changes—sometimes dramatically—people's jobs, responsibilities, tasks, and reporting relationships. Special provisions must be made to deal with these human factors in order to minimize dysfunctional resistance to change. Implemented properly, systems can be highly motivating and enriching to the organizational participants.

STEP 7: EVALUATE AND MAINTAIN SYSTEM

After a new system has been implemented, it is important to review how effectively and efficiently solutions to problems and opportunities have been achieved. Evaluation, therefore, consists of assessing the degree of variation between planned and actual systems performance.

If the new system fails to achieve the design objectives or presents new problems or opportunities, a new SDLC may have to be initiated. If the new system performs satisfactorily, then the system can be maintained at the current operating level until new problems or opportunities arise.

▶ 12.4 STEP 1: IDENTIFY PROBLEMS AND OPPORTUNITIES

Now that we have an overview of the complete SDLC, the remainder of the chapter provides an in-depth review of the first three stages of the SDLC, starting with recognizing problems and opportunities. But before a problem or an opportunity can be analyzed, it must clearly be identified and defined. We will explore first, therefore, concepts pertinent to identifying and defining problems and opportunities. Following the conceptual issues, we will discuss how to define problems, conduct feasibility studies, and form a project team.

CONCEPTS

REACTION AND OPPORTUNISTIC SURVEILLANCE. Managers can take one of two basic approaches to surveillance that are relevant to defining problems and opportunities. These two approaches are called reaction and opportunistic surveillance.

Reaction surveillance involves addressing problems as they arise—a management by exception approach. It is the easiest and most commonly employed technique. For example, if customers begin to complain about the tardiness of order processing, management might react by attempting to resolve the problem. Otherwise, management "leaves well enough alone." In other words, "If it ain't broke, don't fix it."

Opportunistic surveillance continually seeks opportunities that might be beneficial to the organization. Rather than leaving well enough alone, management seeks continual improvement. This is a much more aggressive posture, and it can pay considerable dividends. For example, management may see an opportunity to gain more customers by implementing a new order-processing system that will provide customer deliveries in a way that is superior to that of competitors. Here it might be said, "If it ain't broke, there's still time to 'fix' it."

OBJECT SYSTEM AND INFORMATION SYSTEM. The distinction between an object system and an information system is sometimes subtle but nevertheless important. An **object system** is the physical process of achieving one or more organizational goals. Examples of object systems include manufacturing products and selling merchandise. An **information system** is a physical process that supports an object system in achieving organizational goals. An information system may run *parallel* to the object system in order to provide both documentation and information for decision making pertinent to the management and operation of the object system. In some instances (for example, with military command and control systems and industrial design systems), the object system is merged with the information system. In a manufacturing plant, work orders may be used to document the work flow and production schedules may be used to plan the work flow. In a retail store, sales can be documented by being entered into cash registers or retail terminals, and sales information is used for merchandising decisions.

A helpful and important way to differentiate between object systems and information systems is to keep in mind that without an object system there is no need for an information system. The purpose of an information system is to facilitate the operation of an object system. Indeed, the cost of operating an information system should be offset by the benefits realized when the object system is more efficiently and effectively managed.

FRAMEWORKS FOR STUDYING PROBLEMS AND OPPORTUNITIES. There is a tendency simply to automate old processes rather than to be truly innovative and come up with creative applications of technology. Three high-level, strategic frameworks for recognizing problems and opportunities—competitive strategy, customer resource life cycle (CRLC), and future perfect—were covered in the section on strategic planning in Chapter 11. (Please review these, if necessary, to refresh your memory.) These are powerful tools that should be used by the project team to explore innovative opportunities in the use of technology. In other words, they are not just useful for strategic planning; they should be reused for more detailed analysis during the actual systems development process. A day or two of brainstorming within these frameworks can flesh out a strategic idea into an operational concept.

DEFINING PROBLEMS AND OPPORTUNITIES

Usually, it is not difficult to identify broad problem areas or possible opportunities. Generally, it is more difficult to define, with specificity, the different dimensions or various cause-and-effect relationships that are creating problems or preventing opportunities. For instance, customer demand for faster delivery of orders may be identified as a problem. On the surface, this may appear to be a performance problem related to response time. However, there are many potential causes of the problem.

1. Salespersons fail to turn in customer orders promptly.
2. The order processing department is managed incompetently.
3. Data entry operators give too low a priority to the orders (e.g., they may give higher priority to payroll transactions).
4. The order processing department has a morale problem.
5. There is an insufficient number of data entry operators.
6. Computer programs that process orders have several "bugs" in them, resulting in some orders being processed incorrectly.
7. Computer capacity is insufficient to handle the workload.
8. Information on inventory fluctuations is not timely enough to prevent frequent stock-outs due to poor routing.
9. The inventory manager is not aware of late deliveries because this information is not reported.
10. The credit department does not review customer credit checks until just before orders are to be shipped. Therefore, an order has to be held if any credit questions arise.

Which of these items cause the problem? The preceding list suggests that to ascertain the cause of a problem fully (or the prevention of an opportunity) requires a thorough understanding of both the object system and the information system.

CAUSALITY. The actual cause of a problem can be quite elusive. An inexperienced manager often confuses symptoms with problems. Just because something precedes something else chronologically does not mean that the former caused the latter. For example, a crowing rooster precedes a sunrise, but the rooster does not *cause* the sun to rise.

Similarly, in addressing information systems symptoms, great care has to be taken to identify the real cause of the problem. For example, when a new information system is implemented within an organization, a number of problems may occur and the organization may incorrectly conclude that the information system caused the problems. It may well be, however, that the information system merely revealed problems (like a crowing rooster signals the sunrise) of which the organization was previously unaware.

MAGNITUDE OF PROBLEMS OR OPPORTUNITIES. Problems and opportunities vary in complexity. In many cases, concerns can be addressed with minimal difficulty and time. This usually occurs when the existing system is well understood and problems are rather glaring. Consequently, the appropriate solution is apparent. For example, if the cause is late processing of customer orders due to new salespersons failing to turn in orders promptly, then the problem could be easy to resolve. Management may simply write a memo to the sales manager, explaining the importance of turning in orders promptly and requesting that appropriate action be taken.

More complex problems and opportunities, however, require more comprehensive analysis. For example, if an information system is not providing necessary information or the technology used in an information system is obsolete, problem resolution requires considerably more effort. In such cases, problem resolution or opportunity achievement requires a major overhaul of an existing system or the development of a new one. Major change, however, may not always be *feasible* with available organizational resources.

FEASIBILITY STUDIES

When complex problems and opportunities are to be defined, it is generally desirable to conduct a preliminary investigation called a **feasibility study**. It provides an overview of the problem and generally assesses whether feasible solutions exist—prior to committing substantial resources. During a feasibility study, the project team works with representatives from the departments expected to benefit from the solution. The primary objective of the study is to assess three types of feasibility.

1. *Technical.* Can a solution be supported with existing technology?
2. *Economic.* Is existing technology cost effective (i.e., will the costs be offset by the benefits)?
3. *Operational.* Will the solution work within the organization if implemented?

By intent, the feasibility study is a very rough analysis of the viability of a project. It is also an important checkpoint that should be completed before committing more resources. The feasibility study answers a basic question: is it *realistic* to address the problem or opportunity under consideration?

The final product of a successful feasibility study is a **project proposal** for management. The contents of this report may include, but are not restricted to, the following items.

1. Project name.
2. Problem or opportunity definition.
3. Project description.
4. Expected benefits.
5. Consequences of rejection.
6. Resource requirements.
7. Alternatives.
8. Other considerations.
9. Request for authorization.

JUSTIFYING SYSTEMS. A key part of getting a proposal accepted is justifying it to management. With all of the publicity surrounding the use of information technology for opportunistic or competitive-advantage applications, most information systems professionals are experiencing a combination of excitement and paranoia as they contemplate how to respond. Now that the pressure is on, how exactly should they go about promoting competitive-advantage information systems to top management?

One obstacle is that some systems analysts are shackled by early-1970s thinking, believing that all computing applications have to be cost justified. **Cost justification** involves demonstrating that savings or revenue generated by a new system more than offsets the cost of developing it. As discussed in Chapter 11, common methods of cost justification include **return on investment (ROI)** and **break-even analysis**, depicted in Figure 12.3. ROI is the percentage return computed by ROI = net return ÷ investment (e.g., a $1,000 investment generating a $100 return after one year would net an annual ROI of 10 percent). Break-even analysis is concerned with the point in time at which revenue or savings from investment equals start-up cost. In other words, break-even analysis indicates when the original investment is recouped by additional revenue. Note in Figure 12.3 that when break-even is reached, ROI is 0 percent (i.e., there is no ROI until the original investment is recouped).

Unfortunately, as precise as the formulas for computing break-even analysis and ROI are, considerable judgment is required to come up with these numbers—

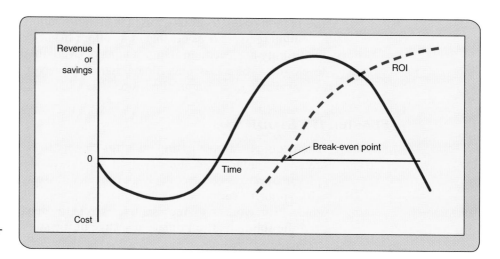

FIGURE 12.3 Break-even analysis and return on investment.

especially benefit numbers—which always makes the analysis somewhat suspect. For example, we generally feel that getting an education is cost justified. But generating the actual costs (including the income foregone while attending school) and benefits (including intangibles such as greater meaning to life) are extremely hard to quantify.

Cost justification of information systems became popular in the late 1960s, when many companies were severely disappointed (and rightly so) with their investments in computer systems. Hard-nosed cost justification was employed to put the brakes on runaway information technology budgets; unfortunately, it also created an infertile environment for future innovation. Enhancements to the way a company operates, such as using systems for competitive advantage, are brought on by entrepreneurial, imaginative thinking that should not be dominated by premature preoccupation with exact cost and benefit justification.

American Hospital Supply's well-known customer order-entry system, for example, was initiated by its marketing staff trying to solve a customer service problem (see Box 12.1). Only later did the company's information management realize the efficiency gains that emerged as a by-product when AHS's order-entry clerical function was eliminated and customers were allowed to place their orders directly.

IT At Work BOX 12.1

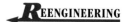

REENGINEERING

AMERICAN HOSPITAL SUPPLY CORPORATION

American Hospital Supply Corporation (now Baxter) found that having salespeople constantly making calls to hospitals within their territories was an expensive way to do business. The company also found it difficult to handle rush orders.

To handle these problems, American Hospital used a provocative approach. Rather than have salespeople take orders from hospitals, the company installed on-line terminals that allowed customers to place orders directly to American Hospital Supply. The role of the salesperson then became one of educating customers about American Hospital Supply products, how to use the terminals, and

how to handle any problems that the customer might have in using a terminal. Consequently, customers were able to be more self-sufficient and place orders more quickly. Also, American Hospital Supply did not have the expense of sending salespeople out merely to take orders; instead, salespeople could concentrate on generating new sales.

Critical Thinking Issues: What other applications are possible now that this system is in place? If this system were designed today, would the respective roles of the salespeople and information management be the same? ▲

The AHS example supports a fundamental concept: if the initial focus is on customer-oriented effectiveness, then efficiency gains are usually a fortunate by-product made possible by the power of information technology. Also, ideas such as improving customer service generally capture management's imagination. If, on the other hand, the initial focus is on cost-cutting efficiency issues that are easier to cost justify, then customer service and effectiveness are usually compromised and the idea has less appeal.

For example, it is much more exciting to talk about a system that allows a pharmacist to check for improper drug combinations automatically than it is to talk about reducing the accounts-receivable clerical staff by 20 percent. The excitement comes not from the appearance of a "cost justification application," but from the appearance of a "good idea." In the case of either AHS or the pharmacy example, before-the-fact estimates of cost and benefits were not precisely determinable. How many more customers will either company gain because of these systems? How many will they keep? How do we know for sure?

With cost justification clearly lacking as a singular, effective way to promote competitive-advantage applications, it is necessary to develop a framework for successfully promoting such applications. One approach involves a three-phase program that can be likened to a political campaign.

1. *Selecting the candidate.* During this stage, a good idea must be developed and thoroughly refined. One approach is to conduct a retreat, such as was discussed in Chapter 11, where users and systems designers go off together for a weekend or so to address the subject without distraction. At such a retreat, it might help to include some customers, and a facilitator who will make sure the focus remains on the competitive-advantage issues.

   If one or more visionary concepts come out of such a session, the battle is half over. If the concepts can be readily cost justified as well, so much the better; but remember that this aspect should not be the only criterion. The concepts selected for further development should be expressed in a crisp, succinct phrase, almost like a campaign slogan. For example, "We are going to be the first car rental company to sell our used cars through an on-line order entry system—instead of just advertising them in the newspaper."

2. *Establishing support.* Management backing and grassroots support are established during this stage. As in a political campaign, differences in opinion on strategic and logistical specifics should be worked out in small groups "behind closed doors" rather than in public. Adjustments, even significant compromises, may be required to gain the constituency necessary for the concept's acceptance.

3. *Inaugurating the winner.* The final stage of promoting competitive applications involves the formal presentation with all appropriate fanfare. Ideally, an initial prototype of the system should be available to demonstrate. By now, it should be said, the system has been informally "wired" for acceptance. Now the time is finally at hand for actual systems development and implementation to begin.

THE PROJECT TEAM

If the project proposal is approved, management generally organizes a **project team** and assigns project responsibility to it. The specific personnel or type of personnel to be included on the project team should be defined under a resource requirements section of the project proposal (see Figure 12.4).

Careful organization of a project team is a prerequisite to good systems analysis. Different types of expertise are required to consider all system variables thoroughly; a system analyst provides primarily computer technology-oriented skills, and representatives from various departments affected by the information system

Project name.

New order processing system

Problem or opportunity definition.

Customers are complaining that they cannot get orders processed. They have to wait for sales representatives to come by to place an order which might take several days.

To send sales representatives by more often will increase our costs too much.

Project description.

Proposed is a new order processing system that will allow customers to place orders directly using an on-line customer order-entry system. Customers can use their personal computers for entering orders.

Customers will be provided with information on inventory availability and alternatives, prices, and shipping schedules.

Besides placing orders, the system can also be used to let customers file complaints, and we can use it to collect survey information from customers.

Benefits.

Estimates are that we will be able to deliver to our customers an average of five days sooner than we or our competition currently can. This increase in customer service and reduction in sales costs should be substantial.

Also, the ability to get complete, accurate, and timely information on customer complaints and surveys will allow us to understand customer needs, preferences, and attitudes better.

Consequences of rejection.

Initial estimates are that the new system will take three to six months to be completely operational. A project team of four to six personnel will be required half-time for the development effort. Budget could run from $500,000 to $750,000.

More accurate resource requirements can be determined once a working prototype of the system is complete. Prototyping could be complete within two to four weeks.

Alternatives.

Besides doing nothing, the main alternative is to purchase a prewritten system or application package that could provide the same functionality as the one proposed. We have found two such systems, but they would require substantial revisions to adapt to our requirements. The expense of doing so exceeds the cost of creating our own system.

Other considerations.

The credit department indicates that the proposed system could greatly enhance cash flow for accounts receivable.

Authorizations.

Manager order processing _____

Sales manager _____

Shipping manager _____

Credit manager _____

Manager information systems _____

Vice president of operations _____

FIGURE 12.4 Project proposal example.

provide the dimensions of their needs and requirements. Project team participants should be given sufficient *release time* from their normal duties to contribute the necessary level of participation to the project. However, release time should be provided only for the duration of the project; upon project completion, the participants should return to their normal duties.

An interesting debate about project teams pertains to who should be the project leader. Some managers contend that a systems analyst should provide the leadership, while others say that this role is better filled by a management-level representative from the departments that will use the system. Projects tend to be completed faster when a systems analyst is in charge, but users are generally more committed to, and more satisfied with, the results of projects when they are directly responsible. When a systems analyst is in charge, users have a tendency to give her too much latitude in designing the system (often because users do not understand much of the technology) and then decide whether or not they like the system *after* it is completed. Unfortunately, the systems analyst may design a system that works but that is not the right system; it does not adequately satisfy the users' information requirements. A case in point is made in Box 12.2. When users are directly responsible for a project, they are inherently more involved in the design of the system. Their involvement improves the probability that the right system is designed, developed, and implemented.

IT At Work   BOX 12.2

DON'T CHANGE IT UNTIL YOU UNDERSTAND IT

In the excitement of implementing new technology, it is often easy to overlook certain capabilities or functions of the old technology and to leave them out of the new system. Such actions result in disillusionment with the new system and nostalgia for the old. Therefore, it is critical to conduct a thorough analysis of the old system before final design decisions are made on the new system.

Consider this simple, noncomputer example of inadequate analysis before implementation of a new technology: hot-air hand dryers in public restrooms. When they were first recommended, everyone seemed to like the idea immediately. It would eliminate the paper waste associated with paper towels, fewer trees would give their all to become paper towels, labor costs for filling paper towel dispensers and emptying trash bins would be reduced, and it would be state-of-the-art technology. So, it was done.

Unfortunately, it was not long before people discovered that certain functions served by those old paper towels were not served by the new system. Specifically, people found it difficult to dry their faces, clean up spills, clean glasses, and blow noses. So, what do we normally find in a restroom with hot-air dryers? Paper towels.

Similarly, when a new computer system is implemented, remnants of the old system may linger on because the designers of the new system overlooked a function that *was* previously provided. It might not have been the most professionally rewarding day of one's career, but if someone had just spent one day in a public restroom analyzing what people used paper towels for, he could have discovered the things paper towels provide that hand dryers do not. Similarly, to design computer systems, we must take the time to do a thorough analysis of the old before bringing in the new.

Critical Thinking Issue: What other new innovations have failed to take into account features that were previously available? ▲

The tasks of identifying and defining a problem or opportunity, and organizing a project team set the stage for the detailed analysis of an existing system. Concepts and techniques of systems analysis are presented in the following section.

▶ 12.5   STEP 2: ANALYZE AND DOCUMENT EXISTING INFORMATION SYSTEMS

Systems analysis is the process of separating a whole into its parts to allow examination of the parts; this leads to an understanding of their nature, function, and interrelationships. Considerable effort is required to conduct the analysis of an information system. This section discusses how to gather the information necessary for analysis—reviewing the object system, defining the decision making associated with the object system, isolating the deficiencies of the object system, and documenting the analysis.

INFORMATION-GATHERING ACTIVITIES FOR SYSTEMS ANALYSIS

The four basic activities used to gather information about an object system and its information system are listed in Table 12.1 and discussed in more depth next.

DOCUMENTATION AND OBSERVATION.   A review of available documentation is a logical starting point when seeking insight into a system. The documentation review allows project team members involved in systems analysis to attain some knowledge of a system before they impose upon other people's time. Unfortunately, documentation seldom completely describes a system, and often it is not up to date. The current operation of the system may differ significantly from how it is described. Therefore, after a review of available documentation, the next logical step is to observe the operation of the system (unless one does not yet exist). Observation provides a more tangible perspective on what is described in the documentation. It also brings to light aspects of the documentation that are incomplete or outdated.

INTERVIEWS AND QUESTIONNAIRES.   After a review of available documentation, those involved in systems analysis can then use interviews or questionnaires to gather additional information. Interviewing techniques and questionnaire design are topics for extensive study. However, a few key concepts should be noted here.

Interviews are generally preferable to questionnaires for information gathering because they allow direct interaction, thorough questioning, and unlimited discussion. Salient issues can be immediately identified (sometimes through "body language") for further questioning. In an interview, not all questions have to be determined in advance (as they do in a questionnaire). However, when information from a large number of people has to be gathered and tabulated, questionnaires are usually preferable for reasons of efficiency.

Two basic formats for questioning are categorized as open-ended and closed-ended. The difference between the two types of questioning is similar to the difference between essay and multiple-choice exams. Open-ended questions allow latitude to the persons responding. Consequently, information gathered from open-ended questions may be creative and rich in content. Examples of open-ended questions are the following.

1. Are there areas of dissatisfaction with the existing information system? If so, what are these areas?
2. Do you have suggestions for improvements if a new system is designed? If so, what are your suggestions?

Table 12.1 Information Gathering Activities

Activity	Explanation
Documentation review	This consists of reviewing recorded specifications that describe the objectives, procedures, reports produced, equipment used, and so on, in an information system.
Observation	This consists of watching the object system and/or the information system in process to note and record facts and events about their operations.
Interviews	This consists of meeting with individuals or groups to ask questions about their roles in and their use of an information system.
Questionnaires	This consists of submitting questions in printed form to individuals to gather information on their roles in and use of an information system.

Structured interviews, with closed-ended questions, are more restrictive in the latitude allowed to a respondent. The respondent must select an answer from available choices. The major advantage of closed-ended questions is that responses are easily quantified for tabulation, which greatly expedites analysis. The most common application of closed-ended questioning involves scaling techniques. Responses are categorized on a scale between two extremes. Examples of such questions are the following.

1. Do you receive your inventory reports on schedule (yes/no)?
2. Is the information in your inventory reports accurate (yes/no)?

Only one question should be asked at a time; for example, asking if an inventory report is accurate and on schedule in one question places the respondent in an awkward position if the report is on time but is not accurate.

Techniques of documentation, observation, interviews, and questionnaires are used in varying degrees during the following steps of analyzing the existing system.

1. Review the object system.
2. Define decision making associated with the object system.
3. Isolate deficiencies in the information system.
4. Document and analyze existing information systems.

These steps of systems analysis are discussed in the remaining sections of this chapter.

REVIEW OBJECT SYSTEM

During this step, project team members have the opportunity to develop a working knowledge of the physical processes associated with the object system under consideration. A clear understanding of the purpose of the object system and of the means used to achieve it should be developed. The project team should develop a thorough understanding of the players and the roles they play. The project team should also make a special effort to become familiar with the vocabulary associated with the object system, minimizing communication problems as the systems analysis progresses.

Some type of procedures manual describing the operation of the object system is usually available. A copy of this manual should be requested from the managers who are responsible for the object system. After the manual has been reviewed, arrange a tour that allows initial observation of the object system in operation. Interviews and, if necessary, questionnaires can be used to complete the review.

DEFINE DECISION MAKING ASSOCIATED
WITH OBJECT SYSTEM

After acquiring an operating knowledge of the object system, the next logical step is to define the decision making associated with managing the object system. A definition of the decision-making system (also known as the **decision system**) provides the framework for determining what information is required. This is one of the most neglected aspects of systems analysis. Since the utility of information is its ability to improve decision making, such negligence is somewhat surprising.

Managers are frequently asked what information they would like to have, or they are offered copies of reports that are currently being produced or will be produced for other managers. This approach tends to encourage managers to ask for more information than they need. Research in the area of decision making and the use of information indicates the following.

1. Decision makers tend to ask for and feel most comfortable with more detailed information than they really need. Moreover, they appear to make better decisions with summarized information and exception reporting.

2. The less knowledgeable decision makers are about the decisions required to manage a process properly, the more information they tend to request (presumably, hoping to find something of value). However, much of the information they request is irrelevant to their decision making.

By basing information requests on the decisions they have to make, managers can be more discriminating in their requests. This reduces the tendency of managers to demand more data than they need. Such overloads are both dysfunctional and expensive.

DIFFICULTY IN DEFINING DECISION SYSTEM. Defining the decision system is a desirable step of systems analysis, and it is not a trivial one. Considerable discipline and effort on the part of managers may be required to define such a system. Managers often make decisions so routinely that it seldom occurs to them how often they make decisions and what types of decisions they make. Consequently, they are understandably tempted to take a "shotgun" approach to defining their information requirements, rather than a more time-consuming but more specific "rifle" approach. The decision-making process will be discussed in more detail in Chapter 15.

DECISION CENTERS. Decisions made in an organization tend to be clustered into decision centers. A **decision center** generally consists of a decision maker, decision procedures, and the activities for which decisions must be made. Accordingly, decisions made in a decision center tend to pertain to the management of a particular organizational process.

Viewing the organization in terms of decision centers is particularly useful in systems analysis. Decision centers are potential areas where organizational processes may be improved by the provision of more relevant, timely, accurate information. In organizational terms, a decision center combined with an activity center constitutes a functional unit or department. Table 12.2 assumes that an existing order-processing system is being analyzed; it shows the decision centers and major decisions likely to exist in the organization.

Another advantage of defining decision centers and major decisions is that the overall profile of decision making and decision-making locations often reveals discrepancies. For example, if salespersons are under the impression that they can commit inventory, but they really cannot, this discrepancy should be cleared up. Otherwise, inventory may be promised to the wrong customers.

If the same decision is being made by two or more decision centers, this, too, should be resolved. Consider, for instance, a situation where all orders must be approved for credit by the credit department before they are sent to the order processing department. However, the order processing department is unaware of this procedure so a second credit check is made, using an exact copy of the credit rating report used by the credit department. Such duplication of effort is not uncommon in organizations. It may go on, unnoticed, until identified by someone aware of what both departments are doing. Requiring that information received by a department be justified for decision making should expose discrepancies and duplications.

ISOLATING DEFICIENCIES IN EXISTING INFORMATION SYSTEM

After defining the decision making associated with managing the object system, the next step is to isolate the deficiencies in the existing information system. This

Table 12.2 **Decision Centers Involved in Order Processing**

Decision center	Activity	Examples of major decisions
Salespersons	Selling merchandise	• Which customers to call on? • What to sell customers? • What is available to sell?
Credit department	Accounts receivable management	• Which customers to allow credit to? • How much credit to allow? • Which customers need past-due notices? • Which customers' credit should be revoked?
Ordering department	Inventory management	• What inventory to stock? • How much inventory to stock? • When to reorder stock? • When to unload slow-moving inventory? • Which customers to allocate available inventory to?
Shipping department	Packing and shipping orders	• What merchandise to send to which customers? • What orders can be shipped together to save delivery cost?

sets the stage for reengineering the process. After the object system has been thoroughly studied through documentation, interviews, or questionnaires, it may appear that defining deficiencies is simply a matter of logically subtracting the decision making information needed from the object system information provided. But, as pointed out previously, identifying true problems and causes is not always linear and/or easy to do; correctly isolating information deficiencies demands both objectivity and persistence.

In the case of the university student at the beginning of this chapter, what exactly *was* the deficiency? In terms of decision making, the various university offices needed *authorization* information for granting reduced fees. Simply concluding that the deficiency of the existing information system was the inability of offices to share information (and therefore reduce duplicate paperwork in three different offices) would not have necessarily met authorization requirements.

Information systems development analysts must always bear in mind the inescapable reality of *change*. An object system is most likely being upgraded or improved even as the analyst is interviewing personnel and reviewing the object system. Similarly, organizational decision-making requirements are constantly undergoing change as the world around the organization (and personnel) changes. Therefore, a simple, linear subtraction of "what we want" from "what we've got" is often hindered because two changing, moving entities are being considered. In this case, the best route may be to establish some common point in the future upon which to extrapolate (not without risk) "what will be needed" and "what will be there"—in order to identify the *projected* deficiencies the new information system will address.

DOCUMENTING EXISTING SYSTEMS

Once the information required from the new system is defined, the next step is to document thoroughly the existing system and the analysis to date—the fourth phase of step two in the overall development life cycle.

Some form of documentation of the existing information system is generally available, and this is the logical starting point for analysis. Narrative documentation is usually too vague and imprecise to ensure that project personnel will accurately understand the system. Therefore, graphical documentation is preferred.

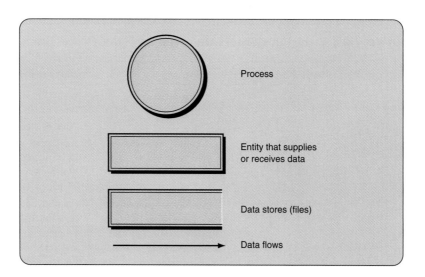

FIGURE 12.5 Data flow diagram symbols.

To illustrate, when receiving complex directions to a geographic location, do you generally prefer verbal directions or a map? The most useful forms of documentation for reviewing an information system are data flow diagrams, flowcharts, and presentation graphics using icons—all of which are structured techniques.

A **data flow diagram (DFD)** uses symbols such as those shown in Figure 12.5 and illustrated in Figure 12.6. DFDs offer an efficient and simple way to show the flow of data in an organization and the data relationships. DFDs can be used as analysis tools if existing documentation does not provide them, or they can be used as design tools. DFDs do not, however, readily show the absolute order of information processing, how data are changed, or temporal relationships. Nevertheless, it is a very straightforward process to document and communicate with DFDs.

A **flowchart** uses symbols and arrows to show processes—the steps and their precise order for receiving, storing, using, and transmitting data. In many cases, flowchart symbols also specify particular types of hardware used, such as a direct storage device as opposed to a sequential storage device. While DFDs show the flow and relationships of data, flowcharts show *how* the data is processed. A flowchart example is shown in Figure 12.7.

Presentation graphics, or custom graphics, is a more elaborate form of documentation that involves the use of pictures to represent objects being por-

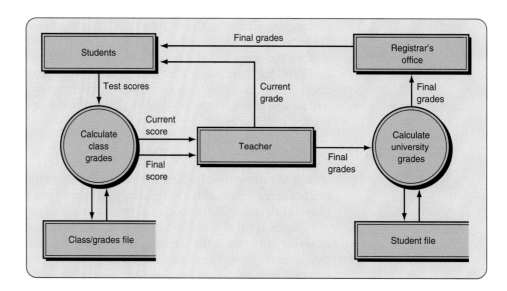

FIGURE 12.6 Data flow diagram student grades example.

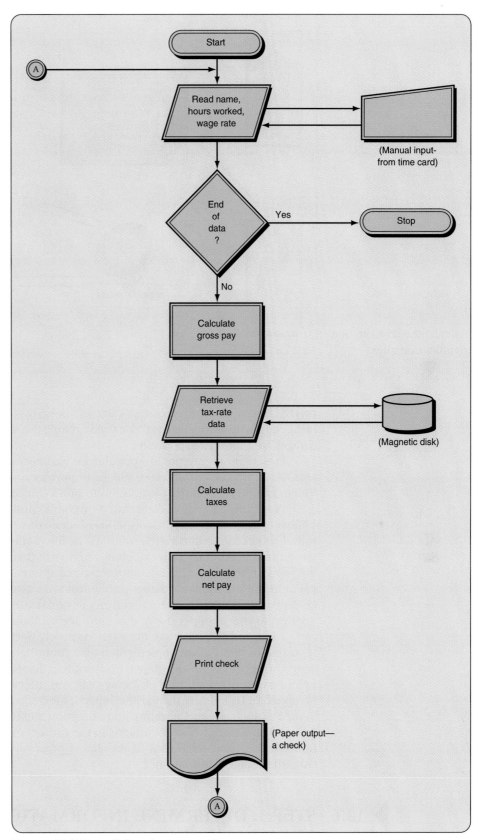

FIGURE 12.7 Payroll flowchart example.

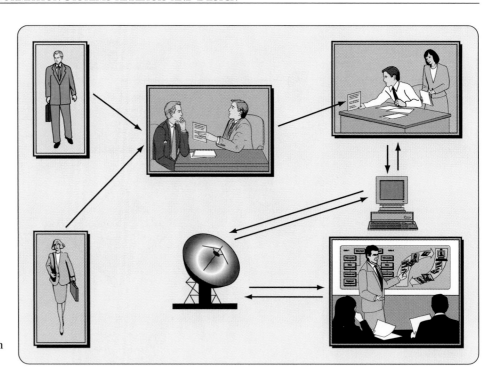

FIGURE 12.8 Presentation graphics examples.

trayed. Figure 12.8 provides an example, showing—graphically—the process of marketing debit cards such as those used for long distance phone calls, city parking garages, and local transportation.

Presentation graphics are popular for management presentation and documentation. Recently, the use of videos to portray a system has become popular. Videos can be particularly meaningful to nontechnical audiences.

Preparing data flow diagrams, flowcharts, and presentation graphics was originally done manually. It was tedious, time consuming, and particularly frustrating when corrections were required. The illustrations shown in Figures 12.6–8 went through several versions before arriving at their publishable forms. One of the tools provided by CASE (computer-aided systems engineering) technology is computer-based graphics to ease the clerical tasks associated with preparing these graphics. Most of the products run on personal computers and include syntax verifiers to check proper use of diagramming symbols.

DFDs and graphics may not exist for poorly documented systems or for systems that have not been implemented on a computer system. In such cases, flowcharts or DFDs must be developed from scratch, that is, from information gathered by observing the operation of the system and interviewing the various persons involved. DFDs indicate the various reports, files, and transaction documents used in an existing system. Collecting and analyzing copies of the various reports, file contents, and transaction documents in the context of the system's flowchart lead to a thorough understanding of the actual processing involved in transforming data into usable information.

▶ 12.6 STEP 3: DETERMINE INFORMATION REQUIREMENTS

Determining **information requirements**, the third step in the system development life cycle, is a critical stage because it concerns whether or not the "right" system is to be developed. Subsequent stages of systems development are concerned with making the system "work right." If the "wrong" system is defined during requirements determination, subsequent efforts are in vain. The system will not be fully utilized, or it will require expensive, time-consuming modification after installation.

There are four general problems in determining information requirements: *single-function systems, information ignorance, individual interviews,* and *unstructured interviews.* These problems and their solutions will be discussed, along with actual cases highlighting solution techniques.

PROBLEMS DETERMINING INFORMATION REQUIREMENTS

SINGLE-FUNCTION SYSTEMS. The first mistake that has historically been made in determining information requirements for information systems is that most systems are viewed as being unifunctional as opposed to cross- or multifunctional. This **single-function system** perspective is far too narrow for most organizations and can create dysfunctional "islands" of systems and information. For example, when developing a new budgeting system, it is easy to focus on what information is needed by the budget managers or budgeting staff members. The problem is that people other than the budgeting staff also use budgeting information. Unfortunately, if the budget department is designing the system, it will likely carry a very strong control orientation as opposed to a general management reporting orientation. This results in budgeting systems that end up being used much like a banking statement simply to reconcile finances. Similarly, many department managers keep their departmental budgets on a departmental computer and simply reconcile them with the "control" statement they receive from the budget department. Due to this phenomenon, up to 60 percent of the data entered into company computers are keyed from reports generated from other computers in the same organization. Box 12.3 illustrates these problems.

IT At Work BOX 12.3

GETTING CONNECTED WITH ACCOUNTING

A marketing vice president for a manufacturing company wanted to categorize costs and revenue by salesperson, customer, and product—since a project could involve more than one salesperson, more than one customer, and more than one product. Unfortunately, the budgeting system only allocated costs by project account number. Only through extensive data collecting from the sales force and the use of spreadsheet software could the information needed be obtained for the vice president.

Some argued that the budgeting department should incorporate the reporting needs of other functional managers in developing their budgeting system. But the all too common argument against this is that it would increase the cost of developing the system. The flaw in this logic is that the increase in costs exists anyway, because other functional managers have to develop their own systems. In the end, the total cost is more than if the systems were developed across the board and shared.

As one marketing vice president said, "The accounting department adds so much overhead to marketing by wanting more and more data categorized in ways that allow them to control and audit us. I need information categorized in ways to help us sell effectively and efficiently. The systems designed by budgeting are not responsive to my needs. Have you ever heard of a company that was successful because it had the best accounting system in the world?"

Critical Thinking Issue: Who should the budgeting department be serving? ▲

Another way to illustrate the need to develop systems cross-functionally is to consider a business process such as order processing. To process orders, salespeople have to decide which customers to call on, what to sell them, and what is available to sell. Credit personnel must decide which customers can have credit and how much, which customers need past-due notices, and which customers' credit should be discontinued. The warehouse must decide what and how much inventory to stock, when to reorder, when to unload slow moving inventory, and to which customers to allocate limited inventory. Shipping must decide such things as what merchandise to send to which customers, what orders can be shipped together to save delivery costs, and when trucks should depart. (These decisions were summarized in Table 12.2, discussed earlier.) In developing a new system, information should be provided so that *all* decisions can be supported.

For example, consider the last decision listed for the ordering department in Table 12.2—"which customers to allocate available inventory to." If the warehouse has five orders but only enough inventory to fill three, it must make a resource allocation decision. Typically, this decision would be made on a first-in-first-out (FIFO) basis. That seems equitable and fair, given the information they have available to them.

However, this approach could result in a terrible decision. What if a customer who does a lot of business with the company really needs this shipment promptly, recently received an order late and was furious about it, is paying a high profit margin on the order, and pays bills promptly? Suppose, in addition, a truck is routed to deliver a shipment to another customer nearby the same afternoon? Because a FIFO decision was made, the inventory is allocated to someone who hardly ever does business with the company, to whom the order is not urgent, who yields a low profit margin, who does not pay bills on time, and for whom a truck is not going into his vicinity for the next three weeks—during which time inventory could have been restocked anyway.

In trying to improve the quality of the decision, factors such as the following should be considered.

▼ How important is each customer to the business?

▼ How promptly does each customer need delivery of the order?

▼ What is the profitability of each order?

▼ What is the credit status of each customer?

▼ What is the shipping schedule for delivery to each customer?

▼ Has the customer recently been upset because a previous order was late?

Note that the information needed to improve decision making in the ordering department comes from *outside* the department. For example, customer need, importance, and profitability would come from sales, credit worthiness would come from credit, and the shipping schedule would come from shipping.

This is a very important concept of information management: most of the information needed to improve decision making within a function will come from *outside* the function. This is why it is so important for an organization to share information if it wants to improve productivity and design information systems that are multifunctional. When an organization learns to share information cross-functionally, employees are empowered to make better and more productive decisions for the organization. The bottom line is that in order to develop a new information system, it is necessary to be aware of all functions that are touched by the information system and be sensitive to their decision-making requirements. Then, a system can be developed that allows information to flow cross-functionally to improve decision making.

As straightforward as the concept of **cross-functional systems** is, many system analysts attempting to develop them complain that employees are very proprietary about "their" functional information and are often unwilling to participate in a system that will "share" information. Recognizing that information is power, employees are not always interested in sharing power—an attitude that

REENGINEERING

...most information needs to be shared *across* functional boundaries is totally dysfunctional. Since information is power, the idea is to empower decision makers by giving them the best information possible. An organization that does not share information cross-functionally ends up with the left hand not knowing what the right hand is doing.

To solve the problem, top management needs to use its leadership and influence to achieve cross-functional design. When a new system design is being undertaken, those functions that are transcended by the new system must have management participation.

INFORMATION IGNORANCE. How do many system analysts go about determining what information managers want from their computer system? Unfortunately, they sometimes simply ask, "What information do you want from the new system?"

A second problem in determining information requirements has to do with the fact that most managers do not know what information they need and end up asking for too much. They give it their best attempt, assuming brilliant computer wizards will sort things out for them. Several months and millions of dollars later, however, when the system is delivered, managers quickly discover that it does not give them the information they need and does give too much of what they don't need. Managers then ask for changes, and the system analyst goes into shock. The costs and time needed to change a system after it is complete are 50 to 100 times higher than making those same changes during the systems design phase. For a custom-built house, for example, consider the cost of adding a bathroom after the house is complete versus the cost of adding a bathroom during the blueprint or design stage. This is one reason why so many needed information system revisions are never implemented, and why, consequently, resulting systems are often a disappointment. A disappointing system can range from a system that only partially fulfills management's requirements (with or without expensive revisions) to one that is totally abandoned, resulting in a million dollar write-off.

Having been victims of management's inability to define information requirements properly, many systems analysts go to Plan B—the "user sign-off." This approach involves asking managers what information they want from a system and then requiring them to sign a document aimed at contractually obligating them to accept the system when they get it. User sign-offs have only marginal political value when systems analysts are battling with management about system revisions, and they do not solve the functional problem—that managers do not know what information they need. A user sign-off is a powerless piece of paper when matched against the fury of top management.

Plan C, sometimes used by systems analysts, is to use the "catalog" approach to information requirements determination. This approach involves showing a manager a wide variety of reports, perhaps requested by other managers or available from a commercial software package. As the manager reviews these reports, she selects the ones believed to be needed. This may seem like a good idea, but it does not work; managers tend to think that all reports will be useful.

In research studies, cosmetically impressive but useless reports have been offered to managers, who demonstrated a high propensity to request them. For example, in one study, production managers were offered 20 different reports. Eight of these reports were deemed useful by a panel of production experts; the remaining reports were useless. Those 12 were thrown in with the 8 reports to see if anyone would take them. Most managers took all 20 reports. What they are generally doing is "playing it safe." Uncertain as to whether they could use the information, they simply requested it all.

In practice, it gets worse. Although a manager requesting information does not use it, the manager who replaces her years later may assume the information has some value. Consequently, she may be found staying late at work, sifting through useless reports, asking the compelling question: "I wonder what my predecessor did with all this information?'' Years of this phenomenon result in *information overload*—managers get lots of information they don't need and can't use.

INDIVIDUAL INTERVIEWS. A third mistake commonly made in determining information requirements occurs when the system design team interviews managers individually rather than in groups, also known as **joint application design (JAD)**. The individual interviewing process places cognitive stress on a manager, stress that hinders his ability to respond adequately to questions.

Consider this scenario: a group of strangers come to you and ask you to tell 10 jokes. Even though you probably know 10 jokes, you might have difficulty recalling them, as most people would. But what if a group of you and your friends are asked *together* to generate jokes? Very likely you and your friends could generate 80, 90, or even 100 jokes. In other words, each person really knows a great deal of jokes, but when asked to come up with them off the top of his head, he would likely have difficulty recalling them. The moral is that group or collective experiences and memory are essential in recalling information. When managers are asked what information they need, they generally mention things they needed recently, not everything they need. Therefore, one reason that the requirements determination should be done as a group or in a joint process is so that the memory of each manager can be pooled to do a more thorough job of recalling key requirements.

A second reason for a joint application design is that, when it comes to developing a new information system, different functional areas of an organization have different agendas. For example, consider the order processing system portrayed in Table 12.2. Each decision center would likely emphasize different design criteria. Sales may view the primary importance of order processing as ensuring prompt and correct delivery of orders to customers. If we were to think of the purpose of order processing from a *group* perspective, we would likely end up with a design criteria that would focus on improving prompt, correct delivery of orders to customers while ensuring credit integrity and facilitating good inventory management, good routing and scheduling of shipments, and so on.

It is difficult to achieve this overall perspective if each manager is interviewed individually. Box 12.4 illustrates the need for joint application design from a cross-functional perspective.

IT At Work BOX 12.4

PUTTING CATALOG SALES IN PERSPECTIVE THROUGH JOINT APPLICATION DESIGN

A direct mail catalogue company was revising its information systems. Prior to the cross-functional design, the credit department viewed its primary goal as ensuring payment from customers. The ideal would be for all customers to make all payments—that is, no credit losses. In an effort to increase its performance in this area, the credit department continually requested more and more information about customers, i.e., credit references, credit bureau checks, and so on, to the point that credit costs were becoming excessive.

Two mistakes can be committed in making a credit decision. The first is to give credit to people who will notpay their bills, and the second is not to give credit to people who will pay their bills. After looking at the problem cross-functionally with joint application design, the organization determined that it was better off not doing any credit checks at all. This rather counterintuitive conclusion was based upon two key understandings generated from the joint application design.

First, the company could send catalogues of only low-priced items to first-time customers. Customers who paid for what they ordered could be upgraded to more expensive catalogues. Those customers who did not pay would, of course, be dropped from any future mailings. In this way, the company was not deciding whether customers would pay based on credit reference material; they knew for a fact, based on their own experience, which customers would or would not pay.

It turned out that the losses from not receiving payment were less than the cost of doing all the credit checks. In other words, the cost of merchandise not paid for was less than the cost of determining whether customers would pay. Information from their own experience was not only more accurate, but it was also less costly than doing the traditional credit reference checking. If credit information requirements had been determined without considering the context of sales management, this insight would not likely have been achieved.

Furthermore, it turns out that people who would generally be categorized as higher credit risks have a greater propensity to purchase from this company's catalogues. Conversely, people who would be considered excellent credit risks tend not to buy anything from their catalogues. This means the company could send out a lot of catalogues to people with excellent credit ratings who seldom make purchases. Therefore, the company would be losing money by shipping catalogues that never generate revenue—they would be better off marketing to those people who would be higher credit risks but would, in fact, pay for things ordered.

Without the perspective provided by a joint application design, it would have been difficult for the credit department to accept that credit checks were not functional to the overall process of making sales and processing orders. Therefore, when determining information requirements, all functions that will be affected should be represented in the same room at the same time.

Critical Thinking Issue: Are there situations where attempting to involve *all* interested parties would *not* be a good idea? ▲

UNSTRUCTURED INTERVIEWS. A fourth problem determining information requirements is that designers usually ask the wrong question: "What information do you need from the new system?" Though this is the obvious question, it is not at all helpful to managers who don't *know* what they need. Many systems analysts assume managers know what they need, while many executives assume systems analysts know what executives need. The problem is that this **unstructured interview** technique is akin to a psychoanalyst talking to a patient lying on a couch and asking, "What type of therapy do you need?" Or a salesperson being an order taker (rather than a problem solver) who asks, "What features do you want?" If patients or customers don't know how to look out for themselves, they are unlikely to get satisfactory solutions. This phenomenon is illustrated in Box 12.5.

IT At Work BOX 12.5

ORDER TAKERS VS. PROBLEM SOLVERS

Jim purchased a home in the country with sufficient land to require a tractor mower, so he set out to purchase one without knowing much about tractor mowers. Jim needed to solve a problem, but he didn't know specifically what his requirements were.

When Jim went into a dealership to purchase a tractor mower, the salesperson asked him what he was looking for and Jim said he was looking for a tractor mower. After that, he found himself in trouble. The next question Jim was asked was what blade width he wanted—a question he was not prepared to answer. Next, he was asked how much horsepower he wanted. Then, "Do you want wide tires, narrow tires, a rear bagger, a side bagger, manual start or electric start?" It turned out that tractor mowers cost between $800 and $2,800, depending on how they are configured. Once the salesperson realized Jim did not know what he was doing, he immediately started pushing the $2,800 unit, suggesting Jim should go first class. For Jim, mowing his yard and "first class" are not two associated concepts. Suspecting that he was being oversold, Jim went to other dealerships. Unfortunately, he encountered the same experience, time after time.

Finally, Jim went into a dealership where the salesperson was not an order taker but a problem solver. He did not ask what features Jim wanted on the lawn mower—he asked other types of questions such as "How big is your yard?" and "How steep is your yard?" He then asked, "What is the terrain like?" He wanted to know if Jim had fences or trees and if Jim wanted his wife to use the tractor mower. Jim answered directly.

With those answers, the salesperson walked over to a tractor mower unit and said, "This is the one you need." When Jim asked him why this particular unit, the salesperson said, "You have a large yard, so you want the widest blade. You need 12 horsepower to drive the widest blade, but you do not need 18 horsepower unless your yard is both big and steep. You want wide tires to keep from slipping into a rut, tilting the blade deck, and scalping the yard. You want a rear bagger so you can mow around the trees and by your fences going one way one time and the other way the next time, so you do not pack the grass. And you want electric start because you've got delusions you are going to get your wife to use it!''

Notice that what the salesperson did was extremely simple. He asked *indirect* questions that backed into Jim's requirements, never specifically asking what features Jim

wanted. Use of indirect questions is the creative skill of the problem solver in sales as opposed to the order taker. Problem solvers creatively determine how to obtain answers to requirements through less obvious, indirect questions. Those designing information systems need to do the same, and executives should request they do so.

Critical Thinking Issue: What skills does it take to be a ''problem solver'' versus an ''order taker?'' ▲

INFORMATION REQUIREMENTS INTERVIEW TECHNIQUES

Straightforward, useful approaches to determining information requirements have been developed through research. Three of such techniques, summarized in Table 12.3 are **business systems planning (BSP), critical success factors (CSF),** and **ends/means (E/M) analysis.** These techniques were discussed in Chapter 11 as *planning* approaches; they are discussed here as *information requirement gathering* techniques. By combining these three different methodologies, a comprehensive, reliable determination of conceptual information requirements can be achieved.

A basic model for determining information requirements using these approaches is portrayed in Figure 12.9. The key is to focus on issues that ''back into'' information requirements. Specific questions asked under each approach will be discussed next. They are summarized in Table 12.4.

BUSINESS SYSTEMS PLANNING (BSP). This approach concentrates on identifying problems and related decisions. Typical BSP interview questions might be the following.

> What are the major problems encountered in accomplishing the purposes of the organizational unit you manage?

For example, in an order processing system, problems include being out of stock too often, allocating limited inventory to the wrong customers, and sending off trucks unaware that another order going to the same destination will be arriving at the dock within the hour.

> What are good solutions to those problems?

For example, better inventory management is required in order to solve the problem of being out of stock too often. To solve the problem of incorrectly allocating orders requires letting the warehouse know the importance of customers, the importance of orders to specific customers, and customer credit status. To solve

Table 12.3 Comprehensive Interview Approaches

Approach	Information system implementation
Specify problems and decisions.	The executive interview portion of business systems planning (BSP).
Specify critical factors.	Critical success factors (CSF).
Specify effectiveness criteria for outputs and efficiency criteria for processes used to generate outputs.	Ends/means analysis (E/M analysis).

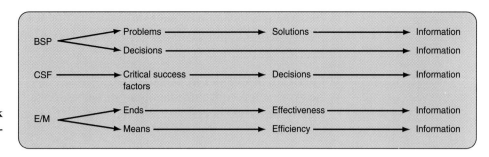

FIGURE 12.9 Framework for information requirements interviews.

the scheduling of truck departure problems requires letting shipping know the destination of orders that are being processed but have not yet arrived at the shipping dock.

How can information play a role in any of these solutions?

For example, to improve inventory management, out-of-stock and below-minimum reporting could be provided electronically, and an automatic reordering system could be implemented. Electronic access to customer importance, importance of order, and credit status could allow the warehouse to make appropriate allocation decisions when inventory is limited. If the shipping department has access to orders received and in process, it can make better decisions about routing and scheduling trucks.

What are the major decisions associated with your management responsibilities?

Major decisions for order processing include deciding which customers to call on and what to sell them. Who receives credit? How much? When should you discontinue credit? What and how much inventory to stock? When to reorder? How to allocate limited inventory? How to schedule and route trucks?

What improvements in information could result in better decisions?

Table 12.4 Summary of Structured Interview Sample Questions

Method	Sample interview questions
Business system planning (BSP)	What are the major problems encountered in accomplishing the purposes of the organizational unit you manage?
	What are good solutions to those problems?
	How can information play a role in any of those solutions?
	What are the major decisions associated with your management responsibilities?
	What improvements in information could result in better decisions?
Critical success factors (CSF)	What are the critical success factors of the organizational unit you manage?
	What actions or decisions are key to achieving these CSFs?
	What information is needed to ensure that critical success factors are under control?
	How do you measure the specific CSFs?
Ends/means (E/M) analysis	What is the good or service provided by the business process?
	What makes these goods or services valuable to recipients or customers?
	What information is needed to evaluate this value?
	What are the key means or processes used to generate or provide goods or services?
	What constitutes efficiency in providing these goods or services?
	What information is needed to evaluate this efficiency?

For example, having customer-order history and information about available inventory could improve decisions about which customers to call on and what to sell them.

CRITICAL SUCCESS FACTORS (CSF). The CSF approach seeks to identify those factors that are critical to the organization's success. Then it focuses information requirements to meet those factors. Typical CSF questions might include the following.

What are the critical success factors of the organizational unit you manage?

Most managers have four to eight of these. For example, critical success factors for order processing include adequate inventory to fill customer orders, prompt order shipment, high percentage of customer payments made, and vendors (suppliers) promptly filling reorders.

What information is needed to ensure that critical success factors are under control?

For example, to determine if adequate inventory is available, management would need summary and exception reports on the percentage of orders filled on time. In addition to overall reports, they should also be categorized by customer and product. To determine if orders are being shipped promptly, management would need to have summary and exception reports on delivery time—both overall reports and reports categorized by customers.

ENDS/MEANS (E/M) ANALYSIS. This approach to determining information requirements is based on desired ends (effectiveness) and available means (efficiency) to achieve the ends. Typical questions to ask using the E/M approach might include the following.

What is the good or service—the "ends"—provided by the business process?

What makes these goods or services valuable to recipients or customers?

What information is needed to evaluate this value—i.e., effectiveness?

What are the key means or processes used to generate or provide goods or services?

For example, the means for order processing include processing orders, processing credit requests, and making shipments.

What constitutes "efficiency" in providing these goods or services?

For example, efficiency for order processing pertains to achieving low transaction costs for orders and credit checks. It would also pertain to minimizing shipment costs.

What information is needed to evaluate this efficiency?

Examples of kinds of information needed to assess efficiency include cost per transaction with historical trends, cost per credit transaction with historical trends, and shipment cost categorized by order, customer, region, and revenue generated.

METHODOLOGY. It is both simple and powerful to use these three methodologies as a basis for indirect questions to obtain a reasonably correct and complete set of information requirements. It is simple because it involves simple components that can be learned by an analyst and a manager in a relatively short time. It is powerful because it is based on fundamental theories of human information processing as well as human strengths and limitations. It also provides a comprehensive set of approaches that are additive in their results.

Interviews have a redundant "safety net" built into them. For example, note that a problem identified in the first set of questions pertains to poor allocation of limited inventory to customers. The need to allocate limited inventory was also identified as a *decision* that must be made. In other words, if the concept of allocating limited inventory was not recalled as a problem, it can still be identified as a decision, and vice versa. This "safety net" effect greatly increases reliability of the structured interview process.

Note that what is generated from the interviews is a profile of conceptual types of information necessary to support an order processing system. For example, the BSP problem "out of stock, below minimum inventory" could be the title of a managerial screen or report. The next part, "automatic reordering of inventory," is a function needed in the new system.

DEFINE INFORMATION CATEGORIES AND MAP INTERVIEWS INTO THEM

Results of interviews need to be converted into information categories. The process of defining information categories from the cross-functional, joint application design interviews is a straightforward process based on **entity/attribute analysis**. *Entities* are defined as persons, places, or things about which information is stored. *Attributes* are the characteristics of these entities. (Entities and attributes were described in more detail in Chapter 8, covering relational data bases.) Customer address is an attribute of customers. We determine entities and attributes by evaluating the information compiled from BSP, CSF, and E/M analysis.

For example, from Table 12.5, the following entities (in italics) and attributes (beneath each entity) can be derived.

Inventory item
Item number
Reorder point

Customer
Customer number
Importance rating
Credit rating

Table 12.5 **Requirements Interview for Order Processing System**

Problems	Solutions	Information
Out of stock too often.	Better inventory management.	Out-of-stock, below-minimum report; automatic reordering of inventory.
Ordering department often allocates limited inventory to the least important customers or to customers with credit problems.	Let ordering department know relative importance and credit status of different customers.	Customer-importance rating and credit rating.
Shipping department often sends off a truck, unaware that another order going to the same destination will be coming to the dock within the hour.	Let shipping department know the destination of orders that are being processed through credit and warehouse.	Shipping destination of orders provided when orders received from customers.

Order
  Order number
  Shipping destination

Entity identifiers (i.e., item number) are automatically added to each entity. Some judgment and interpretation is required to establish entities and attributes. For example, in Table 12.5, the terms *stock* and *inventory* are used as information items to solve the first problem, "Out of stock too often." *Stock* and *inventory* are synonymous, so *inventory item* was selected to represent both concepts. The same was done for *below minimum* and *reorder point*, which means the same thing. The correctness of such interpretations should be confirmed by user management. Also, the exact nature or details of the attributes that are derived from interview results may often not be available from the interviews themselves.

When conceptual information will likely be *computed* from other data or attributes, it is not listed as an attribute. This generally happens when the word *report* or *statistics* is used to describe the information. For example, information required such as "percentage of orders filled on time" involves computation based upon "time promised" and "time delivered."

As you become more experienced, interpretations such as those just illustrated above become more apparent. But remember, mistakes will be caught by subsequent analysis techniques, so do not fret over an inability to achieve perfection during conceptual interpretations.

BUSINESS REENGINEERING

The beginning of the section on analysis stressed the need for understanding something before you change it. Once analysis is complete, understanding should be sought. In fact, a good objective of the analysis phase of system design is to understand the object and information system better than those who work within it. This may seem like an unrealistic objective, but it is not. A major advantage the project team has over those who do the process every day is that the project team can explore the system cross-functionally.

Business reengineering involves the radical change of business process to achieve dramatic improvements in organizational performance. These improvements are made through challenging old ways of doing things and innovating new ways. Business reengineering, as discussed in Chapter 4, is a powerful trend in information systems development used to improve organizational performance and competitiveness.

To begin with, consider the opening case of this chapter. The object and information system need to be reengineered. The first problem is that the same decision is being made three times. The second problem is that it is being made with three separate sources of information, none of which is the correct source. The first issue to resolve is where the decision should be made. Since the business office is the place where the residency issue affects fees, that is the logical place to resolve residency. Where should the information come from? Hint: it already exists. It's whirling around on the university computer disks—the payroll/personnel files where demographic information is stored. What's needed is for the bursar's office to have on-line access to the payroll/personnel file. The student could present a driver's license or some other form of identification, and what took an entire day of her time and a lot of university time could be accomplished in about 10 seconds. That's radical improvement!

Note the need to have cross-functional access to information. In this case, the bursar's office needs access to personnel data. Good information architecture planning (as discussed in Chapter 11) would reveal this need. Another example of business reengineering is discussed in Box 12.6.

IT At Work BOX 12.6

HALLMARK CARDS

At Hallmark Cards, spawning a new line of greeting cards from concept to market took two to three years. Costly revisions to design, lettering, and printing stock were numbering around 50,000 a year. Once products were on the shelves, sales data often arrived too late—sometimes several months too late—to replenish the hot sellers, yank the cold ones, and plan for new lines. The window of opportunity can shut quickly in Hallmark's business; peak retail selling periods for major events such as Valentine's Day last only a few days.

The first reengineering recommendation was to improve the flow of sales data from the Hallmark specialty stores to corporate headquarters. The company outfitted 250 of the independently owned Hallmark stores with computerized point-of-sale systems that use barcode readers to capture detailed information on every purchase. Since then, the company has been getting nearly instantaneous information on what's selling.

Making the torrent of data meaningful to Hallmark management was the next step. Decision support systems, computer programs for key executives that would graphically represent trends in the stores, were created. Knowledge about exactly what was sold yesterday, where it sold, what it sold with, what part of the day it sold, and what display it came out of caused dramatic and exciting changes in Hallmark's business. For instance, the company found that certain products sell better when they are adjacent to other products. In the past, Hallmark would have been leery about suggesting major product and format changes to the retailers; they might have waited 24 months before saying anything. They can now tell retailers what works and what doesn't work with retail, not wholesale, data.

A bigger and more agonizing transformation of Hallmark's business processes happened in their formerly lengthy product development cycle. Analysis found that from the time a concept was given to the creative staff to the time it hit the printing department, there were 25 handoffs. And 90 percent of that time involved work simply sitting in someone's in- or out-basket.

In the summer of 1991, a new line of cards was developed in an entirely different way. Hallmark grouped people together who had been separated by disciplines, departments, floors, and even buildings in order to cut down on the queue time, spur creativity, and end the throw-it-over-the-wall-it's-their-problem cycle. The groupings worked so well that half of the line hit the stores eight months ahead of schedule.

Critical Thinking Issues: What role did point-of-sale technology play in Hallmark's new system? What prevented Hallmark from undertaking the new approach to card design years ago? ▲

Analyzing business reengineering sets the stage for the next four steps in systems development—systems design, development, implementation, and evaluation—which will be covered in Chapter 13.

▶ MANAGERIAL ISSUES

In any system development effort, the following questions must be answered.

1. Search for problems, or take them as they come? Searches can be costly in terms of management time (direct and opportunity) and can lead to morale problems when workers feel that management is "gunning for them." On the other hand, "a stitch in time saves nine"; better to detect a problem early and minimize its effect than react to it later with more serious consequences.

2. Do information systems lead or follow corporate policy? Information systems can provide clear competitive advantages that may put a company in the lead of an industry. Chasing technology—especially rapidly changing technology—can be very costly, however, especially if mistakes are made.

3. How are information systems outlays justified—by reduced costs, increased benefits, or both? Sometimes information technology is needed simply to remain competitive in a changing market.

4. Who leads the information systems project—a systems analyst or an end-user representative? The systems analyst has the best appreciation for what *can be* done; the user has the best appreciation for what *should be* done.

5. How do we make sure an information system serves the corporation, not just part of the firm? How do we deal with requirements that appear dysfunctional? Involving all corporate divisions helps ensure a system will be responsive to corporate needs, but this also increases the likelihood of increasing cost and delaying implementation when divisional disagreements arise.

6. When is radical corporate restructuring of an information system through reengineering necessary? When is it desirable? What are the alternatives? In a rapidly changing market environment, chasing opportunities with incremental changes may never work; choosing the wrong path for a radical restructuring can be just as disastrous. ■

KEY TERMS

Break-even analysis *413*

Business reengineering *434*

Business systems planning (BSP) *430*

Cost justification *413*

Critical success factors (CSF) *420*

Cross-functional system *426*

Data flow diagram (DFD) *422*

Decision center *420*

Decision system *419*

Ends/means (E/M) Analysis *430*

Entity/attribute analysis *433*

Feasibility study *413*

Flowchart *422*

Information requirements *424*

Information system *411*

Joint application design (JAD) *428*

Object system *411*

Opportunistic surveillance *411*

Presentation graphics *422*

Project proposal *413*

Project team *415*

Reaction surveillance *411*

Return on investment (ROI) *413*

Single-function system *425*

Structured interviews *419*

Systems development life cycle (SDLC) *407*

Systems analysis *417*

Unstructured interviews *429*

CHAPTER HIGHLIGHTS *(L-x means learning objective number x)*

▼ The first three steps of the systems development life cycle consist of identifying problems and opportunities, analyzing and documenting existing systems, and determining information requirements (L-1)

▼ To identify problems and opportunities, opportunistic surveillance should be used. Causality of problems needs to be addressed because systems—object *and* information systems—need to be thoroughly understood before attempting to change them. Technical, economic, and operational feasibility studies need to be done, and the proposed project team needs to be cross-functional. (L-2)

▼ Analysis, documentation, observations, interviews, and questionnaires are critical when analyzing existing systems. Reviewing object systems

and defining decision making set the stage for information requirements determination. (L-3)

▼ When documenting systems, graphically oriented diagrams such as data flow diagrams, flowcharts, and models using presentation graphics are the most useful—especially when communicating with management. (L-3)

▼ When determining information requirements, both cross-functional, joint application design and structured interview techniques are key. (L-4)

▼ Business reengineering involves achieving radical performance improvement through radical change, and it is a powerful trend used in information systems development to improve organizational performance and competitiveness. (L-5)

QUESTIONS FOR REVIEW

1. Differentiate between management surveillance actions that are reactionary and those that are opportunistic in orientation. Give examples of each.

2. What is the difference between an object system and an information system?

3. Discuss the fundamental analysis activities for reviewing an object system.

4. Discuss the fundamental analysis activities for defining decision making associated with an object system, analyzing existing information system support of decision making, and isolating deficiencies in an information system.

QUESTIONS FOR DISCUSSION

1. Why might organizations have a tendency to be more reactionary than opportunistic when identifying problems?

2. Why do information systems often get improved without improving the object system?

3. Why is it important to get at the issue of causality when exploring problems associated with a business process?

4. Discuss the importance of understanding a system before changing it.

5. What are the key steps in determining information requirements?

6. Define and discuss business reengineering, in the context of requirements analysis.

5. Why is it important to use cross-functional joint application design for information requirements determination?

6. What role does the structured interview play in information requirements determination?

7. Why is it important to consider business reengineering a part of the analysis process?

EXERCISES

1. Determine and discuss an opportunistic improvement in the admission and registration process that could make attending your university more attractive.

2. Conduct a structured interview for an organizational process—perhaps at your university—using the BSP,

CSF, and E/M analysis questions discussed in the chapter.

3. Drawing from the previous two exercises, discuss how these processes could be reengineered.

GROUP ASSIGNMENT

The essence of JAD—joint application design—is working in groups to achieve a common purpose, even though different points of view are present. Taking the example of the registration system at your university, have members of the group assume the following roles.

▼ Registrar.

▼ Bursar.

▼ Student Aid.

▼ Faculty Advisor.

▼ Campus Computing Services.

▼ Student.

▼ Other interested parties (identify).

With one or more persons in each role, form JAD teams and devise a registration system that will, ideally, improve upon the current system which is in place. Define the problems, solutions, and information in the proposed system. Identify approaches that might be used to obtain the information requirements of the system. As part of the group process, observe the different opinions and points of view that emerge from each of the role players. How are disputed settled? What defines the "best" system?

Minicase 1

REENGINEERING THE UTILITY INDUSTRY

James Coland, having recently moved from Minneapolis to Memphis, needed to acquire telephone and utility services. First, he called the phone company and explained that he wanted telephone service. The phone company asked him about his previous residence and phone number. Mr. Coland provided the information and was asked if he would like the same services that he had on his telephone in Minneapolis. Mr. Coland explained that he

would like everything to remain the same, but was also interested in adding voice mail capabilities. The phone company explained the services that were available and their costs. Mr. Coland agreed to them, and the transaction was completed in less than three minutes.

Next, Mr. Coland contacted the utilities service and explained that he wanted gas and electricity hooked up. He was asked about his residence and given directions to the nearest utility company service office. He was also told that he would need to bring either proof of purchase of residence or a rental agreement, his driver's license, and his social security number as identification. Mr. Coland was somewhat surprised by these requirements, but proceeded to follow the instructions. He went to the service office where he was told to stand in line and fill out an application form. He went to a separate counter, filled out the application form—which included name, address, employer, and other basic demographic information. After completing this information, he stood in a separate line to turn in his form. When the service representative for the utility company received his form, she proceeded to enter all the information into a computer terminal. He was then instructed to provide a $100 cash deposit and was told that his utilities would be hooked up the next day.

Including driving time to and from the service facility as well as the time spent waiting in line (about 25 minutes), Mr. Coland invested two and a half hours out of his work day in order to get his utility services. The only time the service facility was open was during the day between the hours of eight and five o'clock.

Mr. Coland could not help but be struck by the contrast between what was required to establish phone services and utility services. He checked with several colleagues who had recently moved to other cities, and they all had similar experiences. It seemed to everyone that there must be a better way.

Questions for Minicase 1

1. Recognizing that utility companies generally have a monopoly but are nonetheless subject to public pressure if they provide inferior services, do an assessment of the key decisions that have to be made by the utility company and their current processes. You might even construct a data flow diagram of the process. Then, determine what information they really need in order to make their decisions. Also, consider how the process might be reengineered to be more customer driven and more similar to the telephone company's much-less-painful transaction.

2. Discuss how a credit card company might—in an opportunistic fashion—offer customers moving to different cities some type of service in order to minimize the difficulties of getting utilities connected. Providing such a service could be a good strategy, given that the type of person who moves from city to city would probably be an upscale professional customer who might show loyalty to a credit card company that offers a service to minimize the difficulty of relocation.

Minicase 2

INDIVIDUALIZED SYSTEMS

When analyzing a problem for an information systems remedy, system analysts usually work with representatives of organizational groups to tailor a system to the groups' needs. But sometimes analysts have to tailor systems to individual users.

The Institute for Cognitive Prosthetics builds custom computer systems to help head-injury patients overcome very specific problems such as prioritizing items on a list, remembering when to do certain things, and concentrating on a task at hand. Like prosthetic arms and legs, these systems must be custom fit. But because the cognitive processes of these patients are so complicated, the development process itself must be uniquely tailored to each patient. As a result, says Dr. Elliott Cole, "our computing environment is designed around the premise that 5 percent of our work is initial design and 95 percent is modification and enhancement."

When a new patient comes in, Cole analyzes the activities that person wants to perform. "We study the way the individual performs the task, noting those subtasks that the individual can perform easily and those the individual can't perform."

In one case, a woman needed help prioritizing lists after a near-fatal accident. The patient herself eventually came up with the solution, Cole said. "We sat down to design, and after 15 minutes she said, in essence, 'Move out of the way, I have a set of ideas.' And over the next half hour or so, we banged out something that really would work for her."

Questions for Minicase 2

1. Of the three life cycle steps discussed at length in this chapter, which appear to have been done by Dr. Cole and his staff—and which, if any, appear not to be done? Was any one step emphasized over others?

2. Review the summary of structured interview sample questions in Table 12.4. How relevant are these types of questions and the structured interview techniques to this case (ignoring the obvious that each patient is not a business)? Why?

REFERENCES AND BIBLIOGRAPHY

1. Alavik, M., "The Evolution of Information Systems Development Approach: Some Field Observations," *Data Base*, Vol. 15, No. 3, Spring 1984.

2. Blumenthal, S. C., *Management Information Systems: A Framework for Planning and Development*, Englewood Cliffs, NJ: Prentice-Hall, 1969.

3. Bostrom, R. P. "Development of Computer-Based Information Systems: A Communications Perspective," *Computer Personnel*, Vol. 9, No. 4, August 1984.

4. Burns, R. N., and Dennis, A. R., "Selecting the Appropriate Application Development Methodology," *Data Base*, Vol. 17, No. 1, Fall 1985.

5. *Executive's Guide to Computer-Based Information Systems*, Englewood, Cliffs. NJ: Prentice-Hall, 1983.

6. Hall, G., Rosenthal, J., and Wade, J., "How to Make Reengineering Really Work," *Harvard Business Review*, November/December 1993.

7. Hammer, M. and Champy, J., *Reengineering the Corporation*, New York: Harper Business, 1993.

8. Wetherbe, J. C., *Best Practices in Systems Analysis and Design*, St. Paul, MN: West Publishing, 1994.

13

INFORMATION SYSTEMS DESIGN, DEVELOPMENT, IMPLEMENTATION, AND EVALUATION

Chapter Outline

Learning Objectives

After studying this chapter, you will be able to:

1. Explain information systems design objectives, products, and its various approaches.

2. Describe how information systems are developed, tested, and validated—the layered approach, development tools and techniques, quality assurance, and types of testing performed.

3. Discuss the key issues in implementing information systems, including conversion strategy and training as well as the major types of dysfunctional behavior that may occur and guidelines for minimizing them.

4. Describe how to evaluate and continually maintain an implemented information system—its hardware, software, and information.

13.1 A NEW SYSTEM AT SAMSON: BUT DOES IT WORK?

BRIAN SCHROEDER, PRESIDENT and CEO of Samson Shipping, built a lucrative wholesale distribution business. One of the policies he felt very strongly about was that no shipment should ever be made unless it was profitable—the profit generated must exceed the cost of delivering it. If not, orders were to be accumulated until enough revenue was generated to cover delivery costs *and* make a profit.

Jamie Glass managed one of the regional Samson warehouses, doing a very good job and running a very profitable operation. From time to time, however, she had a customer wanting a shipment that was not profitable. Although she would try to explain the corporate policy to customers, customers would explain to her that if they didn't get urgent shipments when they needed them, they would simply find another supplier. This put Jamie in a bind—having to choose between violating corporate policy or risking the loss of crucial customers. Like most managers, she recognized that timely shipments had to be made in order to keep customers; in other words, she would find a way to work around the rules. This never really created a problem for Jamie because the monthly reports on her shipments were something she did in her office with the door closed, using a procedure known as ''creative'' accounting.

A systems analyst, Brad Bounds, was brought in by the CEO to put in an on-line, computer-based inventory order processing and shipment tracking system. At first, the managers thought the new system would be helpful to them. They soon found out, however, that without the flexibility, informality, and privacy of the manual reporting system, managers such as Jamie would be facing computer-generated exception reports every time they made an unprofitable shipment.

The CEO was upset about these exception reports on Jamie and two other managers, Jessie Childs and Scott Jordan. He reprimanded them for violating corporate policy. The three managers then met with Brad and asked him to modify the system, so they could continue to provide customer service, be competitive, and fulfill customer needs. Brad perceived them as wanting to manipulate the system to serve their own purposes. Nevertheless, he explained that the system could be programmed to do whatever needed to be done, but

Warehousing at Samson.

modifications such as they were requesting needed to be approved by Mr. Schroeder. The three managers told Brad to ''forget it.''

The managers then proceeded collectively to sabotage the system by putting in outrageous numbers that made no sense. The system started to generate reports that were as incorrect as those produced when the system was first being tested and the bugs were being worked out. It never occurred to Brad that managers would deliberately sabotage the system, so he kept diligently looking for supposed bugs in the software. Jamie, Jessie, and Scott, meanwhile, began to complain that the system wasn't working correctly and had serious problems. The negative campaigning resulted in the system losing credibility and ultimately being terminated. Brad was terminated along with it.

▶ 13.2 THE SYSTEMS DEVELOPMENT LIFE CYCLE: A REVIEW AND PREFACE

As the foregoing example highlights, good information systems development is much more than finding the fastest, cheapest, most economical machines to gather, store, and report data. There are many more issues to consider—and a good development process can promote success and avoid the problems Samson Shipping faced.

This is the second of two chapters (Chapters 12 and 13) on the systems development life cycle (SDLC). Chapter 12 introduced the seven basic SDLC steps (shown again in Figure 13.1) and detailed the first three: identify problems and opportunities, analyze and document the existing system, and determine the information requirements. This chapter covers the remaining four steps: *design technology and personnel requirements; develop, test, and validate the new system; implement the new system;* and *evaluate and maintain the new system.* We will also consider important behavioral issues in implementing new information systems. As illustrated in the opening case, a system that works right may not necessarily be "right" for the organization, so it is very important that human and behavioral factors be considered when implementing systems.

A REVIEW OF THE SYSTEMS DEVELOPMENT LIFE CYCLE

It is important to recall the primary relationship between the SDLC steps that were discussed in Chapter 12 and those to be discussed here. The first three systems development steps ensure the systems development effort is focusing on the "right things," which are the managerial issues. Subsequent systems development steps (discussed in this chapter) focus on making sure "things are done right"—mainly the technical issues. Another way to think of the two chapters is that Chapter 12 focuses on *what* needs to be done; Chapter 13 focuses on *how* to do it.

It is also important to remember that the SDLC steps are not completely discrete, one-time processes. Rather, the systems development cycle is iterative and evolutionary. The steps in the cycle, however, retain a basic sequential flow from the point of origin of the development cycle—"identify new problems and opportunities." Each step represents a major checkpoint, or milestone, and has identifiable deliverables that symbolize completion. At any step in the cycle, previously unidentified problems and/or opportunities may be discovered. In such cases, it is important to ensure proper integration of a solution to a new problem or opportunity.

Making even a minor change to a system without proper consideration of what has already been accomplished can cause unanticipated and undesirable rippling effects, seriously damaging the operation of the system. Therefore, as Figure 13.1 shows, all steps of the systems development cycle allow return to the

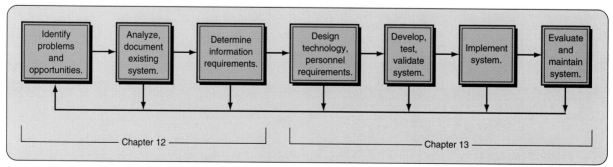

FIGURE 13.1 Systems development life cycle overview.

point of origin. By periodically returning to the first step at any point in the life cycle, the process exhibits a ''spiraling'' or ''whirlpool'' characteristic rather than a purely sequential or ''waterfall'' characteristic.

SYSTEMS DEVELOPMENT: A RAPIDLY EVOLVING ENVIRONMENT

New development tools provide executives with easy-to-use systems.

EMERGING TECHNOLOGY

...object-oriented development promises significant improvements in systems development

The tools, technology, and techniques for systems design and development are evolving rapidly, and emerging best practices for systems development are diverging significantly in form, style, and function from what might be termed *traditional development methods*. In this chapter, we discuss tools and techniques for both traditional development and new development approaches.

As technologies and architectures evolve and advance, so, too, do our tools and techniques for systems development. One of the most important current developments is the emergence of object-oriented development environments, as discussed in Chapter 8. Object orientation moves the developer closer to building systems from interchangeable components instead of building systems line by line with detailed programming languages. Although object orientation is relatively new, it is maturing rapidly and offers the developer new options for building systems through a combination of custom development and assembly with reusable components from software ''libraries.'' Although it is beyond the scope of this book to deal completely with the object-oriented development paradigm, an overview of the object approach to developing systems is covered.

While the key objective of this chapter is to provide an understanding of software development, it would take several more chapters to provide all the operational skills for the techniques discussed. Such detailed training comes from books and courses in systems analysis and design, computer programming, operating systems, networks, CASE tools, and manuals of programming style. However, the material covered in this chapter will allow you to understand the role you might play on a project team, whether you are a user of an information system for a business process or decide to become an information technology professional. Indeed, it is becoming useful for organizational participants to rotate in and out of information technology positions during their career, since this technology is playing such a key role in organizations.

▶ 13.3 STEP 4: DESIGN TECHNOLOGY AND PERSONNEL REQUIREMENTS

Information structuring during information system design is the main focus of this section. **Information systems structure** refers to the structure of information in the *databases* (e.g., logical data structure, data elements, input definitions), the *process structure* (e.g., business rules, logic definitions, algorithms, computation rules), the *presentation mode* (e.g., text, graphical, animation, sound, video), the *presentation style* (e.g., menus, windows, interactive, real time, configurable, natural language), and the *output requirements* (e.g., the context and meaning of the information as presented to the user). For most information system users, structuring the information has the greatest impact on system utility and their jobs.

When structuring information for an information system, a systems designer may not know what specific hardware and software will be best suited to support the system. The degree of uncertainty about the hardware and software platform depends on a number of factors including the scope of the system, the radicalness of the design, and the degree of divergence from the established information technology architecture.

The degree of stability in the technological platform also influences the types of development tools that can be used. Increasingly, development tools are tied to a particular architecture of the technology platform. Thus, if a new technological platform is required, the development team and project management must factor in time for searching, selecting, and learning new tools. The bottom line, as we shall see later in this chapter, is that tools and technologies are related—and decisions about development tools and about technologies are more and more interdependent.

SYSTEMS DESIGN TECHNIQUES AND TECHNOLOGIES

In general, systems design techniques should be as independent of hardware and software as possible, allowing systems specifications to be implemented using whatever hardware and software turns out to be most cost-effective in supporting the information structure. To the degree that design tools and techniques are hardware and software independent, the developer and the business can be less mindful of the interdependencies between the design specification and the ultimate hardware-software environment in which the information system will operate. Moreover, the systems analyst is then less constrained by concerns over types of development tools and can more fully concentrate on developing a design that best satisfies the client's requirements and has the highest fidelity in delivering business results.

In this chapter, a number of sophisticated techniques and technologies are covered. Though organizations may have systems design procedures and computer-aided software engineering (CASE, see Chapter 6) technologies that differ from the procedures presented in this chapter, the differences will generally be cosmetic rather than conceptual in nature.

Before tackling the several sophisticated techniques and technologies, it is helpful to have an understanding of the outcomes or deliverables from the systems design phase of the systems development life cycle. Systems design should generate the following deliverables.

1. *Input definitions* describe input documents and input screens.
2. *Output definitions* describe the printed reports or terminal displays provided by the system. Outputs can be categorized as formal and predefined or informal and ad hoc; the latter requires good anticipation of requirements through the data modeling techniques discussed in this chapter.
3. *Logical data structures* use data modeling to define the various entities, attributes, and relationships within the database designed to support the information system. (This topic was discussed in detail in Chapter 8.)
4. *Data dictionaries* define all the data elements that are inputted, computed, stored, and reported in the information system. This includes the source of each data element, validation logic, processing or computation logic, where each data element is used, and where it is stored.
5. *Logic definitions* graphically define complex processing rules necessary for input, computation, processing, and data storage. Techniques include decision tables and decision trees.
6. *System presentation graphics* portray, in a macro sense, how the overall system is put together. These graphics illustrate information flow, reporting, files, and so forth.

The various design **specifications** (with the exception of presentation graphics) are linked together as illustrated in Figure 13.2, such that the input, computation, logical processing, storage, and reporting of each item of information can be traced forward or backward from its point of origin to its final use. As shown in the figure, and as will be illustrated later in the following section, the

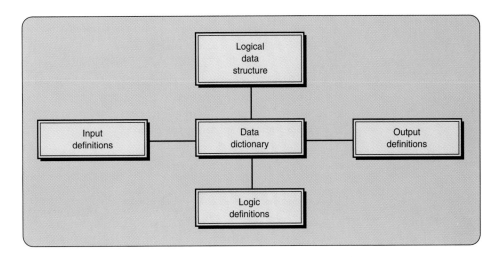

FIGURE 13.2 System design specifications.

data dictionary is the core of design specifications. On completion, the specifications should provide sufficient documentation to guide the generation of software required to operate the system.

The outputs of any system determine the inputs and processes necessary to support the system. Once the output requirements are determined, the system designer can determine what to *include* in the system and how to *structure* it so that outputs can be provided. The process of translating output requirements to determine information inclusion and structure is a two-phase process consisting of a *conceptual* or *logical* phase and a *detailed* phase.

CONCEPTUAL/LOGICAL DESIGN PHASE

The conceptual stage of information requirements was introduced in Chapter 12. A cross-functional joint application design (JAD), in conjunction with structured interviews (using BSP, CSF, and/or E/M analysis), provides a list of the conceptual types of information needed from a system. The same interview used for conceptual information architecture planning is repeated for designing a system during the SDLC. Both high-level managers and operations personnel are also interviewed in order to get more specific details to help design what is to become a production system. The combined results of the interviews with results of data flow diagrams or flowcharts is sufficient for constructing a conceptual or logical data structure—the subjects or entities about which data are to be stored and the relationships among those entities. (For a review of logical data structures, see Chapters 8 and 12.)

DATA DICTIONARY. After creating the conceptual data model, it is a good time to begin the **data dictionary**. Although few of the final data elements will have been identified, and there will not be complete data dictionary information for the data elements, this is not a serious problem. The idea is to define as much as possible (i.e., make partial dictionary entries) for all data elements currently identified. Getting a head start on this documentation makes subsequent design and data dictionary documentation easier to manage. The data dictionary is the core documentation for systems design, development, and subsequent maintenance or modifications. Also, as will be illustrated later, data dictionaries are the cornerstone of automatic program-code generations. Data dictionaries are supported by CASE products, which greatly ease the task of creating and maintaining data dictionaries.

The exact content and format of data dictionary items vary. Most support tools have a fixed set of entries, such as data definitions and format. They also

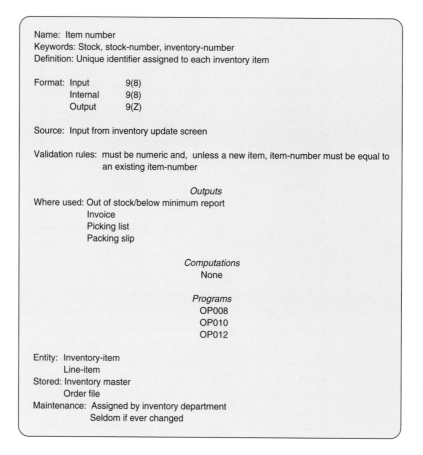

```
Name:  Item number
Keywords: Stock, stock-number, inventory-number
Definition: Unique identifier assigned to each inventory item

Format:  Input        9(8)
         Internal     9(8)
         Output       9(Z)


Source:  Input from inventory update screen

Validation rules:  must be numeric and,  unless a new item, item-number must be equal to
                   an existing item-number

                            Outputs
Where used: Out of stock/below minimum report
            Invoice
            Picking list
            Packing slip


                         Computations
                            None


                          Programs
                           OP008
                           OP010
                           OP012


Entity:  Inventory-item
         Line-item
Stored:  Inventory master
         Order file
Maintenance:  Assigned by inventory department
              Seldom if ever changed
```

FIGURE 13.3 Data element dictionary display.

allow for free-text documentation for other entries desired by the designer. Data dictionary entries are shown in Figure 13.3.

1. **Name.** A unique name assigned to a data element, used to track an element—referred to in an output, input, or decision table—back to the data-element dictionary for a complete description.

2. **Keywords.** This allows an analyst to list other names by which a data element might be referred. CASE products commonly can perform a keyword search for cross-referencing or locating an element.

3. **Format.** Input and output formats define how the data element is formatted, indicating field length and characteristics (e.g., numeric or alphabetic).

4. **Source.** This states where data elements come from—inputs, tables, or computations. Input data elements come directly into the system from an input data stream (e.g., a transaction). Table data elements come from predefined tables (e.g., tax rate tables). Computed data elements are computed from other data elements (e.g., NETPAY = GROSSPAY − TAXES).

5. **Validation rules.** Validation rules reduce data input errors. For example, for an input data element such as DATE, validation might ensure that a date cannot be either later or more than 30 days earlier than today's date.

6. **Where used.** This is a list created to keep track, for control purposes, of each report, computation, and computer program in which a data element is used. The "where-used" list can pinpoint reports and displays that need to be changed when, for example, the definition of a data element has been changed. Also, people receiving reports affected by a change can be identified and alerted to a new procedure, element, or report. During the early and the latter stages of systems design, the specific programs in which a data element is used are often unknown; this will be completed by the programmer during software development.

7. *Entities.* This defines the entity or entities of which the data element is an attribute, determined from the data model. Note that a data element can be an attribute for more than one entity.

8. *Storage.* This defines where (i.e., in what physical file) a data element is stored, although not all data elements are stored in files.

9. *Maintenance.* This describes procedures for updating an element. Some elements are never updated unless there was a mistake (e.g., a social security number or date of birth), some are periodically updated (e.g., a student's grade point average for each semester), and some are occasionally updated (e.g., an address or telephone number).

LOGIC DEFINITION. A key objective of systems design specifications is to avoid narrative descriptions of what a system is to perform, because narrative descriptions tend to be confusing, incomplete, and unreliable. Therefore, various structured techniques have been developed that allow complex logical relationships to be expressed in a nonnarrative form. These techniques are used primarily to describe the following: *input validation logic, computation logic,* and *output processing and reporting logic.*

The main techniques used for logic definitions include decision tables and decision trees—two different techniques aimed at doing essentially the same thing. The theory behind them is that a structured, well-defined logic process will result in more accurate systems design specifications. Each technique accomplishes this in a slightly different way. For the purposes of this discussion, more focus will be placed on decision tables. Once decision tables are understood, it is relatively easy to understand the other techniques and compare their relative values.

Decision tables are powerful, efficient tools for expressing complex logical relationships. A **decision table** is a simple matrix containing columns and rows which are used to define decision relationships. Figure 13.4 illustrates a decision table. Ideally, the format should be implemented on a computer display screen—using CASE technology—for data entry and modification ease.

There are three major components in a decision table: conditions, courses of action, and decision rules. *Conditions* are events or facts that determine the courses of action to be taken. *Courses of action* are processes or operations to be performed under certain conditions. *Decision rules* express the relationships among combinations of conditions and courses of actions.

Decision rules are expressed by making condition entries and course-of-action entries in the matrix provided to the right of condition statements and course-of-action statements. Possible decision rule entries and their definitions are as follows.

Conditions	Decision rules	1	2	3	4	5	6
Courses of action	Decision rules	1	2	3	4	5	6

FIGURE 13.4 Decision table format.

1. *Condition entries*

    Y = Yes, condition statement must apply.

    N = No, condition statement must not apply.

    - = Indifferent, condition statement is irrelevant to the decision table and does not have to be checked.

2. *Course of action entries*

    X = Activate course of action.

    • = Do not activate course of action.

Figure 13.5 shows decision rules for customer billing. Note that a double horizontal line is used to separate conditions from courses of action. If a customer's balance is less than or equal to zero (Decision rule 1, read vertically), no additional conditions are checked and a statement is not printed for the customer. If a customer's balance is greater than zero, but less than his credit limit (Decision rule 2), no additional conditions are checked, and a statement is printed for the customer. If the customer's balance due exceeds his credit limit, then the credit rating is checked; if the credit rating is excellent (Decision rule 3), a statement is printed for the customer. If the credit rating is not excellent (Decision rule 4), a statement is printed and a credit warning message is added to it.

Conditions	Decision rules	1	2	3	4	5	6
Balance due ≤ 0		Y	N	N	N		
Balance due > 0 and ≤ credit limit		–	Y	N	N		
Balance due > credit limit		–	–	Y	Y		
Credit rating excellent		–	–	Y	N		
Courses of action	Decision rules	1	2	3	4	5	6
Do not print statement		X	•	•	•		
Print statement		•	X	X	X		
Add credit warning to statement		•	•	•	X		

FIGURE 13.5 Completed decision table.

DETAILED DESIGN PHASE

Once the conceptual data model is complete and all essential data dictionary entries are made, the detailed phases of information requirements and data structuring can begin. Developing detailed information requirements involves generating exact specifications for all formal required reports and developing a good understanding of ad hoc information requirements to make sure that the data structure contains the necessary entities and data elements. To ensure that detailed requirements are correctly identified, analysts sometimes use *prototyping* discussed below in more detail.

FORMAL REPORTING SPECIFICATIONS. Business or regulatory reporting requirements often stipulate formal reports that must be prepared, such as filings with the Securities and Exchanges Commission. Additionally, executives may require certain summary or exception reports on company or market conditions. These types of standardized, recurring reports require close adherence to report requirements and careful design by developers. A specific example of a formal output that might ultimately be designed for a system is illustrated in Figure 13.6.

Date: 12-06-94		Out of stock/below minimum report					Page 1
Vendor number	Item number	Item description	Stock condition	On hand	Reorder point	Quantity on order	Date ordered
146894	67894220	Hair dryer	Out	0	60	250	12/02/94
792267	68116772	Elect shaver	Below min	20	40	100	12/03/94
406843	46214558	Guitar	Out	0	50	175	12/01/94
787743	22116600	Lamp	Below min	10	40		12/04/94
•	•	•	•	•	•	•	•
•	•	•	•	•	•	•	•

FIGURE 13.6 Out of Stock/Below Minimum Report.

The "Out of Stock/Below Minimum" terminal displays alerts management of stock-out items. This information not only alerts inventory management to the urgency of obtaining more stock from vendors, it also alerts sales personnel to use caution in delivery commitments for those items.

AD HOC REPORTING ABILITY. Some reports are aperiodic or one-time requirements in response to a business situation. These reports are based on ad hoc database inquiries—and will almost exclusively use fourth-generation languages (4GLs) with a relational data model. Examples of popular 4GLs are ACCESS, Q&A, FOCUS, RAMIS, NOMAD, INFO, NATURAL, DB2, and SQL. While designers cannot anticipate *all* ad hoc query and reporting needs, they should consider the most likely ad hoc needs based on present and forecasted future business information needs. Although 4GL languages are relatively easy to use, designers should also anticipate and consider operational and training requirements for those using them.

So how do we make sure we have fully determined the detailed data structure and items to meet formal and ad hoc information reporting requirements? In Chapter 12, it was pointed out that during information requirements determination, the following five mistakes are commonly made.

1. Assuming managers know their information requirements.
2. Failing to ask the right people.
3. Asking people one at a time instead of as a group.
4. Asking the wrong questions.
5. Not allowing users to refine their requirements through trial and error.

The first four mistakes are addressed by techniques covered in Chapter 12 (e.g., cross-functional, joint application development using structured interviews). Mistake number five is the issue here.

Trial-and-error (or experiential) learning is an important part of general problem solving. For example, people use trial and error when they try on clothes before they purchase them, or test-drive cars before making a selection. Trial and error can also be an important part of determining detailed information requirements. Proper analysis *prior* to a trial-and-error process, of course, can substantially reduce the amount of trial-and-error time expended. For example, a fashion consultant could narrow a new wardrobe search and shorten trial and error by asking the customer questions about career, lifestyle, budget, and taste—and by observing physical characteristics. Similarly, the structured interview combined with the analytical tools of data modeling can provide a good approximation of the system, reducing the amount of trial-and-error effort necessary to determine detailed information requirements. The details can then be determined or verified through prototyping or heuristic design.

PROTOTYPING AND HEURISTIC DESIGN. Information systems technology can take advantage of more advanced development techniques for information requirements determination using **heuristic design** or **prototyping**. These two labels describe similar but slightly different approaches to systems development that exploit advanced technologies for using trial-and-error problem solving. Heuristic and prototype development represent major departures from traditional systems development but offer strong and distinctive advantages. Other labels given to the process are *evolutionary* and *iterative* development.

Prototyping and heuristic design techniques emerged in the late 1970s as a solution to the problem of making major revisions to systems after the systems were allegedly complete. Research on systems that had been developed revealed that revision costs were staggering—often exceeding the original development cost several times over. It became clear that it was better to have trial-and-error activity before, rather than after, the final system is built.

This notion of trial-and-error prototyping came from manufacturing, where a prototype product (e.g., a car) is built in a shop (not a factory) and the cycle of testing and modification is repeated several times until the final design is complete. Then, the factory production line is built with reasonable assurance that an acceptable product has been designed. The idea is to avoid building a high-cost factory until the design is right.

A basic model of prototyping or heuristic design is provided in Figure 13.7. As stated at the beginning of this chapter, system design is *output* driven. Accordingly, the initial prototype should focus on the output abilities of the system and the data structure necessary to support them. There is no need during the early stages of the prototype to become preoccupied with detailed specifications or sources of system inputs. Until data structure and data content issues are resolved, concern with details of inputs is premature. Besides the 4GLs and relational database management systems, CASE tools and loosely coupled tool sets have some powerful tools to facilitate the prototyping process. These tools include *menu generators*, *screen generators*, *report generators*, and *code generators*.

1. *Menu generators.* These outline the eventual functions or components of systems (e.g., place order, check on status of order, cancel order) and illustrate how users can branch to various screens and subscreens for data entry or inquiry.

2. *Screen generators.* These are used to format or "paint" desired layouts and the content of a screen using the data dictionary.

3. *Report generators.* These are similar to screen generators in that formats are readily generated in the same fashion, additionally indicating totals, paging, print edits, and sequencing of the system reports.

Using a computer to produce an automobile prototype.

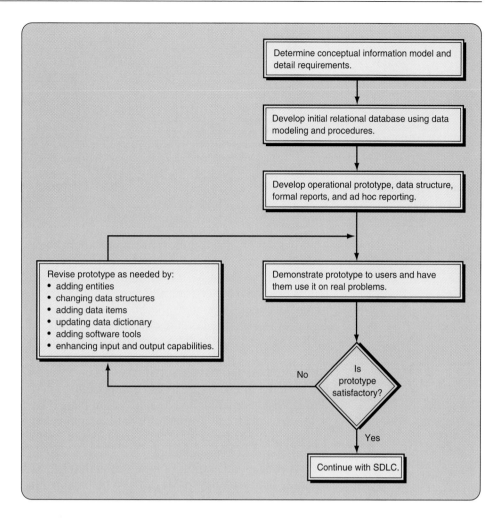

FIGURE 13.7 Model of prototyping or heuristic design.

4. *Code generators.* These allow an analyst to generate modular units of source code from high-level specifications, demonstrate the system, revise specifications, and demonstrate the system again. Code generators play an even bigger role in systems development and are discussed in greater detail in texts on systems analysis and design.

DESIGNING THE INPUT SYSTEM. As users become satisfied with detailed output abilities, *input* design needs can be identified and documented. Due to the on-line interactive nature of most systems, the majority of inputs use the same format as outputs. The format of an output, therefore, can often serve as the format for inputting those required output data elements. For example, consider the customer record display illustrated in Figure 13.8. The data items on the left-hand side of the screen would likely be inputted directly for a new record or modified for an existing record. Whether or not data elements are inputted (as opposed to computed) can be confirmed by checking the SOURCE entry in the data dictionary.

The items on the right-hand side of the screen would likely be computed or generated directly from order transactions (verifiable from the data dictionary). For example, credit rating might be based on evaluation of accounts receivable payment data; or, rather than being computed or derived from other data, it could be inputted based upon a judgment made outside the computer. Again, these are issues documented in the data dictionary and approved by users. At any rate, since the screen format has already been developed for output purposes, it is just as well to use it for input and update purposes.

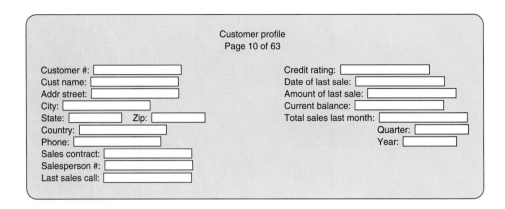

FIGURE 13.8 Customer record display.

Besides on-line inputs, some inputs might come as completed forms, optical-scan sheets, and magnetic ink character recognition data (such as is used on bank checks). These could be transmitted via data communications from other computers or received electronically (e.g., on a floppy disk). In those cases, the document or media format would be defined simply by indicating where the data elements were located on the document or media. Remember, data elements and their input formats are defined in the data dictionary.

GRAPHICS TO DOCUMENT THE OVERALL SYSTEM. The old phrase that "you can't see the forest for the trees" is applicable to design documentation generated during systems analysis and design. To complete system design and allow the forest to be seen, one needs a straightforward, graphical representation of how the overall system is put together. These graphics are useful for documentation and for presentations to management.

A conceptual graphic of a new system is illustrated in Figure 13.9. Graphics for individual screen displays can also be included in management or user documentation. Some on-line outputs also have associated physical documents; for example, invoices and packing slips are paper documents as well as screen displays.

SYSTEM ENCYCLOPEDIA. Keeping track of the presentation graphics, data elements, input and output screens, data flow diagrams, logic definitions, and pro-

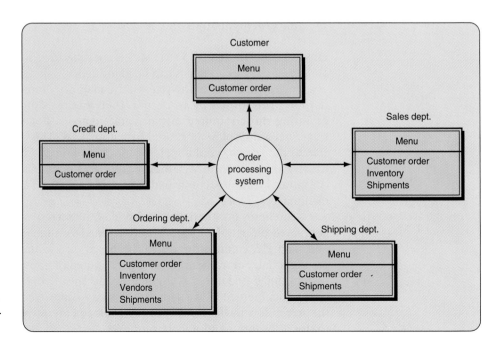

FIGURE 13.9 Conceptual graphic of order-processing system.

gram code (generated from prototyping) is a huge task. To address the problem, many CASE products provide central information repositories, referred to as a **system encyclopedia**. The core of a system encyclopedia is the data dictionary, which links most documentation. Figure 13.10 shows how the data dictionary can be used to keep track of documentation. For each item in an encyclopedia, documentation is kept on who prepared it, when it was prepared, and other useful information.

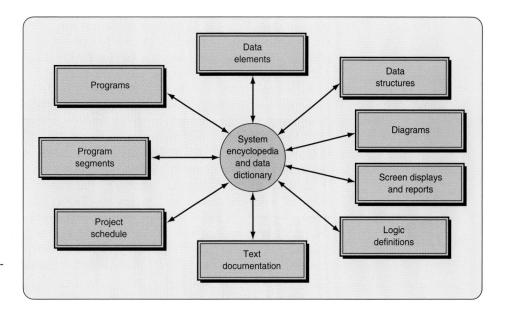

FIGURE 13.10 System encyclopedia for documentation management.

▶ 13.4   STEP 5: DEVELOP, TEST, AND VALIDATE THE NEW SYSTEM

Once system design and design documentation are complete, systems development can proceed. **Systems development** refers to structuring hardware and software to achieve effective and efficient processing of an information system. Since hardware is increasingly available for off-the-shelf acquisition and interconnection, development most often encompasses the structuring or programming of application software that will "command" the hardware. Off-the-shelf software applications are becoming increasingly available that need relatively minor adjustments or configuring to fulfill most, if not all, of the documented information systems requirements. The following discussion, however, assumes that application software (and not individual pieces of hardware) must be created and tested.

Assembling an information system is a major step in the overall systems development process because something *tangible* must be built for developers, users, and corporate sponsors. Up to the point of actually constructing software and hardware, products of labor have been mostly mental—conceptual models and specifications documented in data files, diagrams, and text. System construction, unfortunately, can be *too* important an event. When the demand for a system is especially great, it can be very tempting—in spite of enormous risks—simply to skip SDLC steps 1–4 and start constructing *something* in step 5 (see Figure 13.1). Users can be clamoring for computer-based solutions, management can be chafing at the pace and cost of analysis and design, and developers can be overly eager to apply new technology (and perhaps justify their corporate existence). Like houses and office buildings, however, information systems that are well designed *before* major construction begins are much more likely to be delivered on time, within budget, and useful.

On the other hand, as we saw in the discussion of prototyping and heuristic design, it is usually beneficial to do *some* construction and testing in order to refine requirements determination and design. Therein lies the difference between "traditional" development and emerging development approaches.

The basic premise underlying traditional development approaches is that a system should be thoroughly and exactly specified—through a combination of narratives, diagrams, and formal specification languages—prior to software coding. Traditional development approaches evolved from an era of mainframe technology where computers were accessible only to professionals. Since coding with programming languages was time- and labor-intensive, significant effort was spent creating detailed specifications to ensure that coders had unambiguous and complete requirements from which they could code the business logic and necessary algorithms. Many development organizations and development professionals are now rethinking the traditional development model in view of new technologies, growing user computer literacy, and new organizational demands for faster, more productive, and cheaper development practices.

Newer development approaches are usually based on an information technology environment that is *layered* and that supports cooperative processing—taking advantage of increasing levels of computer power and distributed databases. In contrast to the traditional approach, the emerging development approaches emphasize development speed, inherent self-documentation, high-level programming languages, reusable software components, and an "open" (or common, standardized) systems orientation for compatibility in multivendor environments. Quality and control over the project process and outcomes are created through an emphasis on excellence in executing selected development techniques. These are combined with organizational structures that emphasize small empowered teams that are accountable for organizational or business outcomes, rather than simply system outcomes.

THE LAYERED APPROACH

The **layered approach** to systems development is based on the concept of an information systems development process as the continued unfolding of successive details concerning different layers of hardware and software technology. As illustrated in Figure 13.11, an information system has at least the following layers: (1) presentation, (2) application or business domain logic, (3) database, (4) input and output, and (5) network. Each layer of the application systems architecture plays a specialized role in concert with other layers of the system. During systems development, the development team must work with specialists to create programs supporting each layer, assembling existing components to make the information system exhibit the desired aggregate functionality and behavior.

THE PRESENTATION LAYER. The **presentation layer** is the most visible and ergonomic aspect of an information system. As such, it provides the most vivid image of a system to the user—it is the element that makes the first impression. In fact, the power of the presentation layer to make a positive impression on the user can be used to face-lift an old application by simply replacing the old user interface with a new graphical user interface. Firms can also use an application presentation layer to project an organization's culture by designing in a particular look and feel.

From a development perspective, the systems designer's goal is to create a person-computer interaction pattern that is pleasant to use, efficient, unambiguous, consistent in command structure and response to user requests, error tolerant, and encouraging of user exploration and self-sufficiency. While these are lofty goals, new technologies offer major breakthroughs in person-computer interac-

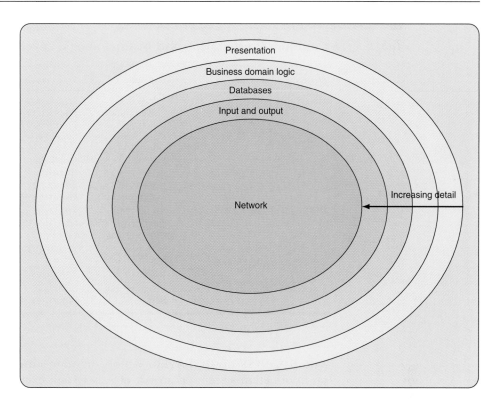

FIGURE 13.11 The systems development layered approach.

tion as was shown by the widespread adoption of the desktop metaphor implemented in popular graphical user interfaces (GUIs). Almost all GUI environments have associated development tools that support rapid prototyping and programming. Table 13.1 provides a summary of major development tools that support various graphical environments.

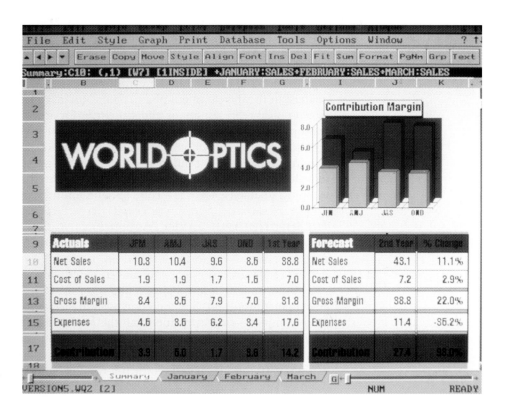

Using logos to produce a unique look.

Table 13.1 **Common Presentation and Business Logic Layer Development Tools**

Presentation Standard	Tool Sets	Programming Languages	Vendors
MS-DOS Windows	Visual Basic	Proprietary Script	Microsoft
	Powerbuilder	Proprietary Script	Powersoft
	Objectview	Proprietary Script	Knowledgeware
	Visualworks	Smalltalk	ParcPlace
	Object Vision	C++	Borland
	PARTS	Smalltalk	Digitalk
	ADW	COBOL	Knowledgeware
	UNIFACE	Proprietary 4GL	UNIFACE
	SQL Windows	Proprietary Script	Gupta
UNIX-OpenLook, MOTIF, etc.	Visual Works	Smalltalk	ParcPlace
	NextStep	Objective C	NeXT
	Glockenspiel	C++	Glockenspiel
	UNIFACE	Proprietary 4GL	UNIFACE
O/S2 Presentation Manager	IEF	COBOL	Texas Instruments
	UNIFACE	Proprietary 4GL	UNIFACE
Macintosh O/S	Visual Works	Smalltalk	ParcPlace
	Serlus	Proprietary OO	Serlus

THE BUSINESS LOGIC LAYER. An organization's **business logic** is the heart of an information system because it directs system execution. Business logic is responsible for computation, data manipulation and transformation, and sequencing of activities within the information system. When the development team is ready to construct the information system, the key challenge is to represent the desired business operations accurately in sequences of computer code.

Constructing the business logic layer entails four elements: (1) encoding algorithms, (2) encoding business rules and logic, (3) structuring and encoding processing sequences, and (4) parsing and delineating activity systems and subsystems in the information system.

THE DATABASE LAYER. Since the inception of computing, database design has been one of the most important development tasks. As discussed in Chapter 12, a considerable amount of time is spent understanding the information needs of an organization and translating these information requirements into appropriate data models. In the development phase, data elements and data models are translated into physical representations and structures for accessing appropriate data at the appropriate time—even under circumstances that were not fully anticipated during the design and development phases. To develop systems at the database layer requires understanding different database management approaches and the interaction of the database management layer with other layers in the system. Developing a database layer is a complex and multidisciplinary task.

THE INPUT/OUTPUT LAYER. As noted many times, output drives design. New presentation layer and database layer tools give systems designers a wide array of display options for information and an increasing range of possibilities for permitting unassisted user access to data stored in databases.

Unfortunately, developing input routines is less intuitive. Although input development tools provide the same level of facilities as those for output, input is more complex—primarily due to all the *boundary* conditions and *editing rules* (as defined in the data dictionary) that must be incorporated into the business logic. Contemporary database management systems help in some ways by automatically editing input routines based on the information stored about the data elements in the database dictionary.

Nonetheless, developing and implementing input definitions, input templates, and input routines must be done carefully to ensure maximum quality and to avoid the old adage: "garbage in, garbage out."

THE NETWORK LAYER. The development process for the fifth and final layer is perhaps the most complex and least understood. Seldom will a systems designer take the lead in developing the **network layer**—the interaction points between the network and the other layers of the systems.

It is also important to realize that with distributed architectures of many computers spread out in an organization, the user and owner of each node in the network must assume a range of management duties not required in the traditional mainframe environment. The systems designer must ensure that users understand these network management issues; a good rule is to make the network layer as simple as possible. To do so, most systems designers rely on network specialists. Developing good working and communication relationships with technical specialists can help avoid misunderstanding and unnecessary conflict.

EMERGING TOOL SETS FOR CONSTRUCTING INFORMATION SYSTEMS

As usual, good tools always help, especially with prototyping and the incremental evolution of the prototype into a production system. Under this approach, the end user and the organizational sponsor of a system are literally involved in physically prototyping and developing a system. Emerging development tools can be classified into three types: (1) *integrated CASE (I-CASE) tools*, (2) *loosely-coupled tool sets*, and (3) *object-oriented development environments*.

Integrated CASE tools support prototyping and reusable systems components, including component repositories and automatic computer code generation. The latest I-CASE tools are actually hybrids that blend traditional development approaches with the latest thinking in development. Since the tools are based partially on traditional approaches, however, they are often less flexible in supporting rapid prototyping when compared to loosely-coupled tool sets and object-oriented development environments.

Loosely-coupled tool sets represent one of the fastest growing and most popular of the new approaches to development tools. Loosely-coupled tool sets are independent tools, developed by different tool vendors, to support one or more information systems architecture layers. Under this scenario, a developer benefits from the best tools for each layer and then assembles and develops components for each layer that are subsequently "hooked" together to produce an operational system. Developers building systems using such tools report that production prototyping is well supported, and development proceeds rapidly with significant client interaction using a prototype to test viability.

The **object-oriented development** paradigm is a significant departure from the past and a tool approach that significantly changes the way development is accomplished. First, object-oriented development (as discussed in Chapter 6) is much more than a programming language or a tool set—it is a perspective or paradigm, a new view of the application domain. Second, successful object-oriented development efforts use an object-oriented development environment that includes an object-oriented programming language (e.g., Smalltalk), a layered object architecture, an object class library that includes a collection of object classes for each layer of the architecture, search tools (e.g., browsers), debuggers, operating system interfaces, and interfaces to other languages and systems. Box 13.1 discusses object-oriented development in more detail.

A Closer Look BOX 13.1

OBJECT-ORIENTED SYSTEMS DEVELOPMENT

The rapid rise of client/server architectures and the accelerated maturation of object-oriented (OO) techniques and tools mean that developers are focusing more on building systems from reused components and commercial libraries of component-based objects than on building everything from scratch. Object-oriented development has many different meanings, but one aspect is clear: object-oriented approaches are based on the need for interchangeable software components (objects) that model the behavior of persons, places, things, or concepts in the real world. In fact, OO approaches are often intuitively understood by managers who can easily map between software objects and real objects that must be managed in the firm.

As a consequence, OO techniques and tools emphasize reusable component building and explicit modeling of real-world behavior in object classes. OO architecture also emphasizes mutual exclusivity among objects and components, so that the functionality and data requirements of each object stand alone. Each object is actually a combination of specific data encapsulated by *methods* that are uniquely capable of acting in the appropriate way on the data when called upon. Hence, each object "knows" how to do the appropriate operations for its data. *Messages* to an object are the "keys" that open the functionality of each object at the appropriate time.

Given the underlying philosophy and operations of an OO system, a developer must use different analysis methods and tools to build such systems. Interestingly, the new OO techniques incorporate many of the structured analysis, data modeling, and top-down development approaches discussed earlier in this chapter.

Some important lessons have been learned developing OO systems. First, OO systems should be developed incrementally and iteratively. It may be cognitively impossible to prespecify the object architecture for the ultimate system before prototyping and learning about the system's desired operation and behavior from the user.

Second, the system architecture evolves over time. After a critical mass of object classes are developed, developers will reconceptualize the object architecture, revise it, rewrite parts of it, and throw away previous components that do not fit the new understanding gained from the incremental-prototype development process.

Third, OO systems require a layered architecture with different types of objects and object behavior for different layers. Most object-oriented systems developed today are composed of object classes for the user-interface layer, applications logic layers, network message layer, and database layer. Specific designs decompose each layer for specialized object classes, depending on the system requirements.

Fourth, OO-based analysis and design techniques and project management approaches are emerging to guide the development process. As OO practice develops, new methodologies will emerge and existing OO methodologies will evolve. In addition, a number of the traditional waterfall methodologies are currently being revamped in order to be more supportive of OO development.

Figure 13.12 illustrates a comprehensive view of the object-oriented development approach. As indicated, two tracks are visible: the top track is oriented to discovering requirements, modeling objects, developing the object architecture, developing prototypes, and extending the system over time. The bottom track emphasizes reusing viable components either developed internally in prior development projects or purchased in the object marketplace. The second track is assembly oriented; developers select and "install" appropriate objects and components. The assembly track requires that development organizations view objects and components as organizational assets that are created, certified, tracked, and monitored for use.

Clearly, a developer has many options for constructing systems—from traditional development methods and tool sets to more advanced object-oriented development environments. Table 13.2 provides a comparison of some of the relative advantages and disadvantages of the different development environments.

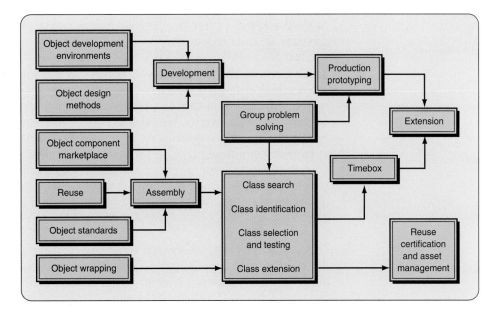

FIGURE 13.12 Overview of object-oriented development approach.

Table 13.2 **Relative Advantages for Development Environments**

Development Environment	Reuse	Speed	Productivity	Platform Independence	Data Independence	Appl. Arch. Compliance
I-CASE	medium	medium	medium	medium-high	medium-high	medium-high
loosely-coupled tool sets	low	medium-high	medium-high	low-medium	low-medium	low
object-oriented	high	medium-high	medium-high	medium-high	n/a	high
traditional	low	low	low	low	low	low

QUALITY ASSURANCE: ATTITUDES AND TECHNIQUES

Whether developing systems using traditional or emerging approaches, one enduring issue transcends all others: *quality*. Quality, or the lack of it, has become a major issue worldwide in virtually all industries. Other than increasing productivity, perhaps no other general management issue has received so much attention. And, as many quality experts are quick to point out, poor quality is a major cause of low productivity. Poor quality can lead to production delays, rework, cost overruns, and unacceptable products.

Application software development has traditionally been one of the most quality-negligent industry activities. The software industry is laced with stories of million-dollar errors on checks printed by computers, lost customer accounts, and on-line systems down for hours or even days. There has been so much emphasis on meeting software development deadlines that there is often little time for quality assurance. It seems, as so often happens in information technology, "urgency drives out quality"; deadlines can become so urgent that the importance of quality is overlooked.

"Street-wise" managers recently have placed greater emphasis on software development quality. Starting with quality-oriented management attitudes, IS organizations have been able to increase quality significantly in software development by focusing on *management attitude*, *design overviews*, and *code inspections*.

MANAGEMENT ATTITUDE. The right place to start with quality is with a management attitude that insists on *economic* quality—quality that is cost-effective. Quality that costs more than it is worth is simply not economic. For example, an on-line system that is working 98 percent of the time may be acceptable for a wholesale distributor's on-line order entry system, and it would not make economic sense to add a second backup computer to provide 99.8 percent uptime. Such reliability, however, would make good economic sense for a major airline with an on-line flight reservation system where even a percentage in gained revenues can more than make up for the cost of improved system hardware.

Quality attitudes can be established with quality standards. Management should establish quality standards that are reflective of their organization's requirements, communicate these attitudes, and then support and reward quality performance.

DESIGN OVERVIEW. A **design overview** consists of a peer evaluation of the designer's overall approach to software development concerning one or more programs in an information system. This overview for quality assurance should be incorporated into IS systems development methodologies.

While peers critique the design, they generally do not offer improvement suggestions; designers respond to criticism with explanations or suggested improvements. If satisfactory responses to criticism cannot be provided at the first meeting, subsequent meetings are scheduled. This process continues until peers are willing to "sign off" on the software design. Once design overviews have been completed, systems designers begin detailed software design to be followed by the *detailed review*, or what IBM calls a *structured walk through*.

During this stage of quality assurance, systems designers step through the logic of their software in a presentation to qualified peers. Peers check for well-structured techniques and top-down design, as well as specific logic. As with a design overview, critiques are made—and, if necessary, an iterative process of explanation and correction is made until peers agree to sign off on the detail design. It is not for the faint-hearted; peer criticism—even when constructive—can seem grueling to system designers. When well orchestrated, however, it can appreciably improve software quality as well as educate programmers in how to write quality software.

CODE INSPECTION. The final stage of quality assurance prior to actually testing a system is **code inspection**. During code inspection, a programmer other than the original coder inspects the program line by line to see if everything seems correct in terms of syntax and correct coding in the particular language. It is the

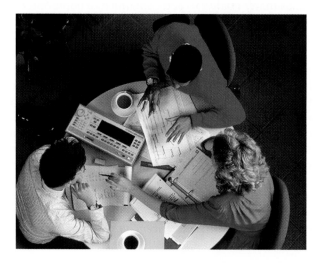

A group conducting a detailed design review.

last inspection before attempting to execute the coding as a whole program. The code inspector will primarily see that coding conventions have been followed and all the "t's are crossed and i's are dotted."

TESTING—A CRITICAL STAGE

During program development, computer program modules are steadily tested by the coder as part of the writing process—sometimes line by line. As the programs are integrated into a total information system software package, overall **testing** of the system becomes possible. When individual modules or programs are tested independently, it is called a **unit test**; when all programs are tested together, it is called a *systems* or an **integrative test**.

Although unit testing is important, integrative testing is a critical stage of the systems development cycle. Integrative testing is the major checkpoint prior to actual implementation or delivery of a system. The consequences of system malfunctions are minimized when they are discovered during integrative testing rather than during or after implementation. In virtually all programs—especially large ones—coding mistakes are an inevitable part of human activity. To that end, testers are *expected* to find mistakes—not simply rubber-stamp the product as "okay."

Good testing actually begins before coding begins—by using the design documentation to design a test plan. This is especially important with large programs containing hundreds, if not thousands, of logic branches where mistakes can easily occur. Unfortunately, very large programs may be physically impossible to test fully mainly because of the number of possible branching permutations; testing tools may be needed to test all possible branches or at least the most critical ones. The testing tools and test data management tools provided by CASE and a programmer's workbench greatly enhance the ability to do high-quality testing in an efficient manner.

The major system processes tested are the following.

1. *Clerical processing.* Data-collection and preparation procedures are performed correctly.
2. *Input processing.* Transactions are checked for errors and applied to the right records in the right files.
3. *Computational processing.* The proper variables are computed, using proper arithmetic.
4. *Logic processing.* Decision rules are executed, using the correct sequencing and branching.
5. *Data accessing.* Data are stored in, and retrieved from, the right locations.
6. *Output processing.* The correct variables are printed in the right places on printouts and displays.

Testing these processes can be accomplished by processing real or fabricated transactions that represent normal and abnormal conditions. Ouputs from transaction processing can be tested by simply checking to see if they are correct. For example, the amount due on a loan can be computed on a calculator and compared to a corresponding output provided by the information system.

An information system must be able to handle exceptions (i.e., abnormal transactions). To test this aspect of the system, transactions that deviate from normal transaction form should be prepared and processed. For example, payroll transactions with invalid department codes, missing social security numbers, pay rates below the minimum wage rate, or hours-worked that exceed the allowable limit should be tested. A properly developed information system should detect such errors and report them.

DEBUGGING. Correcting system malfunctions is called **debugging**. The source of a malfunction can exist anywhere in an information system—during data collection or preparation, during input processing, in the computational or logical processes of one or more computer programs, or at any other point. To debug a malfunction, therefore, its origin must be isolated before the problem can be resolved. The specific location of the malfunction can be isolated by working backward from the output to the input or forward from the input to the output. Once isolated, a system malfunction can be resolved, say, by a change in program code, data collection procedure, or data entry procedure.

VALIDATION. **Validation** ensures that the system meets documented and approved system requirements established during the design stage. This is quite different from testing the system; testing establishes whether the system *works*, while validation establishes whether it does the *right* work when it does work. A software program may not do what it was intended to do even though it executes flawlessly.

Validation should not be done by the testers but rather by analysts who were involved in the design or users who were involved in determining the requirements. It is also sometimes done by independent workers—perhaps by contractors—who can be objective and give stakeholders an honest evaluation prior to system distribution and implementation.

USER-DEVELOPED SYSTEMS

Given the insatiable demand for more and better information to support decision making and operating organizations, it is clear that not enough computer programmers can be trained to handle the entire workload. This situation is similar to the one faced by the telephone company years ago. Had the phone company not automated switchboards as it did, everyone in the work force today would have to be a telephone operator to handle today's telephone workload. Automating switchboards, however, did make all of us telephone operators to some degree; the phone company shifted more and more of the manual workload to telephone users. Today, we only get assistance from a telephone operator when we can't make a call on our own, and often that assistance comes from a computerized operator. Note that there are still telephone operators, but they are able to provide more service per operator than in preautomation days, and costs per transaction have gone down.

The evolution of phone use is analogous to what is happening with computer use. In the early days of computers, computer users were totally dependent on

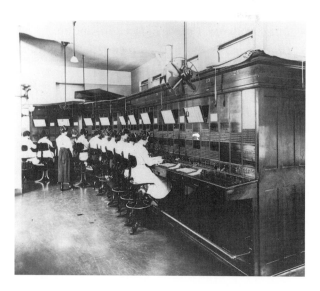

The early days of manual telephone switchboards.

computer technicians. The gradual evolution of *user-friendly* languages and system interfaces is allowing users to do more and more of their own development. The computer technician's role, like the telephone operator's, is becoming one of helping users to help themselves.

With user-friendly, high-level query languages, users can develop software in a day or two to satisfy most of their immediate and ad hoc information requirements, provided that properly collected and organized data are available.

Computer technicians and information systems professionals will still be necessary to manage and control the increasing complexity of hardware, software, and databases needed to support this new environment. But because users will not have to explain to a technician everything they need done; they will be able to access the computer directly, and overall productivity will significantly increase. Professional programmers will still write, edit, and update complex software. Users will program more of the ad hoc ouput programs.

13.5 STEP 6: IMPLEMENT THE NEW SYSTEM

The next-to-final step in developing an information system is **implementation**—putting the developed system into operation. Implementation is not nearly as easy as "plug it in and start it up"; there are serious implementation issues such as *conversion strategy and sequence, user training,* and *behavior*. Implementation, perhaps more than the other development steps, involves a great deal of behavioral consideration to ensure system success. While there certainly are technical issues to consider during this step, the rest of this chapter will emphasize the behavioral factors that can positively or adversely affect information system implementation.

IMPLEMENTATION PLANNING

Unfortunately, one of the least understood and most overlooked issues in information systems development is implementation. Often the biggest error made is postponing implementation planning until it is time to switch from the old system to the new. In Chapter 12, the importance of conducting technical, economic, and operational feasibility studies before developing information systems was discussed. These studies determine if a system is technically feasible and cost justified, and if a system can be implemented in the context of a particular organization using particular employees. To postpone a thorough assessment of the feasibility of implementing a system until after it is designed and developed can cause unfortunate—perhaps unforgiving—consequences. Examples of these consequences, in addition to the case study at the beginning of this chapter, are presented in Box 13.2.

IT At Work BOX 13.2

IMPLEMENTATIONS THAT COULD HAVE BEEN DONE BETTER

A major retail chain developed a new sales entry system using retail terminals. To save cost, the company selected a system that uses keyboard entry of sales price and stockkeeping unit (SKU) numbers instead of selecting the more expensive alternative of optically scanning such information. Technical and economic evaluations had been supportive of the less-expensive system. There was, however, an implementation problem: the stores had high transaction volumes. Thus, when the terminals were installed, long lines formed due to the extra time required to key in the SKU numbers. People waiting in lines became hostile and vocally critical to the sales clerks. In frustration, sales clerks began to use *any* set of SKU keys just to expedite customer orders. This caused many problems for the retail chain, especially when the sales SKU data were used to track inventory.

In another case, an equipment rental company provided its personnel with a decision-support system that took into consideration 80 different variables in preparing customer quotes. The system was developed by technical people and was quite sophisticated. Unfortunately, it was never used. Why? People working at the rental counters felt the system was too complex and difficult to learn for personnel who typically had limited computer exposure. Also, turnover was high in these positions, and managers therefore had little incentive to put forth the effort necessary to teach the system to employees.

Critical Thinking Issue: Why aren't behavioral issues taken into account in developing and implementing information systems? ▲

Allowing system users to experience a new system prior to implementation helps uncover problems before the system becomes set in concrete. (Note the compatibility of this concept with heuristic development and prototyping as discussed earlier in this chapter.) Given that implementation issues should be continuously reviewed during system development, the next issue is preparing for, and actually converting to, the new system. There are two key dimensions to this: *conversion strategy* and *user training*.

CONVERSION STRATEGY

Conversion is the process of changing from the old system to the new system, and it requires careful planning. Conversion methodology can be defined in terms of a continuum ranging from *parallel operation* to *direct cutover* (also called "cold turkey"). In a **parallel conversion**, both the old and new systems are concurrently processed until the new system stabilizes, confirming the reliability of the new system prior to abandoning the old one. In a **direct cutover** conversion, however, using the new system immediately terminates the old system. In practice, the conversion approach used may fall somewhere between parallel and cutover. For example, transactions processed on the old system can be collected for a week and then reprocessed on the new system over the weekend. In this example, parallel processing applies to the transactions processed but not to the time frame in which they are processed.

Parallel processing reduces the risk of implementing a new—but faulty—system; but it has some disadvantages. First, parallel processing is expensive—additional personnel (or overtime) and equipment are often required. For some systems, it is virtually impossible to conduct parallel processing. For example, it is not plausible to parallel process two on-line airline reservation systems.

In direct cutover conversion, rigorous testing of the new system is critical prior to implementation. Where parallel processing is possible, value judgments must be made to assess the trade-offs between risks and costs. Cutover requires much more planning and testing up front—with the users who will suddenly shift from one system to another. Savings from avoiding parallel operations can quickly be eclipsed by losses from cutover to a malfunctioning system or one that users don't understand.

A different dimension to the conversion issue concerns the *scope* of implementation, whether done in parallel or by cutover. The **pilot conversion** approach converts one unit of the business first for a "shake down" before other units are converted. A **phased conversion** approach is an incremental conversion whereby different business units are brought on-line in a stepped sequence. For example, the inventory module of an order processing system can be phased in, followed by accounts receivable, and, finally, order entry.

In implementing a new information system, it is also important to determine the *sequence* in which system segments are converted, generally a function of the following variables.

▼ *Organizational functions:* different departments, branches, plants, or other logical breakdowns.

▼ *Organizational cycles:* normal cycles of organizational activities within organizational functions (e.g., accounting or billing cycles).

It is generally advisable to begin conversion with those segments of the system that appear to offer the least difficulty. For example, the conversion may start with the best-managed and best-organized functions with the shortest cycles. This enhances the probability of initial success, which in turn enhances the credibility and momentum of the new system and its subsequent implementation. Even so, management should attempt to minimize any additional internal or external requirements on the department undergoing conversion. A department is generally disrupted enough during conversion without having to handle the complications of additional disturbances.

The final task of the conversion sequence is to define what will signify the complete implementation of the new system. This definition may vary; but whatever the definition of implementation, it should be agreed upon in advance by organizational members. When the defined implementation has been achieved, the system should be formally approved and accepted, and implementation should be considered complete.

USER TRAINING

Training for a new information system.

Thorough user training is critical to implementing an information system successfully. User training requirements for a new information system can be categorized as either *clerical* or *managerial.* Clerical users must be instructed in how to process transactions. Managers must be informed as to the format and content of reports and workstation displays, as well as how to request reports or make on-line inquiries. Managers also need to understand how programmed decisions are made and how to use any decision-support capabilities.

It is usually advantageous to have representatives (possibly project team members) from the different departments participate in developing user documentation (e.g., user procedures manuals) and in actually training users on the system. Clerical and managerial personnel are often less intimidated by computer technology if a new information system is explained to them and documented for them by someone from their own department rather than by an outside computer technician.

User training frequently overlaps program development, since much of the required training can be accomplished without the use of an actual system. Also, systems tend to be implemented in a modular fashion (e.g., the inventory module of an order processing system may be operational before the order entry module). This allows operational training to be staggered in the sequence in which modules are operationalized. If an early start on user training is possible, it is wise to proceed.

An important emerging trend in training is the concept of just-in-time training. Training in new technology is much like learning a foreign language; "If you don't use it, you lose it." Consequently, training should be scheduled as closely as possible to the time when trainees will begin to use the new system.

BEHAVIORAL CONSIDERATIONS

Serious problems in developing and operating information systems can come from behavioral reactions of those affected by changes brought about by these information systems. Understanding the nature and causes of such behaviors can help management and systems analysts be in a better position to address potential problems properly.

The three most common forms of dysfunctional reaction to newly introduced information systems are *aggression* (physical or nonphysical, intended to disrupt or destroy the system), *projection* (attempts to blame the system for problems not caused by the system), and *avoidance* (defensive reactions by personnel who withdraw from, or ignore, the system). The most dramatic aggression behavior is sabotage. Less dramatic (and more common) behavior occurs in the form of attempts to ''beat the system'' or to disrupt it by outsmarting it. The most common reaction is avoidance by people who are intimidated, frustrated, or simply reluctant to familiarize themselves with the new system and any changes brought about by it.

The three basic organizational groups who are liable to express dysfunctional reactions to a new system are the following:

1. *Operating personnel.* This includes all nonmanagerial personnel except technical staff, further subdivided into nonclerical and clerical (nonclerical personnel provide inputs to the system, clerical personnel process the inputs).

2. *Operating management.* This includes personnel in positions from the first-line supervisor up to and including middle management.

3. *Top management.* This is the senior executive officers of the organization.

Because each group has a somewhat different relationship with information systems, each group is also affected differently by a new system and usually exhibits different behavioral reactions. These reactions are summarized in Table 13.3. General guidelines for minimizing these reactions are listed in Table 13.4.

Table 13.3 **Relationship of Behavioral Groups to Behavioral Patterns**

	Aggression	Projection	Avoidance
Top management			X
Operating management	X	X	X
Operating personnel			
Clerical		X	
Nonclerical	X		

OPERATING PERSONNEL REACTIONS. Nonclerical operating personnel are usually required to provide more input when a new system is installed. As a result, they tend to demonstrate aggressive behavior because of what seems to be increased inconvenience imposed on their daily work activities. For example, salespersons may have to fill out new reports describing the factors that caused the loss of a customer or client. To the salesperson, these reports may appear to be needless, additional work. If salespersons understood how this information could help them focus their efforts, however, they might be less likely to react negatively to the additional input requirements.

Clerical operating personnel are particularly affected by new information systems since their jobs may be changed considerably or even eliminated, and there may be increased work rigidity and time pressure. The usual response to such effects is projection behavior—all undesirable effects and any other ensuing problems are blamed on the computer system and its technicians. Though clerical personnel may want to indulge in avoidance behavior, their low-level positions in the organization tend to make that impractical.

Sometimes a clerical projection reaction is brought on because personnel are the last to know about a new system being developed. This almost secretive atmosphere creates concerns that something bad is about to happen to them. Such concern can be minimized by establishing an atmosphere of openness about forthcoming changes and career security.

Table 13.4 General Guidelines to Minimize Dysfunctional Reactions

1. Identify problems or opportunities that the organization recognizes.
2. Build a good system development cross-functional team with good leadership.
3. Defer changing a business process until it is fully understood.
4. Allow an organization to learn what it really wants through prototyping.
5. Test and validate systems thoroughly prior to implementation.
6. Develop a realistic implementation schedule.
7. Keep the system as simple as possible, provide adequate training, and design systems outputs to fit user needs.
8. Recognize and adjust for any changes in job content resulting from new information systems. In particular, job performance evaluations and the accompanying reward systems should be modified to reflect job changes.

A senior manager explaining the importance of a new system.

The key point is that when information is valuable, those providing it should be sold on the importance of collecting and processing it. This is best accomplished when top management communicates its support of the information system and its use. Top management is usually more effective than technical staff in gaining support for a new information system from operating personnel.

OPERATING MANAGEMENT REACTIONS. Operating management is usually highly affected by new information systems. As a result of the additional information available from new systems, top management is usually more informed about the effectiveness and efficiency of operating managers. This often leads to closer evaluation and control of operating managers' activities. Moreover, many of the decisions previously made by operating managers may be programmed into the new information system. While programmed decisions usually allow operating managers to engage in other more creative and constructive efforts, the overall effect is a change in their job content. Operating managers, therefore, have reason to feel their status or power is threatened, resulting in strong feelings of insecurity. Under these circumstances, reactions of aggression, projection, and avoidance are apt to occur.

To minimize such dysfunctional behaviors, top management should be open about forthcoming changes and include operating management in the design of new information systems. Only top management can convincingly stress that operating managers will play a more challenging and important role in the organization even though some of their decision-making activities will be transferred to the computer system.

TOP MANAGEMENT. Top management is usually less affected by, and concerned with, new information systems than are other groups. Top management may feel some insecurity because a technology they do not understand plays a larger role in their organization, but their high-level positions provide them the option of avoiding new systems. They have little reason to exhibit projection or aggression behavior. Top management is usually more involved with information systems that do more than transaction processing, information providing, and programmed decision making—they are more affected by systems that provide decision support capabilities.

A foremost guideline for overcoming all dysfunctional behavior toward new information systems is to obtain top management involvement and support—but getting top management involved can be difficult. Top-level managers—like most people—are much more comfortable with things they understand. Systems analysts must carefully describe information systems in nontechnical terms when communicating with top management and soliciting their support. Additionally, analysts should stress that information systems projects are consistently more successful from an operational, economical, and technical perspective when top management is involved and supports them. Indeed, eliminating avoidance behavior in top management can contribute significantly to eliminating dysfunctional behavior in the remainder of the organization.

As a final note, the importance of allowing those affected by change to participate in bringing about that change cannot be overemphasized. It is often thought that most people are simply reluctant to accept change. However, this belief is contradicted by the often enthusiastic manner in which people enjoy driving the latest car or having the latest gadgetry. One reason for this apparent contradiction is that people, as consumers, have a great deal of control over such changes—they can decide by their purchasing behavior if they want to accept or reject new products. When things are forced on people, however, they often react quite differently. By allowing organizational personnel to participate in or, even better, to control organizational changes, acceptance and even enthusiasm is much more probable.

▶ 13.6 STEP 7: EVALUATE AND MAINTAIN THE NEW SYSTEM

The final step of the systems development cycle is evaluation and maintenance. It is not a temporary stage like the others; it continues for the life of the newly developed and implemented system. In one sense, it is the perpetual repetition of all the other steps for smaller, incremental changes to the system. The system is evaluated, problems or opportunities are uncovered and analyzed, alternatives are explored and evaluated, and solutions are designed, developed, and implemented—all this is known as "maintenance."

EVALUATION

Like the analysis process described as Step 1 in Chapter 12, **evaluation** provides the feedback necessary to asses the value of a system and its effects on an organization's personnel and business. This feedback serves two functions. First, it provides information about what adjustments may be necessary to the information system. Second, it provides information about what adjustments should be made in approaching future information systems development projects. Information systems should be evaluated like any other organizational function. Outside, independent evaluations are useful, but they are no substitute for an internal manager's judgment. Outside audits should assist management, not do their job.

There are three basic dimensions of information systems that should be evaluated. The first dimension, the *development process*, concerns whether the system was developed properly. The second looks at the *information* being provided. The third evaluation process focuses on evaluating the system's *performance*.

DEVELOPMENT EVALUATION. Evaluation of the development process is primarily concerned with whether the system was developed on schedule and within budget—a rather straightforward evaluation. It requires, however, that schedules and budgets be established in advance and that records are kept of actual performance and costs. Procedures for scheduling and budgeting information systems development were discussed in Chapter 12.

Few information systems have been developed on schedule and within budget. In fact, many information systems have been developed without *any* clearly defined schedules or budgets. A recent survey of 261 software development organizations concluded that about 75 percent had no formal software evaluation process—no measurement of what they do and no way of knowing when and where they are making mistakes. Perhaps the mystique and uncertainty associated with information systems development is to blame for its not being subjected to traditional management control procedures.

With traditional information systems development, an increasing experience base and better understanding of systems development by both technicians and managers have resulted in a greater emphasis on planning and control. With the new trend toward rapid deployment of distributed systems like client/server, however, these lessons may need to be relearned. Otherwise, maintenance costs can balloon on haphazardly designed, coded, documented, and tested systems.

INFORMATION EVALUATION. A good information system performs properly with correct computations, efficiently processed transactions, and on-time reports. A system that merely functions properly, however, may not be a system that is proper for the needs of an organization. An information system should be evaluated in terms of the extent to which its information is relevant or not relevant to the organization's decision making.

This aspect of information system evaluation is difficult and cannot be conducted in the straightforward, quantitative manner used for development evaluations. It is practically impossible to evaluate directly an information system's support of decisions made in an organization—it must be measured indirectly. A viable approach for indirectly measuring and evaluating the information provided by an information system is based on the concept that the more frequently a decision maker's information needs are met by an information system, the more satisfied he or she tends to be with the information system. Conversely, the more frequently that necessary information is not available, the greater the effort (and frustration) required to obtain the necessary information—and hence, the greater the dissatisfaction with the information system. This concept is illustrated in Figure 13.13. Since satisfaction with an information system correlates with the ability of the information system to support decision making, satisfaction can be used as a surrogate to evaluate information provided by an information system.

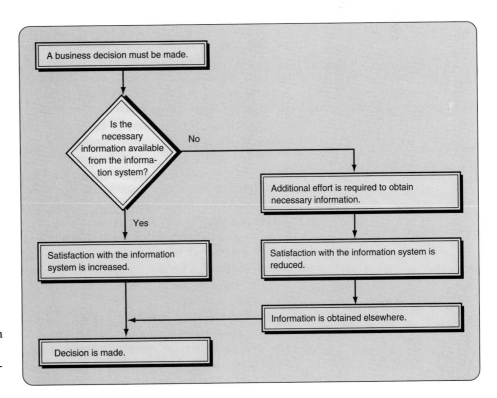

FIGURE 13.13 Relationship between information system support of decision making and user satisfaction.

PERFORMANCE EVALUATION. As stated earlier, a performance evaluation is concerned with how effectively and efficiently the information system is operating. A performance audit collects and evaluates information to answer questions such as the following.

▼ Is the staff adequately trained?

▼ Are state-of-the-art technology and methodology being used?

▼ Are computing and staff resources being adequately utilized?

▼ Is there an information system plan?

▼ Are users satisfied with services?

▼ Does adequate documentation exist for all systems?

▼ Do information systems have an adequate backup and recovery plan?

Ostensibly, a performance audit tends to be an extensive question-and-answer session in which auditors use an exhaustive checklist to evaluate management of an information system and the procedures used. Performance audits are often done because either general management does not feel qualified to do them or management does not want to take the time to become familiar enough with information systems to evaluate their performance. Performance audits can also be used by IT managers to justify their budgets, their performance, or to justify charges made back to customers for services. They can also be used, on the other hand, by top managers to document poor system or IT management performance. Based on the results of evaluation, changes in the system can be made accordingly as part of system maintenance.

MAINTENANCE

All information systems require some modification after development. This can be hardware, information, or software maintenance. Hardware maintenance is straightforward and similar to the common maintenance activities associated with cars and furniture. Information maintenance ensures that incorrect information in databases is ferreted out and corrected, obsolete data are purged, and historic data are archived. "Software maintenance" is a misleading term, however, since software coding does not inherently degrade from use like machined engine parts. But software can have mistakes that need correcting; it does degrade in terms of meeting functional requirements (as the world around it changes); and it does degrade from the accumulation of less-than-perfect modifications. Here, **software maintenance** means all program coding after initial deployment to *correct* coding errors, to *enhance* the functionality of the software, and to *perfect* the maintainability and use of the software. Although not commonly thought of as maintenance, continual education, training, and career development—"maintaining" information systems users, operators, management, and the maintainers themselves—are also essential to a system's success.

Maintenance can be categorized as either scheduled or rescue maintenance. *Scheduled maintenance* is anticipated and can be planned and budgeted for, such as implementing a new inventory coding scheme. *Rescue* or *emergency maintenance* refers to previously undetected malfunctions that are not anticipated but require immediate resolution. A system that is properly developed and tested should have little need for rescue maintenance.

Evaluation and maintenance activities have historically been the lion's share of system life cycle costs—between 40 and 95 percent of information system budgets. Some organizations are "maintenance-bound"; they spend all their efforts maintaining what they have, with no resources left over to develop new information systems. Figure 13.14 illustrates the relationship between the number of implemented systems and the time available for developing new systems. With

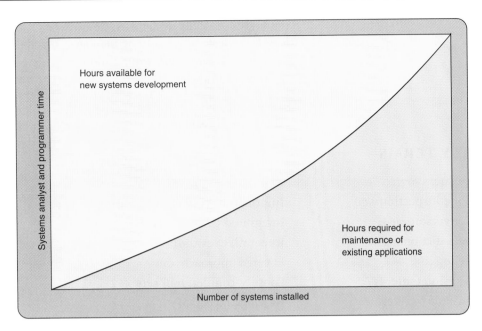

FIGURE 13.14 Relationship between the number of implemented systems and the time available for maintenance and new systems development.

the glowing prospect of a new information system, top management can easily overlook the burgeoning cost of keeping information systems running and meeting evolving corporate information requirements. Management should keep information systems costs in perspective; most often the largest expenses come *after*, not during, development.

▶ MANAGERIAL ISSUES

1. *User involvement.* The direct and indirect users of a system are likely to be the most knowledgeable individuals concerning requirements and which alternatives will be the most effective. Users are also the most affected by a new information system. Information systems analysts and designers, on the other hand, are likely to be the most knowledgeable individuals concerning technical and data managerial issues as well as the most experienced in arriving at viable systems solutions. The right mixture of user involvement and information systems expertise is crucial.

2. *Traditional approaches vs. prototyping.* The traditional development approach stresses detailed, lockstep development with established decision points; prototyping stresses flexible development based on actual use of partially functional systems. Experience has shown that the traditional approach can be better for low-risk, environmentally stable, and technology-simple situations; prototyping is often better under the opposite conditions.

3. *Tool use by developers.* Development tools and techniques can ensure that developers consider all necessary factors and standardize development, documentation, and testing. Forcing their use, on the other hand, may unnecessarily constrain innovation, development efficiency, and personnel productivity.

4. *Quality assurance vs. schedules.* Quality counts in the short term and the long term, but it can lengthen development and increase development costs. Trying to meet tight development schedules can induce poor quality—with even worse schedule, cost, and morale problems.

5. *Behavior problems.* Information systems are primarily for people to use. People may react to new systems in unexpected ways, however, making even

the best technically designed system useless. Changes brought about by information systems need to be managed effectively.

6. *Perpetual development.* Information systems are designed to meet organizational needs. When they don't accurately meet these needs, or these needs change, information systems need to be redeveloped. Developing a system can be a major expense, but perpetually developing a system to maintain its usefulness is usually a much larger expense. ■

KEY TERMS

Business logic *456*

Code inspection *460*

Conversion *464*

Data dictionary *445*

Debugging *462*

Decision table *447*

Design overview *460*

Direct cutover *464*

Evaluation *468*

Heuristic design *450*

Implementation *463*

Information systems structure *443*

Integrated CASE tools *457*

Integrative test *461*

Layered approach *454*

Loosely-coupled tool sets *457*

Network layer *457*

Object-oriented development *457*

Parallel conversion *464*

Phased conversion *464*

Pilot conversion *464*

Presentation layer *454*

Prototyping *450*

Software maintenance *470*

Specifications *444*

Systems development *453*

System encyclopedia *453*

Testing *461*

Unit test *461*

Validation *462*

CHAPTER HIGHLIGHTS *(L-x means learning objective number x)*

▼ Systems design is output driven, moving from a logical design to a detailed design and ending in specifications. (L-1)

▼ Prototyping and heuristic design help ensure correctly identified requirements. (L-1)

▼ Emerging systems development uses a layered approach which includes the presentation layer, the business domain logic layer, the database layer, the input and output layer, and the network layer. (L-2)

▼ Development techniques and tools such as object-oriented programming can significantly increase development productivity. (L-2)

▼ Quality assurance depends on top management attitudes as well as review procedures. (L-2)

▼ Unit and integrative testing and validation are crucial steps to be taken prior to putting a new system into operation. (L-2)

▼ Implementation conversions can be parallel, direct, phased, or pilot. (L-3)

▼ Behavioral dysfunctions such as avoidance, aggression, and projection can be minimized by working closely with operational personnel, operational managers, and top management. (L-3)

▼ Evaluation includes development, information, and performance assessment. (L-4)

▼ Maintenance of hardware, information, and software is commonly the major cost of information systems and is actually the perpetual, cyclic application of all the system development steps for incremental, postimplementation changes. (L-4)

QUESTIONS FOR REVIEW

1. What are the key components of systems design specifications?

2. Why is the data dictionary a key component of systems design specifications?

3. Why is a decision table preferable to a narrative description of logical processes?

4. Why should systems design specifications be "output driven"?

5. What is a data model, and what role does it play in the systems design process?

6. Give a definition of object-oriented systems development, and discuss how it is different from traditional systems development.

7. What is the difference between parallel and direct cutover conversion? Pilot and phased conversions?

8. What types of dysfunctional behavior can be exhibited during implementation of information systems?

9. What are some guidelines for minimizing dysfunctional behavior?

10. What is a performance evaluation, and what role does it play in improving future systems development?

11. What is software maintenance, and why is it necessary?

QUESTIONS FOR DISCUSSION

1. Why is using a heuristic or prototyping process so important to the systems development process? Some traditional systems developers argue that prototyping is a sloppy trial-and-error process for what should be a rigorous analytical process. Debate this issue.

2. What are the fundamental differences between the traditional development approach and emerging development approaches? What do you see are the primary benefits to users of information systems from emerging development approaches? What are the benefits to the systems development staff?

3. Would you think that object orientation is a concept that is more readily embraced by users or developers of information systems?

4. Why do you suppose quality assurance was not a major priority in the early days of systems development? Why has it become so critical in recent time?

5. Consider the implementation problems discussed in Box 13.2, and discuss how the guidelines described in the discussion on implementation might have been used to deal with those issues.

6. Discuss the importance of doing an information evaluation after a system is completed.

7. Discuss the following questions relative to the opening case of the chapter.

   a. What is the real problem that Samson Shipping experienced implementing the information system? Does the problem have anything to do with the policy itself?

   b. What should Brad Bounds have done to deal with the issue of policy before automating the order processing and shipment system?

EXERCISES

1. Get copies of systems design specifications for one or more systems from an organization. (Local companies or your university could be sources.) Look at these specifications, particularly the area of information requirements determination, and see what techniques were used to determine these requirements. Compare the techniques used to the ones discussed in this chapter.

2. Consider the systems design specifications for the systems reviewed in Exercise 1 in terms of design specification, data modeling, software development approach, and approaches for implementation and post-implementation evaluation. List deficiencies and suggested remedies.

3. Arrange to meet with some users of information systems either in organizations close to the university or users of systems within the university itself (e.g., the registrar's office or the business office). Ask them what their major problems were or are with the information systems that have been implemented. Cover such issues as training, scheduling, and the actual conversion process.

GROUP ASSIGNMENT

Divide the class into two groups, information system users and information systems designers. Have the designers make a logical design, based on the users' inputs, of a "homework-assisting information system." Have the users then critique the specifications with recommended changes.

Minicase 1

Liquor-Dispensing Point-of-Sale Terminals

In an attempt to create a new market for point-of-sale technology, NCR developed liquor-dispensing point-of-sale terminals. The notion behind this system was the same as that for many point-of-sale devices: to improve inventory management and minimize "backdoor shrinkage" (theft by employees).

A common problem experienced in many bars is that most transactions are in cash. It is very easy for bartenders to pocket money as well as to give free drinks to friends. Another common problem is that bartenders might take a bottle or two of liquor with them. In response, NCR developed a system which would allow a bar owner to meter specifically how much liquor would go into each type drink. Liquor bottles would be lined up in an overhead rack and all the bartender would have to do is push a button associated with a particular drink (e.g., "Martini''), and the correct amount of liquor would be dispensed, based upon the measure set by management. Inventory would be completely accounted for to the ounce, ''backdoor shrinkage'' could be virtually eliminated, and the dispensed inventory could be matched to the money taken in and would catch bartenders who pocket cash.

This technology was warmly received by bar owners and implemented in a number of hotels and bars around the country. The liquor-dispensing point-of-sale terminals, however, were soon rejected by many bars. Those that rejected the new technology found that bartenders were quitting—refusing to work with the system. Managers had to remove the systems in order to attract and retain bartenders. Further analysis revealed that the typical bartender was getting about 50 percent of his income from keeping some cash and from the large tips received

as a result of providing extra strong drinks to favorite customers.

Questions for Minicase 1

1. What was the underlying problem causing rejection of the system?

2. What would a bar owner or manager have to do in order to be able to retain bartenders? What would be the tax and cost implications to the owner or manager of the bar?

3. What systems analysis and design principles could have revealed these issues prior to a major investment in a new technology that ultimately was rejected by the marketplace?

Minicase 2

Fighting the Software Quality Battle

Superfoods is a national grocery wholesale and retail chain, with company-owned supermarkets as well as franchises. About 40 percent of the supermarkets are owned by Superfoods, and the remaining 60 percent are franchised (and therefore owned by independent operators). However, all supermarkets buy their grocery products directly from Superfoods. Annual Superfoods retail sales exceed $1.8 billion.

A key dimension of Superfoods's franchising ability has been its willingness to share with franchisees the computer system it uses to support its own stores. This allows a rather small grocer to have access to large, sophisticated, point-of-sale-based systems to support sales processing and by-product inventory management. Retail terminals use bar-coding technology to capture inventory and price information, provide financial sales analysis, inventory management, and direct ordering of stock replacement through Superfoods's warehouse outlets.

Although the concept has been well received in the marketplace, much of the software available on the retail terminals, the store-level computers, and Superfoods's central computer has been both error prone and late in availability. To address this problem, Mr. Howard Chervany, vice president of information systems, brought in a new director of systems development, Ms. Alice Gallegos. Ms. Gallegos had an excellent reputation in software management and was often asked to speak on the concepts and techniques she used to manage large software projects.

After arriving on the job and spending a couple of months assessing the situation, Ms. Gallegos realized that the software development group was totally devoid of any

quality assurance processes. She stressed concepts such as design overviews, structured walkthroughs, and code inspection as means of improving software development. She also discussed the notions of problem-and-change management as ways to manage enhancements or corrections to existing software better. Her staff rebelled at the idea of quality assurance concepts and problem-and-change management. They argued that it is just that much more red tape and that it would interfere with their productivity.

One day, Ms. Gallegos called a staff meeting and reviewed her perception of the problem with software development as well as the primary factors contributing to late and error-prone software. She explained that, to rectify the situation, software engineering principles would be enforced and that quality assurance procedures, including design overview, structured walkthroughs and code inspections, would be implemented. The staff mumbled somewhat at the recommendation, but there were no direct arguments against her instructions.

Six months later, Ms. Gallegos observed that software was still late and they were still having error problems. Upon further investigation, she discovered that the staff was collectively ignoring her instructions and not adhering to her quality assurance procedures. She had several one-on-one meetings with key staff people to discuss the problem. They politely responded that they were really just too busy to mess with that ''nonsense.'' They would have done what she wanted, but they just didn't have time with their busy schedules.

Ms. Gallegos called another staff meeting and indicated that she was aware that people were not following software engineering concepts or adhering to quality assurance procedures. She explained that she was putting her foot down on this issue and expected compliance.

The following day, a group of the more veteran systems developers went over her head to the vice president of information systems development and complained that Ms. Gallegos was making a bad situation even worse with her unrealistic demands. At the next management meeting, Mr. Chervany asked Ms. Gallegos why there was so much resistance to the software engineering and quality assurance procedures she was attempting to implement—particularly if they were such good ideas. He stated that he was all for improving software development activities but not at the expense of creating a serious morale problem. He asked her to present the facts supporting what she was trying to implement, so that he could review

them and make a decision. He was not familiar with the concepts, but if they made sense to him, he would support her; if they didn't make sense, he would ask her to come up with a different strategy.

Questions for Minicase 2

1. What should Ms. Gallegos have written in her memo to Mr. Chervany outlining the advantages to good software engineering?

2. What was the underlying problem? Who was more at fault for the resulting situation—Ms. Gallegos, the staff members, or Mr. Chervany? Why?

3. What could Ms. Gallegos have done better to implement the procedures she was advocating?

REFERENCES AND BIBLIOGRAPHY

1. Ackoff, R. L., "Management Misinformation Systems," *Management Science*, December 1967, pp. 147-56.

2. Alter, Steven. "How Effective Managers Use Information Systems." *Harvard Business Review*, November/December 1976.

3. Anderson, N. B., Hedberg, B., Mercer, B., Mumford, E., and Sole, A. *The Impact of Systems Change in Organizations*. Germantown, MD: Sisthoff and Noordhoft, 1979.

4. Andrews, W., "Prototyping Information Systems." *Journal of Systems Management*, September 1983, pp. 16-18.

5. Bell, Simon, *Rapid Information Systems Development*. New York: McGraw-Hill, 1992.

6. Booch, Grady, *Object-Oriented Analysis and Design With Applications* (2nd ed.). Redwood City, CA: Benjamin-Cummings, 1994.

7. Coad, Peter, and Yourdon, Edward, *Object-Oriented Design*, Yourdon Press Computing Series, New York: Prentice-Hall, 1991.

8. Dixon, Robert L., *Winning With CASE: Managing Modern Software Development*, New York: McGraw-Hill, 1992.

9. Ginzberg, Michael J., "Key Recurrent Issues in MIS Implementation Process," *MIS Quarterly*, June 1981.

10. Johnson, James A., *The Software Factory: Managing Software Development and Maintenance*, Wellesley, MA: QED Information Sciences, 1991.

11. Keen, Peter G. W., "Information Systems and Organizational Change," *Communications of the ACM*, Vol. 24, 1981, pp. 24–33.

12. Lucas, Henry C., Jr., *Implementation: The Key to Successful Information Systems*, New York: Columbia University Press, 1981.

13. Wetherbe, James C., and Dickson, Gary W., *Management of Information Systems*, New York: McGraw-Hill, 1984.

CASE DRIVES AN INNOVATIVE SYSTEM

CHRIS SAUER
Fujitsu Centre for Managing IT in Organisations
Australian Graduate School of Management
The University of New South Wales

CASE Drives an Innovative System

Car number plates throughout the state tell travelers that New South Wales is Australia's "premier state." One of the ways in which New South Wales leads the rest of Australia, and indeed most of the rest of the world, is with its prize-winning computer system, DRIVES (standing for DRIver and VEhicle System). DRIVES is an operational transaction-based system which automatically performs the state's vehicle registration and driver licensing activities. It is the highly successful outcome of an innovative development process which started in 1989 and was completed in 1992.

DRIVES is one of the world's largest commercial Unix sites. The application runs to 3 million lines of COBOL procedure division code, all generated by a CASE tool. The database stores details of 3.9 million vehicles and 3.7 million driver's licenses. It services 1,500 terminals and processes 70,000 transactions per day. These transactions generate daily revenue of A$5.5 million (approximately U.S. $4.2 million).

The Problem

The Roads and Traffic Authority (RTA) of New South Wales (RTA) is a state government agency with responsibility for the planning, construction, and maintenance of the state's network of roads. In 1992 and 1993, it had 12,000 employees, and its expenditure was A$1.9 billion (U.S. $1.45 billion). When the RTA was created in 1989 out of a merger of several state government departments, it gained responsibility for registration and licensing. It was immediately faced with a problem. The existing application had been implemented in 1974, so the software was by then antiquated. Largely written in undocumented assembly code, the system had become difficult to maintain. Moreover, the organizational processes which supported the system were expensive. In addition to the network of 138 motor registries through which the public renewed their licenses, made their payments, and carried out administration transactions such as transfer of ownership, there was also a central unit comprising approximately 500 staff devoted to dealing with problems unresolved at the registries and to managing the data inputs and outputs of the existing system. This was a costly overhead.

That the problem was real and immediate was never doubted by the RTA's chief executive, Bernard Fisk, who—emphasizing his point in uncharacteristically idiomatic English—later recalled, "I was dead scared of the existing system falling over." In the political context of a state government with an economic rationalist approach to public administration, there was no question that a cost-effective alternative was required. The system had to be updated on a new technical platform. The economic target which was to justify the new system was the elimination of the 500 jobs that were occupied by the central clerical staff.

Search for a Solution

Once it was agreed, in early 1989, that a new system was needed, Geoff Deacon, the RTA's head of IT, undertook a worldwide search for an existing system which would meet his needs. It was quickly apparent that neither software houses nor comparable authorities elsewhere were able to provide an off-the-shelf solution. The RTA would have to build its own system.

All that was required immediately was for the RTA to assure itself that such a system would be feasible with the technology architecture it had already planned for its other systems. This was to be an open-systems-based mainframe configuration. More precisely, this meant the novel combination of Unix on a Fujitsu mainframe, with Oracle as the database. While there remained some technical issues to clear up, indications were that this would be a good solution.

Laying the Foundations

The CEO clearly signalled the project's priority by dubbing it *DRIVES '90* to indicate his desire that it should be implemented in the following year, and also by appointing his head of IT, Geoff Deacon, as its director.

Deacon set about trying to manage the risk associated with the project by seeking a strategic partner. He hoped that he could persuade a software company to fund some of the development in return for a share in the ownership of the system which might then be sold to similar authorities around the world. The best prospect was a Sydney-based software house called Paxus which could supply technical staff. Paxus was also able to help on another score. To meet the very tight development timetable, a CASE tool was required—even though in 1989 there were no really mature products on the market. However, Paxus had an arrangement whereby it could supply IEF (Information Engineering Framework), a relatively advanced CASE tool from Texas Instruments (TI). It was quickly agreed that the RTA would use Paxus and IEF. In the rush to make progress, a partnership agreement was never finalized, so the RTA ended up bearing all the risk.

Lacking an in-house systems development unit capable of undertaking a project of the magnitude of DRIVES, Deacon set about building up his team with technical staff from Paxus and with some of the RTA's best staff for other key roles such as chief user and change management team leader. The RTA particularly benefited from the fact that Paxus was able to draw on its best suppliers because they were attracted by the state-of-the-art nature of the project technology. Texas Instruments also supplied five consultants to play a leading role in applications development.

The project was organized such that below the project director was a project coordinator with a small support staff. Reporting to the project coordinator were five team leaders. The teams were Development (for the applications); Change Management (for logistics, motor registry refurbishment, and training); Procedures (for defining user procedures and preparing manuals); System Environment (for providing the hardware, systems software, and network infrastructure); and Data Conversion (for converting the records to new formats and cutting over to new database files).

Having thus laid the technical and organizational foundations, the project team was ready for the task of developing the system and preparing the organization in time for an implementation which was planned for early 1991.

Building DRIVES

The cost justification for a new system was based on the elimination of 500 jobs in the central processing department. The main design goal which would permit this saving was for the new system to provide computer-based support for a *one-stop shop operation* in all the motor registries—on any visit to a registry, customers would only have to deal with a single member of RTA staff; and the counter staff could complete all the customer's transactions and solve any problems in the one visit. While the project team was anxious to rationalize the many complex rules and regulations, political sensitivites to the many customer concessions enshrined in prior legislation, com-

bined with the short timetable for development, meant that most of the existing rules had to be retained. In spite of this, administrative procedures certainly were rationalized, one measure of this being the reduction in the number of forms used from 700 to 110.

Planning and controlling the project was undertaken using a computer-based package which was used elsewhere within the RTA for road construction projects. This did not prove satisfactory and was eventually replaced; but planning and controlling was never easy largely because the CASE tool, IEF, was something of an unknown quantity for all the developers, even including TI's own staff, because IEF had never before been used on such a large task.

The end of March 1990 was set as the deadline for the completion of business area analysis; and, true to the old adage that analysis always finishes on time, it did. The resulting data model, however, proved somewhat simpler than that which eventually formed the basis of the implemented system. Several factors influenced this. One was the difficulty of finding top-class business analysts. A second was that, as a result of the merger out of which the RTA had been created, senior managers had a limited understanding of the full scale and complexity of the registration and licensing business. A third was that many of the users whose knowledge formed the basis of the data model were the very same members of the central processing department who stood to lose their jobs as a result of DRIVES. And fourth, the time allowed for analysis was short.

One consequence was that subsequent stages of development were characterized by a continuing revision of the data model. This required informal coordination among the Development staff which was facilitated by their close physical proximity to one another and their strong goal orientation. The final outcome, if not as smoothly achieved as might have been desired, has proved a robust base for DRIVES.

There were two major technical tasks. The first was to ensure that the computing platform was fully defined and would work. George Orr, the System Environment team leader, was responsible for this. His contribution is rated as outstanding by everyone who worked with him. Geoff Deacon rates him "the smartest technical person I've ever had anything to do with" in 25 years in the computing industry. The platform he constructed has proved most successful for the RTA. However, during the early stages of its development, Orr's staff recognized that there might be capacity problems given the volume of processing DRIVES would have to handle. Fujitsu assured the RTA that a more powerful mainframe with a multiprocessor was scheduled for release in time for DRIVES.

The other major technical task was to ensure that the vendor-supplied software worked. Fujitsu was still working on its version of Unix. The CASE tool generated COBOL code on an MVS operating system, not C on Unix as was required, so TI had to convert IEF. This meant that, as an expedient, development had to be carried out on an IBM machine belonging to another state government authority. This generated COBOL code which was then compiled on the Fujitsu machine under Unix. Given this situation, the RTA decided to settle for COBOL source code rather than C.

The vendors, both at this time and later, proved very committed because although they did not have formal partnership agreements, the RTA always treated them as partners and did not lay blame or become adversarial when there were delays or other difficulties. Neville Roach, Fujitsu Australia's managing director, makes the point, ''The RTA didn't treat us in the traditional vendor/buyer adversarial role that many people adopt. When there were some severe stresses, we were all able to get together and say what is it that we can do to help address this problem. If it had been a traditional adversary culture I think we would have ended up with a dispute rather than a resolution.''

Throughout 1990, and indeed throughout the whole project, staff commitment was high—with 70 hour weeks being usual. Even the RTA's own staff who were not paid overtime, worked similarly long hours. By the end of the year, despite his project manager's plans which still aimed for an early 1991 implementation, it became apparent to Geoff Deacon that this was no longer possible. A major stumbling block was data conversion.

At the beginning of 1991, Deacon and his management team undertook a reassessment of the implementation schedule. They split the development and conversion so that the less complex, lower-volume application—licensing—could be implemented sooner, with the more complex, higher-volume application—registration—to be implemented later. They also changed the basis of project control from reporting on detailed tasks to reporting on some 67 critical milestones. This permitted much tighter management control throughout the rest of the project.

Implementation

DRIVES was implemented in 138 motor registries thoughout New South Wales on September 2, 1991, making its first cost savings.

The early days of implementation were not easy for the counter staff. DRIVES was enforcing standard practices where previously there had been local variations. Data problems were causing delays at the counters and queues in the registries. The help desk was swamped with queries. Nevertheless, the front line staff persisted.

Likewise, the DRIVES development team persisted, concentrating on preparing the registration application and converting its data. Processing resources were at full capacity coping with licensing operations, system development and testing, and conversion. The conversion problem was eased by securing temporary capacity from another state government agency. A new, more powerful mainframe was ordered from Fujitsu. Meanwhile the System Environment team continued to try for a 30-machine-transactions-per-second (tps) throughput as its benchmark for processing all the full operational registration and licensing business transactions. Intensive training was conducted, although this proved to be logistically taxing because the applications were not stable and the machine capacity was stretched so that transactions on the training database were sometimes very slow. Also, the motor registries had to continue to provide business-as-usual service, so training in some cases took place before all the application transaction formats had been finalized and sometimes even a couple of months before implementation.

Aware of the continuing pressure from the government to effect the promised savings, Bernard Fisk and Geoff Deacon agreed to implement registation in June 1992 with only 24-tps performance. Initial performance was satisfactory, but there was a changeover period before the largest volume transaction, registration renewals, was required. When it was implemented in mid-August, even though there was a batch version to take the pressure off the on-line system, response times were uncomfortably lengthy. When users ignored the batch renewal transaction and opted for the on-line version, the system slowed to a crawl.

Customer service officers in the motor registries bore the brunt of the public's annoyance at the long queues and slow service. The press, encouraged by the Australian Services Union which was in dispute with the RTA, published highly critical reports. The opposition party's spokesman on transportation issues attacked DRIVES in state parliament.

There was, though, no going back to the old system. The remaining central clerical staff had taken their separation settlements in June. Now, everybody pitched in to make the best they could of the immediate difficulties. Counter staff developed ways of defusing customer dissatisfaction through conversation and explanation, while more seats were installed in the registries to accommodate the queues. Technical staff focused on fine tuning the system. Fujitsu provided more hardware, and their technical staff devoted themselves to preparing a version of Unix which could take advantage of the mainframe's dual processor. The project director invited journalists into the project to see for themselves that the only real problem was a short-term lack of capacity. The CEO and the chief user appeared on a talk radio show to explain the situation. The minister defended the project in parliament, praising the skills and dedication of the RTA's staff.

The system responded to the efforts to tune it, and over the ensuing months performance gradually improved. When Fujitsu's multiprocessor Unix was delivered in January 1993, it brought with it the machine performance the RTA had anticipated. With counter staff now familiar with the application, the RTA was set to reap the benefits of DRIVES.

Set against a total investment in DRIVES of A\$38 million (U.S. \$29 million) with an increased continuing cost of A\$2 million (U.S. \$1.5 million) per year, the A\$20 million (U.S. \$15 million) saving per year on staff costs has given the RTA a net benefit after little over two years of operation. In addition, the RTA has dramatically improved levels of customer service and satisfaction. Furthermore, DRIVES has allowed the RTA to derive a number of other benefits including greater audit control over possible abuse and misuse of information, enhanced management control over registry operations, and opportunities to explore new ways of delivering services to the public. From the technical perspective, not only did the IEF CASE tool permit the system developers to operate at a level of productivity in the top one percentile of all projects, it has also facilitated maintenance and enhancement. In April 1993, a new version of the system, including significant amendments to half the code modules, was implemented without a hitch.

In October 1993, the Australian Information Industries Association recognized the quality and innovative nature of DRIVES by giving the RTA its award for excellence in the application of information technology in a large organization.

Case Study Questions

1. What do you think are the three most important success factors for DRIVES? Why were these important?

2. What major difficulties did the RTA face during development and implementation? How did they solve them?

3. What was innovative about the DRIVES development process? How successful were these innovations?

4. How did the RTA try to manage the risk of using a new development tool and building a new technology platform?

5. What have you learned from DRIVES about using CASE tools?

6. What role did the CEO play? How important was that?

7. From your knowledge of the DRIVES project, what advice would you give to a new project manager undertaking a similarly innovative systems development?

8. Identify a process that was reengineered at RTA and explain the role of IT in the reengineering.

9. What are the major lessons you have learned from this case regarding the system-development process and the major implementation issues.

INFORMATION SUPPORT SYSTEMS (APPLICATIONS)

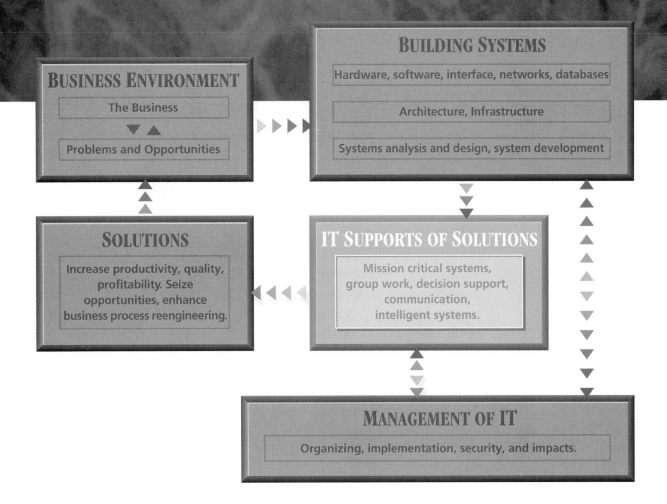

The purpose of IT, as shown in our basic model, is to support solutions to business problems and opportunities. In Parts I and II, we illustrated some solutions and named the enabling technologies, such as expert systems and electronic data interchange. However, we did not elaborate on these technologies. After describing information systems, infrastructure, and the systems development process in Part III, we are now ready to describe the enabling technologies and their implementation in Part IV, which is divided into four chapters.

Chapter 14 describes the support provided by IT to enhance communication within and between organizations. Special attention is given to the support of collaborative work—the work of team members who may be in one or several locations. To compete in the 1990s, it is necessary to provide quality, timely, and inexpensive communication. Several technologies are described in the chapter, including video teleconferencing, E-mail, EDI, work flow, group DSS, voice technologies, and other groupware products. The chapter also describes telecommuting, which can utilize the above technologies, and information superhighways, which enable nationwide and worldwide communication.

Chapter 15 focuses on support technologies for executives and managers. Managerial decision making, especially at the managerial and strategic levels, is becoming more and more complex. Using different tools, IT can provide support to decision making. The chapter concentrates on two types of support. First, the support given to unstructured problems and opportunities is examined under the topic of decision support systems (DSS), which uses a modeling approach to problem solving. Second, the support given to top executives in identifying problems and opportunities, as well as in assessing their importance is covered under the topic of executive information systems (EIS).

Chapter 16 directs attention to the technologies of artificial intelligence, especially to expert systems (ES) and artificial neural networks (ANN). These and other cutting edge technologies use *knowledge* as the primary factor in their systems. The major purpose is the support of knowledge workers in order to increase productivity and quality. The chapter deals primarily with the support provided to mission-critical activities in organizations. Specifically, support is provided to the operational, managerial, and strategic operations of the major functional areas in the organization. It focuses on practical applications, providing solutions for improved productivity and quality and enhancing business processes reengineering.

Chapter 17 describes innovative applications of IT to the major functional areas of the enterprise: accounting/finance, production/operations, marketing, and human resource management. In addition the chapter describes the use of IT in transaction processing systems. Part IV ends with a case describing how the use of multimedia-supported intelligent systems increases productivity in the City of Los Angeles.

Chapter 14—Supporting Communication and Collaborative Work
Chapter 15—Supporting the Manager and Decision Making
Chapter 16—Intelligent Support Systems
Chapter 17—From Transaction Processing to Innovative Functional Support Systems

14

SUPPORTING COMMUNICATION AND COLLABORATIVE WORK

Chapter Outline

Learning Objectives

After studying this chapter, you will be able to:

1. Understand basic communication concepts and their enhancement by IT.

2. Discuss the benefits and limitations of group work.

3. Describe manual and electronic methods for improving the process of group communication and decision making.

4. Explain the various techniques of teleconferencing.

5. Describe electronic mail (E-mail), and other electronic communication services.

6. Define electronic data interchange, and contrast it with E-mail.

7. Describe group decision support systems, their advantages and applications.

8. Describe voice technologies, their advantages and limitations.

9. Explain telecommuting, its advantages and limitations.

10. Describe Lotus Notes.

11. Describe information superhighways and the Internet.

▶ 14.1 THE HARPER GROUP SPEEDS INTERNATIONAL TRADE USING ELECTRONIC DATA INTERCHANGE

THE HARPER GROUP is an international freight moving company that uses IT to support the large amount of cargo it delivers around the world. International trade is complex because it involves customers, customs services, ports, storage companies, and transportation companies. Large amounts of information flow among several trading partners and support services. This information includes orders, biddings, billings, status queries, contracts, payments, and so on.

To improve information flow so that it will move more consistently, freely, and rapidly, and to expedite the movement of cargo, The Harper Group is using electronic data interchange (EDI) technology. EDI links the computers of different organizations, resulting in a paperless flow of routine information.

Let's see how EDI works for Harper. Harper has an EDI arrangement with 500 of its larger customers, one of which is Honda Motor Company of Japan. Honda ships over 300,000 cars and trucks to the United States each year. Harper takes care of all the necessary arrangements, including those involving the U.S. Customs. Harper uses EDI to communicate with U.S. Customs. Nearly 99 percent of all 1,800 Customs brokers conduct most of their business via EDI. Harper can also tap into Honda's computers to deposit or retrieve information required by Customs.

The EDI transaction begins when Honda sends its commercial invoices electronically from its headquarters in Japan to the American Honda offices in Los Angeles (see Figure 14.1). The original information includes details of the cars and parts being shipped, tariff numbers, and the value of each item. The information is then transferred electronically to Harper's mainframe in San Francisco. Harper supplements that data with antidumping information, visas for floor mats and other textiles used in a car, and the name of the freight carrier. The complete files (one order may include several hundred pages of data) are then transferred electronically to U.S. Customs several days before the ship docks in a U.S. port. Customs agents calculate the duty payments and send them to Harper via EDI. Honda's duty payment for each shipment is then transferred electronically from a bank designated by Harper's mainframe to Customs. Finally, Harper bills Honda electronically for its services and is paid via electronic transfer of funds.

Japanese cars waiting to be loaded onto a ship.

Initially, Harper leased the communication links between its headquarters and one customer. As more customers joined, it became more economical to use commercial value-added network services (VANs). These VANs provide all the necessary links between Harper's mainframe, Harper's 10 regional minicomputers, and the customers' computers. As can be seen in Figure 14.1, each VAN is used for a special purpose.

To make the system work, it was necessary to install an EDI translator (described in Section 14.7) between the computers and the communication links (usually telephone lines). A special translator is available for U.S. Customs.

In addition to the EDI, which is used for standard transactions, Harper uses electronic mail to correspond with its clients. Harper has an internal E-mail system and so do its large customers. By using the X.400 gateways, Harper's E-mail is connected with its customers' E-mail.

Overall, this electronic communication system enables cheaper, faster, and more reliable information to flow and support Harper's global business. IT enables Harper to maintain its position as the second largest importer in the United States (Harper filed about 250,000 customs entries in 1993, which gave them about 5 percent of the total U.S. market share). In addition, Harper operates in an industry with thin profit margins, yet its profit margins are substantial and rapidly increasing.

SOURCE: Guglielmo (1992) and *Information Week*, June 20, 1994.

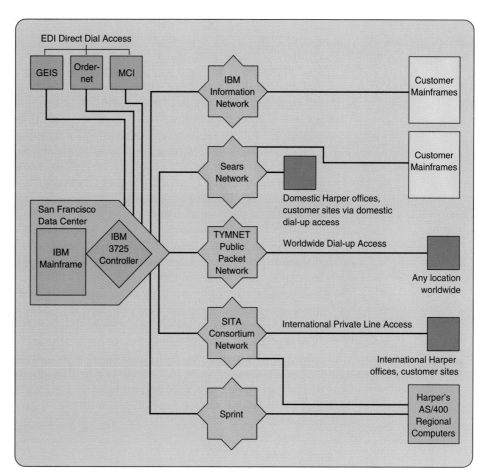

FIGURE 14.1 Using electronic data interchange at Harper Corporation (SOURCE: Guglielmo, 1992, p. 240.)

▶ 14.2 COMMUNICATION NEEDS OF BUSINESS

Chapter 1 introduced some organizational and societal issues that are critical to business today. Several of these issues require that individuals and/or organizations communicate and cooperate in performing their work. An example is Drucker's concept of team-based organizations (1988), where special ad hoc units are assembled to execute special tasks (see also Chapter 4). Similarly, conventionally structured organizations are composed of individuals and units assembled to carry out special missions or to perform certain activities. In either case, participating members may not be in the same location or even working in the same time zone or country. The participants need an efficient and effective way to communicate with each other (locally, nationally, and internationally). Some important organizational trends that require extensive communication are the need to reduce the time-to-market, the need to globalize businesses, and the need to explore both internal and external data continuously and constantly, frequently in real time. These trends point to two important needs.

1. The need for better, faster, and cheaper communication among individuals and organizations.

2. The need to support people who are working together, both in the same and in dispersed locations.

The use of EDI and electronic mail by Harper Corporation, as demonstrated in the opening case, is an example of how companies use IT to improve communication among different organizations involved in international trade. IT provides several other technologies that can be used to improve communication. Improved communication is needed to reduce travel costs; expedite work done by several people at different locations, thus eliminating the need to ship documents and wait for their return; be more responsive to customers by reducing their waiting time for responses; and save time for those individuals who spend a large portion of their time communicating. IT can also enhance communication by integrating different types of media (text, voice, graphics, animation).

Nowadays, without advanced telecommunication systems, it is frequently impossible to continue to do business effectively. For example, suppliers of Sears, Ford, General Motors, and many other large corporations *must* link to these companies through EDI. If not, the suppliers cannot do business with these large corporations, or they are assessed special high fees.

Most managers spend as much as 90 percent of their time communicating. As will be shown in Chapter 15, managers serve as a "nerve center" in the information-processing network, where managers collect, distribute, and process information continuously. Since poor communication means poor management, managers must communicate among themselves and with others. Managers can develop communication networks through which they can influence, inform, control, and inspire. Communication is essential to the success or even the survival of organizations. Unfortunately, there are barriers that can make communication ineffective or inefficient, especially when a large number of people are involved and when some of these individuals are in different locations. A primary purpose of IT is to provide faster, better, and timely communication at a reasonable cost. However, before we see how this is done, let us review some communication concepts.

▶ 14.3 COMMUNICATION CONCEPTS

Communication is an interpersonal process of sending and receiving symbols with messages attached to them. Through communication, people exchange and share information as well as influence and understand each other.

The basic model of communication is shown in Figure 14.2.

The sender encodes a message (voice, text, picture, and so on) and sends it through a channel to a receiver who decodes (interprets) the message. Because of the possibility of many interferences, the receiver may not perceive the meaning intended by the sender. Feedback can help to clarify the content of the message.

FIGURE 14.2 Basic model of communication (Based on Schermerhorn, 1993, p. 474.)

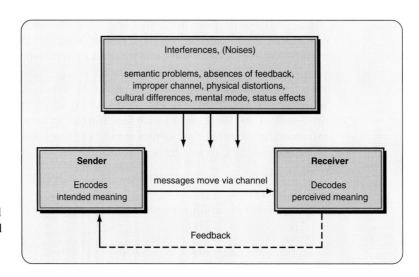

Major concerns of business include the following: that messages be trans-mitted as fast as they are needed, that they are properly interpreted by the in-tended receiver, and that the cost of doing this is reasonable. Communication systems that meet these conditions have several requirements. They must enable two-way communication: messages to flow in different directions simultaneously, and messages to reach people regardless of where they are located. They must also allow people to access sources of information (such as databases). IT can meet these requirements through the electronic transfer of information.

FACTORS DETERMINING USES OF INFORMATION TECHNOLOGIES

Several factors determine the IT technologies that could be used to provide com-munication support to a specific organization or group of users. The major factors are the following.

▼ *Participants.* The number of people sending and receiving information can range from two to many thousands.

▼ *Nature of sources and destinations.* Sources and destinations of information may include people, databases, sensors, and so on.

▼ *Location.* The sender(s) and receiver(s) can be in the same room, in different rooms but in the same location, or in different locations.

▼ *Time.* Messages can be sent at a certain time and received almost simultane-ously. In such a case, communication is **synchronous**. Telephones, tele-conferencing, and face-to-face meetings are examples of synchronous com-munication. **Asynchronous communication**, on the other hand, refers to communication where the receiver gets the message at a different time than it was sent. For example, when you leave a message on an answering machine, you conduct asynchronous communication with the receiver. A fax sent from New York to Tokyo is likely to be read a few hours later due to the different time zones (a 12-hour difference—noontime in New York is midnight in Tokyo).

▼ *Media.* Communication may involve one or several media. As described in Chapter 7, today's IT can handle several types of media such as text, voice, graphics, images, and animation. When several media are used in the same communication system, we call this *multimedia*. Using different media for com-municating can increase the effectiveness of a message, expedite learning, and enhance problem solving, as will be shown in the City of Los Angeles diagnostic system case at the end of Part 4 (Chapter 17). Working with multiple media may, however, reduce the efficiency and effectiveness of the system (speed, capacity, quality) and may significantly increase its cost.

A TIME/PLACE FRAMEWORK

A framework for classifying IT communication support technologies was proposed by DeSanctis and Gallupe (1987). According to this framework, communication is divided into four cells which are shown together with the support technologies in Figure 14.3. The cells are:

1. *Same-time/same-place.* In this setting, participants meet face-to-face in one place and at the same time. An example is a decision room.

2. *Same-time/different-place.* This setting refers to a meeting where the partic-ipants are in different places, but they communicate at the same time. A conference telephone call and video conferencing are examples of such sit-uations.

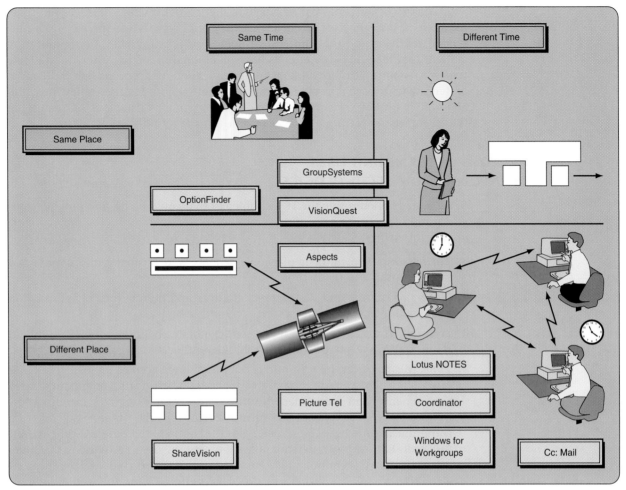

FIGURE 14.3 Time/place communication framework. Shown in each box are representative commercial products. (SOURCE: Chen, 1993. Reproduced with permission.)

3. *Different-time/same-place.* This setting can materialize when people work in shifts. The first shift leaves messages for the second shift.

4. *Different-time/different-place.* In this setting, participants are in different places, and they send and/or receive messages at different times.

14.4 SUPPORTING COLLABORATIVE WORK

As discussed earlier, one of the features of a modern organization is that people collaborate to perform work. Most major decisions in organizations are made by groups of people. Solving complex problems requires the expertise of several individuals, resulting in work groups. In this section, we explore the nature of such work and discuss how IT can be beneficial.

THE NATURE OF GROUP WORK

The term group, or **work group**, refers to two or more individuals who act as one unit in order to perform some task. The group can be permanent or temporary. The group can be in one or several locations, and it can meet concurrently or at different times. A group can be a committee, a review panel, a task force, an executive board, a team, or a department.

Table 14.1 Benefits of Working in a Group

- Groups are better than individuals at understanding problems.
- People are accountable for decisions in which they participate.
- Groups are better than individuals at catching errors.
- A group has more information (knowledge) than any one member and, as a result, more alternatives are generated for problem solving.
- Synergy may be produced, so the effectiveness and/or quality of a group is larger than the sum of what is produced by independent individuals.
- Working in a group may stimulate the participants and the process.
- Group members have their egos embedded in the decision they make, so they will be committed to the implementation.
- The participation of the members in making a decision means less likelihood of their resisting implementation.

SOURCE: Turban, 1993.

Groups can do many things. For example, a group of designers develops a new product, researchers team up to develop new drugs, professors meet to develop appropriate curricula, and artists produce a new film. People can work together on the same document, cooperatively write a book, and even compose a drawing or music jointly. In most groups, though not in all, people make decisions collectively.

For years, people have recognized the benefits of collaborative work. Typical benefits that relate to decision making are shown in Table 14.1. But despite the many benefits of group interaction, the results of people working in groups are not always successful. The reason is that the *process* of collaborative work is frequently plagued with dysfunctions (see Table 14.2). To reconcile the dilemma of having significant benefits on one side and dysfunctions on the other, researchers have developed methods for improving the work of groups.

IMPROVING THE WORK OF GROUPS

For many years, attempts were made to improve the work of groups. If we could eliminate or lessen some of the phenomena that cause the dysfunctions, the benefits would be greatly enhanced. Behavioral scientists, personnel experts, efficiency experts, and others have developed many approaches to solve these problems. Some of the approaches are labeled "group dynamics." Two representative methods are presented next.

Table 14.2 Dysfunctions of Group Process

- Social pressures of conformity ("groupthink") may eliminate superior ideas.
- Time-consuming, slow process (e.g., tendency to repeat what already was said).
- Lack of coordination of the work done by the group.
- Inappropriate influence of group dynamics (e.g., domination of time, topic, or opinion by one or a few individuals; fear to speak; rigidity).
- Tendency of group members to rely on others to do most of the work ("free riders").
- Tendency toward compromised solutions of poor quality.
- Inability to complete a task.
- Large nonproductive time (socializing, getting ready, waiting for people).
- Larger cost of making decisions (many hours of participation, travel expenses, and so on).
- Incomplete or inappropriate use of information.

SOURCE: Turban, 1993.

THE NOMINAL GROUP TECHNIQUE. The **nominal group technique (NGT)**, a typical group dynamic method developed by Delbeck and Van de Ven (see Lindstone and Turroff [1975]), includes a sequence of activities: (1) silent generation of ideas in writing, (2) round-robin listing of ideas on a flip chart, (3) serial discussion of ideas, (4) silent listing and ranking of priorities, (5) discussion of priorities, and (6) silent reranking and rating of priorities. The nominal group process is based on social–psychological research which indicates that this procedure is clearly superior to conventional discussion groups in terms of generating higher quality decisions, a greater quantity of ideas, and an improved distribution of information on fact-finding tasks.

The success of the NGT and similar methods depends considerably on the quality of the facilitator (all group-dynamic approaches require a facilitator) and on the training given to the participants. Also, this approach does not solve several of the dysfunctions of group process such as the fear to speak, slow process, poor planning and organization of the meeting, compromises, and lack of appropriate analysis.

THE DELPHI METHOD. The **Delphi method** was developed by the RAND Corporation as a technological forecasting technique for a group of experts. The intention was to eliminate the undesirable effects of interaction among members of the group. The experts do not meet face-to-face, and they do not know who the other experts are. The method generally begins by having each expert provide an individually written assignment or opinion (e.g., a forecast) along with supporting arguments and assumptions. These opinions are submitted to the Delphi coordinator who edits, clarifies, and summarizes the data. These opinions are then provided as anonymous feedback to the participating experts along with a second round of questions. Questions and feedback continue in writing for several rounds, becoming increasingly more specific, until consensus among the panel members is reached, or until the experts no longer change their positions.

The Delphi method benefits from multiple opinions and group communication among members representing diverse opinions and assumptions. At the same time, it avoids—through anonymity—several negative effects that are often associated with face-to-face solutions, such as dominant behavior, **groupthink** (where people begin to think alike and new ideas are not tolerated), and stubbornness to change one's mind.

Although the Delphi method may encourage some original ideas, it has several limitations. It is slow, expensive, and usually limited to one issue (e.g., technological forecasting or "go"–"no go" decisions).

USE OF INFORMATION TECHNOLOGY—GROUPWARE

The limited success of methods such as the NGT and the Delphi method led to attempts to use information technology to support groups. An emerging name that covers this area is *group support systems* (GSS). The name for the supporting software products is *groupware*.

The term **groupware** refers to software products that support groups of people engaged with a common task or goal. The software provides a mechanism to share opinions and resources. In the computer industry the term *groupware* is known to be very ambiguous. It seems that every vendor tries to manipulate the term to its own advantage, and indeed, there are dozens of products on the market, some of which may not be true groupware. Johansen (1988) has identified 17 different approaches and technologies for computer support of groups. The major group support technologies are discussed in the remainder of this chapter.

▶ 14.5 ELECTRONIC TELECONFERENCING

Teleconferencing refers to the use of electronic communication that allows two or more people from different locations to have a conference. There are several variations of teleconferencing (see LaPlante [1993]). The oldest and the simplest is a telephone conference, where several people talk to each other from three or more locations. Conference calls are available to customers at very low cost. The biggest disadvantage is that they do not allow for face-to-face communication. Also, participants in one location cannot see graphs, charts, and pictures available in other locations. While the latter deficiency can be overcome by using a fax, it is a time-consuming, expensive, and frequently a poor-quality process. One solution is video teleconferencing, where participants can see each other as well as the documents.

VIDEO TELECONFERENCING

In a **video teleconference**, participants in one location can see participants at another location or in several locations. Pictures of the participants can appear on a large screen or on a desktop computer. Originally, video teleconferencing was the transmission of live, compressed TV sessions between two or more points. Video teleconferencing today, however, is a digital technology capable of linking various types of computers. Once conferences are digitized and transmitted over networks, they become a computer application. Therefore, in video conferencing, one can present data, voice, pictures, graphics, and animation (see Figure 14.4).

Video mail is an example of video conferencing as a computer application. Video mail is similar to voice mail; however, the voice/image contents of the video mail can be created from portions of conferences and stored on a file server. It is possible to simultaneously transmit data, voice, and pictures during conferences. It is also possible to work on documents and exchange computer files during conferences. This allows the possibility of high-quality presentations using computer graphics. Video teleconferencing allows several geographically dispersed groups to work together on the same project and communicate by voice simultaneously.

While the first generation of computerized video teleconferencing was conducted in special rooms with large screens, cameras, and coder/recorders, the second generation moved to the worker's desktop, using special equipment such as PC Videophone and LANs. As interactive video moves to the desktop, it becomes

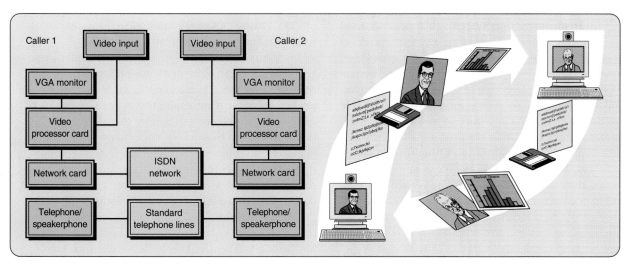

FIGURE 14.4 A typical video teleconference set-up (SOURCE: Yager, 1993, p. 134. Reprinted with permission from the March 1993 issue of BYTE Magazine, © by McGraw-Hill, Inc., New York, N.Y. All rights reserved.)

Table 14.3 **The Benefits of Teleconferencing**

- Providing the opportunity for face-to-face communication for individuals in different locations.
- Providing the possibility of using several types of media to support conferencing.
- Enabling usage of voice (which is more natural than using the keyboard).
- Travel-cost savings have become secondary to the primary reason for teleconferencing: savings in productivity realized by enabling employees to stay at their jobs rather than travel and by eliminating compensatory time taken up while they travel (see Box 14.1).
- Conserving the time and energy of key employees and increasing the speed of business processes (including product development, contract negotiation, and customer service).
- Improving the efficiency and frequency of communications.
- Cost of teleconferencing systems are becoming more affordable, and different types are available to serve every need.
- Messages can be saved in the computer to reconstruct specific parts of a meeting for future purposes.
- Teleconferencing may be used to (1) train end users who are widely dispersed geographically, and (2) hold classes with several instructors and many students at different locations.

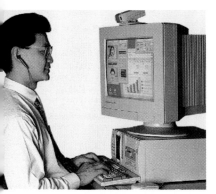

FIGURE 14.5 ShareVision PC 3000, a comprehensive desktop teleconferencing system from Creative Technology, Ltd.

a valuable item that can be used in conjunction with other desktop facilities (see Figure 14.5).

The major benefits of video teleconferencing are given in Table 14.3.

Several factors are limiting the growth of video teleconferencing. These include lack of standards to cost of setup, maintenance, connectivity problems with network security, and network capacity. However, technological developments are reducing the effects of these factors.

Computer programs can enable people at different locations to work together on the same screen, exchanging voice files, spreadsheet analysis, and/or keyed ideas and comments (see Box 14.1).

Several interesting products are marketed by Picture Tel (PCS 100), Fujitsu (Desktop Conferencing), and Creative Technology (ShareVision PC3000). Some of these products use regular telephone lines, and they can run either as stand-alone units or across a LAN.

IT At Work BOX 14.1

VIDEO TELECONFERENCING SAVES MONEY

Bull HN Information Systems (Billerica, MA) used to spend several million dollars a year on travel between its headquarters in Billerica and its Phoenix office. To save money, in 1989 Bull installed a PictureTel System 4000 video teleconferencing unit at the two locations. Bull was then able to greatly increase the number of meetings and contain costs, since no travel was required.

Many other companies reported significant savings. For example, **BASF Corporation's fiber division** (Williamsburg, VA) saves over $1 million a year in travel expenses alone. Video teleconferencing is used not only within one company but also among several companies. For example, **Sun Health Corporation** (Charlotte, NC) purchases supplies for 250 hospitals in 15 states. The member hospitals decided to install video teleconferencing equipment in all hospitals, so they can conduct face-to-face meetings without the need to travel. By the end

of 1993, 22 hospitals were connected to the system which will be gradually available to all 250 hospitals.

In an attempt to cut trips to their offshore drilling sites and their European office in Aberdeen, Scotland, **Global Marine** (Houston, TX) installed Fujitsu's Desktop Conferencing system. One application was to train the IS employees in Aberdeen in a new client/server system that replaced the mainframe. Other applications enable managers at different locations to review contracts, spreadsheets, and proposals. For example, a manager can change a cell value in the spreadsheet and discuss the change with his colleagues in other locations.

Critical Thinking Issues: Is it really necessary to see on a screen the person you are conferencing with? Why not use the inexpensive telephone conferencing? ▲

SOURCE: Condensed from *Computerworld*, May 3, 1993.

Data can be sent *simultaneously* with voice and video. Apart from seeing the person you are talking to (in video colors), the system allows you to create what is called a virtual whiteboard. This means that the two parties can see, simultaneously, changes made to a document "pasted" on an electronic whiteboard.

Take, for example, an advertisement that needs to be cleared by a senior manager. Once the advertisement is scanned into the PC, both parties can see it on the screen. If the senior manager does not like something, he can use a stylus pen and highlight what he wants changed. This makes communications between two parties clearer.

The two parties can also share applications. For example, if party A has a Lotus 1-2-3 (or any other Windows application) screen, party B can make amendments to the document even if party B does not have Lotus 1-2-3.

Applications for desktops go beyond the traditional videoconferencing uses, such as cutting down travel costs. Desktop teleconferencing has many other applications. For example, the product can be used by advertising agencies to show their clients creative concepts and ideas. A client can make amendments on-line that can be seen by the advertising agency presenting clear, immediate communication. Marketeers can also use the product to make remote presentations to customers.

In defense applications, desktop video teleconferencing can be used as a remote surveillance tool because the video camera captures movements which can be tracked by security personnel located elsewhere. The benefit here is that a frame of the video can be captured and enlarged to spot security breaches.

The application in transportation is similar. Traffic officers stationed strategically along highways during peak traffic hours can transmit maps showing congestion areas and decide how to divert traffic.

▶ 14.6   ELECTRONIC MAIL

Electronic mail (E-mail) allows multiple-access communication delivered exclusively on a computer network. With E-mail, a person can send letters to anyone connected to the system. When a message is sent, it enters an individual's "mailbox." The receiver, when connected to the network, is notified that he has mail. The receiver can then read the mail, send a reply, edit the mail, or forward the letter to another person. Some typical capabilities of E-mail are shown in Box 14.2.

A Closer Look BOX 14.2

THE POWER OF E-MAIL

E-mail is more than just mail delivered electronically. Here are some typical capabilities.

▽ Sends anything you create or view on a PC (including pictures and voice).

▽ Contains a good word processing text editor and a spelling checker.

▽ Allows you to color documents in dozens of combinations.

▽ Stores messages.

▽ Retrieves messages from your in-box, bulletin boards, and other electronic devices.

▽ Searches for a document by a keyword.

▽ Uses "return receipt" that notifies you when a recipient reads a message.

▽ Provides priorities of messages.

▽ Prints messages.

▽ Forwards messages.

▽ Sends group reply, that is, replies to everyone who received the current message.

▽ Creates different folders and archives to keep track of your electronic mail.

▽ Allows you to retrieve messages deleted earlier from trash folder.

▽ Creates public bulletin boards where everyone in the organization can post and view messages.

▼ Sends mail to many people, practically to any place in the world that is networked.
▼ Shares text messages and application files across popular computer platforms.

▼ Delivers and receives faxes.
▼ Sends copies of messages (CC:).
▼ Schedule meetings.

E-mail is becoming an important communication tool in many organizations. The primary advantages of E-mail are the following.

▼ The ability to send and receive messages very quickly.
▼ The ability to conduct paperless communication.
▼ The ability to connect to the network from any location that has a telephone line (using a portable computer and a modem). Recently, it became possible to connect to the networks with wireless technologies.
▼ The ability to send messages to many users in a very short time.
▼ The ability to trace any correspondence (who sent, to whom, when, and so on)
▼ The ability to communicate to millions of people, worldwide.
▼ The ability to work with others on the same task.
▼ The ability to rapidly access information stored in databases from many locations.

However, there are limitations of E-mail, such as the following.

▼ The inability to conduct face-to-face communication.
▼ Most E-mails are not very user friendly.
▼ It is necessary to know how to type.
▼ It may involve problems of confidentiality and privacy.

An E-mail system is usually owned by a company. But, E-mail systems "talk" to each other. So, not only can you communicate with the employees of your company (see Box 14.3), but you can also communicate with employees of many other companies, government agencies, and educational institutions.

IT At Work BOX 14.3

REENGINEERING

ENABLED E-MAIL AT HUGHES AIRCRAFT CORPORATION

Hughes Aircraft Corporation is a multinational aerospace and electronic company that employs 25,000 managers and professionals worldwide. A leader in electronics, the company was using more than 10 different E-mail systems. In order to link all its employees, the company embarked on a six-year integration project which ended in a unified E-mail in 1992. Not only are the 25,000 employees linked together, they also are connected with 75,000 employees of General Motors (Hughes' parent company).

The real value of the system is the provision of infrastructure for company-wide applications, streamlining business processes, and speeding the dissemination of critical information. The infrastructure supports what are called mail-enable applications, which provide a focal point to *reengineer business processes*. The E-mail is integrated with a videotext database network that can be accessed for a variety of applications, including electronic routing and approval (ERA). ERA provides electronic forms and routes among employees. The user imports standard information from the database to complete the forms. Thus, the time needed for data entry and approval has been significantly reduced. For example, documents that used to take weeks to get processed, now get processed in minutes (reducing the cycle time). Employees are getting individually tailored information extracted from sources such as *Commerce Business Daily*. People get the right information fast, and they are not charged for the service. On the contrary, they are encouraged to use it as much as possible.

Critical Thinking Issues: How can an E-mail system support an IT infrastructure? ▲

SOURCE: Condensed from *CIO*, January 1992.

E-MAIL ON NETWORKS

E-mail systems were used for many years in the mainframe environment. For example, IBM's PROFS (PRofessional OFfice System) enables employees to communicate all over the world. With today's distributed systems, E-mail is capable of connecting people at different locations who are working on different LANs using different hardware, operating systems, and communication systems. The LAN can be simple, or it can be of the client/server architecture. On E-mail, one can send text, files, graphics, voice or faxes. People can connect to such systems from home or while they are on the road, using regular telephone lines or a form of wireless equipment.

An E-mail system can interface with other E-mail systems, private or public. For example, the Harper's opening case shows us that this company is connected to public systems that operate all over the world, such as MCI MAIL and IBM's X.400. Harper's clients are also connected to the same public systems; therefore, communication is possible among all the companies, regardless of their locations. Even the U.S. government is introducing E-mail (see Box 14.4).

IT At Work BOX 14.4

HOW TO CONVERSE ELECTRONICALLY WITH THE WHITE HOUSE

Try it, you will like it. You can send electronic messages to the White House. Here is how you do it. To the president, use the address: President@Whitehouse.Gov or: Clinton@Whitehouse.Gov. To the vice president: Gore@Whitehouse.Gov. You will get a quick reply, usually from an assistant. Here is a reply sent to one of the authors.

Message 19/19 From   Jul 29 '94
autoresponder@WhiteHouse.Gov   at 12:09 pm

Date: Tue, 29 Jul 94 12:09:38
To: ETURBAN@CSULB.edu

Subject: Your mail has been received

Thank you for sending in your thoughts and comments to the President via electronic mail. We are pleased to introduce this new form of communication into the White House for the first time in history. I welcome your response and participation.

As we work to reinvent government and streamline our processes, this electronic mail experiment will help put us on the leading edge of progress. Please remember, though, this is still very much an experiment.

Your message has been received, and we are keeping careful track of all the mail we are receiving electronically. We will be trying out a number of response-based systems shortly, and I ask for your patience as we move forward to integrate electronic mail from the public into the White House.

Again, on behalf of the President, thank you for your messages and for taking part in the White House electronic mail project.

Sincerely,

Marsha Scott,
Deputy Assistant to the President
and Director of Correspondence

[*You will only receive one automated response per day*]

Critical Thinking Issues: Since the president does not reply in person, why does he need E-mail? What are the benefits to the government? ▲

Several vendors produce E-mail software. Well-known software packages are cc: Mail, Microsoft Mail, WordPerfect Office, InBox, and Quickmail. Windows-based E-mail and mail-enabled applications enterprise-wide are increasing the attractiveness, friendliness, and capabilities of E-mail.

▶ 14.7 ELECTRONIC DATA INTERCHANGE

Harper Corporation, as illustrated in the opening case, uses **electronic data interchange** to communicate electronically with trading partners and supporting services. EDI can be defined as the electronic movement of standard business documents between, or within, firms. EDI uses a structured machine retrievable data format that permits data to be transferred without rekeying. Like E-mail, EDI enables the sending and receiving of messages between computers connected by

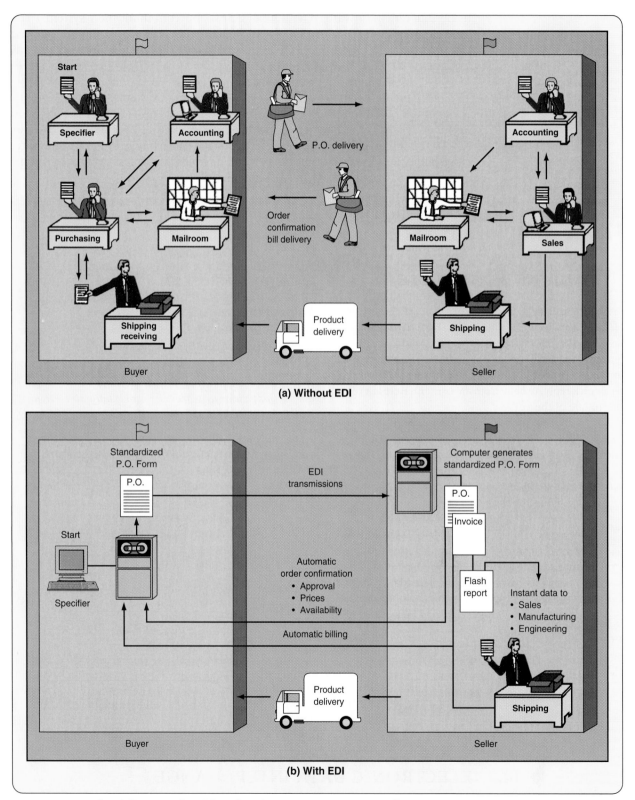

FIGURE 14.6 Order-delivery cycle with and without EDI. (SOURCE: Stalling, 1990.)

a communication link such as a telephone line (see Figure 14.6). However, EDI has some special characteristics.

▼ *Business transactions messages.* As shown in the Harper's case, EDI is used primarily to transfer repetitive business transactions. These include purchase orders, invoices, approvals of credit, shipping notices, and confirmations. In contrast, E-mail is used mainly for nonstandard correspondence.

▼ *Data formatting standards.* Since EDI messages are repetitive, it is sensible to use some formatting standards. Standards can shorten the length of the messages and eliminate data entry errors. In the United States and Canada, data are formatted according to the standards called ANSI X.12. An international standard developed by the United Nations is called EDIFACT. This enables a firm on EDI to share data with those who use the same standards, requiring only one data entry. In contrast, there are no data formatting standards for E-mail since it is usually not formatted.

▼ *EDI translators.* The conversion of data sent into *standard formats* is done by special EDI translators. These translators are programmed to translate to standards such as ANSI X.12. An example of such formatting for Harper Corporation is shown in Figure 14.7.

▼ *EDI uses VAN.* In contrast to E-mail, which uses regular telephone lines, EDI uses a value-added network (VAN). Recall from Chapter 9 that VANs provide high-quality and secured communication at high speeds.

*G*LOBAL PERSPECTIVE

...international standards permit global communication using EDI

HOW DOES EDI WORK?

Let us illustrate how the system works with a hospital example. Information flows from the hospital's information system (see the figure in Box 14.5) into an EDI station which includes a PC, an EDI translator, a modem, and a link to the supplier's mainframe or LAN. From there, the information moves to a VAN via telephone or other communication lines. The VAN transfers the formatted information to the vendor, where the EDI translator converts it to a desired format (or

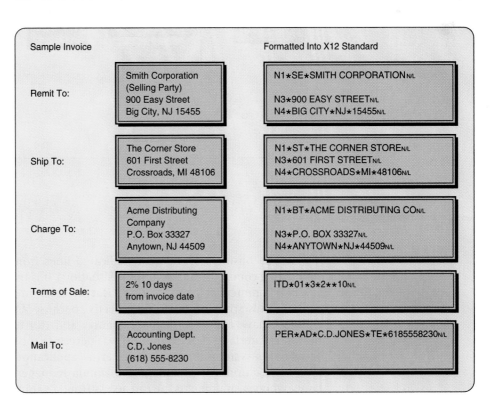

Sample Invoice		Formatted Into X12 Standard
Remit To:	Smith Corporation (Selling Party) 900 Easy Street Big City, NJ 15455	N1*SE*SMITH CORPORATIONN/L N3*900 EASY STREETN/L N4*BIG CITY*NJ*15455N/L
Ship To:	The Corner Store 601 First Street Crossroads, MI 48106	N1*ST*THE CORNER STOREN/L N3*601 FIRST STREETN/L N4*CROSSROADS*MI*48106N/L
Charge To:	Acme Distributing Company P.O. Box 33327 Anytown, NJ 44509	N1*BT*ACME DISTRIBUTING CON/L N3*P.O. BOX 33327N/L N4*ANYTOWN*NJ*44509N/L
Terms of Sale:	2% 10 days from invoice date	ITD*01*3*2**10N/L
Mail To:	Accounting Dept. C.D. Jones (618) 555-8230	PER*AD*C.D.JONES*TE*6185558230N/L

FIGURE 14.7 Translating data to an EDI code. (SOURCE: Guglielmo, 1992, p. 242.)

transmits it as it is). The modems play the usual role of changing digital signals to analog and vice versa.

A Closer Look BOX 14.5

EDI CUTS HOSPITAL COSTS

An average hospital generates about 15,000 purchase orders each year at a processing cost of about $70 per order. The Health Industry Business Communication Council estimates that EDI can reduce this cost to $4 per order, a potential yearly savings of $840,000 per hospital. The required cost ranges between $8,000 and $15,000. This includes purchase of a 486 PC with EDI translator, a modem, and a link to the mainframe-based information system. The hospital can have two or three ordering points. These

are connected to a value-added network (VAN) which connects the hospital to the suppliers. A schematic view of the process is shown in the figure that follows.

The system also can connect the hospital to other hospitals, multihospital systems, or to centralized joint purchasing agencies.

SOURCE: Based on Nussbaum (1992).

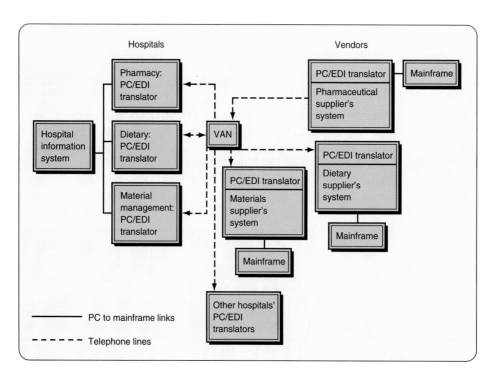

While businesses can lease dedicated lines from telephone companies for conducting communications in some situations, it is usually better to use the services of a commercial VAN. As in the Harper case, one company may use several vendors. This arrangement is cost-effective because VAN vendors work with large volumes, have expertise in maintenance, and can help customers develop the necessary interfaces. For example, it was necessary for Harper to develop interfaces between its system and Honda's internal applications, such as accounting and material requirement planning. If a Honda manager in a certain city wants to know where a shipment is, he can access Honda's shipment tracking system. Hon-

Table 14.4 The Benefits of EDI

- EDI can save a considerable amount of money (see Box 14.5).
- EDI enables companies to send and receive large amounts of information around the globe in real time.
- There are very few errors in the transformed data due to data formatting.
- Information can flow among several trading partners consistently and freely.
- Companies have the ability to access partners' computers to retrieve and store standard transactions.
- EDI fosters true (and strategic) partnership relationships, since it involves a commitment to a long-term investment and the refinement of the system over time.
- EDI creates a complete paperless TPS environment, saving money and increasing efficiency.
- The time for collecting payments can be shortened by several weeks.
- Data may be entered off-line, in a batch mode, without tying up ports to the mainframe.
- When an EDI document is received the data may be used immediately.

da's system interfaces with Harper's system and receives, through the EDI translator, updated information. EDI communication lines are designed for large capacities, high-speed transmission of information, with high security and minimum interferences.

ADVANTAGES AND DISADVANTAGES OF EDI

The use of EDI is rapidly increasing. Many companies use it to change their business processes, while others use it to gain competitive advantage. The major advantages of EDI are summarized in Table 14.4.

Electronic data interchange has its limitations and costs. A company may have to use several EDI translators; the VAN services may be expensive; there could be security problems on the networks; and there could be communication problems with some of the business partners.

▶ 14.8 PUBLIC NETWORK SERVICES AND BULLETIN BOARDS

Public network services, which are accessible via the telephone line, allow people with PCs to access large amounts of specialized information. Some services allow people to execute transactions ranging from buying and selling stocks to transferring money across the country. The services charge a fixed monthly fee and a variable usage fee. The major type of network services, many of which are tied to Internet, follow.

COMMERCIAL DATABASES

An **on-line (commercial) database** service sells access to large (usually nationwide) databases. Such a service can be used to add external data to a corporate information system in a timely manner and at reasonable cost. All that is necessary to retrieve data from such a service is a computer terminal, modem, telephone, password, and payment of some service fees. Sometimes described as a computerized data bank, this form of information supply is becoming extremely popular. Several thousand services* are currently available. Table 14.5 lists representative services.

Directory of Online Databases is a quarterly publication by Cuadra Association, Santa Monica, California (with Elsevier Publishing Company, New York), which provides current information on commercial databases. This directory is also available on-line.

Table 14.5 **Representative Commercial Database (Data Bank) Services**

CompuServe and The Source. This service provides statistical data banks (business and financial market statistics) as well as bibliographic data banks (news, reference, library, and electronic encyclopedias). CompuServe is the largest supplier of such services to personal computer users.

Compustat. Compustat provides financial statistics for more than 12,000 corporations.

Data Resources. This service offers statistical data banks in agriculture, banking, commodities, demographics, economics, energy, finance, insurance, international business, and steel and transportation industries. DRI economists maintain a number of these data banks. Standard & Poor's is also a source for similar information. It offers services under the United States Central Data Bank.

Dow Jones Information Service. This service provides statistical data banks on stock markets, other financial markets and activities, and in-depth financial statistics on all corporations listed on the New York and American stock exchanges, plus 800 other selected companies. Its Dow Jones News/Retrieval system provides bibliographic data banks on business, finance, and general news from *The Wall Street Journal, Barron's,* the Dow Jones News Service, *Wall Street Week,* and the 21-volume *American Academic Encyclopedia.*

Interactive Data Corporation. This statistical data bank distributor covers agriculture, automobiles, banking, commodities, demographics, economics, energy, finance, international business, and insurance. Its main suppliers are Chase Econometric Associates, Standard & Poor's, and **Value Line**.

Lockheed Information Systems. This is the largest bibliographic distributor. Its DIALOG system offers extracts and summaries of more than 150 different data banks in agriculture, business, economics, education, energy, engineering, environment, foundations, general news publications, government, international business, patents, pharmaceuticals, science, and social sciences. It relies on many economic research firms, trade associations, and government agencies for data.

Mead Data Central. This data bank service offers two major bibliographic data banks. Lexis provides legal research information and legal articles. Nexis provides a full-text (not abstract) bibliographic database of more than one hundred newspapers, magazines, newsletters, news services, government documents, and so on. Nexis includes full text and abstracts from *The New York Times* and the complete 29-volume Encyclopedia Britannica. Also provided is the Advertising & Marketing Intelligence (AMI) data bank, and the National Automated Accounting Research System.

SOURCE: Based on Standard & Poor's Compustat Services statistics on financial reports of 6,000 companies.

COMPREHENSIVE INTERACTIVE SERVICES

Several companies provide interactive communication for customers to communicate with vendors. Capabilities range from selling and buying stocks to shopping at certain department stores. A large such service is Prodigy, a joint venture of Sears and IBM. America Online is another large company. Some examples of menus illustrating the capabilities of Prodigy are shown in Figure 14.8.

ELECTRONIC BULLETIN BOARDS

Electronic bulletin boards (EBBs) are public E-mail in which users can leave messages for other people and receive masses of information including large amounts of free software. Some of the EBBs specialize in certain topics, others are general. To access an EBB, you need to be a member and pay a nominal fee. Special interest groups, especially users of specific software (e.g., Lotus 1-2-3), display messages on the boards and exchange experiences about the software. Universities and schools use the EBB to advertise classes and special programs. Downloading software from EBB should be done with care, since some software has been found to be infected with viruses.

▶ 14.9 GROUP DECISION SUPPORT SYSTEMS

Although traditionally most business organizations have been hierarchical, decision making is usually a shared process. Face-to-face meetings among groups of managers are an essential element for reaching consensus. The group may be involved in making a decision or in a decision-related task, like creating a short

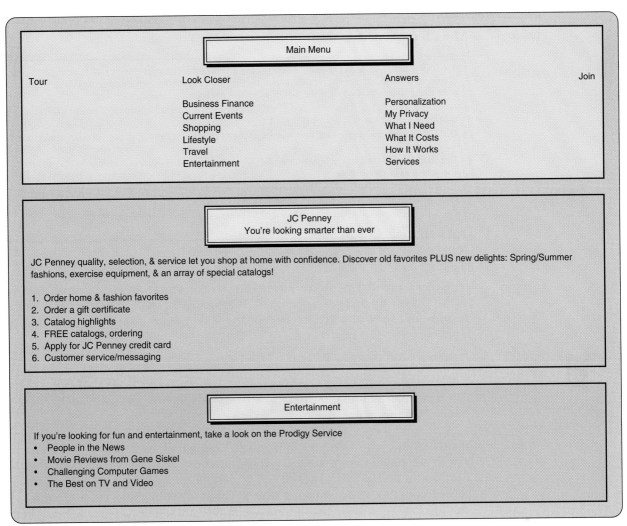

FIGURE 14.8 Representative screens from Prodigy illustrate some of its capabilities. The top part is the main menu; the middle part shows some of the options available once you enter the JC Penney menu. The bottom part designates the submenu of entertainment.

list of acceptable alternatives or deciding on criteria for accepting an alternative. When a decision-making group is supported electronically, the support is referred to as a group decision support system.

WHAT IS A GROUP DECISION SUPPORT SYSTEM?

A **group decision support system (GDSS)** is an interactive computer-based system that facilitates the solution of unstructured problems by a group of decision makers. Components of a GDSS include hardware, software, people, and procedures. These components are arranged to support the *process* of arriving at a decision. Important characteristics of a GDSS, according to DeSanctis and Gallupe (1987), are summarized in Table 14.6.

The goal of GDSS is to improve the productivity of decision-making meetings, either by speeding up the decision-making process and/or by improving the quality of the resulting decisions. This is accomplished by providing support to the exchange of ideas, opinions, and preferences within the group.

GDSS can increase process gains (see Table 14.7) and reduce process losses (such as domination by individuals, fear to speak up, blockage of attention, failure to remember, incomplete task analysis, tendency to compromise, and waste of

EMERGING TECHNOLOGY

...GDSS eliminates traditional obstacles of group decision making

Table 14.6 **The Characteristics of GDSS**

- A GDSS is designed with the goal of supporting groups of decision-makers in their work. As such, the GDSS should *improve* the decision-making process and/or the decision outcomes of groups over those that would occur if the GDSS were not present.
- A GDSS is easy to learn and use. It accommodates users with varying levels of knowledge regarding computing and decision support.
- The GDSS may be designed for one type of problem or for a variety of group-level organizational decisions.
- The GDSS is designed to encourage activities such as generation of ideas, resolution of conflicts, and freedom of expression.
- The GDSS contains built-in mechanisms that discourage development of negative group behaviors, such as destructive conflict, miscommunication, or "groupthink."
- The GDSS is a specially designed information system, not merely a configuration of already existing system components.

SOURCE: Compiled from DeSanctis and Gallupe (1987).

time). Such improvements have been shown in experiments. For example, a study at the University of Arizona resulted in a savings of more than 50 percent per person-hour and a 92 percent reduction in the time required by a team to complete a project.

THE TECHNOLOGY OF GDSS

Like any other information system, a GDSS is composed of hardware, software, people, and procedures.

HARDWARE. Two basic types of hardware configurations can be used by a group. The first configuration involves a **decision room**, a GDSS facility dedicated to electronic meetings and designed as such. The second configuration is basically a collection of PCs, each equipped with keypads for voting and other groupware. The machines can be in one location or in different locations. They are simple to operate. Such PCs are usually part of a network or part of a client/server architecture, use an extensive graphical user interface, and are connected by an E-mail system. This configuration is likely to be the dominating form of GDSSs in the future.

In the first configuration the decision room consists of a large, usually U-shaped table, equipped with 12 to 30 networked and recessed microcomputers to facilitate interaction among participants. A microcomputer attached to a large-

Table 14.7 **Process Gains from Group Decision Support Systems**

- Supports parallel processing of information and idea generation by participants.
- Enables larger groups with more complete information, knowledge, and skills to participate in the same meeting.
- Permits the group to use structured or unstructured techniques and methods to perform the task.
- Offers rapid and easy access to external information.
- Allows nonsequential computer discussion (unlike oral discussions, computer discussions do not have to be serial or sequential).
- Helps participants deal with the larger picture.
- Produces instant, anonymous voting results where people can choose among several methods of voting.
- Provides structure to the planning process, which keeps the group on track.
- Enables several users to interact simultaneously.
- Records automatically all information that passes through the system for future analysis (develops organization memory).

screen projection system is also connected to the network, permitting the display of work done at individual workstations. It also aggregates information from the entire group. Adjacent but separate rooms for doing independent work in smaller groups are equipped with microcomputers that are networked to the microcomputers at the main conference table. The output from smaller group sessions can be displaced on the large "public" screen projector for presentations and can be updated and integrated with planning session results.

A well-known example is the Decision Support Laboratory at the University of Arizona. It is equipped with state-of-the-art workstations, a local-area network, a server, and a "facilitator station" which controls a Barco large-screen projection system (see Figure 14.9). An electronic decision room requires a trained facilitator. The facilitator meets with appropriate personnel before the group meeting in order to discuss the purpose, goal, format, and plans of the session. The success of any GDSS is largely dependent on the quality and skill of such a facilitator.

SOFTWARE. GDSS software is a collection of about a dozen packages, which are integrated as a comprehensive tool kit. Some software can work only in a decision room environment. A typical collection of software for a decision room is shown in Figure 14.10. Newer packages can drive a networked GDSS.

Advanced software packages attempt to support conflict resolution among participants, enable communication with commercial databases, and enable execution of analysis (using quantitative models). Future software may include artificial intelligence capabilities such as intelligent agents.

PEOPLE. The people component of the GDSS includes the group members and a facilitator who is responsible for the smooth operation of the GDSS technology. The facilitator is usually present at all group meetings and serves as the group's "chauffeur," operating the GDSS hardware and software and displaying requested information to the group as needed.

PROCEDURES. The final component of the GDSS consists of procedures that enable ease of operation and effective use of the technology by group members.

FIGURE 14.9 The GroupSystems 24-station decision center, located at the University of Arizona, is used for electronic meetings.

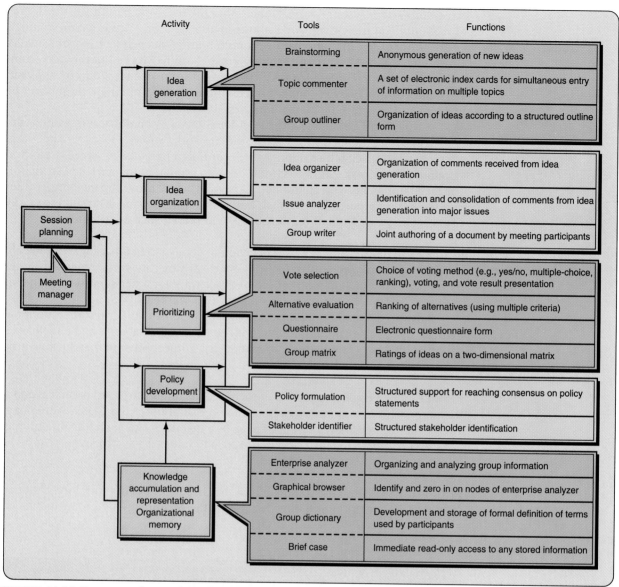

FIGURE 14.10 Structure of typical GDSS software for a decision room. GroupSystems V is a tool kit containing 16 different software tools (right side). These tools are used to support the activities listed on the left side. For example, the brainstorming tool is used to generate ideas. (Courtesy of Ventana Corporation.)

These procedures may apply only to the operation of the hardware and software, or they may extend to include rules regarding verbal discussion among members and the flow of events during a group meeting.

REPRESENTATIVE APPLICATIONS OF GDSS

The Internal Revenue Service used a GDSS to implement quality improvement programs based on participative management in quality teams. The GDSS was helpful in identifying problems, generating and evaluating ideas, and developing and implementing solutions.

San Trans, a Tucson, Arizona, bus company used the University of Arizona GDSS facility to negotiate a labor contract with the Teamsters union, which represents 300 of their blue-collar employees. Management and union representatives met for nine sessions, concluding with a new contract after only 30 hours of electronic meetings. The university's GDSS tools were customized to handle the negotiations.

El Rio Health Care facility of Tucson, Arizona, used the same facility to negotiate a labor contract with their union. The union and management teams had had a history of difficult negotiation. Consequently, occasionally personal animosities surfaced and made the negotiations arduous and lengthy. After 13 sessions that totaled 57 hours in the decision room, the parties reached a mutually agreed-upon contract.

The City of Louisville, Kentucky, used a GDSS to prioritize the 10 most important areas of public education. The prioritization was needed for planning and allocation of resources.

The decision room facility is especially effective in major conflicting decisions such as budget cuts, long range planning, and allocation of resources.

▶ 14.10 OTHER GROUPWARE TECHNOLOGIES

Many other groupware products support the work of groups when the group members are in different locations (see ''Buyers' Guide,'' *PC World*, March 1992). Some of these products enable people to work at the same time. Others allow people to work on the same project at different times (see Box 14.6). Two examples of such products are workflow systems and interactive desktop conferencing.

IT At Work BOX 14.6   **LOBAL PERSPECTIVE**

USING GDSS TO EXAMINE THE FUTURE EUROPEAN AUTOMOBILE INDUSTRY

The automotive industry competes in a global market. Some well-established European companies such as FIAT feel strong competition from Japanese and U.S. manufacturers. In 1990, the automotive industry in Europe established groups of experts in Geneva, Switzerland, and Frankfurt, Germany, and supported these groups with a GDSS named DELWARE. DELWARE incorporates the Delphi forecasting method with a cross-impact analysis (CIA) in an attempt to examine the business environment of the European automobile industry looking toward the year 2000.

The specific task of the experts was to refine their initial estimates about the probability and desirability of 34 business events and trends in Europe. The GDSS enables the experts to achieve this refinement by arriving at a consensus electronically. The project was conducted by the Battelle Memorial Institute which represents the interests of 35 countries.

Communication among the experts was done in an asyncronous mode, since the experts were unable to meet together at specific times. The communication was done by using special GDSS software that enhances the implementation of Delphi and CIA procedures. The results showed a great improvement in communication among the experts who were quickly able to acquire an understanding of the project. The communication was enhanced by oral discussions using the telephone. As a result, the experts agreed on the major business events. The final list is used by the automotive industry in Europe for the purpose of strategic planning.

Critical Thinking Issue: Anonymity is required in a Delphi study and it is provided by a GDSS. Do you need anonymity in this situation? If not, do you need a GDSS or would other information technology do? ▲

SOURCE: Condensed from Vickers (1992).

WORKFLOW SYSTEMS

Workflow software is a powerful business process automation tool that places system controls in the hands of end-user departments. It is highly flexible and can be designed to automate almost any information processing system. Not only does workflow automate business processes, it also provides a quality interface between operating systems. As a result, workflow installations have evolved into enterprise-wide computing solutions at major companies.

There are three types of workflow software: *administrative*—expense reports, travel requests and messages; *ad hoc*—product brochures, sales proposals, and strategic plans; and *production*—credit card mailings, mortgage loans, and insurance claims.

The primary purpose of workflow systems is to provide end users with tracking, routing, document imaging, and other capabilities designed to improve business processes (see Box 14.7).

IT At Work   BOX 14.7

WORKFLOW SOFTWARE AUTOMATES BUSINESS PROCESSES

Bankers Trust Company of New York replaced their manual customer requests system with an automated one. The system is based on Action (from Action Technologies) and it works together with Lotus Notes (see Section 14.13). Cases are placed into Notes, then Action routes the cases to appropriate employees who work on them. The progress in dealing with each request is monitored. Action pays attention to whether the employees complete each task as scheduled. In case of deviations, a reminder is automatically generated. The software tracks every case and knows where it is.

Carold Corporation (a mortgage-banking firm in New York) services about 13,000 loans and about 12,000 insurance policies a year. Scanning related documents and pictures and integrating them with the workflow system greatly increased the productivity of accessing information, conducting analyses, and answering queries.

Critical Thinking Issues: Why is the addition of Action to Lotus Notes beneficial to people working in groups? ▲

SOURCE: Condensed from Sullivan, K. B., "Workflow Applications Can Change the Way of Doing Business, Buyers Say," *PC Week*, April 5, 1993.

There are many workflow software packages on the market. Some are based on E-mail capabilities; others use a shared database or a file on a server that people can log into. The most notable software of the latter category is Lotus Notes (see Section 14.13). Lotus Notes is not just a workflow package; it is an integrated groupware software that has several other capabilities.

▶ 14.11 VOICE COMMUNICATION TECHNOLOGIES

The most natural mode of communication is voice. When people need to communicate with each other from a distance, they use the telephone more frequently than any other device for communication. Communication can now be done with the computer using a microphone and a voice card.

Voice and data can work together to create useful applications. For example, operators of PBXs (see Chapter 9) and other telephone systems are letting callers make simple computer commands through the PBX using interactive voice mail. There is evidence of a large increase in the number and type of voice technologies applications (see Box 14.8).

Voice technologies have the following advantages.

1. Hands-free and eyes-free operations increase productivity, safety, and effectiveness of operators ranging from forklift drivers to military pilots.

2. Voice input eliminates concerns about workers' literacy (users do not have to know how to spell).

3. Certain disabled employees can enter data via voice to command the computer to perform tasks.

IT At Work BOX 14.8

HOW COMPANIES USE VOICE TECHNOLOGIES

1. **Duke Power Company** (Charlotte, NC) has a 24-hour interactive voice response system that addresses questions about fringe benefits via the telephone. (See *Communications News*, March 1993.)

2. **Fleet Services Corporation** allows its 30,000 employees to register for their flexible benefit program via the telephone supported by a voice response system (conducted once each year). (See *Communication News*, March 1993.)

3. **Dixie Electric Management Corporation** uses voice recognition (and interpretation, using ES) of customers who are calling to report downed lines, power outages, or transformer fires. (See *Communication News*, June 1993.)

4. **Toronto Dominion Bank** (Canada) customers can use voice commands to transfer funds between accounts and authorize bill payments. They can request, by voice, that the bank fax copies of interim statements. In addition, they can buy savings bonds, roll over term deposits, and trace checks. Voice orders can be given both in English and French. (Information provided by the bank.)

5. **Bidwell and Company** (Portland, OR) enables customers to find stock prices simply by speaking out the stock symbol.

6. **U.S. West Communications** (Denver, CO) al-

lows customers to say the name of a person they want to call (up to 75 names) rather than dial the number. A voice recognition system will match the name to a phone number and do the dialing for them. (For information, call U.S. West at (303) 896-6942.)

7. Voice terminals in a warehouse provide the following applications (see APICS, May 1993).

▼ *Forklift material movement.* Drivers can send and receive information while operating the forklifts (20 to 50 percent productivity improvement).

▼ *Receiving inspection.* The hands of employees who receive or inspect materials are generally busy. Results of inspection are communicated on-line while inspection is going on.

▼ *Inventory taking and location reporting in floor stack warehouses.* When items are set on the floor, there is no fixed location (such as a fixed storage location). Description of what is available and where the material is located can be done more rapidly and accurately by voice.

▼ *Inventory taking in a refrigerated or dusty warehouse.* Other methods (e.g., reading bar codes) may not work in some environments. ▲

4. Voice terminals are designed for portability. Workers do not have to go to the computer. They can communicate with the computer from their work areas, even when they are on the move.

5. Voice terminals are more rugged in the factory environment than keyboards.

6. It is faster to talk than to keypunch; a person talks about two-and-a-half times faster than he types.

7. Fewer errors in data entry exist as compared to a keyboard data entry.

APPLICATIONS

There are many applications of voice technologies, and many products are available on the market. Here is a sampling.

▼ *Interactive voice recognition.* This is one of the most popular applications. It enables a computer to understand the content of incoming telephone calls. For example, applications 3, 4, 5, and 6 in Box 14.8 involve interactive voice recognition.

▼ *Voice annotation.* This is a combination of recorded voice messages with electronic mail, spreadsheet, and other applications. For example, voice annotation can be used to add comments to documents. Prerecorded voices of experts can

IT At Work BOX 14.9

VOICE MAIL IN A HOTEL

The integrated voice mail system depicted in the figure is self-explanatory. For further details see, *Voice Processing Magazine*, June 1993, pp. 14–16. ▲

1. Call for guest enters the hotel

2. Call goes through PBX

3. PBX checks PMS for guest info

4. PBX transfers call to guest's room

5. After 4 rings no answer, call transfers back to PBX

6. PBX transfers call to voice mail, offers caller choice of either leaving message or marking call "urgent"

7. Voice mail transfers urgent calls to PBX

8. PBX calls guest's cellular phone/pager and transmits caller's phone number. Guest either takes call, or . . .

9. Call is transferred back to guest's voice mailbox

add a background to a document. Users can enter a request for advice or explanations on their PC. A computer program (e.g., Lotus Sound or Remark!) that runs on a dedicated voice server, orders the telephone system to dial the user, who can then pick up the phone to receive recorded instructions. An extension of this application is "timed" voice objects, which are activated in special situations such as during a snowstorm. Voice can be transmitted through the telephone lines and/or across a computer network. Advanced voice annotation systems allow the user to edit the voice messages.

▼ *Automated attendant.* This device transfers calls and monitors them for completion. It streamlines call flow and shortens call hold times. Applications are in call routing, call screening, and receptionist backup.

▼ *Voice mail.* **Voice mail** is a computerized system for storing, forwarding, and routing telephone messages (see Box 14.9). Applications are in message centers with personal greetings, front-end beepers and pagers, departmental messaging, message broadcasting to groups, and emergency notification.

▼ *Audiotext.* Plays and records information in any sequence and/or in response to touch-tone input.

▶ 14.12 TELECOMMUTING

People do not have to work at their company's premises; they can work at home. This phenomenon, called *cottage industry* in the past, is now referred to as **telecommuting** or *teleworking*. Employees can work at home, at the customer's premises, or while traveling, using a computer linked to their place of employment. The first telecommuters were typists and bookkeepers, but now a growing number of professionals do a significant portion of their work at home. Telecommuting, which is used by many corporations in large cities, is also appealing to small entrepreneurs (see Box 14.10).

Telecommuting has potential advantages to the employees, employers, and society (see Table 14.8).

However, there are also potential disadvantages both to employees and the organization. The major disadvantages for the employees are: increased feeling of

---

A Closer Look BOX 14.10

THE VIRTUAL ENTREPRENEUR

While many telecommuters work for other companies, there are people who run their own businesses from home. A third kind of telecommuters are people who work for others in a specially designed telecommuting centers. Henricks (1993) provides the following examples of all three kinds.

▼ Brenda Clamera Brimages develops math textbooks (millions of copies are sold) and manages an ever-shifting stable of writers and designers spread across the country, all from her home.

▼ An ophthalmologist, Dr. J. Garden, examines inmates without traveling the 40 miles to the prison. Instead, she tests eyes using a PC, modem, and video camera, all from her living room.

▼ Frank Cottle has built nine telecommuting centers in southern California where close to 1,000 tenants rent space, computers, faxes, and phones to work with colleagues thousands of miles away.

▼ Michael Kouloaroudis of Brooklyn, New York, gets leads on overseas companies looking for American products. Using one computer and operating from his home, he grossed over $100,000 on one deal alone by selling American-made window air conditioners to Japan.

▼ All 14 employees of Journal Graphics work from home in several states. The company produces transcriptions of broadcast news and talk shows. Employees can relocate as they wish.

Table 14.8 **The Benefits of Telecommuting**

Benefits to the employee
- Less stress (no driving, no office pressure).
- Ability to go to school while working.
- Improved family life (fewer job/family conflicts).
- Opportunity to make more money (if on an incentive plan).
- Save money on lunches, clothes, gas, parking, car maintenance.
- Save commuting time (more leisure time).
- Ability to better control schedule and time.
- Housebound people (single parents of children, handicapped) can be gainfully employed.

Benefits to the organization
- Increased productivity (15 to 50 percent).
- Reduced real estate (or rent) cost.
- Reduced cost of parking lots.
- Retaining skilled employees who otherwise would leave.
- Retaining skilled employees who are not willing to commute (tap remote labor pool, greater staffing flexibility).
- Less paperwork.
- Less absenteeism.
- Fewer labor costs (some people will take lower wages in order to stay home).
- Better interaction of employees with clients and suppliers (work can be done at the customers' sites).
- Effective use of computers and IT.

Benefits to society
- Less air pollution.
- Fewer traffic problems.
- More business to suburbs and rural areas.
- Less use of fossil fuels.

isolation, loss of fringe benefits, lower pay (in some cases), no workplace visibility with the potential of slower promotions, and lack of socialization. The major disadvantages to employers are difficulties in supervising work, potential data security problems, training costs, and high cost of equipping and maintaining telecommuters' homes. Despite these disadvantages, the use of telecommuting is on the increase. Some experts predict that in 10 to 15 years, 50 percent of all work will be done at home, on the road, or at the customer's site.

Almost all groupware technologies can be used to support telecommuting. In addition, the regular and overnight mail, special messengers, and fax are extensively used to support telecommuting.

TELECOMMUTING AND PRODUCTIVITY

Why would productivity go up if people work at home? Strangely enough, reduced absenteeism has been cited by more than one organization as a reason for increased productivity. Paul Ruper, Associate Director of New Ways to Work, claims absenteeism actually can be reduced by telecommuting because of *sort of* illness. He refers to those mornings when an employee wakes up just feeling sort of "blah." The trip to work and a whole day at the office is not going to make him feel any better, so he stays home.

Telecommuting forces managers to manage by results instead of by overseeing. Telecommuting forces both employees and managers to ask some serious questions about the real purpose of a job. This process, although difficult, could make both the manager and employee reduce misunderstandings about work. The employee will have a clear understanding of his responsibilities and will be held accountable for his actions.

Even though many employees are attracted to telecommuting, it is not for everybody and should not be mandatory. Some employees need to work with others and for those employees, telecommuting may not be an option. Also, not all jobs can be done while telecommuting and not all managers can participate.

14.13 INTEGRATED TECHNOLOGIES AND LOTUS NOTES

INTEGRATED TECHNOLOGIES

The technologies presented in the previous sections can be used as stand-alone, independent technologies. However, because these technologies are computer-based, it makes sense to integrate them among themselves and with other computer-based or computer-controlled technologies. In the opening case, Harper Corporation uses E-mail and EDI as well as telephones, fax, and voice mail. Integrating several technologies can save time and money for the users. Therefore, many vendors are developing integrated products. Here are two examples:

▼ PictureTel Corporation formed an alliance with Lotus Development Corporation and developed an integrated desktop video teleconferencing product that uses Lotus Notes. Using the integrated system, Reader's Digest (Pleasantville, NY) has built several applications combined with video teleconferencing capabilities.

▼ Cardiff Software (Solana Beach, CA) developed a fax machine that is integrated with an optical character recognition device and a database. *PC World* uses this product to analyze results of questionnaires that their readers fax to them. When a fax is received, the questionnaire is scanned automatically, and the results are stored in the database.

THE PAPERLESS OFFICE

Technology integration is beneficial in the office, where a large amount of time and paper can be saved. An average office uses 120 pounds of paper per year. The total cost of paper to the U.S. economy is $6.6 billion, and much of this can be saved. For example, forms can be filed and stored electronically in a database, and then transferred through an E-mail. Fax-modem equipment allows you to fax documents straight from your hard disk (you can also receive faxes that will go straight into your hard drive). You can send and receive images. You can even control your office from a distance. For example, it is possible to receive, store, and automatically distribute computerized documents while you are away from your office. All you have to do is command the computer by sending it a fax, and the computer will do the rest (e.g., using PaperWorks from XSoft Corporation). You can send documents (even hand-written ones) to your PC while you enjoy your vacation in Hawaii.

Further reduction in paperwork can be achieved by image and document management. Suppose you need to send a document that includes text and a picture to 50 people. Instead of making 50 copies, you use a scanner to turn the document into a bit-mapped image. You compress the document and store it on a server. The document is then retrievable, even from remote locations, via a network. There is no paperwork except for the original.

Microsoft Corporation developed software, Microsoft at Work, which simplifies communication between a PC, fax machines, printers, copiers, scanners, and telephones. For instance, a worker writing a document on a computer will click on the copying machine icon on Windows and instantly order 100 copies. Another click, and the fax icon will fax the document to a desired location (see Figure 14.11).

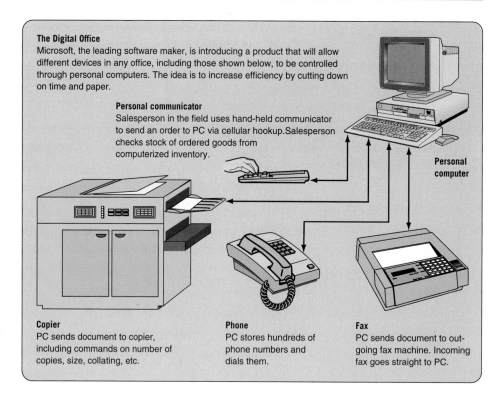

The Digital Office
Microsoft, the leading software maker, is introducing a product that will allow different devices in any office, including those shown below, to be controlled through personal computers. The idea is to increase efficiency by cutting down on time and paper.

Personal communicator
Salesperson in the field uses hand-held communicator to send an order to PC via cellular hookup. Salesperson checks stock of ordered goods from computerized inventory.

Personal computer

Copier
PC sends document to copier, including commands on number of copies, size, collating, etc.

Phone
PC stores hundreds of phone numbers and dials them.

Fax
PC sends document to outgoing fax machine. Incoming fax goes straight to PC.

FIGURE 14.11 The digital office (SOURCE: Courtesy of Microsoft Corporation.)

LOTUS NOTES

WHAT IS LOTUS NOTES? Lotus Notes is a client/server platform for developing and deploying groupware applications. Lotus Notes improves the business performance of people working together by compressing the time and improving the quality of everyday business processes, such as customer service, sales and account management, and product development. Because Lotus Notes offers developers the most efficient platform for building strategic business process applications, these applications provide the greatest impact in reengineering the activities of the organization. Therefore, Lotus Notes is a fast way to create a responsive organization.

Lotus Notes is a robust, secure application development environment through which developers can quickly create cross-platform client/server applications that have immediate impact on the efficiency of business processes. These "knowledge-sharing" applications allow multiple users to manage compound documents, communicate effectively, and take advantage of business process automation over geographically dispersed or even remote locations.

Lotus Notes allows users to access, track, share, and organize document-oriented information. This information can come in multiple formats—text, images, video, and audio—and from various sources—desktop applications, legacy systems, scanners, or faxes.

*E*MERGING TECHNOLOGY

...Lotus Notes enables knowledge sharing

From an organizational standpoint, Lotus Notes leverages a company's investment in technology because it allows the current network, desktop applications, and legacy systems to be combined into strategic, information-based applications.

CHARACTERISTICS OF LOTUS NOTES. According to company's publication (Lotus, 1994), the power of Lotus Notes lies in:

1. Its **Single, Consistent User Interface** to all other people, resources, and information located anywhere on the network.

2. The flexibility to manage **Compound Documents** containing multiple data types from sources such as desktop applications, newsfeeds, scanned images, and legacy systems.

3. Its **Application Development Environment** which allows for the rapid development of workgroup applications.

4. Its **Advanced Security**, offering the flexibility to control access to information down to the field level on an individual document.

5. The use of **Replication** to give all users access to up-to-date information located anywhere within the extended enterprise, including remote locations and users, as well as customers and suppliers.

6. Its **Openness** in terms of support for multiple network and desktop operating systems, desktop applications, external data sources, and messaging systems.

7. The expanding **Industry** of value-added products and services surrounding Notes.

8. Its **Scalability**; that is, its ability to support an organization of any size, from a two user workgroup to an enterprise-wide implementation with tens of thousands of users.

9. Its **Seamless Integration** of the diverse set of client and server elements (user environment, distributed document management, messaging, security, and development environment) required for building custom business process solutions across multiple platforms.

10. Its **Availability**: Lotus Notes is (in 1995) the only integrated platform for quickly developing complete client-server groupware business solutions.

CAPABILITIES OF LOTUS NOTES. Lotus Notes is designed to handle these four main types of applications. In each type, one can find hundreds of specific applications.

1. *Tracking.* This helps users follow what is happening in their business. For example, one may want to track all activities related to a specific customer (agreements, volume of purchase, meetings conducted). Another example is to track all potential candidates for an open position. Yet another application would be to track a specific meeting (prepare agendas, send invitations, prepare minutes). Lotus Notes can be used as an IS *help desk* to track all internal calls from user departments in order to assure speedy response.

2. *Team discussion.* Lotus Notes helps in sharing information and conducting discussions among participants who may be in different locations and at different times (see Box 14.11).

IT At Work BOX 14.11

USING LOTUS NOTES AT PRICE WATERHOUSE

Price Waterhouse (PW) is one of the six largest accounting CPA firms in the United States. In March 1989, PW named Sheldon Laube as the director of information technology. A few months later in a bold, unorthodox move, Laube licensed 10,000 copies of Lotus Notes at a cost of $2 million, while it was still in beta testing. By 1992, Lotus Notes had *fundamentally altered* PW's business processes and brought an end to the chaos that existed in 1989. Here are typical scenes from before Lotus Notes was introduced.

▼ Highly paid associates were shuffling between floors with stacks of paperwork, desperately trying to get sign-offs on top priority products.

▼ Partners in regional offices were struggling to decipher complex accounting rules without the aid of centralized databases.

▼ Out-of-town partners were unable to use local offices to print out data from their three-and-a-half-inch disks.

▼ Partners had to wait weeks to find information about specific tax court rulings.

▼ Local offices adopted their own technology without a strategy for data sharing.

Here is a sample of what Lotus Notes enables PWs employees to do.

▼ View, from inside a database, a collection of the firm's analysis of IRS rulings and opinions.

▼ Share, within hours, all information describing a court ruling and read the ruling itself.

▼ Tap the labors of others by accessing every business proposal PW has submitted to clients since 1989, thus reducing preparation time and improving the chance of winning contracts.

The system, which is built with a client/server architecture, includes about 125 servers and 11,000 PCs residing on PW's worldwide network.

Lotus Notes is a real success. In addition to its information-sharing capabilities, the system is used to create new applications. More than 500 were created by end users and 100 by the IS department. These applications include generation of billing reports and compilation of marketing data by the partners themselves. ''The system puts knowledge in the senior managers' fingertips; that is why they use it,'' commented Laube. Lotus Notes can also put the knowledge of many experts to the service of clients very quickly.

Price Waterhouse was invited to bid on a multimillion dollar consulting job regarding a complex securities trading operation. The proposal was due in four days! The four executives who were needed to write the proposal were in three different states. Not only did they work on the same document with Lotus Notes in the different locations, but they also extracted key components of the proposal from various databases. For example, they pulled resumes of the company's experts from around the world who could be consulted when needed. They also borrowed passages from similar, previously successful proposals. A draft was written, and each executive modified it or made comments. Other executives looked at the proposal via Lotus Notes and contributed valuable suggestions. The proposal was ready on time, and the consulting job was awarded to Price Waterhouse. In addition, the company was awarded a multiple-year contract to audit the complex trading system that they helped create in the initial consulting job.

Notes also changed PW's organizational culture. People that never used computers use them now extensively.

Critical Thinking Issue: How can the use of Lotus Notes eliminate the chaotic scenes that existed before Notes was introduced? Is there any other way to prepare a bid as quickly and economically? ▲

SOURCE: Based on Mehler, M., ''Notes Fanatic,'' *Corporate Computing*, August 1992 and on ''Groupware Goes Boom,'' *Fortune*, December 27, 1993.

---

3. *Broadcasting.* Lotus Notes helps deliver announcements or post information on its bulletin boards. For example, Price Waterhouse's winning team posted requests for help in preparing the bid (Box 14.11). Also, technical notes and tips can be posted so that everyone can benefit from individual expertise.

4. *References.* Lotus Notes helps users to sift through information in the many corporate servers (see Box 14.11).

In addition there are specialized application categories such as the following.

▼ *Things to do.* Lotus Notes reminds individuals or groups about action items that must be completed to keep projects on schedule.

▼ *Contract library.* Lotus Notes can be used as a central repository for all legal contract templates.

▼ *Corporate policy documents.* Lotus Notes maintains and communicates all organizational policy documents to all employees worldwide.

Lotus Notes was designed with three primary business activities in mind: *customer service*, *product development*, and *account management*. For example, in customer service, Lotus Notes can be used to track calls. Each call and its resolution is placed in a common database which informs others of the outcome. With product development, knowledge workers can freely exchange information which could greatly improve productivity and reduce time-to-market. In account management, customer information and action taken can be recorded in a central database which would give all users access to critical information. An illustrative example of how Lotus Notes can be used is shown in Figure 14.12.

EMERGING TECHNOLOGY

...Lotus Notes enable sharing of databases over a network

ADVANTAGES OF LOTUS NOTES. Lotus Notes utilizes information repositories, or databases, that allow users to store and organize information so they can retrieve it. Lotus Notes database capabilities differ from E-mail systems in that they do not require the user to know exactly who the recipient is. Instead, information is forwarded to the appropriate bulletin board. Any user can access the information and read, update, or respond to it.

At the heart of Lotus Notes's success is its distributed document database capability. The following three basic types of databases are used in Lotus Notes.

1. *Discussion databases.* This most common type of database enables users to participate in written meetings. The databases are usually classified by subject.

2. *Document libraries.* This type stores written information normally printed on paper. Databases can be created containing reports, memos, forms, and so on.

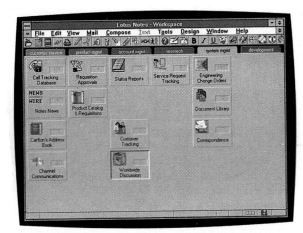

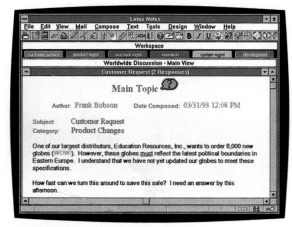

1. This is James' Notes desktop. He uses it to access information and work quickly with people in all departments to solve problems worldwide. James clicks on the Worldwide Discussion application to catch up with important company news. The SmartIcons across the top make it even easier to work in Notes.

2. The field rep in Texas is working on a request from a customer. But to make the sale the product, in this case a globe, has to be changed to reflect the most up-to-date countries and borders. And evidently time is critical. The competition must already be in there pitching.

3. He clicks on the Customer Tracking application to learn more about this customer. The profile includes an attached 1-2-3° spreadsheet. He double clicks the icon to open the spreadsheet and finds that Education Resources is a very large customer that pays its bills.

4. James' next step is to click on the Newswire database for the most up-to-date report on precisely what geographical changes will have to be made on the new globe. And just how extensive they'll be.

5. Once he has the information, he clicks on the Engineering Change Order application to request specific product changes from the plant in North Reading. He links the supporting Newswire information to the E.C.O. It will be easily viewed with a single click of a button.

6. After lunch he opens a document from Ellen in product development who has responded with the necessary changes and scheduling information. The new art was scanned directly through Lotus Notes: Document Imaging from the art department. James approves the art for manufacturing.

7. On the Product Tracking application, all departments involved have confirmed that they can meet the schedule. However, they've cautioned James to be careful about rushing schedules in the future. James uses the Discussion database to acknowledge their comments and thank them for their efforts.

8. Wanting to record and promote the team's accomplishments, James puts together a presentation for senior management in Freelance Graphics. Then he posts the presentation in the Presentation database so everyone can see how the team rearranged the world to save a big account.

FIGURE 14.12 How Lotus Notes supports the business (SOURCE: Advertisement material provided by Lotus Development Corporation.)

3. *Information services.* This type enables users to obtain the latest information about selected topics.

Lotus Notes is software that acts as a group communications environment to allow users to access and create shared information. It provides workgroup E-mail, distributed databases, bulletin boards, text editing, document management and a forms generator, workflow capabilities and various applications development tools, all integrated into an environment with a graphical menu-based user interface. Lotus Notes is used for many applications, including fostering the virtual corporation and similar intercompany alliances.

Lotus's program allows data to be collected, stored, organized, and disseminated among many users on one or several networks. It employs the Windows interface and extensive networks. Lotus Notes works like an organized bulletin board, where information can be found quickly, regardless of its location in an organization.

Lotus Notes can also be used as a *forms generator.* A user can select from many forms. One of Lotus Notes's strongest points is its graphical user interface, which allows users who are already familiar with Windows and OS/2 menu screens to quickly adapt. Overall, Lotus Notes can provide awesome competitive advantage for the users, as was shown in Box 14.11.

DISADVANTAGES OF LOTUS NOTES Lotus Notes is not inexpensive to operate. Ed Catlett, assistant vice president of Johnson & Higgens, an insurance brokerage firm, utilizes Lotus Notes extensively. The firm uses Lotus Notes to exchange information between branch offices and hundreds of insurers worldwide. Catletts says, "You need the people to administer and support the database. You have to have technical people who understand how the servers talk to one another. You have to do disk capacity planning, because you are keeping duplicates of your database in various locations." All this is expensive.

OTHER LOTUS NOTES-RELATED PRODUCTS There are several add-on products available from Lotus and other vendors, such as *document imaging, subscription services,* and *work-flow management.* These include the following.

▼ *Video Notes.* This product allows two Lotus Notes users to conduct real-time, full-motion videoconferencing across a fiber-optic network. The important feature of the product is that it allows users to query and update Lotus Notes and SQL databases.

▼ *AT&T Network Notes.* Notes is available to business users by dialing into an AT&T public network. This will allow users to dial into a network over telephone lines, so they can share documents that include text, image, and video; exchange electronic mail; and replicate documents and files for business partners. AT&T Network Notes will be initially used to access on-line newsletters as well as broadcast news. Eventually AT&T plans to use the interface to sell movies, music CDs, and other products to consumers.

EMERGING TECHNOLOGY

...intelligent agents customize data

▼ *Intelligent agents.* Intelligent agents reside on Lotus Notes servers to filter, abstract, and deliver customized data to users. One drawback to using regular Lotus Notes is that users can be bombarded with information. Sorting relevant information can be very time consuming. The agents allows users to instruct the Lotus Notes server about the information they need. The intelligent agents scans information coming into the server, extract and/or combine data (meeting predefined criteria), and forward the information to the user.

▼ *Competing products.* Two new products compete with Lotus Notes: Touchdown from Microsoft and Novell Groupware from Novell Corporation.

▼ *Notes and the Internet.* Notes now is reachable via the Internet, enabling communication among Notes users in different organizations.

▶ 14.14 INFORMATION SUPERHIGHWAYS AND THE INTERNET

***E*MERGING TECHNOLOGY**

...national information infrastructure

The manner in which we will work and live in the twenty-first century could be determined by a vast web of electronic networks called the **information superhighway**. This system will deliver large amounts of services to our homes, offices, and factories including telephone calls, TV programs and other video images, text, and music (see Figure 14.13). The system will enable students at rural schools to use computers to tap resources at Stanford University, for example, and researchers in a small college in Arkansas to use the power of the supercomputer located at the University of Illinois. The superhighways will allow a doctor to check patients from their homes, and it will let doctors in several remote cities collaborate on a patient's care by immediately sharing his medical history, including X rays and videos from arthroscopic surgery, using multimedia computer screens. Consumers will be able to shop for goods and services all over the world from the comfort of their home. Many more applications for the improvement of society will be realized. All of the technologies described in this chapter and several more may be carried on information superhighways.

Like the railroad system of the nineteenth century and the interstate highway system of the twentieth century, the information highway of fiber-optic cables, satellites, and wireless grids will link millions of computers, telephones, faxes, and other electronic products all over the country and eventually all over the world. The term **electronic or information superhighways** is a catchall name for several different architectures. For example, Vice President Gore envisions a national network of supercomputers linked by fiber optics that will connect universities, hospitals, research institutions, and other organizations that need to share and exchange a vast amount of information. As such, the superhighway will be subsidized and controlled by the government. However, other people envision America's information highway as a *network of networks*, controlled by many companies. The foundation of such a system already exists. Almost 35 million people

VIDEO PHONE: You will be able to conduct a face-to-face conversation from any video phone to others.

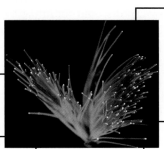

CD-ROM: The utmost multimedia combination at your fingertips for education, entertainment and business.

HDTV: High resolution TV will provide much sharper TV pictures for the viewer's enjoyment.

VIRTUAL REALITY: You will be able to feel the sensation of being in any place you ever wanted to be. Will simulate just about any human activity.

LAPTOP: Powerful and portable. Enables you to work anywhere with wireless telecommunication it is even more useful.

EDUCATION: Children, as well as adults, will be able to learn at home and explore libraries and museums around the globe.

FIGURE 14.13 What the information superhighway can bring to your home

trade information via the Internet, which uses existing telephone lines. However, to rewire America completely with fiber-optic lines that will reach every individual and organization may take 50 years to complete at a cost of $500 billion. Smaller countries will do it much earlier. Singapore, a small island with population of less than three million, will have a national digital network by the year 2000 (see Box 1.5 in Chapter 1). Japan, France, and Germany plan to complete their national networks by 2015.

The superhighway will have two groups of customers. The first group is individuals at home who will shop, bank, work, and entertain themselves without leaving their homes. These customers will pay for the services they get, in a way similar to the way we pay for the telephone or cable TV services. The second group of customers are organizations and businesses. These customers will use the networks for hundreds of applications, several of which are described in this chapter. Companies will conduct important electronic meetings and train employees in many locations simultaneously, using advanced multimedia tools and intelligent computer-aided tutoring.

REENGINEERING

...buying and selling in the information highway

Using the information superhighways, people will be able to see places before they travel to them and even "feel" scenarios (using virtual reality). Students will be able to take classes from home and even create a degree program from courses taken at several universities. Shopping will be changed, not only for individuals who will use home shopping, but also for corporations that will buy directly from producers without the need for retailers and wholesalers. Products will be demonstrated to potential buyers in three dimensions. Frequently, customers will be able to see the various colors, designs, and sizes of the product they wish. Ultimately, customers will be able to interface electronically with designers and order custom-made products. Companies will buy knowledge electronically. Experts and consultants will deliver their services across the world at a small cost.

Building the American information superhighway is not a simple undertaking. In addition to the high cost, and the question of how it will be financed, there are issues and factors that can slow or limit the project, such as technological obsolescence, government regulations, and political considerations for information crossing national borders. The project is also moving slowly because of the many conflicting interest groups, especially telephone companies, cable TV operators, cable manufacturers, and manufacturers of telecommunication hardware and software.

THE INTERNET

While the information superhighway is years away, its predecessor (or basis)—the **Internet**—is growing rapidly. The Internet is the world's largest computer network; it is actually a *network of networks*. It is composed of over 25,000 connected networks with over 2.5 million computers and 25 million users (in 1994). The Internet, which initially served the academic world (e.g., for accessing supercomputers), is now serving the business world as well, providing speedy, low-cost global communication. Several thousand specialty databases are accessed through the Internet. Dialog, one of the largest commercial services that provides database and sophisticated retrieval mechanisms, is also connected to the Internet. Without any fee, you can read books on the Internet whose copyrights have expired. Other books can be reached via the Internet and Online BookStore for a minimal fee. The Internet E-mail is most efficient. It maximizes bandwidth use and permits continuous connection. Users can send messages to groups (many mailing lists are available), including members of specialized news groups. Companies can receive information from experts in narrow specialties. A company can register in any interest group mailing list and get information that flows continuously to members. For example, there is an oil and gas industry list of new explorations. All together, there are about 3,000 news groups that receive messages and news articles according to their specific group profiles.

It is also possible to conduct collaborative work over the Internet. Professionals can write papers jointly, share data, or design new products as a team with members in different locations. Authors and publishers can develop manuscripts very quickly. Also, people can produce business and legal documents as participating members of a team. Companies can retrieve publicly available software from files in the Internet. There are thousands of packages, including some given away free by major vendors.

Lately, large numbers of companies started doing business on the Internet. Digital Equipment Corporation has created an Internet Business Group to help customers and business partners exploit the global network.

WHAT YOU CAN DO WITH THE INTERNET

▼ *Electronic mail.* The simplest use of the Internet connects E-mail of different organizations. For example, you can send a message from your university or place of work to thousands of organizations worldwide. If you have an account with any major on-line service, such as CompuServe, you can use E-mail from your home.

▼ *News group.* The Internet news groups are similar dial-up bulletin board systems. Electronic members are focused around the news group theme. Members of the news group can pose questions or present interesting information.

▼ *Mailing lists.* It is possible to send information not only as public displays on a bulletin board, but to anyone on a specific mailing list.

▼ *Access.* The Internet lets you access remote computers and retrieve files.

▼ *Business activities.* Shopping (e.g., via electronic direct-mail marketing), investing, making reservations, or working together are some business activities you can conduct on the Internet (see Verity [1994]).

▼ *Remote log in with interactive sessions.* This service (which is done by using Telnet) permits remote log in from whatever computer you are using.

▼ *Accessing databases and browsing.* Accessing information in databases is a major theme of the Internet. Using the Internet, you can find information on almost any topic you desire, including related bibliographies. You can browse through news items, "enter" into libraries and catalogs, "visit" a museum, read newspapers or books, or listen to a concert. A variety of tools help you navigate through and reach the resources of the Internet. These are presented next.

ACCESSING THE INTERNET

There are several ways and tools to access the Internet. Some representative systems and tools are the following.

1. *Gopher.* Gopher is a system to access any type of textual information available on the Internet. It is a document delivery system for retrieving documents from the Internet that is based on a set of menus and submenus, and sub–sub menus (many levels). A sample of three menus is shown in Figure 14.14. When you use Gopher, you are running a client program on a client/server system. The client program contacts a Gopher server, asking it to process the information. The Gopher server will use a communication server to find the requested information in one (or more) of the thousands of servers worldwide.

2. *Veronica.* The major limitation of Gopher is that there are thousands of databases, so the user needs to know which servers to search. Veronica is a

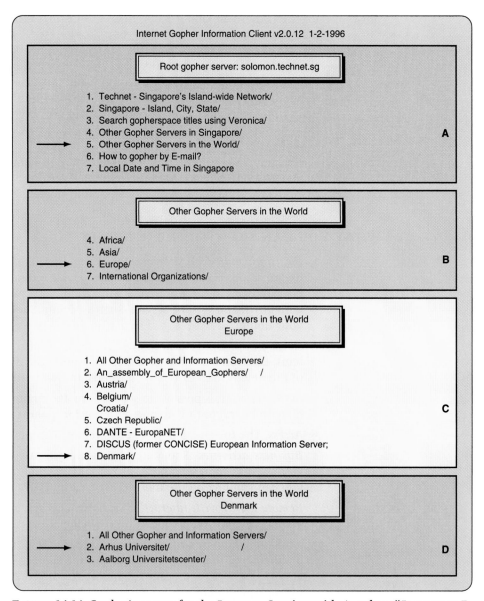

FIGURE 14.14 Gopher's menus for the Internet. Starting with A, select #5; move to B, select #6; move to C, select #8; move to D. By selecting #2, you are at the database of Arhus University. The next submenu will show you the available files at the University.

searchable index of items available via Gopher. Using Veronica, all you need to do is to key in "words to search for." Veronica will search the Internet, looking for all menu items that include the word(s) you specify. Once the search is completed, the user is presented with all relevant menu items. All you have to do is to select the items in the menu that you want.

3. *WorldWide Web.* This is a method for providing distributed information on the Internet. Documents are hypertexted; namely, they are linked to other documents. The hypertext capability enables the user to go from one item to related items without the need to go through menus. This popular access to the Internet is also called WWW or just Web.

4. *Mosaic.* One of the most interesting tools for navigating the Internet is Mosaic. It is a multimedia browser tool which reaches not only text but full color images and sound. It also has hypermedia capabilities, so you can re- trieve a document with a relevant picture and listen to related music. By

clicking on hyperlinks, you can move from one document to a related document across the network. Mosaic (or National Center for Supercomputing Applications, NCSA Mosaics) is part of the worldwide environment. Mosaic is a client/server integrated set of browsers, viewers, servers, gateways, and filters that allow you to approach Internet. A similar tool is NetScape.

5. *Other interfaces.* For other interfaces and features of the Internet, refer to Croninning (1994), Fisher (1992), Kehoe (1993), and Pitter et al. (1995). Also, there are several journals such as *The Internet Business Journal*, *Internet World*, and *Internet Letter*.

DOING BUSINESS ON-LINE

The availability of electronic mail, the Internet, and public network services provides opportunities to conduct business electronically. Resnick (1993) offers guidelines about how to start and conduct such business. For example, one can sell information to people who deal in stocks and real estate. This is called *information brokerage*. Services including advice and execution of transactions. Electronic publishing of on-line directories is another way to reach subscribers. One can sell newsletters to special interest groups, such as members of professional associations.

A large number of potential customers can be reached at a very low cost via the Internet. Therefore, *advertising* on the Internet is becoming popular. In addition, major publishers have put their books on the Internet. Even TV producers envision using the Internet for a pay-per-view service.

For information on the use of the Internet in business, you may want to read *Internet Business Report*, a CHP monthly publication. To reach the publisher on your E-mail, use: lbr@cmp.com

▶ MANAGERIAL ISSUES

Providing timely, relevant, and correct information is a critical factor for the success of almost any organization. In implementing IT to support communication and collaborative work, the following issues may surface.

1. *Privacy and ethics in E-mail.* The increased use of E-mail raises the question of privacy. While letters are sealed, E-mail material is open (unless encrypted). Many organizations are monitoring E-mail, which raises the question of invasion of privacy (see discussion in Chapter 20). Other issues include the use of E-mail for personal purposes and time wasted in sending and receiving material which is not related to work, including electronic junk mail.

2. *Right of free speech.* The dissemination of information via E-mail, the Internet, electronic bulletin boards, and public networks may offend others (e.g., the distribution of pornographic and racial material). But, dissemination of information is a right, according to the U.S. Constitution.

3. *Security of communication.* Communication via E-mail and other technologies raises the issue of the integrity, confidentiality, and security of the data being transferred. The protection of data in networks across the globe is not simple. This topic is addressed in Chapter 19.

4. *Data crossing national borders.* Governments cannot or do not wish to control data that cross their borders via the regular mail. However, it is easier to control data crossing national borders electronically. Such control, which is commonly justified as a protection of citizens' privacy, is sometimes done to preserve jobs. Corporations need to take measures to handle such situations.

5. *Organizational impacts.* Technology-supported communication may have major organizational impacts. For example, Lotus Notes forces people to cooperate and share information. Therefore, its use can lead to significant changes in both organizational culture and the execution of business processes reengineering (see the story of Price Waterhouse in Box 14.11). Further impacts could be on structure and redistribution of organizational power (see Chapter 20). Experiments conducted by Eveland and Bikson (1988) revealed that groups supported by IT differ from groups not supported by IT in their structure and leadership as well as in the way they execute their missions.

6. *The use of a decision room.* A decision room is expensive to build and requires a professional facilitator. (Building a decision room with off-the-shelf components is an option that can reduce the cost at the expense of some capabilities.) In addition, the room may have little utilization, since it is suitable mainly for resolving conflicting decisions, and its use requires a great deal of preparation. Therefore, management should consider renting one.

7. *Importance of business processes reengineering.* As shown in Chapters 3 and 4, BPR can be enhanced by IT. The technologies described in this chapter are extremely useful for the support of team-based organizations, virtual corporations, international trade, shortened time-to-market, and other activities of BPR. Workflow software, for example, can be used to support process redesign.

8. *Which technology to use?* Current events suggest that Lotus Notes may be a structure or foundation that will be used to "hang" proprietary/specialized group-process software—much like the spreadsheet became a platform for analysis-based products. And indeed, Lotus entered a joint venture with AT&T to enable the use of Lotus Notes practically everywhere. It will be interesting to see what further developments will occur now that Lotus Development Corporation has been acquired by IBM.

    The implementation of groupware also raises the question of operating systems. At the time this material was written, Windows for Workgroups (from Microsoft) was the only *operating system* designed specifically to support work groups.

9. *Justification.* The technologies described in this chapter do not come free. For example, Price Waterhouse invested $2 million in Lotus Notes. Some of their competitors are not sure that such an investment is justifiable (many of the benefits are intangible). However, with the introduction of competing products, the price of Lotus Notes will certainly decrease. Also, desktop videoconferencing and inexpensive multimedia equipment encourage the use of videoconferencing. Distributed GDSS and the availability of competing products reduce the cost of the technology. One exception is EDI. It is not a question of justification any more because, in most cases, management *must* use EDI or the company cannot do business with certain of its trading partners.

10. *Ethical issues.* The more information travels on the highways, the more ethical issues may surface. Take, for example, the United States, where several specialized healthcare networks exist such as Telemed, a network which tracks tuberculosis patients so as to prescribe the most suitable drugs. These systems could be abused. How do patients know that they are getting "qualified" network advice? What if personal medical records fall into the wrong hands? The growing advent of computerized networks make medical confidentiality harder to preserve. The problem is how to strike a balance between the benefits of health information systems and their potential ethical problems. ∎

KEY TERMS

Asynchronous communication
487

Communication *486*

Decision room *502*

Delphi method *490*

Electronic bulletin board (EBB)
500

Electronic data interchange
(EDI) *495*

Electronic mail (E-mail) *493*

Group decision support system
(GDSS) *501*

Groupthink *490*

Groupware *490*

Information superhighway *517*

Internet *518*

Lotus Notes *512*

Nominal group technique *490*

On-line database *499*

Synchronous communication *487*

Telecommuting *508*

Teleconferencing *491*

Video mail *491*

Video teleconference *491*

Voice mail *508*

Workflow software *505*

Work group *488*

CHAPTER HIGHLIGHTS *(L-x means learning objective number x)*

▼ There are four settings for supporting communication in meetings: same-time/same-place, same-time/different-place, different-time/same-place and different-time/different-place. (L-1)

▼ Communication is essential to any organization, especially in light of trends such as team-based organization and globalization. (L-1)

▼ There are many benefits to working in groups ("two heads are better than one"), but many dysfunctional behavior can occur in the process of collaborative work. (L-2)

▼ Electronic meeting systems, computer-supported cooperative work, groupware, and other names designate various types of computer support to groups. (L-3)

▼ The Delphi method is a nonelectronic, non-face-to-face method for improving group work that assures anonymity for the participants and provides equal chances to participate. (L-3)

▼ Video teleconferencing utilizes several technologies that allow people to communicate and view each other as well as view and transfer documents. (L-4)

▼ Electronic mail allows quick communication across the globe at minimal cost. (L-5)

▼ Public networks and electronic bulletin boards enable inexpensive communication and dissemination of information. (L-5)

▼ EDI is a special electronic mail that transmits standard transactions (such as purchasing orders) very rapidly and with minimum errors. (L-6)

▼ A group decision support system is usually structured on a LAN and is conducted in a decision room environment with a facilitator. (L-7)

▼ Idea generation is achieved by allowing participants to generate ideas simultaneously and share them, yet keep anonymity. (L-7)

▼ Voice technology can be used to increase productivity and usability of communication. (L-8)

▼ People can work at home supported by distributed GSS, not only as individuals but also as participating team members. (L-9)

▼ Lotus Notes is the major software that supports the work of dispersed individuals and groups. (L-10)

▼ Information superhighways will enable us to integrate voice, text, and other media and bring them interactively into every home, school, and business. (L-11)

▼ The Internet is a network of many major networks. (L-11)

QUESTIONS FOR REVIEW

1. What are some major benefits of working in groups?

2. Are there any major limitations to working in groups?

3. Define a GDSS, and list three of its benefits.

4. Explain the major characteristics of GDSSs.

5. Describe a decision room, and contrast it with other GDSS scenarios.

6. Describe the Delphi method.

7. Define groupware.

8. List the major capabilities of Lotus Notes.

9. List the major capabilities of teleconferencing.

10. Define E-mail, and describe its capabilities.

11. Define EDI, and describe its capabilities.

12. What is the Internet?

13. Define workflow systems.

14. Define telecommuting, and list its major advantages.

15. What are information superhighways?

16. Define voice technology, and list its uses.

17. Explain the benefits of public networks and electronic bulletin boards.

QUESTIONS FOR DISCUSSION

1. Explain why the topic of group work and its support is getting increased attention.

2. How is electronic conferencing related to computers?

3. Explain how the various technologies are integrated in video teleconferencing.

4. Explain the advantages of electronic mail over regular mail.

5. Compare and contrast EDI and E-mail.

6. Explain how EDI works.

7. Explain how workflow software can support decision making.

8. Compare GDSS to noncomputerized group decision making.

9. How can GDSS support creativity?

10. Describe the deficiencies of the nominal group technique and the Delphi method.

11. Explain why there are so few companies that are using decision rooms.

12. Why is Lotus Notes such a successful product?

13. It is said that Lotus Notes can change organizational culture. Explain how.

14. How can computers support a team whose members work at different times?

15. Based on what you know about Lotus Notes, can it support different-time/different-place work?

EXERCISES

1. Prepare a conceptual design of an EDI for a hospital. The hospital conducts its purchases through a special organization which also does purchases for other hospitals (the process is called group purchasing). Purchases are made from several suppliers. Show the PC-to-mainframe links and the telephone lines. The hospital communicates with several other hospitals and with the American Hospital Association.

2. From your own experience or from the vendor's information, list all the major capabilities of Lotus Notes and explain how it can be used to support knowledge workers and managers.

3. Read Mehler's case on Lotus Notes (*Corporate Computing*, August 1992). Explain how Lotus Notes helped in reengineering Price Waterhouse.

4. Find some information about the Internet. Explain its importance for international business and education.

5. The University of Arizona is adopting GroupSystems for use in a distributed mode. Determine which software modules (see Figure 14.11) are especially suitable for a distributed mode.

6. Review the opening case and answer the following questions regarding the EDI.
   a. What benefits are provided to Harper?
   b. What benefits are provided to Honda?
   c. What benefits are provided to U.S. Customs?
   d. Are there any disadvantages to any of the partners?

7. Sears had some problems in 1992 and 1993, regarding dissemination of information that offended people on its Prodigy system. Find material about this (or similar incidents). Use the Internet for your search. Summarize and prepare a report.

8. Harper's CEO said, "We're determined to be an information company. We don't own ships or trucks, but we have always had information. That's the asset we have to market. Therefore we must get a competitive edge in information." Comment on this statement.

9. Compare and contrast E-mail and voice mail.

10. Several employees have complained that whenever they call Jane, a telecommuter, they usually get her answering machine. Furthermore, she will return the calls only the next morning. Jane's productivity at home is very good. Her explanations for not returning the calls seem to be legitimate. So, on one hand, it seems that telecommuting is working well. But other employees are complaining, suggesting that Jane be given a beeper or be told to be at the telephone once every two hours. As a manager, what would you do and why?

GROUP ASSIGNMENT

1. You're are a member of a team working for a multinational finance corporation. Your team's project is to prepare a complex financing proposal for a client within one week. Two of the team members are in Singapore, one is in Seoul Korea, one is in London, and one is in Los Angeles. You cannot get the team members in one place. Your team does not have all the required expertise, but other corporate employees may have it. There are 8,000 such employees worldwide; many of them travel. You do not know exactly who the experts are in your company. Your company never prepared such a proposal, but you know that certain parts of the proposal can be adapted from previous proposals. These proposals are filed electronically in various corporate

databases, but you are not sure exactly where (there are over 80 databases, worldwide). Finally, you will need a lot of external information, and you will need to communicate with your client in China, with investment groups in Japan and New York, and with your corporate headquarters in London.

If the client accepts your proposal, your company will make more than $5 million in profit. If the contract goes to a competitor, you may lose your job.

Your company has all the latest information and communication technologies.

a. Prepare a list of tasks and activities that your team will need to go through in order to accomplish the mission.

b. Describe what information technologies you would use to support the above tasks. Be specific, explaining how each technology can facilitate the execution of each task.

2. The world of the Internet is growing very fast, and it keeps changing. The mission of the group is to report the latest about the Internet. Members of the group will prepare a report which will include the following.

a. New business applications on the Internet.

b. New books about the Internet.

c. Information about new software products related to the Internet.

Also, send a message to the White House and include the reply in your report.

Minicase 1

Nabisco Tracks Attendance Using Voice Technologies

Nabisco's Chicago bakery is the largest bakery in the world. Here is how the company tracks the attendance of some of its employees.

When employees telephone in to inform the company that they cannot come to work, they are directed by a prerecorded voice (interactive voice response) to key in their employee I.D. number. A computer confirms the validity of the number. The caller is then asked for a special identification (a social security number or a special code). This is done for security purposes. Upon confirmation, the caller is presented with a menu of options for selecting an absence code (e.g., illness, death in the family). Finally they are prompted to key in the expected return-to-work date. (A special arrangement for callers that do not have touch-tone telephones involves sophisticated voice recognition systems that request that the caller speak rather than key-in the answers.)

A computer program then updates the daily schedule and presents it to a supervisor (usually on a computer screen). The supervisor makes the necessary changes, calls for additional employees if needed, etc.

The system can also be used for tracking employee responses to working during weekends. Employees are asked by an automated call to give a yes or no response to working on a forthcoming weekend. The list of positive answers is forwarded to the supervisor's screen so a schedule can be made. Then the employees that were selected are called by the system with the details of their schedule. (This case is based on a story in *Communications News*, March 1993, p. 26.)

Questions for Minicase 1

1. Identify the voice recognition and voice synthesis portions of the system.

2. Identify all the tasks carried out by a computer which do not involve voice.

3. What paperwork can be eliminated by such a system?

4. What are the benefits to Nabisco?

5. What are the benefits to the employees?

6. What alternative communication technologies described in this chapter can be used instead of the system described here? Would you recommend any of these; why or why not?

7. Are there any disadvantages to the use of the technology?

Minicase 2

General Mills Reengineers for Electronic Data Interchange

Bob Gaffney, the EDI manager of General Mills (Minneapolis, MN) needed an answer from a transportation company regarding the feasibility of transferring large quantities of Cheerios from a warehouse to a customer.

Naturally, he used the EDI system to transfer a standard request. The company has been using EDI for two years. However, the system was decentralized: the sales, transportation, and warehousing units were practicing EDI independently. As a result, acknowledgements took about 24 hours.

This response time was unacceptable, so it was necessary to change the technology to improve response time. As a part of the corporate reengineering effort, such a change would alter the manner in which General Mills conducted its business. In fact, this change became the strategic goal of the company. The technical goal was to centralize the EDI and to integrate it seamlessly with the company's business applications.

General Mills uses its EDI system for about 5,000 transactions each day. The company is also involved with efficient consumer response (ECR), a program sponsored by the grocery industry to remove unnecessary costs from the food distribution cycle. EDI was found to be a key enabler to making ECR work. Several executives of General Mills are now involved in industry-wide ECR committees.

To build the EDI, the company needed to select VAN suppliers (four are used): to choose EDI translators; to select codes (ANSI X.12 and UCS of the grocery industry); to integrate the EDI with business applications on the mainframe and the LANs, and with communication software internally; and to enlist trading partners (about 400 suppliers and customers). General Mills also helped its

partners to select equipment and vendors for items such as the VAN and EDI translator. Some of the partners had mainframes; others used LANs.

The system has been implemented successfully. It no longer takes 24 hours to get an answer from a trading partner. The shortened response time is now approaching real time.

Questions for Minicase 2

1. Why was the EDI response time 24 hours?

2. How can the EDI facilitate the use of ECR?

3. Why do they need two EDI codes?

4. Why do they need several VAN vendors?

5. Why was it important to select a translator which was VAN independent?

6. Why was "enlisting trading partners" the last step in the process and what difficulties may one encounter in this step?

7. From what you learned about EDI, what kind of transactions can take place between a food manufacturer and its suppliers and customers?

(SOURCE: Based on *Software Magazine*, June 1993.)

Minicase 3

Which Technology to Use?

Marketel is a fast-growing telemarketing company whose headquarters are in Colorado, but the majority of its business is in California. The company has eight divisions, including one in Chicago. (The company just started penetrating the Midwest market.) Recently the company was approached by two large telephone companies, one in Los Angeles and one in Denver, for discussions regarding a potential merger.

Nancy Miranda, the corporate CEO who was involved in the preliminary discussions, notified all division managers on the progress of the discussions. Both she and John Miner, the chief financial officer, felt that an immediate merger would be extremely beneficial. However, the vice presidents for marketing and operations thought the company should continue to be independent for at least two to three years. "We can get a much better deal if we increase our market share," commented Sharon Gonzales, the vice president for marketing. Nancy called each of the division managers and found that six of them were for the merger proposal while two objected to it. Furthermore, she found that the division managers from the West Coast strongly opposed discussions with the Colorado company, while the other managers were strongly against discussions with the Los Angeles com-

pany. Memos, telephone calls, and meetings of two or three people at a time resulted in frustration. It became apparent that a meeting of all concerned individuals was a must. Nancy wanted to have the meeting as soon as possible in spite of the busy travel schedules of most division managers. She also wanted the meeting to be as short as possible. Nancy called Bob Kraut, the chief information officer, and asked for suggestions about how to electronically conduct a conference where the issue is very controversial.

The options are as follows.

1. Use the corporate E-mail. Collect opinions from all division managers and vice presidents; then disseminate them to all parties, get feedback, and repeat the process until a solution is achieved (similar to the Delphi method).

2. Use the corporate EDI in a similar manner. The EDI is more secured than E-mail, and the electronic discussions may involve trade secrets.

3. Fly all division managers to corporate headquarters and have face-to-face meetings until a solution is achieved.

4. Fly all division managers to corporate headquarters. Rent a decision room and a facilitator from the local university for $2,000 per day and conduct the meetings there.

5. Conduct a videoconference. Unfortunately, appropriate facilities exist only at the headquarters and in two divisions. The other division managers can be flown to the nearest division that has equipment. Alternatively, videoconferencing facilities may be rented in all cities.

6. Use a telephone conference call.

Questions for Minicase 3

1. Which of these options would you recommend to management and why?

2. Is there a technology not listed that might do a better job?

3. Is it possible to use more than one alternative in this case? If yes, which technologies would you combine and how would you use them?

REFERENCES AND BIBLIOGRAPHY

1. Applegate, L. M., "Technology Support for Cooperative Work: A Framework for Studying Introduction and Assimilation in Organization," *Journal of Organizational Computing*, Vol. 1, No. 1, 1991.

2. Briere, D., "Groupware: A Spectrum of Productivity Boosters," *Networkworld*, September 16, 1991.

3. Bostrom, R., et al., *Computer Augmented Teamwork: A Guided Tour*, New York: Van Nostrand Reinhold, 1992.

4. Carlyle, R. H., "The Shock of Going Global," *Datamation*, August 1, 1989.

5. Chen, M., *Groupwork and Groupware: A Tutorial* (unpublished); Fairfax, VA: George Mason University, 1993.

6. Cronning, M. J., *Doing Business on the Internet: How the Electronic Highway is Transforming American Companies*, New York: Van Nostrand Reinhold, 1994.

7. Cross, T. B., and H. Raizman, *Telecommuting: The Future Technology at Work*, Homewood, IL: Dow-Jones/Irwin, 1986.

8. DeSanctis, G., and B. Gallupe, "A Foundation for the Study of Group Decision Support Systems," *Management Science*, Vol. 33, No. 5, 1987.

9. Drucker, P. E., "The Coming of the Organization," *Harvard Business Review*, January/February 1988.

10. Ellis, C. A., et al., "Groupware: Some Issues and Experiences (Using Computer to Facilitate Human Interaction)," *Communications of the ACM*, Vol. 34, January 1991.

11. Eveland, J. D., and T. Bikson, "Work Group Structures and Computer Support: A Field Experiment," *Proceedings of Conference on Computer-Supported Cooperative Work*, ACM, 1988.

12. Finholt, T., and L. S. Sproull, "Electronic Groups at Work," *Organization Science*, Vol. 1, No. 1, 1990.

13. Fisher, S., *Riding the Internet*, Carmel, IN: New Riders Publications, 1993.

14. Galagher, J., et al., *Intellectual Teamwork: Social and Technological Foundation of Cooperative Teams*, New York: Lawrence Erlbaum Associates, 1990.

15. Guglielmo, C., "Global Transport," *Corporate Computing*, June/July 1992.

16. Henricks, M., "The Virtual Entrepreneur," *Success*, June 1993.

17. Herniter, B. C., et al., "Computers Improve Efficiency of the Negotiation Process," *Personnel Journal*, April 1993.

18. Hindus, L. A., "What MIS Should Know About Videoconferencing," *Datamation*, August 15, 1992.

19. Hsu, J., and T. Lockwood (eds.), "Collaborative Computing," *Byte*, March 1993.

20. Jessup, L. M., and J. Valacich (eds.), *Group Support Systems: New Perspectives*, New York: Macmillan, 1993.

21. Johnsen, R., *Groupware: Computer Support for Business Teams*, New York: Free Press, 1988.

22. Johnsen, R., "Groupware: Future Directions and Wild Cards," *Journal of Organizational Computing*, Vol. 2, No. 1, 1991.

23. Kehoe, B. P., *Zen and the Art of Internet: A Beginner's Guide*, Englewood Cliffs, N.J.: Prentice-Hall, 1993.

24. Klein, P., "Go with the Flow," *InformationWeek*, March 28, 1994.

25. LaPlante, E., "Teleconferencing," *Forbes ASAP*, September 13, 1993.

26. Lindstone H., and H. Turroff, *The Delphi Method: Technology and Applications*, Reading, MA: Addison-Wesley, 1975.

27. *Lotus Notes—Technical Overview*, Lotus Development Corp., Pub. U134M, 1994.

28. Mockler, R. J., *Computer Software to Support Strategic Management Decision Making*, New York: Macmillan, 1992.

29. Neo, B. S., "The Implementation of an Electronic Market for Pig Trading in Singapore," *Journal of Strategic Information Systems*, December 1992.

30. Nunamaker, J. F., Jr., et al., "Electronic Meeting Systems to Support Group Work," *Communications of the ACM*, July 1991.

31. Nussbaum, G., "EDI: First Aid for Soaring Hospital Cost," *Corporate Computing*, August/September 1992.

32. Pitter, K., et al., *Every Student's Guide to the Internet*, New York: McGraw Hill, 1995.

33. Resnick, R., "Online Business Opportunities Abound," *PC Today*, February 1993.

34. Richter, J., and I. Mesholum, "Telework at Home: The Home and the Organization Perspective," *Human Systems Management*, Vol. 12, No. 3, 1993.

35. Schermerhorn, J. R., *Management for Productivity, 4th ed.* New York: John Wiley and Sons, 1993.

36. Stalling W., *Business Data Communications*, New York: Macmillan Pub. Co., 1990.

37. Turban, E., *Decision Support and Expert Systems*, 3rd ed., Macmillan, 1993.

38. Turban E., and P. Wang, "Telecommuting Management: A Comprehensive Review," *Human Systems Management*, Fall 1995.

39. Verity, J. W., "The Internet: How It Will Change the Way You Do Business," *Business Week*, Nov. 14, 1994.

40. Vickers, B., "Using GDSS to Examine the Future European Automobile Industry," *Futures*, October 1992.

41. Violino, B. and S. Stahl, "No Place Like Home," *Information Week*, February 8, 1993.

42. Yager, T., "Better Than Being There—Desktop Teleconferencing," *Byte*, March 1993.

SUPPORTING THE MANAGER AND DECISION MAKING

Chapter Outline

Learning Objectives

After studying this chapter, you will be able to:

1. Describe the concepts of management, managers, decision making, and computerized support to managers.

2. Analyze the relationship between managers and decision making in light of the decision-making process.

3. Discuss the role of models in decision making.

4. Explain why IT is needed and how it supports managers.

5. Describe the framework for computerized decision support and analyze problems according to the framework.

6. Describe DSS, and analyze their role in management support.

7. Describe EIS, and analyze their role in management support.

8. Compare DSS with ODSS and analyze the major differences.

9. Explain how computers can enhance idea generation.

Case

JEWISH HOSPITAL HEALTHCARE Services (JHHS) is a regional health care provider based in Louisville, KY. It owns and manages seven facilities with a total of 1,0 patient beds and 3,5 employees. The total information management and computer services costs represent approximately 3 percent of the organization's operating budget. According to David Pecoraro, vice president and chief information officer, JHHS made the decision to move into decision support systems (DSS) toward the end of the completion of their first long-range information systems plan. They were finishing their basic information systems installation work in late 1988 and determined that they wanted a higher level of system capability from a management information standpoint.

Currently, JHHS is utilizing various decision-support system applications in the areas of productivity, cost accounting, patient mix, and nursing staff scheduling. These applications are developed with two mainframe DSS development tools: MAPS and Statistical Analysis System (SAS), and PC-based DSS tools such as Lotus 1-2-3.

In early 1992, MAPS became operational. The capabilities of this system include modeling, forecasting, planning, communications, database management systems, and graphics. Based on MAPS, JHHS developed a productivity DSS. Managers can now quickly receive (or generate) reports containing essential information for their decision making. For example, department heads receive four graphs on a single piece of paper to see their departmental productivity, their workload, their hours worked, and the impact of their productivity on salary. Pecoraro's staff has trained all levels of management—from supervisor on up—in the use of the system, so they can see very clearly "a picture of what we produced in the past weeks, what it took to produce it, and what was the cost to the organization."

The JHHS staff is positive about the DSS because it is faster and easier to interpret than the old system. Also, all of the data tie back to the key clinical and financial systems, so there is a high level of trust and credibility in the integrity of the information provided. Implementation of the cost accounting DSS began in 1990. It be-

Jewish Hospital Healthcare Services employees using a DSS tool.

came operational in 1991 and has since become quite valuable to the organization. It is being used for bidding contracts and services, as well as for pricing. The productivity standards are not part of the cost accounting system. However, although the cost accounting system is not linked to the productivity system, the two do share a common database. The cost accounting system is tied to the patient mix system. These systems are used by the product line managers for assistance in formulating and monitoring their business plans.

The SAS was added in 1991. This is a report-generating tool with statistical analysis capabilities. It allows JHHS managers to take both the clinical and financial files from the mainframe to perform analysis on the data. JHHS also has a nursing acuity system on the mainframe where patients are classified by the intensity of their illnesses. These calculations are passed from the mainframe to the nursing staff scheduling system so that, on a daily basis, the nurse managers receive their staffing requirements and a comparison of these to actual staffing levels.

SOURCE: Condensed from the *Journal of Systems Management*, June 1992.

▶ **15.2 MANAGEMENT AND MANAGERS**

The opening case illustrates how the use of a decision support system (DSS) enhanced the *management* of a hospital and helped in increasing its *productivity*. Let us discuss these two important concepts.

Management is a process by which certain goals are achieved through the use of resources (people, money, energy, materials, space, time). These resources are considered to be *inputs*, and the attainment of the goals is viewed as the *output* of the process. The degree of a manager's success is often measured by the ratio between outputs and inputs for which she is responsible. This ratio is an indication of the organization's **productivity**.

$$Productivity = \frac{outputs \ (products, \ services \ produced)}{inputs \ (resources \ utilized)}$$

Productivity (sometimes referred to as efficiency) is a major concern for any organization because it influences the well-being of the organization and its members. Productivity is also a most important issue at the national level. National productivity is the sum of the productivity of all organizations and individuals, and it affects the standard of living, employment level, and economic well-being of a country.

To understand how computers support managers, it is necessary to first describe what managers do. Unfortunately, it is difficult to produce a standard job description for all managers. Managers do many things, depending on their position in the organization, the type and size of the organization, the organizational policies and culture, and the personalities of the managers themselves. Despite this difficulty, there have been many attempts to study what managers do. One of the classical studies was done by Mintzberg (1973), who divided the manager's roles into three categories.

1. *Interpersonal roles:* figurehead, leader, liaison.
2. *Informational roles:* monitor, disseminator, spokesperson.
3. *Decisional roles:* entrepreneur, disturbance handler, resource allocator, negotiator.

Early information systems mainly supported the informational roles; in contrast, the purpose of recent information systems is to support all three roles. In this chapter, we are interested mainly in the support that IT can provide to *decisional* roles. In other chapters (e.g., in the previous one), we presented support to the other roles, especially informational roles.

Table 15.1 presents the findings of a study conducted by McLeod and Jones (1986) regarding how knowledge of the decisional roles of executives can help design executive information systems. The table indicates that most information is used in two roles: handling disturbances and entrepreneurial activities. The per-

---

Table 15.1 **Executive Activities and Information Support**

Nature of Activity (Decision Role)	Information Needed (%)
Handling disturbances. A disturbance is something that happens unexpectedly and demands immediate attention, but it might take weeks or months to resolve.	42
Entrepreneurial activity. Such an activity is intended to make improvements that will increase performance levels. The improvements are strategic and long term in nature.	32
Resource allocation. Managers allocate resources within the framework of the annual and monthly planning tasks and budgets.	17
Negotiations. Managers attempt to resolve conflicts and disputes, either internal or external to the organization. Such attempts usually involve some negotiations.	3
Other Activities.	6

SOURCE: Compiled from McLeod and Jones, 1986.

centages in the table indicate the proportion of people who believe that IT is most critical for that specific activity.

We divide the manager's work, as it relates to decisional roles, into two phases. Phase I is the identification of problems and/or opportunities. Phase II is the decision of what to do about the problems. Figure 15.1 provides a flow chart of this process and the flow of information in it. As shown, information comes from internal and external environments. Internal information is generated from the functional areas. External information comes from sources such as on-line databases, newspapers, industry newsletters, government reports, and personal contacts. Because of the large amount of information available, it is necessary to scan the environment and data sources to find the relevant pieces. Collected information is then evaluated and channeled to quantitative and qualitative analysis, which is carried out by specialists whenever needed. This is basically an interpretation of the information. Then, a decision by an executive or a group is made on whether a problem or opportunity exists. If it is decided that there is a problem, then the problem is transferred as an input to Phase II. There, a decision is made on what to do about the problem. The extensive communication that may take place among executives, managers, and specialists is not shown in the figure. The basic purpose of various *management support systems* (MSS) technologies is to support the tasks of the process of Figure 15.1, as well as to support the specific roles described earlier. In this chapter, attention is given mainly to two MSS technologies: DSS and EIS.

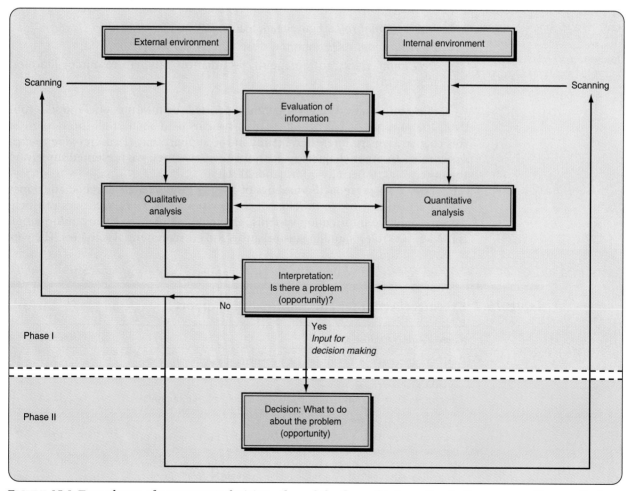

FIGURE 15.1 Two phases of a manager's decision role and the flow of information in the process. (Source: Turban, 1993, p. 396.)

15.3 MANAGERIAL DECISION MAKING

The success of management depends on the execution of managerial functions such as planning, organizing, directing, and controlling. To carry out these functions, managers engage in the continuous process of making decisions.

All managerial activities revolve around decision making. The manager is first and foremost a decision maker (see Box 15.1). Organizations are filled with decision makers at various levels.

A Closer Look BOX 15.1

ABILITY TO MAKE DECISIONS RATED FIRST IN SURVEY

In almost any survey of what constitutes good management, you are likely to find the ability to make clear-cut decisions when needed prominently mentioned. It is not surprising, therefore, to hear that the ability to make crisp decisions was rated first in importance in a study of 6,500 managers in more than 100 companies, many of them large, blue-chip corporations.

As managers entered a training course at Harbridge House, a Boston-based firm, they were asked how important it was that managers employ certain management practices. They also were asked how well, in their estimation, managers performed these practices. From a sta-

tistical distillation of these answers, Harbridge ranked "making clear-cut decisions when needed" as the most important of 10 management practices. From these evaluations, they concluded that only 10 percent of the managers performed "very well" on any given practice.

Ranked second in managerial importance was "getting to the heart of problems rather than dealing with less important issues," a finding that seems to show up in all such studies. Most of the remaining eight management practices were related directly or indirectly to decision making.

SOURCE: Condensed from *Stars and Stripes*, May 10, 1987.

For years, managers have considered decision making a pure art—a talent acquired over a long period of time through experience (learning by trial and error). Management was considered an art because a variety of individual styles could be used in approaching and successfully solving the same type of managerial problems in actual business practice. These styles are often based on creativity, judgment, intuition, and experience rather than on systematic quantitative methods using a scientific approach.

However, this situation is changing. The environment in which management must operate today is becoming turbulent and complex, with a trend toward increasing complexity. Therefore, it is more difficult to make decisions today for two reasons. First, the number of available alternatives is much larger than ever before, due to improved technology and communication systems. More alternatives means that it is more difficult to select one alternative, which is necessary when a decision is made. Second, the cost of making errors can be very large, due to the complexity and magnitude of operations, automation, and the chain reaction that errors can cause in many parts of the organization. Therefore, trial and error may be too expensive. By the same token, however, benefits can be extremely large if correct decisions are made.

As a result of these trends and changes, it is difficult to rely on a trial-and-error approach to management. Managers must become more sophisticated—they must learn how to use the new tools and techniques that are developed in their field. Several of these techniques use a quantitative analysis approach, and they are supported by computers. Some techniques are described in this chapter. Others are described in management science books (e.g., see Turban and Meredith [1994]). Newer computerized techniques that support qualitative analysis are described in the next chapter.

THE PROCESS OF MAKING A DECISION

When making a decision, either organizational or personal, the decision maker goes through a fairly systematic process. Simon (1977) described the process as composed of three major phases: intelligence, design, and choice. A fourth phase, implementation, was added later. A conceptual picture of Simon's modeling process is shown in Figure 15.2. The figure also shows what tasks are included in each phase. There is a continuous flow of information from intelligence to design to choice (bold lines), but at any phase there may be a return to a previous phase.

The decision-making process starts with the intelligence phase, where reality is examined and the problem is identified and defined. In the design phase, a model representing the system is constructed. This is done by making assumptions that simplify reality and by putting the relationships among all variables in writing. The model is then validated, and criteria are set for the evaluation of alternative courses of action that are also being identified. The choice phase involves identifying a proposed solution to the model (not to the problem that it represents). This solution is tested "on paper." Once the proposed solution seems to be reasonable, it is ready for the last phase—implementation. Successful implementation results in solving the original problem. Failure leads to a return to the modeling process.

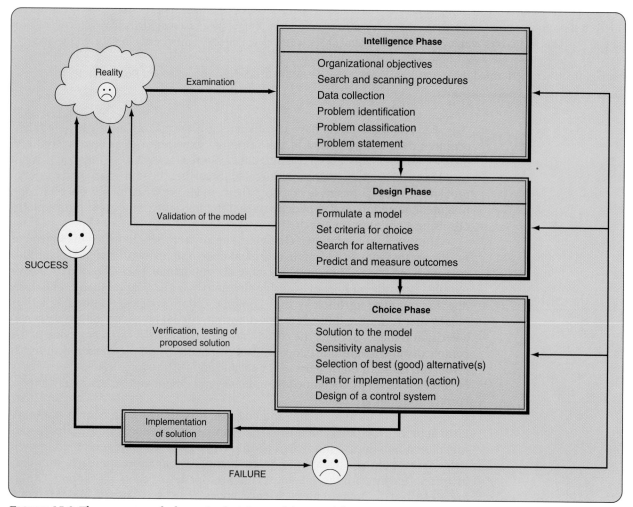

FIGURE 15.2 The process and phases in decision-making/modeling. (Source: Turban, 1993, p. 48.)

MODELS

A major characteristic of decision support systems is the inclusion of a modeling capability. A **model** is a simplified representation or abstraction of reality. It is usually simplified because reality is too complex to copy exactly, and because much of the complexity is actually irrelevant to the specific problem. The basic idea is to perform analysis on a *model* of reality rather than on reality itself. (For the benefits of modeling, see Box 15.2.)

A *Closer Look* BOX 15.2

THE BENEFITS OF MODELS

1. The cost of modeling is much lower than the cost of similar experimentation conducted with a real system.
2. Models enable compression of time. Years of operation can be simulated in minutes (or even seconds) of computer time.
3. Manipulation of the model (changing variables) is much easier than manipulation of a real system. Experimentation is therefore easier to conduct, and it does not interfere with the daily operation of the organization.
4. The cost of making mistakes during a trial-and-error experiment is much less when models are used rather than real systems.

5. Today's environment involves considerable uncertainty. The use of modeling allows a manager to calculate the risks involved in specific actions.
6. The use of mathematical models enables the analysis of a very large, sometimes infinite number of possible solutions. With today's advanced technology and communications, managers frequently have a large number of alternatives from which to choose.
7. Models enhance and reinforce learning and support training.

The representation of systems or problems through models can be done at various degrees of abstraction; therefore models are classified into four groups according to their degree of abstraction.

ICONIC (SCALE) MODELS. An iconic model—the least abstract model—is a physical replica of a system, usually based on a different scale from the original. Iconic models may appear to scale in three dimensions, such as models of an airplane, car, bridge, or production line. Photographs are another type of iconic model, but in only two dimensions. Object-oriented programming and graphical user interfaces are other examples of the use of iconic models.

ANALOG MODELS. An analog model, in contrast to an iconic model, does not look like the real system but behaves like it. These are usually two-dimensional charts or diagrams: that is, an analog model could be a physical model, but the shape of the model differs from that of the actual system. Some examples include organizational charts that depict structure, authority, and responsibility relationships; maps where different colors represent water or mountains; stock market charts; blueprints of a machine or a house; a speedometer; and a thermometer.

MATHEMATICAL (QUANTITATIVE) MODELS. The complexity of relationships in many organizational systems cannot be represented iconically or analogically, or such representations may be cumbersome and time consuming. Therefore, a more abstract model is used with the aid of mathematics. Most DSS analysis is executed numerically using mathematical or other quantitative models.

With recent advances in computer graphics, there is an increased tendency to use iconic and analog models to complement mathematical modeling in decision support systems. For example, visual simulation combines the three types of models.

MENTAL MODELS. In addition to the explicit models described earlier, people frequently use a behavioral mental model.

A **mental model** of a situation is an unworded description of how people think about a situation. The model includes the beliefs, assumptions, relationships, and flows of work as perceived by an individual. For example, a manager's mental model might say that it is better to promote older workers than younger ones and that such a policy would be preferred by most employees.

Mental models are a conceptual, internal representation used to generate descriptions of problem structure, and make predictions of future related variables. They determine the information we use and the manner in which people interpret (or ignore) information. Mental models are extremely important in environmental scanning where it is necessary to determine which information is important. Developing a mental model is usually the first step in modeling. Once people mentally perceive a situation, they may then model it more precisely using another model. Mental models are subjective and frequently change, so it is difficult to document them.

DECISION STYLES

The manner in which decision makers think and react to problems, the way they perceive information, their cognitive response, and their values and beliefs vary from individual to individual and from situation to situation. As a result, people make decisions differently. Although there is a general process of decision making, it is far from standardized. People do not follow the same steps in the same sequence. Furthermore, the emphasis, time allotment, and priorities given to each step vary significantly—not only from one person to another, but also from one situation to the next. The way in which managers make decisions and interact with other people describes their **decision style**. Because decision styles depend on factors described earlier, there are many decision styles. For example, Gordon et al. (1975) identified 40 processes while looking at nine types of decisions, and Mintzberg (1973) identified seven basic styles with many variations.

Two common styles are *analytic* and *heuristic*. People with analytic style employ a planned, sequential approach to decision making; learn by analyzing; place less emphasis on feedback; and use formal rational analysis. They also develop formal, often quantitative models of the situation and try to identify relationships (e.g., similarities) in making inferences.

People with heuristic style learn more by acting than by analyzing situations. They emphasize feedback and use extensive intuition, common sense, spontaneous action, and trial and error. They view the totality of a situation and look for highly visible situational differences when they make inferences.

In addition to analytic and heuristic styles, one can distinguish between *autocratic* and *democratic* styles. There is also the *consultative* style (with individuals or groups). Of course, many combinations and variations of styles exist. For further details on how decision styles relate to DSS and the support provided, see Wedley and Field (1984).

One interesting issue is how to determine a manager's decision style. Several methodologies and questionnaires were developed for this purpose. The Myers–Briggs questionnaire, which attempts to construct a profile of individuals, is one well-known example.

For a computerized system to successfully support a manager, it should fit the decision situation as well as the decision style. Therefore, the system should be flexible and adaptable to different users. Its capability to ask what-if and goal-seeking questions provides flexibility in this direction. Availability of graphics is also desirable in supporting certain decision styles. If an MSS is to support varying styles, skills, and knowledge, it should not attempt to enforce a specific process. Rather, the MSS should help decision makers use and develop their own styles, skills, and knowledge.

▶ 15.4 INFORMATION TECHNOLOGY SUPPORT FOR MANAGERS

In the previous sections we described managers and the tasks that they perform. Two major conclusions were reached. First, managers are executing many tasks; second, the most important task performed by managers is decision making.

In this section, we will attempt to answer four basic questions: (1) Why do managers need the support of information technology? (2) How are the information needs of managers determined? (3) Can one fully automate the manager's job? and (4) What IT aids are available to support managers? (See Box 15.3.)

WHY MANAGERS NEED THE SUPPORT OF INFORMATION TECHNOLOGY

The nature of the decision-making process presented earlier demonstrates the need for information. As a matter of fact, it is impossible to make decisions without information. Information is needed for every step in the decision-making process.

Making decisions while processing information manually is growing increasingly difficult due to the following trends.

▼ The number of alternatives to be considered is increasing, due to innovations in technology, improved communication, and the development of global markets.

▼ Many decisions must be made under time pressure. Frequently, it is not possible to manually process the needed information fast enough to be effective.

▼ Due to increased fluctuations and uncertainty in the decision environment, it is frequently necessary to conduct a sophisticated analysis to make a good decision. Such analysis usually requires the use of IT.

Managers spend a large portion of their time in communication. In some organizations, as much as 80 percent of a manager's time is spent communicating. As was shown in Chapter 14, IT can improve the quality of communication, expedite communication, and help facilitate communication with remote or isolated locations. Executive information systems, for example, can save managers as much as an hour per day on communication and can help in detecting problems and opportunities that otherwise would be missed.

HOW TO DETERMINE THE INFORMATION NEEDS OF MANAGERS

The key to the success of IT is its ability to provide users with the right information at the right time. Finding the information needs of managers is not a simple task. Over the years, there have been many attempts to determine the information needs of IT users. There are several methods for finding managers' information needs (see Box 15.4). Two systematic approaches used with EIS were developed by Wetherbe (1991) and by Watson and Frolick (1992).

IT At Work   BOX 15.3

A DSS FOR PRODUCTION PLANNING IN FINLAND

Dialogos-Team, a consulting company in Espoo, Finland, developed an innovative DSS for production planning (see figure).

Running on Windows, the user-friendly DSS creates a master scheduling plan, and optimizes customer service, inventory value, and production resources. All the data are gathered into the application, which enables the user to manipulate data with interactive graphics. The software enables various simulations. The nucleus of the DSS is the planning window which presents the results of the simulation. This product is used by many multinational corporations, such as by Nest Chemicals, which uses the DSS in Finland, Sweden, and Belgium.

Critical Thinking Issue: How can this DSS help in making decisions for a multinational corporation? ▲

SOURCE: Condensed from *Finnish Trade Review: Look at Finland*, March 1993, p. 9.

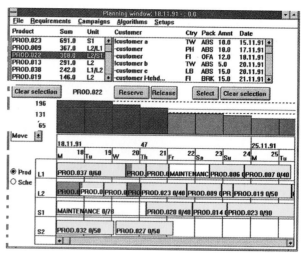

Planning window of the DSS developed by Dialogos-Team.

A Closer Look   BOX 15.4

HOW TO DETERMINE MANAGERS' INFORMATION NEEDS

1. Ask managers to describe the questions they would ask upon their return from a three-week vacation.
2. Use the critical success factors methodology.
3. Interview managers to determine what data they think are most important.
4. List major objectives in their short- and long-term plans, and identify their information requirements.
5. Ask the managers (and especially executives) what information they would least like for their competition to see.
6. Either through an interview or observation process, determine what information is actually used by managers.
7. Provide more immediate, on-line access to their current management reports, and then ask managers how you can better tailor the system to their needs. (Managers are much better at telling you what is wrong with what you have given them than telling you what they need.)
8. Use prototyping.

Wetherbe's approach (1991) consists of a two-phase process (see Figure 15.3). In Phase I, a *structured interview* is conducted to determine managers' perceived information needs. Wetherbe suggested using one of three methods for conducting the structured interviews: IBM's Business System Planning (BSP), critical success factors (CSF), or ends/means analysis (see Chapter 12 for details). In Phase II, a *prototype* of the information system is quickly constructed (in a few days or weeks). The prototype system is shown to the managers who then make suggestions for improvements. The system is modified, and again shown to the managers. Testing and modification go through several rounds until the detailed requirements are established. The *sources* of information are then identified, and the system can be developed.

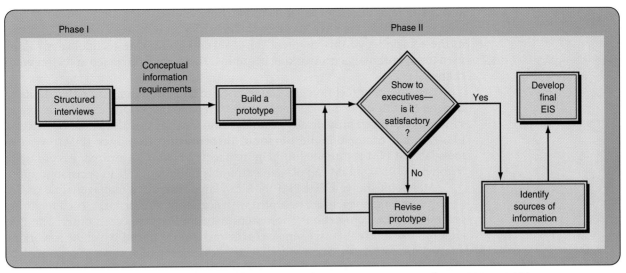

FIGURE 15.3 One approach to finding information needs for an EIS. (Source: Turban, 1993, p. 398.)

The Watson and Frolick approach (1992) is based on the following strategies for *determining* information requirements: *asking* (the interview approach), deriving the needs from an existing information system, *synthesizing* from characteristics of the systems, and *discovering* evolving systems (via prototyping).

CAN ONE FULLY AUTOMATE THE MANAGER'S JOB?

Earlier, we presented a generic decision-making process. Execution of this process involves specific tasks (such as forecasting and evaluating alternatives). The process can be fairly lengthy, which is bothersome for a busy manager. It is not surprising, therefore, that attempts have been made during recent decades to automate many of the steps in this process. Automation of certain steps can save time, increase consistency, and enable better decisions to be made (e.g., by generating and/or examining more alternatives). The more tasks one can automate in the process, the better. If the last statement is correct, one may ask a simple question. Is it possible to completely automate the manager's job? If we find the answer to be affirmative, then we face a second question. Should we do it?

A partial answer to the first question will be given in Section 15.5, where a framework for managerial decision support is presented. In general, it has been found that the job of middle managers is most likely to be automated. Managers at lower levels do not spend much time on decision making. Instead, they supervise, train, and motivate nonmanagers. Therefore, even if we completely automate their decisional role, we cannot automate their jobs. Mid-level managers make fairly routine decisions, and these can be automated. The job of top managers is the least routine and, therefore, the most difficult to automate.

WHAT IT TECHNOLOGIES ARE AVAILABLE TO SUPPORT MANAGERS?

Three major IT technologies have been successfully used to support managers. Collectively, they are referred to as **management support systems** (MSS). First, DSSs have been in use since the mid-seventies, primarily to support analytical, quantitative types of work. Second, EIS is a technology developed in the mid-eighties, mainly to support the informational roles of executives. Lately, the scope and clientele of EIS have expanded to include analysis and communication, and all levels of managers have access to the EIS. DSS and EIS are discussed, in detail, in the remainder of this chapter. Third, several groupware technologies can be used to support managers working in groups. These were discussed in the previous chapter.

Several other technologies can be used to support managers, either alone or integrated with other management support technologies. One example is expert systems, which can provide advice on decision making and also enhance DSS and EIS. Another example is the **personal information manager** (PIM). A set of tools labeled PIM is intended to help managers be more organized. According to Manheim (1989), a PIM can play an extremely important role in decision support.

Manheim showed that PIM tools can support several managerial tasks. For example, most managers are occupied with dozens of routine tasks, each requiring several steps for completion. These steps may conflict with each other. The PIM attempts to capture the user's image of the task (problem) on which he is working on a continuous basis. It provides facilities through which the user can analyze this image and operate on it in ways that will increase his effectiveness. Another example described by Manheim is the support of strategic management, basically as a tool for problem identification.

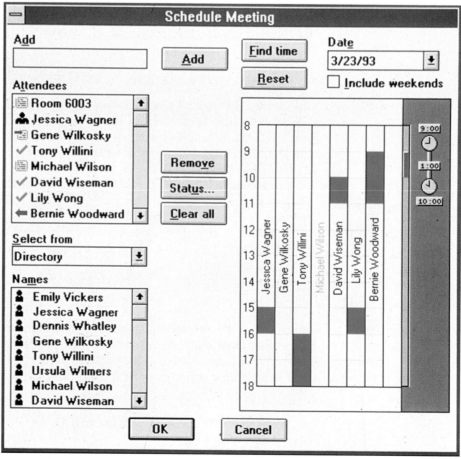

FIGURE 15.4 Lotus's Organizer helps in daily planning. It links related tasks, names, and phone numbers. It includes a to-do list, calendar, address book, note pad, and anniversary reminder. It sounds an alarm to remind you to go to a meeting. Using electronic mail (cc:Mail), invitations to meetings can be sent. Invitees can accept, decline, or delegate to someone else—with a single mouse click.

Representative PIM software includes Agenda and Organizer (from Lotus Development Corporation) and Grand View (from Symantec Corporation). Organizer (see Figure 15.4) is used as a personal assistant to the manager.

▶ 15.5 A FRAMEWORK FOR COMPUTERIZED DECISION SUPPORT

Before describing DSS and EIS, it will be useful to present a classical framework for decision support which was proposed by Gorry and Scott Morton (1971), based on the combined work of Simon (1977, originally 1957) and Anthony (1965). The details are as follows.

The first half of the framework is based on Simon's idea that decision-making processes fall along a continuum that ranges from highly structured (sometimes referred to as *programmed*) to highly unstructured (*nonprogrammed*) decisions. **Structured** processes refer to routine and repetitive problems for which standard solutions exist. **Unstructured** processes are "fuzzy," complex problems for which there are no cut-and-dried solutions.

An *unstructured problem* is one in which none of the three phases—intelligence, design, or choice—is structured. Decisions where some, but not all, of the phases are structured are referred to as **semistructured** by Gorry and Scott Morton. In structured decisions, all phases are structured.

In a structured problem, the procedures for obtaining the best (or good enough) solution are known. Whether the problem involves finding an appropriate inventory level or deciding on an optimal investment strategy, the objectives are clearly defined. Frequent objectives are cost minimization and profit maximization. The manager can use computerized clerical assistance, data processing, or management science models to support structured decisions. In an unstructured problem, human intuition is frequently the basis for decision making. Typical unstructured problems include planning new services to be offered, hiring an executive, or choosing a set of research and development projects for the next year. Semistructured problems fall between the structured and unstructured, involving a combination of both standard solution procedures and individual judgment. Keen and Scott Morton (1978) give the following examples of semistructured problems: trading bonds, setting marketing budgets for consumer products, and performing capital acquisition analysis. Here, a DSS can improve the quality of the information on which the decision is based (and consequently the quality of the decision) by providing not only a single solution but a range of alternatives. These capabilities, which will be described later, allow managers to better understand the nature of problems so they can make better decisions.

The second half of the framework is based upon Anthony's taxonomy (1965), which defines three broad categories that encompass all managerial activities: (1) *strategic planning*—the long-range goals and policies for resource allocation; (2) *management control*—the acquisition and efficient utilization of resources in the accomplishment of organizational goals; and (3) *operational control*—the efficient and effective execution of specific tasks.

Anthony's and Simon's taxonomies are combined in a nine-cell decision support framework (see Figure 15.5). The right-hand column and the bottom row indicate technologies needed to support the various decisions. Gorry and Scott Morton suggested, for example, that for the semistructured and unstructured decisions, conventional MIS, and management science approaches are insufficient. Therefore, they proposed the use of a DSS.

The structured and operational control-oriented tasks (cells 1, 2, and 4) are being performed by low-level managers, whereas tasks in cells 6, 8, and 9 are the responsibility of top executives. This means that DSS, EIS, expert systems, and neural net computing are often applicable for top executives and professionals tackling specialized, complex problems.

COMPUTER SUPPORT FOR STRUCTURED DECISIONS

Structured and some semistructured decisions, especially of the operational and managerial control type, have been supported by computers since the 1950s. Decisions of this type are being made in all functional areas, especially finance and operations management.

Problems that are encountered fairly often have a high level of structure. It is therefore possible to abstract, analyze, and classify them into standard classes. For example, a "make-or-buy" decision belongs to this category. Other examples are capital budgeting (e.g., replacement of equipment), allocation of resources, distribution of merchandise, and inventory control. For each standard class, a prescribed solution was developed through the use of mathematical formulas. This approach is called management science/operations research and is also executed with the aid of computers (see Turban and Meredith [1994]).

The management science approach adopts the view that managers can follow a fairly systematic process for solving problems. Therefore, it is possible to use a scientific approach to managerial decision making. This approach, which also centers around modeling, involves the following steps:

1. *Defining* the problem (a decision situation which may deal with a setback or with an opportunity).
2. *Classifying* the problem into a standard category.
3. *Constructing* a mathematical model that describes the real-life problem. (See Box 15.5.)
4. *Finding* potential solutions to the modeled problem and evaluating them.
5. *Choosing* and recommending a solution to the problem.

Type of Decision	Type of Control			Support Needed
	Operational Control	Managerial Control	Strategic Planning	
Structured	Accounts receivable, order entry [1]	Budget analysis, short-term forecasting, personnel reports, make-or-buy analysis [2]	Financial management (investment), warehouse location, distribution systems [3]	MIS, Management science models, Transaction processing
Semistructured	Production scheduling, inventory control [4]	Credit evaluation, budget preparation, plant layout, project scheduling, reward systems design [5]	Building new plant, mergers and acquisitions, new product planning, compensation planning, quality assurance planning [6]	DSS
Unstructured	Selecting a cover for a magazine, buying software, approving loans [7]	Negotiating, recruiting an executive, buying hardware, lobbying [8]	R & D planning, new technology development, social responsibility planning [9]	DSS ES Neural Networks
Support Needed	MIS, Management science	Management science, DSS, EIS, ES	EIS, ES, Neural Networks	

FIGURE 15.5 Decision support framework. Technology is used to support the decisions shown in column at the far right and in the bottom row.

A Closer Look BOX 15.5

ABOUT MODELING AND MODELS

All models are comprised of three basic components: decision variables, uncontrollable variables (and/or parameters), and result (outcome) variables (see figure below). These components are connected by mathematical relationships. In a nonquantitative model, the relationships are symbolic or qualitative.

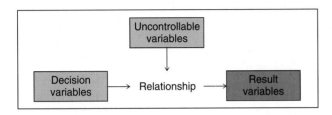

The results (or outcome) of decisions are determined by (1) the decision being made; (2) other factors that are uncontrollable by the decision maker; and (3) by the relationships among variables.

RESULT VARIABLES. These variables reflect the level of effectiveness of the system; that is, they indicate how well the system performs or attains its goals. The result variables are considered, mathematically, to be *dependent variables*.

DECISION VARIABLES. Decision variables describe the alternative courses of action. For example, in an investment problem, investing in bonds is a decision variable. In a scheduling problem, the decision variables are people and jobs. The values of these variables are determined by the decision maker. Decision variables are classified mathematically as *independent variables* (or unknown variables). An aim of DSS is to find good enough, or possibly the best, values for these decision variables.

UNCONTROLLABLE VARIABLES OR PARAMETERS. In any decision situation there are factors that affect the result variables but *are not under the control* of the

decision maker. These factors can be either fixed, and then they are called parameters, or they can vary, and then they are called variables. Examples are the prime interest rate, a city's building code, tax regulations, and prices of utilities. Most of these factors are uncontrollable because they emanate from the environment surrounding the decision maker. These variables are also classified as *independent variables* since they affect the dependent (result) variables.

INTERMEDIATE VARIABLES. Intermediate variables are any variables necessary to link the decision variables to the results. Sometimes they reflect intermediate outcomes. For example, in determining machine scheduling, spoilage is an intermediate variable while total profit is the result variable (spoilage affects the total profit).

The components of a quantitative model are tied together by sets of mathematical expressions such as equations or inequalities.

EXAMPLE: A simple financial-type model may look like this: $P = R - C$, where P stands for profit, R stands for revenue, and C stands for cost. Another well-known financial-type model is a present-value model, which may look like this:

$$P = \frac{F}{(1 + i)^n}$$

where:

P = the present value
F = a future single payment in dollars
i = interest rate
n = number of years

Using this model, one can find, for example, the present value of a payment of $100,000, to be made five years from today, considering 10 percent interest rate, to be:

$$P = \frac{100,000}{(1.1)^5} = \$62,110$$

MANAGEMENT SCIENCE

Modeling involves the transformation of a real-world problem into a standard structure. A list of representative, structured **management science** problems and tools is given in Box 15.6. Software packages for such models are available in computer stores. Using the software, it is possible to solve such problems very quickly.

Managerial problems that are not structured cannot be solved by standard models. These are usually the more difficult and important problems (of the managerial control and strategic planning nature). Such problems require the use of a DSS.

A Closer Look BOX 15.6

REPRESENTATIVE STRUCTURED MANAGEMENT SCIENCE PROBLEMS AND TOOLS

Problem	Tool
Allocation of resources	Linear, nonlinear programming
Project management	PERT, CPM
Inventory control	Inventory management models
Forecasting results	Forecasting models, regression analysis
Managing waiting lines	Queuing theory, simulation
Transporting and distributing goods	Transportation models
Matching items to each other	Assignment models
Predicting market share and other dynamically oriented situations	Markov chain analysis, dynamic programming, simulation

15.6 DECISION SUPPORT SYSTEMS—AN OVERVIEW

The concepts involved in **decision support systems** (DSS) were first articulated in the early 1970s by Scott Morton under the term *management decision systems*. He defined such systems as "interactive computer-based systems, which help decision makers utilize *data* and *models* to solve unstructured problems" (1971). It should be noted that DSS, like MIS and other MSS technologies, is a content-free expression (i.e., it means different things to different people). Therefore, there is no universally accepted definition of DSS. It can be viewed as an approach or a philosophy rather than a precise methodology. However, a DSS has certain recognized characteristics that will be presented later.

Now, let us examine a typical case of a successfully implemented DSS, as shown in Box 15.7.

The case demonstrates some of the major characteristics of a DSS. The risk analysis performed first was based on the decision maker's initial definition of the situation, using a management science approach. Then the executive vice president, using his experience, judgment, and intuition, felt that the model should be modified. The initial model, although mathematically correct, was incomplete. With a regular simulation system, a modification would have taken a long time, but the DSS provided a very quick analysis. Furthermore, the DSS was flexible and responsive enough to allow managerial intuition and judgment to be incorporated into the analysis.

How can such a thorough risk analysis be performed so quickly? How can the judgment factors be elicited, quantified, and worked into the model? How can the results be presented meaningfully and convincingly to the executive? What is meant by "what-if" questions? Answers will be provided in the forthcoming sections.

First, let us review some reasons for the increased use of DSS. Firestone Tire and Rubber Company explained its reasons for implementing DSSs as follows:

1. The company was operating in an unstable economy.
2. The company was faced with increasing foreign and domestic competition.
3. The company encountered increasing difficulty in tracking numerous business operations.

IT At Work BOX 15.7

THE HOUSTON MINERALS CASE

Houston Minerals Corporation was interested in a proposed joint venture with a petrochemicals company to develop a chemical plant. Houston's executive vice president responsible for the decision wanted analysis of the risks involved in areas of supplies, demands, and prices. Bob Sampson, manager of planning and administration, and his staff built a DSS in a few days by means of a specialized planning language. The results strongly suggested that the project should be accepted.

Then came the real test. Although the executive vice president accepted the validity and value of the results, he was worried about the potential downside risk of the project, the chance of a catastrophic outcome. Sampson explains that the executive vice president said something like this:

I realize the amount of work you have already done, and I am 99 percent confident with it. But, I would like to see

this in a different light. I know we are short of time and we have to get back to our partners with our yes or no decision.

Sampson replied that the executive could have the risk analysis he needed in less than one hour. "Within 20 minutes, there in the executive boardroom, we were reviewing the results of his "what-if" questions. Those results led to the eventual dismissal of the project, which we otherwise would probably have accepted."

Critical Thinking Issue: Why do you think that the "what-if" analysis reversed the initial decision? ▲

SOURCE: Based on material provided by Comshare Corp.

4. The company's existing computer system did not support the objectives of increasing efficiency, profitability, and entry into profitable markets.

5. The data processing department could not begin to address the diversity of the company's needs or management's ad hoc inquiries, and business analysis functions were not inherent within the existing systems.

In Firestone's case, the existing information systems were not sufficient to support the company's critical response activities, described in Chapter 1. However, there are also other reasons why companies are using DSSs (see Table 15.2).

A DSS can provide a competitive advantage to companies. For example, American Airlines is using a DSS to increase productivity, reduce maintenance costs, and improve revenues (see Box 15.8).

Another reason for the development of DSSs is the end-user computing movement. End users are not programmers and therefore they require easy-to-use construction tools and procedures. These are provided by DSSs.

A DSS can support individuals, but it can also support groups. Since many major decisions in organizations are group decisions, it only makes sense to try

Table 15.2 The Justification for DSS

Factors	Cited by (%)
Accurate information is needed.	67
DSS is viewed as an organizational winner.	44
New information is needed.	33
Management mandated the DSS.	22
Timely information is provided.	17
Cost reduction is achieved.	6

SOURCE: Compiled from Hogue and Watson (1985).

IT At Work BOX 15.8

A DSS FOR IMPROVING PRODUCTIVITY AND PROFITABILITY

The airline industry is one of the most competitive businesses. Global competition, high investment, regulation by various countries, and price wars are causing profits to dwindle and forcing some airlines out of business. Being a large airline does not necessarily provide advantages, especially where maintenance is concerned. American Airlines has 10 different fleet types (as compared to one in Southwest Airlines). Each aircraft goes through 30 different maintenance checkups. Some checkups involve overhaul checks and rebuilding, which are lengthy and expensive (up to $1 million). Every day that an aircraft is not in service costs the airline additional money (lost revenue). For American Airlines, maintenance scheduling of 600 airplanes is a nightmare.

Starting with a five-year plan for major overhauls, planning is becoming a critical activity. The planning process is complex because of limited maintenance facilities and resources (e.g., hangars, equipment), government safety requirements, and delays in arrival to the maintenance shops (e.g., due to weather condition). The DSS takes all of the above factors into consideration. It allows the user to generate a maintenance plan and perform various "what-if" analyses. Once a plan is selected, it is subject to continuous changes, since planners need to react quickly to the rapidly changing maintenance-planning environment. The DSS includes many models, ranging from standard linear programming optimization to complex mathematical programming and simulation.

Utilization of the DSS helped American Airlines to: 1) improve productivity, 2) reduce (and avoid) maintenance costs by as much as $454 million over the active life of just the 227 wide-body aircrafts, and 3) generate revenues by reducing the time that airplanes are not flying.

A five-year plan, which took weeks to generate manually, takes 1 to 10 minutes with the DSS (each type of aircraft has its own plan, and each plan includes the resource utilization as well).

Critical Thinking Issues: Without the DSS, would American Airlines have been able to grow or compete? What could happen as a result of poor planning? ▲

SOURCE: Based on Gray, D. A., "Airworthy-Decision Support for Aircraft Overhaul Maintenance Planning," *OR/MS Today*, December 1992.

---

and make such decisions more effective. As discussed in the previous chapter, the technologies of group support system (GSS) can be utilized to improve the *communication* and *process* of people working together. One aspect of a GSS is a group decision support system (GDSS), where computerized support is aimed at supporting a group assembled to make a specific decision, usually in a specially designed decision room. This topic was discussed in Chapter 14, Section 14.9.

 ## 15.7 CHARACTERISTICS AND CAPABILITIES OF DSS

Because there is no consensus on what constitutes a DSS, there is obviously no agreement on the characteristics and capabilities of DSS. The following is as an ideal set. Most DSSs have only some of the following attributes.

1. A DSS provides support for decision makers, mainly in semistructured and unstructured situations, by bringing together human judgment and computerized information. Such problems cannot be solved (or cannot be solved conveniently) by other computerized systems or by management science.

2. Support is provided for various managerial levels, both to individuals and groups, ranging from top executives to line managers.

3. A DSS provides support to several interdependent and/or sequential decisions. This is important because many decisions are interrelated.

4. A DSS supports all phases of the decision-making process—intelligence, design, choice, and implementation—as well as a variety of decision-making processes and styles. This is a powerful capability, making the DSS very useful.

5. A DSS is adaptive over time. The decision maker should be reactive when using the DSS, able to easily confront changing conditions quickly, and adapt the DSS to meet changes. In semistructured and unstructured problems, changes can occur very rapidly.

6. A DSS is easy to construct (even by end users) and use. User-friendliness, flexibility, strong graphic capabilities, and a dialogue language that resembles English can greatly increase the usability of DSS.

7. A DSS promotes learning, which leads to new demands and refinement of the system, which leads to additional learning, and so forth. There is a continuous process of developing and improving the DSS.

8. A DSS usually utilizes models (standard, and/or custom made). The modeling capability enables experimenting with different strategies under different configurations. Such experimentation can provide new insights and learning.

9. Advanced DSSs are equipped with a knowledge component that enables the efficient and effective solution of very difficult problems.

10. A DSS includes easy execution of sensitivity analysis. Such analysis can increase the confidence of the decision maker in the modeling and the DSS. Most DSSs include a "what if" sensitivity analysis; some also include "goal seeking." These are discussed next.

SENSITIVITY ANALYSIS: "WHAT-IF" AND GOAL SEEKING

Sensitivity analysis refers to the study of the impact that changes in one (or more) parts of a model have on other parts. Usually, we check the impact that changes in input variables have on output variables. Sensitivity analysis attempts to help managers when they are not certain about the accuracy or relative importance of information.

The topic of sensitivity analysis is extremely important in DSS because (1) it enables flexibility and adaptation to changing conditions and to requirements of different decision-making situations, and (2) it provides a better understanding of the model and the problem it purports to describe. It may increase the confidence of the users in the model, especially when the model is not so sensitive to changes. Two popular types of sensitivity analysis are *"what-if"* and *goal seeking.*

"WHAT-IF" ANALYSIS. A model builder makes predictions and assumptions regarding the input data, many of which deal with assessment of uncertain futures. When the model is solved, the results depend on these data. **"What-if" analysis** attempts to check the impact of a change in the input data on the proposed solution. For example, *what* will happen to the total inventory cost *if* the cost of carrying inventories increases by 10 percent? Or, *what* will be the market share *if* the advertising budget increases by 5 percent?

Assuming the appropriate user interface, managers can easily ask the computer these types of questions. Furthermore, they can repeat the questions and change the percentages or any other data in the question.

GOAL SEEKING. **Goal-seeking analysis** attempts to find the value of the inputs necessary to achieve a desired level of output. It represents a "backward" solution approach. For example, let us say that an initial analysis yielded a profit of $2 million. Management wants to know what sales volume would be necessary to generate a profit of $2.2 million.

A computer printout of goal-seeking dialogues is shown in Figure 15.6. The user wants to determine the per-unit selling price necessary to achieve a net gain (before tax) of $130,000 for each of the subsequent years in a multiyear income

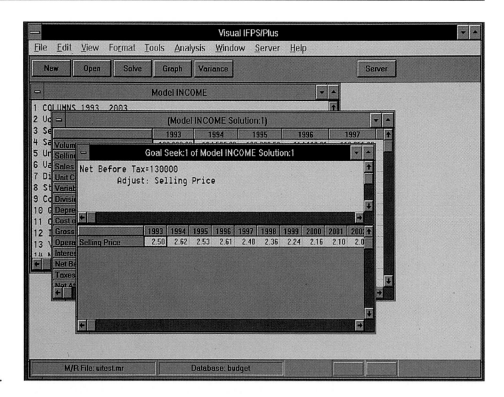

FIGURE 15.6 Goal-seeking dialogue conducted with IFPS Plus software.

model. The computer calculates the necessary price (per unit) for each of the years in a planning document. The program allows the user to find the values of several variables to be adjusted when several goals are involved.

▶ 15.8   THE STRUCTURE, COMPONENTS, AND DEVELOPMENT OF A DSS

A DSS is composed of several components as illustrated in Figure 15.7. Every DSS consists of at least the data management, user interface, and model management components. A few advanced DSSs also contain a knowledge management component.

1. ***Data management.*** Data management includes the *database(s)*, which contains relevant data for the situation, managed by a *database management system* (DBMS).

2. ***User interface (or human–machine communication) subsystem.*** The user can communicate with and command the DSS through this subsystem.

3. ***Model management.*** This includes a software package with financial, statistical, management science, or other quantitative models that provide the system's analytical capabilities and an appropriate software management package to manage the models.

4. ***Knowledge management.*** This subsystem can support any of the other subsystems or act as an independent component, providing knowledge for the solution of the specific problem. This component is available in only a few DSSs.

These components constitute the software portion of the DSS. They are housed in a computer and can be facilitated by additional hardware and software pieces. Finally, the user is considered to be a part of the system. Researchers assert that some of the unique contributions of DSSs are derived from the interaction between the computer and the decision maker (user).

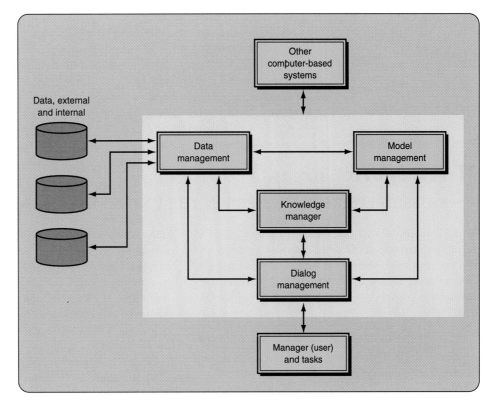

FIGURE 15.7 Conceptual model of a DSS shows four main software components facilitated by other parts of the system. (Source: Turban, 1993, p. 91.)

DATA MANAGEMENT SUBSYSTEM

The data management subsystem is similar to any other data management system. The necessary data flow from several sources and are extracted prior to their entry to the DSS database. In some DSS, there is no separate DSS database, and data are entered into the DSS as needed.

MODEL MANAGEMENT SUBSYSTEM

The model management subsystem of the DSS has several elements: model base; model base management system; modeling language; model directory; and model execution, integration, and command.

The *model base* contains all the models and the models' building blocks that are used to develop applications or run the system. The role of the **model base management system** (**MBMS**, see Box 15.9) is analogous to that of a DBMS.

A Closer Look BOX 15.9

MAJOR FUNCTIONS (OR CAPABILITIES) OF THE MBMS

▼ Creates models easily and quickly, either from scratch, existing models, or the building blocks.

▼ Allows users to manipulate models so that they can conduct experiments and sensitivity analyses, ranging from "what-if" to goal-seeking analysis.

▼ Stores and manages a wide variety of different types of models in a logical and integrated manner.

▼ Accesses and integrates the model building blocks.

▼ Catalogs and displays the directory of models.

▼ Tracks models, data, and application usage.

▼ Interrelates models with appropriate linkages through the database.

▼ Manages and maintains the model base with management functions analogous to database management: store, access, run, update, link, catalog, and query.

Modeling languages are used to write (to program) specific models, while a *model directory* lists all the models stored in the model base. Finally, *model execution, integration and command* is a program that helps in executing these activities.

The model base may contain standard models (such as financial or management science) and customized models. Many DSS are integrated with management science and other modeling systems. Such integration both enhances data management and allows the incorporation of judgment (see Box 15.10).

IT At Work BOX 15.10

 **G**LOBAL PERSPECTIVE

A DSS HELPS RESEARCHERS IN THE UNITED KINGDOM

ICI Pharmaceutical, a U.K.-based firm, uses a DSS to support strategic decision making in a research and development environment. It also helps managers to form and communicate perceptions, and to manage organizational change. The decisions supported by the DSS are:

▼ Selecting an appropriate portfolio of research projects.

▼ Monitoring project development and changing allocation of resources when needed.

▼ Making the appropriate evaluations of progress.

Prior to the use of the DSS, the company used a combination of management science models (e.g., linear programming), cost–benefit analysis, and internal consultants, to manage their R&D portfolio. The main problem with this approach was the inability to incorporate the large amount of data into an integrated decision. The

DSS, which complements existing models, overcomes the data problem and, in addition, provides a computer-supported judgmental model that allows deeper analysis. In addition, the DSS facilitates the process of quantifying individual preferences and gives scope to an easy exchange and comparison of information. The DSS also helps in building a sense of teamwork. One of the models used is that of the Analytical Hierarchy Process (see Saaty [1990]). The DSS also uses several other quantitative tools, including probability time curves. The incorporation of several simple judgment models makes the DSS most effective.

Critical Thinking Issues: How can one DSS incorporate several models and a large amount of data into an integrated system? How can sensitivity analysis incorporate judgment? ▲

SOURCE: Condensed from Islei et al. (1991).

KNOWLEDGE MANAGEMENT SUBSYSTEM

Many unstructured and semistructured problems are so complex that they require expertise in addition to the regular DSS capabilities for their solutions. Such expertise can be provided by an expert system. Therefore, the more advanced DSSs are equipped with a component called *knowledge management*. Such a component can provide the required expertise for solving some aspects of the problem and/or provide knowledge that can enhance the operation of the other DSS components.

EMERGING TECHNOLOGY

...expert systems help in making smarter decisions

The knowledge management component is composed of one or more expert systems. Like data and model management, knowledge management software provides the necessary execution and integration of the expert system. The capabilities of this component are discussed in Chapter 16.

Decision support systems that include such a component are referred to as an intelligent DSS, a DSS/ES, or a knowledge-based DSS.

COMMUNICATION MANAGEMENT SUBSYSTEM: THE USER INTERFACE

The communication component of a DSS is the software and hardware that provide the user interface for DSS. The term *user interface* covers all aspects of the communications between a user and the DSS. Some DSS experts feel that user interface is the most important component because much of the power, flexibility, and ease-of-use characteristics of DSS are derived from this component. One of the major reasons why managers have not used computers and quantitative analyses to the extent that these technologies have been available is an inconvenient user interface.

The communication subsystem is managed by software called **user interface management system** which was described in Chapter 7.

THE USER

The person faced with the problem or decision that the DSS is designed to support is referred to as the *user*, the *manager*, or the *decision maker*. These terms fail to reflect, however, the heterogeneity that exists among users and usage patterns of DSS (see Box 15.11). There are differences in the positions users hold, the way in which a final decision is reached, the users' cognitive preferences and abilities, and ways of arriving at a decision (decision styles).

A DSS has two broad classes of users: managers and staff specialists (like financial analysts, production planners, and market researchers).

A Closer Look BOX 15.11

WHO USES DSS?

Decision makers can use DSS in two ways. In a *terminal mode*, the decision maker is the direct user of the system. In an *intermediary mode*, the decision maker uses the system through intermediaries, who perform the analysis and interpret and report the results. The decision maker does not need to know how the intermediary used the system to arrive at the requested information.

The use of an intermediary allows the manager to benefit from the DSS without actually having to use the keyboard. Some managers resist using the keyboard, and until speech recognition devices become economical, there will continue to be some resistance to the terminal mode.

There are three types of intermediaries that reflect different types of support for the manager.

  1. *Staff assistant.* This person has specialized knowl-

edge about management problems and some experience with decision-support technology.

  2. *Expert tool user.* This person is skilled in the application of one or more types of specialized problem-solving tools. The expert tool user performs tasks for which the problem solver does not have the necessary skills or training.

  3. *Business (system) analyst.* This person has a general knowledge of the application area, formal business administration education (not computer science), and considerable skill in DSS construction tools.

Another type of intermediary is the *facilitator* in a group DSS (see Chapter 14).

SOURCE: Based on Alter, 1980, p. 115.

BUILDING A DSS AND TECHNOLOGY LEVELS

The development process of DSS is similar to the development of any other application, except that the process involves *prototyping*. In DSS terminology, this is described as an **iterative approach**, which involves a series of short construction steps with immediate feedback from users on issues ranging from the correct information needs to the way the output is to be presented. The iterative approach, according to Courbon et al. (1980), involves four activities:

  1. *Select an important subproblem.* The user and the builder jointly identify a subproblem for which the initial DSS is constructed. The subproblem should be small enough so that the nature of the problem, the need for computer-based support, and the nature of that support are clear.

2. *Develop a small but usable system to assist the decision maker.* No major system analysis or feasibility analysis is involved. The system should, out of necessity, be simple.

3. *Evaluate the system and improve it; then evaluate it again.* At the end of each cycle, the system is evaluated by the user and the builder. The evaluation mechanism is what keeps the cost and effort of developing a DSS consistent with its value.

4. *Refine, expand, and modify the system in cycles.* Subsequent cycles expand and improve the original version of the DSS. All the analysis-design-construction-implementation-evaluation steps are repeated in each successive refinement.

This process is repeated several times until a relatively stable and comprehensive system evolves. The interaction between the user, the builder, and the technology is extremely important in this process. Note that user involvement is very high. There is a balance of effort and cooperation between the user and the builder: the user takes the lead in utilization and evaluation activities, while the builder is stronger in design and implementation phases. The user plays a joint and active role, in contrast to conventional system development where the user frequently operates in a reactive or passive role.

There is also a disadvantage to this iterative process. When such an approach is used, the gains obtained from cautiously stepping through each of the system's life-cycle stages might be lost. These gains include a thorough understanding of the information system's benefits and costs, a detailed description of the business's information needs, an information system design that is easy to maintain, a well-tested information system, and a well-prepared group of users.

TECHNOLOGY LEVELS

A useful framework for understanding DSS construction issues was devised by Sprague and Carlson (1982), who identified three **technology levels of DSS**: specific DSS, DSS generators, and DSS tools (see Figure 15.8).

1. *Specific DSS.* The "final product," or the DSS application that actually accomplishes the work, is called a **specific DSS**. For example, the Houston Minerals case presented earlier used a specific DSS for analyzing a joint venture.

2. *DSS generators (or engines).* A **DSS generator** is an integrated package of software that provides a set of capabilities to build a specific DSS quickly, inexpensively, and easily. A popular microcomputer-based generator is Lotus 1-2-3. A generator possesses diverse capabilities—ranging from modeling,

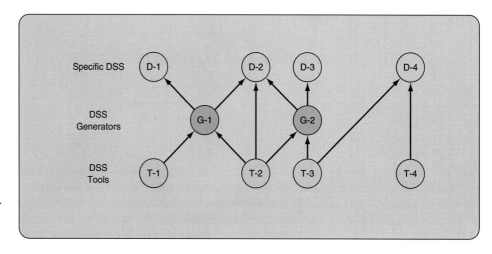

FIGURE 15.8 The three levels of DSS technology provide a framework for constructing DSS applications. (Source: Turban, 1993, p. 115.)

report generation, and graphical display to performing sensitivity analysis and risk analysis. These capabilities, which have been available separately for some time, are integrated into an easy-to-use package. Most end-user-developed DSS are constructed with DSS generators. Some well-known generators are Express, Excel, Focus, QuattroPro, and IFPS Plus. Some generators are designed for specific DSS categories, such as financial and manufacturing.

3. *DSS tools.* At the lowest level of DSS technology are the software utilities or tools. These elements facilitate the development of either a DSS generator or a specific DSS. Examples of **DSS tools** are programming languages, graphics, editors, query systems, random number generators, and spreadsheets.

The use of DSS generators is extremely helpful in constructing specific DSS and enabling them to quickly adapt to changes. Using generators can save a significant amount of time and money, thus making a DSS financially feasible. Constructing DSS only with tools, without generators, can be a very lengthy and expensive proposition, especially if the tools themselves need to be developed.

▶ 15.9   ORGANIZATIONAL DECISION SUPPORT SYSTEMS

Some decision support systems provide support throughout large and complex organizations (e.g., see Box 15.12). The major benefit of such systems is that many organizational members become familiar with computers, analytical techniques, and DSS.

IT At Work   BOX 15.12

GLOBAL PERSPECTIVE

A DSS IN THE EGYPTIAN CABINET

The Egyptian cabinet is the highest executive body in Egypt. It is composed of thirty-two ministries, each responsible for one department (e.g., labor, energy, education). The cabinet is headed by the prime minister and, as a body, deals with country-wide policies and strategic issues. The cabinet also includes four ministerial committees assisted by staff. The cabinet makes extremely important decisions (see the process in the diagram on the next page) in areas ranging from economic infrastructure to education. Most difficult are the decisions regarding allocation of scarce resources. Many of the issues are complex and require considerable preparation and analysis. Furthermore, due to conflicting interests, there are frequent disagreements among the ministries.

The cabinet must work with the parliament and many governmental agencies. There are also links between the cabinet and external agencies, ranging from universities to international bodies. It makes sense to support decision making in the Egyptian cabinet with some computer-based information system, but it is difficult to do. The reason is that many decisions are made by groups, the composition of the decision makers is frequently changing, decisions are made at various locations, and the participants use different methodologies and styles.

THE CABINET INFORMATION AND DECISION SUPPORT CENTER (IDSC). To properly support the information needs of the cabinet, a special center was created. The IDSC was guided by three strategic objectives:

1. Develop information and support systems for the cabinet.

2. Support the establishment of end-user managed information and decision support centers in the thirty-two ministries.

3. Encourage, support, and initiate IS projects that would accelerate the development of Egyptian governmental ministries and agencies.

To achieve these objectives, a tri-level architecture was conceived, including the IDSC level, the national level, and the international level. Obviously, extensive national and international telecommunication support is required for such a system. The center started in 1985 and grew to about 200 employees by 1989. Dozens of specific DSS applications were constructed, both for ad hoc and repetitive decisions; several of them were highly interrelated. Examples of specific DSS are the following:

1. ***Customs tariff policy formulation DSS.*** This system involved six ministries, so coordination was difficult and diversity of opinions played a major role in many decisions. The DSS helped to achieve consistent tariff structure and increased government revenue (yet minimized the burden on low income families).

2. ***Debt management DSS.*** Egypt relies on foreign debt (about 5,000 loans valued at $40 billion in the early 1990s). The purpose of the DSS was to manage this debt. This included, for example, how best to

schedule payments, decide on appropriate refinancing, and simulate how the debt is going to look in the future.

Critical Thinking Issues: Why are there several specific DSSs in an organizational DSS? How does this ODSS relate to GDSS? ▲

SOURCE: H. El Sherif and O. A. Sawy, "Issue-Based Decision Support Systems for the Egyptian Cabinet." Reprinted by permission from the *MIS Quarterly*, Volume 12, Number 4, December 1988. Copyright 1988 by the Society for Information Management and the Management Information Systems Research Center at the University of Minnesota.

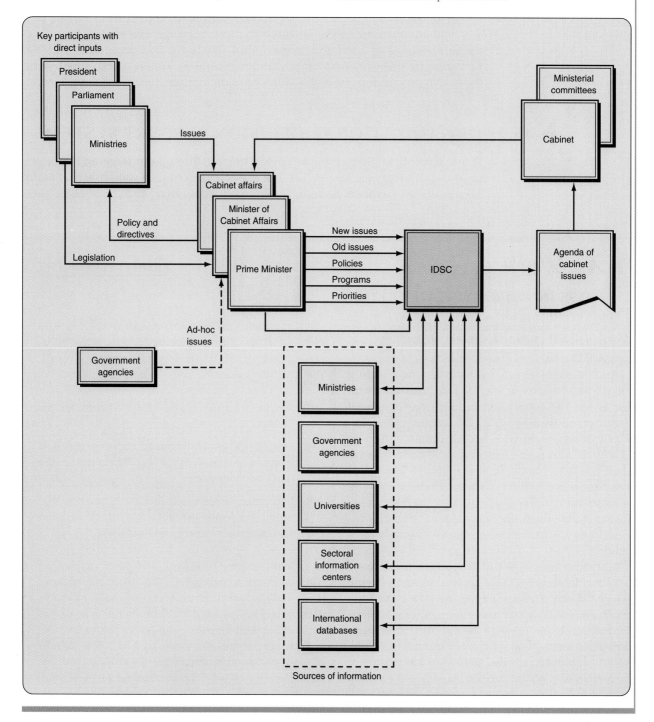

The **organizational decision support system (ODSS)** was first defined by Hackathorn and Keen (1981), who distinguished between three levels of decision support: individual, group, and organization. They maintained that computer-based systems can be developed to provide decision support for each of these levels. They perceived an ODSS as one that focuses on an organizational task or activity involving a sequence of operations and actors (e.g., developing a divisional marketing plan, capital budgeting). Furthermore, they said that each individual's activities must mesh closely with other people's work. The computer support was seen primarily as a vehicle for improving communication and coordination, in addition to that of problem solving.

George (1990) summarized the following common characteristics of ODSS.

▼ An ODSS is an organizational activity that affects several organizational units or corporate problems.

▼ An ODSS cuts across organizational functions or hierarchical layers.

▼ An ODSS almost necessarily involves computer-based technologies and may also involve communication technologies.

 ## 15.10 EXECUTIVE INFORMATION AND SUPPORT SYSTEMS—AN OVERVIEW

The majority of personal DSSs support the work of professionals and middle-level managers. Organizational DSSs provide support primarily to planners, analysts, and researchers or to managers. Rarely do we see a DSS used directly by top- or even middle-level executives. One of the reasons is that DSS does not meet the executives' needs (see the Hertz case, Box 15.13).

IT At Work BOX 15.13

AN EXECUTIVE INFORMATION SYSTEM AT HERTZ CORPORATION

THE PROBLEM. Hertz, the largest company in the car rental industry, competes against dozens of companies in hundreds of locations. Several marketing decisions must be made almost instantaneously (e.g., whether to follow a competitor's price discount or not). These decisions are decentralized and are based on information about cities, climates, holidays, business cycles, tourist activities, past promotions, competitors' behavior, and customers' behavior. The amount of information is huge, and the only way to process it is to use a computer. The problem faced by Hertz was how to provide accessibility to such information and use it properly.

THE INITIAL SOLUTION—A DSS. A DSS was developed in 1987 to allow fast analysis by executives and managers. The system was constructed on the corporate mainframe with a DSS generator (System W from Comshare). The DSS was very helpful in analyzing information. But when a marketing manager had a question, he had to go to a staff assistant, tell that person what was needed, and then wait for the result. There were some

other problems with the system. The staff assistants were not always available, sometimes there were misunderstandings, and quite often managers needed answers to additional questions. All of these situations made the process lengthy and cumbersome. When time is of the essence, late information is useless to the manager. The need for a better system was obvious.

THE EIS. In 1988, Hertz decided to add an EIS—a PC-based system used as a companion to the DSS. The EIS was built with Commander EIS (also from Comshare). The combined system gave executives tools to analyze the mountains of stored information and make real-time decisions without the help of assistants. The system is extremely user-friendly and is maintained by the marketing staff. Since its assimilation into the corporate culture conformed to the manner in which Hertz executives were used to working, implementation was no problem.

Executives can now manipulate and refine data to be more meaningful and strategically significant to them. Further, workload on the mainframe programming resources has been reduced, since the EIS allows executives to draw information from the mainframe, store the needed data on their own PCs, and perform a DSS-type analysis without tying up valuable mainframe time. The people at Hertz feel that the EIS creates synergy in decision making. It triggers questions, a greater influx of creative ideas, and more cost-effective marketing decisions.

Critical Thinking Issue: Why was the DSS insufficient by itself, and how did the addition of the EIS make it effective? ▲

SOURCE: Condensed from O'Leary, M., "Putting Hertz Executives in the Driver's Seat," *CIO*, February 1990.

An **executive information system** (EIS), also known as an **executive support system** (ESS), is a technology emerging in response to situations such as shown in Box 15.13. Generally, there are several factors that drive the need for EIS. They are listed in Box 15.14.

A Closer Look BOX 15.14

WHY EIS?

Watson et al. (1991) arranged the factors that create the need for executive information systems in a descending order of importance:

External
▼ Increased competition.
▼ Rapidly changing environment.
▼ Need to be more proactive.
▼ Need to access external databases.
▼ Increasing government regulations.

Internal
▼ Need for timely information.
▼ Need for improved communications.
▼ Need for access to operational data.
▼ Need for rapid status updates on different activities.
▼ Need for increased effectiveness.
▼ Need to be able to identify historical trends.
▼ Need for access to corporate databases.
▼ Need for more accurate information.

The terms *executive information systems* and *executive support systems* mean different things to different people. Furthermore, in many cases, the terms are being used interchangeably. The following definitions, based on Rockart and DeLong (1988), distinguish between EIS and ESS.

▼ *Executive information system (EIS).* An EIS is a computer-based system that serves the information needs of top executives. It provides rapid access to timely information and direct access to management reports. EIS is very user friendly, is supported by graphics, and provides "exceptions reporting" and "drill down" capabilities. It is also easily connected with on-line information services and electronic mail.

▼ *Executive support system (ESS).* An ESS is a comprehensive support system that goes beyond EIS to include analysis support, communications, office automation, and intelligence (see Box 15.15).

▶ 15.11 CAPABILITIES AND BENEFITS OF EIS

Executive information systems vary in their capabilities and benefits. They can be classified according to four areas: quality of information provided by the EIS, the user interface, the technical capabilities provided, and the general benefits. The following EIS capabilities are of special interest.

IT At Work BOX 15.15

AN ESS IN THE PERSIAN GULF WAR

The Second Marine Aircraft Wing had to plan its activities in the fast-changing political and military environment of the Persian Gulf War. The commanding general and his staff of about 100 people needed large amounts of information, such as personnel availability, logistics status, and aviation weather conditions and forecasts. Getting all this information via telephones and paper reports was a slow and possibly inaccurate task.

Using RediMaster (from American Information Systems), a local area network, and information downloaded from a mainframe and PCs, an ESS was constructed. The ESS included E-mail, calendar, word processing, spreadsheet, graphics software, and anything else that could be used to support the commanders.

By mid-January 1991, when the war started, the system was up and running, and the commanding general was able to receive on-line, real-time reports on subjects ranging from target lists to casualty reports. Indeed, computer technology such as ESS contributed to the success of Desert Storm.

Critical Thinking Issue: Why was this considered an EIS and not a DSS? ▲

SOURCE: Condensed from information provided by the vendor.

DRILL DOWN

**E MERGING TECHNOLOGY**

...An EIS offers immediate access to detailed, timely information, improving analysis and decision making.

The capability called **drill down** provides details of any given information. For example, an executive may notice a decline in corporate sales in a daily (or weekly) report. To find the reason, the executive may want to immediately see the sales in each region, without the need of programmers. If a problematic region is identified, the executive may want to see further details (e.g., by product or by salesperson). In certain cases, this drill down process may continue into several levels of detail. To provide such capability, the EIS may include several thousand menus, submenus, and sub-submenus. Drill down can be also achieved by direct query of databases.

CRITICAL SUCCESS FACTORS AND KEY PERFORMANCE INDICATORS

As discussed in Chapter 11, the critical factors that must be considered in attaining the organization's goals are called **critical success factors (CSF)**. Such factors can be strategic, managerial, or operational, and they are derived mainly from three sources: organizational factors, industry factors, and environmental factors. Success factors can be at the corporate level as well as other levels (division, plant, department). Sometimes it is necessary to consider the CSFs of individual employees.

Critical success factors, once identified, can be monitored, measured, and compared to standards. Each CSF can be measured by one or several **key performance indicators**, a sample of which is provided in Box 15.16 on page 556. The left side of the box lists CSFs; the right side lists the indicators.

STATUS ACCESS

In the **status access** mode, the latest data or reports on the status of key indicators can be accessed at any time. The relevance of information is important here. Emphasis is placed on the latest data. This may require daily or even hourly operational tracking and reporting. In extreme cases, real-time reporting may be required. Although status access allows executives to pursue the information requested (e.g., to conduct a drill down), it is usually not geared to data manipulation or analysis.

A Closer Look BOX 15.16

TYPICAL KEY PERFORMANCE INDICATORS

CSF	Key performance indicators
Profitability	Profitability measures for each department, product, region, etc. Comparisons among departments, and products comparisons with competitors.
Financial	Financial ratios, balance sheet analysis, cash reserve position, rate of return on investment.
Marketing	Market share, advertisement analysis, product pricing, weekly (daily) sales results, customer sales potential.
Human Resources	Turnover rates.
Planning	Corporate partnership ventures, growth/share analysis.
Economic Analysis	Market trends, foreign exchange values, industry trends, labor cost trends.
Consumer Trend	Consumer confidence level, purchasing habits, demographical data.

TREND ANALYSIS

In analyzing data, it is extremely important to identify trends. Are sales increasing? Is market share decreasing? Is the competitor's share of the market declining against ours? The executive likes to examine trends, especially when changes in data are detected. **Trend analysis** can be done using forecasting models, which are included in many ESS, or the executive can activate an adjacent DSS to conduct the trend analysis.

AD HOC ANALYSIS

Executive support systems provide for **ad hoc analysis** capabilities instead of merely providing access to the data analysis. Executives can use the ESS to do creative analysis on their own. Executives may even select the programming tools to be used, the outputs, and the desired presentation of information. Several new tools provide for ad hoc analysis, which is sometimes called **on-line analysis processing** (OLAP).

EXCEPTION REPORTING

Exception reporting is based on the concept of *management by exception*. According to this concept, an executive should give attention to significant deviations from standards. Thus, in exception reporting, an executive's attention will be directed only to cases of very bad (or very good) performance. This approach saves considerable time for both producers and readers of reports.

▶ 15.12 DEVELOPMENT OF AN EIS AND ENTERPRISE EIS

Like any other information system, an EIS can be developed in-house, or it can be purchased. If developed in-house, it can be programmed from scratch, or it can be developed with special productivity tools. For example, Interactive Images (Woburn, MA) sells an EIS generator called EASEL. Comprehensive sets of tools are provided by several vendors such as Comshare, SAS, Pilot Executive, and Information Builders.

The process of building an ESS can be very lengthy and complex. General phases are similar to those used in other information systems, but the process may be more complex.

The EIS building tools are conceptually similar to DSS generators. They allow quick construction of specific EIS. For example, Commander EIS is a modular EIS generator which includes several basic modules as shown in Figure 15.9.

In recent years, the EIS has been enhanced with relational and multidimensional analysis and presentation, friendly data access, user-friendly graphical interface, imaging capabilities, hypertext, E-mail, and modeling. These are helpful for any executive. However, it is important to remember that a most important goal is to provide an *overall solution* to specific enterprise problems. One can distinguish two types of EIS: (1) the one designed especially to support top executives, and (2) the EIS that is intended to serve a wider community of users (see Box 15.17).

The executive-only EIS can be part of the enterprise-wide system. As such, EIS will become less strictly defined, and EIS applications will embrace a range of products targeted to support professional decision makers throughout the enterprise. For this reason, some people define the acronym EIS to mean *enterprise* information systems, or everybody information systems.

There is a trend to deliver EIS-style technology (such as superb graphics and accessibility to data) to a large community of users. As such, the traditional EIS becomes a general enterprise support system. It should be clear that an information-delivery application designed for a small number of top executives must be different in some respects from an information-delivery application designed for a broad cross section of managers and analysts throughout the corporation.

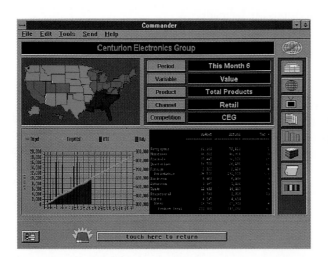

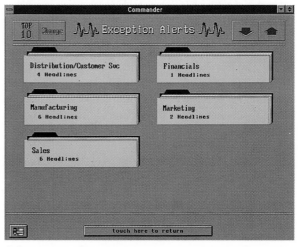

FIGURE 15.9 Sample screens from Commander EIS—a modular system for generating an executive information system.

IT At Work BOX 15.17

AN ENTERPRISE EIS HELPS A MULTINATIONAL BANKING CORPORATION

The Hong Kong and Shanghai Banking Corporation is the 10th largest bank in the world. The bank has been expanding very rapidly, buying banks all over the world. It is a true international corporation that holds banks in many countries in Asia, Europe, and North America. In the mid-1970s, the company introduced computers in their Hong Kong operations, mainly to improve their regular transactions. Efficient data processing is critical to the success and survival of any bank. Anytime an acquisition was made, the holding company had to convert existing information systems to match that of the parent company. This is a difficult task due to technological and cultural differences.

In the 1980s, competition became more intense due to the deregulation of banking in the United States and an increased trend for free trade. Also, banks faced competition from other financial institutions such as credit companies and brokerage houses. The result was that making money on loans (interest income) became very

difficult. Banks, however, have many other products such as letters of credits, credit cards, and investment management. Substantial profits can be made from such products and services. Recognizing the opportunity, the Hong Kong Bank developed a sophisticated profitability EIS and DSS. The system monitors performance and profitability for every bank, branch, and department in the organization. In addition, profitability is tracked by product and by customer. The system enables the bank to identify weak and strong areas, and make operational and strategic decisions accordingly. Also, the bank can provide special services to its most valuable customers and increase productivity by transferring technology and knowledge to weak areas. As a result, the Hong Kong Bank became the most profitable large bank in the world.

Critical Thinking Issue: How can the system identify weak and strong areas, and what kind of subsequent decisions can be made? ▲

SOURCE: Private communication with a bank employee (1995).

Finally, in order to save the executive's time in conducting a drill down, finding exceptions, and identifying trends, an intelligent EIS has been developed. Automating these activities not only saves time but also assures that the executive will not miss any important indications in a large amount of data (see Box 15.18).

A Closer Look BOX 15.18

AN INTELLIGENT EIS

Using intelligent software agents (see Chapter 16), Comshare Inc. was able to automate several tasks of an EIS. Specifically, the software can filter through databases or other electronic sources and glean important, relevant information for executives. The information is delivered in a form that is actionable. The software is an expert system that attempts to find irregular things, or exceptions, and then apply special rules to these exceptions. Of special interest is the Exception Monitor, which supplements Comshare's Commander EIS. It has three components:

1. *Monitor Builder.* This component allows the user to specify the exception-detecting rules. That is, to specify what is an exception, or what needs to be detected.

2. *Exception engine.* This software detects variances, data relationships, patterns, and trends according to the specifications of the Monitor Builder.

3. *Desktop alerting.* This component sends messages to users alerting them to the exceptions.

Exception Monitor can save a considerable amount of time in informing executives. It can be designed to follow all the critical success factors and key performance indicators. It provides answers to questions such as why, where, and when exceptions are happening.

SOURCE: *Comshare Exception Reporting* (1994).

▶ 15.13 SUPPORTING IDEA GENERATION AND CREATIVITY

Many decision theory models assume that alternative courses of action are known to the decision makers or are very easy to generate. Although this assumption is probably correct in many structured decisions, there are many semistructured and unstructured situations for which alternative courses of action are not known in advance. DSS deal with such situations. Therefore, it is frequently necessary to generate ideas that are processed and evaluated by the DSS. To generate good ideas, people need to be creative.

In the past, it was believed that an individual's creative ability stemmed primarily from personality traits such as inventiveness, independence, individuality, enthusiasm, and flexibility. However, several studies have indicated that individual creativity can be learned and improved, and it is not as much a function of individual traits as once believed. This understanding has led innovative companies to recognize that the key to fostering creativity may be the development of an idea-nurturing work environment. Idea-generation methods and techniques, to be used by individuals or in groups, are consequently being developed.

Manual methods of **idea generation** (such as brainstorming) can be very successful in certain settings. However, there are circumstances where such an approach is either not economically feasible or not possible. For example, manual methods will not work or will not be effective in the following situations involving group creativity sessions:

1. There is a poor facilitator (or there is no facilitator).
2. There is no time to conduct a proper idea-generation session.
3. It is too expensive to conduct an idea-generation session.
4. The subject matter is too sensitive for a face-to-face idea-generation session.
5. There are not enough participants, the mix of participants is not optimal, or there is no climate for idea generation.

Manual methods designed to facilitate individual creativity may not work for all individuals or in all types of situations. In such cases, it makes sense to electronically induce idea generation.

IDEA-GENERATION SOFTWARE

Idea-generation software is designed to help stimulate a single user or a group with new ideas, options, and choices. The user does all the work, but the software encourages and pushes just like a personal trainer. Although idea-generation software is still relatively new, there are several packages on the market. The cost ranges from $100 to $600 per package. Representative products are Brainstorm (from Mustang Software), Creative Whackpack (from Creative Think), IdeaFisher (from IdeaFisher Systems), and Think Tank (from Living Videotext).

Various approaches are used by idea-generating software to increase the flow of ideas to the user. One package (IdeaFisher) is unique in that it has an associative lexicon of the English language that cross-references words and phrases (see Box 15.19). These associative links, based on analogies and metaphors, make it easy for the user to be fed words related on some level to a given theme.

Some software packages use questions to prompt the user toward new, unexplored patterns of thought (see Box 15.19). This is especially useful to help users break out of cyclical thinking patterns, break mental blocks, or deal with bouts of procrastination. Creative Whackpack uses a 64-card deck that provides techniques to "whack" the user out of habitual thought patterns.

Idea-generation software for groups works somewhat differently from such software for individuals. As shown in Chapter 14, participants in groups create

A Closer Look BOX 15.19

IDEAFISHER USES ASSOCIATION

The first component of IdeaFisher is called the QBank. Questions in QBank are organized to assist the user in more accurately formulating the exact problem that she is trying to solve. A series of "modification" questions encourage the user to branch into different lines of thought, and a series of "evaluation" questions help the user to test and compare the quality of "winning" ideas with the original objective. This list of central ideas can then be used to decide what to pursue first in the IdeaBank and what to save for later.

IdeaBank is a database of over 60,000 idea words, concepts, and associations. The result is a cross-reference power of more than 705,000 direct idea associations and an infinite number of secondary (linked) associations. The potential number of associations triggered in the user's mind may easily reach into the millions. The inclusion of polar opposites stimulates an ever-larger group of associations that would never have otherwise occurred to the user.

IdeaBank also lets users add personal associations and phrases to Topical Categories or to create their own Topical Categories, filled with thoughts from personal knowledge along any subject line (i.e., products, customers or competition).

The third component of the system, the Notepad, allows the two databases to work efficiently together. This frees the user to focus on productive efforts in selecting alternative lines of thought, maximizing the number of quality ideas, and selecting the best ones. The ways these components all work together provides the uniqueness of the system.

---

ideas simultaneously. The ideas are shown one at a time to each participant, stimulating electronic discussion or generation of more ideas. A large number of ideas is generated in a short time. These ideas are organized, debated, and prioritized by the group, all electronically.

The benefits of creativity enhancement afforded by idea-generating software are numerous. The competitive advantage of the tool is realized across all industry spectrums because of the many new ideas and approaches that result from its use (see Box 15.20). It acts as a catalyst to generate alternative solutions which help operations run more efficiently. When fresh ideas are infused into the operation

---

IT At Work BOX 15.20

BRAINSTORMING BUSINESS PROBLEMS USING IDEAFISHER

▼ **CEC Instruments** (San Dimas, CA) used the Idea-Fisher software to cope with shrinking military contracts. In order to survive, the company was looking to the commercial market. Using IdeaFisher, Jim Shenk, manager of contracts, realized that CEC had overlooked an expanding market for its technical instruments in the commercial aviation market. (SOURCE: Condensed from *Alaska Airlines Magazine*, June 1992, p. 11.)

▼ **Clayton Lee**, an inventor in Houston, TX reduced the manufacturing costs of a new product (Jupiter) from $2,000 to $100 per unit. As a result, the market for the product widened enormously. In addition, IdeaFisher was used to modify existing products by relieving the inventor of having to think up all the questions that he should be asking himself. (SOURCE: Condensed from *Invent*, May 1991, p. 21.)

▼ **Inforcomp Corporation** (Oceanside, CA) used the software to introduce a cost-reduction program to a daily newspaper (*The Tribune*). The software enabled the company to overcome resistance to the introduction of a new budgeting system. The software also enabled consultants to market and promote new programs to management. (SOURCE: Condensed from *I/S Analyzer*, September 1991, pp. 13-14.) ▲

and when dealing with clients, improved solutions for business problems will result.

▶ MANAGERIAL ISSUES

1. *Intangible benefits.* Most MSS are difficult to justify because they generate mostly intangible benefits, such as the ability to solve problems faster. While the cost of small systems is fairly low and justification is not a critical issue, the cost of a medium-to-large MSS can be very high. Standard accounting methodologies of cost–benefit analysis, where many intangible benefits exist can be used.

2. *Documenting personal DSS.* Many employees develop their own DSS to increase their productivity and quality. It is advisable to have an inventory of these DSSs and make certain that appropriate documentation and security measures exist. In such cases, if the employee leaves, then the productivity tool remains.

3. *Security.* DSS and EIS may contain extremely important information for the livelihood of the organization. Taking appropriate security measures is a must (see Chapter 19). The problem is that when end users build a DSS, they frequently ignore appropriate security measures. Management must remember that end users are not professional systems builders. For this reason, there could be problems with data integrity and the quality of the systems developed.

4. *Ready-made commercial DSS.* With the decreased cost of system development, it is possible to find more and more specific DSSs sold off the shelf. While the DSS may not fit the organizational need exactly, it may fit fairly well. It is sometimes advisable to change business processes to fit a commercially available DSS rather than to build one. Also, some vendors are willing to modify their standard software to fit the customer's needs.

5. *Intelligent DSS.* Introducing intelligent agents into a DSS can greatly increase its functionality. The intelligent component of a system such as American Express's Credit Card Authorizer can be less than 3% of the entire authorization system (the rest is DSS, databases, and telecommunications). Yet, the benefits of the system are incredible.

6. *Organization culture.* The more people recognize the benefits of DSS and the more support is given to it by top management, the more the DSS will be used. If the organization's culture is supportive, hundreds of applications will be developed.

7. *Ethical issues.* Corporations with management support systems may need to address some serious ethical issues due to the potential impacts on employment and individuals. For example, a company developed a DSS to help people compute the financial implications of early retirement. However, the DSS developer did not include the tax implications, resulting in incorrect retirement decisions. In addition, there was no information about psychological and social impacts.

Other issues include using information in the MSS that may violate the privacy of certain individuals or sharing of information, a frequent situation in organizational and group DSSs. Here, individuals may be exposed to sensitive information that they should keep secret.

Another important issue is human judgment, which is frequently used in DSSs. Human judgment is subjective, and therefore, it may lead to unethical decision making. The company should provide an ethical code (see Chapter 20) for DSS builders.

KEY TERMS

Ad hoc analysis *558*

Critical success factors *557*

Decision styles *536*

Decision support systems (DSS) *544*

DSS generator *552*

DSS tools *553*

Drill down *557*

Exception reporting *558*

Executive information system (EIS) *556*

Executive support system (ESS) *556*

Goal-seeking analysis *547*

Idea generation *561*

Iterative (development) approach *551*

Key performance indicators *557*

Management *530*

Management science *543*

Management support systems (MSS) *539*

Mental model *536*

Model *535*

Model base management system *549*

Online transaction processing *558*

Organizational decision support system (ODSS) *555*

Personal information managers (PIM) *540*

Productivity *530*

Semistructured *541*

Sensitivity analysis *547*

Specific DSS *552*

Status access *558*

Structured *541*

Technology levels (of DSS) *552*

Trend analysis *558*

"What-if" analysis *567*

Unstructured *541*

User interface management system *551*

CHAPTER HIGHLIGHTS *(L-x means learning objective number x)*

▼ Managerial decision making is synonymous with the whole process of management.(L-1)

▼ In making decisions, one should consider multiple goals and sensitivity analysis issues. (L-2)

▼ Models enable fast and inexpensive experimentation with systems. They can be iconic, analog, or mathematical. (L-3)

▼ Decision making is becoming more and more difficult due to the trends discussed in Chapter 1. Information technology enables managers to make better and faster decisions. (L-4)

▼ Decision making involves four major phases: intelligence, design, choice, and implementation. (L-5)

▼ DSSs can improve the effectiveness of decision making, decrease the need for training, improve management control, facilitate communication, save costs, and allow for more objective decision making. (L-6)

▼ The major components of a DSS are the database and its management, the model base and its management, and the friendly user interface. An intelligent (knowledge) component can be added. (L-6)

▼ The data management subsystem includes a DSS database, a DBMS, a data directory, and a query facility. (L-6)

▼ The model base includes standard models and models specifically written for the DSS. (L-6)

▼ Custom-made models can be written with third- or fourth-generation languages. End-user DSS are usually written with fourth-generation languages. (L-6)

▼ A DSS can be used directly by managers, or it can be used via intermediaries. (L-6)

▼ There is a trend to integrate DSS and EIS to an ESS. Thus, an ESS is basically an EIS with analysis capabilities. (L-7)

▼ Finding the information needs of executives is a very difficult process. Methods such as CSF and BSP are effective, especially if they are followed by prototyping. (L-7)

▼ "Drill down" is an important capability of EIS. It allows an executive to look easily and very quickly at various levels of details. (L-7)

▼ Organizational DSS deals with decision making across functional areas and hierarchical organizational layers, and it operates in a distributed environment. (L-8)

▼ Idea generation can be enhanced by electronic software, which uses associations, identification of patterns, and other well-known techniques to support idea generation. (L-9)

QUESTIONS FOR REVIEW

1. Describe the major roles of managers.

2. Define the executive's interpersonal, informational, and decisional roles.

3. Explain the phases of intelligence, design, and choice.

4. What are programmed vs. unprogrammed problems? Give one example of each in the following three areas: finance, marketing, and personnel administration.

5. Explain "what-if" analysis, and provide an example.

6. What is goal-seeking analysis? Provide an example.

7. Give two definitions of DSS.

8. Briefly define the major components of a DSS.

9. List some of the major functions of a MBMS.

10. What is the major purpose of the user interface system?

11. List the major classes of DSS users.

12. Describe the idea of technology levels.

13. Define DSS generators, and discuss their objectives.

14. What is the difference between an EIS and an ESS?

15. What are some of the pressures for the creation of an EIS?

16. What are the major benefits of an EIS?

17. Explain "drill down," and list its advantages.

18. Explain electronically supported idea generation.

QUESTIONS FOR DISCUSSION

1. What could be the major advantages of a mathematical model that would be used to support a major investment decision?

2. Your company is considering opening a branch in China. List typical activities in each phase of the decision (intelligence, design, choice, and implementation).

3. A hospital desires to know what level of demand for its services will guarantee an 85 percent bed occupancy. What type of sensitivity analysis should the hospital use and why?

4. Some experts believe that the major contribution of a DSS is to the implementation of the decision and not to the intelligence, design, or choice. Why is this so?

5. How is the term *model* used in this chapter? What are the strengths and weaknesses of modeling?

6. List some internal data and external data that could be found in a DSS for a company's selection of an investment stock portfolio.

7. List some internal and external data in a DSS that will be constructed for a decision regarding the expansion of a hospital.

8. If a DSS is employed in finding answers to management questions, what is the EIS used for?

9. Explain how the approach of critical success factors is used in an interviewing approach for finding information needs.

10. American Can Company announced in early 1986 that it was interested in acquiring a company in the health maintenance organization (HMO) field. Two decisions were involved in this act: (1) the decision to acquire an HMO, and (2) the decision of which one to acquire. How can a DSS and an EIS be used in such a situation?

11. Why can't a conventional MIS fulfill the information needs of executives?

12. Why is it so difficult to find the information needs of managers? List a few approaches that can be used to discover the information needs of managers.

13. Explain how critical success factors are measured in your company.

14. What are the major benefits of integrating EISs and DSSs?

15. Discuss the differences between an ODSS and a DSS.

16. Explain how IT can facilitate idea generation. What are its advantages over manual facilitation?

17. How can each of Simon's phases of decision making be supported through information acquisition and use?

EXERCISES

1. Susan Lopez was promoted to the position of director of the transportation department in a medium-size university. She controlled the following vehicles: 17 sedans, 15 vans, and 3 trucks. The previous director was fired because there were too many complaints about not getting vehicles when needed. Susan was told not to expect any increase in budget for the next two years (no replacement or additional vehicles). Susan's major job was to schedule vehicles for employees, and to schedule maintenance and repair of the vehicles. Currently, all this is accomplished manually.

   Your job is to advise Susan regarding the possibility of using a DSS to improve this situation. Susan has a 486 PC, Lotus 1-2-3, Paradox, and Harvard Graphics, but she is using the computer only for word processing. Prepare:

   a. A justification for the use of the proposed DSS, namely, what this DSS can do to improve Susan's job.

   b. Describe the decision variables, result variables, and independent variables of the DSS model.

   c. Which of the existing computing resources will be used for the DSS, and what for?

GROUP ASSIGNMENT

1. Development of an ESS is proposed for your university. Identify the organization structure of the university and its existing information system. Then, group members should identify and interview several potential users of the system. In the interview, you should check the need for such a system and convince the potential user of the benefit of the system.

2. The group should identify current DSS tools and proceed to a computer store to see some of these products.

The group then makes an evaluation summary of at least four products:

a. An integrated spreadsheet (such as Lotus 1-2-3).
b. An integrated DBMS.
c. A data access (for EIS) tool such as LightShip, Forest and Trees, Impromptu, or Visual Basic.
d. Multidimensional presentation, such as PowerPlay, CA Compete, or Commander Prism.

Minicase 1

Executive Support to Teleglobe Canada

Teleglobe Canada provides the communication link between Canada and all other countries in the world. In the late 1980s, Teleglobe was privatized and became regulated by the Canadian Radio and Telecommunications Commission. At the same time, the company had to report to the parent company in great detail about finance, operations, and marketing activities. Frequently, the parent company asked for information from managers after their assistants left or even called managers at home. The pressures were mounting.

The corporate president, Jean-Claude Delome, was interested in quick access to data and improved communications even before the privatization. The company had excellent functional MIS, but management wanted a system that showed trends, patterns, and comparisons. So, Delome requested development of a system which would do just that, "a system that will sit on the top of the company databases." Teleglobe had information architecture in place with three layers: strategic planning, management control, and operations control. Each of these layers was comprised of numerous systems, but the three layers did not interact easily among themselves. To accommodate the president, the MIS department decided to build an additional layer to address corporate-level issues, such as profits and costs, networks and facilities, rates and tariffs (which are constantly changing), service profitability, and capital investment. They also wanted to provide modeling capabilities and "what-if" analysis.

The MIS department took the following steps:

1. Looked at the company mission goals and objectives.

2. Prepared a list of critical success factors which distilled the numerous objectives and priorities identified in Step 1.

3. Selected a "champion" for the project—the finance department.

4. Decided to develop an EIS, using Commander EIS (from Comshare).

5. Developed an EIS prototype for the finance department.

6. Improved the prototype and expanded the EIS to all other parts of the company.

7. Developed a total of 30 EISs, all using the same information, but with the presentation customized to fit the needs and even the personality of each user.

8. The system's capabilities were basically those shown in Fig. 15.9. The system became a success. The EIS changed the company and the managers, who became more efficient.

Questions for Minicase 1

1. Which pressures presented in Chapter 1 can be identified in this case?

2. Which concepts discussed in Chapter 2 can be identified in this case?

3. Why was the EIS needed? Why not use the existing MIS and add a DSS?

4. It was felt that the use of CSFs tied to the corporate mission and objectives was the key to the success of the EIS. Why is this so?

5. Review the development process used in this case. Identify the things that you like and dislike, and comment.

6. It is time now for upgrading the EIS. Based on what you learned in this text and on information you acquired from other sources (vendors, publications), what would you suggest be done now?

SOURCE: This case is based on Comshare Publication # 337352.

Minicase 2

A Decision Support System—Or Is It?

John Young is the general manager of a small electric utility company in Colorado. John was concerned with the large number of customer complaints. Complaints were received by the customer relations department and distributed to the appropriate departments for consideration. Each complaint was investigated, and a response was provided either orally or in writing to the complainant.

John completed a course in decision support systems and learned to program with Lotus 1-2-3. As a part of the course, he constructed a customers' complaint DSS. The system was installed recently. Its database includes information about each complaint (a copy of), who is handling it, when it was assigned to an individual department, when it was resolved, and how it was resolved (a copy of the letter to the customer or a copy of the telephone conversation with the customer).

John was very proud of the system. He felt that it increased his control and, because everything is documented, people would handle complaints more effectively. One morning, he had the following conversation with his assistant, Nancy Gray, who also completed a DSS course.

John: What do you think about the success of my DSS?

Nancy: The system works fine, but I am not sure that this is a DSS.

John: You know that I designed it myself. The system is user friendly. I can find the status of any complaint and compute, if necessary, how long it took to solve the complaint.

Nancy: This is all great, but what specific decisions do you support?

John: Well, this information can be used by me to decide, for example, on rewards for those who handle the complaints most effectively.

Nancy: How?

John: I am not sure. I may conduct comparisons.

Questions for Minicase 2

1. Is John's system a DSS? Why or why not?

2. If it is not a DSS, what is necessary to make it a DSS?

REFERENCES AND BIBLIOGRAPHY

1. Alter, S. L., *Decision Support Systems: Current Practice and Continuing Challenge*, Reading, MA: Addison-Wesley, 1980.

2. Anthony, R. N., *Planning and Control Systems: A Framework for Analysis*, Cambridge, MA: Harvard University Graduate School of Business Administration, 1965.

3. Bergerson, F., et al., "Top Managers Evaluate the Attributes of EIS," in *DSS 91 Transactions*, Manhattan Beach, CA, 1991.

4. Carter, G. M., et al., *Building Organizational Decision Support Systems*, Cambridge, MA: Academic Press, 1992.

5. Couger, J. D., et al., "Enhancing the Creativity of Reengineering," *Information Systems Management*, Spring 1994.

6. Courbon, J. C., et al., "Design and Implementation of DSS by an Evaluation Approach," unpublished working paper, 1980.

7. Elam, J., and A. Mead, "Can Software Influence Creativity?" *Information Systems Research*, January/March 1990.

8. George, J. F., "The Conceptualizations and Development of Organizational DSS," unpublished working paper, Department of Management Information Systems, University of Arizona, 1990.

9. Gillan, C., and K. McPherson, "EIS: A White Paper," *Computerworld* Supplement, October 26, 1992.

10. Gordon, L. A., et al., *Normative Models in Managerial Decision Making*, New York: National Association of Accounting, 1975.

11. Gorry, G. A., and M. S. Scott Morton, "A Framework for Management Information Systems," *Sloan Management Review*, Vol. 13, No. 1, Fall 1971.

12. Gray, P. (ed.), *Decision Support and Executive Information Systems*, Englewood Cliffs, NJ: Prentice-Hall, 1994.

13. Hackathorn, R. D., and P. G. W. Keen, "Organizational Strategies for Personal Computing in Decision Support Systems," *MIS Quarterly*, September 1981.

14. Hogue, J. T., and H. J. Watson, "Current Practices in the Development of Decision Support Systems," *Information & Management*, May 1985.

15. Holtman, C. (ed.), *Executive Information Systems and Decision Support*, London: Chapman & Hill, 1993.

16. Islei, G., et al., "Modeling Strategic Decision Making and Performance Measurement at ICI Pharmaceutical," *Interfaces*, November/December 1991.

17. Keen, P. G. W., and M. S. Scott Morton, *Decision Support Systems: An Organizational Perspective*, Reading, MA: Addison-Wesley, 1978.

18. McLeod, R. Jr., and J. W. Jones, "Making Executive Information Systems More Effective," *Business Horizons*, September/October 1986.

19. Mallach E. G., *Understanding Decision Support Systems and Expert Systems*, Burr Ridge, IL.: Richard D. Irwin, 1994.

20. Manheim, M. L., "Toward True Executive Support: Managerial and Theoretical Perspective," in *DSS 89 Transactions*, San Diego, CA, 1989.

21. Mintzberg, H., *The Nature of the Managerial Work*, New York: Harper & Row, 1973.

22. Rockart, J. F., and D. DeLong, *Executive Support Systems*, Homewood, IL: Dow Jones–Irwin, 1988.

23. Saaty, T. C., *Decisions for Leaders: The Analytic Hierarchy Process*, Pittsburgh, PA: University of Pittsburgh Press, 1990.

24. Scott Morton, M. S., *Management Decision Systems: Computer Based Support for Decision Making*, Cambridge, MA: Harvard University, Division of Research, 1971.

25. Simon, H., *The New Science of Management Decisions*, rev. ed., Englewood Cliffs, NJ: Prentice-Hall, 1977.

26. Sprague, R. H., and E. D. Carlson, *Building Effective Decision Support Systems*, Englewood Cliffs, NJ: Prentice–Hall, 1982.

27. Sprague, R. H., and H. J. Watson (eds.), *Decision Support Systems*, 3rd ed., Englewood Cliffs, NJ: Prentice-Hall, 1993.

28. Turban, E., *Decision Support and Expert Systems*, Englewood Cliffs, NJ: Prentice-Hall, 3rd edition 1993, 4th edition 1995.

29. Turban, E., and J. Meredith, *Fundamentals of Management Science*, 6th ed., Homewood, IL: Richard D. Irwin, 1994.

30. Watson, H. J., and M. Frolick, "Determining Information Requirements for an Executive Information System," *Information System Management*, Spring 1992.

31. Watson, H. J., et al., "Executive Information Systems: A Framework for Development and a Survey of Current Practices," *MIS Quarterly*, March 1991.

32. Watson, H. J., et al., *Executive Information Systems*, New York: Wiley, 1992.

33. Watson, H. J., et al., *Building Executive Information Systems*, New York: John Wiley & Sons, 1996.

34. Wedley, W. K., and R. H. C. Field, "A Predecision Support System," *Academy of Management Review*, October 1984.

35. Wetherbe, J. C., "Executive Information Requirements: Getting It Right," *MIS Quarterly*, March 1991.

36. Young, L. F., *Decision Support and Idea Processing Systems*, Dubuque, IA: William C. Brown, 1988.

▶16

INTELLIGENT SUPPORT SYSTEMS

Chapter Outline

Learning Objectives

After studying this chapter, you will be able to:

1. Describe artificial intelligence and compare it with conventional computing.

2. Describe the characteristics, structure, benefits, and limitations of expert systems.

3. Explain the process of building expert systems, and compare it with the process of building conventional, computer-based information systems.

4. Analyze the suitability of business problems to be solved with expert systems or related artificial intelligence technologies.

5. Describe the major characteristics of natural language processing and voice technologies.

6. Distinguish between neural computing and other computer-based technologies.

7. Describe the major features of fuzzy logic.

▶ 16.1 LIFE IN THE TWENTY-FIRST CENTURY

THE FOLLOWING FEW scenarios demonstrate how people will live and work in the twenty-first century.

Driving to Work

Today when you drive to work or school, you follow a routine process. You start the car and move it into the street; you try to avoid accidents; you start fighting traffic ("all those people who do not know how to drive"); and finally, you are on the freeway, speeding not to be late. "Sorry," the officer says. "You were speeding." ("Everybody is speeding. Why me?") Finally you arrive at your destination, tired and stressed. For a moment, you close your eyes and say to yourself, "My job is in the marketing department. I am not a paid driver. I wish I could afford a limo." Good news. Your wish may soon come true.

Tomorrow, you will enter your Autonomous Land Vehicle (ALV). You will say, "Go to work, car," and slip into the back seat. The car will then start itself, open the garage door, back out into the street, and carefully drive itself to work. You can fully relax in the back seat, watch TV, sip coffee, or just take a nap.

A fantasy of a commuter? Not for very much longer. Prototypes developed by Carnegie Mellon University (Pittsburgh) and in Munich, Germany, are driving by themselves in city traffic at about 30 miles per hour.

Next time you pass a car without a driver, or get passed on the road by one, smile and wave—you have just seen the future zip by.

SOURCE: Condensed from *AI Expert*, September 1991 and April 1994.

Shopping

You return from work, and there is no food in your place. A friend told you about shopping from home using your computer; you can see pictures of the products, compare prices, click on the items you want to order, and authorize payment by giving your secret password. A delivery is made within an hour. This is not actually such a big deal. As a matter of fact, you do not have to wait for the twenty-first century. Such systems have been in operation since the early 1990s. However, not many shoppers use them. They want to have the good feeling of touching what they buy. For this, you *may* have to wait for the twenty-first century, when *virtual reality* becomes economically feasible. The technology will allow you to "walk through" a supermarket (or other store), "pick up" an item, and "put it" in the shopping cart. When you finish, you go to the checkout and pay. All this will be done, of course, from your living

Prototypes for Autonomous Land Vehicles are already being tested. (SOURCE: Communication of the ACM March 1994 pg. 5 and AI Expert Sept. 1991.)

room, but you will have the feeling of being in the supermarket and touching supermarket items.

Vacation

Work and shopping are not much fun. How about taking a trip to Hawaii? We mean a real trip, not through virtual reality. Of course, you can do this today. But who is going to do all the research on hotels, airlines, and so on, and save you lots of money? You can try to do it yourself, use a travel agent (which may not be the best), or call upon your **intelligent agent**. Here is how the process will work.

Step 1. You turn on your PC and enter your destination, dates, budget available, special requirements, and desired entertainment.

Step 2. Your computer will dispatch an agent that will "shop around," entering the regular telephone network (using General Magic's Telescript software) and communicating electronically with the databases of airlines, hotels, and other vendors.

Step 3. Your agent attempts to match your requirements against what is available, negotiating with the vendors' agents. These agents may activate other agents to make special arrangements, cooperate with each other, activate multimedia presentations, or make special inquiries.

Step 4. Your agent returns to you within minutes with one or more recommendations. You have a few questions; you want modifications. No problem. Within a few minutes, it is a done deal. No waiting in telephone lines; no mistakes by people. Once you

approve the deal, the agent will make the reservations and even report to you about any changes.

How do you communicate with your agent? By voice, of course.

SOURCE: Condensed from *Fortune*, June 24, 1994.

16.2 INTELLIGENT SYSTEMS AND ARTIFICIAL INTELLIGENCE

The scenarios of the twenty-first century may seem like a dream, but it is only a question of how long before they become reality. Many other scenarios are on the drawing boards of research institutions and technology-oriented corporations worldwide. Common to all these scenarios is that each will include intelligent computer systems. **Intelligent systems** describe the various commercial applications of artificial intelligence (AI). The field of intelligent systems (also known as knowledge-based systems) is expanding rapidly. A major management consultant, A.D. Little, estimates that by the year 2000, 15 to 20 percent of all computer applications will be intelligent systems, sometimes referred to as smart computers.

The fundamentals of the major intelligent systems and the support they provide are the subject of this chapter.

DEFINITIONS

Artificial intelligence (AI) is a term that encompasses many definitions (see Turban [1992]). Most experts agree that AI is concerned with two basic ideas. First, it involves studying the thought processes of humans; second, it deals with representing those processes via machines (computers, robots, and so on).

One well-publicized definition of AI is as follows: artificial intelligence is behavior by a machine that, if performed by a human being, would be called *intelligent*. Winston and Prendergast (1984) list three objectives of artificial intelligence: (1) make machines smarter (primary goal), (2) understand what intelligence is (the Noble laureate purpose), and (3) make machines more useful (the entrepreneurial purpose).

Let us explore the meaning of the term *intelligent behavior*. Several abilities are considered to be signs of intelligence:

▼ Learning or understanding from experience.

▼ Making sense out of ambiguous or contradictory messages.

▼ Responding quickly and successfully to a new situation (different responses, flexibility).

▼ Using reason to solve problems and direct conduct effectively.

▼ Dealing with perplexing situations.

▼ Understanding and inferring in ordinary, rational ways.

▼ Applying knowledge to manipulate the environment.

▼ Recognizing the relative importance of different elements in a situation.

Although AI's ultimate goal is to build machines that will mimic human intelligence, the capabilities of current intelligent systems (commercial AI products) are far from exhibiting any significant success. Nevertheless, intelligent systems are getting better with the passage of time, and they are currently useful in conducting many tasks that require some human intelligence.

An interesting test to determine if a computer exhibits intelligent behavior was designed by Alan Turing (a British AI pioneer)—the **Turing Test**. According to this test, a computer could be considered "smart" only when a human interviewer, conversing with both an unseen human being and an unseen computer, could not determine which was which (see Figure 16.1).

Definitions of AI presented up to this point concentrate on the notion of intelligence. According to another definition, artificial intelligence is the branch of computer science that deals with ways of representing knowledge using symbols rather than numbers and rules of thumb (or heuristics) rather than algorithms for processing information. Let us explore the meaning of this definition.

1. *Numeric vs. symbolic.* Computers were originally designed to process numbers. People, however, tend to think symbolically; our intelligence seems to be based, in part, on our mental ability to manipulate symbols rather than just numbers. Although **symbolic processing** is at the core of AI, this does not mean that AI does not involve math. But, the *emphasis* in AI is on manipulation of symbols.

2. *Algorithmic vs. nonalgorithmic.* An **algorithm** is a step-by-step procedure with well-defined starting and ending points that is guaranteed to reach a solution to a specific problem. Many human reasoning processes, however, tend to be nonalgorithmic. In other words, our mental activities consist of more than just following logical, step-by-step procedures. Again, while AI is primarily a nonalgorithmic approach, it may use algorithms occasionally.

3. *Heuristics.* People frequently use **heuristics** (or rules of thumb), consciously or otherwise, to make decisions. By using heuristics, one does not have to completely rethink what to do every time a similar problem is encountered.

KNOWLEDGE AND AI

AI is frequently associated with the concept of knowledge. Although a computer cannot (as yet) have experiences or study and learn as the human mind can, it can use knowledge given to it by human experts. Such knowledge consists of facts,

FIGURE 16.1 The Turing test

concepts, theories, heuristic methods, procedures, and relationships. Knowledge is also information that has been organized and analyzed to make it understandable and applicable to problem solving or decision making. The collection of knowledge related to a problem (or an opportunity) to be used in an intelligent system is organized and stored in a **knowledge base**.

INTELLIGENT AGENTS

EMERGING TECHNOLOGY

...intelligent agents help human beings make educated decisions

An intelligent agent is a software routine attached to other software for the purpose of executing special tasks that require some intelligence. In Section 16.1, we described the role of an intelligent agent in finding information, evaluating it, and acting on behalf of a human master. Some agents—which are small expert systems or other intelligent systems—are already in commercial use. For example, Wizards is a built-in package in Microsoft's spreadsheet Excel 5.0 (and higher). The Wizard "watches" users and offers suggestions on how to improve the operations they do when using Excel. Both Microsoft and Lotus are introducing intelligent agents into many of their products. Of special interest are the agents in Lotus Notes (discussed in the previous chapter), which help Notes users to access databases.

Intelligent agents are expected to play a major role for navigators of the Internet and the forthcoming information superhighway. Working with networks requires knowledge of protocols, formats, procedures, dictionaries, and several other not-so-user-friendly items. The more networks we have, the more users will be using them and the more guidance they will need.

Intelligent agents can also be used for business intelligence such as spying on a competitor.

▶ 16.3 ARTIFICIAL VS. NATURAL INTELLIGENCE

The potential value of artificial intelligence can be better understood by contrasting it with natural, or human, intelligence.

According to Kaplan (1984), AI has several important commercial advantages over natural intelligence.

▼ AI is more *permanent*. Natural intelligence is perishable from a commercial standpoint, because workers may take knowledge with them when they leave their place of employment or they may forget their knowledge. AI, however, is permanent as long as the computer systems and programs are unchanged.

▼ AI offers *ease of duplication and dissemination*. Transferring a body of knowledge from one person to another usually requires a lengthy process of apprenticeship; some expertise can never be duplicated completely. However, when knowledge is embodied in a computer system, it can be copied from that computer and easily moved to another computer, even across the globe.

▼ AI can be *less expensive* than natural intelligence. There are many circumstances in which buying computer services costs less than having corresponding human beings carry out the same tasks.

▼ AI, as a computer technology, is *consistent and thorough*. Natural intelligence is erratic because people are erratic; they may not perform consistently.

▼ AI can be *documented*. Decisions made by a computer can be easily documented by tracing the activities of the system. Natural intelligence is difficult to document; for example, a person may reach a conclusion but at some later date be unable to re-create the reasoning process that led to that conclusion or to even recall the assumptions that were a part of the decision.

Natural intelligence however, does have several advantages over AI.

▼ Natural intelligence is *creative*, whereas AI is rather uninspired. The ability to acquire knowledge is inherent in human beings. But with AI, tailored knowledge must be built into a carefully constructed system.

▼ Natural intelligence enables people to benefit from and directly use *sensory experiences*. Most AI systems must interpret information collected by sensors, thus providing people with indirect sensory experiences.

▼ Perhaps most important, human reasoning is always able to make use of a wide *context of experiences* and bring that to bear on individual problems. In contrast, AI systems typically gain their power by having a very narrow focus.

Computers can be used to collect information about objects, events, or processes. Of course, computers can process large amounts of information more efficiently than people can. People, however, do some things instinctively that have been very difficult to program into a computer. They recognize relationships between things, sense qualities, and spot patterns that explain how various items interrelate.

Photographs are nothing more than collections of minute dots. Yet without any conscious effort, people discover patterns that reveal faces and other objects in photos. Similarly, one of the ways that humans make sense of the world is by recognizing relationships and patterns that help give meaning to the objects and events they encounter. If computers are to become more human-like, they must be able to make the same kinds of associations among the qualities of objects, events, and processes that come so naturally to people.

CONVENTIONAL VERSUS AI COMPUTING

Conventional computer programs are based on algorithms. An algorithm is a mathematical formula or sequential procedure that will lead to a solution. The algorithm is converted into a computer program that tells the computer exactly what operations to carry out. The algorithm then uses data such as numbers, letters, or words to solve problems.

AI software is based on symbolic representation and manipulation. In AI, a symbol is a letter, word, or number that represents objects, processes, and their relationships. Objects can be people, things, ideas, concepts, events, or statements of fact. Using symbols, it is possible to create a knowledge base that contains facts, concepts, and the relationships among them. Then various processes are used to manipulate the symbols in order to generate advice or a recommendation for solving problems.

The major differences between AI computing and conventional computing are shown in Table 16.1.

Table 16.1 Conventional vs. AI Computing

Dimension	Artificial Intelligence	Conventional Programming
Processing	Mainly symbolic	Primarily algorithmic
Nature of input	Can be incomplete	Must be complete
Search approach	Heuristic (mostly)	Algorithms
Explanation	Provided	Usually not provided
Focus	Knowledge	Data, information
Maintenance and update	Relatively easy, due to modularity	Usually difficult
Reasoning capability	Yes	No

DOES A COMPUTER REALLY THINK?

Knowledge bases and search techniques certainly make computers more useful (see Box 16.1), but can they really make computers more intelligent? The fact that most AI programs are implemented by search and pattern-matching techniques leads to the conclusion that computers are not really intelligent. You give the computer a lot of information and some guidelines about how to use this information. Using the information and guidelines, the computer can then come up with a solution. But all it does is test the various alternatives and attempt to find some combination that meets the designated criteria. So the computer appears to be "thinking" and often gives a satisfactory solution. Dreyfus and Dreyfus (1988) feel that the public is being misled about AI—its usefulness is overblown and its goals are unrealistic. They claim that the human mind is just too complex to duplicate.

Nevertheless, despite criticism, AI methods can be extremely valuable. AI techniques can make computers easier to use and make knowledge available to the masses.

A Closer Look BOX 16.1

POTENTIAL BENEFITS OF ARTIFICIAL INTELLIGENCE

▼ AI makes the use of computers very friendly.

▼ AI enables easy accessibility to databases.

▼ AI helps to solve problems which cannot be solved by conventional computing.

▼ AI helps to solve problems with incomplete or unclear data.

▼ AI helps in handling the information overload (e.g., by summarizing information for us).

▼ AI forces us to convert information to knowledge; and knowledge is power!

▶ 16.4 THE ARTIFICIAL INTELLIGENCE FIELD: INTELLIGENT SYSTEMS

EMERGING TECHNOLOGY

...several applied AI technologies

The development of machines that exhibit intelligent characteristics involves several sciences and technologies, ranging from linguistics to mathematics (see the roots of the tree in Figure 16.2). Artificial intelligence, in itself, is not a commercial field. It is a science and a technology. It is a collection of concepts and ideas that are appropriate for research but cannot be marketed. However, AI provides the scientific foundation for several growing commercial technologies. The major intelligent systems are expert systems, natural language processing, speech understanding, robotics and sensory systems, fuzzy logic, neural computing, computer vision and scene recognition, and intelligent computer-aided instruction. In addition, a combination of two or more of the above is considered a hybrid intelligent system. These are illustrated in Figure 16.2 (as the branches of the tree), and some are discussed next.

EXPERT SYSTEMS

Expert systems are computerized advisory programs that attempt to imitate the reasoning processes of experts in solving difficult problems. They are in use more than any other applied AI technology. Expert systems are of great interest to organizations because they can increase productivity and augment workforces in specialty areas where human experts are becoming increasingly difficult to find and retain or are too expensive to use. Expert systems are discussed in Sections 16.5 through 16.12 of this chapter.

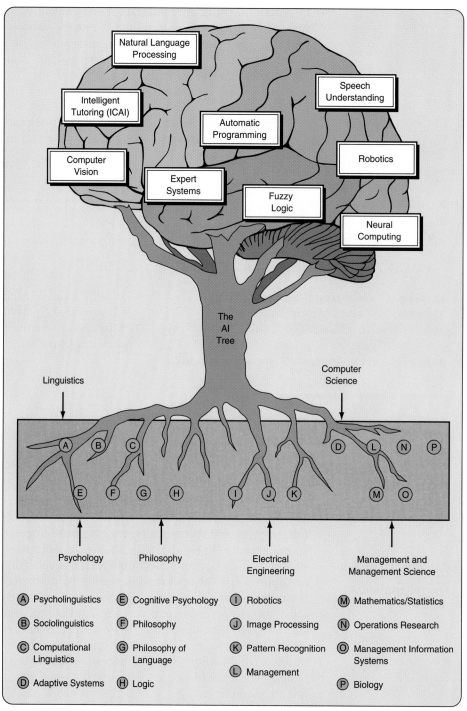

FIGURE 16.2 The disciplines of AI (the roots) and the major applications. (SOURCE: Adapted from Cercone, N., and G. McCalba, "Artificial Intelligence: Underlying Assumptions and Basic Objectives," *Journal of the American Society for Information Science*, September 1984, and from G. S. Tuthill, *Knowledge Engineering*, Blue Ridge Summit, PA: TAB Books, 1990.)

NATURAL LANGUAGE PROCESSING

Natural language technology gives computer users the ability to communicate with the computer in their native languages. This technology allows for a conversational type of interface, in contrast to using a command or other special computer language. Limited success in this area is typified by systems that can recognize and interpret written sentences relating to very restricted topics.

The field of **natural language processing** (discussed in more detail in Section 16.13) is divided into the following two subfields:

▼ Natural language *understanding* investigates methods of allowing a computer to comprehend instructions given in ordinary English (or other human language), so that computers can understand people.

▼ Natural language *generation* (also known as voice synthesis) strives to have computers produce ordinary English language so that people can understand computers more easily.

SPEECH (VOICE) UNDERSTANDING

Speech understanding is the recognition and understanding by a computer of a *spoken* language (see Section 16.13). It is a process that allows someone to communicate with a computer by speaking to it. The term *speech recognition* is sometimes applied only to the first part of the process: recognizing words that have been spoken without necessarily interpreting their meanings. The other part of the process, in which the meaning of the speech is ascertained, is called **speech understanding.** The process of speech understanding attempts to translate what a human speaks into individual words and sentences understandable by the computer.

ROBOTICS AND SENSORY SYSTEMS

Sensory systems, such as vision systems and signal processing systems, combined with AI define a broad category of systems generally referred to as **robotics.** A robot is an electromechanical device that can be programmed to perform manual tasks.

Not all of robotics is considered to be part of AI. A robot that performs only the actions that it has been preprogrammed to perform is considered to be a "dumb" robot, possessing no more intelligence than, say, an elevator. An "intelligent" robot includes some kind of sensory apparatus, such as a camera, that collects information about the robot's operation and its environment. The intelligent part of the robot allows it to *interpret* the collected information and *respond* and adapt to changes in its environment, rather than just to follow instructions "mindlessly."

Robots combine sensory systems with mechanical motion to produce machines of widely varying abilities. Robotics are used mainly in welding, painting, and simple material handling. Assembly-line operations, particularly those which are highly repetitive or hazardous, are beginning to be performed by robots (see Box 16.2).

COMPUTER VISION AND SCENE RECOGNITION

Visual recognition has been defined as the addition of some form of computer intelligence and decision making to digitized visual information received from a machine sensor. The combined information is then used to perform, or control, such operations as robotics movement, conveyor speeds, and production-line

IT At Work BOX 16.2

*E*MERGING TECHNOLOGY

HOSPITAL ROBOTS INCREASE QUALITY AND EFFICIENCY

If you go to a hospital and see a robot dispensing medicine to patients, do not be alarmed. The robot, armed with a gripper, picks up medications from a storage cell and delivers them to bar-coded patient bins. The bins are then brought by hospital technicians to the nursing floors and administered to the patients.

A large hospital dispenses about 12,000 doses of medicines per day. When done manually, the dispensing involves human errors, sometimes as much as 1 percent a day. An error may kill a patient. The robot (developed by Automated Healthcare) does not make mistakes. Furthermore, the robot keeps track of the dispensed drugs through an inventory control system built into its own software. It also increases efficiency by calculating the shortest paths for medication pickup and delivery.

Critical Thinking Issue: If you were in a hospital, would you be comfortable having a robot select your medication? ▲

SOURCE: Condensed from *ComputerWorld*, January 11, 1993.

A Closer Look BOX 16.3

*E*MERGING TECHNOLOGY

USE OF COMPUTER VISION IN QUALITY CONTROL

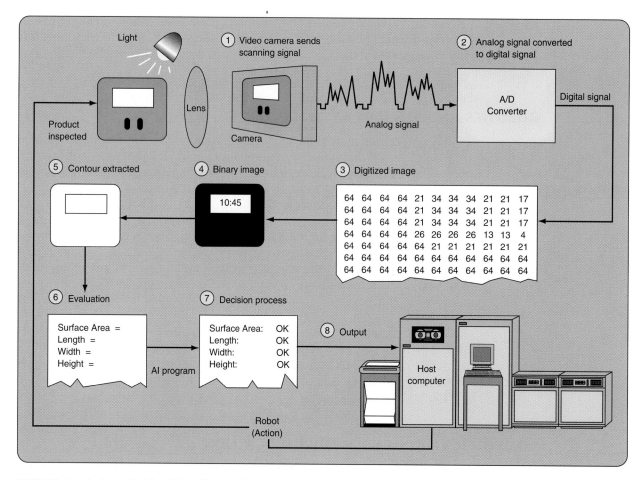

SOURCE: *Introduction to Machine Vision*, Allen-Bradley Publication 2805–2.1, 1985, pp. 1–3.

quality. The basic objective of computer vision is to interpret scenarios. Computer vision is used extensively in performing industrial quality control (e.g., inspection of products).

Box 16.3 illustrates how information collected by a camera (a sensor) is digitized and interpreted by a computer AI program. The computer then instructs a robot to take an action such as removing a defective product.

INTELLIGENT COMPUTER-AIDED INSTRUCTION

Intelligent computer-aided instruction (ICAI) refers to machines that can tutor humans. To a certain extent, such a machine can be viewed as an expert system. However, the major objective of an expert system is to render advice, whereas the purpose of ICAI is to teach.

Computer-assisted instruction (CAI), which has been in use for several decades, brings the power of the computer to bear on the educational process. Now AI methods are being applied to the development of *intelligent* computer-assisted instruction systems in an attempt to create computerized "tutors" that shape their teaching techniques to fit the learning patterns of individual students.

ICAI applications are not limited to schools; as a matter of fact, they have found a sizable niche in the military and corporate sectors. ICAI systems are being used today for various tasks such as problem solving, simulation, discovery, learning, drill and practice, games, and testing. Such systems are also used to support people with physical or learning impairments.

MACHINE LEARNING

Automated problem solving has been a target for generations, long before computers were invented. After computers were developed, they were used to solve structured problems using quantitative models. Complex problems, however, cannot be solved by such models. Instead, specialized knowledge is needed. Such knowledge can be provided, in some cases, by expert systems (ES). However, the use of ES is limited by such factors as its rule structure, difficulties in knowledge acquisition, and inability to learn from experience. For situations where an ES is inappropriate, we use a different approach called **machine learning**. Machine learning refers to a set of methods that attempt to teach machines to solve problems or to support problem solving by analyzing (learning from) historical cases.

This task, however, is not simple. One problem is that there are many models of learning. Sometimes it is difficult to match the learning model with the type of problem that needs to be solved. Two methods of machine learning, *neural computing* and *fuzzy logic*, are described in Sections 16.14 and 16.15.

OTHER APPLICATIONS

AI can be applied to several other tasks such as automatic computer programming, summarizing news, and translation from one language to another. The ultimate aim of automatic programming is a computer system that can develop programs by itself, in response to and in accordance with the specifications of a program developer. Some computer programs "read" stories in newspapers or other documents and make summaries in English or in other languages (see Box 16.4). This helps in handling the information-overload problem.

Computer programs are able to translate words and simple sentences from one language to another. For example, a package called LOGUS is used for translating from English to German (and German to English).

IT At Work BOX 16.4

GENERAL ELECTRIC'S SCISOR ANALYZES FINANCIAL NEWS

General Electric's Research and Development Center has developed a natural language system called SCISOR (System for Conceptual Information Summarization, Organization, and Retrieval) which performs text analysis and question answering in a constrained domain. One application of this system is in analyzing financial news. SCISOR automatically selects and analyzes stories about corporate mergers and acquisitions from an on-line financial service, Dow Jones. It is able to process news at 10 seconds per story. First, it determines if the story is about a corporate merger or acquisition. Then, it selects information such as the target, suitor, and price per share. The system also allows the user to browse and ask questions such as, "What was offered for Polaroid?" or "How much was Bruck Plastics sold for?" The schematic of this answer retrieval process is shown in the accompanying diagram.

This application demonstrates how natural language processors can be used in the knowledge acquisition mode, selecting specific types of articles from a universe of financial news. It also uses a processor as a database interface to permit questioning using ordinary language. Its effectiveness was demonstrated in testing when it proved to be 100 percent accurate in identifying all 31 mergers and acquisitions stories that were included in a universe of 731 financial news releases from the newswire source.

Critical Thinking Issues: What is the benefit of analyzing financial news by a machine? How does it relate to database inquiries? ▲

SOURCE: Condensed from *Management Accounting*, October, 1989.

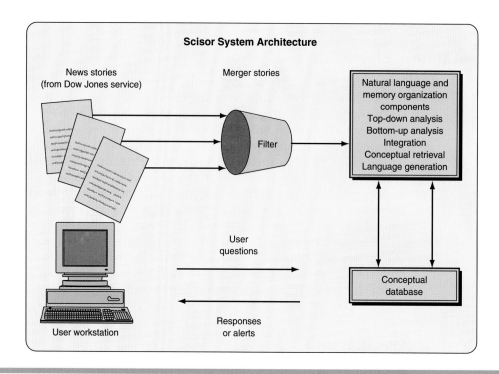

▶ 16.5 WHAT IS AN EXPERT SYSTEM?

When an organization has a complex decision to make or a problem to solve, it often turns to experts for advice. These experts have specific knowledge and experience in the problem area. They are aware of alternative solutions, chances of success, and costs that the organization may incur if the problem is not solved. Companies engage experts for advice on such matters as equipment purchase, mergers and acquisitions, and advertising strategy. The more unstructured the situation, the more specialized (and expensive) is the advice. Expert systems (ES) are an attempt to mimic human experts (see Box 16.5).

IT AT Work BOX 16.5

GENERAL ELECTRIC'S EXPERT SYSTEM MODELS HUMAN TROUBLESHOOTERS

THE PROBLEM. General Electric's (GE) top locomotive field service engineer, David I. Smith, had been with the company for more than 40 years. He was the top expert in troubleshooting diesel electric locomotive engines. Smith was traveling throughout the country to places where locomotives were in need of repair, to determine what was wrong, and advise young engineers about what to do. The company was very dependent on Smith. The problem was that he was nearing retirement.

TRADITIONAL SOLUTION. GE's traditional approach to such a situation was to create apprenticeship teams that paired senior and junior engineers. The pairs worked together for several months or years, and by the time the older engineers finally did retire, the younger engineers had absorbed enough of their seniors' expertise to carry on troubleshooting or other tasks. This practice proved to be a good short-term solution, but GE still wanted a more effective and dependable way of disseminating expertise among its engineers and preventing valuable knowledge from retiring with people like David Smith. Furthermore, because railroad service shops are scattered all over the world, it is not economically feasible to keep an expert on a permanent base in each and every location.

GE decided to build an expert system to solve the problem by modeling the way a human troubleshooter works. The system builders spent several months interviewing Smith and transferring his knowledge to a computer. The computer programming was prototyped over a three-year period, slowly increasing the knowledge and number of decision rules stored in the computer. The new diagnostic technology enables a novice engineer or technician to uncover a fault by spending only a few minutes at the computer terminal. The system can also explain to the user the logic of its advice, serving as a teacher. Furthermore, the system can lead users through the required repair procedures, presenting a detailed, computer-aided drawing of parts and subsystems and providing specific how-to instructional demonstrations.

The system is based on a flexible, human-like thought process, rather than rigid procedures expressed in flowcharts or decision trees.

The system, which was developed on a minicomputer but operates on microcomputers, is currently installed at every railroad repair shop served by GE, thus eliminating delays, preserving Smith's expertise, and boosting maintenance productivity.

Critical Thinking Issue: If an expert system can replace David Smith, why not replace all experts in the world with expert systems? ▲

Typically, an ES is a decision-making software that can reach a level of performance comparable to—or even exceeding that of—a human expert in some specialized and usually narrow problem areas. The basic idea behind an ES is simple. *Expertise* is transferred from an expert (or other sources of expertise) to the computer. This knowledge is then stored in the computer. Users can call on the computer for specific advice as needed. The computer can make inferences and arrive at a conclusion. Then, like a human expert, it advises the nonexperts and explains, if necessary, the logic behind the advice. ES can sometimes perform even better than any single expert (see Box 16.6).

Let us discuss the major concepts involved in an expert system in order to better understand its capabilities. These concepts were referred to in Box 16.5.

EXPERTISE AND KNOWLEDGE

Expertise is the extensive, task-specific *knowledge* acquired from training, reading, and experience. Knowledge enables experts to make better and faster decisions than nonexperts in solving complex problems. It takes a long time (usually several

IT At Work BOX 16.6

AN EXPERT SYSTEM BEATS TEN WALL STREET HOUSES

Macro World Investor is an expert system that makes buy/sell recommendations for traders on Wall Street. The system, which sells for $899, analyzes the relationship between economic trends, price movements, and financial fundamentals. This ES outperformed the ten best investment firms as ranked by *The Wall Street Journal* (see the April 21, 1989 issue). A complementary package is used for economic forecasting. Both packages run on a PC. (SOURCE: Based on a story in *AI Week*, July 1, 1989.)

Expert systems are not the only ones that beat professional traders. The newspaper *Expressen* (Stockholm, Sweden) gave the equivalent of $1,250 each to five stock analysts and a chimpanzee named Ola. They were told to make as much money as they could on the stock market. While the stock experts carefully considered their portfolios, Ola made his choice by throwing darts at names of companies listed on the Stockholm stock exchange. One of the chimp's darts hit Forsheda, a small diversified company whose stock rose 44 percent over the month. So, the chimp won, making $190 profit in one month (August 3 to September 3, 1993). A suggestion has been made that the chimp now compete against the expert system.

Critical Thinking Issue: Is the expert system powerful enough to beat the chimpanzee? ▲

---

years) to become an expert. Expertise is distributed in organizations in an uneven manner. A few senior or top experts possess more knowledge than junior experts. Figure 16.3 demonstrates a typical distribution of knowledge in an organization.

The objective of an expert system is to transfer expertise from an expert to a computer and then on to other humans (nonexperts). This process involves four activities: *knowledge acquisition* (from experts or other sources), *knowledge representation* (in the computer), *knowledge inferencing*, and *knowledge transfer* to the user.

Knowledge acquisition involves obtaining knowledge from experts or from documented sources. Through the activity of knowledge *representation*, acquired knowledge is organized in one of several possible configurations and stored, electronically, in a knowledge base. A unique feature of an expert system is its ability to reason. Given that the necessary expertise is stored in the knowledge base and that the program has accessibility to databases, the computer is programmed so

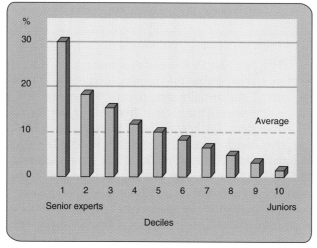

FIGURE 16.3 Distribution of expertise: percent successes achieved per decil. A senior expert possesses about 30 times more expertise than a junior expert. (SOURCE: Adapted from Augustine, N. R., "Distribution of Expertise," *Defense Systems Management*, Spring 1979.)

that it can make inferences. The inferencing is performed in a component called the **inference engine**. The inference results in a piece of advice or a recommendation for novices. Thus, the expert's knowledge, has been *transferred* to users. A unique feature of an ES is its ability to explain its advice or recommendation. The explanation and justification is done in a subsystem called the *justifier* or the *explanation subsystem*.

▶ 16.6 BENEFITS AND LIMITATIONS OF EXPERT SYSTEMS

During the past few years, the technology of expert systems has been successfully applied in thousands of organizations worldwide to problems ranging from AIDS research to the analysis of dust in mines (see Box 16.7 for illustrative applications).

IT At Work BOX 16.7

 **G LOBAL PERSPECTIVE**

INNOVATIVE EXPERT SYSTEMS—A SAMPLER

Of the many innovative expert systems on the market, the following are of particular interest.

TARA: An Intelligent Assistant for Foreign Traders. Foreign exchange currency traders cannot afford to think over multimillion-dollar situations for long. They must examine large quantities of data; consider historical trends; determine what is relevant; and, many times in the course of a day, make the ever-critical decision to buy or sell. The decisions must be made very quickly, frequently within minutes. Prediction is a high-risk, high-reward job, where even the best traders are pleased with being right 60 percent of the time. At Manufacturers Hanover Trust, an expert system called the Technical Analysis and Reasoning Assistant (TARA) was built to assist foreign currency traders. (SOURCE: Schorr and Rappaport [1989].)

Pitch Expert. This large system was implemented in Kraft pulp mills in Canada to analyze and diagnose problems associated with pitch dirt and pitch deposition. The solution to the problems which Pitch Expert is helping to solve requires special expertise, which must be up-to-date. When experts are unavailable, or when the experts are not fully trained, losses occur. These losses are estimated at $80 million annually in Canada. The system increases productivity in close to 40 Canadian mills rep-

resenting over 20 companies. Savings are estimated at $22 million annually.

The system is used also for training employees. Since the problems of pulp mills are similar, the system is used not only by 20 Canadian companies but also by companies in other countries. (SOURCE: Condensed from *AI Magazine*, Fall 1993.)

Analyst: An Advisor for Financial Analysis for Automobile Dealerships. One of the services General Motors (GM) offers to approximately 12,000 domestic GM dealerships (and affiliates) is inventory financing. This service is also known as wholesale or "floor plan" financing. In exchange for funds, dealers must adhere to a set of rules, the most important of which is to promptly pay GM as vehicles are sold. Adherence is analyzed at least annually. The process of analyzing a dealership is, in essence, financial risk analysis. An expert system was developed to expedite analysis, specifically to predict a dealership's likely performance until the next scheduled review. The system also recommends credit lines and suggests ways to reduce risk. (SOURCE: Schorr and Rappaport [1989].)

Critical Thinking Issue: Is there anything common to these three systems? ▲

THE BENEFITS OF EXPERT SYSTEMS

Why have ES become so popular? It is because of the large number of capabilities and benefits ES provide? A few of these are described next.

INCREASED OUTPUT AND PRODUCTIVITY. ESs can work faster than humans. For example, a system called XCON has enabled Digital Equipment Corporation (DEC) to increase fourfold the production preparation of minicomputers which are customized for their clients. Thus, DEC is using a *mass customization* approach in their production.

INCREASED QUALITY. ES can increase quality by providing consistent advice and reducing the error rates. For example, XCON reduced the error rate of configuring computer orders from 35 percent to 2 percent.

CAPTURE OF SCARCE EXPERTISE. The scarcity of expertise becomes evident in situations where there are not enough experts for a task, where the expert is about to retire or leave the job (as in case of Box 16.5, General Electric Company), or where expertise is required over a broad geographic location (see Box 16.8).

IT At Work BOX 16.8

GLOBAL PERSPECTIVE

KNOWLEDGE TRANSFER TO REMOTE LOCATIONS

One of the greatest potential benefits of ES is its ease of transference across international boundaries. An example of such a transfer is an eye-care ES (for diagnosis and recommended treatment) developed at Rutgers University in conjunction with the World Health Organization. The program has been implemented in Egypt and Algeria, where serious eye diseases are prevalent but eye specialists are rare. The program is rule-based, runs on a microcomputer, and can even be operated by a physician's assistant or nurse.

Critical Thinking Issue: If this ES works as indicated, do we really need eye doctors? ▲

OPERATION IN HAZARDOUS ENVIRONMENTS. Many tasks require humans to operate in hazardous environments. ES that interprets information collected by sensors enables workers to avoid hot, humid, or toxic environments, such as a nuclear power plant that has malfunctioned.

ACCESSIBILITY TO KNOWLEDGE AND HELP DESKS. Expert systems make knowledge (and information) accessible to many people in several locations. People can query systems and receive advice. One area of applicability is in support of help desks.

RELIABILITY. ES are reliable. They do not become tired or bored, call in sick, or go on strike; and they do not talk back to the boss. ES also consistently pay attention to all details and do not overlook relevant information and potential solutions.

INCREASED CAPABILITIES OF OTHER COMPUTERIZED SYSTEMS. Integration of ES with other systems makes the other systems more effective; the integrated systems cover more applications, work faster, and produce higher-quality results.

ABILITY TO WORK WITH INCOMPLETE OR UNCERTAIN INFORMATION. In contrast to conventional computer systems, ESs can work with incomplete information, like human experts. The user can respond with a "don't know" or "not sure" answer to one or more of the system's questions during a consultation, and the ES will still be able to produce an answer, although it may not be a certain one.

PROVISION OF TRAINING. ES can provide training. Novices who work with ES become more and more experienced. The explanation facility can serve as a teaching device, and so can notes that may be inserted into the knowledge base.

ENHANCEMENT OF PROBLEM SOLVING CAPABILITIES. ES enhance problem solving by allowing the integration of top experts' judgments into analysis. Problem solving is also enhanced by the integration of expertise of several experts. Thus, one can solve problems where the required scope of knowledge exceeds that of any one individual (see Box 16.9).

IT At Work BOX 16.9

AUTOMATED MARKETING ANALYSIS AT OCEAN SPRAY CORPORATION

Ocean Spray Cranberries is a large, fruit-processing cooperative of fruit growers. Ocean Spray needed data to determine the effectiveness of its promotions and advertisements, and to be able to strategically respond to its competitors' promotions. The company also wanted to identify trends in consumer preferences for new products and pinpoint marketing factors that might be causing changes in the selling level of certain brands and markets. The company buys marketing data from InfoScan. InfoScan collects data, using bar code scanners, in a sample of 2,500 stores nationwide. The data for each product include sales volume, market share, distribution, and price information. Information about promotions (sales, advertisements) is also collected. The amount of data provided to Ocean Spray on a weekly (and soon on a daily) basis is overwhelming (about 100 to 1,000 times more data items than Ocean Spray used to collect on its own).

All the data are deposited in the corporate database. In 1993, it was estimated to contain about 600 million numbers and was growing at a rate of 100 million numbers per year. To analyze the vast amount of data, the company developed a DSS. Although it is used primarily by analysts, the managers and salespeople of Ocean Spray requested a system that would be easy and fast to use. The solution was another information system called CoverStory. CoverStory is an expert system. CoverStory summarizes information in accordance with user preferences. It interprets data processed by the DSS, identifies trends, discovers cause–effect relationships, presents hundreds of displays, and provides any information required by the decision makers. This system alerts managers to key problems and opportunities. Ocean Spray has found that it is simply impossible to run the business without this system.

Critical Thinking Issues: Why does Ocean Spray need 1000 times more data? What is the role of the expert system in analyzing this data? ▲

SOURCE: Condensed from *Interfaces*, Nov./Dec. 1990, pp. 29–38.

ELIMINATION OF THE NEED FOR EXPENSIVE EQUIPMENT. In many cases, a human must rely on expensive instruments for monitoring and control. Using ES one can perform the same tasks with lower-cost instruments because of the ability to investigate the information provided by instruments more thoroughly and quickly. Alternatively, if we have a complex piece of equipment, an ES can make it easier to operate.

FLEXIBILITY. ES can offer flexibility in both service and manufacturing industries. For example, DEC tries to make each computer order fit the customer's needs as closely as possible. Before XCON, DEC found it increasingly difficult to do this because of the variety of customer requests.

THE LIMITATIONS OF EXPERT SYSTEMS

Available ES methodologies are not always straightforward and effective. Here are some problems that have slowed the commercial spread of ES.

▼ Knowledge to be captured is not always readily available.

▼ Expertise is hard to extract from humans.

▼ The approach of each expert to a situation may be different, yet correct.

▼ It is hard, even for a highly skilled expert, to abstract good situational assessments when he is under time pressure.

▼ Users of expert systems have natural cognitive limits, so they may not use the benefits of the system to the fullest extent.

▼ ES work well only in a narrow domain.

▼ Most experts have no independent means of checking whether their conclusions are reasonable or correct.

▼ The vocabulary, or jargon, that experts use for expressing facts and relations is frequently limited and not understood by others.

▼ Help in building ES is frequently required from knowledge engineers who are rare and expensive—a fact that could make ES construction rather costly.

▼ Lack of trust by end users may be a barrier to ES use.

▼ Knowledge transfer is subject to several perceptual and judgmental biases.

In addition, expert systems may not be able to arrive at conclusions (especially in early stages of system development). For example, even the fully developed XCON cannot fulfill about 2 percent of the orders presented to it. Finally, expert systems, like human experts, sometimes produce incorrect recommendations. Some of these limitations are lessening with the second generation of ES.

▶ 16.7 COMPONENTS OF AN EXPERT SYSTEM

The following components may exist in an expert system: knowledge base, inference engine, blackboard (workplace), user interface, explanation subsystem (justifier), and knowledge refining system. Their relationships are shown in Figure 16.4, and a brief description of each component follows.

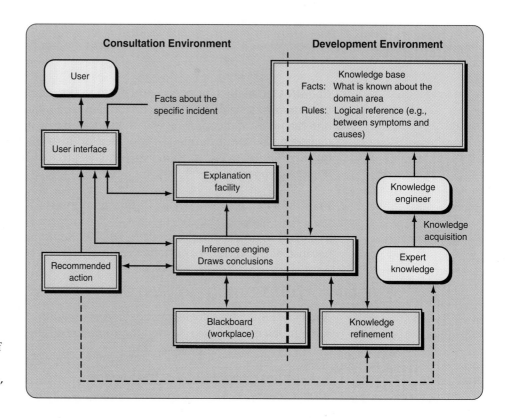

FIGURE 16.4 Structure of an expert system. (SOURCE: Turban, 1993, p. 473.)

KNOWLEDGE BASE

The knowledge base contains knowledge necessary for understanding, formulating, and solving problems. It includes two basic elements: (1) *facts*, such as the problem situation and theory of the problem area, and (2) special heuristics or *rules* that direct the use of knowledge to solve specific problems in a particular domain.

INFERENCE ENGINE

The "brain" of the ES is the inference engine, also known as the *control* structure or the rule interpreter (in rule-based ES). This component is essentially a computer program that provides a methodology for reasoning and formulating conclusions. The major functions of the inference engine include the following.

▼ Determining which rules will be used.

▼ Presenting the user with a question, whenever needed.

▼ Adding the answers to the ES memory.

▼ Inferring a new fact from a rule.

▼ Adding the inferenced fact to the memory.

BLACKBOARD

The **blackboard** is an area of *working memory* set aside for the description of a current problem, as specified by the input data; it is also used for recording intermediate results. It is a kind of database.

USER INTERFACE

Expert systems manage communication between the user and the computer. This communication could best be carried out in a natural language, usually presented as questions and answers and sometimes supplemented by graphics. Future interfaces will include voice understanding and synthesis.

EXPLANATION SUBSYSTEM (JUSTIFIER)

The ability to trace responsibility for conclusions to their source is crucial both in the transfer of expertise and in problem solving. The explanation subsystem can trace such responsibility and explain the ES's behavior by interactively answering questions such as the following.

▼ *Why* was a certain question asked by the expert system?

▼ *How* was a certain conclusion reached?

▼ *Why* was a certain alternative rejected?

▼ *What* is the plan to reach the solution? For example, what remains to be established before a final diagnosis can be determined?

KNOWLEDGE REFINING SYSTEM

Human experts have a **knowledge refining** system; that is, they can analyze their own performance, learn from it, and improve it for future consultations. Similarly, such evaluation is necessary in computerized learning so that the program will be able to analyze the reasons for its success or failure. This can lead to improvements that result in a better knowledge base and more effective reasoning.

Such a component is not available in commercial expert systems at the moment, but it is being developed (based on machine learning techniques) in experimental ES.

▶ 16.8 HOW ARE EXPERT SYSTEMS DEVELOPED?

Constructing an ES may be done in two different ways. Either one *builds* all (or some) of the components described in the previous section, or one *acquires* all the components *except the content* of the knowledge base which must be built. The latter option is known as building an expert system with a *shell*. That is, all the components of the ES, except the knowledge base, are fairly generic. Therefore, they can be reused for different expert systems. The knowledge is the content, or the ''inside'' of the shell. Using shells, we can build systems much faster and with less programming skills. Building an ES with a shell, however, has limitations: the builder is constrained by the features of the shell so he has less flexibility. In addition, one can buy a ready-made ES off the shelf. But, the number of such ES is limited and they can be used only for generic applications.

KNOWLEDGE ENGINEERING

The process of building expert systems by either of the previous approaches is described as **knowledge engineering**. The process includes the following five activities: *knowledge acquisition, knowledge validation, knowledge representation, inferencing,* and *explanation.* (see Figure 16.5)

1. *Knowledge acquisition.* Knowledge is acquired from human experts, books, documents, sensors, or other sources such as computer files. The knowledge may be specific to the problem domain and the problem-solving situation, it may be general knowledge (e.g., knowledge about business), or it may be **metaknowledge** (knowledge about knowledge). By the latter, we mean information about how experts use their knowledge to solve problems.

2. *Knowledge validation.* Knowledge is validated and verified (e.g., by using test cases) until its quality is acceptable.

3. *Knowledge representation.* The acquired knowledge is organized in an activ-

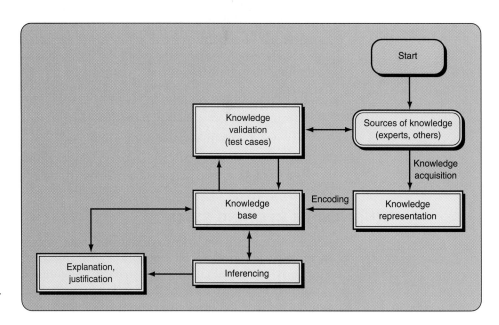

FIGURE 16.5 Process of knowledge engineering. (SOURCE: Turban, 1993, p. 511.)

ity called knowledge representation. This activity involves preparation of a "knowledge map" and encoding the knowledge into the knowledge base.

4. *Inferencing.* Inferencing involves the design of software that will enable the computer to make inferences based on knowledge that a user has regarding a specific problem and then provide advice to the user.

5. *Explanation.* The design of an explanation is provided by an explanation facility. For example, this includes programming the ability to answer questions like *why* a specific piece of information is needed by the computer or *how* a certain conclusion was derived by the computer.

THE DEVELOPMENT PROCESS

Because an ES is basically computer software, its development follows a software development process using a prototyping approach. The various tasks that are encountered in building an ES are organized into six phases as shown in Figure 16.6. Notice that the process is cyclical; that is, you may return to previous phases. The prototyping (called *rapid prototyping* in ESs) is in the core of the process.

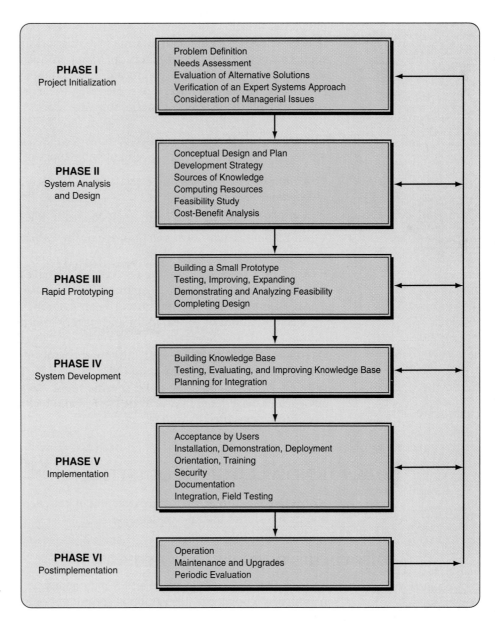

FIGURE 16.6 Schematic view of the ES development life cycle. (SOURCE: Turban, 1993, p. 633.)

PARTICIPANTS IN THE DEVELOPMENT PROCESS

Several humans usually participate in the development of an expert system. But at minimum, there is a builder (the knowledge engineer) and there is an expert.

THE EXPERT. The expert is a person who has special knowledge, judgment, experience, and methods as well as the ability to apply these talents to give advice and solve problems. It is the expert's job to provide knowledge about how he accomplishes the task that the ES will perform. The expert knows which facts are important and understands the meaning of the relationships among facts. In diagnosing a problem with an automobile's electrical system, for example, an expert mechanic knows that fan belts can break and cause the battery to discharge. Directing a novice to check the fan belt and interpreting the meaning of a loose or missing belt are examples of expertise. When more than one expert is used, situations can become difficult if the experts disagree.

THE KNOWLEDGE ENGINEER. The knowledge engineer helps the expert(s) structure the problem area by interpreting and integrating human answers to questions, drawing analogies, posing counter examples, and bringing conceptual difficulties to light. She is usually also the system builder. The shortage of experienced knowledge engineers is a major bottleneck in ES construction. To overcome this bottleneck, ES designers are using productivity tools (e.g., special editors), and research is being conducted on building systems that will bypass the need for knowledge engineers. In some cases, the expert can act as the knowledge engineer with the support of special software tools.

THE USER. Most computer-based systems have evolved targeted to a single-user mode. In contrast, an ES has several possible types of users.

▼ A nonexpert client seeking direct advice. In such a case, the ES acts as a *consultant* or *advisor*.

▼ A student who wants to learn. In such a case, the ES acts as an *instructor*.

▼ An ES builder who wants to improve or increase the knowledge base. In such a case, the ES acts as a *partner*.

▼ An expert. In such a case, the ES acts as a *colleague* or an *assistant*. For example, an ES can provide a "second opinion," so the expert can validate his judgment. An expert can also use the system as an assistant to carry on routine analysis of computations or to search for and classify information.

OTHER PARTICIPANTS. Several other participants may be involved in an ES. For example, a *system builder* may assist in integrating the ES with other computerized systems. A *tool builder* may build specific tools. *Vendors* may provide tools and advice, and *support staff* may provide clerical and technical help. Note that several roles can be executed by one person.

▶ 16.9 KNOWLEDGE ACQUISITION

Knowledge acquisition is the extraction of knowledge from sources of expertise and its transfer to the knowledge base.

DIFFICULTIES IN KNOWLEDGE ACQUISITION

The fact that the knowledge in an ES may appear in several sources is only one reason why knowledge acquisition is considered one of the most difficult phases (perhaps *the* most difficult phase) of building an expert system. The following are some other major difficulties of acquiring knowledge.

EXPRESSING THE KNOWLEDGE. To solve a problem, a human expert executes a two-step internal process. First, the expert inputs relevant information about the problem into his brain. Second, the expert uses inductive, deductive, or other problem-solving approaches with the information. The result (output) is a recommendation on how to solve the problem. An expert may have difficulty describing this process to a knowledge engineer, or the expert may describe the process inaccurately.

TRANSFER TO A MACHINE AND REPRESENTATION. Knowledge is transferred to a machine where it must be organized in a particular manner. The machine *requires* the knowledge to be expressed explicitly at a lower, *more detailed* level than humans use. Human knowledge exists in a compiled format. A human expert usually does not remember all the intermediate steps used by his brain in transferring or processing knowledge.

NUMBER OF PARTICIPANTS. In a regular transfer of knowledge, there are two participants: sender and receiver. In ES, there could be four (or even more) participants: expert, knowledge engineer, system designer (builder), and user. The more participants involved, the more difficult is the acquisition.

STRUCTURING THE KNOWLEDGE. In an ES, it is necessary to elicit not only the knowledge, but also its structure. We have to represent the knowledge in a structured way (e.g., as rules). This may be a difficult task.

OTHER REASONS. Several other reasons add to the complexity of transferring knowledge.

▼ The experts automate some of their processing and are not able to explain how they solve certain problems.

▼ The experts may lack time, be unwilling to cooperate, or change their behavior when they are observed and/or interviewed.

▼ The system builders have a tendency to collect knowledge from one source, but relevant knowledge may be scattered across several sources. Also builders may attempt to collect documented knowledge rather than use experts. Thus the knowledge collected may be incomplete.

▼ It is difficult to recognize specific knowledge when it is mixed up with irrelevant data; it is also difficult to test and refine it.

▼ Problematic interpersonal communication factors may exist between the knowledge engineer and the expert.

To overcome these difficulties, it is necessary to use a structured process to acquire knowledge, which is described next.

METHODS OF KNOWLEDGE ACQUISITION

The basic model of knowledge acquisition portrays teamwork in which a knowledge engineer mediates between the expert and the knowledge base. The knowledge engineer elicits knowledge from the expert, refines it with the expert, and represents it in the knowledge base. The elicitation of knowledge from the expert can be done in one of the following approaches.

Manual methods are basically structured around some kind of an interview. The knowledge engineer elicits knowledge from the expert and/or other sources and then codes it in the knowledge base. The process is shown in Figure 16.7. Manual methods are slow, expensive, and sometimes inaccurate. Therefore, the trend is to automate the process.

Semiautomatic methods are divided into two categories: (1) those intended to support experts by allowing them to build knowledge bases with little or no help from knowledge engineers (Figure 16.7, Part b), and (2) those intended to help knowledge engineers by allowing them to execute necessary tasks in a more efficient and/or effective manner.

In *automatic methods*, the roles of expert, knowledge engineer, and builder are combined. For example, the induction method shown in Figure 16.7 (Part c) can be administered by a system analyst. The role of the expert is minimal and there is little need for a separate knowledge engineer. However, the term automatic may be misleading. There is always going to be a human builder, but there may be little or no need for a separate knowledge engineer or expert.

KNOWLEDGE ACQUISITION FROM MULTIPLE EXPERTS

In many cases, builders tend to build ES for a very narrow domain in which expertise is clearly defined. In such a case, it is easy to find one expert. However, in certain cases, there could be a need for **multiple experts**, especially when a complex ES is constructed or when expertise is not particularly well defined.

The major purposes of using multiple experts are (1) to broaden the coverage of proposed solutions (i.e., the solutions complement each other), and (2) to combine the strengths of different approaches of reasoning.

When multiple experts are used, there are often differences of opinion and conflicts that have to be resolved. Conflicts can arise because experts follow different lines of reasoning derived from their backgrounds and experiences.

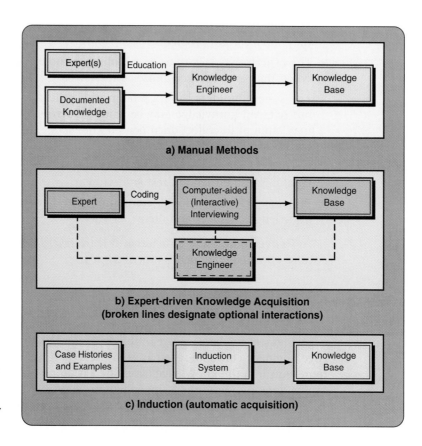

FIGURE 16.7 Methods of knowledge acquisition. (SOURCE: Turban, 1993, pp. 519–520.)

VALIDATION AND VERIFICATION OF THE KNOWLEDGE BASE

Knowledge acquisition involves quality control aspects that appear under the terms *evaluation, validation,* and *verification.* These terms are frequently confused, mixed up, or used interchangeably. We use the definitions provided by O'Keefe et al. (1987).

Evaluation is a broad concept. Its objective is to assess an expert system's overall value. In addition to assessing acceptable performance levels, it analyzes whether the system would be usable, efficient, and cost-effective.

Validation is the part of evaluation that deals with the performance of the system (e.g., how it compares to experts). Simply stated, validation refers to building the "right" system, that is, substantiating that the system performs with an acceptable level of accuracy.

Verification refers to building the system "right," that is, substantiating that the system correctly implements its specifications.

▶ 16.10 KNOWLEDGE REPRESENTATION

Once knowledge is acquired, it must be organized in one or more configurations. The knowledge in the knowledge base may be organized differently from that in the inference engine through a variety of knowledge representation schemes. The two most common representation methods are described: *production rules* and *frames.*

PRODUCTION RULES

The concept of **production rules** was developed by Newell and Simon (1973) for their model of human cognition. The basic idea of these systems is that knowledge is presented as rules in the form of condition–action pairs: "IF this condition occurs, THEN some *action* will (or should) occur." Expert systems whose knowledge is represented solely as production rules are referred to as **rule-based systems**.

Rules may appear in different forms. Some examples include the following.

▼ *IF condition THEN action.* For example:
IF your income is high, THEN your chance of being audited by the IRS is high.

▼ *Action IF condition.* For example:
Your chance of being audited is high IF your income is high.

▼ *More complex rules.* For example:
IF your credit rating is high AND your salary is more than $30,000 OR your assets are more than $75,000, AND your pay history is not poor, THEN approve a loan of up to $10,000, and list the loan in category B. The action part may include additional information: THEN approve the loan and refer to an agent.

The IF side of a rule may include dozens of IFs. The THEN side may include several parts as well.

Two types of rules are common in AI: knowledge and inference. Knowledge rules, or *declarative rules,* state all the facts and relationships about a problem domain. Inference rules, or *procedural rules,* advise on how to solve a problem, given that certain facts are known.

FRAMES

A **frame** is a data structure that includes all the relevant knowledge about a particular object. This knowledge is organized in a special hierarchical structure that

```
┌─────────────────────────────────────────────┐
│  ┌───────────────────────────────────────┐  │
│  │        Automobile Frame               │  │
│  └───────────────────────────────────────┘  │
│                                              │
│   Class of:  Transportation                  │
│   Name of Manufacturer:  Audi                │
│   Origin of Manufacturer:  Germany           │
│   Model:  5000 Turbo                         │
│   Type of car:  Sedan                        │
│   Weight:  3300 lb.                          │
│   Wheelbase:  105.8 inches                   │
│   Number of doors:  4 (default)              │
│   Transmission:  3-speed auto                │
│   Number of wheels:  4 (default)             │
│   Engine:  (Reference Engine Frame)          │
│     • Type:  In-line, overhead cam           │
│     • Number of cylinders:  5                │
│   Acceleration (procedural attachment)       │
│     • 0-60:  10.4 seconds                    │
│     • Quarter mile:  17.1 seconds, 85 mph    │
│   Gas mileage:  22 mpg average (procedural attachment) │
│                                              │
│  ┌───────────────────────────────────────┐  │
│  │          Engine Frame                 │  │
│  └───────────────────────────────────────┘  │
│                                              │
│   Cylinder bore:  3.19 inches                │
│   Cylinder stroke:  3.4 inches               │
│   Compression ratio:  7.8 to 1               │
│   Fuel system:  Injection with turbocharger  │
│   Horsepower:  140 hp                        │
│   Torque:  160 ft./LB                        │
└─────────────────────────────────────────────┘
```

FIGURE 16.8 Frame describing an automobile. (SOURCE: Turban, 1993, p. 566.)

permits knowledge processing. Frames are basically an application of *object-oriented programming* for AI and ES.

Frames, as in *frames of reference*, provide a concise, structural representation of knowledge in a natural manner. In contrast to other representation methods, the values that describe one object are grouped together into a single unit called a frame. Thus, a frame encompasses complex objects, entire situations, or a management problem as a single entity. The knowledge in a frame is partitioned into slots. A slot can describe declarative or procedural knowledge.

A typical frame describing an automobile is shown in Figure 16.8. Note the slots describing attributes, such as name of manufacturer, model, origin of manufacturer, type of car, number of doors, engine, and other characteristics.

▶ 16.11 HOW DO EXPERT SYSTEMS MAKE INFERENCES?

Once an ES is completed, it is disseminated to users either by sending them a disk or making the ES available on a network. The user turns on the system to start a dialogue with the computer via the user interface. A simple interface includes an exchange of questions and answers. A sample of a question-and-answer dialogue regarding the purchasing of a car is given in Box 16.10.

Notice that the computer asks questions and the user provides answers. However, the user can also ask questions, such as "why" and "how," and the answers are provided by the computer. The dialogue in Box 16.10 ended with a specific recommendation. The numbers in the column labeled "value" are the confidence levels (on a scale of 0 to 10). Working with ES software, it is frequently possible to conduct a sensitivity analysis. Thus, the user can change some of the input data and see how the new recommendations compare with the old ones. The results in Box 16.10 show the current values vs. the previous (before the change was completed).

IT At Work BOX 16.10

HOW TO SELECT AN ADVERTISEMENT MEDIA— A SAMPLE OF AN ES CONSULTATION

This prototype system will attempt to provide recommendation(s) on the advertising mix so as to maximize the client's product exposure in the market. Presently, the system only makes recommendations on two types of advertising media: television and newspaper.

Sample Printout of Consultation

```
EXSYS Pro ══════ You may select ONLY ONE value ══════

        Client prefer
          1   Only TV media
          2   Only Newspaper media
          3   More TV media
          4   More Newspaper media
          5   No preference indicated




                     ▮ ►► Why_


Enter the value number<s> or select with arrow keys and press <ENTER>
WHY  QUIT  <H>-help  Memo <F10>
```

The user asks the computer *why* (why you need this information). The computer answers by displaying the pertinent rule (#1).

```
EXSYS Pro ══════ RULE NUMBER: 1 ══════

  IF:
       <1> Client prefer ONLY TV media
  THEN:
          All budget on TV - Confidence=8/10

  NOTE:  The client is always right. We should always try to meet the
  client's expectations. If the client prefers only TV as the
  advertising medium for product exposure, we should accomodate it.




IF line # for derivation <K>-known data  <C>-choices
↑or↓ - prev. or next rule <J>-jump  <H>-help <F10>-Memo <ENTER>-Done:
```

```
EXSYS Pro ════════════════════════════════════

     Please input a value for the variable

     ┌─────────────────────────────────────────┐
     │ Please enter the size of the client's budget │
     └─────────────────────────────────────────┘
               ▮ ►► 80000_



WHY   QUIT  <H>-help  Memo <F10>  <Ctrl-U>Undo
```

Once all questions are answered by the user, the expert system displays the recommendations:

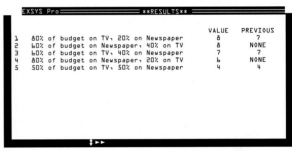

```
EXSYS Pro ═══════════ **RESULTS** ═══════════

                                            VALUE   PREVIOUS
  1   80% of budget on TV, 20% on Newspaper    8       7
  2   60% of budget on Newspaper, 40% on TV    8      NONE
  3   60% of budget on TV, 40% on Newspaper    7       7
  4   80% of budget on Newspaper, 20% on TV    6      NONE
  5   50% of budget on TV, 50% on Newspaper    4       4


              ▮ ►►

All choices <A> only if >1 <G>  Print <P>  Change/rerun <C>
Rules used <line #> Quit/save <Q> Help <H> Memo <F10> Done <D>
```

Note: Print-outs generated with EXSYS PRO (from EXSYS Corporation). ▲

To use a knowledge base, we need a computer program that will enable us to access the knowledge for the purpose of making inferences for problem solving. This program is an algorithm that controls some reasoning processes, and it is usually referred to as the inference engine. In rule-based systems, it is also referred to as the rule interpreter. This program directs the search through the knowledge base. The process may involve the application of inference rules. The program decides which rule to investigate, which alternative to eliminate, and which attribute to match.

▶ 16.12 APPLICATIONS OF EXPERT SYSTEMS

Expert systems are in use today for many applications in all types of organizations. ES are especially useful in ten generic categories, which are displayed in Table 16.2.

Table 16.2 **Generic Categories of Expert Systems**

Category	Problem Addressed
1. Interpretation	Inferring situation descriptions from observations
2. Prediction	Inferring likely consequences of given situations
3. Diagnosis	Inferring system malfunctions from observations
4. Design	Configuring objects under constraints
5. Planning	Developing plans to achieve goal(s)
6. Monitoring	Comparing observations to plans, flagging exceptions
7. Debugging	Prescribing remedies for malfunctions
8. Repair	Executing a plan to administer a prescribed remedy
9. Instruction	Diagnosing, debugging, and correcting student performance
10. Control	Interpreting, predicting, repairing, and monitoring system behavior

The following four examples illustrate the diversity and nature of applications.

EXAMPLE 1: RUSSIAN TRADE ADVISOR

GLOBAL PERSPECTIVE

...how to trade with the former Soviet Union

PROBLEM. The economic and political changes in what used to be the Soviet Union may provide an opportunity for many companies to trade with Eastern Europe. However, there is little expertise in Western countries on what is really going on in Russia and other countries of the former Soviet Union. So while there are opportunities, there are also risks. The situation is clouded by a stream of incomplete, frequently contradictory, and even incorrect data. Business people want quick and reliable advice, but it is rarely available. (The U.S. Department of Commerce is flooded with such requests.)

SOLUTION. An expert system was developed by Deloitte and Touche, a management consulting firm. The major objective of the system is to provide advice on trade opportunities and licensing requirements for medium- to high-technology products. The system started as an advisory service to the company's consultants. Now it is marketed (for a fee) to potential traders. Also, the ES deals with export licensing requirements and provides a facsimile of an export license application (displayed on the screen with instructions about how to complete it). The system, which includes several knowledge bases, is supported by hypertext that helps navigating through the complex forms.

USE. The system is very user friendly; it is based on simple sets of menus. The market is divided into 12 sectors, each matched with potential products. The system assesses the opportunities for general classes of products and for specific ones. Then, potential buyers are identified, as well as procedures for making contacts. Explanations are provided on request. Several other types of valuable information are provided by the system. (SOURCE: Condensed from Szuprowicz [1991].)

EXAMPLE 2: TICKET AUDITING AT NORTHWEST AIRLINES

PROBLEM. When Northwest Airlines (NWA) acquired Republic Airlines, its volume of operations increased to 50,000 tickets per day. These tickets needed to be audited by comparing a copy of each ticket against fare information including commissions. There are about 40,000 separate agreements between NWA and various travel agents. The travel agents report the commissions, but not how they were computed. Manual comparison was slow and expensive. Therefore, only *samples* of the tickets (about 1 percent) were audited. The sample indicated an error rate of about 10 percent (usually a loss to the airline).

SOLUTION. A ticket-auditing ES was built during 1990 and 1991. All tickets are scanned electronically and stored in a database. Another database stores all the fares and commission agreements. Then the expert system goes to work. The system first determines the correct fare, using 250 rules. Then, the most favorable commission to the agents is determined. Any discrepancy results in a report to the agent, with a debit or credit and an appropriate explanation. The system also provides information for marketing, contract management, planning, and control.

RESULTS. The system initially processed 70,000 tickets each night on a SUN workstation. Furthermore, future growth can be handled easily. The reduction in agent errors saves NWA about $10 million annually. (SOURCE: Condensed from Smith and Scott [1991].)

EXAMPLE 3: CREDIT CLEARING HOUSE— DUN & BRADSTREET CORPORATION

PROBLEM. The Dun and Bradstreet credit clearing house provides risk analysis to manufacturers, wholesalers, jobbers, and marketers in the apparel industry. Credit rating and specific credit amounts are recommended for each of about 4,000 customers. Dun & Bradstreet maintains and updates a database of credit rating on approximately 200,000 businesses, and the apparel industry is only a portion of it. Customers of Dun & Bradstreet used to complain about inaccuracies (it is difficult to update the material constantly), inconsistencies (different interpretations by different risk analysts), and slow response time.

SOLUTION. An expert system was developed using ART IM from Inference Corporation. The system is capable of handling more than 90 percent of all requests, using its almost 1,000 rules and the accompanying databases.

RESULTS. Response time has been reduced from about three days to several seconds, and the recommendations generated are very consistent. Also, as soon as there are changes in the retailers' data, the expert system reevaluates the implications on credit worthiness and informs its clients, if needed. Similar systems are in operation in other business units at Dun & Bradstreet. (SOURCE: Condensed from Neuquist [1990].)

EXAMPLE 4: DUSTPRO—ENVIRONMENTAL CONTROL IN MINES

PROBLEM. The majority of the 2,000 active mines in the United States are medium or small sized. They cannot afford a full-time dust control engineer, whose major job is to reevaluate and reassign facilities each time operating conditions change. However, if a dust control engineer is not readily available, the mine must be shut down until an expert arrives. Experts are expensive but so is downtime, so this can be costly. Operating without appropriate testing and interpretation of results is a violation of federal regulations.

SOLUTION. DustPro is a small rule-based system developed by the U.S. Bureau of Mines. It includes about 200 rules and was developed with a Level 5 shell (from Information Builders) on a microcomputer. It took about 500 hours to develop the system. The system is now in operation in more than 200 mines.

SYSTEM CHARACTERISTICS. DustPro advises in three areas: control of methane gas emission, ventilation in continuous operations, and dust control for the mine's machines. Data on air quality is entered manually. The user interface is very friendly. The system is composed of 13 subareas of expertise, and the average consultation time is 10 to 15 minutes.

SYSTEM USE. DustPro, through a series of questions, determines what types of ventilation are used, what the dust standard is, and which type of mine is most affected by the dust. Then, the system can advise the operators what to do if problems are suspected. The system and its variants are used at the U.S. Bureau of Mines Pittsburgh Research Center to diagnose problems telephoned in by mine operators. This saves bureau staff time and travel expense. Also, the staff can respond more quickly and devote more time to research and development. The system is so successful that more than ten countries have requested permission to use it in their mines. (SOURCE: Condensed from an Information Builders publicity publication.)

▶ 16.13 NATURAL LANGUAGE PROCESSING AND VOICE TECHNOLOGY*

Natural language processing (NLP) refers to communicating with a computer in English or whatever language you may speak. Today, to tell a computer what to do, you type in commands by the keyboard. In responding to a user, the computer outputs message symbols or other short, cryptic notes of information.

To use a computer properly, you must learn the commands, languages, and jargon. This usually takes considerable time and practice. Then you need to remember everything. This is the main reason why computers have been called unfriendly. Menus and icons with pointing devices like light pens, the mouse, and touch screens help. But they are not perfectly natural.

Many problems could be minimized or even eliminated if we could communicate with the computer in our own languages. We would simply type in directions, instructions, or information. Better yet, we would converse with the computer using voice. The computer would be smart enough to interpret the input, regardless of format.

To understand a natural language inquiry, a computer must have knowledge to analyze and then interpret the input. This may include linguistic knowledge about words, domain knowledge, common sense knowledge, and even knowledge about the users and their goals. Once the computer understands the input, it can take the desired action.

In addition to *natural language understanding*, there is also *natural language generation*. Once the computer takes action, it will usually provide some output. In many cases, it is desirable to provide that output in a natural language. For that reason, the computer must be able to generate appropriate natural language. The easiest way to do this is to provide "canned" sentences, phrases, paragraphs, or other outputs.

In this section, we are going to talk about *natural language processing* software—programs that understand and generate natural language inputs and outputs. We will also cover the practical applications of such software. Finally, *voice recognition* systems will be considered.

NATURAL LANGUAGE PROCESSING SOFTWARE

Presently, two major techniques are used in NLP programs: *key word analysis* (pattern matching) and *language processing* (syntactical and semantic analysis). Other methods, such as the use of neural computing, will not be covered here.

---

*SOURCE: Based, in part, on Frenzel, 1987.

KEY WORD ANALYSIS (PATTERN MATCHING)

In **pattern matching**, the NLP program searches through an input sentence looking for selected **key words** or phrases. Once a key word or phrase is recognized, the program responds with specific "canned" responses.

Alternatively, the program may actually construct a response, based on a partial reply coupled with the key words or selected phrases from the input. The program recognizes very specific inputs that it uses to construct an output response or initiate some other action.

The program usually starts by displaying a message on the screen to elicit an input response from the user. Next, the program scans the input text searching for key words. The program can tell where one word ends and another begins by looking for spaces and punctuation marks. As each word is identified, it is used in pattern-matching processing that compares the word to a list of *prestored words* and phrases.

Each word in the input text is matched against those in the key word directory stored in the program. Two possibilities exist. The first is that no key word is located. If that is the case, the program is set up to respond with one or more stock messages (e.g., "please rephrase your input"); then the process continues for all key words. This process may continue for several iterations until an appropriate word is recognized. As a result, an appropriate output response is selected or developed and sent to the user. An early key word matching program is ELIZA. Using ELIZA, it is easy to see both the capabilities and the limitations of NLP (see Box 16.11).

A Closer Look BOX 16.11

PORTION OF A CONVERSATION WITH ELIZA

* HOW DO YOU DO.
   PLEASE TELL ME YOUR PROBLEM.

** My problem is artificial intelligence.

* YOUR PROBLEM IS ARTIFICIAL INTELLIGENCE—THAT'S INTERESTING.

** Well actually, the real problem is a subfield of artificial intelligence called natural language.

* I AM NOT SURE I UNDERSTAND YOU FULLY.

** That is the problem, getting a program to understand.

* PLEASE GO ON.

** How can I get a program to comprehend what I tell it in plain English?

* WHY DO YOU ASK?

** That is the source of my problem.

* WHY DO YOU SAY YOUR PROBLEM?

** Well, it is not my problem exclusively, but I still have it.

* DOES THE FACT THAT YOUR PROBLEM IS NOT EXCLUSIVELY YOURS SUGGEST ANYTHING ELSE TO YOU?

** Not at all.

* DOES THAT HAVE ANYTHING TO DO WITH THE FACT THAT YOUR PROBLEM IS ARTIFICIAL INTELLIGENCE?

** It sure does.

* WHAT DOES THAT SUGGEST TO YOU?

** If I understood AI well enough, I wouldn't have such a problem with natural language understanding.
   etc, etc, etc.

* = ELIZA; ** = client

LANGUAGE PROCESSING (SYNTACTIC, SEMANTIC, AND PRAGMATIC ANALYSIS)

Although key word pattern matching is a widely used technique, its usefulness is restricted because it simply cannot deal with the large variations that occur in using natural languages. The most obvious and straightforward approach to the problem is to perform a detailed analysis of the syntax and semantics of an input statement. In this way, the exact structure of an input sentence and its meaning can be determined. Of course, this is easier said than done. Even sophisticated systems for analyzing syntax and semantics fall short of the job, because *there are too many words with multiple meanings* (such as *can*, *will*, and *class*) and an enormous number of ways to put these together to form sentences.

Syntax analysis looks at the way a sentence is built—the arrangement of its components and their relationships. Syntactic processes analyze and designate sentences to make clear the grammatical relationships between words in sentences. *Semantics* is concerned with assigning meaning to the various syntactic constituents. *Pragmatics* attempts to relate individual sentences to one another and to the surrounding context.

APPLICATIONS OF NATURAL LANGUAGE PROCESSING AND SOFTWARE

Natural language processing programs have been applied in several areas. The most important are: human–computer interfaces (mainly to databases), abstracting and summarizing text, grammar analysis, translation of a natural language to another natural language (e.g., English to German), translation of a computer language to another computer language, speech understanding, and composing letters (see Box 16.12).

By far the most dominant use of NLP is in interfaces, or "front-ends," for other software packages. Such *front-end interfaces* are used to simplify and improve

---

A Closer Look BOX 16.12

EMERGING TECHNOLOGY

COMPOSING LETTERS BY MACHINE

The functional breakdown of Ombudsman, a product that was an intelligent correspondence generation (ICG) in composing documents is diagrammed below.

Critical Thinking Issues: What is the benefit of composing a letter by a machine? Would you prefer that a machine write your letters?

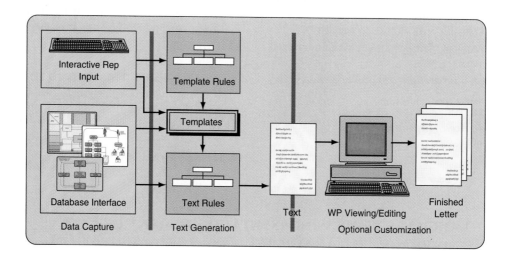

(SOURCE: Courtesy of Cognitive Systems, New Haven, CT.)

communications between application programs and the user. The natural language front-end allows the user to operate the applications programs with everyday language.

Although natural language front-ends are being created for a wide variety of application programs, their most common use is with DBMS. An example of a commercial package is INTELLECT (from Trinzic Corporation previously AI Inc.); see Box 16.13. A popular PC-based product is Paradox (from Borland International Corporation). This product combines NLP and DBMS.

IT At Work BOX 16.13

 **GLOBAL PERSPECTIVE**

APPLICATION OF INTELLECT AT BRITISH GAS

British Gas is a large natural gas provider; it serves two million customers in the United Kingdom. In less than three months, the company wrote 25 different management information applications with INTELLECT. The systems ranged from quality assurance to customer inquiry handling, as well as accounting and legal systems. Of special interest is a system for the personnel director that allows a broad overview of staffing levels and requirements.

"It is as quick to use as any fourth-generation language on the market and is efficient in its use of machine resources," comments Dudley, the director of information systems. "We were also impressed by both the simplicity of the syntax and the privacy and access control aspects of the product."

The ultimate goal is for senior managers to be able to ask any question they want and receive an answer from the computer using INTELLECT's capabilities. New systems at British Gas are designed to remove the need for regular printed reports and to enable users to produce their own information in the format they find most useful.

Critical Thinking Issue: Does using INTELLECT mean that you can conduct a conversation with a machine? ▲

(SOURCE: Publicly disclosed information from Trinzic Corporation.)

SPEECH (VOICE) RECOGNITION AND UNDERSTANDING

Speech or **voice recognition** is the process of having the computer recognize normal human speech. When a speech recognition system is combined with a natural language processing system, the result is an overall system that not only recognizes voice input but also *understands* it.

Speech recognition is a process that allows one to communicate with a computer by speaking to it. The term *speech recognition* is sometimes applied only to the first part of the process—recognizing words that have been spoken without necessarily interpreting their meanings. The other part of the process, where the meaning of the speech is ascertained, is called *speech understanding*. It may be possible to understand the meaning of a spoken sentence without actually recognizing every word and vice versa.

ADVANTAGES OF SPEECH RECOGNITION

The ultimate goal of speech recognition is to allow a computer to understand the natural speech of any human speaker at least as well as a human listener could understand it. In addition to the fact that this is the most natural method of communication, speech recognition offers several other advantages.

▼ *Ease of access*—Many more people can speak than type. As long as communication with a computer depends on developing typing skills, many people may not be able to use computers effectively.

▼ *Speed*—Even the most competent typists can speak more quickly than they can type. It is estimated that the average person can speak twice as quickly as a proficient typist can type.

▼ *Manual freedom*—Obviously, communicating with a computer through typing occupies your hands. There are many situations in which computers might be useful to people whose hands are otherwise occupied, such as product assemblers, pilots of military aircraft, and busy executives.

▼ *Remote access*—Many computers are set up to be accessed remotely by telephones. If a remote database includes speech recognition capabilities, you could retrieve information by issuing oral commands into a telephone.

▼ *Accuracy*—In typing information, one is prone to make mistakes, especially in spelling. These are minimized with voice input.

VOICE SYNTHESIS

The technology by which computers speak is known as **voice synthesis**. The synthesis of voice by computer differs from a simple playback of a prerecorded voice by either analog or digital means. As the term synthesis implies, sounds that make up words and phrases are constructed electronically from basic sound components and can be made to form any desired voice pattern.

The current quality of synthesized voice is very good, but the technology remains somewhat expensive. The anticipated lower cost and improved performance of synthetic voice in the near future will encourage more widespread commercial applications. Opportunities for its use will encompass almost all applications that can provide an automated response to a user, such as enquiries by employees pertaining to payroll and benefits. Several banks already offer a voice service to their customers, informing them about their balance, which checks were cashed, and so on.

▶ 16.14   NEURAL COMPUTING

The tools of AI have been mostly restricted to sequential processing and to only certain representations of knowledge and logic. A different approach to intelligent systems involves constructing computers with architecture and processing capabilities that mimic certain processing capabilities of the brain. The results are knowledge representations based on massive parallel processing, fast retrieval of large amounts of information, and the ability to recognize patterns based on experience. The technology that attempts to achieve these results is called **neural computing** or **artificial neural networks** (ANNs).

BIOLOGICAL AND ARTIFICIAL NEURAL NETWORKS

Artificial neural networks are biologically inspired. Specifically, they borrow ideas from the manner in which the human brain works. The human brain is composed of special cells called **neurons**. Estimates of the number of neurons in a human brain cover a wide range—up to 100 billion—and there are more than a hundred different kinds of neurons. Neurons are separated into groups called networks. Each network contains several thousand neurons that are highly interconnected. Thus, the brain can be viewed as a collection of neural networks.

The ability to learn and react to changes in our environment requires intelligence. Thinking and intelligent behavior are controlled by the brain and the central nervous system.

EMERGING TECHNOLOGY
...mimicking the human brain

An artificial neural network (ANN) is a model that emulates a biological neural network. Today's neural computing uses a very limited set of concepts from biological neural systems. The concepts are used to implement software simulations of massive parallel processes that involve processing elements (also called artificial neurons or neurodes) interconnected in a network architecture. The artificial neuron receives inputs that are analogous to electrochemical impulses which biological neurons receive from other neurons. The output of the artificial neuron corresponds to signals sent out from a biological neuron. These artificial signals can be changed, similar to the change occurring in the human brain. Neurons in an ANN receive information from other neurons or from external sources, perform transformation on the information, and pass on the information to other neurons or external outputs.

The manner in which information is processed by an ANN depends on its structure and on the algorithm used to process the information.

COMPONENTS AND STRUCTURE OF ANN

An ANN is composed of artificial neurons (referred to as neurons); these are the **processing elements** (PEs). Each of the neurons receives input(s), processes the input(s), and delivers a single output. This process is shown in Figure 16.9.

Each ANN is composed of a collection of neurons that are grouped in layers. A typical structure is shown in Figure 16.10. Note the three layers: input, intermediate (called the hidden layer), and output. Several hidden layers can be placed between the input and output layers.

Similar to biological networks, an ANN can be organized in several ways; that is, neurons can be interconnected in different ways. In processing information, many of the processing elements perform their computations at the same time. This **parallel processing** resembles the way the brain works, and it differs from the serial processing of conventional computing.

PROCESSING INFORMATION IN THE NETWORK

Once the structure of a network is determined and the network is constructed, information can be processed. Several concepts related to processing are important.

Each *input* corresponds to the value of a single attribute. For example, if the problem is to decide on the approval or disapproval of a loan, an attribute can be income level, age, or ownership of a house. All inputs—including qualitative at-

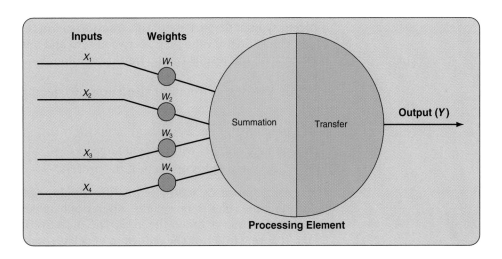

FIGURE 16.9 Processing information in an artificial neuron. (SOURCE: Turban, 1993, p. 686.)

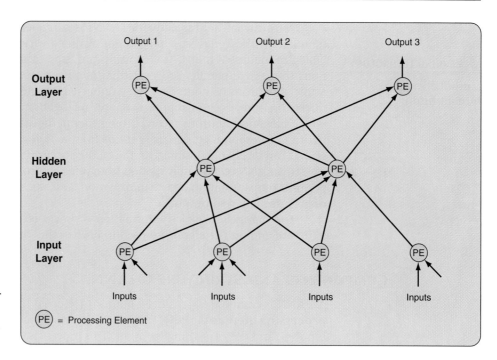

FIGURE 16.10 Neural network with one hidden layer. (SOURCE: Turban, 1993, p. 687.)

tributes, voice, or pictures—must be preprocessed into binary (0 and 1) equivalencies. Examples of inputs to neural networks are graphics, digitized images, voice patterns, digitized signals from monitoring equipment, and coded data from loan applications.

The *output* of the network is the solution to a problem. In the case of the loan application, for example, it may be "yes" or "no." The ANN assigns numeric values, for example, $+1$ for "yes" and 0 for "no." The purpose of the network is to compute the values of the outputs.

A key element in an ANN is the *weight*. Weights express the *relative strength* (or importance) of the initial entering data, or the various connections that transfer data from layer to layer. Weights are crucial; it is through repeated adjustments of weights that the network "learns."

The *summation function* finds the weighted average of all input elements entering into each processing element. The summation function computes the internal stimulation of the neuron. Based on this level, the neuron may or may not produce an output. The relationship between the internal stimulation level and the output are expressed by *transformation (transfer) functions*, and there are several different types. The purpose of this transformation is to modify the output levels to some meaningful value (e.g., between zero and one). Once the transformation is completed, the results can be translated into operational terms (such as "yes" and "no").

An ANN learns from its experiences. A typical process of learning involves three tasks:

1. Compute outputs.
2. Compare outputs with desired targets.
3. Adjust the weights and repeat the process.

The learning process starts by setting the weights randomly at some levels or by following some rules to do so. The difference between the actual output (Y) and the desired output is called the *delta*. The objective is to minimize the delta (or better, reduce it to zero). The reduction of delta is done by incrementally changing the weights.

HARDWARE AND SOFTWARE

Although neural computing is structured to run on parallel processing, it is considerably more inexpensive and simple to run it on a single processor. Current neural network applications use software simulations with a single processor expedited by the use of special acceleration boards. Thus, applications can even run on a PC. In the future, it will be economically feasible to run some ANNs on parallel processors.

BENEFITS AND APPLICATIONS OF NEURAL NETWORKS

The value of neural network technology includes its usefulness for **pattern recognition**, learning, classification, generalization, and abstraction, as well as the interpretation of incomplete and noisy inputs.

Neural networks have the potential to provide some of the human characteristics of problem solving that are difficult to simulate using the logical, analytical techniques of DSS or even expert systems. For example, neural networks can analyze large quantities of data to establish patterns and characteristics in situations where rules are not known. Neural networks may be useful for financial applications such as measuring stock fluctuations for determining an appropriate portfolio mix. These features have thus far proven to be difficult for the symbolic/logical approach of traditional AI.

Neural networks have several other benefits:

▼ *Fault tolerance.* Since there are many processing nodes, damage to a few nodes or links does not bring the system to a halt.

▼ *Generalization.* When a neural network is presented with an incomplete or previously unseen input, it can generate a reasonable response.

▼ *Adaptability.* The network learns in new environments. The new cases are used immediately to retrain the program and keep it updated.

Beyond its role as an alternative computing mechanism, neural computing can be combined with other CBIS to produce powerful hybrid systems. Such integrated systems include models, databases, expert systems, and other technologies to produce computerized solutions to complex problems.

In general, ANNs do not do well at tasks that are not done well by people. For example, speedy arithmetic and data processing tasks are not suitable for ANNs and are best accomplished by conventional computers. Specific areas of business that are well suited to the assistance of ANNs include the following:

▼ *Financial services*—identification of patterns in stock market data and assistance in bond trading strategies.

▼ *Loan application evaluation*—judging worthiness of loan applications based on patterns in previous application information.

▼ *Solvency prediction*—assessing the strengths and weaknesses of corporations and predicting possible failures.

▼ *Credit card information*—fast detection of fraud from purchasing patterns (see Box 16.14).

▼ *Airline forecasting*—prediction of seat demand after training with historical data; rapid modification by retraining with new data as they become available.

▼ *Evaluation of personnel and job candidates*—matching personnel data to job requirements and performance criteria; it allows flexibility and tolerance of incomplete information.

▼ *Resource allocation based on historical, experiential data.*—finding allocations that will maximize outputs.

IT At Work BOX 16.14

FIGHTING CREDIT CARD FRAUD WITH NEURONS

Credit card losses cost American banks several billion dollars each year. Almost all credit card fraud involves counterfeit cards, use of stolen cards, and fraudulent credit card applications. In the past, card issuers have tried to curtail their losses with software programs based on statistical regression.

"The problem is that these kinds of programs have never allowed for higher vacation spending, holiday splurges, or emergency expenses," said Ted Crooks of HNC Corporation "You save for that lifetime trip, and when you get there, your credit might be cut off because the bank's program thought you to be a conservative spender."

When legitimate customers are denied credit, the danger for the bank is that their cardholders will switch to another card for the transaction—and then maybe forever. The only other solution banks had was to ignore the fraud.

To curtail fraud and improve banks' response to cus-

tomers, HNC has developed Falcon, a neural network product. Falcon passes each transaction as input to the neural network, which decides on the probability of fraud, scores it, and returns the result to the merchant in real time. The bank sets the threshold of probability, including making the decision about when a human analyst should be summoned.

"The beauty of Falcon is that it not only looks at transactions, it looks at the *nature* of transactions. It looks at the *relationships* among information," Crooks said.

The Falcon approach offers broad protection against 90 percent of all potential fraud. It is especially effective for lost or stolen cards, where quick response is essential.

Critical Thinking Issue: What is the advantage of Falcon over a simpler check against the balance in the database? ▲

SOURCE: Condensed from "Application Watch," *AI Expert*, March 1993.

▶ 16.15 FUZZY LOGIC

...handling inexact information for profit through fuzzy logic

Fuzzy logic deals with uncertainty. This technique, developed by Zadeh (1988) simulates the process of human reasoning by allowing the computer to behave less precisely and logically than conventional computers do.

The thinking behind this approach is that decision making is not always a matter of black and white, true or false; it often involves gray areas and the term *maybe*. In fact, creative decision-making processes are often unstructured, playful, contentious, and rambling.

Fuzzy logic can be advantageous for the following reasons:

▼ *It provides flexibility.* Rigid thinking can often lead to unsatisfactory conclusions. You have locked yourself into a set pattern. Make allowances for the unexpected, and you can shift your strategy whenever necessary.

▼ *It gives you options.* If you are confronted with a number of possibilities, you will need to consider them all. Then, using facts *and* intuition ("highly unlikely" or "very good"), you can make an educated guess. Even computers are learning to use such rules of thumb.

▼ *It frees the imagination.* At first, you may feel that something simply cannot be done—all the facts conspire against it. Why not try asking yourself, "What if . . . ?" Follow another avenue, and see where you end up. You may make a better decision.

▼ *It is more forgiving.* When you are forced to make black-and-white decisions, you cannot afford to be wrong. When you are wrong, you lose completely. The other way is more forgiving. If you figure something is 80 percent gray, but it turns out to be 90 percent gray, you are not going to be penalized very much.

▼ *It allows for observation.* Literal-minded computers have been known to come up with some peculiar results. For example, when one user instructed her computer to come up with information on smoking in the workplace, the computer diligently churned out an article on a smoked salmon-processing plant. A little fuzzy logic might have helped the computer make a more intelligent choice.

▼ *It shortens systems' development time.*

▼ *It decreases systems' maintainability.*

▼ *It uses less expensive hardware than systems that do similar things.*

▼ *It handles control or decision-making problems which are not easily defined by mathematical models.*

According to Barron (1993), productivity of decision makers using fuzzy logic can improve 3,000 percent.

EXAMPLE: INTERNATIONAL INVESTMENT MANAGEMENT: STOCK SELECTION

𝒢LOBAL PERSPECTIVE

...investing wisely in global markets using fuzzy logic

An international investment company is using a combined fuzzy logic and ANN system (called FuzzyNet) to forecast the expected returns from stocks, cash, bonds, and so on in order to determine the optimal allocation of assets. Since the company invests in global markets, it is necessary to determine the credit worthiness of various countries and estimated performances of key socioeconomic ratios. Then, it must select specific stocks based on company, industry, and economic data. The final stock portfolio must be adjusted according to the forecast of foreign exchange rates, interest rates, and so on—which are handled by a currency exposure analysis. The integrated network architecture of the system is shown in Figure 16.11. As can be seen, the integrated system includes the following technologies:

1. *Expert system.* The system provides the necessary knowledge for both country and stock selection (rule-based system).

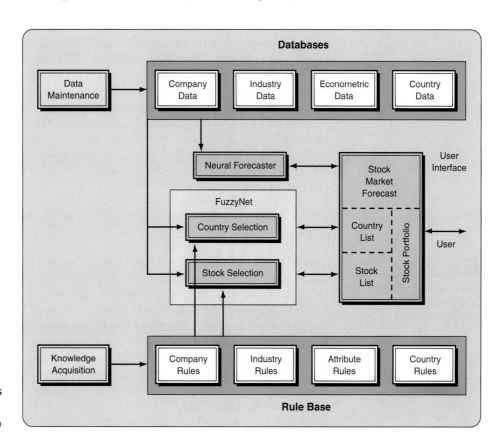

FIGURE 16.11 FuzzyNet's architecture. (SOURCE: Wong et al., 1992, p. 48.)

2. *Neural network.* The neutral network conducts a forecasting, based on the data included in the database.

3. *Fuzzy logic.* The fuzzy logic supports assessment of factors for which there are no reliable data. For example, the *credibility* of rules in the rule base is given only as a probability. Therefore, the conclusion of the rule may be expressed either as a probability or as a degree of fuzzy membership.

The rule base feeds into the FuzzyNet, along with data from the database. The FuzzyNet is composed of three modules: membership function generator, fuzzy information processor, and back-propagation neural network. The modules are interconnected; each performs a different task in the decision process. By using several tools, it is possible to handle a broader range of information and solve more complex problems.

▶ 16.16 INTELLIGENT SYSTEMS SUPPORT FOR KNOWLEDGE WORKERS, AND SELF-DIRECTED TEAMS

Intelligent systems can support the work of many diverse employees, both blue-collar and white-collar. Any job that can be improved with expertise can be enhanced with AI technologies. However, two groups of employees merit special attention: knowledge workers and self-directed teams.

KNOWLEDGE WORKERS

As described in Chapter 2, **knowledge workers** perform three major roles. First, they monitor and interpret the ever-expanding external knowledge for the organization. Intelligent systems can help by summarizing news and other information, and by assisting in the interpretation of information. Second, knowledge workers act as internal consultants. Intelligent systems can expedite the analysis required. Frequently, knowledge workers need information support or database searches. These can be enhanced by intelligent systems. Finally, knowledge workers act as change agents. Since most workers are not experts on change management, they can get help from expert systems.

In many cases, the traditional hierarchical management approach is not effective for large numbers of knowledge workers. Organizations are restructuring their companies to create flatter organization or organizations composed of many self-directed teams. Many of the employees in the self-directed teams are knowledge workers.

SELF-DIRECTED TEAMS

*R*EENGINEERING

...self-managed teams equipped with computerized expertise

Several times in this book, we have mentioned the concept of self-directed work teams which are empowered to do all their tasks. Ideally, such teams have the technical skills and authority needed to manage themselves. In practice, this is rarely true. Teams, like any organizational unit, need help from experts from time to time. Also, team members need to be continuously trained to keep up with changing technologies. Expertise is expensive and may sometimes be inaccessible. Therefore, it makes sense to equip the teams with computerized expertise. This is where intelligent systems play a major role.

An example of such an arrangement is in the city of Los Angeles (see the Part IV case for more details), where the service level management section of the Information Systems Department is an autonomous team responsible for troubleshooting problems in 12,000 workstations citywide. The team is supported by an intelligent system which includes an expert system supported by hypertext and video images. The system has doubled members' productivity, increased quality, and provided advice, especially to junior members of the team.

▶ MANAGERIAL ISSUES

The implementation of intelligent systems is an extremely important yet difficult task in organizations.

Heightened Expectations. There is *too much expectation* and hope associated with these technologies. People do not understand them and do not know how to build and maintain them. As a result, there is a very large failure rate (some people estimate it at 85 percent). Once systems fail, management gets discouraged. As a result, they may miss important opportunities and lag behind the competition. This can be even more risky than building systems that fail.

Acquiring Knowledge. Intelligent systems are built up on experts' knowledge. How to acquire this knowledge is a major problem. It is not only the technical issues discussed earlier, but there is also the motivational issue. How can an expert be motivated to contribute his knowledge?

System Acceptance. The acceptance of intelligent systems by the IS department and the integration of such systems with mainstream IT is a critical success factor. There are psychological, social, technical, and political reasons for the IS department to reject the new technologies. Without the cooperation of the IS department, these systems are likely to fail.

System Integration. Intelligent systems can succeed as stand-alone systems, but they have a broader area of applications when integrated with other CBIS. This is another reason why the IS department must cooperate. Such hybrid systems are complex, but if they are successful, the rewards can be enormous.

System Technologies. In a period when the role of intelligent systems is growing and expected to reach 20 percent of all IT applications by the end of the decade, it is critical for any prudent management to closely examine the technologies and their business applicability.

Ethical Issues. Finally, there can be ethical issues related to the implementation of expert systems and other intelligent systems. The actions performed by an expert system can be unethical, or even illegal. For example, the expert system may advise you to do something that will hurt someone, or invade the privacy of certain individuals. ■

KEY TERMS

CHAPTER HIGHLIGHTS *(L-x means learning objective number x)*

▼ The primary objective of AI is to build computers that will perform tasks that can be characterized as intelligent. (L-1)

▼ The major characteristics of AI are symbolic processing, use of heuristics instead of algorithms, and application of inference techniques. (L-1)

▼ AI has several major advantages over people: it is permanent; it can be easily duplicated and disseminated; it can be less expensive than human intelligence; it is consistent and thorough; and it can be documented. (L-1)

▼ The major application areas of AI are expert systems, natural language processing, speech understanding, intelligent robotics, computer vision, and intelligent computer-aided instruction. (L-1)

▼ Knowledge engineering involves acquisition, representation, reasoning (inference), and explanation of knowledge. (L-2)

▼ Expert system technology attempts to transfer knowledge from experts and documented sources to the computer, in order to make the knowledge available to nonexperts for the purpose of solving difficult problems. (L-2)

▼ The major components of an ES are a knowledge base, inference engine, blackboard, user interface, and explanation subsystem. (L-2)

▼ The inference engine, or thinking mechanism, is a program of using the knowledge base, a way of reason with it to solve problems. (L-2)

▼ Expert systems, like human experts, can make mistakes. (L-3)

▼ Knowledge acquisition, especially from human experts, is a difficult task due to several communication and information-processing problems. (L-3)

▼ Validation and verification of the knowledge base are critical success factors in ES implementation. (L-3)

▼ Production rules take the form of an IF-THEN statement, such as: IF you drink too much, THEN you should not drive. (L-3)

▼ A frame is a holistic data structure based on object-oriented programming technology. (L-3)

▼ The ten generic categories of ES are interpretation, prediction, diagnosis, design, planning, monitoring, debugging, repair, instruction, and control. (L-4)

▼ Expert systems can provide many benefits. The most important are improvement in productivity and/or quality, preservation of scarce expertise, enhancing other systems, coping with incomplete information, and providing training. (L-4)

▼ Natural language processing (NLP) provides an opportunity for a user to communicate with a computer in day-to-day spoken language. (L-5)

▼ Speech recognition enables people to communicate with computers by voice. There are many benefits to this emerging technology. (L-5)

▼ Neural computing attempts to mimic the manner in which the brain works. (L-6)

▼ Neural systems are composed of processing elements called artificial neurons. They are interconnected; and they receive, process, and deliver information (usually in binary code). A group of connected neurons forms an artificial neural network. (L-6)

▼ Fuzzy logic is a technology that helps analyze situation under uncertainty. The technology can also be combined with an ES and ANN to conduct complex predictions and interpretations. (L-7)

QUESTIONS FOR REVIEW

1. What is the Turing Test?
2. List the major advantages that artificial intelligence has over natural intelligence.
3. List the major disadvantages of artificial intelligence compared with natural intelligence.
4. Define a knowledge base.
5. List three capabilities of an ES.
6. Explain how an ES can distribute (or redistribute) the available knowledge in an organization.
7. Define the major components of an ES.
8. A knowledge base includes facts and rules. Explain the difference between the two.
9. Which component of ES is mostly responsible for the reasoning capability?
10. What is the function of the justifier?
11. Who are the potential users of ES?
12. List the ten generic categories of ES.
13. Describe some of the limitations of ES.
14. What are the steps in the knowledge engineering process?

15. What is metaknowledge?

16. Contrast knowledge acquisition with knowledge representation.

17. List several sources of knowledge.

18. Compare declarative and procedural knowledge.

19. Give four reasons why knowledge acquisition is difficult.

20. What are the major difficulties of knowledge acquisition from multiple experts?

21. Define evaluation, validation, and verification of knowledge.

22. Describe a natural language and natural language processing.

23. What are the major advantages of NLP?

24. Distinguish between NLP and natural language generation.

25. The use of NLP as an interface to DBMS is gaining popularity. Explain how NLP increases the accessibility to databases.

26. List the major advantages of voice recognition.

27. What is an artificial neural network?

28. How do weights function in an artificial neural network?

29. What are the major benefits and limitations of neural computing?

30. Define fuzzy logic, and describe its major features and benefits.

QUESTIONS FOR DISCUSSION

1. A major difference between a conventional decision support system and an ES is that the former can explain a "how" question whereas the latter can also explain a "why" question. Discuss.

2. Obtain an access to ELIZA, and run a conversation with it. After about 12 to 15 questions and answers, stop. What are the major limitations of ELIZA that you observed?

3. It is said that language processing is far more effective than key word search. Why?

4. What is the difference between voice recognition and voice understanding?

5. Assume that you are to collect knowledge for one of the following systems. What sources of knowledge would you consider?
   a. An advisory system on equal opportunity hiring situations in your organization.
   b. An advisory system on investment in residential real estate.
   c. An advisory system on how to prepare your federal tax return (Form 1040).

6. Discuss examples of production rules in three different functional areas (e.g., marketing, accounting, and so on).

7. Compare and contrast neural computing and conventional computing.

8. Compare and contrast numeric and symbolic processing techniques.

9. Compare and contrast conventional processing with artificial intelligence processing.

10. Fuzzy logic is frequently combined with expert systems and/or neural computing. Explain the logic of such integration.

11. Describe how IT can fulfill the information needs of a knowledge worker.

12. Describe the support given to self-directed teams by ES.

EXERCISES

1. Read the knowledge acquisition session that follows, and complete exercises a and b:

   a. List the heuristics cited in this interview.
   b. List the algorithms mentioned.

   KNOWLEDGE ENGINEER
   (KE):   You have the reputation for finding the best real estate properties for your clients. How do you do it?
   EXPERT: Well, first I learn about the client's objectives.
   KE: What do you mean by that?
   EXPERT: Some people are interested in income, others in price appreciation. There are some speculators, too.
   KE: Assume that somebody is interested in price appreciation. What would your advice be?

   EXPERT: Well, I would first find out how much money the investor can put down and to what degree he can subsidize the property.
   KE: Why?
   EXPERT: The more cash you put as a down payment, the less subsidy you will need. Properties with high potential for price appreciation need to be subsidized for about two years.
   KE: What else?
   EXPERT: Location is very important. As a general rule, I recommend looking for the lowest-price property in an expensive area.
   KE: What else?
   EXPERT: I compute the cash flow and consider the tax impact by using built-in formulas in my calculator.

2. Sofmic is a large software vendor. About twice a year, Sofmic acquires a small specialized software company. Recently, a decision was made to look for a software company in the area of neural computing. Currently, there are about 15 companies that would gladly cooperate as candidates for such acquisitions.

   Bill Gomez, the corporate CEO, asked that a recommendation for a candidate for acquisition be submitted to him within one week. "Make sure to use some computerized support for justification, preferably from the area of AI or neural computing," he said. As a manager responsible for submitting the recommendation to Gomez, you need to select a computerized tool for conducting the analysis. Respond to the following points:

   a. Prepare a list of all the tools that you would consider.
   b. Prepare a list of the major advantages and disadvantages of each tool, as it relates to this specific case.
   c. Select a computerized tool.
   d. Mr. Gomez does not assign grades to your work. You make a poor recommendation and you are out. Therefore, justify your recommendation.

3. Table 16.2 provides a list of ten categories of ES. Compile a list of 20 examples, two in each category, from the various functional areas in an organization (accounting, finance, production, marketing, personnel, and so on).

4. Debate: Computers can be programmed to play chess. They are getting better and better and soon may beat the world champion. Do such computers exhibit intelligence? Why or why not?

5. Debate: Prepare a table showing all the arguments you can think of that justify the position that computers cannot think. Then, prepare arguments that show the opposite.

6. Debate: Bourbaki (1990) describes Searle's argument against the use of the Turing Test. Summarize all the important issues in this debate.

7. Debate: Lance Eliot made the following comment in *AI Expert* (August 1994, p.9):

   "When you log-on to the network, a slew of agents might start watching. If you download a file about plant life, a seed company agent might submit your name for a company mailing. Besides sending junk mail, such spying agents could pick up your habits and preferences and perhaps make assumptions about your private life. It could note what days you get onto the system, how long you stay on, and what part of the country you live in. Is this an invasion of your privacy? Should legislation prevent such usage of intelligent agents? Perhaps network police (*more* intelligent agents) could enforce proper network usage."

   Prepare arguments to support your perspective on this issue.

8. Give five examples where voice recognition can be applied, and list the benefit(s) in each case. Be specific.

GROUP ASSIGNMENT

Find recent application(s) of intelligent systems in an organization. Each group member is assigned to a major functional area. Then, from a literature search, material from vendors, or industry contacts, he should find two or three recent applications (within the last six months) of intelligent systems in this area. The group will submit the following reports.

1. One-page abstract of the applications in each functional area.

2. Analysis of the similarities and differences among the applications across the functional areas. A possible arrangement is to look at the underlying technology (e.g., compare the use of ANN in marketing against finance or management).

Minicase 1

Rules of Thumb Schedule Trains in Paris

One of France's busiest train stations is the Gare de l'Est in Paris. Trains are parked at 30 platform tracks, and then they are funneled onto six mainline tracks. Over 1,100 trains come and go every day, including some fast trains that cruise at a speed close to 200 miles per hour! That's a train every thirty seconds during busy periods.

Scheduling trains at the platforms is a complex logistical problem experienced by any large train station. In Paris, the scheduling is especially difficult. Traffic levels are near the theoretical maximum. Each train must be assigned one of 640 possible routes into and out of the station. Local and long distance trains share the same plat-

form assignments. One single delayed train can cause a chain reaction during rush hours that reverberates through the schedule for as long as four hours afterwards. When a track or platform must be taken out of service for repairs, as many as 250 trains each day may have to be diverted. The scheduling problem is currently handled by dispatchers who have solved these daily problems manually for scores of years. Only specialists at the Gare de l'Est have the skills to reroute these trains without creating delays—skills that derive from 10 to 15 years of experience working at the station.

The number of possible solutions to such problems is astronomical. As in chess, the combinations of all possible moves and countermoves are so numerous that there is no satisfactory algorithmic solution to this problem. To enumerate all possible solutions using a powerful computer may take days to execute. Yet, in the real world of railroading, a solution is needed in minutes.

Until now, the solution has been for human experts to use rules of thumb—heuristics—to give a working solution. It may not always be the absolute best, but it is still satisfactory. These rules are enunciated as constraints that say what may and may not be done in terms of train routes; they also consider the effects of any changed route on all the others. The basic rule in railroading, for example, is that two trains must not occupy the same track at the same time. The first corollary is that, on a single track, no train must pass another from either direction. These are rules that *must never* be violated. Other rules can be relaxed, such as: "Don't assign a train to a platform until the previous debarkees have fully cleared the platform." This rule *may be relaxed* to solve pressing problems.

The deficiencies of a manual system are the following:

1. Some dispatchers get sick from time to time, placing an extreme amount of pressure on the remaining dispatchers.

2. Due to time constraints, dispatchers can run through limited numbers of possible arrangements for both planning and rerouting, so the best arrangements may be missed.

3. On holidays, when extra trains are needed, it is necessary to relax some rules. Working under time pressure, dispatchers are not always relaxing the most appropriate rules.

4. Employees are filling out paper documents manually. This process is lengthy.

5. Some dispatchers make mistakes, which may cause significant delays.

6. Preparation of the daily planning takes too much time, especially when repairs are scheduled.

7. The scheduling issue creates a limit on the traffic flow.

8. Preparation of the semiannual timetable takes a long time.

9. Unnecessary delays may develop when the dispatchers cannot work fast enough to handle emergencies.

Adding more dispatchers is an expensive solution that does not solve several of the problems cited earlier. In late 1988, it became clear to management that a computerized support was needed. Among the proposals made, there was one that suggested the use of an expert system.

As a result, a system was built in 1989 and has run successfully since then. It works with a combination of rules and object-oriented programming. When the system is needed, it is used interactively by dispatchers. When a problem develops, the ES subdivides it into subproblems. Then, possible routes are examined quickly. If a potential conflict between trains is indicated, appropriate recommendations for its resolution are provided. The program starts in a batch mode and applies its rule base automatically, listing any situation it cannot solve. Then the dispatcher, in an interactive mode, attempts to solve the problem with the machine.

Questions for Minicase 1

1. A preliminary study concluded that DSS or MIS would not be correct approaches. Why?

2. The possibility of using neural computing was examined, but quickly discarded. Why?

3. Which of the nine deficiencies listed earlier *cannot* be removed by an expert system and why?

4. Can this system be transferred to manage train schedules in train stations in other countries? Why or why not?

5. Explain how the improvements are achieved. What is the role of dispatchers now? Do we need dispatchers at all?

6. The ES output was designed so it would look exactly the same as that of the manual system. What is the logic of such a design?

SOURCE: Based on information provided by Texas Instruments.

Minicase 2

Can an Expert System Enhance the Image of a Bank?

The following are two positions regarding the use of an ES in a bank.

Position A:

If you saw the classic science fiction film *2001: A Space Odyssey*, you might remember the astronaut saying, "Open the pod bay door, HAL." That was the computer's name, the HAL 2000. HAL replies, "I'm sorry, Dave. I can't do that."

HAL could say things like that. He had artificial intelligence. Well, there's a computer in your future. When you go into the bank and ask for a loan, it might just say to you, "I'm sorry Dave. I can't do that." The First National Bank of Chicago uses an ES to make lending decisions. The AI program has about 250 rules.

When you come in for a loan, the less-experienced lending officer types your information into the system. The computer asks questions to clarify a few points. Then, it recommends whether or not you get the loan.

Using AI to diagnose illnesses, locate petroleum deposits, or play chess (as many of the programs are designed to do) seems like a sensible thing. But making a loan is based on a list of criteria, and one is that the bank wants to reduce its exposure to risk.

Banks have been trying to shake their cold, impersonal image for years. They have taken out the steel bars at teller windows and developed a more sensitive business style. Now, along comes a cold, calculating computer that will never understand, or be able to take into account, people's personal situations. A couple with a new child on the way won't get a home improvement loan for a room addition because the computer says the bank wants to "reduce its exposure" to those kinds of loans.

Computers can't think; they can't feel; and so far, they cannot reason. Don't get me wrong; I like computers, and I use them every day. But it's *how* they're used that's important.

Position B

Many banks are busily developing ES that capture the experience of their top loan officers in sizing up loan applicants. These capture not just the formulas loan officers use to analyze the applicant's financial statements and the condition of the applicant's industry, but also the subjective factors—the loan officers' "sixth sense"—which lead them to grant a loan to an applicant who looks questionable on paper or to turn down an applicant who looks

good. These allow junior loan officers to draw on the expertise of the most successful lenders as advisory systems.

Furthermore, loan officers must have at their fingertips an enormous amount of constantly changing data—on industry conditions, interest rates, tax law, credit ratings of the applicant's customers, and so on. Systems that make the latest data available, coupled with heuristic rules, provide a service that easily pays for itself and provides better and quicker service to the clients.

There is a concern that lenders would put too much reliance on a dumb system and lose the human element. But from experience so far, reality seems to be the opposite. Bankers who do not use computers and are unsure of their ability to make good decisions tend to be too conservative and turn down potentially good loans. This costs the bank just as much as granting poor loans. So, these expert loan advisers allow more people to make better decisions. As a result, banks keep their clients happy and improve their own profitability.

Question for Minicase 2

1. Based on the material present in this chapter, whose position is stronger: A or B? Why?

2. You are hired by a bank to convince customers that ES are great. What arguments, in addition to position "B," would you use?

3. Suggest how certain information technologies can support the ES to make it more humanized.

4. How can an ES capture the "sixth sense" of a loan officer?

SOURCE: Position A is based on *The Orange County Register*, February 17, 1986. Position B is based on Van Horn [37] pg. 194.

REFERENCES AND BIBLIOGRAPHY

1. Austin, S., "Genetic Solution to XOR Problems," *AI Expert*, December 1990.

2. Barron, J. J., "Putting Fuzzy Logic into Focus," *Byte*, April 1993.

3. Benabsat, I., and J. S. Dhaliwal, "A Framework for the Validation of Knowledge Acquisition," *Knowledge Acquisition*, Vol. 1, No. 1, 1989.

4. Berghel, H., et al., "An Expert System for Managing Toxicological Studies," *Expert Systems: Planning Implementation Integration*, Spring 1991.

5. Bonissone, P. P., and H. E. Johnson, Jr., "Expert System for Diesel Electric Locomotive Repair," *Human Systems Management*, Vol. 4, 1985.

6. Bourbaki, N., "Turing, Searle, and Thought." *AI Expert*, July 1990.

7. Burns, H., et al., *The Evolution of Intelligent Tutoring Systems: Evolutions in Design*, Hillsdale, NJ: Lawrence Erlbaum, 1991.

8. Dreyfus, H., and S. Dreyfus, *Mind Over Machine*, New York: Free Press, 1988.

9. Edmonds, R. A., *A Guide to Expert Systems*, Englewood Cliffs, NJ: Prentice-Hall, 1988.

10. Frenzel, L., *Crash Course in AI and Expert Systems*, Indianapolis: Howard W. Sams, 1987.

11. Gallant, S. I., *Neural Network Learning and Expert Systems*, Cambridge, MA: MIT Press, 1993.

12. Grefenstette, J., "Optimization of Control Parameters for Genetic Algorithms," *IEEE Transactions on Systems Management and Cybernetics*, Vol. 16, No. 1, 1982.

13. Goonatilade, S., and S. Khebbal, *Intelligent Hybrid Systems*, New York: Wiley, 1994.

14. Hart, A., *Knowledge Acquisition for Expert Systems*, 2nd ed., New York: McGraw-Hill, 1992.

15. Hecht-Nielsen, R., *Neurocomputing*, Reading, MA: Addison–Wesley, 1990.

16. Johnson, G., *Machinery of the Mind: Inside the New Science Of Artificial Intelligence*, New York: Time Books, 1992.

17. Kaplan, S. J., "The Industrialization of Artificial Intelligence: From By-Line to Bottom-Line," *AI Magazine*, Summer 1984.

18. Kosko, B., *Fuzzy Thinking: The New Science of Fuzzy Logic*, Englewood Cliffs, NJ: Prentice-Hall, 1993.

19. Koza, J., *Genetic Programming*, Cambridge, MA: MIT Press, 1992.

20. McGraw, K. L., and B. K. Harbison–Briggs, *Knowledge Acquisition, Principles and Guidelines*, Englewood Cliffs, N.J.: Prentice-Hall, 1989.

21. Medsker, L., and J. Liebowitz, *Design and Development of Expert Systems and Neural Computing*, New York: Macmillan, 1994.

22. Milheim, W. D., "Computer-Based Voice Recognition: Components, Applications, and Guidelines for Use," *Performance Improvement Quarterly*, Vol. 6, No. 1, 1993.

23. Motada, H., "Second-Generation Expert Systems," *IEEE Expert*, April 1994.

24. Newell, A., and H. Simon, *Human Problem Solving*, Englewood Cliffs, NJ: Prentice-Hall, 1973.

25. Newquist, H. P. III, "No Summer Returns," *AI Expert*, October 1990.

26. O'Keefe, R. M., et al., "Validating Expert System Performance," *IEEE Expert*, Winter 1987.

28. Rich, E., and K. Knight, *Artificial Intelligence*, 2nd ed., New York: McGraw-Hill, 1991.

29. Schorr, A., and A. Rappaport, *Innovative Applications of Artificial Intelligence*, Menlo Park, CA: AAAI Press, 1989.

30. Shapiro, S. C. (eds.), *Encyclopedia of Artificial Intelligence* 2nd ed., New York: Wiley, 1992.

31. Smith, R., and C. Scott, *Innovative Applications of Artificial Intelligence #3*, Menlo Park, CA: AAAI Press/MIT Press, 1991.

32. Szuprowicz, B. O., "The Soviet Union Trade Advisor," *Expert Systems*, Spring 1991.

33. Trippi, R., and E. Turban (eds.), *Neural Computing Applications in Investment and Financial Services*, Chicago: Probus, 1993. 2nd ed., 1996.

34. Turban, E., *Decision Support and Expert Systems* 3rd ed., New York: Macmillan, 1993. 4th ed., Prentice Hall 1995.

35. Turban, E., *Expert Systems and Applied AI*, New York: Macmillan, 1992.

36. Turban, E., and M. Tan, "Methods for Knowledge Acquisition from Multiple Experts," *International Journal of Applied Expert Systems*, Vol. 1, No. 2 1993.

37. Van Horn, M., *Understanding Expert Systems*, Toronto: Bantam Books, 1986.

38. Winston, P. H., and K. A. Prendergast (eds.), *The AI Business*, Cambridge, MA: MIT Press, 1984.

39. Wong, F. S., et al., "Fuzzy Neural Systems for Stock Selection," *Financial Analysts Journal*, January/February, 1992.

40. Zadeh, L., "A Fuzzy Logic," *Computer*, April 1988.

41. Zadeh, L., "Fuzzy Logic, Neural Networks, and Self Computing," *Communications of the ACM*, March 1994.

42. Zadehi, F., *Intelligent Systems for Business: Expert Systems with Neural Networks*, Belmont, CA: Wadsworth, 1993.

17

FROM TRANSACTION PROCESSING TO INNOVATIVE FUNCTIONAL SYSTEMS

Chapter Outline

Learning Objectives

After studying this chapter, you will be able to:

1. Relate functional areas and business processes to the value chain model.

2. Describe traditional functional systems.

3. Describe the transaction processing system and how it is supported by IT.

4. Describe the support provided by IT to the production/operations area.

5. Describe the support provided by IT to the marketing and sales area.

6. Describe the support provided by IT to the human resource management area.

7. Discuss integrated information systems.

17.1 INFORMATION TECHNOLOGY BENEFITS BUSINESS PROCESSES AT PYRO INDUSTRIES

PYRO INDUSTRIES IS a small manufacturer based in Burlington, WA. The company manufactures one product in one plant: a special stove designed to replace or augment a home central heating system. The product is sold through distributors and authorized dealers in several U.S. states and Canadian provinces. The rapidly growing company concentrates on manufacturing, while marketing is done through dealers.

Initially, Pyro developed some basic accounting software modules to support its routine business processes. These included purchase order and accounts receivable modules. The company wanted to integrate these modules with other software, such as the ones supporting manufacturing and sales. Thus, in 1990, Pyro purchased accounting, manufacturing, and marketing software from one vendor, Macola (of Marion, OH). This vendor has several other business processes modules. At that time, Pyro discontinued its "homegrown" custom-written programs for accounting and inventory control. (Prior to this purchase, the payroll and some other transactions were done manually.)

The company reengineered its manufacturing processes by introducing additional software—MRP II. MRP II is a production planning and scheduling software that is integrated with marketing and finance. The reason for selecting such a sophisticated information system was the need for more information to manage the fast-growing company. Independent functional information systems were unable to properly support business processes which crossed several functional areas. MRP II enabled the company to complete back-order fulfillment every day, rather than being logged back one to two weeks, and to conduct very detailed analyses. For this type of business, it is necessary to keep track of all sales orders and to know what orders are not filled. Such knowledge enables the company to provide customers with better information about the status of their orders and eliminate duplicate shipments.

In 1993, the system was used daily by 35 employees. During 1994, Pyro placed 75 workstations on a LAN and attached additional manufacturing modules for supporting additional processes, such as quality assurance. The integrated software helps the company to reengineer its manufacturing from a traditional manufacturing philosophy to that of just-in-time. The integrated soft-

Integrated software supports business processes from accounting to shipping.

ware allows Pyro to optimally schedule its finished goods, subassemblies, and parts production in order to minimize running out of stock and production line stoppages. The software also allows Pyro to test new product line capacities, run simulated (trial) work orders through the shop floor to identify potential bottlenecks, minimize inventories, and maximize customer service. The MRP II software supports a vendor certification program so that the company does business only with reliable vendors. In addition, Pyro can monitor inventory levels and match work, purchases, and customer orders against the production schedule. Any minor adjustments to incoming raw material shipments can be made before potential problems arise. Finally, the program provides all the necessary documentation for placing vendors on a daily shipment schedule.

A tangible benefit of the system is the annual savings of $50,000 to $75,000 (from increased sales due to customer satisfaction). Also, the payroll preparation process was cut from four to two days. Several intangible benefits were materialized as well. Customer satisfaction increased and so did employee satisfaction. Despite the fast growth, there was no need to add another person in the shipping department. And finally, a shop floor control software module reduced the staff by one employee.

SOURCE: Condensed from McCormack, J. S., "Growth . . . That's the Name of the Game—Pyro Industries, Inc.," *APICS*, May 1993.

▶ 17.2 BUSINESS PROCESSES, THE VALUE CHAIN, AND THE FUNCTIONAL AREAS

The opening case of Pyro Industries points to some interesting issues regarding implementation of information technology.

▼ IT supported the routine processes of a manufacturing company, enabling it to be efficient and effective and to satisfy its customers.

▼ The software helped the modernization and reengineering of the company's major business processes.

▼ The software supports several business processes. Some software modules are supporting only one process, while others support several.

▼ The company's major applications were in manufacturing processes. However, the same vendor provides ready-made accounting, marketing, and finance software modules, which were *integrated* with the manufacturing module and with each other.

▼ IT can be beneficial to small companies as well as large ones.

The manufacturing, accounting, marketing, and finance departments are the major functional areas of Pyro and other manufacturing companies. Traditionally, information systems were designed to support the functional areas by increasing their effectiveness and efficiency. However, as discussed in Chapter 4, the traditional functional hierarchical structure may not be the best for many modern organizations. This is because certain business processes may involve activities that are performed in several functional areas. Suppose a customer wants to buy a particular product that is stored in the corporate warehouse. An order arrives at the marketing department; then credit is approved by finance. Operations will prepare the product; the shipping department will deliver it. Accounting will bill the customer, and finance may arrange for insurance. In such a case, the customer may not be properly served, and the cost of doing business can be very high. In addition, in the traditional structure, IT is usually organized along functional areas rather than business processes. As a result, one may experience problems in both performing business processes and supporting them with IT.

One possible solution is to reengineer the organization. For example, create teams, with each responsible for performing a complete business process. Then, it will be necessary to adopt appropriate information systems applications for the reengineered processes. In other cases, the use of IT creates a change in the business processes and organizational structure. However, many companies do not need to be reengineered; they do well with incremental improvements and ad hoc problem solving as problems occur. Before demonstrating the role of IT in all the above situations, we will relate Porter's value chain model to the functional areas and to business processes.

THE VALUE CHAIN MODEL, FUNCTIONAL AREAS, AND BPR

The **value chain** model, introduced in Chapter 2 (Figure 2.7), views activities in organizations as either primary (reflecting the flow of goods and services) or secondary (supporting primary activities). There are five primary activities:

▼ *Inbound logistics:* raw material handling (in a manufacturing firm).

▼ *Operations:* machinery, assembling, testing.

▼ *Outbound logistics:* warehousing and distribution of finished goods.

▼ *Marketing and sales:* advertising, promotion pricing, channel relation.

▼ *Service:* installation, repair, parts.

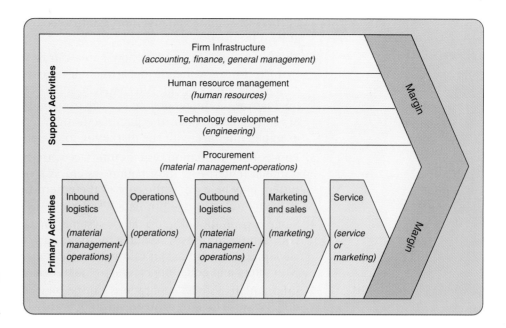

FIGURE 17.1 Typical functional areas mapped on the value chain of a manufacturing company.

These primary activities are supported by the following secondary activities: *procurement, technology development, human resource management,* and *firm infrastructure.*

The organizational structure of firms is intended to support these activities. However, the structure may not be a complete fit, either with the value chain or with business processes. As discussed in Chapter 4, most organizations have a hierarchical structure which resulted from principles such as division of labor and specialization. Figure 17.1 attempts to map the typical functional departments on the value chain structure. Each of the functional departments developed its own supporting information system. However, as indicated earlier, a complete business process may involve activities traditionally done in several functional areas. For example, a purchase may involve operations, finance, procurement, and marketing. The functional information systems may not be effective in supporting business processes that cross functional lines.

Two approaches can be used to handle this problem. First, reengineer the information systems themselves, so they will fit processes more closely. Second, permit an integration of all functional systems, such that it will be easy to build applications from databases, models, or other components which exist in separate functional areas.

In this chapter, we will demonstrate—via several innovative applications—the manner in which information systems support traditional functional areas and typical incremental improvement efforts. We also will illustrate how support is rendered to existing business processes and to their reengineering. Finally, the software integration issue is discussed.

▶ 17.3 MAJOR CHARACTERISTICS OF A FUNCTIONAL INFORMATION SYSTEM

The hierarchical organizational structure involves functional areas. These are supported by functional information systems that share five major characteristics.

1. As shown in the opening case, a functional information system is comprised of several smaller information systems (or modules) that support specific activities performed by each functional area. For example, computerized pro-

duction scheduling and inventory control support the manufacturing system at Pyro Industries.

2. The submodules in any functional area can be integrated (as in the case of Pyro) to form a coherent departmental functional system, or they can be completely independent. Alternatively, some of the applications within each module can be integrated across departmental lines, while others cannot. Several applications in the manufacturing information system of Pyro, for example, interface with the marketing information system.

3. Functional information systems interface with each other to form the organizational (enterprise) information system. A specific functional information system may be used as the core of the enterprise information system, such as the manufacturing information system in the Pyro case.

4. Some organizational information systems interface with the environment. For example, a human resource information system collects data about the labor market and transmits information to federal agencies about compliance with safety and equal-opportunity regulations and guidelines.

5. Information systems applications can be viewed as supporting three traditional ways of looking at an organization's activities: operational, managerial, and strategic levels of an organization.

A model of the information systems in the production/operations area is provided in Figure 17.2. Some of these applications are discussed in Section

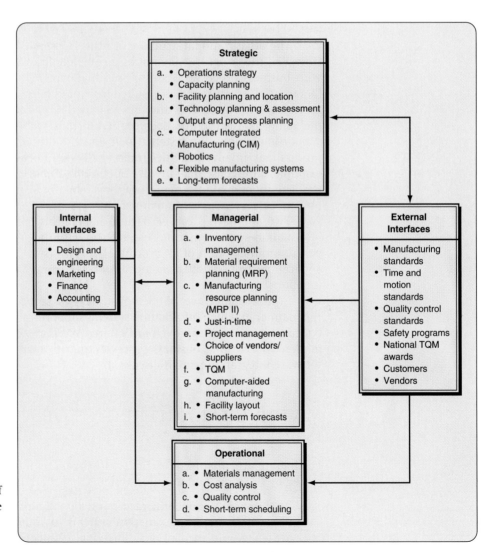

FIGURE 17.2 A model of information systems in the production/operations functional area.

17.6. The information systems of other functional areas have the same basic structure. Note that in each case, the information systems applications are classified into operational, managerial, and strategic levels. Information systems interface with other functional information systems and with external information systems. These information systems applications receive much of their input from the corporate *transaction processing system.*

17.4 TRANSACTION PROCESSING

As described in Chapter 2, the **transaction processing system (TPS)** is the backbone of an organization's information systems. The TPS supports routine business activities such as monitoring, collecting, storing, processing, and disseminating information for all mission-central business transactions.

Business transactions occur when a company produces a product or provides a service. For example, to produce toys, a manufacturer needs to buy materials and parts, pay for labor and electricity, build toys, ship toys to customers, bill customers, and collect money. A bank that maintains the company checking account must keep the account balance up-to-date, disperse funds to back the checks written, accept deposits, and mail a monthly statement. Each transaction may generate additional transactions. For example, purchasing materials will change the inventory level, and paying an employee reduces the corporate cash on hand. Because of their routine and repetitive nature, such business processes are fairly easy to computerize. An organization may have one integrated TPS or several, one for each specific business process. In the latter case, the systems should interface with each other.

OBJECTIVES OF TPS

The primary goal of TPS is to provide all the information needed by law and/or organizational policies to keep the business running properly and efficiently. Some specific objectives include the following: to allow for efficient and effective operation of the organization (efficient use of resources, attainment of organizational goals), to provide timely documents and reports, to increase the competitive advantage of the corporation, to provide the necessary data for tactical and strategic systems such as DSS applications, to assure accuracy and integrity of data and information, and to safeguard assets and security of information. It should be emphasized that TPSs are the most likely candidates for reengineering, and that TPSs are the most justifiable in terms of tangible benefits of IT investments.

CHARACTERISTICS OF TPS

By reviewing the characteristics of TPS, one may better understand how IT can support the mission critical activities of an organization. The characteristics of a TPS are provided in Table 17.1.

ACTIVITIES AND METHODS OF TPS

The overall role and major activities of TPS for a manufacturing organization were shown in Chapter 2 (see Figure 2.7). A similar diagram can be drawn for a service or government organization. Regardless of the specific data processed by a TPS, a fairly standard process occurs (see Figure 17.3).

First, data are collected by people or sensors and entered into the computer via any input device. Generally speaking, organizations try to automate the TPS **data entry** as much as possible because of the large volumes involved. Next, the system processes data in one of two basic ways: *batch* or *on-line processing.* In **batch**

Table 17.1 The Major Characteristics of TPS

- *Large amounts of data* are inputted, processed, and outputted.
- *The sources of data are mostly internal, and the output is intended mainly for an internal audience.* This characteristic is changing since distribution of output reports as well as accessibility to databases may involve trading partners.
- The TPS processes information on a *regular* and *repetitive* basis: daily, weekly, biweekly and so on.
- *Large storage* (database) capacity is required.
- *High processing speed* is needed due to the high volume.
- *Historical orientation of information* is prevalent. TPS basically monitors and collects past data.
- *Structured format* exists in the input and output data. Since the processed data are fairly stable, they are formatted in a standard fashion.
- *High level of detail* is usually observable, especially in input data but often in output as well.
- *Low computation complexity* (simple mathematical and statistical operations) is usually evident in TPS.
- *A high level of accuracy, data integrity, and security* is needed. Sensitive issues such as privacy of personal data are strongly related to TPS.
- *High reliability is required.* The TPS can be viewed as the blood line of the organization. Interruptions in the flow of TPS data can be fatal to the organization.
- *Inquiry processing is a must.* TPS frequently enables users to interactively query files and databases (on-line and in real time).

processing, transactions are collected as they occur, placing them in groups or batches. The batches are then prepared and processed periodically (e.g., every night or once a week). In **on-line processing**, data are processed as soon as a transaction occurs. For example, when an item such as a toy is sold in a store, the POS terminal immediately notifies the inventory system, which triggers a change in the inventory level. The sale of the toy causes other files to be updated in real time (e.g., cash on hand or a departmental sales file). In addition, a *hybrid system* (combination of batch and on-line) can collect the data as they occur, but process them at specified intervals. For example, as can be seen in Figure 17.4, sales at POS terminals are entered into the computer as they occur; however, they are processed only during evenings.

The data of a TPS are stored in two types of files: *transaction* and *master*. The **transaction file** contains the individual transactions that took place during a specified time. A purchase order from a vendor or the receivable account of a specific client on a given date may be included in a particular transaction file. The information in the transaction files is updated every time a transaction occurs. A **master file** is a permanent group of records, such as a master purchase order file

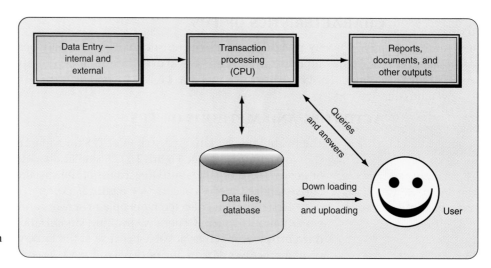

FIGURE 17.3 The flow of information in transaction processing.

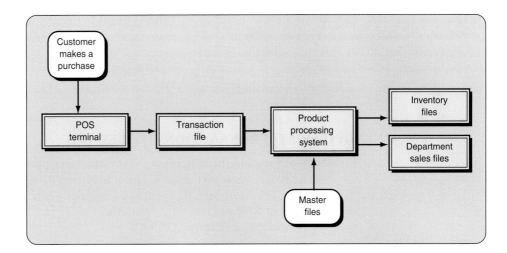

FIGURE 17.4 A hybrid TPS.

or a master inventory file. These files are updated periodically (e.g., once each day or week) to make them current. Data from the transaction and master files enter the *product processing system* and are transferred, after processing, to the inventory or sales files.

MODERN TPS

Transaction processing systems may be fairly complex, involving customers, vendors, telecommunications, and different types of hardware and software. Traditional TPS are centralized and run on a mainframe. However, large savings can be realized when innovations such as on-line transaction processing (OLTP) are created on a client/server architecture, or when customers are allowed to enter data into the TPS or query it directly (see Box 17.1).

IT At Work BOX 17.1

MODERNIZING THE TPS CUTS DELIVERY TIME AND SAVES MONEY

The **3Es Company** (Des Moines, IA) is a middle-size wholesaler of electrical equipment ($50 million annual sales). Until 1993, the company delivered sales receipts and paper orders by hand to the order entry department, where they were keyed into a mainframe computer. Back orders took about two weeks to fill, and employees had no way of knowing if an item was in stock or how much time was needed to get it from producers.

The new system is centered around an NCR 3550 mainframe. 3Es created a database containing purchasing information, and ordering patterns and histories of all its 2,200 customers. Customers now transmit their orders electronically via modems and PCs (the company is considering an electronic data interchange system). The customers can query their accounts electronically, 24 hours a day, from any location. The savings has been significant. Ninety percent of all back orders are now filled in three to five days instead of two weeks. Also, employees

are freed from responding to customers' queries and from administrative work.

Moving TPS to customers is being done by several other companies. For example, **Grossman's** (a retailer in Braintree, MA) replaced all of its POS terminals with a network of 700 PCs (486-based). The network rings up sales, updates inventory, and keeps customers' histories at 125 stores. The PCs automatically record stock from a remote database and trace out-of-stock items available at other stores. This way, customers can get unavailable items within hours. The $3 million investment is expected to pay for itself in less than two years. Employees do not have to count inventory or order merchandise any longer. They can use the time saved for more productive tasks.

Several companies outsource their transaction processing. For example, **Citgo Petroleum** must process more than 2.5 million credit card transactions each year.

Using a network, these transactions are transferred to **JC Penney's Business Services** subsidiary for processing. JC Penney has 40,000 other customers for whom they perform transaction processing.

Critical Thinking Issue: How do you feel about outsourcing transaction processing activities? ▲

SOURCE: Condensed from *InformationWeek*, May 24, 1993.

REENGINEERING TRANSACTION PROCESSING

Many of the published success cases of **business process reengineering** (BPR) deal with transaction processing. This is because TPS usually involve large volumes and most TPS have been in operation for many years. One of the most publicized examples of BPR in TPS is the accounts payable project at Ford Motor Company (see Hammer and Champy [1993]).

CASE: FORD MOTOR COMPANY. As part of their productivity improvement program, Ford management put its accounts payable department—along with many other departments—under the microscope in search of ways to cut costs. Accounts payable employed more than 500 people. Management thought that by streamlining processes and installing new computer systems, it could reduce the head count by some 20 percent. This was an improvement, but it was not dramatic enough to help Ford achieve its goals.

Ford managers ratcheted up their goal: perform accounts payable with 100 clerks. Analysis of the existing system revealed that when the purchasing department wrote a purchase order, it sent a copy to accounts payable. Later, when material control received the goods, it sent a copy of the receiving document to accounts payable. Meanwhile, the vendor also sent an invoice to accounts payable. If the purchase order, receiving document, and invoice matched, then the accounts payable department issued a payment. Unfortunately, there were many cases of mismatching.

The department spent most of its time on mismatches—instances where the purchase order, receiving document, and invoice disagreed. In these cases, an accounts payable clerk would investigate the discrepancy, hold up payment, generate documents, and generally gum up the works.

One way to improve things might have been to help the accounts payable clerk investigate more efficiently. But a better choice was to *prevent* the mismatches in the first place. To that end, Ford instituted "invoiceless processing." Now when the purchasing department initiates an order, it enters the information into an online database. It doesn't send a copy of the purchase order to anyone. When the goods arrive at the receiving dock, the receiving clerk checks the database to see if the goods correspond to an outstanding purchase order. If so, she accepts them and enters the transaction into the computer system. (If she can't find a database entry for the received goods, or if there is a mismatch, she simply returns the order.)

Under the old procedures, the accounting department had to match 14 data items among the receipt record, the purchase order, and the invoice before it could issue payment to the vendor. The new approach requires matching only four items—part number, unit of measure, and supplier code—between the purchase order and the receipt record. The matching is done automatically, and the computer prepares the check, which accounts payable sends to the vendor (or electronic transfer is done). There are no invoices to worry about since Ford has asked its vendors not to send them. Figure 17.5 illustrates the reengineered system as compared to the old one.

Ford didn't settle for the modest increases it first envisioned. It opted for a radical change and it achieved dramatic improvement: a 75 percent reduction in head count, not the 20 percent it would have achieved with a conventional program. And since there are no discrepancies between the financial record and phys-

REENGINEERING
———————▶
...for 75% labor reduction

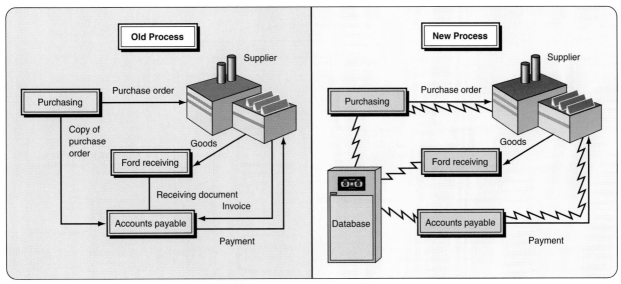

FIGURE 17.5 Ford's accounts payable reengineered. The old process is shown on the left. Using an on-line database, the process was reengineered with IT, reducing head count by 75 percent and improving accuracy. (Purchasing orders and payments are done either electronically or with paper, depending on the supplier.)

ical record, material control is simpler, receipts are more likely to be correct, and financial information is more accurate.

▶ 17.5 TRANSACTION PROCESSING TASKS

Transaction processing exists in all functional areas. However, most processes are in the accounting/finance areas, as shown in Figure 17.6. The major components of a TPS and its processes are the following:

▼ **The ledger.** The entire group of accounts maintained by a company is collectively referred to as the ledger. In one place, the ledger keeps all information about changes in specific account balances. Companies may use various kinds of ledgers, but every company has a **general ledger**. A general ledger contains all the assets, liabilities, and owners' equity accounts. Maintaining the general ledger involves a large number of simple transactions and is an ideal application area for computers.

▼ **Order processing.** Orders for goods and/or services may flow to a company electronically, be entered by phone, or come in on paper. Salespeople in many companies enter orders using portable computers from the client's site. Orders can also be internal—from one department to another. An example is Otis Elevator Company, where employees enter maintenance and parts orders using wireless hand-held computers (see Box 17.2). A computerized system receives, summarizes, and stores the orders. Order processing can be reengineered, for example, with a GPS, as shown in Box 17.3. An example of applying IT to sales order processing is shown in Figure 17.7. In some cases, orders to warehouses and/or manufacturing are issued automatically. An EDI system would be especially useful in such a case. A computerized system can track sales by product, by zone, or by salesperson. This information is used, for example, in an EIS.

▼ **Accounts Payable and Receivable.** Accounts payable and receivable list the credit, debit, and balance of each customer or vendor. The information is generated from sales journals or purchase orders. The accounts are updated periodically. They are considered subsidiaries of the general ledger and usually are maintained by the same software. Analysis of accounts receivable can help identify a customer's credit rating and compute the risks of the account not

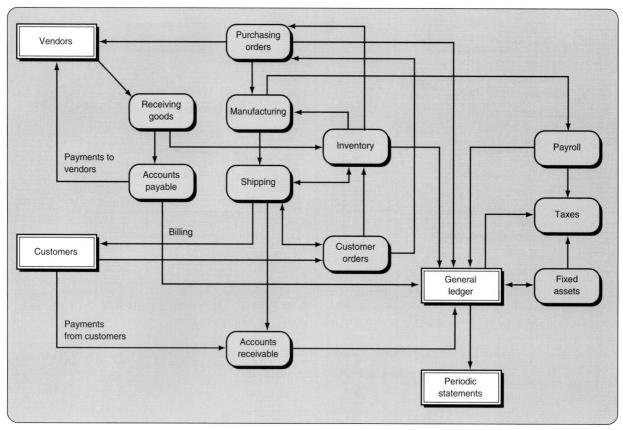

FIGURE 17.6 Overview of the major business transactions in the accounting area.

being paid. Accounts receivable can also assist in making decisions about when to send a reminder notice for payments, transfer the account to a collection agency, or declare a debt as a loss (aging of debt report). Accounts payable also generates the information necessary to make payments to vendors.

▼ **Receiving and Shipping.** Whenever goods are received or shipped, transactions are created. For example, when items are shipped, customers need to be billed,

IT At Work BOX 17.2

EMERGING TECHNOLOGY

HAND-HELD COMPUTERS AND WIRELESS COMMUNICATION AT OTIS ELEVATOR COMPANY

Using hand-held (notebook) computers, Otis field service technicians communicate instantly with the company's host computer in Farmington, CT. They communicate about on-site technical assistance, ordering parts, and job dispatching. Previously, field workers were forced to leave the work site, search for a working phone, call the home office, wait on hold, call again, and waste large quantities of time. Now, using a wireless network, communication can be initiated from a location as remote as an elevator shaft. The use of hand-held computers has greatly increased productivity by reducing repair time. Customer satisfaction has also been increased

due to faster service. The wireless network is provided by ARDIS, a partnership of IBM and Motorola. ARDIS is part of a new generation of wireless telephones, called "personal communication services." It enables communication from places where cellular telephones are ineffective, such as tunnels. By using computers, documents can be viewed, images can be examined, and problems can be diagnosed quickly—even from a distance.

Critical Thinking Issue: If wireless communication is good for elevator repair persons, can it be useful for *all* repair persons? ▲

SOURCE: Information provided by Otis Elevator Company.

IT At Work BOX 17.3

TAXIS IN SINGAPORE ARE DISPATCHED BY SATELLITE

As of 1996, taxis in Singapore are tracked by a GPS, which is comprised of 24 satellites. It was originally set up by the U.S. government for military purposes and now is also used for commercial purposes. A GPS allows its users to get an instant fix on a geographical position. How does the system work? Customer orders are received by telephone and fax. Frequent users enter orders by keying in a PIN number in the telephone, which identifies them automatically. This computerized system is connected to the GPS. Once an order is received, the system finds a vacant cab nearest the caller, and a display panel in the taxi alerts the driver to the address of the caller. The driver has five seconds to push a button and accept the order. If he does not, the system automatically searches out the next nearest taxi for the job.

The system completely reengineered customer order processing. First, customers do not have to wait a long time just to get an operator (a situation that exists during rush hours, rain, or any other time of high demand for taxis). The transaction time for processing an order is much shorter, thus freeing up the operator. Second, taxi drivers are not able to pick and choose which trips they want to take, since the system will not provide the commuter's destination. This reduces the customer's average waiting time significantly, while minimizing the travel distance of empty taxis. Third, the system increases the capacity of the human operators by ten fold (1,000 percent), providing a competitive edge to the cab companies that use the system. Fourth, frequent commuters get priority, since they are automatically identified.

Critical Thinking Issues: What kind of priorities can one give to frequent customers? Is it a good idea to assign a taxi to a customer without considering the destination? ▲

inventories need to be updated, and the general ledger is modified. When items are received, a confirmation is generated to accounts payable, so payments can be made and inventories can be updated. If goods received are deemed substandard, then adjusting transactions are made and the goods are returned to the vendor.

▼ *Inventory on hand.* There are several types of inventories in organizations. According to Weygandt et al. (1993), inventory consists of many ready-to-sell items in a merchandising enterprise. In a grocery store, canned foods and dairy products are inventory items. In manufacturing companies, there are three categories of inventory: finished goods, work in process, and raw materials. The

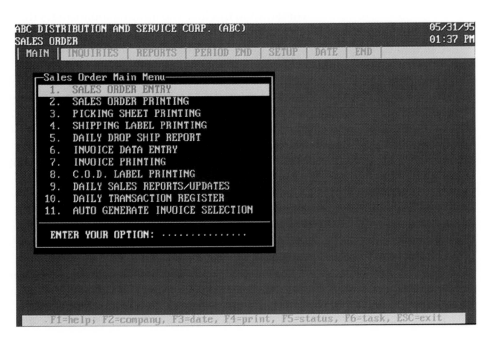

FIGURE 17.7 Information technology support to the sales ordering process.

accounting function must determine the number of units of inventory in each category that are owned by the company on the date that a financial (or tax) statement is prepared. To determine inventories, companies must count, weigh, or measure each kind of inventory on hand and record the results. Information technology can be used to expedite this process. For example, in Chapter 14 we illustrated how a computerized voice technology is used in taking inventory. Scanning bar codes on packages is another common computerized inventory counting method.

▼ *Periodical reports and statements.* Many periodical reports and statements are generated by the TPS. These include external reports to the SEC (such as K-10s), IRS, and other state and federal agencies. Many internal periodical reports are also produced daily, weekly, monthly, and annually. Cash-flow statements, payroll summaries, productivity summaries, and sales figures are just a few examples.

▼ *Fixed assets management.* Organizations own a large amount of fixed assets such as buildings, cars, and machines. These assets depreciate over time. It is necessary to keep a record of the original cost of each item, the depreciation rate used for tax purposes, the improvements made in the asset, and the book value of each asset. When an asset is sold, the company may incur a gain or a loss on the sale. All these are recorded and are part of fixed assets management. An asset may go through dozens or hundreds of changes during its life. Also, the total of all assets need to be periodically computed. Information systems can execute such transactions effectively and efficiently.

▼ *Payroll.* Preparing the periodic payroll was one of the first applications of computers in business. Preparing payroll is a routine computer job that involves computing gross salary during a given period and determining appropriate deductions and reductions (taxes, insurance, contributions). Most payroll programs will calculate the net pay, and some even print checks. Many companies use outsourcing for payroll. Outsourcers use powerful computers to prepare payroll in the most efficient manner. For those that do not like to outsource, there exist dozens of ready-made payroll packages, many of which run on PCs and sell for as little as $100. (You may get one for free on the Internet.)

▼ *Personnel files and skills inventory.* The human resources department in any organization is responsible for keeping a personal file for each employee. All information about a person, beginning with his application for employment, is contained in this file. The information includes the skills and experience of the employee, the test taken and passed by the employee, and performance evaluations over time. In addition, the file includes the employee's preferences for relocation and for changing his current job. When the personnel files are computerized, it is easy to identify qualified employees within the company to fill open positions. Using computerized search, it is also easy to identify employees for promotion, transfer, special training programs, and layoffs. Many companies allow employees to update their own personal files (e.g., change address), saving clerical labor and reducing errors in data entry.

▼ *Government reports.* The human resource department is responsible for the completion of several standard state and federal reports. These reports indicate compliance with laws and regulations involving employees. Both scheduled and ad hoc reports go to agencies such as the Equal Employment Opportunity Commission (EEOC), Occupational Safety and Health Administration (OSHA), Immigration and Naturalization Service (INS), and Employment Standards Administration (ESA).

In the near future, it is expected that such reports will be filed electronically through telecommunications channels, similar to the manner in which SEC financial reports are received from companies and the IRS accepts tax returns.

▼ *Salary and benefits administration.* Employees' contributions to their organizations depend on the rewards they receive, such as salary, bonuses, and other benefits. Managing the benefits system can be a complex task, due to its many components and the tendency of organizations to allow employees to choose and trade off benefits ("cafeteria style"). In some organizations, employees can learn about benefits and/or register for specific benefits using networks and voice technology. In large companies, using computers for benefit selection can save a tremendous amount of labor, waiting time, and aggravation.

Providing flexibility in selecting benefits is viewed as a competitive advantage in large organizations. It can be successfully implemented when supported by computers. Some companies have automated benefits enrollments. Employees call in and select desired benefits from a menu. The system specifies the value of each benefit and the available benefits balance of each employee.

Analyzing the monetary value of fringe benefits is important for management in structuring the benefits plan and negotiating employment contracts with unions. Trading off benefits is common in labor–management negotiations. Therefore, management uses computers to develop DSS models, which assess the effectiveness of certain compensation and benefit plans. Appropriate benefits management requires expertise that can be provided by expert systems.

▶ 17.6   MANAGING PRODUCTION/OPERATIONS AND LOGISTICS PROCESSES

The production and operations management (POM) function in an organization is responsible for the processes that transform inputs into useful outputs (see Figure 17.8). The POM area is very diversified, in comparison to the other functional

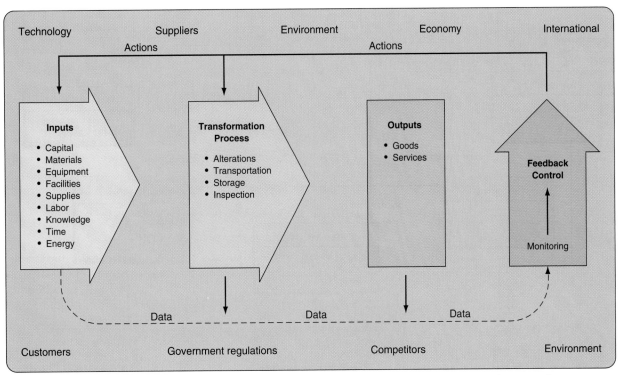

FIGURE 17.8 The operations process transforms inputs into useful outputs. (SOURCE: Meredith, J. R., *The Management of Operations*, 4th Ed., New York: John Wiley & Sons, Inc. Copyright 1992, p. 10. Reprinted by permission of John Wiley and Sons, Inc.)

areas, and so are the supporting information systems. It also differs considerably among organizations. For example, manufacturing companies use completely different processes than service organizations, and a hospital operates much differently from a university. Some of these processes are so complex that they are described in separate books (e.g., quality control and project management are the sole subjects of several books).

An example of the complexity of the field is shown in Figure 17.9. As seen in the figure, the POM is interrelated to finance and sales (on the left), engineering and design (on the right), and purchasing and logistics (warehousing, on the bottom). Certain processes may involve several or all of these activities. In this chapter, we will introduce some of these activities and the IT tools that are used to support them. These activities are the following:

(a) In-house logistics and material management.

(b) Planning production/operations.

(c) Automating design work and manufacturing.

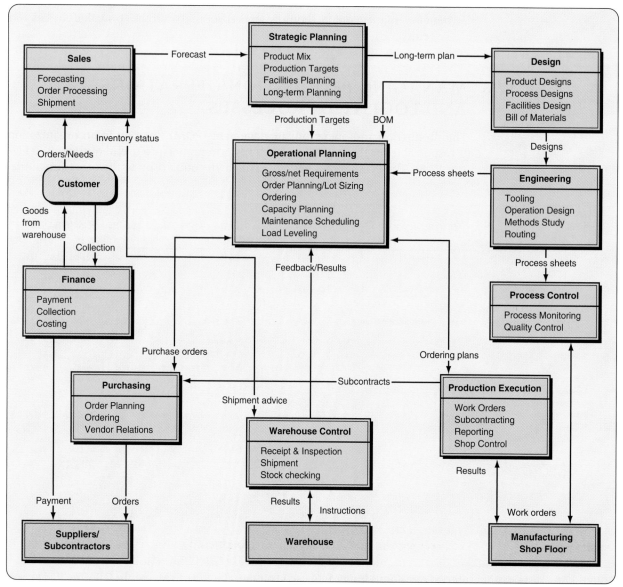

FIGURE 17.9 The manufacturing process and its interactions with related processes. (SOURCE: Narayanan et al., 1993, p. 52.)

(d) Moving from mass production to mass customization.

(e) Computer-integrated manufacturing (CIM).

IN-HOUSE LOGISTICS AND MATERIAL MANAGEMENT

Logistics management is related to ordering, purchasing, inbound logistics, and outbound logistics activities. Logistics activities are a good example of processes that cross several primary and support activities in the value chain. The purchasing agent decides—with functional area people—what, where, and when to buy. Prices are negotiated with suppliers, and materials (and parts) are ordered and received. The materials received are inspected for quality and then stored. While in storage, they need to be maintained. The materials are then distributed to those who need them. Some materials are disposed of when they become obsolete or when their quality is unacceptable.

All these activities can be supported by information systems. For example, placing orders can be done with EDI. Inspection can be supported by scanners and voice technologies, and distribution and material handling can be performed by robots. Large warehouses use robots to bring materials and parts from storage whenever needed. The parts are stored in bins, and the bins are stocked one above the other, similar to the way safe deposit boxes are organized in banks. Whenever a part is needed, the storekeeper keys in the part number. The mobile robot travels to the part's "address," takes the bin out of its location (using magnetic force), and brings the bin to the storekeeper. Once a part is taken out of the bin, the robot is instructed to return the bin to its permanent location. In intelligent buildings in Japan, robots bring files to employees and return them for storage; and, in some hospitals, robots dispense medicine.

QUALITY CONTROL. Quality control systems that are stand-alone systems or part of a total quality management (TQM) system provide information about the quality of incoming material and parts, as well as the quality of in-process semifinished products and finished products. Such systems record the results of all inspections. They also compare actual results to standards. Quality data may be collected by sensors and stored in a database for analysis. Periodic reports are generated (e.g., percentage of defects, percentage of rework needed), and comparisons are conducted between departments.

Standard quality control information systems are available from several vendors (e.g., HP and IBM) for executing standard computations such as preparing control charts. After the data are recorded, it is possible to use expert systems to make interpretations and recommend actions.

INVENTORY MANAGEMENT. Inventory Management deals with decisions about how much inventory to keep. Overstocking can be expensive; so is the lack of sufficient inventory. Three costs play important roles in inventory decisions: the cost of maintaining inventories, the cost of ordering (a fixed cost per order), and the cost of not having inventory when needed (the shortage or opportunity cost).

Two basic decisions are made by operations: when to order and how much to order.

These decisions are supported by inventory models, such as the economic order quantity (EOQ) model. These models attempt to minimize total inventory-relevant cost. Dozens of models exist, because inventory scenarios can be diverse and complex. For example, discounts are given for purchasing in large quantities. Demand for parts can fluctuate in a sporadic manner, and delivery times vary. A large number of commercial inventory software packages are available at low cost.

Once decisions about how much to order and when are made, an information system can be used to track the level of inventory for each item that management wants to control. When the inventory falls to a certain level, called the **reorder point**, the computer automatically generates a purchase order. In some cases, the order is transferred electronically to a vendor, or to the manufacturing department if restocking is done in-house.

Computerized inventory systems are usually used in incremental improvements. However, they can be a segment in a large-scale BPR.

PLANNING PRODUCTION/OPERATIONS

Because of the complexity of production/operation processes and their interrelationship with other processes, it is necessary to provide extensive planning. This planning is supported by IT. Some major areas of planning and their computerized support are the following:

MATERIAL REQUIREMENTS PLANNING (MRP). The previously described logistics inventory systems were designed for individual items for which the demand is completely independent. However, in manufacturing systems, the demand for some items can be interdependent. For example, a company may make three types of chairs that all use the same legs, screws, bolts, and nuts. Thus, the demand for screws for example, depends on the shipment schedule of all three types of chairs. The plan for acquiring (or producing) parts, subassemblies, or materials in such a case is called **material requirements planning (MRP)**. MRP is usually computerized because of the complex interrelationship among many products and their components, and the need to change the plan each time a delivery

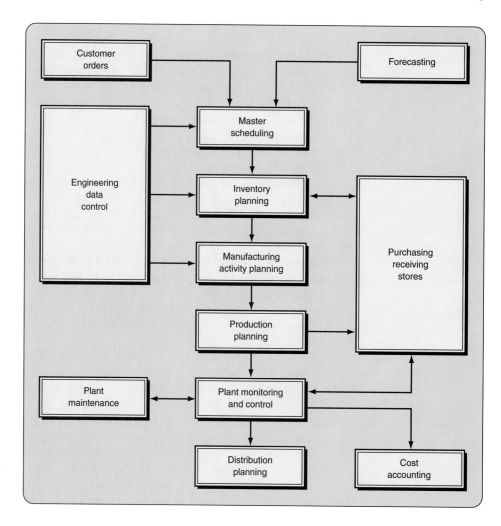

FIGURE 17.10 A typical MRP II system and its modules. (SOURCE: Meredith, J. R. *The Management of Operations*, 4th Ed., New York: John Wiley and Sons, Inc., p. 480. Copyright 1992. Reprinted by permission of John Wiley and Sons, Inc.)

date or quantity ordered is changed. Many MRP packages are available commercially. MRP deals only with production scheduling and inventories. But a more complex process will also involve allocation of resources. In such a case, a more complex, integrated software is available—MRP II.

MANUFACTURING RESOURCE PLANNING (MRP II). Computerized scheduling systems are frequently tied to other functional areas. **Manufacturing resource planning (MRP II)** is an *integrated* computer system that connects the regular MRP to other functional areas (see Figure 17.10). In addition to the output of MRP, MRP II determines the costs of parts and the cash flow needed to pay for parts. It also estimates cost of labor, tools, equipment repair, and energy. Finally, it provides a detailed, computerized budget.

As shown in Figure 17.10, the forecasted and actual customer orders enter the master schedule, which drives the production system. Another major input to the production process is the engineering database, which includes bills of material, engineering designs, drawings, and other information required to manufacture and assemble products. The right hand side of the figure shows the actual building stage, where plant monitoring and control operations take place. This function receives additional information and generates information for plant maintenance. Cost accounting data are also collected at this stage. The process is completed with *distribution planning*.

Other company functions can also be tied to this system. Information about when items will be purchased and products will be delivered, is needed so that the finance department can prepare cash flow projections. The human resource department can project hiring and layoff requirements. Finally, the marketing department can determine up-to-date customer delivery times and purchasing lead times. MRP II software is available commercially. An example of the use of MRP II is shown in Box 17.4. It allowed Lipton Company to smooth out the peaks and valleys that had been whipsawing production levels.

IT At Work BOX 17.4

 **E**MERGING TECHNOLOGY

LIPTON MAINTAINS QUALITY AND PRODUCTIVITY USING MRP II

Thomas J. Lipton Company (Englewood, NJ) is a large international food processor (known for its tea products). Food processing is a very competitive global industry where many government regulations must be observed and rigorous quality control programs must satisfy not only the government, but also consumers. European, Japanese, and American companies are all struggling for market share.

Lipton's prime supplier of packaging materials is Stone Container Corporation, so an electronic data interchange (EDI) system was established between the two companies. Soon, many of Lipton's customers (e.g., supermarkets) were added. The EDI enabled Lipton to increase its service level to the customers by an order of magnitude. The EDI was part of a major change of Lipton's information system, moving from a mainframe to a client/server architecture based on a minicomputer. Incidently, this change was part of the strategy of Lipton's parent company—moving to an open system. The parent company, Unilever, an Anglo-Dutch conglomerate, is in a process of placing all their 120 companies on client/server architectures.

The collaboration between Lipton's headquarters staffs and operations management at its plants enables sharper planning and tighter delivery schedules. A key goal at Lipton is to smooth out the peaks and valleys that have whipsawed production levels. Orders will always skyrocket for holidays and summer vacations, but it's possible to "annualize" those oscillations through the integration of planning, inventory control, sales forecasts, shortened lead times, and faster order processing. A pilot project was done at Lipton's Independence, MO, plant in which production-line data were uploaded into higher-level MIS functions for integration with plant accounting and business systems. This facilitates the development of an executive information system (EIS) to give top management real-time access and on-line decision support for plant operations.

Today, availability of the latest information makes Lipton more flexible and responsive to shifting consumer preferences. It can more freely pursue a quick response strategy unfettered by outmoded computer architecture. Lipton wants shortened production lead times, decreased changeover times, and improved supply chain management. It sees its Unix-based MRP II as essential for those efforts.

"Shelf wars" for prominent positioning on store aisles and shelves come into play in the world of retail grocery distribution and sales. Lipton's reliance on MRP II ena-

bles it to offer competitively priced premium foods and beverages with no compromise in its century-old tradition for quality.

Critical Thinking Issues: How is MRP II related to EDI, and what kind of planning strategy is used by Lipton? ▲

SOURCE: Condensed from Sykes C., "Lipton Maintains Quality Image with Strategic Shift to Unix-based MRP II," *APICS*, May 1993.

GLOBAL PERSPECTIVE

...Toyota develops just-in-time system

JUST-IN-TIME SYSTEMS. MRP systems are conceptually related to (or can even be a part of) the **just-in-time (JIT)** concept (developed by Toyota Motor Company in Japan). JIT is an attempt to *minimize waste* of all forms (space, labor, materials, energy, and so on), *continually improve* processes and systems, and *maintain respect* for all workers. For example, if materials and parts arrive at a workstation exactly when needed, then there is no need for inventory (saving space, material handling, cost), there are no delays in production, and there is no idle production facilities.

Just-in-time is achieved by the use of several technologies and management techniques (elements of JIT) that enable production to move as fast as possible without interruption. The major elements include low inventories, small lot sizes, fixed production rates, extensive preventative maintenance and quick repairs, few but reliable vendors, high-quality material and work, quick changes (setups), multifunctional and skilled workers, cooperative spirit (among departments, employees, and management), encouragement for a problem-solving environment, continual innovation and improvements, and a *pull system* for moving goods (where the control of moving work is determined backwards, from the last workstation to previous stations). Other elements are standardized outputs, moderately utilized capacity, and participative management.

Implemented JIT systems have resulted in significant benefits. These range, for example, from reducing production time from 15 days to 1 day (at Toyota), to reducing cost by 30 to 50 percent and, at the same time, increasing quality.

Some or even all elements of JIT can be executed manually. However, the use of IT to support even some of the elements may result in significant enhancement of JIT, especially when complex systems are involved. For example, using EDI can greatly enhance implementation, especially when international business partners are involved. HP Manufacturing Management II (from Hewlett-Packard Company) is a software program that supports multilocation tracking and JIT component ordering; extensive MRP and inventory control execution; and interfaces to financial management, budgeting, and CAD/CAM applications. Control Manufacturing (from Cincom Systems) supports multiple location JIT inventory control, as well as MRP, cost management, and production scheduling. It interfaces with several databases and is fully integrated with accounting and financial planning components. JIT systems are often interrelated to computerized project management systems.

PROJECT MANAGEMENT. A *project* is usually a one-time effort. It is composed of many interrelated activities, costs a substantial amount of money, and lasts for weeks to years. The management of a project (planning, organizing, and control) is complicated because of the following characteristics.

▼ Most projects are unique undertakings; and, therefore, there is little prior experience.

▼ Uncertainty exists due to the long completion times.

▼ There could be significant participation of outsiders, which is difficult to control.

▼ There are extensive interactions among participants.

▼ Projects often carry high risk but also provide high profit potential.

The management of projects is enhanced by project management tools such as the Program Evaluation and Review Technique (PERT) and Critical Path Method (CPM). These tools are easily computerized, and indeed there are dozens of commercial packages on the market.

SHORT-TERM SCHEDULES. Operations managers schedule jobs and employees on a daily and weekly basis. Information systems can be used to support such scheduling. For example, paper-based bar (or Gantt) charts can be computerized. Computerized charts can utilize colors to allow presentation of more information. Some complex scheduling situations are supported by DSS and even by expert systems (see Box 17.5).

IT At Work BOX 17.5

UNITED AIRLINES USES COMPUTERS TO SCHEDULE GATE ASSIGNMENTS

Assigning airplanes to gates in large airports is a complex job. Frequently, the gate controllers have to accommodate as many as 40 planes in less than 30 minutes. Changes are made constantly, due to weather conditions, mechanical problems, or other interferences. The old system used magnetic display bars, which had a tendency to fall on the floor. United Airlines now uses an expert-systems-based scheduling system at its major airports. It displays all the information of the old system, and much more. The system has a superb graphic display; aircraft are shown as bars with different colors. The length of the bar indicates the length of time the aircraft is scheduled to occupy the gate. Other displays tell the controllers the nature of the flight (flight number, arrival and departure time, present fuel load, and much more). The system ensures that aircraft are not assigned to the wrong kind of gate and contains an explanation if a gate is inappropriate for a certain aircraft.

The system provides input to zone controllers who are responsible for fueling, baggage handling, catering services, crew management, and so on. Changes are accomplished much faster, and a next-day schedule is expedited by about five hours each day. The system does many other things. For example, it alerts the controllers to airplanes that are on the ground, but whose gates have not been assigned. Similar systems are used by all major airlines.

Critical Thinking Issues: Why is assigning airplanes to gates a complex task? Why are graphics so important? ▲

SOURCE: Based on *Artificial Intelligence Letter*, Austin, TX: Texas Instruments, January 1988.

AUTOMATING DESIGN WORK AND MANUFACTURING

An important activity in the value chain is the design of products, services, or processes. Design is a lengthy process that may take years. IT has been successfully used in cutting the time required for design. Following are descriptions of representative information technologies (condensed from Zachary and Richman [1993]) that can be used:

COMPUTER-AIDED DESIGN. Computer-aided design (CAD) is a system that enables drawings to be constructed on a computer screen and subsequently stored, manipulated, and updated electronically. Most CAD systems allow the designer to draw a model of the design using a set of simple geometric figures (such as lines and circles) in two-dimensional modeling that form a 3-D drawing. Such figures may be brought to the screen and resized, reoriented, partially trimmed, or otherwise adjusted to create the desired drawing. In other words, each more complex part in the design is broken down into a set of simpler figures that, when appropriately positioned, create a graphic image of the whole part. The use of different colors in different portions of the design display helps make drawings even clearer and easier to understand. Another aspect of CAD graphics that substantially enhances clarity is the fact that a drawing may be rotated so the designer can view it from different angles. The ability to rotate or cause movement in the design allows testing for clearances and frequently leads to a major reduction in the cost of prototyping.

Having access to a computerized design database makes it easy for a designer to quickly modify an old design to meet new design requirements—an event that occurs quite frequently. This enhances designer productivity; speeds up the design process; reduces design errors resulting from hurried, inaccurate copying; and reduces the number of designers needed to perform the same amount of work. It also means that the designers can focus on doing work that is mostly nonroutine, while the CAD system does most of the routine work. Another advantage associated with a CAD database is that all of the designs are based on the same standards: standard primitives, standard colors, and other standard design rules. This reduces unpleasant surprises for a designer attempting to modify a previous design that might, under a manual system, be based on a different set of rules or assumptions than the one(s) he is following. CAD systems can reduce design time significantly and increase its quality (see Box 17.6).

IT At Work BOX 17.6

REENGINEERING DESIGN AT KODAK

Kodak Corporation was in dire trouble. One of its main competitors, Fuji, announced that it would come out soon with a new product, the disposable camera, which had the potential of garnering huge market share. This camera could be purchased for a nominal retail cost. Once the film had been shot by its purchaser, the camera would be returned to a developer, who would break down the parts and send them back to the manufacturer. Kodak had no comparable product, and its product development cycle was estimated to take 70 weeks to create such a competitive product. Kodak's business process needed changing to enhance its time-to-market capability. Like many processes, Kodak's development process was, primarily, sequential. First, the camera body designers had to do their work; then, it was forwarded to the shutter designers; then, to the film advance mechanism department, and so on. Kodak tried to use parallel processes. However, quite often, parts wouldn't fit together. A change in design in any part of the process would affect its overall integration, and communicating these ongoing changes were often "hit-and-miss."

Kodak greatly enhanced its time-to-market cycle and changed its business process by instituting two information technologies: (1) CAD/CAM and (2) integrated product design database. These combined systems resulted in increasing Kodak's productivity. Much of the dramatically improved results came from the integrated database. This system allowed each group of independent designers to view others' changes or improvements and factor those revisions into their own work.

Significant time reductions occurred, since the revisions were identified immediately and could be integrated instantaneously. They no longer had to experience the frustrating realization at the very end of the entire process that parts wouldn't fit together. Kodak was able to reduce its time-to-market to 38 weeks, almost half of its previous capability. In addition, Kodak's tooling and manufacturing costs were reduced by 25 percent from former levels. The manufacturing staff could now review the design process while still in the design process, allowing them to offer valuable cost-effective suggestions. The shorter design time allowed Kodak to offer its products in the U.S. market before Fuji had a chance to do so.

Information technology enabled successful reengineering to take place. In this case, integrated databases allowed a completely new process to materialize, now called *concurrent manufacturing*. This new process has spread to the automotive and aircraft manufacturing industries because it is very effective in reducing time-to-market, eliminating costly changes due to last-minute recovery of others' revisions, and integrating cost-saving manufacturing ideas into the design phase.

Critical Thinking Issues: Think about examples where integrated databases can reduce the time-to-market by 50% or more. ▲

SOURCE: Condensed from Hammer and Champy (1993).

COMPUTER-AIDED ENGINEERING. Computer-aided engineering (CAE) enables engineers to do complex engineering analysis on the computer. Once CAD work has been completed, a designer can use CAE to analyze the design and determine if it will work the way the designer thought it would. For example, if a circuit design simulation shows that the circuit produces a few unanticipated and undesired outputs, some redesign is clearly necessary.

With any kind of CAE, detailed engineering analysis provides data that may be useful when actually manufacturing the product. Such data not only include product specifications, but also process information on the design of tools or moulds and programs used for controlling the motions of numerical control (NC) machines or robots. Thus, a database created as a result of CAD/CAE may then be used to support computer-aided manufacturing (CAM).

COMPUTER-AIDED MANUFACTURING. Computer-aided manufacturing (CAM) encompasses the computer-aided techniques that facilitate planning, operation, and control of a production facility. Such techniques include computer-aided process planning, numerical control part programming, robotics programming, computer-generated work standards, MRP II, capacity requirements planning and shop-floor control. When CAD is feeding information to CAM, the combined system is referred to as CAD/CAM.

MOVING FROM MASS PRODUCTION TO MASS CUSTOMIZATION

One of the most innovative concepts of the Industrial Revolution was *mass production*. In mass production, a company produces a large quantity of an identical, standard product, under close supervision. The product is then stored for future distribution to many customers. Because the concept of mass production results in a low cost, products are relatively inexpensive and sold in department or specialty stores. The concept of mass production was adapted to thousands of products, ranging from simple watches to major appliances (such as TV sets and washing machines) to vehicles and computers. Because of increased competition, manufacturers may provide several models (e.g., regular and deluxe). The basic idea, however, is to manufacture a large quantity of goods which are placed in inventory and then sold to unknown customers.

A major change in manufacturing developed with the rise of the automobile, which was initially produced in pure mass production. Due to increased competition, customers were able to select "options," such as an air conditioner or automatic transmission. Manufacturers collected the customized orders. Once they accumulated enough similar orders to justify manufacturing the customized product, they produced the item. The result was a waiting time of several weeks or even months. Today's customers are not willing to wait so long.

*R*EENGINEERING

...Mass customization keeps production costs low while maximizing customer satisfaction

As discussed in Chapters 1, 3, and 4, **mass customization** may be essential to the survival of companies in the 1990s. The basic idea is to enable a company to produce large volumes (mass), yet to customize the product to the specifications of individual customers (e.g., see Pine [1993]). Mass customization enables a company to provide flexible and quick responsiveness to a customer's needs, at a low cost and with high quality. Mass customization is made possible by allowing fast and inexpensive production changes, by reducing the ordering and sales process, by shortening the production time, and by using prefabricated parts.

To implement mass customization, a company must (1) turn its work processes into modules and (2) create an architecture for linking the modules, to allow them to swiftly merge in the best sequence required to produce the final products or services (see Box 17.7).

To successfully coordinate the process modules, a company must have the ability to support these features:

1. *Instantaneous.* The module processes must be linked together as quickly as possible; this implies a sophisticated IT system such as groupware and work flow.
2. *Costless.* The linkage system should not add a significant cost to the product or service. The use of flexible manufacturing, a computerized approach described in the next section, can help.
3. *Seamless.* A dynamic network virtually creates instant teams to support each customer; this process must appear seamless to the customer.
4. *Frictionless.* Worker modules must come together immediately without the benefit of ever having met; there can be no friction in the creation process.

IT At Work   BOX 17.7

 **R**EENGINEERING

BALLY REENGINEERED ITSELF TO MASS CUSTOMIZATION

Bally Engineered Structures of Bally, PA, had been established in 1933 as a producer of custom-made, insulated products for commercial and industrial uses. When the market matured in the 1970s, Bally found itself competing in a price-sensitive market, and the company developed into a mass production operation in order to reduce cost. Mass production resulted in a lower cost and standard products. By the beginning of the 1990s, the competition shifted from an emphasis on price to price-and-customized products. In order to develop a stronger company for future growth, Bally (which employs 400 people) established new goals. They included: (1) customizing of products to suit the needs of the individual customers, (2) developing new products, (3) delivering products to customers faster than the competition, and (4) reducing the overall manufacturing and administrative costs. These goals required a massive reengineering of the manufacturing process and other company processes.

In order to accomplish the new goals, the company utilized a computer-driven intelligent system to reengineer sales and ordering processes, which were composed of 86 tasks conducted sequentially and could take from five to seven weeks. The first step involved a redesign of the sales and order entry system. This allowed salespeople to access information directly from the AS/400 via their own personal computers. Salespeople are able to provide customer requirements, receive price quotations, identify order status and shipment information, receive specification drawings, and communicate with anyone in the company through the electronic mail system. The system also allows for controlled access to a company personnel database. For example, managers can identify employees with specific expertise. As a result, the sales and ordering process was reduced to less than 20 tasks and took from one to two weeks.

Another computer-related improvement of the AS/400 system was the direct input of customer configu-

rations into a CAD system. From the initial design, bills of materials were generated and copies could be sent via fax machine directly to the customer. This also allowed the elimination of a complex system of checking and comparing the components. Every employee now has access to all data needed for his job, and unnecessary paperwork has been minimized. As a result, the number of customer options has soared from 12 to 10,000, making Bally a true user of *mass customization*. Ultimately, Bally plans to eliminate all paperwork related to the manufacturing process, which will continue to be done at reduced costs and improved lead times. Bally also developed a computerized network that links sales representatives, customers, production people, and suppliers into one system which shares information across the entire value chain.

Without mass customization, Bally would be a struggling company fighting to cut prices with other competitors. However, today the company has a leading position, with 12 to 15 percent of the $400 million U.S. market. Utilization of the computer to maintain this leading position is viewed as reengineering, followed by continuous, incremental improvements. The future holds even more changes, such as information networks that will connect the company with customers and suppliers. But the ultimate goals continue to be increased product diversification, improved quality and service, and lowered manufacturing costs.

Critical Thinking Issues: How much more are you willing to pay for a customized rather than a standard product, and why is mass customization better than regular customization? ▲

SOURCE: Condensed from Pine, B. J. II and T. W. Pietrocini, "Standard Modules Allow Mass Customization at Bally Engineered Structures," *Planning Review*, July/August 1993, pp. 20–22.

An important point here is that mass customization involves not only the operations function but also marketing and sales, personnel, and finance. An example can be seen in the case of Bally (Box 17.7). The information systems of Bally cross traditional department lines.

Another example of mass customization is Digital Equipment Corporation's computerized configuration system, which was described in Chapter 4. This system was supported by expert systems that enabled customers to receive customized midrange computers at a competitive price and in shortened delivery times.

FLEXIBLE MANUFACTURING SYSTEMS. A **flexible manufacturing system (FMS)** refers to a group of machines designed to provide the flexibility of individual machines, yet handle high-quantity intermittent processing requirements. They save space, provide high consistency and quality, use little manual labor, and increase capacity. Virtually unmanned, these systems include a series of identical machining centers; an automated, computer-controlled materials-handling system; and other possible peripherals, such as a wash station, coordinate measuring machine, grinders, storage rack, robots, and loading/unloading stations. The materials management system is typically a series of automated vehicle carts used for transporting pallets of materials that are guided by a tow line or rails. The FMS is supervised by a computer, which interfaces with the plant computer when it needs additional data or when it is feeding data back. FMS is especially effective in a computer-integrated manufacturing environment.

COMPUTER-INTEGRATED MANUFACTURING (CIM)

Computer-integrated manufacturing (CIM) is a concept or philosophy concerning the implementation of various integrated computer systems in factory automation. CIM has three basic goals.

▼ *Simplification* of all manufacturing technologies and techniques.

▼ *Automation* of as many of the manufacturing processes as possible by integrating many information technologies. A list of such automated systems is provided in Figure 17.11.

▼ *Integration and coordination* via computer hardware and software of all aspects of design, manufacturing, and related functions.

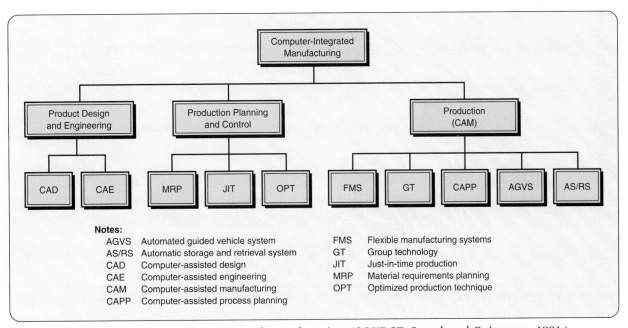

FIGURE 17.11 Essentials of computer-integrated manufacturing. (SOURCE: Saraph and Guimaraes, 1991.)

THE CIM MODEL. All of the hardware in the world will not make a computer-integrated manufacturing system work if it does not have the support of the people designing, implementing, and using it. According to Kenneth Van Winkle, manager of manufacturing systems at Kimball International, a furniture manufacturer, "Computer technology is only 20 percent of CIM. The other 80 percent is the *business processes* and *people.*" In order to bring people together and formulate a workable business process, CIM must start with a plan. This plan comes from the CIM Model. The CIM Model conceptually describes the CIM vision and architecture as directed from the top levels of the business. This model is then communicated to the functional and operational managers and to the technical engineers and scientists. Then, with the approval and support of upper management, the CIM vision can be implemented from the bottom up.

The CIM Model is derived from the CIM Enterprise Wheel developed by the Technical Council of the Society of Manufacturing Engineers (see Figure 17.12). There are five fundamental dimensions of the wheel. The outer circle represents

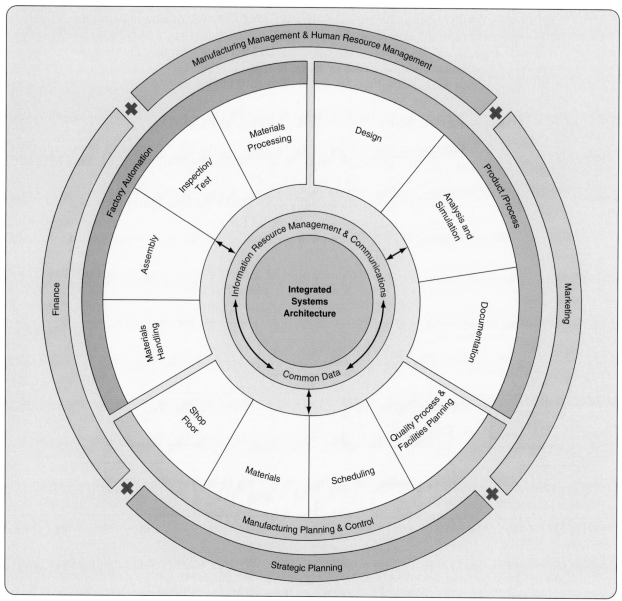

FIGURE 17.12 The CIM model, integration of all manufacturing activities under unified management. (SOURCE: Society of Manufacturing Engineers, Dearborn, Michigan. Reproduced with permission.)

general business management. The inner circle represents four major families of processes that make up a CIM: *(1) product and process definition, (2) manufacturing planning and control, (3) factory automation,* and *(4) information resource management.* Each of these five dimensions is a composite of more specific manufacturing processes, and each dimension is interrelated with the others. Thus, when planning a CIM system, no dimension can be ignored. The hub of the wheel represents the IT resources and technologies necessary for the integration of CIM. Without an integrated plan, trying to implement a CIM would be next to impossible. This is the reason for many CIM failures in the early stages of computer integration. There must be communication, data sharing, and cooperation among the different levels of management and functional personnel.

The major advantages of CIM are its comprehensiveness and flexibility. This is especially important in BPR, where processes are completely restructured or eliminated. Without CIM, it may be necessary to invest large amounts of money in changing existing information systems to fit the new processes.

▶ 17.7 MANAGING MARKETING, DISTRIBUTION, AND SERVICE PROCESSES

CHANNEL SYSTEMS

The term **channel systems** refers to all the systems involved in the process of getting a product or service to customers and dealing with all customers' needs. The complexity of channel systems can be observed in Figure 17.13, where six major systems are interrelated.

Channel systems can link and transform marketing, sales, supply, and other activities and systems. Added market power comes from the integration of channel systems with the corporate functional areas. Information technology, as will be shown in this section and is shown throughout the text, plays an extremely important role in supporting these systems. The problem is that a change in any of the channels may affect the other channels. Therefore, the supporting information systems must be coordinated or even integrated.

Of the many channel systems' activities, only a few are described here. They are organized into four groups:

(a) The customer is king.   (c) Distribution channels.
(b) Telemarketing.   (d) Marketing management.

THE CUSTOMER IS KING

In Chapters 1 through 4, we emphasized the increasing importance of customers, the trend for customization, and the trend toward consumer-based organizations. Therefore, it is essential today for companies to know more about customers and to treat the customer as king. New and innovative products and services, successful promotions, and superb customer service are becoming a necessity for many organizations. These can be supported by IT. In this section, we will present illustrations of how IT supports customer-oriented activities. Several additional examples are given in other chapters of this book.

CUSTOMER PROFILES AND PREFERENCE ANALYSIS. Information about existing and potential customers is critical for the success of many corporations. Therefore, sophisticated information systems are developed to collect data regarding customers, demographics (ages, sex, income level), and their likes and dislikes (see Box 17.8). These data are stored in a corporate database or in special marketing databases for future analysis and use. For example, the opening case in Chapter 1 (7-Eleven) is centered around collecting information about customers.

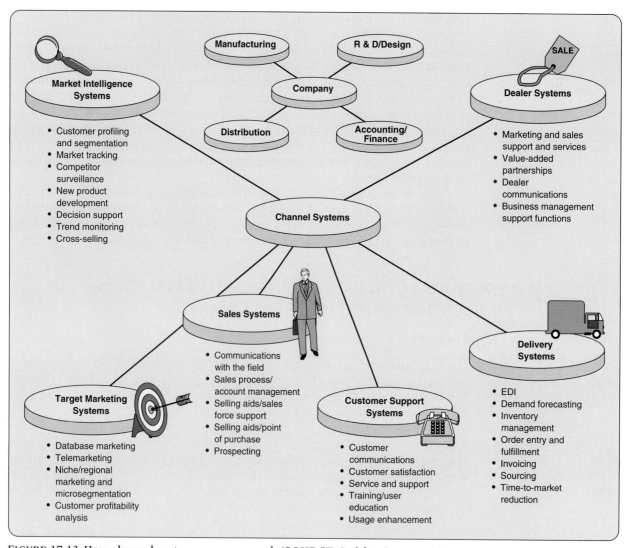

FIGURE 17.13 How channel systems are composed. (SOURCE: *Insights,* Summer 1989, p. 5.)

IT At Work BOX 17.8

GLOBAL PERSPECTIVE

FINNISH NEURAL NETWORKS HELP IN CUSTOMER ANALYSIS

Infomarket Corporation (Lappeenranta, Finland) developed a neural network-based application for customer analysis. It enables a retailer, retail chain, or other seller to analyze its customer structure on the basis of purchasing behavior.

Modern supermarkets are visited by tens of thousands of customers every week, buying thousands of different brands of goods. It is, therefore, difficult to obtain up-to-date information concerning the actual purchasing behavior of customers. Yet, accurate information on customers' purchases is registered in the checkout terminals of stores. This information is analyzed on a daily basis by Infomarket's neural network. The system provides the retailer's management with a concrete picture of the

structure of customer classes, the retailer's shares of the sales in the region and the demand for different goods in different customer classes. The network also analyzes the impact of various promotions and price variations. Finally, the program makes it possible to compare and analyze the performance of resalers and sales agents. The neural software is often more accurate and faster than traditional statistical methods. The software is in use in many countries worldwide.

Critical Thinking Issue: Can you visualize how a neural network works here? In what other businesses can similar systems be used? ▲

SOURCE: Condensed from *Finnish Trade Review,* March 1993.

PROSPECTIVE CUSTOMER LISTS AND MARKETING DATABASES. A reliable customer database is critical for many businesses. While some businesses are selling their products through outlets (such as department stores), others try to reach customers directly at their homes. Even companies that sell through outlets need to know something about customers and their preferences. IT can help create customer databases of both existing and potential customers (see Cameron and Targett, [1992]). It is possible today to purchase computerized lists from several sources (see Chapter 20 for a discussion of customers' privacy issues related to such lists) and then merge them electronically. Once prospective customer lists are stored electronically, they can be easily accessed and sorted by any desired classification for direct mailing or for telemarketing.

Several U.S. retailers ask customers to tell them only the zip code in which they live. This way the retailers do not get involved in privacy issues, yet they get valuable information. This information is matched with the items purchased. Using geographical information systems (GIS), for example, retailers can make better decisions about where to open new branches and outlets. Again, the objective is to make customers happy. These examples illustrate how business decisions are being driven by existing customers. However, to maintain existing customers and to gain new ones, advertising and sales efforts are necessary.

CUSTOMER INQUIRY SYSTEMS AND AUTOMATED HELP DESK. Organizations are flooded with inquiries from customers. These can amount to thousands per day. The usual way to handle inquiries is to establish a help desk that answers the telephone, E-mail, faxes or face-to-face inquiries. Many of these help desks are clogged, resulting in considerable waiting time. An automatic voice system is useful in some cases, while in others the customer wastes a lot of time moving from one voice menu to another and not being properly served. Information technology can provide several alternative solutions to the problem. For example, some companies use expert systems to expedite the search for information. This speeds up the work of the help desk employees. A more sophisticated solution is to enable customers to electronically enter the corporate database and find the answers by themselves. The use of *intelligent agents* (see Chapter 16) is expected to completely reengineer the manner in which customer inquiry systems operate.

*E*MERGING TECHNOLOGY

...Expert systems help customers help themselves

TELEMARKETING

Telemarketing is playing an increasing role in our society. It is an integral part of some reengineering projects and is heavily backed by information technologies.

WHAT IS TELEMARKETING? **Telemarketing** is a marketing process that uses telecommunications and information systems to execute a marketing program for customers who want to shop from their homes (see Box 17.9). Operationally, telemarketing can be done in several ways, such as telephone calls generated by computer programs and computer-generated messages delivered by voice technologies. A telemarketing process can be divided into five major activities: advertisment and reaching customers, order processing, customer service, sales support, and account management, all of which are supported by IT.

Telemarketing benefits include generating leads, gathering information, providing information, help in selling, improving cash flow, and enhancing customer service (see Box 17.10). The capabilities as well as the limitations of telemarketing are summarized in Table 17.2 on page 645.

Despite its limitations, telemarketing is growing very fast, especially when the computer is used interactively by the customer. The Internet, for example, is becoming a prime telemarketing vehicle. The number of telemarketing employees in the United States is expected to double from four million in 1995 to eight million by the year 2000. Many new jobs are being created by such systems.

A Closer Look BOX 17.9

THE ROLE OF COMPUTERS IN HOME SHOPPING

Home shopping via television is a fast growing business (see *BusinessWeek*, July 1993, and *Forbes*, May 23, 1993). Viewers observe a special TV channel that displays products; and if interested, they call and order, using a credit card to pay. The orders are entered into computers as soon as they are received by the telephone operators. Such entry helps to determine whether to continue with the advertisement of an item or to discontinue advertising. (TV time is very expensive; if an item is not selling well the advertising should be stopped.) In addition, the computer entry triggers an order to the warehouse, instructions regarding shipment, and a bill sent to the credit card company. In a few years, customers will be able to home shop interactively from their TV via computers. This is done interactively so shoppers can request information about *any* desired products and buy them. This is in contrast to home shopping via TV, where you can buy only what is presented on the TV screen. Computerized home shopping can be done by using services such as America Online, Prodigy, and the Internet.

DISTRIBUTION CHANNELS

DISTRIBUTION CHANNELS MANAGEMENT. Organizations can distribute their products and services through several available delivery channels. For instance, a company may use its own outlets or distributors. In addition, the company needs to decide on the transportation mode (e.g., trains, planes, trucks). Deliveries can be accomplished by the company itself or by a trucker, or the entire delivery process can be subcontracted (see the Harper case in Chapter 14). DSS models are frequently used to support this type of decision. Once products are in the distribution channels, they need to be monitored and tracked. Fast and accurate delivery times guarantee high customer satisfaction and repeat business. Some of the most sophisticated tracking systems are used by Federal Express, UPS, and other large transportation companies (see Box 17.11).

IT At Work BOX 17.10

E MERGING TECHNOLOGY

HUMANA INCREASES SALES PRODUCTIVITY BY 345 PERCENT

Humana is a large health care provider which owns and manages hospitals and other health care facilities. As part of its marketing programs, the company uses telemarketing to arrange appointments with senior citizens interested in a variety of Medicare plans. Humana also sells memberships in a seniors association and conducts advertisements to recruit employees. More than 20 agents are now using an advanced marketing information system which enables them to do the following.

▼ Compile a list of customers from several sources (prospect database, responses to direct mail, responses to advertisements, responses to point-of-purchase displays, and so on).

▼ Process the list by a minicomputer to qualify prospects and set up appointments for field representatives to meet with prospects.

The system is based on off-the-shelf software integrated with Humana's hardware and telecommunications system.

The results are as follows:

▼ A 345 percent increase in outgoing calls per hour.

▼ A 180 percent increase in contacts handled by agents.

▼ A significant increase in leads generated by the telemarketing employees.

Critical Thinking Issue: How can telemarketing increase outgoing calls so much? How do you feel about being approached by an unexpected marketing call? ▲

SOURCE: Condensed from *Voice Processing Magazine*, March 1993.

Table 17.2 **Capabilities and Limitations of Telemarketing**

Capabilities
- Order processing allows customers to buy at their convenience.
- Message-on-hold feature is effective in informing customers about a company's products and services. It is the least expensive form of company advertisement, but can be the most effective.
- Telemarketing reduces operating costs; cuts number of salespersons, including their travel expenses, entertainment costs, and travel time.
- Telemarketing is a versatile and cost-effective method to increase sales, manage accounts, and make the outside sales force more productive.
- Sales support improves the effectiveness and efficiency of the sales force.
- Customer service features allow customers to voice their concerns and gain ongoing support after purchasing products. The result is a positive image and a loyal customer.
- Telemarketing can collect information about customer needs and wants, quickly, inexpensively, and accurately.

Limitations
- Cost of telemarketers, commissions, training, equipment, and telephone can be very high, depending on scope of the operation and its overall objectives.
- It is difficult to find good telemarketers.
- Negative image—telemarketing is seen by many as illegitimate and a nuisance.
- The combination of unlisted telephone numbers, devices that enable people not to accept calls, and telephone answering machines presents telemarketing companies with difficulties reaching people.

IMPROVING SALES AT RETAIL STORES. The home shopping alternative puts pressure on retailers to offer more products in one location and provide better service to the customer (remember, the customer is king). The increased number of products and the customers' desire to get more information while at the store results in a need to add many salespeople. This increases cost. Also, long lines are in evidence in some stores. Using information technology, it is possible to improve the situation by reengineering the checkout process (as illustrated in Box 17.12).

MARKETING MANAGEMENT

Many marketing management activities are supported by computerized information systems. Here are some representative examples of how this is being done.

IT At Work BOX 17.11

 **REENGINEERING**

COSMOS—FEDERAL EXPRESS TRACKING SYSTEM

Whenever you mail a package by Federal Express, your package is under constant surveillance. When a package is picked up, a hand-held scanner data entry device reads the bar code with the package identification number. The person who picks up the package adds details about the sender, receiver, and type of delivery. This information is transferred from the device to the corporate database. From that point on, the bar code on the package is read any time there is a change in the distribution channel. For example, this occurs when the van unloads the package at the city's center or when the package is loaded on an airplane. Using COSMOS, Federal Express is able to tell a customer the location of the package at any time. The system also records when, where, and by whom the package was received.

The system was so successful that it is now used by many major shippers in the industry. Furthermore, within a short time, many companies outside the United States have seen the system and been inspired to develop similar systems in their own countries.

In a process reengineering effort, Federal Express now permits its customers to go on-line electronically, access COSMOS, and find the status of every package in real time.

Critical Thinking Issue: Who benefits from such tracking and why? ▲

IT At Work BOX 17.12

TANDY CORPORATION REENGINEERS SHOPPING PROCESSES

In order to keep aisles from getting clogged with shopping carts and checkout lines from becoming too long, Tandy Corporation introduced a wireless portable system in their large Incredible Universe stores.

Each Incredible Universe store has 15,000 or more different products, ranging from refrigerators to computers. To manage such a store, Tandy joined forces with IBM and Grid Systems Corporation to create a unique information support system.

Here is how the system works. When a customer enters the store she receives a smart card. To make a purchase, the shopper presents the card to a sales representative, who runs a bar code reader attached to a PalmPad computer over the card and then scans the bar code reader over the UPC on the desired appliance or other product (see figure). Pricing, inventory status, product options, and service (warranty) options, as well as delivery schedules, then appear on the PalmPad screen. It is visible to the sales representatives and to the customer. When a customer decides to buy an item, the information is transmitted from the wireless PalmPad to a PC, which is connected to a LAN and to the IBM store control information system. When the customer finishes shopping, she presents the card to the cashier; the bill appears in a split second; and the customer can pay cash or use a credit or debit card. The payment processing time takes less than 1 minute compared with 5 to 10 minutes in an ordinary store. (This time *includes* working on warranties and making shipping arrangements for home deliveries for large items.)

Tandy sales reps use a pen-based system to supply customers with up-to-date information on purchasing options.

The new process enables Tandy to accommodate more than 50,000 customers per store per month, and the customers are happy. Furthermore, the system allows management to run the store at a low cost.

Critical Thinking Issue: Small retail stores cannot afford to provide such a service. Will they be able to compete? ▲

SOURCE: Condensed from *ComputerWorld*, July 19, 1993.

PRICING OF PRODUCTS OR SERVICES. Sales volumes are largely determined by the price of the products or services. The price is also a major determinant of profit. Pricing is a difficult decision, and prices may need to be changed frequently. For example, in response to price changes made by competitors, a company may need to adjust its prices or take other actions. Many companies are using **On-line Analytical Processing** (OLAP) to support these and other marketing decisions.

SALESPERSON PRODUCTIVITY ANALYSIS. Salespersons differ from each other; some excel in selling certain products, while others excel in selling to a certain type of customer or in a certain geographical zone. This information, which is usually collected in the marketing TPS, can be analyzed, using a comparative performance system, where sales data by salesperson, product, region, and even the time of day can be compiled. Actual current sales can be compared to historical data and to standards. Multidimensional spreadsheet software (such as CA Compute from Computer Associates) and other OLAP can be used to facilitate this type of analysis. Assignment of salespersons to regions and/or products and the calculation of bonuses can also be supported by this system.

PRODUCT/CUSTOMER PROFITABILITY ANALYSIS. In deciding on advertisement and other marketing efforts, it is frequently important to know the profit contribution of certain products or services. Similarly, it is valuable to know how much profit the company derives from each customer, product, or service. In Chapter 15, we demonstrated how this is done by Hong Kong Bank. Profitability information can be derived from the cost-accounting system. Identification of profitable customers and the frequency with which they interact with the organization can be derived from special promotional programs, such as the frequent flyer programs used by airlines and hotels (see Box 17.13). Both the operations and the analysis of such programs are fully computerized. For example, profit performance analysis software is available from Comshare. It is designed to help managers assess and improve the profit performance of their line of business, products, distribution channels, sales regions, and other dimensions critical to managing the enterprise. Northwest Airlines uses expert systems and DSSs to check the profitability of more than 40,000 programs they have for calculating commissions to travel agents.

IT At Work BOX 17.13

A FREQUENT FLYER PROGRAM

Anyone can register in a frequent flyer program. Once you accumulate a certain number of miles, you are eligible to receive a free ticket. Mileage can also be accumulated by renting a car, staying in a hotel, using a long-distance telephone company, or just using a credit card. Customers who fly frequently are classified as elite or preferred customers and collect special bonuses, ranging from free upgrades to first class, to 50 percent extra mileage. Below is a typical monthly statement of a frequent flyer account. Having millions of registered members, frequent flyer programs could not have become a reality without the aid of a supporting information system.

FREQUENT FLYER STATEMENT (mileage summary).

SUMMARY DATE:	05/08/93	MILES WITH NO EXPIRATION DATE:	5500
AADVANTAGE NUMBER:	HR20670	MILES EXPIRING ON - 12/31/94:	21331
PROGRAM-TO-DATE MILES:	166135	- 12/31/95:	40014
YTD GOLD/PLAT QUAL MLG:	19656	- 12/31/96:	35998
		TOTAL AVAILABLE AWARD MILEAGE:	102843

TRANSACTION DATE	TRANSACTION DESCRIPTION	MILEAGE	BONUS MILES	TOTAL ACCUM MILEAGE
03/02/93	AA 813 Y DFW LGB	1221		1221
03/02/93	AA 719 Y FLL DFW	1118		1118
03/19/93	AA 506 Y DFW LIT	303	197	500
03/19/93	AA 464 Y LGB DFW	1221		1221
03/19/93	AV 4 DY LITTLE ROCK AP AR	500		500
03/23/93	AA 461 Y DFW LGB	1221		1221
03/23/93	AA 659 Y LIT DFW	303	197	500
03/19/93	MCI LONG DISTANCE SERVICE		570	570
04/19/93	MCI LONG DISTANCE SERVICE		885	885
04/05/93	CITIBANK CARD PURCHASES		4015	4015

Critical Thinking Issue: The major beneficiaries of such a program are employees who accumulate miles while traveling for business, but redeem the mileage for vacations. Should the business reclaim these miles? ▲

LEARNING ABOUT COMPETITORS. Frito-Lay learns constantly about their competitors. Each time a Frito-Lay employee delivers goods to a specific store, he surveys the shelves to see what and how many products are available from the competition. This information, collected by hand-held computers, is entered into the corporate database and is used for decision making about prices, advertisements, changes in products, and the like. As discussed in Chapters 3 and 14, companies use a variety of information technologies to learn about their competitors.

SALES ANALYSIS AND TRENDS. The marketing TPS collects sales figures that can be segregated by an EIS along several dimensions. Such segregation is done for early detection of problems and opportunities, usually by searching for trends. For example, if sales of a certain product show a continuous decline in a certain region but not in other regions, one may want to investigate the declining region. Similarly, an increasing sales volume of a new product, if it is found to be statistically significant, calls attention to an opportunity. This application demonstrates the reliance of an EIS on the TPS.

An interesting computerized technology that can support this type of analysis is a geographical information system (GIS). Using existing maps at various levels of detail, a marketing manager can learn a lot about the company's customers and competitors, and experiment with potential strategies (see Box 17.14).

IT At Work BOX 17.14

 **E**MERGING TECHNOLOGY

BANKS USING GEOGRAPHICAL INFORMATION SYSTEMS (GIS) TO SUPPORT MARKETING

Banks are using GIS for plotting the following situations.

▼ Branch and ATM locations.

▼ Customer demographics (e.g., residence, age, income level) for each product of the bank.

▼ Traffic patterns (in terms of business activities).

▼ Geographical area served by each branch.

▼ Market potential.

▼ The banks' strengths and weaknesses—against the competition.

▼ Branch performance.

A GIS is used as a geographic spreadsheet that allows managers to model business activities and perform "what-if" analyses (e.g., close a branch, merge branches, what if a competitor opens a branch). The maps consolidate pages of analysis. Representative pioneering banks are First Florida Bank (Tampa, FL), Marion Bank (Philadelphia, PA), and NJB Financial (Princeton, NJ).

Critical Thinking Issue: How can a GIS indicate a bank's strengths and weaknesses against the competition? ▲

SOURCE: Condensed from Radding A., "Going with GIS," *Bank Management*, December 1991.

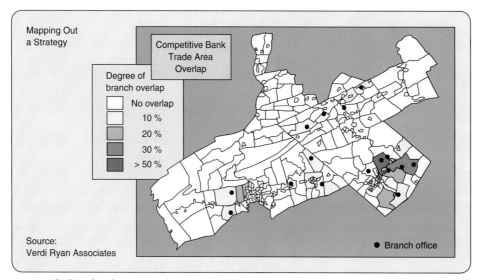

A GIS helps bank map where it's strong—and weak—against the competition.

DEMAND AND PRICE FORECASTS. Forecasts of demand for products and services are essential for corporate planning and budgeting. Demand forecasts are also used for decisions regarding pricing and advertising. Demand forecasting is the driving information for production scheduling, capacity planning, and other enterprise decisions. Forecasting activities are frequently done with specially constructed DSS models. However, particular forecasts in marketing may involve a qualitative analysis, which is not provided by a DSS. For example, certain technological developments, competitors' actions, and changes in consumer preferences cannot be supported by a quantitative DSS approach and need the support of a group of experts which may use group-support technology.

NEW PRODUCTS, SERVICES, AND MARKETS PLANNING. In our highly competitive world, innovation is the key to success and survival. Innovation means continuous introduction of new, improved products and services, and development of new markets. However, such ventures can be expensive and risky. An important question to ask about a new product or service is, "Will it sell?" An appropriate answer involves careful analysis, planning, and forecasting. These can best be executed with the aid of IT because of the large number of determining factors and uncertainties that may be involved. This is clearly in the DSS arena, where market research, simulation, and detailed marketing analysis are integrated to support critical decisions.

BUSINESS ALLIANCES. Increased competition and the complexity of some technological systems encourage marketing alliances and joint ventures. The success of such **business alliances** depends on careful analysis of the strengths and contributions of each partner. Marketing partnerships are popular among international corporations and are usually supported by IT from inception. IT provides for communication links among partners, transfer of funds across international borders, and control and evaluation of the partnership. Examples of such information technology support are EDI and **electronic markets**. Electronic markets enable buyers and sellers to exchange information regarding prices, locate availability of goods, and make payment arrangements; all are done rapidly and at a very low cost. Also, they provide wide exposure to buyers and sellers worldwide (see Box 17.15).

A Closer Look BOX 17.15   **LOBAL PERSPECTIVE**

ELECTRONIC MARKETS: AN OPPORTUNITY FOR BUSINESS ALLIANCES AND INTERNATIONAL TRADE

Electronic markets allow buyers and sellers to exchange information about market prices and product offerings through a computerized system. Electronic marketing replaces traditional systems of intermediaries; it forces sellers to form cooperative arrangements with new IT-based intermediaries or with other sellers or service providers to sponsor a new electronic market.

One of the first large electronic markets is that of Reuters Holdings PLC. This service enables money dealers to complete foreign currency exchange transactions through one of over 170,000 Reuter Video terminals in 78 countries. An extension of this market for trading in futures and future options was launched in 1988 by Reuters and the Chicago Mercantile Exchange. This system offers 24-hour-a-day access to the global futures markets.

The first electronic market on the Internet, called CommerNet, was launched in fall 1994. It enables customers to purchase goods and services and do banking electronically. Companies can solicit bids, place orders directly from manufacturers, bid on contracts, and collaborate over the network in designing products. For example, a computer manufacturer that buys goods electronically can then sell the finished products to customers worldwide over the network. CommerNet is a joint venture of a large bank (Bank of America) and computer manufactures (Apple, Sun Microsystem, and Hewlett–Packard).

▶ 17.8 MANAGING HUMAN RESOURCE SYSTEMS: FROM RECRUITMENT TO EMPOWERMENT

Due to recent developments in database management systems and client/server architecture, there is increasing evidence that human resource information systems (HRIS) are indeed spreading (e.g., see Lederer and Licker [1992], and Broderick and Boudreau [1992]). Initial HRIS applications were mainly related to TPS. However, recently we have seen considerable computerization activities in the managerial and even the strategic areas (see Meinert and Davis [1989], and Byun and Suh [1994]). One of the most comprehensive HRIS is that of Federal Express (see Minicase 1 at the end of this chapter).

Managing human resources is a complex job that starts with the hiring of an employee and ends with his retirement or other form of departure. It includes several processes; a few of them are described in this chapter.

(a) Recruitment.

(b) Human resource maintenance and development.

(c) Human resource planning.

(d) Empowerment of employees.

(e) Teams.

RECRUITMENT

Recruitment involves finding employees, testing them, and deciding which ones to hire. While some companies are flooded with thousands of applicants, in other cases it is difficult to find the right people. Information systems can be very helpful in both cases. Here are some examples.

POSITION INVENTORY. Large organizations need to fill vacant positions frequently; therefore, they maintain a file that lists all open positions in the organization. Open positions are categorized by job title, geographical area, task content, and skills required. The total list of vacant positions is referred to as a position inventory. Like any other inventory, this one is updated each time a transaction occurs.

An advanced computerized position inventory system enables the list to be current and to be viewed by any employee, usually from any location, at any time. In addition, it is possible to match openings to available personnel (as reflected in the personnel files). Valuable information can be generated by analyzing the position inventory and its changes over time; e.g., one can find those jobs with high turnover. This information can support related decisions, such as promotions, salary administration, and training plans.

EMPLOYEE SELECTION. The human resource department is responsible for screening of job applicants. Screenings, evaluations, and selections must be done in compliance with state and federal regulations. In addition to filing a form, candidates may take tests and go through interviews. All this information needs to be evaluated. In order to expedite the evaluation process and assure consistency in the selection, companies use information technologies such as expert systems. For an example, see Box 17.16.

HUMAN RESOURCE MAINTENANCE AND DEVELOPMENT

Once employees are recruited, they are part of the corporate human resource pool. This pool needs to be maintained and developed. Some activities supported by IT are the following:

IT At Work   BOX 17.16

CYDSA USES AN EXPERT SYSTEM TO ASSESS FUTURE PERFORMANCE OF CANDIDATES

The human resource department of CYDSA, a large company in Mexico, administers a behavioral profile test to measure the capabilities of individuals under consideration for employment. The test results were analyzed manually by experts appropriate for the positions to be filled. Results are divided into three categories: candidate style, candidate values, and candidate thought preferences. Due to the large number of applicants, the many locations of the corporation, and the high level of expertise required for the analysis, it was very difficult to execute a quality analysis in a timely manner. To overcome these problems, an expert system was developed that includes eleven knowledge bases.

The basic objective of the system is to assess the candidates' directional initiative, potential performance problems, and supervision effectiveness. Analysis of an average applicant, which takes an hour when it is done manually, can be performed in about five minutes when supported by the expert system. The system is available via satellites to all corporate sites through electronic networks.

Critical Thinking Issue: What are the benefits of this expert system to CYDSA? How would you feel if your job application were assessed by a machine for a yes-or-no decision? ▲

SOURCE: Condensed from Terashima, H. Sehusi, "An Expert Systems for Describing Human Behavior in Work Environments," In: Cantu-Ortiz F. J. (Ed), *Operational Expert Systems in Mexico*, New York, NY: Pergamon Press, 1991.

PERFORMANCE EVALUATION. Most employees are evaluated periodically by their immediate supervisors. Others are evaluated by peers or subordinates. Evaluations are usually recorded on forms and can be keyed in or scanned into the information system. Once digitized, evaluations can be used to support many decisions, ranging from rewards to transfers to layoffs. Using such information manually is a tedious and error-prone job. Analysis of employees' performances can be done with the help of expert systems, which provide an unbiased and systematic interpretation of performance over time.

Evaluating professors on-line is done in several universities. The evaluation form appears on the screen, and the students fill in this form. Results can be tabulated in minutes.

TRAINING AND HUMAN RESOURCE DEVELOPMENT. Employee training and retraining is an important activity of the human resource department. Major issues are planning classes and tailoring specific training programs to meet the needs of the organization and employees. Sophisticated human resource departments build a development plan for each employee. IT can support the planning, monitoring, and control of these activities by using work flow and project management applications.

IT also plays an important role in training. Some of the most innovative developments are in the areas of intelligent computer-aided instruction (ICAI) and application of multimedia support for instructional activities. Instruction can be provided on-line at different sites of an organization (see Box 17.17).

TURNOVER, TARDINESS, AND ABSENTEEISM ANALYSES. Replacing employees can be an expensive proposition (replacing a skilled employee may cost as much as $25,000). Therefore, it is important to learn why employees leave. The same is true for tardiness and absenteeism. Data on these issues are collected in the payroll system and personnel files. By using DSS models, for example, it is possible to identify causes and patterns as well as to assess the impact of programs that aim to reduce turnover, tardiness, and absenteeism.

IT At Work BOX 17.17

ON-LINE MULTIMEDIA SUPPORTS TRAINING AT PIZZA HUT

*E*MERGING TECHNOLOGY

Many companies, especially in the restaurant business, cannot afford to have their key managers occupied with extensive classroom training. Also, travel and accommodation costs may be high if training is out of town. To solve this problem, Pizza Hut created an on-site computerized multimedia training program. The program includes computer-based training modules and is supported by video and hard-copy material. Computer-based training is used mainly to teach complex topics such as analysis skills and decision making. The training involves hands-on experience using the Automated Restaurant Management System program and other computerized applications for restaurants. Even though 70 percent of all trainees have never used computers before, the success has been overwhelming. Pizza Hut also provides an on-line certification given to managers after they pass a computerized test.

Critical Thinking Issue: How do you feel about learning without teachers? ▲

SOURCE: Condensed from *ComputerWorld*, March 4, 1991.

HUMAN RESOURCE PLANNING AND MANAGEMENT–LABOR NEGOTIATIONS

Managing human resources in large organizations involves extensive planning. Here are some examples of how IT can help.

PERSONNEL PLANNING. In preparing the corporate strategic plan, it is often necessary to include a personnel component. The human resource department forecasts requirements for people and skills. Then, the department needs to plan how to find (or develop from within) sufficient human resources. In some geographical areas, it may be difficult to find particular types of employees. The same may be true for companies that need to staff offices in foreign countries.

Large companies develop qualitative and quantitative workforce planning models. Such models can be enhanced if IT is used to collect, update, and process the information. An integral part of such planning is the use of multidimensional computerized forecasting models.

SUCCESSION PLANNING. Replacement of top managers can be a difficult, lengthy, and expensive process. Therefore, prudent corporations prepare long-range plans for replacement of departing managers, especially for those whose departure times are known, e.g., due to retirement. In some cases, the succession plan includes a contingency plan for replacing executives whose departure times are unknown. The plan, which includes selection and training, protects against sudden departures. Expert systems have been successfully used to support succession planning.

LABOR–MANAGEMENT NEGOTIATIONS. A labor–management negotiation can take several months, during which time employees present to management a large number of demands. During negotiations, both sides need to make concessions and trade-offs. Large companies (e.g., USX-Steel, Pittsburgh, PA) have developed computerized DSS models that support such negotiations. The models can simulate financial and other impacts of fulfilling any demand requested by the employees, and they can provide answers to queries in a matter of seconds. Another information technology that has been used successfully in labor–management negotiations is GDSS. The use of GDSS helped improve the negotiation climate and considerably reduced the time needed for reaching an agreement.

EMPOWERMENT OF EMPLOYEES

In previous chapters, we mentioned **empowerment** several times. Empowerment, as related to BPR, suggests a radical change in the way organizations operate. However, empowerment means different things to different people, and it has been practiced for several decades. What is new is the role that IT plays in enabling extensive and comprehensive empowerment. Many organizations find it useful to empower their employees, either as individuals or when they are working in autonomous teams. Such empowerment is viewed by many as an important trend for successful organizations; it is a typical building block in many reengineering efforts and can be supported by information technology.

REENGINEERING

...is supported by empowerment

Empowerment, according to Webster's dictionary, is giving legal or moral power or authority. *Power* is defined as a capacity for action. Empowerment means giving each employee the authority (and responsibility) to make the company more successful and, in the process, to upgrade the employee's job. According to Ripley and Ripley (1992), empowerment is a *concept*, a *philosophy*, a set of *behavioral practices*, and an *organizational program*. As a concept, empowerment is the vesting of decision making or approval authority to employees where, traditionally, such authority was a managerial prerogative. Empowerment as a philosophy and set of behavioral practices means allowing self-managing teams and individuals to be in charge of their own career destinies, as they meet and exceed company and personal goals through a shared company vision. Empowerment as an organizational program involves giving permission to the total workforce to unleash, develop, and utilize their skills and knowledge to their fullest potential for the good of the organization as well as for themselves. It also involves providing the framework in which this can be done.

The empowerment program of Trane Air Conditioner (Macon, GA), according to Garwood (1991), is aimed at the following goals:

1. Increase motivation to reduce mistakes and have individuals take more responsibility for their own actions.
2. Increase the opportunity for creativity and innovation.
3. Assist the continuous improvement of process, product, and service.
4. Improve customer satisfaction by having the employee closest to the customer make rapid, relevant decisions.
5. Increase employee loyalty, while at the same time reducing turnover, absenteeism, and illness.
6. Increase productivity by increasing employee pride, self-respect, and self-worth.
7. Use peer pressure and self-managing team methods for employee control and productivity.
8. Relieve middle and upper management from being "control dogs" and from doing lower level tasks, thereby allowing them more time to do strategic planning—focusing on achieving more market share and customer satisfaction.
9. Increase the bottom line by such methods as reducing waste and building quality, while meeting customer requirements.
10. Increase upper management time for development of strategy plans.
11. Reduce the excessive need for quality assurance personnel, lawyers, and historian accountants.
12. Maintain and increase competitiveness.

RELATIONSHIP TO INFORMATION TECHNOLOGY. Empowerment can be enhanced with IT. Perhaps IT's most important support to empowerment is provision of the right information, at the right time, at the right quality and cost. A client/

server architecture based on open systems can provide cognitive capabilities to users so they can be empowered by traveling along networks to get the information they need. Availability of information is necessary, but it may not be sufficient. To be fully empowered means to be able to make decisions. Quick and correct decisions require knowledge. Knowledge is scarce in organizations, and it is usually provided by specialists. Accessibility to such knowledge may not be easy or cheap. To empower employees means to increase the demand for knowledge, since many employees become empowered to make decisions. Expert systems and other intelligent systems can play a major role in providing knowledge to the empowered employees.

Empowered employees are expected to perform better. To do so, they may need new tools. Information technology can provide tools that will enhance the creativity and productivity of employees, as well as the quality of their work, as was shown in Chapters 14 through 16. These tools can be special applications for increasing creativity, spreadsheets for increasing productivity, and PDAs to improve communication.

Finally, empowerment may require training. People need more skills or higher levels of skills. Self-directed teams, for example, are supposed to contain all the necessary skills to achieve a goal. When organized, teams may require training, which can be enhanced by IT. For example, we showed how companies provide on-line training, use multimedia, and even apply intelligent computer-aided instruction. Levi Strauss & Company uses a program called Training for Technology, which aims at training people to use the skills and tools they need in order to be able to find information and use it properly.

EMPOWERMENT OF CUSTOMERS, SUPPLIERS, AND BUSINESS PARTNERS. In addition to empowering employees, companies are empowering their customers, suppliers, and other business partners. For example, Levi Strauss allows its textile suppliers to access its database, so that the suppliers know exactly what Levi Strauss is producing and selling. Thus, suppliers know what the company needs and when, and can ship supplies in a JIT manner. The company is using a similar approach with all its suppliers.

𝓡EENGINEERING

...Levi Strauss empowers suppliers to aid JIT delivery

TEAMS

According to a lead article in *Fortune* magazine, corporate America is having a love affair with teams (see Dumaine [1994]). This issue was alluded to in Chapter 4, when BPR was discussed as it related to restructuring of organizations. A survey conducted by The Center for Effective Organizations at the University of Southern California showed that 68 percent of the largest corporations in America are using self-managed teams. However, the survey also showed that only 10 percent of the employees are in such teams. These figures suggest that while most companies use teams, they are not replacing the hierarchical organizational structure with the flat team-based structure as proposed in Chapter 4. This is because: (1) not all organizations can be structured as team-based organizations, (2) not all processes should be converted to team-based processes, and (3) transforming organizations takes a long time.

Whether teams are all over the organization or only in some part of it, they can be extremely valuable. Types of teams include the following: (1) permanent or work group teams (usually multiskilled) which are **self-managed teams** and conduct the routine work of the organization; (2) **problem-solving teams** (usually multidisciplinary, multiskilled) established for the purpose of solving a specific problem and then dismantated; (3) **quality circles** which meet intermittently to find and solve workplace-related problems; (4) **management teams** consisting mainly of managers from different functional areas, whose major objective is to coordinate the work of other teams; and (5) **virtual teams**, where members in

𝓡EENGINEERING

...teams are transforming the organization

different places, frequently members of different organizations, communicate via computers. In all of these cases, IT plays a critical role in empowering team members and providing the necessary communication links among teams. An illustrative case is provided next.

GLOBAL PERSPECTIVE

...IT supports team building in Canada

CASE: HOW GE OF CANADA SUPPORTS ITS TEAMS WITH IT. One of the most publicized examples of a company that transformed itself to a self-directed team structure is GE Canada (see Applegate and Cash [1989]). Because the company was relatively small (360 employees) and in the financial services industry, it was easier to reengineer. The company is now composed of 20 teams that are heavily supported by IT.

The steering committee that planned the BPR recognized from the beginning that IT would be a critical factor in the transformation—for communication among teams, for information sharing, and as a tool to support the work of team members. Here are some of the IT applications.

1. Since all secretarial and administrative resources were eliminated, it was necessary to provide productivity software support applications (such as word processing and electronic calendars).

2. Special applications were written for user-friendly access to databases. For example, an on-line access to financial data was created to facilitate data analysis by payroll and control teams. Downloading data from the mainframe was made simple and easy.

3. Employees were empowered to make their own travel arrangements by electronically accessing airline and hotel availability information and electronically making reservations. (GE has an agreement with a large travel agency that allows these activities.)

4. Robots were installed to deliver mail and supplies.

5. E-mail, voice mail, and fax were made available to all employees.

6. Training in spreadsheet software (Lotus 1-2-3) and in downloading data to the spreadsheet was provided.

7. Special hardware and software requested by specific teams for improving productivity, quality, or communication was provided (e.g., scanners, imaging technology). As a matter of fact, employees were encouraged to find ways in which IT could be of help.

The results of the GE transformation were dramatic indeed. The number of employees was reduced by 40 percent, while the productivity of the group and its quality (especially in terms of customer service) were drastically improved.

▶ 17.9 INTEGRATING FUNCTIONAL SYSTEMS AND COMMERCIAL SOFTWARE PACKAGES

For many years, most IS applications were developed in the functional areas, independent of each other. Many companies developed their own customized systems in functional areas that dealt with standard procedures to execute transaction processing/operational activities in the functional areas. These procedures are fairly similar, regardless of where they are being performed. However, today there is a trend to buy commercial, off-the-shelf functional applications. The smaller the organization, the more attractive such an option is. Indeed, several hundred commercial products are available to support each of the major functional areas. For extensive coverage of accounting packages, see Crane (1992). For software for sales and marketing, see Stephens (1993). Development tools are now available to build custom-made applications in a specific domain. For example, there are software packages for building financial applications, a hospital pharmacy management system, and a university student registration system.

However, the trend to reengineer business processes and to cross functional lines requires different kinds of information systems. Matching business processes with a combination of several functional off-the-shelf packages may be a solution in some areas, but not in all. An integrated accounting system is shown in Box 17.18. This system can interface with other functional areas. For example, it was shown in the Pyro opening case that it is possible to integrate manufacturing, sales, and accounting software. Similarly, in the case of Mark III (Minicase 3 in Chapter 3), the company integrated all its functional information systems. However, combining existing packages may not be practical or effective in many cases. To build applications that will easily cross functional lines and reach separate databases requires new approaches such as client/server architecture.

IT At Work BOX 17.18

M.A.S. 90 EVOLUTION/2: GENERAL ACCOUNTING

M.A.S. 90 is a product of the State of the Art, Inc. (Irvine, CA). M.A.S. 90 is a collection of standard accounting modules (the "wheel" in the diagram) that are supported by communication and inquiry modules (right side). The user can integrate as many of the modules as needed for the business. On the left side, there is a list of other business processes/functional applications with which the accounting applications can interface. The software can run on several hardware platforms, including LANs. Each module has a menu of 10 to 20 routines, and it can produce 15 to 30 different reports. ▲

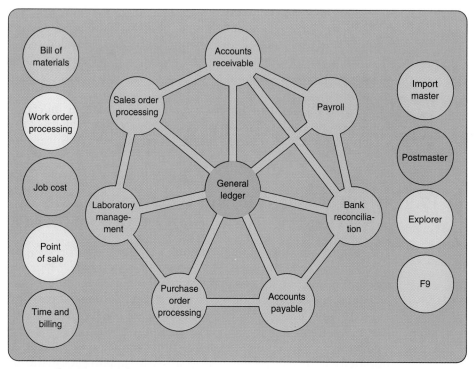

Integrated accounting/business software (Courtesy of the State of the Art, Inc.).

Information systems integration tears down barriers among departments and between departments and corporate headquarters. Various functional managers are linked together to an enterprise-wide system. A proposal of a structure for such an information system was developed by Yakhou and Rahali (1992) and it is shown in Figure 17.14. There is data sharing as well as joint execution of business processes across functional areas, allowing individuals in one area to quickly and easily provide input to another area. Integrated information systems can be done not only in a small company like Pyro, but also in large, even multinational corporations (see Box 17.19).

One example of such integration is a class of commercially available software called Customer-Oriented Manufacturing Management System (COMMS). This type of software is designed for manufacturing organizations. The software is an extension of MRP II which integrates several functional areas. COMMS products are offered by more than 30 vendors.

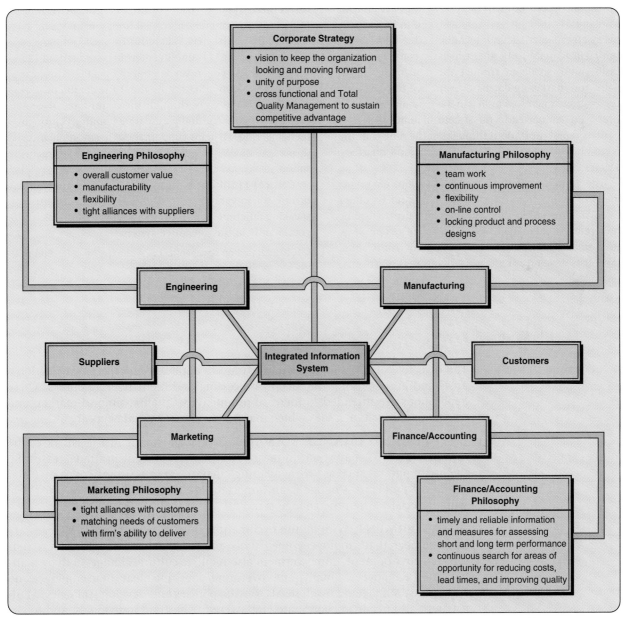

FIGURE 17.14 Integrated information systems—sharing data and business processes across functional lines. (SOURCE: Yakhou and Rahali, 1992. Reprinted from APICS–The Performance Advantage, Dec. 1992, p. 36.)

IT At Work BOX 17.19

INTEGRATED CLIENT/SERVER SYSTEM AT EUROPCAR

Recent reengineering of Europcar Interent, the largest European-based car rental agency, resulted in changing the structure of the entire organization, in addition to changing everyday work processes and methods. To support these changes, the company combined 55 different mainframe and minicomputer systems into a single client/server center known as Greenway. Located at corporate headquarters near Paris, the $400 million system combines data from nine different countries within Europe.

Certain aspects of the project were outsourced, while as many as 40 engineers were assigned to perform the necessary manual data integration. The pilot project started in January 1993, after which the conversion process began to accelerate through the remainder of 1993. Sales and marketing databases went live in March; the reservation systems went live in May; administrative offices were connected to the system in June; and lastly, various rental car stations throughout the nine countries were phased onto the system by the second quarter of 1994.

The 55 independent systems had various data types, many of which were incompatible. Europcar was interested in integrating their business practices, customer preferences, and related data into a single system. However, to complicate matters, the company had to simultaneously develop a uniform set of business practices, or

corporate standards, to support the new single business entity. Furthermore, Europcar had to consider the variety of languages spoken in the nine countries involved, as well as different currencies and cultures.

Key business processes—including reservations, billing, fleet management, cost control, and corporate finance—were all integrated into Greenway. Several customer benefits now include (1) no time delays since clerks no longer have to manually verify credit cards or calculate bills, (2) reservation desks linked to airline reservation systems like SABRE or Amadeus, and (3) corporate customers managed from one location.

Training on the new system for Europcar employees was conducted at 37 training centers in increments of 225 users per week. Greenway is utilized by 3,000 Europcar employees at 800 offices throughout the continent. Europcar originally grew through the acquisition of geographically and culturally disparate entities. Through reengineering, IT helps support these business alliances to present more of a multicountry team-based organization.

Critical Thinking Issues: What are some of the difficulties of integrating 55 systems from nine countries speaking different languages? What functional areas can you identify in the integrated system? ▲

SOURCE: Based on Greebaum, J., "A Bumpy Road for Europcar," *InformationWeek*, February 7, 1994.

▶ MANAGERIAL ISSUES

The objective of this chapter is to illustrate IS applications in various functional areas and in supporting transaction processing and reengineering efforts. These applications are intended to increase productivity, quality, time-to-market, and customer satisfaction. Issues which may be important to managers are as follows:

LAYOFFS AND CHANGE MANAGEMENT. As shown in the GE case, the introduction of IT may result in massive layoffs (40 percent in the GE case). So the use of phrases such as "reengineering" may result in resistance to change and in morale problems. Change is an important issue that management must deal with, especially when the change is radical.

EMPOWERMENT. With all the excitement about empowerment, it is necessary to remember that employees need tools and knowledge to succeed in a self-directed environment. Empowerment also requires cultural change, both by managers and employees. Finally, empowerment does not mean that employees do everything. Management still needs to issue policies and develop strategies. Management also needs to coordinate empowered teams and individuals, and to exercise controls. IT tools, such as Lotus Notes, can be helpful in supporting management's role in empowering employees.

INTEGRATING INFORMATION SYSTEMS. Integration of information systems used to be a major problem in many organizations. While client/server and open systems solve some of the technical difficulties, there are still problems of integrating different types of data and procedures used by functional areas. Also, there is an issue of information sharing, which may contradict existing practices and culture.

TRANSACTION PROCESSING. Transaction processing may not be an exotic application, but it deals with the core processes of the organization, with the mission-central activities. Also, transaction processing collects the information needed for most other applications. Therefore, the TPS must receive top priority in resource allocation. This, however, should not be at the expense of innovative applications which are needed to sustain competitive advantage and profitability.

THE CUSTOMER IS KING. In implementing IT applications, management must remember the importance of the customer, whether external or internal. Some innovative applications that are intended to increase customers' satisfaction are difficult to justify in a traditional cost–benefit analysis. Here, too, corporate culture is important. Empowering customers to enter into a corporate database can make customers happy (since they get quick answers to their queries) and can save money for a company. But, it may be resisted because of security concerns.

FINDING INNOVATIVE APPLICATIONS. New tools such as Lotus Notes, enable the construction of many applications that can increase productivity and quality. Finding opportunity for such applications can best be accomplished co-operatively by end users and the IS department. ■

KEY TERMS

Batch processing *622*

Business alliances *649*

Business process reengineering *624*

Channel systems *641*

Computer-aided design (CAD) *635*

Computer-aided engineering (CAE) *637*

Computer-aided manufacturing (CAM) *637*

Computer-integrated manufacturing (CIM) *639*

Data entry *621*

Electronic markets *649*

Empowerment *653*

Flexible manufacturing systems (FMS) *639*

General ledger *625*

Inventory management *631*

Just-in-time (JIT) *634*

Management teams *654*

Manufacturing resource planning (MRP II) *633*

Mass customization *637*

Master file *622*

Material requirement planning (MRP) *632*

On-line analytical processing (OLAP) *646*

On-line processing *622*

Problem-solving teams *654*

Quality circles *654*

Reorder point *632*

Self-managed teams *654*

Telemarketing *643*

Transaction file *622*

Transaction processing system (TPS) *621*

Value chain *618*

Virtual teams *654*

CHAPTER HIGHLIGHTS *(L-x means learning objective number x)*

▼ The major business functional areas are accounting, finance, production/operations, marketing, and human resource management. (L-1, L-2)

▼ Information systems applications can support many functional activities. Considerable software is readily available on the market for much of this support. (L-2)

▼ The backbone of most information systems applications is the transaction processing system. (L-3)

▼ Transaction processing systems support the routine, mission-central operations of the organization. (L-3)

▼ The major area of IT support to production/operation is in logistic and inventory management; e.g., MRP, MRP II, JIT, CAD, CAM, mass customization, and CIM. (L-4)

▼ Channel systems deal with all activities related to customer orders, sales, advertisement and promotion, market research, customer service, and product and service pricing. (L-5)

▼ All issues related to personnel and people's development are supported by human resource information systems. These issues include employee selection, hiring, performance evaluation, salary and benefit administration, training and develop-

ment, labor negotiations, and manpower planning. (L-6)

▼ Integrated information systems are necessary in order to assure effective and efficient execution of activities in parts of the value chain and in business processes. (L-7)

QUESTIONS FOR REVIEW

1. What is a functional information system?
2. List the major characteristics of a functional information system.
3. What are the objectives of a TPS?
4. List the major characteristics of a TPS.
5. Distinguish between batch and on-line TPS.
6. Define a general ledger and how it is supported by IT.
7. Define mass customization.
8. Describe the managerial applications of finance and accounting.
9. Describe MRP.
10. Describe MRP II.
11. Describe CAD. Explain CAE and CAM.
12. Define CIM, and list its major benefits.
13. Define channel systems.
14. What is telemarketing?
15. Define JIT, and list some of its benefits.
16. Explain human resource information systems.
17. Describe empowerment.
18. List and describe various types of teams.

QUESTIONS FOR DISCUSSION

1. Why is it logical to organize IT applications by functional areas?
2. Describe the role of a TPS in a service organization.
3. Why are TPSs a major target for reengineering?
4. Which functional areas are related to payroll, and how does the relevant information flow?
6. Relate CAD to CAE and to CAM.
7. It is said that in order to successfully use MRP, it must be computerized. Why?
8. The Japanese are implementing most of the components of JIT without computers. Discuss the various elements of JIT, and comment on the potential benefits of computerization.
9. Conduct some research on MRP and MRP II, and discuss the relationship between these two products.
10. Describe how IT enhances mass customization.
11. Describe the role of computers in CIM.
12. Explain how flexible manufacturing systems are related to JIT and how IT can foster such a relationship.
13. Explain how IT can make the customer a king.
14. Why are information systems so critical to sales order processing?
15. Explain how IT can enhance telemarketing.
16. Geographical information systems are playing an important role in supporting marketing and sales. Provide some examples not discussed in the text.
17. How can IT enhance empowerment of employees? of suppliers? of vendors?
18. Marketing databases play a major role in channel systems. Why?
19. How can IT support the work of teams?
20. Discuss the need for software integration.
21. Human resource information systems (HRIS) are a newcomer to the area of computer-based information systems. There are many routine applications in this area that could have easily been computerized long ago. Speculate on the reasons for the delay in introducing HRIS.

EXERCISES

1. Prepare a flow diagram (similar to Figure 17.6) that shows the role of a TPS in a hospital.
2. Federal Express's COSMOS system (see Box 17.11) collects information that is used to answer customers' queries regarding the location of packages. The information in the databases is also used by Federal Express for several other purposes, especially for supporting important corporate marketing decisions. Prepare a list of three to

five applications that Federal Express can develop with information collected by COSMOS.

3. The chart shown in Figure 17.9 portrays the flow of routine activities in a typical manufacturing organization. Explain in what areas IT can be most valuable.
4. Review the empowerment goals listed in Section 17.8. List the information technologies that can enhance each of the goals. Explain how the technologies can help.

GROUP ASSIGNMENTS

1. Visit a large company in your area and identify its channel systems. Prepare a diagram that will show the six components of Figure 17.13. Then find how IT supports each of those components. Finally, suggest improvements in the existing channel system that can be supported by IT technologies which are not in use by the company today.

2. Preparing an advertising program for a client is a long process, involving many individuals and groups. The process starts with a work order generated by an executive account and distributed to a creative services department, which prepares the concepts of the program and layouts. The layouts must be approved, distributed, and filed. Cost estimates must be prepared by the art director, production manager, and media planner. The client must approve the program and the cost. Then, final art must be prepared and again approved by the client. Finally, supplier purchase orders must be created. All this is done manually, creating a paper nightmare.

Your group acts as a consultant to Young and Rubicam, one of the nation's largest advertising agencies. The company wants to improve quality, productivity, and customer service by using IT. Cost of IT is not a problem.

Prepare a report that will include:

a. Material on the advertisement business and on Young and Rubicam.
b. A diagram that shows how you envision the execution of an advertising program.
c. A list of information technologies that can be used to improve the advertising program process.
d. Explain how each of the technologies is going to be used and be specific.
e. In your opinion, is your proposal a BPR proposal? Why or why not?
f. For each technology proposed, find a vendor who distributes the technology. Get information about the cost and the possible integration of the various technologies.

Minicase 1

Federal Express's Organizational Effectiveness System

Federal Express Corporation (Memphis, TN) revolutionized the quick-delivery business. This company, which employs about 100,000 people worldwide, is a leader in the use of IT. One of its most innovative systems is an organizational effectiveness system called PRISM. First implemented in the early 1980s to support personnel activities, the system evolved into an advanced, multitechnology management information system that assures the health and well-being of the corporation by allowing it to be flexible and responsive.

PRISM provides managers with the ability to electronically input and access data pertaining to their subordinates. PRISM is primarily an advanced and comprehensive HRIS. It provides over 300 different screens to its users, covering almost all areas of human resource management. The system is constructed around core applications. These include functions such as fringe benefit management, employment verification, position control, EEOC (Equal Employment Opportunity Commission) management, hiring, retirement, and training.

The system allows the personnel department to concentrate on developing, not just tracking, corporate human resources. It influenced and reengineered all internal human resources and other business processes within Federal Express, such as processing job applications; hiring employees; processing benefits; and employee assessment, training, safety, and retirement. PRISM is also connected to external organizations such as government agencies (affirmative action, safety) and to benefits and retirement plan providers. Almost all input data is entered directly by users. Employees across the world are empowered to view and maintain their personal data 24 hours a day. They can select and change benefits from a menu. They can, for example, log on to PRISM to electronically schedule and then take appropriate tests.

PRISM has interfaces with other information systems within Federal Express, such as the drug testing system, the aircrew assignment system, and the corporate safety system.

Federal Express was founded on the concept of "people $\rightarrow$ service $\rightarrow$ profit." Because PRISM has a positive impact on employees, both service and profits have improved. PRISM enables a more adaptive, responsive, and flexible organization that provides Federal Express with a strategic advantage. However, the company does not target competitors, buyers, or customers. Instead, PRISM enhances the organization's flexibility so the company can respond quickly and effectively to changes in the marketplace and facilitate change management.

Finally, PRISM frees managers from clerical and operational tasks, so they can devote more time and energy to planning, organizing, motivating, and controlling.

Questions for Minicase 1

1. Identify the interfaces to the environment described in this case.

2. Why doesn't PRISM target competitors, buyers, or customers?

3. Is it a good idea to allow employees to maintain their own personal files? Why or why not?

4. It is said that PRISM provides a strategic advantage. Describe how it is done.

5. Do you think that Federal Express is taking the right approach? Why or why not?

SOURCE: Based on Palvia P. C. et al., "A Key to Organizational Effectiveness at Federal Express Corporation," *MIS Quarterly*, Sept. 1992.

Minicase 2

Functional Information Systems at Argot International

Argot International is a medium-sized company in Peoria, Illinois with about 2,000 employees. The company manufactures special machines for the agribusiness industry, both for farms and food processing plants. The company buys materials and components from about 150 vendors in six different countries. They also buy special machines and tools from Japan. Products are sold either to wholesalers (about 70) or directly to clients (from a mailing list of about 2,000). The business is very competitive.

The company has the following information systems in place: financial/accounting, marketing (primarily information about sales), engineering, research and development, and manufacturing (CAM). These systems are independent of each other, and only the financial/accounting systems are on a LAN.

The company is having profitability problems. Cash is in high demand and short supply, due to strong competition from Germany and Japan. It is proposed that the company investigate the possibility of using information technology to improve the situation. However, the vice president of finance objects to the idea, claiming that most

of the tangible benefits of information technology are already being realized.

Questions for Minicase 2

You are hired as a consultant to the president. Use the knowledge acquired in this text to respond to the following.

1. Prepare a list of potential applications of information technologies that you think could help the company. Divide them into "very important" and "important."

2. From the description of the case, would you recommend any telecommunication arrangements? Be very specific. Remember, the company is in financial trouble.

3. In your opinion, how should the data be processed and managed in such a company? Would you recommend a supercomputer, mainframe, other arrangements? Should a DBMS be used? Is an object-oriented database appropriate (and for what use)?

Minicase 3

Electronic Pig Auctioning in Singapore

Pork is the main meat item consumed by about 2.5 million Chinese in Singapore. To meet this demand, there is a need for between 2,000 and 3,000 pigs every day. The pigs are raised on about 120 farms, mostly in Malaysia, although some are in Indonesia. The business used to be controlled by 4 out of 23 importers. Prices were set by the major importers, allowing them to make substantial profits at the expense of the consumers.

In order to protect customers, the government decided to change pig trading by using open electronic auctions. This idea was adapted from Taiwan, where a similar system was working successfully. The pig trading is done in a system called Hog Auction Market (HAM). As in any auction, bidders are competing against each other by placing bids. Refer to Figure 17.15 to see how the bidding is conducted.

On the left side of the figure are the pigs. On the right side are the bidders. Importers bring pigs into the auction area where data (such as the type of pig) are entered into the computer. Using a lottery, the sequence of auctioning is determined. Then, the pigs are washed (guess who is considered to be the cleanest country in the world), marked for identification, and weighed. (The weight is automatically recorded by a computer). At that point, everything is ready for the auction. About 40 bidders, licensed by the government, enter the area and pay the necessary participation fees.

When a pig is ready to be auctioned, its ID number, type, weight, and starting price are displayed on a large screen visible to all bidders. The pig is moved to a track where it can be visually assessed by bidders. The bids are executed by pressing a ''bid'' button, signifying that the bidder is willing to pay the displayed price. If two or more bidders press buttons, the price is automatically raised by $0.02 per kilogram. The process continues until only one bidder remains. Once a bid is awarded, the computer checks the adequacy of funds, and the successful bidder gets his pig. Using computers makes the process very efficient. A pig is shown for five seconds or less before it is sold.

The system helped to increase the quality of meat, since pigs are now being sold individually. Commission

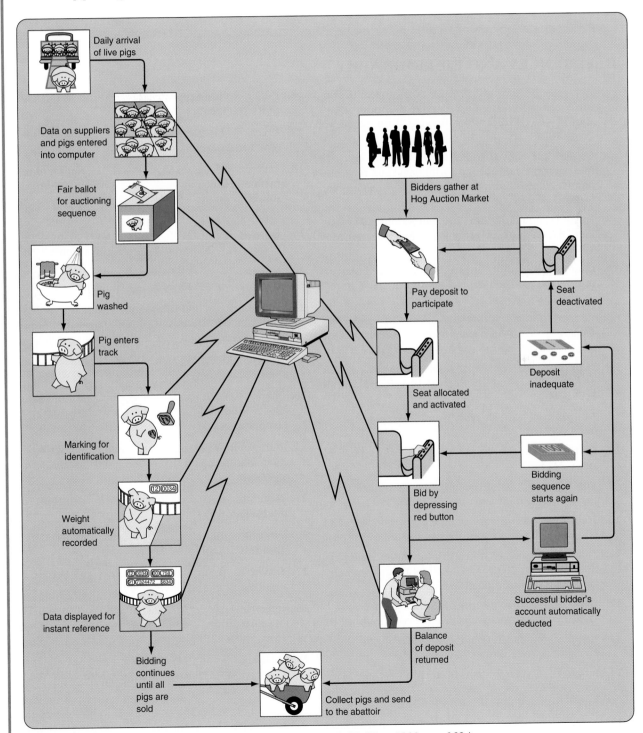

FIGURE 17.15 The electronic hog auctioning process. (SOURCE: Neo, 1992, pg. 283.)

was dropped from between 7 and 10 percent to 3 percent. Farmers are being paid in three days instead of three to four weeks. Most importantly, the consumers are paying about 20 percent less (prices dropped from $2.80 to $2.30 per kilogram).

Questions for Minicase 3

1. Is this a BPR? Why or why not?

2. What specific information technologies are involved in the systems?

3. What are the advantages over a no-auction system?

4. What are the advantages over a manual auction system?

5. Who are the major beneficiaries of the system?

SOURCE: Condensed from Neo, B.S., "The Implementation of an Electronic Market for Pig Trading in Singapore," *Journal of Strategic Information System*, December 1992.

REFERENCES AND BIBLIOGRAPHY

1. Applegate, L. M., and J. J. Cash, "GE Canada: Designing a New Organization," Harvard Business School Case #9-189-138, Boston: Harvard Business School Press, 1989.

2. Broderick, R., and J. W. Boudreau, "Human Resource Management, Information Technology, and the Competitive Edge," *Academy of Management Executives*, Vol. 6, No. 2, 1992.

3. Byun, D., and E. H. Suh, "Human Resource Management Expert Systems Technology," *Expert Systems*, May 1994.

4. Cameron, R., and D. Targett, "Computerized Marketing Databases: Their Role Now and in the Future," *Journal of Information Technology*, Vol. 7, 1992.

5. Carme, E., et al., "Labor–Management Contract Negotiations in an Electronic Meeting Room: A Case Study," *Group Decisions and Negotiations*, Vol. 2, 1993.

6. Clark, D. G., *Marketing Analysis and Decision Making: Text and Cases with Lotus 1-2-3*, Redwood City, CA: Scientific Press, 1987.

7. Dumaine B., "Trouble with Teams," *Fortune*, September 5, 1994.

8. Crane, R., "Accounting Systems," *Computerworld*, February 24, 1992.

9. Von Ohsen C., "Implementing CIM in a Small Company," *Industrial Engineering*, November 1992.

10. Elaison, A., *On-line Business Computer Applications*, 2nd ed., Chicago: Science Research Associates, 1987.

11. Eldon, Y. L., et al., "Marketing Information Systems in the *Fortune* 500 Companies," *Journal of Management Information Systems*, Summer 1993.

12. Garwood, R., "Empowerment: No Longer a Luxury," *Production and Inventory Management Review*, April 1991.

13. Hammer, M., and J. Champy, *Reengineering the Corporation*, New York: Harper Business, 1993.

14. Inoue, Y., "Expert Systems in Human Resource Management: A Survey," *International Journal of Applied Expert Systems*, Vol. 1, No. 3, 1994.

15. Katzenback, J. R., and D. K. Smith, *The Wisdom of Teams*, Boston: Harvard Business School Press, 1993.

16. Kotler, P., *Marketing Management*, 8th ed., Englewood Cliffs, NJ: Prentice Hall, 1994.

17. Krebs, V. E. "How Artificial Intelligence Assists HR Managers," *Personnel*, Vol. 64, No. 9, 1987.

18. Lederer, A. L., and Licker, P. S., "The Impact of Information Technology on the Management of Human Resources," *Journal of Management Systems*, Vol. 4, No. 2, 1992.

19. Lopes, P. F., "CIM II: The Integrated Manufacturing Enterprise," *Industrial Engineering*, November 1992.

20. Malone, T. W., et al., "The Logic of Electronic Markets," *Harvard Business Review*, May/June 1989.

21. Meinert, D. B., and Davis, D. L. "Human resource decision support system (HRDSS)," *Information Resources Management Journal*, Vol. 2, No. 1, Winter 1989.

22. Meredith, J. R., *The Management of Operations*, 4th ed., New York: Wiley, 1992.

23. Moriarty, R. T., and G. S. Swartz, "Automation to Boost Sales and Marketing," *Harvard Business Review*, January/February 1989.

24. Narayanan, V., et al., "Simulation: A Tool for Production Planning and Execution," *Information Technology—Journal of SCS*, April 1993.

25. Neumann, S., *Strategic Information Systems*, New York: Macmillan, 1994.

26. Pine, B. J. II, *Mass Customizations*, Boston: Harvard Business School Press, 1993.

27. Rands, T., "Information Technology as a Service Operation," *Journal of Information Technology*, Vol. 7, 1992.

28. Roberts, J. W., "Systems Support of Just-In-Time Manufacturing," *Journal of Information Systems Management*, Winter 1990.

29. Ripley, R. E., and M. J. Ripley, "Empowerment, the Cornerstone of Quality," *Management Decisions*, Vol. 30, No. 4, 1992.

30. Saraph, J. V. and T. Guimaraes, "The Role of IS in Manufacturing Automation," *Journal of Information Systems Management*, Winter 1991.

31. Schumann, M., et al., "Predicting Market's Response," *Information Strategy: The Executive's Journal*, Winter 1990.

32. Smith, S., and W. Swinyard, *Marketing Models with Lotus 1-2-3*, Homewood, IL: Richard D. Irwin, 1988.

33. Staiti, C., "Customers Drive New Manufacturing Software," *Datamation*, November 15, 1993.

34. Stephens, S., "What to Do About Sellware?" *Voice Processing Magazine*, March 1993.

35. Trippi, R., and E. Turban, *Neural Computing in Investment*, Chicago: Probus, 1993. 2nd ed., 1996.

36. Tyler, T. C., "Sales and Marketing Software," *Sales and Marketing Management*, December 1992. (A list of about 1,000 commercial software packages is included on p. 61.)

37. Von Ohsen, C., "Implementing CIM in a Small Company," *Industrial Engineering*, November 1992.

38. Weygandt, J. J., et al., *Accounting Principles*, New York: Wiley, 1993.

39. Wilkinson, J. *Accounting Information Systems: Essential Concepts and Applications*, New York: John Wiley and Sons, Inc., 1989.

40. Yakhou, M., and B. Rahali, "Integration of Business Functions: Roles of Cross-Functional Information Systems," *APICS*, December 1992.

41. Zachary, W. B., and E. Richman, "Building an Operations Management Foundation That Will Last: TQM, JIT, and CIM," *Industrial Engineering*, August 1993.

EXPERT SYSTEMS IMPROVE THE TROUBLESHOOTING OF THE CITY OF LOS ANGELES COMPUTER HARDWARE*

Introduction

Los Angeles' computerized environment consists of a vast array of stand-alone as well as networked computer workstations. The city's Information Systems Department (ISD) installs and maintains about 13,000 workstations, larger computers, peripherals, and communication for the workstations. Many of these workstations have multiple users (3 to 5); thus about 35,000 employees are working with computers.

When a city employee—the client—experiences a problem on a computer device, the ISD is called. This call sets in motion an orderly diagnosis, tracking, and resolution of the problem. The city has organized employees responsible for this process into a three-level tracking system which includes (1) a first-level help desk unit (see

*SOURCE: Based on Clarke et al. (1994).

the figure below) that initially receives the trouble call and solves most simple problems, (2) a second-level unit that provides detailed diagnosis and traking of problems *not solved* at the first level, and (3) a third-level unit that solves problems *not solved* at level two. The second-level unit is called the Service Level Management Section (SLMS). It receives a description of the problem needing attention, either by phone or through a mainframe-based problem-tracking network (NETMAN), accessed also by the first-level help desk area. SLMS attempts to diagnose the problem and resolve it, or hand difficult problems over to the third-level unit for final resolution. At all times, the problem is tracked by NETMAN and managed by SLMS to its complete resolution, including end-user follow-up. Thus, at all times, the client has complete and accurate information as to the status of any problem under investigation.

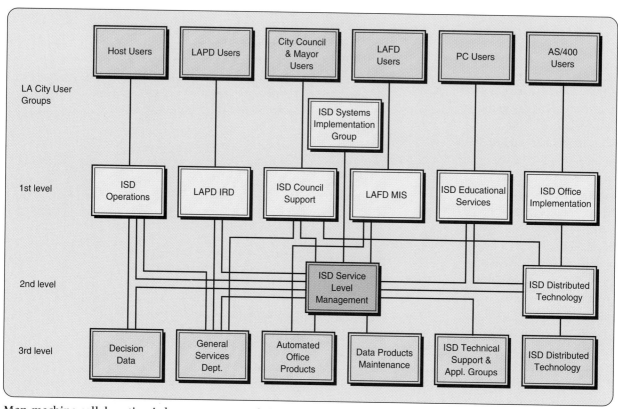

Man-machine collaboration is key to success or failure.

The Problem

Obviously, managing problems in a complex environment, such as that of a very large city, requires knowledge of and experience with almost every computer type and configuration. Investigating, assigning, tracking, and resolving client computer problems quickly are challenging and necessary elements of any large, computerized environment. The problem faced by SLMS in 1989 was that the demand for their services exceeded the unit's capacity. Thus, when a service was not provided, the client workstation was not working, affecting one or more employees.

SLMS has a relatively small staff of computer professionals responsible for managing an immense amount of technology that is expanding and getting more complicated daily. Due to budgetary problems, the staff is not able to increase. The problem is further complicated by a constant rotation of personnel in this area. In addition, the department is faced with changing training requirements which are necessary to meet the needs of a rapidly changing computer environment. The number of problem incidents received by SLMS each month in 1994 was about 1,300 for an eight-hour shift, and the number is growing rapidly as more users, equipment, and applications are being added on a daily basis. Thus, the business of problem resolution at SLMS is becoming increasingly more difficult.

The Solution

The SLMS staff has envisioned a tool that would help reduce the time required to solve computer problems and increase the reliability of the solutions. They realized that if they did not prepare for the future workload, the operation of this area would become less and less productive and the level of service provided to clients would deteriorate. SLMS concluded that a computer-based problem-determination expert system would be the most cost-effective solution. It was further recognized that the task in the problem-solving process that would receive the greatest impact by such a system would be the problem diagnosis step. The average time spent on this step has been about 16 minutes per problem. Expert systems have proven to be an excellent aid to the execution of this task (see Ford, [1990]).

The SLMS organization has developed such a system using Trinzic's 1st CLASS ES tool kit. The system is called the Automated Workstation Expert System Of Maintained Equipment (AWESOME). The first phase of AWESOME came on-line in December of 1990. An innovation introduced in AWESOME is the support of the expert system with multimedia. Specifically, the integrated system includes hypermedia and on-line video images.

The Integrated System

AWESOME, is a PC-based system that aids in all aspects of problem diagnostics. The following features are included.

▼ Problem diagnostic advice provided by the ES.

▼ Access to supporting information (phone numbers, client departments, technical manuals, and support-level communications) via a hypertext capability.

▼ Provision of information pertaining to all ISD problem determination knowledge (provided by both the explanation capability of the ES and the hypertext system).

▼ Video images and device-specific information are available for all supported devices.

The Role of Video Images

AWESOME makes extensive use of video images to aid in problem diagnosis, including images of all supported devices, control panels, keyboards, and cable configurations. These images play a very important role in AWESOME's diagnostic procedure for two reasons. First, images increase the productivity of SLMS's employees by expediting diagnosis time. Second, any communication between the client and SLMS may involve a discussion about the application of operating procedures or the investigation of a certain part. Such communicative troubleshooting in an ES environment can be greatly expedited with the use of images (see Thompson, [1991]).

The video images, used by all SLMS employees, provide valuable troubleshooting information at all levels of experience. In adition to video images, graphical screens help the SLMS staff navigate through diagnostic procedures.

The Role of Hypertext

Hypertext works in much the same way as a system of index cards. Information is entered on an initial hypertext card which pops up like a window. On this information card, there are "buttons"—highlighted word(s) that can be "clicked" on to bring up additional, overlaid cards. Thus, further investigation of highlighted topics is possible. The information on the cards covers topics about the clients, equipment used, technical manuals for all equipment, diagnostic procedures, and any other relevant information. In this way, hypertext allows the SLMS employee to breeze through large amounts of information to find whatever is needed for quick diagnosis.

Hypertext is used mainly by the less experienced employees. It helps them to quickly find possible causes of problems. More experienced employees use hypertext as a timesaving device. Using hypertext, they do not have to check notes or remember minute details any longer.

The use of multimedia in AWESOME is both objective and subjective. All problems can be presented pictorially (as with a video still image of the device) so that intelligent interaction with the client can take place ("Can you see the red button near the access plate," for example). The objective portion allows the multimedia to be integrated with a formal set of rules presented according to what troubleshooting is recommended. The hypertext portion which is subjective, besides being part of the formal presentation of troubleshooting rules, allows quick access to important information supplementing this effort ("You should contact your data processing coordinator to help you get this part; she is Mary and her phone number is 4721," for example).

All of the previously mentioned activity works hand in hand to build a total picture of the problem, so that troubleshooting professionals can make the best decision on what avenue of resolution to take.

Implementation

The area of application for AWESOME is computer technical support. This includes the diagnosis and resolution of any technical problems on all mainframe-attached computer workstations and their communications to this mainframe in the city environment. AWESOME also serves as an information repository, including telephone numbers, critical position and technical support contacts, chain of command, and so on. The system was implemented in five phases from 1992 to 1994.

Cost-Benefit Analysis

The overall cost-benefit analysis of this project was an exercise in recognizing what productivity improvement could be rendered from AWESOME. The improvement was compared against the fixed and variable costs relevant to the application.

Fixed costs included the cost of the purchased package as well as costs for research, development, the video imaging subsystem, and implementation with the SLMS programming staff. These initial costs have proven to be a great bargain for the city of Los Angeles.

Future Considerations

Within the ISD, service level management and network operations were (in 1994) the only two help desk agencies using AWESOME. It is hoped that all citywide system support activities will use this product. AWESOME can be easily modified to include other information and features needed in order to make it as useful for other groups as it has been for SLMS. For this to happen, the following conditions are essential.

▼ High-level coordination with all citywide system support groups to facilitate installation and maintenance of this product.

▼ Citywide recognition of expert system standards of development, training, and usage.

Managerial Decision Support Systems

The existing system does not include any managerial decision support. However, as the communication and reporting systems are maturing, a vast amount of information is accumulating which can be utilized by a DSS quickly and at low cost. The following are some DSS projects under consideration:

▼ Analysis of all requests for help in order to detect patterns of problems. This may help the identification of poor equipment, poor training, or unqualified employees.

▼ Analysis of the time spent on problem diagnosis, determination, and correction. This may help in assigning employees to tasks in the best possible manner.

▼ Screen sharing between clients and SLMS employees as part of a distributed group support system.

▼ Correlation between type and amount of computer usage and types of problems.

Reengineering the Business Processes

The solution provided by the multimedia-supported expert system is impressive, but it is only good for a few years. The increased demands on SLMS as well as budgetary constraints will soon make the system ineffective. Therefore, the city of Los Angeles is looking at possible reengineering of all their processes. One idea is to provide end users in the various city departments with intelligent, user-friendly, troubleshooting software. Several vendors (e.g., IBM and Compaq) already provide customers with such packages. Such an on-line system could eliminate all (or most) of the level 1 initial screening. So level 1 could be eliminated or combined with level 2. Transferring tasks to end users is a major strategy of BPR.

Case Study Questions.

1. Which organizational and technological trends are evidenced in this case?

2. Why was an expert system selected? Why not a DSS or a neural net computing system?

3. How can the use of hypertext increase productivity and quality?

4. How can the use of video images increase productivity and quality?

5. Identify all the communication links in this case. Can they be enhanced? How?

6. Explain how the proposed DSS could identify poor equipment or a poor training program.

7. Which information technologies can enhance communication between the city departments, which are on 24-hour schedule, and SLMS, which is on an 8 hour schedule.

8. Does videoconferencing make sense in such an environment? If so, where and how? If it does not, why not?

9. Continuous improvements in new equipment reduce the need for units such as SLMS. However, in the case of the city of Los Angeles, it is expected that the demand for SLMS services will increase, at least during the next 5 to 10 years. Why is this so?

10. Should the existing system, which increased productivity by at least 50 percent, considered reengineering? Why or why not?

11. Can you envision any other DSS applications that are not described here but could be beneficial for the city?

References and Bibliography

CLARKE, D. E., et al., "Integrating Expert Systems and Multimedia for Improved Troubleshooting of the City of Los Angeles' Computer Hardware," *Expert Systems with Applications*, July 1994.

FORD, B., "An Expert Diagnostic System Using Multimedia," *Expert Systems: Planning, Implementation, Integrations*, Vol. 2, No. 3, 1990, pp. 19–24.

FUERST, W. L., et al., "Expert Systems and Multimedia: Examining the Potential for Integration," *Journal of MIS*, Spring. 1995

THOMPSON, D., "Imaging Meets Expert Systems," *AI Expert*, Vol. 6, No. 11, 1991, pp. 24–32.

PART V

MANAGING INFORMATION TECHNOLOGY

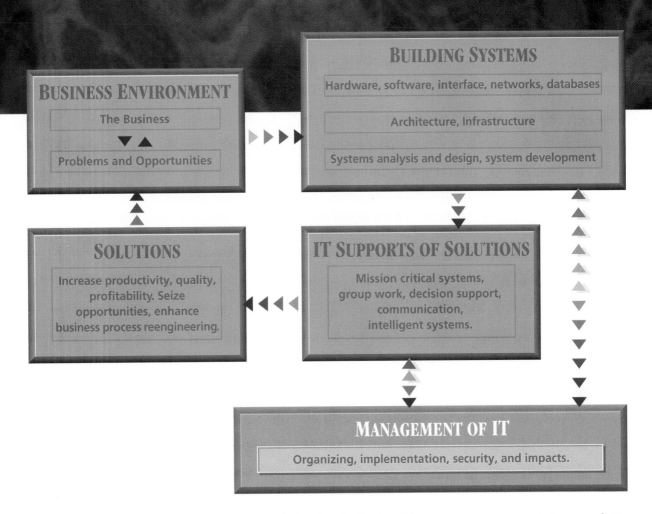

BUSINESS ENVIRONMENT

The Business

▼ ▲

Problems and Opportunities

BUILDING SYSTEMS

Hardware, software, interface, networks, databases

Architecture, Infrastructure

Systems analysis and design, system development

SOLUTIONS

Increase productivity, quality, profitability. Seize opportunities, enhance business process reengineering.

IT SUPPORTS OF SOLUTIONS

Mission critical systems, group work, decision support, communication, intelligent systems.

MANAGEMENT OF IT

Organizing, implementation, security, and impacts.

The last part of this book deals with some management issues of IT. Information is an important asset in many organizations; in others, it may be critical. Therefore, information should be managed appropriately. The problem is that information resources are scattered all over the organization and are managed by several entities. Also, information is flowing to and from organizations.

This part opens with *Chapter 18*, which deals with the *organization* of information resources. Main issues involve the relationship between the IS department and decentralized end users. In addition, the chapter deals with the internal structure of the IS department and with end-user computing.

Protecting information resources is becoming very difficult because many companies have a large number of systems scattered all over, and there is a need to protect information flowing in internal and external networks.

Chapter 19 deals with the issues of computer security and crime. The chapter presents an overview of the hazards faced by information systems and the major actions that can be taken against them. Also, there is a discussion of ways to plan for a disaster and how to recover from it.

The book ends with an overview of the major impacts of IT on organizations. *Chapter 20* is divided into the following topics: ethical issues in IT, impact on individuals, impact on organizations, impacts on society, and the future of IT.

Part V ends with the case of Otis elevator, a world-leading manufacturer and server of elevators. The case, which serves also as an integrative case for the entire book, describes how Otis used IT to reengineer itself. The case also demonstrates the diversified applications of the use of IT, which are part of Otis's corporate culture.

Chapter 18—Organizing Information Resources
Chapter 19—Control and Security of Information Systems
Chapter 20—Impact of Information Technology on Individuals, Organizations and Society

ORGANIZING INFORMATION RESOURCES

Chapter Outline

Learning Objectives

After studying this chapter, you will be able to:

1. Discuss possible reporting locations for IS.

2. Distinguish the issues pertinent to centralizing or decentralizing IS.

3. Describe the role of IS leadership.

4. Define different internal structures for IS.

5. Describe the structure of a virtual IS organization.

6. Describe the relationship between end users and the IS department.

7. Describe the role of the information center in an organization.

8. Describe the role of the steering committee in an organization.

▶ 18.1 SUCCESSES AND FAILURES OF INFORMATION SYSTEMS IN FOUR ORGANIZATIONS

THE FOLLOWING ARE four cases of successes and failures of information systems as witnessed by the authors. The companies requested to be anonymous and will be referred to as Firms A through D.

Case A: Organizing for a Complex Worldwide Financial System

Firm A is a large company that operates worldwide. In 1992, the firm's computing was centralized except for the minicomputers located at job sites around the world. In that year, the controller determined that existing accounting and financial information systems were inadequate. Working with the IS department and an outside accounting firm, he further determined that the current systems could not be salvaged. A major project was mounted to design, develop, and procure a worldwide accounting and financial information system.

A project team to plan the new system was organized within the controller's department. The project team was staffed originally with people from the accounting (consulting) firm's management services staff, from other outside consultants, and from people carefully selected from the central IS staff. In general, the latter were the "pick of the crop" and represented the younger, more innovative staff members. Additionally, many members of the design staff employed on the project team were carefully selected from the controller's organization.

The project team established a management advisory group (MAG) consisting of several of the firm's top executives. This committee was to oversee the management of the project and represent the project to the senior management of the firm. A technical advisory group (TAG) was also created. This committee consisted of two internal IS persons and four experts from outside the firm. The TAG was to meet quarterly and advise the MAG on the technical viability of the project.

In late 1991, the project team presented a complete project description, proposal, and cost analysis for comment by the TAG. It was estimated the system development would take 3 years and cost $46 million (in constant 1993 dollars) without including any equipment costs. These figures showed a substantial rate of return from carrying out the project. Equipment would consist of job site computers, regional computers, and a central host computer. Communications would require some satellite links. The project was approved by the firm's senior management.

Man-machine collaboration is key to success or failure.

One of the early tasks of the project team was to select a supporting computer system, systems software, and, where appropriate, applications software. In every case, the selections were fully documented, commented upon by TAG, and approved by the MAG.

The equipment selection and procurement decision was a major one. At the time the project was initialized, a mainframe was used as the central host computer for both engineering and scientific purposes. The project team spent approximately six months gathering information about whether using additional mainframe equipment or client/server architecture would be more suitable for the project. The team recommended the client/server, and their recommendation was seconded by the TAG, approved by the MAG, and accepted by the firm's executive council. A similar decision process was used for systems software (database management system, operating systems, and so on) as well as applications software.

Note that in Firm A, control was passed from IS to the user-dominated project team. There was a well-developed plan in place, and the systems development function was decentralized to the user organization. Procurement decision making was formally done, which included cost–benefit analysis, and outside parties were used as consultants. Standards for equipment and software were established early in the project.

In summary, this case represents a project that is very large, extremely complex, and excellently managed. A variety of technical and political issues surfaced, which were studied and resolved. This project is proceeding according to schedule and corporate management is pleased.

Case B: Don't Underestimate Leadership

Firm B is a large regional newspaper organization. For several years the company had considered building a computer system to support subscriber management, newspaper delivery, billing, and accounting. They hired two consulting firms to study their system, neither of which was satisfactory to management. Both consultants had followed a study approach based on IBM's Business Systems Planning (BSP), which identified general information requirements and systems priorities. A third study was commissioned from a well-known national consulting firm. Based on this organization's report, a commitment was made to initiate the computer system. The forecast was that this project would last about two years and cost approximately $10 million.

Like Firm A, this organization created a project organization headed by a user. In this case, the user was an accountant. This project team also included consultants from a computer vendor as well as from the vendor supplying the database management system used in the project. Also on the project team were staff drawn from the data processing department and from user organizations. As with Firm A, these were generally the best people available.

Also like Firm A, new computing equipment was involved in this project. In this case, however, instead of the computer involved in the project being a supplement to the firm's existing equipment, the system was a replacement for what the firm already had. As a result, in addition to new systems being built for the project, *conversion* of old programs was also necessary for the old systems.

A commercially available system development methodology was selected and utilized throughout the project. As the project proceeded, it became apparent that the project leader (the accountant) never fully adapted to the IS environment and was not comfortable in his position. He had a great deal of trouble dealing with the large number of vendors involved in the project and began to have conflicts with the manager of IS concerning equipment issues. In addition, the IS staff were constantly being interrupted to consider issues involved with the system conversion.

As the project progressed, it began to get badly behind schedule so the scope of the project was reduced to meet the schedule. The project leader became totally dependent upon one of the IS staff on the project team in making estimates of time and cost for the revised project. These schedules began to slip as well. Meanwhile, the general business climate in which the newspaper was operating began deteriorating badly and cost control became the paramount consideration. The team was continually pressed to hold to cost and time schedules. When additional slippages occurred, the firm's senior management decided to discontinue the project and disbanded the project team.

Although the situation is remarkably similar to the one described at Firm A, we have a situation where one was a success and the other was a failure. In both cases, the scope of the project was difficult to estimate and thus the project was changed as it went along. However, A was structured to manage these changes; B was not.

Case C: Failing to Organize the Users Can Lead to Failure

Firm C is a large agricultural cooperative listed in the *Fortune* 500 organizations. As such, it is widely distributed geographically and managerially decentralized. Acquisitions have recently increased the size and complexity of this organization.

Computing had been largely centralized at the corporate headquarters, but one or two remote divisions have had their own IS staffs and equipment (minicomputers). After a consulting study in the early 1990s, a management system was established to make computing more effective.

The firm's IS department utilized several procedures for ensuring user involvement in system design and development. User liaison was accomplished by having business systems managers in each organizational unit and by insisting that a user act as the project manager for each major project. A full system of charge-out was employed, and a very detailed systems development life cycle is now in place.

A central information systems organization (the IS department), originally created in 1970, has evolved through a series of mainframe products and introduced a charge-back system to charge users for the use of computing resources. User organizations have complained that the charge-back system has penalized them for the inefficiency of the IS department. Although the firm's IS department had been totally responsible for procurement decisions regarding the central hardware, it has had little success controlling proliferation of other types and kinds of equipment throughout the organization. Acquisitions have resulted in several incompatible systems but do not account for all of the diversity.

The remote users have argued that the central IS department has not been providing efficient and effective service. These users have proposed that they be able to acquire their own client/server systems. Over the objections of the central IS department, they have been allowed to obtain equipment and begin hiring programming staffs. At present, the firm has several types of IBM computers, as well as equipment manufactured by Apple, Sun Microsystems, and Digital Equipment Corporation. The variety of PCs are continually proliferating among the users. The central IS group is unhappy about this situation and is trying to find out what computers are in the organization by taking an equipment inventory.

All this proliferation has occurred despite the presence of a detailed information systems plan which has substantial user input from the user organizations through the business systems managers. The vice president of information systems, after 11 years in the position, has left to take a job with another firm.

Despite a very formal planning and management system, this firm is not properly managing its computing resources. The high turnover of IS employees, the high levels of user dissatisfaction, and the attitude of senior management all reflect problems with Firm C's use of its computing resources.

Case D: CEO and VP of IS Partnership Leads to Success and Promotion

Firm D is a nationwide automobile leasing company that is a subsidiary of a financial corporation. After several years of severe trouble with its IS department, an incoming chief executive officer (CEO) appointed a new vice president of information systems. A dramatic turnaround occurred in the three years following these changes.

During the turnaround period, this firm's centralized IS department went on to a formalized planning system. They also went through a conversion of their computing systems from mainframes to client/servers. Both these experiences were very positive for the IS department and the users.

The new VP of information systems had formerly been head of the company's small operations research unit, which was located in the IS department. This person had a very good reputation among the users for being responsive to their needs and able to give them quick solutions to their problems. The CEO installed the new VP in the office next to his. After a short period, the VP of information systems contracted outside consultants to conduct a study of the IS department in order to identify its strengths and weaknesses. A large part of this study involved the attitudes of both the users and IS personnel.

Soon after the completion of the study, a user training program was conducted for the firm's senior management, again using outside resources. The CEO attended all the sessions, which showed his interest in information systems. After the conclusion of this training, similar sessions were held for the firm's middle managers.

In 1992, it became apparent that, in order to meet the competition, the firm would have to implement new information systems for automated customer check-in and check-out at its 1,000 national rental offices. The decision to develop the system was made primarily because the competition had (or was developing) such a system and because cost savings and "better management information" could be demonstrated.

As with Firms A and B, a project team was set up, but in this case the team was located within IS. Heavy user involvement was obtained in the system design as a formal strategy. Also, like Firm A, this firm had a formal project and information systems plan. The development staff was organized into groups attached to specific user organizations.

About a year after the IS department had been under the management of the new VP, an incident occurred that sent a message concerning the CEO's attitude toward IS. The CEO had become aware that one division and its management were very resistant to the new computerization project. After several discussions, the CEO fired the division head and replaced him with the executive to whom the IS department had been reporting, the controller. This manager immediately began to work with IS on computer projects within the division. At the time of this personnel change, the CEO established that the VP of IS would report directly to him. Overall, this firm changed a very troublesome computer situation into one that was very positive, all in a period of three years.

18.2 FITTING INFORMATION SYSTEMS INTO THE ORGANIZATION

Some of the most important decisions made in association with an organization's use of computing resources concern the *acquisition, organization,* and *motivation* of information systems personnel to perform their duties. Decisions in each area, of course, must deal with a number of important issues and trade off a number of factors.

The cases described previously provide us with a rich environment in which to examine the organizational, staffing, and motivational issues associated with information systems management. Clearly, issues of IS planning and control, equipment selection, and project control are also involved. In this chapter, however, we will focus on four major issues: *organization, IS leadership, and the relationship between the IS department and the rest of the organization*. These issues are also important features of the situations described in the cases. First, let us consider the organizational issues associated with IS. Two considerations are paramount: (1) how the IS function fits into the overall organization, and (2) how the IS function is internally structured. Decisions in each of these areas are related to specific issues or problem areas.

A major decision that must be made by senior management is where a central IS department is to report. Partly for historical reasons, the most common place to find the IS function is in the accounting or finance organization. In this situation, IS normally reports to the controller or the vice president of finance. One may alternatively find the IS department reporting to one of the following: (1) a vice president of administration, (2) the senior executive of an operating division, (3) an executive vice president, (4) the CEO. In the latter case, the **chief information officer (CIO)*** usually carries the title of vice president. The actual title may be vice president of IS, vice president of administrative services, or vice president of information resources. Four possibilities are shown in Figure 18.1.

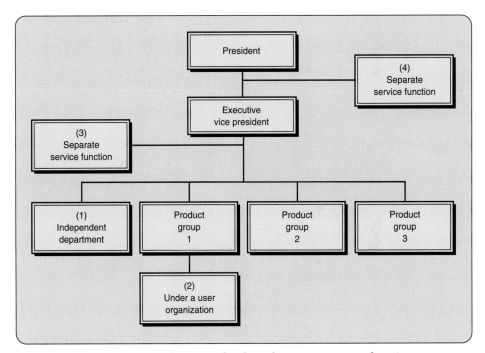

FIGURE 18.1 Four alternative locations for the information systems function.

The title of CIO and the position to whom this person reports reflect, in many cases, the support being shown by executive management for the IS function. This issue is covered in more detail in what follows. Note, however, that Firm D, in one of the successful situations described in the opening case, used the reporting relationship to signify the CEO's strong support for IS to the overall organization.

The reporting relationship of the IS function is also important, in that it reflects the focus of the function. If IS reports to the accounting or finance area,

---

*To show the importance of the IS area, some organizations call the director of IS a *CIO*, Chief Information Officer, similar to Chief Financial Officer (CFO) and Chief Operating Officer (COO). Typically, only senior vice presidents receive such titles. CIOs exist mainly in organizations that are heavily dependent on IT, such as banks, insurance companies, and airlines.

there is often a tendency to emphasize accounting or finance applications at the expense of those in the marketing, production, and logistical areas. To be most effective, the IS function needs to take as broad a view as possible. When the information function is given the title of information resources management or administrative services, it is common that the organization has the charter to do much more than just provide information system services. In these instances, the department usually involves itself in planning and providing total information services for the entire organization.

GUIDELINES

There are two important guidelines associated with placing IS into the overall organization. The first of these follows from the fact that there appears to be a relationship between the reporting level and the success of the function IS. It has been the authors' experience that the level of IS success is greatly enhanced in cases in which the CEO considers the IS function an integral part of the business and chooses to emphasize this fact by having the function report directly to the top of the organization.

The second guideline is that it is far better to have the information systems function report to the VP of administration, chief information officer, or director of information resources management than to have the information systems function report to a specific function such as accounting. There are two reasons for this. The first was already mentioned—the IS function needs to have as broad a perspective as possible regarding systems priorities. The second reason is that, with technology moving so fast and in so many directions, it is important to take more than just the IS perspective. New and related technologies such as data communications, graphics, expert systems, and word processing illustrate this situation.

▶ 18.3 THE CENTRALIZATION–DECENTRALIZATION OF INFORMATION RESOURCES

In the modern computing environment, it is desirable to distribute equipment and data throughout the organization. We frequently see this type of distribution with distributed or client/server processing. It is also possible to distribute the development function and management control of the development process throughout the organization.

All the firms in the opening cases except B involved the distribution of computing hardware, and Case A depicted a situation in which organizational data was distributed. Cases A and B described instances of the development process being distributed to the user organization. In both cases, a project development team was created and reported to the user organization in the function addressed by the project. In Case D, a project team was created but was housed within the IS organization. None of these case studies involved a situation in which a permanent development staff is housed within a user organization, although this approach is becoming more common.

The fact that the case studies describe one instance of the successful decentralization of the development function (Case A), one instance of an unsuccessful decentralization of the development process (Case B), and one instance of the successful use of a project team within the central IS organization (Case D) shows that there is nothing about decentralizing or not decentralizing that will guarantee success or failure. The important thing to note about the decentralization of the development process is that the option exists; and, if properly performed, it may offer advantages in the building of very large systems.

Case C involved a situation in which many systems (relatively unsuccessful in terms of user acceptance) were developed centrally. This case also involved the development of systems by programming staff located in geographically decentralized organizational components. In this situation, there was a profusion of computer equipment involved as well as the use of a variety of developmental practices. Whereas the development of systems by the central IS staff was "highly managed," there was little central control of the **decentralized IS** computing activity. Senior management basically said that the decentralized units could do anything they pleased with systems that were particular to only one unit.

Case C describes a situation in which an attempt was made to provide **centralized IS** computing in a geographically and managerially decentralized organization. The company tried to do this with a central development staff and centralized equipment for some systems, using a highly managed approach. At the same time, it gave decentralized units complete autonomy to do as they pleased regarding purely local applications. The case study certainly shows that the central systems were less than successful. We also know of at least one situation in which a desirable integration of two local systems was impractical because of incompatible equipment and software. Firm C was faced with a difficult organizational problem from a computing standpoint. Although it tried hard, it generally failed to place computing effectively into the organization with which it had to work.

There are several summary comments that can be made regarding the centralization–decentralization of computing personnel and management control of the systems development process. One is that overall decisions as to whether development will be distributed are not made by the IS manager. In most cases, these decisions are made by senior management, and they determine the environment within which the IS manager must operate. Certainly, in Firms A and B, this was the case. Similarly, the centralization–decentralization pattern of development encountered in Case C was the result of a decision made by executive management.

In addition, it is folly to completely give up on central planning and control of the information systems function. To simply say that subunits, which in many cases represent large-scale profit centers, can do as they please regarding equipment and development practices is to shirk a senior management responsibility. Chapter 11 illustrates the need for centrally coordinated planning to ensure good strategic and information architecture planning.

Finally, decentralization of resources (especially systems personnel) is neither doomed to failure nor a prescription for success. Depending upon the situation, this action can be very effective, but the personnel involved must be carefully selected; and a managerial system must be in place to coordinate with the central IS function and with overall corporate activities.

ADVANTAGES AND DISADVANTAGES

Both the centralization and decentralization of the IS department have certain advantages and disadvantages. It is worthwhile reviewing some of the arguments for each of the approaches. As you read, keep in mind that the strengths of one tend to be the weaknesses of the other.

ARGUMENTS FOR CENTRALIZATION

1. It is much easier to consolidate financial and operating data for reporting and evaluation purposes. Without centralization, consolidation is usually obstructed by incompatibilities of different systems, system designs, and data formats.
2. It is easier to attract and manage computer professionals in a centralized system. Centralization, moreover, reduces the impact of both shortages and turnover of development personnel by permitting a larger staff. In addition,

the larger staff provides a greater opportunity to include specialists such as capacity planners or data communications experts.

3. Top management can more easily control operating divisions which use uniform information reporting systems. When units develop their own reporting systems individually, there are usually discrepancies in data used, data definitions, and reporting formats. Through centralized systems, uniformity can be maintained.

4. There is frequently an economy of scale to be gained by centralizing the IS staff. Efficiencies are afforded by reduction in duplication of effort and better control of allocation of systems analysis and programming activities.

ARGUMENTS FOR DECENTRALIZATION

1. The IS staff is closer to local problems and gets to know the business of the user better than if the staff were located elsewhere. In general, the argument is that the users are more satisfied with these systems than they are with those developed centrally because their needs are better met.

2. Computer equipment and local staff can be more responsive to both developmental and operational requirements when they are decentralized to user departments. User departments have more discretion in scheduling their resources than do centralized groups. They do not have to compete with other departments for resources.

3. It is much easier to control costs when computer resources are decentralized to user departments. This condition tends to make the user department managers more sensitive to cost–benefit considerations because the computing costs directly affect the profitability of their departments.

OVERALL RECOMMENDATIONS

The following guidelines are helpful in making a decision about whether to centralize or decentralize.

Centralized IS resources tend to be best suited to the following situations:

1. Information systems for top level management (e.g., executive information systems).

2. Organization wide, homogeneous functions such as payroll, personnel, and common accounting functions.

3. Work that does not require rapid response time can be done more economically on a centralized basis.

4. Organizational functions that are too small to justify appropriate computing equipment and/or staff.

5. Situations where integration of information technically requires centralized processing (e.g., airline reservations).

Decentralized IS resources tend to be best suited to the following situations:

1. Situations where rapid and flexible response time for development and/or production is required.

2. Situations where the systems are unique and heterogeneous to a decentralized operation (e.g., a conglomerate may own several companies that are in different businesses).

3. Information systems for which there is no compelling reason to centralize (e.g., a stand-alone inventory system).

The four companies described in the opening cases had different approaches to the centralization–decentralization situation. Firm D was very successful using a centralized format. Firm A was successful in taking a partially decentralized approach in that it used a project team. Firm B, taking a similar approach, failed.

Firm C totally failed to match its computing organization to its overall organizational structure. This lack of success can be partially attributed to the fact that it tried to employ a centralized IS organization under conditions of extreme organizational decentralization.

A large retail organization, facing similar organizational circumstances, has taken a decentralized approach and has been highly successful. This organization has separate divisions in the department store business, the discount business, and the specialty business (e.g., bookstores). The firm argues that because the divisions are different in design, merchandise offerings, and market orientations, they need total autonomy. These conditions and philosophy have resulted in separate, freestanding computing organizations which have been highly successful. Firm C would have been a more successful computer user had it adhered to a similar approach for the relationship between the IS function and the overall organization.

▶ 18.4 LEADERSHIP FOR INFORMATION SYSTEMS AND THE CHIEF INFORMATION OFFICER

In order to succeed with IT and to avoid failure, it is useful to examine the emerging leadership role of the IS department and its chief.

To understand the role of the CIO in an organization, it is beneficial first to understand the changing role of the information systems department. This changing role, portrayed in Table 18.1, indicates a transformation from a technical, low management level to a strategic, upper management position.

The changing role of the department points to the changing role of its chief and to the fact that the CIO is becoming an important member of the organization's top management team.

THE ROLE OF THE CIO

The role of the CIO depends on the role of the IS department and is determined by many factors ranging from the type of industry to the size of the organization. In a survey conducted in 1992, it was found that the prime role of the CIO is to align IT with the business strategy (see Table 18.2).

This changing role of the CIO reinforces our previous comment that the CIO is entering the top management level, especially in organizations that greatly depend on IT. Therefore, the relationship between the CIO and the CEO is becoming critical, as shown in opening Case D. Information technology has become a stra-

---

Table 18.1 **The Information Systems Leadership Role**

Traditional Major IS Functions
- Technical (sometimes business) design and programming.
- Project management.
- Operations.
- Staff activities (consulting, planning, education, and so on).

Newly Critical Functions in the Late 1980s and 1990s
- Design and programming of increasingly complex "mission critical" systems.
- Infrastructure development and maintenance (computers, networks, software, and data).
- Education of line management to its responsibilities.
- Education of IS management concerning the business.
- Proactive use of business and technical knowledge to "seed" the line with innovative ideas concerning effective uses of information technology.

SOURCE: Rockart (1988), pp. 57–64.

Table 18.2 **The Roles of the CIO**

CIOs were asked to name their top priority in helping to improve their organizations' efficiency and performance. The results are:

Align technology with the business strategy	24%
Implement state-of-the-art solutions	12%
Provide and improve information access	12%
Enhance customer service	9%
Create links within the organization	7%
Train and empower employees	7%
Create links with external customers	6%
Enhance current systems	4%
Support business reengineering	4%
Act as change agent/catalyst	4%
Educate business units about IT	3%
Evaluate emerging technologies	3%
Implement standard systems and architecture	3%
Others	2%

SOURCE: Kiely (1992), p. 30. Reprinted through the courtesy of *CIO*. © 1992 CIO Communications Inc.

tegic resource for many organizations. Coordinating this resource requires strong leadership and cooperation within the organization. Therefore, the CIO–CEO relationships are crucial for effective, successful utilization of IT.

Two factors stand out in those organizations that tend to be successful computer users: the high degree of support shown for the IS department by the organization's senior management, and the consequent image the IS department has in the organization. In the case studies, Firm D is a classic example of this situation. Recall that the CEO took a number of actions to show support for the IS department and enhance its image.

REENGINEERING

...changing the corporate hierarchy to reflect the role of IT.

Some of these actions are obvious, and others are more subtle. Among the more obvious are (1) putting the IS VP's office next to the CEO's, (2) supporting an executive training series in IS and attending the sessions in an uninterrupted manner, and (3) elevating the head of IS to a vice president level reporting directly to the CEO instead of to the controller. Less obvious is that the CEO of Firm D used the organizational reward system to show support for IS. The fact that a division head who was not supportive of IS was replaced received considerable notice in the organization. Budget commitment to the IS department, plus the undertaking of a major IS project affecting the entire organization, are other signs of support for IS in the case of Firm D. Overall, management support and image enhancement provided in Firm D are among the best ever observed by the authors. This situation, coupled with good management on the part of the IS vice president, was greatly responsible for one of the most dramatic turnarounds we have seen in an organization's IS success.

GUIDELINES

The attitudes and actions of senior management regarding the IS department are extremely important to its success. Unfortunately, it is simple to preach about the sorts of things that management "ought to do." It is quite another thing to bring about the proper actions. Here we identify some of the sorts of actions that would be beneficial on the part of senior management:

1. Place the IS department in the organization in such a way that it is visible, has access to senior management's attention, and is located so as to have a broad perspective regarding the organization's information needs.

2. Provide adequate resources for the IS department.

3. Give time and effort to IS issues facing the organization. In other words, become involved with IS planning, policy, and control issues.

4. Use the organizational reward system for those individuals and their sub-units.

5. Select an IS manager who is a skilled manager, and make this person a part of the senior management team.

The three ''external'' issues regarding the IS organization—the reporting relationship, the degree of centralization–decentralization, and the amount of support shown for the function by top management—are all associated with IS success. However, the decisions involved in these areas are, in general, made by senior management, not by IS managers. It is important therefore that senior management appreciate the importance of these decisions and be made aware of the guidelines that have been offered.

▶ 18.5   THE BASIC ORGANIZATIONAL STRUCTURE OF THE INFORMATION SYSTEMS DEPARTMENT

Once the relationship of IS to the organization is addressed, the next important managerial issue regarding IS is that of structuring the IS department. This must be done keeping in the mind the issues of managerial efficiency and overall effectiveness of the unit (especially with serving the needs of the users). Whereas issues of the relationship between the IS function and the overall organization are often beyond the IS manager's purview, decisions involving the internal structure of the department are usually made by the IS manager. A common basic structure of an information system department is shown in Figure 18.2. Note that the computer operations function and the systems development function report to the director of information systems.

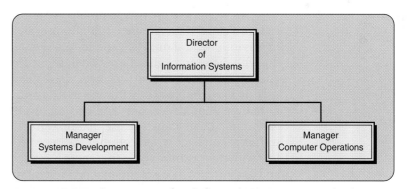

FIGURE 18.2 Basic structure of an information systems organization.

There are instances in which development and computer operations are separated into different parts of the organization, but this is relatively uncommon. The argument favoring such a structure is that computer operation is much like a factory and should be run as such. Thus, as a departure from systems development, the operations function needs a completely different type of management and should report to a different manager. The discussion that follows will assume that the more normal basic structure shown in Figure 18.2 is employed.

The **internal structure** of the information systems organization must cope with a number of situations. One involves the trade-off between managerial flexibility and efficiency and service to the user. Another is the issue of maintaining existing systems and providing for evolution of these systems as user needs change and/or new external requirements become apparent. A third concerns the monitoring of the information systems function by the overall organization, setting priorities for the organization, and aligning the information systems planning with overall organizational directions. In addition, there are several other organizational issues that do not fit in any one category.

MANAGERIAL EFFICIENCY VERSUS USER SERVICE

From an efficiency standpoint, an IS manager would probably prefer to structure the development function as shown in Figure 18.3. (We are assuming here that one group acts as analysts and another group does the programming.) The beauty of this organization is that it is very flexible. If new systems development requirements come along, it is easy to assign persons from the analysis and programming pool to do the job. The difficulty, especially from a user perspective, is that the analysts and programmers assigned to their project may have no experience with the problem or no familiarity with the user's area. In addition, they are often an unknown quantity, since they may not have worked before with this user.

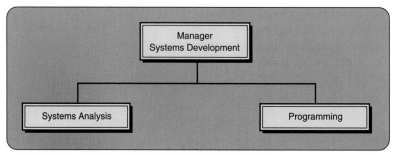

FIGURE 18.3 Information systems organization structured for managerial flexibility.

An attempt to ease these problems has resulted in an extension of the structure in Figure 18.3. Another subunit, user liaison, has been added. The persons in this unit, who should be experienced senior analysts, are responsible for working with the user organizations to determine their information needs and with the analysts and programmers to meet these needs. Typically, one person from the user liaison group works with one user organization. In this way, the liaison gets to know the user's business and becomes well known to persons in the user organization. In addition, the user liaison can translate business problems into more technical language when communicating with the systems developers. One problem with this organization is that there is often confusion about the responsibilities and authority of the user liaison and the responsibilities and authority of the users or systems personnel. Another problem is that this system is very dependent on the skills of each user liaison.

Another organizational form that has been used to try to balance managerial need and user requirements is a matrix organization, as shown in Figure 18.4. In a matrix organization, there is a pool of programmers and there is a pool of analysts. These people report to supervisors with titles such as manager of programming and manager of analysis, respectively. In addition there is a subunit composed of project leaders. These people report to a manager with a title such as manager of project development. When a new project comes along, it is assigned to a project leader who negotiates with the manager of analysis and the manager of programming to form a project team. A programmer or analyst is typically involved with one project at a time, but a project leader may be involved with as many as three projects at the same time. Project leaders tend to work with partic-

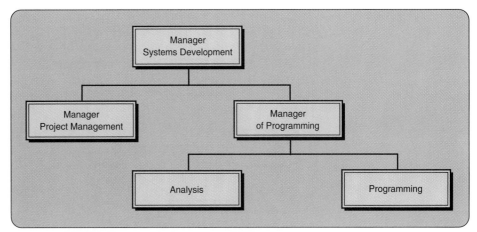

FIGURE 18.4 Information systems organization in matrix form.

ular user organizations, but the analysts and programmers do not. This organizational form is very efficient, but it has the disadvantage that each analyst and programmer has two bosses (because each reports to a project leader for project-related matters and to the manager of their function for overall matters). Performance is evaluated by the functional manager with input from project leaders with whom an individual has worked. This system has great potential for difficulties when conflicts arise.

Large IS departments may have a fairly complex structure as shown in Minicase 1. It is interesting to note that this structure has been changed several times over the last 25 years. A possible forthcoming change is toward an end-users-oriented structure and a virtual IS organization.

END-USER ORIENTED STRUCTURE AND THE VIRTUAL IS ORGANIZATION

Figure 18.5 shows an end-user-oriented structure which could be prominent in future IS organizations. This is a functional organization in which analysts and programmers are grouped into teams to service a particular user group. Each team has diverse skills among its members. As discussed in Chapter 4, some organizations and information technology organizations are moving toward self-directed permanent or temporary teams. A team may not have all the skills it needs but may bring in a "virtual team member" for specialized skills on an "as needed" temporary basis (see Fig. 18.6). Such a structure is referred to as a *virtual IS organization* (see Minicase 2).

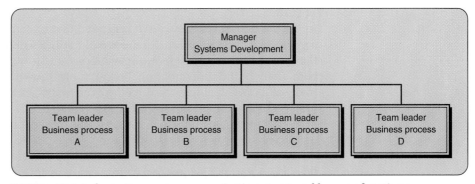

FIGURE 18.5 Information systems organization structured by user functions.

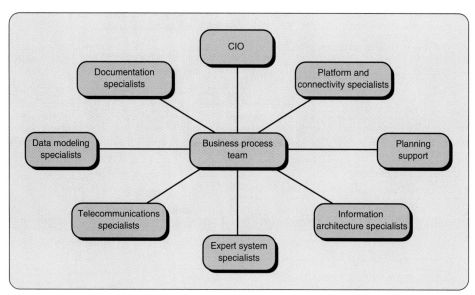

FIGURE 18.6 Model of business process team drawing from specified sources for virtual team member.

The **virtual IS organization** can be arranged in several configurations, some of which are described in Box 18.1.

The virtual arrangement can be difficult to manage in the sense that slack resources may exist in one team while another is overloaded. The shortcoming is balanced by the fact that over time, the systems development personnel become very familiar with the function they are serving. Furthermore, by working together on many projects, they form many strong interpersonal relationships, which usually work well to ease problems of communication and systems implementation.

Before leaving this topic, it should be noted that special project teams are often formed for very large projects. In the case studies, Firms A, B, and C in the opening section all used this approach. Another organizational form not specifically discussed, because of the assumption of the existence of a centralized information systems function, is to place the analysis and programming functions in the user organization. This is really a variant of the functional structure, generally brought on by a poorly managed, unresponsive IS function. This has been a recent trend, but in the authors' opinion should be approached with caution. Unless good plans and standards are in place, and the user organization is very familiar with managing data processing, many difficulties—not the least of which is cost escalation—can occur when systems development is distributed.

ANALYSIS AND PROGRAMMING

In the previous discussion, it was assumed that one group performed the systems analysis and another group did the programming. This is only one way of dividing the systems development task. Another, obviously, is to have people who perform both analysis and programming. Research has shown that both systems involve a trade-off between efficiency and effectiveness. When the functions are separated, projects tend to be performed more efficiently, as they come in closer to cost and time estimates. On the other hand, using the separate functions also tends to produce systems with less satisfied users.

Another issue to keep in mind involves career paths. Frequently, it is the practice to start people in programming and, over time, move them into analysis. However, the problem-solving-skills associated with successful performance as a

A Closer Look BOX 18.1

THE VIRTUAL IS ORGANIZATION

Virtual IS organizations are emerging in several different forms, but generally the central IS staff works with departmental IS (end-user computing), business managers, outside vendors, and even corporate customers. This changes the nature and culture of the traditional IS hierarchical structure to a more open, interactive structure (see the figure below).

Some characteristics of the new structure are the following:

▼ *IS personnel*, particularly those involved in application development, are incorporated into the business units, sometimes even reporting directly to the business managers.

▼ *The boundary of the virtual IS organization* doesn't end at the company's walls; vendors and customers may be part of the team, as well.

▼ *The rest of the virtual IS organization* is coming to rely on what is left of central IS functions to develop an overall technical architecture that meets the needs of the entire corporation.

▼ *Central IS plays a prominent role as technology scouts*, scouring the stream of new products and technologies for those most suitable for the company.

The structure is fluid and changing.
SOURCE: Condensed from Moad (1994). Figure reprinted with permission of *DATAMATION* magazine, February 1, 1994. © 1994 by Cahners Publishing Company.

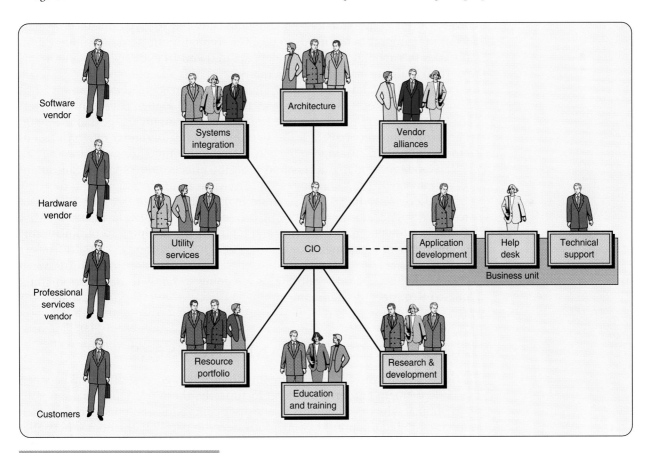

systems analyst has little to do with programming skills. Thus, we may question whether good programmers can be good analysts. Evidence is building that suggests that the keys to successful systems analysis involve expertise in problem solving, interpersonal communication, and organization. It may be that analysts should be specially recruited and have different training from those who have had a career writing computer programs. Some organizations are hiring MBAs who are not IS majors and training them to be system analysts on a just-in-time, as-needed basis.

MAINTENANCE

Another problem, whose resolution will affect the IS internal organization chart, is maintaining existing systems. There are two major alternatives for performing this function. The first is to have the person or persons who developed the system be responsible for correcting any errors that show up after the system is put into operation. These people would also modify the system as changes occur due to new user needs or business requirements. The second approach to dealing with system change is the creation of a separate maintenance function to handle any system modifications except foreign changes. Sometimes such a function is carried out in the systems development subunit, and sometimes in the systems operations subunit.

Both approaches to performing systems maintenance have advantages and disadvantages. Having the systems developers do their own maintenance is efficient. Because of their familiarity with the system, they can more easily make modifications. The difficulty is that if these persons know they will be doing their own maintenance, they tend to keep some of the documentation in their heads. Further, if this is the practice and someone leaves, it is very difficult for a new person to figure out what needs to be done to modify the system. Another difficulty with this approach is that developers can spend an excessive amount of time performing routine maintenance. In many cases, this allocation of time is difficult to track, and, therefore, the organization does not recognize the amount of its resources being allocated to maintenance as opposed to new development.

Having a separate maintenance function has the disadvantage that the maintenance programmers have a lot of learning to do each time a new task is encountered. Further, although some people enjoy maintenance programming and are very good at it, many others find it boring after a time. Some organizations use maintenance programming as a first-year training assignment for new programmers. Advantages of a separate maintenance group are that it tends to force good system documentation on the part of developers, it makes for easy accounting of maintenance activity, and it buffers the organization against losing key development personnel.

On balance, the advantages of a separate maintenance function outweigh the disadvantages. Some organizations are going so far as to outsource maintenance to a contract programming group.

▶ 18.6 THE IS DEPARTMENT AND END USERS

The four opening cases allude to the importance of a good relationship between the IS department and **end users**; unfortunately, these relationships are not always optimal. The developments of end-user computing and outsourcing, which were discussed in Chapter 11, were motivated—in part—by the poor service that end users felt they received from the IS department. Conflicts occur for many reasons, ranging from the fact that priorities of the IS department may differ from that of the end users to a simple lack of communication. An example of such conflict is illustrated in Box 18.2.

Generally, the IS organization can take one of the following four approaches toward end-user computing.

1. *Sink or swim.* Don't do anything—let the end user beware.
2. *Stick.* Establish policies and procedures to control end-user computing so that corporate risks are minimized.

IT At Work BOX 18.2

THE DEPARTMENT OF TRANSPORTATION

The Department of Transportation in Minnesota had come across a hybrid PC system that would allow road surveys to be accomplished with less time and effort, and greater accuracy. The system would require two people to conduct a survey instead of the normal three, and because of the precision of the computer-based system, the survey could be done in half the time.

The department ran into a problem because the Information Systems Department for the State of Minnesota had instituted standards for all PCs that could be purchased by any state agency. Specifically, a particular brand of IBM PC was the only PC purchase allowed, without going through a special procedure. The red tape, as well as the unwillingness of the Information Systems Department to allow any deviation from the standard, caused a great deal of frustration.

As a last resort, the Department of Transportation simply procured the hybrid PC and camouflaged the transaction as engineering equipment for conducting surveys. From that point on, they decided that they would do what they needed to do to get their jobs done, and the less the Information Systems Department knew about what they were doing, the better. When asked why they behaved this way, the administrator of the Department of Transportation simply said, "We have to do it this way because the Information Systems Department will either try to stop or hold up for a long period of time any decision we want to make because they just are not familiar enough with the issues that we are facing in our department."

Critical Thinking Issue: What are the organizational risks when the Transportation Department takes this attitude? ▲

3. *Carrot.* Create incentives to encourage certain end-user practices that reduce organizational risks.
4. *Support.* Develop services to aid end users in their computing activities.

Each of these responses presents the IS executive with different opportunities for facilitation and coordination.

The *sink-or-swim* response is the default action. It does nothing to increase the level of end-user computing or improve its quality. All of the risks mentioned in Chapter 11 apply, while the benefits to end users and the IS department are solely a function of end-user efforts.

The restrictive *stick* response forces coordination at the cost of some computing opportunities. Many of the risks associated with end-user computing could be reduced by effective policies, standards, and procedures. These same policies, standards, and procedures are likely to reduce the incentives for end users to do their own computing (lead times are increased, user control and flexibility are reduced, and development costs are higher).

The *carrot* response motivates end users to reduce risks to the firm associated with their computing. By allowing end users to retain their computing freedom, it encourages them to work in proper, consistent ways, but it does not provide a complete program of support.

The *support* response is designed to increase end-user computing through the provision of services. These services are carefully designed to increase beneficial computing and foster coordination. As long as end users are able to choose to use or not to use services, they retain control over their computing activities and thus view services positively. Their having a choice also provides a check on the IS department, because services that focus too much on coordination and not enough on facilitation will simply not be used.

Each type of response is appropriate in some situations, but a combination of responses is necessary for management on a broad scale. The next section describes an organized approach to defining these combinations.

18.7 SERVICE SUPPORT LEVELS AGREEMENTS

An effective approach to managing end-user computing must achieve both facilitation and coordination. Service support levels do this by (1) defining computing responsibilities, (2) providing a framework for designing support services, and (3) allowing end users to retain as much control as possible over their own computing.

Service support levels are formal agreements regarding the division of computing responsibility between end users and the IS department. Such divisions are based on a small set of critical computing decisions that are made by *end-user management*. The way managers make these decisions commits them to accept certain responsibilities and to turn over others to the IS department. Since end-user management makes the decisions, they are free to choose the amount and kind of support they feel they need. This freedom to choose provides a check on the IS department. If the IS department is to meet its objectives of coordinating and facilitating end-user computing, it must develop and deliver support services to meet these needs.

An approach based on service support levels offers several other advantages. First, it reduces "finger pointing" by clearly specifying responsibilities. When a microcomputer malfunctions, everyone knows who is responsible for fixing it. Second, it provides a structure for the design and delivery of end-user services by the IS department. This structure allows a range of support options to be provided from a common pool of services. For example, the same consultant can have clearly specified duties at each support level. Third, incentives are created for end users to improve their computing practices, thereby reducing computing risks to the firm. By clearly stating what has to be done to qualify for better IS service, end-user management is in a better position to make trade-offs in its computing decisions. Finally, it provides a means for the IS department to coordinate end-user computing. The same staff people who provide support services also monitor and report on end-user activities. Some end-user computing will remain outside these coordination efforts, but those activities are recognized to be the responsibility of end-user managers.

Establishing service support levels requires four steps.

1. Defining levels.
2. Dividing computing responsibility at each level. (This issue was discussed in Chapter 11.)
3. Designing service support levels.
4. Implementing service support levels.

The process of establishing and implementing service support levels may be applied to each of the principle computing resources: hardware, software, and data.

 ## 18.8 THE INFORMATION CENTER

An interesting change in organizational structure related to computer technology is the introduction of the **information center** (IC)*. The concept was conceived by IBM, Canada, as a response to the increased number of end-user requests for new computer applications. This demand created a huge backlog in the IS department, and users had to wait several years to get their systems built.

---

*Sometimes spelled *information centre* because of its Canadian origins. Other names for similar organizational units are *information resource center* and *users' service center*.

Information centers are groups of employees specially trained in the use of building tools and applications software. The IC's primary task is to provide fast turnaround on user requests for information, data analyses, special reports, and other one-time information needs.

This subunit is set up to help users get certain systems built quickly and provide tools that can be employed by users to build their own systems. The concept of the IC, furthermore, suggests that the few persons working as a team or as individuals in the center should be especially oriented toward the user in their outlook. This attitude should be shown in the training provided by the staff at the center and in the way the staff helps users with any problems they might have.

One medium-sized high-technology company has even used its reward system to encourage the use of new tools. This company employs an information center within its IS function (other companies place the center in functional areas or in staff departments such as industrial engineering). Users who take classes in the tools provided by the center and become "certified" in their use receive a $500 bonus. Another large firm provides a fourth-generation language to its users through its information center. If the use of a 4GL is "one shot," the IS function does not care how inefficient the user may be. But, if the use becomes repetitive, then the personnel of the information center will work with the user to streamline the application in order to make use of the software more efficient.

The information center is also an ideal way to encourage the use of PCs and to manage their proliferation. Certain PCs can be designated for support, training classes can be held in their use, software for them can be made available, and an agreement can be made to help users who have trouble with the supported PCs. This approach can be a major key in effectively controlling the proliferation of PCs throughout the organization.

The information center can also be used as a place to house a few "commandos," or "guerrilla warriors" who can be available to build important user systems very quickly. These systems, frequently stand-alone decision support systems, can be constructed by the staff of the information center much more quickly than can systems built with traditional software and systems development methods. Because of the impact of such systems and the rapidity with which they can be made available, the information systems function often gets a very good reputation in the user community.

PURPOSES AND ACTIVITIES

The three main functions of an IC are (1) to provide assistance to end users in dealing with computing problems, (2) to provide general technical assistance, and (3) to provide general support services. Each function should fulfill the requirements shown in Box 18.3.

STAFFING

Information centers should be staffed by people with the following attributes:

▼ Business knowlege (such as MBAs).

▼ Analytical skills.

▼ Current knowledge of software development packages.

▼ Current basic hardware knowledge.

▼ Knowledge of where to go to find needed information.

▼ Patience and enthusiasm.

▼ Good interpersonal communication skills.

A Closer Look BOX 18.3

REQUIREMENTS OF INFORMATION CENTERS

End-user computing:

▼ Training and education.

▼ Assisting in software (application) development.

▼ Developing prototype programs.

▼ Providing debugging assistance.

▼ Identifying networking requirements.

▼ Consulting with the user to determine if a particular application is appropriate for end-user development.

▼ Providing a formal means for users' communication with management and with the traditional data processing staff.

▼ Cooperating with database administrators to improve access to shared data resources.

▼ Generating a catalog or library of existing applications for future use.

Technical assistance:

▼ Providing guidance in the selection of hardware and software.

▼ Helping in the selection and evaluation of application

packages, DSS generators, ES shells, and other building tools.

▼ Assisting in software installation and updates.

▼ Assisting in using query and report languages and/or packages.

▼ Assisting in the installation and use of hardware.

▼ Assisting in the installation and use of communication devices.

▼ Establishing database (or file) backups, recovery, and archive guidelines.

General support services:

▼ Providing clearing house functions for receiving and disseminating information on relevant personal computing issues.

▼ Establishing a "hotline" for interrupt-driven user requests for information on software, hardware, or application systems.

▼ Chairing user group meetings on a regular and ad hoc basis.

SOURCE: Compiled from *Jacobson and Cardullo (1983)*.

▼ Programming skills (especially in 4GLs).

▼ Drive and motivation to complete programs without direct supervision.

▼ End-user and service orientation.

PROBLEM AREAS

The purposes and activities of the IC staffed with this kind of people present a utopian vision: users get the information they need, when they need it; the data processing department is freed from mundane programming to work on important projects. As for other managers and professionals in an organization, there is a wealth of information that can be easily tapped for the benefit of the corporation. All of this is coordinated at the IC, where users and IC personnel work together to meet everyone's needs. Reality, however, may be quite different. Although many tend to agree that the IC is the best way to control and capitalize on the sweep of new information technology, it is evident that many organizations have also found that the path to the utopian vision is a rocky one. The following are some potential problem areas in IC operations:

▼ Opposition comes from the IS department if the IC is not under their control (e.g., power struggle and ego problems).

▼ Users do not have enough computer knowledge, yet they set up their own IC. This may result in low-quality service.

▼ Corporate management anticipates that the IC will be an expensive new unit with its hardware and software. Because it is difficult to conduct a cost–benefit analysis of an IC, management may be reluctant to establish one.

▼ There may be resistance from non-computer-oriented users who fear that the IC will help only computer-oriented users.

▼ Security problems (e.g., more company data in more hands) may develop.

▼ A struggle about to whom the IC should report and who should control it may occur.

▼ Senior management support may be lacking.

▼ Staffing the IC with individuals who do not possess the specified attributes discussed earlier may be a problem.

▼ Potential backlog of IC-developed or -assisted applications can occur.

▼ Proliferation of PCs may have resulted in "uncontrolled" purchases, which may mean supporting multiple vendors' products and incompatibility of equipment.

▼ There can be a redundancy of effort if IC operations are not coordinated (several IC-like groups may emerge and duplicate one another's efforts).

The importance of ICs may diminish in the future as users become more computer literate, development tools become more friendly, hardware becomes more reliable, and intelligent diagnostic and training tools provide some of the services provided by ICs.

▶ 18.9   THE STEERING COMMITTEE AND CONSULTANTS

The company described in opening Case C is an example of a very highly managed information systems organization. Yet the situation described was not a successful one. One of the management tools used by Firm C was a corporate **steering committee**. A group of senior managers, representing various organizational units, was set up to establish information systems priorities and to ensure that the information systems function was meeting the needs of the enterprise. This group was not successful in achieving these objectives. The problem with the steering committee was that it met quarterly, and simply "blessed" the actions and recommendations made by the vice president of information systems. In effect, they never made the commitment to perform the tasks they should have performed as a high-level committee.

Despite the fact that the situation described here is typical of what many companies have experienced when they have attempted to set up corporate steering committees to oversee the information systems function, others have used such a committee very successfully, such as the firm in Case A. What is the difference? There are two key reasons why some committees are successful and others are not. The first is associated with the support-and-image issue discussed previously. It is vitally important that the most senior member of the steering committee be committed to the organization's successful use of computing resources and show this commitment by words and deeds. If the senior member of the committee, frequently the CEO or a senior vice president, has taken the time to understand the responsibilities regarding IS and exercise this knowledge in the steering committee, then a major step toward a successful IS experience has been taken. The proper signals by this corporate sponsor or mentor to the others in the organization will enhance the importance of the information systems function. One very simple way to do this is by appropriate participation in the steering committee.

The second reason that some steering committees are successful is that they do the proper things and do them well. The typical duties of the steering committee (also discussed in Chapter 11) are as follows:

1. *Direction setting.* This means to work on linking the corporate strategy with the computer strategy. Planning is the key activity.

2. *Rationing.* The committee approves the allocation of resources within the information systems organization.

3. *Structuring.* The committee deals with how the IS function is positioned in the overall organization. The issue of centralization–decentralization of IS resources must be resolved.

4. *Staffing.* Key IS personnel decisions involve a consultation-and-approval process. The selection of the CIO is of paramount importance.

5. *Communication.* It is important that information regarding IS activities flows freely.

6. *Evaluating.* The committee should establish performance measures for the function and see that they are met.

The most successful IS steering committees typically are supported by a good staff. These committees react well to the plans and actions of others but do not work especially well in developing plans and actions. Thus, their activities are frequently iterative in nature. Material is presented to the committee, modifications are requested and made, and the committee reacts again. Often several cycles are involved.

The firm described in Case A effectively used both an IS corporate steering committee and a major project steering committee (referred to as the management action group). One source of input to the latter group in their deliberations was the evaluation and recommendations made by the technical advisory group (a small group of systems experts composed of persons from outside the company).

CONSULTANTS (OUTSIDE ADVISORS)

One tactic successfully used by organizations is the use of outside experts in an advisory capacity that differs from the typical consultant's role. The technical advisory group used to advise the management action group in Case A is an example of this sort of arrangement. These advisory groups are small, typically three or four persons. Each person is a recognized expert, and all may come from different outside sources. Some may be consultants, some may be professors, and some may be experts from noncompeting firms. These groups most often give advice and counsel to the head of IS, to a corporate steering committee, or to the head of a large project team.

The outside advisory group typically meets only once for each project, usually for two or three days, and reviews an entire project for the IS function itself. In some cases, they spend a good deal of time getting reports from project personnel or IS managers on the state of affairs. At the conclusion of their meeting, they draft a formal report on both the strengths and weaknesses of the project or function they are evaluating. These outside experts can provide great comfort to nontechnical managers regarding the health and/or risks of a project. Expect to see more use of these small groups in IS organizations in the future.

▶ MANAGERIAL ISSUES

The following are the major issues related to this chapter.

1. *To whom should the IS department report.* This is an important issue and is related to the issue of the degree of IS decentralization and to the role of the CIO. Reporting to a functional area may introduce biases in providing IT priorities to that department, which may not be justifiable.

2. *How much to decentralize the information resources.* This policy issue can backfire if done improperly. Determining the degree of decentralization involves many factors, some of which have contradicting impacts. For example,

more decentralization means more innovative opportunities for end users, but less control by the IS department on resources, which may result in duplication and waste.

3. *Who needs a CIO?* This is a critical question that is related to the role of the CIO as a senior executive in the organization. Giving a title without authority can damage the IS department and its operation. Asking the IS director to assume a CIO's responsibility, but not giving the authority and title, can be just as damaging. Any organization that is heavily dependent on IT should have a CIO.

4. *How to organize the IS department.* There are many possibilities. However, the department's organization should depend on its role, its size, and the degree of importance of IT to the organization. Also, the corporate strategy of outsourcing IS services needs to be considered. Lately there is a trend to use both permanent and temporary teams (sometimes virtual teams) as the core of the IS department. If the IS department is ineffective and/or inefficient, the entire organization is at risk.

5. *End users are friends, not enemies, of the IS department.* The relationship between end users and the IS department can be very delicate. In the past, IS departments were known to be insensitive to end-user needs. This created a strong desire for end-user independence, which can be both expensive and ineffective. Successful companies develop a climate of cooperation and friendship between the two parties.

6. *Using various instruments to improve end-user/IS department relationships.* The use of an information center, service support level agreements, and a steering committee can be very helpful in improving end-user/IS department relationships. But, such instruments can be expensive and inefficient. Careful analysis is needed to determine if and how to use such instruments.

7. *Using consultants.* It can be very helpful to use a consultant, but it can also be very frustrating. Good management of the relationship with consultants is a must.

8. *Ethical issues.* The reporting relationship of the IS department can result in some unethical issues. If the IS department reports, for example, to the finance department, the finance department may misuse information about individuals or other departments. ■

KEY TERMS

Centralized IS *679*

Chief information officer (CIO) *677*

Decentralized IS *679*

Information center *690*

Internal IS structure *683*

Service support levels *690*

Steering committee *693*

Virtual IS organization *686*

CHAPTER HIGHLIGHTS *(L-x means learning objective number x)*

▼ IS reporting locations can vary, but a preferred location is to senior management. (L-1)

▼ IS can be centralized or decentralized, depending on the nature of the organization. (L-2)

▼ There are alternative IS structures; however, a team approach, focusing on business processes, is becoming more common. (L-4)

▼ In many organizations, there are conflicts between the IS department and end users. (L-6)

▼ Service-support-level agreements can reduce conflicts between IS and end-user. (L-6)

QUESTIONS FOR REVIEW

1. What are possible reporting locations for IS?

2. Why has IS historically reported to finance or accounting departments?

3. What are considerations for centralizing or decentralizing IS?

4. What are the internal structures for IS presented in the chapter?

5. What is a virtual IS structure?

6. What are some traditional responses to end-user computing, and what are their limitations?

7. Discuss the service support levels and the role they play in end-user computing.

8. What are the most important services to end users from an information center?

QUESTIONS FOR DISCUSSION

1. What is a desirable location for IS to report to and why?

2. Consider the four cases in the beginning of the chapter, and discuss the pros and cons of IS being centralized or decentralized in each case.

3. Why is a team approach focusing on business processes preferable? Consider Chapter 4 and the information architecture discussed in Chapters 10–13 in your discussion.

4. Explain why many of the IC problems disappear when the IC is funded by users.

5. Given that troubleshooting, consulting, and training rank as the most important services provided by an information center, what types of hours and availability should the information systems department consider having for end-user computing support?

EXERCISES

1. If you have worked in an IS organization, discuss the reporting location and internal structure of the IS group.

2. What would you consider to be the critical success factors of Case A in the beginning of the chapter?

3. What were the factors resulting in success for Case D in the beginning of the chapter?

4. Drawing from this and other chapters in the book, what recommendations would you make that could have avoided the failures of Cases B and C?

GROUP ASSIGNMENT

The class is divided into groups. Each group will visit an IS department and present the following in class: an organizational chart of the department; a discussion on the department's CIO (director) and her reporting status; information on a steering committee (composition, duties); information of service support levels; and a report on the extent of IT decentralization and end-user computing in the company.

Minicase 1

Centralized Information System at Mead Corporation

Mead Corporation (Dayton, OH) is a large U.S. paper and forest products company. Mead also is in the information business, as the owner of LEXIS (legal on-line research service) and NEXIS (a news information retrieval service). The central IS department used to report to a vice president of operations and was called Information Service. Due to the large size of Mead, the company is decentralized. Several of its divisions have an option to have their own IS departments or to use the centralized IS department for corporate-wide applications. In 1980, management realized that it was necessary to reorganize the IS function. The old structure included six departments in the information service organization: operations, telecommunications, technical services, system development, operational systems, and operations research (for system analysis). There was a need for a corporate-wide network, as well as for information resources planning and control and for handling decision support applications. The function was relocated, so its CIO reports directly to the CEO. After two additional reorganizations, the department organizational structure looks like the following.

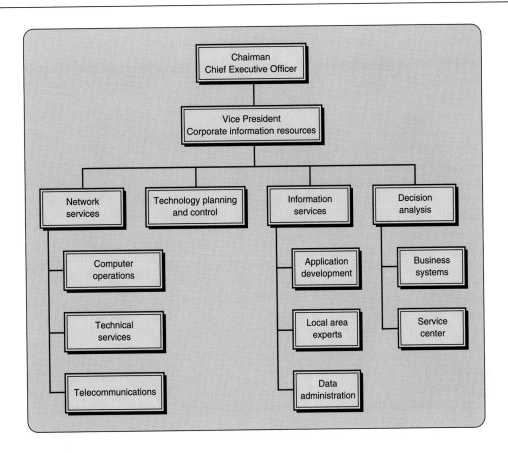

The 1990's organization shifted emphasis from end-user computing and small systems to building infrastructure and integrating application development. A major task has been to permit end-user applications and large scale business systems to cross fertilize each other.

Mead is using extensive IT planning. Recently, it shifted attention to the support of BPR at Mead. Mead is using IT to build superhighways of information rather than simply accelerate business processes. Mead also changes its relationships with its own customers, so it will be easy to do business with Mead. EDI and terminals at customers' sites are some examples.

A basic tactic of Mead is to retain central control of the IT infrastructure and distribute responsibility for building and maintaining applications in the business units. Yet, as the use of information technology has changed, Mead's centralized IS department has reorganized to focus on those new uses. Notice that the name of the centralized department has been changed to the Information Resources Department.

Questions for Minicase 1

1. Trace the changes in the centralized IS department, and relate them to the material discussed in this chapter.

2. Evaluate relationships between the centralized IS departments and end users as described in this case.

3. Analyze the tactic of centralized control over the infrastructure, and decentralized authority over building and maintaining applications.

4. Review Mead's current organizational structure. What unique feature exists in this structure?

5. Based on what you have learned in this chapter, is there anything that you would recommend for the next change in the structure?

SOURCE: This minicase was condensed from Sprague and McNurlin (1993). The figure was reproduced with permission from Barbara McNurlin.

Minicase 2

The Dilemma of the Departed Programmer

Mark had been working as a production coordinator for an association's research journal for the past five years. During that time, he developed strong editorial and journalistic skills, and had mastered his job quite well. He had, in fact, outgrown his position and was interested in seeking new and different challenges. So he took a couple of courses in programming and became quite proficient in the C++ programming language. He approached his managers about taking over some of the programming within the operation of the journal; this would include financial as well as subscription management types of issues. The journal department had been unable to get any direct support from the central IS group, so the opportunity to use Mark's skills at basically no extra cost was quite appealing.

During the next couple of years, Mark developed some fairly elaborate systems and the department became quite dependent on them for its day-to-day operations. Mark was happy because he found his expanded responsibilities to be both challenging and rewarding, and he was upgrading his skills to improve his marketability.

The following year, Mark decided to market his skills—combining both journalism and computer programming—and was able to land a very good position working in a software product development company.

Soon after he left, the journal department wanted to make modifications to the systems Mark had developed. They had no one in the department who could provide the programming skills necessary in C++. The management of the journal went to the central IS group asking for some assistance; at that time, they found out that the organization did not use C++ programming for any of its software development activity and did not have the expertise available to help the department. The manage-

ment of the journal department protested that they needed such skills and asked IS why they didn't have them available. The IS group explained that there was a plethora of languages out there and that it was unrealistic and impractical to expect them to be proficient in all of them. They further explained that the journal department should have checked with the central IS group before selecting a language for developing their systems. The management of the journal department protested to senior management, saying IS was being totally unresponsive.

The result was a major shouting match between the journal department and the central IS group, and senior management had to come up with some way to reconcile the situation.

Questions for Minicase 2

1. Based on what you know now, what could have been done to prevent this incident?

2. What kind of reconciliation can be used now in this specific case?

3. Discuss how the opportunities and pitfalls of end-user computing pertain to this case of the departed programmer.

4. Discuss how service support levels could have been helpful in avoiding the problem that occurred after Mark left.

5. Suppose an organization has instituted the service support level concept. An end user, unaware of these policies, proceeds either formally or informally to develop some type of application and ends up in the same type of predicament described in this case. How should the IS department respond to such a situation?

REFERENCES AND BIBLIOGRAPHY

1. Applegate, L. M., and J. J. Elam, "New Information Systems Leaders: A Changing Role in a Changing World" *MIS Quarterly*, December 1992.

2. Davis, F. D., "Perceived Usefulness, Perceived Ease of Use, and User Acceptance of Information Technology," *MIS Quarterly*, September 1989.

3. Davis, S. A., and R. P. Bostrum, "Training End Users: An Experimental Investigation of the Role of the Computer Interface and Training Methods," *MIS Quarterly*, Vol. 17, No. 1, March 1993.

4. Feeny D. F., et al., "Understanding the CEO/CIO Relationship" *MIS Quarterly*, December 1992.

5. Freedman, D., "Reengineering the Turf," *CIO*, November 15, 1992.

6. Fuller, M. K., and E. B. Swanson, "Information Centers as Organizational Innovation," *Journal of Management Information Systems*, Vol. 9, No. 1, Summer 1992.

7. Hammond, L. W., "Management Consideration for an Information Center," *IBM Systems Journal*, Vol. 21, No. 2, 1982

8. Hershey, G., and D. Kizzier, *Planning and Implementing End-User Information Systems*, Cincinnati: South Western Publishing Company, 1992.

9. Grupe, F. H., "Problem Solving Models that Build Effective Relationships with your Users," *Journal of Systems Management*, March 1994.

10. Gupta, Y. P., "The Chief Executive Officer and the Chief Information Officer: The Strategic Partnership," *Journal of Information Technology*, Vol. 6, 1991.

11. Jacobson, H., and J. Cardullo, "Information Centers: Boon or Bane," *Management Technology*, Sept., 1983.

12. Jarvenpaa, S. L., and B. Ivas, "Executive Involvement and Participation in the Management of Information Technology," *MIS Quarterly*, June 1991.

13. Kiely, T., "The Shape of Excellence," *CIO*, August 1992.

14. Leitheiser, R. L., and J. C. Wetherbe, "Service Support Levels: An Organized Approach to End-User Computing," *MIS Quarterly*, Vol. 10, No. 4, December 1986.

15. Mirani, R., and W. R. King, "Impacts of End-User and Information Center Characteristics on End-User Computing Support," *Journal of Management Information Systems*, Vol. 11, No. 1, 1994.

16. Moad, J., "Welcome to the Virtual IS Organization," *Datamation*, February 1, 1994.

17. Moynihan, T., "What Chief Executives and Senior Managers Want from Their IT Department," *MIS Quarterly*, March 1992.

18. Napier, H. A., "Peer Evaluation Selects Professionals," *Journal of Systems Management*, January 1980.

19. Rockart, J. F., "The Line Takes the Leadership—IS Management in a Wired Society," *Sloan Management Review*, Summer 1988.

20. Shah, H. U., et al., "Bridging the Cultural Gap Between Users and Developers," *Journal of Systems Management*, July 1994.

21. Sprague, R. H., and B. C. McNurlin, *Information Systems Management in Practice*, Englewood Cliffs, N.J.: Prentice Hall, 1993.

22. Stephens, C. S., et al., "Executive or Functional Manager? The Nature of the CIO's job," *MIS Quarterly*, December 1992.

19

CONTROL AND SECURITY OF INFORMATION SYSTEMS

Chapter Outline

Learning Objectives

After studying this chapter, you will be able to:

1. Recognize the various threats to computing facilities.

2. Distinguish between computer crimes and accidental damage to information systems.

3. Analyze the major countermeasures (controls) and their functions.

4. Describe and compare general and application controls.

5. Discuss the difficulties of implementing controls.

6. Describe the role of information systems auditing.

7. Describe the potential impacts of a disaster and the planning for disaster recovery.

8. Explain how to protect a personal computer against internal and external threats.

9. Have a vision of control and security management in the '90s.

10. Analyze implementation from a cost-benefit point of view.

19.1 THE BOMBING OF THE WORLD TRADE CENTER

ON FRIDAY, FEBRUARY 26, 1993, a bomb ripped apart the subbasement of the 110-story World Trade Center in New York City. The bombing, which killed 6 people and injured over 1,000, forced an evacuation of the huge office complex. Hundreds of financial firms were thrown into a state of chaos because they could not return to the huge office building for several weeks. Most of these companies faced the enormous and unprecedented task of restoring their networked distributed computer systems in order to resume business.

The problem was further complicated because those companies that used distributed systems relied on LANs. In contrast with mainframe environments, where companies typically have standard procedures and a plan for recovery from disasters (see Section 19.10), the users of LANs are generally unprepared. The problem in a distributed environment is that it is not enough to find a recovery site with backup systems—an approach typically used in mainframe environments. Instead, it is necessary to find office space where workers can reestablish their networks to enable continuous transactions. This means it is necessary to equip a temporary space with computers (primarily PCs), communication lines, and LANs. In addition, the employees need full office support, ranging from telephone lines and faxes to duplicating machines. To prepare ahead of time for a disaster involving a distributed system may require costly arrangements.

Fortunately for those companies that had planned ahead for such a disaster, the transition was fairly smooth, even though they were operating in a distributed environment. For example, Dean Witter Financial Services Group enacted a contingency plan, using an office equipped with PCs set aside earlier for emergency use. By the following Monday, the company was running business as usual (see picture).

Other corporations were less fortunate. Some restored their networks but could not secure telephone

Dean Witter Reynolds' temporary set-up after the World Trade Center bombing.

lines. Others had problems with their networks and, in some cases, even their contingency plans were not effective. For example, several companies with arrangements for a temporary site as a backup to their mainframe operations had problems either accessing the tapes from the vaults in the World Trade Center building or finding the tapes contaminated by smoke particles.

Disaster recovery experts say that most of the companies were simply unprepared, but the situation was especially severe for LAN-based companies. Ken Brill, president of a data-center infrastructure consulting company in Santa Fe, NM, summarized the situation: "I can protect a 20,000-square-foot data center, but how do I safeguard a million square feet of office space?"

SOURCE: Based on a story in *InformationWeek,* see McPartlin and Panettieri (1993).

 19.2 A KEY ISSUE FOR MANAGEMENT

Throughout this book, we have seen that information systems are used to increase productivity and help achieve quality. Most large, many medium and even some small corporations in the United States today are strongly dependent on IT. Their information systems have considerable strategic importance. On the other hand, as illustrated in the World Trade Center case, information systems can become a dangerous problem when they break down. The actions of people or of nature may cause an information system to function in a way different from what was planned. In such cases, damage may occur. It is important, therefore, to know how to ensure the continued operation of an IS and what to do if the system breaks down.

The opening case and incidents described in the next section point to some critical issues regarding information systems control and security. These include the following:

▼ Many hazards, some accidental and others intentional, threaten information systems.

▼ Computer crimes, criminals, and motives for committing crimes are many and varied.

▼ Damage to information systems can be substantial, both tangible and intangible.

▼ Major targets that are susceptible to conspiracies and attacks include data, hardware, networks, software, and other computing facilities.

This chapter concentrates on these and several other issues, which can be described under the scope of information systems control and security.

Information systems control and security deals with the protection of computing facilities from deliberate or accidental threats that might cause unauthorized modification, disclosure, or destruction of data or programs. It also concerns protecting the computing facilities (as well as the data) from degradation or from nonavailability of services. Some terminology of the field is described in Box 19.1.

A Closer Look BOX 19.1

INFORMATION CONTROL AND SECURITY TERMINOLOGY

Backup—An extra copy of the data and/or programs kept in a secured location(s).

Decryption—Transformation of scrambled code into intelligible data after transmission.

Encryption—Transformation of data into scrambled code prior to its transmission.

Exposure—The harm, loss, or damage that can result if something has gone wrong in an information system.

Fault tolerance—The ability of an information system to continue to operate (usually for a limited time and/or at a reduced level) when a failure occurs.

Information system controls—The procedures, de-

vices, or software that attempt to ensure that the system performs as planned.

Integrity (of data)—A guarantee of the accuracy, completeness, and reliability of data. System integrity is provided by the integrity of its components and their integration.

Threats (or hazards)—The various dangers to which a system may be exposed.

Risk—The likelihood that a threat will materialize.

Vulnerability—Given that a threat exists, the susceptibility of the system to harm caused by the threat.

The more organizations depend on computers, the more important security becomes. Organizations whose systems are properly controlled and secured could have a significant advantage over organizations that lack such controls. Therefore, information systems control and security is a topic of prime concern to senior management. Estimates concerning losses from the theft of tangible and intangible assets, destruction of data, embezzlement of funds, and fraud range from $10 billion to $50 billion annually. Some incidents are illustrated next.

▶ ## 19.3 INCIDENTS OF INFORMATION SYSTEMS BREAKDOWNS

In the opening case, we illustrated the danger faced by businesses that are dependent on computers when a disaster strikes. Information systems, however, can be damaged for many other reasons. The following incidents illustrate representative cases of breakdowns in information systems.

INCIDENT 1

Stanley Mark Rifkin obtained the electronic transfer code for Security Pacific Bank in Los Angeles, where he was previously employed as a consultant. In the fall of 1978, posing as a branch manager, he called from a public telephone and used the code to transfer $13 million from the bank to a Swiss bank account. By the time the fraud was brought to Security Pacific's attention (by the FBI), Rifkin had flown to Switzerland, converted the funds to diamonds, and returned to the United States. Only when Rifkin boasted of the feat to an ex-girlfriend (whom he was trying to impress) was he identified, convicted, and sentenced to prison.

INCIDENT 2

A Tarrant County, TX jury found Donald Gene Burleson, age 40, guilty of harmful access to a computer, a third-degree felony with a maximum penalty of 10 years in prison and a $5,000 fine.

"As far as I know, it's the first case of this type (computer virus prosecution) in the nation," said Assistant District Attorney Davis McCown. Jurors were told that Burleson planted a virus in the computer system that was used to store records at USPA & IRA Company, a Fort Worth-based insurance and brokerage firm. (A virus is a computer program, often hidden in what seems to be normal computer software, that instructs the computer to change or destroy information.)

McCown told the jury that the virus was programmed like a time bomb and was activated two days after Burleson was fired from his job. The virus eliminated 168,000 payroll records, which resulted in a one-month delay in issuing employee payroll checks. (SOURCE: condensed from *Stars and Stripes*, September 22, 1988.)

INCIDENT 3

Federal regulations introduced in 1985 prohibit telephone companies from charging for any telephone call shorter than two seconds. The previous limit had been one second; therefore, it was necessary to reprogram the billing computers. A programming error at Pacific Bell (now Pacific Telesis) classified many regular long distance calls as being less than two seconds. As a result, more than 1.6 million Californians made long distance calls during a period of three months in 1986 and were not charged for them.

The error, which caused a $30 million loss in revenue, was discovered during a routine audit during which the volume of paid calls was found to be less than the volume of actual completed calls.

As you might expect, the customers' joy was short-lived. Once discovered, the company fixed the error and billed customers for all the unpaid calls.

INCIDENT 4

On Sunday, May 8, 1988, a fire disabled a major Illinois Bell switching center in Hinsdale, IL. The outage affected the voice and data telecommunications of more than one-half million residents and hundreds of businesses, during a period ranging from two days to three weeks. The major effects on businesses were the following:

▼ Dozens of banks were hindered in cashing checks and transferring funds.

▼ At least 150 travel agencies were hindered in their ability to make reservations and print tickets.

▼ About 300 automated teller machines were shut down.

▼ Most of the cellular phone and paging systems in the area were disrupted.

▼ Hundreds of companies were hindered in their communications, both inside and outside the immediate area.

The business cost was conservatively estimated to be $300 million.

INCIDENT 5

For almost two weeks in the spring of 1993, a seemingly legitimate automated teller machine (ATM) operating in a shopping mall near Hartford, Connecticut, gave customers apologetic notes that said "sorry, no transactions are possible." Meanwhile, the machine recorded the card numbers and the personal identification numbers that hundreds of customers entered in their vain attempts to make the machine dispense cash.

On May 8, 1993, while the dysfunctional machine was still running in the shopping mall, thieves started tapping into the 24-hour automated teller network in New York City. Using counterfeit bank cards encoded with the numbers stolen from the Hartford customers, the thieves removed about $100,000 from the accounts of innocent customers. The criminals were successful in making an ATM machine do what it was supposedly *not* designed to do: breach its own security by recording bank card numbers together with personal security codes. Diebold, the nation's largest manufacturer of ATMs, would not offer any theories on how the crime was committed, which was the first of its kind—for fear of encouraging copycat efforts.

INCIDENT 6

...a software bug knocks out Singapore's telecommunications

On October 12, 1994, at 11:31 AM, two-thirds of Singapore's telecommunication system was knocked out of business. Telephones, fax machines, wireless telephones, pagers, and credit cards were useless. The disruption lasted about five hours. Hundred of thousands of people were affected.

What happened? Singapore is expanding its telecommunication system. In order to cope with increased demand, a new computer software was installed.

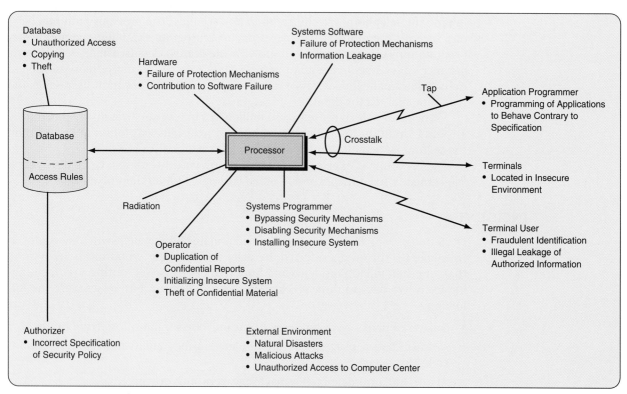

FIGURE 19.1 Security threats. (SOURCE: Gallegos and Wright, 1988, p. 12.)

But, the new software was unable to do its job. A software bug corrupted one of two common channel signaling systems that link the country's 28 telephone exchanges. Within minutes the problem spread to 26 exchanges. Unfortunately, there were no software backups. A complete disaster was prevented only because the older system was running side-by-side with the new one. The deputy president of Singapore Telecom, Mr. Lee, said that this sort of thing should not happen. "Unfortunately," he added, "with computer software, a certain amount of risk has to be taken, and it is the job of Singapore Telecom to make sure that this risk is kept at a minimum."

▶ 19.4 SYSTEM VULNERABILITY AND HAZARDS

Information systems are made up of many components that may be in several locations. Thus, each information system is vulnerable to many potential **hazards**. Figure 19.1 presents a summary of the major threats to the security of an information system. This figure, along with the incidents just described, illustrate that the hazards may be accidental, such as errors or natural disasters, or they may be intentional, such as theft, viruses, and malicious attacks on a computer center. Intentional hazards can be serious due to the large number of potential computer criminals, both internal and external to the organization. These criminals have various motives, which are difficult to anticipate.

The **vulnerability** of an information system is demonstrated in Figure 19.2, which identifies 11 vulnerable points that require protection. As an illustration, Figure 19.3 shows specific potential threats and controls in one of these 11 points (data collection). In Figure 19.1 we show a typical computer system and identify

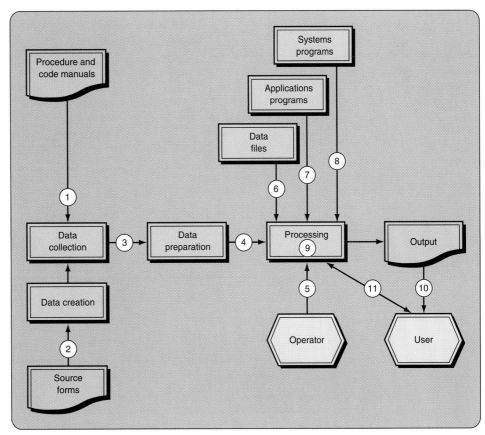

FIGURE 19.2 Vulnerable points in the various stages of information processing (boxes) and control locations (circles). (SOURCE: Hussain and Hussain, p. 190.)

areas that are considered to be security threats. Here are some specific threats to information systems:

1. Loss, theft, or corruption (change) of data.
2. Inappropriate use of data (e.g., manipulating inputs).
3. Theft of mainframe computer time.
4. Theft of equipment and/or programs.
5. Errors in handling, entering, processing, transferring, or programming data.
6. Equipment malfunctions.
7. Accidental or malicious damage to computer resources.
8. Destruction from viruses and similar attacks.

These threats to information systems can be divided into three major categories: *human errors, environmental hazards,* and *computer crimes.*

Several computer problems result from **human error.** Errors can occur in the design of the hardware and/or information system. They can also occur in the programming, testing, data collection, data entry, authorization, and instructions. Human errors contribute to the vast majority of control- and security-related problems in many organizations.

Environmental hazards include earthquakes, severe storms, floods, tornados, power failures, fires (the most common hazard), defective air-conditioning, and water cooling system failures. In addition to damage from combustion, computer resources can incur damage from other elements that accompany fire, such as smoke, heat, and water. Such hazards may disrupt normal computer operations and result in long waiting periods and exorbitant costs while computer programs and data files are recreated. The third category receives the most publicity—*computer crimes.*

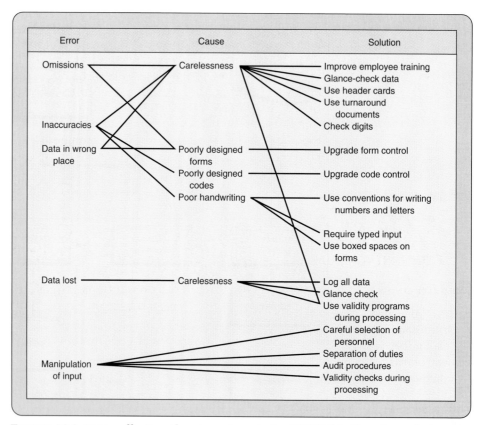

FIGURE 19.3 Data collection threats and controls (SOURCE: Hussain and Hussain, p. 195.)

▶ 19.5 COMPUTER CRIMES

Parker (1981) distinguishes between *computer abuse, computer crime*, and *computer-related crime*. **Computer abuse** is any intentional act involving computer or technology use in which a victim suffered, or could have suffered, a loss. **Computer crime** involves *illegal* computer abuse which is prosecutable under any computer-crime laws—state or federal (see Box 19.2). **Computer-related crime** is a crime in which the computer is used as a tool for executing the crime.

A Closer Look BOX 19.2

REPRESENTATIVE FEDERAL LAWS DEALING WITH COMPUTER CRIME

According to the FBI, an average robbery involves $3,000; an average white-collar crime involves $23,000; but an average computer crime involves about $600,000. The following are some federal statutes dealing with computer crime.

▼ Counterfeit Access Device and Computer Fraud Act (passed in October 1984).
▼ Computer Fraud and Abuse Act (1986).
▼ Computer Security Act of 1987.
▼ Electronic Communications Privacy Act of 1986.
▼ Electronic Funds Transfer Act of 1980.

TYPES OF COMPUTER CRIMES AND CRIMINALS

Computer crimes can occur in four ways. First, the computer can be the *target* of the crime. For example, a computer may be stolen or destroyed, or data may be destroyed by a virus. Second, the computer can be the *medium* of the attack by creating an environment in which a crime or fraud can occur. For example, false data are entered into a computer system to mislead individuals examining the financial condition of a company. Third, the computer can be the *tool* by which the crime is perpetrated. For example, a computer is used to plan a crime, but the crime does not involve a computer. Fourth, the computer can be used to *intimidate* or deceive. For instance, a stockbroker stole $50 million by convincing his clients that he had a computer program with which he could increase their earnings by 60 percent per month. In many ways, computer crimes resemble conventional crimes (see Box 19.3).

A Closer Look BOX 19.3

COMPARING CRIMES

Computer crime

▼ Use of computers to embezzle funds or assets.
▼ Destruction or alteration of software or data.
▼ Unauthorized access to and/or theft of software, equipment, or data.
▼ Unauthorized use of computers and computer services.

Conventional crime it resembles

▼ Embezzlement.
▼ Vandalism and fraud.
▼ Theft or trespassing.

▼ Petty theft, embezzlement, or joyriding.

SOURCE: Extracted from "Report on Computer Crime," U.S. Office of Technology Assessment and the American Bar Association, 1984.

Crimes can be performed by *outsiders* who penetrate a computer system (frequently via communication lines) or by *insiders* who are authorized to use the computer system but are misusing their authorization. **Hacker** is the term often used to describe outside people who penetrate a computer system. A **Cracker** is a malicious hacker who may represent a serious problem for a corporation. Computer and security experts agree that the likelihood of threats from outsiders is much less than that from insiders. For example, Allen (1977) found that in only 5 out of 89 cases were outsiders involved. Computer criminals, whether insiders or outsiders, have a distinct profile and are driven by several motives (see Box 19.4). Ironically, many employees fit this profile, but only some of them are criminals. Therefore, it is difficult to defend information systems, especially when criminals use unique attack methods.

A Closer Look BOX 19.4

THE COMPUTER CRIMINAL—PROFILE AND MOTIVATION

The profile

Sex: White males between the age of 19-30 with no criminal record. (Women tend to be accomplices.)

Occupation: Application programmer, system user, clerical personnel, student, or manager.

IQ: High IQ, bright, personable, and creative.

Appearance: Outwardly self-confident, eager, and energetic.

Approach to work: Adventurous, willing to accept technical challenge, and highly motivated.

The motivation

Economic: Urgent need for money (e.g., due to extravagant lifestyle, gambling, family sickness, or drug abuse).

Ideological: Deceiving the establishment is viewed as fair game because "the establishment deceives everyone else."

Egocentric: Beating the system is fun, challenging, and adventurous. Egocentricity seems to be the most distinguishing motive of computer criminals.

Psychological: Getting even with the employer who is perceived by the employee as cold, indifferent, and impersonal.

Other: The employee views himself as a "borrower" of software, for example, not a thief.

SOURCE: Based on Bologna (1987).

METHODS OF ATTACK

Two basic approaches are used in deliberate attacks on computer systems: data tampering and programming techniques.

Data tampering ("data diddling") is the most common approach and is often used by insiders. It involves entering false, fabricated, or fraudulent data into the computer, or changing or deleting existing data. For example, to pay for his wife's drug purchases, a savings and loan programmer transferred $5,000 into his personal account and tried to cover up the transfer with phony debit and credit transactions.

Computer criminals also use *programming techniques* to modify a computer program, either directly or indirectly. For this crime, programming skills and knowledge of the targeted systems are essential. **Programming fraud** schemes appear under many names (see Box 19.5). The most publicized attack method is the use of a **virus**. A virus receives its name from the program's ability to attach itself to other computer programs, causing them to become viruses themselves (infection). With infection, a virus can spread throughout a computer system in one or several organizations (see Figure 19.4). Due to the availability of public-domain software and widely used public networks, viruses can be spread to many

A Closer Look BOX 19.5

PROGRAMMING FRAUD SCHEMES

Programming Technique	Definition
Virus	Secret instructions inserted into programs (or data) that are innocently run during ordinary tasks. The secret instructions may destroy or alter data, as well as spread within or between computer systems.
Worm	A program which replicates itself and penetrates a valid computer system. It may spread within a network, penetrating all connected computers.
Trojan horse	An illegal program, contained within another program, that "sleeps" until some specific event occurs, then triggers the illegal program to be activated and cause damage.
Salami slicing	A program designed to siphon off small amounts of money from a number of larger transactions, so the quantity taken is not readily apparent.
Super zapping	A method of using a utility "zap" program that can bypass controls to modify programs or data.
Trap door	A technique that allows for breaking into a program code, making it possible to insert additional instructions.

businesses (see Box 19.6). Viruses are not limited to one country, they are known to spread all over the world (see Box 19.7). For further discussion of viruses and software, see Section 19.12.

When a virus is attached to a legitimate software program, the program becomes infected without the owner of the program being aware of the infection. Therefore, when the software is used, the virus spreads, causing damage to that program and possibly to others. Thus, the legitimate software is acting as a *Trojan horse*. The name Trojan horse originated from a legendary story about a large

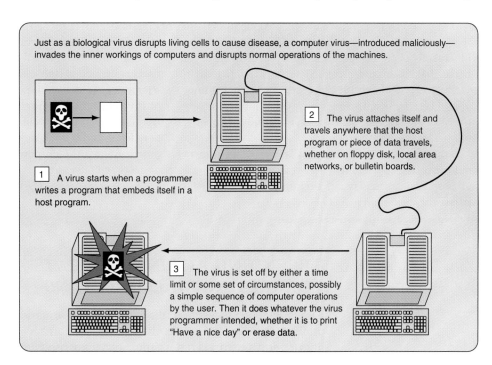

FIGURE 19.4 How a computer virus can spread. (SOURCE: Courtesy of Thumbscan.)

hollow wooden horse filled with Greek soldiers, which was given as a gift to the city of Troy, whose walls were too strong for the Greek army to conquer. Unsuspecting, the citizens of Troy wheeled the horse inside the gates. Later that night, the Greek soldiers emerged from the horse, opened the gates for their fellow soldiers, and attacked the enemy from within the city to win the war.

IT At Work BOX 19.6

VIRUS ON NETWORKS

In November 1988, a computer virus spread through a Department of Defense communications network that linked computers in military complexes and university campuses. The virus, planted by a Cornell University graduate student (see Exercise 4), did not destroy data on the computers' data files. But it did take up memory and slowed down processing on the computers by repeatedly reproducing itself. John McAfee, director of the

Computer Security Industry Association in Santa Clara, California, estimated the damage to be at least $97 million (including one million hours to restore the memory). The student was caught and convicted of this crime.

Critical Thinking Issue: If a student can cause such damage, would you ever be able to trust a computer that is connected to a network? ▲

A Closer Look BOX 19.7

 **GLOBAL PERSPECTIVE**

INTERNATIONAL ASPECTS OF SECURITY AND VIRUSES

Computer crimes are spreading throughout the world (see Scherizen [1993]). Some of the most notorious viruses were developed internationally and transmitted across several continents. The *Michelangelo* virus was first reported in April 1991 in Sweden and the Netherlands. It is set to go off in many countries every March 6, the birthday of the Renaissance painter and sculptor. The virus attacked about 30,000 PCs in 1992 worldwide, creating hysteria in the business community. It became a *cause célèbre* for the vulnerability of our computerized society. The hysteria got people shaken up and increased security awareness. In March 1993 and March 1994, the virus caused only minor damage because people were ready. Other internationally known viruses are the *Pakistani Brain*, *nVir* from Germany, and the *Jerusalem* virus from Israel.

In the Netherlands, hackers now face up to six years in jail for hacking a system that serves a common use, such as a hospital database. For entering any other secured data system, the maximum penalty is four years.

According to the Oct. 26, 1992, issue of *Computerworld*, foreign governments are trying to steal corporate secrets. Nations that are active in economic espionage are China, France, Japan, Israel, Russia, Sweden, Switzerland, and the United Kingdom. In his best seller, *The Cuckoo's Egg*, Cliff Stoll describes how he electronically tracked down German hackers who were breaking into computers at American and European military and defense industry-related sites to steal information for the KGB.

According to *BusinessWeek*, August 1, 1988, German hackers created a club called the Chaos Computer Club (Hamburg, Germany) to promote creative chaos, such as uncovering a security hole in the videotext system of the German telephone system. The club publishes a weekly newsletter and a book on tips about breaking into computer systems. The purpose is to make people aware and protect themselves against break-ins.

▶ 19.6 DEFENDING AGAINST THREATS AND CORRECTING MALFUNCTIONS

Knowing about major potential threats to information systems is important, but understanding ways to defend against these threats is equally critical. Defending information systems is not a simple or inexpensive task for the following reasons:

▼ Hundreds of potential threats exist.

▼ Computing resources may be situated in many locations.

▼ Information assets are controlled by many individuals.

▼ Computer networks can be outside the organization and difficult to protect.

▼ Rapid technological changes make some controls obsolete as soon as they are installed.

▼ Many computer crimes are undetected for a long period of time, so it is difficult to "learn from experience."

▼ People tend to violate security procedures because the procedures are inconvenient.

▼ Many computer criminals who are caught often go unpunished (no deterrent effect).

▼ The amount of computer knowledge necessary to commit computer crimes is usually minimal.

▼ The cost of preventing hazards can be very high. Therefore, most organizations simply cannot afford to protect against all possible hazards.

▼ It is difficult to conduct a cost–benefit justification for controls before an attack occurs.

Therefore, organizing an appropriate defense system is one of the major activities of any prudent IS or functional manager who controls information resources.

Protection of IT is accomplished by inserting controls—defense mechanisms—which are intended to *prevent* accidental hazards, *deter* intentional acts, *detect* problems as early as possible, *enhance damage recovery*, and *correct problems*. Controls can be integrated into hardware and software during the system development phase (a most efficient approach). They can also be implemented once the system is in operation or during its maintenance. The important point is that defense should stress **prevention**; it does no good after the crime. Since there are many threats, there are also many defense mechanisms. In this section, some representative controls are described.

Controls are designed to protect all the components of an information system. Specifically, controls protect data, software, hardware, and networks.

DEFENSE STRATEGIES (HOW DO WE PROTECT?)

There are several types of strategies that can be used to defend an information system. The selection of a specific strategy depends on the objective of the defense and the perceived cost-benefit.

The following are the major **defense strategies:**

1. *Prevention and deterrence.* Prevent the threat from occurring. For example, properly designed controls will not allow errors to occur, will deter criminals from attacking the system, and better yet will deny access to unauthorized people. It is frequently more economical to prevent an undesirable act, through **deterrence**, than to detect and correct it at a later date.

2. *Detection.* Detect the malfunction early. In such cases, it is important to detect the malfunction as early as possible. It may not be economically feasible to prevent all hazards, and preventive measures may not work. Therefore, unprotected systems are vulnerable to attack. Like a fire, the earlier it is detected, the easier it is to combat, and smaller is the damage. **Detection** can be performed in many cases by using special diagnostic software.

3. *Limitation.* Minimize losses once a malfunction has occurred. Users typically want their systems back in operation as quickly as possible. This can be ac-

complished by including a *fault-tolerant system* that permits operation in a degraded mode until full recovery is made. If a fault-tolerant system does not exist, a quick and expensive recovery must take place.

4. *Recovery.* Plan to fix a damaged information system as quickly as possible. Replacing rather than repairing components is one way for fast recovery.

5. *Correction.* Correct damaged systems to eliminate the problem or at least minimize the chance of it occurring again. Sometimes it is necessary to introduce improved controls to prevent reoccurring problems.

Remember that controls cost money and, in most cases, it is better to use only a limited number of controls. It is basically a question of economics, since it is senseless to invest two dollars to prevent the loss of one. Therefore, a careful cost–benefit analysis is needed for each control (see Section 19.11).

TYPES OF CONTROLS

Controls play different roles in the defense of a computer system. A typical highly-secured system is shown in Figure 19.5. Defense is geared against insiders (inside line) and outsiders (outside line). Note the physical shield that the user must pass through (follow the footsteps). The nonphysical (logical, administrative) controls are shown by solid lines with arrows. There are many other types of controls; some are intended to protect against human errors, while others are designed to protect against natural forces.

Information system controls can be divided into two major groups: general (system) controls and application controls. **General controls** are established to protect the system regardless of the specific application. For example, protecting

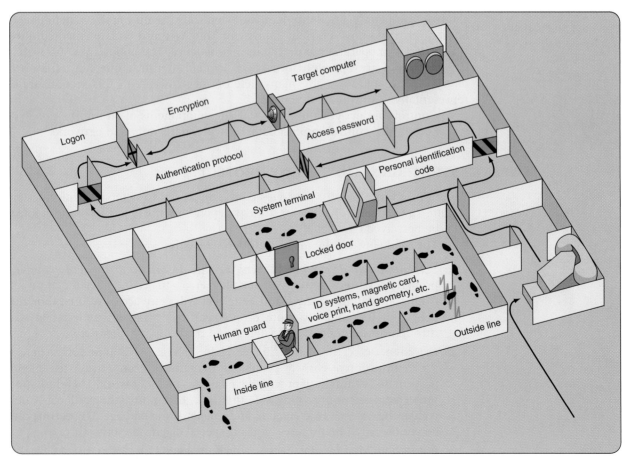

FIGURE 19.5 The defense. (SOURCE: *Discover*, November 1983, p. 34.)

hardware and controlling access to the data center are independent of the specific application. Major categories of general controls are physical controls, access controls, data security controls, communications (networks) controls, and administrative controls. Details are provided in Section 19.7.

Application controls are safeguards that are intended to protect specific applications. Details are provided in Section 19.8. The IS controls, regardless of their nature, can be viewed as providing layers of security mechanisms (or barriers).

▶ 19.7 GENERAL CONTROLS

There are many types of general controls, ranging from physical controls to administrative controls. Some are described next.

PHYSICAL CONTROLS

Physical security refers to the protection of computer facilities and resources. This includes protecting physical property such as computers, data centers, software, manuals, and networks (see Box 19.8).

A Closer Look BOX 19.8

PHYSICAL CONTROL INCIDENTS

It is easy to steal computer parts. Roberto Gomez depended on building security guards to protect the PCs in his department. He thought that the guards would challenge any person seen removing a computer from the job site. He realized the error in his thinking when he discovered that a thief had removed all of the internal boards of several PCs. It cost more than $5,000 to replace the boards, which could have been easily concealed in a briefcase or a purse. Thieves are especially interested in 486 and Pentium chips.

Stealing laptops for sensitive data. Thieves have been busy lately in almost every large city in the world. The target is laptop computers. Thieves reportedly have special success at hotels and conference rooms in convention centers. While the computers themselves may bring only several hundred dollars each, the thieves are apparently more interested in the trade secrets and other sensitive data stored on the hard disks. One way to protect trade secrets and other sensitive data is to make sure that the information is always encrypted. A small chip added to a computer restricts unauthorized users from using the computer.

(SOURCE: For the first incident, private communication; for the second incident, *Internal Auditor*, February 1993.)

Physical security is the first line of defense and usually the easiest to construct. Physical security provides protection against most natural hazards as well as against some human hazards. Appropriate physical security may include several controls such as the following:

1. Appropriate design of the data center. For example, the site should be noncombustible and waterproof.
2. Shielding against electromagnetic fields.
3. Good fire prevention, detection, and extinguishing systems.
4. Emergency power shutoff, and backup batteries, which must be maintained in operational condition.
5. Sprinkler system, water pumps, and adequate drainage facilities. A better solution is fire-enveloping Halon gas systems.

6. Properly designed, maintained, and operated air-conditioning systems.

7. Motion detector alarms that detect physical intrusion.

ACCESS CONTROL

Access control is the restriction of unauthorized user access to a portion of a computer system or to the entire system. To gain access, a user must first be *authorized*. Then, when the user attempts to gain access, she must be *authenticated*. Access to a computer system basically consists of two steps: (1) access to the system, and (2) access to specific commands, transactions, privileges, programs, and data within the system. Access control software is commercially available for large mainframes, minicomputers, personal computers, local area networks, and dial-in communications networks.

Access procedures match every valid user with a unique user identifier (UID). They also provide an authentication method to verify that users requesting access to the computer system are really who they claim to be. User identification can be accomplished when each user is identified by the following:

▼ Something only the user *knows*, such as a password.

▼ Something only the user *has*, for example, a magnetic card or a token.

▼ Something only the user *is*, such as a signature, voice, fingerprint, or retinal (eye) scan. **Biometric controls** are finding increased application as an authentication method in sophisticated installations (see Box 19.9).

A *Closer Look* BOX 19.9

◀ EMERGING TECHNOLOGY

BIOMETRICS

Biometric technology is defined as an "automated method of verifying the identity of a person, based on physiological or behavioral characteristics." The most common biometrics are the following.

▼ **Fingerprints.** Each time a user wants access, he is identified by matching a fingerprint against a template containing the authorized person's fingerprints (see photo).

▼ **Hand geometry.** Similar to fingerprints, except the verifier uses a television-like camera to take a picture of the user's hand. Certain characteristics of the hand (e.g., finger length and thickness) are electronically compared against the information stored in the computer.

▼ **Blood vessel pattern in the retina of a person's eye.** A match is attempted between the pattern of the blood vessels in the back-of-the-eye retina which is being scanned and a prestored picture of the retina.

▼ **Voice.** A match is attempted between the user's voice and the voice pattern stored on templates.

▼ **Signature.** Signatures are matched against the prestored authentic signature. This method can supplement a photo-card ID system.

Fingerprint identification control system.

▼ **Keystroke dynamics.** A match of the person's keyboard pressure and speed against prestored information.

(SOURCE: Based on Sherman, R. L., "Biometrics: The Right Look Can Open Doors," *Security Management*, October 1992.)

DATA SECURITY CONTROLS

Data security is concerned with protecting data from accidental or intentional disclosure to unauthorized persons, or from unauthorized modification or destruction. Data security functions are implemented through operating systems, security access control programs, database/data communications products, recommended backup/recovery procedures, application programs, and external control procedures. Data security must address the following issues:

▼ Confidentiality of data. ▼ Critical nature of data.
▼ Access control. ▼ Integrity of data.

Two basic principles should be reflected in data security.

1. *Minimal privilege.* Only the information a user needs to carry out an assigned task should be made available to him.
2. *Minimal exposure.* Once a user gains access to sensitive information, he has the responsibility of protecting it by making sure only people whose duties require it obtain knowledge of this information while it is being processed, stored, or in transit.

Data integrity is the condition that exists as long as accidental or intentional destruction, alteration, or loss of data *does not* occur. It is the preservation of data for its intended use.

COMMUNICATIONS (NETWORK) CONTROLS

Several controls are available to protect the communication networks against outside threats. Most common are communications access control systems, encryption methods, and cable testers. An access control system guards against unauthorized dial-in attempts. **Encryption** methods guard against the alteration of data and against viewing select information during transmission and reception.

Many companies use an access protection strategy that requires authorized users to "dial in" with a preassigned personal identification number (PIN). This strategy may be enhanced by a unique and frequently changing password. A communications access control system authenticates the user's PIN and password. Many security systems proceed one step further and accept calls only from designated telephone numbers. The system breaks the original connection and calls the user back at the number where that user is expected to be. Such access control systems never allow incoming calls to directly gain access to the computer system.

Encryption involves encoding regular digitized text into unreadable scrambled text or numbers and decoding it upon receipt (see Figure 19.6). Encryption accomplishes three purposes: (1) identification (helps identify legitimate senders and receivers), (2) control (prevents changing a transaction or message), and (3) privacy (impedes eavesdropping). A widely accepted encryption algorithm is the Data Encryption Standard (DES), produced by the U.S. National Bureau of Standards. Many software products are available for encryption. Encryption can be further enhanced by *traffic padding*. A computer generates random data that are intermingled with real data, making it virtually impossible for an intruder to identify the true data.

A popular defense of LANs is troubleshooting. For example, one can use a *cable tester* to find almost any fault that can occur with LAN cabling. Another protection can be provided by *protocol analyzers*, which allow the user to inspect the contents of information packets as they travel through the network. Recent analyzers use *expert systems*, which interpret the volume of data collected by the analyzers. Some companies offer integrated LAN troubleshooting (a tester and an intelligent analyzer). One such product is LAN Meter (from Fluke Corporation).

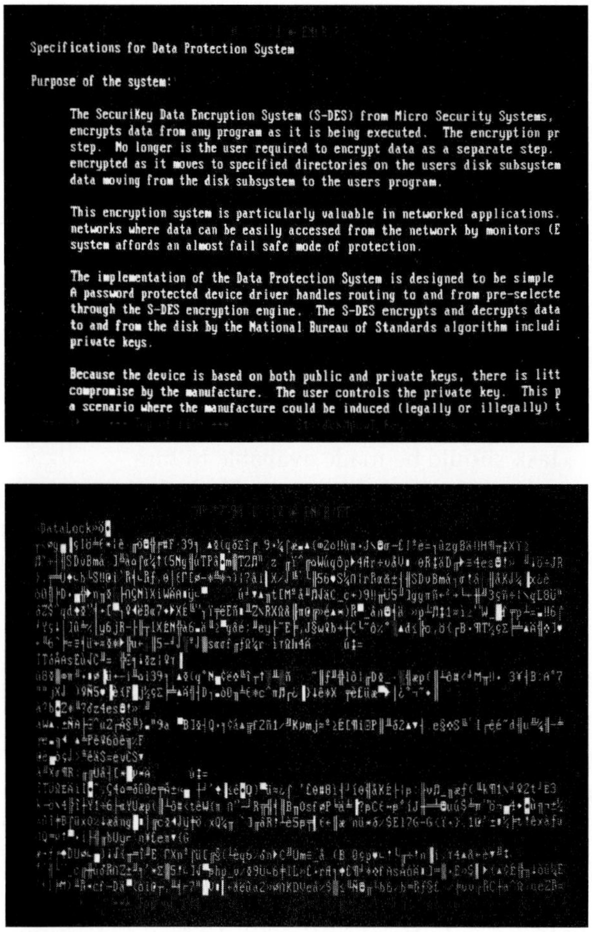

FIGURE 19.6 Encryption of data as executed by Securi-Data, the DEC encryption device. The encryption and decryption are accomplished through hardware and software special procedures.

ADMINISTRATIVE CONTROLS

Administrative controls refer to management whose objective is to increase computer security. While the previously discussed controls were technical in nature, administrative controls deal with issuing guidelines and monitoring compliance with the guidelines. Several administrative controls can be established to enhance security and reduce errors. Representative examples include the following:

▼ Appropriate selection, training, and supervision of employees, especially in accounting and information systems.

▼ Fostering company loyalty.

▼ Immediately revoking access privileges of dismissed, resigned, or transferred employees.

▼ Requiring periodic modification of access controls (e.g., passwords).

▼ Developing programming and documentation standards (to make auditing easier and to use the standards as guides for employees).

▼ Insisting on security bonds or malfeasance insurance for key employees.

▼ Instituting separation of duties (see Box 19.10).

▼ Holding periodic random audits of the system.

OTHER GENERAL CONTROLS

Several other types of controls are considered general. Representative examples include the following:

A Closer Look BOX 19.10

SEPARATION OF DUTIES

Many functions are performed by data center employees such as: control clerk, computer operator, data (tape) librarian, data entry employee, systems analyst, database administrator, internal auditor, programmers (development, maintenance), security administrator, terminal operator, telecommunication technician, users (of various kinds), trainer, help center employee, and trouble-shooter.

In large organizations one or more individuals may be assigned to each function. However, in small organizations, some of these functions must be combined into one job. When one person is responsible for several tasks, there is a greater chance for either intentional crime and/or accidental error in the system. Therefore, organizations may want to *separate* and divide the computer functions among individuals as much as possible, subject to physical, economical, technological, and organizational constraints.

▼ *Programming controls.* Errors in programming may result in costly problems (e.g., see Incident 3 in Section 19.3). Causes include the use of incorrect algorithm or programming instructions, carelessness, inadequate testing and configuration management, or lax security. Controls include training, establishing standards for testing and configuration management, and enforcing documentation standards.

▼ *Misunderstandings or misinterpretations.* Manuals are often a source of problems because they are difficult to interpret or may be out of date. Accurate writing, standardization updating, and testing are examples of appropriate documentation control.

▼ *System development controls.* System development controls assure that a system is developed according to established policies and procedures. Conformity with budget, timing, security measures, and quality and documentation requirements must be maintained.

▶ 19.8 APPLICATION CONTROLS

General controls are intended to protect the computing facilities and provide security for hardware, software, data, and networks. However, general controls do not protect the *content* of each specific application. Therefore, application controls need to be used. These controls are frequently built into the applications (e.g., they are part of the software) and are usually written as validation rules. For example, a simple rule can be the following: "In totaling numbers, sum each row, then sum each column; the grand total of the columns and rows must be the same."

Application controls can be classified into three major categories: *input controls*, *processing controls*, and *output controls*.

INPUT CONTROLS

Input controls are designed to prevent data alteration or loss. Data are checked for accuracy, completeness, and consistency. Input controls are very important; they prevent the GIGO (garbage-in, garbage-out) situation. Examples of input controls are the following:

▼ *Completeness.* Items should be of a specific length, (e.g., nine digits for a social security number). Addresses should include a street, city, state, and zip code.

▼ *Format.* Formats should be a standard form. For example, sequences must be preserved (zip code comes after an address).

▼ *Range.* Only data within a specified range are acceptable. For example, zip code ranges between 10,000 to 99,999, the age of a person cannot be larger than 120, and hourly wages cannot exceed $30.

▼ *Consistency.* Data collected from two or more sources need to be matched. For example, in medical history data, males cannot be pregnant. *Check totals* are a useful methodology in which intermediate totals are checked. *Hash totals* use various algorithms to check data before and after transmission. For example, the algorithm sums the data row by row and column by column even though the units are not of the same dimension (e.g., adding $1000 + 52 days + 200 units + 60 lb. equals a "hash" total of 1312). Then, the derived total is compared with the keyed-in hash total.

PROCESSING CONTROLS

Processing controls assure that data are complete, valid, and accurate when being processed and that programs have been properly executed. Typical controls are the following:

▼ *Double processing.* Executing the same task using two different programs (e.g., one written in COBOL, the other in FORTRAN).

▼ *Sequencing.* The computer can be programmed to call attention to anything that is out of order (e.g., missing data).

▼ *Transaction counts.* The number of transactions processed is compared against the number of transactions inputted.

▼ *Software support.* Many input, processing, and output controls are provided by special software packages known as *performance monitoring systems.* Such software protects the data and programs from many threats.

These programs allow only authorized users to access certain programs or facilities and monitor the computer's use by individuals.

OUTPUT CONTROLS

Output controls ensure that the results of computer processing are accurate, valid, complete, and consistent. It is necessary to study the nature of common output errors, the causes of such errors, and possible controls to deal with problems. Also, it is necessary to assure that outputs are sent only to authorized personnel.

▶ 19.9 AUDITING INFORMATION SYSTEMS

Controls are established to insure that information systems work properly. Controls may be installed in the original system, or they can be added on by the IS department, end users, or others (e.g., vendors) once a system is in operation. Installing controls is necessary but not sufficient. It is also necessary to answer questions such as the following: Are controls installed as intended? Are they effective? Did any breach of security occur? If so, what actions are required to prevent reoccurrences? These questions need to be answered by independent and unbiased observers. These observers perform the information system *auditing* task.

An **audit** is an important part of any control system. In an organizational setting, it is usually referred to as a regular *examination* and *check* of financial and accounting records and procedures. Auditing is executed by specially trained professionals who may be internal employees or external consultants. In the information system environment, auditing can be viewed as an additional layer of controls or safeguards.

TYPES OF AUDITORS AND AUDITS

Two types of auditors (and audits) can be observed: *internal* and *external*. An *internal auditor* is usually a corporate employee who is not a member of the IS department. The auditor can be an individual who reports directly to the CEO, the vice president of administration, or a member of the controller's office. Information systems auditing is usually a part of the accounting internal auditing and is frequently done by corporate internal auditors. Some large corporations have internal audit committees that report directly to the board of directors. Some portions of IS auditing are done by members of the IS department. Their major concern is quality control, and ensuring that systems function as intended.

An *external auditor* is a corporate outsider. This type of audit reviews the findings of the internal audit and the inputs, processing, and outputs of information systems. The external audit of information systems is frequently a part of the overall external auditing performed by a certified public accounting (CPA) firm. External audits of information systems are usually much more limited in scope than internal ones.

The scope of information systems auditing (which used to be called electronic data processing [EDP] auditing) can be very broad in nature and is outside the scope of this book. Auditing looks at all potential hazards and controls in information systems. It focuses attention on topics such as new systems development, operations and maintenance, data integrity, software application, security and privacy, disaster planning and recovery, purchasing, budgets and expenditures, chargebacks, vendor management, documentation, insurance and bonding, training, cost control and productivity. Several guidelines are available to assist auditors in their jobs. SAS No. 55 is a comprehensive guide provided by the American Institute of Certified Public Accountants (see *The Journal of Accountancy*, September 1990). Also, guidelines are available from the Institute of Internal Auditors, Orlando, Florida.

Auditors attempt to answer questions such as these:

▼ Are there sufficient controls in the system?

▼ Which areas are *not* covered by controls?

▼ Which controls are *not* necessary?

▼ Are the controls implemented properly?

▼ Are the controls effective; that is, do they check the output of the system?

▼ Is there a clear separation of duties?

▼ Are there procedures to assure compliance with the controls?

▼ Are there procedures to assure reporting and corrective actions in case of violations of controls?

Two types of audits are used to answer these questions. The *operational audit* determines whether the IS function is working properly. The *compliance audit* determines whether controls have been implemented properly and are adequate.

HOW IS AUDITING EXECUTED?

There are many procedures for IS auditing. They can be classified into three categories: auditing *around* the computer, auditing *through* the computer, and auditing *with* the computer.

Auditing around the computer means verifying processing by checking for known outputs using specific inputs. Therefore, it is assumed that there is no need to check the processing if the correct output is obtained. The best usage for this approach is for systems that produce a limited range of outputs. This approach is fast and inexpensive, but it may give false results. For example, two errors may compensate for each other, resulting in correct output.

In the approach of *auditing through the computer,* inputs, outputs, and processing are checked. This approach is more complex and is usually supported by special tools. Some methods used by auditors are reviewing program logic, test data, and controlling processing and reprocessing.

Auditing with the computer means using a combination of client data, auditor software, and client and auditor hardware. It allows the auditor to perform tasks such as simulating payroll program logic using live data.

Auditors use several tools to increase their effectiveness and efficiency. Typical tools are checklists, formulas, and charts. These can be executed manually or computerized. Several computer programs are available to support the auditor's job. These include programs for testing, summarizing, sampling, and matching. Generalized Audit Software (GAS) is a set of programs designed to support auditing.

SOURCES OF INFORMATION FOR AUDITOR'S REPORTS

Auditors gather information from sources such as samples of inputs and outputs, interviews with end users and information systems employees, application programs tested using the auditor's data, and reviews of previous audit reports.

Audit results are presented in special reports submitted to the audit committee. These reports call attention to weaknesses and deficiencies and suggest possible remedies. They also highlight positive aspects of the system. Some reports are very comprehensive and include detailed analysis and recommendations.

Often it is necessary to trace a transaction through each processing step (when, where, by whom, and so on). The procedure (or document) that describes such tracing is called an **audit trail**. In manual systems it is fairly easy to conduct an audit trail. However, in computerized systems, this may not be so easy. One task of auditing is to provide procedures for audit trails and to execute them when needed.

Auditors and security consultants may try to break into a computer system, in what is called a *simulated attack,* in order to find weak points in the system (see Box 19.11). In some cases, companies hire famous hackers to do the job.

A Closer Look BOX 19.11

"HACKERS" AUTHORIZED TO BREAK INTO THE STATE OF ILLINOIS INFORMATION SYSTEM

Auditors for the State of Illinois issued a public statement on July 1, 1993, in which they notified the State that they were successful in their mission of breaking into the Central Computer Facility which serves 109 state agencies. The auditors pulled off their mission with "disturbing ease." An authorized hacker, operating from a remote location, was able to break into the system, and read, modify, and delete data such as payroll and prison records. Real hackers could have altered the security structure and negated system integrity. The security system, which was thought to be satisfactory, was enhanced immediately and all known security flaws were fixed.

▶ 19.10 IMPLEMENTING CONTROLS AND DISASTER PLANNING

Implementing controls in an organization can be a very complicated task, particularly in large, decentralized companies where administrative controls may be difficult to enforce. Lee (1990) suggests that EDP auditing be expanded to include end-user computing. An interesting question is whose responsibility is it to implement controls? Hutt (1988) outlines the role of management in planning and enforcing controls. Of the many issues involved in implementing controls, two are described here: planning and organizing, and disaster recovery planning.

PLANNING AND ORGANIZING

A comprehensive control and security management program must begin with the establishment of a formal, documented, organization-wide **security policy**, endorsed by the highest levels of management in the organization. An example of such a program, composed of five parts, was developed by Fine (1983) (see Table 19.1).

Fine's *total computer security* can be envisioned as a horizontal beam supported by eight pillars. The pillars are the five management issues of Table 19.1 and three technical issues: *physical security*, *control*, and *system security*. These three support the integrity and confidentiality of an organization's information systems.

Each of the program's pillars must be carefully planned and properly managed. This may not be a simple task, since each of the pillars is fairly broad. For example, the responsibility pillar includes 15 topics (see Table 19.2), each of which can be further broken down into several subtopics.

Developing a security policy begins with a detailed analysis of current equipment, functions performed, data contained, ease of access, security devices, and potential losses. Following this analysis, a policy can be drafted that will focus on employees as well as other assets (hardware, software, and data). Any security policy developed should deal with threats proactively, not just reactively. For each identified threat, the policy should describe not only the necessary protection, but also the actions to be taken if the threats materialize. Stringent policies, surprise audits, and strenuous **security awareness** programs are excellent ways of protecting the company's information systems.

The structure of the security unit depends on the size and structure of the organization and the importance of its information systems. In large organizations, there might be an IS security manager who is in charge of a staff of security administrators. The security manager and security administrators typically form a

---

Table 19.1 **A Framework for a Comprehensive Control and Security Program**

- *A defined and documented computer security policy.* This part specifies the scope and direction of the company's involvement in computer security.
- *Standards and procedures.* These are the detailed, day-to-day guidelines that should be followed during any type of IS operation or activity. They are designed to help protect the firm's computing assets from most security threats.
- *An assignment of responsibility for computer security.* Division of responsibility among the computer security unit, IS department, personnel department, and top management is outlined in this section of the program.
- *A personnel security program.* This part includes procedures for employees' employment cycles, from preemployment to postemployment. This program should address areas such as preemployment screening and background checks, condition of employment agreements, security training, bonding, employee morale, and employee termination procedures.
- *A complete asset-threat inventory.* The inventory provides a set of safeguards designed to protect a firm's computing assets against predetermined potential threats. It includes identification and valuation of assets, identification of potential threats, risk assessment, identification of potential safeguards, selection of safeguards, adoption of a contingency plan, testing of the contingency plan, an auditing plan, and ongoing computer security evaluation.
- *Introduction of user awareness program.* A key to any successful security program is user security awareness. A formal security awareness program can be very beneficial. Companies use posters, fliers, videos, and even special events and promotions to increase awareness.

SOURCE: Based on Fine (1983).

Table 19.2 **Responsibilities of the IT Security Function**

1. Vulnerability assessments.
2. Control recommendations.
3. Compliance checking.
4. Assistance in control implementation.
5. User and management education.
6. Development of security policies, standards, and guidelines.
7. Participation in systems development efforts.
8. Contingency planning.
9. Special user-specific consulting and research.
10. Security administration (e.g., user IDs, passwords, and clearance levels).
11. System breach investigation and prosecution assistance.
12. Establishment and maintenance of accountability and responsibility.
13. Documentation of a targeted, secured computing environment.
14. Representation of the organization at external meetings (e.g., security standard-setting meetings).
15. Evaluation and selection of systems security-related products and services.

SOURCE: Based on Wood (1990).

centralized security unit, supported by a network of decentralized security coordinators residing in user departments. In smaller organizations, the director of the IS department may be in charge of security.

Security administration is also the responsibility of line managers, who should be familiar with the security policy. Line managers are responsible for protecting all resources in their possession and for ensuring that employees are aware of and abide by established security policies and procedures.

DISASTER RECOVERY PLANNING

An important element in any security system is the **disaster recovery** plan. A disaster may result from many causes. These can be divided into natural causes and those caused by people. Natural causes include earthquakes, fire, flood, hurricanes, ice storms, lightning, sand storms, snow, and tornadoes. Human causes include blackouts (power failure), communication outages, explosions (bombing), fire (arson), gas leaks, labor strikes, oil leaks, power fluctuations, riots, radioactive fallout, structural failure, and sabotage. Destruction of all (or most) of the computing facilities can cause significant damage. Therefore, it is difficult for an organization to obtain insurance for its computers and information system without showing a satisfactory disaster prevention and recovery plan.

Disaster recovery is the chain of events linking planning to protection to recovery. The following are some key thoughts by Knoll (1986):

▼ The purpose of a recovery plan is to keep the business running after a disaster occurs. Both the IS department and line management should be involved in preparation of the plan. Each function in the business should have a valid recovery capability plan.

▼ Recovery planning is part of asset protection. Every organization should assign responsibility to management to identify and protect assets within their spheres of functional control.

▼ Planning should focus first on recovery from a total loss of all capabilities.

▼ Proof of capability usually involves some kind of test. The test is the most important vehicle for keeping the recovery plan current.

▼ The plan should be kept in a safe place; copies should be given to all key managers; and the plan should be audited periodically.

▼ All critical applications must be identified and their recovery procedures addressed in the plan.

▼ The plan should be written so that it will be effective in case of disaster, not just in order to satisfy the auditors.

Disaster recovery planning can be very complex, and it may take several months to complete (see Butler [1992]). Using special software, the planning job can be expedited (see Box 19.12).

IT At Work BOX 19.12

PC-BASED SOFTWARE PROVIDES A USEFUL DISASTER PLAN

Hurricane Hugo hit Charleston, South Carolina, on Friday, September 20, 1989. Electrical power was knocked out for nine days. However, Heritage Trust Credit Federal (a credit union) resumed normal operation by the following Tuesday.

The credit union had developed a disaster recovery plan supported by a battery operated, PC-based software (Recovery Pac, from Computer Security Consultants, Ridgefield, CN). Both internal and external auditors were involved in the plan. When a disaster occurred, the software was to be activated. The software tracks the crisis and suggests the best method of handling it. The software

is flexible enough to guide users through problems that have not been anticipated in the tests or the original plan.

Other representative software products include the Total Recovery Planning system and PANAMAX. For a comprehensive list of risk and recovery planning software, see *Computerworld*, March 13, 1989; *Data Center Manager*, January/February 1990, p. 40; *Networking Management*, June 1992, p. 25; *InfoWorld Direct*, May 1993, p. 42; and *Software Magazine*, June 1993, pp. 67–68.

Critical Thinking Issue: What would have been the situation if there were no recovery plan in place? ▲

Disaster avoidance, a relatively new aspect of disaster planning, is oriented toward prevention. The idea is to minimize the chance of avoidable disasters occurring (such as fire or other human-caused threats). For example, many companies use a device called uninterrupted power supply (UPS), which provides power in case of a power outage.

In the event of a major disaster, it is often necessary to move the computing facility to another **backup** location. Two major alternatives exist. External *hot-site* vendors provide access to a fully configured backup data center (see Box 19.13). External *cold-site* vendors provide empty office space with special flooring, venti-

---

IT At Work BOX 19.13

TWO BROKERAGE COMPANIES COPE WITH AN EARTHQUAKE

On the evening of October 17, 1989, a major earthquake hit San Francisco, California, and Charles Schwab and Company was ready. Within a few minutes, the company's disaster plan was activated. Programmers, engineers, and backup computer tapes of October 17th transactions were flown on a chartered jet to Carlstadt, New Jersey. There, a hot-site was provided by Comdisco Disaster Recovery Service. The next morning, the company resumed normal operation.

Montgomery Securities on the other hand had no backup recovery plan. On October 18, the day after the quake, the traders had to use telephones rather than computers to execute trades. Montgomery lost revenues of $250,000 to $500,000 during this one day.

Critical Thinking Issues: Why is it so important for a brokerage house to have a recovery plan? Is it just because of the loss of revenues? ▲

SOURCE: Based on a story in *BusinessWeek*, November 13, 1989.

lation, and wiring. In an emergency, the stricken company moves its own (or leased) computers to the site.

One of the simplest ways to protect information systems is by backing up data and programs and keeping the backups in a safe place.

Physical computer security is an integral part of a total security system. Cray Research, a leading manufacturer of supercomputers, has incorporated a corporate security plan as described in Box 19.14.

IT At Work BOX 19.14

A CORPORATE SECURITY PLAN IN ACTION

The corporate data center (Eagan, MN) is used not only for its own needs but also as a showcase and demonstration site for customers and researchers. The corporate security plan covers:

▼ Electrical power (protection, backup)

▼ Air-conditioning

▼ Fire protection and alarms

▼ Heating

Corporate computers are monitored automatically and controlled centrally. *Graphic displays* show both normal status and disturbances. All the devices controlled are represented as *icons* on floor-plan graphics. These icons can change colors (e.g., green means normal, red

signifies a problem). The icons can flash as well. Corrective action messages are displayed whenever appropriate. The alarm system includes over 1000 alarms. Operators can be alerted, even at remote locations, in less than one second.

The security system is also integrated with a productivity monitoring and cost-effectiveness system concerning the buildings. Cost issues are addressed by looking at specific information such as the possibility of reducing energy costs in the data center, reducing maintenance and operations costs, and assuring an optimal power usage.

Critical Thinking Issue: Why is a security system tied with a productivity system? ▲

▶ 19.11 RISK MANAGEMENT AND COST–BENEFIT ANALYSIS

It is not economical to guarentee protection against every possible threat. Therefore, an IT security program must provide a process for assessing threats and deciding which ones to ignore, reduce, or eliminate. Installation of control measures is based on a balance between the cost of controls and the need to reduce or eliminate threats. Such analysis is basically a **risk management** approach, which helps identify threats and select cost-effective security measures.

Major activities in the risk management process can be applied to existing systems as well as to systems under development. These are summarized in Figure 19.7 on page 723.

RISK MANAGEMENT ANALYSIS. Risk management analysis can be enhanced by the use of software packages. A sample computation that can be executed by such software is shown here:

$$\boxed{\text{Expected Loss} = P1 \times P2 \times L}$$

where:

$P1$ = probability of attack

$P2$ = probability of successful attack

L = Loss occurring if attack is successful.

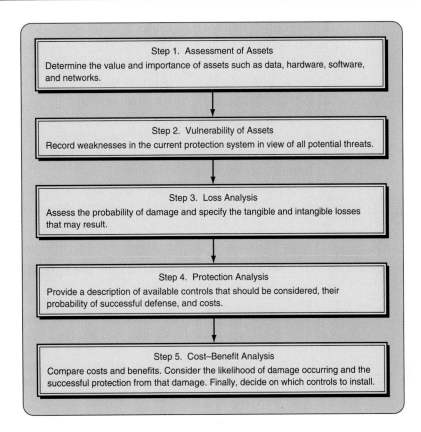

FIGURE 19.7 The risk management process.

Example:

$$P1 = .02$$
$$P2 = .10$$
$$L = 1,000,000$$

Then expected loss = $2000

The expected loss can then be compared against the cost of preventing it. The value of these software programs is not only in their ability to execute computations, but also in their ability to provide a structured, systematic framework for ranking both threats and controls.

HOW MUCH TO SECURE? The National Computer Security Center (NCSC) of the Department of Defense published a book containing guidelines for security levels. The government uses these guidelines in its requests for bids on jobs where vendors must meet specified levels. The seven levels are shown in Figure 19.8.

▶ 19.12 HOW TO PROTECT PERSONAL COMPUTERS

Even though the PC at home or work is fairly safe, it still needs some protection. Major external threats are power surges during electrical storms, and viruses. If your PC is networked, additional protection is necessary against both viruses and break-ins. The following are recommended actions for protecting your PC.

REDUCING THE RISK OF A VIRUS ATTACK

Simple procedures can reduce the risk of a virus entering your PC.

▼ Install a reliable antivirus protection package on your machine (if it does not have a built-in one), and scan all disks before use.

▼ Use only "shrink-wrap" copies of all software. (Shrink-wrap copies are original vendor copies obtained directly from the vendor or a reliable distributor).

▼ Do not download software from bulletin boards or other on-line services to hard disks. Download to a floppy disk, and test it thoroughly.

▼ Always plug your PC into a surge protector.

▼ Do not use public domain software or shareware, even if it is obtained from an associate, unless it has been properly tested.

▼ Do not exchange programs between computers at work and computers at home. Only exchange data or text.

▼ Perform regular backups of the data stored on your computer. "Write-protect" all disks and backup media, and store the disks in a secured place.

▼ Always boot from a hard disk; or, boot from a write-protected disk.

▼ Be on the lookout for symptoms of a virus infection.

Some operating systems (e.g., DOS 6.0, Windows 3.1 or higher) include a built-in virus detecting mechanism. Alternatively, you can install virus detecting software that can check computer drives.

The following is a typical message that was displayed by a program called SCAN when the author's computer was attacked by a virus attached to software given to him by a colleague:

> ***SCAN 3.7V64 Copyright 1994-95 by McAfee Associates.***
> *Scanning for known viruses.*
> *Scanning B:\COMMAND.COM*
> *Found Yankee Doodle Virus [Doodle]*
> *Disk B: contains 1 directories and 34 files.*
> *Found 2 files containing viruses.*

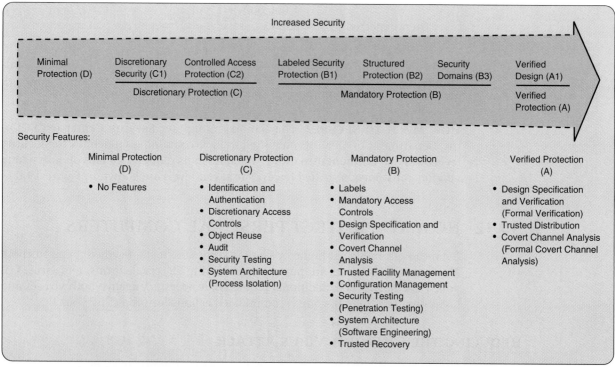

FIGURE 19.8 The NCSC level of securities is considered an excellent guideline for determining an appropriate level of security. (SOURCE: Chokhani, 1992, P. 68. Copyright 1992, Association for Computing Machinery Inc.)

PROTECTING AGAINST LOSS OF DATA

The major *internal threat* is loss of data. Make sure that you save data properly and frequently, and do not let others play with your PC. (A year's worth of data and programs were destroyed in a few minutes when a novice student assistant accidently reformatted the hard disk of one of the authors' computers. Luckily, a backup was available).

TAKING CARE OF PHYSICAL ELEMENTS

Do not neglect the physical controls. Make sure the disks are clean and handled according to the manufacturer's specifications. Take the same care with your hardware; your computer does not like coffee, orange juice or even water, especially on its keyboard, so be careful. These are other good practices to follow:

▼ Remove disks from the computer when the computer is not in use.

▼ Keep disks away from electrical or magnetic fields, dust, and heat. (You may be surprised to know that your telephone and your microwave generate magnetic fields that may destroy data!)

▶ 19.13 CONTROL AND SECURITY IN THE 1990S

In the global business world of the '90s, computer control and security are receiving increased attention. Several important trends include the following:

INCREASING THE RELIABILITY OF SYSTEMS

The objective here is to use **fault tolerance** to keep the information systems working, even if some parts fail. Compaq Computer and other PC manufacturers provide a feature that stores data on more than one disk drive at the same time. So, if one disk fails or is attacked, the data are still available. Some new personal computers include a built-in battery that is automatically activated in case of power failure. According to a 1994 Dataquest survey, 63 percent of all U.S. corporations have battled computer viruses. Therefore, the latest technologies need to be employed to protect against viruses (see Box 19.15).

EXPERT SYSTEMS FOR EARLY DETECTION

Detecting early intrusion is extremely important, especially for classified information and financial data. Recent research cites the use of expert systems for this purpose (see Box 19.16).

EXPERT SYSTEMS IN AUDITING

Expert systems are used also to enhance the task of IS auditing. For example, expert systems evaluate controls and analyze basic computer systems.

ARTIFICIAL INTELLIGENCE IN BIOMETRICS

Expert systems, neural computing, voice recognition, and fuzzy logic can be used to enhance the capabilities of biometric systems.

A Closer Look BOX 19.15

THE SOFTWARE SOLUTIONS

Leading antivirus companies are offering an increasingly sophisticated range of products to help companies combat the latest virus threats. These products typically use three main techniques to combat viruses: *scanners, monitors*, and *integrity checkers*. Briefly, here's how they work.

Scanners, the oldest antivirus technology around, employ a database of known viruses and their characteristics and constantly check new software against it. The problem is that a pure scanner can't detect viruses that aren't in its database. Consequently, few people use a pure scanner today. Instead, scanning is combined with heuristics and other artificial intelligence techniques to catch unknown viruses and thus make systems more secure.

Monitors were the next step in virus protection. They employ a "terminate resident and stay" (TRS) program that constantly looks for, and thwarts, suspicious activities, such as attempts to write to executable files or to the boot sector on MS-DOS machines. The problem with both software and hardware monitors is false alarms. It is very hard for a program to tell whether a write-to-disk is legitimate 100 percent of the time. And because monitors use TRSs, they can sometimes conflict with other programs in mem-

ory. Almost all modern antivirus programs combine scanning and monitoring, and increasingly they go beyond that.

The latest wrinkle in antivirus software is the **integrity checker**. A typical integrity checker, like Central Point Software's Anti Virus; Untouchable, from Baton Rouge; or Symantec Corporation's Norton Anti-Virus, scans all files in the system and calculates a check sum for each. Then it creates a database of check sums and checks them regularly. If a file is ever changed, the check sum will change, thereby alerting the antivirus program of a possible virus attack.

Another thing many modern antivirus programs can do is remove viruses and repair damaged files. When the repair works, it means that the infected PC doesn't have to be rebuilt from a low-level hard disk format following a virus attack. But repairing is a tricky process and not always successful. In order to do it effectively, the antivirus program usually has to know the specific virus that infected the system. Otherwise, it can't be sure exactly what the virus changed and, therefore, cannot repair the file.

SOURCE: Condensed from *Datamation*, May 1, 1993, p. 54.

A Closer Look BOX 19.16

INTRUSION DETECTING EXPERT SYSTEMS

A new approach to computer and network security involves the use of artificial intelligence technologies and especially expert systems. Several research institutions (e.g., SRI International, Menlo Park, CA) develop expert systems for their clients. The new approach, called intrusion **detecting systems**, is especially suitable for local area networks and client/server architectures. This approach compares users' activities on a workstation network against historical profiles and analyzes the significance of any discrepancies. The purpose is to detect security violations. The

approach is pursued by several government agencies (e.g., Department of Energy and the U.S. Navy) and large corporations (e.g., Citicorp, Rockwell International, and Tracor).

The system detects other things as well, for example, compliance issues. People tend to ignore security measures (20,000–40,000 violations were reported each month in a large aerospace company in California).

SOURCE: Based on Kerr (1990).

EXPERT SYSTEMS FOR DIAGNOSIS AND PROGNOSIS

Expert systems can be used to diagnose troubles in computer systems and to suggest solutions. The user provides the expert systems with answers to questions about symptoms. The expert system uses its knowledge base to diagnose the source(s) of the trouble. Once a proper diagnosis is made, a restoration suggestion is provided by the computer.

SMART CARDS

Smart card technology can be used to protect PCs on LANs. An example is Excel MAR 10 (from MacroArt Technology, Singapore). The smart card offers six safety levels. These include identification of authorized user, execution of predetermined programs, authentication, encryption of programs and files, encryption of communication, and generation of historical files. This product can also be integrated with fingerprint facility. The user's smart card is authenticated by the system using signatures calculated with a secret key and the encryption algorithm.

▶ MANAGERIAL ISSUES

Security is a top management concern. It includes the following:

1. Responsibilities for security should be assigned in all areas. It is important to make sure that people know who is responsible and accountable for what.

2. Security awareness programs are important for any organization that is heavily dependent on IT. Such programs should be corporate wide and supported by senior executives.

3. Monitoring security measures and assuring compliance with administrative controls are essential to the success of any security plan. For many people, following administrative controls means additional work, which they prefer not to do.

4. Too many controls can be too expensive. Conducting a cost–benefit analysis and determining the appropriate level of controls are important management tasks.

5. Auditing information systems should be institutionalized into the organizational culture. You do it not because your insurance company may ask for it, but because it can save you considerable amounts of money. On the other hand, overauditing is not cost effective.

6. Disasters may occur in almost any place and at any time. If your organization is heavily dependent on information, it is advisable to plan for disasters, so a quick recovery is assured.

7. Like any virus, a computer virus can cause major damage. An appropriate amount of "vaccination" is the most cost-effective approach to the problem. ■

KEY TERMS

CHAPTER HIGHLIGHTS *(L-x means learning objective number x)*

▼ Data, software, hardware, and networks can be threatened by many internal and external hazards. (L-1)

▼ The damage to an information system can be caused either accidentally or intentionally. (L-2)

▼ There are many potential computer crimes; some resemble conventional crimes (embezzlement, vandalism, fraud, theft, trespassing, and joyriding). (L-2)

▼ Computer criminals are driven by economic, ideological, egocentric, or psychological factors. Most of the criminals are insiders, but outsiders (such as hackers, crackers, and spies) can cause major damage as well. (L-2)

▼ A virus is a computer program, hidden within a regular program, that instructs the regular program to change or destroy data and/or programs. (L-2)

▼ Information systems are protected with controls such as security procedures, physical guards, or detecting software. (L-3)

▼ The purpose of controls is to assure that an information system will operate as intended. (L-3)

▼ Controls are used for *prevention, deterrence, detection, recovery*, and *correction* of information systems. (L-3)

▼ General controls include physical security, access controls, data security controls, communication (networks) controls, and administrative controls. (L-4)

▼ Biometric controls are used to identify users by checking physical characteristics of the user (e.g., fingerprints, retina of the eye). (L-4)

▼ Encrypting information is a useful method for protecting transmitted data. (L-4)

▼ Application controls are usually built into the software. They protect the data during input, processing, or output. (L-4)

▼ Determining the proper controls is an exercise in risk management. Both formulas and software are available. (L-5)

▼ A detailed internal or external IT audit may involve hundreds of issues and can be supported by both software and checklists. (L-6)

▼ Disaster recovery planning is an integral part of effective control and security management. (L-7)

▼ Protecting your PC is fairly easy, especially if security software is used. (L-8)

▼ Expert systems and built-in components will help in reducing the risk of computer malfunctions. (L-9)

▼ It is extremely difficult and expensive to protect against all possible threats. Therefore, it is necessary to use cost–benefit analysis to decide how many and which controls to adopt. (L-10)

QUESTIONS FOR REVIEW

1. Define controls, threats, vulnerability, and backup.
2. What is the purpose of a control system?
3. Name the major vulnerability points in a computerized system.
4. Describe the major threats to a computerized system.
5. What is computer crime?
6. List the four major categories of computer crime.
7. What is the difference between hackers and crackers?
8. Describe the profile of a computer criminal.
9. Describe the major motivations of computer criminals.
10. Distinguish between criminal acts of input tampering and programming techniques.
11. Explain a virus, a worm, and a Trojan horse.
12. Describe prevention, deterrence, detection, limitation, recovery, and correction.
13. List five factors that make it difficult to protect an information system.
14. Distinguish between general controls and application controls.
15. What is the difference between authorized and authenticized users?
16. Explain encryption.
17. What does separation of duties mean?
18. Define check totals and hash total.
19. Distinguish between internal and external auditing.
20. Distinguish between auditing around, through, and within the computer.
21. What is a security policy?
22. Define and describe a disaster recovery plan.
23. What do "hot" and "cold" sites for recovery mean?
24. List and briefly describe the steps involved in risk analysis of controls.

QUESTIONS FOR DISCUSSION

1. Why should information control and security be a prime concern to management?

2. Find an article or story on a computer virus and describe the life cycle of that virus.

3. Compare the computer security situation with that of insuring a house.

4. Why is it sometimes necessary to have several biometrics in a single information system?

5. Explain how encryption can protect an information system.

6. Describe how IS auditing works and how it is related to traditional accounting and financial auditing.

7. Review Fine's total security framework. Explain the need for all eight pillars.

8. Some insurance companies will not insure a business unless the firm has a computer disaster recovery plan. Explain why.

9. Explain why risk management should involve the following elements: threats, exposure associated with each threat, risk of each threat occurring, cost of controls, and assessment of their effectiveness.

10. List the major measures suggested to protect a PC. Which ones would you tend to ignore? Why?

11. It was suggested recently to use viruses and similar programs in wars. What is the logic of such a proposal? How can it be implemented?

EXERCISES

1. The daily probability of a major earthquake in Los Angeles is .0007. The chance of your computer center being damaged during a quake is 5 percent. If the center is damaged, the average estimated damage will be $1.6 million.

   a. Calculate the expected loss (in dollars).

   b. An insurance agent is willing to insure your facility for an annual fee of $15,000. Analyze the offer, and discuss it.

2. View the movie *Wargames* or *The Net*. Relate the contents of this chapter to the movie.

3. Espionage in general and industrial espionage in particular can be supported by computers. Find some material on this topic and summarize it.

4. Robert T. Morris, a computer wizard and graduate student at Cornell University, introduced a damaging program to thousands of computers and on the Arparet network. He was fined $10,000, sentenced to three years of probation, and ordered to perform 400 hours of community service and to pay the cost of his probation supervision. This verdict caused a debate, which lingered for three years. It finally reached the U.S. Supreme Court which refused to hear the case (see *Computerworld*, January 29, 1990; May 7, 1990; May 14, 1990, and October 14, 1991). In your view, is the punishment too high, too low, or just right? Why?

5. Expert systems can be used to analyze the profile of computer users. This may enable better intrusion detection. Should an employer notify employees that their usage of computers is being monitored by an expert system (see *Datamation*, February 1, 1990)?

6. Ms. M. Hsieh worked as a customer support representative for the Wollongong Group, a small software company (Palo Alto, CA). She was fired in late 1987. In early 1988, Wollongong discovered that someone was logging onto its computers at night via a modem and had altered and copied files. During investigation, the police traced the calls to Ms. Hsieh's home and found copies there of proprietary information valued at several million dollars. It is interesting to note that Ms. Hsieh's access code was canceled the day she was terminated. However, the company suspects that Ms. Hsieh obtained the access code of another employee. (SOURCE: Based on *BusinessWeek*, August 1, 1988, p. 67.)

   a. How was the crime committed? Why were the controls ineffective? (State any relevant assumptions)

   b. What can Wollongong do in order to prevent similar incidents in the future?

7. In May 1989, a massive computer crash caused the SABRE Passenger Reservation Service System of American Airlines to be idle for 13 hours. It was determined that the program was erroneously changed by another program. The altered information erased critical storage data on IBM 3080 disk drives. Thus, the erroneous program "walked through" SABRE's memory, stripping away the digital labels on each disk volume. This resulted in the inability to address any of SABRE's disk drives. (SOURCE: Based on Bozman, J.R., "Run Away Program Gores SABRE," *Computerworld*, May 22, 1989, p. 1.)

   a. What kind of problem is described in this case?

   b. The SABRE reservation system is one of the largest in the world. How is it possible that its controls were ineffective?

   c. How could this problem have been avoided?

8. Refer to the opening case to this chapter. You were hired as a consultant to one of the financial services companies that were evacuated from the World Trade Center. The company asked your advice on the following:

   a. Should they continue their work with networks or use a centralized mainframe? Which is easier to protect?

   b. Will the companies that return to the World Trade Center need to prepare for potential disasters?

   c. How can they calculate the amount of money that they should invest in disaster planning and recovery management?

GROUP ASSIGNMENT

The group is to be divided into two parts. The first part will interview students and business people and record the experiences they have had with computer problems. The second group will visit a computer store (read the literature or use the Internet) to find out what software is available to fight computer problems. Then, the group will prepare a presentation in which they describe the problems and identify which of the problems could have been prevented with the use of commercially available software.

Minicase 1

Hacker Convicted

Kevin David Mitnick had to spend a year in jail without parole. However, as a result of a plea bargain deal, the 25-year-old Mitnick was relieved of paying fines. His electronic excursions and his "addiction to hacking" allegedly cost the Digital Equipment Corporation (DEC) $4 million in damages.

Mitnick was arrested in the Fall of 1988, for stealing a long-distance security software source code from DEC. His arrest captured national headlines. On March 15, 1989, he pleaded guilty to "possession of unauthorized telephone access devices" and to "computer fraud." The computer fraud count dealt with Mitnick's access to a DEC VAX system and his misappropriation of a security software system.

In order to gain prison release in a year, Mitnick had to agree to a three-year supervised probation; compliance with all federal, state, and local laws; and psychiatric counseling as recommended by the probation office. He also agreed "not to use telephones illegally to access computers or violate any state, federal, or local law."

During his imprisonment, Mitnick was not even allowed unsupervised access to a prison pay phone. He was permitted to dial only telephone numbers authorized by the U.S. Attorney. Mitnick was described as "a guy who couldn't get through a day without breaking into a computer somewhere."

Questions for Minicase 1

1. As manager of IT security, what measures would you install to prevent a hacker such as Mitnick from accessing your organization's computer system?

2. What computer crime legislation was applicable in this case, and why?

3. How will jail sentences, as proposed in this case, affect other computer hacking incidents? Will it deter future hacking?

4. In your view, is Mitnick's punishment too severe, not severe enough, or just right?

Note: Mitnick was described as the "most wanted computer hacker in the world" when he violated his probation and eluded federal authorities for 2 years. During this period he stole more than 20,000 credit card numbers and millions of dollars. He was arrested in February 1995 after federal agents used smart monitoring equipment to locate his apartment.

Minicase 2

How Much Disaster Preparation Is Enough?

On December 3, 1990, it was virtually impossible to find a hotel room in the 50-mile radius around New Madrid, Missouri. Apparently, the news media (teams of reporters, camera people, and news personnel) were waiting for the major earthquake predicted by Iben Browning. This earthquake never occurred.

The following discussion took place a few days later at the headquarters of MidAmerica Transit of Memphis, TN, not far from New Madrid.

John (director of information services): I told you this Iben is crazy, and so is all the media hype. It cost us $26,000 to prepare against something that never oc-

curred. Last year we had the same problem with a "maybe flood." It cost us over $15,000 to make people ready. Our employees are tired of these disaster preparations. The chance of a disaster is so low that we'd be much better off to ignore them.

Nancy (vice-president of finance): We are lucky that Browning was wrong. Even with all the preparation, we would have suffered irreversible damage if a major earthquake occurred. You know that our company is heavily reliant on computers and networks. We would lose hundreds of thousands of dollars if a disaster strikes.

John: We are paying too much for something that has close to zero chance of occurring.

Nancy: Remember what happened on October 17, about six weeks ago, to those companies in San Francisco that were not ready for the earthquake? Do not forget that a major flood around the Mississippi River is predicted for next spring.

John: This is true, but many companies find that this kind of insurance is simply too expensive. So they do not do any major preparation. I can use the money to increase productivity and reduce the number of employees by one or two. We do too much contingency planning.

Larry (vice president of administration): Have we ever conducted a detailed analysis of this issue?

Nancy: No. There are too many unknown factors.

There are several different possible disasters, and no one can really predict how much damage there will be.

Questions for Minicase 2

You were hired as a consultant to MidAmerica Transit.

1. Would you recommend John's approach of not doing any major preparation? Or would you support Nancy's position? Why?

2. You were asked to prepare a detailed analysis of the situation for Larry. Outline the steps that you would follow.

3. What difficulties would you encounter in executing the steps in #2?

Minicase 3

Flyhigh Corporation

Flyhigh is a large aerospace corporation (fictitious name, real incident) that regularly performs projects for the military and other government organizations. A virus attack that caused significant damage resulted in an investigation. The investigation revealed the following:

▼ While there are clear instructions not to use common names (such as Smith, Lee, or Brown) as passwords, these names are in use.

▼ While there are clear instructions to change passwords once a month, many people neglect to do so. In fact, some employees have not changed their password for more than a year.

▼ Violations are especially prevalent among top managers and top scientists. The higher the individuals are in the organizational hierarchy, the more likely it is that they will ignore the instructions.

▼ In the past, notices were mailed to violators, but most of the notices were ignored.

▼ The responsibility for security issues is decentralized.

The database administrator is responsible for security in the IS department and for the LAN. Various individuals were assigned responsibility in users' departments, mainly for microcomputers. However, some departments do not have anyone formally assigned for computer security, while others do not have any formal procedures regarding security management.

Questions for Minicase 3

1. What do you suggest should be done about the violators?

2. Would you change the responsibility scheme (structure)? How?

3. The actual loss to the corporation from the virus attack is estimated at $1,600,000. Should somebody be punished? Justify your answer, if punishment is recommended. What should it be, and who should be punished?

REFERENCES AND BIBLIOGRAPHY

1. Adam, J. A., "Threats and Countermeasures (for Networks)," *IEEE Spectrum*, August 1992.

2. Allen, B., "The Biggest Computer Frauds: Lessons for CPA," *Journal of Accountancy*, May 1977.

3. Baker, R., *Computer Security Handbook*, 2nd ed., Blue Ridge Summit State: TAB Books, 1991.

4. Banton, E., and J. Roseberger, "Determining Your Information Systems Vulnerability to Viruses," *Journal of Systems Management*, May 1991.

5. Bock, I. B., and J. F. Schrage, "Computer Viruses: Over 300 Threats to Microcomputing and Still Growing," *Journal of Systems Management*, February 1993.

6. Bologna, J., "Computer Crime: The Who, What, Where, When, Why, and How," *Data Processing and Communication Security*, Vol. 10, No. 1, 1987.

7. Brancheau, J. C., and J. Wetherbe, "Key Issues in Information Systems Management," *MIS Quarterly*, March 1987.

8. Butler, J., "How to Stay in Business When Disaster Strikes," *Software Magazine*, August 1992.

9. Chokhani, S., "Trusted Product Evaluation," *Communications of the ACM*, July 1992.

10. Coderre, D. G., "Computer Assisted Auditing Tools and Techniques," *Internal Auditor*, February, 1993.

11. Fine, L. H., *Computer Security–A Guide for Management*, London: Heinemann, 1983.

12. Fites, P., et al., *The Computer Virus Crisis*, New York: Van Nostrand Reinhold, 1989.

13. Ford, J. C., "Expert Systems in Auditing" in Umbaugh. R. E. (ed.) *Handbook of MIS Management*, Boston, Auerbach Publishers, 2nd ed. 1991.

14. Freedman, D. H., "The Goods on Hacker Hoods," *Forbes ASAP*, September 13, 1993.

15. Hayman, A., and E. Oz, "Integrating Data Security into the System Development Life Cycle," *Journal of Systems Management*, August 1993.

16. Hussain, K. M. and D. Hussain, Managing Computer Resources. Homewood, Ill., 2nd ed., IRWIN, 1988.

17. Hutt, A. E., "Management Role in Computer Security," in Hutt A. E., et al., (eds.); *Computer Security Handbook*, New York, McMillan, 1988.

18. I/S Analyzer, "How to tighten security and ease security administration in an enterprise computing environment," *I/S Analyzer*, June 1995.

19. Kerr, S., "Using AI to Improve Security," *Datamation*, February 1, 1990.

20. King, J., "Lessons from Hell (Dealing with Natural Disasters)," *Computerworld*, June 29, 1992.

21. Knoll, A. P., *Disaster Recovery: An Organization View*, IBM Information Systems Management Institute, Chicago, IL, 1986.

22. Lee, D. R., "Changing Responsibilities for Audit and Security Information Resources," *Information Executive*, Spring 1990.

23. Loch, K. D., et al., "Threats to Information Systems: Today's Reality, Yesterday's Understanding," *MIS Quarterly*, June 1992.

24. McPartlin, J. P., and J. C. Panettieri, "Towers Without Power," *InformationWeek*, March 8, 1993.

25. Melford, R. J., "Network Security," *Internal Auditor*, February 1993.

26. Mungo, P., and B. Clough, *Approaching Zero: The Extraordinary Underworld of Hackers, Phreakers, Virus Writers and Keyboard Criminals*, New York: Random House, 1993.

27. Murphy, M. A., and A. L. Parker, *Handbook of EDP Auditing* 2nd ed., Boston: Warren, Gorham, & Lamont, 1991.

28. Parker, D. B., *Manager's Guide to Computer Security*, Reston, NJ: Reston Publishing Company, 1981.

29. Pauchant T., et al., "The Dial Tone Does Not Come From God!" *Academy of Management Executive*, Vol. 6, No. 3, 1992.

30. Roberts, R., and P. Kane, *Computer Security*, Greensboro, NC: Computer Book Publishers, 1989.

31. Sherizen, S., "The Globalization of Computer Crime and Information Security," *Computer Security Journal*, Vol. 8, No. 2, 1993.

32. Somerson, P., "Spy-Proof Your PC," *PC Computing*, September 1992.

33. Stallings, W., "A Network Security Primer," *Computerworld*, January 29, 1990.

34. Steinberg, R. M., and R. N. Johnson, "Implementing SAS No. 55 in a Computer Environment," *Journal of Accountancy*, August 1991.

35. Uehling, M. D., "Cracking the Code," *Popular Science*, January 1993.

36. Violino, B., and P. Klein, "Security Users Still Struggle to Manage 'LANarchy,'" *InformationWeek*, March 7, 1994.

37. Warman, A. R., *Computer Security Within Organizations*, London: Macmillan, 1993.

38. Wood, C. C., "Principles of Secure Information System Design," *Computers and Security*, September 1990.

20

IMPACTS OF INFORMATION TECHNOLOGY ON ORGANIZATIONS, INDIVIDUALS, AND SOCIETY

Chapter Outline

Learning Objectives

After studying this chapter, you will be able to:

1. Understand the major impacts of information technology on organizations, individuals, and society.

2. Describe the major ethical issues related to information technology, and identify situations in which they occur.

3. Explain the various aspects of privacy and its possible invasion by organizations or individuals using information technology.

4. Describe the potential dehumanization of people by computers and other potential negative impacts of information technology.

5. Describe the major impacts of information technology on structure, power, jobs, supervision, and decision making in organizations.

6. Evaluate the potential negative impacts of information technology on health and safety.

7. Describe some of the major societal impacts of information technology.

8. Describe the negative and positive impacts of information technology on employment levels.

9. Discuss the future of information technology.

▶ 20.1 SOFTWARE DILEMMA AT AGRICO, INC.

AGRICO (DES MOINES, IA) manages over 350 farms in several midwestern states. The company has four regional offices, and it uses several arrangements of property management. For example, Agrico leases land owned by the company to farmers, then sells the crops and shares the revenue with the farmers. Agrico sells large quantities of agricultural products on the Chicago Commodities Market.

Prior to 1987, Agrico outsourced most of its computer services. However, due to the growth of its business and its reliance on information, the company decided to build its own IS department. Unfortunately, Agrico was unable to find an off-the-shelf software package. After advertising its needs, the company received several bids and selected AMR, a small software company in Omaha, Nebraska, to develop its information system. AMR only had 12 customers, 10 employees, and one product: an integrated farm management software package. While the basic software was similar, AMR provided customizations for each customer.

Agrico and AMR signed an agreement that specified that the *source code* (see Chapter 6) would be maintained in escrow with a third party for backup and accessibility purposes. Due to frequent modifications, Agrico needed to have access to the code for "viewing listings necessary to test the system." In addition, since AMR is a very small company, Agrico needed to have access to the code in the event that AMR had problems. Agrico found that there were several variations of the code (because of the other 11 clients).

AMR delivered the *object code* (see Chapter 6) to Agrico. Agrico requested that the source code be placed in escrow. Rogers, AMR's president, claimed that Agrico should be satisfied with his backup plan, according to which he occasionally took computer tapes to his bank's vault in Omaha.

However, Agrico had no independent way to verify that the source code in the vault was indeed Agrico's and that it was a current version. Due to the importance of the information for Agrico and its 350 customers, it became critical for Agrico to be assured that the source code would be in a true escrow location. Rogers, however, refused to do so. He was afraid that placing the code with a third party would put his own survival at risk because an unauthorized person could copy the software and then compete with AMR. Since AMR is small and basically has one product, the company's survival is dependent on the security of that product. Agrico

Farmers put their trust in Agrico's management.

was very upset, but it was unable to change vendors because it had already invested time and money in the software. Also, AMR was still the best vendor. Consequently, the two companies were in dispute. Legal experts advised Agrico that the contract was not clear on the location of the escrow.

Because of the large development efforts, AMR assigned a full-time employee, Jane Seymour, to work at Agrico's premises. She was aware of the dispute and was very uncomfortable because of the situation.

In May 1987, Agrico's vice president of information systems entered the computer room. Jane Seymour was on her dinner break. The source code was left on the computer screen (either deliberately or accidently). The vice president immediately called the president of Agrico and asked, "Should I copy the source code to tape? We only have one hour; an immediate decision is needed." Agrico's president called his lawyer, who advised him that copying the software might be illegal, and if he should be caught, he could be sued by AMR.

While the president did not want to do something illegal, he felt that Agrico was entitled to get the code as an assurance for the survival of AMR and the safety of the client's assets.

SOURCE: Condensed from "Agrico, Inc.—A Software Dilemma," Harvard Business School Case #9-189-085, Boston: Harvard Business School Press, 1989.

20.2 DOES INFORMATION TECHNOLOGY HAVE ONLY POSITIVE EFFECTS?

The decision faced by Agrico's president is a major one; it can determine the future of the company. Such a decision is typical of a new type of situation created due to the use of IT. Information technology has drastically and rapidly affected the way the world does business. The changes IT has brought have had an effect on private and public organizations as well as on employees, customers, clients, and society. Indeed, everyone—from the living room to the boardroom—has been touched in some way by IT. However, not everyone likes computers and IT, and even those who do, may not like them at times (see Box 20.1).

A Closer Look BOX 20.1

SOME GOOD REASONS TO HATE COMPUTERS

▼ They cost too much.

▼ They break down all the time.

▼ You can't fix them by whacking them a few times with a hammer.

▼ The different brands are incompatible.

▼ They take up too much desk space.

▼ They become obsolete five minutes after you leave the store.

▼ They don't understand plain English.

▼ Electronic bulletin boards never have enough thumbtacks.

▼ You have to know how to type to use them.

▼ They lose your data every time there is an electrical storm in the western hemisphere.

▼ They give off radiation that may cause cancer, but we won't find out until we all have it.

▼ They have three-pronged plugs, and it is a two-pronged world.

▼ There are too many kinds to choose from.

▼ Our grandparents never had them, and they got along just fine.

▼ They're taking away people's jobs.

▼ They don't do anything the average person needs.

▼ They think the world can be reduced to strings of ones and zeros.

▼ Storing words on disks never made any sense, and it never will.

▼ Five cables sticking out of an appliance is cruel and unusual punishment.

▼ Computer furniture is uncomfortable and looks lousy around the house.

▼ Instruction manuals are written by illiterate sadists.

▼ When they sell you a $500 computer, they forget to mention that you have to spend another $1,500 in order to do anything with it.

▼ How can you respect any machine controlled by a mouse?

▼ It hurts your back to sit in front of one for a long time.

▼ They don't make good conversation at parties.

▼ When you make a mistake using one, you can't blame it on anybody.

▼ Worst of all, the guy down the street has a better one than I do.

SOURCE: Compiled from Gutman D., "43 Good Reasons to Hate Computers," *The Miami Herald*, August 18, 1989.

Concern about technology's effect on people, organizations, and society is not new. Philosophical arguments of the British intellectual class concerning the effects of the Industrial Revolution on society were expressed over 120 years ago by Samuel Butler. In his book *EREHWON*, (*nowhere* spelled backwards), a man loses his way in a strange land and wanders into a society that has rejected machines. The people froze technology at a predetermined level and outlawed all further technological development; they made a conscious decision to reject technology. While there are many philosophical, technological, social, and other differences between that society and our own, there are many people who believe that humankind is threatened by the evolution of technology. Our society, however, has not rejected technology. In contrast, we recognize that computers and technology are essential to maintaining and supporting our culture as we know it. We are in a symbiotic relationship with technology. As such, we must be aware of its effect on us as individuals and as members of organizations and society.

In previous chapters, attention has been given to the manner in which information systems are being justified, constructed, used, and maintained. Such systems can benefit organizations in many ways: productivity can be increased, quality of services can be assured, organizations can become more responsive to their customers, and organizations can solve complex problems that benefit their employees and/or customers. As illustrated, information systems, in many cases, are composed of a human-machine team. In all of these discussions we assumed that members of an organization would reap the fruits of new technology and that computers have had no major negative impact on people, organizations, and society. The benefits to all have been demonstrated repeatedly, and the question of potential negative effects seldom arose.

Nevertheless, information technology *has* raised a multitude of negative issues, ranging from illegal copying of software programs to planned surveillance of employees' electronic mail files. Health and safety issues are of major concern as well as the impact of IT on employment level and quality of life. In this concluding chapter, some of these issues will be discussed, especially the impact of IT on organizations, individuals, and society.

▶ 20.3 ETHICAL ISSUES

Ethics is a branch of philosophy that deals with what is considered to be "right" and "wrong." In one of the oldest codes of ethics, the Ten Commandments, clear specifications are given about what an individual should and should not do. Over the years, philosophers have proposed many ethical theories and propositions, but what is unethical is not necessarily illegal. In most instances, an individual faced with an ethical decision is *not* considering whether or not to break the law. In today's complex environment, the definitions of "right" and "wrong" are not always clear (see the Agrico case and Table 20.1 pg. 739). A debate is also occurring about *who* should teach ethics. Some people believe that families and schools should teach ethics, not companies. Others believe it is the duty of a company to develop a code of ethics to guide its employees. The spread of IT has created many new ethical situations. For example, the issue of a company monitoring electronic mail is very controversial (47 percent of the readers of *InformationWeek* believe companies have the right to do so, 53 percent disagree). Obviously, there are major differences among companies and individuals with respect to what is right and wrong.

There are also differences regarding ethics among different countries. What is unethical in one culture may be perfectly acceptable in another. Many Western countries, for example, have a much higher concern for individuals and their rights to privacy than some Asian countries. (In Asia, more emphasis is placed on society or groups than on individuals.)

Many companies and professional organizations develop their own codes of ethics. A **code of ethics** is a collection of principles intended as a guide for members of a company or an association (See Oz, 1994). For a discussion of the code of the Association for Computing Machinery (ACM), see Anderson, et al. (1993).

The diversity of IT applications and increased use of the technology have created many ethical issues. An attempt to organize these issues into a framework was undertaken by Mason (1986), who categorized ethical issues into four groups: privacy, accuracy, property, and accessibility. Each group has its own major concerns.

▼ *Privacy.* Collection, storage, and dissemination of information about individuals.

Table 20.1 What Is Right and What Is Wrong?—A Self-Assessment.*

Scenario	The behavior is (vote for one only)		
	Unethical	Not unethical	Not ethics issue
1. A software developer continued to work on a project, even though he knew that using the software would produce incorrect results. It was not because the program was bad, but because some part of the input information could not be trusted.	( )	( )	( )
2. A programmer developed "profiles" of potential customers from publicly available information. He sold the list to mail-order firms. Some of the profiles were inaccurate; consequently people received numerous pieces of junk mail and unsolicited telephone calls.	( )	( )	( )
3. Management allowed employees to use computer services for approved personal purposes, then monitored usage without employees' knowledge.	( )	( )	( )
4. The president of a software development company marketed a tax advice program, knowing it had bugs. As a result, some users filed incorrect tax returns and were penalized by the IRS.	( )	( )	( )
5. A computer scientist worked on two research projects for developing systems. He diverted funds from one project to another, completing both projects successfully.	( )	( )	( )

*A self-assessment is a question-and-answer procedure. Participants are exposed to a set of scenarios and asked to express opinions by voting on three options: unethical, not unethical, or not an ethics issue.

SOURCE: Extracted from Weiss (1990).

▼ *Accuracy.* Authenticity, fidelity, and accuracy of information collected and processed.

▼ *Property.* Ownership and value of information.

▼ *Accessibility.* Right to access information and payment of fees to access it.

Representative questions and issues in each category are listed in Table 20.2. Of these, the issue of privacy is discussed in detail in the next section.

▶ 20.4   INFORMATION PRIVACY

Privacy means different things to different people. A former U.S. Supreme Court Justice, Potter Stewart, said the following about pornography, which could be applied to privacy: "I cannot define it, but I know it when I see it." It is common to identify four states of privacy: (1) solitude—an individual's desire to be left alone, away from outside interference; (2) intimacy—the state of privacy one wants to enjoy from the outside world; (3) anonymity—a person's wish to be free from external surveillance; and (4) reserve—an individual's desire to control information about himself.

In general, privacy is the right to be left alone and the right to be free from unreasonable personal intrusions. A definition of information privacy, according to Agranoff (1992), is the "claim of individuals, groups, or institutions to determine for themselves when, and to what extent, information about them is communicated to others."

Table 20.2 **A Framework for Ethical Issues**

Privacy	*Accuracy*
• What information about oneself should an individual be required to reveal to others? • What kind of surveillance can an employer use on its employees? • What things can people keep to themselves and not be forced to reveal to others? • What information about individuals should be kept in databases, and how secure is the information there?	• Who is responsible for the authenticity, fidelity, and accuracy of information collected? • How can we ensure that information will be processed properly and presented accurately to users? • How can we ensure that errors in databases, data transmissions, and data processing are accidental and not intentional? • Who is to be held accountable for errors in information, and how is the injured party compensated?
Property	*Accessibility*
• Who owns the information? • What are the just and fair prices for its exchange? • Who owns the channels of information? • How should one handle software piracy (copying copyrighted software). • Under what circumstances can one use proprietary databases? • Can corporate computers be used for private purposes? • How should experts who contribute their knowledge to create expert systems be compensated? • How should access to information channels be allocated?	• Who is allowed to access information? • How much should be charged for permitting accessibility to information? • How can accessibility to computers be provided for employees with disabilities? • Who will be provided with equipment needed for accessing information? • What information does a person or an organization have a right or a privilege to obtain—under what conditions and with what safeguards?

SOURCE: Compiled from Mason (1986).

Privacy has long been a legal and social issue in the United States and many other countries. The right to privacy is recognized today in virtually all U.S. states and by the federal government, either by statute or common law (see Table 20.3 for a list of federal privacy legislation). The definition of privacy can be interpreted quite broadly. However, according to Freedman (1987), the following two rules have been followed fairly closely in past court decisions.

1. The right of privacy is not absolute. Privacy must be balanced against the needs of society.

2. The public's right to know is superior to the individual's right of privacy.

These two rules show why it is difficult, in some cases, to determine and enforce privacy regulations.

GLOBAL PERSPECTIVE

...international views on privacy differ widely

There are major differences among countries with respect to privacy regulations. Some countries (e.g., Sweden and Canada) have very strict laws; others have none. For example, Italy, Belgium, Spain, Portugal, and Greece lack legislation protecting an individual's right to control personal data in governmental or commercial databases. This obstructs the flow of information among countries in the European Community with controls to those without controls. To overcome this problem, the European Community Commission issued guidelines to all its country members regarding the rights of individuals to access information about themselves and the right to correct errors.

The complexity of collecting, sorting, filing, and accessing information *manually* from several different agencies was, in many cases, a built-in protection

Table 20.3 **Privacy Legislation**

Name	Content
Fair Credit Reporting Act, 1970	Allows individuals to access information that credit bureaus (e.g., TRW) maintain. Individuals can correct inaccuracies.
Freedom of Information Act, 1970	Permits individuals to access any information about themselves stored by the federal government.
Privacy Act of 1974	Prohibits the government from collecting information secretly. Information collected must be used only for a specific purpose. It can be used for other purposes only with the consent of the individual. Individuals can access and correct this information.
Right to Financial Privacy Act of 1978	Guards the safety of data in financial institutions. People must be notified if the government wants access to the data.
Electronic Communications Privacy Act of 1986	Prohibits private citizens from intercepting data communication without authorization.
Computer Matching and Privacy Act of 1988	Regulates the matching of computer files by state and federal agencies.

against misuse of information. It was simply too expensive, cumbersome, and complex to do it. However, personal computers, powerful software, large databases, and upgraded "communication highways" have created an entirely new dimension to accessing data. The inherent power in systems that can access vast amounts of data could be used for the good of society. For example, by matching records with the aid of a computer, it is possible to eliminate or reduce fraud, government mismanagement, tax evasion, welfare cheats, family support filchers, employment of illegal aliens, and so on. The question is: what price must every individual pay, in terms of a loss of privacy, so that the government can better apprehend criminals?

Unfortunately, the same system that helps the government could be used to blacklist innocent citizens. For example, people who have filed workers compensation or product-liability lawsuits or have used legitimate benefits extensively (such as health care) could be blacklisted by providers and denied benefits. These decisions may be made without an individual even knowing the basis for them.

Some representative issues of privacy are discussed next.

ELECTRONIC SURVEILLANCE

According to the American Civil Liberties Union (ACLU), monitoring computer users—**electronic surveillance**—is a major problem. The ACLU estimated that in 1987, four to six million computer users were monitored without their knowledge. While the issue of surveillance is one of the most extensively debated privacy issues, the practice is still widely used (see Box 20.2).

According to Beth Givens, project director for the Privacy Rights Clearinghouse at the University of California, San Diego, employees have very limited protection against employers' surveillance. Although several legal challenges are now underway, the law appears to support employers' rights to read electronic mail and other electronic documents. Legislation now before the U.S. Congress attempt to at least require employers to inform employees that their on-the-job activities might be monitored electronically.

A Closer Look BOX 20.2

COMPANIES SPY ON EMPLOYEES

A survey conducted by *MacWorld* magazine in May 1993 indicated that about 22 percent of all employers engage in surveillance of employee computer files, electronic mail files, and voice mail boxes. Among companies with more than 1,000 employees, the figure rises to 30 percent. Only 18 percent of the companies have written policies on elec-

tronic privacy, and 35 percent said that it was "never acceptable" to eavesdrop electronically on employees. Most surprising is that in less than one-third of the cases of such surveillance, employees were warned about such a possibility.

SOURCE: Compiled from *MacWorld*, May 1993.

PERSONAL INFORMATION IN DATABASES

Information about individuals is being kept in many databases. When you apply for a new telephone, for example, you may be asked to fill in a two-page questionnaire. The questionnaire is reviewed and then stored in a database. Perhaps the most visible locations of such records are credit reporting agencies (e.g., TRW, Equifax, and TransUnion). Other places where personal information might be stored are with banks and financial institutions; cable TV, telephone, and utilities companies; employers; apartments and equipment rental companies; hospitals; schools and universities; supermarkets, retail establishments, and mail-order houses; government agencies (e.g., Internal Revenue Service, Census Bureau, your municipality); libraries; and insurance companies.

There are several concerns about the information you provided to these record keepers. Under what circumstances will personal data be released? Do you know where the records are? Are these records accurate? Can individuals change inaccurate data? How long will it take to exercise a change? How are the data used? To whom are such data given or sold? How secure are the data against unauthorized people?

Having information stored in many places increases the chance that the information is inaccurate, not up-to-date, or not secured properly. Here are some examples of potential problems.

▼ An entire city in New England was unable to get financing. An investigation discovered that all the taxpayers were wrongly labeled as people who had failed to pay their property taxes.

▼ Landlords refuse to rent apartments to individuals frequently because of errors in databases (e.g., mixing up people with the same or similar names).

▼ People experience difficulties in financing or refinancing homes because of delayed or even incorrect information in databases.

▼ Totalitarian governments exercise tight control. For example, it is rumored that execution occurrences in certain countries are related to a national information system that singles out individuals who oppose their governments.

▼ Individuals may be fired from their jobs when management discovers private information on the E-mail that may not be related to work.

▼ Confidential information such as about the health status or sexual preference of an individual may have a negative impact on hiring, promotion, and other personnel decisions.

To assist individuals in the control of personal records it is possible to use the services of a commercial company. For example, Privacy Guard Corporation advises individuals about how to protect their rights, and it monitors several databases.

Some companies do attempt to protect the privacy of individuals (see Box 20.3). One problem with databases, however, is that they are used to compile different mailing lists. Such lists are sold to various vendors, who then call upon people as potential customers. The customers may not appreciate the intrusion of vendors.

IT At Work BOX 20.3

AMERICAN EXPRESS PROTECTS THE PRIVACY OF ITS CUSTOMERS

American Express (AmEx) was one of the first financial service companies to adopt a formal privacy policy regarding information about its customers. These policies restrict disclosure of data to those with a "business need" to see it. AmEx also gives its customers the choice not to receive promotional material. However, AmEx is using its vast database internally to generate lists for mass mailings and specialized promotions.

Stephen Cone, senior vice president for direct marketing, uses sophisticated mathematical models to sift through billions of bits of data to predict what products a person might be interested in. For example, all information—from the original application to each card transaction—is accessed to build individual profiles. These profiles can be used to determine marketing strategies, generate a list of potential customers, and so on.

From purchased lists, AmEx compiles a list of every potential cardholder in America. The records note every solicitation AmEx has ever sent to each person. The lists also contain demographic data and lifestyle indicators. AmEx produces many specialized models from this data. For example, AmEx has a "who's moving" model that is extremely valuable because people who are relocating tend to make several other changes at the same time. The company also has a "lifestyle" model that decides which solicitation letters to send to a prospect. The effect of this selective, direct marketing tool is that response rates are up 10 to 20 percent over previous years.

Even though AmEx does not rent out its list, it does enter into joint ventures with merchandising companies that conduct several thousand promotions a year. They offer everything from invitations to local pizzerias to solicitations for potential buyers of luxury cars. AmEx can pinpoint the cardholders that are most likely to respond to each offer.

American Express has realized that information about actual consumer behavior is extremely valuable. How a consumer spends her money is a better measure of her needs and desires than any marketing survey could ever be.

Critical Thinking Issues: Do you think that what AmEx is doing is ethical? How would you feel as a customer? What can you do if you are unhappy? ▲

SOURCE: Based on Hansell, S., "Getting to Know You," *Institutional Investor*, June, 1991.

INFORMATION ON BULLETIN BOARDS

There is an ever-increasing number of **electronic bulletin boards**, both nationally and within corporations. It is estimated that in 1993 there were 13 million users of over 55,000 commercial bulletin boards. One problem is how to keep owners of bulletin boards from disseminating information that may be offensive to readers (see Box 20.4). The difficulty in addressing this problem is the conflict between freedom of speech, privacy, and ethics. An interesting issue is the increased hard-core pornography that is available from bulletin boards (see Elmer–Dewitt, 1995).

TRANSFER OF DATA ACROSS INTERNATIONAL BORDERS

Several countries restrict the flow of personal data across their borders (e.g., Canada, Brazil). These countries usually justify their acts as protecting the privacy of their citizens. (Other justifications are property protection and economics.) The

A Closer Look BOX 20.4

PRODIGY BANS BIAS NOTES FROM ITS ELECTRONIC BULLETIN BOARD.

Prodigy operates one of the largest electronic bulletin boards in the United States. Two types of messages can be transmitted: public messages, which are posted by individuals and/or organizations, and private messages, which are sent usually by one individual to another (or to several individuals). On July 31, 1992, it was discovered that Prodigy carried two antisemetic statements disseminated by one individual to many recipients.

Prodigy has a policy of free expression of ideas on its network. However, at the same time, the company has an explicit policy banning its millions members from posting public messages that are "obscene, profane, or otherwise offensive references." The company screens the publicly carried notes, but they do not check the content of each private person-to-person electronic message. Prodi-

gy's position stirred controversy. This episode has raised a question regarding the limits of free speech on the computer network. It also raised the question of Prodigy's responsibility to prevent those notes that offend other people.

The company said it would try to reconcile the two policies which seem to be inconsistent. Prodigy also said that its case is similar to that of any city when it decides what movies and books are acceptable. In January 1993, Prodigy closed down its "frank discussion" channel when the language used by some participants got a little too frank for the owners of the company (IBM and Sears).

SOURCE: Condensed from stories in *USA Today, The Wall Street Journal, The New York Times,* and *Chicago Tribune* during the early part of August, 1992.

transfer of information in and out of a nation without knowledge of the authorities or individuals involved raises a number of privacy issues. Whose laws have jurisdiction when records are in a different country for reprocessing or retransmission purposes? For example, if data are transmitted by a Polish company through an American satellite to a British corporation, whose laws control what data and when? Questions like these will become increasingly more complicated and common as time goes on. Governments must make an effort to develop laws and standards to cope with the rapidly increasing rate of information technology in order to solve some of these privacy issues.

PRIVACY CODES

One way to improve the privacy situation is to develop **privacy policies** (codes), which can help organizations avoid legal problems. In many corporations, senior management has begun to understand that with the ability to collect vast amounts of personal information on customers, clients, and employees comes an obligation to ensure that the information—and, therefore, the individual—is protected. A sample of privacy policies is shown in Box 20.5.

▶ 20.5 IMPACTS ON ORGANIZATIONS

Utilization of computers may result in many changes in organizations. Some of the major potential impacts, which are discussed in this chapter, are in the areas of structure, authority, power, job content, employee career ladders, supervision, and the manager's job. A brief description of each follows.

STRUCTURE

FLATTER ORGANIZATIONAL HIERARCHIES. IT allows increased productivity of managers, an increased **span of control** (the number of employees per supervisor), and a decreased number of experts (because of expert systems). It is reasonable to assume, then, that *fewer* managerial levels will exist in many organizations;

A Closer Look BOX 20.5

PRIVACY POLICY BASICS

These three concepts help define information privacy.

Data collection.

▼ Data should be collected on individuals only to accomplish a legitimate business objective.

▼ Data should be adequate, relevant, and not excessive in relation to the business objective.

▼ Individuals must give their consent before data pertaining to them can be gathered. Such consent may be implied from the individual's actions (e.g., applications for credit, insurance, or employment).

Data accuracy.

▼ Sensitive data gathered on individuals should be verified before it is entered into the database.

▼ Data should be accurate and, where and when necessary, kept current.

▼ The file should be made available so the individual can ensure that the data are correct.

▼ If there is disagreement about the accuracy of the data, the individual's version should be noted and included with any disclosure of the file.

Data confidentiality.

▼ Computer security procedures should be implemented to provide reasonable assurance against unauthorized disclosure of data. They should include physical, technical, and administrative security measures.

▼ Third parties should not be given access to data without the individual's knowledge or permission, except as required by law.

▼ Disclosures of data, other than the most routine, should be noted and maintained for as long as the data are maintained.

▼ Data should not be disclosed for reasons incompatible with the business objective for which they are collected.

SOURCE: Condensed from Agranoff (1992).

there will be fewer staff and line managers. This trend is already evidenced by the continuing phenomenon of the ''shrinking size of middle management.''

Flatter organizational hierarchies will also result from reduction in the total number of employees as a result of increased productivity and from the ability of lower-level employees to perform higher-level jobs (e.g., by using ES). As one example, consider the 1985 Bank of America's reorganization and the 1991 Citicorp's reorganization, each of which resulted in a smaller corporation, larger span of control, and a much flatter structure. A main cause for the downsizing of many organizations is the increased use of computers.

STAFF-TO-LINE RATIO. The ratio of staff to line workers has increased in most organizations as computers replace clerical jobs, and as the need for information systems specialists increases. Expansion of IT, and especially ES, may reverse this trend. Specifically, the number of professionals and specialists could *decline* in relation to the total number of employees in the organizations.

SPECIAL UNITS. Another change in organizational structure is the possibility of creating a technology center, a DSS department, a management support department, and/or an AI department.

CENTRALIZATION OF AUTHORITY

The relationship between computerized systems and the degree of centralization of authority (and power) in the organizations that these systems serve has been debated extensively, especially since the introduction of microcomputers. It is still difficult, however, to establish a clear pattern. For example, the introduction of ES in General Electric's maintenance area increased the power of the decentralized units because they became less dependent on the company's headquarters. On the other hand, ES can be used as a means of increasing control and centralization.

Computer-based information systems can support either centralization or decentralization of electronic information processing within an organization. Although information systems are usually established *after* an organizational structure is completed, it is quite possible that a new or modified information system will change the organizational structure and/or the degree of decentralization.

Because of the trend toward smaller and flatter organizations, centralization may become more popular. However, this trend could be offset by specialization in more decentralized units. Whether extensive use of IT will result in more centralization or decentralization of business operations and management may depend on top management's philosophy.

POWER AND STATUS

Knowledge is power—this fact has been recognized for generations. The latest developments in computerized systems are changing the power structure within organizations. The struggle over who will control the computers and information resources has become one of the most visible conflicts in many organizations, both private and public. Expert systems, for example, may reduce the power of certain professional groups because their knowledge will become public domain. On the other hand, individuals who control AI application teams may gain considerable prestige, knowledge, power, and status. As a result, there is a **power redistribution** in many organizations. Managers and employees who control IT are likely to gain power at the expense of others.

JOB CONTENT

One major impact of IT is on the content of many jobs in both private and public organizations. **Job content** is important not only because it is related to organizational structure, but also because it is interrelated with employee satisfaction, compensation, status, and productivity. Changes in job content occur when work is redesigned, especially when business process reengineering (BPR) is attempted.

ROLE AMBIGUITY AND CONFLICT. Changes in the job content may result in opportunities for promotion and employee development. But these changes could create problems of role conflict and **role ambiguity**, especially in the short run. In addition, there may be considerable resistance to changes in roles, primarily on the part of managers who favor a noncomputerized information systems.

EMPLOYEE CAREER LADDERS

Increased use of IT in organizations could have a significant and somewhat unexpected impact on career ladders. Today, many highly skilled professionals have developed their abilities through years of experience, holding a series of positions that expose them to progressively more difficult and complex situations. The use of IT and especially ES may "block out" a portion of this learning curve. However, several questions remain unaddressed. How will high-level human expertise be acquired with minimal experience in lower-level tasks? What will be the effect on compensation at all levels of employment? How will human resource development programs be structured? What career paths will be offered to employees?

CHANGES IN SUPERVISION

The fact that an employee's work is performed on-line and stored electronically introduces the possibility for greater electronic supervision. For professional employees whose work is often measured by completion of projects, "remote supervision'' implies greater emphasis on completed work and less on personal contacts. This emphasis is especially true if employees work in geographically dispersed locations away from their supervisors. In general, the supervisory process may become more formalized, with greater reliance on procedures and measurable outputs than on informational processes.

OTHER CONSIDERATIONS

Several other personnel-related issues could surface as a result of using IT. For example, what will be the impact of IT on job qualifications, on training requirements, and on worker satisfaction? How can jobs involving the use of IT be designed so that they present an acceptable level of challenge to users? How might IT be used to personalize or enrich jobs? What can be done to make sure that the introduction of IT does not demean jobs or have other negative impacts from the workers' point of view? What principles should be used to allocate functions to people and machines, especially those functions that can be performed equally well by either one? Should cost or efficiency be the sole or major criterion for such allocation? All these and even more issues could be encountered in any system implementation.

THE MANAGER'S JOB

The most important task of managers is making decisions. IT can change the manner in which many decisions are being made and consequently change the managers' jobs (see Box 20.6). The impact of IT on decision making can be many; the most probable areas are listed here:

▼ Automation of routine decisions.

▼ Less expertise required for many decisions.

▼ Less reliance on experts to provide support to top executives.

▼ Power redistribution among managers.

▼ Support to complex decisions, making them faster and with better quality results.

A Closer Look BOX 20.6

HUBER'S PROPOSITIONS ABOUT COMPUTERS' IMPACTS ON DECISION MAKING

According to George Huber, the use of computer-assisted communication technologies leads to the following organizational changes:

1. A large number and variety of people participating as decision sources.
2. A decrease in the number and variety of people participating in traditional face-to-face communication.
3. Less time in meetings.
4. Better chance that a particular organizational level will make a particular decision.
5. Greater variation across the organization in the levels at which a particular type of decision is made.
6. Fewer organizational levels involved in authorizing actions.

7. Fewer intermediate information nodes within the organizational information processing network.
8. Fewer levels involved in processing messages.
9. More frequent development and use of databases.
10. More rapid and accurate identification of problems and opportunities.
11. Organizational intelligence (e.g., scanning, monitoring) that is more accurate, comprehensive, timely, and available.
12. Higher-quality decisions.
13. Shorter time required to authorize actions.
14. Shorter time required to make decisions.

SOURCE: Compiled from Huber (1990).

Many managers have reported that the computer has finally given them time to "get out of the office and into the field." (It is claimed that executive information systems [EIS] can save an hour a day for every user.) They also have found that they can spend more time planning activities instead of "putting out fires." Another aspect of the management challenge lies in the ability of IT to *support* the decision process in general and strategic planning and control decisions in particular. IT could change the decision-making process and even decision-making styles. For example, information gathering for decision making will be done much more quickly. Most managers currently work on a large number of problems simultaneously, moving from one to another as they wait for more information on their current problem or until some external event "interrupts" them. IT tends to reduce the time necessary to complete any step in the decision-making process. Therefore, managers will work on fewer tasks during each day but complete more of them. The reduction of start-up time associated with moving from task to task could be the most important source of increased managerial productivity.

Another possible impact on the manager's job could be a change in leadership requirements. What are generally considered to be good qualities of leadership may be significantly altered with the use of IT. For example, when face-to-face communication is replaced by electronic mail and computerized conferencing, leadership qualities attributed to physical appearance could be less important.

Even if managers' jobs do not change dramatically, the methods that managers use to do their jobs will. For example, an increasing number of CEOs no longer use intermediaries; instead, they work directly with computers. Once voice understanding is economically feasible, we may see a real revolution in the manner in which computers are used by managers.

► 20.6 IMPACTS ON INDIVIDUALS

Information systems affect individuals in various ways. What is a benefit to one individual may be a curse to another. Some of the ways that IT may affect individuals, their perceptions and behaviors, will be considered next.

JOB SATISFACTION

Although many jobs may become substantially more "enriched" with IT, other jobs may become more routine and less satisfying, For example, Argyris (1970) predicted that computer-based information systems would reduce managerial discretion in decision making and thus create dissatisfied managers.

DEHUMANIZATION

A frequent criticism of traditional data processing systems is their negative effect on people's individuality. Such systems are criticized as being impersonal; they **dehumanize** and depersonalize activities that have been computerized. Many people feel a loss of identity; they feel like "just another number" because computers reduce or eliminate the human element that was present in the noncomputerized systems.

While the major objective of new IT technologies such as DSS is to increase productivity, they also create *flexible* systems that can allow individuals to input their opinions and knowledge. These technologies attempt to be people oriented and user friendly.

Kaltnekar (1991) has suggested that one can pose the question of whether IT exists for the sake of people or whether people exist for the sake of the technology. He addressed the issue of the importance of achieving a balance between technology and the significance of the person in an organization. He also posed the question of whether IT is just one organizational function or whether the organization is a function of IT. Technical solutions to organizational problems can easily subvert the need to consider relationships among people in an organization. He stated that the basic requirement for system development is the recognition that all work processes be designed because of people and for people. Hardware and software accomplish many difficult tasks previously performed by people. This enables people to devote time to more creative tasks. Now, however, ES and AI are replacing people in the creative arena. People have become dependent on technology and may become a mere link in the chain. Kaltnekar says, "... one faces a half-serious yet worrying question: will there be any place for man in the future automated world?"

PSYCHOLOGICAL IMPACTS

One example of a psychological impact resulting from the widespread use of home computers is that home computers threaten to have an even more isolating influence than was created by television. If people are encouraged to work and shop from their living rooms, then some unfortunate psychological effects—such as depression and loneliness—could develop. Another example is distance learning. Children can be schooled at home through IT, but the lack of social contact could be damaging.

▶ 20.7 IMPACTS ON HEALTH AND SAFETY

Computers and information systems are part of the job environment. Therefore, they may adversely affect our health and safety. To illustrate, we will discuss the effects of three issues: job stress, video display terminals, and long time use of the keyboard. The protection against such problems is shown in Box 20.7.

JOB STRESS

Job stress is caused by many factors. With the onset of computerization, many workers feel out of place in their positions. They see computers executing many of the tasks they used to do, so they are unsure of their future place in the organization. Management does not usually discuss such changes with workers, and management seldom makes changes in the affected job descriptions. Consequently, these individuals are left without a clear understanding of what their jobs are supposed to be and what they are supposed to do (i.e., increased role ambiguity).

Another factor that causes job stress is an increase in workload and/or responsibilities. Although computerization has benefitted organizations by increasing productivity, it has also created an ever-increasing workload. Workers feel overwhelmed and start feeling anxious about their jobs and their performances. These feelings of anxiety can affect workers' productivity. Management's responsibility is to help alleviate these feelings by redistributing the workload among workers or hiring more individuals. Sometimes training is necessary. Also, it is management's responsibility to design jobs properly and to initiate retraining programs. If these problems are not faced, an organization will be inefficient. It will have a computer system capable of doing the work needed, but it will not have the individuals capable of doing their work.

REPETITIVE STRAIN INJURIES

Exposure to *video display terminals* (VDTs) raised the issue of risk of radiation exposure, which has been linked to cancer and other health-related problems. For

A Closer Look BOX 20.7

ERGONOMIC PRODUCTS PROTECT COMPUTER USERS

Many products are available on the market to improve working conditions for people who spend much of their time with a computer. The following pictures are representative examples.

(a) Wrist support.

(b) Back support.

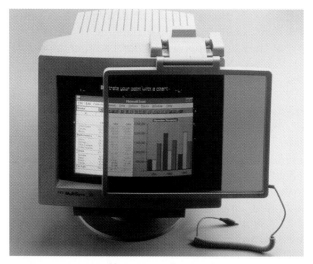

(c) Eye-protection filter (optically coated glass filter).

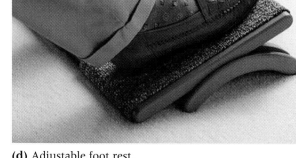

(d) Adjustable foot rest.

SOURCE: Based on information taken out of vendors' catalogs.

example, lengthy exposure to VDTs has been blamed for miscarriages in pregnant women. However, results of the research done to investigate this charge have been inconclusive. It is known that exposure to VDTs for long periods of time can affect an individual's eyesight. Other potential hazards, though not direct results of the VDT, are backaches due to long or inappropriate sitting in front of computers and muscle tension in peoples' fingers and wrists. *Carpal tunnel syndrome* is a pernicious and painful form of repetitive strain injury that affects the wrists and hands. It has been associated with the long-term use of the keyboard. Repetitive strain injuries can be very costly to corporations. According to Cone (1994), there have been more than 2,000 lawsuits against computer manufacturers and employers. For example, a lawsuit against IBM filed in 1994 requested $11.5 million for inappropriate design of a keyboard that caused carpal tunnel syndrome.

LESSENING THE NEGATIVE IMPACT ON HEALTH AND SAFETY

Designers are aware of the potential problems associated with prolonged use of computers. Consequently, they have attempted to design a better computing environment. Research in the area of **ergonomics** (or human factors) provides guidance for designers. For instance, ergonomic techniques focus on creating an environment for the worker that is well lit and comfortable. Devices such as antiglare screens have helped alleviate problems of fatigued or damaged eyesight, and chairs that contour the human body have helped decrease backaches.

OTHER IMPACTS

Individuals can be affected by computerization in many ways. Actually, computers change the manner in which people live, work, learn, and entertain themselves. Interaction between individuals and computers are so numerous that entire volumes can be written on the subject. An overview of such interactions is provided by Kanter (1992) and illustrated in Figure 20.1 pg. 752. The figure shows the individual circled by electronic transfer of money (to be used in home shopping and smart cards) that allows purchase of products and services. These are organized in the intermediate ring as six systems (consumer, education, and so on). Finally, the outer ring gives some examples of specific products or services in each system.

▶ 20.8 SOCIETAL IMPACTS

The societal implications of IT will be far reaching. Use of IT already has had many direct beneficial effects on society—solving complicated human and social problems such as medical diagnosis, computer-assisted instruction, government program planning, environmental quality control, and law enforcement. Problems in these areas could not have been solved economically—or at all—without IT. This section describes several representative impacts.

OPPORTUNITIES FOR PEOPLE WITH DISABILITIES

Integration of some AI technologies such as speech recognition and vision recognition into a CBIS could create new employment opportunities for people with disabilities. For example, those who cannot type would be able to use a voice-operated typewriter, and those who cannot travel could work at home. Boeing Company is developing several ESs to help employees with disabilities perform a variety of useful tasks.

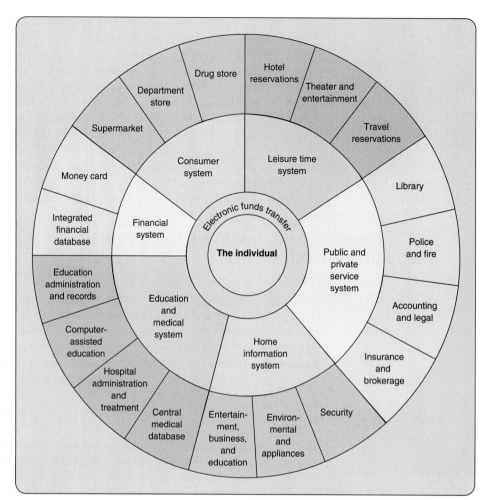

FIGURE 20.1 Information system and the individual. (SOURCE: Kanter, Jerome, *Managing With Information*, 4th Ed. © 1992, p. 350. Reprinted with permission of Prentice-Hall, Upper Saddle River, New Jersey.)

FIGURE 20.2 Enabling disabled people to work with computers. (SOURCE: Lazzaro [1993].)

A PC for a blind user, equipped with an Oscar optical scanner and a braille printer, both by TeleSensory. The optical scanner converts text into ASCII code or into proprietary word processing format. Files saved on disk can then be translated into braille and sent to the printer. Visually impaired users can also enlarge the text on the screen by loading a TSR software magnification program.

FIGURE 20.2 (continued)

The deaf user's PC is connected to a telephone via an Ultratec Intele-Modem Baudot/ASCII modem. The user is sending and receiving messages to and from someone at a remote site who is using a telecommunications device for deaf people (right).

This motor-disabled person is communicating with a PC using a Pointer Systems optical head pointer to access all keyboard functions on a virtual keyboard shown on the PC's display. The user can "strike" a key in one of two ways. He can focus on the desired key for a user-definable time period (which causes the key to be highlighted), or he can click an adapted switch when he chooses the desired key.

Adaptive equipment permits people with disabilities to perform ordinary tasks with computers. In Figure 20.2, one can see a PC for a deaf user, a PC for a blind user, and a PC for a motor-disabled person. Effective July 26, 1994, companies with as few as 15 employees have been mandated to comply with the Americans with Disabilities Act. This act requires companies to take reasonable steps to assure that employees with disabilities will be able to work with specially-adapted computers as well as with other equipment.

CHANGING ROLE OF WOMEN

IT is changing the "traditional" role of women in the workplace. The opportunity to work at home (see Chapter 14 for a discussion on telecommuting and the need for less travel due to teleconferencing) helps women with young children assume more responsible managerial positions in organizations. This could lead to better pay for women who can devote more attention to business while they still carry on duties at home.

IMPROVEMENTS IN HEALTH CARE

EMERGING TECHNOLOGY

...Expert systems help individuals to be healthier and wealthier

IT has caused major improvements in health care delivery ranging from better and faster diagnoses to expedited research and development of new drugs, to more accurate monitoring of critically ill patients. One technology that has made a special contribution is artificial intelligence. AI supports various tasks carried out by physicians and other health-care workers. Of special interest are expert systems that support diagnosis of diseases and the use of machine vision in enhancing the work of radiologists. Recently, surgeons started to use virtual reality to plan complex surgeries.

HELP FOR THE CONSUMER

Several IT products are in place, and many more will be developed, to help the layperson perform tasks that are skilled or tasks that are undesirable. TaxCut is an expert system product that can help in tax preparation; Willmaster is an ES that helps a layperson draft a simple will; and Wines on Disk advises the consumer how to select wines. Intelligent robots will clean the house and mow the lawn. These and many other improvements can contribute to an increased quality of life.

QUALITY OF LIFE

On a broader scale, IT has implications for the **quality of life**. An increase in organizational efficiency may result in more leisure time for workers. The workplace can be expanded from the traditional nine-to-five job at a central location to twenty-four hours-a-day at *any* location. This expansion provides a flexibility that can significantly improve the quality of leisure time, even if the total amount of leisure time is not increased. Our health and safety can also be improved, since robots can work in uncomfortable or dangerous environments (see Box 20.8).

IT At Work BOX 20.8

EMERGING TECHNOLOGY

NEW TASKS FOR ROBOTS

CALIFORNIA ROBOTS HIT THE ROAD.* While driving in California, one can see signs that say "Robots Working." The California Transportation Department and the University of California at Davis have developed robotic road-maintenance systems that save money, reduce congestion, and prevent worker accidents. The first robo-repairer, which is operated by only one employee, uses lasers to spot cracks between the pavement and the shoulder. It then dispenses the right amount of patch material.

Caltrans Corporation is testing an unmanned machine, based on technology developed for the military, that would combine a hovercraft and a video camera to inspect bridges. Other highway robots restripe traffic lanes and identify hazardous materials from a safe dis-

tance. Caltrans project manager, Thomas West, says such machines may be critical to keeping roads in good shape to handle the ever-increasing traffic.

ROBOTS CLEAN TRAIN STATIONS IN JAPAN.* With growing amounts of rubbish to deal with at Japanese train stations and fewer people willing to work as cleaners, officials have started turning the dirty work over to robots. Since May 1993, the Central Japan Railway Company and Sizuko Company, a Japanese machinery maker, have been using two robots programmed to vacuum rubbish. A railway official said the robots, which are capable of doing the work of 10 people, have been operating two or three days a week at the Sizuko station in central Japan. The robots measure about 1.5

meters wide and 1.2 meters long. The railway and Sizuko spent 200 million yen ($2 million) to develop the machines and are planning to program them for other tasks, such as sweeping and scrubbing (robots are even being used to clean cemeteries).

More than any other country, Japan has made extensive use of robots in industry. It also uses them to assist the blind and the elderly as well as to diagnose some illnesses.

Critical Thinking Issues: If robots are so productive, what will be the impact on unemployment when more tasks will be robotized? What will people do when robots take over? ▲

*SOURCE: Based on "California Robots May Soon Hit the Road," *BusinessWeek*, December 7, 1992.

**SOURCE: Based on "Robots Used to Clean Train Station in Japan," *The Sunday Times* (Singapore), June 6, 1993.

The automated crack sealing machine developed by the California Department of Transportation and the University of California, Davis.

SOCIAL RESPONSIBILITY

Organizations need to be motivated to utilize IT to improve the quality of life in the workplace. They should design their IT to minimize negative working conditions. This challenge relates not only to companies that produce IT hardware and software but also to companies that use these technologies. Increased exposure to the concepts and actual use of IT will bring pressure on public agencies and corporations to employ the latest capabilities for solving social problems outside the workplace as well. This is part of the organization's **social responsibility**. At the same time, conflicting public pressures may rise to suppress the use of IT because of concerns about privacy and "big brother" government. Computer applications can benefit society in many ways. Here are some examples.

▼ Searching for missing children is enhanced by electronic imaging and fax. High-quality photos plus text can be sent from the Center for Missing and Exploited Children to many fax machines and to portable machines in police cars. Of special interest is the support given by computers in a California kidnapping case (see Box 20.9), which improved the quality of fax transmission and increased the number of people exposed to the announcements.

▼ A sick person who needs help can activate a small transistor that is worn on a necklace. A computer chip automatically activates the telephone to notify an operator who can contact the emergency service or a physician.

IT At Work BOX 20.9

INFORMATION HIGHWAYS TRACING KIDNAPPERS

On October 1, 1993, America was shocked by the abduction of 12-year old Polly Kloss from a slumber party at her home in Petaluma, California. While Polly was only one of 4,500 children missing annually, her case received tremendous publicity due to the unusual nature of the abduction. Normally, the authorities distribute blurry black-and-white snapshots of the victim in the neighborhood of the missing child. The police usually use fax machines that turn out poor reproductions of pictures for dissemination. But this time, over 7 million high-quality pictures of Polly and an FBI sketch of the kidnapper turned up in millions of households, on electronic bulletin boards, and in many other places. This time, computers were used to disseminate the information using the Internet.

Polly's picture and the FBI sketch were scanned into the Internet and several other networks. From there, the information was transmitted to several hundred electronic bulletin boards. In addition, eight computers sent the images via computer fax to grocery stores and transportation hubs around the country at a rate of 1,000 pictures per minute (see picture).

Since it was the first application of computers for the purpose of distributing high-quality information nationwide, it took about two weeks to complete. The knowledge gained through this experience will enable the National Center for Missing and Exploited Children to solicit

The FBI notice posted on the Internet to help find a kidnapping victim.

the help of millions of searchers for lightening-fast searches.

Critical Thinking Issue: Can similar efforts be made to search for all 4500 missing children each year? ▲

SOURCE: Based on Smolowe, J., "A High-Tech Dragnet," *Time*, November 1, 1993.

▼ A geographical information system helps the San Bernadino Sheriff's Department in visualizing crime patterns and allocating resources.

▼ A computerized voice mail system is used in Rochester, New York, so that homeless and other needy people can find jobs, access health care resources, and gain independent living skills.

▼ IT provides many devices for disabled people. Examples include a bilingual notebook computer for blind students, a two-way writing telephone, a robotic page turner, a hair brusher, and a hospital-bedside video trip to the zoo.

INTERNATIONAL IMPLICATIONS

As a result of advancements in information technology, such as the increased speed of communications and information flow, we are living in a shrinking world. In fact over 25 years ago, Marshal McLuhan coined the term "global village" to refer to this very concept.

Transborder data flows can impact the very world order in which we live (see Box 20.10). This is occurring due to the ease with which information can be distributed to large numbers of people in a short time span. The power of the

A Closer Look BOX 20.10

GLOBAL PERSPECTIVE

THE ISSUES OF DATA TRANSFER ACROSS INTERNATIONAL BORDERS

Moving information across international borders, also known as transborder data flow (TBDF) has several global impacts. It is difficult to control the flow of data, but some goverments are attempting to do it. The major issues that affect TBDF are the following.

Security issues.

▼ *National security.* Databases may contain classified information relevant to national security. Transfer of such data outside the country may jeopardize the country's security.

▼ *Organizational security.* Similar to national security, an organization's security may be at risk. France, for example, requires that every database maintained in that country be registered with the government, so classified material can be monitored.

▼ *Personal security.* A major issue is privacy. Sweden, Canada, France, and Brazil have strict privacy laws. These countries require that information be processed within their borders as much as possible. The problem is that this may increase the cost of processing. Also, privacy laws differ from one country to another.

Sovereignty issues.

▼ *National sovereignty.* Some countries prefer that hardware, software, and networks used be made in their country.

▼ *Economic sovereignty.* Some countries want information to be processed within their boundaries to increase employment and improve the balance of payments.

▼ *Cultural sovereignty.* Many countries want to maintain their cultural identities. They are afraid of what is described as "electronic colonialism." They can control what is shown on television, but it is difficult to control what is on the Internet or on a bulletin board.

Technical issues.

▼ *Data vulnerability and accuracy.* This issue is similar to what was described in Chapter 19. However, due to global flows, the problems may be more acute.

▼ *Technical standards.* There are no global technical standards for transmitting information across borders. Communication infrastructures differ from one country to another.

Developing issues.

▼ *Legal and regulatory issues.* Every country has its own legal system regarding national, organizational, and personal flow and use of data and information.

▼ *Intellectual property.* Transfer of data may violate intellectual property laws with regard to copyrights, patents, licenses, and copying of software. There is an issue of different laws in different countries as well as enforcement of such laws.

▼ *Developing countries.* Many so-called Third World nations have fears regarding the use of information flowing to their territories. Also, they lack communication infrastructure.

---

media is growing as a result of cable television, electronic publishing, and networking through computer modems.

Many countries, whether willingly or unwillingly, are being somewhat Westernized as a result of information flowing freely across borders about Western ways-of-life and values. This has the potential to fuel the fires of political unrest, especially in nondemocratic countries. Facsimile, computer disks, electronic publishing, tape recorders, and other forms of information technology could assist the masses in planning revolts. How these advancements in technology are viewed, therefore, would depend upon which side of the coin—figuratively speaking—one's affiliations are on.

THE ROLE OF MANAGEMENT

The potential impacts of IT discussed in this chapter raises the issue of what management can do about all the changes. How do we anticipate the broad societal effects of IT and the things it makes possible? What can we do to ensure that people's attitudes toward IT are well founded and that their expectations about what these systems can do are accurate? How do we determine the potential positive and negative effects of IT before they become realities? One of the most important issues for managers to consider is the impact of IT on employment.

▶ 20.9 INFORMATION TECHNOLOGY AND EMPLOYMENT

The major attribute associated with automation is the replacement of people by machines. From its inception in the eighteenth century, automation has caused many people to lose their jobs. Naturally, many people rejected or objected to automation. Butler's work of fiction, described in Section 20.2, is an example of the concern people have about automation; so is the classic Charlie Chaplin movie *Modern Times*. This movie attempted to show how machines displace people and how work can be dehumanized in a factory.

No doubt many people *have* been displaced by automation, but many more have gained employment due to automation. Machines replaced muscle power in the Industrial Revolution; in the Information Revolution, machines are replacing both muscle and brain power. The increase in productivity provided by computers leads to lower costs and prices for products and services. Computers encourage competition, which leads to further decline in prices. Lower prices mean higher demand which, in turn, creates more jobs. The computer industry itself has created millions of new jobs.

Unemployment has been one of the major concerns of developing countries. However, during the past decade, this concern has spread to industrialized countries as well (see Box 20.11). The high unemployment rate in the United States in 1992 was one of the major factors in the 1992 presidential election. In 1994, the United Nations conducted a special investigation to study unemployment, which continues to increase in many countries.

A Closer Look BOX 20.11

WILL COMPUTERS CAUSE JOBLESSNESS?

When the level of built-in intelligence reaches critical mass, jobs could swiftly disappear, leaving all but a privileged few out of work. Indeed, it is now possible to see that the desire for efficiency could mean that virtually every job is automated out of existence. The amount of work already replaced by computers is obvious, and increasing IT power will accelerate the process. This is a frightening enough prospect in itself. If human beings stay on the same road and marry computers with other technologies, however, there is an even greater possibility of humans themselves being replaced. People must decide now what level of intelligent technology is consistent with humanity and a high quality of life, delineating the border between people-friendly tools and destructive replacements. It is hoped that the warning is heard and that people will choose rightly to deprive IT of its power.

SOURCE: Condensed from Ceramalus (1993).

Due to difficult economic times, increased global competition, demands for customization, and increased consumer sophistication, companies have had no choice but to increase their investments in IT. In addition, computers are becoming "smarter" and more capable as time passes. The idea of replacing people with machines is increasing rapidly. For this reason, some people believe that society is heading toward **massive unemployment**. The remaining part of this section presents the major arguments of two opposing factions: people who believe that massive unemployment is coming (see Box 20.11) and those who believe that this is not going to happen.

ARGUMENTS THAT SUPPORT MASSIVE UNEMPLOYMENT

Kalman Toth, author of *The Workless Society* (1990), predicted that by 2010 there will be massive unemployment—the entire U.S. workforce replaced by machine intelligence. He believes that people currently making a living from computers will be replaced by what he refers to as silicon magnetic intelligence (SMI). Eventually, SMI will be able to drive trucks and perform other tasks through development of a stationary body-based intelligence augmented by a visual pattern processed through a video camera. By adding hearing and speech to an artificial intelligence device that already can see, SMI units could take over unlimited human jobs.

While Toth's predictions may seem to be imaginative, a group of economists (Peitchins [1983] and Noble Prize winner, Wassily Leontief [1986]), presents the following supporting arguments.

1. The need for human labor will be reduced significantly because of computers (productivity increases of 1000 percent or more will be realized by using CBIS).

2. The required skill levels of people performing many jobs with the help of IT will be low.

3. IT will affect both blue- and white-collar employees (professionals and managers) in all sectors, including service industries and high-technology companies. In the past, service industries and the high-technology sector absorbed employees displaced by computers in other sectors.

4. In the past few years, especially in the early 1990s, several industries—ranging from banking and insurance to computer and automotive industries—have laid off millions of employees.

5. Industry, government, and services already have a substantial amount of **hidden unemployment**; that is, companies retain many employees who are not needed or fully utilized due to humanitarian reasons, union pressures, or government policies.

6. Unemployment levels have grown steadily in the past decade in spite of increased computerization.

7. The per capita amount of goods and services that people can consume is limited, and sooner or later, it may stop growing. Therefore, the idea that the economy can produce without limit (and create jobs) is highly questionable.

8. Many organizations are reengineering their operations in an effort to remain competitive or to stay within budgets. This will reduce the demand for labor even further.

ARGUMENTS CONTRADICTING MASSIVE UNEMPLOYMENT

While the arguments for massive unemployment in the future are rather convincing, there are many people, including another Nobel Prize winner, Herbert Simon (1977), who believe that IT *will not* cause massive unemployment. Instead, IT will continue to create new jobs and even increase the overall employment level. Their primary arguments are the following.

1. Historically, automation has always resulted in increased employment by creating new occupations.

2. Unemployment is higher in nonindustrialized countries than in industrialized ones.

3. Work, especially the professional and managerial kind, can always be expanded, so there will be work for everyone.

4. The task of converting to automated factories and offices is complex and may take several generations.

5. Many tasks cannot be fully automated (e.g., top management, nursing, marriage counseling, surgery, the performing arts, and the creative arts).

6. Machines and people can be fully employed, each where the comparative advantage is strongest.

7. Real wages may be reduced; however, people will have income from other sources (assuming that the government will control the distribution of wealth). Therefore, people will have enough money to spend and thus will help create more jobs.

8. The cost of goods and services will be so low that the demand for them will increase significantly. Automation will never catch up with the increased demand.

This debate about how IT will affect employment raises a few other questions. Is some unemployment really socially undesirable? (People could have more leisure time.) Should the government intervene more in the distribution of income and in the determination of the employment level? Can the "invisible hand" in the economy, which has worked so well in the past, continue to be successful in the future? Will IT make most of us idle but wealthy? (Robots will do the work, and people will enjoy life.) Should the issue of income be completely separated from that of employment? The answers to these questions will be provided in part by the developments in future IT.

▶ 20.10 THE FUTURE OF INFORMATION TECHNOLOGY

Over the next 30 to 40 years, the world population seems almost certain to double to 10 to 11 billion people. Most of these people will be more educated than their parents, and they will want to live as affluently as do most people in the United States. Society will be pressured to provide education, health and social services, and a clean environment to all these people. People will need jobs, and countries will need highways, telecommunication lines, and large quantities of food.

To some, technology is a great opportunity (see Bellamy's utopian book *Looking Backward* [1989]). To others, technology is viewed as a threat (see Huxley's *Brave New World* [1932]).

The purpose of this concluding section is to summarize some predictions regarding the future of information technology. Its impact on people, organizations, and society is too speculative to deal with and, thus, will be left to authors such as Bellamy and Huxley.

TECHNOLOGICAL DEVELOPMENTS

Technological developments will accelerate in the future. Here are some specifics.

Chip technology will progress as more transistors are placed on one chip.

Storage will be larger and will access faster; compression methods will increase today's capacity fivefold or more in about five years.

Telecommunication will expand to more networks, more capacity (ATM switches), more speed, and more wireless communication.

Information superhighways will foster the integration of computer, television, and other facilities in every home and business.

Object-oriented approach will become widely accepted for building information systems.

Graphical user interface will be used in most information systems.

Distributed and cooperative computing will be common in most organizations.

Client/server architecture will be most popular in middle-size to large-size corporations.

Emerging technologies such as neural computing and other machine learning technologies will be introduced into many applications, and in many cases they will be integrated with other CBIS.

Intelligent agents will improve accessibility to databases as well as software development and use. They will be able to learn from experience and act as personal assistants to managers.

Speech recognition is being improved with every improvement in microprocessing power and increased computer memory. Computers will increase their vocabulary through experience.

Software development time will be shorter and less expensive due to CASE tools, object-oriented programming, and prototyping.

End-user computing will continue to grow with or without the cooperation of the information system department.

The success of these technological developments depends, of course, on research efforts such as shown in Box 20.12.

A Closer Look BOX 20.12

WHAT HITACHI'S LABS ARE HATCHING

Hitachi is a Japanese diversified-technological company that combines some of the capabilities of General Electric, AT&T, and IBM. This multinational giant has extensive laboratories, several of which are in the United States. The following are some of its IT-related research projections.

3 to 5 years

▼ Neural networks on silicon chips that mimic learning and pattern-recognition faculties of the human brain.

▼ Multimedia offices where computers have high-resolution screens and hi-fi audio that can also double as videoconference terminals.

5 to 10 years

▼ Handheld computers that obey handwritten or voice commands and exchange information over radio waves.

▼ Virtual reality technology that allows users on a network to meet and interact in computer-simulated environments.

10 to 20 years

▼ Superconducting chips, packing 100 times more data and 10 times the speed of today's chips.

▼ Neural computers made of tens of thousands of powerful microprocessors, combining optical and electronic circuits that are able to learn and reason.

▼ Translation software for any of the world's languages.

▼ Underground magnetic levitation conveyors linked by software for distribution of goods in congested cities.

More than 20 years

▼ Biocomputers whose organic materials can repair themselves like living creatures.

▼ Intelligent cities, with homes and offices wired with fiber optics that send voice, image, and computer data and are run by electronic control centers.

SOURCE: Condensed from *BusinessWeek*, September 28, 1992.

INFORMATION SYSTEMS APPLICATIONS

Improvements in technology will result in new and improved applications in almost every field of science, business, medicine, education, and government. Innovative applications will surround us. What we see today is only the beginning. The only limit will be imagination. Soon, we will be able to write a whole handbook of computer applications in each field or even subfield.

Consider the forecasts depicted in Boxes 20.12 and 20.13. While some of the technological developments are forecasted to occur before the year 2000, wide-range acceptance of these developments in terms of applications will take place a decade later. Historically, a gap of about 10 years occurs between the initial availability of a technology and its wide-spread use. (It took more than 10 years before ATMs started to appear in supermarkets.) This gap is a result of barriers such as

---

A Closer Look BOX 20.13

A DELPHI FORECAST OF INFORMATION TECHNOLOGY

Information technologies will grow far more sophisticated in the next few years, but social acceptance of some information services is likely to lag behind technical capabilities, according to a recent Delphi poll of experts.

Eleven authorities on technology were asked for estimates of the year in which a particular milestone would take place, as well as the likelihood of its occurrence. The accompanying chart lists mean estimates for these forecasts.

Milestone	Year of occurrence	Probability (0-1.0)
Sophisticated software programs are developed for personalized teaching, managing medical care, total control of all corporate operations, and so on.	1996	.95
Expert systems are commonly used to make routine decisions in business, engineering, medical diagnosis, and other fields.	1998	.88
Access to library materials via computer is more convenient and less expensive than going to the library.	2000	.87
Optical computers enter the commercial market.	2000	.86
Small computers about the size of a writing pad are commonly used by most people to manage their personal affairs and work.	2002	.85
Voice-access computers permit faster, more convenient interaction between humans and machines.	2002	.84
Education is commonly conducted by using computerized teaching programs and interactive TV.	2002	.69
Public networks permit anyone access to libraries of data, electronic messages, video teleconferencing, common software programs, and so on.	2003	.84
Routine parts of most software are generated by machine.	2003	.82
Parallel processing using multiple chips becomes dominant.	2003	.71
Computer programs have the capacity to learn by trial and error in order to adjust their behavior.	2004	.86
Teleconferencing replaces the majority of business travel.	2006	.40
Half of all goods in the United States are sold through computer services such as Prodigy.	2007	.43
Half of all U.S. workers perform parts of their jobs partially at home using computer systems.	2009	.52

SOURCE: Halal, W. E., "The Information Technology Revolution," from *The Futurist*, July/August 1992. Reproduced with permission from THE FUTURIST, Bethesda, Maryland.

resistance to change; lack of support from top management; difficulties in justifying intangible benefits; and technological problems of integration and interfacing different technologies, databases, and networks.

▶ MANAGERIAL ISSUES

Management attention must be directed to the social, psychological, ethical, and legal issues surrounding IT. Ignoring these issues could cause litigation and/or disturbances at work. Here are some points to consider:

1. Lawsuits against employers because of repetitive strain injuries are on the increase. Employees are suing employers under the federal Disabilities Act. Because this law is new, any court involvement may be very costly.

2. Multinational corporations face different cultures in the different countries in which they are doing business. What might be ethical in country A may be unethical in country B. Therefore, it is essential to develop a country-specific ethics code in addition to a corporate-wide one. Also, managers should realize that in some countries there is no legislation specifically concerned with computers and data.

3. Issues of privacy, ethics, social responsibilities, and so on may seem to be indirect to running a business. Such an attitude may have been correct in the past, but it may be incorrect in the future. Ignoring such issues may hinder the operation of many organizations.

4. Due to the rapid technological development, management will have to address complex issues such as these:

    a. Which technologies to use when and to what extent.
    b. Which vendors to use and how to control them.
    c. How to best use IT.
    d. To what degree a company should be a leader in developing IT.
    e. How to manage the proliferation of IT in organizations, and how to reconcile the differences between end users and the IS department.
    f. What IT architecture to use, and when to reengineer information systems.

The ability to manage IT properly in the future will provide management with unparalled opportunities to make their organizations effective and efficient in our turbulent and competitive world. ■

KEY TERMS

Code of ethics *738*	Hidden unemployment *759*	Privacy policies *744*
Dehumanization *748*	Job content *746*	Quality of life *754*
Electronic bulletin boards *743*	Job stress *749*	Role ambiguity *746*
Electronic surveillance *791*	Massive unemployment *758*	Social responsibility *755*
Ergonomics *750*	Power redistribution *746*	Span of control *744*
Ethics *738*	Privacy *739*	

CHAPTER HIGHLIGHTS *(L-x means learning objective number x)*

▼ The major negative impact of IT is in the area of ethics, invasion of privacy, unemployment, and dehumanization. (L-1)

▼ The major positive impact of IT is its contribution to employment of the disabled, improvements in

health, delivery of education, fighting crimes, and improvement of the environment. (L-1)

▼ Ethical issues can be classified into categories of privacy, accuracy, property, and accessibility. (L-2)

▼ Major privacy issues are electronic surveillance, keeping personal information in a database (accuracy and accessibility issues), dissemination of offensive information on bulletin boards, and assuring the right to privacy. (L-3)

▼ Computers may have several negative impacts on certain individuals. Dehumanization is a major concern that needs to be overcome by proper design and planning. (L-4)

▼ Information technology can make organizations flatter and change authority, job content, and status of employees. As a result, the manager's job and methods of supervision and decision making may drastically change. (L-5)

▼ Computers can increase health risks for human eyes, backs, bones, and muscles. Ergonomically designed computing facilities can greatly reduce the risks associated with computers. (L-6)

▼ Many positive social implications can be expected from IT. They range from providing opportunities to the disabled to reducing people's exposure to hazardous situations. (L-7)

▼ In one view, IT will cause massive unemployment because of increased productivity, reduced required skill levels, and the potential reduction of employment in all sectors of the economy. (L-8)

▼ In another view, IT will increase employment levels because automation makes products and services more affordable, and so demand increases; and the process of disseminating automation is slow enough to allow the economy to adjust to information technologies. (L-8)

▼ Quality of life, both at work and at home, is likely to improve as a result of IT. (L-8)

▼ The technological part of IT will continue to develop at an accelerated rate. Computers will be much faster and cheaper, and they will possess massive storage capabilities. (L-9)

▼ Object-oriented programming, graphical user interface, distributed processing, and client/server architecture are some of the most important developments of IT in the immediate future. (L-9)

QUESTIONS FOR REVIEW

1. Explain why IT may have negative effects on people.

2. Define ethics.

3. What are the four categories of ethics as they apply to IT?

4. Explain why some people object to computerization.

5. Define the four states of privacy: solitude, intimacy, anonymity, and reserve.

6. Why do the government and corporations use surveillance?

7. Why is there so much information about individuals in databases?

8. Explain the potential ethical issues involved in using electronic bulletin boards.

9. Describe the content of a "code of ethics" (for privacy).

10. What are some of the major impacts of IT on individuals?

11. Describe some of the potential risks to human health caused by extensive use of computers.

12. List the major societal impacts of IT that are described in this chapter, and categorize each of them as either negative or positive.

13. Present the major arguments of those who believe that IT will result in massive unemployment.

14. Present the major arguments of those who believe that IT will *not* result in massive unemployment.

15. Describe the following organizational impacts: flatter organizations, increased span of control, power redistribution, supervision, and decision making.

QUESTIONS FOR DISCUSSION

1. There are three ways to alert employees that information in their computers is under observation: (1) notify all employees upon recruitment that they may be observed while working on their computers, (2) notify employees once a year that they may be under surveillance, or (3) alert employees by a light or visible message on the computer screen (each time the computer is turned on) that they may be under observation. Which alternative would you prefer and why?

2. The Internal Revenue Service (IRS) buys demographic market research data from private companies. This data contains income statistics which could be compared to tax returns. Many U.S. citizens feel that their rights within the realm of the privacy act are being violated; others just say that this is an unethical behavior on the part of the government. Discuss.

3. Clerks at the 7-Eleven stores (see the case in Chapter 1, Section 1) enter information regarding customers (sex, approximate age, and so on) into the computer. This information is then processed for improved decision making. Customers are not informed about this nor are they asked for permission. (Names are *not* keyed in). Are the clerks' actions ethical?

4. Many hospitals, health maintenance organizations (HMO's), and federal agencies are converting or plan

to convert all patients' medical records from paper to electronic storage (using imaging technology). Once completed, electronic storage enables quick access to most records. However, the availability of these records in a database and on networks may allow people, some of whom are unauthorized, to view one's private data. To protect privacy fully may cost too much money and/or considerably slow accessibility to the records. What policies could health care administrators use in such situations? Discuss.

5. Northeast Utilities (Hartford, CT) has its meter readers gather information about services needed on its customers' homes, such as a driveway or fence requiring repairs. They then sell the data to companies that would stand to gain from the information. Customers are then solicited via direct mail, telemarketing, and so on, for the services that the meter readers record as being needed. While some customers welcome this approach, others consider it an annoyance because they are not interested in the particular repairs. Northeast Utilities was rated as the number one company of the "top 100 most effective users of IT" by *Computerworld* in 1988. Assess the value of the company's IT against the potential negative effects of adverse public reaction.

6. IT may have both positive and negative effects at the same time and in the same situation. Give two examples of each, and explain how to reconcile such situations.

7. Explain why there are such diverse opinions regarding specific ethical issues even within the same company.

8. It is said that IT has raised many new privacy issues. Why is this so?

9. Discuss the various aspects of relationships between IT and surveillance.

10. Several examples in this chapter illustrate how information about individuals can help companies improve their businesses. Summarize all the examples provided in this chapter, and explain why they may result in invasion of privacy.

11. Robots are used in California and Japan to support transportation (see Box 20.7). At the same time, they may take jobs away from people. Describe all the considerations that management will be faced with when it needs to decide whether or not to use robots.

12. Explore the effects of the Americans with Disabilities Act as it relates to IT.

13. Explain why organizations are becoming flatter and what the implications are on management practices.

14. In what ways is the manager's job changing as a result of extensive use of IT?

15. Review Huber's 14 propositions (see Box 20.6). Describe cases from your own experience that relate to these propositions.

16. Opening a regular (paper) letter while being delivered in the company mail is a violation of the law. But opening E-mail is not. Discuss.

17. Is ethics relative?

18. Why do many companies and professional organizations develop their own codes of ethics?

19. What are the two major rules of privacy? Why do these rules make privacy issues difficult to enforce?

20. What are the major privacy issues in information technology?

EXERCISES

1. An information security manager had access to corporate E-mail. She routinely monitored the contents of electronic correspondence among employees. She discovered that many employees are using the system for personal purposes. Some messages were love letters, and one dealt with a plan for homosexual relations. Other messages related to a football betting pool. The security manager prepared a list of the employees, with samples of their messages, and gave them to management. Some managers punished their employees. The employees objected to the monitoring, claiming that they should have the same right of privacy as they had using the company's interoffice mail system.
   a. Is monitoring of E-mail by managers ethical?
   b. Is the use of E-mail by employees for personal communication ethical?
   c. Is submission of a list of abusers by the security manager to management ethical?
   d. Is punishing the abusers ethical?
   e. What should the company do in order to rectify the situation?

2. Review the opening case on Agrico.
   a. Identify all of the ethical issues involved in this case.
   b. Advise Agrico's president as to what action to take, and justify your recommendation.
   c. Assume that Jane left the software on the screen deliberately; is her behavior ethical or not?

3. Eugene Wang resigned his job at Borland Corporation, a large software company, in September 1991 to join Symantec Corporation (a competitor). On the day he announced his resignation, Wang allegedly sent 12 computer messages to Symantec containing sensitive Borland Corporation secrets including their long-term plan for new products. The messages were received, according to police records, at Symantec's headquarters in Cupertino, California.

   Symantec's chairman was indicted by a grand jury after being accused of receiving stolen property and of conspiracy. Wang was charged with conspiracy and trade-secret law violations.

   While the case is still in courts, there are some interesting observations.

   ▼ Borland Corporation was roundly criticized in the industry for drawing the police into what has traditionally been considered private dispute between corporations.

▼ Ironically, Borland was able to read the coded messages sent by Mr. Wang by using a software developed by Peter Norton division of Symantec Corporation.

▼ Mr. Wang decided to sue Borland, claiming that his privacy was violated by tapping his electronic mail.

▼ Symantec Corporation called the charges unfounded, and a lawyer specializing in computer litigations said that trade-secret theft can be difficult to prove since it is difficult to define such secrets.

▼ The high-technology community is interested in the case because it has focused attention on issues of trade secrecy and corporate loyalty.

▼ Symantec filed a lawsuit claiming the Borland was abus-

ing the legal system in order to drive down Symantec's stock price, but on the day of the indictment, both stocks' prices climbed (about 5 percent for Borland, 10 percent for Symantec).

Evaluate the case, and express your position regarding the following issues.

a. Privacy rights in electronic mail.

b. Should the police have been involved in this case?

c. If Symantec is going to be found not guilty on the charges, is their action ethical?

SOURCE: Based on a story in the *Los Angeles Times*, March 5, 1993, pp. D2–D7 and in the *Orange County Register*, March 6, 1993, p. C2.

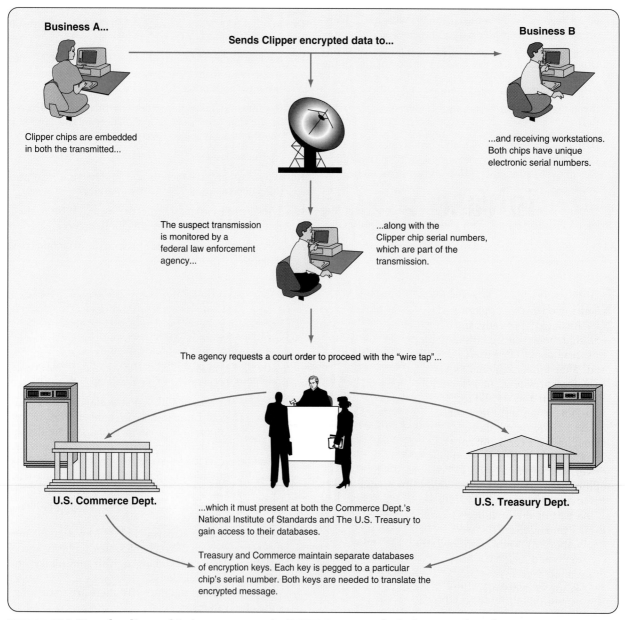

Business A...

Sends Clipper encrypted data to...

Business B

Clipper chips are embedded in both the transmitted...

...and receiving workstations. Both chips have unique electronic serial numbers.

The suspect transmission is monitored by a federal law enforcement agency...

...along with the Clipper chip serial numbers, which are part of the transmission.

The agency requests a court order to proceed with the "wire tap"...

U.S. Commerce Dept.

U.S. Treasury Dept.

...which it must present at both the Commerce Dept.'s National Institute of Standards and The U.S. Treasury to gain access to their databases.

Treasury and Commerce maintain separate databases of encryption keys. Each key is pegged to a particular chip's serial number. Both keys are needed to translate the encrypted message.

FIGURE 20.3 How the clipper chip is meant to work. (SOURCE: From Thyfault, M., et al., "The Data Security Furor," *InformationWeek*, February 14, 1994, p. 12.)

GROUP ASSIGNMENT

According to Denning (1993), a leading researcher on data security, personal privacy must be balanced against our collective interest in law and order. Denning supports proposed legislation which would require providers of electronic communications services and PBX operators to do the following: (1) ensure the government, in real time, that the communications signals of individual(s) named in a court order can be monitored and transferred to a remote government monitoring facility and (2) ensure that this will be done without detection by the subject and without degradation of service. Monitoring will be done by a special clipper chip, a microprocessor that is linked to a telephone or data terminal, so federal agents can unscramble coded messages (see Figure 20.3).

Opponents of the proposed legislation raise the following concerns.

▼ The proposal would hold back technology and stymie innovation.

▼ It will jeopardize security and privacy—first, because the remote monitoring capability would make the system vulnerable to attack and, second, because the intercept capability itself would introduce a new vulnerability into the systems.

▼ Implementing the intercept could harm the competitiveness of the United States.

▼ The cost of implementing the intercept might not justify the benefits.

▼ It is not clear who must comply with the proposed legislation and what compliance means.

QUESTIONS FOR GROUP ASSIGNMENT

a. Find the status of the proposed federal legislation.

b. Divide the group into pro and con subgroups.

c. Prepare presentations to the class by each subgroup.

d. Prepare a summary statement.

Minicase 1

How Private is E-Mail?

Southeast Transport is a medium-sized transportation company operating in Florida, Georgia, and South Carolina. Business was steady, and both the management team and shareholders were satisfied. Rumors, however, began to spread about drug use in the corporate headquarters and some of its regional offices. Jeff Mendelson, the corporate president, had a policy of ignoring rumors. However, on May 17, he received a call from the largest shareholder (an insurance company) notifying him that an anonymous letter alleged that drug use was spreading throughout the company and that several managers were involved. The shareholder felt that drug use, especially by drivers and dispatchers, could jeopardize the well-being of the corporation. Jeff decided to conduct a secret, internal investigation.

As part of the investigation, management monitored E-mail and voice mail (without letting the employees know about it). They confirmed drug use in several departments and regional offices as well as the involvement of some managers. They also found that a married manager in the IS department was having an affair with one of his subordinates. (Such an affair may be viewed as sexual harassment under the corporate guidelines).

The corporate executives were debating on whether to use the E-mail data as evidence in either or both of the incidents. They were unable to reach a decision. Some executives felt that the evidence should not be used at all because the company did not have a clear policy regarding the private use of E-mail or the monitoring of messages. Others felt that it was not illegal to collect the data, and the data should be used.

Questions for Minicase 1
As a consultant, respond to the following.

1. What would you advise the CEO to do and why?

2. What recommendations would you make with respect to corporate policies regarding the private use of E-mail and the monitoring of employees?

3. Some people argue that not notifying employees about the monitoring created an unethical situation. Others say that, in this case, it was perfectly ethical to monitor? What do you think?

Minicase 2

American Stock Exchange Seeks Wireless Trades

In April 1993, the American Stock Exchange (Amex) introduced a pilot project to test the use of handheld computers in trading. Previous attempts by the Chicago Board of Trade and by the Chicago Mercantile Exchange were not successful. Experiments are still being conducted. Amex is using simple, off-the-shelf equipment instead of the highly customized terminals used by the Chicago exchanges. The project is the first in a series designed to make Amex a paperless trade floor.

Omer F. Sykan, director of technical planning at Amex, said that the biggest benefit is to get a real-time position analysis to the 462 members of the exchange. Experiments are being done with two different devices. One device is used by market specialists to transmit option trades to a PC-based risk analysis system. The second device is used for equity (stocks) trading.

Wireless technologies are expected to be faster and more cost-effective than the paper-and-pencil trading mechanism in use for the past 200 years. In the old system, specialists scribble their trades on an order slip. Then, a clerk manually enters the data into the computer. If the markets are moving rapidly, the information that the clerk gathers from the floor is often obsolete by the time it is put into the computers. Handheld devices transmit information instantaneously.

While the devices are extremely easy to use, they are not welcomed by many traders. "Us old guys are faster than most of these computers," says Jack Maxwell, a veteran of 26 years with Amex. "To hell with it; I don't need the handhelds." Attitudes of traders like Maxwell are a big problem facing expanded use of computers.

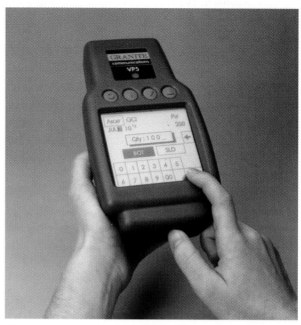

The American Stock Exchange's hand-held computer.

Questions for Minicase 2

1. As a consultant to Amex, you need to identify the problems of implementing the handheld computers. How would you **approach** your case?

2. The President of Amex is considering laying off traders like Maxwell. Would you support this decision or not?

3. Find the status of the computerization that is going on in several stock and commodity exchanges. (Search the library and the Internet for material published in the last six months.)

4. How would you convince a trader who may soon lose his job to use the new device?

SOURCE: Based on *Computerworld*, May 17, 1993, p. 6 and *The Wall Street Journal*, July 19, 1993, p. C1

REFERENCES AND BIBLIOGRAPHY

1. Agranoff, M. H., "Controlling the Threat to Personal Privacy," *Journal of Information Systems Management*, Vol. 8, No. 3, Summer 1992.

2. Anderson, R. E., et al., "Using the New ACM Code of Ethics in Decision Making," *Communication of the ACM*, February 1993.

3. Argyris, C., "Resistance to Rational Management Systems," *Innovation*, November 10, 1970.

4. Bellamy E., *Looking Backward: 2000–1887*, Boston Mass: Houghton, Mifflin, 1989.

5. Bogumil, W. A., Jr., and V. G. Gupta, "Information Systems and Americans with Disabilities Act," *Information Systems Management*, Summer 1993.

6. Butler, S., *EREWHON, or, Over the Range*, (1923, Reprint) Shrewsbury Edition, New York: AMS Press, 1972.

7. Breuer, J. E., "If We Dump Middle Management and Empower Whoever is Left, Will the Bottom Line Take Care of Itself?" *Inform*, Vol. 5, No. 5, May 1991.

8. Ceramalus, N., "The Treat of Workless Future," *Management-Auckland*, November 1993.

9. Kuczka, S., "Kids, Computers, and Porn," *Chicago Tribune*, August 6, 1993.

10. Clark, D., *Computers at Risk: Safe Computing in the Information Age*, Washington, DC: National Research Council, 1990.

11. Cone, E., Keyboard Injuries: Who Should Pay? *InformationWeek*, January 27, 1994.

12. Dejoie, R., et al., *Ethical Issues in Information Systems*, Boston: Boyd and Fraser, 1991.

13. Denning, D. E., "To Tap or Not To Tap," *Communications of the ACM*, March 1993.

14. Denning, D. E., "Forum," *Communications of the ACM*, June 1993.

15. Elmer-Dewitt, P., "On the Screen Near You: Cyberporn," *Time*, July 3, 1995.

16. Flaherty, D., *Protecting Privacy in Surveillance Societies*, Chapel Hill, NC: University of North Carolina Press, 1989.

17. Freedman, W., *The Right of Privacy in the Computer Age*, New York: Quorom Books, 1987.

18. Gardner, E. P., et al., "Job Stress and the VDT Clerical Worker," *Human Systems Management*, April 1988.

19. Halal, W. E., "The Information Revolution," *The Futurist*, July/August, 1992.

20. Hamel, G., and C. K. Prahalad, *Computing for the Future*, Boston: Harvard Business School Press, 1994.

21. Hartley, R. F., *Business Ethics: Violators of the Public Trust*, New York: Wiley, 1993.

22. Huber, G. P., "A Theory of the Effects of Advanced Inforamtion Technologies on Organizational Design, Intelligence, and Decision Making," *Academy of Management Review*, Vol. 15, No. 1, 1990.

23. Huxley, A., *Brave New World*, London Chatto and Williams, 1932.

24. Johnson, D. G., *Computer Ethics* 2nd ed., Englewood Cliffs, NJ: Prentice-Hall, 1993.

25. Kaltnekar, Z., "Information Technology and the Humanization of Work," *Management Impacts of Information Technology: Perspectives on Organizational Change and Growth*, Harrisburg, PA: Idea Group Publishing, 1991.

26. Kanter, J., *Managing with Information*, 4th ed. Englewood Cliffs, NJ: Prentice-Hall, 1992.

27. Kraut, R., et al., "Computerization, Productivity, and Quality of Life," *Communications of the ACM*, February 1989.

28. Lazzaro, J. J., "Computers for the Disabled," *BYTE*, June 1993.

29. Leontief, W., *The Future Impact of Automation on Workers*, Oxford: Oxford University Press, 1986.

30. Mason, R. "Four Ethical Issues of the Information Age," *MIS Quarterly*, March 1986.

31. Oz, E., *Ethics for Information Age*, W. C. Brown Communications, Inc: New York, 1994.

32. Palvia S., et al., (eds.), *The Global Issues of Information Technology Management*, Harrisburg, PA: Idea Group Publishers, 1992.

33. Partridge, D., "Social Implications of AI," in *AI Principles and Applications*, Ed. M. Yazdani, New York: Chapman and Hall, 1988.

34. Peitchins, S. G., *Computer Technology and Employment*, New York: St. Martin's Press, 1983.

35. Pinsonneault, A., and K. Kraemer, "The Impact of Information Technology on Middle Managers," *MIS Quarterly*, September 1993.

36. Port, O., et al., "The Keys to the Future Special Report," *Business Week*, June 13, 1994.

37. Schuler, D., "Social Computing—Special Section," *Communications of the ACM*, January 1994.

38. Scott Morton, M. (ed.), *The Corporation of the 1990s*, Oxford: Oxford University Press, 1991.

39. Simon, H., *The New Science of Management Decisions*, Englewood Cliffs, NJ: Prentice-Hall, 1977.

40. Snepp, F., and W. Kalbacker, "No Place to Hide," *Playboy Magazine*, Vol. 40, No. 4, 1993.

41. Toth, K., "The Workless Society," *The Futurist*, May–June, 1990.

42. Wagner, I., "A Web of Fuzzy Problems: Confronting the Ethical Issues," *Communications of the ACM*, June 1993.

43. Weiss, E. A. (ed.), "Self-Assessment Procedure XXII—Ethical Issues." *Communications of the ACM*, November 1990. (Compiled from a report by D. B. Parker et al., SRI International.)

44. Wells-Branscomb, A., *Who Owns Information? From Privacy to Public Access*, New York: Basic Books, 1994.

OTIS ELEVATOR PIONEERING INFORMATION TECHNOLOGY

Otis Elevator (Farmington, CT) is the world's largest elevator company (23 percent market share, $5 billion sales, 1995). It serves buildings as tall as 110 stories (The World Trade Center), and it is organized into four geographic divisions: North America, Latin America, Pacific Area, and European Transcontinental Operations.

The international elevator industry is very competitive; the major manufacturers are Otis, Westinghouse, Dover, Montgomery, Schindler, U.S. Elevator, and Fujitec. Because elevator sales are directly correlated to the building cycle, they are also cyclical. However, the service market is very stable. Elevator manufacturers often accept a low margin on the sale of an elevator in order to obtain the service contract, since service accounts for a significantly higher portion of profits.

The service market attracts many participants because of its steady demand and high profitability. Consequently, thousands of elevator service companies exist, including many small companies devoted exclusively to elevator service. These companies can service elevators from almost any manufacturer, since all elevators made prior to the introduction of microprocessor-based elevator control systems use similar electromechanical technology.

An elevator service company is selected on the basis of *responsiveness, quality,* and *price.* As a building ages and competition for tenants increases, the cost of service often becomes a major consideration, and the lowest bidder receives the service contract. Many elevator manufacturers offer discounts for long-term service contracts in an effort to attract and maintain service customers.

North American Operations (NAO) is the second largest division of Otis Elevator. Branch offices (250) and smaller field offices report to district offices, which bear profit and loss responsibility. Field offices handle both sales and service, and they range in size from 1 or 2 people in outlying areas to as many as 100 people in large metropolitan areas.

History of Otis Information Services

The year 1982 was one of transition for NAO's information services area. With a cost reduction program completed, management was willing to spend money on IT and began to assess the ability of information services to improve the quality of its maintenance service.

The initial task was to establish a centralized customer service department to accept customer requests for elevator maintenance during nonworking hours. Otis and other elevator service companies were at that time, using commercial *answering agencies* to receive such calls. Otis supplied its answering agencies with a duty roster from which to select an agency mechanic to dispatch to the customer. In small cities, the *same* answering agency was commonly used by several elevator service companies.

Customers assess the quality of an elevator company's service mainly by its responsiveness to calls. Although Otis received assurances from the local answering agencies that they would promptly notify Otis of customer callbacks, this was often not done. As a result, customers were unhappy.

By August 1982, a centralized customer service system, named OTISLINE, had been successfully piloted in a major Eastern market, and Otis management decided to implement a North American customer service center to dispatch service mechanics. An IBM 3083 mainframe and other hardware and communication equipment were installed to support OTISLINE.

Most of the 2,300 service mechanics employed by NAO in 1983 were assigned routes and were responsible both for callbacks from customers and for preventive maintenance for specific elevators. NAO calculated that reducing callbacks for each installed elevator by one call a year would save OTIS $5 million annually.

OTISLINE not only improved the quality of NAO's customer service; it also *changed* the way NAO did business. The OTISLINE system affected almost all of NAO's business functions, including information services, customer service, service mechanic dispatching and control, and service marketing and engineering. In addition, its infrastructure has been used to support applications that enhance the productivity of elevator sales representatives and service mechanics.

The OTISLINE application in the 1990s is a part of NAO's Service Management System (SMS), *an integrated database management system.* Prior to OTISLINE, the SMS database contained the *customer master file* (customer name, building locations, contract information) and other information that was used to monitor and control the service business, such as route information and service price estimating data. With OTISLINE, the SMS was expanded to include all maintenance activities for elevators under a service contract. Some applications—such as service price estimating—were improved, and new applications—such as billing—were added.

The database prior to centralization included static customer information. The new centralized database added data on sales call management, route management, service performance measurement, cost estimation, and building information. The system produced weekly reports on the status of each branch office. It also produced reports on the frequency of breakdowns by elevator, type of elevator, or other permutation requested by management. Every month, 20 top financial managers receive an 80-page book that includes 570 graphs depicting every major financial indicator in the company. This takes the place of cumbersome spreadsheets and unmanageable documents and charts. In addition, Otis managers can access a database of 40,000 reports without leaving Microsoft's Excel, using macros and a user-friendly menu that acts as doorway into the Excel-based executive information system which is used by 45 top executives.

OTISLINE supplies the company with valuable information that did not exist under the old system. For example, it is possible to determine whether an elevator broke down because of design problems or because of improper service. The system also identifies weak and strong components in elevators. Hence, the company is able to adjust its spare parts inventory and predict breakdowns before they occur. This, in turn, reduces the number of customer callbacks. The data collected by OTISLINE are a valuable source of information for engineers and elevator designers. Parts susceptible to frequent breakdowns are redesigned. In addition, because OTISLINE identifies frequency of breakdowns by elevator type, the engineering group is able to study why certain elevator models are superior to others.

The OTISLINE application was designed to enable the OTISLINE dispatcher to respond to a customer in *less than a minute* by giving the dispatcher a local display and providing short database paths to the necessary information. The system tracks both service-call time and service time. As a result, the company was able to reduce custromers' wait time. The average arrival time of the service person to the site has been reduced to 76 minutes, and the service time was reduced to 75 minutes. (From a total of 4 to 6 hours prior to OTISLINE.)

Because of the strategic nature of the OTISLINE application, a large portion of the information services budget was earmarked for its support. The data center operations budget was also increased significantly to support OTIS-LINE's stringent response time and performance requirements. Emergency calls coming in from elevators are recognized by OTISLINE, and the dispatcher is alerted.

The dispatcher can then work with the callers to expedite the dispatch of a service mechanic. As a result, the capabilities of front-line workers (both dispatchers who answer the service calls, and technicians) have been changed. Dispatchers are trained to deal with passengers under stress when they are trapped in elevators.

The earthquake that hit Los Angeles in January 1994 provides a good example of how OTISLINE works in an emergency. As soon as the first call came in to OTISLINE operators reporting both the earthquake and the fact that some passengers were trapped inside elevators, Otis officials put together a crisis team. About 40 OTISLINE operators were assembled to take emergency calls and dispatch repairmen from the Los Angeles area to free trapped passengers. Otis reported that all of the 17 passengers who were trapped inside elevators were freed within half an hour or less after their emergency calls were taken.

OTISLINE presented Otis Elevator with an opportunity to differentiate itself from the competition by adding new services. They are described briefly in the following.

Contract Tracking

Managing over 60,000 contracts with customers worldwide is no simple job. Special software was developed for use by construction superintendents, the sales force, the contract management group, schedulers, shop floor people, regional management, and regional field operations staff. When Otis sells an elevator, a contract number is assigned by the system which launches the contract management process, including contract tracking. The elevator and its options are described and submitted electronically for processing, and manufacturing parts are specified for fabrication using order information and the bills of material. Each contract has various status reports indicating where it is in the process and what work remains to be done. Using a nearby terminal, a superintendent requests a shipping date, so that the elevator components arrive when they are needed. All work is accomplished and information is exchanged between job site, processing, and manufacturing via contract tracking screens. Everyone assigned to the contract can log on the system to check its status and to see if the previous party has completed his work.

The system cannot be abused or manipulated; each activity or task can only be completed on today's date. The contract status summary screen shows every detail of the project: high-level components manufactured and shipped, a task summary, scheduled and actual completion dates of each task, and early warning indications where and when people need to be assigned to the contract or if some specific engineering still needs to be finished. These early warnings have proven to be very helpful.

The contract tracking system knows how long it takes to complete specific tasks, for example manufacturing and paperwork. If a job captain has not allocated enough time, the system will highlight this discrepancy. If a too-ambitious completion date is specified, the system will accept it but won't guarantee that the task will be finished on that date. In addition, the system tracks actual elapsed times for completion, so it is possible to accurately measure performance and productivity.

Otis has done more training for contract tracking than for any other system in its history. It is evolving from its project management origins into a strategic management evaluation tool that adds another information dimension to understanding how to conduct business. Otis is now working on a system of just-in-time manufacturing, where elevators arrive on site just as they are ready for installation. This is due to the success of the Contract Tracking system.

Remote Elevator Monitoring (REM)

Otis uses REM, an application by which a microprocessor monitors the elevator's control system and logs performance statistics directly onto a distant computer. A master unit (black box), installed in the building machine room, sends messages over a dedicated telephone line to OTIS-LINE. Functions with abnormal performance readings are corrected during regular maintenance. If a shut-down occurs, the REM system allow Otis to determine, through a bidirectional telephone link between the elevator cab and OTISLINE, whether passengers are trapped in that elevator.

The black box monitors hundreds of elements in each elevator. A service repairman connects a personal computer to the black box and ties both units into a telephone link directly to company headquarters in Connecticut. In about ten minutes, the data collected are analyzed, the problem is diagnosed, and a recommended course of action is transmitted to the job site.

The great advantage of REM is its ability to identify problems before an elevator is out of service. Service mechanics can adjust running elevators to keep them operating at maximum performance levels, and NAO can handle specific problems before customers are even aware of them.

REM has an external and internal impact. Introduced as an additional customer service, it serves as a diagnostic tool which automatically feeds the shared company database. It enables preemptive maintenance (striving for the goal of zero callbacks) and thus reduces maintenance and service costs and improves customer satisfaction. With REM, there should eventually be no breakdowns because an employee should be able to be on-site before breakdowns occur.

Mobile Communication

Regular cellular telephones may not work from certain elevator shafts. A high-quality mobile communication system, called ARDIS (Advanced Radio Data System) is used at Otis. A wireless network enables an effective two way-radio link to receive dispatch messages, order parts, check deliveries, and close service calls without leaving the customer site. The radio network provides instant, wireless data transmission between mobile, portable, or laptop computers and host computers.

Otis Elevator is the first international user of ARDIS. This puts all of North America at Otis' fingertips. Before ARDIS, field mechanics had to use a one-way pager. Once a mechanic is paged, he must call OTISLINE's 24-hour service to speak with a customer service representative who would tell him what the problem was on the next job, where it occurred, and the possible cause. With that system, the mechanic would have to leave the site he was at to find a telephone; but with ARDIS the mechanic can stay at his current site and assess the situation from there. The key benefit is that if the situation is not an emergency, he can stay put and finish the current job.

Field mechanics at Otis are using Motorola's KDT 840 portable data terminal to send and receive messages. With the KDT unit, an Otis dispatcher can call the mechanic; the mechanic can acknowledge receipt of the call and give the dispatcher his estimated time of arrival. The dispatcher can then call the customer and relate the message. This is very helpful in emergency cases.

Fuzzy Logic

In Otis's research towers, elevators that possess artificial intelligence capabilities are being tested. Some of these systems are already capable of recording and regularly updating rates of elevator use at various locations and times, using the technology of fuzzy logic. If you are the only person waiting on the 27th floor of a building and the elevator system knows that the 33rd floor is usually busy at that time, the elevator will bypass you to serve the greater number of people likely to be waiting on the 33rd floor. The elevator continues to keep track of the demands made on it from other floors. If an unacceptable amount of time goes by and the elevator door has not opened on the 27th floor, the system will drop its priority on efficiency and rescue the lonely summoner.

Soon elevators will be able to view waiting areas with optical systems. A camera will be able to see a group of people waiting in the lobby of a large building with several elevators and route the required number of elevators to handle the crowd.

Marketing Service

The Service Management System (SMS) portion of OTISLINE contains information on all installed Otis elevators in North America. The OTISLINE facility is used to identify customers whose service contracts are not with Otis. The OTISLINE dispatcher finds out when the current elevator maintenance contracts expire and produces a list of prospective customers which is distributed monthly to the service sales representatives in the appropriate areas. Although relatively simplistic, this was a capability that Otis only activated in 1994.

Otis Scheduled Maintenance (OSM)

Otis developed a software package, Otis Scheduled Maintenance (OSM), that optimizes maintenance scheduling utilizing distributive processing to link the OTISLINE mainframe with branch-office PCs and field personnel's KDTs. OSM allows supervisors and examiners to jointly develop appropriate maintenance schedules and routines for all maintenance activities. The OSM software uses this input to schedule the daily work of each maintenance mechanic. Then, the mechanics type in their dates worked, actual times, and other relevant information for each activity when the work is completed. Supervisors, together with their mechanics, then evaluate performance and adjust maintenance schedules based on actual experience.

New Business Processes Systems

Several business applications were introduced in 1994. The first one is SALVE, a support system used by sales representatives in their negotiations with customers from the initial contact to the booking stage. Once an order has been booked, it is forwarded to SAGA, a contract management system which creates and maintains the sales order. Information gained from SALVE and SAGA serves as input to STAR, the purchasing and supplier management system. SAFRAN-N,S,K handles invoicing and other accounting functions related to modernization as well as sales of new equipment. SYGECO handles accounts receivable. SAFRAN-O, handles the billing of maintenance services. The new Otis systems improve productivity since bills are prepared on a quarterly basis for the 60,000 contracts to maintain 130,000 elevators.

These new systems were designed for supporting business processes (e.g., negotiation), as opposed to the previous systems which targeted specific activities in one functional area, such as repairs or sales. SALVE, for example, supports the negotiation process up to the booking stage. The same software is used for both new equipment and services sales. This is a big change from the old system where employees managed operations by activity. For example, for "new sales," there was one type of management and for "repairs" there was another type. There was no global view of what was done per elevator. The previous architecture required specialized sales organizations for new equipment and for maintenance. Salesmen now have the flexibility to receive a mixed portfolio of activities.

From the sales force perspective, the major benefit of SALVE is the drastic reduction of lead time. The processing time from obtaining a signed customer order to forwarding the material form to the factory has been reduced from one month to 48 hours. Moreover, the salesperson is in a stronger bargaining position with the customer since she has a complete record of previous negotiations and contracts with the customer, thanks to SALVE. From the management perspective, SALVE offers two main advantages. First, orders get to the factory quicker. Second, unlike in the past when too many customized units were sold, there are now more sales of standard products because the salesperson can bring the customer to the product line through the new information technology.

Conclusion

Since the implementation of OTISLINE, Otis elevators offices throughout the world have taken the initiative to make the system better. Each branch office has taken the IT infrastructure and tried to mold it to the individual characteristics of their areas of responsibility. As Otis moves in to new world markets, the technology will continue to grow and make further advances. As people are trained to make their work easier and be able to more quickly serve the customer base, they will continue to become more innovative and less resistant to change. This makes the future for IT and Otis Elevator brighter and more profitable.

Case Study Questions

1. Describe how Otis IT supports specific business processes.

2. What pressure(s) contributed to the creation of OTIS-LINE?

3. How does IT provide a competitive advantage to Otis?

4. What role was played by the database(s)?

5. How are customer service processes supported by IT?

6. How are manufacturing processes supported by IT?

7. How is IT supporting the maintenance of elevators?

8. Why is contract management considered a critical success factor, and how is it supported by IT?

9. How does IT support emergency situations?

10. What support is provided by IT to marketing and sales?

11. Describe the advantages of the newest business processes support systems.

Case Study Group Assignment

1. From your own experiences, list improvements that you would like to see as a user of an elevator. Then, identify the Otis IT systems that can support such improvements. Prepare a report to a management of a large hotel where people complain about the elevators, and explain why management should consider Otis's services.

2. Identify an elevator service company in your area that competes with Otis but does not use computer technology (or uses it only for traditional data processing applications). Interview the president to find out what the company knows about Otis's services and what the company is doing, or plans to do, in order to compete with Otis. Prepare a summary of the interview, and then comment on the strategy proposed by the service company.

References and Bibliography

HAMILTON, R., "System Sorts Data Deluge," *Computerworld*, March 16, 1992.

JELASSI, T., "Gaining Business From Information Technology," *European Management Journal*, March 1993.

O'NEIL, J., and K. OSTROFSKY, "Otis Elevator: Managing the Service Force," Harvard Business School Case #9-191-213, Boston: HBS Press, October 21, 1992.

SAMLI, A., et al., "What Presale and Postsale Services Do You Need to be Competitive," *Industrial Marketing Management*, February 1992.

SENN, J. A., "Debunking the Myths of Strategic Information Systems," *Business*, October–December 1989.

SHIPMAN, A., "Otis Seizes the High Ground," *International Management*, November 1992.

STODDARD, D., "OTISLINE (A)," Harvard Business School Case #9-186-304, Boston: HBS Press, 1986 (with teaching note #5-187-0866, 1988).

▶ INTRODUCTION TO INTERNATIONAL CASE STUDIES

Information technology, as seen throughout this book, is becoming pervasive in organizations regardless of their location. Furthermore, many companies today operate in several countries, and their supporting information systems are critical to their success and survival.

Throughout the book we repeatedly illustrated the global nature of IT (follow the "Global Perspective" icons). In the concluding part of this book we present five case studies written by IT experts in five different countries. The purpose of these cases is to illustrate the common elements of information systems, regardless of where they are developed. However, cultural, economic, and political characteristics introduce some particular issues and factors that need to be considered.

Case #1. The first case presents TradeNet, an international trading system that enables Singapore to effectively compete against other countries in southeast Asia where labor and resources are considerably less expensive. The case traces the development of this complex system, where partnership between various government agencies and industry is critical. Thirteen important lessons are drawn, some of which are universal while others are particular for Singapore.

Case #2. The second case describes an important management decision: the outsourcing of IT at the corporate level of a multinational corporation, with headquarters in the United Kingdom. The outsourcing decision was made in order to reduce costs to compete in a weak global economy. Decentralization of operations and reengineering both justified outsourcing at that time. But the controversial issue of outsourcing as a corporate strategy is raised in the case.

Case #3. The restructuring of another multinational corporation, Digital Equipment Corporation, is the subject of case #3. Here, the U.S. corporation empowered its European subsidiary to manage its sales, service, logistics, and manufacturing in Europe. The case describes the retooling of the IT to support the company's restructuring. Of interest is the information need at the Swiss headquarters, and the degree of centralization vs. decentralization of the information resources (see Chapters 4 and 18).

Case #4. In a bold pioneering move, a regional bank in Korea downsized its information system to a client/server architecture by using software from a small unknown vendor in Taiwan. The case describes the system development process and how IT increased the profitability of the bank.

Case #5. Public organizations also utilize IT to improve their operations, and the success of government is increasingly dependent on the appropriate use of technologies. Such a situation is illustrated in the case of the Brazilian government, where reengineering was needed to stop the runaway inflation and to restructure a high foreign debt. The case vividly illustrates the important role that IT can play in public organizations.

TRADENET:
Singapore's Computerization of International Trade*

BOON SIONG NEO
Nanyang Technological University, Singapore

Introduction

Singapore, a tiny island with a population just under 3 million is the 17th largest trader in the world (over US$200 billion in 1994). At any given time there are more than 800 vessels in its port, the busiest in the world. Changi international airport is the largest and busiest in Southeast Asia. Located in the southern tip of the Malaysian peninsula at the entrance to the Malacca Straits, Singapore is used by many traders as a hub for trans-shipping goods among vessels and among aircraft. The country provides an ample free tax zone to attract international traders. Over 700 shipping companies do business in Singapore. Since trade is a significant component of Singapore's economy, the government decided to support trade by providing the most efficient services to the international trading community, at competitive prices.

In order to attain this objective, Singapore is using the most sophisticated information technology (IT) applications. For example, the intelligent systems of its port are considered to be among the most innovative in the world. However, the most known IT system, and the one that plays a most significant role in Singapore's trade is TradeNet.

TradeNet is an EDI system that links over 12,000 traders (an increase from 1,000 in 1990), support companies and government agencies that are involved in Singapore's international trade, for the purpose of exchanging trade documents electronically. Through TradeNet, companies and agencies can submit, directly from their computers, documents, such as trade declarations, which state the nature, source and destinations of products; and permits which are needed to be approved by governnment agencies.

A document can be sent to all relevant bodies and returned with approvals in about 15 minutes. This once took between 2–4 days. The documentation processing cost has been reduced by more than 20% and in some cases by as much as 50%. Overall, TradeNet saves more than $600 million a year. And it is only the beginning. Recently, (at the end of 1995), TradeNet went interactive. This reduced the processing time to about 2.5 minutes. The interactive system allows the processing of documents in real-time, instead of being collected and sent out later in batches as was the case until 1995.

But, TradeNet is much more than just a vehicle for improving transfer of documents. It is a facilitator of international trade and a foundation upon which several national networks are constructed.

Commitment to the TradeNet Idea

International trade is characterized not only by the physical movement of goods across national boundaries, but also by the unwieldy, voluminous, and costly paperwork that accompanies it, containing data that facilitate the physical goods movement (e.g., destination), show ownership, describe attributes of the goods, and whether they meet governmental requirements (e.g., whether they are high-technology goods that may be prohibited from export to certain countries). A 1985 study by the Swedish Trade Procedures Council showed that the costs of trade processing and documentation were between four to seven percent of invoice value. For trade-dependent Singapore, the opportunity was obvious: a half percentage point cost reduction in trade paperwork would mean a saving of almost US$1 billion annually!

In Singapore, the government requires that trade documents be prepared and submitted to a number of agencies for clearance before goods may be imported or exported. There are 20 government agencies requiring documentation for specific categories of goods, although up to three agencies' approvals are the norm for any one commodity. The trade documents were in paper form, and were often hand-delivered to, and collected from,

*Source: Neo, B. S., ''Managing New Information Technologies: Lessons from Singapore's Experience with EDI'', *Information & Management*, Vol. 26, 1994, pp 317–326. Modified by the author. Reproduced by permission of *Information & Management* and the author.

government agencies in many geographically dispersed locations. Further, although there was substantial overlap in the type of information required, each government agency had its own document with its own format. This meant that a trader often needed to enter the same data in different formats in several documents to satisfy the requirements of various government departments and agencies. The number of trade documents averages about 10,000 per day. The complexity of document flows required for international trade in Singapore is illustrated in Figure 1.

From the traders' view, the clearance of documents was endured as a necessary evil, slowing down the movements of goods and tying up labor that was in short supply in the tight Singapore labor market. From the view of the government agencies, the handling of trade documents was tedious, with one agency having as many as 100 clerks to process, key in, and approve the documents.

This trade documentation problem led several government agencies to initiate a search for solutions; this inevitably pointed to IT as a major option. In 1984, the Port of Singapore Authority implemented a system to link port users to it for the purpose of submitting and clearing sea manifests. In 1985, the Civil Aviation Authority of Singapore initiated a study to examine trade clearance for air

cargo, and recommended the development of a common computer system for the air freight industry. In December 1985, the Ministry of Trade and Industry implemented a new trade processing system that computerized the front-end data entry for trade documents and speeded up the reporting of trade statistics. In the same year, the Telecommunication Authority (responsible for all telephone networks) together with AT&T conducted a market study and concluded that there were opportunities to exploit value-added networks, especially in facilitating international trade. These attempts were largely confined to areas within the ambit of each agency's charter and expertise. The solutions that were proposed or implemented were not linked, and by themselves did not constitute, an adequate solution to the trade processing problem.

Recognizing the need for a coordinated effort to resolve the trade documentation problem, a multi-agency Committee for the Integration of Documents and Procedures was formed in February 1986 to look for solutions to simplify and integrate trade procedures in order to speed up the clearance of cargoes and to generate accurate and timely trade information. The committee submitted its report in June 1986, and recommended the development and implementation of an on-line community trading system called TradeNet. With this, multiple trade forms

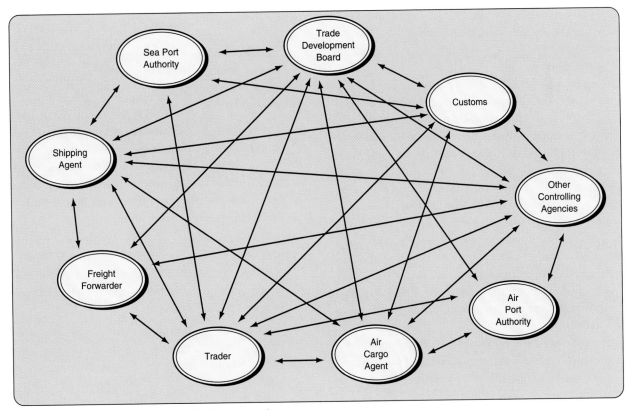

FIGURE 1 Typical document flow for import and export.

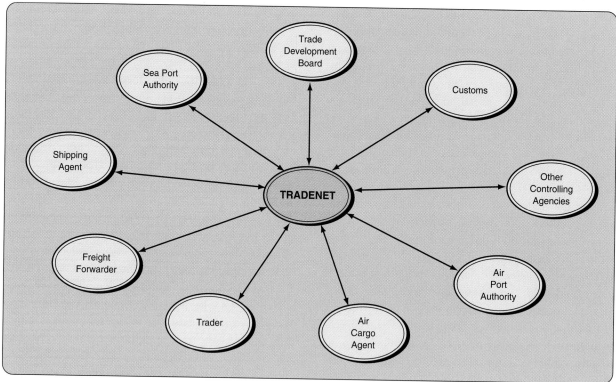

FIGURE 2 Document flow in TradeNet.

would be consolidated into a single document, which would be submitted electronically to the relevant government agencies. In contrast to the paperwork web, the proposed document flow scheme in TradeNet is simple, as illustrated in Figure 2.

The potential of TradeNet in enhancing Singapore's international competitiveness was highlighted as a strategic goal. There was considerable excitement about the possibility for a trader to make a single electronic trade document submission that would be routed to as many agencies as required. By providing fast turnaround and making it easy, convenient, and cost effective for traders to do business, Singapore would be able to attract more companies to make investments as well as set up their regional headquarters within her borders. TradeNet was seen as a new way of doing business in the global arena, and Singapore would be among the pioneers in simplifying trade processing (other countries, like Hong Kong, had proposed similar ideas but progress toward implementation had stalled).

The issue of how Singapore may be more internationally competitive had caught the attention of the nation at that time, because Singapore was suffering its first major economic recession since independence and was experiencing negative growth for the first time in twenty years.

There was much public and political debate on ways to reduce costs to make Singapore more competitive.

The government's commitment to the strategic project was underscored when the Prime Minister announced a deadline of January 1989 for implementation, allowing two years to develop the system. Four major lessons may be drawn from this:

1. The *trigger* for Singapore's consideration of new IT solutions was a specific *business problem*. It did not result from a general scanning of new IT developments. Such a problem-directed search process improves the likelihood that the new ITs would be relevant in meeting business needs.

2. Sustaining a strategic IT effort requires a *vision* that goes beyond the original problem that triggered its consideration. TradeNet *evolved* into an idea that would enhance the global competitiveness of Singapore as a trading nation.

3. The TradeNet solution requires the *cooperation* of multiple government agencies and an *integration* of their efforts. Having a strong sponsor like the government was important but not sufficient for success. Earlier efforts by individual government statutory boards did not result in an acceptable solution. In today's com-

petitive environment, inter-organizational collaboration is often required in major strategic moves, including the adoption of new ITs.

4. The government's approval was given for the TradeNet *idea*, and not a particular technological platform. The public announcement focused on the *conceptual solution* without a premature commitment on any particular technology. Coupling a technological platform to a proposed solution may stifle creativity in finding more appropriate technologies to meet the business needs. This was important in TradeNet's case, because the recommended technological platform initially was not EDI-based.

The Technological Decision

After the approval for TradeNet was given, an executive committee, comprising the CEOs of various government agencies, trade associations and major user firms, was set up to gather support for the system and to oversee its progress. A project team was also formed to define, develop, and implement the proposed system. The team completed the functional specifications for the system in

February 1987 and began the search for a technical solution.

The prior solution involved a large mainframe computer with on-line linkages to traders to allow the submission of trade documents for clearance. The search for alternative solutions took two forms: first, a request for information (RFI) was sent to prospective vendors to find out the products and services available to meet the requirements of the functional specifications; second, the project team visited several seaport and airport installations in Japan, Sweden, Holland, the UK and the USA. They saw both on-line and EDI-based systems. On their return, and on studying the 23 responses to the RFI, the project team proposed the adoption of an EDI-based approach.

At the time that the project team was considering the technical solution, the number of trade documents processed was about 10,000 per day. As immediate approval for import/export permits was not required, an EDI-based solution seemed to best meet the operational requirements at an acceptable price: the cost of providing on-line service to handle the peak workload would have been prohibitive. The project team submitted a technical paper

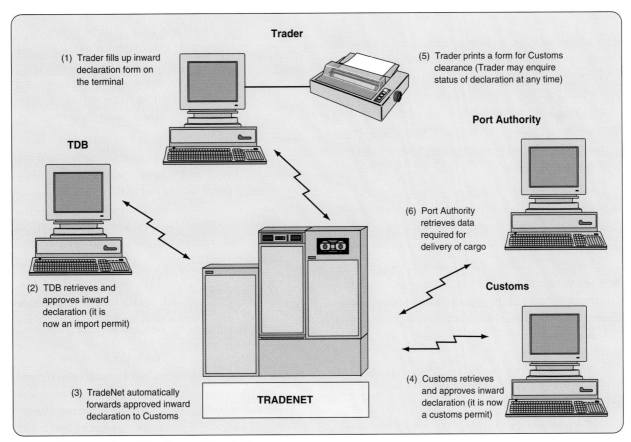

FIGURE 3 Electronic trading through TradeNet.

to the executive committee recommending EDI for TradeNet.

As illustrated in Figure 3, a trader would fill an inward declaration document on a local terminal or personal computer. Once completed, the TradeNet computer is accessed via a modem and telephone line and the form is transmitted to the system. The Trade Development Board retrieves the form and approves it by entering a password and then transmits the form back to the TradeNet system. This then becomes the import permit for the trader, which can be retrieved from TradeNet. The inward declaration is also automatically forwarded to Customs for retrieval and approval, and then transmitted back to the trader. The same information may therefore be retrieved by all authorized parties who need it for operational or reporting purposes.

A planned educational program was launched to expose the business community to EDI. Seminars for managers and executives were organized periodically, with key government leaders and prominent CEOs of government agencies invited to give the opening speeches. EDI success stories from other countries were highlighted. The press was fed with information on a regular basis to keep the public informed. Four major lessons may be drawn from the decision to invest in EDI as a new technology to Singapore:

5. Adopting new ITs requires *exposure to new information and new ways* of doing business. The RFI and overseas visits were instrumental in confirming the match between Singapore's processing requirements with the features of EDI technology.

6. An influential person who would champion the new IT is a critical factor in its adoption. TradeNet had two *influential champions*.

7. Once adopted, new ITs must be *marketed* to the intended clientele and users. A carefully planned and coordinated *publicity and educational effort* was instrumental in preparing the trading community to accept the new technology.

8. The adoption of a new IT is facilitated when users can *apply it immediately and inexpensively* to resolve a business problem. The business community could see its value immediately.

The Delivery Organizational Structure

Once the approval for the TradeNet project was given, there was a need to determine an appropriate organization to develop and implement the system. Which government agency should be responsible for TradeNet? The Trade Development Board (TDB) was championing the simplification and integration of trade procedures and documentation, but did not even have its own computer services department. The National Computer Board (NCB), the lead agency in government computerization, had the technical expertise, but did not have knowledge of international trade transactions. At that time, the CEOs of both TDB and NCB met and decided to "join hands." They shared similar views on the importance of the proposed TradeNet project. According to one, "we knew each other well and we could work together." Breaking away from past practice, the government assigned the TradeNet project to both TDB and NCB collectively. The TDB-NCB partnership was born, with TDB's CEO chairing the executive committee and co-opting the key government agencies and trade associations to support the project. The NCB provided the project team, and worked with key users to define the system requirements.

During 1987, consensus was building towards setting up a new private company to run TradeNet. It could give all major interested parties a stake and provide the needed incentives to ensure TradeNet's utilization and success. Also, EDI technology had potential beyond trade processing and the new company could spearhead development of other applications. Finally, the company could be a vehicle to ensure financial accountability. Approval for a new company to operate TradeNet was given after an internal feasibility study in early 1988 showed that it was financially viable. In March 1988, a new for-profit company, Singapore Network Services (SNS), was set up, with an initial capitalization of S$24 million. TDB took 55% ownership, with the remaining shares taken up by the agencies responsible for the port, civil aviation, and telecommunication network, each owning 15% of SNS's shares. Three important lessons are:

9. *Partnership* between business and IT people is critical for the successful development of strategic systems. Each party will not have the requisite knowledge and expertise to proceed successfully by itself. The importance of the TDB-NCB partnership to TradeNet's success was recognized when the Society for Information Management gave its Partners-in-Leadership award to TradeNet in 1989.

10. An integrated system requires the *cooperation* of interested parties into the delivery structure to ensure its support and success. Each major interested party should be given a stake. The executive committee, and the formation of SNS were important delivery mechanisms in TradeNet's success.

11. The *focused effort* that a separate business organization could give to the exploitation of a new IT would speed up its application and *diffusion*. The formation of SNS was instrumental in the rapid growth and development of other EDI applications in Singapore. EDI applications are now available for the medical, legal, and other business communities.

Selection of a Vendor

The decision to adopt an EDI-based system narrowed the number of qualified vendors. After careful scrutiny of the 23 responses, only three vendors were qualified: IBM, McDonnell Douglas Information Systems, and GE Information Services. IBM and McDonnell Douglas had also proposed strategic ties with local software houses for the project. All three were already operating EDI networks in other countries. A Request for Proposal (RFP) or tender was provided to the three shortlisted companies in mid-1987. After the responses were received in August 1987, there were intensive discussions with the three vendors, including on-site overseas visits by the project team.

IBM, with a local software house, Computer Systems Advisers (CSA) as subcontractor, was selected as the vendor for TradeNet. A US$ 10 million contract was signed with SNS in April 1988. IBM, departing from its normal practice, agreed to license its proprietary EDI system, the Information Exchange, to SNS and to adapt it to meet the requirements. It also agreed to allow SNS to operate it as a value-added network (VAN) service provider in Singapore and provide all necessary support toward that end. IBM and CSA worked out an acceptable plan that would implement TradeNet in phases. The tender price was not the primary criterion in SNS's selection of IBM. Two further lessons may be added:

12. *Specific criteria* must be set in selecting vendors for critical systems. The vendor must be able to meet the firm's *strategic objectives*. IBM met both SNS's objectives of timing and technology transfer, and was awarded the contract.

13. In adopting new ITs and embarking on major critical system projects, vendor selection is a *major policy decision*. Once a vendor is selected, organizational dependence on it tends to grow as personnel develop skills and expertise around the vendor's platforms and products. IBM and CSA were able to obtain substantial advantage from the publicity given to TradeNet. CSA's growth was boosted by the TradeNet contract, and in 1990, IBM formalized its strategic relationship with CSA by taking up equity interest in this local software house.

Results of Singapore's EDI Implementation

The impacts of the active management approach to the adoption of EDI in Singapore can be assessed by examining four areas: project management, user adoption, business productivity, and diffusion of EDI applications.

Project Management

TradeNet performed extremely well from a normal project management criteria: time and cost targets. TradeNet went "live" in January 1989—on time. There was little variation from the cost estimates of the feasibility study, based on the contract awarded to IBM. In terms of system performance, 97% of all trade documents processed through TradeNet are now approved by the relevant government agencies within 15 minutes of submission, compared to the two-day turnaround time needed previously.

User Business Productivity

User trading firms have reported substantial savings in labor and inventory holding costs, with 20 to 30 percent savings in documentation overhead. TradeNet's round-the-clock operation and pre-clearance procedures allow traders to process the necessary trade documents prior to the physical arrival of their goods, which could then be moved out of the air or sea ports immediately, without going through a warehouse pending clearance. Trading firms that were already computerized could transfer the necessary data from their own systems directly to TradeNet, eliminating duplicate data entry and reducing errors.

Diffusion of EDI Applications in Singapore

SNS has since built new services on the basic EDI engine; these cater to the diverse needs of other industry sectors, including MediNet for the healthcare community, LawNet for the legal community, and other generic services for interorganizational linkage between manufacturers, retailers, suppliers, and financial institutions. For example, hospitals are now able to transmit medical claims electronically to the Central Provident Fund for approval; manufacturers and retailers can transact by sending quotations, purchase orders, invoices and tenders electronically, and settle their payments through the electronic payment system offered by the banks.

International links to the United States, Europe, and Japan are also provided. There can be no international trade on a proprietary system, and therefore the internationally-accepted EDI-FACT standard was adopted for TradeNet. Now, global business connectivity is a reality for EDI users in Singapore via GEIS (General Electric Information Services), providing access to more than 5000 users worldwide; SITA (Societe International de Telecommunications Aeronautiques), providing access to more than 25,000 airlines, freight forwarders, and custom administrators; and Fujitsu, providing access to 18,000 users in Japan. Links to other international networks are being negotiated.

Instant access to information for decision-making is also available to TradeNet subscribers. Databases are provided through third party connections (e.g., linkage with PortNet provides freight forwarders direct access to shipping and vessel schedules and makes it possible to book port services directly through the same terminal connection). The StarNet community system at the air cargo complex in the Changi International Airport also provides for efficient cargo tracking and communication between airlines, cargo handlers, and freight forwarders.

A firm can now integrate its trade processing requirements with other business communication requirements. In Singapore, EDI is no longer exclusively associated with trade documentation, it is seen as an enabling technology for communication with business partners anywhere in the world.

Case Study Questions

1. Review the advantages of EDI (Chapter 14) and justify the use of EDI here over E-mail.

2. Why is TradeNet superior to the prior solution (a large mainframe with online linkages to traders)?

3. How does TradeNet enhance the competitiveness of Singapore in international trade? (Relate to Chapter 3).

4. Identify the factors that facilitate the success of TradeNet.

5. Why was cost not considered a major factor in awarding the contract?

6. Is the process of selecting EDI in line with the process of system development suggested in Chapters 12 and 13?

7. What have you learned from this case regarding the process of new technology adoption?

8. Review the reasons for the vendor's selection. What are the major lessons provided by the case? Do you agree or disagree? Why?

9. Explain why TradeNet is no longer exclusively associated with trade documentation, but it is seen as an enabling technology for communication in international trade.

10. Some people argue that a problem-directed approach (Lesson 1) is inferior to a search for problems using proven technologies. The logic is that the latter helps organizations discover problems that they do not know about. Debate.

11. Identify political, economical, and cultural factors cited in the case and assess their impact on TradeNet.

PILKINGTON PLC:
A Major Multinational Outsources Its Head Office Information Technology Function*

LESLIE WILLCOCKS
Templeton College, Oxford, United Kingdom

GUY FITZGERALD
University of London, United Kingdom

Introduction—A Difficult Business Climate

Pilkington Plc is a major international company supplying flat and safety glass and related products worldwide to a range of industries. In 1992 Pilkington had revenues of £2.6 billion ($US 4b. approx.) and a profit before taxation and after exceptional items of £77 million ($US 110m.), This compared with a profit of £152 ($US 228m.) on similar revenues the previous year. The Group operates globally through its regionally-based operating companies. In the face of declining profits and a nearly world-wide business slump, the Pilkington board ordered cost reductions across the Group. In this context the Group Head Office (HO), based at St. Helens in the United Kingdom (UK), was one target for large headcount reductions. This was to be done by focusing on core activities only, outsourcing as many services as possible, or devolving services into the operating companies or business divisions.

IT—A Candidate For Outsourcing

In the 1991-2 period Pilkington considered the outsourcing of IT/IS Head Office services. Bill Limond, Head of Group Information Systems, explains:

"... the decision resulted from the need to support the reorganization which was taking place in Head Office—one target was to reduce numbers; the result was a reduction from about 500 people to about 180 ... the rationale behind this being a 'back to the knitting' type of philosophy."

As far as the IT/IS function was concerned a number of options were considered. The first, recommended by external consultants, was to retain the IT function during the HO change program and then wind the function down when the changes had gone through. Another option was to form a stand-alone IT/IS company that would then sell its services back to Head Office as well as on the open market. Both were rejected as risky, with particular doubts about the financial viability of the latter. A big question was whether HO IT underpinned Pilkington business strategy in a critical way, or indeed significantly differentiated the company from its competitors in the marketplace. The options, and the pattern of sourcing decisions made by companies about their IT, are shown in Figure 1.

In the end it was decided that HO IT, as least the technology and service elements, represented a 'useful commodity' as far as Pilkington was concerned. Therefore a proposal to 'total' outsource all Head Office IT operations and development to a large supplier was made:

"This is not traditional facilities management we are talking about (where only mainframe operations are outsourced); this was business-led IT restructuring, right sizing applications from mainframe to local area networks, critical to the future of the business. There was about 75–80% development in the contract and about 20–25% machine minding in the FM sense." (Tony Rickels, IS manager).

Total outsourcing refers to IT services costing more than 80% of the formal IT budget being handed over to third party management. At Pilkington it involved transferring virtually all HO IT staff, and selling all existing HO operational IT assets (worth £400,000 or $600,000 approx.) to the vendor. This included the IBM mainframe. However, it is interesting to note that none of the manufacturing IT in the operating companies was outsourced at this stage. Expenditure on IT in manufacturing plants amounted to over £50 million ($75m.) a year worldwide.

The Total Outsourcing Route

Total outsourcing was not the only option open to Pilkington management. They could have used the maturing IT/IS services market by 'contracting in' service firms to

---
*Acknowledgment: Our sincere thanks to Pilkington plc and the managers we interviewed for their help and cooperation in helping the prepare the details, and making this case possible. The case is prepared as a basis for classroom discussion only.

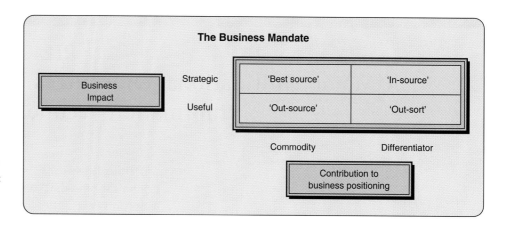

FIGURE 1 IT: Business Contribution and Sourcing Decisions (SOURCE: Feeny, Willcocks, and Fitzgerald, 1993)

work as resources alongside in-house IT staff and under Pilkington management direction, either on short-term contracts or on a preferred supplier basis. The company could have chosen a selective outsourcing approach, only 'contracting out' to third party management some of the IT activities, for example mainframe processing.

However, the IT/IS management hoped to achieve several objectives through taking the 'total' approach. Outsourcing to a prime contractor enables the internal IT/IS management to focus on the strategic concerns, leaving the day-to-day management and service delivery to the contractor. Also it would permit a transitional period during which the outsourcing vendor would manage aging systems and equipment. This would give time for the development of new systems, including office and network systems and special applications being moved from the mainframe to a PC network. Thirdly, outsourcing would permit a site move, including, where appropriate, the transfer of non-HO applications to business units. These included pensions, investments, training, accounts, and payroll systems. Fourthly, outsourcing IT would also, hopefully, bring in wider, relevant expertise from a large vendor while also providing enhanced career opportunities for the company's IT staff, job security, and a broadening of their skills.

The Outsourcing Deal

In January 1992 a £4 million ($6m.) two year contract was signed with EDS-Scicon, with a target to move off the IBM mainframe by December 1993. EDS would be responsible for running the mainframe and also for developing distributed local area networks and related business applications. However, interestingly, despite the general emphasis on cost savings, Pilkington IT/IS managers still decided to invest capital in, and retain ownership of, the new infrastructure once it had been built.

EDS had been on a short-list of four vendors. There were several selection criteria. One was multi-vendor

expertise—Pilkington had different technological bases throughout the Group, and also wanted to retain flexibility about how future equipment requirements could be serviced. The vendor also had to have financial stability, location flexibility, wide geographic support across the world to match the company's own spread, networking expertise, and depth and breadth in technical support. Finally and critically, there had to be a close relationship with the vendor, together with good terms and conditions of employment and career opportunities for transferred staff. EDS—as the largest single IT service provider in the world—seemed capable of meeting all these criteria. Although all this implied a long-term 'strategic alliance' type relationship nevertheless the initial contract was short term for discrete, head office systems only.

Managing the Outsourcing Risks

A major feature of this outsourcing arrangement was the critical requirement to reduce risks commonly associated with 'total outsourcing'. A two year contract with an option to renew was negotiated as a way of providing the necessary flexibility. This seemed to provide the possibility of a long term relationship but also an escape route if things did not work out. Many CIOs fear irreversibility of contract or the high switching costs often connected with long term total outsourcing deals. Bill Limond explains:

"We are dealing with a terrific amount of change within the business and within HO itself. We didn't know what it was going to look like at the end. . . . A long contract would have been quite inappropriate here, there is too much change involved. But in any case I think one wants to retain a certain amount of negotiating independence, especially given the background of that change. Some of our other operations have gone into longer term contracts and we have reservations about them."

A critical concern was to avoid staffing problems and resentment. All staff were unionized but employee relations problems were avoided. 37 staff moved to the vendor on the same conditions or better, 3 retired and 3 key staff were retained at HO, while operations research staff were absorbed into other parts of the company. A great deal of attention was given to communicating with staff, in November 1991, what was going to happen, and providing individual discussions with the vendor. Much of this was handled by the in-house IS manager, Tony Rickels, who, in February 1992, accepted the option of joining the vendor as Account Manager for the contract once it had been signed. This meant that staff who knew the business, including their ex-company manager, would be largely responsible for delivering the contract. There were strengths and weaknesses in this approach. Much depended on the additional expertise and training introduced by the vendor, and also whether career opportunities opened up at EDS for ex-Pilkington staff who wanted them. In other outsourcing deals vendors have been known to transfer the more skilled ex-staff to other, more lucrative contracts. Pilkington could have reduced this risk by retaining the employment contracts of its systems developers but instead felt it could depend on the quality of the relationship with the vendor.

The contract was tight in its contractual terms, including pay and conditions, penalties, arbitration, and termination arrangements. Interestingly, the first 90 days of the contract were spent securing the service and defining and agreeing on service levels. This went against the normal advice in outsourcing deals, namely to agree on service levels before signing any outsourcing contract. For existing operations the vendor service levels became built around the quality provided previously by the in-house function. Because of uncertainties surrounding HO reorganization and IT needs, a lot more flexibility was left on benchmarks for the development part of the outsourcing. In practice it was mainly done by resource level—what a maximum complement of 37 staff could be expected to achieve—with deliverables and dates being monitored and agreed during contract performance by a monthly steering group. This was not wholly satisfactory but was the best that could be achieved in a fluid IT-development environment.

Reshaping In-House Capability

It was felt that risk could be further reduced by retaining certain key activities, skills and roles in-house. A team of 6 IT/IS professionals remained in Group HO. Two were involved mainly with the contract and the relationship with EDS, and the rest were involved with international group-wide IT/IS strategies, including a person dedicated to telecommunications, and two to information technol-

ogy policy, standards and developments. Bill Limond, responsible for Pilkington international IT/IS strategy, explains the logic behind these arrangements:

"You have to distinguish very clearly between the strategy, direction, control and defining information and communication needs on the one hand, and the service provision of information systems and technology on the other.... A very important aspect of what we were doing was certainly not to outsource management and control, and above all the direction and strategy.... You have also got to retain an informed buyer expertise, but it doesn't need to be terribly deep into the technology. It needs to be deep enough to understand what the potential is of the technology, and what the pitfalls are."

This fitted in with the recent overall Pilkington focus on retaining core competencies, including control over strategy, while streamlining the rest. On IT/IS, Pilkington retained critical capability to set strategy, maintain common standards and view IT/IS integration possibilities across the Group, together with the ability to identify the IT/IS needs of business managers. Contract management and regular monitoring of vendor performance were also identified as critical. This arose partly from disappointing experiences with outsourcing in other subsidiaries where such skill had not been retained.

'Rightsizing' to Local Area Networks

In January 1994 Pilkington became one of the first UK corporations to switch off its Head Office mainframe as a result of a downsizing project. The IBM 4381 was replaced with distributed Novell-based local area networks (LANs) supporting IBM PS/2s and an RS/6000 Unix server for application support. The project began in late 1991, cost over £3 million ($US 4.6m.) and had been managed throughout by the services company EDS as part of the outsourcing arrangement. The mainframe was no longer appropriate for the restructured head office. The new infrastructure was designed to provide flexible, reliable and cost-effective support for Group functions and users at Brussels, St. Helens, Lathom and London offices, as well as for the operating companies communicating with them. Pilkington standardized on Microsoft Office software for their global communications. The software package included electronic mail, word processing, spreadsheets and graphics, and facilitates electronic exchange of data and complex documents around the Group.

Up to the end of 1994 the decisions on IT at Pilkington Head Office would seem to have worked out. The outsourcing contract saved some £1.25 million ($1.85m.) over two years. The company had been able to migrate its systems while reducing significantly the size of the HO IT function. The ongoing GHQ IT costs have been halved. The new systems saved Pilkington from having to make a £1 million ($1.5m.) mainframe upgrade, and at the same time accelerated many routine tasks. For example, Group monthly financial consolidations now ran twice as fast, cutting a full day out of the Board reporting timetable. There was a developing relationship with the vendor who also saw the possibilities of further business throughout the Group. The outsourcing agreement was renewed for another two years in early 1994. By mid-1994 the vendor, EDS, had come to use Pilkington HO as a reference site for other potential outsourcing customers.

Looking to the Future

However, as for many other companies that had outsourced IT, several outstanding questions remained for Pilkington. The company had seemingly successfully outsourced HO operations, at least for the short term. But were the critical capabilities retained in-house enough to see it through another contract? Should it eventually bring IT back in-house, perhaps in an easier business climate, now that a difficult organizational restructuring and technological transition had been managed? Or should more of its IT be outsourced? If so, should Pilkington develop a long-term strategic partnership with EDS, or were there advantages in looking for another or additional suppliers? Jo Boyers, manager in the HO IT/IS team, highlights a final issue for Pilkington:

> *"You are continually trying to take the initiative because IT is becoming an increasingly strategic element in business. There's a lot more being spent on it. A lot more than people realize. Companies are realizing that they have got to be ahead of their competitors on IT use, but at the same time they have to control their expenditure."*

As for other companies, if Pilkington chose to go further down the outsourcing route it would now need to bring off the difficult balancing act of combining what advantages came from outsourcing IT with achieving the increased competitiveness and strategic support that IT had the potential to provide.

Case Study Questions

1. Detail the reasons for the total outsourcing decision at Pilkington. Do you think the decision makes the most sense or was there an equally or more viable alternative?

2. From your reading of the case, what do you think are the major business, technical and economic factors a company needs to take into account when making an IT sourcing decision?

3. According to Willcocks and Fitzgerald (1995): "In IT never outsource a problem." Clearly for Pilkington the LAN development was a problem. The company had insufficient in-house expertise to develop the systems itself, but also at the beginning of the contract had less than a clear idea of what the systems should look like, and the information needs they would serve. Why was outsourcing the development work not a disaster?

4. What in-house capability did Pilkington retain? Was this enough? Were there advantages in keeping in-house greater technical expertise?

5. Consider the questions at the end of the case, and the problem posed by Jo Boyers. What directions would you recommend for Pilkington? Give reasons for your answers.

6. Identify any cultural, economic, or political factors that are relevant to this case.

References and Bibliography

1. Feeny, D., Willcocks, L. and Fitzgerald, G. (1993). "Strategies For IT Management: When Outsourcing Equals Rightsourcing." In Rock, S. (ed.) *A Director's Guide to Outsourcing IT*. Institute of Directors/IBM, London.

2. Huber, R. (1993). "How Continental Bank Outsourced Its Crown Jewels." *Harvard Business Review*, January–February, pp. 121–129.

3. Lacity, M. and Hirschheim, R. (1993). *Information Systems Outsourcing: Metaphors, Myths and Realities*. John Wiley and Sons, Chichester.

4. Lacity, M., Hirschheim, R. and Willcocks, L. (1994). "Realizing Outsourcing Expectations: Incredible Expectations, Credible Outcomes." *Information Systems Management*, Fall, pp. 7–18.

5. Willcocks, L. and Fitzgerald, G. (1993). "Markets as Opportunity? Case Studies in Outsourcing Information Technology and Services," *Journal of Strategic Information Systems*, Winter, Vol. 2, No. 3, pp. 223–242.

6. Willcocks, L. and Fitzgerald, G. (1995). "The Changing Shape of the Information Systems Function." in Earl, M. (ed.), *Information Management—The Organizational Dimension*. Oxford University Press, Oxford.

DIGITAL EQUIPMENT CORPORATION[1] INTERNATIONAL: Fitting Information Technology Architecture to Competitive Restructuring

Donald Marchand
International Institute of Management Development, Switzerland

Kimberly A. Bechler
Research Associate, International Institute for Management Development, Lausanne, Switzerland

In July 1991, Peter Cook, Director, European Information Systems for Digital Equipment Corporation International (Europe), was reviewing the company's restructuring plan—designed to enable the organization to respond more capably to market demands. Cook needed to determine the extent to which IT decision-making should be centralized or decentralized; how to bridge the gap between business needs and IS deliverables; how to strike a balance between standardization (enabling sharing of information across the organization) and customization to each profit-and-loss group's own needs; and how to build a flexible IT architecture that could both respond to today's business requirements and accommodate radical changes in tomorrow's business structure.

Digital International (Europe)

Digital Equipment Corporation established overseas sales and distribution in the late 1960s, which eventually led to the founding of Digital Equipment Corporation International (Europe) as a wholly-owned company in 1979. Digital International adopted a management structure similar to that of Digital US. The company's matrix structure was built around key functional managers and geographic regions. Within the regions, country managers maintained overall responsibility for coordinating business activities. (*See Figure 1, Pre-Structuring Organization Chart*). Digital managed its business—along five dimensions: customer, geography, application/industry, product, and function/process. The challenge was one of overall optimization—to integrate and balance all five dimensions.

Digital Europe was comprised of two major functional parts: Sales & Service (S&S) and Logistics & Manufacturing (L&M). Sales & Service operated as subsidiary units, each managed by a country general manager and by a functional group structure based in Geneva, Switzerland, where Digital's European headquarters was located. S&S subsidiaries were responsible for selling, support, service, in-country distribution and logistics, and profit and loss. The Logistics & Manufacturing organization comprised the manufacturing plants and European distribution organization. L&M managed the manufacturing plants, central distribution and logistics as far as the port of entry, and operated on a standard cost basis.

Digital's Restructuring

The driving force behind Digital's restructuring was an increasing recognition that the firm needed to adapt more rapidly to changes in the market. The market increasingly demanded integrated solutions to problems—that is, customers wanted customization, software, and integration. Digital needed to be able to play the role of integrator.

In 1990, Digital began a restructuring plan which created three types of entrepreneurial business structures: product creation units (PCU); applications/industry business units (IBU); and account business units (ABU). The PCU was responsible for engineering, manufacturing, design, and production. The IBU provided specific services that were designed to link products with solutions which met customer needs. Both the PCU and the IBU sold its products and services to the ABUs. The ABU had various options to satisfy their customers. They could buy both IBU and PCU services, buy only products from the PCU, or they also had the freedom to go outside DEC for products and services. The ABUs would only pay for the principal costs that added value. With this new restructuring,

---

[1]This case is a condensed version of the Digital Equipment Corporation International (Europe) A & B case studies, prepared by Research Associate Cathy B. Huycke with the assistance of Peter R. Cook, under the supervision of Professors Michael D. Oliff and Donald A. Marchand.

Copyright © 1994 by the International Institute for Management Development (IMD), Lausanne, Switzerland.

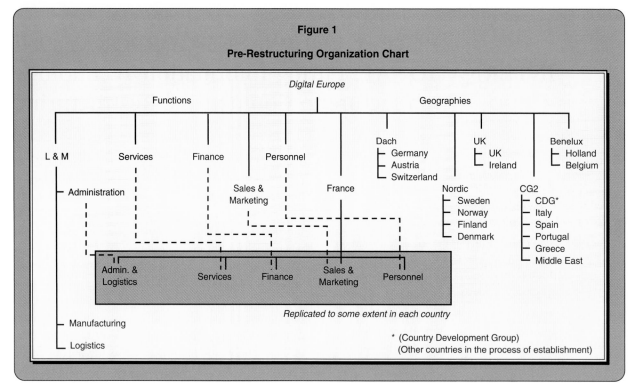

FIGURE 1

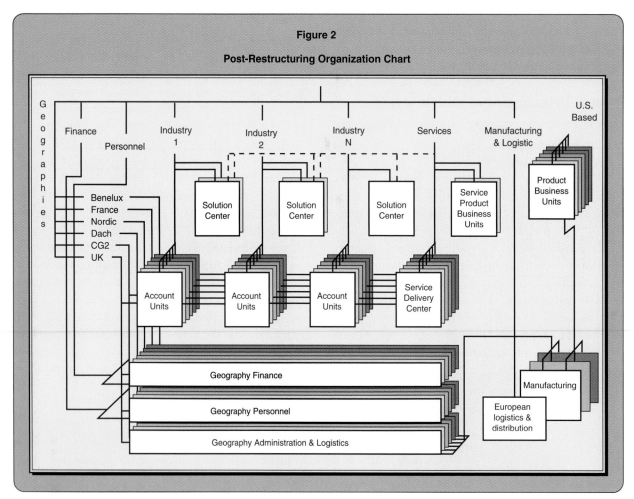

FIGURE 2

only the ABUs operated with profit and loss responsibility. The PBUs and IBUs operated at value-added cost.

In theory, the ABU paid a negotiated rate with the PBU and IBU. But, in practice, with 200 ABUs in Europe and 50–60 PBUs, it was likely that all would not negotiate different rates. According to Cook, "The system operated much like a market. Although there were price lists, those ABUs that had very big deals operated outside these lists." (*See Figure 2, Post-Restructuring Organization Chart.*) Digitals "infrastructure"—i.e., finance, human resources, manufacturing, logistics, etc.—continued to operate on a centralized basis. The future impact of the restructuring plan on this part of the company was still not clear.

Cook wanted to ensure a balanced approach to addressing customer needs and the development of products and application solutions. The sharing of applications and skill sets across customers was critical to maintaining flexibility.

Digital Europe's IS Resources

Digital's information systems (IS) were structured like the rest of the organization, with the basic separation into the field (Sales & Service) and manufacturing (Manufacturing & Logistics). (*See Figure 3, Pre-Restructuring IM&T Organization Chart.*) Historically, field IS had been driven strongly by the area IS organizations which developed basic functional systems. They were then implemented in the subsidiaries. Within the subsidiaries, there were user support and operations groups. Area development and maintenance were done in the subsidiaries but under area control.

Plants, however, were mainly autonomous—each plant had the complete capability to create, implement, support, and operate its own information systems. On a scale of 0% (full autonomy) to 100% (central support), the plants historically had been 5% and the field 85%. Cook believed that neither amount was perfect. What was the ideal mix of autonomy/central support for facilitating more sharing and economy-of-scale benefits in the plant IS organization? How could the subsidiaries' "ownership" of their systems be increased?

Starting in 1989, field IS was "vendorized" (i.e., sold at value-added cost, no profit was realized) to the service organization which, in turn, delivered the same services—

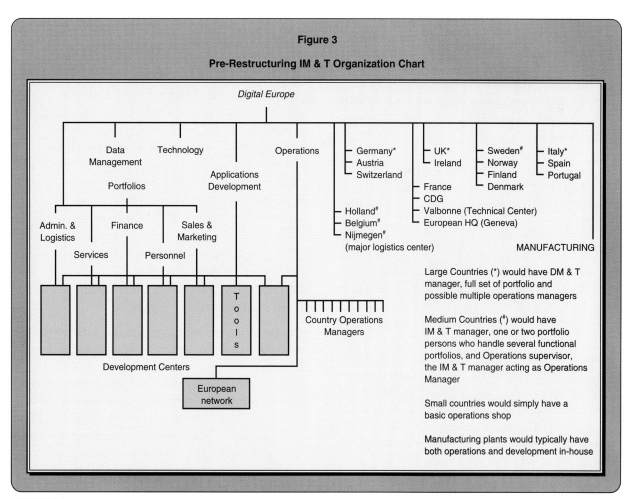

FIGURE 3

consulting, advice, design, development, implementation, operation, support, and maintenance—to external customers. Within the plants, this "vendorization" had not occurred, as the plants were geographically fairly isolated from Digital's customers. Electronic data interchange (EDI) was used to link the organization internally and externally.

Technically, the IS architecture was based on Digital's successful proprietary computer operating systems and communications network, which had supported them through the 1980s. This was being extended to an open systems, multivendor base using Digital's emerging network standard, NAS, as the framework for integration.

Cook believed that the evolving role of the IS department was "to articulate the future state for users; to communicate and steer users away from the blind alleys in technology and business processes; and to provide support, advice, and consulting services to help users make the transition to new technologies."

Peter Cook's IT Strategy

To accommodate the changes in company activities and business processes generated by Digital's restructuring, Peter Cook developed a new IT strategy. Key elements of Cook's IT strategy included a "governance model", designed to balance centralization/decentralization forces; a reconfigured IS Group to bridge the gap between business needs and IS deliverables; balancing the flexibility versus economies of scale trade-offs to minimize total company IS costs; and scenario analysis planning, to operate better under uncertainty.

The Governance—Market Economy Model: Balancing Centralization/ Decentralization Forces

Cook described the rationale for his "governance model" approach:

> If we fail to decentralize the company's IT design methods, for a company that is functionally decentralized we run into *central planning*, which results in conflict. However, if we have highly centralized functions with a decentralized design process, we go into a phase of scarce resources and ineffectiveness, as we always re-invent the wheel every time we design something. The ideal approach is the *governance model*. This model uses a combination of *free market forces*, which are self-interest driven, and a *set of laws and rules*. The laws don't tell you what to do, but what *not* to do. It relies on the *free market* to tell you what to do.

Setting the "Laws": The philosophy of setting the laws was "to control what was necessary to control." Peter Cook

adopted standards covering data management, transaction messaging, and the technical framework for operating systems and hardware. Data management standards were used to ensure that the data supplied by the application could be used by the corporate-wide management information systems. Transaction message standards were used to ensure that transaction traffic generated by the application could be correctly handled by the rest of the global computing system. Technical framework standards—the technical architecture of the operating systems and hardware—were used to ensure that applications built in one location could be successfully reused in other places without the need for major changes to the technical infrastructure, and that intercommunication was technically possible.

"Guiding the Market": Within the framework of standards, operational "entrepreneurial" units could choose whatever application they wanted that met their needs and conformed to standards. Applications already created by other groups were available "free of charge," while new development projects would cost the operational units money. The advantage of this approach was that it placed the decision-making close to the business unit level, while ensuring that strategic plans and directions (in both business process and IT areas) could be managed at the cooporate level by setting appropriate standards and guidelines.

Cook believed the best solution was a combination of "centrally" produced packages with local selection and customization. The ideal solution was to structure applications composed of modules, each implementing a "business primitive," which could be assembled like LEGO pieces to build systems to meet local needs. The business primitive was the smallest component of the function, representing a highly specific activity at the task level—for example, checking credit status.

The Challenge—Bridging the Gap between IT Business Needs and IT Design Via IS Organizational Re-Configuration

Within the newly configured IS group, there were three sub-functions: User Services, Systems House and an architecture, strategy, and standards group (IM&T). (*See Figure 4, Post-Restructuring IM&T Organization.*) User Services and "System House" were the components that had been vendorized; IM&T remained centralized. The role of the "Systems House" was to develop and deliver customized solutions for particular entrepreneurial groups and to institutionalize the standardization process.

Digital's objective was to have User Service Group (USG) focused on providing internal users with the systems they required to perform their functions in the company. The USG subcontracted or purchased applications expertise from the Systems Houses which were specialized in particular applications, such as customer administration, management information and decision support, data warehouses, and fiscal and accounting systems. The IM&T group was responsible for maintaining the standards and architectures within which the USGs and Systems Houses created their solutions.

The net result of this reconfiguration of the IS group was that Cook was able to reduce his resource base of operators by 30%.

Maximizing Resources: Economies of Scale (EOS) versus Local Flexibility

Cook described the trade-offs between EOS and local flexibility:

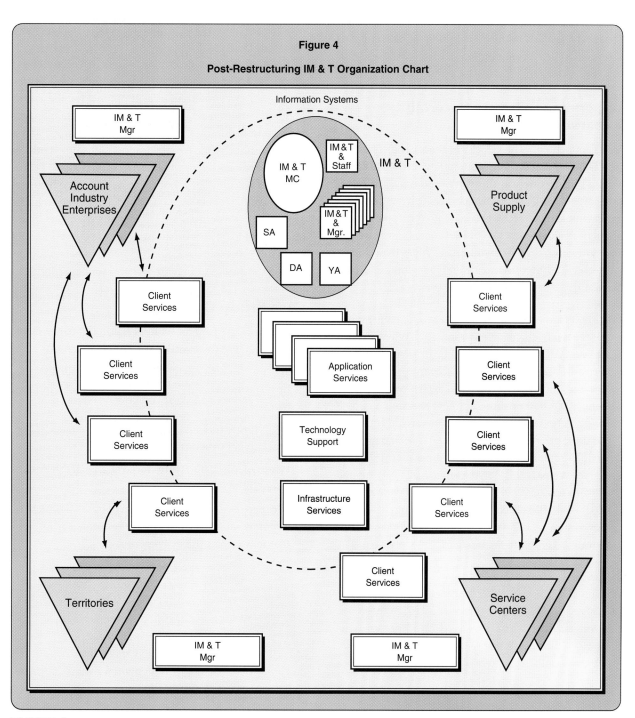

Figure 4

Post-Restructuring IM & T Organization Chart

FIGURE 4

We've analyzed our activities to decide where we do and do not want EOS. The driver is the conflict between saving IS money and saving the overall company money. If Digital has one huge data centre in the middle of Europe doing everything the company needs, I can reduce the IS cost substantially. The price to the business, however, is high as it will need to adapt to my standard environment. If it is laissez-faire, I end up with a very high IS cost, but the business benefits because every system is customized to user requirements. The objective is not to minimize the IS budget as a proportion of the company's budget, but to minimize the *total cost* to the organization for delivering information. It's a compromise.

Responding to Future Uncertainty—Scenario Analysis

Cook commented, "The velocity of change is increasing." Cook believed that the most appropriate method to create systems architecture was through *scenario analysis*. To get some level of consistency, Digital used the scenario of four architectures: data, technical, systems (i.e., applications modules), and business. Cook believed that the slowest to change was the systems architecture, while the business and technology architectures were changing at an ever increasing speed.

> We build a systems architecture that is hopefully stable under rapidly changing environments. When we create a model, rather than testing it against business needs, we test against possible scenarios—which may be a long way from the business needs. We attempt to identify the two or three business decisions that will have a radical impact on our systems architecture. We use these business architecture scenarios to design the modules or at least to list the modules that will be required. We pass this down as the legal structure and allow the entrepreneurial units to build whatever they need within the systems architecture using these modules—knowing full well that, once the world changes, we can re-configure the modules.

Value added from IT is based on the business manager's ability to see business change. I want to build an architecture that will adapt to all possible scenarios. We need the architecture and systems that can respond to external forces.

Cook knew that the configuration of the new IT architecture needed to be able to support an organization that was highly decentralized in terms of its ABU focus and also centralized in terms of corporate-wide activities such as manufacturing, finance, human resources, etc. With the restructured company, the country management unit was no longer in place as a focal point for general management as well as IS.

Cook needed to determine where decisions about specific functions should be made—should they be decentralized or centralized? Was it optimal for the entrepreneurial units to decide on functionality, data management, transaction messaging, hardware platforms, and a technical framework for application software—both its development and deployment? Or should Cook be responsible for some or all of these decisions? Which approach would enable Digital to build a better IT architecture, one that would respond to ongoing change with the most flexibility? If restructuring were to be a continually changing process, how could IS accommodate shifts in business strategies or organizational reconfigurations?

Case Study Questions

1. What are the benefits of a centralized IS department, and what are the benefits of a decentralized IS?

2. What is the relationship between the corporate structure and IS structure, and what is the problem faced by Cook?

3. What forces (drivers) caused Digital to change its organizational structure?

4. Which of the changes introduced by Digital can be considered BPR?

5. Are there any cultural, economic, political, or other environmental factors unique to the European location that may impact the delivery of IT?

FROM A DINOSAUR TO A CHAMELEON:
Transformation of a Korean Bank

YOUNG MOO KANG
Dong-A University, Korea

The Kwangju Bank is a regional bank that is located in Kwangju City Korea. Kwangju City is located in the southern part of Korea and has a population of 1.2 million. In 1989, the bank had 44 branches and 1,170 employees with a deposit volume of 850 million dollars. The bank had been in trouble over the years. In particular, 1989 was a very bad year for the Kwangju Bank. It had lost 43.8 million dollars in a foreign exchange fraud. Furthermore, it had to stop banking services for 32 hours due to computer problems. There had been rumors that the bank was in such a serious financial situation that the bank was attributing its inability to execute transactions to computer breakdowns.

In June 1989, Mr. Song Byungsoon was brought in as the new chairman of the board for the bank. He had an excellent track record as a leader in the industry, with new ideas and a driving force. He had been chairman of the board of the Citizens National Bank in 1980 and president of the Office of Bank Supervision and Examination in 1983. The Citizens National Bank is one of the largest banks in Korea. The Office of Bank Supervision and Examination is a government financed organization that supervises financial activities of all banks. Clearly more than qualified for the position, Mr. Song was considered the best person for rescuing the bank from troubled waters.

Mr. Song is well known in the banking industry for his vision and willpower. For instance, within only one-and-a-half months after his inauguration as chairman of the board of the Citizens National Bank, Mr. Song had designed and implemented a credit card system that was the first in Korean banking history.

After a year as chairman of the board of the Kwangju Bank, Mr. Song had restored the banks health and eliminated the red ink on its balance sheets. The results were so remarkable that his story was published in the British *Financial Times*. Since then, the Kwangju Bank has grown steadily over the years. During the last 5 years, the total assets have increased by 4.6 times, with bank accounts being 52% and trust accounts 48%. The deposit volume has increased by 4.7 times. The number of branches has increased from 44 to 112. The bank has 1.5 million customers. During a peak period, about 650,000 transactions are processed each day. However, the number of employees has grown to only 1,867 from 1,170 during the last 5 years. Now, the bank has established itself as an aggressive and energetic regional bank in Korea. Among the 10 Korean regional banks, the Kwangju Bank has the highest growth rate in deposits and the second highest growth rate in net income in 1994.

How was this dramatic change possible? What are the critical factors for the success? Mr. Song says that the most critical action was the downsizing of information systems with the reengineering of banking processes. Let us look at how the bank's information systems were downsized and reengineered.

Reasons for Initiating the Bank Information System Project

Kwangju Bank's original information system was developed about 10 years ago. The hardware was purchased from a U.S. hardware vendor. The software was licensed from a Japanese application package vendor and modified by a Korean software firm. When the system was implemented, it was considered a reasonably efficient system. However, support from the vendors was not satisfactory. Frequently, the bank could not respond to the market quickly because the information system was too rigid and did not provide proper support. Furthermore, the system had completely stopped several times.

The bank's top executives decided to overhaul the information systems. The bank spent 7.6 million dollars during the second half of 1990 and the first half of 1991 in order to upgrade the bank's online transaction processing (OLTP) system. However, in the summer of 1991, the vendor who supplied the bank's OLTP system notified the bank that it could not provide maintenance service after May 31, 1993. The vendor suggested the bank upgrade the host computer in order to guarantee the maintenance service. However, the upgrade would have cost 11.3 million dollars.

Disturbed at this information, Mr. Song investigated the problem thoroughly. He concluded that downsizing

793

the OLTP system was the best long-term solution for the bank. He thought that the bank should learn how to play in the global market. However, the Kwangju Bank was too weak to compete against foreign banks from the U.S., Europe and Japan. Furthermore, the bank operations were hindered by its computer systems and computer vendors. The bank could not set its own business strategies because the information systems could not support them. On the other hand, the expenditure on information systems was growing faster than the increase in the bank's income.

If the above trends were not corrected quickly, the Kwangju Bank would not survive. However, the centralized information system could not be reformed easily without drastic measures. Mr. Song concluded that the time had arrived to completely rebuild the information system and prepare the way to utilize information technology. He requested CHNO Consulting, one of Korea's leading consulting firms, to investigate the possibilities of downsizing the bank's information systems.

The idea of downsizing information systems attracted the attention of U.S. and European companies in the late '80s and early '90s. However, no bank in the world had successfully downsized its OLTP system yet. The OLTP system is the bank's most critical system because it is directly linked to the customer's financial interests. Any minor problems in the system will seriously affect the bank's credibility. Therefore, downsizing a bank's OLTP system is an innovative, but highly risky project that no one had successfully implemented before. However, Mr. Song decided to build an information system the bank could depend on by fully utilizing all available information technology.

Objectives of the New Information System

Before undertaking the project, the bank needed to have clear objectives for the new information system. Since Mr. Song's inauguration as chairman of the board, he strongly emphasized that the way of doing business should be changed dramatically in order to survive in the new global market. He believed that the information system should be flexible enough to facilitate developing new products, support the bank's new business strategy, actively serve customers wherever they are, and give the bank control over the future of the information system.

In the past, the bank information systems were developed from the bank's perspectives, not from the customer's. Therefore, the old information systems were designed to manage master files and process accounts based on loans and deposits, not individual customers.

However, the new information systems should attract customers by helping them manage their financial interests more conveniently. Therefore, the new information systems should be able to provide banking services wherever and whenever the customers want. In other words, the information system should support commercial banking, home banking, self-service terminals, automatic teller machines and electronic "wallets." Additionally, the new information systems should be flexible enough to help the development of new products and the making of more effective banking decisions.

Characteristics of the New Information System

How could the new information system support the above objectives? The client/server model was adopted in order to make the information system flexible. The interface between servers and clients in a client/server model made it easier for the bank to develop and implement new strategies and products. For example, new components or functions could be added to either the servers or the clients without worrying about ill effects to the other side.

Furthermore, customer databases were distributed to regional servers in order to maximize local autonomy and minimize processing time and risk of total system failure. The system used open systems architecture in order to be independent of vendors, achieve flexibility, and minimize maintenance and upgrade costs. The timetable for developing the new information system is summarized in Table 1.

Technical Components of the New Information System

In developing centralized information systems, computer vendors are typically in charge of selecting, implementing, testing and installing the hardware and software. On the other hand, in developing client/server systems, project

Table 1 Timetable of the Information System Development Project

Stages	Time
Formation of project team	June 1991
Basic design	March 1992
Detailed design, selecting vendors	June 1992
Commissioning development	August 1992
Implementation, partial testing	February 1993
Integrated testing, system tuning	May 1993
Parallel testing, user training	September 1993
Completing system conversion	January 1994

teams have the freedom of selecting various components by themselves. However, project teams are also fully responsible for the outcomes.

Finding an appropriate OLTP middleware was the most crucial part in selecting technical components. The Unix operating systems (OS) that the project team decided to use did not provide the necessary security controls for real-time operations, which are essential in banking operations. The Unix OS also did not allow clients to invoke services across multiple servers. Furthermore, the Unix OS did not allow the different servers to cooperate with other servers when they need access to resources that are not local.

However, OLTP Monitor middleware guarantees the integrity of all activities within and across servers. There are several well known OLTP middeware available on the market such as Tuxedo's ATMI and /WS or Encina's Transactional RPS. However, there were no reports on using the above products for bank OLTP systems.

After extensive investigations, the project team found an OLTP middleware called CStalk. This middleware was developed by a Taiwanese company called RPTI and had been used in an online banking system.

It was a highly risky decision for the Kwangju Bank to choose a little known software company as a supplier of the crucial component in the system. However, after visits to RPTI and a Taiwanese bank which had implemented CStalk, Mr. Song became confident about CStalk. Eventually, Mr. Song's decision proved to be right.

Outline of the New Information System

The Kwangju Bank has 7 regional centers and 112 branches. The new information system, which has a distributed client/server architecture, consists of a regional center server for each regional center, a branch server for each branch, and numerous clients. Each regional server serves about 15-20 branches.

The regional center server consists of an HP 9000/70 with 256 MB main memory and two 6 gigabyte hard disks. It uses Oracle DBMS. Each regional center maintains its regional account master files and customer databases on its server. The regional center server also processes transactions and certain online activities performed within its region. Therefore, the regional center server functions as a database server and an application server for the region.

Among the seven regional servers, three servers are located in Seoul and two other cities and four other servers are located at the headquarters. The headquarters server handles the common tasks that are applied to all regions. In other words, it works as a server for functions such as foreign exchange, commercial banking, home banking, information management for senior managers, and office automation.

All servers are remotely monitored, security checked, and operated unattended. At each regional center, dual servers with dual databases are employed in order to maximize reliability. Because of the distributed multiserver dual architecture, the impact of any malfunction will be localized to a very limited area.

On the other hand, each branch uses SUN Sparc-10 as its branch server. Its main tasks are totalization and transaction approval operations.

For client computers, the bank uses 386 or 486 microcomputers instead of the dedicated teller terminal. This approach provides the bank with more power and flexibility and costs only one-sixth of the cost of a dedicated terminal. There are about 1,100 client computers which have passbook printers and card readers. Additionally, there are 170 automatic teller machines and numerous CDs each with a self-service passbook printer.

The systems use the Unix operating system. Communications within a regional center or a branch use a LAN with TCP/IP. Communications between regional centers use 1Mbps T1 service. On the other hand, communications between regional centers and branches use 56Kbps leased lines. Figure 1 shows components of the new information system.

Application Programs Reengineering

During the information system design stage, the project team evaluated all the application programs. The programs had been created in a piecemeal way without an overall blueprint. Consequently, it was very difficult and costly to maintain or modify the programs. Furthermore, it is very hard to create new programs efficiently in response to the rapidly changing market environment.

In order to overcome these problems, the project team integrated, simplified or removed transaction processes whenever possible. Results were impressive. From the 3,000 original transaction processes, only 400 transaction processes were kept. Additionally, 200 new processes were created based on the customers' requests.

Furthermore, the project team utilized commercial software packages whenever possible. It lets packages handle an average of 10 back-office activities out of 13 activities per process. The reengineering project which has simplified transaction processes by using commercial packages, has dramatically reduced the cost of program development from 12.5 million dollars to 2.5 million dollars.

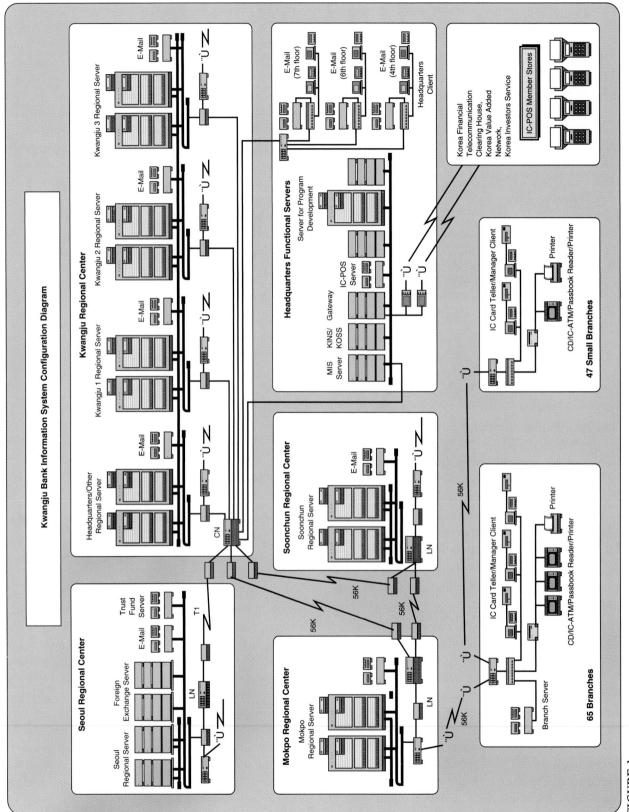

FIGURE 1

Success Factors of the Information System Project

The most important success factor in the project was the chairman of the board's vision and strong leadership. There were numerous obstacles and doubts from various sources when the bank started the information system downsizing project. The vendors who supplied mainframe-based systems tried to obstruct the project in order to protect their current and potential markets. Senior staff at the Kwangju Bank computer center were cynical about the project because they were not comfortable with the new technology.

Furthermore, academicians who were commmissioned to evaluate the project concluded that it was too risky to undertake since the technology was not mature enough. Therefore, the general feeling on the project was very pessimistic to say the least. However, Mr. Song firmly believed that downsizing the information system was the best solution and that the technical problems associated with the project were solvable.

Benefits from the New Information System

It has been more than one year since the new information system was implemented. The bank has experienced many benefits from the new system. Those benefits can be grouped into two: benefits for the customers and those for the bank.

First, customers get better service in terms of timeliness and quality. For example, the transaction processing speed has been improved significantly from 4-6 seconds to 0.7-2.0 seconds per transaction. The bank is able to serve customers 24 hours a day and 7 days a week instead of the usual 8 hours.

Customers also have more financial services to choose from because new product development cycles have been significantly shortened from months to weeks.

Second, the bank was able to reduce expenses with better performance and pursue new business strategies more effectively. The new open information system provides greater flexibility and freedom from vendor domination and allows easier adoption of new technology.

For example, the maintenance and operating expenses for the new information system have been slashed to one-third of those of the old system. The number of information center staff has been reduced from 120 to 60. In case of trouble, the old system had to be completely shut down and required significant repair time. However, if there is a malfunction in the new system, only the defective part needs to be stopped for repair. All in all, Mr. Song's vision has been realized.

Case Study Questions

1. Relate the bank's problems to its computer system.

2. Relate the change in the computer system to the bank's reengineering.

3. Why was the client/server approach better than the upgrading of the mainframe?

4. What was the significance of global competition in the IT decisions?

5. What are the risks and opportunities of downsizing an OLTP in a bank?

6. How is the new system supporting the decentralization of operations?

7. Discuss the issues relating to software development and applications.

8. Identify cultural, economic, or political factors that are relevant to this case.

9. Did the business process reengineering have to accompany the new information systems development? Why or why not?

MANAGING PUBLIC INFORMATION SYSTEMS DEVELOPMENT

NICOLAU REINHARD
RONALDO ZWICKER
University of Sao Paulo, Brazil

1. Introduction—The Secretary of the Treasury

The Brazilian Federal Government has around 600,000 employees (excluding state-owned companies) and is responsible for around 10% of the country's IT spending. In 1985 the country went through significant political changes: a civilian president took office under a democratic regime. At this time Brazil was renegotiating its foreign debt of US$ 80 billion, with the involvement of the IMF. Reducing government size and deficit, and controlling and giving more transparency to public spending became a political priority. For this purpose Congress created the Secretary of the Treasury (ST) in the Ministry of Economics and Finance (MEF). This new Secretary would accumulate the functions of financial management, internal and foreign debt control, internal control and auditing, and accounting for all federal government agencies. (In this text the term "Agency" is used for any organization directly controlled by the federal government.) The Minister of Economics and Finance at that time was a very prestigious and charismatic person, mainly due to the (short-lived) success of his economic stabilization program. A young, dynamic and politically well-connected economics professor became the first Secretary of the Treasury, bringing with him a number of competent and motivated executives from other government agencies to the newly formed ST.

The ST, however, had no effective control mechanisms for the prescribed functions: Ministries and other agencies had financial autonomy to execute the budget approved by Congress and could be controlled only through the aggregate cash flow, local auditing or accounting statements that would be available with a delay of 6 to 9 months, and therefore without managerial effectiveness.

2. The SIAFI Project

The Secretary then decided to centralize the financial administration for the whole government through a centralized accounting, control and funds transfer system: Agencies would still have financial and budget autonomy, but all transactions would only be effective after being recorded in the system. This would be enforced by the fact that all payments to creditors would be made only through the system. Resources would be distributed to agencies through limited drawing rights against ST's Central Treasury Banking Account. This system would allow the auditors to control transactions on-line, and, if necessary, stop undue payments in time. It would also allow a better cash-flow management, because of the complete knowledge of accounts payable. The system would also control Treasury-guaranteed government debt, at the federal, state and municipal levels.

The system, to be called SIAFI (an acronym for Integrated System for Financial Administration, in Portuguese), would give the ST total control over government spending, which was completely against the prevailing decentralization and liberalization tendencies of the new government. The Secretary obtained the budget to pay directly for the whole system, including equipment and installation for all other agencies. For many users this would be their first contact with a computerized on-line system. Other users would have to substitute their existing control systems for the new one. SIAFI would also require significant changes in operational procedures and strongly impact employment at the agencies, since all accounting and reporting functions would now be performed automatically by the system. It was estimated that the system would eliminate 1,000 clerical jobs, requiring also new skills for accountants, auditors and financial and planning officers.

The Data Processing Company (referred to as the Company in this case), an organization owned by the MEF, submitted a proposal to build an innovative distributed system, based on locally produced minicomputers. This system would be state-of-the-art and would take one year for project development and two more years to be implemented. The Secretary, however, considered the political timing to be unique and required the system to be operational in 7 months, that is, at the beginning of the next fiscal year. A team with members from the Secretary and the Company presented another viable alternative: a mainframe-based centralized system, using Adabas as the DBMS and a network with SNA architecture linking all users in the capital and provinces to the Company's operating centers. This proposal had many disadvantages: lower performance, high communication cost, lower availability, besides being based on an aging technology. This, however, was also its strength: since the proposed technology was already used for all other major applications in the Company, the infrastructure was already there, with trained staff at all levels. The system would run on an existing mainframe that would soon have to be upgraded.

The team had only halfhearted support from the Company's upper management, that saw the advanced solution as a unique opportunity for modernization. This conflict eventually led the Ministry to intervene later in the Company and appoint a member of the ST team to become its new president. The project was nevertheless started under the leadership of a department manager of the ST and addressed all major problems: revision of norms and regulations, system specification, infrastructure, training, user and technical support, etc. The people involved understood this project to be a unique professional opportunity and challenge; others however viewed it with disbelief.

SIAFI system became operational in 6 months (in the form of a functional prototype). Usually long processes for the acquisition of equipment (terminals, microcomputers, communications controllers, etc.) were expedited, political contacts were used to secure the large number of data lines (in permanent short supply in the country) and other infrastructure resources. The team also promoted the required changes in regulations and legislation and obtained the support from groups that would be affected (accountants and financial and planning officers) by securing them training programs and new career perspectives, besides extensive nation-wide user training. This task was made easier because the Secretary had the normative power for most changes and used his political influence to secure the others. Agencies were instructed to relocate workers that would be displaced by the system. Special attention was given to public relations to maintain a positive image of the project in all ranks of Government and isolate resisting groups. Strong support also came from the high courts that control government activities.

On January 2nd, 1987, the system was officially installed, although with many problems: many of the 1,200 terminals were not fully operational (specially in remote parts of the country), users had many questions about procedures, and the system had low performance. These problems were eventually solved and the system stabilized around 10 months later.

The total implementation cost for the first phase of the project was US$ 30 million. This investment was returned in the 4 first months of operation, due to savings in interest paid by the government, because of the centralized cash flow operation. During the period of implementation the project employed a total of 350 people (both from the ST and the Company), that was later reduced to a permanent staff of around 100. The initial software development team had 64 members, with 27 analysts and programmers remaining for maintenance. The yearly budget for the system has grown from US$ 40 to 95 million (in 1995).

Overall the system was considered to be one of the greatest successes of a public information system in Brazil. Besides the operational savings, the system gave transparency to government action that has been instrumental in improving effectiveness and responsiveness to Congress, having played a major role in some recent political crises. Both the Secretary and his principal project manager left the ST after some time to work for the private sector and as consultants to international agencies.

SIAFI has since been expanded, both in computational power and communications network. In 1992 the Social Security Administration was included in the system by presidential decree, leading to a sharp increase in the size and usage of the system. The present dimension of SIAFI is shown in Table 1.

Table 1 SIAFI (the figures are for 1994)

Direct nodes	5,100
Connected nationwide networks	30
Users	
active passwords	76,000
organizational units	11,000
Documents recorded (per year)	11,000,000
Transactions (per month-average)	24,000,000
Response time (average)	4 seconds
Transaction types available	670
Transaction cost (average)	30 cents

The evolution of SIAFI usage and performance for the last 8 years is shown in Table 2.

SIAFI presently runs on an IBM 9021/962 mainframe (310 MIPS, 768 MB and 416 GB disks). The network uses around 2,000 leased data lines (not including the connected networks).

The system has been augmented with functions for planning and budgeting, managerial control and is linked to other centralized government systems (personnel, etc.). Some of these modules compete with systems from other ministries (the conflict is most evident with the

Table 2 SIAFI usage and performance
(averages)

Year	Transaction/month (in millions)	Response time (in seconds)
1987	5.0	19.0
1988	8.8	8.8
1989	11.1	8.7
1990	12.3	5.0
1991	13.3	5.3
1992	17.8	5.0
1993	20.5	5.3
1994	20.6	3.9

budgeting system from the Ministry of Planning). The original SIAFI emphasized only the operational transactions, that had to be used by the agencies. The added management support modules, to be used on a voluntary base, have been adopted very slowly.

SIAFI has also been used as a model for several other countries. In fact some of the initial team members are now working for international agencies to implement these systems.

3. Other Centralized Control Systems Projects

Soon after the implementation of SIAFI, the same team undertook another ambitious project to centralize the control of the largest item in government spending: Personnel, responsible at that time for 80% of the budget. Public jobs are a source of political power and their irregularities are strongly visible to public opinion. The ST is responsible for controlling these expenses, although the control of personnel policies belongs to the Ministry of Administration. This ministry was operating a reporting system that did not provide timely and complete information, but had been working for some time on a new decentralized system that was not as coercive as the one proposed by the ST, although better aligned with the prevailing political orientation.

The system proposed by the ST, to be called SIAPE (for Integrated System for Personnel Administration) was designed to centralize all payroll payments and provide users with other functions for human resources administration. Users, still responsible for their payrolls, would therefore be forced to keep the personnel databases at the Secretary permanently updated. Eliminating redundant functions would also bring operational savings. The system would be a significant improvement because of the general lack of integrated human resources systems in the ministries.

The project team of this system, similar to SIAFI, and designed to share the same infrastructure, was continually in trouble. The team with members from the ST and the EDP company had difficulties in concluding the specification process because of the large number of special conditions and constant changes in norms and procedures. Nevertheless the system was implemented by decree in a significant number of ministries, but was continually plagued by poor data quality.

SIAPE was seen by users as a control system that would allow the ST to enforce Government policies related to compensation, pay increases, promotions, etc. The lack of control had until then reduced the effectiveness of these policies, leading to constant budget overruns and administrative irregularities. Many users (understandably) resisted the implementation of the system. After 2 years the project was handed over to the Ministry of Administration, where it had never been well accepted, and only after an intense political action at the President's level, in 1993, was the use of the payroll module made mandatory in all remaining government agencies. SIAPE's other modules (human resources management, etc.), have never been implemented, although the software has been operational since 1992. The Ministry of Administration considers the design of these modules to be inadequate and has planned to redesign them.

The EDP company that operates the system has had a difficult time in receiving payment for the operation of SIAPE (not solely due to budget shortages), but cannot stop providing the services because of the strategic importance of the payroll.

SIAPE, in its present state is a simple payroll system, although it can identify irregularities and stop undue payments. It has a limited use for managerial control and planning, because of its inability to support payroll projections, analysis of compensation policies, manpower and career planning, performance evaluation, etc.

Recently, some ministries, including the MEF, have developed their own human resources systems, with interfaces to SIAPE payroll. There are constant pressures to discontinue the whole SIAPE system.

A few years later, the same team of the ST started a new project in another area of strategic importance to the control of government spending: purchases of goods and services and materials administration (SIASG, for Integrated System for Management of General Services). This area, despite heavy regulations, is a constant source of problems that regularly makes the news. The system would be of great benefit to the government due to standardization, economies of scale and its usefulness in promoting industrial policies, besides the possibility of control of operational procedures. Some ministries have their own systems, which they even have shared with other agencies. The project, however, never went beyond the preproject phase in the ST and was, after some time, also handed over to the Ministry of Administration, which has the responsibility for control and normatization in this area. Although the project has not yet been implemented, there have been some advances: the development (without implementation) of a codification and a comprehensive catalog of materials and services, a centralized suppliers directory and a central exchange for materials among agencies. This system, too, is not high on the Ministry priority list, because of budget shortages and lack of human resources to manage the project.

Both projects, SIAPE and SIASG, are designed to be integrated operationally with SIAFI and would, together, constitute the backbone of the integrated control system that would help in achieving the effectiveness and efficiency of government action.

The existing technical infrastructure has also been used for some other support systems, like a successful electronic mail system that is used for administrative transactions and fast broadcast of new norms and regulations to agencies and the public interfacing with government. ST is also considering to give the public limited access rights to aggregated data of SIAFI.

4. The New Challenge

In January 1995 a new president took office and invited the former Secretary of the Treasury and his principal project manager at that time, to participate in the new government as, respectively, Vice-Minister of Planning and Vice-Minister of Finance. Balancing the budget, reducing the size of government are still top priorities to control inflation (for which the structuring systems are highly strategic instruments). The political process resulting from governing with a coalition of political parties, regional disparities and local interests add to the complexity of the problem.

Possible alternatives include the unification of the Ministry of Planning Budget system with SIAFI, providing resources and support for SIAPE and SIASG, etc. The strongest constraints are not financial, but political and managerial.

For the systems themselves, there remain the challenges of technical actualization, integration with other systems, and having them become widely used planning and management control instruments. One project, for

which government is seeking World Bank funding is the development of a new client/server architecture for SIAFI with a centralized server for operational transactions and clients in the ministries with copies of the relevant databases and appropriate tools for management applications, to be developed centrally or locally by individual users. In a later phase the servers for transaction processing and data storage should also be distributed. This infrastructure would also be shared by the other systems. Although SIAFI itself is beyond question, the ST has had difficulty in justifying the proposed changes and the investments in the other centralized control systems.

Case Study Questions

1. Discuss the importance of scheduling the deliverables (systems functions) to the success of a project.

2. Discuss the importance of identifying the resources required for the project (both tangibles and intangibles) and their "owners".

3. Discuss the importance of having measurable goals for a project. How should one establish the (politically) most meaningful measures?

4. Discuss the risk of using innovative technologies in large interorganizational systems projects.

5. Are there differences in Information Systems success factors between public organizations and private companies? Are there differences in project management strategies between turbulent environments and stable environments? Between strategic applications and support functions?

6. What can be done to increase the survival rate of operational transaction-processing systems in turbulent environments? Are they different from those of decision-support systems?

7. Discuss the relationship between the reorganization of the government and supporting IT.

8. What are the political and economic implications of the success of the government changes supported by IT?

9. Read some material about the economic, political, and cultural environment in Brazil. Then point to issues relevant to this case.

10. Identify issues in this case that are similar to those of TradeNet.

GLOSSARY

Action language is the user's action (e.g., input data, query, etc.) in communication.

Ad hoc reports are issued in reply to a request, in contrast with periodical reports.

An **algorithm** is a step-by-step procedure to achieve a solution (the closest solution).

American National Standard Code for Information Interchange (ASCII) is a standard for encoding alphanumeric symbols into bits, made common with personal computers.

Analog signals are continuous waves that "carry" information by altering the characteristics of the waves.

Analysis graphics provide the ability to convert previously analyzed data, such as statistical data, into graphic formats like bar charts, line charts, pie charts, and scatter diagrams.

The **analytic engine** was designed by Charles Babbage as an advanced mechanical calculator, the forerunner of the modern computer, but never built due to the poor manufacturing capabilities in the 1840s.

Application controls are designed to protect specific applications.

An **application program** is a set of computer instructions written in a programming language, the purpose of which is to provide functionality to a user.

Application systems (see application program).

An **arithmetic/logic unit (ALU)** performs all arithmetic and logic comparison operations for a central processing unit.

Artificial intelligence (AI) is a subfield of computer science concerned with symbolic reasoning and problem solving.

Artificial neural network (ANN) is a computer technology attempting to build computers that will operate like a human brain. The machines possess simultaneous data storage and work with ambiguous information.

An **assembler** is a systems software program that translates an assembly language program into machine language.

Assembly language is a low-level language but slightly more user-oriented than machine language, representing machine language instructions and data locations in primary storage using mnemonics which people can more easily use.

In an **asynchronous transmission**, only one character is transmitted or received at a time, with each character preceded by a start bit and ended with a stop bit that let the receiving device know where a character begins and ends.

An **attribute** is column or field of data about an entity.

An **audit** is a regular examination or check of systems, their inputs, outputs, and processing.

An **audit trail** lists all changes made to a file for checking or control purposes.

A **backup** is a copy of software or data.

Backward error correction (BEC) entails going "back" to the sender and requesting retransmission of the entire data stream or a particular part if it can be identified.

Bandwidth refers to the range of frequencies available in any communication channel; in general, the higher the bandwidth, the more information can be transmitted simultaneously.

Bar code scanners read or scan bar codes, including Universal Product Codes (UPCs), on merchandise and transmit the data to a computer.

BASIC (**B**eginners **A**ll-purpose **S**ymbolic **I**nstruction **C**ode) is a popular programming language on millions of personal computers, including Visual BASIC.

Batch processing processes inputs at fixed intervals as a file and operates on it all at once; interactive (or on-line) processing operates on a transaction as soon as it occurs.

A **bit** (or **b**inary dig**it**) is the smallest unit processed in a computer; numerically, a 1 or a 0.

A **black box** is a common term for a device known for its input and output but not how it performs a function internally.

Break-even analysis indicates when an original investment is recouped by additional revenue.

A **bus** is a channel or "highway" through which information is passed in an electronic form.

In a **bus** topology, nodes are arranged along a single length of cable that can be extended at the ends.

Business alliances are different forms of cooperation between two or more business partners (e.g., joint venture).

Business functions are functional areas such as accounting, finance, manufacturing and marketing.

Business logic directs system execution and entails four elements: encoded algorithms, encoded business rules and logic, structured and encoded processing sequences, and parsed and delineated activity systems.

A **business process** is a collection of activities that take one or more kind of inputs and create an output.

Business process reengineering (BPR) is a methodology for introducing a fundamental change in specific business processes, usually supported by an information system.

Business systems planning (BSP) concentrates on identifying problems and related decisions, based on business processes and data classes.

A **byte** is a number of bits used to represent one alphanumeric character; commonly eight bits in most computers.

C is a high-level procedural language that is considered more transportable than other languages; a C program written for one type of computer can generally be run on another type of computer with little or no modification.

C++ is an extension of the programming language C.

Cache memory is temporary, very fast, digital storage for a central processor.

CD-ROM (**c**ompact **d**isc-read **o**nly **m**emory) is a secondary digital storage medium that uses laser-made pits in plastic to represent bits.

Cellular radio technology is a radio-based communications system using defined geographic service areas with each area then subdivided into hexagonal cells.

A **central processing unit (CPU)** is the "brains" of a computer—controlling all computational, input, output, and storage activities.

Centralized computing puts all processing and control authority within one computer to which all other computing devices respond.

A **centralized database** has all related files in one physical location.

Channel systems is a network of the materials and product distribution system within an organization, and between the organization and its suppliers and customers.

Chargeout systems treat the MIS function as a service bureau or utility charging organizational subunits for providing MIS services with the objective of recovering (or partially recovering) MIS expenditures.

A **Chief Information Officer (CIO)** is the director of the IS department in large, organization, analogous to a CEO, COO, or CFO.

A **circuit switched** network is composed of shared, analog channels used mainly for low-speed, intermittent transmissions used by many parties one at a time.

An object's **class** defines all the messages to which the object will respond, as well as the way the objects of this class are implemented.

Client/server architecture is a type of distributed architecture where end-user PC's (clients) request services or data from designated processors or peripherals (servers).

A computer processing unit **clock** provides a steady electronic pulse which all other units can use to stay in syncopation.

COBOL (**Co**mmon **B**usiness **O**riented **L**anguage) is a high-level language developed for the business community to make its instructions approximate the way they would be expressed in natural English.

Code inspection is the final stage of quality assurance prior to actually testing a system, when a program is inspected line-by-line to see if everything seems correct in terms of syntax and correct coding in the particular language.

A **code of ethics** is a group of ethical behavior rules developed by organizations or by a professional society.

Common carriers are businesses that supply high-speed voice and data communication services.

Communications software allows computers to exchange data over circuits.

Competitive advantage is an advantage over a competitor such as lower cost or quicker deliveries.

The **competitive forces model** is a business framework depicting the five forces in a market (e.g., bargaining power of customers).

Competitive strategy focuses on general corporate strategy concerning the new competitors, existing competitors, substitute products, buyers, and suppliers.

A **compiler** translates a high-level language program to object code.

Complex instruction set computer (CISC) is a computer that uses a complete set of instructions that can be used to direct the CPU.

A **computer** is an electronic device capable of storing and manipulating data and instructions.

Computer-aided design (CAD) software allows designers to design and "build" production prototypes in software, "test" them as a computer object under given parameters, compile parts and quantity lists, outline production and assembly procedures, and then transmit the final design directly to milling and rolling machines.

Computer-aided engineering (CAE) enables engineers to execute complex engineering analysis on a computer.

Computer-aided manufacturing (CAM) software uses a digital design such as that from a CAD system to directly control production machinery.

Computer architecture is the arrangement of computer components and their relationships.

Computer crime is using a computer to steal, embezzle, or defraud.

Computer graphics present data in two or virtual three-dimensional form such as bar charts, histograms, pie charts, or grids on a display screen or plotter to highlight data variations.

Computer integrated manufacturing (CIM) software is embedded within each automated production machine to produce a product.

A **computer system** is composed of hardware (physical equipment, media, and attached devices), software (coding that manipulates the hardware), procedures, personnel, and data.

Contingency management is a management concept that claims that there is no best way to manage; rather, the best management approach is contigent on the situation or characteristics of an organization.

The **control unit** interprets and carries out instructions contained in computer programs, and controls input and output devices and the data transfer processes from and to memory.

Conversion is the process of changing from an old system to a new system.

Cooperative processing teams two or more geographically dispersed computers to execute a specific task.

Cost justification involves demonstrating that savings or revenues generated by the new system more than offset the costs of developing it.

Cost leadership is the ability of a company to produce quality products at the lowest cost in its industry group.

Critical success factors (CSF) are those few things that must go right in order to ensure the organization's survival and success.

Cross-functional systems are organizational units that cross functional lines; instead of being specialized, they are generalists units that can complete an entire process.

Cross-functional teams (see cross-functional systems).

Customer-oriented (or **customer-focused**) organizations treat customers as their first priority; everything else is derived from customers.

Customer resource life cycle (CRLC) concentrates on the relationship to the customer as the key to achieving strategic advantage.

Data are raw facts that can be processed into accurate and relevant information.

Data communications is the process of exchanging data or information electronically.

Data confidentiality makes sure that data are protected and accessible only to authorized people.

A **data definition language** is used to define the link between the logical and physical views of a database.

A **data dictionary** is a comprehensive list or collection of information, usually arranged alphabetically, giving the form, function, meaning, and syntax of the data in a database.

Data encryption is encoding data so that they cannot be understood unless they are decoded; used to protect data from unauthorized users.

A **data-flow diagram (DFD)** uses symbols to show the flow of data in an organization and data relationships for analysis or as a design tool.

Data inconsistency is data redundancy without data consistency.

Data independence allows data fields to be added, changed, and deleted from a database without necessarily affecting existing application programs.

Data integrity is the accuracy and accessibility of data.

The **data manipulation language** provides users with the ability to retrieve, sort, display, and delete the contents of their databases.

Data redundancy is information that is duplicated within a system.

Data repositories contain information about a system that can be used, for example, by CASE tools.

Data tampering is deliberately entering false data, or changing and deleting true data.

A **database** is a collection of files serving as a data resource for computer-based information systems.

A **database administrator** is someone responsible for ensuring that a database fulfills users' business needs—functionality and from the data itself.

A **database management system (DBMS)** is a software program (or group of programs) that manages and provides access to a database.

Debugging is correcting system malfunctions.

Decentralized computing breaks centralized computing into functionally equal parts with each part essentially a smaller, centralized subsystem.

A **decision center** generally consists of a decision maker, decision procedures, and an activity for which decisions must be made.

A **decision room** is an arrangement for a group DSS in which terminals are available to some or all participants.

A **decision support system (DSS)** is a computer-based information system that combines models and data in an attempt to solve semistructured problems with extensive user involvement.

A **decision system** provides the framework for determining what information is required.

A **decision table** is a simple matrix containing columns and rows that are used to define decision relationships.

Decision trees are graphical aids to chart decision choices with conditions.

Dehumanization is making people operate more like machines, instead of making machines operate more like people.

The **Delphi method** is a qualitative forecasting methodology using anonymous questionnaires in several iterations to find consensus.

Demodulation is the conversion of data from analog to digital format.

A **design overview** consists of a peer evaluation of the designer's overall approach to software development concerning one or more programs in an information system.

Desktop publishing uses sophisticated word processing software for textual output that resembles professional typesetting.

A **dialog system** is hardware and software that provides a user interface.

The **difference engine** was a mechanical device devised by Charles Babbage in 1812 to perform numeric calculations.

Differentiation (of product or service) is a strategy of gaining competitive advantage by providing a product (or service) of the same cost and quality as a competitor, but with some additional attribute(s), that makes it different from the competition.

Digital signals are discrete on–off pulses that convey information in terms of 1s and 0s—just like the central processing unit in computers.

Direct cut-over is a system implementation strategy of completely shutting down an old system and then completely starting up the new system.

A **disaster avoidance plan** is a comprehensive plan to avoid a controllable catastrophe in the corporate information systems.

A **disaster recovery plan** is a plan to operate an IS area after a disaster (such as an earthquake) and to restore the functioning of the systems.

A **diskette** or floppy disk is a relatively soft, plastic platter coated with ferric material for storing data as magnetized spots.

Distributed computing breaks centralized computing into many, semi-autonomous computers that may not be (and usually aren't) functionally equal.

A **distributed database** has complete copies of a database, or portions of a database, in more than one location.

Downsizing an application is rehosting or reengineering a mainframe application to mini- or microcomputers.

Drill-down is the ability to investigate information in increasing detail; e.g., find not only total sales, but also sales by region, by product, or by saleperson.

A **DSS generator** is a computer software package that provides the capabilities to quickly build a specific DSS.

DSS tools are software utilities that facilitate DSS development.

Economic order quantity (EOQ) is a basic formula to predict the quantity of an item to order to maintain a given inventory level under specified deplenishment rates.

An **electrically erasable PROM (EEPROM)** is a semiconductor memory device that can be altered in the field by applying electrical pulses.

Electronic bulletin boards are public-access electronic mail message centers where authorized people can leave messages for everyone to read (e.g., interest groups in Internet).

Electronic data interchange (EDI) is a computer-to-computer direct communication of standard business transactions between or among business partners.

An **electronic form** is a paperless form that appears on a computer's screen and is filled in electronically by a user.

Electronic funds transfer (EFT) is the transmission of funds, debits and credits, and charges and payments electronically between banks and their customers.

Electronic mail (e-mail) is computer-based messages that can be electronically manipulated, stored, combined with other information, and exchanged with other computers.

Empowerment is providing employees with sufficient resources and authority to make the necessary decisions to accomplish tasks.

Encapsulation is the term used to describe the fact that an object contains all the data and operations necessary to carry out some action.

End-user computing is the use or development of information systems by the principal users of the systems' outputs or by their staffs.

Ends/Means Analysis (E/M Analysis) determines information requirements based on desired ends (effectiveness) and available means (efficiency) to achieve the ends.

Enterprise-wide systems (or enterprise computing) are information systems that are used throughout a company or enterprise.

Entity-attribute analysis is the process of defining information categories from the cross-functional interviews based on entities and their information attributes.

The **environment** (of a system) are elements that lie outside a system but have an impact on the system's performance.

An **erasable PROM (EPROM)** is a semiconductor memory device that can be programmed and erased using ultraviolet light.

Entities are people, places, or things about which we want to collect, store, and maintain information.

Ergonomics is the science of adapting machines and work environments to people.

Executive information systems (EIS) are specifically designed to support executive work.

An **executive support system (ESS)** is an executive information system that includes some analytical and communication capabilities.

An **expert support system** is an expert system that supports problem solving and decision making.

An **expert system (ES)** is a computer system that applies reasoning methodologies or knowledge in a specific domain to render advice or recommendations—much like a human expert.

Expertise is the set of capabilities that underlies the performance of human experts, including extensive domain knowledge, heuristic rules that simplify and improve approaches to problem solving, metaknowledge and metacognition, and compiled forms of behavior that afford great economy in skilled performance.

Extended Binary Coded Decimal Interchange Code (EBCDIC) is a standard scheme for encoding alphanumeric characters into bits; most common on mainframes.

An **external database** is a database wholly outside the organization but accessible via communications.

Fault-tolerance is the ability to continue operating satisfactorily in the presence of faults.

A **feasibility study** seeks an overview of a problem and a rough assessment of whether feasible solutions exist prior to committing resources.

Feedback is information flowing from an outcome (or result) to the decision maker controlling a system or process.

Fiber optic cables consist of thousands of very thin filaments of glass fibers which can conduct light pulses generated by lasers at transmission frequencies that approach the speed of light.

A **field** is a unique type of information or characteristic about an entity.

A **file** is a group of data with some form of commonality.

Flattened organizations have a reduced managerial staff or fewer levels of management, and a larger span of control.

A **flowchart** uses symbols and arrows to show processes—the steps and their precise order for receiving, storing, using, and transmitting data.

FORTRAN (**For**mula **Tran**slator) is an algebraic, formula-type procedural language developed primarily to meet typical scientific processing requirements.

Forward error correction (FEC) uses knowledge about a message stream and mathematical algorithms to allow a receiver to correct received data streams without having to go back to a sender.

Four-stage model of planning is a generic information systems planning model based on four major, generic activities: strategic planning, information requirements analysis, resource allocation, and project planning.

Fourth-generation languages (4GL) are nonprocedural programming languages that allow users and professional programmers to specify the results they want and let the computer determine the sequence of instructions that will accomplish those results.

Frames are a knowledge representation scheme that associates one or more features with an object.

A **front-end processor** is a specialized computer that manages all routine communications with peripheral devices.

Full-duplex transmission uses two circuits for communications—one for each direction simultaneously.

Functional information systems serve a particular functional area (such as marketing or manufacturing information systems).

Future perfect is a concept based on the premise that technology will get perfect and that, therefore, companies should develop a business vision of perfection based on giving customers what they want anytime, anyplace, anywhere.

Fuzzy logic is a way of reasoning that can cope with uncertain or partial information; a characteristic of human thinking and some expert systems.

A **Gantt chart** is a planning technique that, like PERT, graphically provides a list of tasks to be performed and when they are to start and finish—but do not show sequential dependencies.

General controls are physical, access, communication, administrative, and data security controls aimed at protecting a system in general rather than specific applications.

A **general ledger** is the entire group of accounts maintained by an organization.

Geographical information systems use spatial data such as digitized maps, and can combine this data with other text, graphics, icons, and symbols.

Global business drivers are entities that benefit from global economies of scale and add value to a global business strategy.

Goal-seeking (analysis) is asking what values certain variables must have in order to attain desired goals.

A **graphical user interface (GUI)** is an interactive, user-friendly interface in which icons and similar graphical devices enable a user to control a computer.

A **group DSS (GDSS)** is an interactive, computer-based system that facilitates finding solutions to semistructured problems by using a set of decision makers working together as a group.

Group support systems (GSS) support the working of groups (e.g., communication and decision making).

Groupthink is a situation where people think alike and new ideas are not tolerated.

Groupware is a generic term for several computerized technologies and methods that aim to support the work of people working in groups.

Hackers are people who illegally or unethically access a computer system.

A **half-duplex** transmission uses only one circuit but it is used in both directions—one direction at a time.

Handwriting recognition is the ability to recognize letters and numbers written by hand.

Hardcopy documents are more-or-less permanent documents on media other than electrical based, usually on paper with ink.

A **hard disk** is a hard, metal platter coated with a material that can be magnetized in spots to represent bits, primarily for secondary storage.

Hardware is the physical equipment, media, and attached devices used in a computer system.

Heuristic design or prototyping is an approach to systems development that exploits advanced technologies for using trial-and-error problem solving.

The **hierarchical model** relates data by structuring data into an inverted "tree" in which records refer to a senior field and any number of subordinate fields (i.e., one "parent" and several "children").

A **hierarchical organization** is a traditional multilevel structure, like a military command, with each level supervising the level below it.

Hypermedia combines several types of media such as text, graphics, audio, and video linked by association.

Hypertext is textual data that is linked with other, related textual data.

Icons are pictures of features or functions that can be graphically "selected" for execution.

Image processing systems receive, store, manage, and distribute images.

An **image technology** receives images of documents, stores them, and retrieves them when needed.

An **index** is an ordered listing of certain fields to aid a DBMS in locating particular records quickly.

Indexed sequential access method is a combination or compromise between indexed blocks of data arranged sequentially within each block.

Industry Standard Architecture (ISA) is the most common system architecture, based on a 16-bit central processor and a 16-bit bus.

An **inference engine** is the part of an expert system that performs a reasoning function.

Information is data that are processed or operated on by a computer.

An **information architecture** is a conceptualization of the manner by which information requirements are met by the system.

Information centers train and support business users with end-user tools, testing, technical support information, and standard certification.

An **information infrastructure** is the physical arrangement of hardware, software, databases, networks, and so forth.

Information requirements are those items of information needed by information systems users for decision making.

An **information system** is a physical process that supports an object system by providing information to achieve organizational goals.

The **information superhighway** is a national information infrastructure to interconnect computer users.

Information systems controls are used to counter computer hazards (such as crime and human errors).

Information technology (IT) is the technology component of an information system, or the collection of the entire systems in an organization.

Information technology architecture is the field of study and practice devoted to understanding and deploying information systems components in the form of an organizational infrastructure.

An **information warehouse** is a decision-support tool for collecting information from multiple sources and making that information available to end users in a consolidated, consistent manner.

Infrared communications uses red light below what is commonly visible to humans, but light nonetheless that can be modulated or pulsed for conveying information.

Inheritance is a feature of objects where subclasses inherit the behaviors and attributes defined by its superclass as well as any additional behaviors and attributes of its own.

An **input device** is a computer system component that accepts data from the user (e.g., a keyboard or mouse).

Inputs are the resources introduced into a system for transformation into outputs.

An **input/output (I/O) device** transfers data into or out of a computer.

An **instruction set** is a set of instructions a CPU can execute.

Integrated CASE tools support prototyping and reusable systems components, including component repositories and automatic computer code generation.

Integrated circuits are interconnected layers of etched semiconductor materials forming electronic transistor circuit units with "on–off" positions that direct the electrical current passing through them.

Integrative tests examine all of the programs together as a system.

Intelligent agents are expert or knowledge-based systems embedded in computer-based information systems (or their components).

Intelligence support systems are intelligent systems designed to support knowledge workers.

Intelligent systems include a knowledge component, such as an expert system or neural network.

Interactive software allows a user to alter the sequence or flow of information.

Interfaces interact with a user, accepting commands and displaying the results generated by other portions of the computer system.

The **internal IS structure** is the organizational structure of an IS department.

Internet is a self-regulated network of computer networks connecting over 25,000 networks with over 2.5 million computers and 25 million users.

An **interpreter** is a compiler that translates and executes one source program statement at a time.

IT outsourcing is using outside vendors to create, maintain, or reengineer IT architectures and systems.

A **job** is a unit of work within a program.

A **job control language (JCL)** is a special computer language that allows a systems professional to communicate with the operating system.

Joint application design (JAD) is a process to determine information requirements from team interviews of managers as a group process.

A **joystick** is a hand-grip device used to position a cursor.

Just-in-time (JIT) is a concept in which material and parts arrive at a work place when needed, minimizing inventory, waste, and interruptions.

A **key** is a symbol or group of symbols used to reference other, related data.

Key performance indicators (KPI) are specific measures of the critical success factors in an executive information system.

Knowledge is the understanding, awareness, or familiarity acquired through education or experience.

Knowledge acquisition extracts and formulates knowledge derived from various sources, especially from experts.

A knowledge base is a collection of facts, rules, and procedures organized into schemas.

Knowledge engineering (KE) captures human knowledge and places it into a computer system where it is used to solve complex problems normally requiring a high level of human expertise.

Knowledge representation is a formalism for representing facts and rules in a computer about a subject or a specialty.

Knowledge workers are people who use knowledge as a significant part of their work responsibility.

Laser printers are nonimpact printers that produce high-quality printed output.

A layered approach to systems development is based upon the concept of an information systems development process as the continued unfolding of successive details concerning different layers of hardware and software technology in the information system.

Legacy systems are older systems that have become central to business operations and may be still capable of meeting these business needs; they may not require any immediate changes, or they may be in need of reengineering to meet new business needs.

A light pen is a special input device using a light-sensing mechanism to detect and send signals to a computer; typically used for selecting items from a computer-screen menu.

A local area network (LAN) is a system for interconnecting two or more closely located communicating devices supporting full connectivity so that every user device on the network has the potential to communicate with any other device.

The logical view, or user's view, of a database represents data in a format that is meaningful to a user and to the software programs that process that data.

Long-range planning is a corporate or IT plan for five years or longer.

Loosely coupled toolsets are independent tools, developed by different tool vendors, to support one or more information systems architecture layers.

Lotus Notes is a commercial workflow and groupware software package that also provides application developers an environment for quickly creating cross-platform client/server applications.

Machine language is the internal representation of instructions and data in binary format for direct processing by a central processing unit.

A macro, from the Greek meaning "large," refers to a single instruction or formula that combines a number of other simpler instructions.

Magnetic tape is a plastic ribbon coated on one side with an iron-oxide material that can be magnetized by electromagnetic pulses for storing data.

Mainframe computers are relatively large computers built to handle very large databases, thousands of user terminals with fast response times, and millions of transactions.

Management information systems (MIS) are designed to provide past, present, and future routine information appropriate for planning, organizing, and controlling the operations of a functional area in an organization.

Management support systems (MSS) are three major IT technologies designed to support managers: decision support systems, executive support systems, and groupware technologies.

Master–slave network architectures consist of a master (or "host") computer that controls all computer processing and all work performed by "slave" devices.

A master file is the main collection of records relating to a specific application area.

Menu interaction allows users to conduct a dialogue with a computer by using menus.

A method (in an object-oriented model) is an operation, action, or a behavior an object may undergo.

Metaknowledge is knowledge about knowledge; knowledge in an expert system about how the system operates or reasons.

Microcomputers are the smallest and least expensive category of general-purpose computers; also known as **micros** and **personal computers**.

Microwave systems are used to transmit very high-frequency radio signals in a line-of-sight path between relay stations spaced approximately 30 miles apart (due to the earth's curvature).

Middleware is systems software that can translate client requests into a form that certain servers can better understand, translate server response into a form clients can better understand, monitor system performance, and can aid developers by providing an intermediary "layer" between application programs and system software.

Milestones, or checkpoints, are established to allow periodic review of progress so that management can determine if a project merits further commitment of resources, if it requires adjustments, or if it should be discontinued.

A minicomputer is a relatively smaller, cheaper, and more compact computer that performs the same functions as a larger, mainframe computer, but to a more limited extent.

MIPS is an acronym for **m**illions of **i**nstructions **p**er **s**econd; used for measuring computer processing power.

Mission central operations are the routine, core operations of a business, such as receiving orders and fulfilling them.

A model base is a collection of preprogrammed quantitative models (e.g., statistical, financial, optimal) organized as a single unit.

A model base management system (MBMS) is a software program to establish, update, and use a model base.

A modem is a device that **mo**dulates and **dem**odulates signals.

Modulation is the conversion of data from digital to analog format.

A mouse is a handheld device with one or more selection buttons used to move a cursor on a computer screen and make selections.

Multimedia is the combination of at least two media for input or output of data; these media can be audio (sound), voice, animation, video, text, graphics, and/or images.

A multiplexor is an electronic device that allows a single communications channel to simultaneously carry data transmissions from many sources.

Multiprocessing involves more than one processor within a computer for processing more than one program simultaneously.

Multiprogramming involves two or more application modules or programs placed into main memory at the same time, but executed one at a time (i.e., concurrently).

A natural language interface lets a user retrieve data with simple, human languagelike (e.g., English) commands.

A natural language processor (NLP) is an knowledge-based user interface that allows the user to carry on a conversation with a computer-based system in much the same way as he or she would converse with another human.

A network is a telecommunications system that permits the sharing of resources such as computing power, software, input/output devices, and data.

The **network layer** identifies the interaction points between the network and the other layers of a system.

The **network model** creates relationships among data through a linked-list structure in which subordinated records can be linked to more than one parent.

A **node** is a device on a network with the ability to exchange control and data transmissions with other nodes on the network.

A **nonprocedural language** is a high-level language that allows the programmer to specify the desired result without having to specify the detailed procedures needed for achieving the result; also called a fourth-generation language.

Normalization is a method for analyzing and reducing a relational database to its most parsimonious or streamlined form for minimum redundancy and maximum data integrity—as well as best processing performance.

An **object** is similar to an entity in that it is the embodiment of a person, place, or thing.

Object-oriented development is based on interchangeable software components (objects) that model the behavior of persons, places, things, or concepts in the real world.

An **object-oriented model** consists of objects, attributes (characteristics that describe the state of that object), and methods (an operation, action, or a behavior the object may take on).

Object-oriented programming (OOP) models a system as a set of cooperating objects.

An **object program** is the set of instructions produced after translating a source program into machine language.

An **object system** is a physical process whose purpose is to achieve one or more organizational goals.

Office automation systems (OAS) are used to increase the productivity of office workers and the quality of office work.

On-line data entry inputs data directly to and is immediately used by a computer.

An **open system** is a computer system that permits the use of a wide range of software and hardware by many vendors.

The **Open Systems Interconnection (OSI)** standard is a seven-layer protocol using peer-to-peer communications at each layer for well-defined functions.

Operating system software supervises the overall operation of a computer, including such tasks as monitoring the computer's status, handling executable program interruptions, and scheduling of operations.

Opportunistic surveillance continually seeks opportunities that might be beneficial to the organization.

An **optical character reader (OCR)** is an input device that scans textual data.

Optical scanners scan text and graphics forms for input to a computer system.

An **organizational DSS (ODSS)** is a network DSS that serves people at several locations.

Organizational information requirements analysis (OIRA) is a model for information systems planning that ensures various information systems and databases can be integrated to support decision making and operations.

Organization transformation is a radical change in an organization involving structure, culture, and the manner in which business is conducted.

Outputs are the completed products or services of a system.

An **output device** is the part of a computer system that produces processed data or information.

In a **packet switched network**, data are broken into groups (called packets) of characters to which control information has been added at the beginning and the end of the group for transmission over various circuits, for reassembly at the final destination.

Parallel conversion is a process of converting from one information system to a newer system by using both systems concurrently until the new system is demonstrably stable and reliable.

Parallel processing is executing several processing instructions at the same time (in parallel) rather than one at a time (serial or sequential processing).

Parity bits are character or control codes that are like check-sums that are verified at the receiving end of a transmission to determine whether bits were lost during the transmission.

Pascal is a high-level procedural language, named after the French mathematician Blase Pascal, with power, flexibility, and a self-documenting structure that makes it an attractive choice for academic, business, and scientific applications.

Peer-to-peer network relationships stress processing on an equal basis among all processors, sharing devices and data on a mutual basis.

A **pen-based system** is a small computer that can accept input from a stylus or pen; commonly used for filling out forms or taking notes.

Periodic reports are routine reports executed at predetermined times (in contrast with ad hoc reports).

Personal information manager (PIM) is a software package for a manager's personal use combining the features of project management software and desktop organizers.

Program evaluation and review technique (PERT) is a planning and control tool representing the network of tasks in diagram form required to complete a project, establishing sequential dependencies and relationships among the tasks.

Phased conversion is switching from an old system to a new system in phases throughout an organization.

The **physical view** of a database deals with the actual, physical arrangement and location of data in the direct access storage devices.

Pilot conversion is switching from an old system to a complete, new system in parts of an organization, one part at a time.

A **plotter** is a printing device that produces high-quality line drawings by moving either pens or electrostatic charges over paper.

Pointers link subordinates and parents in the network database model by linking physical storage addresses.

Point-of-sale (POS) terminals are input devices used in retail establishments to enter data when and where a transaction is made.

Portability means that the same software can be run on many different computers.

Presentation graphics, or custom graphics, is a form of documentation that involves the use of pictures that are representative of the objects being portrayed.

The **presentation layer** arranges and displays data for users and is the most visible and ergonomic aspect of an information system.

Primary activities are the core organizational activities in Michael Porter's value chain model.

A **primary key** is a record identifier, a field that uniquely identifies a record and thus distinguishes it from all other records in the file.

Primary storage, or main memory, stores data and code for the CPU.

A private branch exchange (PBX) is a privately owned and operated circuit switching device that allows many internal users to share external communications circuits, routes incoming calls, and provides limited internal communications services.

A private line is an analog or digital line that is rented exclusively to one customer for voice or data communications.

Problem-solving (or project) teams are created for a specific purpose (e.g., solve a problem) and then disbanded.

Procedural languages require a programmer to specify, step by step, exactly how the computer must accomplish a task.

Production rules are knowledge formalized into "rules" containing an IF part and a THEN part.

Productivity is the ratio of outputs (results) to inputs (resources utilized).

Programming languages are the basic building blocks for all software, allowing people to tell computers what to do and the means by which systems are developed.

Project planning is the fourth stage of the model for information systems planning, providing an overall framework with which the system development life cycle can be planned, scheduled, and controlled.

Process innovation is an approach in business process reengineering by which radical changes are made through innovations.

A computer processor is a device that processes inputs into outputs.

A programmable ROM (PROM) is a semiconductor memory device that can be programmed once (and only once).

A project proposal for management is the product of the final stage of a successful feasibility study.

A project team is assigned project responsibility for system development, often under the resource requirements section of a project proposal.

A communications protocol is a set of rules or limits in language usage and flows of speech in order to ensure some level of mutual understanding.

Prototyping is an approach to systems development that exploits advanced technologies for using trial-and-error problem solving.

Pull-down menus are submenus that appear when one selects a certain item in a higher level menu.

Quality circles are groups of employees whose objective is to increase quality in their work area by solving problems jointly and introducing change.

Query-By-Example (QBE) allows users to choose easily which table(s) to ask questions of, select the fields to be included in the answer, and then enter an example of the data wanted.

A query language is a programming language provided as part of a DBMS for easy access to the data in the database.

The three R's of reengineering are redesign, retool, and reorchestrate.

Random-access memory (RAM) is digital storage or memory that can be directly written to and read.

Reaction surveillance involves addressing problems as they arise—a management by exception approach.

Read-only memory (ROM) is digital storage or memory that can be read directly.

In the real-time business processing system, controls and information processing must be synchronized with an actual occurrence of events.

With real-time processing, there is no perceived delay between sending an inquiry and receiving a response.

Records are subsets of data about an entity; an instance or occurrence of an entity.

Reduced instruction set computer (RISC) is a CPU based on a very small set of instructions "hard-wired" into the CPU, while less frequently used instructions are kept in software.

Reengineering is the introduction of fundamental and radical changes to a process; the complete restructuring of an existing system.

Registers are specialized, high-speed memory areas for storing temporary results of ALU operations as well as for storing certain control information.

The relational model is based on the concept of tables to capitalize on the concept of having simple rows and columns of data.

Relations are tables of entities with corresponding attributes and tuples.

Resource allocation is the third stage of the model for information systems planning, consisting of developing the hardware, software, data communications, facilities, personnel, and financial plans needed to execute the master development plan defined in an OIRA.

Response management is the strategy of responding to competitors or market developments rather than being a leader.

Return on investment (ROI) is the percentage return computed by ROI = net return ÷ required investment.

In a ring topology, nodes are arranged along the transmission path so that a signal passes through one station at a time before returning to its originating node; the nodes form a closed circle.

Robotics is the science of using a machine (a robot) to perform manual functions without human intervention.

A rule-based system is a system in which knowledge is represented in terms of rules (e.g., a system based on production rules).

Secondary storage stores data in a format that is compatible with the data stored in primary storage, but provides space for storing and processing large quantities of software and data for long periods.

Sectors are divisions of storage tracks; addressable concentric rings on magnetic, secondary storage disks used for storing data.

Self-directed teams make their own decisions and have authority (and responsibility) to execute specific tasks.

Sensitivity analysis studies the effect of a change in one or more input variables on a proposed solution.

Semistructured processes involve problems where some, but not all, phases are structured or routine.

Sequential database access starts at the beginning of the database, examining each record in turn until the one sought is found.

A shell is a complete expert system stripped of its specific knowledge.

A simplex data transmission uses one circuit in one direction only.

Smart cards are storage mediums the size of a credit card that contain a microprocessor capable of recording and storing information.

Softcopy documents are on media that is electrical based and easily changed, such as magnetic diskettes or in a computer primary memory.

Software is instructional coding that manipulates the hardware in a computer system.

Software maintenance is all program coding after initial deployment to correct coding errors, enhance the functionality of the software, and perfect the functioning of the software.

A source program is a set of programming instructions written in a user-oriented language.

Specifications provide sufficient documentation to guide the creation of software required to operate a system.

Computer spreadsheet software transforms a computer screen into a ledger sheet, or grid, of coded rows and columns.

Information system stages of growth are six commonly accepted stages that all organizations seem to experience in implementing and managing an information system from conception to maturation.

A star network has a central node that connects to each of the other nodes by a single, point-to-point link.

A steering committee is composed of key managers representing major functional units within the organization to oversee the IS function, to ensure that adequate planning and control processes were present, and to direct IS activities in support of long-range organizational objectives and goals.

Strategic alliances are business alliances among companies that provide strategic benefits to the partners.

Strategic information systems (SIS) are information systems that provide, or help to provide, strategic advantage.

Strategic planning, the first stage of the planning model, aligns IS strategic planning with overall organizational planning by assessing organizational objectives and strategies, setting the IS mission, assessing the environment, and setting IS policies, objectives, and strategies.

Structured processes involve routine and repetitive problems for which standard solutions exist.

Structured query language (SQL) is a common database definition and manipulation language using a simple, textual format.

Supercomputers have the most processing power of computers generally available.

Support activities do not add value directly to a firm's product or service under consideration but support the primary activities that do add value.

The supervisor is a control program that is that part of the operating system and acts as an overall coordinating program.

Switching costs are costs incurred when a company changes a supplier (or other business partner).

Symbolic processing uses symbols, rather than numbers, combined with rules of thumb (or heuristics) to process information and solve problems.

In a synchronous transmission, blocks of characters, preceded by unique bits, are sent over a communications link in a continuous bit stream while data transfer is controlled by a timing signal initiated by the sending device.

A system is a set of elements that acts as a single, goal-oriented entity.

System development refers to the structuring of hardware and software to achieve the effective and efficient processing of information.

System development life cycle (SDLC) is a model for developing a system based on traditional problem solving with sequential steps and options for revisiting steps when problems appear.

A system encyclopedia, in many CASE products, provides a central information repository, the core of which is the data dictionary.

System software is a set of instructions that act as the intermediary between the computer hardware and application programs.

System utilities are programs that have been written to accomplish common tasks such as sorting records or copying disk files onto magnetic tape for backup.

Telecommunication generally refers to all types of long-distance communication through the use of common carriers, those businesses which supply high speed voice and data communication services.

Time sharing allows a number of users to operate concurrently with the same CPU, with each user commanding the CPU for a certain length of time.

Time to market is the time from the start of the development of a product (idea) until the time when the product is ready to be sold in the market place.

A toolkit is a collection of software tools that automates one type of software task or one phase of the software development process.

A topology is a physical arrangement of communications devices; an architecture.

Total quality management (TQM) is an organization-wide effort to improve quality and make it the responsibility of all employees.

Touch screens enable a user to select entries and choose commands by simply making manual contact with a screen.

Track balls are input pointing and selection devices resembling an inverted "mouse."

Tracks are addressable concentric rings on magnetic, secondary storage disks used for storing data.

Transaction files are all the changes made or to be made to a master file.

A transaction processing system processes an organizations basic business transactions such as purchasing, billing, and payroll.

Transistors, also known as solid-state devices or semiconductors, are small, fast, and cheap electronic switches.

A tuple is a row or record of data about an entity.

Turing tests, named after the English mathematician, Alan Turing, are designed to measure the degree of a computer's "intelligence" by seeing if a human, by asking questions and reading the answers, can identify whether the correspondent is a human or a computer.

A unit test is when individual modules or programs are tested independently.

Unstructured processes involve problems none of which is routine or repetitive; they are "fuzzy," complex problems for which there are no cut-and-dried solutions.

Upsizing an application is moving a PC application or reengineering it to a mainframe.

User interfaces facilitate communications between a user (a person) and an information system and may be tailored uniquely for an individual.

Validation ensures that a system meets documented and approved system requirements established during the design stage.

Value added networks are communications providers that add communications services to existing, common carriers.

Value systems in Michael Porter's value chain model include suppliers, distributors, and buyers (all with their own value chains).

Videoconferencing is a multiple-way, real-time television session.

Virtual corporations may operate from various locations, usually through telecommunications, without a permanent headquarters.

A virtual machine is a computer system that appears to a user as being a real computer but, in fact, has been created by the operating system.

Virtual memory (VM) allows a program to execute as if primary memory were larger than it actually is.

Virtual reality is a pseudo-3D interactive technology which provides a user with a feeling that he or she is physically present in a computer-generated world.

A virus is software that can damage or destroy data or software in a computer.

Voice mail is digitized spoken messages that is stored and transferred electronically to receivers.

Voice recognition is the ability of a computer to understand the meaning of spoken words.

Voice synthesis transforms computer output to voice or audio output.

Wand readers are handheld optical readers for scanning data.

"What-if" analysis seeks to determine what the effect will be of changing some of the input data.

A white box is a device whose internal processes are known to a user.

Wide area networks (WANs) are networks that generally span distances greater than one city and include regional networks such as telephone companies or international networks such as global communications services providers.

A word is a logical grouping of bits in memory and for data transmission over the bus.

Word processing software allows a user to manipulate text rather than just calculate and manipulate numbers.

Workflow systems use group support software for scheduling, routing, and monitoring specific tasks throughout an organization.

Workstations are relatively small computers that provide a high level of performance; they are typically based upon a RISC architecture and providing both very high speed calculations and high-resolution color displays.

WORM (**w**rite **o**nce, **r**ead **m**any) is a technology using plastic platters like CD-ROMs that can be written to once and then read or accessed often.

WYSIWYG (**w**hat **y**ou **s**ee **i**s **w**hat **y**ou **g**et) means that material displayed on a computer screen will look exactly—or almost exactly—as it will look on a printed page.

PHOTO CREDITS

Chapter 1

Opening Case: Courtesy 7-Eleven Japan Co., Ltd. Figure 1.3: Courtesy Hewlett Packard. Figure 1.6: Tom Lubevitch. *Page 19:* Courtesy Research Data Worldwide. *Page 21:* Courtesy Port of Singapore Authority. *Page 24:* Courtesy of International Business Machines Corporation.

Chapter 2

Opening Case: Courtesy Panhandle Eastern Corp. Figure 2.2: Courtesy Panhandle Eastern Pipe Line Company. Figure 2.3: Courtesy American Airlines. *Page 44:* Courtesy Heimann Systems Co. Figure 2.8: Courtesy Lotus Development Corp. *Page 57:* BYTE Magazine, June 1993.

Chapter 3

Opening Case: Courtesy Caterpillar Inc. *Page 97:* Robot Aided Manufacturing Center, Inc.

Chapter 4

Opening Case: Alvis Upitis/The Image Bank.

Chapter 5

Opening Case: Courtesy Boss Studio. Figure 5.1: Brian Lovell/The Picture Cube. Figure 5.2: Courtesy Sperry Univac, Division of Sperry Corp. Figure 5.4: Courtesy Apple Computers. Figure 5.5: Courtesy Mainframe Hardware. Figure 5.6: Courtesy of International Business Machines Corporation. Figure 5.7: Courtesy Hewlett Packard. Figure 5.8: © Sun Microsystems. Figure 5.9 (top): Courtesy Compaq. Figure 5.9 (bottom left): Courtesy of International Business Machines Corporation. Figure 5.9 (bottom right): Courtesy Hewlett Packard. Figure 5.10: Frank Pryor /Courtesy Apple Computers. *Page 170:* © GEM Plus. Figure 5.14: Courtesy USDA Computer Center. Figure 5.15: Courtesy Conner Peripherals. *Page 177:* Courtesy of Sony Electronics Inc. Figure 5.16: Courtesy Verbatim. *Page 179:* Courtesy Storage Technology Corp.

Chapter 6

Opening Case: Courtesy of Cypress Semiconductor Corp. Figure 6.4: Courtesy Lotus Development. Figure 6.5: Courtesy Lotus Development Corporation. Figure 6.6: Courtesy Microsoft. Figure 6.7: Courtesy RISO, Inc. Figure 6.8: Courtesy Wordperfect, Inc. Figure 6.9: Courtesy Computervision Corporation. Figure 6.10: Courtesy of International Business Machines Corporation. Figure 6.11: Courtesy Sterling Software.

Chapter 7

Opening Case: Courtesy of United Services Automobile Association. Figure 7.3: Courtesy Penstock, Inc. *Page 235:* Courtesy of International Business Machines Corporation. Figure 7.6: Courtesy Great Plains Software. Figure 7.8: Courtesy Lotus Development Corp. Figure 7.10: Courtesy Asymetrix Corp. *Page 251:* Courtesy Looking Glass Software, Inc. *Page 253:* Courtesy MapInfo, Troy NY. Figure 7.11: Courtesy NEC Corporation (Japan). *Page 264:* Courtesy Dallas Area Rapid Transit.

Chapter 8

Opening Case: Courtesy Dell Computer Corporation. *Page 273:* Steven Peters/ Tony Stone Images/ New York, Inc. *Page 278:* Courtesy Microsoft. *Page 280:* Courtesy of International Business Machines Corporation. *Page 288:* Courtesy Wang Laboratory.

Chapter 9

Opening Case: Edward Caldwell. *Page 300:* Greg Pease/Tony Stone Images/ New York, Inc. *Page 300:* Courtesy AT&T. *Page 303:* Courtesy Motorola.

Page 307: Courtesy Hayes Microcomputer Products, Inc. *Page 326:* Courtesy Wordperfect, Inc.

Chapter 10

Opening Case: Frank Herholdt/Tony Stone Images/ New York, Inc. *Page 340:* Mitch Kezar/Tony Stone Images/ New York, Inc. *Page 346:* Charles Gupton/ Stock, Boston. *Page 351:* Courtesy of International Business Machines Corporation. *Page 354:* Bruce Ayres/Tony Stone Images/ New York, Inc.

Chapter 11

Opening Case: Ron Sherman/Tony Stone Images/ New York, Inc.

Chapter 12

Opening Case: Tony Freeman/PhotoEdit.

Chapter 13

Opening Case: Courtesy of International Business Machines Corporation. *Page 443:* Tim Brown/Tony Stone Images/ New York, Inc. *Page 450:* Courtesy GM Corporation. *Page 460:* Courtesy Hewlett Packard. *Page 462:* Courtesy AT & T Bell Laboratories. *Page 465:* Tim Brown/Tony Stone Images/ New York, Inc. *Page 467:* Mark Richards/PhotoEdit.

Chapter 14

Opening Case: Richard Kalvar/Magnum Photos, Inc. Figure 14.5: Courtesy of Creative Technology. Figure 14.9: Ventana Corp., Group Systems V/ University of Arizona Center for the Management of Information. Figure 14.12: Lotus Development Corporation. Figure 14.13 (clockwise from top right): Courtesy of International Business Machines Corporation, Courtesy Sony Pictures Entertainment Company, Courtesy Apple Computers, Courtesy Toshiba, L. Felzmann/Matrix International, Inc., Gabe Palacio/Leo de Wys, Inc. Figure 14.13 (center): Blair Seitz/Photo Researchers.

Chapter 15

Opening Case: Courtesy Jewish Hospital Healthcare Services. *Page 538:* Courtesy Dialogos-Team Oy. Figure 15.4: Courtesy Lotus Development Corp. Figure 15.6: Courtesy Comshare, Inc. Figure 15.9: Courtesy Comshare, Inc.

Chapter 16

Opening Case: The Robotics Institue/ Carnegie Mellon University. Figure 16.1: Van Horn, Understanding ES p.131

Chapter 17

Opening Case: George Disario/The Stock Market. Figure 17.7: Courtesy State of The Art, Inc. *Page 646:* Courtesy Tandy Corporation.

Chapter 18

Opening Case: Charles Thatcher/Tony Stone Images/ New York, Inc.

Chapter 19

Opening Case: Courtesy Eileen Hilloch/Dean Witter Reynolds, Inc. *Page 714:* Courtesy Startek Engineering, Inc. Figure 19.6: Courtesy Micro Security Systems, Inc.

Chapter 20

Opening Case: Jack K. Clark/Comstock, Inc. *Page 751:* Courtesy WorkSmart/ ErgoView Technologies. *Page 755:* Courtesy U. C. Davis. *Page 756:* James Keyser. *Page 768:* Courtesy Granite Communications.

NAME INDEX

ORGANIZATIONS INDEX